BIOETHICS AND PUBLIC HEALTH LAW

ASPEN PUBLISHERS

BIOETHICS AND PUBLIC HEALTH LAW

Second Edition

David Orentlicher
Samuel R. Rosen Professor of Law
Indiana University School of Law, Indianapolis

Mary Anne Bobinski
Dean and Professor of Law
University of British Columbia Faculty of Law

Mark A. Hall
Fred D. and Elizabeth L. Turnage Professor of
Law and Public Health
Wake Forest University

Law & Business

AUSTIN   BOSTON   CHICAGO   NEW YORK   THE NETHERLANDS

Aspen Publishers
Attn: Permissions Department
76 Ninth Avenue, 7th Floor
New York, NY 10011-5201

To contact Customer Care, e-mail customer.care@aspenpublishers.com, call 1-800-234-1660, fax 1-800-901-9075, or mail correspondence to:

Aspen Publishers
Attn: Order Department
PO Box 990
Frederick, MD 21705

Printed in the United States of America.

1 2 3 4 5 6 7 8 9 0

ISBN 978-0-7355-7004-7

Library of Congress Cataloging-in-Publication Data

Orentlicher, David, 1955-
 Bioethics and public health law / David Orentlicher, Mary Anne
Bobinski, Mark A. Hall. — 2nd ed.
  p. cm.
 Includes bibliographical references and index.
 Author's names appear in different order in previous ed.; Mark A. Hall name appears first.
 ISBN 978-0-7355-7004-7 (alk. paper)
 1. Public health laws — Moral and ethical aspects — United States — Cases. 2. Bioethics — United States. I. Bobinski, Mary Anne. II. Hall, Mark A., 1955- III. Title.

 KF3775.A7H34 2008
 344.7304 — dc22

                                                                2007049155

About Wolters Kluwer Law & Business

Wolters Kluwer Law & Business is a leading provider of research information and workflow solutions in key specialty areas. The strengths of the individual brands of Aspen Publishers, CCH, Kluwer Law International and Loislaw are aligned within Wolters Kluwer Law & Business to provide comprehensive, in-depth solutions and expert-authored content for the legal, professional and education markets.

CCH was founded in 1913 and has served more than four generations of business professionals and their clients. The CCH products in the Wolters Kluwer Law & Business group are highly regarded electronic and print resources for legal, securities, antitrust and trade regulation, government contracting, banking, pension, payroll, employment and labor, and healthcare reimbursement and compliance professionals.

Aspen Publishers is a leading information provider for attorneys, business professionals and law students. Written by preeminent authorities, Aspen products offer analytical and practical information in a range of specialty practice areas from securities law and intellectual property to mergers and acquisitions and pension/benefits. Aspen's trusted legal education resources provide professors and students with high-quality, up-to-date and effective resources for successful instruction and study in all areas of the law.

Kluwer Law International supplies the global business community with comprehensive English-language international legal information. Legal practitioners, corporate counsel and business executives around the world rely on the Kluwer Law International journals, loose-leafs, books and electronic products for authoritative information in many areas of international legal practice.

Loislaw is a premier provider of digitized legal content to small law firm practitioners of various specializations. Loislaw provides attorneys with the ability to quickly and efficiently find the necessary legal information they need, when and where they need it, by facilitating access to primary law as well as state-specific law, records, forms and treatises.

Wolters Kluwer Law & Business, a unit of Wolters Kluwer, is headquartered in New York and Riverwoods, Illinois. Wolters Kluwer is a leading multinational publisher and information services company.

To the memory of Prof. Herman I. Orentlicher, for his commitment
to "neutral skepticism," rigorous standards, and,
above all, decency.
—D.O.

To my partner Holly and our daughter Anna, and to my parents, for their
encouragement.
—M.A.B.

To Larry C. Hall, Ph.D., for showing me the joys of an academic life.
—M.A.H.

To Bill Curran, for his guiding light.

Summary of Contents

Contents

2

■

The Treatment Relationship *91*

3

■

The Right and "Duty" to Die   **229**

4

■

Organ Transplantation: The Control, Use, and Allocation of Body Parts

6

■

Public Health Law 579

Preface

The Content and Organization of This Book

This book contains the materials from *Health Care Law and Ethics* (7th ed., 2007) that are focused on bioethics and public health law. As the larger casebook nears its half-century anniversary, we pause to reflect on the remarkable metamorphosis of health care law, from a subspecialty of tort law to a mushrooming academic and practice field whose tentacles reach into myriad scholarly disciplines and areas of substantive law. Each of the book's six prior editions reflects an important stage in this evolutionary growth. Health care law originated as a separate field of professional practice and academic inquiry during the 1960s, when the first edition of the casebook was published. Under the somewhat grandiose label of "medical jurisprudence," the primary focus at first was on medical proof in all kinds of criminal and civil litigation, on medical malpractice actions against physicians, and on public health regulation. The principal concern was how traditional bodies of legal doctrine and practice — such as criminal, tort, and evidence law — should apply in medical settings.

During the 1970s, bioethics became a major additional area of concern as a consequence of the right-to-die movement spawned by the *Quinlan* case, and the focus on individual autonomy contained in the informed consent doctrine and the landmark decision on reproductive decisionmaking in Roe v. Wade. Law courses during this and earlier periods were taught under the heading of "law and medicine."

In the 1980s economic and regulatory topics formed the third component of health care law, as exemplified by the increasing application of antitrust laws to the health care industry, and the growing body of legal disputes under Medicare and Medicaid. This newer dimension accelerated its growth into the 1990s with the spread of HMOs and other managed care organizations, which propelled various corporate and contractual restructurings. These newer topics found their way into courses described as "health law." New developments present continuing challenges to each of these areas of health care law and ethics. In the new millennium, biotechnology, consumer-driven health care, medical confidentiality, and bioterrorism are examples of emerging issues that receive increased attention in this new edition.

This path of development has resulted in an academic discipline defined more by an accretion of topics drawn from historical events than by a systematic conceptual organization of issues. Each of the four major branches — malpractice, bioethics, public health, and financing/regulation — stands apart from the others and is thought to be dominated by a distinct theme. The principal concern of malpractice law is quality of care; bioethics is concerned with individual autonomy; public health poses the rights of patients against the state; and the primary focus of financing and regulatory law is access to care and the cost of care. As a consequence, health care law has yet to become a truly integrated and cohesive discipline.[1] It is largely the creature of history and not of systematic and conceptual organization.

Our major ambition in the casebook is to remedy this state of disarray. This field has reached a stage of maturity that calls for stepping back and rethinking how all of its parts best fit together as a conceptual whole. In our view that conceptual whole is best organized according to the fundamental structural relationships that give rise to health care law. These relationships are:

1. The patient-physician relationship, which encompasses the duty to treat, confidentiality, informed consent, and malpractice
2. State oversight of doctors and patients, which encompasses the right to die, reproductive rights, physician licensure, and public health
3. The institutions that surround the treatment relationship, encompassing public and private insurance, hospitals and HMOs, and more complex transactions and organizational forms

We develop the traditional themes of quality, ethics, access, and cost throughout each of these three divisions. We also address cutting-edge and controversial topics such as AIDS, genetics, managed care, and rationing, but not as discrete topics; instead, we integrate these developments within a more permanent, overarching organizational structure that is capable of absorbing unanticipated new developments as they occur.

In deciding which topics to present in each section, and in what depth, our basic guide has been to focus on the essential attributes of the medical enterprise

---

[1] This disarray is reflected by the ongoing confusion over competing names for the field. Although "law and medicine" and "health care law" appear to signify the same topic, the first term is understood to mean older-style malpractice subject matter, and the second term is used to refer to newer economic and regulatory issues. Paradoxically, whereas "health care law" and "health law" might be thought to signify somewhat different fields — the latter not restricted to medical treatment and therefore encompassing public health issues — in fact they are taken to mean the same thing.

that make it uniquely important or difficult in the legal domain. Health care law is about the delivery of an extremely important, very expensive, and highly specialized professional service. If it were otherwise, this book would likely not exist. Some lawyers and scholars maintain that there is no unifying concept or set of ideas for health care law; rather, it is merely a disparate collection of legal doctrines and public policy responses, connected only by the happenstance that they involve doctors and hospitals in some way — much as if one were to offer a course on the law of green things or the law of Tuesdays.[2] It would be far more satisfying to find one or more organizing principles that explain not only what makes the disparate parts of health care law cohere, but also why that coherence distinguishes health care law from other bodies of integrated legal thought and professional practice.

We believe those organizing principles can, in part, be found in the phenomenology of what it is to be ill and to be a healer of illness. These two human realities are permanent and essential features that distinguish this field from all other commercial and social arenas. They permeate all parts of health care law, giving it its distinctive quality and altering how generic legal doctrine and conventional theories of government respond to its problems and issues. Health care law might still be worth studying even without these unique attributes of medical encounters, but it is much more engaging and coherent because of them. It is these attributes that give rise to an interrelated set of principles that justify classifying health care law as a coherent and integrated academic and professional discipline. For additional discussion, see The History and Future of Health Care Law: An Essentialist View, 41 Wake Forest L. Rev. 347 (2006).

Accordingly, we stress the essential attributes of medical encounters throughout these materials by incorporating insights from other academic disciplines and theoretical perspectives. Behavioral disciplines such as psychology, sociology, and anthropology help to illuminate the nature of medical knowledge and the lived experience of illness, dependency, and trust as they occur in real-life medical encounters. Findings from health services research published in the health policy literature create a stronger empirical and theoretical base for exploring health care law, one that better exposes its broad social impact. Analytical disciplines, such as economics and moral and political theory, create the foundation for understanding developments in financing, regulation, and bioethics. And the perspectives of feminist, communitarian, and critical race theory demonstrate the limitations of conventional analytical models and help us understand how health care law must evolve to accommodate viewpoints and concerns that have been excluded in the past.[3]

---

[2] For a similar claim relating to cyberlaw, see Frank H. Easterbrook, Cyberspace and the Law of the Horse, 1996 U. Chi. Legal F. 207, 207–208 (1996).

[3] For additional discussion of the overall content of health care law and approaches to teaching it, see Symposium, Rethinking Health Law, 41 Wake Forest L. Rev. 341 (2006); Symposium, The Field of Health Law: Its Past and Future, 14 Health Matrix 1 (2004); American Society of Law and Medicine Task Force on Health Law Curricula, Health Law and Professional Education, 63 U. Det. L. Rev. 245 (1985); William J. Curran, Titles in the Medicolegal Field: A Proposal for Reform, 1 Am. J.L. & Med. 1 (1975); Symposium, Teaching Health Law, 38 J. Leg. Educ. 485 (1988); Symposium, 6 J. Health Admin. Educ. 221 (1988); Clark Havighurst, American Health Care and the Law: We Need to Talk!, 19(4) Health Aff. 84 (July 2000).

In the first chapter, we have collected background and introductory readings that are relevant to a number of discussions throughout the book, as well as to several different approaches to teaching the course. These are intended for teachers and students to draw on selectively when and where they see fit.

The death of Bill Curran, the original author of the casebook, left us with a considerable burden to shoulder. Although Prof. Curran was involved in the conceptual reorganization of these materials, he was unable to contribute to their selection and editing. Still, his presence is felt in every part of these materials through the inspiration of his mentoring, his friendship, and his vast body of work.

We intend that this book will continue to serve as more than a teaching tool, and will prove useful as an ongoing resource for conducting research in health care law. To that end we provide substantial bibliographic notes in each section. Also, we have created a dedicated World Wide Web site to serve this book: www. health-law.org. It contains interesting background materials, updates of important events since publication, additional relevant topics that were excluded due to space constraints, and links to other resources on the Internet.

The following is a bibliography of resources and readings that relate to research in health care law generally. Additional bibliographic references that relate to particular parts of health care law can be found at pages 73, 230, 591.

Treatises and Texts: Barry Furrow et al., Health Law (2d ed. 2001); Mark A. Hall, Ira Mark Ellman, and Daniel S. Strouse, Health Care Law and Ethics in a Nutshell (2d ed. 1999); Michael MacDonald et al., Treatise on Health Care Law; John H. Robinson, Roberta M. Berry & Kevin McDonnell, eds., A Health Law Reader: An Interdisciplinary Approach (1999); World Health Organization, International Digest of Health Legislation.

Health Care Law Journals and Recurring Symposia: American Journal of Law and Medicine (Boston Univ.); Annals of Health Law (Loyola-Chicago); DePaul Journal of Health Care Law; Food, Drug and Cosmetic Law Journal; Health Law & Policy Abstracts and Public Health Law Abstracts (SSRN online journals); Health Matrix (Case Western Univ.); Houston Journal of Health Law & Policy; Indiana Health Law Review (Indiana Univ. Indianapolis); Journal of Contemporary Health Law and Policy (Catholic Univ.); Journal of Health & Biomedical Law (Suffolk); Journal of Health and Hospital Law (St. Louis Univ., AHLA); Journal of Health Care Law & Policy (Univ. of Maryland); Journal of Law and Health (Cleveland-Marshall); Journal of Law, Medicine and Ethics (ASLME); Journal of Legal Medicine (So. Illinois Univ.); Medical Trial Technique Quarterly; Journal of Medicine and Law; St. Louis Univ. Law Journal; Seton Hall Law Review; Quinnipiac Health Law Journal; Whittier Law Review; Yale Journal of Health Policy, Law and Ethics.

Leading Medical, Industry, and Health Policy Journals: American Journal of Public Health; American Medical News (AMA); Health Affairs (published by Project Hope); Health Care Financing and Delivery (SSRN online journal), Health Care Financing Review (DHHS); Health Economics, Policy and Law (Cambridge Press); Health Services Research; Inquiry (published by Excellus, a Blue Cross plan in Rochester, New York); Hospitals and Health Networks (AHA); Journal of the American Medical Association; Journal of Health Politics, Policy and Law; Medical Care; Milbank Memorial Fund Quarterly; Modern Healthcare; New England Journal of Medicine.

Health Law Societies, Digests, and Newsletters: ABA Forum on Health Law (newsletter); American College of Legal Medicine (Milwaukee, journal); American Society of Law, Medicine, and Ethics (Boston, two journals); BNA Health Law Reporter (D.C., weekly); American Health Lawyers Association (D.C., monthly digest and newsletter, bimonthly journal); Specialty Law Digest: Health Care Law (monthly).

Acknowledgments

This manuscript could not have been prepared without the thoughtful advice of our colleagues who commented on drafts and gave us suggestions for revision (especially Bill Brewbaker, Seth Chandler, Judy Failer, Hank Greely, David Hyman, Eleanor Kinney, Jack Nelson, Mark Pescovitz, Phil Peters, and Dan Strouse), without the diligent help of those students and staff who assisted us over the past few years (Sarah Batut, Chet Chea, Nathan Childs, Tyler Hall, Sarah Harbottle, Laura Hermer, David Higgins, Faith Long Knotts, James Martin, Michael Schrader, and Betsy Segal), and without the superhuman patience of our families (who, curiously, wish to remain anonymous). Finally, we thank the authors and publishers who granted permission to use each of the excerpts of copyrighted material in these readings.

David Orentlicher
Mary Anne Bobinski
Mark A. Hall

January 2008

BIOETHICS AND PUBLIC HEALTH LAW

1

Introduction

The following two overview cases and the accompanying notes are intended to introduce issues and themes that are pursued in different parts of this book. You are not expected to retain their analyses and holdings at this point; you only need to get a sense of the range of topics that are covered in different courses that might be taught from this book.

The readings that follow these cases introduce background information and overarching perspectives that are important for understanding the legal issues developed throughout this book. Although lifted out of their respective contexts, we present them at the outset because they raise cross-cutting themes that cannot be cabined within a single chapter. Therefore, it will be necessary to revisit these readings from time to time throughout the course.

A. OVERVIEW CASES

IN RE BABY K
16 F.3d 590 (4th Cir. 1994)

[Read the excerpt at page 338.]

Notes: Rationing, Justice, and the Doctor-Patient Relationship

1. *Introduction to Complexity.* How many different issues can you identify in the *Baby K* case? There are many problems raised by the case, most of which are not overtly addressed in the opinion. The complexity of health care issues is one of the major themes of this book. A wide range of philosophical debates and legal rules can be implicated by the facts (and frailties) of human biology. This creates a variety of lenses through which to view any case.

One method of studying the health care system is purely *descriptive*, looking at how health care providers and patients *actually* interact. How does the legal system respond to the problems created by biological frailty and the development of medical knowledge? Another focus is normative: How *should* providers and patients interact, and how *should* the legal system regulate health care relationships?

Under either the descriptive or the normative approach, health care interactions implicate one or more of four different sets of legal or ethical analysis. (1) We can look at the doctor-patient relationship in terms of legal duties and liabilities, focusing on whether the health care provider met her professional obligations to her patient under malpractice or fiduciary law. (2) We can also consider broader philosophical issues such as what is the proper realm of patient autonomy, and what is a provider's *moral* duty to act for the benefit of the patient ("beneficence"). (3) A medical case can also implicate broader societal issues, such as whether third-parties or the state in general has a stake in the treatment decision. This focus falls in the realm known as public health law, and implicates constitutional issues. (4) Finally, the medical encounter can be viewed through an organizational or economic lens, which focuses on who pays for the treatment and what institutional constraints are created by the setting in which treatment is provided. Can you identify how each of these four perspectives might be pertinent to *Baby K*?

Despite the variety of issues encountered in this book and the diversity of perspectives, there is a fundamental coherence to health care law. It lies in the fundamental nature of illness and the healing encounter. To use a common metaphor, imagine we are in a dark room with a mysterious object. We can use all of our other senses to determine the nature of the object: smell, taste, touch, etc. Although each person's sensory experiences might be very different, the fundamental nature of the object remains the same.

2. *What Really Happened in* Baby K? Baby K, whose name was Stephanie Keene, ultimately lived for two and a half years in a pediatric nursing facility. She died in the emergency room of Fairfax Hospital in Fairfax, Virginia—the same hospital in the *Baby K* case—after being taken there by ambulance for the sixth time. Her anencephaly had been diagnosed by ultrasound during the sixteenth week of her gestation, and her mother, Contrenia Harrell, decided to carry her to term, believing (according to press accounts) that "'all life is precious'" and that God would guide Stephanie's life. Other local hospitals reportedly refused to accept a transfer of Baby K shortly after her birth.

Baby K's medical bills ultimately reached almost $1 million. They were covered in part by her mother's insurance with an HMO and in part by Medicaid. These financing systems are described in sections C.1 and C.3. They often do not pay the full costs of treatment. Nevertheless, hospital officials stated that the costs of Baby K's care were not a factor in the hospital's lawsuit. Even so, the hospital may have been thinking about the implications of the case for future patients, and the cost of caring for patients like Baby K are likely to be an issue for other hospitals as health insurers increasingly employ capitation rates for reimbursement, and as Medicare and Medicaid continue to limit their reimbursement rates.

The readings in section C.2 discuss the growing crisis over health care spending, and section D.2 discusses the importance of having an accurate understanding of how these cases arise in the real world. Do any of these additional facts and speculations alter your instincts about who should make the treatment decision for a patient like Baby K? Do you think the insurers should have a stake in the decision? Would it be reasonable to tell Baby K's mother she can insist on treatment but not on payment, thereby remaining liable for the bills? If she still insisted on treatment, but the hospital knew she could never pay, should it still have to treat?

3. *A Medical Miracle?* Some might scoff at Ms. Harrell's reported belief in a medical miracle, but one may in fact have occurred here. As the court noted, anencephalic children generally do not live very long; fewer than 10 percent of such children survive more than a week. Baby K may be the longest lived child with anencephaly. Rather than a miracle, however, her length of life may indicate that the general lack of aggressive treatment for anencephalic children results in their actual lifespans being considerably shorter than their potential lifespans. The readings in section B.3 give more insight into why patients look to physicians for miracles, and how doctors decide what care is most beneficial.

4. *Unusual or Typical?* The *Baby K* case involves a fact situation that is the converse of the typical court case involving life-sustaining treatment. Such cases usually involve physicians who insist on treatment over the objections of the patient or the patient's family. That is what happened in 1976 in the case of Karen Quinlan, the first "right-to-die" case, and in 1990 in the case of Nancy Cruzan, the first "right-to-die" case before the U.S. Supreme Court. (Both of these cases are discussed in Chapter 5.) Yet, the *Baby K* situation may become more typical as the result of greater pressures on physicians to limit medical costs. The care of dying patients is an obvious place to look for cost savings. Does this suggestion contravene our deeply-treasured value of individual autonomy? Does this value hold the same force when society's resources are at stake? If care were terminated for Baby K, would the result be to force sacrifices by society's most vulnerable to benefit the comfortable or well-to-do? These perspectives are developed further in section D.3.

5. *The Court's Decision.* Do you agree with the majority's or the dissent's analysis of EMTALA? Note that, as the majority opinion indicates, EMTALA was passed in response to hospitals' refusing to provide care to patients who had neither insurance nor personal resources with which to pay for emergency care. Despite this legislative history, EMTALA has been interpreted to preclude refusals of emergency care on grounds other than the patient's inability to pay. Do you think Congress intended for EMTALA to require treatment of anencephalic children with ventilators? If Ms. Keene also had a cardiac defect that required open heart surgery to repair, and she were brought to the emergency room because of distress related to the heart condition, do you think the court would have required the hospital to perform the surgery? If not, then how can the court require the hospital to provide a ventilator for anencephalic children? Compare Bryan v. Rectors and Visitors of the University of Virginia, 95 F.3d 349 (4th Cir. 1996) (rejecting an EMTALA claim against hospital

after physicians withheld resuscitative treatment from a hopelessly ill patient who suffered a heart attack and died).

Concerns about principle go both ways in this case. It is accepted practice to give anencephalic infants artificial nutrition and hydration through feeding tubes, as was done for Baby K. Is there any principled or practical distinction that justifies giving artificial feeding but refusing artificial breathing? If you can see such a distinction, should it be the sole province of physicians to apply, or is it a distinction that only patients and family can draw? See Chapter 2 for further discussion of this and other aspects of EMTALA and of patients' rights to decide.

As n.2 of the *Baby K* opinion indicates, the lower court found that withholding a ventilator would also violate the Rehabilitation Act of 1973 and the Americans with Disabilities Act of 1990. Both of these Acts prohibit discrimination against persons on account of their disabilities. As the court suggested, one could argue that Baby K was being denied treatment of her respiratory problems on account of her having the disability of anencephaly. Is this an appropriate way to characterize what was going on in the *Baby K* case? Why do you think the appellate court preferred to decide this case on the basis of an unlawful denial of emergency care rather than on the basis of unlawful disability discrimination?

6. *The Hospital's and the Physicians' Decision.* Inasmuch as the costs of Ms. Keene's care were fully reimbursed by the insurers, why do you suppose the hospital and the physicians were unwilling to provide emergency ventilatory treatment to Ms. Keene? After all, the treatment was life-sustaining, and it was clearly desired by Ms. Keene's mother. Do you think it was appropriate for the physicians to try to override the wishes of Ms. Keene's mother?

7. *Rationing Decisions.* This case is very much about the role of the courts in rationing health care. Was the majority correct to take a "hands off" attitude about the social policy implications of its decision? The precedent it set clearly makes it more difficult for health care providers to withhold care on the grounds that the care is not worth its cost. Are courts well situated to making decisions of this type? Are they better situated than legislatures? The need to ration medical resources is one of the themes that run throughout this book. As introduced in section D.4, rationing entails two broad sets of inquiries: What substantive criteria should determine what type of care is provided or withheld? What procedural mechanisms should be used to make these decisions?

■ **IN RE A.C.**
573 A.2d 1235 (D.C. App. 1990)(en banc)

[Read the excerpt at page 480.]

Notes: The Patient vs. the State

1. *Duties to Third Parties.* Although it was A.C. who sought treatment, her providers obviously were concerned about the effects of her decisions on her fetus. Was the fetus a patient of theirs as well, or did it have the legal status of any other

"third party" who might be affected? What duties should physicians owe to third parties to protect them from infection or to warn them of dangers their patients might pose? Note that, often times, as in *A.C.*, it is not possible to protect third parties without infringing duties to the patient. Here, the providers breached both their duty of confidentiality, by going to the courts, and their duty to honor their patient's treatment requests. Obviously, these were extraordinary circumstances, but they give us occasion to consider what other situations justify a similar sacrifice of a patient's interest to pursue a broader social good.

2. *Consent to Treatment.* Physicians must typically obtain the consent of their patients before performing surgery, even beneficial surgery. This aspect of the interaction between A.C. and her providers is a key factor in the court's analysis. What does it mean to determine whether a patient has "consented" to treatment? The trial court initially found that it was not clear whether A.C. had decided "whether the baby should live or die." Wouldn't it be possible to want the baby to live without wanting to undergo invasive surgery that would hasten one's own death? A.C. expressed her views again after learning of the initial court order permitting the cesarean section. Her health care providers disagreed about whether she had reached a truly competent and informed decision. The court again ordered the operation. The appellate court suggests that the trial court failed to conduct an appropriate analysis of the consent issue. What should the trial court have done?

3. *The Role of the "State."* The hospital argued that judicial intervention was necessary to protect the interests of the viable fetus, even if this would diminish A.C.'s life expectancy. In a sense, the hospital was attempting to assert the interests of the state in the protection of life. Thus, this case implicates the struggle between an individual's right to guide her own health care and the state's right to limit individual liberty to protect the public health. Note that the court's rejection of state intervention is not absolute. The court suggests that the state's interest in the protection of life will only "rarely" justify forced medical treatment. You know, for instance, that there is a right to refuse life-sustaining treatment. But there are also several prominent examples of the rare exception. One that springs to mind is mandatory vaccination. Another, more threatening, example relates to state concern over whether pregnant women are endangering the health of their fetuses. Consider also mandatory autopsies, and various options for retrieving organs for transplant.

The conflict between individual liberty and public health lurks in the background of many other health care interactions. Rather than forcing treatment, the state can limit treatment options. For instance, it has attempted to ban abortions, and it regulates which pharmaceutical drugs can be used. Also, the state requires licensing of physicians who intend to practice medicine. Should there be a constitutional right to receive treatment from alternative healers who do not qualify for a medical license?

The ethical dimension of these debates is usually framed in terms of protecting individual autonomy. Because the theme of autonomy is so central to much of this book, it is given special attention in section D.2. The readings collected there question whether individual autonomy is always the correct analytical model, considering the embedded dependence of patients on their families, physicians, and society. These readings also question how capable and willing patients actually are to act as autonomous agents when they are desperately ill. Consider how these readings would apply to someone like A.C.

When the state exercises coercive authority to protect public health, there is a risk that those it chooses to burden are less socially and politically empowered than those it chooses to protect. Do the facts in *A.C.* justify this kind of radical critique? See the readings in section D.3.

B. THE NATURE OF MEDICAL PRACTICE

The remainder of this chapter contains introductory and background materials that relate broadly to several or all portions of the book. The readings are diverse and introduce a wide range of challenging ideas and important information. You should read through the assigned parts at the outset, and then come back to individual excerpts as they become relevant to the discussion of particular legal topics in your course.

We begin with a description of the human condition of illness and the professional practice of medicine, since these are what distinguish health care law from other fields of legal study. It is essential throughout this book to have some appreciation of the impact that illness has on how people function, the intricacies of medical decisionmaking, and how doctors and patients interact. To focus your thoughts on these issues, reflect on your own experiences with medical care, and consider the following list of popular "misconceptions" (developed by Alain Enthoven). What observations and evidence emerge from these readings to rebut or qualify each of these commonly held notions?

1. The doctor should be able to know what conditions the patient has, to answer the patient's questions precisely, and to prescribe the right treatment. If the doctor isn't, that is incompetence or even malpractice.
2. For each medical condition, there is a "best" treatment. It is up to the doctor to know about that treatment and to use it. Anything else is unnecessary surgery, waste, fraud, or underservice.
3. Medicine is an exact science. Unlike 50 or 100 years ago, there is now a firm scientific base for what the doctor does. Standard treatments are supported by scientific proof of efficiency.
4. Medical care consists of standard products that can be described precisely and measured meaningfully in standard units such as "inpatient days," "outpatient visits," or "doctor office visits."
5. Much of medical care is a matter of life and death or serious pain or disability.
6. More medical care is better than less care.
7. People have no control over the timing of their need for medical care. Whatever care is needed is needed right away.

1. Doctors and Hospitals

■ HEALTH CARE PAST AND PRESENT
Robert Rhodes
Health Care Politics, Policy, and Distributive Justice: The Ironic Triumph (1992)*

Death before the nineteenth century was an ever-looming presence in our ancestors' thoughts and a frequent visitor to their families. They feared it and had little control over it. Sudden death was as central to attitudes prior to the twentieth century as the cemetery was to every village and town. . . .

Resignation and fatalism toward natural occurrences characterize preindustrial societies, just as a sense of self-direction and control characterize modern society. . . . Modern societies have faith that they can control the future. A futurist orientation allows for savings, capital formation, long periods of education, and life-styles that deny instant gratification for future health. Preindustrial conditions do not reward such faith. . . . Uncontrollable natural or supernatural forces took away life, and one needed to reconcile one's fate to the four horsemen of the apocalypse: disease, famine, pestilence, and drought.

The twentieth century represents perhaps the clearest triumph of science over fatalism. . . . The modern hospital, the professionalism of physicians and nurses, and effective pharmaceuticals, have dramatically altered mortality rates and improved the quality of life in postindustrial states.

For those entering a hospital prior to 1900, the probability of treatment helping, rather than harming, would be less than fifty-fifty, and the odds would be considerably poorer prior to 1870. Today, we identify hospitals as technologic citadels of sophisticated medical practice. But their preindustrial origins were as religious and charitable institutions for the hopelessly sick and poor. They were places to comfort the indigent dying.

For the first three quarters of the nineteenth century, medical personnel were not in charge of hospitals. . . . In the main, hospitals at that time were places for the homeless poor and insane to die. The affluent classes were treated at home. For a variety of reasons, however, hospitals became central to medical practice and education between 1870 and 1910.[6] . . .

[T]he development of the medical profession parallels particular developments of the hospital. This is especially true of surgery, which enjoyed a dramatic increase of prestige and precision during this time. Technological advances played a major role in changing surgery. Before painkilling drugs, surgical methods in the first half of the nineteenth century depended upon powerful and swift physicians whose craft and tools were closer to the corner butcher. Mortality rates of about 40 percent followed amputation.

Three developments altered the brutality and mortality rates and allowed abdominal surgery, which was rarely performed prior to 1890. Dentist William Morton's demonstration of ether at Massachusetts General Hospital in 1846 ushered in a means of eliminating pain and allowed more careful and delicate

---

[6] Paul Starr, The Social Transformation of American Medicine 151 (1982).

surgery. Joseph Lister's discovery of antisepsis in 1867 gradually led to new procedures during surgery to prevent infection. However, antisepsis was poorly understood. Lister's technique was based on the use of carbolic acid spray, but his methods were adopted only over a long period of time. Fatal infections continued even after using the spray because antiseptic procedures were not followed carefully until after 1880. Soon, sterile procedures were properly followed and surgery rapidly expanded. Finally, the development of the X-ray in 1895, along with other diagnostic tools, opened the way for abdominal surgery for appendicitis, gallbladder, and stomach ulcers. Thoracic surgery and surgery of the nervous and cardiovascular systems developed in the early 1900s.

TRIUMPH AND TRAGEDY

By 1950, the cliché a "medical miracle" had rich meaning. Infant mortality rates in the United States were fewer than 15 per 100,000 births, down from 300 or so per 100,000 at the turn of the century. Pneumonia, once whispered by medical staff who witnessed the suffering of the dying to be the "old man's relief," now was easily controlled with penicillin. Infectious diseases in particular dramatically declined in the first half of the twentieth century. Improvement in health was a triumph of modernity, and part of that triumph was a consequence of modern medicine. There is, however, much debate about the weight of medicine's contribution, compared to other modern factors. . . .

Our dramatic advances in health are also related to improved nutrition, lifestyle, and education, as well as to medical advancements. The literature of health care points, in particular, to . . . proper diet, minimal tension, absence of smoking or heavy drinking, daily exercise, and a life-style that provides low-risk factors for accidents. Advances in health and longevity are more closely tied to higher income, better diets, and especially greater education than to advances in medicine. . . .

Yet, American perception of well-being is closely identified with medicine. Paradoxically, much of the public's present disenchantment with medicine is the consequence of this identification. Modern medicine has advanced to the frontiers of preserving life, but only by increasingly more expensive therapies and diagnoses to preserve life "on its margins." That is, additional expenditures and efforts to treat disease produce diminishing results in proportion to the effort. We are just beginning to learn that our scientific capacity to triumph over illness, physical anomalies, and death, on many occasions with medical miracles, brings with it a special brand of tragedy.

We have become totally modern. No more can we explain death and suffering as a consequence of fate. It is our medicine, or lack of it, that denies death and suffering. We know we must choose who receives scarce resources and who does not. No longer can we attribute to fate or to God the responsibility for making life-and-death decisions. Yet, these life-and-death decisions involve very expensive procedures and technologies and often contribute only marginally to extending life. Examples are well known and regularly make front-page newspaper drama: organ transplants, aggressive treatment of terminal patients, neonates under 750 grams, or long-term comatose patients.

These new choices challenge our basic values and frequently produce conflict. . . . Conflict is father to politics and law, and politics determines who gets what, when, and how. Conflict also forces moral reassessment of traditional attitudes and postures, including the justice question: "Who *should* get what, when and how."

How do we distribute health care? How should we? How does political power within the present economic system determine the distribution of health care? These questions obviously spill over the boundaries of economics, politics, sociology, law, medicine, history, and philosophy. In particular, looming over the politics of health care is a sense of the tragic, as well as the majestic. Tragedy points to human endeavors that are virtuous and honorable, yet carry the seeds of their own downfall. Our efforts to lessen the suffering and lengthen the lives of Americans through accessible, affordable, quality health care represent the best of our traditions and have been, on balance, an American success story. Sometimes we fall short in that effort because some group is unreasonably left behind in the political shuffle. The [45] million Americans who [have] no health coverage represent[] such a group. At other times, our very success leads to exasperating dilemmas of bioethics and distributive justice that would cross the eyes of a Solomon. Our dilemma over public financing for costly organ transplants at the expense of other badly needed programs or continued aggressive treatment of comatose or terminally ill loved ones are poignant, modern examples. It is here where triumph merges with tragedy.

■ DOCTORS, PATIENTS, AND HEALTH INSURANCE: THE ORGANIZATION AND FINANCING OF MEDICAL CARE
Herman Miles Somers & Anne Ramsay Somers
1961

. . . The popular conception of the doctor-patient relationship is a mixture of fact and fancy. Until World War II the general practitioner family doctor was still in the majority. The one-to-one relationship of a personally chosen physician — where economic and other factors permitted any choice — with his patient was the most common form of medical practice. In big cities the doctor had an office, usually mahogany and leather, sparsely equipped with simple diagnostic aids, a few surgical tools, and some antiseptic drugs. But, especially in rural areas and suburbs, he was more often found in the homes of his patients doing his rounds, working at the bedside of the sick and injured. His black bag held almost all his equipment. His records were kept partly in a small notebook, mostly in his mind and heart. He appeared indefatigable, compassionate, and available wherever and whenever needed. . . .

This doctor of the past has been idealized in story, picture, and legend. . . . Despite its apparent anachronisms, the picture still appeals to people's sentiments — even to those fully aware of its use as a public relations device. It has the warmth and intimate concern that no hypodermic needle — no complex of steel and tubing — can replace, however effective they may be. Although medical miracles are now performed successfully between strangers, doctors and patients both believe that the absence of continuity, personal concern, and individual attention are detrimental to the best medical care. This is not without foundation.

The origin of the "traditional" doctor-patient relationship reaches deep into the past. From the beginning of medical history, the practicing physician has been part priest, part technician, part personal or family counselor. In early days, when medicine had very little in the way of scientific knowledge to rely on, it was inevitable that the subjective priestly element should be dominant. . . .

In modern times medicine has become more scientific. But the traditional reliance on mystical forces and a highly authoritarian doctor-patient relationship persists to a degree unknown in other contemporary human relations. . . . The relationship of citizen and state, of employer and employee, of teacher and pupil, parent and child, even of husband and wife, have undergone profound and acknowledged changes as a result of the technological and socio-economic trends of the past few centuries. But there is no general acknowledgment or acceptance of the significant change that has, in fact, been taking place in the doctor-patient relationship. Of the manifold and complex reasons, only a few of the more important can be noted here.

First and basic is the persistence — in spite of scientific progress — of large elements of uncertainty and fear regarding illness and medical care which are conducive to continued reliance on hope, faith, confidence and other subjective factors on the part of both doctor and patient. "Honor thy physician because of the need thou hast of him." So said apocryphal Ecclesiastes to the Hebrews thousands of years ago. And still, today, patients yearn to have confidence in their doctors, to idealize them, to endow them with superhuman powers. Talcott Parsons, the Harvard sociologist, reconciles the use of such subjective factors — the use of "modern magic" — with the scientific basis of modern medicine by calling it a "functional bias."

> The basic function of magic is to bolster the self-confidence of actors in situations where energy and skill *do* make a difference but where, because of uncertainty factors, outcomes cannot be guaranteed. This fits the situation of the doctor, but in addition on the side of the patient it may be argued the *belief* in the possibility of recovery is an important factor in it. If from purely a technical point of view both the individual doctor and the general tradition are optimistically biased it ought to help. . . . Of course this argument must not be pressed too far.

As the boundaries of medical ignorance and uncertainty are pushed back, one would expect this resort to supra-scientific factors to decline, and, indeed, it has in the case of bacterial and other diseases where the cause and cure are clearly established. But the reduced role of subjective factors in the treatment of specific cases has been more than offset by an increasing interest in the role of the emotions in illness. A widespread increase in psychotherapy and psychosomatic medicine has renewed the emphasis on a personal doctor and a personal doctor-patient relationship of a type that permits knowledge of the "whole [person]." . . .

Moreover it is now widely believed that illness, *per se*, tends to create — even in the most intellectual of patients — an attitude of dependence, of "regression" to helplessness, and perhaps to childlike behavior. . . . In this state, confidence in the authority and benevolence of the doctor, as well as in his scientific knowledge and technical skill — the now-familiar "father-image" — is generally desired and often desirable.

Finally, there is the impenetrable mystery of death. The physician's relation to this event — however helpless he in fact may be — has endowed him, in the eyes of centuries of patients, with an aura of the mystery. To the extent that the physician identifies himself with this priestly role and takes on himself the burden associated therewith, or at least appears to do so through the gravity of his personal demeanor and behavior, his supra-scientific role continues to be respected and perpetuated, reinforcing in the eyes of individual patients and society at large his status as a dispenser of increasingly scientific medicine.

■ COMPETING SOLUTIONS: AMERICAN HEALTH CARE PROPOSALS AND INTERNATIONAL EXPERIENCE
Joseph White
1995

America's systems for delivering and paying for medical care are notably more complex than those of most other countries. Many doctors work in more than one hospital, making governance of medical staffs difficult; specialists are harder to coordinate because there are more of them; and the proliferation of forms of managed care means rapid change in patterns of gatekeeping and referral.

PHYSICIANS

American doctors go through extensive training to work long hours for high pay. The typical medical school program requires, after four years of college, four more years of "undergraduate" medical education. During the final two years, students receive some clinical training. Virtually all graduates then must complete some graduate medical education in order to be licensed to practice medicine. This education is obtained in residency programs, mainly in hospitals affiliated with medical schools. Normally only one year of residency (as an intern) is needed for licensure, but up to eight years (for neurosurgeons) may be required for certification as a specialist.

. . . Given the length of their training and the size of their debts, it is understandable that most physicians feel entitled to incomes that are much higher than those of most other Americans. . . . [The median physician salary is about $200,000, roughly five times that of the average American worker. The range across specialties is broad. Pediatricians and general practitioners typically earn around $150,000, common medical specialists (cardiology, dermatology, anesthesiology) are in the $225,000-$300,000 range, while heart surgeons and brain surgeons can earn well over $500,000. Some doctors earn substantially more from entrepreneurial activities such as medical patents and investments in various health care organizations.]

An unusually high proportion of American doctors are trained to specialize. Fewer than 10 percent of American doctors [call] themselves general practitioners (GPs), the standard term for primary care physicians. But because a specialist such as a family practitioner, internist, pediatrician, or obstetrician-gynecologist may be a person's regular physician, between 33 and 40 percent of physicians (depending on who is counting) are mainly primary care providers. [Specialists who receive several years of extra training and pass additional exams are designated as "Board Certified," meaning that they comply with voluntary, private standards set by the American Specialty Boards, which operate under the auspices of the AMA. At one time, board certification was relatively rare, but now the vast majority of new doctors obtain certification. About two dozen boards now exist, covering not only standard specialties but also areas of general practice such as family medicine and internal medicine.] . . .

Two-thirds of physicians practice in offices, the vast majority with admitting privileges to a hospital. Many practice in more [than one hospital] (for example, a nice suburban hospital for simple cases, and a high-tech academic medical center for difficult ones). Hospitals therefore must compete for admissions by making those physicians happy, such as by having the fanciest equipment. . . .

INSTITUTIONAL CARE

Long-term or chronic care, especially for the aged, is a complicated system on its own, and the potential expenses of long-term care are so great that it is highly unlikely that any reform will do much about it. [Therefore, the focus here is] on the costs of the current American health care system, of which one major component is hospital services for acute care.

The American supply of hospitals is dominated by private nonprofit hospitals — many owned by religious organizations. [About two-thirds] of hospital beds [are] provided by the nonprofits, 10 percent by the for-profit sector. The rest, just over a quarter of the beds, [are] in federal, state, or local facilities. It is hard to identify much difference between the behavior and efficiency of the for-profit and private nonprofits. If private institutions are more efficient, the savings go largely or entirely to investors.

Americans spend a great deal of money on hospitals: [about 40 percent] of all spending on patient care. But . . . the hospital is not as dominant a provider as it once was or still is in other countries. Hospitals and doctors tried to avoid regulation by moving care to ostensibly freestanding ambulatory care facilities. Examples include kidney dialysis units, and radiology group practices with close relations with hospitals. Some payers encouraged the shift, believing those facilities would be cheaper. . . .

Back in the traditional hospitals, the nature of care depends greatly on hospitals' relationships with doctors and medical schools, and on hospitals' catchment areas — the areas from which they get most of their patients. . . .

A suburban hospital can generally provide sophisticated care, such as cardiac bypass surgery, but it is not as likely to have clinical professors who are able to provide extremely specialized care for "interesting" cases. All hospitals want the most advanced equipment, but the academic medical centers must have it for research and training. These centers rely heavily on residents and interns for delivery of care and, most important, are likely to have a much lower-class population of patients.

Many of the [academic medical centers] are in inner cities. They are likely to have large outpatient departments to train the students (residents) and serve the local population, which feeds into the inpatient wards; the emergency room not only gets emergencies but also serves as an outpatient clinic for some for the population. All of this is the good news: If a major teaching hospital is in the inner city, then either a large and endowed institution or a state government pays for some care for the inner-city poor.

When local hospitals receive little funding for education, poor populations must frequently rely on a hospital financed by a strapped city or county budget. Such hospitals — for example, Cook County in Chicago, Boston City, and Charity in New Orleans — have interns and residents to do the work because of their relationship with a training program, but nowhere near the resources of a freestanding university hospital. All hospitals in the inner city try to convince Medicare that they deserve an extra subsidy for treating a poorer, less-insured, and often sicker population. The federal government calls these disproportionate share payments. One of the huge issues for American health care reform is what will happen to the academic medical centers and the remaining urban public hospitals if payment systems allow competing insurers to favor hospitals that are less expensive because they have lesser teaching and subsidy burdens.

Another major issue is how a bias toward specialized, high-technology medicine, created in part by how medical education is financed and how physicians are paid, is reinforced by arrangements for capital investment in American medicine. There are hardly any measures in place to prevent a "medical arms race" among hospitals that seek the most advanced technology in order to attract physicians and generate revenue. . . .

Because for years insurers would pay whatever physicians and hospitals billed, and hospitals relied on physicians to provide patients, hospitals competed for patients by having the best equipment, and insurers ended up paying for excess treatments and higher charges per treatment. At one time also physicians could refer patients to any specialist they wished, and patients could go directly to a specialist without referral.

The rise of managed care and of more aggressive bargaining by insurers has begun to change this basic pattern. Insurers have become more likely to refuse to approve a given service or to insist on a lower price. Hospitals still need to attract physicians by offering the best equipment, however, so they are caught between the demands of doctors and payers. Meanwhile insurers are limiting choice of and access to specialists by building closed panels, in which a person covered by a plan either cannot use or must pay a surcharge to use any provider who is not on special contract to the plan. A patient might find that her doctor of 20 years' standing is no longer part of her insurance plan; a physician might find that many of his patients can afford referral only to three nephrologists whom he does not know. One of the key issues in reform is whether these new restrictions on choice of physician are necessary.

▮ DOCTORS, PATIENTS, AND HEALTH INSURANCE: THE ORGANIZATION AND FINANCING OF MEDICAL CARE
Herman Miles Somers & Anne Ramsay Somers
1961

[T]he conflict between [hospital] medical staff and [hospital] management has become both sharper and more open in recent years. The roots of this conflict—the basic dichotomy in hospital organization—go back to eighteenth century Britain and the establishment of the Anglo-American tradition of voluntary hospitals. There was no such dichotomy in medieval days when hospitals were operated, with little medical assistance, by monastic orders for the sick poor. There is generally no such duality in the major Continental hospitals which are usually run, with unquestioned authority, by full-time chiefs of medical services. The distinguishing feature of the Anglo-American voluntary hospital, however, has been its use by private physicians for private patients with little or no accompanying administrative or financial responsibility. . . .

Recent developments—the hospital's changing role, its increase in size, complexity, utilization, cost, and its greatly altered financial base—have intensified the inherent instability of this administrative structure. . . . Lay influences on hospital administration and policy are clearly increasing. Ultimate policy responsibility has always rested with lay trustees. Traditionally, they limited their oversight to balancing the books. With the tremendous increase in hospital costs, however, this single concern has led to increasing surveillance over the hospital's total functioning, including the organization of the medical staff. The hospital administrator, traditionally an untrained individual content to play a fairly subservient role and socially outranked by doctor and trustee alike, is being transformed into a professional with increasing self-confidence and authority. . . .

At the same time the hospital has become an indispensable workshop for the modern physician, who finds it virtually impossible to practice good medicine without hospital affiliation. The hospital is the center of his professional world, and he is acknowledged to be its key figure. Fully 40 percent of private physician income is now earned in the hospital. Naturally he wants "his" institution equipped with the latest scientific and technological facilities. But the doctor's relationship to the hospital is peculiarly ambiguous. As a rule he assumes neither administrative nor financial responsibility. Yet, in practice, his is the most powerful voice in the organization. He alone admits and discharges patients; he alone can diagnose, prescribe, and treat patients—still the chief purpose for which the hospital exists. With his high professional status, he may, in most hospitals, countermand administrative orders and defy lay authority with relative impunity. The result is the confusing duality that prevails today throughout the hospital system, public and private. . . .

It is sometimes proposed that hiring the medical staff on a salary or contract basis would increase the doctors' sense of responsibility for hospital administration and help clarify lines of accountability. It could integrate the administrative structure without restricting professional integrity. This is the general pattern in a few of the nation's best hospitals, such as the Henry Ford in Detroit and the Cleveland Clinic Hospital. Most of the profession is, however, vigorously opposed to such practice, alleging "hospital domination," "lay control," or the "corporate practice of medicine." Some hospitals have taken a middle road — employing full-time medical directors (this is frequently the practice in government hospitals) and in a few instances, full-time chiefs of medical services. This too is generally frowned on by physicians in private practice. . . .

Many hospital spokesmen, however, content themselves with pleading for physician cooperation in assuring some responsibility for hospital operations and costs. . . . But such recommendations are usually set in a purely hortatory context. It is not clear how such preachments are to influence the individual doctor. The "medical staff" of which he is a member is in most instances simply a term for the collectivity of physicians authorized to practice in a particular hospital. The staff can be as disciplinary an instrument as it chooses to be, but in most places it has chosen minimal responsibility. . . . By and large the staff still prefers not to interfere with the practices of the individual physician.

■CLINICAL DECISION MAKING FROM THEORY TO PRACTICE
David M. Eddy
1996

Medical practice is in the middle of a profound transition. Most physicians can remember the day when, armed with a degree, a mission, and confidence, they could set forth to heal the sick. Like Solomon, physicians could receive patients, hear their complaints, and determine the best course of action. While not every patient could be cured, everyone could be confident that whatever was done was the best possible. Most important, each physician was free, trusted, and left alone to determine what was in the best interest of each patient.

All of that is changing. . . . Now physicians must deal with second opinions, precertification, skeptical medical directors, variable coverage, outright denials, utilization review, threats of cookbook medicine, and letters out of the blue chiding that Mrs. Smith is on two incompatible drugs. Solomon did not have to call anyone to get permission for his decisions. What is going on?

What is going on is that one of the basic assumptions underlying the practice of medicine is being challenged. This assumption is not just a theory about cholesterol, antiarrhythmia, or estrogens. This assumption concerns the intellectual foundation of medical care. Simply put, the assumption is that whatever a physician decides is, by definition, correct. The challenge says that while many decisions no doubt *are* correct, many are not, and elaborate mechanisms are needed to determine which are which. Physicians are slowly being stripped of their decisionmaking power.

Notes: Doctors and Hospitals

1. *History and Description.* For general histories and descriptions of the health care delivery system, see David Smith & Arnold Kaluzny, The White Labyrinth: A

Guide to the Health Care System (2d ed. 1986); Harry A. Sultz & Kristina M. Young, Health Care USA: Understanding Its Organization and Delivery (2d ed. 1999). For more extensive historical accounts of the transformation of hospitals and their role in modern medicine, see Guenter B. Risse, Mending Bodies, Saving Souls: A History of Hospitals (1999); Charles Rosenberg, The Care of Strangers (1987); David Rosner, A Once Charitable Enterprise (1982); Rosemary Stevens, In Sickness and in Wealth: American Hospitals in the Twentieth Century (1989).

2. *The Two-Headed Monster.* The unique structure of American hospitals, in which doctors are independent but essential to their financial well-being, has been described as "attractive as a two-headed monster" and as "stable as a three-legged stool." See H. L. Smith, Two Lines of Authority are One Too Many, 84 Modern Hosp. 59 (March 1955). This division of authority is mirrored throughout the organizational structure of the health-care system. For instance, hospitals, unlike any other business organization, are required by state licensure laws and private accreditation standards to have *two* sets of corporate bylaws, one for the hospital administration and a second for the medical staff. Similarly, health insurance traditionally pays hospitals separately from doctors, as reflected in the distinctions between Blue Cross (hospital insurance) and Blue Shield (physician insurance) and between Medicare Part A and Part B.

3. *Power Relationships in Medicine.* Medical sociologists and organizational theorists have produced a rich literature discussing the role of physicians within medical institutions. Leading examples are Eliot Freidson, Doctoring Together (1975); Eliot Freidson, Profession of Medicine (1970); Paul Starr, The Social Transformation of American Medicine (1982); Jeffrey Harris, The Internal Organization of Hospitals: Some Economic Implications, 8 Bell J. Econ. 467 (1977). For an exploration of how these insights illuminate a variety of legal doctrines and public policy debates, see Mark A. Hall, Institutional Control of Physician Behavior: Legal Barriers to Health Care Cost Containment, 137 U. Pa. L. Rev. 431 (1988) ("Because the law absorbs and reflects the values and relationships of traditional medicine, it has codified the ethic of professional dominance, effectively shielding physicians from the institutional influence contemplated by revolutionary changes in health care policy."); Sara Rosenbaum, The Impact of United States Law on Medicine as a Profession, 289 JAMA 1546 (2003).

2. The Culture of Medicine

■ MAGIC OR MEDICINE? AN INVESTIGATION OF HEALING AND HEALERS*
Robert Buckman & Karl Sabbagh
1995

Despite the enormous variety of their forms and formats and their lack of any apparent common ingredient, every interaction between a patient and a

---

healer shares a common structure. In each consultation, (1) the patient comes to the healer with an idea that something is wrong. (2) The healer then tries to find out what the cause of the problem is and (3) makes some intervention—a drug, a spell, a recommendation or something else. After the consultation, (4) the patient (or society on the patient's behalf) rewards the healer for his or her time and trouble. Finally, (5) there is some measure of the outcome of the consultation, something that wouldn't have happened if the consultation hadn't taken place. This might be a measurable improvement (or deterioration) in some physical parameter of the illness or a subjective sense of feeling better (or worse).

And that is all there is to it. In all its guises, in all cultures and in all languages, those are the basic steps in what appears to be a complex and varied first dance between patient and healer which forms the basis of the relationship between them. As a means of analyzing the patient-doctor/healer relationship in greater detail, we propose to start by examining . . . [the first] component of the consultation. . . . This leads to a . . . conclusion that some may find surprising, namely that the exact definition of what constitutes a disease or an illness is determined not by biology but by society. Certainly, there is a class of health problems that are seen in a similar way in all societies. For instance, if a previously fit man suddenly clutches his chest, looks white and sweaty and is acutely short of breath even at rest, then in Western society we would say that this man has probably had a heart attack, and we would prove it with ECGs and blood tests. It might be that in another society that episode is regarded as a visitation from a malevolent spirit, but even so it would be recognized as a serious, acute and unheralded problem—albeit a visitation, not a myocardial infarct.

However, not all diseases are as clear-cut as a heart attack. Some are far more difficult to define and pigeon-hole and are classified differently in different societies. In Germany, for example, doctors prescribe six times the amount of heart drugs per person than in England or France. This is not because of a greater incidence of coronary artery disease in Germany—in fact, there is less of it than in France—and it clearly has no effect on death rates since the mortality from all forms of heart disease is the same in all countries. One of the major reasons is that the German language doesn't have a way of distinguishing heart problems from any other kind of chest pain. . . .

[T]he English and the Americans don't attribute vague chest pains to the heart unless there's some solid evidence for genuine heart disease. Thus *Herzinsuffizienz* is an illness-label that is almost exclusive to Germany—hence, perhaps, the excessive prescription of heart drugs. In the same way, in France, a large number of nonspecific symptoms are attributed to a *crise de foie*—a "crisis of the liver." In fact, approximately 80 percent of problems attributed to a crisis of the liver are actually migraine. And most of the rest are minor gastrointestinal conditions. . . . Similarly, in the American medical view, minor illnesses are much more likely to be ascribed to (unspecified) viral illnesses. This is in line with the prevailing mood of the times in America in which disease is seen as an external invasive threat and there is a predilection for diagnosing infections since they can often be dealt with actively and quickly. . . .

Now consider a common event (in many lives)—a hangover. We all expect a hangover if we drink excessively; so is a hangover an expected consequence of ordinary life or is it a disease? Whether or not it is a disease, is it an illness? What about bereavement? We expect to be sad after the death of someone we love — if the bereaved person cries continuously for a week, is that an illness? If he or she cries for six months, is that an illness? And what about adolescence? In Montana, a change in financing of private hospitals led to many general hospitals quickly changing themselves into psychiatric hospitals. Unfortunately, there were not enough patients to fill them, so there was a sudden epidemic of new diagnoses. Teenagers who had falling grades at school were now diagnosed as psychiatrically disturbed (with a major advertising campaign to get the point across to the parents) and were admitted to a hospital — at four times the rate that occurred in neighboring Utah. . . .

These [examples] again emphasize the partly arbitrary — and rather parochial — definitions of disease and illness. Each society decides for itself at the time what are legitimately regarded as diseases or illnesses. Those definitions vary from culture to culture. Furthermore, those conditions that we regard as normal today may be diagnosed as illnesses tomorrow.

■ THE TYRANNY OF HEALTH*
Faith T. Fitzgerald
331 New Eng. J. Med. 196 (1994)

There has recently been much in both lay and medical literature on the promotion of healthy lifestyles. Once upon a time people did not have lifestyles; they had lives. Those lives were filled with work and play, battle and respite, excitement and boredom, but principally with the day-to-day struggle for existence, centered largely around the family, birth, death, disease, and health. What is the difference between a lifestyle and a life? Central to it, I believe, is the concept that lifestyle is something one chooses, and life is something that happens to one. This distinction will affect the future of medicine, and certainly health care reform, in this country. The emphasis on healthy lifestyles, although salutary in many ways, has a very dark side to it and has led to the increasing peril of a tyranny of health in the United States. To explain the potential dangers of the emphasis on healthy lifestyles, I here review the concept of health and its role in the fabric of our society.

A healthy lifestyle is said to be essential to the promotion of wellness. What is wellness? In 1946, the World Health Organization, largely in revulsion against the activities of Nazi physicians and the creatures who worked with them, redefined health as "a state of complete physical, mental, and social well being, and not merely the absence of disease or infirmity." This has become known as "wellness," a highly desirable state. A well or healthy person is one who is not only physically whole and vigorous, but also happy and socially content. What a good idea! . . .

Concurrently, and perhaps naively, both the lay public and the medical profession began to confuse the ideal of health with the norm for health. That is, we went from "Wouldn't it be great to have this be the definition of health" to "This *is* the definition of health." Having accepted the view that health should be a

---

perfect state of wellness, we went on to declare that it was. But if one accepts the idea that physical vigor and emotional and social contentment are not only desirable, but also expected, there is a problem. If health is normal, then sickness and accidents are faults. Who or what is at fault varies: environmental pollution, for example, or government plots, doctors themselves, diet, radon, or political bias. We now act as if we really believe that disease, aging, and death are unnatural acts and all things are remediable. All we have to do, we think, is know enough (or spend enough), and disease and death can be prevented or fixed. . . .

In his paper "Medical Nemesis," Illich[2] wrote in 1974 that classifying all the troubles of humanity as medical problems is actually antithetical to true health, in that it limits the ability of people to learn to cope with pain, sickness, and death as integral parts of life. Health, he maintained, is not freedom from the inevitability of death, disease, unhappiness and stress, but rather the ability to cope with them in a competent way. If this is true, then the more medicine and society direct individual behavior, the less autonomous, and therefore the less healthy, the individual may become.

We must beware of developing a zealotry about health, in which we take ourselves too seriously and believe that we know enough to dictate human behavior, penalize people for disagreeing with us, and even deny people charity, empathy, and understanding because they act in a way of which we disapprove. Perhaps the health care crisis could be resolved, in part, if we [health care professionals realized that] . . . we cannot fix everything (though we do some things marvelously well), nor can our patients—no matter how intelligent or attentive—prevent all disease and death. We may be trying to do too much and thus diluting an awareness and application of what we can do well.

■ THE MACHINE AT THE BEDSIDE*
Stanley Joel Reiser & Michael Anbar
1984

Technology has altered significantly the form and meaning of the medical relationship. It allows us to direct our vision and attention to variables singled out by it as significant. Thus, stethoscopes increase the significance of chest sounds, X-rays of anatomic shadows, electrocardiograms of waves on a graph, computers of printouts, dialysis machines of chemical balances, and so forth. Such evidence is important for diagnosis and therapy, and the more precisely it can be stated, the more valuable it becomes. In comparison, evidence given by patients, and altered by its passage through the prism of their experience and personality, has seemed to the technological age of the past two centuries less substantive, accurate, and meaningful as a basis for clinical decisionmaking and actions. Increasingly, practitioners encounter patients for relatively brief and intermittent periods—such as the consultant visiting a hospitalized patient whom he or she has never before met. In such visits the technical aspects often dominate, for there is no time or prior relationship to determine much about who the patient is, or what the patient thinks about the illness or the needs it engenders. And even in

---

[2] Illich I. Medical nemesis. Lancet 1974;1:918-21.

medical relationships that are not so discontinuous, technological measurements and measures tend to crowd out other dimensions of evaluation and therapeutics. To speak so of the attention focused on the technological features of practice does not diminish their great significance and benefit. Rather, it points out that they do not encompass all critical aspects of diagnosis or treatment. . . .

From the beginning of their introduction in the mid-nineteenth century, automated machines that generated results in objective formats such as graphs and numbers were thought capable of purging from health care the distortions of subjective human opinion. They were supposed to produce facts free of personal bias, and thus to reduce the uncertainty associated with human choice. This view, held by both practitioners and patients, stimulated the intense use of these devices, sometimes to excess. This excess has been characterized by overreliance on technologically depicted features of illness, inadequate understanding of the capabilities and limits of machines and the information they generate, and relative inattention to those aspects of medicine learned by inquiry into the patient's experiences and views. Machines can seem so accurate, so right. They can make us forget who made them, and who designed into them — with all the possibilities of human frailty and error — the programs that dictate their function. They can make us forget the hands and minds behind their creation; they can make us forget ourselves.

Notes: The Social Construction of Disease

1. *Is Anyone Healthy?* Students, especially younger ones, often fail to appreciate the extent to which health issues pervade society. According to one survey, in a typical *month* 80 percent of adults report some type of medical symptom, 20 percent visit a doctor, 6 percent visit an alternative (nontraditional) health care provider, and 4 percent go to a hospital. Larry Green et al., The Ecology of Medical Care Revisited, 344 New Eng. J. Med. 2021 (2001). See also Nortin M. Hadler, The Last Well Person (2004); Clifton Meador, The Last Well Person, 330 New Eng. J. Med. 440 (1994).

2. For additional views on the meaning of health and illness and the impact of medical technology, see Nancy King et al. (eds.), The Social Medicine Reader (2d ed. 2005); R.A. Deyo & D.L. Patrick, Hope or Hype: The Obsession with Medical Advances and the High Cost of False Promises (2005); Robert A. Aronowitz, Making Sense of Illness: Science, Society, and Disease (1998); Daniel Callahan, False Hopes: Why America's Quest for Perfect Health Is a Recipe for Failure (1998); Rene Dubos, Man, Medicine and Environment (1968); Michel Foucault, The Birth of the Clinic (1963); David Mechanic, Symptoms, Illness Behavior, and Help Seeking (1982); Roy Porter, The Greatest Benefit to Mankind (1998); David Rothman, Beginnings Count: The Technological Imperative in American Health Care (1997); Wm. B. Schwartz, Life Without Disease: The Pursuit of Medical Utopia (1998); Susan Sontag, Illness as Metaphor (1988); Richard A. Miller, Extending Life: Scientific Prospects and Political Obstacles, 80(2) Milbank Q. (2002); Lars Noah, Pigeonholing Illness: Medical Diagnosis as a Legal Construct, 50 Hastings L. Rev. 241 (1999); Talcott Parsons, The Sick Role and the Role of the Physician Reconsidered, 53 Health & Soc'y 257

(1975); Symposium, 21(2) Health Aff. (Mar. 2002); Symposium, 20(5) Health Aff. (Sept. 2001); Symposium, 25 J. Med. & Phil. 519 (2000); Developments, Medical Technology and the Law, 103 Harv. L. Rev. 1519 (1990).

3. *The Phenomenology of Sickness and Healing*

■ MAKING MEDICAL SPENDING DECISIONS*
Mark A. Hall
1997

THE ONTOLOGICAL ASSAULT OF ILLNESS

Illness is frequently described as an "ontological assault." It undermines one's personal identity by attacking the fundamental unity of mind and body. In a state of health, our body is part of an integrated sense of self that responds instinctively to our will and serves our inner purposes almost effortlessly. When illness strikes, our body becomes an enemy of self. It does not respond as we wish and its frailties dominate our conscious thoughts. Illness strikes at one of our most fundamental assumptions in everyday life — that we will continue to exist and function much as we have in the past. Serious illness shatters our "primordial sense of invulnerability."[3]

The profound incapacitating effect of this assault on our very being is much more debilitating than any of life's other major disruptions, whether they be divorce, incarceration or impoverishment. Physician and philosopher Edmund Pellegrino observes correctly that:

> In no other deprivation is the dissolution of the person so intimate that it impairs the capacity to deal with all other deprivations. The poor man can still hope for a change of fortune, the prisoner for a reprieve, the lonely for a friend. But the ill person remains impaired even when freed of these other constraints on the free exercise of his humanity.[4]

Consider also this account by a philosopher and patient who herself suffers from a severe chronic illness, multiple sclerosis:

> The most deeply held assumption of daily life is the assumption that I, personally, will continue to be alive and it is in light of this assumption that one engages in daily activities. The onset of illness, however, brings one concretely face-to-face with personal vulnerability. . . . Thus, the person who is ill . . . is unable readily to fit illness into the typified schema used to organize and interpret experience. . . . One finds oneself preoccupied with the demands of the here

---

[3] Silberman 1991. In addition to the sources cited in the following notes, see Pellegrino 1979; Pellegrino and Thomasma 1981; Cassell 1982; Cassell 1985; Kleinman 1988.
[4] Pellegrino 1982, at 159.

and now, confined to the present moment, unable effectively to project into the future.[5]

In addition to these profound internal effects, . . . when ill we are often immobilized and confined to bed in a prone position and subjected to mind-altering medications. This compromises our physical ability to act and deliberate and places us in a psychological state of dependency. Treatment also compromises physical integrity and exposes us to singular vulnerability by giving physicians unprecedented access to our bodies and personal histories. Treatment requires us to expose every part of ourselves, down to our very blood and guts, while we remain prostrate or unconscious.

Typically, when ill, we do not resist what would otherwise be viewed as utterly repugnant invasions and vulnerabilities. Sickness returns us to an infantile state where our strongest desire is usually to be cared for and to be relieved of the responsibility and anxiety of deciding and acting.[6] "Such sick people . . . may plausibly prefer not to take on any kind of work, much less the fierce, foreign, and forbidding labor of medical decisions."[7] This is true even for the most knowledgeable of patients—physicians themselves. Franz Ingelfinger, M.D., long time editor of the eminently prestigious New England Journal of Medicine and an expert in diseases of the esophagus, found himself in a dilemma of how best to treat his own difficult case of cancer of the esophagus. His doctors, respecting their patient's world renowned expertise, were leaving this vexing decision to him:

> As a result, not only I but my wife, my son and daughter-in-law (both doctors), and other family members became increasingly confused and emotionally distraught. Finally, when the pangs of indecision had become nearly intolerable, one wise physician friend said, "What you need is a doctor." . . . When that excellent advice was followed, my family and I sensed immediate and immense relief.[8] . . .

[M]y description of the real experience of illness applies to simple and serious conditions alike. Sickness does not have to be life threatening for it to profoundly affect thinking and functioning. A bad flu bug, a relentless shooting pain, a case of food poisoning, an inconsolable child, or even an unexplained lump or a persistent bad cough can have these menacing and incapacitating effects at least to some degree. Even if this state of mind is the exception in medical treatment encounters, it nevertheless is the dominant explanation of why the medical system exists. . . . Medical ethics and health care policy should have its primary focus on the quintessential features of the treatment relationship even if those features account for only a fraction of [medical] decisions.

---

[5] Toombs 1992, at 21, 69.
[6] On this regression to infancy caused by sickness, see Burt 1979; Somers and Somers 1961, at 459-60.
[7] Schneider 1997.
[8] Ingelfinger 1980.

THE MYSTICAL POWER OF HEALING

[The condition of illness is only half of the story in a medical encounter. We must also understand something about the experience of healing. Modern medicine thinks of healing as occurring mainly through biochemical processes activated by medical interventions chosen based on diagnostic analysis and professional experience.] . . . Much of medicine is of this rational quality, but [this account ignores] an essential nonrational component of medicine. . . . This essential component is the mystical power of healing. By this, I mean the hidden elements of the treatment encounter that result in healing through what might be termed charismatic or self-healing means. The power of healing I refer to is the dimension of doctoring that enables physicians to confer relief through spiritual or emotional means akin to those used by parents or priests.[9]

Before alienating the skeptical reader entirely, let me illustrate with an everyday example from my own experience. Last year when my six-year-old daughter was suffering from a common ear ache, her distress brought her to inconsolable tears while waiting more than an hour to be seen by the doctor. I convinced a nurse to take her temperature, give her an aspirin, and say a few kind words of reassurance. Instantaneously, my daughter felt much better, far quicker than any possible pharmacological effect could have taken hold. I was puzzled by this abrupt improvement until I had my own excruciating ear ache a few weeks later and experienced exactly the same sort of instantaneous relief as soon as the doctor examined me and wrote a prescription. Knowing that I was in the good hands of a trained professional who offered the prospect of relief produced in me a sense of exhilaration and a release of anxiety accompanied by a pronounced improvement of my symptoms. This instantaneous recovery might be attributed simply to excessive nerves or to a more complex type of placebo effect but, however labeled or explained, it was effective. The pain was not just more bearable; it went away.

Researchers and physicians have documented countless similar examples of mundane and miraculous relief caused by a largely nonscientific or "nonspecific" process of healing.[10] This placebo effect is not limited to purely psychological states, bizarre conditions, especially susceptible patients, or to manipulative physicians. This effect has been documented in the treatment of diabetes, cancer, and heart disease, for instance, and without the physicians even intending to cause the effect. In one scientific study, two sets of patients were subjected to different surgical operations to treat angina (chest pain), one that performed the standard chest operation, and the other that only pretended to do so by cutting the skin under anesthesia. Both the sham and the real procedure produced equal relief of physical symptoms.[11] A review of other surgical and medical procedures once firmly believed to be effective but later discarded as entirely unfounded led one author to speculate that placebo healing effects may be present to a significant extent in 70 percent of clinical encounters.[12]

---

[9] On the prevalence of the image of physician as parent or priest, see May 1983.
[10] In addition to the sources in the following notes, see Spiro 1986; Brody 1980.
[11] Beecher 1961.
[12] Roberts 1993; Roberts 1995.

Those who have studied this nonspecific healing effect conclude that it pervades medicine, both in modern times and in prescientific and primitive cultures.[13] This is because the effect is connected more to the intervention of the healer than it is to the particular therapeutic agent used. Put another way, the doctor himself is a therapeutic agent, regardless of the actual effectiveness of the particular drug or procedure.[14] In each culture and each era, there has been a prevailing theory of medical treatment, many of which are pure fantasy if not dangerous, yet remarkably few have been proven to be wholly without benefit. Doctors and healers have been universally respected throughout the ages and across primitive and advanced societies; we can only assume that most of them have offered some form of relief despite the now apparent quackery they once practiced. Indeed, it has often been commented that the history of medicine until this century has been the history of the placebo effect. Now that medicine has a firm scientific foundation, this mystical or charismatic element has been surpassed by technological skill, but it will never be entirely displaced. One of the prominent trends in modern medicine is the revival of both popular and scientific interest in these poorly understood domains of caring for patients through alternative or holistic schools of medicine.[15]

The best scientific explanation for this charismatic healing effect is that the process of treatment, and not its specific content, has universal benefit for many or most illnesses, regardless of the specific physiological effects of the treatment. The treatment process has this universal healing power by virtue of the archetypal characteristics that activate the patient's own healing mechanisms — mechanisms that are still largely undiscovered and unexplained. This is best demonstrated by the fact that the basic structure of the treatment encounter is remarkably the same across all systems of medicine, including Western, Eastern, religious, herbal, and primitive. In each of these belief systems, society recognizes the healing powers of a professional elite (physicians or shamans), who administer personally to the patient with physical touching and healing agents (drugs or herbs), often in a dramatic and cathartic ritualistic setting (surgery or exorcism) specially designed for the purpose (hospital or bonfire). In the process, patients feel cared for (nurses or mystics), they are given an explanation for their condition (diagnosis or demonization) that is consistent with their prevailing belief system (scientific medicine or spirit worship), and they are assigned tasks of self care in which they take responsibility in part for their own improvement (dietary regimen or prayer).[16]

These many symbolic structural elements are thought to activate patients' internal healing powers through a variety of psychological channels. A patient who knows someone is devoted to caring for him is able to release the dread and anxiety that may be heightening discomfort and weakening the body's resistance. Believing in the power of the healer may enable the patient to regress to an earlier, more infantile state of mind that enhances this release and the resulting comfort. This confidence in the healer is elevated by the healer's status in society,

---

[13] Turner et al., 1994; Moerman 1983; Brody 1980.
[14] Suchman & Matthews 1988; Houston 1938.
[15] Cohen 1995; Moyers 1993; Frohoch 1992; Siegel 1986; Cousins 1979; Siegel 1986.
[16] The leading work developing this explanation is Frank 1973. See also Brody 1992; Novack 1987; Spiro 1986.

his invocation of methods consistent with that society's belief system, and his offering an explanation of the otherwise troubling and disorienting disease that makes sense to the patient. And, this belief is further cemented by the ritualistic and dramatic elements of laying on of hands, taking of medication, climactic performance, and hallowed setting. . . .

Critical to this healing power is the patient's confidence and trust in the healer. "The image of omnipotence is an essential component of the healer."[17] The healer appears able to activate the patient's own healing mechanisms because the patient turns himself over both in mind and body to the healer. "A patient's hope and trust lead to a 'letting go' that counteracts stress and is often the key to getting well."[18] Psychiatrists, starting with Freud, have described this phenomenon as "transference," in which patients foist on their healers qualities they formerly attributed to their parents in infancy when parents were viewed as all powerful and all knowing. "Deep in patients' unconscious, physicians are viewed as miracle workers, patterned after the fantasized all-caring parents of infancy. Medicine, after all, was born in magic and religion, and the doctor-priest-magician-parent unity that persists in patients' unconscious cannot be broken."[19] . . .

I hasten to concede that none of these assertions are known with any degree of empirical confidence. We are forced into this highly speculative reading of anecdotal accounts from physicians, anthropologists, and ethnographic researchers since empirical testing of this nonspecific healing power is very difficult and has not been widely attempted.[20] Nevertheless, many informed observers and patients view the charismatic dimension of healing as fundamental to the treatment relationship.[21]

[PARTIAL BIBLIOGRAPHY]

Beecher, H. (1961). "Surgery as Placebo," 176 JAMA 1102.

Brody, H. (1992). The Healer's Power (New Haven, CT: Yale Univ. Press).

Brody, H. (1980). Placebos and the Philosophy of Medicine: Clinical, Conceptual, and Ethical Issues (Chicago: Univ. of Chicago Press).

Burt, R.A. (1979). Taking Care of Strangers: The Rule of Law in Doctor-Patient Relations (New York: The Free Press).

Cassell, E.J. (1991). The Nature of Suffering and the Goals of Medicine (Oxford Univ. Press).

Cassell, E.J. (1985). The Healer's Art (MIT Press).

Cassell, E.J. (1982). "The Nature of Suffering and the Goals of Medicine," 306 New Eng. J. Med. 639.

Cohen, M.H. (1995). "A Fixed Star in Health Care Reform: The Emerging Paradigm of Holistic Healing," 27 Ariz. St. Law J. 79.

---

[17] Cassell 1985, at 141. See also Cassell 1991.

[18] Siegel 1986.

[19] Katz 1984, at 142-47, 192. See also Burt 1979.

[20] There are some scattered scientific studies demonstrating the placebo effect and the effect of certain of these healing rituals, but no scientific studies exploring what ingredients make this process work . . . [or are counterproductive].

[21] E.g., Brody 1992; Katz 1984; Burt 1979.

Cousins, N. (1979). Anatomy of an Illness as Perceived by the Patient: Reflections on Healing and Regeneration (New York: W.W. Norton).

Frank, J.D. (1973). Persuasion and Healing: A Comparative Study of Psychotherapy (Baltimore: Johns Hopkins Univ. Press).

Frohoch, F.M. (1992). Healing Powers: Alternative Medicine, Spiritual Communities, and the State (Univ. Chicago Press).

Houston, R. (1938). "The Doctor Himself as a Therapeutic Agent," 11 Annals Int. Med. 1415.

Katz, J. (1984). The Silent World of Doctor and Patient (New York: The Free Press).

Kleinman, A. (1988). The Illness Narratives: Suffering, Healing, and the Human Condition (Basic Books).

Ingelfinger, F. (1980). "Arrogance," 303 New Eng. J. Med. 1507.

Moerman, D.E. (1983). "Physiology and Symbols: The Anthropological Implications of the Placebo Effect," in The Anthropology of Medicine, eds. L. Romanucci-Ross, et al. (Prager).

Moyers, B. (1993). Healing and the Mind (Doubleday).

Novack, D.H. (1987). "Therapeutic Aspects of the Clinical Encounter," 2 J. Gen. Intern. Med. 346.

Pellegrino, E.D. (1982). "Being Ill and Being Healed," in The Humanity of the Ill, ed. V. Kestenbaum (Univ. Tennessee Press).

Pellegrino, E.D. (1979). "Toward a Reconstruction of Medical Morality: The Primacy of the Act of Profession and the Fact of Illness," 4 J. Med. & Philo. 32.

Pellegrino, E.D. and Thomasma, D.C. (1981). A Philosophical Basis of Medical Practice (Oxford Univ. Press).

Roberts, A.H. (1995). "The Powerful Placebo Revisited: Magnitude of Nonspecific Effects," 1 Mind/Body Med. 35-43.

Roberts, A.H., et al. "The Power of Nonspecific Effects in Healing," 12 Clin. Psychol. Rev. 375.

Schneider, C.E. (1997). The Practice of Autonomy: Patients, Doctors, and Medical Decisions (forthcoming, Oxford Univ. Press).

Schneider, C.E. (1994). "Bioethics with a Human Face," 69 Ind. Law J. 1075-1104.

Siegel, B.S. (1986). Love, Medicine & Miracles (Harper & Row).

Silberman, C. (1991). "From the Patient's Bed," 13 Health Management Q. 12.

Somers, H.M. and Somers, A.R. (1961). Doctors, Patients and Health Insurance: The Organization and Financing of Medical Care (Washington, D.C.: Brookings Institution).

Spiro, H.M. (1986). Doctors, Patients, and Placebos (New Haven: Yale Univ. Press).

Suchman, A.L. and Matthews, D.A. (1988). "What Makes the Doctor-Patient Relationship Therapeutic? Exploring the Connexional Dimension of Medical Care," 108 Ann. Intern. Med. 125.

Toombs, S.K. (1992). The Meaning of Illness, A Phenomenological Account of the Different Perspectives of Physician and Patient (Boston: Kluwer Academic Publishers).

Turner, J.A., Deyo, R.A. and Loeser, J.D., et al. (1994). "The Importance of Placebo Effects in Pain Treatment and Research," 271 JAMA 1609-1614.

Notes: The Power of Medicine and the Vulnerability
of Patients

1. *Illness.* Does your own experience with illness confirm or rebut the incapacitating and dehumanizing effects described by Mark Hall? Consider the additional accounts, both analytical and narrative, on the Web site for this book, www.health-law.org. For additional descriptions and analyses of the phenomenology of illness, see Howard Brody, Stories of Sickness (1987); Kathy Charmaz, Good Days, Bad Days: The Self in Chronic Illness and Time (1991); Norman Cousins, The Healing Heart (1983); David M. Frankford, Food Allergy and the Health Care Financing Administration: A Story of Rage, 1 Widener L. Symp. J. 159 (1996); Marsha Garrison & Carl Schneider, The Law of Bioethics 1-5 (2003); Michael C. Dohan, Reflections on a Bone Marrow Transplant, 132 Annals Internal Med. 587 (2000). Discussing how issues of trust and vulnerability affect a number of issues in health care law, see Mark A. Hall, Law, Medicine and Trust, 55 Stan. L. Rev. 463 (2002); Robert Gatter, Faith, Confidence, and Health Care: Fostering Trust in Medicine Through Law, 39 Wake Forest L. Rev. 395 (2004).

2. *Doctors, Patients, and Placebos.* These readings explain that the placebo effect is not isolated to a few psychologically susceptible individuals or conditions. It permeates medical encounters and typifies the doctor-patient relationship in ways that scientific medicine tends to ignore or deny. The mere encounter with a doctor appears to activate internal, self-healing mechanisms across a wide range of medical conditions, regardless of the actual treatments rendered. In short, doctors do not just administer placebos; they *are* placebos. Considering this, should the FDA deny approval for a drug because it acts "only" as a placebo? How does a doctor obtain informed consent from a patient when he knows the treatment is partially or totally intended to invoke a placebo effect? For additional discussion, see Kathleen M. Boozang, The Therapeutic Placebo: The Case for Patient Deception, 54 Fla. L. Rev. 687 (2002); Anne Harrington, The Placebo Effect: An Interdisciplinary Exploration (1997); The Science of the Placebo (Harry A. Guess et al. eds., 2002). See generally Amitai Aviram, The Placebo Effect of Law: Law's Role in Manipulating Perceptions, 75 Geo. Wash. L. Rev. 54 (2006) (discussing how, "like the placebo effect of medicine, a law may impact social welfare beyond its objective effects by manipulating the public's subjective perception of the law's effectiveness").

3. *Alternative and Conventional Healers.* There is now widespread social interest in alternative healing, both as a separate area of professional practice and as a component of conventional scientific practice. For further exploration, see Thomas A. Droege, The Faith Factor in Healing (1991); B. O'Connor, Healing Traditions: Alternative Medicine and the Health Professions (1995); Michael H. Cohen, Complementary and Alternative Medicine: Legal Boundaries and Regulatory Perspectives (1998); Barbara L. Atwell, Mainstreaming Complementary and Alternative Medicine in the Face of Uncertainty, 72 UMKC L. Rev. 593 (2004); Symposium, 31 J.L. Med. & Ethics 183 (2003); Michael H. Cohen & Mary C. Ruggie, Integrating Complementary and Alternative Medical Therapies in Conventional Medical Settings, 72 U. Cin. L. Rev. 671-729 (2003); Joseph A. Barrette, The Alternative Medical Practice Act, 77 St. John's L. Rev. 75 (2003); James A. Bulen, Complementary and Alternative Medicine: Ethical and Legal Aspects of Informed Consent to Treatment, 24 J. Leg. Med. 331 (2003); Kathleen M. Boozang, Is the

Alternative Medicine? Managed Care Apparently Thinks So, 32 Conn. L. Rev. 567 (2000).

4. *Therapeutic Jurisprudence.* Consider the various implications these provocative readings have for law and public policy. Do they alter conventional legal notions about who should control decisionmaking in the treatment encounter? Do they suggest that health insurance should more freely cover untested or unorthodox therapies? When disputes arise over treatment decisions or insurance coverage, are patients capable of aggressively pursing their legal rights? Are patients capable of acting as informed consumers in a medical marketplace in which they evaluate the costs and benefits of different treatment options? Questions like these are addressed by a branch of legal thought known as "therapeutic jurisprudence," which views law as a therapeutic agent. This perspective asks whether normal social and behavioral assumptions realistically fit the medical arena, and whether legal rules do a good job of fostering the therapeutic goals of medicine. For leading examples, focused mainly on mental health and criminal law, see David B. Wexler, Therapeutic Jurisprudence: The Law as a Therapeutic Agent (1990); David Wexler & Bruce Winnick, Essays in Therapeutic Jurisprudence (1991); Law in a Therapeutic Key (David B. Wexler & Bruce J. Winnick eds., 1996); Marshall B. Kapp, The Law and Older Persons: Is Geriatric Jurisprudence Therapeutic? (2003). For an attempt to further develop this perspective in health care law, see Hall, supra, 55 Stan. L. Rev. 463 (2002).

4. The Nature of Medical Judgment

▓ VARIATIONS IN PHYSICIAN PRACTICE: THE ROLE OF UNCERTAINTY*
David M. Eddy**
3 Health Affairs 74, No. 2 (Summer 1984)

. . . An analysis of procedure rates for Medicare patients in 13 large metropolitan areas in the United States showed that for more than half the procedures studied, the rates varied more than 300 percent between the areas with high and low rates. Another study that compared utilization rates in 16 large communities in four states found more than threefold differences between the highest and lowest rates for heart bypass, thyroid, and prostate surgery; fivefold differences for specific back and abdominal surgeries; sevenfold differences for knee replacements; and almost 20-fold differences for carotid endarterectomies. . . . In Vermont, the chance of having one's tonsils removed as a child are 8 percent in one community and 70 percent in another. In Iowa, 15 percent of the men younger than 85 years in one region have had prostatectomies compared with more than 60 percent in another. In Maine, the chance of hysterectomy by the age of 70 years varies across communities from less than 20 percent to more

** Dr. Eddy is a physician researcher, formerly on the faculty of Duke University, and now a consultant in Jackson Hole, Wyoming. The first paragraph is taken from a later work, Clinical Decision Making: From Theory to Practice (1996).

than 70 percent.[11] While some of the variations might be explained by differences in disease incidence, available resources, and patient preferences, it is impossible to explain all of them. . . .

Why do physicians vary so much in the way they practice medicine? At first view, there should be no problem. There are diseases — neatly named and categorized by textbooks, journal articles, and medical specialty societies. There are various procedures physicians can use to diagnose and treat these diseases. It should be possible to determine the value of any particular procedure by applying it to patients who have a disease and observing the outcome. And the rest should be easy — if the outcome is good, the procedure should be used for patients with that disease; if the outcome is bad, it should not. Some variation in practice patterns can be expected due to differences in the incidence of various diseases, patients' preferences, and the available resources, but these variations should be small and explainable.

The problem of course is that nothing is this simple. Uncertainty, biases, errors, and differences of opinions, motives, and values weaken every link in the chain that connects a patient's actual condition to the selection of a diagnostic test or treatment. This [reading] describes some of the factors that cause decisions about the use of medical procedures to be so difficult, and that contribute to the alarming variations we observe in actual practice. It examines the components of the decision problem a physician faces, and the psychology of medical reasoning, focusing in particular on the role of uncertainty. Finally, it suggests some actions to reduce uncertainty and encourage consistency of good medical practice.

Uncertainty creeps into medical practice through every pore. Whether a physician is defining a disease, making a diagnosis, selecting a procedure, observing outcomes, assessing probabilities, assigning preference, or putting it all together, he is walking on very slippery terrain. It is difficult for nonphysicians, and for many physicians, to appreciate how complex these tasks are, how poorly we understand them, and how easy it is for honest people to come to difference conclusions.

Defining a Disease

If one looks at patients who are obviously ill, it is fairly easy to identify the physical and chemical disorders that characterize that illness. On the other hand, a large part of medicine is practiced on people who do not have obvious illnesses, but rather have signs, symptoms, or findings that may or may not represent an illness that should be treated. Three closely related problems make it difficult to determine whether or not a patient actually has a disease that needs to be diagnosed or treated.

One problem is that the dividing line between "normal" and "abnormal" is not nearly as sharp as a cursory reading of a textbook would suggest. . . .

A second problem is that many "diseases," at least at the time they are diagnosed, do not by themselves cause pain, suffering, disability, or threat to life. They are considered diseases only because they increase the probability that something else that is truly bad will happen in the future. . . .

---

[11] Wennberg J. Dealing with medical practice variation: a proposal for action, Health Aff. 1984; 3:6.

The difficulty of defining a disease is compounded by the fact that many of the signs, symptoms, findings, and conditions that might suggest a disease are extremely common. If a breast biopsy were performed on a random sample of senior citizens, fully 90 percent of them could have fibrocystic disease. If obesity is a disease, the average American is diseased. By the time they reach seventy, about two-thirds of women have had their uteruses removed. . . .

Given these uncertainties about what constitutes a disease, it should not be surprising that there are debates about the definitions of many diseases, and when there is agreement about a definition, it is often blatantly and admittedly arbitrary. A quick review of the literature reveals multiple definitions of glaucoma, diabetes, fibrocystic disease of the breast, coronary artery disease, myocardial infarction, stroke, and dozens of other conditions. Morbid obesity is defined as 100 percent above the ideal weight. But what is "ideal," and why 100 percent? The lesson is that for many conditions a clinician faces, there is no clear definition of disease that provides an unequivocal guide to action, and there is wide room for differences of opinion and variations in practice. . . .

[E]ven when sharp criteria are created, physicians vary widely in their application of these criteria — in their ability to ask about symptoms, observe signs, interpret test results, and record the answers. The literature on "observer variation" has been growing for a long time. . . . A group of experts compiled 100 electrocardiogram tracings, 50 of which showed myocardial infarctions, 25 of which were normal, and 25 of which showed some other abnormality (according to the experts). These EKGs were then given to ten other cardiologists to test their diagnostic abilities. The proportion of EKGs judged by the ten cardiologists to show infarcts varied by a factor of two. If you had an infarct and went to physician A, there would be a 28 percent chance the physician would have missed it. If you did not have an infarct and went to physician B, there would be a 26 percent chance that physician would have said you had one. . . .

Thirteen pathologists were asked to read 1,001 specimens obtained from biopsies of the cervix, and then to repeat the readings at a later time. On average, each pathologist agreed with himself only 89 percent of the time (intraobserver agreement), and with a panel of "senior" pathologists only 87 percent of the time (interobserver agreement). Looking only at the patients who actually had cervical pathology, the intraobserver agreement was only 68 percent and the interobserver agreement was only 51 percent. The pathologists were best at reading more advanced disease and normal tissue, but were labeled "unsatisfactory" in their ability to read the precancerous and preinvasive stages.

Similar studies have been reported for the presence of clubbing of the fingers, anemia, psychiatric disease, and many other signs, symptoms, and procedures. Even if there were no uncertainty about what constitutes a disease and how to define it, there would still be considerable uncertainty about whether or not a patient has the signs, symptoms, and findings needed to fit the definition.

SELECTING A PROCEDURE

The task of selecting a procedure is no less difficult. There are two main issues. First, for any patient condition there are dozens of procedures that can be ordered, in any combination, at any time. The list of procedures that might be included in a workup of chest pain or hypertension would take more than a page, spanning the spectrum from simply asking questions, to blood studies, to X-rays. Even for highly specific diagnostic problems, there can be a large choice of procedures. For example, if a woman presents with a breast mass and her physician wants to know its approximate size and architecture, the physician might contemplate an imaging procedure. The choice could include mammography, ultra-sonography, thermography, diaphanography, computed tomography, lymphography, Mammoscan, and magnetic resonance imaging. A physician who chose mammography would still have to decide between xeromammography and film mammography, with several brands being available for the latter. There are about a dozen procedures that apply the principles of thermography. And why should a diagnostic workup be limited to one test? Why not follow a negative mammogram with a computed tomogram (or vice versa)? For the detection of colorectal cancer, a physician can choose any combination of fecal occult blood tests (and there are more than a dozen brands), digital examination, rigid sigmoidoscopy, flexible 30 cm sigmoidoscopy, flexible 60 cm sigmoidoscopy, barium enema (either plain or air contrast), and colonoscopy. These choices are not trivial. Most procedures have different mechanisms of action and a long list of pros and cons. Different brands of fecal occult blood tests have very different sensitivities and specificities, and film mammography and xeromammography differ in their radiation exposure by a factor of about four. These procedures are for relatively well-defined diseases; imagine the problems of selecting procedures to evaluate symptoms like fatigue, headache, or fever that can have about a dozen causes. . . .

In theory, much of the uncertainty just described could be managed if it were possible to conduct enough experiments under enough conditions, and observe the outcomes. Unfortunately, measuring the outcomes of medical procedures is one of the most difficult problems we face. The goal is to predict how the use of a procedure in a particular case will affect that patient's health and welfare. Standing in the way are at least a half dozen major obstacles. The central problem is that there is a natural variation in the way people respond to a medical procedure. Take two people who, to the best of our ability to define such things, are identical in all important respects, submit them to the same operative procedure, and one will die on the operating table while the other will not. Because of this natural variation, we can only talk about the probabilities of various outcomes — the probability that a diagnostic test will be positive if the disease is present (sensitivity), the probability that a test will be negative if the disease is absent (specificity), the probability that a treatment will yield a certain result, and so forth.

One consequence of this natural variation is that to study the outcomes of any procedure it is necessary to conduct the procedure on many different people, who are thought to represent the particular patients we want to know about, and then average the results. . . . Some diseases are so rare that, in order to conduct the ideal clinical trials, it would be necessary to collect tens of thousands, if not hundreds of thousands, of participants. A good example concerns the frequency of the Pap smear. One might wonder why the merits of a three-year versus one-year frequency cannot be settled by a randomized controlled trial. Because of the low frequency of cervical cancer, and the small difference in outcomes expected for the two frequencies, almost one million women would be required for such a study. . . .

Finally, even when the best trials are conducted, we still might not get an answer. Consider the value of mammography in women under fifty, and consider just one outcome—the effect on breast cancer mortality. Ignore for the time being the radiation hazard, false-positive test results, inconvenience, financial costs, and other issues. This is one of the best-studied problems in cancer prevention, benefiting from the largest (60,000 women) and longest (more than 15 years) completed randomized controlled trial, and an even larger uncontrolled study involving 270,000 women screened for five years in 29 centers around the country. Yet we still do not know the value of mammography in women under 50. The first study showed a slight reduction in mortality, but it was not statistically significant. The larger study suggested that mammography has improved since the first study, and that it is now almost as good in younger women as in older women, but the study was not controlled and we do not know if "almost" is good enough. Even for women over 50, where the first study showed a statistically significant reduction in breast cancer mortality (of about 40 percent at ten years), there is enough uncertainty about the results that no fewer than four additional trials have been initiated to confirm the results. These trials are still in progress.

Unable to turn to a definitive body of clinical and epidemiological research, a clinician or research scientist who wants to know the value of a procedure is left with a mixture of randomized controlled trials, nonrandomized trials, uncontrolled trials, and clinical observations. The evidence from different sources can easily go in different directions, and it is virtually impossible for anyone to sort things out in his or her head. Unfortunately, the individual physician may be most impressed by observations made in his or her individual practice. This source of evidence is notoriously vulnerable to bias and error. What a physician sees and remembers is biased by the types of patients who come in; by the decisions of the patients to accept a treatment and return for follow-up; by a natural desire to see good things; and by a whole series of emotions that charge one's memory. On top of these biases, the observations are vulnerable to large statistical errors because of the small number of patients a physician sees in a personal practice. . . .

Now assume that a physician can know the outcomes of recommending a particular procedure for a particular patient. Is it possible to declare whether those outcomes are good or bad? Unfortunately, no. The basic problem is that any procedure has multiple outcomes, some good and some bad. The expected reduction in chest pain that some people will get from coronary artery bypass surgery is accompanied by a splitting of the chest, a chance of an operative mortality, days in the hospital, pain, anxiety, and financial expense. Because the outcomes are multiple and move in different directions, tradeoffs have to be made. And making tradeoffs involves values.

Just as there is a natural variation in how each of us responds to a medical procedure, there is a variation in how we value different outcomes. The fact that General Motors alone produces more than 50 distinct models of automobiles, not to mention dozens of options for each model, demonstrates how tastes about even a single item can vary. Imagine the variation in how different people value pain, disability, operative mortality, life expectancy, a day in a hospital, and who is going to feed the dogs. . . .

[B]ecause decisions about procedures are typically made by physicians on behalf of their patients, the physicians must infer their patients' values, and keep them distinct from their own personal preferences. This raises the second problem, communication. It is difficult enough to assess one's own values about the outcomes of a complicated decision (think about switching jobs); consider having someone else try to learn your thoughts and do it for you. The room for error in communications can be appreciated by returning to the experiment in which four physicians asked 993 coal miners about cough, shortness of breath, pain, and sputum. The variation in their reports of responses to a simple question like, "Do you have a cough?" was large [from 150 to 300 percent variation in reporting the symptom present]; imagine a question like, "How do you feel about operative morality?"

PUTTING IT ALL TOGETHER

The final decision about how to manage a patient requires synthesizing all the information about a disease, the patient, signs and symptoms, the effectiveness of dozens of tests and treatments, outcomes and values. All of this must be done without knowing precisely what the patient has, with uncertainty about signs and symptoms, with imperfect knowledge of the sensitivity and specificity of tests, with no training in manipulating probabilities, with incomplete and biased information about outcomes, and with no language for communicating or assessing values. If each piece of this puzzle is difficult, it is even more difficult for anyone to synthesize all the information and be certain of the answer. It would be an extremely hard task for a research team; there is no hope that it could occur with any precision in the head of a busy clinician. Hence the wide variability in the estimates physicians place on the values of procedures.

[A] final example document[s] how difficult it is to combine information from many sources to estimate the value of a particular procedure. . . . A survey of 1,000 11-year-old schoolchildren in New York City found that 65 percent had undergone tonsillectomy. The remaining children were sent for examinations to a group of physicians and 45 percent were selected for tonsillectomy. Those rejected were examined by another group of physicians and 46 percent were selected for surgery. When the remaining children were examined again by another group of physicians, a similar percent were recommended for tonsillectomy, leaving only 65 students. At that point, the study was halted for lack of physicians.

CONSEQUENCES

The view of anyone who wants a close look at the consequences of different medical procedures is, at best, smoky. Some procedures may present a clear picture, and their value, or lack of it, may be obvious; putting a finger on a bleeding carotid artery is an extreme example. But for many, if not most medical procedures, we can only see shadows and gross movements. We usually know the direction in which various outcome measures can move when a medical activity is undertaken, but we typically do not know the probabilities they will move in those directions, or how far they will move. We certainly do not know how a particular individual will respond. Words like "rare," "common," and "a lot" must be used instead of "one out of 1,000," or "seven on a scale of one to ten."

There is also a strong tendency to oversimplify. One of the easiest ways to fit a large problem in our minds is to lop off huge parts of it. In medical decisions, one option is to focus on length of life and discount inconvenience, pain, disability, short-term risks, and financial costs. A physician can also draw on a number of simplifying heuristics. Anyone uncomfortable dealing with probabilities can use the heuristic, "If there is any chance of (the disease), the (procedure) should be performed." If one cannot estimate the number of people to be saved, one can use the heuristic, "If but one patient is saved, the effort is worthwhile." If one cannot contemplate alternative uses of resources that might deliver a greater benefit to a population, there is the heuristic, "Costs should not be considered in decisions about individual patients." There is a general purpose heuristic, "When in doubt, do it." Or as one investigator wrote, "An error of commission is to be preferred to an error of omission." Unfortunately, a large number of incentives encourage simplifications that lead to overutilization. It is time-consuming, mentally taxing, and often threatening to colleagues for a physician to undertake a deep analysis of a confusing clinical problem. A physician is less likely to be sued for doing too much than too little. Most physicians' incomes go up if they do more, and go down if they do less. Hospitals get to fill more beds and bill for more procedures, laboratories collect more money for services, and companies sell more drugs, devices, and instruments. The more that is done, the more the providers win. The losers are patients, consumers, and taxpayers—anyone who has to undergo a valueless procedure or pay the bill.

In the end, given all the uncertainties, incentives, and heuristics, a physician will have to do what is comfortable. If it is admitted that the uncertainty surrounding the use of a procedure is great, and that there is no way to identify for certain what is best, or to prove that any particular action is right or wrong, the safest and most comfortable position is to do what others are doing. The applicable maxim is "safety in numbers." A physician who follows the practices of his or her colleagues is safe from criticism, free from having to explain his or her actions, and defended by the concurrence of colleagues.

Notes: Medical Decisionmaking

1. *The Nature of Medical Judgment.* An even better sense of medical decisionmaking can be had from examining a range of particular medical cases. To some extent, this is possible by reading the cases in this book, but for the most part the intricacies of the medical decisions are described in only an abbreviated fashion. A good example of one, full-length case discussion, which illustrates many of the dimensions of uncertainty of judgment described by David Eddy, is provided on the Web site for this book, www.health-law.org. For additional readings on the nature of medical judgment, see Kathryn Montgomery, How Doctors Think (2006); Jerome Grupman, How Doctors Think (2007); Atul Gawande, Complications: A Surgeon's Notes on an Imperfect Science (2002); Kathryn Hunter, Doctors' Stories: The Narrative Structure of Medical Knowledge (1991).

2. *Medical Terminology.* Prior editions of this book contained information about medical terminology, medical science, and anatomy. Lawyers who practice in this field must eventually acquire a fair amount of medical knowledge, and

many law students enjoy learning something about a different profession's specialized vocabulary. Others see medical terminology as an obstacle to understanding what's really happening in these cases. We have chosen to cater to the latter group; our feeling is that if you end up working in this field, you will have plenty of opportunity to learn the terminology later. Here, when cases contain uncommon medical terms, we will define them for you. If we fail to do so, most terms used in this book are contained in better-quality general dictionaries. For those who want more specialized information, here is a sampling of medical dictionaries, some written especially for lawyers and others for medical professionals or for the lay public: Dorland's Illustrated Medical Dictionary; Slee's Health Care Terms; Taber's Cyclopedic Medical Dictionary.

■ LAW AND MEDICINE
William J. Curran
1st ed. 1960

There may have been a time when doctors and lawyers had much in common, but today their environments are radically divergent and the problem of mutual understanding is a real one. The doctor is trained in a dynamic and experimental science, he is seeking truth in a physical world. He is steeped in the practical judgment, though he avoids generalization. The lawyer, on the other hand, lives within the generalities of the law. The courts apply justice through the advocacy system and seek truth through the burden of proof. When the doctor or other medical person comes into contact with the courts and lawyers, he is often mystified and is generally impatient with the conservatism of the courts in accepting the advances of science. The lawyer often does not seem to the doctor to be seeking truth, but only to place blame.

Most lawyers are Aristotelian in method, if not in philosophy. So are law students by the time they are seniors. That is to say, they work from settled principles on stated fact situations. While they are seeking the results of their deductive logic, their facts remain unchanged. This is not the case in science and in medicine. The scientist seeks truth within the scientific method. The physician is also an experimentalist, an empiricist. At times, however, he does not like being called a scientist, particularly when he is treating a patient. Then he may prefer the title of artisan — but still an empirical artisan.

The failure to understand the basic difference in method between doctors and lawyers is often a stumbling block to greater cooperation between the two professions. It often leads the lawyer into error in presenting the medical issues in a legal action. It may seem obvious that a lawyer should understand the physician's methods as well as his conclusions. Yet, when the attorney accepts a case and prepares it for trial, he tends not to do this. If his client has a back injury, he is interested only in the doctor's conclusions in regard to that injury. He may study the basis for the physician's conclusions in regard to this case, but he rarely does anything more until the next case comes along when again he is interested only in *that* injury. . . .

■ PHYSICIANS VERSUS LAWYERS: A CONFLICT OF CULTURES
Daniel M. Fox*
AIDS and the Law (H. Dalton & S. Burris eds., 1987)

If we are to move in the direction of cooperation rather than conflict, we must understand the roots of the antagonism between the professions and the contemporary forces that threaten to deepen it.

I emphasize physicians' antagonism to lawyers, because I suspect that most lawyers are not normally antagonistic toward physicians. Physicians, on the other hand, believe they are being taken advantage of by lawyers who do not understand medicine or value it properly. They are, moreover, mortified because the conflict is usually displayed in public settings controlled by lawyers — court proceedings and legislative hearings.

The conflict between physicians and lawyers, though it is rooted in the modern history of the two professions, has become more intense in recent years as the authority most people accord to physicians has diminished. Some physicians accuse lawyers of helping to undermine public confidence in them by mindlessly pursuing malpractice litigation. Many attribute their rising premiums for malpractice insurance to the work of greedy and unscrupulous lawyers. Physicians often blame lawyers for the mass of regulations that burden them. In an astonishing display of professional bigotry, the new president of the Association of American Medical Colleges told a medical school graduating class in June 1986, "We're swimming in shark-infested waters where the sharks are lawyers."

To most physicians, adversarial proceedings are an ineffective and irrational method for resolving conflict. Where Anglo-American lawyers presume that a person accused of a crime is innocent until proven guilty in a court of law, physicians believe it is dangerous to make any presumption before examining evidence. Similarly, most physicians do not understand the history or the logic of lawyers' claim that formalized conflict between plaintiffs and defendants in a courtroom or around a table resolves disagreements with reasonable equity and preserves social peace.

Physicians are trained to rely on two methods of addressing conflicts about data and their interpretation. The first method is the assertion of authority from the top of a hierarchy in which power is derived from knowledge. The second method is peer review-discussion to consensus among experts of roughly equal standing and attainment. Both methods, the hierarchical and the consensual, rest on the assumption that truth is best determined by experts. . . .

Note: Law vs. Medicine: A Culture Clash

Here are some additional perspectives on the differences and commonalities between doctors and lawyers:

---

* Daniel Fox is widely known and published in the health care public policy field. He is the president of the Milbank Memorial Fund, and he previously held various positions in academics and government.

> Doctors and lawyers are not alike, either by disposition, or by education, or in practice. Even though the basic objectives of our two professions are the same, namely, to serve society, the education and practice of each are worlds apart. . . . The adversary system squeezes the doctor into roles and settings with which he is unfamiliar and in which he is ineffective. . . . The adversary system, as effective as it may be in achieving justice, is clearly ineffective in establishing truth in medicine. Charles G. Guild, III, M.D., Lawyers Doctors and Medical Malpractice: A Surgeon Reacts, *in* E. D. Shapiro et al., Medical Malpractice (2d ed. 1966).

> If a doctor were called on to treat typhoid fever he would probably try to find out what kind of water the patient drank, and clean out the well so that no one else could get typhoid from the same source. But if a lawyer were called on to treat a typhoid patient he would give him thirty days in jail, and then he would think that nobody else would ever dare to drink the impure water. If the patient got well in fifteen days, he would be kept until his time was up; if the disease was worse at the end of thirty days, the patient would be released because his time was out. As a rule, lawyers are not scientists. They think that there is only one way to make men good, and that is to put them in such terror that they do not dare to do bad.

Meyer Levin, Compulsion (1956) (taken from the defense attorney's closing argument to the jury).

For additional books and articles that illustrate differences of professional approach, ethical principles, and cultural values between lawyers and physicians (not necessarily with that intention in mind), see J. Katz, The Silent World of Doctor and Patient (1984); Peter Jacobson & Gregg Bloche, Improving Relations Between Attorneys and Physicians, 294 JAMA 2083 (2005); William M. Sage, The Lawyerization of Medicine, 26 J. Health Pol. Pol'y & L. 1179 (2001); Alan A. Stone, Law's Influence on Medicine and Medical Ethics, 312 New Eng. J. Med. 310 (1985).

C. THE HEALTH CARE FINANCING AND DELIVERY SYSTEM

The readings in this section describe the economic and regulatory forces that shape how health care is delivered in the United States. All of us have some exposure to the world of medicine but few law students have reason to understand the intricacies of this financing and delivery system and how it has developed. This understanding is essential in a course that focuses on the full range of legal and public policy issues pertaining to the delivery and payment for medical care. Those issues have naturally taken shape according to the structural components and historical growth of the health care sector and its various institutions.

We begin with a rudimentary overview of the history of health insurance and of the principal events that have shaped its development. Included in this is a discussion of whether there is a "crisis" in American medicine. We finish with an introduction to more recent innovations such as HMOs. As you read through this alphabet soup of actors, institutions, and acronyms, rather than memorizing all the details, try to construct a coherent story line of how the health care sector took shape over time and how its various pieces interconnect at present. You don't need to master all the details now, for they will reemerge throughout the course, but it will be easier to remember them at the end if you have an initial framework to attach them to.

1. Insurance and Regulation

▮ U.S. HEALTH CARE COVERAGE AND COSTS: HISTORICAL DEVELOPMENT AND CHOICES FOR THE [FUTURE]*
Randall R. Bovbjerg, Charles C. Griffin & Caitlin Carroll**
21 J.L. Med. & Ethics 141 (1993)

American health policy today faces dual problems of too little coverage at too high a cost. Our combined system of private and public financing leaves about one seventh of the population without insurance coverage from any source. At the same time, the coverage Americans do have costs ever-larger shares of our country's productive capacity, well above what other countries pay and what many people, health plans, businesses, and governments want to pay. This "paradox of excess and deprivation"[2] results from the incremental approach the U.S. has taken to solving incompatible policy goals of widening health insurance coverage while trying to control costs and maintain a high level of quality. This essay examines the American record over the past 60 years in pursuing this incremental approach and draws from it lessons for the current effort to reform the system.

PRE-1929: ERECTING MEDICAL INFRASTRUCTURE AND ESCHEWING NATIONAL HEALTH INSURANCE

Neither medicine nor health coverage was very advanced prior to the Great Depression.[3] Accustomed to the medical miracles of the late twentieth century, one tends to forget that nineteenth century doctors could do little for patients, and hospitals were mainly charity wards where the poor went to die. Medical practice was totally unregulated, and competing theories of disease and treatment flourished. Antiseptic surgery developed only in the latter part of the century. At that same time, local, state, and national medical associations began to promote professional standards (of their own design) as well as the enactment of state

---

* Reprinted with the permission of the American Society of Law, Medicine & Ethics. Updated by the editors of this book to reflect recent developments.

** The authors are, respectively, Senior Research Associate, Health Policy Center, The Urban Institute: Economist, The World Bank; and Research Assistant, The Urban Institute. Bovbjerg's name is pronounced "Boh-berg."

[2] Alain Enthoven and Richard Kronick, A Consumer-Choice Health Plan for the 1980s, 320 New Eng. J. Med. 29 (1989).

[3] Joseph A. Califano, Jr., America's Health Care Revolution: Who Lives? Who Dies? Who Pays? (New York: Random House, 1986); Paul Starr, The Social Transformation of American Medicine (New York: Basic Books, 1982); Edward Shorter, The Health Century (New York: Doubleday, 1987); Rosemary Stevens, In Sickness and in Wealth: American Hospitals in the Twentieth Century (New York: Basic Books 1989).

licensure requirements. By 1912, it could be said that "for the first time in human history, a random patient with a random disease consulting a doctor chosen at random stands a better than 50/50 chance of benefiting from the encounter."[4]

By the 1920s, today's familiar patterns of accreditation and licensure were set for medical education, medical practice, and hospitals. Doctors practiced almost exclusively as solo, office-based practitioners on a fee-for-service basis. Physicians treated their own patients in hospitals, rather than referring them to hospital-based specialists, often salaried, as in much of Europe. Community-based, voluntary hospitals were well established in most of the country, with not-for-profits dominant, basically serving as workshops for community physicians. Still, for most Americans, illness, injury, and early death were more to be suffered than helped by a doctor, much less insured against.

A good thing, too, for insurance coverage was virtually nonexistent, whether private or public. True, some private insurers were willing to write a kind of "health insurance," but only covering loss of income from disability, not physician or hospital bills. Historically, insurance theory — and commercial insurers — thought the term *health insurance* an oxymoron. The reason was that sickness, or more precisely, the use of medical services, was not believed to be an "insurable risk." . . .

Insurance may also have seemed less important because expenses for available care were not large relative to typical incomes. The average day in a hospital cost only a few dollars, and physicians did not charge — or earn — large amounts. . . . In short, in the era before health insurance, when patients themselves paid for almost all health care, the medical economy behaved much like the rest of the economy and was small relative to the whole. All together, the nation spent only about 3.5 percent of gross [domestic] product (GDP) on health care (Table 1).

1929-1940: ENTER HEALTH INSURANCE

Then came the birth of the "Blues," the true beginnings of health insurance as we now know it. . . . Blue Cross plans were organized by hospital associations, typically at the state level. The first Blues-style hospital plan started in 1934 with special New York enabling legislation. Very quickly, physicians followed suit, organizing their own Blue Shield plans, first for in-hospital surgical care, then for medical services as well. Blues plans had unique service areas, not competing with one another, and had strong ties to hospital associations and medical societies. . . . [8] By 1938, 1.4 million Americans were enrolled in 38 Blue Cross plans. Only after the hospitals and the Blues proved the market viable did ordinary insurers begin to write coverage for medical bills. . . .

---

[4] This contemporaneous pronouncement came from Harvard Professor L. Henderson, calling the year 1912 "a Great Divide." Quoted in Richard Harris, A Sacred Trust (New York: New American Library, 1966), 5.

[8] Odin W. Anderson, Blue Cross Since 1929 (Cambridge, MA: Ballinger Publishing Co., 1975); Sylvia Law, Blue Cross: What Went Wrong? (2d ed.) (New Haven: Yale University Press, 1976); Paul Starr, The Social Transformation of American Medicine (New York: Basic Books, 1982).

Table 1
The Rising Tide of Medical Costs: 1929-[2005]

Time period	Health care share of GDP at end of period (percent)	Annual growth in real health care dollars, per capita (percent)
1929	3.5	—
1929-1940	4.0	1.4
1940-1950	4.5	4.0
1950-1960	5.3	3.6
1960-1970	7.3	6.5
1970-1980	9.1	3.8
1980-1990	12.2	4.4
1990-2000	14.1	~4.5
2001-2005	16.0	~4

These early Blues, followed by commercial plans, set the pattern for health coverage that still dominates U.S. health financing. Patients were given "free choice of provider" (able to use almost any provider, not limited to contracted doctors or hospitals), with relatively low out-of-pocket cost at the time of service. Providers received retroactive fee-for-service payment (not an advance salary, capitation, or contracted amount) for all services they deemed "medically necessary." Risk pooling and financing came from insurers acting as "third parties," at a remove both from patients (first parties) and from providers (second). . . .

At first, there was no cost problem, for when coverage reached few people, benefit and payment levels were low, and medical technology did not exist to provide very sophisticated care. There appears to have been virtually no appreciation for how expensive this mode of operation would ultimately prove to be.

Blues plans were publicly perceived to have a more social role than "ordinary" insurance. Their not-for-profit status, chartered as "hospital (and medical) service corporations," rather than as insurance companies, reflect this perception. . . . In hindsight, the Blues also reflected the economic and professional self-interest of medical providers, seeking to strengthen private practice, institutionalize fee-for-service billing, and promote fiscal and clinical independence from outside control. They helped strengthen providers as private entrepreneurs. . . .

THE 1940S [AND 1950S]: WORKPLACE GROUPS: GREAT LEAP FORWARD

Private health insurance took a great leap forward in the 1940s. The economy moved back to full employment, manufacturing surged, and urbanization accelerated. It became rather common for manufacturing workers, especially through unions, to seek group health coverage as a fringe benefit of employment. . . . The tax treatment of fringe benefits encouraged employment group coverage. IRS administrative decisions, later codified in the Internal Revenue Code of 1954, deemed such benefits taxable neither to employer nor employee. Hence, through workplace insurance, health services could be prepaid with pre-tax dollars, reducing the cost of private coverage by savings on tax otherwise due. As tax levels rose, this tax subsidy became a more valuable benefit. . . .

The federal government supplied some health services, but only to identifiably "federal" populations. For example, the armed services, veterans, and the merchant marine all had dedicated hospitals; and the Indian Health Service operated on reservations. Interestingly, federal coverage of these populations was achieved predominantly through direct service delivery operations rather than through the financing of purchases from private providers. At the local level, states and municipalities also ran some hospitals and medical clinics. Local institutions often specialized in tuberculosis or mental health care, but some also provided general acute care, notably cities' public general hospitals. Most hospital care, however, remained the province of not-for-profit community hospitals.

This era also brought heavier public subsidy to the mainly private suppliers of care. Immediately after the war, the federal Hill-Burton Act made available grants to expand and modernize hospital capacity, which had suffered during the war. Soon thereafter, federal grants were also made available for medical education. In addition, with the post-war enlargement of the National Institutes of Health, federal policy greatly expanded support for basic research. . . .

The 1950s brought health coverage to much of the middle class through a combination of private action and the tax subsidy. By 1960, over two thirds of Americans had private coverage, but over 55 percent of personal health spending still came from patients' own pockets rather than from insurance coverage. . . .

The beginnings of price increases were becoming visible, though without being considered a major problem. . . . As one example, the average hospital expense/day was only $7.98 in 1950, but rose to $16.46 in 1960. . . .

THE 1960S [AND 1970S]: ENTER BIG GOVERNMENT, INCREMENTALLY

The sixties were marked by further incremental expansion of coverage, with most attention paid to expansion of government-subsidized care for those omitted by private coverage (the poor, the frail, the aged) through the intervention of federal medical entitlement programs. The theory was that beneficiaries would be entitled to medical service. An emerging reality was that providers were entitled to collect what they wanted from government. The decade began with John F. Kennedy's newly activist leadership seeking a "New Frontier" that included federal medical coverage, at least for the elderly. Strong opposition came from fiscal conservatives and from medical interest groups, spearheaded by the AMA [American Medical Association], which supported voluntary private insurance. Opponents objected on the ground that "socialized medicine" would ultimately allow federal bureaucrats to control clinical decisions in medicine (as well as medical incomes). . . .

After President Lyndon B. Johnson's landslide victory in 1964, federally funded *Medicare* was enacted to provide conventional third-party coverage for the aged (those within the Social Security system and past retirement age) and the disabled (those unable to work). The program was patterned on the Blues, with automatic entitlement to Part A hospital coverage (parallel to Blue Cross) and voluntary enrollment in Part B physician and other coverage (Blue Shield). The state-federal *Medicaid* program was created, almost as an afterthought, to cover what one might call the "deserving" poor (basically those unable to work by virtue of age, blindness, or disability). Medicaid built on the Kerr-Mills precedent of state discretion operating within a federal set of rules. . . .

By virtue of the vastly increased public role in financing coverage as well as continued growth in private coverage, the pattern of U.S. health spending shifted markedly. Whereas in 1960 over half of total health spending was still met by patients' direct out-of-pocket payments, by 1970 the patient's share had dropped to only 35 percent, while the federal share doubled to over 20 percent. . . .

Medicare essentially adapted Blues' reimbursement principles to public payment; the prime objective was to give beneficiaries access to private providers. The program was created as a third party outside medical transactions, responsible for reimbursing hospitals for their "reasonable costs" retrospectively and physicians for their actual submitted bills. . . . Superimposing this public largesse on top of existing payment mechanisms favorable to providers understandably failed to promote cost-conscious tradeoffs between value and cost of services.

This decade of greatly subsidized demand and provider-driven payment spurred further hospital expansion and upgrading, as well as the entry of many new physicians, as manpower policy simultaneously responded to a perceived "physician shortage." Medical price rises became much larger than the general rate of inflation. Average hospital expense per day, for example, rose from $16.46 in 1960 to $53.95 in 1970. As one early-seventies commentator noted, the price of a hospital room in the early 1950s was about that of a good hotel, but by end of the 1960s, hospital prices had left hotels well behind. Usage of services also increased. . . .

Much of the 1960s growth was intentional, especially for serving the elderly and others previously without coverage. Such expansion continues to seem desirable from today's perspective. In hindsight, however, a key problem was not mere price increases and new benefits to encourage new services, but rather the "blank check" fashion in which expanded coverage was removed entirely from disciplined evaluation of the benefit obtained from new services. Neither public nor private payers made any attempt to signal *how much* new care was enough, either through payment rules and incentives or through explicit provisions about benefits or utilization of care. Medical "need" was once thought to set a natural limit on services; in fact, "need" is an expansive, not a limiting concept. All signals were for more of everything: scientific research and technological innovation, insurance benefits, and clinical services. Given free rein, medical care can expand enormously as we have since learned. Additional care can almost always offer some level of legitimate benefit to some patients. . . .

By the end of the 1960s, the basic patterns of U.S. health care delivery and financing were set: Private hospitals and physicians delivered most health care.

Employers voluntarily provided private insurance to workers. Governments provided public insurance to those too old or unable to work (through public plans modelled on the private ones). All plans retrospectively reimbursed provider-set charges or costs. Each plan paid separately for its own financing, based on its own experience. Generous fee-for-service reimbursement encouraged even more services, with no built-in controls on price or utilization. . . .

[T]he 1970s became the first decade of "cost containment." Health prices were frozen (along with all others), then regulated by federal wage and price controls under President Nixon's "Economic Stabilization Program." Health controls were kept on for some months after others were lifted, and costs were effectively held down. Thereafter, inflation returned with a vengeance. There were so many manifestations of increased cost consciousness in the public sector that only the highlights can be mentioned. For example, a single 1972 omnibus bill strengthened federal health planning regulation, required utilization/quality review of Medicare hospitalizations, and limited the allowed annual growth of prevailing Medicare physician fees. Two years later, the National Health Planning Act required states, under threat of losing all federal health monies, to regulate hospital growth through certificates of need. Also in 1974, the HMO Act, sought reform reflecting a mix of regulation and market-oriented approaches. Many state governments also experimented with "prospective reimbursement" or hospital "rate setting" to control hospital costs, which were (and are) the largest share of health spending. In sharp contrast, the private sector response to rising costs was more muted. . . .

Costs continued to grow rapidly. The medical care CPI again outpaced the CPI for all items. Real medical spending outgrew real GDP by a factor of two, down slightly from the 1960s' two and a half. By 1980, health's share of GDP reached 9.1 percent (Table 1). . . .

THE 1980s: EVERY PLAN FOR ITSELF, AS COSTS RISE AND COVERAGE DROPS

The 1980s began with the self-consciously conservative administration of Ronald W. Reagan, who was philosophically committed to a limited federal role in health care. Still, there were expectations of an actively "pro-competitive" federal reform that would promote private coverage and private economizing. Academic and other theorists had developed such ideas, which were encouraged by the "privatizing" rhetoric of the new administration. . . . Probably the decade's most significant federal action came in 1983, when the administration and Congress collaborated in creating a Prospective Payment System (PPS) for inpatient hospital services under Medicare. In place of retrospective cost-based reimbursement, hospitals were to be paid fixed amounts per case, with rates set in advance for each of nearly 500 types of case, called "DRGs." Under this scheme, each institution is at financial risk for each case; a hospital earns no more for spending more and is able to keep the balance if it spends less. . . .

Some states experimented further with prospective payment for hospitals, either regulating only Medicaid rates or also covering most or all other payers. . . . Other states took market-oriented approaches: Arizona solicited competitive bids for HMO-like plans to cover its first-ever Medicaid program enrollees and California negotiated special hospital discounts for its Medicaid recipients' care through "selective contracting."

The private sector also showed new aggressiveness in attempting to contain costs during the 1980s. . . . Most significantly but with more difficulty, firms increasingly sought to move toward "managed care" and away from open-ended coverage of whatever services doctors and patients choose. Managed care includes not merely HMOs but also new entities called "PPOs" or other plans with limitations on what physicians and what services could be used. . . .

The U.S. has thus tried a mélange of different strategies for cost containment, both regulatory and market-oriented in nature. But all have been incremental (e.g., "managed care" for particular plans, administered prospective pricing for Medicare hospital payments) rather than system-wide (e.g., budgetary limits, restructured rules on insurance choice and pricing). And all have their weaknesses . . . and powerful opponents.

With regard to health care coverage, the 1980s saw the first-ever drop in percentage of the population with coverage, driven by a drop in private health insurance coverage. For 1990, the total share of the population with private coverage dropped 5-10 percentage points. . . .

Many factors helped cause the decline in private coverage, but two were paramount: rising costs and declining insurance pooling. First, the continuing rise in health care costs has made insurance premiums too high to continue to attract new purchasers. . . . Second, risk pools have continued to disaggregate, as more and more firms self-insure and experience rating spreads to ever-smaller groups. This continuing trend means that firms with high-risk employees or a bad year of experience can no longer count on insurance to spread these costs. These problems are worst in the "small group" insurance market (often defined as under 50 or 25 employees). . . . Even those with large-group coverage fear for their coverage. Not only has corporate "downsizing" cost many employees their jobs, but cost-containment has led to sudden medical cutbacks as well. . . .

Some cost-containment efforts did help moderate the rate of growth in health spending, especially for hospital care. . . . Nonetheless, medical spending continued to grow rapidly. During the 1980s, real health care spending grew at 4.4 percent a year, over two and a half times as fast as real GDP, just as in the fast-growth 1960s. Health therefore consumed fully 12.2 percent of GDP in 1990, a total of $666 billion or about $2,566 per capita. . . .

[I]n the 1960s, U.S. health care spending was not far out of line with that of other developed countries, given the higher level of U.S. national income. Since then, especially in the 1980s, U.S. spending as a share of GDP has increased rapidly, whereas other countries' growth has been more controlled. Other developed countries all faced what they considered unacceptable cost increases in the 1970s and 1980s, but almost all implemented social limits on further growth, with significant success. The result is that the U.S. spends far more on health care than any other developed nation. . . .

ENTERING THE [NEW CENTURY]: OMINOUS TRENDS IN COST AND COVERAGE

Health spending is about to grow right off the charts, thanks to the magic of compound interest. The projections are truly staggering for policymakers worried about the federal deficit, workers' earnings, or international competitiveness — and these are not the worst-case scenarios, just extrapolations of current trends. For the year [2005, health spending reached 16 percent of GDP (Table 1), some $2 trillion or about $6,700 per capita], according to federal statisticians. . . . As disquieting as these statistics are, [this] century's "out years" (as budgeters call them) will be even worse: Health's share of GDP is projected to climb to some [20 percent in 2015], mostly paid by government. Such projections assume continuation of today's trends in price inflation, growth in utilization and intensity of services, growth and aging of the population, and other factors. Such numbers greatly inspire reformers. . . .

Where are we headed next? That is the subject of much discussion . . . on Capitol Hill. . . . The political and practical backing for some change seems strong. But we end on a rather pessimistic note. This situation has existed before. Very high expectations attended earlier debates [on national health insurance], yet earlier reform plans all ended as incremental changes to the same basic system. Recent experience shows, however, that a failure to fundamentally reform the system will only put off the day of reckoning, and not for long, as the tide of rising costs continues to erode the gains made over the last four decades. The underlying question is whether the current crisis will conquer the historic inertia of the payment system, which now nurtures a huge economic sector of politically active people. . . .

Health Coverage by Source, 2005

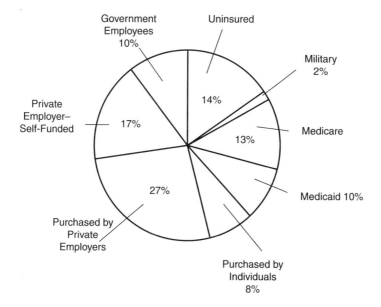

■ THE SAD HISTORY OF HEALTH CARE COST CONTAINMENT AS TOLD IN ONE CHART
Drew E. Altman & Larry Levitt
21(2) Health Affairs 9 (March 2002)*

What [this] Exhibit shows is that no approach our nation has tried, over the past thirty-five years, to control health costs has had a lasting impact. When Medicare and Medicaid passed in the mid-1960s, the new public programs took some of the burden of health spending off of the private sector, but only temporarily. By the late 1960s the rate of increase in private health spending per capita shot up. In the early 1970s wage and price controls had a dramatic impact on health care costs. But again, the impact was short-lived, and the rate of increase in private health spending rose dramatically after a few years. When President Jimmy Carter threatened tough cost containment regulation in the late 1970s, the health care industry organized what it called the "Voluntary Effort." The rate of increase in per capita private-sector health spending fell rapidly but then bounced back within a few years. Managed care and the threat of the Clinton health care reform plan appeared to have had a dramatic impact on the rate of increase in private health spending in the mid-1990s, but by the late 1990s it was on the rise again, reaching double-digit rates of increase by 2001. . . .

Exhibit 1
Annual Change in Private Health
Spending Per Capita (Adjusted for Inflation), 1961-2001

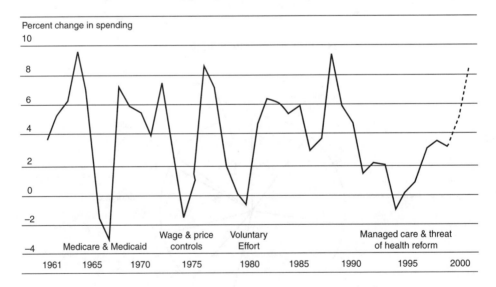

* Reprinted with the permission of Project Hope.

Some believe that we will not get a handle on health care costs as a nation until we are ready to make tough decisions about rationing medical care. An equally plausible scenario is that the apparent failure of all approaches reflects the American people's uncontainable desire for the latest and best health care, and that what we will do in the future is try small things that will work at the margin, complain a lot, but ultimately pay the bill.

2. The Crisis in Coverage and Spending

■ THE FUTURE OF THE AMERICAN HEALTH CARE SYSTEM
Henry T. Greely*
3 Stan. L. & Pol'y Rev. 16 (1991)

It was the best of times, it was the worst of times, it was the age of wisdom, it was the age of foolishness, it was the epoch of belief, it was the epoch of incredulity, it was the season of Light, it was the season of Darkness, it was the spring of hope, it was the winter of despair, we had everything before us, we had nothing before us, we were all going direct to Heaven, we were all going direct the other way — in short, the period was so far like the present period, that some of its noisiest authorities insisted on its being received, for good or for evil, in the superlative degree of comparison only.

Like Dickens's *ancien régime*, today's American medicine is a study in vivid contrasts. Infant mortality in the United States has just reached a record low; the revolution in genetics holds out the promise of unbelievably detailed knowledge of the human organism; successful surgery is performed on fetuses still in the womb; and hearts, livers, lungs, and bone marrow of others recall to life men and women otherwise doomed. Yet [almost one American in six] has no health insurance coverage; . . . emergency rooms throughout the country are filled to overflowing, when they are not closing their doors for good; an American admitted to a hospital has better than one chance in about thirty of being injured there; and Americans living in the worst slums have life expectancies below those of the residents of some of the poorest countries in the world. American medicine is everywhere triumphant, but everywhere in rags. . . .

The coming crisis in the American health care system is amply illustrated [by] the problems in access, cost and quality that will make health policy the leading domestic policy issue of [our time]. The problem of access to health care is stated simply: An estimated [48] million Americans are not covered by any private or governmental health insurance plan. Although coverage is not the same as access, neither are the two divorced. People without health coverage are left to rely on hospital emergency rooms and, where available, public clinics for most of their care. Their access is rationed largely (and effectively) by inconvenience and waiting time. . . .

Cost of a service cannot be considered without also considering the quality of the service received. Measuring quality in health care is difficult, but two general problems, one actual and one perceived, are apparent in American medicine.

---

* Professor of Law, Stanford University.

The actual problem is that health care is an uncertain science and the hospital a dangerous place. This commonplace truth recently took on renewed importance as the Harvard Medical Practice Study published its powerful review of the quality of medical care in New York hospitals. . . . Projecting the percentages across the country leads to the conclusion that about 1.5 million people are injured in hospitals by their medical care each year; about 400,000 of these people are injured by negligence. . . .

The perceived problem with quality is more subtle. Americans have longer—and healthier—life spans than ever before, but we do not *feel* healthy or well cared for. In the midst of unprecedented health, we perceive ourselves in unprecedented danger. Some of this may result from expectations that have outstripped reality; some may be from the frequent and frequently conflicting stories of new health threats—threats in food, water, air, and even in the imperceptible fluctuating electromagnetic fields of modern life. Each new study produces news stories, anxiety, and confusion.

Access, costs, and quality are all meaningless without some grounds for comparison, but medical comparisons are very difficult. Different countries deliver health care in different ways. What is satisfactory to one country's citizens and what is feasible in one country's political system may prove worthless in another's. Nonetheless, for whatever their value, we can make some comparisons. . . . [The United States spends 75 to 100 percent more per capita on health care than does Canada, France, Germany, and many northern European and Scandinavian countries, and 150 to 300 percent more per capita than England, Japan, Spain, and several other European countries.]

It is hard to know what those funds buy in terms of health because health is a product of so much more than medical care. Nevertheless, the casual observer can see no reason to believe that Americans are healthier than citizens of other rich countries; our life expectancy and infant mortality statistics show that, at least in some respects, we are less healthy.

In its technical brilliance, American health care is unsurpassed. Its best care would have seemed miraculous just a few years ago. But the bad side of American health care is very bad, and there is reason to think that it will get worse before it gets better. For one thing, the coming years will see a further increase in both the number of the elderly in the population and their percentage of the population. The growth will be particularly great among those over 85, the people most likely to make heavy use of the medical system. New technology, for which one can almost always read "expensive" new technology, continues to invade medicine. . . .

An outside observer might conclude that America's greatest domestic problem over the next decade will be something other than health care—education, poverty, racism, crime, and the decaying infrastructure are some of the many possibilities. But, unlike those issues, the problems of the health system will soon reach a condition where the middle class will demand that something *must* be done. The nature and timing of the collapse cannot be predicted, but like the *ancien régime* a little more than 200 years ago, it is increasingly clear that the system cannot continue indefinitely.

■ WHY CONSERVATIVES DON'T TALK ABOUT AMERICA'S HEALTH SYSTEM
Democratic Study Group, U.S. House of Representatives
1991

Even though the United States devotes a far larger share of its GDP to health care than any other of the 23 industrialized countries, it does not rank similarly high in terms of the basic indicators of health status. Rather, the standing of the United States ranges from somewhere below the middle (life expectancy for women) to close to the bottom (infant mortality).

Despite our high level of health care spending, the United States ranks 21st out of the 23 industrialized countries in terms of infant mortality — ahead of only Portugal and Greece. . . . The United States ranks *18th* among the 23 industrialized countries in terms of life expectancy for males — again despite the high level of health care spending in the United States. . . .

Like infant mortality, life expectancy is also clearly linked to socioeconomic status, and there is a much lower male life expectancy among the disproportionately poor black population in the United States. However, even the life expectancy for white males in the United States is lower than the male life expectancy in 13 of the 23 industrialized countries (including such diverse countries as France, Greece, Australia, and Canada). . . . For women, life expectancy in the United States ranks 15 out of 23. Countries with a higher female life expectancy than the United States include Spain, Greece, Canada, France, West Germany, and Sweden. . . .

While Americans are spending considerably more for health care than citizens of other industrialized countries — and may well be getting less for what we spend — it is nevertheless possible that Americans simply prefer the particular style of medicine and health care delivery that has developed in the United States. That is, we might be paying more than West Europeans, but getting in return a system with which we are satisfied.

A good indication of whether the level of satisfaction with the health care system is, in fact, higher in the United States than abroad is provided by . . . comparisons between attitudes in the United States and Canada. . . . [These] two nations have generally similar cultures and lifestyles but rather different health care systems (the Canadian system being a publicly funded program of universal health insurance [that spends about 45 percent less per capita]). . . .

[T]he level of satisfaction with health care services received was significantly higher in Canada than in the United States: 67 percent of Canadians stated they were *very* satisfied with the health care services they had received during the last year, compared to only 35 percent in the United States. Further, 18 percent of Americans surveyed were actually *dis*satisfied with the health care services they had received, while only 5 percent of Canadians were similarly dissatisfied. . . .

The data presented in this section suggest that the health care crisis in the United States is *not* the inevitable result of modern medicine. Rather, West European nations, Canada, and Japan all manage to spend significantly smaller fractions of their GDP on health care than the United States, while simultaneously providing broader access to health care than is available in this country.

Further, citizens of these other industrialized nations seem to receive at least as much (and generally more) health care services in the form of doctor visits and hospital stays as received by Americans. Overall health status in these other nations seems no worse (and generally better) than in the United States, and Western Europe appears to be ahead of the United States in addressing major health problems such as heart attacks and breast cancer.

■ DANGEROUS MEDICINE: A CRITICAL ANALYSIS OF CLINTON'S HEALTH PLAN
Doug Bandow*
1993

In his [1993] State of the Union speech the president stated that "our government will never again be fully solvent until we tackle the health-care crisis." . . . If one took his rhetoric seriously one would think that people were dying in droves due to inadequate medical care. . . . The theme of "crisis" has been repeated endlessly by [political] aides, legislators, journalists, and analysts. Yet there is, demonstrably, no *crisis*. Problems, yes. Serious problems, yes. But a "crisis," no.

Indeed, if you become seriously ill, there is no better nation in which to become sick than the United States. America's death rate, perhaps the best measure of access to and quality of care, is among the lowest, and often *the* lowest, for most major illnesses. In some cases the differences are quite dramatic: You are twice as likely to die from a hernia or intestinal obstruction in Sweden than in the U.S., three times as likely to die from an ulcer in Great Britain than in America, and seven times as likely to die from prostate disease in Sweden than in the U.S.

This is not to say that American *health* is equal to that elsewhere. Infant mortality and life expectancy lag behind those of many other industrialized states, but that reflects serious social pathologies absent from many other nations. For example, the U.S. has many problems characteristic of Third World states in its inner cities. . . . [O]verall health figures are dramatically affected by America's high rates of homicide, drug use, and AIDS. . . . In short, if Americans survive to enter a nursing home, their life expectancy rises to the longest in the world. The fact that many do not survive is not a fault of the present health care system — nor will it be affected by health care "reform."

American medicine is particularly good at treating the injured and sick because it rewards research and innovation, and utilizes the latest medical techniques and technologies. The pharmaceutical industry, for instance, is one of America's most competitive businesses internationally. American companies have developed a larger share of significant new drugs than any other nation. These products actually reduce total health care costs by cutting the need for surgery and other expensive alternative procedures. Naturally, these products also save lives and ameliorate suffering for millions of people.

---

* The author was a senior fellow at the Cato Institute, which is known for its libertarian and free market public policy positions.

Compared to other nations the U.S. also makes available more high-tech devices and procedures. . . . America has four times as many open-heart surgeries as Germany and six times as much radiation therapy and eight times as many magnetic resonance imaging [machines] as Canada. . . . American physicians, with a universe of modern technology at their fingertips, are the envy of the world's physicians. . . .

[S]pending/GDP ratios alone do not demonstrate the existence of a problem, let alone a crisis. There is no "right" amount of money to spend on health care and comparisons with other nations help little. Based on purchasing-power parities (rather than misleading exchange-rate measurements), America has the highest standard of living in the world: the U.S. gross domestic product per capita is more than 55 percent higher than that of Western Europe, 35 percent more than in Australia, 28 percent greater than in Japan, and 11 percent higher than in Canada. There is nothing strange, then, about Americans devoting an increasing share of their incomes on medical attention as they grow more prosperous. Surely there is at least as much justification for spending a marginal dollar on health as on a nicer car, more recreation, or another beer.

Notes: The Crisis in American Medicine

1. *The Perpetual Crisis.* American medicine has been declared to be in a "crisis" since at least the early 1960s. See Marion Sanders, The Crisis in American Medicine (1961). Can things really be all that bad if they've been like this so long? Another self-proclaimed iconoclast who doesn't think we are necessarily spending too much on health care is the highly-respected health economist Joseph P. Newhouse, An Iconoclastic View of Health Cost Containment, Health Aff., Supp. 1993, at 152. Harvard economist David Cutler claims that increased medical spending over the past several decades has produced increases in average health that are worth several times more than their aggregate costs. David M. Cutler, Your Money or Your Life: Strong Medicine for America's Health Care System (Oxford Univ. Press, 2004). For a counter argument and evidence, see Elliott S. Fisher, Medical Care: Is More Always Better?, 349 New Eng. J. Med. 1665 (2003); Nortin M. Hadler, The Last Well Person (2004). See generally Symposium, 22(1) Health Aff. 1 (Jan. 2003).

Even if there is not a "crisis," there is still clearly a serious problem in American medicine. In case you're still not convinced, consider the following additional facts, opinions, and anecdotes.

Medicine, like many other American institutions, suffered a stunning loss of confidence in the 1970s. Previously, two premises had guided government health policy: first, that Americans needed more medical care — more than the market alone would provide; and second, that medical professionals and private voluntary institutions were best equipped to decide how to organize those services. . . . In the 1970s this mandate ran out. The economic and moral problems of medicine displaced scientific progress at the center of public attention. Enormous increases in cost seemed ever more certain; corresponding improvements in health ever more doubtful. The prevailing assumptions about the need to expand medical care were reversed: The need now was to curb its apparently insatiable appetite for resources. In a short time, American medicine seemed to pass from stubborn shortages to irrepressible excess, without ever having passed through happy sufficiency. [Paul Starr, The Social Transformation of American Medicine 379 (1982).]

Studies indicate that at least 25 percent of the money we spend on health care is wasted. . . . Millions of unnecessary procedures and tests are performed each year. Almost half the coronary bypasses, the majority of cesarean sections, and a significant proportion of many other procedures, such as pacemaker implants and carotid endarterectomies, are unnecessary or of questionable value. A former editor of the Journal of the American Medical Association is convinced that more than half of the forty million medical tests performed each day "do not really contribute to a patient's diagnosis or therapy." Doctors order many procedures and tests to protect themselves from potential medical malpractice liability. Some procedures are performed because doctors simply do not know the precise circumstances under which many procedures work. [Joseph A. Califano, Rationing Health Care: The Unnecessary Solution, 140 U. Pa. L. Rev. 1525 (1992).]

How much does an overnight stay at a Virginia hospital cost? . . . A year ago, Mr. Shipman, a 43-year-old former furniture salesman from Herndon, Va., experienced severe chest pains during the night. . . . Suspecting a heart attack, doctors first performed a cardiac catheterization to examine and unblock the coronary arteries. Then, they inserted a stent, a small metal device that props open a blocked artery so the blood flows better to the heart. Lacking health insurance, Mr. Shipman . . . checked himself out of the hospital against medical advice. Since then, Mr. Shipman and his wife, Alina, have received hospital bills totaling $29,500. . . . In addition, there were other bills: some $1,000 for the ambulance trip, $6,800 from the cardiologist who performed the stent procedure, and several thousand dollars for the local emergency-room visit. In all, the two-day health crisis left the Shipmans saddled with medical bills totaling nearly $40,000. Once solidly middle class, the couple says the debt triggered a gradual unraveling of their lives. "Middle class or not, when you have a bill of $37,000 hanging over your head, that's all you think about," says Ms. Shipman. . . . "You eat, sleep and breathe that bill." [Lucette Lagnado, Anatomy of a Hospital Bill, Wall St. J., Sept. 21, 2004, at B1.]

In May of 2002, a panel of experts . . . released a report documenting . . . [that] the long-term uninsured face a twenty-five percent greater likelihood of premature death than do insured Americans. Institute of Medicine, Care Without Coverage (National Academy Press, Washington, D.C., 2002). . . . In sum, an estimated 18,000 Americans, six times the number killed in the attacks of September 11, die annually because they are uninsured. . . . The uninsured [also] . . . face, day by day, the risk of imminent financial disaster. Medical expenses are one of the leading causes of bankruptcy in the United States. Melissa B. Jacoby, Teresa A. Sullivan, and Elizabeth Warren, Rethinking the Debates Over Health Care Financing: Evidence from the Bankruptcy Courts, 76 New York University Law Rev 387 (2001). . . . Lack of health insurance is among the greatest threats to financial security that Americans currently face. [Timothy Jost, Disentitlement: Health Care Entitlements and the Threats That They Face (2003).]

There is no U.S. health care system. What we call our health care system is, in daily practice, a hodgepodge of historic legacies, philosophical conflicts, and competing economic schemes. Health care in America combines the tortured, politicized complexity of the U.S. tax code with a cacophony of intractable political, cultural, and religious debates about personal rights and responsibilities. Every time policymakers, corporate health benefits purchasers, or entrepreneurs try to fix something in our health care system, they run smack into its central reality: the primary producers and consumers of medical care are uniquely, stubbornly self-serving as they chew through vast sums of other people's money. Doctors and hospitals stumble their way through irresolvable conflicts between personal gain and ethical responsibilities; patients struggle with the acrimony and anguish that accompany life-and-death medical decisions; consumers, paying for the most part with everybody's money but their own, demand that the system serve them with the immediacy and flexibility of other industries; and health insurers are trapped in the middle, trying to keep everybody happy. A group of highly imaginative, energetic people armed with the world's largest Mark-n-Wipe board could not purposefully design a more complex, dysfunctional system if they tried. It is a $1.3 trillion per year fiasco narrated with moral shrillness and played out one competing anecdote after another. [J.D. Kleinke, Oxymorons: The Myth of a U.S. Health Care System 1 (2001).]

2. *More Facts and Figures*. One way to put health care spending in context is to realize that it accounts for a larger portion of our gross domestic product than any other sector of the economy — more than housing, food, or transportation. Another way to capture the economic impact is to realize that the annual cost for private health insurance in 2006 averaged more than $11,000 for a family or $4000 for an individual. The following graph provides additional detail about historical spending levels for the health care sector.

National Health Spending, Selected Years

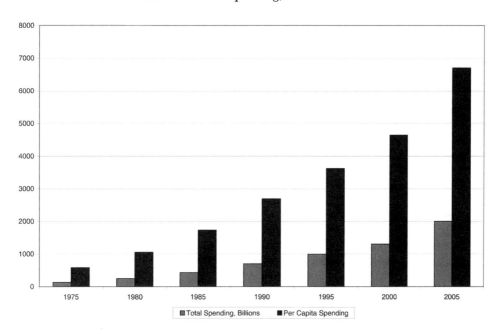

For more readings that describe the evolution of the health care financing and delivery system and the various public policy problems it currently faces, see the series of articles in the New England Journal of Medicine starting with John K. Iglehart, The American Health Care System: Expenditures, 340 New Eng. J. Med. 70 (1999); David Mechanic, The Truth About Health Care: Why Reform Is Not Working in America (2006); Julius B. Richmond & Rashi Fein, The Health Care Mess: How We Got into It and What It Will Take to Get Out (2005); Paul Krugman & Robin Wells, The Health Care Crisis and What to Do About It, 53 N.Y. Review of Books No. 5 (March 23, 2006). A fascinating account of the early history of health insurance is Herman Somers & Anne Somers, Private Health Insurance, 46 Cal. L. Rev. 376, 508 (1958).

There is seemingly an endless appetite for facts and figures about the U.S. health care delivery system. Those who wish more, or more recent, numbers can find them in the annual editions of the American Hospital Association's *Hospital Statistics*, in the annual reports of the Medicare Payment Advisory Commission (MedPac), in periodic issues of *Health Affairs* and on the Web pages for the U.S. Census Bureau and the Centers for Medicare and Medicaid Services (CMS), which are linked to the Web page for this book, www.health-law.org.

3. *International Comparisons.* According to one analysis, the poor U.S. performance on aggregate health statistics is not due to major differences in health habits or lifestyles, since the United States ranks in the middle or toward the top in fat, alcohol, and cigarette consumption, and its health rankings remain low even when comparing only the white population and when excluding automobile deaths. Instead, this author argues that the lower U.S. rankings are due in large part to the relatively inadequate system of primary care physicians and the overuse of high-risk procedures. Barbara Starfield, Is U.S. Health Really the Best in the World?, 284 JAMA 483 (2000). Another prominent study found that the British are much healthier than Americans in all major disease areas, such as diabetes, heart disease, stroke, lung disease, and cancer, even after controlling for all relevant sociodemographic factors. J. Banks, M. Marmot, et al., Disease and Disadvantage in the United States and England, 295 JAMA 2037 (2006). Considering a broad range of indicators of health status and health care access, the World Health Organization ranked the U.S. health care system thirty-seventh in the world. See also Cathy Schoen et al., U.S. Health System Performance: A National Scorecard, 25 Health Aff. w457 (Sept. 2006).

3. Changes in Financing and Delivery Systems

■ MEDICARE AND THE AMERICAN HEALTH CARE SYSTEM: 1996 REPORT TO CONGRESS
Prospective Payment Assessment Commission

National health care expenditures . . . increased at more than twice the economywide rate of inflation since 1975. . . . Recently, however, the increase in health care spending has slowed. . . . The recent changes in health care expenditure trends are due partly to pressure exerted by private payers. Employers that purchase coverage for employees and their dependents increasingly are demanding health insurance products that control their outlays yet preserve quality. This pressure has resulted in a shift toward managed care plans, which often have benefit packages that are similar to or more generous than traditional indemnity insurance, but at lower prices. Like indemnity offerings, managed care plans receive a premium for assuming the financial risk of providing a defined set of benefits for each person. Unlike traditional indemnity insurers, though, these plans attempt to constrain expenditures by playing an active role in the delivery of services. . . .

The most common managed care models are health maintenance organizations (HMOs), preferred provider organizations (PPOs), and point-of-service (POS) plans. In a traditional HMO plan, subscribers must receive their care from a limited group of providers. PPO and POS subscribers may not be subject to the same level of plan oversight as in HMOs: Generally they may go to any provider, but their out-of-pocket payments are lower if they choose participating providers that give the insurer discounted rates. . . .

Managed care plans use a variety of techniques to control their costs. First, they actively seek providers with lower-cost practice patterns and offer them a defined patient base in exchange for favorable payment rates. By limiting the number of providers or by creating strong financial incentives to choose certain ones, managed care plans influence which providers subscribers will use. Through this selective contracting, managed care plans can substantially affect providers' revenues. Plans' bargaining positions are strongest in areas with excess provider capacity. Providers that choose not to participate or that are not selected by the managed care plan may experience a decline in their patient volume.

In addition, managed care plans often use discounted fee-for-service rates to control their costs. They also use per case, per day, or per person payments to shift some of the financial risk of treating patients to providers. Per case or per day payments are generally made to hospitals, whereas per person payments are more often made to physicians, predominately primary care practitioners. These payment methods reward providers for delivering care efficiently, discouraging unnecessary service use.

A per person, or capitation, payment system is the most comprehensive way to shift financial risk to providers. Under capitation, providers receive a prepaid sum to furnish a defined set of services to a plan's enrollees. This creates a monetary incentive for physicians to limit patients' use of services (or encourage preventive services) because the physician receives the same payment regardless of the volume or intensity of care, or even if no care is provided at all. Many managed care plans also require primary care physicians to act as "gatekeepers" to specialty care or hospital services. Under these arrangements, the primary care physician must preauthorize any services a patient receives. While these physicians usually do not bear the full financial risk for the additional services, delegating the gatekeeping function enables managed care plans to use financial incentives to limit referrals. . . .

Hospitals are seeking alternative revenue streams by broadening the scope of services they offer and competing for patients with other types of providers, [such as outpatient departments. By 1995], ... outpatient services represented 28.8 percent of total hospital revenue. Similarly, a growing number of hospitals are venturing into the post-acute care market, where payments are still dominated by fee-for-service methods. Hospitals are developing skilled nursing facilities (SNFs) or are using acute care beds as swing beds to provide skilled nursing services. In addition, they are establishing their own rehabilitation units and home health agencies. ...

Along with controlling their costs and seeking alternative revenue sources, hospitals are attempting to broaden (or maintain) their market share by securing a patient base through arrangements with other providers or managed care plans. Such arrangements have the potential to make overall service delivery more efficient and provide patients with a continuum of care. In 1994, for instance, 21 percent of community hospitals participated in health networks — groups of hospitals, physicians, other providers, insurers, or community agencies that coordinate and deliver a broad spectrum of services. Anecdotal evidence suggests that most hospitals have some type of arrangement, such as joint ventures or informal alliances, with other providers. Entering into arrangements with physicians is an increasingly popular strategy for hospitals. Such relationships can bolster a hospital's ability to secure managed care contracts. ...

The long-term effects of the changing environment on hospitals are still unclear. ... Hospitals traditionally have been viewed as the hub of the health care system and often have the capital reserves necessary to finance collaborations with other providers. Those that aggressively pursue such arrangements not only can improve their chances of being the hospital of choice for inpatient services, but also can exert more influence over medical practice decisions. In areas where managed care systems exert more control, however, hospitals may be viewed as cost centers with little input into delivery decisions.

PHYSICIANS

Historically, physicians determined not only which services would be provided, but where those services would be delivered. These decisions generally were made with little accountability for costs. Managed care is changing this. ... One indication of the level of financial pressure physicians are facing is the [reduced growth] in physician income. ... Some physicians are responding to the intensified pressures by selling their practices to hospitals or managed care organizations, and becoming employees of those entities. In 1990, nearly 70 percent of physicians reported they were self-employed. By 1995, this share had dropped to 55 percent. ...

Because physicians generate the demand for hospital services, they have leverage to assume a leadership role in arrangements with other providers. As health care funds become more and more limited, physicians — especially those who deliver primary care services — have an opportunity to play a larger part in deciding how those dollars will be distributed. ...

■ THE HEALTH CARE REVOLUTION: REMAKING MEDICINE IN CALIFORNIA*

Barbara Marsh
L.A. Times, Aug. 31, 1995

To find out where the nation's health care system may be headed, ask anybody in San Diego. San Diegans know more than most Americans about managed care, which controls costs by limiting consumer choice. About two-thirds of insured San Diego residents were enrolled in health maintenance organizations last year—one of the highest levels in the country. "Every other major city and county in the country will be facing within five years the situation we are facing today," predicts Dr. Robert Ross, the county's health director. . . .

The system apparently pleases the healthy majority of consumers with access to doctors and hospitals at affordable prices. But those with unusual, chronic or serious illnesses often fail to benefit. Many San Diegans can't switch health plans because their employers offer only one. And consumers find it extremely difficult to fight a system that gives doctors financial incentives to minimize treatment. . . .

Surveys suggest that San Diegans generally are satisfied with their health care. . . . San Diegans were especially pleased with the quality of their care and the minimal paperwork involved. Eighty-five percent said they would recommend their doctor to a friend. . . .

Of course, managed care in San Diego—like elsewhere—isn't the result of a consumer revolt. It arose because employers threw up their hands at the rising costs of employee health care. In the late 1970s, an unusually active group of large employers—including defense and aerospace contractors, retailers, banks and local schools—got together to brainstorm ways to rein in double-digit increases in health benefits. The group even launched its own network of hospitals and physicians offering services at rates below traditional insurance plans. So employers couldn't have been more receptive when HMOs rushed into the market in the early 1980s. . . .

And many local hospitals, clinics, physicians and other providers have merged to form or align themselves with four vast systems that deliver managed care: HealthCare System, Scripps Health Corp., UCSD Healthcare and Kaiser. Experts predict more consolidation. . . .

Here as elsewhere, managed care has created an excess of specialist physicians. Many are fleeing San Diego for places still unpenetrated by HMOs. One day late in June, with a moving van parked outside his office, Dr. Steven Kotner fought back tears as he told how HMOs had lured away his patients with cheap insurance prices. "The majority would have stayed with me if they could," he says. His wife Andy, who managed his practice, defiantly lifts her chin to add, "They want us in Tennessee!"

Meanwhile, primary physicians, the workhorses of managed care, shoulder the patient burden. Dr. Laura Nathanson, a family practitioner in Encinitas, says it's tough to keep track of the terms of her patients' 18 different health plans. Her practice employs two staffers to keep up with the plans' ever-changing lists of approved providers, so patients won't get charged for services that aren't covered.

When she's on call at night, Nathanson keeps three separate lists of approved test centers, hospitals and emergency rooms so she can direct patients to the right place. "I routinely tell patients, 'Don't go anywhere—even to Nordstrom's—unless you've had your visit authorized,'" she jokes. . . .

Consumer advocates say people here generally understand little about what they're buying when they join an HMO. Jeanne Ertle, executive director of San Diego Neighbor to Neighbor, a local activist group, says consumers don't carefully compare benefits, co-payments, or deductibles. "Ultimately, it's the bottom line," says Ertle. "Which one can they afford?" . . . So HMOs and managed care get mixed reviews from today's San Diegans. As the nation continues to wrestle with health care reform, the ambiguities will only deepen.

Managed care, for instance, has yet to tackle the problem of San Diego's growing population of uninsured residents. . . . Five years ago, Celia Martinez, who cares for a paralyzed invalid, says she applied for insurance through Kaiser's plan for individuals. The 63-year-old woman, who stands 5 foot 4 and weighs 200 pounds, says Kaiser refused to allow her to join because she weighs too much. Earlier this summer, Martinez broke her arm, couldn't work for six weeks—and found herself having to arrange a payment plan for the care she received through UCSD Medical Center. "When it comes to California, they don't help you," she says. "You don't get no help. Everything is pay, pay, pay." . . .

■ TRANSCRIPT OF INTERVIEW WITH JAIME ROBINSON, Ph.D.[*]
Lehman Brothers Industry Expert Conference Call Series
May 17, 2002

As we go into the new decade, the insurance industry is reevaluating whether it wants to be America's method of health care cost control. It's found that this is a very difficult and very unappreciated job. It appears to the public that there is a tradeoff between corporate profits and individual health care, which is a very, very bad image for the industry. The insurers now want to have a completely different image, which is helping the consumer make health care choices. . . .

I think the battle is over and the providers won. The health plans don't really want to get in there and second-guess doctor decision-making. That just proved to be a turf where the providers were very strong, and had the support of the patients and the regulators. . . . There is a lot of lousy medicine being practiced out there that the insurance companies could detect, and could clean up, but they could never convince anybody that they're doing it for the right reasons rather than simply for their own profits.

They've essentially abandoned that role. Increasingly they want to see themselves as a financial services company, like a Fidelity, [which manages investment funds for retirement accounts.] . . . Fidelity offer[s] a stock fund and a bond fund and a mixed fund and employees can allocate their savings across these however they want [with the help of] some decision support tools. . . . The health

---

[*] Prof. Robinson is a health economist at the University of California at Berkeley. Reprinted with the permission of Prof. Robinson and Lehman Brothers.

plans want to do that on the health plan side. "We have our PPO product and our HMO product and our Medical Savings Account product and we're not going to try to force people to pick one or the other. We're going to give them choices. We're going to give them information about the different products, about their prices, about access and about quality. We're going to give them Internet based decision support and tools, and we're going to let them choose. After that, what happens is between the patient and their doctor and their hospital. We, the insurance company, are not going to be responsible for that." . . .

One of the reasons that the insurance industry wants to get out of managed care and go back to being like the financial services industry is that it wants to stop being continually compared to the tobacco industry. It doesn't want to be the second most hated industry in America. The industry needs to re-brand itself as a consumer friendly decision support and information industry rather than something that's trying to save money for corporations.

Notes: Managed Care vs. Consumer-Driven Care

1. *Managed Care Is Here to Stay.* Despite fierce resistance by many doctors and some patients, managed care is here to stay, and, indeed, has become the dominant form of insurance. However, enrollment has shifted rather dramatically in recent years from tightly managed HMO plans to PPO and POS plans that give patients more options. Regardless of the form managed care takes, it raises a host of legal, ethical, and regulatory issues that are explored throughout this book. For now, consider these broad inquiries: Are you concerned that insurers are interfering with medical judgment by deciding what treatments to pay for? Would you be more comfortable with a regime that let physicians and patients decide for themselves, but rewarded physicians for saving money or punished them for being excessive? Or, is the answer to make patients pay much more out of pocket so that they regulate their own spending decisions?

2. *Consumer-Driven Care.* For a fuller account of Prof. Robinson's views, see The End of Managed Care, 285 JAMA 2622 (2001), where he observes:

> [The following] problems will plague a consumer-driven health care system. First, despite the widespread dissemination of information, . . . even the most sophisticated and Internet-enabled consumer . . . will face significant obstacles in understanding the quality and even the true price of health insurance and health care services. . . . [C]onsumers vary enormously in their financial, cognitive, and cultural preparedness to navigate the complex health care system. The new paradigm fits most comfortably the educated, assertive, and prosperous and least comfortably the impoverished, meek, and poorly educated. . . . Finally, the emerging era will make transparent and render difficult the redistribution of income from rich to poor that otherwise results from the collective purchasing and administration of health insurance.

The consumer-driven movement is occurring in several different ways. One is simply to *increase co-payments and deductibles* significantly, even for HMOs, which traditionally have imposed only minimal cost-sharing obligations on patients. The second is for employers to contribute only a fixed amount toward the cost of health insurance (*defined contribution*) and let employees shop for whatever coverage they want, rather than pay for all or most of the cost of a group policy that the employer selects. A complementary approach is for the government to subsidize insurance through a *tax credit* that operates like a voucher. Third, insurers are adopting an approach to provider contracting known as *tiered networks*:

> Health plans, employers and hospitals are returning to notions of preferred providers and health plans. . . . The basic notion involves dividing hospitals and groups of physicians so that even though all of them may be listed in that thick provider directory, not all are created equal. For example, a hospital may say that 10 of 12 hospitals in an area are on a preferred list. If an enrollee is admitted to one of those hospitals no co-payment or deductible is required. But if the same enrollee goes to one of the two local hospitals that are not on the preferred list ("affiliated hospitals"), they are required to pay a deductible or co-payment of anywhere from $100 to $400 per day. These arrangements are referred to as "tiering" of providers. . . . Under certain systems, [providers] may set their own price and decide for themselves whether they want to be in the low, medium or high tier. . . .
>
> The move to tiering is partly a response to a change in the economic balance of power between health plans and providers. . . . In the early days of managed care, health plans did not contract with all hospitals and clinics. Instead, they offered a limited panel of providers the promise of more patients in exchange for discounted prices. Soon the sales people took over and decided that very broad provider networks were needed in order to match the competition, resulting in the extensive network overlap that now exists. . . . Many hospitals [then] used their newly found leverage to exit from [managed care] contracts. . . . By establishing tiers of providers, some health plans have returned to the old notion of identifying certain hospitals as preferred. At this point, that preference is based on pricing, although health plans say that they want to reach a point where tiering of hospitals and clinics would be based on measures of quality. Allan Baumgarten, Tiering Approaches for Health Plans: Incentives and Information for Consumers (June 17, 2002).

See also Symposium, W3 Health Aff. 135 (March 2003). Other examples of increased consumerism are prescription drug manufacturers' much more aggressively advertising directly to consumers rather than only to physicians, and the wealth of medical and health insurance information now available on the Internet. Consumer-driven ideas are being applied even to the Medicaid program for the poor. Jeb Bush, Market Principles: The Right Prescription for Medicaid, 17 Stan. L. & Pol'y Rev. 33 (2006).

The pros, cons, and legal implications of consumer-driven health care are being extensively debated and analyzed. For a sampling of the literature, see Regina Herzlinger, ed., Consumer-Driven Health Care: Implications for Providers, Payers, and Policymakers (2004); Timothy S. Jost, Health Care at Risk: A Critique of the Consumer-Driven Movement (2007); Malcom Gladwell, The Moral-Hazard Myth, New Yorker (Sept. 8, 2005); James C. Robinson, Reinvention of Health Insurance in the Consumer Era, 291 JAMA 1880 (2004); John V. Jacobi, Consumer-Driven Health Care and the Chronically Ill, 38 U. Mich. J.L. Reform 531 (2005); Amy B. Monahan, The Promise and Peril of Ownership Society Health Care Policy, 80

Tul. L. Rev. 777 (2006); Marshall B. Kapp, Patient Autonomy in the Age of Consumer-Driven Health Care, 2 J. Health & Biomed. L. 1 (2006); Haavi Morreim, High-Deductible Health Plans: New Twists on Old Challenges from Tort and Contract, 59 Vand. L. Rev. 1207 (2006); Mark A. Hall, Paying for What You Get, and Getting What You Pay For, 69 Law & Contemp. Probs. 159 (Autumn 2006); Peter D. Jacobson & Michael R. Tunick, Consumer-Directed Health Care and the Courts: Let the Buyer (And Seller) Beware, 26(3) Health Aff. 704 (June 2007); Symposium, 39 Health Serv. Res. 1049 (2004); Symposium, 24(6) Health Aff. (Dec. 2005); Symposium, 25(6) Health Aff. w516 (2006); Symposium, 28 J. Leg. Med. 1 (2007).

For a good overview of managed care generally, see Peter Kongstvedt, Managed Care: What It Is and How It Works (2d ed. 2002); Jacob S. Hacker & Theodore R. Marmor, How Not to Think About "Managed Care," 32 U. Mich. J. L. Reform 661 (1999). For additional discussion of broad changes in the health care system, see Understanding Health System Change: Local Markets, National Trends (Paul B. Ginsburg & Cara S. Lesser eds., 2001); John K. Iglehart, Changing Health Insurance Trends, 347 New Eng. J. Med. 956 (347).

3. *The Onslaught of Acronyms.* Regrettably, the health care field is overrun with acronyms. Since 1970 or so, no new institution or phenomenon seemingly can exist in medicine without being known primarily by its three-to-five-letter abbreviation. Most of the specialized organizational terms and acronyms you will encounter in these readings are collected and defined in the glossary at page 673 for convenient reference throughout the semester.

D. MORAL AND POLITICAL THEMES

The remainder of this chapter addresses various analytical theories that give greater depth to our understanding of health care law and public policy. Most of these analytical frameworks spring from some branch of moral and political theory that addresses fundamental questions of social justice, such as how best to distribute scarce medical resources, and whose decision over medical treatment should govern when there is conflict. Necessarily, this must be a grab bag of somewhat disconnected lines of thought drawn from many different intellectual disciplines—primarily philosophy, economics, and political science. This is due to what Einer Elhauge below calls the "paradigm pathology" of health care law: Although this field may have a core set of concerns, it lacks a dominant analytical mode. In classic fields of law such as contracts or torts, most people seem at least to be asking the same sorts of questions, even if they don't arrive at the same answers. Health care law has so many interdisciplinary, intellectual currents that courts and scholars sound at times like the mythical builders of the Tower of Babel. Some order can be brought to this mélange of ideologies by categorizing different and competing "paradigms" of thought. As Clark Havighurst explains in the second reading in this section, the dominant paradigm in past decades has been professionalism, and this is the one to which all the contenders respond. Rather than attempt any neat packaging of the contenders, for they are still very untidy, try to identify which currents of thought are consistent with and opposed to the professionalism paradigm, and in what ways. Then, try to articulate how different paradigms would answer the fundamental questions of social justice mentioned above (who gets which resources, and who decides).

1. Competing Paradigms

■ ALLOCATING HEALTH CARE MORALLY*
Einer Elhauge**
82 Cal. L. Rev. 1449 (1994)

Health law policy suffers from an identifiable pathology. . . . [I]t employs four different paradigms for how decisions to allocate resources should be made: the market paradigm, the professional paradigm, the moral paradigm, and the political paradigm. . . . [R]ather than coordinate these decisionmaking paradigms, health law policy employs them inconsistently, such that the combination operates at cross-purposes.

This inconsistency results in part because, intellectually, health care law borrows haphazardly from other fields of law, each of which has its own internally coherent conceptual logic, but which in combination results in an incoherent legal framework and perverse incentive structures. In other words, health care law has not — at least not yet — established itself to be a field of law with its own coherent conceptual logic, as opposed to a collection of issues and cases from other legal fields connected only by the happenstance that they all involve patients and health care providers.

In other part, the pathology results because the various scholarly disciplines focus excessively on their favorite paradigms. Scholars operating in the disciplines of economics, medicine, political science, and philosophy each tend to assume that their discipline offers a privileged perspective. This leads them either to press their favored paradigm too far or to conceptualize policy issues solely in terms of what their paradigm can and cannot solve.

Instead, health law policy issues should be conceived in terms of comparative paradigm analysis. Such analysis focuses on the strengths and weaknesses of the various decisionmaking paradigms, determining which is *relatively* better suited to resolving various decisions, and then assigning each paradigm to the roles for which it is best suited. . . .

Luckily, this is a mode of analysis in which legal scholars, as cross-disciplinary generalists, have some plausible claim to comparative scholarly advantage. Unluckily, it is hard and arduous. Nevertheless, it offers the promise that health law scholars will provide insights into health policy that so far have been missed. In a field as intellectually new as modern health law, it should hardly be surprising that this task has only begun.

** Professor of Law, Harvard University.

◼ THE PROFESSIONAL PARADIGM OF MEDICAL CARE: OBSTACLE TO DECENTRALIZATION*
Clark C. Havighurst**
30 Jurimetrics J. 415 (1990)

The thesis of this article is that, despite all the organizational and financial changes that occurred in the health care sector in the 1980s, we still cannot fight the battle for efficiency effectively because we are saddled as a society with a particular paradigmatic conception of the medical care enterprise. The source of this paradigm is a deep-seated belief, long fostered by the medical profession, that medical care is not a commodity, that its characteristics are scientifically determined, and that decisions concerning it must be entrusted exclusively to professionals. That this paradigm is ideologically attractive and contains some significant kernels of truth simply complicates the problem of adapting it to accord with current economic realities.

The professional paradigm of the medical enterprise is a venerable one, stemming from the days early in this century when the medical profession rose to what sociologist Paul Starr has called a position of "cultural authority, economic power, and political influence."[8] Although its tenets are nowhere officially set down, some of them can be deduced from the profession's performance during the era when it exercised rather complete hegemony over health care and its financing. Judging from that experience, the profession's ideology has included the following themes:

- medical care should be evaluated only on the basis of safety and efficacy;
- cost considerations should not enter into medical decisionmaking because counting costs implies both a willingness to trade off a patient's welfare against other societal needs and a tolerance for differences based on ability to pay;
- decisions on the appropriate utilization of medical services should be based exclusively on scientific evidence and expert opinion;
- although patient preferences should be honored under the principle of informed consent, there is no similar urgency about giving people opportunities to express their preferences qua consumers, with cost differences in view; and
- professional norms alone should set the limits of a physician's judgment.

Under these general principles, the role of payers was long limited to ensuring that professional norms were followed, so that only care that was virtually useless or positively harmful was excluded. . . .

---

* Copyright © 1990, American Bar Association. Reprinted by permission. All rights reserved.
** Professor of Law, Duke University.
[8] P. Starr, The Social Transformation of American Medicine 5 (1982).

The professional paradigm derives much of its force from the egalitarian ideal in medicine — the belief that every citizen is entitled to medical care of the same quality and that "two-tier" medicine is unthinkable. Even though society has not seen fit to adopt an egalitarian policy by accepting either the heavy tax burden or the stringent rationing necessary to achieve it, the egalitarian ideal colors much thinking about medical care. Indeed, even in the absence of any actual legal or contractual entitlement, a powerful entitlement mentality must be confronted by anyone seeking to economize in the provision of health services. The professional paradigm generally supports this view of things, while the profession as a whole resists most of the measures that would be necessary to create an affordable, truly egalitarian system. There is here a marriage of convenience — between physicians' desires to resist infringements on their clinical freedom and a particularly extreme view of the requirements of social justice.

The scientific character of medicine has also provided vital support for the professional paradigm. Indeed, the success of the medical profession in establishing its scientific character in the early part of the century — in the Flexner Report,[9] for example — laid the groundwork for its claim of exemption from market forces and for its autonomy as a profession. Once medical care was viewed as the application of science to human problems rather than as a commercial service to be bought and sold in market transactions, the profession was able to resist most of the pressures that naturally arose and to head off, by effective lobbying or collective action, market developments that might have threatened its hegemony. . . .

Residues of the professional paradigm can be found in many places but are particularly significant in the legal system. Not only does the law tend to defer to the medical profession's presumed scientific authority on many points, but it is often administered with an egalitarian mentality that tends to define issues in terms of abstract rights. Indeed, the law frequently goes to great lengths to avoid appearing to concede that some persons might ever have a legal or even a contractual right to better medical care than someone else. This refusal to recognize the reality that some consumers might choose, or wish to choose, to purchase more or better health care than others — or have a lesser entitlement because of inability or unwillingness to pay — greatly complicates efforts to economize in the private sector. It also raises, perhaps inappropriately, the cost to government of providing for those who cannot support themselves. As long as the legal system does not acknowledge inequality or recognize efforts to escape the costly standards implicit in the professional/scientific/egalitarian paradigm, neither self-supporting consumers nor taxpayers are in a good position to economize on health care by refusing to buy too much of a good thing.

---

[9] A. Flexner, Medical Education in the United States and Canada (Carnegie Foundation for the Advancement of Technology, Bull. No. 4, 1910).

2. Ethics and Empiricism

■ THE PRACTICE OF AUTONOMY: PATIENTS, DOCTORS, AND MEDICAL DECISIONS
Carl E. Schneider*
1998

Bioethicists, like lawyers, live in danger of what I once called "hyper-rationalism." Hyper-rationalism has both a methodological and a substantive aspect. As a method, [h]yper-rationalism is essentially the substitution of reason for information and analysis. It has two components: First, the belief that reason can reliably be used to infer facts where evidence is unavailable or incomplete, and second, the practice of interpreting facts through a narrow set of artificial analytic categories. Hyper-rationalism, in other words, tempts us to believe that we can understand how people think and act merely by reasoning, and not by investigating. Hyper-rationalism seductively justifies discussing human behavior without investigating how people actually behave. Hyper-rationalism is the conceptualist's revenge for the world's complexity. . . .

In bioethics, as in many other areas of human thought, these assumptions see people as operating in remarkably rational ways. They hold that people deliberate explicitly about their situations, that they do so in predominantly rational terms, that they are autonomy maximizers, and that they have well-worked-out agendas which they need autonomy to fulfill. They see people primarily as makers of decisions reaching out for control over their lives. . . .

For one thing, the assumptions of hyper-rationalism can lead us into a tendency to see human nature and conduct as verging on the uniform. . . . As empiricists in fields ranging from sociology to psychology to anthropology have been at pains to show, this view exaggerates human rationality and understates the role of social and cultural factors in patient's lives. . . .

Hyper-rationalists' . . . picture of human nature is too simple, too disembodied, to be convincing. They present a bloodless, flat, distant, abstract, depersonalized, impoverished view of the way people think, feel, and act, of the social circumstances in which people live, of the ethical lives they lead. And hyper-rationalism's simplifications are particularly injurious in bioethics, a field that treats people in their least rational moments, in their most emotional travails, in their most contextual complexity.

Hyper-rationalism, of course, has its uses. It promotes the kind of generalization that frees courts and commentators to reason logically about the normative problems that are, after all, one of their central concerns. And some simplification of life's complexity is necessary if human problems are to be dealt with practically and promptly, if comprehensible rules are to be devised, if useful precedent is to be developed, if institutions are to function smoothly. But we should want to insinuate as much of that complexity as possible into normative discourse. A failure to do so perilously distances norms from the people and circumstances they seek to govern.

---

* Professor of Law, University of Michigan.

This is a peril with which law is all too familiar. Indeed, one of the most illuminating bodies of modern legal writing is the scholarship which makes sport of the idea (that seems so natural and right to lawyers and law professors) that the law makes rules and that people know about them, accept them, and respond to them in a considered, rational, and even acquiescent way.[2] . . .

One of the great truths about law is that with unnerving frequency, it fails to achieve the effects intended for it, and sometimes quite fails to have any effect at all. Some of the most fascinating modern legal scholarship reminds lawyers how removed their talk is from the world's ken. That literature reveals that, to the lawyer's chagrin, businesses resist using contracts, ranchers do not know what rules of liability govern damage done by wandering cattle, suburbanites do not summon the law to resolve neighborhood disputes, engaged couples do not know the law governing how they will own property when they marry, citizens repeatedly reject the due process protections proffered them, and, what is worse, all these people simply don't care what the law says.

Much the same can be said of many of the law's recent bioethical reforms. There is evidence that as few as 10 percent of us have made an advance directive, that only a quarter of us have signed an organ donor card (despite the swarms of us who say we want to be donors), that even competent patients are not widely consulted about do-not-resuscitate orders, that doctors have reduced informed consent to one more bureaucratic chore, and that plaintiffs rarely win informed consent suits.

What is going on here? Well, of course, lots of things. But central among them is society's enormous complexity and the narrow relevance of the law to it. People are enticed by many pressures beyond those the law creates. They have their own agendas and, more important, their own normative systems. The law writes rules, but the governed—when they know the rules—often have the incentives, time, and energy to avoid them.

Consider advance directives. They offer an apparently irresistible way of speaking in one of life's greatest crises. Yet people spurn them. They do so because they have their own lives to lead. Momentous as the crisis may be, it will generally not seem urgent until it arrives. People resist contemplating their own mortality. They heartily dislike and don't easily understand legal forms; they find them obscure and darkly imagine how they might be misused. For that matter, people may doubt that they will be used at all. Further, many people have trouble envisioning their circumstances years into the future or how they would respond to those hypothetical circumstances. And I suspect that people expect that decisions about their welfare would in any case fall to people they trust—to their families. In short, advance directives were formulated and promoted by people—bioethicists, lawyers, and doctors, for instance—who know what they want to do through them and keenly want to do it. But many of us are not clear about what we want and about whether getting it is worth the costs.

In short, while the language of the law may have penetrated into the bosom of society, it must still, in quotidian life, compete with the many other languages that people speak more comfortably, more fluently, and with much more

---

[2] The next five paragraphs constitute an interpolation excerpted from another publication by the same author, Bioethics in the Language of the Law, 24 Hastings Center Rep., No. 4 (July 1994).

conviction. These are languages of religion and morality, of love and friendship, of pragmatism and social accommodation, of custom and compromise. The danger for bioethicists, then, is believing too deeply that law can pierce the Babel, can speak with precision, can be heard. . . .

This literature, then, should alert us to the dangers of hyper-rationalism, to the perils of believing pure ratiocination can allow us to understand how people will conceive of their problems, organize their lives, resolve their disputes, and respond to legal norms. But what is the antidote to hyper-rationalism? There are several. For instance, [Howard] Brody writes that philosophy of medicine "can indeed advance by . . . abstract discussions; but it can advance only so far. At some point we will require a richer context for the discussion to proceed fruitfully. This context can be provided by stories of sickness." . . .

We need, then, to inhabit all the mansions available in the house of bioethics. And among the least inhabited of those mansions is that of empirical research. Such research offers a breadth, rigor, and precision of understanding that is available in no other way. It provides a disciplined way of reviewing our assumptions and a systematic means of identifying neglected issues. In sum, empirical research provides a fruitful means of obtaining a more detailed, complex, and acute understanding of what patients want, think, and do which can deepen — and darken — our understanding of bioethical problems.

■ MEDICAL LAW AND ETHICS IN THE POST-AUTONOMY AGE
Roger B. Dworkin*
68 Ind. L.J. 727 (1993)

Patient autonomy has long been the dominant rhetorical value in American medical law and medical ethics. It has been far less dominant in fact. Now, developments in genetics raise serious questions about the scientific validity of the assumptions on which autonomy-based law and ethics rest, and new attention to the values of civic republicanism, community, and inclusiveness raises questions about the extent to which the dominance of autonomy is desirable. Yet a move away from autonomy is frightening, especially when no one can be sure what will take its place. In this essay, I shall examine in a preliminary way the extent to which autonomy really dominates our medical law and ethics, the extent to which reformulation seems desirable in light of scientific developments and changing values, and the direction medical law and ethics might safely move in a post-autonomy age.

RHETORIC AND REALITY

Autonomy can mean a number of different things. To the liberal individualist (that is, the typical American), it means the ability and the opportunity to choose one's course of action and to act to effectuate one's choice. It means freedom from constraint as long as one's behavior does not injure others.

---

* Professor of Law, Indiana University School of Law — Bloomington.

It tends not to recognize the extent to which most actions, even the most apparently private ones, have an impact on others,[2] and the more apparently private an activity is, the more liberal individual autonomy insists that it not be regulated.

Concern for patient autonomy in the liberal individualist sense dominates the rhetoric of American medical law and medical ethics. Cardozo's dictum that "[e]very human being of adult years and sound mind has a right to determine what shall be done with his own body"[3] is ubiquitous. The entire law of informed consent is premised on the dominance of patient autonomy over competing values, including the value of good medical care. Abortion law, right-to-die law, and even some wrongful birth and life opinions are explained textually as reflecting respect for patient autonomy. . . .

Yet, in reality, autonomy does not seem to be as dominant a value as rhetoric would suggest.

. . . Of course, the law allows autonomy to be sacrificed when important public needs are at stake. Thus, compulsory vaccination laws are plainly valid. However, their existence does not really challenge autonomy's dominant position. It simply demonstrates that even a dominant value must sometimes be sacrificed for the public good.

Often, however, autonomy yields in the face of less clearly public concerns. The most obvious rejections of autonomy are professional licensure statutes and the regulation of drugs and medical devices by Congress and the Food and Drug Administration. Licensure and the control of allegedly beneficial medicines and devices are designed to protect persons from themselves, that is, to paternalistically prevent individuals from autonomously making bad choices. . . .

The law does not honor the freely entered into agreements of doctors and patients. The law of tort, not contract, determines the quality of medical care to which a person is entitled, and a patient may not contract away the right to receive reasonable care. A patient's informed consent to receive medical care does not exempt a health care provider from liability if a consented to risk occurs through negligence. . . .

At first blush, autonomy may seem to be the primary value underlying the Supreme Court's abortion jurisprudence. However, . . . under *Roe*, abortion may be regulated after the end of the first trimester to the extent necessary to protect maternal health. Further, the Court allowed states to prohibit anybody other than doctors from performing abortions even during the first trimester, a restriction that can only be understood as reflecting a paternalistic concern for maternal well-being. . . .

To some extent, right-to-die law reflects a real concern for individual autonomy, yet here too the law remains unwilling to go where the autonomy principle would push it. . . . A patient may effectively ask not to be resuscitated and perhaps not to be fed, but a request for a lethal injection will not be honored. Refusal to honor such a request is inconsistent with a law based on patient autonomy. Patient autonomy has even less to do with right-to-die cases about

---

[2] See generally Mary Ann Glendon, Rights Talk (1991).
[3] Schloendorff v. Society of N.Y. Hosp., 105 N.E. 92, 93 (N.Y. 1914).

patients who have never been competent and once-competent patients who did not express their treatment desires before becoming incompetent. . . .

New drug regulation, injury compensation law, informed consent cases, abortion decisions, right-to-die law, and organ transplantation decisions all demonstrate that American medical law, even as it has developed in the heyday of liberal individualism, is not nearly as autonomy-centered as it claims to be. If that is true, what can we expect as liberalism loses its lustre and science challenges its foundations? . . .

Unlike liberal individualism, a second possible meaning of autonomy is rooted not so much in choice as in being let alone. It is a physical concept rather than an intellectual one. If you touch me or eavesdrop on me, you have injured my autonomy by invading my space. If you actually do something to change my body, you have injured my autonomy by changing the very constitution of what I am. This view might be called physical essentialist autonomy. . . .

[E]xtreme cases, like those involving incompetent persons, make plain the insufficiency of that approach. However, the approach is also inadequate for competent persons. Choice making is a characteristic of healthy persons, but it is not their only characteristic. We must be cautious not to factually overrate even healthy persons' abilities to choose and not to ethically overvalue that capacity. Overvaluation risks dehumanizing incompetent persons and creating an ethical vacuum if and when we learn that healthy persons' abilities to choose are more constrained than we like to think. . . .

Liberal individualist autonomy and physical essentialist autonomy thus seem to impale us on the horns of a dilemma. A third approach to autonomy would treat the individual as dominant, but attempt to avoid the failings of both liberal individualism and physical essentialism. This approach would be rooted in respect for the individual as a complete being. It would deviate from common linguistic meanings of the word *autonomy* by focusing neither on the freedom to choose and act nor on the freedom from physical intrusion. It would simply be an approach that put the interests of the person most affected by an action or proposed action first. It would be a highly realistic approach because it would examine what really happens to a person. Thus, it could avoid resort to rhetorical fictions (like liberal individualism) and sacrifice of a person's well-being to someone else's principles (like physical essentialism). Such an approach might be called respectful paternalism. It would be paternalistic because it would involve someone making decisions for somebody else, presumably in that person's best interest. It would be respectful because it would consider the real impact of an action on the person affected, thus avoiding the imposition of one's principles on another to her detriment, and because it would consider the preferences and choices of the affected person, to the extent they can be ascertained, as part of the decisionmaking process. . . .

This weak version of autonomy seems an improvement over either of the other two approaches. Yet it is not without its shortcomings. By focusing solely on the individual, respectful paternalism, like all forms of autonomy, ignores both reality and important personal and social interests. All autonomy-centered approaches ignore the fact that nobody is autonomous. Everybody lives in groups — families, workplaces, clubs, labor unions, towns, states, countries — and almost everything that affects one person affects others as well.

Insights offered by feminist,[54] republican,[55] and communitarian[56] scholars have demonstrated the impoverishment of an exclusively individual rights based approach to social issues, and developments in genetics cast doubt on the factual underpinnings of such an approach. . . .

The same point can be made in every area of bioethics: Pregnant women have fetuses, mates, and parents. . . . Persons with healthy organs may have siblings with unhealthy ones. Potential surrogate mothers may have husbands, preexisting children, the new child, men with whom they have contracted and those men's wives, all of whom are affected by the surrogate mother's behavior. Dying persons have families with both emotional and financial needs.

Autonomy-based systems undervalue those other persons' needs. They assume that it is possible to ascertain who is most affected by an action or condition and then allow that person's interests to trump all others. The factual assumption is true sometimes, but only sometimes. Who is most affected by a decision about whether to use a kidney from an incompetent "donor" to save a dying competent sibling with end stage renal disease? Who is most affected by a decision whether to perform a cesarian section delivery that may shorten the life of a terminally ill, episodically competent pregnant woman by a few days in order to run an x percent chance of saving her fetus? . . .

[M]odern genetics compounds the difficulties by simultaneously reemphasizing the poverty of autonomy-based approaches and highlighting the risks in surrendering the focus on individuals. . . . Genetic medical practice challenges the conventional notion of the individually based doctor-patient relationship. Genetic medicine only makes sense if it is understood as a family-centered, rather than an individually focused form of medical practice. Typically, physicians and other genetic counsellors are consulted by couples who want to learn their risk of having a child with a genetic disease, by couples and their already affected children, or by persons who seek information about their own health based on the condition of their relatives. Each of these situations requires learning about one person to help another. Each may present the diagnostician with information about persons whom he has never seen and may raise serious questions about his obligations. To what individual does the doctor owe a duty when tests of husband, wife, and child reveal that the husband is not the child's father? What are the doctor's duties when diagnosis of a person present in the doctor's office necessarily informs him that relatives of that person are at risk for developing avoidable colon cancer or having a child with hemophilia? In a profession whose raison d'être is doing family studies to reveal family information, these questions cannot be answered by thoughtless recitation of tired slogans about the doctor owing an exclusive obligation to his patient. Indeed, often it is not even clear who the patient is.

Modern genetic research compounds the inadequacy of the individual autonomy model by rekindling the debates between free will and determinism and between nature and nurture. As scientists map the human genome, they

---

[54] E.g., Leslie Bender, A Lawyer's Primer on Feminist Theory and Tort, 38 J. Legal Ed. 3 (1988).

[55] E.g., Michael J. Sandel, Liberalism and the Limits of Justice (1982).

[56] E.g., Glendon, supra note 2.

increasingly discover not only the genes for well-known genetic diseases, but also uncover the genetic roots of a wide variety of diseases and behaviors that are often not thought of as genetic. What does it mean to talk of an autonomous individual if the individual's genotype predisposes him to alcoholism, schizophrenia, crime, cancer, or heart disease? To the extent that most American law and ethics are based on assumptions about personal moral accountability, modern genetics throws those legal and ethical positions into question.

However, . . . [r]ecognizing that there are limits to what individuals can do or control is not a concession to total determinism. The danger of modern genetics, like the danger of the old eugenics, is that society will mistakenly believe it proves more than it does and use it as an excuse to injure further those who are already disadvantaged. Thus, again, the challenge is to incorporate new understandings in a way that moves away from the excesses of individual autonomy and its frequent inability to help solve problems, without legitimating imposition on underdogs. How is that to be done?

RESPECT FOR ALL INDIVIDUALS

I suggest that a useful way to begin would be (1) to refocus our rhetoric and our rules away from concern for individual choice and toward respect for individuals, while (2) recognizing that individuals live in groups whose individual members deserve respect too. In other words, we should combine what I have called respectful paternalism with respect for all affected members of society. Respect for individuals requires valuing their apparently freely made choices, even if we do not always follow them. Respect for individual affected members of society recognizes the reality of the social condition but reduces risks of imposition by insisting on finding real impacts on real persons before those interests may be weighed against others. Respect for all individuals rejects as unacceptably dangerous a focus on the alleged interests of society as a whole. . . .

In determining an individual's interests, his ability to choose and the negative impact of taking that away from him are relevant. . . . To put it differently, the choices of competent persons are worth points in the legal and ethical calculus. However, choices do not end the inquiry. They may be illusory; the person may no longer be aware of them; and other people count too. Therefore, the way to make a decision is to consider what is best for everyone concerned, while specifically assigning a value to choices in order to avoid running roughshod over affected persons. . . .

Perhaps the approach suggested here can be made clearer by applying it to a few examples. . . .

Respect for all affected individuals would require that before consenting to treatment patients be given the amount of information that a person who cared about their well-being (including their psychological and dignitary well-being) would give them — not the amount a hypothetical reasonable doctor would provide or a reasonable patient would want. Conversation with close family members of the patient and some attention to their desires would be relevant as well. Failure to provide adequate information under such a vague standard should be viewed as an ethical lapse. Whether it makes sense also to treat it as a tort is beyond the scope of this essay.

Terminally ill patients who are incompetent and have expressed no choices about withholding or withdrawing medical care deserve respect. They retain an interest in dignity and in avoiding unnecessary suffering. However, their loved ones' interests are also strong and should be accorded great weight. Suffering from watching a close relative die a prolonged death is real. On the other hand, the anguish of believing one was premature in letting the loved one die is real as well. Respect for relatives requires that they be accorded significant discretion in deciding whether to allow the patient to die. The doctor's sense that he is wasting his time in a futile exercise is probably worth something, especially if the patient is past suffering and the family is split. An identified salvable patient's need for the dying person's hospital bed is also relevant. A generalized concern about not wasting resources is not. Society cannot be allowed to solve its health care cost crisis by running roughshod over its sickest members.

Medical law and ethics based on individual autonomy are rooted in fiction and ignore important values. The salutary role of the autonomy focus is that it avoids state imposition and abuse of the weak. As the illustrations here suggest, an approach rooted in respect for all individuals would avoid fiction and increase the chance of sound results by considering all relevant persons and values in each case, while keeping the door to state imposition and abuse of the powerless tightly closed.

Notes: Medical Ethics and Professionalism

1. *Competing Paradigms.* In Resuscitating Professionalism: Self-Regulation in the Medical Marketplace, 66 U. Mo. L. Rev. 341 (2001), Prof. Gail Agrawal develops a forceful and nuanced case for reinvigorating the professional paradigm, but with a new focus on how physicians can play a constructive role in containing costs and allocating limited medical resources. On professionalism generally, see Eliot Freidson, Professionalism: The Third Logic (2001).

In The Invention of Health Law, 91 Cal. L. Rev. 247 (2003), Prof. Gregg Bloche critiques the economic rationality paradigm and proposes an approach to health care law that is a more "pragmatic adaptation to health care's particularities" that recognizes "feelings of being cared for, respect for personal dignity, and the deepened sense of community that health care can bring about."

For additional discussion of competing paradigms in health law, see Symposium, Rethinking Health Law, 41 Wake Forest L. Rev. 341 (2006); Symposium, The Field of Health Law: Its Past and Future, 14 Health Matrix 1 (2004).

2. *Bioethics and Law.* For additional insightful discussions of the individual rights paradigm and the proper role of law in deciding issues of medical ethics, see George Annas, Standard of Care: The Law of American Bioethics (1993); Roger Dworkin, Limits: The Role of Law in Bioethical Decision Making (1996); Jerry Menikoff, Law and Bioethics: An Introduction (2001); David Rothman, Strangers at the Bedside: A History of How Law and Bioethics Transformed Medical Decisionmaking (1992); Susan A. Channick, The Myth of Autonomy at the End-of-Life, 44 Vill. L. Rev. 577 (1999); Charity Scott, Why Law Pervades Medicine: An Essay on Ethics in Health Care, 14 Notre Dame J.L. Ethics & Pub.

Pol'y, 245 (2000); Michael H. Shapiro, Is Bioethics Broke? On the Idea of Ethics and Law "Catching Up" with Technology, 33 Ind. L. Rev. 17 (1999); Rebecca Kukla, Conscientious Autonomy: Displacing Decisions in Health Care, 35(2) Hastings Center Rep. 34 (March 2005).

Bioethics has spawned an immense mulitidisciplinary literature, much of which is cited in the portions of this book where it is relevant. These are the leading general and comprehensive sources: **Journals:** Bioethics Reporter; Bioethics; Cambridge Quarterly of Health Care Ethics; Kennedy Institute of Ethics Journal; Hastings Center Report; Issues in Law and Medicine; Journal of Clinical Ethics; Journal of Medical Ethics; Journal of Medical Humanities and Bioethics; Journal of Medicine and Philosophy; and the general medical and legal journals listed in the preface. **Treatises and Monographs:** T. Beauchamp & J. Childress, Principles of Biomedical Ethics (5th ed. 2002); Baruch A. Brody et al., Medical Ethics: Analysis of the Issues Raised by the Codes, Opinions & Statements (2001); J. Childress & R. Gaare, BioLaw: A Legal and Ethical Reporter on Medicine, Health Care, and Bioengineering; H. Tristram Englehardt, The Foundations of Biomedical Ethics (2d ed. 1996); Bernard Gert et al., Bioethics: A Return to Fundamentals (1997); Nancy Jecker, Albert Jonsen & Robert Pearlman, Bioethics: An Introduction to the History, Methods and Practice (1997); A. Jonsen, M. Siegler & W. Winslade, Clinical Ethics: A Practical Approach to Ethical Decisions in Clinical Medicine (5th ed. 2002); David Orentlicher, Matters of Life and Death: Making Moral Theory Work in Medical Ethics and the Law (2002); W. Reich, Encyclopedia of Bioethics; Robert Veatch, A Theory of Medical Ethics (1981).

3. *The Attack on "Principlism."* The conventional way to frame issues of medical ethics is in terms of autonomy vs. beneficence and to ask which of these two principles is more appropriate and to what degree in particular cases. This approach grew primarily out of the foundational work of Tom Beauchamp and James Childress at Georgetown University's Kennedy Institute of Ethics and at the University of Virginia, and is presented in their now classic *Principles of Biomedical Ethics.* This framework has become so dominant that it is sometimes referred to as the "Georgetown mantra." But this approach's ordering of discussion according to mid-level principles has come under attack in recent years from several directions.

Some argue that principles are too abstract and so the focus should be on a more intuitive or pragmatic analysis of individual cases. This is known as "casuistry." Others argue that resort to primarily these two principles is too arbitrary or ad hoc and not sufficiently founded in rigorous philosophical analysis. Still others advance a "virtue ethics," which holds that we must look not only at the rightness or goodness of an action but also the character of the actor, in order to identify and cultivate good moral traits such as honesty and compassion.

Beauchamp and Childress respond that their principles framework is more malleable than their critics recognize and so is capable of adapting to all of these competing positions. For more insight into this debate, see Nancy S. Jecker et al., Bioethics: An Introduction to the History, Methods and Practice (1997); Edmund D. Pellegrino & David C. Thomasma, The Virtues in Medical Practice (1993); Symposium: Emerging Paradigms in Bioethics, 69 Ind. L.J. 945 (1994); Edmund Pellegrino, The Metamorphosis of Medical Ethics, 269 JAMA 1158 (1993).

4. *Empiricism and Narratives*. Whichever philosophical or analytical camp one hails from, all agree that ethical debate is greatly enhanced with good empirical information. So are legal and public policy debates. That is why we try to provide as much insightful empirical data as we can throughout the notes in this book. For other general overviews of empirical work relevant to health care law and ethics, see Susan Wolf, Shifting Paradigms in Bioethics and Health Law: The Rise of a New Pragmatism, 20 Am. J. L. & Med. 407 (1994); Symposium, 31 Ind. L. Rev. 1 (1998).

Empiricism can also take a more anecdotal form. There is growing interest in understanding legal and public policy problems through the rhetorical device of narrative. See, e.g., Robin West, Narrative, Authority & Law (1993). Telling personal stories can be a powerful way to demonstrate how law actually affects people in real lives. Several compelling examples are cited in the bibliography at pages 26-27. For a gripping account by a law professor who underwent a heart transplant, of why advance directives should not be conclusive, see Louis J. Sirico, Jr., Life and Death: Stories of a Heart Transplant Patient, Real Prop. Prob. & Tr. J. 554 (2002). For additional narratives, see Elizabeth A. Pendo, Images of Health Insurance in Popular Film: the Dissolving Critique, 37 J. Health L. 267 (2004); Stacey A. Tovino, Incorporating Literature into a Health Law Curriculum, 9 J. Med. & L. 213 (2005); Kathryn Hunter, Doctors' Stories: The Narrative Structure of Medical Knowledge (1991); Dena Davis, Tell Me a Story: Using Short Fiction in Teaching Law, 47 J. Legal Educ. 240 (1997); Sidney Watson, In Search of the Story: Physicians and Charity Care, 15 St. Louis U. Pub. L. Rev. 353 (1996). Narrative approaches have also been criticized as excessively anecdotal and tending to be misrepresentative. See David A. Hyman, Patient Dumping: Lies, Damned Lies, and Narrative, 73 Ind. L.J. 797 (1998).

3. Postmodern Critical Theory

■ SLAVERY, SEGREGATION AND RACISM: TRUSTING THE HEALTH CARE SYSTEM AIN'T ALWAYS EASY! AN AFRICAN AMERICAN PERSPECTIVE ON BIOETHICS*
Vernellia R. Randall**
15 St. Louis U. Pub. L. Rev. 191 (1996)

. . . Just like the rest of America, the African American community is facing a number of bioethical issues including: abortion, disparate health status, racial barriers to access to health care, racial disparities in medical treatment, the Human Genome Project and genetic testing, organ transplantation, AIDS, physician assisted suicide and right to die, reproductive technology, and violence.

---

* This article is reprinted with permission, copyright © 1996, St. Louis University.

** Vernellia Randall is a Professor of Law at the University of Dayton School of Law. In addition to her legal training, Professor Randall has her B.S.N. and M.S.N. and worked for over a decade as a nurse.

Unlike the dominant American group, African Americans view these issues through an additional screen of fear and distrust. It is this fear and distrust that causes us to believe that the principles of bioethics: autonomy, beneficence, nonmaleficence, and justice, won't protect our community from mistreatment and abuse. . . .

African Americans have been experimented on without consent, thus violating the principle of autonomy. We have been treated and experimented on in ways which have caused us harm, thus violating the principles of nonmaleficence and beneficence. We have been given different treatment and provided different access to health care, thus violating the principle of justice. At best, the judgment in applying the articulated principles has been exercised fairly consistently in a manner which disadvantages and harms African Americans. . . .

Eurocentric bioethics focuses on the individual, ignoring the interests of others who are intimately affected, such as the family and the community. This focus on the individual is based on a philosophy that regards the self, and only the self, as the end per se. However, the African American perspective views this reliance on ethical egoism to be misplaced. African Americans believe that "it takes a whole village" to raise a child, and thus, at a minimum, African Americans view ethical egoism to be contradictory to the raising of healthy children. Furthermore, even as adults, none of us function as islands; we all must rely on others for, at a minimum, reaffirmation of our self-assessment.

Second, Eurocentric bioethics embraces Kantian ethics, which are antithetical to Afrocentric bioethics. Kantian ethics require universal norms and an impartial perspective, which is inattentive to relationships and community. Kantianism privileges abstract reasoning over virtue, character, and moral emotions. Kantian ethics maintain that the only way we can morally constitute ourselves is by free and rational choice. It is the exclusivity of that claim that is troubling. African Americans believe that we morally constitute ourselves not only through free and rational choice but also through our parents and our community.

Third, Eurocentric bioethics tends to view the patient or research subject generically, without attention to race, gender, or insurance status. As a result, the development of laws and bioethical principles, discourse, and practices are informed by the values and beliefs of one group: white, middle-class, males.

Eurocentric bioethical principles such as autonomy, beneficence, and informed consent do not have the same force when viewed through the African American bioethical perspective of distrust. These principles leave considerable room for individual judgment by health care practitioners. The flaw of a principle-based paradigm is that very judgment. The application of the principles will be subject to other values held by the society. In a racist society (such as ours), the judgment is often exercised in a racist manner.

Thus, Eurocentric bioethics has adopted rules and has applied them with little, if any, concern for how race or other characteristics affect the working of the rules. In fact, numerous studies have documented a disparity between traditional bioethical practice and the needs of minority populations. For instance, African Americans notably differ from European Americans, both in their unwillingness to complete advance directives and in the desires expressed regarding life-sustaining treatment. Substantially more African Americans and Hispanics "wanted their doctors to keep them alive regardless of how ill they were, while more . . . whites agreed to stop life-prolonging treatment under some circumstances. . . . "

The implication for the African American community is the failure of bioethical problem-solving to take into consideration those factors important to solving problems in the African American community. Most of the problem-solving has been at odds with the affirmation of the African American individual and the African American community. In fact, for the most part, mainstream bioethicists have consistently neglected to comment on the social ills or injustices such as "the [African Americans'] enslavement, the injustices and discrimination they have suffered, the stereotyping of their language and culture, and their disadvantaged economic, political, educational, and health status." As a result of this lack of affirmation, or, this oppression, we are in danger of losing our own perspectives — our own gifts. . . .

African Americans face the health care system with anxiety, fear, and disaffection. Such anxiety, fear, and distrust will not be alleviated until bioethics constructs a practical, ethical approach to the anxiety and fear which would lead to community empowerment. Such a practical approach would require behaviors such as: reinstatement of community hospitals; assuring urban perinatal health care; encouraging traditional lay-midwifery; and reestablishing the extended family. However, such practical approach must be based on not only on the traditional Eurocentric principles but also on:

- recognizing the needs of the community and not just the individual self;
- formulating bioethical and legal solutions involving both the family and the community;
- aggressively training health care providers and institutions about the African American perspective, thus making the barrier of distrust easier to overcome;
- eliminating the disparities in health status;
- aggressively reducing the existing disparities in health care delivery in the African American community.

■ THE COLONIZATION OF THE WOMB
Nancy Ehrenreich*
43 Duke L.J. 492 (1993)

Science has been called the religion of modern times, and probably only a fool would attempt to convince a reader, in the course of a law review article no less, that medicine, the form of science most widely used by the consuming public, is not "scientific." Yet that is what I must do here, for central to my argument is the notion that medicine is a hegemonic discourse — that it is laden with value choices and beliefs that masquerade as truth, nature, and biological "fact." My argument will be limited, however, to that part of medicine that deals with women and their reproductive processes, and I will not attempt to prove my point — a rather misguided effort anyway in an argument premised on profound skepticism about

---

* Nancy Ehrenreich is a professor at the University of Denver College of Law.

the notion of empirical proof itself—so much as to present a substantial amount of material suggestive of it. . . .

The scientific world view is accepted by scientists and laypeople alike. It is a belief system that denies its own reality as a world view, believing instead that it is a series of truths about knowing and controlling the unpredictable world we live in. . . . Through the use of the scientific method, it is thought, science can continually test and perfect the knowledge it acquires, moving ever closer to a "true" understanding of the world and the individuals who occupy it. . . . In the area of medicine, this theme of controlling nature is particularly evident. Technological advances have totally transformed what we mean by life and death, allowing tiny babies to survive and prosper after premature births and the elderly or those with permanent brain damage to exist (if not exactly "live") far beyond anything previously thought possible. Technology is extolled for enabling physicians to overcome "imperfections" in a woman's reproductive organs by removing eggs from ovaries, fertilizing them in petri dishes, and then returning them to the uterus. Physicians correct bad eyesight, replace torn ligaments, set broken bones, refashion hearts. Central to our notion of medicine is its role in controlling and transforming our bodies.

Upon examination, it can be seen that this view strongly associates science with many of the same terms that are traditionally associated with men; whereas, the opposite of science (anything that is unscientific) is associated with opposed and feminized terms. Science is thought to be an objective, neutral, rational, fact-based method of controlling nature, whereas non-"scientific" forms of knowledge are usually stigmatized as superstition and ignorance and thought to be based on subjective, biased, and emotional assessments of reality. Non-science is also clearly associated with women: the phrase "old wives' tale," for example, makes quite explicit the cultural equation between bad health care and women, simultaneously defining women's knowledge as nonscientific and dismissing it as erroneous. Moreover, women are seen not only as the source of dangerous medical advice but also as the sites of dangerous disease and decay. In short, . . . women are often treated as the prototypical embodiment of the natural world that science exists to control.

I can imagine many readers arriving at this point only to say, "So what? Medicine and science are, generally, objective and rational. Of course they are imperfect and will continually improve, but they are nevertheless as close as we can get to a neutral and accurate understanding of the world." Many recent writings, however, have fundamentally challenged that confidence in medical knowledge. . . .

[T]hings are actually much more complicated. I will start from the fundamental assumption, long accepted in the social sciences, that biological science is a product of culture, rather than an entity existing separate and apart from the world it attempts to know. In other words, the very categories through which medical scientists comprehend the world are themselves the product of the culture in which they live. Medicine is a social construct, rather than a set of "truths" about the world. To accept this premise is not to say that medicine is "wrong" or that it never works but that its understanding is partial, its truths contingent.

Applying this insight to the reproductive context, I will contend, therefore, that the field of obstetrics is not a domain in which experts use generally unchallengeable "facts" about human reproduction to facilitate the birthing process, but rather that it is an arena of struggle over the role(s) of women in society and indeed over the meaning of the word *woman*. Before turning to that broader point, however, I must first add one last piece of the picture of how Western dualisms operate in the realm of medicine by discussing how the reproductive process itself is perceived. . . .

As many writers have pointed out, medicine (as practiced in the United States) conceives of female reproductive processes, from menstruation to childbirth to menopause, as pathological, disease-like conditions that need to be controlled to prevent them from harming the women in whose bodies they occur (or, in the case of childbirth, the fetuses those women are carrying). . . . Childbirth itself is also seen as a dangerous, pathological, and unpredictable medical event. The role of the physician during labor is conceptualized, therefore, as imposing control and predictability on this process (and, hence, on the women through whom it is played out). Physicians "manage" the labor, performing various interventions to ensure that it proceeds along the lines of "normal" births, lines that are derived by averaging the wide range of patterns that labor actually follows among different women into a standardized set of "stages" with their own prescribed durations and symptomatology. In addition, successful childbirth has increasingly become equated with only the production of a "perfect" product, a child free of infection or disabilities. . . .

Protecting a fetus often entails imposing certain risks on the woman carrying it; a cesarean section, for example, is at least twice as likely as a vaginal birth to result in the death of the mother. Yet this risk becomes irrelevant if the cultural norm already prescribes that she be willing to sacrifice anything and everything for her children (born or unborn). Given that norm, it is easy for the doctor to either (1) assume that she is a good mother and therefore not consider her preferences very much during labor, on the assumption that she would want to sacrifice for her child, or (2) assume that she is a bad mother and therefore not consider her preferences very much during labor, on the assumption that she has no right to have them respected. . . .

In recent years, however, the medical model of reproduction has come under sustained attack by a burgeoning (at the beginning, primarily white) women's health movement. . . . [T]here are essentially three ways in which such sets of opposing terms are usually criticized. First, one can argue that the dualisms unfairly stereotype members of the low status group. That is, they are inaccurate: most white women are not passive, most African-Americans are not lazy, and so on. Those presenting a parallel challenge to the medical model claim that it unfairly stigmatizes alternative birthing approaches as less scientific or successful than traditional medicine. Second, one can argue that the dualisms elevate traits that are actually unenviable and socially destructive and disparage traits that are good and valuable. Thus, for example, relational feminists have contended that pure logic is not necessarily superior to intuitive understanding and that striving for self-sufficiency may be less laudable than recognizing human interdependence, and race theorists have suggested that contextual facts and narrative are as powerful conceptual tools as abstract analytics. In the reproductive context, this criticism takes the form of an effort to elevate alternative birthing strategies, arguing that they are actually better—both in terms of quality of care and in terms of human fulfillment—than the traditional approach.

The third critique of Western dualisms, and the one that is most important to my argument, alleges that the distinctions the dualisms draw are themselves incoherent. That is, in any particular instance, it will not be readily apparent whether an individual's reaction to her circumstances is rational or emotional, active or passive. What seems absolutely illogical to one person, for example, might indeed seem perfectly rational to another. Because of this indeterminacy of meaning, the act of labeling conduct as one or the other is facilitated by unstated (and perhaps unconscious) assumptions that reflect and reinforce power disparities in society. In other words, the dualisms do not represent or identify "real" differences in the world but rather serve as vehicles for the deployment of social power.

I mean two things by this assertion. First, the power to decide what is rational (or whatever) and what is not devolves upon those with power in the society at large. Because their visions of the world are those most often conveyed through societal institutions such as law, the media, and schools, it is their interpretations of a particular incident that will seem most "true." Second, that power to name, to interpret the world, legitimates the position of the dominant group to which it belongs as well as that group's oppression of others. The consistent application of the dominant terms of the dualisms to those in power and the devalued terms to a variety of "others" reinforces negative images of those others that then seem to justify their subordination. Relying on these insights, much of the critical feminist and critical race theory scholarship in the last several years has been directed at revealing the ways in which the dominant belief system's interpretation of the world prevents judges from seeing the behavior and concerns of women (of all colors) or people of color (of both sexes) as rational, responsible, and legitimate. . . .

II. LAW AND MEDICINE AS MUTUALLY LEGITIMATING DISCOURSES AND PRACTICES

. . . Legal authorities in general pay great deference to medical expertise. The most obvious example of this deference, of course, is the retention of a custom standard to define medical malpractice. . . . In the area of reproduction, this judicial deference to medical authority is particularly marked. . . . This judicial tendency to subsume women's interest in controlling their reproductive capacities within physicians' right to practice medicine reflects a similar attitude in the society at large. . . .

When considered in light of the sets of associations previously described, law's great deference to medicine is perhaps not surprising. . . . [L]aw is associated with many of the same traits as medicine. Both are thought to be neutral and objective pursuits, devoid of personal bias or subjective self-interest. Both are seen as coldly rational—as based on facts and rules, rather than opinions and values. Moreover, both are seen as controlling people: Whereas medicine controls their physical bodies, law controls the body politic, providing a peaceful means for resolving disputes that otherwise might dissolve into warfare. Put another way, medicine controls physical nature, whereas law avoids a social "state of nature." Finally, both fields are populated by elite white men who enjoy very comfortable incomes and high status. Given these affinities, judicial trust in the medical profession to make dispassionate and value-free decisions in individual cases is not surprising. . . .

Notes: Feminist and Critical Race Theory

1. *Constructive or Confrontational?* Some readers will find this style of analysis disturbing and threatening. Leslie Bender explains, however, that the aim of much critical analytical writing is to enlighten and sensitize:

> [T]here are many feminist analyses and perspectives, of which my arguments are only one. . . . Because many readers are unaware of the extensive writing and theorizing within feminism and from feminist premises about every kind of subject, they think feminist is a label meaning "political struggles for women's rights." Certainly feminist means that but it also means more. Some themes in feminist ethics are challenges to the values and conceptions of human natures and human interactions that dominate our current discourses in law, medicine, and ethics. Some feminist theorizing emphasizes the need to value and focus on care, compassion, responsiveness, responsibility, conversation, and communication, as well as learning to listen closely to others and to pay attention to others' needs, regardless of their differences from our own. I write in that tradition. Feminist ethics also challenges power structures and systemic biases in law and ethics that undervalue or disregard the perspectives and experiences of all women in differing ways and of men of subordinated statuses, whether subordinated by structures of race, class, sexual identity, some other identity-based classification, or some combination thereof. Feminism seeks to reconstruct our understandings and practices in ways that more closely respond to the needs of those people in their daily lives . . . [and] dying processes.

A Feminist Analysis of Physician-Assisted Dying and Active Euthanasia, 59 Tenn. L. Rev. 519 (1992).

2. *Discrimination in Treatment.* Radical critiques of the medical establishment have considerable empirical as well as philosophical and political support. Researchers have demonstrated disturbing ethnic, gender, and socio-economic disparities in treatment patterns for patients with similar conditions. This discrimination can sometime take the form of the absolute denial of care. More often, treatments are not pursued aggressively for some patients as for others. See Leslie Laurence & Beth Weinhouse, Outrageous Practices: The Alarming Truth About How Medicine Mistreats Women (1994); Institute of Medicine, Unequal Treatment: Confronting Racial and Ethnic Disparities in Health Care (2002); Council on Ethical and Judicial Affairs, Black-White Disparities in Health Care, 263 JAMA 2344 (1990); Symposium, 9 J. Health Care L. & Pol'y 1-135 (2006); Symposium, 48 St. Louis U. L.J. 1 (2003); Symposium, 29 Am. J.L. & Med. 151-421 (2003); Symposium, 353 New Eng. J. Med. 727 (2005); Symposium, 1 Yale J. Health Pol'y L. & Ethics (2001); Symposium, 40(1) Med. Care 1 (Supp. 2002). For a provocative challenge to this large body of evidence, claiming that it fails to

account for legitimate factors that might explain patterns of disparate treatment, such as differing patient preferences, medical conditions, or prognoses, see Sally Satel, "PC" M.D.: How Political Correctness Is Corrupting Medicine (2001).

Several articles analyze what legal actions might result from the documented pattern of differential treatment of minorities. See Mary A. Crossley, Infected Judgment: Legal Responses to Physician Bias, 48 Vill. L. Rev. 195 (2003); Michael Shin, Redressing Wounds: Finding a Legal Framework to Remedy Racial Disparities in Medical Care, 90 Cal. L. Rev. 2047 (2002); Larry J. Pittman, A Thirteenth Amendment Challenge to Both Racial Disparities in Medical Treatments and Improper Physicians' Informed Consent Disclosures, 48 St. Louis U. L.J. 131 (2003); Symposium, 9 DePaul J. Health Care L. 667 (2005); Symposium, 9 DePaul J. Health Care L. 905 (2006).

Should doctors take race into account at all in deciding how best to treat patients? Critics argue that skin color is an imperfect proxy for genetic or environmental factors that are relevant to choosing the best treatment for each patient. For policy and legal analysis, see Symposium, 34 J.L. Med. & Ethics 483 (2006); Erik Lillquist and Charles A. Sullivan, The Law and Genetics of Racial Profiling in Medicine, 39 Harv. C.R.-C.L. L. Rev. 393 (2004); Sharona Hoffman, "Racially-Tailored" Medicine Unraveled, 55 Am. U. L. Rev. 395-456 (2005) ("'race-based' medicine might violate numerous anti-discrimination provisions contained in federal law, state law, and federal research regulations and guidelines"); and articles by Jonathan Kahn in 4 Yale J. Health Pol'y L. & Ethics 1 (2004); 15 S. Cal. Interdisc. L.J. 105 (2005); and 92 Iowa L. Rev. 353 (2007).

3. *Discrimination in Research.* The history of medical research reveals a disturbing pattern of discrimination against racial and ethnic minorities, women, and the poor. See page 227. In this country, the Tuskegee experiments—in which researchers studied the long-term effects of infection with syphilis by withholding treatment from a group of African American males—provide a particularly vivid example of unethical conduct. See James H. Jones, Bad Blood (1993). Medical researchers also have discriminated against women. Researchers argued that excluding women was justified by the potential risks their research might present in the event of pregnancy, even if the women used birth control or were beyond child-bearing years. Researchers also argued that women did not make good research subjects because their biological differences might cloud the research findings.

Unfortunately, the routine exclusion of women from research trials meant that women with life-threatening illnesses might be denied access to potentially helpful experimental treatments. It also resulted in flawed research: If one believes the contention that female biology might alter research results, then excluding women from research must produce incomplete results. Finally, the exclusion of pregnant, or potentially pregnant, women from research (1) denies many women access to potentially helpful experimental treatments, (2) values fetal interests over maternal interests, and (3) means that new treatments will not have been proven to be safe for pregnant women or their fetuses. Widespread criticism of these practices has led to some significant congressional reforms, including a presumption that federally funded research would include subjects who were women and members of racial or ethnic minorities. See Rothenberg, supra.

4. *Outsider Jurisprudence*. Feminist critique, critical race theory, and critical legal studies are flourishing in health care law, as they are elsewhere in legal analysis. See, e.g., Symposium, Deconstructing Traditional Paradigms in Bioethics: Race, Gender, Class, and Culture, 15 St. Louis U. Pub. L. Rev. 183 (1996). Leading **critical legal scholars** are David Frankford and Gregg Bloche. Examples of their work include their Measuring Health Care: Political Fate and Technocratic Reform; 19 J. Health Pol. Pol'y & L. 647 (1994) (Frankford); Privatizing Health Care: Economic Magic to Cure Legal Medicine; 66 S. Cal. L. Rev. 1 (1992) (Frankford); The Invention of Health Law, 91 Cal. L. Rev. 247 (2003) (Bloche); Beyond Autonomy: Coercion and Morality in Clinical Relationships, 6 Health Matrix 229 (1996) (Bloche). Professors Dorothy Roberts and Lisa Ikemoto have been especially prominent scholars on **critical race theory**. Examples of their work include Killing the Black Body: Race, Reproduction, and the Meaning of Liberty (1997) (Roberts); The Genetic Tie, 62 U. Chi. L. Rev. 209 (1995) (Roberts); The Fuzzy Logic of Race and Gender in the Mismeasure of Asian Women's Health Needs, 65 U. Cin. L. Rev. 799 (1997) (Ikemoto); In the Shadow of Race: Women of Color in Health Disparities Policy, 39 U.C. Davis L. Rev. 1023 (2006) (Ikemoto). See also Michele Goodwin, Black Markets: The Supply and Demand of Body Parts (2006); Frank M. McClellan, Is Managed Care Good for What Ails You? Ruminations on Race, Age and Class, 44 Vill. L. Rev. 227 (1999); David B. Smith, Health Care Divided: Race and Healing a Nation (1999); Vernellia Randall, Racist Health Care: Reforming an Unjust Health Care System to Meet the Needs of African-Americans, 3 Health Matrix 127 (1993). **Feminist critique** is multidisciplinary, but is especially rich with respect to reproductive issues. For a broad introduction, see articles published in Symposium, Feminist Bioethics, 26 J. Med. & Phil. 339 (2001); Symposium, New Perspectives on Women, Health & Law, 3 Tex. J. Women & L. 1-402 (1994). See also Susan M. Wolf, Feminism & Bioethics: Beyond Reproduction (1996); Leslie Bender, Teaching Feminist Perspectives on Health Care Ethics and Law: A Review Essay, 61 U. Cin. L. Rev. 1251 (1993); Mary Anne Bobinski & Phyllis Griffin Epps, Women, Poverty, Access to Health Care, and the Perils of Symbolic Reform, 5 J. Gender, Race, & Just. 233 (2002); Karen H. Rothenberg, New Perspectives for Teaching and Scholarship: The Role of Gender in Law and Health Care, 54 Md. L. Rev. 473 (1995); Symposium, 9 Duke J. Gender L. & Pol'y 1 (2002).

4. Distributive Justice

▮ UNCOMPENSATED HOSPITAL CARE: RIGHTS AND RESPONSIBILITIES*
Uwe Reinhardt**

While honest economists long ago despaired of developing an overarching theory of distributive justice, political philosophers continue to hammer away at

---

* This reading is excerpted from the first chapter of a book by this title edited by F. Sloan, J. Blumstein & J. Perrin (1986). Reprinted with permission of Johns Hopkins University Press.

** The author, a professor of economics at Princeton University, is a prominent writer and speaker on health care public policy. His first name is pronounced "oo-veh."

the problem. The several distinct theories of distributive justice emerging from these efforts are elegant in their internal logic, and eminently stimulating even to a skeptic. In the end, however, that literature fails as a guide towards a universally acceptable principle of justice. On the contrary, it persuades one that there cannot possibly be such a principle. For however tight the internal logic of any particular philosopher's theory of justice may be, that logic is ultimately anchored on some overarching value for which that author claims primacy on purely subjective grounds. Collectively, the political philosophers writing on the subject teach us that justice, like beauty, rests in the eye of the beholder.

Libertarian philosophers, for example, elevate individual liberty to the status of the single, overriding social value to which all other values are subordinate, and which can never justly be traded off against any subordinate value. Implicit in the libertarian's concept of "liberty" is the tenet that the individual is entitled to dispose of his or her possessions as he or she sees fit. Extreme versions of the theory — articulated, for example, in Robert Nozick's Anarchy, State, and Utopia (1974) — hold that any governmental infringement on this presumed property right is ipso facto unjust. Thus, to tax one person's wealth in order to finance another person's health care is unjust, as is a policy that compels physicians or privately owned facilities to render health care to designated individuals. In the libertarian's credo, it is the health care provider's right to determine whom to serve and whom not to serve, and also what price to exact for health services rendered. Health care providers must find this a comforting credo.

Diametrically opposed to the libertarian credo are the various theories of distributive justice espoused by egalitarian philosophers. Egalitarian philosophers elevate "equal respect for all individuals" or "equality of opportunity" to the overriding value of a just society to which all other values — among them individual liberty — are deemed subordinate. Equality of opportunity, argue these philosophers, requires as a minimum that all members of society have equal access to certain basic commodities, access to which determines an individual's range of opportunities and measure of self-respect. Health care, along with food, shelter, and education, is among these basic commodities.

The entitlements implicit in the egalitarian tenet seem rather open-ended, and as recent history in this country has shown, they certainly are. Egalitarians, however, do not glibly ignore resource constraints. They merely argue that, in the face of such constraints, need, rather than ability to pay, should be the basis for rationing. Clearly this theory of justice implies redistribution of the sort libertarians consider coercive and hence unjust.

One's own predilections aside, it is certainly no more logically compelling to let equal opportunity triumph completely over individual liberty than it is to do the reverse. Indeed, outside the ivory tower any prevailing sense of justice is apt to be an amalgam in which each of the pure theories is somewhat compromised. While purist philosophers may deplore such compromises, policymakers must not only countenance them but actively lead in forging the amalgam.

A remarkable and unique feature of American health policy has been its attempt to accommodate simultaneously both the egalitarian and the libertarian theories of justice in their extreme purity. No other nation in the industrialized West has been quite so bold, or quite so naive, as to attempt that feat. Ironically, no other nation finds itself, in the mid-1980s, with the unsolved problem of uncompensated indigent care at the center stage of its health policy debate. There appears to be a casual link between schizoid thinking on the ethical plane and impotence at the level of policy.

Throughout the postwar period, and possibly even earlier, our policies on the distribution of health care have been firmly rooted in the egalitarian credo: It has been a widely shared notion that health care in the United States should be distributed on the basis of medical need rather than ability to pay. Furthermore, with appeal to the overarching principle of "equal respect for all individuals," it has generally been held (at least in public debate) that the nation should aim for equality in the process of health care—that there should be equity in the so-called amenities accompanying the delivery of health care, including the travel and wait time during access and the degree of free choice among providers. Politicians of all ideological stripes have supported these tenets (at least none has openly questioned them), and health care providers have endorsed them as well.

Cynics may argue that no one seriously entertained these lofty maxims and that they were recited by politicians mainly for public consumption. Some glaring remaining inequalities in access to health care may be cited to buttress that case. But a fair reading of health legislation during the 1960s and 1970s should persuade even a skeptic that public policy in those years was motivated by a genuine desire to move the country closer to an egalitarian distribution of health care. By the end of the 1970s, few policy analysts and even fewer public officials still questioned the proposition that access to all medically necessary and technically feasible health care on equal (process) terms is one of an American citizen's basic rights.

The pursuit of an egalitarian health care system is, of course, not a uniquely American phenomenon. Most other industrialized nations have shared that goal, and some of them seem to have been rather more successful than have we in approaching it. A uniquely American phenomenon, however, has been the endeavor to extract an egalitarian distribution of health care from a delivery system still firmly grounded in libertarian principles.

To be sure, our health care delivery system does not measure up in all respects to a libertarian's dream. Some individual liberties are being compromised by government for the sake of quality control, and even the staunchest defenders of the libertarian credo, America's physicians, have from time to time enlisted the government's coercive power to protect their economic turf through occupational licensing. We share such infringements with other modern societies. But in no other modern society espousing egalitarian principles for the distribution of health care have physicians and hospitals been quite so free as they have in the United States to organize their facilities as they see fit, to practice medicine as they see fit, and to price their services as they see fit. In these realms, libertarian principles have prevailed, and every legislative attempt to compromise them for the sake of cost control or greater equity in distribution has, until very recently, been beaten back successfully, with overt appeals to the libertarian credo. "If you want an egalitarian distribution of health care," providers have said, "we endorse it heartily, and we shall do our best to bring it about—but for a fee, and we want that fee to be reasonable as we define that term."

Libertarian and egalitarian purists wrestle with one another in any democratic society. The politician's task, as noted earlier, is to fashion from this struggle a sustainable social compromise. It is on that count that American health policy has performed poorly relative to other democracies. For, in seeking to cater to both extremes among notions of distributive justice, American policymakers have bestowed upon the nation a maze of public health programs that make a Rube Goldberg contraption appear streamlined by comparison.

There has been extraordinarily generous public health insurance coverage for some services and for some individuals—replete with completely free choice of providers by patients and with virtually open-ended reimbursement formulas for providers, . . . entitlements that have, on occasion, bordered on handing providers the key to the public treasury. . . . Yet, attempts to curb that flow of public funds into private treasuries have always been decried and, until very recently, rejected as an intolerable, regulatory infringement on private liberties.

Congressional respect for this peculiar conception of "liberty" naturally carried the danger of turning any federal health program into a fiscal hemorrhage. Too timid to prevent that outcome through controls on providers, our politicians have pursued the next logical policy to contain public health budgets: They simply have left glaring gaps in health insurance coverage, particularly for the near poor and the unemployed (whose health insurance coverage typically ceases with employment). . . . [O]ne would be hard put to identify any other industrialized society today that would still visit upon an unemployed worker's family, already down on its luck in so many material and emotional ways, the added anxiety and potential real hardship of going without health insurance coverage. It happens only in America.

It has become fashionable to attribute our long-standing failures in this area to a streak of meanness in the American character. Having lived both outside and inside this nation, I do not accept that interpretation. The special genius of nations who have long settled these problems lies not in their citizens' superior character, but lies, as noted, in a political process capable of forging a more stable ethical foundation for their health care systems. In all of these nations, the providers of health care enjoy fewer liberties than do their American counterparts. But in addition, a good many of these countries—for example, the United Kingdom, West Germany, France, Switzerland, and Holland—have been rather more tolerant of some degree of tiering in their health systems than have the champions of egalitarianism in the United States. Perhaps the time has come for Americans, too, to debate more openly—and without the customary rancor and slander—just what are the essential ingredients of a just health care system.

Note: Social Justice

Theories of social justice relevant to health care delivery are pursued further in Chapter 2.A.1. For additional readings, see Madison Powers & Ruth Raden, Social Justice: The Moral Foundations of Public Health and Health Policy (2006); Norman Daniels, Donald Light & Ronald Caplan, Benchmarks of Fairness for Health Care Reform (1996); Larry Palmer, Law, Medicine and Social Justice (1989); Kevin P. Quinn, Viewing Health Care as a Common Good: Looking Beyond Political Liberalism, 73 S. Cal. L. Rev. 277 (2000); Jennifer Prah Ruger,

Health, Capability and Justice: Toward a New Paradigm of Health Ethics, Policy and Law, 15 Cornell J.L. & Pub. Pol'y 403 (2006).

For extensive analysis of the distributive aspects of health care law, finance, and policy, see Clark C. Havighurst and Barak D. Richman, Symposium, Health Policy's Fourth Dimension, 69(4) Law & Contemp. Probs. 1 (Autumn 2006), in which the lead authors argue that:

> [because] the legal and regulatory environment of U.S. health care has been structured according to the perceptions and preferences of [social and political] elites, . . . significant social-justice issues are raised by the American legal system's many ways of making families of modest means, if they want health coverage, pay for especially costly versions of it. . . . [T]he health care system's systematic exploitation of the many for the benefit of the privileged few has been either overlooked, underestimated, or conveniently ignored by analysts and policy-makers. . . . Specifically, we see a seemingly well-meant but essentially destructive policy bias—assiduously cultivated by the health care industry and shared by many commentators and policy analysts—in favor of more and better health care for all with only nominal regard for how much it costs or who bears the burden, . . . thereby maintaining a system that is rigged against the true interests of the political majority. Clark C. Havighurst and Barak D. Richman, Distributive Injustice(s) in American Health Care, 69(4) Law & Contemp. Probs. 7 (Autumn 2006).

■ PATIENT POWER: SOLVING AMERICA'S HEALTH CARE CRISIS
John C. Goodman & Gerald L. Musgrave
1992

The potential demand for health care is virtually unlimited. Even if there were a limit to what medical service can do (which, over time, there isn't), there is an almost endless list of ailments that can motivate our desire to spend. About 83 million people suffer from insomnia, 70 million have severe headaches, 32 million have arthritis, 23 million have allergies, and 16 million have bad backs. Even when the illnesses are not real, our minds have incredible power to convince us that they are.

Consider the case of an 80-year-old man who suffered from the condition of "slowing down." Despite the physician's counsel that the condition was perfectly normal at age 80, the patient and his wife went on a literal shopping spree in the medical marketplace. As the physician explained to the *New York Times:*

> A few days ago the couple came in for a follow-up visit. They were upset. At their daughter's insistence they had gone to an out-of-town neurologist. She had wanted the "best" for her father and would spare no (Medicare) expense to get it. The patient had undergone a CAT scan, a magnetic resonance imaging, a spinal tap, a brain-stem evoke potential and a carotid duplex ultrasound. No remediable problems were discovered. The Medicare billing was more than $4,000 so far; . . . they were emotionally exhausted by the experience and anxious over what portion

of the expenses might not be covered by insurance. I have seen this Medicare madness happen too often. It is caused by many factors, but contrary to public opinion, physician greed is not high on the list. I tried to stop the crime, but found I was just a pawn in a ruthless game, whose rules are excess and waste. Who will stop the madness? . . .

◼ MAKING MEDICAL SPENDING DECISIONS: THE LAW, ETHICS, AND ECONOMICS OF RATIONING MECHANISMS*
Mark A. Hall

When we are ill, we desperately want our doctors to do everything within their power to heal us, regardless of the costs. Medical technology has advanced so far, however, that literal adherence to this credo for every human frailty would consume much more than our country's entire economic output,[1] and, in the process, cause economic collapse. . . . Any workable system for financing and delivering health care must face the fundamental problem of how best to allocate limited medical resources among competing beneficial uses. Someone, somewhere must decide which items of potential medical benefit are not worth the cost. . . .

It is sometimes thought that medical advances will eventually reduce medical spending by making people fundamentally healthier, but this assumption is equally flawed. Medical needs are inherently limitless because aging and illness are a permanent feature of the human condition. Much beneficial medical care results in people living to an older age where they are more frail and succumb to more chronic and expensive diseases. This does not mean we should suppress these innovations, only that the drive to conquer all forms of illness is ultimately doomed to failure. The course of history over this century demonstrates that, as medicine advances, so do both medical needs and medical spending.

For these various reasons, most policy analysts recognize that rationing in some form is desirable and inevitable. Every spending decision is necessarily a rationing decision simply because resources devoted to one person or one use are not available for someone or something else. If wants are limitless and resources are finite, it is impossible to maintain that rationing is avoidable in all its forms.

We have always rationed health care resources on a massive scale, only according to irrational and unjust principles.[12] Presently, we ration health care by denying it to those unfortunate individuals who lack insurance either because

---

* Copyright © 1997, Oxford University Press. Reprinted with permission.

[1] The U.S. gross domestic product per capital is about $23,000. To see how easy it would be to spend this amount each year on maximal health care, consider that it costs about this same amount on average simply to incarcerate a prisoner (not counting the costs of building new prison space). See also Lamm, R. D., "Rationing of Health Care: Inevitable and Desirable," 140 U. Pa. L. Rev. 1511, 1512 (1992) ("[A] French study asked how much it would cost to give all the health care that is 'beneficial' to each citizen. The answer was five-and-one-half times the French gross national product.").

[12] Fuchs, V.R., "The 'Rationing' of Medical Care," 311 New Eng. J. Med. 1572 (1984); Rosenblatt, R.E., "Rationing 'Normal' Health Care: The Hidden Legal Issues," 59 Texas L. Rev. 1401-1420 (1981).

their employer does not provide it or because their level of poverty has not yet fallen to the desperate level required for Medicaid eligibility.[13] At the same time, we heavily subsidize health insurance for the upper and middle classes through a regressive tax policy that excludes from an employee's income the value of insurance premiums contributed by employers. Moreover, for those who are fully insured, we devote vast resources to save lives and restore health once an illness or accident occurs, but we spend only microscopic amounts in comparison on basic safety, health education, and health prevention measures. . . .

The haphazard and unprincipled basis on which rationing presently occurs effectively rebuts another argument raised by critics of rationing, namely, that rationing should occur only under numerous, morally demanding conditions that presently do not exist. These critics impose unattainably Utopian prerequisites to rationing, such as developing ethically unassailable and scientifically valid rationing criteria, insisting on their strict egalitarian application throughout all strata of society, and first eliminating all wasteful spending, both within medicine and elsewhere in society. These demands ignore the fact that any systematically thought-out rationing scheme, however flawed, is far superior to the thoughtless and inhumane way in which many uninsured people are now treated. A more considered form of resource allocation is the first step, not the last, toward social equity and broad-based reform.[16] Only with some better approach to rationing will minimally acceptable access to health care become affordable for everyone.

Despite these many powerful arguments, it is still controversial to speak in terms of rationing health care. In order to avoid drawing the fire of those who oppose any use of this term, I will instead lean towards the more neutral terminology of resource allocation or spending decisions. I will not entirely refrain from the "R" word, however. Its emotional baggage can help to dramatize the pervasive necessity of making medical spending decisions. Despite their differing emotional content, both rationing and allocation can fairly be used in the generic sense that refers to either implicit or explicit denial of marginally beneficial medical treatment out of consideration for its cost. . . .

[R]egardless of the overall structure of a health care financing and delivery system, [w]hether it is regulatory or competitive, public or private, we are plagued by two basic issues: (1) Who should decide what care is not worth the costs, and (2) what criteria of benefit should be used to make this determination? The second of these problems is the one that has received more attention to date. Numerous volumes have been written on questions such as whether the short supply of transplantable organs should be distributed based simply on random draw or who has been waiting the longest, or instead based on elaborate concepts of medical need or medical benefit.[23] This literature also gives extensive thought to routine

---

[13] In 1992, the poverty line for a family of four was $14,335. Medicaid eligibility often is set at less than half the poverty level and, in some states, may be set at less than one-quarter the federal poverty level.

[16] See generally Callahan, D., "Rationing Health Care: Will it be Necessary? Can it be Done Without Age or Disability Discrimination?," 5 Issues in Law & Med. 353 (1989); Callahan, D., "Meeting Needs and Rationing Care," 16 Law Med. & Health Care 261 (1988).

[23] The leading general discussions are found in AMA Council in Ethical and Judicial Affairs, "Ethical Considerations in the Allocation of Organs and Other Scarce Medical Resources Among Patients," 155 Archives Internal Med. 29 (1995); Blank, R.H., Rationing Medicine (1988); Churchill, L.R., Rationing Health Care in America: Perceptions and Principles of Justice (1987); Kilner, J.F., Who

medical technologies. It explores whether medical resources generally should be rationed according to age or instead according to some more quantitative formula for effectiveness or value. Others before me have debated at length whether medical benefit should be defined by the number of lives saved, the length of life, the quality of life, or some more intermediate goal such as diagnostic certainty, and whether judgments about people's social worth can be prevented from tainting these concepts.

These are tremendously fascinating and important questions deserving of continuing inquiry, but they avoid what I see as a more fundamental question: Who should be the rationing decisionmaker? . . . [M]edical sociologist David Mechanic [f]irst articulated that health care spending decisions can be made through three fundamentally different mechanisms. Cost-sensitive treatment decisions can be made by patients, by physicians, or by third parties—primarily private and governmental insurers but also various regulatory or review organizations. Elsewhere in our economy, cost/benefit trade-offs are usually made through the purchasing decisions of individual consumers. For example, nutrition resources are allocated at both the macro and micro levels through the aggregation of countless individual decisions of how much food to buy, of what quality, and from what source. This simple market mechanism is not generally available or desirable for health care because of the unpredictability of illness and the complexities of medical judgment. . . . [W]e purchase insurance rather than pay out of pocket because we want to protect ourselves from the uncertain costs of health care and the anxiety of making spending decisions under the strain of serious illness. Moreover, even without insurance, patients make few of their medical decisions themselves because the complexity of treatment compels us to delegate extensive authority to our doctors. . . .

Insurers, either private or governmental, can make medical spending decisions through cost-sensitive rules about what treatment they will pay for. Until recently, this has seldom happened, but in 1994 Oregon became the first state to attempt explicit rule-based rationing for all of medicine. Oregon ranked over 600 condition-treatment pairings (e.g., surgery for appendicitis) according to their medical effectiveness, for purposes of allocating limited Medicaid funding. Elsewhere in this country, efforts are under way to develop a host of much more detailed and nuanced clinical practice guidelines, which could also serve as rule-based tools for third-party resource allocation. In addition to insurers' payment rules, spending decisions can be imposed by other parties who are similarly outside the doctor-patient relationship. Courts, citizen groups or other ideal democratic processes, and physician administrators who review the work of treating doctors are each able to set limits or give directions on how medical resources are spent. . . .

The third fundamental alternative for allocating medical spending authority is for physicians to incorporate cost considerations into their clinical judgment. Authorizing physicians to make cost/benefit trade-off decisions at the bedside

---

Lives? Who Dies?: Ethical Criteria in Patient Selection (1990); Winslow, G.R., Triage and Justice (1982). An early general discussion is contained in Note, "Scarce Medical Resources," 69 Colum. L. Rev. 620 (1969). The most recent treatment is the cogent and comprehensive analysis by Elhauge, E., "Allocating Health Care Morally," 82 Cal. L. Rev. 1449 (1994). For a thorough discussion of rationing criteria used commonly throughout society, see generally Elster, J., Local Justice: How Institutions Allocate Scarce Goods and Necessary Burdens (1992).

differs from centralized, rule-based rationing because it individualizes spending decisions to the circumstances of each patient, and it operates through professional incentives rather than bureaucratic authority. Bedside rationing, however, fundamentally compromises physicians' role-based ethic, which . . . traditionally requires doctors to provide all care that offers any benefit, regardless of its cost. Physician bedside rationing is rendered even more controversial by the use of financial incentives to motivate doctors' performance. . . .

As can be seen from this summary, most of this book is taken up with what Edward Rubin terms a "microanalysis of social institutions," one that seeks to assess the relative strengths, weaknesses, and characteristics of alternative mechanisms for allocating health care resources, drawing from both political economics and social theory. . . . Accordingly, I will not be wedded to a particular analytical framework or ideological perspective. I will undertake a pragmatic analytical critique, one that seeks to clarify for each rationing mechanism its basic rationale, its inherent limits, the evidence supporting both views, the potential for harm or manipulation, and the accommodations needed to make it work.

Notes: Health Care Rationing; Institutional Analysis

1. Other aspects of rationing, which is perhaps the most important health care policy issue of our times, are explored in Chapters 2.A.3 and 4.C. See the footnotes above for cites to several multidisciplinary sources. See also Henry J. Aaron & Wm. B. Schwartz: Can We Say No? The Challenge of Rationing Health Care (2005); Norman Daniels & James Sabin, Setting Limits Fairly: Can We Learn to Share Medical Resources? (2002); Einer Elhauge, The Limited Regulatory Potential of Medical Technology Assessment, 82 Va. L. Rev. 1525 (1996); David Eddy, Health System Reform: Will Controlling Costs Require Rationing Services?, 272 JAMA 324 (1994); Symposium, 59 Tex. L. Rev. 1345 (1981); 60 Tex. L. Rev. 899 (1982).

2. *Comparative Institutional Analysis.* The approach Mark Hall takes to analyzing health care rationing is known as "comparative institutional analysis" or as "legal process theory." It is an approach that is well suited to analyzing numerous legal and public policy issues, in health care and elsewhere, and so it is employed throughout this book. Its focus is not so much on what the correct answer is, but on what are the best (or least worst) institutions and processes for arriving at an answer. This approach compares the strengths and weakness of various institutions and processes within the judicial system, the private sector, the public sector, the nonprofit sector, and professional groups, among others. An excellent example of institutional choice analysis applied to problems in health policy is Russell Korobkin, The Efficiency of Managed Care "Patient Protection" Laws: Incomplete Contracts, Bounded Rationality, and Market Failure, 85 Cornell L. Rev. 1 (1999). See also William M. Sage, Unfinished Business: How Litigation Relates to Health Care Regulation, 28 J. Health Pol. Pol'y & L. 387 (2003); Ezekiel Emanuel, Choice and Representation in Health Care, 56 Med. Care Res. & Rev. 1 (1999). See generally Neil Komesar, Imperfect Alternatives: Choosing Institutions in Law, Economics and Public Policy (1995); Edward Rubin, The New Legal Process, The Synthesis of Discourse, and the Microanalysis of Institutions, 109 Harv. L. Rev. 1393 (1996).

2

The Treatment Relationship

Ordinarily, the patient-provider relationship is a consensual one to which both parties must agree. Therefore, an individual physician may, generally speaking, refuse to accept patients for any reason or for no reason. The same is true to a lesser extent for hospitals and other institutions. But this general freedom of contract is limited in several important ways. Hospitals may not turn patients away in emergencies until they have at least stabilized the patient's condition. Neither may doctors or hospitals refuse patients for certain discriminatory reasons, such as the patient's race, sex, or HIV-status. While historically a physician's freedom to turn away patients found its limitations primarily in the law, the growth of formal arrangements between managed care health plans and physicians means that a provider's obligation to treat is being increasingly defined by the private agreements among the patient, insurance plan, and provider. The following materials explore the origins of, and limits on, this freedom of contract between providers and patients.

A. THE DUTY TO TREAT

1. *The Duty to Accept Patients*

■ HURLEY v. EDDINGFIELD
59 N.E. 1058 (Ind. 1901)

BAKER, Justice.
The appellant sued appellee for $10,000 damages for wrongfully causing the death of his intestate. The court sustained appellee's demurrer to the complaint, and this ruling is assigned as error.

91

The material facts may be summarized thus: At and for years before decedent's death appellee was a practicing physician at Mace, in Montgomery county, duly licensed under the laws of the state. He held himself out to the public as a general practitioner of medicine. He had been decedent's family physician. Decedent became dangerously ill, and sent for appellee. The messenger informed appellee of decedent's violent sickness, tendered him his fee for his services, and stated to him that no other physician was procurable in time, and that decedent relied on him for attention. No other physician was procurable in time to be of any use, and decedent did rely on appellee for medical assistance. Without any reasons whatever, appellee refused to render aid to decedent. No other patients were requiring appellee's immediate service, and he could have gone to the relief of decedent if he had been willing to do so. Death ensued, without decedent's fault, and wholly from appellee's wrongful act. The alleged wrongful act was appellee's refusal to enter into a contract of employment. Counsel do not contend that, before the enactment of the law regulating the practice of medicine, physicians were bound to render professional service to every one who applied. The act regulating the practice of medicine provides for a board of examiners, standards of qualification, examinations, licenses to those found qualified, and penalties for practicing without license. The act is a preventive, not a compulsive, measure. In obtaining the state's license (permission) to practice medicine, the state does not require, and the licensee does not engage, that he will practice at all or on other terms than he may choose to accept. Counsel's analogies, drawn from the obligations to the public on the part of innkeepers, common carriers, and the like, are beside the mark. Judgment affirmed.

■ WILMINGTON GENERAL HOSPITAL v. MANLOVE
174 A.2d 135 (Del. 1961)

SOUTHERLAND, Chief Justice.

This case concerns the liability of a private hospital for the death of an infant who was refused treatment at the emergency ward of the hospital. The facts are these:

On January 4, 1959, Darien E. Manlove, the deceased infant, then four months old, developed diarrhea. The next morning his parents consulted Dr. Hershon. They asked whether the medicine they had for him was all right and the doctor said that it was. In the evening of the same day Mrs. Manlove took the baby's temperature. It was higher than normal. They called Dr. Hershon, and he prescribed additional medication (streptomycin), which he ordered delivered by a pharmacy.

Mrs. Manlove stayed up with the child that night. He did not sleep. On the morning of January 6th the parents took the infant to Dr. Hershon's office. Dr. Thomas examined the child and treated him for sore throat and diarrhea. He prescribed a liquid diet and some medicine. . . .

On the morning of January 7th (a Wednesday) [the infant's] temperature was still above normal — 102. Mr. and Mrs. Manlove determined to seek additional medical assistance. They knew that Dr. Hershon and Dr. Thomas were not in their offices on Wednesdays, and they took their infant to the emergency ward of the Wilmington General Hospital.

There is no real conflict of fact as to what occurred at the hospital. The parents took the infant into the reception room of the Emergency Ward. A nurse was on duty. They explained to the nurse what was wrong with the child, that is, that he had not slept for two nights, had a continuously high temperature, and that he had diarrhea. Mr. Manlove told the nurse that the child was under the care of Dr. Hershon and Dr. Thomas, and showed the nurse the medicines prescribed. The nurse explained to the parents that the hospital could not give treatment because the child was under the care of a physician and there would be danger that the medication of the hospital might conflict with that of the attending physician. The nurse did not examine the child, take his temperature, feel his forehead, or look down his throat. The child was not in convulsions, and was not coughing or crying. There was no particular area of body tenderness.

The nurse tried to get in touch with Dr. Hershon or Dr. Thomas in the hospital and at their offices, but was unable to do so. She suggested that the parents bring the baby Thursday morning to the pediatric clinic.

Mr. and Mrs. Manlove returned home. Mrs. Manlove made an appointment by telephone to see Dr. Hershon or Dr. Thomas that night at eight o'clock. At eight minutes past three o'clock in the afternoon the baby died of bronchial pneumonia. . . .

It was assumed by both parties below that the hospital was a private hospital and not a public one — that is, an institution founded and controlled by private persons and not by public authority. The trial court disagreed, finding a quasi-public status in the receipt of grants of public money and tax exemptions. . . . Hence, the court concluded, liability may be imposed on the defendant in an emergency case.

We are compelled to disagree with the view that the defendant has become a public (or quasi-public) hospital. It is admitted (although the record does not show it) that it is privately owned and operated. We find no dissent from the rule that such a hospital is a private hospital, and may, at least in the absence of control by the legislature, conduct its business largely as it sees fit. . . .

Moreover, the holding that the receipt of grants of public money requires the hospital to care for emergency cases, as distinguished from others, is not logical. Why emergency cases? If the holding is sound it must apply to all the hospital services, and that conclusion, as we shall see, is clearly unsound. . . .

We are of opinion that the defendant is a private and not a public hospital, in so far as concerns the right of a member of the public to demand admission or treatment. What, then, is the liability of a private hospital in this respect?

Since such an institution as the defendant is privately owned and operated, it would follow logically that its trustees or governing board alone have the right to determine who shall be admitted to it as patients. No other rule would be sensible or workable. Such authority as we have found supports this rule. "A private hospital owes the public no duty to accept any patient not desired by it, and it is not necessary to assign any reason for its refusal to accept a patient for hospital service." 41 C. J. S. Hospitals §8, p.345. . . .

. . . Does that rule apply to the fullest extent to patients applying for treatment at an emergency ward? . . .

It may be conceded that a private hospital is under no legal obligation to the public to maintain an emergency ward, or, for that matter, a public clinic. But the maintenance of such a ward to render first-aid to injured persons has become a well-established adjunct to the main business of a hospital. If a person, seriously hurt, applies for such aid at an emergency ward, relying on the established custom to render it, is it still the right of the hospital to turn him away without any reason? In such a case, it seems to us, such a refusal might well result in worsening the condition of the injured person, because of the time lost in a useless attempt to obtain medical aid. Such a set of circumstances is analogous to the case of the negligent termination of gratuitous services, which creates a tort liability. Restatement, Law of Torts, "Negligence," §323. . . .

As above indicated, we are of opinion that liability on the part of a hospital may be predicated on the refusal of service to a patient in case of an unmistakable emergency, if the patient has relied upon a well-established custom of the hospital to render aid in such a case. . . .

Applying this rule here, we inquire, was there an unmistakable emergency? Certainly the record does not support the view that the infant's condition was so desperate that a layman could reasonably say that he was in immediate danger. The learned judge indicated that the fact that death followed in a few hours showed an emergency; but with this we cannot agree. It is hindsight. And it is to be noted that the attending physician, after prescribing for the child one morning before, did not think another examination that night or the next morning was required. If this case had gone to the jury on the record here made, we would have been required to hold that it was insufficient to establish liability. We cannot agree that the mere recitation of the infant's symptoms was, in itself, evidence of an emergency sufficient to present a question for the jury. Before such an issue could arise there would have to be evidence that an experienced nurse should have known that such symptoms constituted unmistakable evidence of an emergency. . . .

The possibility that the case might turn on additional evidence respecting the matters we have touched upon was not considered either by the court or counsel. In the circumstances we think the case should go back for further proceedings. We should add, however, that if plaintiff cannot adduce evidence showing some incompetency of the nurse, or some breach of duty or some negligence, his case must fail. Like the learned judge below, we sympathize with the parents in their loss of a child; but this natural feeling does not permit us to find liability in the absence of satisfactory evidence.

For the reasons above set forth the order denying summary judgment is affirmed, without approving the reasons therefor set forth in the court's opinion.

■ SOPHIE'S CHOICES: MEDICAL AND LEGAL RESPONSES TO SUFFERING
Lois Shepherd*
72 Notre Dame L. Rev. 103 (1996)

[U]nprecedented claims to rights based on the avoidance of suffering are being made and recognized in courts and legislatures. The basis of such appeals is a belief that the suffering imposed by nature need not be tolerated and that such

* Law professor at Florida State University. Reprinted with permission. Copyright © 1996, Notre Dame Law Review, University of Notre Dame. The editors and Aspen Law Books are required to state that they bear any responsibility for any errors that may have occurred in reprinting or editing this excerpt.

suffering instills in the suffering individual a right to relief. Suffering thus becomes a sufficient condition for a right. There need be no tortfeasor nor any societally caused harm, nor any inequality for a suffering individual (or such individual's advocate) to claim relief. . . . In such instances the basis of the rights espoused is the principle that people should not be required to suffer when the means are available to end or altogether avoid such suffering. . . .

I think we can look at a number of possible reasons why there is pressure to talk about and recognize rights based in suffering. . . . [W]e appear to be developing a collective conscience, a shared empathy, and a feeling of responsibility for the welfare of others, especially in matters of health. As this collective conscience develops in a country whose jurisprudence gives great deference to individual rights, there is a developing sense that in matters of social welfare we have certain rights. These certain "positive" rights are rights *to* certain goods or services, rather than simply rights to non-interference with respect to obtaining such goods or services. This plays out in the health care arena in an incrementally emerging right to health care. This right emerges in those situations when our collective conscience cannot turn away — when the suffering is acute and visible — such as when a patient arrives at the emergency room in need of immediate attention. . . .

[C]hanges in the legal culture reflect a heightened public awareness and appreciation of others' suffering. This may be due, in part, to the fact that historical distinctions between public and private have blurred, so that, according to Hannah Arendt, the two realms "constantly flow into each other like waves in the never-resting stream of the life process itself."[155] Concerns that were originally and exclusively the province of the family, where the necessary tasks for the survival of life took place, have become a "collective" concern. We are now a "collective of families economically organized into the facsimile of one super-human family." . . .

In the collective conscience, we share not only a growing awareness of the suffering, and especially the visible suffering, of others, but a growing sense of responsibility to help others avoid avoidable suffering. We find conceptual support for this heightened social responsibility in such theories as the feminist ethic of care. The ethic of care requires attending to responsibilities and relationships, rather than attending to rights and fairness (the ethic of justice). Rather than learning and then applying abstract principles, such as equality, reciprocity, and property rights that have universal applicability (since all are grounded in an ethic of justice), an individual or society acting under the ethic of care would seek responses that are appropriate to the particular case.

Much of the recent work on the ethic of care is an outgrowth of Carol Gilligan's 1982 work, *In a Different Voice,* in which she presents her empirical findings that women and men tend to reason about moral problems from different approaches. . . . Gilligan writes:

> The moral imperative that emerges repeatedly in interviews with women is an injunction to care, a responsibility to discern and alleviate the "real and recognizable trouble" of this world. For men the moral imperative appears as an injunction to respect the rights of others and thus to protect from interference the rights to life and self-fulfillment.

---

[155] Hannah Arendt, The Human Condition 33 (1958).

Whether there are gender differences in moral reasoning or not, . . . we continue to move along the path of a collective conscience in matters of health. [T]he responsibility we feel for the care of others becomes duty, and in the language of advocacy for recognition and adherence to that duty, we see constant recourse to the familiar language of rights. To give proper weight to a concern within our rights-based constitutional framework, there is pressure to . . . create new, unprecedented expectations of rescue-like behavior.

■ WIDEMAN v. SHALLOWFORD COMMUNITY HOSPITAL
826 F.2d 1030 (11th Cir. 1987)

HILL, Circuit Judge.

This case presents the novel question of whether a county government's alleged practice of using its emergency medical vehicles only to transport patients to certain county hospitals which guarantee the payment of the county's medical bills violates a right protected by the federal constitution. We hold that such a practice, even if proved, would not violate any established constitutional right. . . .

I. BACKGROUND

The facts underlying this case are undeniably tragic. On April 12, 1984, Toni Wideman, who at the time was four months pregnant, began experiencing abdominal pain. She called her obstetrician, Dr. John Ramsey, who instructed her to come immediately to Piedmont Hospital. Ms. Wideman called the 911 emergency telephone number in DeKalb County and requested an ambulance to take her to Piedmont. Three employees of the DeKalb County Emergency Medical Service (EMS) responded to this call. Ms. Wideman claims that she again informed the EMS employees to take her to Piedmont where her doctor was waiting, but they refused and, instead, took her against her wishes to Shallowford Community Hospital. After a substantial delay, during which the attending physician at Shallowford spoke by phone with Dr. Ramsey, Ms. Wideman was transferred to Piedmont. At that point, however, Dr. Ramsey was unable to stop her labor, and Ms. Wideman gave birth to a premature baby, named Ebony Laslun Wideman, who survived for only four hours. . . .

. . . It seems that both parties, as well as the district court, have assumed that the alleged policy violates a cognizable constitutional right, which the plaintiffs characterize as their right to the provision of essential medical treatment and services by the county.[3] However, . . . the proper resolution of this case

---

[3] The constitutional right alleged by the plaintiffs arguably may be characterized as the much more specific right to the medical care and services of their choice. Ms. Wideman was provided with medical care in this case; indeed, she was rushed to a hospital in an ambulance provided by the county. Her claim appears to be that she should have been able to direct the ambulance wherever she wanted to go. For purposes of our analysis, however, we shall consider the plaintiffs' alleged constitutional right as they have characterized it.

requires us first to determine whether the Constitution grants a right to medical care and treatment in these circumstances. . . .

III.A. EXISTENCE OF A CONSTITUTIONAL RIGHT TO ESSENTIAL MEDICAL CARE

Beginning from the broadest prospective, we can discern no general right, based upon either the Constitution or federal statutes, to the provision of medical treatment and services by a state or municipality. If such a right exists at all, it must derive from the Fourteenth Amendment's due process clause, which forbids a state to deprive anyone of life, liberty or property without due process of law. The due process clause, however, has traditionally been interpreted as protecting certain "negative liberties," i.e., an individual's right to be free from arbitrary or discriminatory action taken by a state or municipality. This circuit has recognized the "well established notion that the Constitution limits the actions the states can take rather than mandating specific obligations." Bradberry v. Pinellas County, 789 F.2d 1513, 1517 (11th Cir. 1986). . . .

Two Supreme Court decisions dealing with access to abortions also support our conclusion that there is no general right to medical care or treatment provided by the state. In Maher v. Roe, 432 U.S. 464 (1977), two indigent women brought suit challenging a Connecticut regulation prohibiting the funding of abortions that were not medically necessary. The plaintiffs argued under the Fourteenth Amendment that the state regulation impinged on their constitutional right to an abortion, as recognized in Roe v. Wade, 410 U.S. 113 (1973). The Court upheld the state regulation, concluding that *Roe* did not declare an unqualified constitutional right to an abortion; rather, that case declared a woman's right to be protected from unduly burdensome interference with her freedom to decide whether to terminate her pregnancy. Significantly, in reaching this result, the Court noted that "the Constitution imposes no obligation on the states to pay the pregnancy-related medical expenses of indigent women, or indeed to pay any of the medical expenses of indigents." *Maher*, 432 U.S. at 469 (footnote omitted).

The Court's subsequent decision in Harris v. McRae, 448 U.S. 297 (1980), reinforced the constitutional distinction between requiring the state to provide medical services and prohibiting the state from impeding access to such services. The plaintiffs in *Harris* challenged the constitutionality of the Hyde amendment, which denied public funding for certain medically necessary abortions, as violating their due process liberty interest in deciding whether to terminate a pregnancy. The Supreme Court held that although the liberty protected by the due process clause prohibits unwarranted government interference with freedom of choice in the context of certain personal decisions, "it does not confer an entitlement to such funds as may be necessary to realize all the advantages of that freedom." . . . More recently, the Court has interpreted *Maher* and *Harris* as standing for the proposition that, "as a general matter, the state is under no constitutional duty to provide substantive services for those within its border." Youngberg v. Romeo, 457 U.S. 307, 317 (1982).

Several court of appeals decisions have addressed the issue of whether a state or municipality has a duty under the Fourteenth Amendment to provide various protective services to its citizens. Almost without exception, these courts have concluded that governments are under no constitutional duty to provide police, fire, or other public safety services. . . .

B

That there exists no such general right to the provision of medical care and services by the state, however, does not end our inquiry. Both the Supreme Court and various circuit courts have indicated that the existence of a "special custodial or other relationship" between an individual and the state may trigger a constitutional duty on the part of the state to provide certain medical or other services. In these special circumstances, the state's failure to provide such services might implicate constitutionally protected rights.

For example, the Supreme Court has held that the Eighth Amendment prohibition against cruel and unusual punishments, applicable to the states via the Fourteenth Amendment, requires states to provide medical care for those whom it is punishing by incarceration. . . . Similarly, the Court has held that an involuntarily committed mental patient retains . . . a clear Fourteenth Amendment right "to adequate food, shelter, clothing, and medical care." *Youngberg*, 457 U.S. at 315 . . .

Following this rationale, a constitutional duty can arise only when a state or municipality, by exercising a significant degree of custody or control over an individual, places that person in a worse situation than he would have been had the government not acted at all. Such a situation could arise by virtue of the state affirmatively placing an individual in a position of danger, effectively stripping a person of her ability to defend herself, or cutting off potential sources of private aid. The key concept is the exercise of coercion, dominion, or restraint by the state. . . .

In the present case, we conclude that DeKalb County did not exercise a degree of coercion, dominion, or restraint over Ms. Wideman sufficient to create a "special relationship," . . . The county did not force or otherwise coerce her into its ambulance; it merely made the ambulance available to her, and she entered it voluntarily. Ms. Wideman's physical condition at the time might have required her to seek immediate medical help, and that need might have induced her to make use of the service provided by the county, hoping that she could convince the EMS employees to take her where she wanted to go. Her physical condition, however, cannot be attributed to the county. . . . Therefore, the county was under no affirmative constitutional duty to provide any particular type of emergency medical service for her. . . .

. . . Because the Constitution does not require municipalities to provide any emergency medical services at all, it would be anomalous indeed to hold them liable for providing limited services which happen to be less extensive than a particular citizen may desire. . . .

Notes: The Differing Obligations of Physicians and Hospitals; Hospitals as Quasi-Public Facilities

1. *The "No Duty" Rule.* As the *Hurley* court suggests, physicians are not obligated to provide care to a particular patient unless they have agreed to do so.

A standard characterization of this principle appears in Oliver v. Brock, 342 So. 2d 1, 3 (Ala. 1976):

> A physician is under no obligation to engage in practice or to accept professional employment, but when the professional services of a physician are accepted by another person for the purposes of medical or surgical treatment, the relation of physician and patient is created. The relation is a consensual one wherein the patient knowingly seeks the assistance of a physician and the physician knowingly accepts him as patient. The relationship between a physician and patient may result from an express or implied contract, either general or special, and the rights and liabilities of the parties thereto are governed by the general law of contract. . . . 61 Am. Jur. 2d, Physicians, Surgeons, and Other Healers, §96.

This "no duty" rule is consistent with tort law's normal "Good Samaritan" doctrine, which does not require individuals, even professionals, to come to the aid of strangers in distress. A physician's *ethical,* as opposed to legal, duty is somewhat more demanding, however. The American Medical Association's Principles of Medical Ethics state that a "physician shall, in the provision of appropriate patient care, except in emergencies, be free to choose whom to serve. . . ." Council on Ethical and Judicial Affairs, Code of Medical Ethics: Current Opinions with Annotations xv (2006-2007). Why couldn't this ethical pledge be converted into an implied promise that physicians make to the public at large? See William E. May, Medical Ethics: Code and Covenant or Philanthropy and Contract?, 5(6) Hastings Center Rep. 29 (1975). Doesn't the public rely on physicians as much as they do on hospital emergency rooms? Consider especially Dr. Eddingfield's status as the plaintiff's family physician. Despite these qualms, *Hurley* is still thought to state the prevailing law for physicians.

2. *Triggering a Treatment Relationship.* A physician's complete freedom to refuse treatment exists only if a treatment relationship has not been initiated. We discuss below what actions constitute the initiation of treatment; but here, the fact that Dr. Eddingfield may have treated Mr. Hurley in the past did not suffice, because the law considers treatment relationships to coincide with "spells of illness." Thus, once a patient recovers from an illness or stops seeking treatment, a new treatment relationship must be formed in order to invoke a duty of continuing treatment. See, e.g., Castillo v. Emergency Medicine Associates, 372 F.3d 643, 648-652 (4th Cir. 2004).

Consider how this issue might come out differently when the patient receives medical care from a health maintenance organization (HMO). In this regard, see Hand v. Tavera, 864 S.W.2d 678 (Tex. Ct. App. 1993) (holding that "when the health-care plan's insured shows up at a participating hospital emergency room, and the plan's doctor on call is consulted about treatment or admission, there is a physician-patient relationship between the doctor and the insured").

3. *The Hospital's Duty.* Despite the reluctance of the *Manlove* court to find a duty to treat, it is considered a groundbreaking case in that it paved the way for other courts to make more definitive findings of hospital liability for the refusal of emergency care. See, e.g., Stanturf v. Sipes, 447 S.W.2d 558 (Mo. 1969) (hospital may be liable for refusing to treat frostbite victim who could not post $25 deposit); Mercy Medical Center v. Winnebago County, 206 N.W.2d 198 (Wis. 1973) ("It

would shock the public conscience if a person in need of medical emergency aid would be turned down at the door of a hospital"); but see Campbell v. Mincey, 413 F. Supp. 16 (N.D. Miss. 1975) (no obligation of hospital emergency room to care for pregnant woman in labor). Many states impose a requirement of open emergency rooms by statute or regulation. See Waxman & Dorn, States Take the Lead in Preventing Patient Dumping, 22 Clearinghouse Rev. 136 (1988). See generally Karen Rothenberg, Who Cares? The Evolution of the Legal Duty to Provide Emergency Care, 26 Hous. L. Rev. 21 (1989); Judith L. Dobbertin, Note, Eliminating Patient Dumping: A Proposal for Model Legislation, 28 Val. U. L. Rev. 291, 321-331 (1993); Annot., 11 A.L.R. Fed. 683 (1972).

How do you explain the fact that hospitals have a duty to provide emergency care to all who seek it while physicians are under no such obligation? Arguably, it does not make sense to expect physicians to be available at all times, while hospitals can reasonably be expected to always have someone staffing their emergency rooms. But what about just expecting physicians to be available during their regular office hours for emergencies? Can't doctors factor into their scheduling the possibility of emergencies? Don't they in fact already do that? Is part of the issue that physicians may not necessarily have the expertise for any emergency patient that comes though the door? Suppose the physician is a dermatologist and is confronted with a cardiac emergency. Is there anything the doctor reasonably could do besides call 911?

Hospitals, too, may be able to limit their obligation according to their capacity or expertise. Suppose a hospital has no emergency room because it specializes in elective surgeries. Or suppose the emergency room is full? When this happens, hospital emergency departments often place themselves on "drive- by" status, which means they alert ambulances not to stop there. One court held this was permissible in the case of a child who consequently suffered brain damage, even though the hospital had treated the child many times in the past and had encouraged his parents to pass up other closer hospitals and come there if he had serious problems. Davis v. Johns Hopkins Hospital, 622 A.2d 128 (Md. 1993).

4. *The Meaning of Reliance.* Why is the *Manlove* reliance theory limited to just emergency care? Observe the court's reasoning that "such a refusal [of treatment] might well result in worsening the condition of the injured person, because of the time lost in a useless attempt to obtain medical aid." Presumably, this is true only in a very serious or "unmistakable" emergency. It might be possible, however, to argue for other types of reliance. Suppose, for instance, that a prospective patient chose to live in the community because of the presence of a hospital, and it would thereby frustrate his or her reliance if the hospital could deny care in nonemergencies as well as emergencies. Such patients may have a psychological reliance but no *detrimental* reliance in the sense of a material change in one's position for the worse.

Where reliance is detrimental, should the patient have to demonstrate actual reliance in the particular case, rather than reliance being assumed? The *Manlove* court appeared to treat only the detriment part as requiring proof, not the psychological expectation. Should we presume that patients always legitimately expect emergency rooms to be open to them? Consider, for instance, Guerrero v. Copper Queen Hospital, 537 P.2d 1329 (Ariz. 1975), which found that a hospital in a border town owned by a local mining company had a duty to render emergency aid to two severely burned Mexican children who were injured in their home across the border.

5. *Physicians "On Call."* *Hurley* and *Manlove* appear consistent because one is about doctors and the other is about hospitals. But does it make sense for hospitals to have a duty to accept emergency patients if the doctors who work there are free to refuse treatment? Courts have resolved this problem by holding that a doctor who is "on call" for a hospital emergency room voluntarily undertakes the hospital's greater duty of care. The leading decision is Hiser v. Randolph, 617 P.2d 774 (Ariz. 1980). At 11:45 P.M. one night, Bonita Hiser came to the emergency room at Mojave County General Hospital in a semi-comatose condition arising out of an exacerbation of her juvenile onset diabetes. Along with the seven other doctors in the area, Dr. Randolph took turns as the on-call physician for the emergency room, a duty for which he was paid $100 per 12-hour shift, and he was on call when Mrs. Hiser came to the hospital. When the emergency room nurse called Dr. Randolph, he refused to come in. He claimed this was because he lacked the expertise to treat diabetes, but there was also evidence that his refusal was based on personal animosity toward Mrs. Hiser or the fact that Mrs. Hiser's husband was a lawyer. Mrs. Hiser died because of the delay in treatment. The court found that Dr. Randolph breached his duty of care arising from his status as an on-call physician. According to the court,

> the obviously intended effect of the [hospital's] bylaws and rules and regulations was to obligate the emergency room doctor "on call" to provide emergency treatment to the best of the doctor's ability to any emergency patient of the hospital. Under these circumstances, the lack of a consensual physician-patient relationship before a duty to treat can arise has been waived by the signatory doctors.

But see Childs v. Weis, 440 S.W.2d 104 (Tex. Ct. App. 1969) (physicians on emergency call were under no specific duty to see all patients who presented themselves to the emergency room).

A similar analysis is possible for HMO physicians. See St. Charles v. Kender, 646 N.E.2d 411 (Mass. Ct. App. 1995) (HMO subscriber is a third-party beneficiary of an HMO's contracts with its physicians; contract was breached when physician failed to return patient's calls for an appointment). In Hand v. Tavera, 864 S.W.2d 678 (Tex. Ct. App. 1993), Lewis Hand went to the Humana Hospital (Village Oaks) emergency room because of a three-day headache. He also had high blood pressure, and his medical history revealed that his father had died of an aneurysm. The emergency room physician was able to control Mr. Hand's blood pressure and headache temporarily with medication but ultimately concluded that Mr. Hand should be admitted to the hospital. Hospital admissions required the approval of another physician under the Humana Health Care Plan, so the emergency room physician called Dr. Robert Tavera, the physician responsible that evening for authorizing admissions of Humana patients. Dr. Tavera decided that Mr. Hand should be treated as an outpatient. A few hours after returning home, Mr. Hand suffered a stroke. The trial court granted Dr. Tavera summary judgment on the ground that no patient-physician relationship had been formed, but the appellate court held that a patient-physician relationship existed by virtue of Mr. Hand's membership in the Humana Health Care Plan and Dr. Tavera's designation "as the doctor acting for the Humana plan that night." As the court observed, "Hand paid premiums to Humana to purchase medical care in advance of need . . . and Tavera's medical group agreed to treat Humana enrollees in exchange for the fees received from Humana. In effect, Hand had paid in advance for the services of the Humana plan doctor on duty that night, who happened to be Tavera, and the physician-patient relationship existed."

6. *The Quasi-Public Status of Hospitals.* Another basis for imposing a duty to treat, distinct from the reliance theory, is the assertion that physicians or hospitals owe duties to the public at large simply by virtue of their having chosen to become licensed health care providers. It is a version of this argument that the *Hurley* court rejects with the cryptic comment that "analogies, drawn from the obligations to the public on the part of innkeepers, common carriers, and the like, are beside the mark." In ancient common law, certain occupations and businesses were considered to be "common callings," meaning that they could not turn away customers without a good reason. Innkeepers and public transport ("common carriers") were the classic examples. The reasons for these heightened public service duties were the importance of the service, the monopoly status of the business, and the support it received from the government. See Charles Burdick, The Origin of the Peculiar Duties of Public Service Companies, 11 Colum. L. Rev. 514, 616, 742 (1911); O. W. Holmes, Jr., Common Carriers and the Common Law, 13 Am. L. Rev. 40 (1879). In modern times, these "businesses affected with a public interest" are the public utilities (electric, phone, trains, etc.), and common law duties of public service have been supplanted by overt government regulation. This body of common law has therefore become somewhat archaic, but it is still sometimes invoked against trade associations or labor unions that refuse membership. See generally, Comment, Judicial Intervention in Admission Decisions of Private Professional Associations, 49 U. Chi. L. Rev. 840 (1982); Developments, Judicial Control of Actions of Private Associations, 76 Harv. L. Rev. 983 (1963).

This body of law has been used to characterize hospitals as "quasi-public" facilities for purposes of giving *physicians* rights of access to their medical staffs. Considering that patients are the ultimate customers for whom public benefit is intended, shouldn't this analogy have even more application to them? It would be ironic indeed to insist on physician access but deny patient access. Nevertheless, the *Manlove* court rejected this view. In other states, more recent decisions have been more receptive to the quasi-public characterization. For instance, in Thompson v. Sun City Community Hospital, 688 P.2d 605 (Ariz. 1984), the court found that a cause of action exists against a hospital that stabilized a patient with a severed artery and then transferred him for financial reasons. The court based the duty to treat on the general public policy embodied in hospital licensing regulations and private accreditation standards. Also, in Payton v. Weaver: 182 Cal. Rptr. 225 (Cal. App. 1982) the court suggested in dictum that this public service theory could be used to impose a community-wide obligation on kidney dialysis centers to share the burden of treating an unwanted disruptive patient. Cf. A. J. G. Priest, Possible Adaptation of Public Utility Concepts in the Health Care Field, 35 Law & Contemp. Probs. 839 (1970).

7. *The Private Status of Physicians.* Reconsider the situation of physicians. Why shouldn't medical practice by physicians be considered a "common calling" or a quasi-public service? Indeed, it turns out that, in fifteenth-century English law, physicians were included on the list of common callings along with blacksmiths and other important professions. Perhaps today the missing ingredient is that a physician rarely has a local monopoly; usually there are several in town. But not always. One court found a common law duty to treat where the sole physician practice group in town refused to accept a patient who had filed a complaint against one of the doctors in the group. Leach v. Drummond Medical Group, 192 Cal. Rptr. 650 (Cal. Ct. App. 1983).

In a few state statutes, regulatory law imposes some limited duties on physicians to provide care for patients. In Massachusetts, for instance, physicians, as a condition of being licensed, must agree to charge Medicare patients no more than Medicare's "reasonable charge." This has been held not to violate the constitutional rights of physicians. Dukakis v. Massachusetts Medical Society, 815 F.2d 790 (1st Cir. 1987).

8. *Paying vs. Indigent Patients.* Perhaps this body of law is not more developed because doctors and hospitals rarely turn away patients who can pay. For patients who cannot pay, the public service theory is usually no help, since the common law never required common callings to serve people for free. Only the reliance theory reaches this result, but it is restricted to severe emergencies, those in which the patient is worse off for having made a futile attempt to secure service. Only in Arizona have courts used a public service theory to impose a duty to treat patients who cannot pay, and there too the duty is limited to emergency care. (Should it be?)

9. *Enforcement of Public Rights.* For patients who cannot pay, regulatory law places hospitals under somewhat greater duties than the common law to treat both emergency and nonemergency patients, but these public law duties are limited and are not enforceable by individual patients. The federal Hill-Burton Act (42 U.S.C. §291) requires hospitals who have received construction grants under the Act to provide 3 percent of their care to indigent patients for 20 years. See James Blumstein, Court Action, Agency Reaction: The Hill-Burton Act as a Case Study, 69 Iowa L. Rev. 1227 (1984); Kenneth Wing, The Community Service Obligation of Hill-Burton Health Facilities, 23 B.C. L. Rev. 577 (1982). Construction funding under the Act ceased a number of years ago, however, so few hospitals are still under this obligation, and even when the law was in effect individual patients could not easily enforce it. See generally AHA v. Schweiker, 721 F.2d 170 (7th Cir. 1983); Rand E. Rosenblatt, Health Care Reform and Administrative Law: A Structural Approach, 88 Yale L.J. 243 (1978).

Another source of relevant law is charitable tax exemption. Nonprofit hospitals are considered to be "charities" that are exempt from property and income tax. Part of this charitable status includes an obligation to treat some patients for free. Federal law restricts this free-care obligation to emergency patients, as do most states, but a few states are beginning to require hospitals to devote a certain percentage of their overall services to patients who cannot pay. Once again, however, this is a community service obligation owed to the public at large, not to individual patients, and so it cannot be enforced very easily by private

action. Finally, the Joint Commission on Accreditation of Healthcare Organizations (JCAHO) private accreditation standards require hospitals to accept patients
without regard to "source of payment," but this is interpreted to mean accepting
all patients with some source of payment (e.g., not turning away Medicaid
patients) rather than a duty to accept patients who cannot pay.

This leaves us with the following patchwork of laws: for physicians, no
common law duty to treat, even in emergencies. For hospitals: (1) a common law
duty to treat emergency patients regardless of payment, but only in severe
emergencies; (2) common law and regulatory duties to treat all patients who can
pay; but (3) no enforceable duty to treat nonemergency or mild emergency
patients who cannot pay. This set the stage for enactment of a new federal statute,
the Emergency Medical Treatment and Active Labor Act (EMTALA), discussed in
the *Burditt* case at page 106.

Notes: Moral and Constitutional Rights to Health Care

1. *Moral Rights to Treatment.* The discussion of legal rights to treatment surely
must be informed by how our society views moral rights to health care. While Lois
Shepherd argues that we are evolving toward a more caring community (page 94),
what message does society send when the law limits the right to treatment so
narrowly as to encompass only serious emergencies? Does the emergency care
limitation suggest that we are trying to limit care to the most compelling needs
and to avoid people demanding too much care (emergencies being thought of as
unpredictable)? This might be seen as a partial embodiment of the "rescue
principle," which declares that the strongest ethical demand in medicine is to help
those in greatest need. In this regard, the moral dimension of medicine is
stronger than in any other commercial arena, because there is no equivalent
requirement that grocers, restaurants, or hotels provide their services for free to
people in dire straits. What justifies this distinction? Is it that if food and housing
were available on demand, it would be too easy to abuse the privilege? But what
kinds of incentives for patients does a right only to emergency care generate? Is
the reluctance of the courts to find even broader rights to health care a reflection
of the difficulty in deciding who to hold responsible for vindicating these rights?
Or perhaps it reflects the difficulty in defining what a right to health care would
include. Consider in this regard the difference between defining a right to
housing and a right to health care.

The moral issue can also be debated from a broader, social perspective. So
far, we have thought only about whether patients have a right to demand
treatment from particular doctors and hospitals. Even where they do not have
these private rights, perhaps they have a claim to a more public right, one that
society as a whole owes to provide minimally decent health care to all. We
currently recognize this claim to basic social support for education and to a more
limited extent for food and housing. But for health care, there is no national safety
net. Medicaid coverage provides health insurance for the poor, but less than half
of those living in poverty are eligible. Almost 47 million Americans have no health
insurance of any kind. Perhaps this social inequity is politically and morally
sustainable only because private hospital emergency rooms exist as a last resort for

those without insurance. Could it be, then, that the heightened private law duties of hospitals have weakened our nation's public law commitment to health care access? See Mark A. Hall, The Unlikely Case in Favor of Patient Dumping, 28 Jurimetrics 389 (1988). For an argument that private law duties tend to undermine voluntary charity, see Richard Epstein, Mortal Peril: Our Inalienable Right to Health Care? (1997). For responses to Epstein, see Symposium: Is America's Health Care System in Mortal Peril?, 1998 U. Ill. L. Rev. 683.

2. *Positive vs. Negative Liberty.* If there is a moral right to health care generally, it is clearly not vindicated as a substantive due process right by the U.S. Constitution. *Wideman* is a classic statement of the principle that the Bill of Rights embodies primarily negative, not positive, liberties, that is, it is concerned mainly with freedoms from government imposition, not rights to government assistance. Thus, the Constitution becomes relevant to health care when the government bans treatment choices or forces treatment, but not when it simply declines to assist in obtaining treatment. In this regard, the U.S. Constitution differs markedly from constitutional models in Europe.

Wideman was followed by an important Supreme Court opinion confirming its general analysis in this regard. In DeShaney v. Winnebago County Department of Social Services, 489 U.S. 189 (1989), the Court held that no constitutional violation occurred in a case where a child was left with permanent brain damage when a state social services agency failed to intervene aggressively enough to prevent child abuse. The state had received several reports of severe beatings by the father. The Court reaffirmed "that the due process clauses generally confer no affirmative right to governmental aid," and it reasoned that the state agency had not assumed a "special relationship" with the child by virtue of having made some ineffectual efforts to protect him since the agency did nothing to make him more vulnerable to the danger. See also Archie v. Racine, 847 F.2d 1211 (7th Cir. 1988) (en banc) (§1983 action not maintainable for city rescue service's negligent failure to dispatch ambulance; no constitutional right to treatment exists).

3. *Institutional Responsibilities of Mental Hospitals.* An exception to this negative liberty principle exists for individuals over whom the state has control, and it has generated significant litigation with respect to mental hospitals. An early, highly influential decision addressing the constitutional right to treatment in the context of state institutionalization is Judge Frank Johnson's remarkable order taking direct charge over the administration of Alabama's state mental hospital because of its persistent failure to provide any meaningful form of treatment. Wyatt v. Stickney, 325 F. Supp. 781 (M.D. Ala. 1971), 344 F. Supp. 373 (M.D. Ala. 1972). See also O'Connor v. Donaldson, 422 U.S. 563 (1975) (civil commitment to psychiatric hospital invalid without treatment); Comment, Wyatt v. Stickney and the Right of Civilly Committed Mental Patients to Adequate Treatment, 86 Harv. L. Rev. 1282 (1973). In Thomas S. v. Morrow, 781 F.2d 367 (4th Cir. 1986), the court found a constitutional duty to provide community-based mental health services in order to ensure the availability of a least restrictive means of treatment for patients that would otherwise have to be involuntarily committed. In Olmstead v. L.C., the U.S. Supreme Court found a duty under the Americans with Disabilities Act for states to place individuals with mental disabilities in less restrictive community settings rather than in institutions. 527 U.S. 581 (1999).

Prisoners are another class of persons who gain certain rights to health care by virtue of their confinement. There, the rights rest also in the Eighth Amendment's prohibition against cruel and unusual punishment.

4. *Equal Protection.* In Maher v. Roe, 432 U.S. 464, 469-470 (1977), discussed in *Wideman*, the Court identified another possible source of a constitutional duty to treat: "The Constitution imposes no obligation on the states to pay . . . any of the medical expenses of indigents. But when a state decides to alleviate some of the hardships of poverty by providing medical care, the manner in which it dispenses benefits is subject to constitutional limitations." For example, in Memorial Hospital v. Maricopa County, 415 U.S. 250 (1974), the Court struck down Arizona's requirement of a year's residence in a county as a condition of receiving nonemergency medical care at county expense as infringing on the right to travel. Might a state be subject to an equal protection attack for funding some procedures but not others? See Doe v. Colautti, 592 F.2d 704 (3d Cir. 1978) (finding no violation of the equal protection clause when Pennsylvania's medical assistance program provided less generous benefits for psychiatric care than for general medical care).

5. *Legislative Mandates.* In Harris v. McRae, 448 U.S. 297 (1980), another abortion funding case discussed in *Wideman*, the Court addressed a nonconstitutional theory for compelling government funding of health care. States that participate in Medicaid are, generally speaking, required to fund most medically necessary forms of treatment. Beal v. Doe, 432 U.S. 438, 444 (1977). Although *McRae* found this statutory requirement to be inapplicable to abortions, in other cases the medical necessity mandate has proved to be an effective tool for obtaining Medicaid coverage. Ellis v. Patterson, 859 F.2d 52 (8th Cir. 1988) (requiring reasonable funding once a state decides to provide coverage for liver transplants); Rush v. Parham, 625 F.2d 1150 (5th Cir. 1980) (requiring funding for sex change operations in certain circumstances). However, there is no statutory requirement that Medicaid be funded at a level sufficient to cover all people who need it.

■ BURDITT v. U.S. DEPARTMENT OF HEALTH AND HUMAN SERVICES
934 F.2d 1362 (5th Cir. 1991)

REAVLEY, Circuit Judge.

Hospitals that execute Medicare provider agreements with the federal government pursuant to 42 U.S.C. §1395cc must treat all human beings who enter their emergency departments in accordance with the Emergency Medical Treatment and Active Labor Act (EMTALA), 42 U.S.C. §1395dd. Hospitals and responsible physicians found to have violated EMTALA's requirements are subject to civil money penalties. [This case is an appeal by Dr. Burditt of a $20,000 fine assessed against him by the Department of Health and Human Services. EMTALA also provides for a private cause of action, with prevailing plaintiffs entitled to monetary damages from the offending hospital and appropriate equitable relief. Damages may not be recovered from physicians in a private cause of action, however.] . . .

I.A. FACTS

Mrs. Rosa Rivera arrived in the emergency room of DeTar Hospital in Victoria, Texas at approximately 4:00 p.m. on December 5, 1986. At or near term with her sixth child, she was experiencing one-minute, moderate contractions every three minutes and her membranes had ruptured. Two obstetrical nurses, Tammy Kotsur and Donna Keining, examined her and found indicia of labor and dangerously high blood pressure. Because Rivera had received no prenatal care, and had neither a regular doctor nor means of payment, Kotsur telephoned Burditt, who was next on DeTar's rotating call-list of physicians responsible for such "unaligned" obstetrics patients. Upon hearing Rivera's history and condition, Burditt told Kotsur that he "didn't want to take care of this lady" and asked her to prepare Rivera for transfer to John Sealy Hospital in Galveston, Texas, 170 miles away. Burditt agreed to call back in five to ten minutes.

Kotsur and Keining told the nursing supervisor, Jean Herman, and DeTar's administrator, Charles Sexton, of their belief that it would be unsafe to transfer Rivera. When Burditt called back, Keining told him that, according to Sexton's understanding of hospital regulations and federal law, Burditt would have to examine Rivera and personally arrange for John Sealy to receive her before he could legally transfer her. Keining asked Burditt for permission to start an intravenous push of magnesium sulfate as a precaution against convulsive seizures. Burditt told Keining to begin administering this medication only if Rivera could be transported by ambulance. . . .

Burditt arrived at approximately 4:50 to examine Rivera. He confirmed her blood pressure to be the highest he had ever seen, 210/130, and he assumed that she had been hypertensive throughout her pregnancy. As the experienced head of DeTar's obstetrics and gynecology department, Burditt knew that there was a strong possibility that Rivera's hypertension would precipitate complications which might kill both Rivera and her baby. He also knew that the infants of hypertensive mothers are at higher-than-normal risk of intrauterine growth retardation. He estimated that Rivera's baby was six pounds — less than normal weight — and arranged her transfer to John Sealy, a perinatal facility better equipped than DeTar to care for underweight infants. . . .

At approximately 5:00, Herman showed Burditt DeTar's guidelines regarding EMTALA, but he refused to read them. Burditt told Herman that Rivera represented more risk than he was willing to accept from a malpractice standpoint. Herman explained that Rivera could not be transferred unless Burditt signed a DeTar form entitled "Physician's Certificate Authorizing Transfer." Burditt asked for "that dang piece of paper" and signed his name under the following:

> I have examined the patient, _____, and have determined that, based upon the information available to me at this time, the medical benefits reasonably expected from the provision of appropriate medical treatment at another medical facility outweigh the increased risks to the patient's medical condition from effecting [the] transfer. The basis for my conclusion is as follows: _____

Burditt listed no basis for his conclusion and remarked to Herman that "until DeTar Hospital pays my malpractice insurance, I will pick and choose those patients that I want to treat."

Burditt then went to care for another unaligned patient, Sylvia Ramirez, while the nurses arranged Rivera's transfer. They found another obstetrical nurse, Anita Nichols, to accompany Rivera to John Sealy. Burditt returned to the nurses' station and stayed there from 5:30 to 6:18. He never again examined Rivera or asked about her medical condition, though he inquired several times about the status of her transfer. Burditt delivered the Ramirez baby at 6:22. Afterward, Nichols told him the results of her examination of Rivera and informed him that the ambulance had arrived. Based exclusively on Nichols' statements, Burditt concluded that Rivera's condition had not changed since his examination two hours before. Burditt did not reexamine Rivera though he saw her being wheeled to the ambulance. He did not order any medication or life support equipment for Rivera during her transfer.

Nichols delivered Rivera's healthy baby in the ambulance approximately 40 miles into the 170-mile trip to John Sealy. She directed the driver to nearby Ganado Hospital to get a drug called pitocin to staunch Rivera's bleeding. While there, Nichols telephoned Burditt, who ordered her to continue to John Sealy despite the birth. Instead, per Rivera's wishes, Nichols returned Rivera to DeTar, where Burditt refused to see her because she failed to proceed to John Sealy in accordance with his instructions. Burditt directed that Rivera be discharged if she was stable and not bleeding excessively. A DeTar official pressed Burditt to allow Dr. Shirley Pigott to examine Rivera. Rivera stayed at DeTar under Pigott's care for three days and left in good health. . . .

II.A.1. Screening

Because Rivera presented herself to DeTar's emergency department and a request was made on her behalf for care, EMTALA required DeTar to

> provide for an *appropriate* medical screening examination *within the capability of the hospital's emergency department* to determine whether or not an emergency medical condition . . . exists or to determine if the individual is in active labor. . . .

42 U.S.C. §1395dd(a) (emphasis added). The parties agree that DeTar appropriately screened Rivera and discovered that she had an "emergency medical condition" — severe hypertension — within the meaning of 42 U.S.C. §1395dd(e)(1).[3]

---

[3] EMTALA defines "emergency medical condition" as

> a medical condition manifesting itself by acute symptoms of sufficient severity (including severe pain) such that the absence of immediate medical attention could reasonably be expected to result in —
>   (A) placing the patient's health in serious jeopardy,
>   (B) serious impairment to bodily functions, or
>   (C) serious dysfunction of any bodily organ or part.

42 U.S.C. §1395dd(e)(1) (Supp. IV 1987).

II.A.2. Emergency Medical Condition and Active Labor

Patients diagnosed with an "emergency medical condition" or "active labor" must either be treated or be transferred in accordance with EMTALA. Burditt claims that Rivera received all of the care that she was due under EMTALA because he stabilized her hypertension sufficiently for transfer and she was not in active labor when she left DeTar for John Sealy.

II.A.2.a. Unstable Emergency Medical Condition

Rivera's blood pressure was 210/130 at 4:00 and 5:00. This was the last reading known to Burditt before he facilitated her transfer. Nurses also measured her blood pressure as 173/105 at 5:30, 178/103 at 5:45, 186/107 at 6:00, and 190/110 at 6:50. Experts testified that Rivera's hypertension put her at high risk of suffering serious complications, including seizures, heart failure, kidney dysfunction, tubular necrosis, stroke, intracranial bleeding, placental abruption, and fetal hypoxia. This is substantial, if not conclusive evidence that Rivera entered and exited DeTar with an emergency medical condition.

Burditt argues that he fulfilled EMTALA's requirements with respect to Rivera's hypertension by "stabilizing" it, or

> provid[ing] such medical treatment of the condition as may be necessary to assure, within reasonable medical probability, that no material deterioration of the condition is likely to result from [a] transfer. . . .

42 U.S.C. §1395dd(e)(4)(A). He claims that the magnesium sulfate that he ordered for Rivera has an antihypertensive effect that complements its primary anticonvulsive purpose.

Development of any of the possible complications could have killed or seriously injured Rivera, her baby, or both, and thus would constitute a "material deterioration" under 42 U.S.C. §1395dd(e)(4)(A). Any deterioration would "result" from transfer in that Rivera would have received better care for any complication at DeTar than in the ambulance. Thus, Burditt could not have stabilized Rivera unless he provided treatment that medical experts agree would prevent the threatening and severe consequences of Rivera's hypertension while she was in transit. [The HHS appeals board] could properly disregard Burditt's testimony and accept that of all other testifying experts in holding that Burditt provided no such treatment, and thus did not stabilize Rivera's emergency medical condition. . . .

II.A.2.b. Active Labor

EMTALA defines "active labor" as labor at a time when

> (B) there is inadequate time to effect safe transfer to another hospital prior to delivery, or
> (C) a transfer may pose a threat [to] the health and safety of the patient or the unborn child.

42 U.S.C. §1395dd(e)(2)(B)-(C). This statutory definition renders irrelevant any medical definition of active labor. . . .

Burditt challenges the ALJ's finding that, at approximately 5:00, there was inadequate time to safely transfer Rivera to John Sealy before she delivered her baby. Dr. Warren Crosby testified that, based on Burditt's own examination results, Rivera would, more likely than not, deliver within three hours after Burditt [made the decision to transfer her to] John Sealy. . . . Burditt does not challenge [the] conclusion that the ambulance trip from DeTar to John Sealy takes approximately three hours. We therefore hold that [the HHS appeals board] properly concluded that Rivera was in active labor under 42 U.S.C. §1395dd(e)(2)(B).

The ALJ also found that Rivera was in active labor under clause C at the time Burditt examined her. There is always some risk of a vehicular accident in transit, so transfer always "may" pose a threat to the health and safety of the patient or fetus. . . . We believe that Congress intended clause C to extend EMTALA's . . . protection to women in labor who have any complication with their pregnancies regardless of delivery imminency. Because better medical care is available in a hospital than in an ambulance, whether a transfer "may pose a threat" under 42 U.S.C. §1395dd(e)(2)(C) depends on whether the woman in labor has any medical condition that could interfere with the normal, natural delivery of her healthy child. Under the statutory language, a woman in labor is entitled to EMTALA's . . . protections upon a showing of possible threat; it does not require proof of a reasonable medical probability that any threat will come to fruition. . . .

The record overwhelmingly confirms that Rivera's hypertension could have interfered with a normal delivery, and she was thus in active labor under 42 U.S.C. §1395dd(e)(2)(C). . . .

II.A.3. Treat or Transfer

Upon discovery of active labor or an emergency medical condition, EMTALA usually requires hospitals to treat the discovered condition. Under certain circumstances, however, EMTALA allows hospitals to transfer patients instead of treating them. 42 U.S.C. §1395dd(b)(1)(B). . . . [The court went on to find that Burditt had not satisfied the requirements under EMTALA for a transfer before stabilization. Under EMTALA, transfer is permitted if the patient requests transfer *or* the physician has certified in writing that the medical benefits of transfer outweigh the increased risks to the patient. In addition, the receiving hospital must be capable of providing the needed treatment and must have agreed to accept the transfer. Finally, the transfer must occur with appropriate personnel and transportation, including appropriate life support measures. While Burditt had obtained consent from John Sealy before the transfer, he had not reasonably concluded that the benefits of transfer outweighed the risks nor had he arranged for the transfer with appropriate personnel and transportation.]

II.C. EMTALA's CONSTITUTIONALITY

As his final attempt to escape [liability], Burditt claims that EMTALA effects a public taking of his services without just compensation in contravention of the Constitution's Fifth Amendment.

Assuming *arguendo* that professional services constitute property protected by the takings clause, Burditt has not shown that EMTALA effects a taking.

EMTALA imposes no responsibilities directly on physicians; it unambiguously requires hospitals to examine and stabilize, treat, or appropriately transfer all who arrive requesting treatment. Its provision for sanctions against physicians who knowingly violate its requirements is merely an enforcement mechanism that does not alter its explicit assignment of duties.

Governmental regulation that affects a group's property interests "does not constitute a taking of property where the regulated group is not required to participate in the regulated industry." Whitney v. Heckler, 780 F.2d 963, 972 (11th Cir.), *cert. denied*, 479 U.S. 813 (1986).

Two levels of voluntariness undermine Burditt's taking assertion. Only hospitals that voluntarily participate in the federal government's Medicare program must comply with EMTALA. Hospitals must consider the cost of complying with EMTALA's requirements in deciding whether to continue to participate in the Medicare program.

Second, Burditt is free to negotiate with DeTar or another hospital regarding his responsibility to facilitate a hospital's compliance with EMTALA. Thus, physicians only voluntarily accept responsibilities under EMTALA if they consider it in their best interest to do so. Accordingly, Burditt's claim under the takings clause is without merit. . . .

Notes: The Federal Patient Dumping Statute

1. *Historical Background*. Congress passed the Emergency Medical Treatment and Active Labor Act (EMTALA) as part of the Consolidated Omnibus Reconciliation Act of 1986 (COBRA), in response to the perception that state law was too weak to prevent widespread patient dumping. While EMTALA, or COBRA, has worked better than previous legal efforts, in part because of the private right of action, there are still concerns that patient dumping persists at unacceptable levels. One scholar argues, however, that

> EMTALA is a virtual catalogue of how to get a statute wrong. First, generalize from unrepresentative anecdotal evidence in identifying the problem. Draft the statute sloppily, and leave the most important words undefined or defined too broadly. Finance the resulting open-ended entitlement with an unfunded mandate imposed on private parties. . . . [Design the enforcement system] to reward the wrong people. Finally, apply the statute even after the world on which it depended has vanished. Any one of these problems would be bad enough in isolation, but their combined effect is devastating to the interests EMTALA was intended to protect. David A. Hyman, Dumping EMTALA: When Bad Laws Happen to Good People (1998) (not yet published).

As you read the following notes, see if you can determine why someone might reach such a conclusion. Nevertheless, Prof. Hyman acknowledges that

> the statute is wildly popular across the entirety of the political spectrum and among such disparate interest groups as physicians, advocates for the poor, [academics,] and consumer groups. Unlike many reforms, EMTALA does not

create a new administrative bureaucracy; it does not favor the interests of the well-connected against the less fortunate; its on-budget costs are modest; and it seems to be no more intrusive than is absolutely necessary to accomplish its objectives. David A. Hyman, Patient Dumping and EMTALA: Past Imperfect/Future Shock, 8 Health Matrix 29 (1998).

For further discussion of these and other aspects of EMTALA, see Russell Korobkin, Determining Health Care Rights from Behind a Veil of Ignorance, 1998 U. Ill. L. Rev. 801; Sara Rosenbaum, Bruce Siegel, & Marsha Regenstein, EMTALA and Hospital "Community Engagement": The Search for a Rational Policy, 53 Buff. L. Rev. 499 (2005); Karen Rothenberg, Who Cares? The Evolution of the Legal Duty to Provide Emergency Care, 26 Hous. L. Rev. 21 (1989); Dana E. Schaffner, Note, EMTALA: All Bark and No Bite, 2005 U. Ill. L. Rev. 1021; Lawrence E. Singer, Look What They've Done to My Law, Ma: COBRA's Implosion, 33 Hous. L. Rev. 113 (1996); Annot., 104 A.L.R. Fed. 166 (1991).

Dr. Michael Burditt was the first physician fined for an EMTALA violation, and his actions were vigorously defended by the Texas Medical Association. For a critical view of the Fifth Circuit's decision in the *Burditt* case, see David Hyman, Lies, Damned Lies, and Narrative, 73 Ind. L.J. 797, 824-832 (1998).

2. *Screening and Stabilizing.* EMTALA creates two distinct duties. First, the duty to screen patients is triggered by their arrival at the hospital, and it ceases if it is determined they are not in what the statute defines as an "emergency" condition. Second, if they are in an emergency condition, then the hospital must stabilize them. (The statutory requirements are similar for patients in active labor.) Most litigation has arisen at the first stage, in cases where patients claim the hospital failed entirely to evaluate or recognize their emergency condition. But that is not our main concern here. Our concern is, if there clearly is an emergency, how far does the duty to treat extend? Do hospitals have to perform bypass surgery after they halt a heart attack? Although *Burditt* found that "stabilizing" care was not rendered in that case, what about other typical situations? Consider whether the outcome would be any different under EMTALA than it was under this state law decision: Joyner v. Alton Ochsner Medical Foundation, 230 So. 2d 913 (La. Ct. App. 1970) (auto accident victim did not "require immediate admission" after stabilizing care was rendered, despite "multiple deep facial lacerations, a possible head injury, traumatic damage to the teeth and multiple bruises and contusions of the body, resulting in considerable loss of blood"). Consider whether the duty to treat under EMTALA is as strong as it is under this state law decision: Thompson v. Sun City Community Hospital, 688 P.2d 605 (Ariz. 1984) (a cause of action exists against a hospital that stabilized a patient with a severed artery and then transferred him for financial reasons). Is the federal statute any more demanding than the *Manlove* reliance theory? See generally M. Hall, The Unlikely Case in Favor of Patient Dumping, 28 Jurimetrics J. 389 (1990) ("In the great majority of cases, the federal standard will do nothing to prevent patient dumping. . . . Even for those patients who do require stabilization prior to transfer, the federal law will result only in a delay in the transfer."); Kenneth R. Wing & John R. Campbell, The Emergency Room Admission: How Far Does the "Open Door" Go?, 63 U. Det. L. Rev. 119 (1985).

According to the Eleventh Circuit, the stabilization requirement of EMTALA applies only when a hospital discharges a patient or transfers the patient to another hospital. Harry v. Marchant, 291 F.3d 767 (11th Cir. 2002) (en banc). See also Bryan V. Rectors and Visitors of the University of Virginia, 95 F.3d 349, 352 (4th Cir. 1996) (also observing that the stabilization requirement of EMTALA is defined in terms of transfer or discharge).

In its requirement to stabilize emergency patients, EMTALA does not require the impossible. If a hospital does not have the facilities or personnel necessary to fully stabilize a patient, and the patient must be transferred to a more sophisticated hospital to receive needed care, the first hospital can transfer the patient to the more sophisticated hospital without violating EMTALA. The transferring hospital must do all it can to stabilize the patient's condition, but it need not to what it cannot do. Cherukuri v. Shalala, 175 F.3d 446 (6th Cir. 1999) (absolving physician at small rural hospital after the physician transferred two patients who needed surgery to stop internal bleeding from an automobile accident).

3. *The Patient's Indigency.* While the passage of EMTALA was motivated by concerns about private hospitals "dumping" indigent or uninsured patients on public hospitals, the statutory language imposes no requirement that patients show that they were denied emergency services because of indigency or lack of insurance. See 42 U.S.C. §1395dd(a) ("if any individual . . . comes to the emergency department . . . , the hospital must provide for an appropriate medical screening examination within the capability of the hospital's emergency department"). Accordingly, courts have generally held that it is irrelevant why a person did not receive an appropriate screening exam or, if an emergency was identified, why a person did not receive stabilizing care before discharge or transfer. As one court observed, "[EMTALA] applies to any and all patients, not just to patients with insufficient resources." Brooker v. Desert Hosp. Corp., 947 F.2d 412, 415 (9th Cir. 1991). *Accord* Summers v. Baptist Medical Center, 91 F.3d 1132 (8th Cir. 1996); Gatewood v. Washington Healthcare Corp., 933 F.2d 1037, 1040 (D.C. Cir. 1991).

The Supreme Court addressed the motive question in the context of EMTALA's stabilization requirement and rejected any need to show an improper motive. Roberts v. Galen of Virginia, Inc., 525 U.S. 249 (1999). The Court "express[ed] no opinion" on the need to show an improper motive for a claim of inappropriate medical screening.

Perhaps the most controversial extension of EMTALA beyond economic discrimination occurred in the *Baby K* case. In In re Baby K, 16 F.3d 590 (4th Cir. 1994), parents of an anencephalic child sought ventilatory treatment of their child during periodic bouts of respiratory distress. After the second of three such episodes, the hospital sought judicial permission to withhold the ventilator when the child next came to the emergency room. In the view of the hospital, it was medically and ethically inappropriate to ventilate the child given her limited life expectancy, her total absence of consciousness, and the futility of treatment at improving her condition. According to the hospital, the only appropriate treatment for the child was the treatment "it would provide other anencephalic infants—supportive care in the form of warmth, nutrition, and hydration." The court rejected the hospital's argument. It observed that EMTALA requires stabilizing treatment in the event of a medical emergency, and the child's respiratory distress met EMTALA's definition of a medical emergency. If there was to be an exception for "futile" care under EMTALA, Congress would have to write that exception into the statute. The court's opinion in *Baby K* is presented in Chapter 3 and discussed in Chapters 1 and 3.

The *Baby K* decision raises serious questions about the ability of society to contain health care costs. If the hospital in the case could not deny a ventilator to an anencephalic child, how could any emergency medical care be withheld on the ground that its high costs were not justified by its minimal benefit? Is there a distinction between the economic or other discrimination prohibited by EMTALA and the denial of care that results when a hospital is concerned about the limits of society's resources?

Perhaps in recognition of these concerns, the Fourth Circuit limited the impact of *Baby K* two years later. In Bryan v. Rectors and Visitors of the University of Virginia, 95 F.3d 349 (4th Cir. 1996), an EMTALA claim was brought on behalf of a patient who died of a heart attack after her physicians decided that "no further efforts to prevent her death should be made." Twenty days before the heart attack, the patient had been admitted to the hospital in respiratory distress. Eight days before the heart attack, apparently because of the hopelessness of the patient's condition, her physicians decided to withhold further life-sustaining treatment, including cardiopulmonary resuscitation, in the event of a cardiac arrest. When she suffered her heart attack, no efforts were made to prevent her death. According to the court, there was no EMTALA violation because EMTALA "was intended to regulate the hospital's care of the patient only in the immediate aftermath of the act of admitting her for emergency treatment and while it considered whether it would undertake longer-term full treatment or instead transfer the patient to a hospital that could and would undertake that treatment." Id. at 352.

4. *Preventive Dumping.* There has been concern that hospitals would try to evade their EMTALA obligations by dumping patients before they reach the emergency room. For example, when called by a paramedic or emergency medical technician who is transporting a patient by ambulance, the emergency room staff might direct the ambulance to another hospital. Early cases suggested that hospitals would have considerable freedom to prevent patients from reaching the emergency room. See Miller v. Medical Center of Southwest Louisiana, 22 F.3d 626 (5th Cir. 1994) (hospital not liable under EMTALA for refusing to accept the transfer of a patient who needed specialized emergency care beyond the capabilities of the transferring hospital); Johnson v. University of Chicago Hospitals, 982 F.2d 230 (7th Cir. 1992) (hospital not liable for diverting an ambulance to another hospital).

Subsequent amendment of the EMTALA regulations and case law interpreting the amendment have limited the ability of hospitals to engage in preventive dumping. Under one regulation, patients have come to the hospital's emergency room for purposes of EMTALA once they have reached any part of the hospital's property, including a hospital-owned ambulance service. 42 C.F.R. §489.24(b) (2007) (applied in Hernandez v. Starr County Hospital District, 30 F. Supp. 2d 970 (S.D. Tex. 1999); Preston v. Meriter Hosp., Inc., 700 N.W.2d 158 (Wis. 2005)). The same regulation permits hospitals to divert non-hospital-owned ambulance services if the emergency department "does not have the staff or facilities to accept any additional emergency patients." 42 C.F.R. §489.24(b)(4). The Ninth Circuit has interpreted this provision to mean that a hospital violates EMTALA when it diverts a non-hospital-owned ambulance in the absence of an inability to provide treatment for the patient. Arrington v. Wong, 237 F.3d 1066 (9th Cir. 2001). See Caroline J. Stalker, Comment, How Far Is Too Far?: EMTALA Moves from the Emergency Room to Off-Campus Entities, 36 Wake Forest L. Rev. 823 (2001).

Note that there is some ambiguity to §489.24(b). Although the regulation seems to limit the ability of hospitals to divert non-hospital-owned ambulances, it also states that "[a]n individual in a non-hospital-owned ambulance off hospital property is not considered to have come to the hospital's emergency department even if a member of the ambulance staff contacts the hospital by telephone or telemetry communications and informs the hospital that they want to transport the individual to the hospital for examination and treatment."

A related question is whether patients must come to the emergency department, as opposed to other parts of the hospital, to trigger EMTALA. As indicated, under 42 C.F.R. §489.24(b), EMTALA is triggered when a patient is anywhere on the hospital's property. Thus, a First Circuit decision emphasizes the point that a hospital's duty to stabilize before transfer applies to any patient in the hospital, "regardless of how that person enters the institution or where within the walls he may be when the hospital identifies the problem." Lopez-Soto v. Hawayek, 175 F.3d 170, 173 (1st Cir. 1999) (observing that the stabilization requirement of EMTALA applies to an individual who "comes to a hospital" and holding that EMTALA applies when a pregnant woman is admitted to the maternity ward and taken to the operating room for a cesarean section, and her infant is born with respiratory distress and needs emergency care).

5. *Dumping After Admission to the Hospital.* Courts disagree as to whether EMTALA's stabilization requirement continues to apply once the patient has been admitted to the hospital. Cases have arisen in which patients were admitted to the hospital for treatment and, after a few or more days of treatment, been transferred to another hospital or discharged before their illness was fully treated. Some courts have concluded that the obligation to stabilize persists throughout the patient's hospitalization. See Thornton v. Southwest Detroit Hospital, 895 F.2d 1131 (6th Cir. 1990); Lee v. Alleghany Regional Hospital Corporation, 778 F. Supp. 900 (W.D. Va. 1991); Smith v. Richmond Memorial Hospital, 416 S.E.2d 689 (Va. 1992).

Other courts have concluded that the stabilization requirement ceases upon the patient's admission to the hospital. Bryan v. Rectors and Visitors of the University of Virginia, 95 F.3d 349, 352 (4th Cir. 1996); James v. Sunrise Hospital, 86 F.3d 885 (9th Cir. 1996); Bryant v. Adventist Health Systems/West, 289 F.3d 1162 (9th Cir. 2002). Note that in *Bryan* and *Bryant*, the courts were deciding about the stabilization requirement for care rendered during the patient's hospital stay and not in the context of a transfer or discharge. Hence, it is not surprising that the courts were especially concerned about converting state malpractice claims into federal EMTALA claims. See note 6, infra.

In *Bryant*, the Court observed that the stabilization requirement would not cease upon the patient's admission to the hospital "if a patient demonstrates in a particular case that inpatient admission was a ruse to avoid EMTALA's requirements." 289 F.3d at 1169. A federal district court invoked that point in a case in which a patient was sent home after admission but before his injuries had been stabilized. Morgan v. North Mississippi Medical Center, Inc., 403 F. Supp. 2d 1115, 1130 (S.D. Ala. 2005). Although the court denied the hospital's motion to dismiss the EMTALA claim, it ultimately concluded on summary judgment that the hospital had not engaged in a ruse to avoid EMTALA's requirements when it admitted the patient. Morgan v. North Mississippi Medical Center, Inc., 458 F. Supp. 2d 1341 (S.D. Ala. 2006).

In a final rule that took effect in 2003, the Centers for Medicare and Medicaid Services took the position that a hospital's obligations cease once the patient has been admitted to the hospital as an inpatient. 42 C.F.R. §489.24(d)(2).

6. *Appropriate Medical Screening.* In interpreting EMTALA's requirement of an "appropriate medical screening examination," courts have recognized an important tension between ensuring access to emergency care for all persons and creating a federal cause of action for charges of malpractice in the emergency room. If a person is sent home from the emergency room after a physician wrongly concludes that there is no serious health problem, the mistaken diagnosis may reflect either the negligent provision of care or the purposeful denial of care. A hospital trying to evade its EMTALA obligations might do so by giving undesired patients short shrift when screening them. At the same time, patients who have been injured by malpractice may try to bring their claim under both state tort law and federal EMTALA law, thereby increasing their potential recovery, gaining access to a federal forum and its quicker judgments, and increasing its bargaining power with the hospitals by virtue of the latter's possible loss of its participation in Medicare. EMTALA claims are often appended to state tort claims when people sue for injuries allegedly caused by inadequate emergency care. Singer, supra, 33 Hous. L. Rev. at 118 & n.22.

Courts have consistently stated that EMTALA cannot be used to bring claims for medical malpractice, and they have tried to distinguish between a denial of care and the negligent provision of care by looking at whether the hospital screened the patient in the same way it screens similarly situated patients. As the D.C. Circuit explained, the issue is whether the hospital "conform[ed] its treatment of a particular patient to its standard screening procedures. . . . [A]ny departure from standard screening procedures constitutes inappropriate screening." Gatewood v. Washington Healthcare Corporation, 933 F.2d 1037, 1041 (D.C. Cir. 1991). Similarly, the Fourth Circuit has stated that EMTALA's screening requirement is designed to prevent "disparate treatment." Vickers v. Nash General Hospital, Inc., 78 F.3d 139, 143 (4th Cir. 1996). Hospitals are obligated only to "apply uniform screening procedures to all individuals coming to the emergency room." In re Baby K, 16 F.3d 590, 595 (4th Cir. 1994). *Accord* Correa v. Hosp. San Francisco, 69 F.3d 1184 (1st Cir. 1995); Summers v. Baptist Medical Center, 91 F.3d 1132, 1138 (8th Cir. 1996); Repp v. Anadarko Municipal Hospital, 43 F.3d 519, 522 (10th Cir. 1994); Holcomb v. Monahan, 30 F.3d 116, 117 (11th Cir. 1994).

The Sixth Circuit has adopted a similar standard, although it has indicated that the departure from the hospital's standard screening procedures must have resulted from some invidious motive like bias against the patient on the basis of "race, sex, politics, occupation, education, personal prejudice, drunkenness, spite . . . distaste for the patient's condition (e.g., AIDS patients). . . . " Cleland v. Bronson Health Care Group, Inc., 917 F.2d 266, 271-272 (6th Cir. 1990); Roberts v. Galen of Virginia, 111 F.3d 405, 408-409 (6th Cir. 1997), *rev'd in part*, 525 U.S. 249 (1999). Even if the Sixth Circuit requires some invidious motive, would it ever be difficult to find a bias lurking that would be unacceptable under the *Cleland* standard? Perhaps not often, but see Garrett v. Detroit Med. Ctr., 2007 U.S. Dist. LEXIS 17584 (E.D. Mich. Mar. 14, 2007) (dismissing patient's EMTALA claim on grounds that the defendant hospital transferred the patient to a hospital so he could be treated at a hospital that was "in-network" for his insurance).

Despite the courts' admonition that EMTALA does not create a federal malpractice cause of action, there inevitably will be some overlap between EMTALA claims and malpractice claims. Do you see how a requirement that hospitals provide all patients with their standard screening procedures amounts to requiring that the hospitals provide nonnegligent care? See Demetrios G. Metropoulos, Note, Son of COBRA: The Evolution of a Federal Malpractice Law, 45 Stan. L. Rev. 263 (1992).

As the preceding discussion indicates, courts have interpreted the requirement of an appropriate screening examination as an equal treatment right rather than an entitlement right. But isn't EMTALA a statute that grants an entitlement rather than a right of equal treatment? Is there a way to define appropriate screening examination as an entitlement without turning it even more clearly into the equivalent of nonnegligent care?

2. Wrongful Reasons to Reject Patients

While physicians or hospitals may, for most patients, refuse to treat for "good" reasons (such as inability to pay), or even for no particular reason, they may not deny care for the wrong reasons. For example, the federal civil rights acts make it unlawful for physicians and hospitals that receive federal money (such as Medicare and Medicaid) to discriminate on the basis of a patient's race, sex, religion, disability or other enumerated characteristics. On the other hand, without a statute that specifically prohibits the particular reason for discrimination, morally problematic denials of care are generally permissible, as the *Walker* case at page 127 demonstrates. When a patient is protected from discrimination by a civil rights statute, may a physician nevertheless refuse to treat on grounds of religious belief? The California Supreme Court has granted certiorari to answer that question for a patient denied fertility services, allegedly on the basis of her sexual orientation. North Coast Women's Care Medical Group, Inc. v Superior Court, 2006 Cal. LEXIS 8074 (2006).

The following materials focus on disability discrimination as the most recent and controversial form of statutory prohibition. In so doing, we do not mean to neglect the obvious importance of race and gender discrimination laws. At one time in our country's history, it was commonplace, especially in the South, for hospitals to refuse admission to blacks. These and other forms of overt discrimination have now largely disappeared as the result of various prohibitions contained in federal and state regulatory law, as well as in the hospital industry's own private accreditation code. See generally Sara Rosenbaum et al., U.S. Civil Rights Policy and Access to Health Care by Minority Americans, 57 Med. Care Res. & Rev. 226 (2000).

Serious concerns remain, however, over more subtle forms of racial and gender bias in the delivery of health care services. One form occurs in the location of health care facilities, which in inner cities are sometimes older, less accessible, or not as well equipped. See Daniel K. Hampton, Note, Title VI Challenges by Private Parties to the Location of Health Care Facilities: Toward a Just and Effective Action, 37 B.C. L. Rev. 517 (1996). Discrimination can also arise in individual treatment decisions. Numerous studies have documented that physicians treat blacks, and sometimes women, differently for the same medical conditions. For instance, blacks are less likely than whites to receive a kidney transplant, coronary artery bypass surgery, or other major surgical procedures. See page 80. Others respond that these studies are not as conclusive as they may appear because of real or possible differences in income, medical considerations, biological factors, and patient preferences. For more discussion, see page 81.

No cases have yet arisen that attack differential treatment patterns as forms of racial or gender discrimination, but when they do, they will confront the problems of which medical justifications are permissible and the extent to which courts will inquire into the complexities of medical judgment. The outcome of these questions undoubtedly will be influenced by how the courts have resolved similar disputes over disability discrimination.

The analysis of discrimination under disability statutes is inherently complicated. Often a person's disability is relevant in deciding whether the person is a candidate for treatment. For example, it would not make much sense to transplant a kidney or liver into a patient dying of cancer. As we will see, unlawful denials of care can occur both from a refusal to treat at all or a refusal to provide certain kinds of care after the patient-physician relationship is formed.

■ UNITED STATES v. UNIVERSITY HOSPITAL
729 F.2d 144 (2d Cir. 1984)

PRATT, Circuit Judge.

. . . Baby Jane Doe was born on October 11, 1983 at St. Charles Hospital in Port Jefferson, New York. She was suffering from multiple birth defects, the most serious of which were myelomeningocele, commonly known as spina bifida, a condition in which the spinal cord and membranes that envelop it are exposed; microcephaly, an abnormally small head; and hydrocephalus, a condition characterized by an accumulation of fluid in the cranial vault. In addition, she exhibited a "weak face," which prevents the infant from closing her eyes or making a full suck with her tongue; a malformed brain stem; upper extremity spasticity; and a thumb entirely within her fist.

As a result of the spina bifida, the baby's rectal, bladder, leg, and sensory functions were impaired. Due to the combination of microcephaly and hydrocephalus, there was an extremely high risk that the child would be so severely retarded that she could never interact with her environment or with other people.

At the direction of the first pediatric neurosurgeon to examine her, the baby was immediately transferred to University Hospital for dual surgery to correct her spina bifida and hydrocephalus. Essentially, this would entail excising a sac of fluid and nerve endings on the spine and closing the opening, and implanting a shunt to relieve pressure caused by fluid build-up in the cranial cavity. The record indicates that these dual, corrective surgical procedures were likely to prolong the infant's life, but would not improve many of her handicapping conditions, including her anticipated mental retardation.

After consulting with several physicians, nurses, religious advisors, a social worker, and members of their family, the parents of the baby decided to forego the corrective surgery. Instead, they opted for a "conservative" medical treatment consisting of good nutrition, the administration of antibiotics, and the dressing of the baby's exposed spinal sac.

Litigation surrounding Baby Jane Doe began on October 16, when A. Lawrence Washburn, Jr., a Vermont attorney unrelated to the child and her family, commenced a proceeding in New York State Supreme Court seeking appointment of a guardian ad litem for the child and an order directing University Hospital to perform the corrective surgery, [contending that failure to do so would violate Section 504 of the Rehabilitation Act of 1973, 29 U.S.C. §794.] . . .

. . . The Appellate Division found that the "concededly concerned and loving parents have made an informed, intelligent, and reasonable determination based upon and supported by responsible medical authority." As the court elaborated:

> The record confirms that the failure to perform the surgery will not place the infant in imminent danger of death, although surgery might significantly reduce the risk of infection. On the other hand, successful results could also be achieved with antibiotic therapy. Further, while the mortality rate is higher where conservative medical treatment is used, in this particular case the surgical procedures also involved a great risk of depriving the infant of what little function remains in her legs, and would also result in recurring urinary tract and possibly kidney infections, skin infections and edemas of the limbs.

Thus, the Appellate Division determined that the parents' decision was in the best interest of the infant and that there was, therefore, no basis for judicial intervention. . . . [The Appellate Division's decision was affirmed by the New York Court of Appeals, but on the ground that the trial court had abused its discretion in permitting the case to go forward. The Court of Appeals observed that (a) Mr. Washburn (the petitioner) had no direct interest in the case (b) Mr. Washburn had not contacted the State Department of Social Services, which had primary responsibility under state law for initiating child abuse proceedings and (c) the trial court had failed to seek the Department of Social Service's assistance.

Meanwhile, as the state court proceedings were unfolding, HHS received a complaint that Baby Jane Doe was being denied medical treatment because of her handicap. In response to the complaint, HHS obtained the record of the state court proceedings and, after personal review by the Surgeon General, requested the infant's medical records from the hospital. When the hospital refused to provide the records, HHS brought its case in federal court, alleging that the hospital was violating Section 504 of the Rehabilitation Act. The federal district court granted summary judgment for the hospital on two grounds: first, the hospital refused to operate on Baby Jane Doe, not because of her handicap, but because her parents did not consent to the procedures; and second, the parents' refusal of treatment was reasonable given the medical options. The federal government appealed, resulting in this opinion.]

To focus more sharply on this central issue, it is first necessary to examine the theory upon which the government predicates its [claim]. The theory rests on two premises. First, the government draws a distinction between decisionmaking based on a "bona fide medical judgment," which without definition it concedes to be beyond the reach of §504, and decisionmaking based solely on an individual's handicap, which it argues is covered by §504. Second, the government identifies Baby Jane Doe's microcephaly, which the record indicates will result in severe mental retardation, as the handicapping condition. From these premises, the government reasons that if a newborn infant suffering from spina bifida and hydrocephalus, but not microcephaly, would receive treatment or services that differ from those provided to an infant suffering from all three defects, or alternatively, if the hospital would seek a state court order compelling surgery in the former case, but not in the latter, then a violation of §504 would have been established. . . .

With this unsettled regulatory background in mind, we turn to the statutory language, which is fundamental to any issue of statutory construction. Section 504 provides in pertinent part as follows:

> No otherwise qualified handicapped individual in the United States, as defined in section 706(7) of this title, shall, solely by reason of his handicap, be excluded from the participation in, be denied the benefits of, or be subjected to discrimination under any program or activity receiving federal financial assistance.

Under 29 U.S.C. §706(7)(B), "the term 'handicapped individual' means . . . any person who (i) has a physical or mental impairment which substantially limits one or more of such person's major life activities, (ii) has a record of such an impairment, or (iii) is regarded as having such an impairment." . . .

[We] next consider whether [Baby Jane Doe] possibly can be considered an "otherwise qualified" handicapped individual or to have been "subjected to discrimination" under §504. These two issues are intertwined.

The leading cases construing the "otherwise qualified" criterion of §504 have involved allegedly discriminatory denials of admission to certain educational programs. Southeastern Community College v. Davis, 442 U.S. 397 (1979); Doe v. New York University, 666 F.2d 761 (2d Cir. 1981). In that context, this court in Doe v. New York University recognized that

> it is now clear that [the phrase "otherwise qualified handicapped individual"] refers to a person who is qualified *in spite of* her handicap and that an institution is not required to disregard the disabilities of a handicapped applicant, provided the handicap is relevant to reasonable qualifications for acceptance, or to make

substantial modifications in its reasonable standards or program to accommodate handicapped individuals but may take an applicant's handicap into consideration, along with all other relevant factors, in determining whether she is qualified for admission. [Id. at 775 (emphasis in original).]

Doe establishes that §504 prohibits discrimination against a handicapped individual only where the individual's handicap is unrelated to, and thus improper to consideration of, the services in question. As defendants here point out, however, where medical treatment is at issue, it is typically the handicap itself that gives rise to, or at least contributes to, the need for services. Defendants thus argue, and with some force, that the "otherwise qualified" criterion of §504 cannot be meaningfully applied to a medical treatment decision. Similarly, defendants argue that it would be pointless to inquire whether a patient who was affected by a medical treatment decision was, "solely by reason of his handicap, . . . subjected to discrimination."

The government's answer to both these arguments is that Baby Jane Doe can be viewed as suffering from not one, but multiple handicaps. Indeed, the crux of the government's case is that her microcephaly is the operative handicap, and that the requested records are necessary to determine whether she has been discriminated against solely for that reason.

Despite its superficial logic, the government's theory is flawed in at least two respects. First, the government's view of "otherwise qualified" is divorced from the statutory language. As the mainstream of cases under §504 exemplifies, the phrase "otherwise qualified" is geared toward relatively static programs or activities such as education, employment, and transportation systems. As a result, the phrase cannot be applied in the comparatively fluid context of medical treatment decisions without distorting its plain meaning. In common parlance, one would not ordinarily think of a newborn infant suffering from multiple birth defects as being "otherwise qualified" to have corrective surgery performed or to have a hospital initiate litigation seeking to override a decision against surgery by the infant's parents. If Congress intended §504 to apply in this manner, it chose strange language indeed.

Second, in arguing that Baby Jane may have been "subjected to discrimination" the government has taken an oversimplified view of the medical decisionmaking process. Where the handicapping condition is related to the (conditions) to be treated, it will rarely, if ever, be possible to say with certainty that a particular decision was "discriminatory." It is at this point that the analogy to race, relied on so heavily by the dissent, breaks down. Beyond the fact that no two cases are likely to be the same, it would invariably require lengthy litigation primarily involving conflicting expert testimony to determine whether a decision to treat, or not to treat, or to litigate or not to litigate, was based on a "bona fide medical judgment," however that phrase might be defined. Before ruling that congress intended to spawn this type of litigation under §504, we would want more proof than is apparent from the face of the statute.

The legislative history, moreover, indicates that congress never contemplated that §504 would apply to treatment decisions of this nature. . . . [According to t]he Senate Report accompanying the 1974 amendments:

... Section 504 was enacted to prevent discrimination against all handicapped individuals . . . in relation to federal assistance in employment, housing, transportation, education, health services, or any other federally-aided programs. Examples of handicapped individuals who may suffer discrimination in receipt of federally-assisted services . . . are as follows: physically or mentally handicapped children who may be denied admission to federally-supported school systems on the basis of their handicap; handicapped persons who may be denied admission to federally-assisted nursing homes on the basis of their handicap; those persons whose handicap is so severe that employment is not feasible but who may be denied the benefits of a wide range of federal programs. . . .

S. Rep. No. 1297, supra at 6388-6389.

This passage provides the best clue to congressional intent regarding §504's coverage of "health services." As Judge Gesell noted in American Academy of Pediatrics v. Heckler, 561 F. Supp. at 401:

The legislative history . . . [on this subject] focuses on discrimination against adults and older children and denial of access to federal programs. As far as can be determined, no congressional committee or member of the House or Senate ever even suggested that section 504 would be used to monitor medical treatment of defective newborn infants or establish standards for preserving a particular quality of life. No medical group appeared alert to the intrusion into medical practice which some doctors apprehend from such an undertaking, nor were representatives of parents or spokesmen for religious beliefs that would be affected heard. . . .

We are aware, of course, that "where the words and purpose of a statute plainly apply to a particular situation, . . . the fact that the specific application of the statute never occurred to Congress does not bar us from holding that the situation falls within the statute's coverage." United States v. Jones, 607 F.2d 269, 273 (9th Cir. 1979), *cert. denied*, 444 U.S. 1085 (1980). Here, however, the government's theory not only strains the statutory language but also goes well beyond congress's overriding concern with guaranteeing handicapped individuals access to programs or activities receiving federal financial assistance. Further, the situation in question is dramatically different in kind, not just in degree, from the applications of §504 discussed in the legislative history. . . .

This void in the legislative history is conspicuous for another reason. Prior to the enactment of the Rehabilitation Act, Congress had passed a number of measures limiting federal involvement in medical treatment decisions. For example, the very first section of the Medicare law, . . . codified at 42 U.S.C. §1395, . . . provides that "nothing in this subchapter shall be construed to authorize any federal officer or employee to exercise any supervision or control over the practice of medicine or the manner in which medical services are provided." . . .

In view of this consistent congressional policy against the involvement of federal personnel in medical treatment decisions, we cannot presume that Congress intended to repeal its earlier announcements in the absence of clear evidence of congressional intent to do so. . . .

In the present case, Baby Jane Doe has been treated in an evenhanded manner at least to the extent that the hospital has always been and remains willing to perform the dual, corrective surgeries if her parents would consent. Requiring the hospital either to undertake surgery notwithstanding the parents' decision or alternatively, to petition the state court to override the parents' decision, would impose a particularly onerous affirmative action burden upon the hospital. . . .

WINTER, Circuit Judge, dissenting.

Since I believe that §504 applies to the provision of medical services to handicapped infants, I respectfully dissent. . . . Section 504 . . . states with as much clarity as is reasonably possible that in some circumstances recipients of federal financial assistance may not differentiate between individuals on grounds that one or more is handicapped. . . . Although modern courts frequently rely upon legislative history to reach results at odds with the seemingly plain language of a statute, only the most compelling reasons should induce a court to override statutory language because the legislative history is silent on a particular point. Such compelling circumstances might exist in the present case if Congress had no reason to address the questions at hand when it enacted §504. It hardly needs stating that the underlying issues brim with political and moral controversy and portend to extend the hand of the federal government into matters traditionally governed by an interaction of parental judgment and state authority. Were I able to conclude that Congress had no reason to address these issues in its consideration of §504, I would concur with the majority on the grounds that specific consideration by the Congress of this political and moral minefield would be appropriate before applying the statute as written.

However, such a conclusion is untenable since §504 is no first step into a hitherto uncharted legal wilderness. As the Senate Report stated:

> Section 504 was patterned after, and is almost identical to, the antidiscrimination language of section 601 of the Civil Rights Act of 1964, 42 U.S.C. 2000d-1 (relating to race, color, or national origin), and section 901 of the Education Amendments of 1972, 42 U.S.C. 1683 (relating to sex). The section therefore constitutes the establishment of a broad government policy that programs receiving federal financial assistance shall be operated without discrimination on the basis of handicap.

S. Rep. No. 1297, 93d Cong., 2d Sess., *reprinted* in 1974 U.S. Code Cong. & Ad. News 6373, 6390. Section 504 was thus enacted against a background of well understood law which was explicitly designated as a guide to interpretation. Congress was persuaded that a handicapped condition is analogous to race and that, so far as the administration of federal financial assistance is concerned, discrimination on the basis of a handicap should be on statutory par with discrimination on the basis of race.

Once §504's legislative heritage is acknowledged, the "void" in the legislative history is eliminated and the many issues raised by defendants with regard to medical decisions, parental judgments and state authority simply evaporate. The government has never taken the position that it is entitled to override a medical judgment. Its position rather is that it is entitled under §504 to inquire whether a judgment in question is a bona fide medical judgment. While the majority professes uncertainty as to what that means, application of the analogy to race eliminates all doubt. A judgment not to perform certain surgery because a person is black is not a bona fide medical judgment. So too, a decision not to correct a life threatening digestive problem because an infant has Down's Syndrome is not a bona fide medical judgment. The issue of parental authority is also quickly disposed of. A denial of medical treatment to an infant because the infant is black is not legitimated by parental consent. Finally, once the legislative analogy to race is acknowledged, the intrusion on state authority becomes insignificant. . . .

Bragdon v. Abbott, 524 U.S. 624 (1998). Invoking the Americans with Disabilities Act's (ADA's) protection from discrimination based on disability, a woman with HIV infection challenged her dentist's refusal to fill her cavity unless he performed the procedure in a hospital. (The woman, Sidney Abbott, would have been responsible for the cost of using the hospital's facilities.) Important issues in the case were whether HIV infection constitutes a disability for purposes of the ADA and whether the dentist could nevertheless justify denying treatment in his office to protect himself from becoming infected with HIV during the procedure. (The ADA generally tracks the framework of the Rehabilitation Act's protection against discrimination based on disability but expands to more people the protection of the Rehabilitation Act.)

The Court concluded that Ms. Abbott's HIV infection constituted a disability under the ADA on the ground that HIV infection is a "physical . . . impairment that substantially limits one or more . . . major life activities." 42 U.S.C. §12102(2)(A). According to the Court, HIV infection is a physical impairment from the moment of infection because the virus immediately begins to damage an infected person's white blood cells and because of the severity of the disease. As to whether HIV infection substantially limits a major life activity, the Court observed that it might have identified many major life activities substantially limited by HIV infection. Since Ms. Abbott claimed that HIV infection substantially limited her ability to have children, the Court restricted its inquiry to that life activity. As an activity "central to the life process itself," reproduction constitutes a major life activity, wrote the Court. Moreover, HIV infection substantially limits reproduction in two ways: "First, a woman infected with HIV who tries to conceive a child imposes on the man a significant risk of becoming infected. . . . Second, an infected woman risks infecting her child during gestation and childbirth. . . . " The Court also noted that, even though the risk of transmission of HIV from mother to infant could be reduced by treatment to 8 percent, such a risk of transmitting a fatal disease rose to the level of a substantial limitation.

As to whether the dentist could defend his insistence on treatment at a hospital, he would have to show that Ms. Abbott "pose[d] a direct threat to [his] health or safety. . . ." 42 U.S.C. §12182(b)(3), with direct threat defined as "a significant risk to the health or safety of others that cannot be eliminated by a modification of policies, practices, or procedures or by the provision of auxiliary aids or services." Id. In assessing whether the dentist's fear of HIV transmission was objectively reasonable, "the views of public health authorities, such as the U.S. Public Health Service, CDC, and the National Institutes of Health, are of special weight and authority. The views of these organizations are not conclusive, however. A health care professional who disagrees with the prevailing medical consensus may refute it by citing a credible scientific basis for deviating from the accepted norm." The Court remanded the case for consideration of the dentist's defense of a direct threat to his health if he were to fill Ms. Abbott's cavity in his office instead of a hospital.

On remand, the First Circuit found in favor of Ms. Abbott. The court concluded that, because of the availability of universal precautions to prevent transmission of HIV infection from patient to dentist, the dentist could not justify his denial of treatment in terms of the need to protect himself from becoming infected with HIV. Abbott v. Bragdon, 163 F.3d 87 (1st Cir. 1998), *cert. denied*, 526 U.S. 1131 (1999). (Universal precautions are measures that health care providers are supposed to take with every patient to prevent the spread of infectious diseases like HIV and hepatitis. Examples of universal precautions are the wearing of gloves and other protective attire by health care providers, the use of special wastebaskets to dispose of used needles, and sterilization of medical instruments after each use.) The First Circuit decided that once physicians take universal precautions, no significant risk of HIV transmission remains.

■ GLANZ v. VERNICK
756 F. Supp. 632 (D. Mass. 1991)

MAZZONE, Judge.

In April, 1989, plaintiff's decedent, Raymond Vadnais, brought this suit alleging discrimination in violation of §504 of the Rehabilitation Act of 1973 (the "Act"), 29 U.S.C. §794. . . . The allegations in the complaint can be briefly summarized as follows. In December, 1986, defendant Dr. Vernick saw Mr. Vadnais at the Ear, Nose, and Throat Clinic (the "ENT Clinic") at Beth Israel Hospital and treated him for severe pain in the right ear, at first by prescribing antibiotics and ear drops. In January, 1987, Dr. Vernick diagnosed a perforation in Mr. Vadnais's right ear and, at Mr. Vadnais's third visit, recommended surgery to repair the perforation. After Mr. Vadnais agreed to undergo surgery, Dr. Vernick learned that Mr. Vadnais was infected with HIV and in March, 1987, informed Mr. Vadnais that he would not perform the operation. The ear condition persisted, causing severe pain and discomfort, while Mr. Vadnais continued the ineffective use of antibiotics and ear drops.

In August, 1988, Dr. Yale Berry, unaware of Mr. Vadnais's HIV status, performed the surgery, curing Mr. Vadnais's ear problem. Subsequently, Mr. Vadnais brought this lawsuit seeking . . . compensatory damages for the pain and suffering and emotional distress caused by the delay in receiving corrective surgery, along with punitive damages and attorney's fees. . . .

Count I of the complaint charges that Dr. Vernick, . . . by refusing to perform surgery, unlawfully discriminated against Mr. Vadnais because of his handicap, HIV seropositivity, in violation of §504 of the Rehabilitation Act. . . .

Section 504 states in pertinent part that "no otherwise qualified handicapped individual in the United States . . . shall, solely by reason of his handicap, be excluded from the participation in, be denied the benefits of, or be subjected to discrimination under any program or activity receiving federal financial assistance. . . . " 29 U.S.C. §794.

The defendants argue that summary judgment is appropriate for several . . . reasons. . . . [including] the ground that Mr. Vadnais was not "otherwise qualified" for elective ear surgery. They argue that it is proper for a doctor to consider a patient's handicap in determining whether a patient is qualified for surgery. On the basis of this argument, they conclude that Mr. Vadnais was not "otherwise qualified" for surgery because his HIV disease increased his risk of infection, and, furthermore, that the court should defer to the doctor's determination that it was in his patient's best interest to postpone surgery.

The defendants cannot be faulted for considering Mr. Vadnais's handicap in determining whether he was "otherwise qualified" for surgery. In School Bd. v. Arline, 480 U.S. 273, 287-289 (1987) [reprinted in Chapter 6], the Supreme Court held that the defendant school board could consider the risks posed by the plaintiff's contagious disease (tuberculosis) in determining whether she was otherwise qualified to teach school. It follows that, in the present case, the defendants can take into account the risks imposed—both on the patient and on themselves—by the prospect of surgery on an HIV-positive patient. Of course, if they properly conclude that there are risks, they must also consider whether it is possible to make reasonable accommodations to enable the patient to undergo surgery despite those risks.

As the Court made clear in Arline, the "otherwise qualified" determination requires an individualized inquiry and appropriate findings of fact. With respect to the defendants' assertions about the risks of surgery, the facts are in dispute. The defendants contend that surgery was postponed because Dr. Vernick thought that Mr. Vadnais was "AIDS positive," because the proposed ear surgery was elective, and because it would pose significant risks to the patient. In addition, they offer Dr. Berry's statement in his deposition that he would not have performed the surgery had he known that Mr. Vadnais had AIDS. The plaintiff offers the contradicting evidence that Mr. Vadnais was HIV-positive and had not yet been diagnosed as having AIDS when surgery was refused. Moreover, Dr. Vernick in answers to interrogatories and Dr. Berry in his deposition stated that they do not consider HIV seropositivity alone as a disqualifying factor for surgery. Based on the evidence that the plaintiff has produced, facts are certainly available to warrant the conclusion that Mr. Vadnais was "otherwise qualified" for surgery. Moreover, the defendants have not produced any evidence that reasonable accommodations could not have been made.

There is some merit to the argument that the court should defer to a doctor's medical judgment. Cf. Arline, 480 U.S. at 288 ("courts normally should defer to the reasonable medical judgments of public health officials" when conducting "otherwise qualified" inquiry). Accepting this argument at face value, however, would completely eviscerate §504's function of preventing discrimination against the disabled in the healthcare context. A strict rule of deference would enable doctors to offer merely pretextual medical opinions to cover up discriminatory decisions. The evidentiary approach to §504 cases discussed in Pushkin v. Regents of the Univ. of Colo., 658 F.2d 1372 (10th Cir. 1981), properly balances deference to sound medical opinions with the need to detect discriminatory motives. The plaintiff must first make out a prima facie case that he was otherwise qualified for surgery, and only then does the burden shift to the defendant to show that the plaintiff's handicap made him unqualified. The plaintiff, however, must still be given an opportunity "to prove either that the reason given by defendants is a pretext or that the reason . . . 'encompasses *unjustified* consideration of the handicap itself.'" *Leckelt*, 714 F. Supp. at 1385 (citing *Pushkin*, 658 F.2d at 1387) (emphasis added). . . .

■ WALKER v. PIERCE
560 F.2d 609 (4th Cir. 1977)

BRYAN, Senior Circuit Judge.

Violation of their civil rights was laid in this action for damages and declaratory and injunctive relief by Virgil Walker and Shirley Brown, black females, to Clovis H. Pierce, the attending obstetrician at the Aiken County Hospital in South Carolina for sterilizing them, or threatening to do so, solely on account of their race and number of their children, while they were receiving medical assistance under the Medicaid program. . . .

Centering the controversy is the policy previously announced and constantly pursued in practice by the doctor, testified to by him as follows:

> My policy was with people who were unable to financially support themselves, whether they be on Medicaid or just unable to pay their own bills, if they were having a third child, to request they voluntarily submit to sterilization following the delivery of the third child. If they did not wish this as a condition for my care, then I requested that they seek another physician other than myself.

There is no question of his professional qualifications or experience.

As drawn by the plaintiffs, he is the arch-offender. The accusation is incursion upon their constitutional rights of privacy, due process of law and equal protection of the law as well as of their statutory privileges against discrimination on account of their race and color, all by subjecting or threatening the plaintiffs as citizens of the United States with involuntary sterilization. . . .

Virgil Walker had completed the seventh grade, was separated from her husband and was receiving Aid to Families with Dependent Children and Medicaid benefits. Expecting her fourth child, she first went to Pierce on January 7, 1972. During this consultation, he discussed family planning and his sterilization policy. Walker refused to consent. The issue again came up at the second visit and she again declined. Walker testified that Pierce threatened to have her state assistance terminated unless she cooperated. She called another doctor, but he was not taking new patients.

On February 4, 1972, Spears, a Department of Social Services caseworker assigned to Walker, received a note from Pierce's office asking that he talk with Walker about sterilization. Thereupon, Spears, according to his testimony, spoke with her on February 17th, offering to get her a second doctor. On the other hand, Walker stated that Spears had said there was nothing he could do. Then she returned to Pierce and subsequently signed a consent form for sterilization.

Her fourth child was delivered at the Aiken County Hospital April 16, 1972 by Dr. Billy Burke, an obstetrician who substituted for Pierce on occasion. Burke discussed tubal ligation with Walker. Her response was that she did not want additional children and understood that it would be a permanent sterilization. Two more consent forms were then signed. Pierce performed the operation April 17, 1972. She protested no further because, she said, it would have been futile.

Walker's hospital bills and doctor's fees were paid by Medicaid. Under the South Carolina plan operated by the Department of Social Services, the patient-physician relationship is one of free choice for both parties. The physician, under no contract with the state, simply submits his bill when treatment is concluded to the Medicaid insurance carrier instead of the patient. . . .

We perceive no reason why Dr. Pierce could not establish and pursue the policy he has publicly and freely announced. Nor are we cited to judicial precedent or statute inhibiting this personal economic philosophy. Particularly is this so when all persons coming to him as patients are seasonably made fully aware of his professional attitude toward the increase in offspring and his determination to see it prevail. At no time is he shown to have forced his view upon any mother. Indeed, quite the opposite appears. In the single occasion in this case of a sterilization by this doctor, not just one but three formal written consents were obtained — the first before delivery of the fourth child and two afterwards. . . .

[The court also held that Dr. Pierce was not a state actor and therefore could not be found to have violated his patients' constitutional rights.]

Notes: Discriminatory Denials of Care

1. *Subsequent Developments.* In the end, the parents in *University Hospital* agreed to have a shunt implanted to drain the fluid in their daughter's brain, although the surgery was delayed because of an infection that was likely related to the opening in her spine. The child, Keri-Lynn, has done much better than predicted. Although she is confined to a wheelchair, she can talk, and she attends a school for developmentally disabled children. At age 20, she had attained a first or second grade level of scholastic achievement. Experts continued to disagree as to whether surgery to close Keri-Lynn's spine would have improved her outcome. Jamie Talan, A Fighter's Spirit; 20-year-old Keri-Lynn — Baby Jane Doe — Beat Steep Odds, Newsday, October 13, 2003, at A3; B. D. Colen, What Ever Happened to Baby Jane Doe?, 24(3) Hastings Center Rep. 2, 2 (1994).

2. *The Americans with Disabilities Act. University Hospital* and *Glanz* were decided under the Rehabilitation Act, which applies only to federally funded programs or services and federal executive agencies. Since those cases, the Americans with Disabilities Act (ADA) has gone into effect, and its provisions apply to all nonfederal providers of health care services, public or private. The statutory language of the ADA was designed to track the Rehabilitation Act and court decisions interpreting that Act.

For further discussion of the ADA and denials of health care, see Carl H. Coleman, Conceiving Harm: Disability Discrimination in Assisted Reproductive Technologies, 50 UCLA L. Rev. 17 (2002); Mary A. Crossley, Of Diagnoses and Discrimination: Discriminatory Nontreatment of Infants with HIV Infection, 93

Colum. L. Rev. 1581 (1993); E. Haavi Morreim, Futilitarianism, Exoticare, and Coerced Altruism: The ADA Meets Its Limits, 25 Seton Hall L. Rev. 883 (1995); David Orentlicher, Destructuring Disability: Rationing of Health Care and Unfair Discrimination Against the Sick, 31 Harv. C.R.-C.L. L. Rev. 49 (1996); Philip G. Peters, Jr., When Physicians Balk at Futile Care: Implications of the Disability Rights Laws, 91 Nw. U. L. Rev. 798 (1997); and Philip G. Peters, Jr., Health Care Rationing and Disability Rights, 70 Ind. L. J. 491 (1995).

3. *Definition of Disability.* As indicated by the Supreme Court in *Bragdon*, one has to determine whether a person is in fact disabled under the ADA or Rehabilitation Act before deciding whether there has been unlawful discrimination on account of disability. Until recently, it did not seem to be very difficult for plaintiffs to prove that they were disabled under the ADA. Disability can be shown not only by the presence of a disabling condition but also by a history of a disabling condition or by showing that one is regarded by others as having a disabling condition. 42 U.S.C. §12102(2). Moreover, the legislative history indicated that the judgment whether a patient is disabled should be made assuming that no treatment is provided. Thus, even if a patient's disabling symptoms could be alleviated with medication, the patient would still be considered disabled under the ADA. H.R. Rep. No. 485(II), 101st Cong., 2d Sess., at 52 (1990).

In 1999, the Supreme Court raised the bar on the definition of disability by holding that a person is not actually disabled if medications or medical devices can alleviate the disabling symptoms. Moreover, the Court established a relatively high threshold for showing that one is disabled because of being "regarded as having" a disabling condition. Sutton v. United Air Lines, 527 U.S. 471 (1999).

In *Sutton*, the plaintiffs had been denied jobs as commercial airline pilots because of poor eyesight even though glasses or contact lenses would give them 20/20 vision or better. Because the plaintiffs were not visually impaired with corrective lenses, they could not claim to be actually disabled. As to the "regarded as being disabled" inquiry, the Court observed that the airline only declined to hire them as commercial airline pilots. Because many other jobs were still open to the plaintiffs, including regional pilot or pilot instructor jobs, they were not regarded as being substantially limited in their employment opportunities.

As *Bragdon* suggests, satisfying the definition of disability in the health care context will likely not be as demanding as in the employment context.

For a very helpful discussion about defining disability, see Mary Crossley, The Disability Kaleidoscope, 74 Notre Dame L. Rev. 621 (1999).

4. *When Denial of Treatment Is Discriminatory.* What standard does the *Glanz* court suggest for deciding whether a denial of care constitutes unlawful discrimination on the basis of disability? What theories does the *University Hospital* court use to find no unlawful discrimination when medical care is withheld from a severely disabled newborn? Which of the different approaches do you think makes the most sense?

Note that, while the court's decision in *University Hospital* rested in part on the fact that Baby Jane Doe's parents agreed to the withholding of care, there is much more to the opinion. In addition, another court reached the same result as *University Hospital* in a case in which the parents charged that the physicians' treatment recommendations were biased by the presence of the child's severe disability and that the physicians failed to disclose their bias when obtaining the parents' consent to withhold care. Johnson v. Thompson, 971 F.2d 1487, 1493-1494 (10th Cir. 1992) (citing *University Hospital* for the proposition that, "[w]here the handicapping condition is related to the condition(s) to be treated, it will rarely, if ever, be possible to say . . . that a particular decision was 'discriminatory.'"). There are other reasons to discount parental agreement. As Judge Winter observed in his *University Hospital* dissent, parental agreement does not necessarily vitiate a discrimination claim. The parents may not be adequately representing the child's interests.

Both *Glanz* and *University Hospital* take the view that a person's disability can be a relevant consideration in the person's access to health care. If a disability affects the benefit that the patient can receive from health care, then the disability can be a factor in deciding how to treat the patient. But that leaves most disabled persons subject to denials of health care. The immune system compromise of an HIV-infected person, for example, will have wide-ranging effects on that person's response to medical or surgical therapy. Crossley, supra, at 160. Indeed, the argument in *Glanz* that Mr. Glanz's HIV infection would predispose him to infection would apply to any HIV-infected patient undergoing surgery. How do we consider the effects of a person's disability without discriminating unfairly against that person? What if it is true that a disabled person would not gain as much benefit from treatment as a nondisabled person? Is an appropriate analogy the educational services that states are required to provide in the primary public schools for children with disabilities? See New Mexico Association for Retarded Citizens v. New Mexico, 678 F.2d 847, 854-855 (10th Cir. 1982) (requiring special education to ensure that children with disabilities receive an education appropriate to their needs).

Rather than avoiding the care of certain patients by claiming that the patient is not a candidate for care (as in *University Hospital* or *Glanz*), physicians might claim that the patient needs to be referred for more specialized care. In Lesley v. Chie, 250 F.3d 47 (1st Cir. 2001), the U.S. Court of Appeals for the First Circuit addressed a disability discrimination claim in the context of a physician's referral of the patient to a more specialized colleague. In *Lesley,* the court considered "the extent to which a court should defer to a physician's claim that he lacks the experience, knowledge, or other prerequisites necessary to address the medical conditions that allegedly prompted his referral of a patient to another physician." The case arose after an obstetrician referred an HIV-infected, pregnant woman to another hospital for drug therapy designed to prevent transmission of HIV to the woman's child. The other hospital had a special Women and Infants HIV Program. The court found no Rehabilitation Act violation, writing,

> Under the Rehabilitation Act, a patient may challenge her doctor's decision to refer her elsewhere by showing the decision to be devoid of any reasonable medical support. This is not to say, however, that the Rehabilitation Act prohibits unreasonable medical decisions as such. Rather, the point of considering a medical decision's reasonableness in this context is to determine whether the decision was unreasonable in a way that reveals it to be discriminatory. In other words, a plaintiff's showing of medical unreasonableness must be framed within some larger theory of disability discrimination. For example, a plaintiff may argue

that her physician's decision was so unreasonable — in the sense of being arbitrary and capricious — as to imply that it was pretext for some discriminatory motive, such as animus, fear, or "apathetic attitudes." See, e.g., Howe v. Hull, 874 F. Supp. 779, 788-89 (N.D. Ohio 1994) (under ADA, jury could find doctor's diagnosis that plaintiff had extremely rare disorder requiring transfer was pretextual, where patient only had an allergic drug reaction, and doctor did not mention the rare disorder in requesting the transfer but only mentioned plaintiff's HIV-status). Or, instead of arguing pretext, a plaintiff may argue that her physician's decision was discriminatory on its face, because it rested on stereotypes of the disabled rather than an individualized inquiry into the patient's condition — and hence was "unreasonable" in that sense. [Id. at 55.]

   To what extent are the costs of care relevant to the analysis? If Baby Jane Doe's care cost thousands instead of hundreds of thousands of dollars, should that make a difference in deciding whether disability discrimination occurred? If you think social costs are relevant, then why does the denial of care by Dr. Pierce seem more troubling than the withholding of care from Baby Jane Doe? Wasn't he also concerned primarily about social costs? Is his decision worse because it was directed toward only the poor, or because welfare status is correlated with race? Or is it that sterilization is reminiscent of discredited eugenic social policies of the past?

   5. *Infectious Patients.* As *Bragdon* indicates, an outright denial of care on account of the person's HIV status is unlawful disability discrimination. However, *Bragdon* and *Glanz* also indicate that the freedom of a physician to deny care on the basis of a patient's infected status depends not only on whether the infection affects the patient's ability to benefit from treatment but also on the risk to the physician of becoming infected from the patient. How should the risk be taken into account? What if an orthopedic surgeon refuses to operate on an HIV-infected (or hepatitis-infected) patient on the grounds that orthopedic surgery is "bloody" and involves exposure to sharp edges of bone as well as to sharp surgical instruments? What if the surgeon already provides care to a significant number of HIV-infected patients and the surgeon is trying to have a child? Should it matter whether the denial of care is for elective rather than essential surgical procedures? Consider a dermatologist who refuses to perform a hair transplant on an HIV-infected person on the ground that the procedure invariably causes significant bleeding from the patient's scalp. It is important to note that the circuit courts disagree on exactly when a risk is serious enough to be "significant." for a discussion of the different standards, see Onishea v. Hopper, 171 F.3d 1289, 1296-1299 (11th Cir. 1999) (interpreting "significant risk" in the context of a Rehabilitation Act case).

   Concerns about discrimination against HIV-infected physicians are discussed at pages 199-200.

3. Rationing and Discrimination

   This section examines whether it is desirable or permissible for insurance providers to exclude some medical conditions or treatments by assessing which medical needs are most demanding and what treatments work the best. The public policy focus here is on how health care resources might be better allocated, and the legal focus is on disability discrimination. As you read this section, realize that, in a world of limited resources, insurance cannot pay for all beneficial medical care that anyone might need. The problem, then, is which approach to limiting insurance benefits makes the most sense, and whether discrimination law allows sensible health care public policy to emerge from either market or political forces.

■ ALEXANDER v. CHOATE
469 U.S. 287 (1985)

Justice MARSHALL delivered the opinion of the Court.

. . . Faced in 1980-1981 with projected state Medicaid costs of $42 million more than the state's Medicaid budget of $388 million, the directors of the Tennessee Medicaid program decided to institute a variety of cost-saving measures. Among these changes was a reduction from 20 to 14 in the number of inpatient hospital days per fiscal year that Tennessee Medicaid would pay hospitals on behalf of a Medicaid recipient. Before the new measures took effect, respondents, Tennessee Medicaid recipients, brought a class action for declaratory and injunctive relief in which they alleged, inter alia, that the proposed 14-day limitation on inpatient coverage would have a discriminatory effect on the handicapped. Statistical evidence, which petitioners do not dispute, indicated that in the 1979-1980 fiscal year, 27.4 percent of all handicapped users of hospital services who received Medicaid required more than 14 days of care, while only 7.8 percent of nonhandicapped users required more than 14 days of inpatient care.

Based on this evidence, respondents asserted that the reduction would violate §504 of the Rehabilitation Act of 1973 . . . [which] provides: "No otherwise qualified handicapped individual . . . shall, solely by reason of his handicap, be excluded from the participation in, be denied the benefits of, or be subjected to discrimination under any program or activity receiving Federal financial assistance." 29 U.S.C. §794. . . .

[The] major thrust of respondents' attack was directed at the use of any annual limitation on the number of inpatient days covered, for respondents acknowledged that, given the special needs of the handicapped for medical care, any such limitation was likely to disadvantage the handicapped disproportionately. . . . [T]he Medicaid programs of only ten states impose such restrictions.[4] Respondents therefore suggested that Tennessee follow these other states and do away with any limitation on the number of annual inpatient days covered. Instead, argued respondents, the state could limit the number of days of hospital coverage on a per-stay basis, with the number of covered days to vary depending on the recipient's illness (for example, fixing the number of days covered for an appendectomy); the period to be covered for each illness could then be set at a level that would keep Tennessee's Medicaid program as a whole within its budget. . . .

---

[4] As of 1980 the average ceiling in those states was 37.6 days. Six states also limit the number of reimbursable days per admission, per spell of illness, or per benefit period.

The first question the parties urge on the Court is whether proof of discriminatory animus is always required to establish a violation of §504 and its implementing regulations, or whether federal law also reaches action by a recipient of federal funding that discriminates against the handicapped by effect rather than by design. . . . Discrimination against the handicapped was perceived by Congress to be most often the product, not of invidious animus, but rather of thoughtlessness and indifference — of benign neglect. . . . For example, elimination of architectural barriers was one of the central aims of the Act, yet such barriers were clearly not erected with the aim or intent of excluding the handicapped. . . .

At the same time, the position urged by respondents — that we interpret §504 to reach all action disparately affecting the handicapped — is also troubling. Because the handicapped typically are not similarly situated to the nonhandicapped, respondents' position would in essence require each recipient of federal funds first to evaluate the effect on the handicapped of every proposed action that might touch the interests of the handicapped, and then to consider alternatives for achieving the same objectives with less severe disadvantage to the handicapped. The formalization and policing of this process could lead to a wholly unwieldy administrative and adjudicative burden. . . .

To determine which disparate impacts §504 might make actionable, . . . [we must strike] a balance between the statutory rights of the handicapped to be integrated into society and the legitimate interests of federal grantees in preserving the integrity of their programs: While a grantee need not be required to make "fundamental" or "substantial" modifications to accommodate the handicapped, it may be required to make "reasonable" ones. . . .

[A]n otherwise qualified handicapped individual must be provided with meaningful access to the benefit that the grantee offers. The benefit itself, of course, cannot be defined in a way that effectively denies otherwise qualified handicapped individuals the meaningful access to which they are entitled; to assure meaningful access, reasonable accommodations in the grantee's program or benefit may have to be made. In this case, the 14-day limitation will not deny respondents meaningful access to Tennessee Medicaid services or exclude them from those services.

The new limitation does not invoke criteria that have a particular exclusionary effect on the handicapped; the reduction, neutral on its face, does not distinguish between those whose coverage will be reduced and those whose coverage will not on the basis of any test, judgment, or trait that the handicapped as a class are less capable of meeting or less likely of having. Moreover, it cannot be argued that "meaningful access" to state Medicaid services will be denied by the 14-day limitation on inpatient coverage; nothing in the record suggests that the handicapped in Tennessee will be unable to benefit meaningfully from the coverage they will receive under the 14-day rule.[22] The reduction in inpatient coverage will leave both handicapped and nonhandicapped Medicaid users with

---

[22] The record does not contain any suggestion that the illnesses uniquely associated with the handicapped or occurring with greater frequency among them cannot be effectively treated, at least in part, with fewer than 14 days' coverage. In addition, the durational limitation does not apply to only particular handicapped conditions and takes effect regardless of the particular cause of hospitalization.

identical and effective hospital services fully available for their use, with both classes of users subject to the same durational limitation. . . .

To the extent respondents further suggest that their greater need for prolonged inpatient care means that, to provide meaningful access to Medicaid services, Tennessee must single out the handicapped for more than 14 days of coverage, the suggestion is simply unsound. At base, such a suggestion must rest on the notion that the benefit provided through state Medicaid programs is the amorphous objective of "adequate health care." But Medicaid programs do not guarantee that each recipient will receive that level of health care precisely tailored to his or her particular needs. Instead, the benefit provided through Medicaid is a particular package of health care services, such as 14 days of inpatient coverage. That package of services has the general aim of assuring that individuals will receive necessary medical care, but the benefit provided remains the individual services offered — not "adequate health care."[23] . . .

Section 504 does not require the state to alter this definition of the benefit being offered simply to meet the reality that the handicapped have greater medical needs. To conclude otherwise would be to find that the Rehabilitation Act requires states to view certain illnesses, i.e., those particularly affecting the handicapped, as more important than others and more worthy of cure through government subsidization. Nothing in the legislative history of the Act supports such a conclusion. Cf. Doe v. Colautti, 592 F.2d 704 (3d Cir. 1979) (state may limit covered-private-inpatient-psychiatric care to 60 days even though state sets no limit on duration of coverage for physical illnesses). Section 504 seeks to assure evenhanded treatment and the opportunity for handicapped individuals to participate in and benefit from programs receiving federal assistance. The Act does not, however, guarantee the handicapped equal results from the provision of state Medicaid, even assuming some measure of equality of health could be constructed. . . .

We turn next to respondents' alternative contention . . . that all annual durational limitations discriminate against the handicapped because (1) the effect of such limitations falls most heavily on the handicapped and because (2) this harm could be avoided by the choice of other Medicaid plans that would meet the state's budgetary constraints without disproportionately disadvantaging the handicapped. Viewed in this light, Tennessee's current plan is said to inflict a gratuitous harm on the handicapped that denies them meaningful access to Medicaid services. . . .

On the contrary, to require that the sort of broad-based distributive decision at issue in this case always be made in the way most favorable, or least disadvantageous, to the handicapped, even when the same benefit is meaningfully and equally offered to them, would be to impose a virtually unworkable requirement on state Medicaid administrators. Before taking any across-the-board action affecting Medicaid recipients, an analysis of the effect of the proposed change on the handicapped would have to be prepared. Presumably, that analysis would have to be further broken down by class of handicap — the change at issue here, for example, might be significantly less harmful to the blind,

---

[23] . . . [W]e express no opinion on whether annual limits on hospital care are in fact consistent with the Medicaid Act. . . .

who use inpatient services only minimally, than to other subclasses of handicapped Medicaid recipients; the state would then have to balance the harms and benefits to various groups to determine, on balance, the extent to which the action disparately impacts the handicapped. In addition, respondents offer no reason that similar treatment would not have to be accorded other groups protected by statute or regulation from disparate-impact discrimination.

It should be obvious that administrative costs of implementing such a regime would be well beyond the accommodations that are required. . . . As a result, Tennessee need not redefine its Medicaid program to eliminate durational limitations on inpatient coverage, even if in doing so the State could achieve its immediate fiscal objectives in a way less harmful to the handicapped. . . .

■ WILL CLINTON'S PLAN BE FAIR?
Ronald Dworkin*
New York Review of Books, Jan. 13, 1994

Some critics deny that health-care rationing is really necessary: They argue that if the waste and greed in the American health-care system were eliminated, we could save enough money to give men and women all the medical treatment that could benefit them. But . . . the greatest contribution to the rise in medical costs in recent decades has been the availability of new, high-tech means of diagnosis, like magnetic resonance imaging and new and very expensive techniques like organ transplants and, on the horizon, monoclonal-antibody treatment for cancer. . . . Many politicians and some doctors say that much of the new technology is "unnecessary" or "wasteful." They do not mean that it provides no benefit at all. They mean that its benefit is too limited to justify its cost, and this is an argument for rationing, not an argument that rationing is unnecessary. . . . So we cannot . . . avoid the question of justice: What is "appropriate" medical care depends on what it would be unfair to withhold on the grounds that it costs too much. That question has been missing from the public debate. . . .

For millennia doctors have paid lip service, at least, to an ideal of justice in medicine which I shall call the rescue principle. It has two connected parts. The first holds that life and health are, as René Descartes put it, chief among all goods: Everything else is of lesser importance and must be sacrificed for them. The second insists that health care must be distributed on grounds of equality: that even in a society in which wealth is very unequal and equality is otherwise scorned, no one must be denied the medical care he needs just because he is too poor to afford it. These are understandable, even noble, ideals. They are grounded in a shared human understanding of the horror of pain, and, beyond that, of the indispensability of life and health to everything else we do. The rescue principle is so ancient, so intuitively attractive, and so widely supported in political rhetoric, that it might easily be thought to supply the right standard for answering questions about rationing. . . .

In past centuries, however, there was not so huge a gap between the rhetoric of the rescue principle and what it was medically possible for a community to do.

---

* Professor of Law, New York University.

But now that science has created so many vastly expensive forms of medical care, it is preposterous that a community should treat longer life as a good that it must provide at any cost — even one that would make the lives of its people barely worth living. . . .

The rescue principle does have something helpful, though negative, to say about the other question of justice, which is how health care should be distributed. It says that if rationing is necessary, it should not be done, as it now largely is in the United States, on the basis of money. But we need more positive advice: What should the basis of rationing be? The egalitarian impulse of the principle suggests that medical care should be distributed according to need. But what does that mean — how is need to be measured? Does someone "need" an operation that might save his life but is highly unlikely to do so? Is someone's need for life-saving treatment affected by the quality his life would have if the treatment were successful? Does the age of patient matter — does someone need or deserve treatment less at 70 than a younger age? Why? How should we balance the need of many people for relief from pain or incapacity against the need of fewer people for life-saving care? At one point the procedures of an Oregon commission appointed to establish medical priorities ranked tooth-capping ahead of appendectomy, because so many teeth can be capped for the price of one operation. Why was that so clearly a mistake? We need a different, more helpful statement of ideal justice. . . .

[A] more satisfactory ideal of justice in health care [is] the "prudent insurance" ideal. We should allocate resources between health and other social needs, and between different patients who each need treatment, by trying to imagine what health care would be like if it were left to a free and unsubsidized market [under transformed social conditions in which people were better informed and wealth was distributed more equitably]. . . . We can speculate about what kind of medical care and insurance it would be prudent for most Americans to buy, for themselves, . . . and we can use those speculations as guidelines in deciding what justice requires now — in deciding, for example, which medical tests and procedures are "necessary and appropriate." . . . Of course, any judgment about what most prudent people would do is subject to exceptions: some people have special preferences, and would make very different decisions from those many other people would. . . . But it seems fair to construct a mandatory coverage scheme on the basis of assumptions about what all but a small number of people would think appropriate, allowing those few who would be willing to spend more on special care to do so, if they can afford it, through supplemental insurance. . . .

■ HEALTH CARE RATIONING AND DISABILITY RIGHTS
Philip G. Peters, Jr.*
70 Ind. L.J. 491 (1995)

. . . Any criterion suggested for rationing health care will be controversial. The stakes are high and no popular or ethical consensus has emerged. But allocation

---

* Ruth L. Hulston Professor of Law, University of Missouri-Columbia.

decisions are omnipresent and their continuation is inevitable. . . . Americans have never been willing to pay for all the health care that is of any conceivable benefit, nor are they likely to do so in the future. Unfortunately, the existing mechanisms for deciding who receives what care are blunt and often irrational or unfair, reflecting the influence of wealth, employment, habit, cost, and power. . . . Common sense tells us to give priority to services that do the most good. As a result, an approach which would eliminate only the least beneficial or least cost-effective treatments has considerable potential appeal. It offers both the promise of maximizing health care outcomes from limited resources and the surface allure of scientific objectivity and nonpartisan neutrality. . . .

But rationing the least effective care has a dark side beneath its veneer of objectivity. Any health care allocation scheme which attempts to maximize health care outcomes by giving priority to the most effective treatments has the potential to disfavor disabled patients and others, such as the elderly and the frail, whose quality of life is most impaired or whose conditions are most resistant to cure. As a result, the use of effectiveness criteria to allocate health resources may be challenged as violating society's commitment to equality in general, and to protection of those with the greatest need in particular.

The resolution of this conflict between efficiency and equality has dramatic implications for health policy. . . . It arises whenever effectiveness or cost-effectiveness is used by health care providers or insurers to determine which treatments to provide or insure. Those instances range from bedside decisions by clinicians to macroallocation decisions by benefit plans about coverage of conditions such as AIDS, infertility, or mental illness. In each setting, allocations based on medical utility have the potential to disfavor some patients on the basis of their disability. . . .

I. [EFFECTIVENESS MEASURES AND THE OREGON EXPERIMENT]

Health economists have worked for decades on methodologies for calculating both the effectiveness and the cost-effectiveness of health care expenditures.[11] Originally utilized to compare the value of different treatments for the same disease, these methods were later used to compare the cost-effectiveness of treatments for different diseases. Cost-effectiveness calculations have the appeal of incorporating outcomes research, patient preferences, and expected costs into a rational and potentially sophisticated scheme for maximizing health care outcomes from the available resources. . . .

Theoretically, at least, calculating the effectiveness of a medical service is relatively straightforward. This calculation involves both an estimate of the likely

---

[11] The history of Quality-Adjusted Life Years ("QALYs") is briefly described in John La Puma, Quality-Adjusted Life Years: Ethical Implications and the Oregon Plan, 7 Issues L. & Med. 429, 433-434 (1992) (expanding upon John La Puma & Edward F. Lawlor, Quality-Adjusted Life-Years: Ethical Implications for Physicians and Policymakers, 263 JAMA 2917 (1990)). American researchers initially derived the methodology from operations research in engineering and mathematics, using it in the health care setting to measure the tradeoff between survival and quality of life that is implicated by some treatment choices such as conservative care versus aggressive care. See id. The British, most notably Alan Williams, then borrowed the concept as a way of suggesting priorities in their national health care system. . . . More recently, QALYs have been calculated for a number of treatments in the United States. . . .

outcomes and an assignment of value to those outcomes. The value assigned to an outcome is determined by the impact which the treatment is expected to have on a patient's quality of life. That value is then adjusted to reflect the probability and duration of the expected benefit.[12] The product of this calculus is a single unit which expresses the number and quality of additional years that the treatment is likely to confer. These outcome units have been called both Quality-Adjusted Life Years ("QALYs") and Well Years. . . .

The theoretical value of these calculations cannot be overstated. They provide a common unit of measurement which permits treatments for different diseases to be compared on the basis of their expected benefit or their cost-effectiveness.[16] Using QALYs or their equivalents, comparisons can be made between such disparate treatments as AZT, autologous bone marrow transplants, infertility treatments, mammography screening, early CT scans for head pain, and heroic care for patients in persistent vegetative states. . . .

As the health economist David Hadorn has emphasized, reliable cost-effectiveness data will help health care providers minimize human suffering to the maximum extent possible with the resources society allocates to health care.[17] . . . Current insurance and clinical practices often make the same kinds of calculations regarding treatment value and cost, albeit in a more intuitive manner. . . . QALYs can help improve the process, making it more rational and, therefore, more just. . . .

QALYs may also help health decisionmakers to avoid what David Eddy has called "rationing by meat ax." By excluding the least effective treatments for conditions that ordinarily are covered by insurance, savings could be generated to fund more comprehensive coverage of treatments for conditions such as mental health that are typically excluded or restricted. Blanket restrictions on treatments for infertility or mental health, for example, could be replaced by narrower exclusions of only those treatments which are least effective.

In addition, the exclusion of whole groups of uninsured persons from programs such as Medicaid could be replaced by the exclusion of marginally effective care. Oregon, for example, replaced a Medicaid system in which a six-year-old child was eligible when a seven-year-old was not, in which pregnant

---

[12] . . . Milton C. Weinstein & William B. Stason, Foundations of Cost-Effectiveness Analysis for Health and Medical Practices, 296 New Eng. J. Med. 716, 718-719 (1977).

[16] . . . John Rawles includes several helpful illustrations of comparisons based on cost-effectiveness:

> For example, a patient with severe arthritis of the hip who is unable to work and is in severe distress scores a quality of life of 0.7. . . . His expectation of life of ten years is reduced to seven quality adjusted life years. Successful hip replacement, by eliminating disability and distress, restores 3 QALYs to his total, at an average cost of pounds sterling750 per QALY.
>
> Another example is a patient with renal failure undergoing renal dialysis twice a week in hospital for a year. He is unable to work and suffers moderate distress with a quality of life of 0.9. However, hemodialysis is life-saving, so every year adds 0.9 to the number of QALYs he would otherwise enjoy, at a cost of pounds sterling14000 per QALY.

John Rawles, Castigating QALYs, 15 J. Med. Ethics 143, 144-145 (1989).

[17] David C. Hadorn, Setting Health Care Priorities in Oregon: Cost-Effectiveness Meets the Rule of Rescue, 265 JAMA 2218, at 2225 (1991) (describing the original Oregon methodology and the modifications undertaken before submission to the federal government for approval). . . .

women had coverage but other women did not, and in which single adults with children were covered but those without children or with a spouse were excluded. In its place, the state has instituted a system [described below] that provides protection for [all people below the poverty line] by prioritizing the treatments covered.[24] ... This explicit attention to the difficult choices is in marked contrast to current practices, such as those of physicians who use neutral terms such as "futility" to mask intuitive judgments about the value of treatment to the patient. ...

But measurement of medical effectiveness also presents serious methodological and ethical problems which must be surmounted before its use expands. The methodological problems arise both from the difficulty of obtaining adequate data about outcomes, benefits, and costs and also from predictable issues of study design. Problems of this kind contributed to the failure of Oregon's initial attempt to prioritize medical treatments entirely on the basis of net benefit. ...

In order to calculate a treatment's medical effectiveness, analysts must estimate its probable outcome and then place a value on that outcome. Both steps could disfavor disabled patients. When outcomes are taken into account, patients with preexisting disabilities, such as diabetes, cancer, or pulmonary disease, could be disfavored because they often have more difficulty fighting unrelated illnesses (comorbidity) than patients who are otherwise healthy.[36] For example, diabetes reduces the probable effectiveness of some treatments for serious heart ailments. Unchecked alcoholism, another disability, could interfere with the success of organ transplantation. ...

In addition, seriously disabled patients could be disfavored when values are placed on treatment outcomes. For example, QALY use disfavors lifesaving care for patients who are expected to be disabled after treatment, because saving the life of a disabled person with an impaired quality of life will theoretically generate fewer quality-adjusted life years than saving the life of a person whose quality of life after treatment would be better. ...

The chance that disabled patients will fare unfavorably in QALY calculations is further accentuated by the risk that the scales used to measure quality of life will unfairly underestimate the quality of life of disabled persons. This was precisely the federal government's criticism of the Oregon quality of life measurements.

---

[24] Norman Daniels, Is the Oregon Rationing Plan Fair?, 265 JAMA 2232 (1991); David M. Eddy, What's Going on in Oregon?, 266 JAMA 417, 419 (1991). Compare the approach of Missouri, which spent nearly $1 million keeping Nancy Cruzan alive in a persistent vegetative state, while providing Medicaid for only 40 percent of its citizens below the poverty level. Leonard M. Fleck, Just Health Care Rationing: A Democratic Decisionmaking Approach, 140 U. Pa. L. Rev. 1597, 1611 (1992).

[36] See, e.g., David C. Hadorn, The Problem of Discrimination in Health Care Priority Setting, 268 JAMA 1454, 1457-1458 (1992) (noting poorer outcomes commonly associated with de facto disabilities such as severe diabetes or cancer); David Orentlicher, Rationing and the Americans with Disabilities Act, 271 JAMA 308, 310 (1994) (recognizing that patients with pulmonary disease are poor candidates for coronary bypass surgery). In another example, an HMO denied payment for a $170,000 liver transplant requested by an e-antigen positive hepatitis-B patient due to the high rate of reinfection of e-antigen positive patients and the liver shortage. Barnett v. Kaiser Found. Health Plan, Inc., Health Care Facility Mgmt. (CCH) ¶22,594 (N.D. Cal. 1993). The HMO's eight-member advisory board had concluded that transplantation was not an appropriate medical treatment for the patient's condition. The federal district court ruled that the HMO had not abused its discretion in considering this factor, even though transplantation might be the patient's only chance of survival. The disability rights laws were apparently not addressed.

Yet, until the Oregon plan was submitted for federal government approval, no public attention had been called to the discriminatory potential of prioritization on the basis of medical effectiveness. Although the Oregon plan was vilified on other grounds (principally that only poor people would be asked to make sacrifices to help fund an expansion of health care coverage for other poor people),[43] virtually no public debate on disability rights had occurred. As a result, the [first] Bush administration's rejection of the plan because of discrimination against patients with disabilities surprised most observers and caused some speculation that the administration had simply used the disability rights issue to derail a proposal which it found objectionable for other reasons. . . .

Oregon's initial ranking of treatments in May, 1990, was based on a pure cost-effectiveness analysis, but problems with that list[44] induced the Oregon Health Services Commission to abandon that list and produce another one in April, 1991, using a more intuitive, multifactorial methodology. Nonetheless, considerations of effectiveness continued to play a crucial role . . . at three junctures. First, the Commission divided all treatments into one of seventeen different categories and then ranked these categories. A sampling of the categories illustrates the methodology: "acute fatal, treatment prevents death with full recovery" (ranked #1); "maternity care" (#2); "acute fatal, treatment prevents death without full recovery" (#3); "comfort care" (#7); "acute nonfatal, treatment causes return to previous health state" (#10); and "infertility services" (#15). These rankings gave priority to treatments which produced complete cures over those which ordinarily produce only partial recovery. In this way, the Commission retained a blunt measure of effectiveness in its ranking process. The Commission also considered cost-effectiveness as one of many factors used to create and rank these categories.

---

[43] See, e.g., Alexander M. Capron, Oregon's Disability: Principles or Politics?, Hastings Ctr. Rep., Nov.-Dec. 1992, at 18, 19; Charles J. Dougherty, Setting Health Care Priorities: Oregon's Next Steps, Hastings Ctr. Rep., May-June 1991, at Supp. 1; Michael J. Garland, Justice, Politics and Community: Expanding Access and Rationing Health Services in Oregon, 20 L. Med. & Health Care 67, 69, 74-77 (1992); Hadorn, Setting Health Care Priorities, supra n.17, at 2224; Paul T. Menzel, Some Ethical Costs of Rationing, 20 L. Med. & Health Care 57, 62 (1992); W. John Thomas, The Oregon Medicaid Proposal: Ethical Paralysis, Tragic Democracy, and the Fate of a Utilitarian Health Care Program, 72 Or. L. Rev. 47, 51-52, 127-128 (1993).

[44] . . . In David Eddy's view, Oregon's inability to estimate accurately either costs or benefits precluded reliance on its initial list. Categories of services and outcomes were defined too broadly. For example, "trouble speaking" could range from mild lisp to mutism. Duration of treatment benefits was poorly differentiated. Cost data were incomplete or inaccurate. And the list generated serious doubts whether the values assigned to treatment outcomes, especially lifesaving treatments, had been accurately measured. David M. Eddy, Oregon's Methods: Did Cost-Effectiveness Analysis Fail?, 266 JAMA 2135 (1991); David M. Eddy, Oregon's Plan: Should It Be Approved?, 266 JAMA 2439 (1991).

Counter-intuitive rankings resulted from these problems. Reportedly, "burn over large areas of the body" scored the same as an "upset stomach." Michael Astrue, then-general counsel of the Department of Health and Human Services, was startled that treatments for ectopic pregnancies and appendicitis were ranked below some dental caps and splints for temporomandibular joint disorder. Michael J. Astrue, Pseudoscience and the Law: The Case of the Oregon Medicaid Rationing Experiment, 9 Issues L. & Med. 375, 379 (1994); see also Hadorn, Setting Health Care Priorities, supra n.17, at 2219 (suggesting that the results were the "inevitable consequence" of cost-effectiveness analysis). . . . Unwillingness to accept the implications of cost-effectiveness analysis, especially for the prioritization of noncritical care over life-extending care, may also partially explain the adverse reaction to this list. . . .

Second, the Commission used QALYs to rank treatments within the 17 categories.[51] Third and finally, the Commissioners reviewed the resulting list and adjusted some of the rankings using their "professional judgments and their interpretation of the community values." The Commissioners imposed a "reasonableness" test upon themselves, taking into account effectiveness and cost along with other factors such as public health impact, incidence of condition, and social costs. The result was a ranking of 709 treatments of which 587 were to be funded in the first year. . . .

[T]he Department of Health and Human Services ("HHS") announced that Oregon had been denied a waiver [of the usual Medicaid coverage requirements] because its plan violated the Americans with Disabilities Act ("ADA"). . . . HHS specifically identified two instances in which disabilities had been impermissibly taken into account: (1) the ranking of alcoholic cirrhosis of the liver (#690) below other cirrhoses (#366) and (2) the ranking of extremely low birth weight babies (#708) below heavier babies (#22).

Oregon denied that it had violated the ADA, but nevertheless complied with HHS's demands. Approval was not granted until Oregon had eliminated quality of life data from its formal methodology and had abandoned the separate classification of alcoholic cirrhosis and low birth weight babies. In addition, the newly elected Clinton administration insisted that Oregon no longer disfavor infertility treatments. In March, 1993, the Oregon Commission approved a new list which was based first on mortality and then, as a tie-breaker, on cost considerations. It was then adjusted by the Commission to reflect community values, such as a preference for preventive services and a dislike for medically ineffective care. The plan took effect on February 1, 1994.

This exchange between Oregon and the federal government has dramatic implications for health policy. Oregon's capitulation has cast a shadow over similar endeavors by other states. In its wake, considerable confusion exists about the permissible role of effectiveness in allocating health resources. . . . Alexander Morgan Capron, an . . . advocate of rationing, was . . . dire in his assessment. "As some form of rationing is an inevitable part of all health insurance," he concluded, "the ADA roadblock to rational prioritization of services by their expected benefit should be of grave concern to us all."[70]

Was the federal government correct? Exactly what limits do the disability rights laws place on the use of effectiveness criteria? Answering these questions requires a basic understanding of the disability rights laws.

---

[51] Benefits were measured using Dr. Robert M. Kaplan's Quality of Well-Being ("QWB") sale. Using the results of a random telephone poll of 1,001 Oregon households in which respondents were asked to rank 23 symptoms and 6 levels of functional impairment, the Commission assigned a value to various states of health, such as requiring a wheelchair or having severe burns. The benefits associated with each treatment were then calculated by using the values for the various outcomes provided by the telephone survey and weighting those values to reflect the probability of their occurrence. Expected outcomes were ascertained by polling practitioners. Outcomes (such as death or return to former health) were estimated five years after treatment. Net benefit (QWB) scores were derived by comparing the QWB score without treatment to the QWB score with treatment. The Commission multiplied the expected QWB by the duration of the benefit (thereby obtaining a measure of quality-adjusted life years or QALYs). In most cases, duration was the patient's life expectancy.

[70] Capron, supra note 43, at 20.

II. FEDERAL DISABILITY RIGHTS LAW

A. THE BASIC PARADIGM

Two federal statutes protect disabled individuals from improper discrimination in health care decisionmaking: The Rehabilitation Act of 1973 and the more recent Americans with Disabilities Act of 1990 ("ADA"). . . . Although the ADA is much more detailed than the Rehabilitation Act and the wording of the various titles of the ADA are slightly different, the basic paradigm of the two federal laws protecting disability rights can be briefly summarized. Section 504 of the Rehabilitation Act bars discrimination by any program receiving federal financial assistance or any executive agency against an "otherwise qualified" individual with a disability "by reason of her or his disability." The ADA extends this prohibition against discrimination "on the basis of" disability to state programs and private entities that do not receive federal funding.[74]

Federal law defines disabled persons as individuals who have a "physical or mental impairment which substantially limits a major life activity," "who have a record of such an impairment," or who are "regarded as having such an impairment." The regulations list examples such as blindness, mental retardation, emotional illness, cancer, heart disease, and HIV infection. . . .

Because functional impairment may affect a person's qualifications for some benefits, the laws governing disability rights permit consideration of a person's disability if the condition legitimately affects that person's ability to meet the essential eligibility requirements. This basic structure is quite different from civil rights legislation governing race because race is presumed to be irrelevant.

While acknowledging that disabilities are sometimes relevant, Congress also recognized that their consideration would often result in the exclusion of disabled persons who could become qualified with modest modifications of policies or practices. To prevent this, Congress required that a reasonable effort be made to accommodate the needs of disabled persons before concluding that they are ineligible. By conferring on people with disabilities this right to affirmative assistance, Congress endorsed, at least in a limited way, an egalitarian approach to distributive justice which allocates extra resources for those persons with the greatest need.[83] . . . To summarize this basic paradigm, a disabled person is qualified to receive health benefits or services if, with reasonable accommodation, she is able to meet the "essential" or "necessary" eligibility criteria. . . .

When the issue is joined, as it was in Oregon, the statutory terms *essential* and *necessary* seem sufficiently elastic to permit courts to consider whether medical utility is a permissible basis for disfavoring disabled patients. In effect, courts would be deciding whether the objective of maximizing health outcomes is an

---

[74] See 42 U.S.C. §12101(a)(14).

[83] As federal district court Judge Devine poignantly observed, this provision charts a course between the extremes of no assistance for overcoming disabilities (social Darwinism) and unlimited assistance. Garrity v. Gallen, 522 F. Supp. 171, 207 (D.N.H. 1981). . . . See Wendy E. Parmet, Discrimination and Disability: The Challenges of the ADA, 18 L. Med. & Health Care 331, 336 (1990) (describing the ADA as an entitlement program placed on the private sector); Peter M. Shane, Structure, Relationship, Ideology, or, How Would We Know a "New Public Law" If We Saw It?, 89 Mich. L. Rev. 837, 862 (1991) (describing the ADA as "social welfare legislation" and not simply an "antidiscrimination" law). . . .

"essential" program objective within the meaning of the equal opportunity laws. . . . HHS did exactly this in responding to the Oregon waiver request. . . .

While the legal status of rationing based on effectiveness is still uncertain, underwriting exclusions based on anticipated cost have express congressional sanction. In the ADA, Congress authorized benefits plans to engage in "the legitimate classification of risk."[97] As a result, plans remain free to consider how various disabilities influence a person's risk of death or illness. This exclusion permits risk-bearing health plans (but not necessarily practicing physicians) to consider the anticipated cost of treating various disabilities. However, the statutory exemption for underwriting practices does not appear to sanction the use of QALYs or other measures of a given treatment's effectiveness. Unlike restrictions based on underwriting risks, eligibility restrictions based on effectiveness are not based on the risk of subscriber illness and its predicted cost. They are based, instead, on predicted outcomes. Patients whose care is relatively ineffective are not necessarily any more costly or financially risky than other patients. . . . As a result, only the cost portion of cost-effectiveness analysis has clear statutory blessing, and even then only when it is part of an underwriting process. . . .

Until the courts rule on this issue, it is possible . . . that employers will be flatly prohibited from adopting health benefits plans that discriminate on the basis of disability for nonunderwriting reasons. . . . [To overcome this objection, employers and insurers will need to establish that] the use of effectiveness criteria is vital to the goal of maximizing health outcomes from fixed resources. . . .

Notes: Rationing Insurance Benefits; Disability Discrimination; Cost-Effectiveness Studies

1. *The Scope of Disability Discrimination Laws.* The potential impact of disability discrimination law on many aspects of medical decisionmaking is only gradually coming to light. This is because many medical conditions qualify under the broad definition of "disability," explained on page 129, not just stereotypical "handicaps." That being the case, it is difficult to arrive at an understanding of these statutes that would keep courts and agencies from micromanaging medical decisions and medical institutions. Observe how hard the *Choate* Court struggles simply to rule that a facially neutral restriction on coverage is not discriminatory. The *Choate* precedent has nothing to say, however, about coverage and treatment restrictions that target specific diseases and treatments. It is these restrictions whose legality is still very much in doubt.

---

[97] The ADA permits "underwriting risks, classifying risks, or administering such risks." 42 U.S.C. §12201(c)(2);? . . . Bernard B., 528 F. Supp. at 132-133 (holding that an insurance company did not discriminate under §504 in choosing to exclude mental health benefits from a minimum coverage plan), *aff'd*, 679 F.2d 7 (2d Cir. 1982).

The restrictions must not be a subterfuge and, unless the plan is self-insured, must comport with state law. The exemption applies to any "organization covered" by the ADA which has a "bona fide benefit plan." This very likely includes publicly funded health plans which use underwriting calculations to predict risks and shape coverage. . . .

It is also important to realize how many activities and programs the discrimination laws cover. Section 504 covers federal government jobs, programs, and contractors. The ADA covers state and private entities. It is divided into several titles, each of which covers different realms of activity (employment, transportation, public accommodations). The most obvious application to private health insurance is through the employment title, since insurance is an employment benefit. It is also possible, however, to construe insurance as a public accommodation. The public accommodations title is usually thought of as requiring only physical access to places of business, but some courts initially interpreted this title to require businesses to design their products and services to accommodate disabilities. Regarding insurance, this might mean that not only the refusal to sell insurance but also the terms of coverage would be subject to ADA scrutiny. Several circuit courts, however, have rejected this interpretation, holding instead that the public accommodations title was not intended to "require a seller to alter his product to make it equally valuable to the disabled." Doe v. Mutual of Omaha Insurance Co., 179 F.3d 557 (7th Cir. 1999). See also Parker v. Metropolitan Health, 121 F.3d 1006 (6th Cir. 1997) (en banc). As a consequence, courts have upheld caps of $10,000 on payment for AIDS treatment, when they are in insurance plans not purchased by employers (and therefore not subject to the employment discrimination portion of the ADA). See generally Sharona Hoffman, AIDS Caps, Contraceptive Coverage, and the Law, 23 Cardozo L. Rev. 1313 (2002); Jeffrey S. Manning, Are Insurance Companies Liable under the Americans with Disabilities Act?, 88 Cal. L. Rev. 607 (2000); Luke Sobota, Does Title III of the ADA Regulate Insurance?, 66 U. Chi. L. Rev. 243 (1999); Comment, 28 Am J.L. & Med. 107 (2002).

2. *Excluding Specific Diseases.* If disease-specific restrictions, like those in McGann v. H & H Music, constitute disability discrimination under employer-based insurance, what about other more common, less objectionable restrictions? In *Choate* the Supreme Court cited approvingly a Second Circuit opinion holding that the limitation of mental health coverage does not violate §504. See also Modderno v. King, 82 F.3d 1059 (D.C. Cir. 1996) (disparity in coverage of mental health treatment is not disability discrimination; to rule otherwise would be "to invite challenges to virtually every exercise of the [insurer's or employer's] discretion with respect to the allocation of benefits amongst an encyclopedia of illnesses"). But what is the difference between AIDS restrictions and mental health restrictions? Could it be the fact that many mental health patients are not disabled, whereas all AIDS patients are? Then what about the exclusion of experimental cancer treatment? See Henderson v. Bodine Aluminum, 70 F.3d 958 (8th Cir. 1995) (denying expensive new therapy for breast cancer is potentially discrimination based on disability type where the plan covers this treatment for other cancers and there is evidence it works for breast cancer). But see Lenox v. Healthwise of Kentucky, 149 F.3d 453 (6th Cir. 1998) (no ADA violation in excluding coverage for heart transplants). See Jane Korn, Cancer and the ADA: Rethinking Disability, 74 S. Cal. L. Rev. 339 (2001).

Are these distinctions made any easier by the Supreme Court's "meaningful access to benefits" test? Meaningful access to which benefits? To the particular item of treatment being sought or to insurance coverage generally? See Doe v. Chandler, 83 F.3d 1150 (9th Cir. 1996) (limiting welfare for disabled recipients but not for dependent children does not discriminate against the disabled because state may craft different benefits for different programs). Even if it is conceded that meaningful access exists at a threshold level, does this justify discrimination above the threshold? For an argument that these distinctions fail to adequately protect against disability discrimination through disparate impact, see D. Orentlicher, Destructuring Disability: Rationing of Health Care and Unfair Discrimination against the Sick, 31 Harv. C.R.-C.L. L. Rev. 51 (1996). According to another law professor, "the ADA is an inadequate and even inept tool for resolving whether we should tolerate cost-conscious [insurance] policies" because its concepts are so poorly suited for articulating and understanding the underlying social policy debate. Mary A. Crossley, Medical Futility and Disability Discrimination, 81 Iowa L. Rev. 179 (1995). For additional discussion of ADA issues generally and in insurance coverage and medical care, see Alexander Abbe, "Meaningful Access" to Health Care and the Remedies Available to Medicaid Managed Care Recipients under the ADA and the Rehabilitation Act, 147 U. Pa. L. Rev. 1161 (1999); Mary Crossley, Medicaid Managed Care and Disability Discrimination Issues, 65 Tenn. L. Rev. 419 (1998); Mary Crossley, Becoming Visible: The ADA's Impact on Health Care for Persons with Disabilities, 52 Ala. L. Rev. 51 (2000); Mary Crossley, The Disability Kaleidoscope, 74 Notre Dame L. Rev. 521 (1999); Maxwell J. Mehlman et al., When Do Health Care Decisions Discriminate against People with Disabilities?, 22 J. Health Pol. Pol'y & L. (Dec. 1997).

3. *Medicaid Coverage.* Many of the decisions discussed require Medicaid to fund controversial procedures such as sex-change operations and liver transplants for former alcoholics are reasoned in terms of handicap discrimination, even though they are based on the Medicaid statute. They reason that the basic standard of rationality and nonarbitrariness required by the Medicaid statute prevents covering a medically beneficial treatment for some conditions but not for others. Therefore, Medicaid must either exclude the treatment altogether or selectively exclude it under generic criteria such as medically necessary or experimental. See, e.g., Salgado v. Kirschner, 878 P.2d 659 (Ariz. 1994) (unreasonable to cover liver transplant only for children; medically relevant factors, not age alone, should determine coverage).

Imagine that you are in charge of allocating limited government health care funds. Where, if anywhere, would you want to set limits? Would you fund a liver transplant for a patient whose recovery is only 50 percent certain? For a patient with only partial liver dysfunction whose life is not at stake? For an alcoholic? Would you support lung transplants for cigarette smokers? Heart transplants for overeaters? If the legislature appropriated an additional $5 million to use at your discretion, would you choose (1) a large expansion in low-cost prenatal care, which would help decrease the high costs of caring for premature births, or (2) a few expensive organ transplants, or (3) some of both? Which of these decisions would handicap discrimination principles allow? On transplant funding issues generally, see Lisa Deutsch, Medicaid Payment for Organ Transplants: The Extent of Mandated Coverage, 30 Colum. J.L. & Soc. Probs. 185 (1997); Clark Havighurst & Nancy King, Liver Transplantation in Massachusetts: Public Policymaking as Morality Play, 19 Ind. L. Rev. 955 (1986); Schuck, Government Funding for

Organ Transplants, 14 J. Health Pol., Pol'y & L. 169 (1989); Note, 79 Minn. L. Rev. 1232 (1995); Note, 89 Nw. U. L. Rev. 268 (1994).

4. *Actuarial Justification.* The analysis under the ADA is complicated by the specific exception in the Act for health insurance benefits. As Philip Peters indicates, however, this exclusion is limited to cost-based restrictions by insurers. (Ironically, Oregon dropped these legally defensible factors early on because of the political backlash from the public and from physicians.) Also, the protection of underwriting does not apply if a restriction is found to be a "subterfuge" for disability discrimination, for instance, if the purpose is to make the job unattractive for disabled workers. The EEOC's interpretive guidelines suggest that solid actuarial justification is necessary to avoid a "subterfuge" characterization for disease-specific restrictions, and, moreover, that similarly costly conditions must be equally restricted. But see Leonard F. v Israel Discount Bank, 199 F.3d 99 (2d Cir. 1999) (rejecting EEOC's interpretation of "subterfuge"). See generally Bonnie Tucker, Insurance and the ADA, 46 DePaul L. Rev. 915 (1997).

5. *"Fundamental Alteration."* Public and private insurers also have the potential defense, discussed in *Choate*, that removing particular coverage restrictions would be unreasonably costly or would fundamentally alter the nature of the product or program. This is the defense on which Philip Peters rests most of his justification for effectiveness analysis in the remainder of his article. (Additional excerpts can be found on the Web site for this book, www.health-law.org) But this issue is also largely untested in the courts. In contrast with *Choate*, see Olmstead v. L.C., 527 U.S. 581 (1999) (finding a potential ADA violation where state Medicaid plan covered long-term hospitalization for mental illness but not less restrictive community placement options, and suggesting that it would not be a "fundamental alteration" to require the state to expand its coverage if doing so can be "reasonably accommodated" without straining the budget for other mental health services); Lovell v. Chandler, 303 F.3d 1039 (9th Cir. 2002) (finding an ADA violation where the state expanded eligibility for Medicaid up to three times the poverty level but excluded disabled participants from the increased eligibility parameters, even though the state said this was all it could afford). See Sara Rosenbaum, *Olmstead v. L.C.*: Implications for Medicaid and Other Publicly Funded Health Services, 12 Health Matrix 93 (2002).

6. *Race or Gender Discrimination.* Insurance restrictions can be challenged under other discrimination statutes besides disability. Suppose, for instance, that an excluded disease category has a disproportionate impact on blacks. Most commentators conclude that this alone is not sufficient without some indication of racial animus or subterfuge. More compelling, however, is the argument that a treatment exclusion has a categorical effect on only one gender. In Newport News Shipbuilding v. EEOC, 462 U.S. 669 (1993), the Court held that an employer violates Title VII's prohibition of sex discrimination by providing more generous pregnancy benefits to female employees than to the wives of male employees. See also Arizona Governing Comm. v. Norris, 463 U.S. 1073 (1983) (pension plans must be equal for men and women even though women's cost more because they live longer). Similarly, would the exclusion of fertility treatment such as in vitro fertilization constitute either gender or disability discrimination? Saks v. Franklin Covey Co., 316 F.3d 337 (2nd Cir. 2003) (no, because infertility is not always a disability, and plan excluded fertility treatment for both men and women). In a

split decision, a court of appeals ruled that exclusion of all forms of contraception pills, procedures, or devices, used by both men and women, does not constitute sex discrimination. In re Union Pacific Railroad Employment Practices Litigation, 479 F.3d 936 (8th Cir. 2007). See generally Lisa Kerr, Can Money Buy Happiness? An Examination of the Coverage of Infertility Services under HMO Contracts, 49 Case W. Res. L. Rev. 559 (1999); Carl Coleman, Conceiving Harm: Disability Discrimination in Assisted Reproductive Technologies, 50 UCLA L. Rev. 17 (2002). For a related issue, see L. Dechery, Do Employer-Provided Insurance Plans Violate Title VII When They Exclude Treatment for Breast Cancer?, 80 Minn. L. Rev. 945 (1996); Christine Nardi, When Health Insurers Deny Coverage for Breast Reconstructive Surgery: Gender Meets Disability, 1997 Wis. L. Rev. 778.

Among the various controversies concerning what health insurance should cover, debates about contraception and sexual health have been especially lively following the introduction of Viagra, the impotence pill for men. Viagra was easily covered by traditional health insurance because it addresses a physical dysfunction often caused by health problems such as heart disease or side effects from medication. However, Viagra is also prescribed in more discretionary situations to enhance sexual performance, especially among elderly men, for whom a decline in sexual vitality is an expected consequence of aging. Rather than drawing age-based lines or crafting sexual performance indicators that would be hard to defend or administer, insurers simply capped the number of Viagra pills permitted per month. (One wonders how they arrived at the cutoff.) See Alison Keith, The Economics of Viagra, 19(2) Health Aff. 147 (Mar. 2000). The coverage of Viagra highlights the inequities of not covering contraceptives for women, which are similarly important to sexual health. Because fertility is a normal condition, blocking fertility does not fit within the traditional insurance concepts of treatment for illness or disease. Nevertheless, many insurers have agreed to include contraceptive coverage, and some state legislatures have mandated the same. For a good overview of this debate, see Hazel Glenn Beh, Sex, Sexual Pleasure, and Reproduction: Health Insurers Don't Want You to Do Those Nasty Things, 13 Wis. Women's L.J. 119 (1998); David Chavking, Medicaid and Viagra: Restoring Potency to an Old Program?, 11 Health Matrix 189 (2000); Sharona Hoffman, AIDS Caps, Contraceptive Coverage, and the Law, 23 Cardozo L. Rev. 1315 (2002). Comment, 35 Tulsa L.J. 399 (2000). For an analysis from the perspective of sex discrimination law, see Sylvia Law, Sex Discrimination and Insurance for Contraception, 73 Wash. L. Rev. 363 (1998). For a constitutional analysis, see Note, 54 Vand. L. Rev. 451 (2001). Regarding moral criteria generally, see Sharona Hoffman, Unmanaged Care: Towards Moral Fairness in Health Care Coverage, 78 Ind. L.J. 659 (2003); Norman Daniels & James E. Sabin, Setting Limits Fairly: Can We Learn to Share Medical Resources? (2000); Jennifer Prah Ruger, Health, Capability and Justice: Toward a New Paradigm of Health Ethics, Policy and Law, 15 Cornell J.L. & Pub. Pol'y 403 (2006).

Civil rights discrimination statutes apply to government programs as well, under Title VI. These statutes have had less effect. A series of public interest lawsuits have attempted to block cities from closing public hospitals in low-income communities, finding that the disparate impact on minorities does not constitute prohibited discrimination. See, e.g., Bryan v. Koch, 627 F.2d 612 (2d Cir. 1980);

NAACP v. Wilmington Medical Center, 657 F.2d 1322 (3d Cir. 1981). See generally Marianne Lado, Breaking the Barriers of Access to Health Care: A Discussion of the Role of Civil Rights Litigation, 60 Brook. L. Rev. 239 (1994); Sidney Watson, Reinvigorating Title VI: Defending Health Care Discrimination — It Shouldn't Be So Easy, 58 Ford. L. Rev. 939 (1990).

7. *Who Decides Medical Effectiveness?* Assuming fair and nondiscriminatory measures of medical effectiveness can be devised, who should apply them? Philip Peters' discussion of QALYs is purposefully somewhat abstract in this regard, because QALYs can be used by any number of decisionmakers to tailor medical decisions. Doctors can use them to trim costs incrementally at the bedside; employers, insurers, and the government can use them to limit the benefit packages they are willing to pay for; and courts can use them to resolve disputes over what those benefit packages actually promise. These notes are focused on the second set of decisionmakers. The two cases that follow focus on the courts. Physicians as decisionmakers are considered throughout these materials, including under informed consent, malpractice, and financial incentive payments.

8. *Medical Effectiveness Measures.* It is important to distinguish among ordinary medical effectiveness, cost-effectiveness analysis, and cost-benefit analysis. Ordinary effectiveness determines simply whether a medical procedure works at all or whether it works better than another for the same condition. Cost-effectiveness analysis asks how much it costs to achieve an increment in health improvement. QALYs were devised in order to have a common measure of health improvement other than simply number of lives or years of life saved. A generic unit of health improvement then allows comparisons between totally different treatments and disease conditions, such as determining whether prenatal care is a more cost-effective use of medical resources than are liver transplants. The comparative analysis can help determine the best use of limited funds, but it cannot tell us what total health expenditures should be, that is, whether to do *both* prenatal care and liver transplants, or *neither* and instead spend the money on education or housing. If that decision is to be made quantitatively, it requires a cost-benefit analysis, which compares the cost of medical procedures with their benefit in terms of dollars. This is obviously much more controversial since it requires that a value be placed on human life and suffering. It is important to stress that none of the techniques surveyed by Philip Peters goes this far. They only ask, comparatively, whether one benefit is greater than another, not whether the expenditure is worth it at all.

For example, it has been estimated that the cost of administering Pap smears, which detect cervical cancer, is roughly $5,000 per additional year of life expectancy for testing every three years but $200,000-400,000 per year of life saved for annual testing. Does this tell you conclusively which should be funded? Which would you choose as a patient paying out-of-pocket? As a gynecologist? As a Medicare bureaucrat? See Sarah Feldman, How Often Should We Screen for Cervical Cancer?, 349 New Eng. J. Med. 1495 (2003) (recommending testing every three years after a series of negative one-year exams). Are these decisions made any easier by comparing these cost-effectiveness ratios with those for other treatments? "[An] analysis compar[ing] the costs and outcome of heart transplantation with those of conventional care for congestive heart failure yield[ed] a figure of $23,000 [to $33,700] per added year of life [for heart transplants]. . . . By comparison, in 1984 dollars, coronary-artery bypass grafting cost about $10,000 per added year of life, [and] hemodialysis for [kidney failure] about $32,000. . . . Treatment of [AIDS] costs about $140,000 per case." Cassells, Heart Transplantation: Recent Policy Developments, 315 New Eng. J. Med. 1365, 1366 (1986). See generally P. J. Neumann. Using Cost-Effectiveness Analysis to Improve Health Care: Opportunities and Barriers (2005). For broader discussions of the use of cost-benefit analyses in legal and regulatory settings generally, see Matthew Adler & Eric Posner, Cost-Benefit Analysis: Legal, Economic, and Philosophical Perspectives (2001); Symposium, 29 J. Legal Stud. 837 (2000).

Several times over the past twenty years, CMS has proposed to include cost-effectiveness criteria in deciding what treatments are covered by Medicare, but so far it has failed to adopt such a rule. See Susan B. Foote, Why Medicare Cannot Promulgate a National Coverage Rule: A Case of *Regula Mortis*, 27 J. Health Pol. Pol'y & L. 707 (2002); Jacqueline Fox, Medicare Should, but Cannot, Consider Cost: Legal Impediments to a Sound Policy, 53 Buff. L. Rev. 577 (2005); Peter J. Neumann et al., Medicare and Cost-Effectiveness Analysis, 353 New Eng. J. Med. 1516 (2006).

9. *Rationing Criteria.* QALYs are objectionable on other moral grounds besides disability discrimination. As discussed most forcefully by David Hadorn and John Harris, cited by Peters, the mathematics of QALYs mean that it is equally as valuable to save ten years from one person's life as it is to save one year of life for ten people. This utilitarian logic does not fit most people's intuitions. See John Taurek, Should the Numbers Count?, 6 Phil. & Pub. Aff. 293 (1977). On the other hand, if we are to avoid use of rationing criteria that contain any controversial value judgments, we would have to adopt completely arbitrary rationing criteria such as a simple lottery, or treating whoever asks first. Most people would view these "neutral" criteria as even more irrational and objectionable. Einer Elhauge, Allocating Health Care Morally, 82 Cal. L. Rev. 1449 (1994). Prof. Gregg Bloche argues that health care law and policy is in a "confused, even chaotic state" because it assumes that medical resources can be allocated in a "systematically rational manner," which is not feasible or even desirable considering differing values, limitations on human rationality, and inconsistent understandings about what rationality means or requires. Instead, he urges an "inelegant" approach that "defines our aims more modestly, consistent with a picture of rationality as limited by context, discontinuous across different settings, and changeable with time." Gregg Bloche, The Invention of Health Law, 91 Cal. L. Rev. 247 (2003).

10. *Social Values.* Those who advocate more explicit rationing of limited resources usually object to the fact that our society spends too much on heroic, high-tech rescue efforts for those who are visibly threatened with death or disability at the same time that we neglect inexpensive preventive measures that would keep the situation from arising in the first place. This is known as the paradox of "statistical versus identifiable lives," or as the "rescue ethic," and it exists not only in medicine but in other social arenas such as traffic safety and high-risk recreational activity. If the thrust of this argument is to spend more on prevention, few would disagree, but if the thrust is to spend less on heroic measures, the argument is met with the following response:

I will risk my life on the roads to do nothing more than secure a bag of potato chips, not to mention take the risk of eating them simply for fleeting gustatory sensations. But should I come up short in the potato chips v. life lottery, and suffer either a car or a cardiovascular accident, I do not expect society to respond by saying, "Well, tough luck, but you made an open-eyed trade-off here." No, I expect EMTs to rush to the scene and pound on my chest and speed me to the hospital in reckless disregard of the laws set down to reduce the risk faced by other travelers in search of potato chips and other goods. This social response, I am suggesting, can be seen as a way of marking the fact that our lives are shot through with incommensurable values, and that we have to wind our way through them in a way that does its best to acknowledge their separate significance.

J.L. Nelson, Publicity and Pricelessness: Grassroots Decisionmaking and Justice in Rationing, 19 J. Med. & Phil. 333 (1994). In a similar vein, Calabresi and Bobbitt explain that rationing is more socially acceptable when the tragic choices are hidden from view, as they are when the harms are merely statistical, than when identifiable victims of rationing can clearly be seen. G. Calabresi & P. Bobbitt, Tragic Choices (1978). Does this suggest to you that we satisfy a social value when we spend much more on rescues than on prevention, or does it mean that social policy is wrong?

11. *Kidney Dialysis.* Health care rationing issues first came to the public's attention when kidney dialysis was developed in the late 1960s. Moved by the plight of patients dying from kidney failure who could not afford this expensive treatment, Congress in 1973 expanded Medicare to cover virtually all costs for dialysis (and later for kidney transplants), for anyone afflicted with "end stage renal disease" (ESRD), i.e., kidney failure—regardless of whether they were elderly or disabled. This is the only time Congress has enacted a disease-specific insurance program, and may well be the last time. Congress drastically underestimated the costs of this program, which now runs several billion dollars a year and has spawned a huge industry in dialysis clinics. In contrast, British doctors, because of severe overall funding limits, generally do not order dialysis for older patients and those with other serious illnesses. See generally, J. Iglehart, The End Stage Renal Disease Program, 328 New Eng. J. Med. 366 (1993); H.B. Southern, Medicare's End-Stage Renal Disease Program: Its Development and Implications of Health Care Policy, 26 Harv. J. on Legis. 225 (1989); Note, 26 Harv. J. on Legis. 225 (1989).

12. *Oregon's Rationing List.* It is fascinating to observe how Oregon's bold approach actually functioned when implemented in real-world settings. Subsequent evaluation reveals that the list has not generated substantial savings. Many of the items eliminated from funding are fairly "small ticket," are requested only rarely, or were not covered in the first place. In other instances, physicians have been able to obtain coverage by recharacterizing the patient's condition as being more serious. Also, many Oregon Medicaid patients are covered by HMOs in which physicians are paid a capitation payment rather than fee-for-service, so physicians often provide the service even when they are not required to if it is relatively inexpensive. Accordingly, Oregon's expansion of Medicaid eligibility has been financed mostly by increased taxation and legislative appropriations, not by savings from The List. The main impact of the list, according to the following reviews, is its use as a political tool to secure more funds from the legislature.

Symposium, 24 J. Health Pol. Pol'y & L. 151 (1999). Another study, however, found that more than 12 percent of Oregon Medicaid recipients have been denied a needed medical service due to the rationing list. Half of these people managed to get the service in any event, either by paying for it themselves or by receiving charity care. On balance, Oregon's Medicaid recipients were found to be as satisfied with their health care and to have better access to care than other low-income people who had private insurance. Janet B. Mitchell & Fred Bentley, Impact of Oregon's Priority List on Medicaid Beneficiaries, 57 Med. Care Res. & Rev. 216 (2000). Since then, however, enrollment has declined substantially because Oregon began to charge sliding scale premiums for people who did not meet the most stringent poverty guidelines, prompting many of the poor and near-poor to drop coverage, resulting in an enrollment mix that is much more like traditional Medicaid in other states. Jonathan Oberlander, Health Reform Interrupted: The Unraveling of the Oregon Health Plan, 26(1) Health Aff. W96 (Dec. 2006). This author concludes that "the faltering of health reform . . . [after the state] invested two decades of efforts in moving toward universal coverage reminds us just how hard it can be for states to build and sustain large-scale coverage expansions."

For further discussion of the Oregon scheme and the legality of QALYs under the ADA, see Kevin P. Quinn, Viewing Health Care as a Common Good: Looking Beyond Political Liberalism, 73 S. Cal. L. Rev. 277 (2000); W. John Thomas, The Oregon Medicaid Proposal: Ethical Paralysis, Tragic Democracy, and the Fate of a Utilitarian Health Care Program, 72 Or. L. Rev. 47, 135-145 (1993); Note, 83 Geo. L.J. 2697 (1995); Comment, 31 Hous. L. Rev. 265 (1994); Note, 93 Colum. L. Rev. 1985 (1993); Note, 106 Harv. L. Rev. 1296 (1993); Symposium, 1 Health Matrix 135 (1991).

13. *Additional Readings on Rationing.* It is impossible to overemphasize the importance of health care rationing as an aspect of health law and policy. Other aspects of this issue, perhaps the most perplexing of the health care policy issues of our time, are explored in Chapter 1.D.4. For further elaboration of moral and public policy objections to and defenses of QALYs and other criteria for rationing, see Larry Churchill, Rationing Health Care in America (1987); Frances Kamm, Morality and Mortality (1993); John Kilner, Who Lives? Who Dies? (1990); Paul Menzel, Strong Medicine: The Ethical Rationing of Health Care (1990); Eric Rakowski, Taking and Saving Lives, 93 Colum. L. Rev. 1063 (1993); Matthew D. Adler, QALYs and Policy Evaluation: A New Perspective, 6 Yale J. Health Pol'y, L. & Ethics 1 (2006).

Problem: Allocation Choices in a Public Program

You are CEO of a municipal hospital, funded by the county, looking at next year's budget. This forces you to make tough allocation decisions. Due to your brilliant administrative leadership, the hospital managed to treat all patients who requested service last year, and it still has a $5 million surplus left over. After receiving recommendations from a task force, you have to choose among these three options:

(1) Return the money to the county to help them avoid an anticipated property tax increase.

(2) Buy one Very Big Fancy Machine (VBFM), which, over the course of its five-year useful life, will treat 100 patients a year, with a 1 percent better chance of saving their life compared with existing technologies. In other words, the machine is expected to save five lives at a cost of $1 million/life. On average, each person saved will live for ten more years. (Imagine a machine that helps resuscitate patients in the emergency room.)

(3) Buy 5,000 Really Simple Little Things (RSLTs), which have a 1 percent chance to extend life one year for each person who uses one. In other words, this will provide one additional year for 50 people, at a cost of $100,000 per person. (Imagine an expensive drug that does a better job of delaying but not preventing death from cancer.)

Now, suppose you learn that patients treated with the VBFM will be left bed ridden and debilitated but fully conscious, whereas RSLT patients are left ambulatory but in pain and with diminished mental capacities. Unfettered by the ADA, (since it applies to public hospitals) what do you do? Realizing, however, that the ADA might apply, does it potentially force you to change your mind? What factors determine what effect the ADA might have?

B. INFORMED CONSENT

1. Goals, Aspirations, Policies

In Chapter 1.B.3 and in the introduction to this chapter we explained the obvious fact that the physician-patient relationship is characterized by a huge imbalance of power, owing to the vulnerability of illness and treatment and physicians' vastly superior knowledge and skills. This power imbalance may be further accentuated by economic and cultural factors. See Chapter 1.D.3. What should the medical and legal response be to these inequalities in the physician-patient relationship? Historically, or perhaps apocryphally, a patient's reverence for her physician was a source of comfort and an important underpinning to the psychology of a cure. A wide range of factors — perhaps among them the anti-establishment views of the 1960s, the consumer movement of the 1970s, the startling advances and lingering failures of medical progress, and the expansion of specialties such as "bioethics" and "health law" — have combined to challenge the authority and supremacy of the physician. The most prominent legal tool used by those seeking to reform the physician-patient relationship is the doctrine of informed consent. It is believed that requiring physicians to provide more information to their patients will help to redress the power imbalance problems created by the inequality of knowledge. As you read the materials on informed consent, consider how effective the law has been, or conceivably could be, in accomplishing this reformist mission. Consider also what model the reformists envision for the ideal patient-physician interaction, and whether all (or many) patients actually subscribe to that model.

▮ PATIENT-CENTERED MEDICINE: A PROFESSIONAL EVOLUTION
Christine Laine & Frank Davidoff*
275 JAMA 152, 152-153 (1996)

In the past, physicians commonly withheld diagnostic information from patients with patients' tacit consent. Hippocrates advocated "concealing most things from the patient while you are attending to him . . . revealing nothing of the patient's future or present condition." . . . The attitude[] of Hippocrates . . . would undoubtedly get [him] into trouble today. Patients increasingly expect to know not only their diagnoses, but also details of pathophysiology, treatment options, and prognosis. . . . Patients expect and often demand information that used to be only within physicians' reach, and physicians increasingly expect to share such information with patients.

The transformation in attitudes surrounding disclosure of diagnoses is particularly striking when one considers cancer. . . . A 1961 study . . . revealed that . . . 90 percent of physicians surveyed preferred not to tell cancer patients their diagnoses. . . . [B]y 1979 . . . 97 percent of physicians surveyed preferred to disclose a diagnosis of cancer. . . .

Beyond "honesty is the best policy," the argument for informing patients is that information enables patients to participate in medical decisions. In more physician-centered days, physicians would decide what was best for their patients, and patient participation was limited to compliance with physicians' orders. As medicine becomes more patient centered, participation begins with the patient helping to decide what the physician will order, and the emphasis shifts from compliance to participation.

▮ RETHINKING INFORMED CONSENT
Peter H. Schuck**
103 Yale L.J. 899, 900-905 (1994)

The doctrine requiring physicians to obtain a patient's informed consent before undertaking treatment is relatively young, having first appeared in a recognizable, relatively robust form only in 1957.[1] Yet the values that underlie the doctrine have an ancient pedigree. The consent norm had occupied a prominent and honored place in our legal thought for many centuries before the courts began to develop a jurisprudence of informed consent in health care.[2] Also well established

---

* Dr. Laine is Senior Deputy Editor, and Dr. Davidoff is now an Editor Emeritus, at the Annals of Internal Medicine, published by the American College of Physicians. Dr. Lane is also affiliated with the Division of Internal Medicine at Jefferson Medical College, Thomas Jefferson University.

** Reprinted by permission of The Yale Law Journal Company and Fred B. Rothman & Company. The author is the Simeon E. Baldwin Professor of Law at Yale Law School.

[1] See Jay Katz, The Silent World of Doctor and Patient 48-84 (1984); see also Ruth R. Faden & Tom L. Beauchamp, A History and Theory of Informed Consent 235-273 (1986).

[2] See, e.g., Ford v. Ford, 10 N.E. 474, 475 (Mass. 1887) [assault defined in part by absence of consent].

was the cognate notion that consent must be informed or knowledgeable in some meaningful sense if we are to accord it legal or moral significance. . . .

The doctrine of informed consent in health care shared in the more general expansion of American tort liability that proceeded well into the 1980s and that now appears to have stabilized. Everyone, it seems, favors the principle of informed consent; it is "only" the specific details and applications of the doctrine that arouse serious debate. In order to map and enlarge this debate, it is useful to distinguish three different versions of informed consent doctrine. The first is the letter and spirit of the doctrine as developed primarily by courts — the law "in books." The second is the doctrine as imagined, feared, and often caricatured by some physicians — the law "in the mind." The third version, a consequence both of the gap between the first two and of other situational constraints, is the doctrine as actually practiced by clinicians — the law "in action." (Of course, there are almost as many laws-in-action as there are distinct physician-patient relationships.)

Most commentators on informed consent deploy one or more of these versions of the law. Generally (and crudely) speaking, these commentators fall into two camps: idealists and realists. Informed consent idealists — primarily some judges and medical ethicists — advocate a relatively expansive conception of the physician's obligation to disclose and elicit information about risks and alternatives.[18] More specifically, the idealists tend to define informed consent law's pivotal concepts — materiality of risk, disclosure, alternatives, and causation — broadly and subjectively from the perspective of the individual patient rather than that of the professional, while defining the law's exceptions to the duty narrowly. Perhaps most important, idealists emphasize the qualitative dimension of physician-patient interactions concerning treatment decisions. They insist that these interactions be dialogic rather than authoritative, tailored to the individual patient's emotional needs and cognitive capacities rather than formulaic, aimed at maximizing patient autonomy and comprehension rather than mere information flow, and sensitive to the distortions that can be created by power differentials between physician and patient.

The idealists employ a distinctive rhetorical strategy. Capitalizing on the universal support for the principles and goals of informed consent, they point to the often striking difference between the law in books and the law in action — a difference that I call the "informed consent gap." The existence of this gap, they argue, shows that the law in action falls far short of the law in books. Since the law that they think should be in the books is often even more demanding, the true gap is wider still. The problem, then, is not so much the law in books, which tends to demand too little of physicians; rather, it is the laws in action and in the mind. For the idealist, therefore, the goal of reform must be to close the informed consent gap by conforming the law in action, at the very least, to the law now in books.

The realists — primarily practicing physicians — harbor a different vision of informed consent.[20] Although they emphatically do not contest the principle and

---

[18] See, e.g., Canterbury v. Spence, 464 F.2d 772, 787 (D.C. Cir. 1972) (principle of informed consent requires that physician disclose information that reasonable patient would wish to know in making treatment decisions); Truman v. Thomas, 611 P.2d 902, 906-907 (Cal. 1980) (patient must be apprised of risks of not undergoing treatment, even if she has refused treatment); see also Katz, supra note 1, at 48-84.

[20] Perhaps the most articulate of the realists is Dr. Thomas P. Duffy. See Thomas P. Duffy, Agamemnon's Fate and the Medical Profession, 9 W. New Eng. L. Rev. 21 (1987) (reviewing and

goals of informed consent, they do question whether most patients really desire the kind of dialogue that the idealists propose. They also question whether, whatever patients desire, the gains in patient autonomy and improved outcomes produced by the dialogue are worth the additional time, money, and needless patient anxiety and confusion that informed consent may entail. Like the idealists, many realists employ a characteristic rhetoric. Rather than master the doctrinal details of the informed consent law in books, they point instead to the law in their minds, which they can easily caricature in order to demonstrate the law's folly. Although some realists do not concede that the law in action actually deviates from the law in their minds, many others readily admit that a gap does in fact exist. To them, however, this gap simply demonstrates how impractical the idealists' vision is and why it cannot be implemented in the demanding world of contemporary clinical practice.

In a real sense, then, informed consent idealists and realists argue past one another, producing a debate that is oblique and inconclusive rather than pointed and fruitful. For several related reasons, it is time to revisit this debate. These reasons include the intense public concern about rising health care costs, the bureaucratization of the physician-patient relationship, and the organization of health care delivery into units with some degree of market power over providers. Is the informed consent gap to be deplored or tolerated? Should physicians' legal obligations to disclose be further expanded, retained in their present form, or reduced? . . .

Notes: The Theory and Practice of Informed Consent

1. *Using Legal Rules to Foster Autonomy.* Peter Schuck suggests that informed consent idealists seek to promote individual autonomy while informed consent realists argue that the goals of complete individual autonomy cannot be met, at least not without great cost. As you read the following materials, identify the interests protected by the informed consent doctrine. A number of commentators have concluded that the doctrine fails to protect individual interests or to promote individual autonomy. See, e.g., Jay Katz, Informed Consent—Must It Remain a Fairy Tale?, 10 J. Contemp. Health L. & Pol'y 69 (1993).

Should we blame the law for this shortcoming, or is it inherently incapable of regulating the subtle and minute interactions between doctors and patients? Dr. Jay Katz, one of the law's most visionary and respected advocates of heightened informed consent, believes that "the radically different climate of physician-patient decisionmaking . . . cannot be implemented by judicial, legislative, or administrative orders." Jay Katz, The Silent World of Doctor and Patient 228 (1984). Similarly, a prestigious blue-ribbon ethics commission recognized that

---

criticizing Jay Katz's approach). Dr. Sherwin Nuland advances a more moderate realist position in his . . . book. See Sherwin B. Nuland, How We Die: Reflections on Life's Final Chapter 258-261, 265-267 (1994) (distinguishing inter alia, between family physicians, who can and should engage in meaningful informed consent dialogue with patients, and specialists, who cannot realistically be expected to do so).

further evolution of legal standards toward a firmer protection of individual self-determination in medical decisions must be tempered by a recognition of the law's limits as an instrument of social control. . . . [T]he Commission is concerned that efforts to draw the law further into regulating the subtler aspects of relations between patients and health care professionals may prove ineffective, burdensome and ultimately counterproductive. President's Commission for the Study of Ethical Problems in Medicine and Biomedical and Behavioral Research, Making Health Care Decisions: A Report on the Ethical and Legal Implications of Informed Consent in the Patient-Practitioner Relationship 30, 204, 252 (1982).

For a critique of the current system of patient autonomy and the physician-patient fiduciary relationship see Roger B. Dworkin, Getting What We Should from Doctors: Rethinking Patient Autonomy and the Doctor-Patient Relationship, 13 Health Matrix 235 (2003); M. Greg Bloche, The Invention of Health Law, 91 Cal. L. Rev. 247 (2003). For a discussion and critique of new models of "shared decisionmaking" in health care, see Carl E. Schneider, Void for Vagueness, Hastings Center Rep. 10 (Jan.-Feb. 2007).

2. *Informed Consent in Practice.* Also consider the problems raised by the implementation of the doctrine. The process of health care decision making described in narratives by physicians often suggests the irrelevance of the legal framework. See, e.g., Atul Gawande, Complications: A Surgeon's Notes on an Imperfect Science (2002). Has the process of providing informed consent through signed consent forms become as ritualized and meaningless as the exchange of a peppercorn in land transactions? Empirical studies often cast doubt on the efficacy of the practice of informed consent. In one pathbreaking article, Alan Meisel & Loren H. Roth reviewed the empirical data on informed consent. Alan Meisel and Loren H. Roth, Toward an Informed Discussion of Informed Consent: A Review of the Empirical Studies, 25 Ariz. L. Rev. 265 (1983). They found that few patients understood or remembered what they had been told about their medical condition and treatment options. Other research confirms these findings. In one typical study, patients facing either anterior cervical fusion or lumbar laminectomy were given a training session on the procedures by a neurosurgeon and a clinical nurse specialist with a master's degree in neurosurgery. D. A. Herz, J. E. Looman, & S. K. Lewis, Informed Consent: Is It a Myth?, 30 Neurosurgery 453 (1992). Patients were given a "simple" written test immediately after the training session; the mean patient score was only 43.5 percent. Six weeks later, the mean test score dropped to 38.4 percent. The authors concluded that health care providers "cannot necessarily expect accurate patient or family recall or comprehension. Fulfillment of the doctrine of informed consent by neurosurgeons may very well be mythical." See also A. M. Adams & A. F. Smith, Risk Perception and Communication: Recent Developments and Implications for Anaesthesia, 56 Anaesthesia 745 (2001).

There are a number of explanations for the gap between disclosure and comprehension/retention. Patients are often sick or emotionally vulnerable at the time of the disclosure; information may be presented in a highly technical and incomprehensible fashion; patients may not have the intelligence or educational background necessary to understand medical information; and patients may not feel able to ask important follow-up questions. See, e.g., S. J. Philipson, M. A. Doyle, S. G. Gabram, C. Nightingale & E. H. Philipson, Informed Consent for Research: A Study to Evaluate Readability and Processibility to Effect Change, 43 J. Investig. Med. 459 (1995) (96 percent of consent forms studied found to have readability levels higher than the target level of an eighth grade reading ability). Despite these problems, patients often report that they are satisfied with the informed consent process. See, e.g., F. W. Verheggen, R. Jonkers & G. Kok, Patients' Perceptions on Informed Consent and the Quality of Information Disclosure in Clinical Trials, 29 Patient Educ. Couns. 137 (1996). Informed consent issues are particularly salient in developing countries. See Michael T. Krosin et al., Problems in Comprehension of Informed Consent in Rural and Peri-Urban Mali, West Africa, Clinical Trials 306 (2006).

3. *Information That Is Harmful: Genetics and HIV.* Information is not always welcome. Some types of information may increase anxiety and decrease enjoyment of life without appreciably adding to decisionmaking ability. See Karen Rothenberg, Breast Cancer, the Genetic "Quick Fix," and the Jewish Community, 7 Health Matrix 97 (1997). Imagine a genetic condition associated with the early onset of severe dementia and death for which there is no effective preventive treatment. How many people would want to know how and when they are going to die? But how do you ask whether someone wants to know this without tipping them off to the truth? One solution to this dilemma is to have a more elaborate informed consent process before giving the test, in which patients are told that the information obtained might be upsetting or might affect their ability to obtain life or health insurance or threaten their job security. Then patients could choose not to be tested at all. See Consensus Statement, Genetic Testing for Susceptibility to Adult-Onset Cancer: The Process and Content of Informed Consent, 277 JAMA 1467 (1997); American Society of Clinical Oncology, Policy Statement Update: Genetic Testing for Cancer Susceptibility, 21 J. Clin. Oncol. 2397 (2003). This expansive approach to pretest counseling obviously would put a crimp in the approach that many clinicians take toward routine testing, in which screening tests are done without any notice at all, much less with elaborate informed consent.

Advances in genetics raise an additional dilemma, noted by Roger Dworkin in his article excerpted at page 67. If one patient wants the information and consents to testing, does this invade the privacy of family members who may not want to know the information or even to have the information created? Again, they might suffer either psychological effects or adverse financial effects from insurance or employment. Dworkin argues that genetic medicine requires us to adapt our individual autonomy model of informed consent so that it becomes more family-centered. How would one obtain consent from an extended family? Is agreement by every competent adult required, or only a critical mass, or only a single family matriarch or patriarch?

4. *Do Patients Want Decisional Autonomy?* Several commentators have argued that patients want to be informed but do not actually want to make their own health care decisions. Carl Schneider, a law professor at the University of Michigan, after reviewing empirical studies of patient interest in medical decisionmaking, concluded:

Taken as a whole, these studies surveyed a considerable variety of populations—from the perfectly well to the dangerously sick. They asked patients about their own conditions and about hypothetical illnesses. They framed their respondent's choices in a variety of ways. And their virtually universal conclusion was that, while patients commonly wish to be informed about their medical circumstances, at least a quite substantial number of them did not want to make their own medical decisions, or perhaps even to participate in those decisions in any very significant way. . . .

One might suppose that if patients were ever to assert their decisional authority it would be after hearing the alarming recitation of risks that characterizes the process of informed consent. Yet a number of studies of that process "strongly suggest that refusals attributable to disclosures are rarely, if ever, seen." Similarly, a study of why patients refuse treatment found an average of 4.6 refusals per 100 patient days. The reasons for refusal were complex, and generally there was more than one "cause" per patient. But two kinds of reasons stood out: first, a failure to tell the patient about the purpose of what was proposed; second, psychological factors, prominently including "characterological factors" (for example, using a refusal to accept treatment as a way of expressing a wish to be cared for) and "other psychoses." While the first of these causes reconfirms the wish for information we have so frequently encountered, neither of them is inconsistent with a reluctance to take control of medical decisions. And the dog that did not bark in the night is the absence of any significant number of patients who heard a doctor's recommendation and reached a different conclusion on the merits.

Carl E. Schneider, Bioethics with a Human Face, 69 Ind. L.J. 1075, 1097, 1099 (1994). Professor Schneider also noted significant evidence that "the more severe a patient's illness, the less likely the patient is to want to make medical decisions." Id. at 1101. See also Carl E. Schneider, The Practice of Autonomy: Patients, Doctors, and Medical Decisions (1998), which is excerpted at page 65.

5. *Individual Autonomy as a Cultural Norm.* Some have argued that the law in this area represents an obsession with Western values and norms that seem less relevant to those from other cultures. For cultural and comparative perspectives on the doctrine, see Leslie J. Blackhall et al., Ethnicity and Attitudes Toward Patient Autonomy, 274 JAMA 820 (1995); Joseph A. Carrese & Lorna A. Rhodes, Western Bioethics on the Navajo Reservation: Benefit or Harm?, 274 JAMA 826 (1995); Lawrence O. Gostin, Informed Consent, Cultural Sensitivity, and Respect for Persons, 274 JAMA 844 (1995); Frances H. Miller, Denial of Health Care and Informed Consent in English and American Law, 18 Am. J.L. & Med. 37 (1992); Kristina Orfali & Elisa J. Gordon, Autonomy Gone Awry: A Cross-Cultural Study of Parents' Experiences in Neonatal Intensive Care Units, 25 Theoretical Med. 329 (2004).

6. *Individual Autonomy and Medical Research.* Commentators have been particularly concerned with the role of informed consent in medical research. See, e.g., George J. Annas, Questing for Grails: Duplicity, Betrayal and Self-Deception in Postmodern Medical Research, 12 J. Contemp. Health L. & Pol'y 297 (1996); Ruth R. Faden & Tom L. Beauchamp, A History and Theory of Informed Consent 151-232 (1986). The issue is explored in greater depth in section B.5.

7. *Informed Consent vs. Traditional Malpractice.* Despite academic interest, informed consent theories play a role in a relatively small percentage of claims against physicians, at least as measured by opinions published in computerized databases such as Westlaw. As you read these materials, consider the role that

informed consent theories appear to play in traditional malpractice litigation. Of what relevance is it that informed consent claims are rarely brought alone but are most often seen in cases where plaintiffs also are asserting traditional negligence claims?

8. *The Spectrum of Informed Consent Standards.* Both courts and legislatures have participated in the redefinition of the roles in the physician-patient relationship. They have responded to the inequality in knowledge between providers and patients in at least four distinct ways. Some jurisdictions, about half in fact, use some version of a "professional malpractice" standard, under which physicians are required to disclose to patients that information which would have been disclosed by the reasonable, minimally competent physician. A substantial number of states use the "material risk" or "reasonable patient" standard, which requires disclosure of risks that a reasonable patient would consider to be material in making a medical treatment decision. A small number of jurisdictions take an even more protective approach, requiring disclosure of information that a particular patient (as contrasted with a "rational" patient) would have wanted to make his or her decision. Finally, courts seeking tools to regulate the nature of the physician-patient relationship have recently turned to fiduciary law as a source of additional disclosure obligations for physicians.

9. *Additional Commentaries.* The literature in this area is voluminous. Some particularly useful law review commentaries (in addition to those cited in Schuck's article) include Jamie Staples King & Benjamin W. Moulton, Rethinking Informed Consent: The Case for Shared Medical Decision-Making, 32 Am. J.L. & Med. 429 (2006); Sheldon F. Kurtz, The Law of Informed Consent: From "Doctor Is Right" to "Patient Has Rights," 50 Syracuse L. Rev. 1243 (2000); Grant H. Morris, Dissing Disclosure: Just What the Doctor Ordered, 44 Ariz. L. Rev. 313 (2002); William M. Sage, Regulating Through Information: Disclosure Laws and American Health Care, 99 Colum. L. Rev. 1701 (1999); Marjorie Maguire Schultz, From Informed Consent to Patient Choice: A New Protected Interest, 95 Yale L.J. 219 (1985). For a classic attack on the fundamental theory of informed consent liability, see Richard Epstein, Medical Malpractice: The Case for Contract, 1976 Am. Bar. Found. Res. J. 87. The major treatise is Fay A. Rozovsky, Consent to Treatment: A Practical Guide (2000). There are several important books on the subject, including Carl E. Schneider, The Practice of Autonomy: Patients, Doctors, and Medical Decisions (1998); Ruth R. Faden & Tom L. Beauchamp, A History and Theory of Informed Consent (1986); Jessica W. Berg et al., Informed Consent: Legal Theory and Practice (2001). For general discussions of informed consent, see George P. Smith, II, The Vagaries of Informed Consent, 1 Ind. Health L. Rev. 109 (2004); and Annot., 88 A.L.R. 3d 1008 (1978).

2. The Competing Disclosure Standards

■ CANTERBURY v. SPENCE
464 F.2d 772 (D.C. Cir.), cert. denied, 409 U.S. 1064 (1972)

[Appellant Canterbury, a 19-year-old clerk-typist who had experienced persistent back pain, sought care from Dr. Spence. Dr. Spence conducted a number of tests to determine the cause of the back pain and eventually recommended that Canterbury undergo a laminectomy. According to the court, Canterbury "did not raise any objection to the proposed operation nor did he probe into its exact nature." Dr. Spence spoke with Canterbury's mother by telephone. She asked "if the recommended operation was serious and Dr. Spence replied 'not any more than any other operation.'" It is unclear whether Mrs. Canterbury consented to the operation before it took place; she did sign a consent form afterward. The laminectomy was performed without any apparent difficulties. During the recovery period, however, hospital personnel failed to assist Canterbury during the process of voiding, and Canterbury fell out of his bed while attempting to void. Canterbury developed signs of partial paralysis a few hours after the fall, which were only partially improved by another operation.]

At the time of the trial . . . [he] required crutches to walk, still suffered from urinal incontinence and paralysis of the bowls, and wore a penile clamp. . . . [H]e [had] held a number of jobs, but had constant trouble finding work because he needed to remain seated and close to a bathroom. The damages appellant claims include extensive pain and suffering, medical expenses, and loss of earnings.

Appellant filed suit in the district court on March 7, 1963, four years after the laminectomy and approximately two years after he attained his majority. The complaint stated several causes of action against each defendant. Against Dr. Spence it alleged, among other things, negligence in the performance of the laminectomy and failure to inform him beforehand of the risk involved. Against the hospital the complaint charged negligent postoperative care in permitting appellant to remain unattended after the laminectomy, in failing to provide a nurse or orderly to assist him at the time of his fall, and in failing to maintain a side rail on his bed. . . .

At the close of appellant's case in chief, each defendant moved for a directed verdict and the trial judge granted both motions. . . . The judge did not allude specifically to the alleged breach of duty by Dr. Spence to divulge the possible consequences of the laminectomy.

We reverse. The testimony of appellant and his mother that Dr. Spence did not reveal the risk of paralysis from the laminectomy made out a prima facie case of violation of the physician's duty to disclose which Dr. Spence's explanation did not negate as a matter of law. . . .

Suits charging failure by a physician[6] adequately to disclose the risks and alternatives of proposed treatment are not innovations in American law. They date back a good half-century, and in the last decade they have multiplied rapidly. There is, nonetheless, disagreement among the courts and the commentators on many major questions, and there is no precedent of our own directly in point. For the tools enabling resolution of the issues on this appeal, we are forced to begin at first principles.

The root premise is the concept, fundamental in American jurisprudence, that "[e]very human being of adult years and sound mind has a right to determine

---

[6] Since, there was neither allegation nor proof that the appellee hospital failed in any duty to disclose, we have no occasion to inquire as to whether or under what circumstances such a duty might arise.

what shall be done with his own body. . . . "[12] True consent to what happens to one's self is the informed exercise of a choice, and that entails an opportunity to evaluate knowledgeably the options available and the risks attendant upon each. The average patient has little or no understanding of the medical arts, and ordinarily has only his physician to whom he can look for enlightenment with which to reach an intelligent decision. From these almost axiomatic considerations springs the need, and in turn the requirement, of a reasonable divulgence by physician to patient to make such a decision possible.[15]

A physician is under a duty to treat his patient skillfully but proficiency in diagnosis and therapy is not the full measure of his responsibility. The cases demonstrate that the physician is under an obligation to communicate specific information to the patient when the exigencies of reasonable care call for it. . . .

A reasonable revelation in these respects is not only a necessity but, as we see it, is as much a matter of the physician's duty. It is a duty to warn of the dangers lurking in the proposed treatment, and that is surely a facet of due care. It is, too, a duty to impart information which the patient has every right to expect. The patient's reliance upon the physician is a trust of the kind which traditionally has exacted obligations beyond those associated with arms length transactions. His dependence upon the physician for information affecting his well-being, in terms of contemplated treatment, is well-nigh abject. As earlier noted, long before the instant litigation arose, courts had recognized that the physician had the responsibility of satisfying the vital informational needs of the patient. More recently, we ourselves have found "in the fiducial qualities of [the physician-patient] relationship the physician's duty to reveal to the patient that which in his best interests it is important that he should know." We now find, as a part of the physician's overall obligation to the patient, a similar duty of reasonable disclosure of the choices with respect to proposed therapy and the dangers inherently and potentially involved.

This disclosure requirement, on analysis, reflects much more of a change in doctrinal emphasis than a substantive addition to malpractice law. It is well established that the physician must seek and secure his patient's consent before commencing an operation or other course of treatment. It is also clear that the consent, to be efficacious, must be free from imposition upon the patient. It is the settled rule that therapy not authorized by the patient may amount to a tort—a common law battery—by the physician. And it is evident that it is normally impossible to obtain a consent worthy of the name unless the physician first elucidates the options and the perils for the patient's edification. Thus the

---

[12] Schloendorff v. Society of New York Hospital, 211 N.Y. 125, 105 N.E. 92, 93 (1914). . . .

[15] In duty-to-disclose cases, the focus of attention is more properly upon the nature and content of the physician's divulgence than the patient's understanding or consent. Adequate disclosure and informed consent are, of course, two sides of the same coin—the former a sine qua non of the latter. But the vital inquiry on duty to disclose relates to the physician's performance of an obligation, while one of the difficulties with analysis in terms of "informed consent" is its tendency to imply that what is decisive is the degree of the patient's comprehension. As we later emphasize, physician discharges the duty when he makes a reasonable effort to convey sufficient information although the patient, without fault of the physician, may not fully grasp it. . . .

physician has long borne a duty, on pain of liability for unauthorized treatment, to make adequate disclosure to the patient.[36] . . .

Duty to disclose has gained recognition in a large number of American jurisdictions, but more largely on a different rationale. The majority of courts dealing with the problem have made the duty depend on whether it was the custom of physicians practicing in the community to make the particular disclosure to the patient. . . . We agree that the physician's noncompliance with a professional custom to reveal, like any other departure from prevailing medical practice, may give rise to liability to the patient. We do not agree that the patient's cause of action is dependent upon the existence and nonperformance of a relevant professional tradition.

There are, in our view, formidable obstacles to acceptance of the notion that the physician's obligation to disclose is either germinated or limited by medical practice. To begin with, the reality of any discernible custom reflecting a professional consensus on communication of option and risk information to patients is open to serious doubt. We sense the danger that what in fact is no custom at all may be taken as an affirmative custom to maintain silence, and that physician-witnesses to the so-called custom may state merely their personal opinions as to what they or others would do under given conditions. . . . Respect for the patient's right of self-determination on particular therapy demands a standard set by law for physicians rather than one which physicians may or may not impose upon themselves.

More fundamentally, the majority rule overlooks the graduation of reasonable-care demands in Anglo-American jurisprudence and the position of professional custom in the hierarchy. . . .

There is . . . no basis for operation of the special medical standard where the physician's activity does not bring his medical knowledge and skills peculiarly into play. . . .

[T]he physician's duty to disclose is governed by the same legal principles applicable to others in comparable situations, with modifications only to the extent that medical judgment enters the picture. We hold that the standard measuring performance of that duty by physicians, as by others, is conduct which is reasonable under the circumstances.

Once the circumstances give rise to a duty on the physician's part to inform his patient, the next inquiry is the scope of the disclosure the physician is legally obliged to make. The courts have frequently confronted this problem but no uniform standard defining the adequacy of the divulgence emerges from the decisions. . . .

The larger number of courts, as might be expected, have applied tests framed with reference to prevailing fashion within the medical profession. . . .

---

[36] We discard the thought that the patient should ask for information before the physician is required to disclose. Caveat emptor is not the norm for the consumer of medical services. Duty to disclose is more than a call to speak merely on the patient's request, or merely to answer the patient's questions; it is a duty to volunteer, if necessary, the information the patient needs for intelligent decision. The patient may be ignorant, confused, over-awed by the physician or frightened by the hospital, or even ashamed to inquire. See generally Note, Restructuring Informed Consent: Legal Therapy for the Doctor-Patient Relationship, 79 Yale L.J. 1533, 1545-1551 (1970). . . .

In our view, the patient's right of self-decision shapes the boundaries of the duty to reveal. That right can be effectively exercised only if the patient possesses enough information to enable an intelligent choice. The scope of the physician's communications to the patient, then, must be measured by the patient's need, and that need is the information material to the decision. Thus the test for determining whether a particular peril must be divulged is its materiality to the patient's decision: All risks potentially affecting the decision must be unmasked. And to safeguard the patient's interest in achieving his own determination on treatment, the law must itself set the standard for adequate disclosure.

Optimally for the patient, exposure of a risk would be mandatory whenever the patient would deem it significant to his decision, either singly or in combination with other risks. Such a requirement, however, would summon the physician to second-guess the patient, whose ideas on materiality could hardly be known to the physician. That would make an undue demand upon medical practitioners, whose conduct, like that of others, is to be measured in terms of reasonableness. Consonantly with orthodox negligence doctrine, the physician's liability for nondisclosure is to be determined on the basis of foresight, not hindsight; no less than any other aspect of negligence, the issue on nondisclosure must be approached from the viewpoint of the reasonableness of the physician's divulgence in terms of what he knows or should know to be the patient's informational needs. . . .

From these considerations we derive the breadth of the disclosure of risks legally to be required. The scope of the standard is not subjective as to either the physician or the patient; it remains objective with due regard for the patient's informational needs and with suitable leeway for the physician's situation. In broad outline, we agree that "[a] risk is thus material when a reasonable person, in what the physician knows or should know to be the patient's position, would be likely to attach significance to the risk or cluster of risks in deciding whether or not to forego the proposed therapy."

The topics importantly demanding a communication of information are the inherent and potential hazards of the proposed treatment, the alternatives to that treatment, if any, and the results likely if the patient remains untreated. The factors contributing significance to the dangerousness of a medical technique are, of course, the incidence of injury and the degree of the harm threatened. A very small chance of death or serious disablement may well be significant; a potential disability which dramatically outweighs the potential benefit of the therapy or the detriments of the existing malady may summons discussion with the patient.

There is no bright line separating the significant from the insignificant; the answer in any case must abide a rule of reason. Some dangers — infection, for example — are inherent in any operation; there is no obligation to communicate those of which persons of average sophistication are aware. Even more clearly, the physician bears no responsibility for discussion of hazards the patient has already discovered, or those having no apparent materiality to patients' decision on therapy. . . .

No more than breach of any other legal duty does nonfulfillment of the physician's obligation to disclose alone establish liability to the patient. An unrevealed risk that should have been made known must materialize, for otherwise the omission, however unpardonable, is legally without consequence.

Occurrence of the risk must be harmful to the patient, for negligence unrelated to injury is nonactionable. And, as in malpractice actions generally, there must be a causal relationship between the physician's failure to adequately divulge and damage to the patient.

A causal connection exists when, but only when, disclosure of significant risks incidental to treatment would have resulted in a decision against it. The patient obviously has no complaint if he would have submitted to the therapy notwithstanding awareness that the risk was one of its perils. On the other hand, the very purpose of the disclosure rule is to protect the patient against consequences which, if known, he would have avoided by foregoing the treatment. The more difficult question is whether the factual issue on causality calls for an objective or a subjective determination. . . .

It has been assumed that the issue is to be resolved according to whether the factfinder believes the patient's testimony that he would not have agreed to the treatment if he had known of the danger which later ripened into injury. . . .

In our view, this method of dealing with the issue on causation comes in second-best. It places the physician in jeopardy of the patient's hindsight and bitterness. It places the factfinder in the position of deciding whether a speculative answer to a hypothetical question is to be credited. It calls for a subjective determination solely on testimony of a patient-witness shadowed by the occurrence of the undisclosed risk.

Better it is, we believe, to resolve the causality issue on an objective basis: in terms of what a prudent person in the patient's position would have decided if suitably informed of all perils bearing significance. If adequate disclosure could reasonably be expected to have caused that person to decline the treatment because of the revelation of the kind of risk or danger that resulted in harm, causation is shown, but otherwise not. The patient's testimony is relevant on that score of course but it would not threaten to dominate the findings. . . .

In the context of trial of a suit claiming inadequate disclosure of risk information by a physician, the patient has the burden of going forward with evidence tending to establish prima facie the essential elements of the cause of action, and ultimately the burden of proof — the risk of nonpersuasion — on those elements. . . . The burden of going forward with evidence pertaining to a privilege not to disclose, however, rests properly upon the physician. . . .

We now delineate our view on the need for expert testimony in nondisclosure cases. . . .

The guiding consideration our decisions distill, however, is that medical facts are for medical experts and other facts are for any witnesses — expert or not — having sufficient knowledge and capacity to testify to them. It is evident that many of the issues typically involved in nondisclosure cases do not reside peculiarly within the medical domain. Lay witness testimony can competently establish a physician's failure to disclose particular risk information, the patient's lack of knowledge of the risk, and the adverse consequences following the treatment. Experts are unnecessary to a showing of the materiality of a risk to a patient's decision on treatment, or to the reasonably, expectable effect of risk disclosure on the decision. These conspicuous examples of permissible uses of nonexpert testimony illustrate the relative freedom of broad areas of the legal problem of risk nondisclosure from the demands for expert testimony that shackle plaintiffs' other types of medical malpractice litigation. . . .

This brings us to the remaining question . . . whether appellant's evidence was of such caliber as to require a submission to the jury. [T]he evidence was clearly sufficient to raise an issue as to whether Dr. Spence's obligation to disclose information on risks was reasonably met or was excused by the surrounding circumstances. Appellant testified that Dr. Spence revealed to him nothing suggesting a hazard associated with the laminectomy. His mother testified that, in response to her specific inquiry, Dr. Spence informed her that the laminectomy was no more serious than any other operation. When, at trial, it developed from Dr. Spence's testimony that paralysis can be expected in 1 percent of laminectomies, it became the jury's responsibility to decide whether that peril was of sufficient magnitude to bring the disclosure duty into play. There was no emergency to frustrate an opportunity to disclose, and Dr. Spence's expressed opinion that disclosure would have been unwise did not foreclose a contrary conclusion by the jury. There was no evidence that appellant's emotional makeup was such that concealment of the risk of paralysis was medically sound. Even if disclosure to appellant himself might have bred ill consequences, no reason appears for the omission to communicate the information to his mother, particularly in view of his minority. The jury, not Dr. Spence, was the final arbiter of whether nondisclosure was reasonable under the circumstances. . . .

Reversed and remanded for new trial.

CULBERTSON v. MERNITZ
602 N.E.2d 98 (Ind. 1992)

KRAHULIK, Justice.

Roland B. Mernitz, M.D., (Appellee-Defendant) seeks transfer from the Court of Appeals' reversal of a summary judgment entered in his favor. Culbertson v. Mernitz (1992), Ind. App., 591 N.E.2d 1040. The issue squarely presented in this petition is whether expert medical testimony is required to establish the standard of care of health care providers on the issue of informed consent. . . .

The facts of the case are as follows. Dr. Mernitz first saw Patty Jo Culbertson on March 28, 1988. Her chief complaint was that of uncontrollable leakage of urine and discharge from the vagina. After performing a physical examination, Dr. Mernitz . . . recommend[ed] . . . that she . . . undergo a surgical procedure known as a MMK [Marshall Marchetti Krantz] procedure in order to suspend the bladder and either a hysterectomy or cryosurgery to freeze the infected tip of the cervix. Dr. Mernitz contends that he advised her of the general risks of any surgery, viz. infection, bleeding, and death, and that, with respect to the bladder suspension, he explained to her the risk that the procedure could fail and the possibility that she would be unable to void. . . . Both parties . . . agree that Dr. Mernitz did not advise her of a risk that the cervix could become adhered to the wall of the vagina.

Following this office visit, Mrs. Culbertson decided to proceed with the bladder suspension and cryosurgery. She was admitted to the hospital and underwent these procedures. Post-surgically, Mrs. Culbertson's cervix adhered to the wall of her vagina. Dr. Mernitz prescribed medication for this condition, but Mrs. Culbertson became dissatisfied with his care and saw another surgeon who eventually performed a total abdominal hysterectomy, bilateral salpingo-oophorectomy which involves the removal of both ovaries, and another bladder suspension.

Following this surgery, Mr. and Mrs. Culbertson filed a proposed complaint against Dr. Mernitz with the Indiana Department of Insurance in four counts. . . . Count II alleged that Dr. Mernitz failed to inform Mrs. Culbertson of the alternatives to surgery and the inherent risks and complications of surgery. . . .

A medical review panel was convened and, after submission of evidence to it, issued its written opinion. . . . With respect to the informed consent issue alleged in Count II, the panel ruled:

> The Panel determines that [Dr. Mernitz] did not advise [Mrs. Culbertson] of the complication of cervical adhesion to the vagina; the Panel further determines that such non-disclosure does not constitute a failure to comply with the appropriate standard of care, as such complication is not considered a risk of such surgery requiring disclosure to the patient.

The Culbertsons filed their civil action in a complaint that mirrored the allegations of the proposed complaint. After answering this complaint, Dr. Mernitz moved for summary judgment relying on the expert opinion issued by the medical review panel. The Culbertsons did not file an affidavit or other evidence in opposition to the motion for summary judgment, but argued to the trial court that the "prudent patient" standard should be utilized in evaluating informed consent claims. The trial court entered summary judgment [for the defendants]. . . . [W]e must determine the role, if any, played by expert medical opinion in resolving claims of medical malpractice premised upon a failure to obtain an informed consent.

The courts, historically, have established the standard of care required of physicians when treating patients. The law requires that a physician treating a patient possess and exercise that degree of skill and care ordinarily possessed and exercised by a physician treating such maladies.

. . . In order for a lay jury to know whether a physician complied with the legally prescribed standard of care, expert testimony has generally been held to be required. This requirement was premised on the logical belief that a non-physician could not know what a reasonably prudent physician would or would not have done under the circumstances of any given case. Therefore, an expert familiar with the practice of medicine needed to establish what a reasonably prudent physician would or would not have done in treating a patient in order to set before the jury a depiction of the reasonably prudent physician against which to judge the actions of the defendant physician. An exception was created in cases of res ipsa loquitur on the premise that in such cases a lay jury did not need guidance from a physician familiar with medical practice as to what was required of a reasonably prudent physician because the deficiency of practice "spoke for itself." Kranda v. Houser-Norborg Med. Corp., 419 N.E.2d 1024, 1042 (Ind. App. 1981). This was the settled law of most American jurisdictions, including Indiana, prior to the early 1970s when two cases on the opposite coasts carved out an additional exception to the requirement of expert medical testimony in the area of "informed consent." [The court summarized Cobbs v. Grant, 8 Cal. 3d 229 (1972), and Canterbury v. Spence, 464 F.2d 772 (D.C. Cir.), cert. denied, 409 U.S. 1064 (1972).]

INFORMED CONSENT IN INDIANA JURISPRUDENCE

[The court reviewed Indiana case law and concluded that Indiana followed the medical malpractice standard in informed consent cases. Under this standard, physicians are required to disclose that which the reasonably careful, skillful and prudent physician would disclose under the same or similar circumstances. In general, medical expert testimony will be required to determine whether a physician has violated her duty, "unless the situation is clearly within the realm of laymen's comprehension."]

Resolution of the issue of the necessity of expert medical testimony in informed consent cases depends on whether the issue is viewed through the eyes of the physician or the patient. When viewed through the eyes of the physician, it is easy to see that a physician should not be required to guess or speculate as to what a hypothetical "reasonably prudent patient" would "need to know" in order to make a determination. A physician should only be required to do that which he is trained to do, namely, conduct himself as a reasonably prudent physician in taking a history, performing a physical examination, ordering appropriate tests, reaching a diagnosis, prescribing a course of treatment, and in discussing with the patient the medical facts of the proposed procedure, including the risks inherent in either accepting or rejecting the proposed course of treatment. From a physician's viewpoint, he should not be called upon to be a "mind reader" with the ability to peer into the brain of a prudent patient to determine what such patient "needs to know," but should simply be called upon to discuss medical facts and recommendations with the patient as a reasonably prudent physician would.

On the other hand, from the patient's viewpoint, the physician should be required to give the patient sufficient information to enable the patient to reasonably exercise the patient's right of self-decision in a knowledgeable manner. Viewed from this vantage point, the patient does not want the medical profession to determine in a paternalistic manner what the patient should or should not be told concerning the course of treatment. Thus, such a patient would view the reasonably prudent physician standard as destroying the patient's right of self-decision and, impliedly, placing such decision under the exclusive domain of the medical profession. While this viewpoint may or may not have been justified in 1972 when *Canterbury* and *Cobbs* were decided, a review of medical ethics standards of care in 1992 should assuage this fear.

The 1992 Code of Medical Ethics, as prepared by the Council on Ethical and Judicial Affairs of the American Medical Association, sets forth the medical profession's standard on informed consent. It reads as follows:

> The patient's right of self-decision can be effectively exercised only if the patient possesses enough information to enable an intelligent choice. The patient should make his own determination on treatment. The physician's obligation is to

present the medical facts accurately to the patient or to the individual responsible for his care and to make recommendations for management in accordance with good medical practice. The physician has an ethical obligation to help the patient make choices from among the therapeutic alternatives consistent with good medical practice. Informed consent is a basic social policy for which exceptions are permitted (1) where the patient is unconscious or otherwise incapable of consenting and harm from failure to treat is imminent; or (2) when risk-disclosure poses such a serious psychological threat of detriment to the patient as to be medically contraindicated. Social policy does not accept the paternalistic view that the physician may remain silent because divulgence might prompt the patient to forego needed therapy. Rational, informed patients should not be expected to act uniformly, even under similar circumstances, in agreeing to or refusing treatment.

We recognize this statement as a reasonable statement on the issue of informed consent. There is no need to change Indiana law on this issue. We therefore hold that, except in those cases where deviation from the standard of care is a matter commonly known by lay persons, expert medical testimony is necessary to establish whether a physician has or has not complied with the standard of a reasonably prudent physician.

In the present case we cannot say that the risk of the adherence of the cervix to the vaginal wall is a matter commonly known to lay persons. Therefore, the Culbertsons needed to provide expert medical testimony to refute the unanimous opinion issued by the medical review panel in order to present a material issue of fact as to what a reasonably prudent physician would have discussed concerning this proposed surgery. Without the presentation of such expert medical opinion, the trial court could only conclude that there was no genuine issue of material fact and that summary judgment should be entered for Dr. Mernitz.

[Justice Dickson's dissenting opinion is omitted.]

Notes: Competing Disclosure Standards

1. *The Objective Patient-Centered Standard vs. the Professional Standard.* Why did the *Canterbury* court reject the professional standard of disclosure? One criticism of the malpractice standard is that it measures the scope of required disclosures by customary practice rather than by the patient's need to know. The *Culbertson* court considered and rejected this argument, noting that the 1992 Code of Medical Ethics promulgated by the American Medical Association recognizes a physician's duty to provide information to patients. Does *Canterbury*'s material risk standard provide any significant additional protections given current norms of medical practice? A recent empirical study suggests that informed consent claims are more likely to succeed in jurisdictions that have adopted the "patient-centered" standard of disclosure. David M. Studdert, et al., Geographic Variation in Informed Consent Law: Two Standards for Disclosure of Treatment Risks, 4 J. Empirical Studies 103 (2007).

2. *The Implications of Canterbury's Patient-Centered or Material Risk Standard.* How are providers to know whether a risk should be deemed material? Is there any way for a physician to make this determination before providing care for the

patient or before litigating the issue? What factors does the court suggest are relevant to the determination of materiality? How would you advise a physician who is considering whether to inform patients about the following risks associated with a particular type of cosmetic surgery: (1) a 0.01 percent risk of death from anesthesia; (2) a 1 percent risk of severe bleeding that would require a blood transfusion (which carries additional risks, ranging from fever to heart failure to transmission of HIV); (3) a 3 percent risk of postoperative infection (which would require treatment by antibiotics, which carry a small risk of adverse reactions); (4) a 5 percent risk of nerve damage that could lead to localized paralysis and/or loss of sensation; and (5) a 10 percent risk that the cosmetic flaw will not be significantly improved.

Some legislatures have provided "safe harbors" for physicians. In Texas, for example, a Medical Disclosure Panel determines what disclosures should be made for certain types of procedures. Physicians disclosing risks pursuant to the Panel's guidelines enjoy a rebuttable presumption that their informed consent obligations have been met. Failure to follow the guidelines creates a rebuttable presumption of negligence. Tex. Civ. Prac. & Rem. Code §74.106 (2006).

3. *The Professional Disclosure Standard: The Dominant Rule.* About half of the states still follow the "professional" malpractice standard of disclosure rule in informed consent cases. In some states, the standard has been adopted by the courts; in others it has been imposed by the legislature. Jamie Staples King & Benjamin W. Moulton, Rethinking Informed Consent: The Case for Shared Decision-Making, 32 Am. J.L. & Med. 429, 493-501 (2006) (state-by-state summary). In these jurisdictions, medical practice determines whether a particular type of information will be disclosed to patients. The standard protects physicians from liability so long as they disclose that which would be disclosed by the reasonably prudent physician under like or similar circumstances. In *Culbertson,* the court suggests that the professional malpractice standard will protect individual autonomy because it incorporates the view that individuals must be given enough information to make intelligent decisions. Was Mrs. Culbertson given enough information in this case?

4. *The Subjective Patient-Centered Disclosure Standard.* Note that the material risk standard requires the disclosure of information that a reasonable person would consider material in making a determination about treatment. In most circumstances, physicians are not required to provide information about risks that might be considered significant by an individual patient. The *Canterbury* court recognizes this potential defect but finds that the imposition of a subjective disclosure standard would pose an "undue burden" on a physician—unless the physician knows of the patient's idiosyncratic views. See, e.g., Lugenbuhl v. Dowling, 676 So. 2d 602 (La. Ct. App. 1996); Robert Gatter, Informed Consent and the Forgotten Duty of Physician Inquiry, 31 Loy. U. Chi. L.J. 557 (2000). The overwhelming majority of those jurisdictions that use the "material risk" standard have followed the *Canterbury* approach by measuring the scope of disclosure by the objective patient. But cf. Macy v. Blatchford, 8 P.3d 204 (Or. 2000) (evidence of sexual relationship between physician and patient relevant to determine whether physician had met his statutory duty to "explain" proposed treatment because of the possible impact of the relationship on the patient's ability to understand).

5. *Expert Testimony under the Material Risk and Professional Disclosure Standards.* In jurisdictions following the professional disclosure standard, testimony by medical experts obviously will be required to determine whether the defendant met the standard of care. Will a plaintiff in a "material risk" jurisdiction be able to avoid this requirement? Testimony by medical experts will still be required to provide the fact finder with information about the nature and degree of risk associated with particular treatments. Experts may also be needed to help the fact finder determine whether the harm suffered by the plaintiff was caused by the procedure or by the plaintiff's underlying injury. See Annot., 52 A.L.R.3d 1084 (1973).

6. *Whose Duty? Disclosure as a "Professional" Rather Than "Institutional" Obligation.* Another important consequence of the doctrinal origins of the informed consent claim is that its application has been restricted to a limited range of health care professionals. See, e.g., Foster v. Traul, 120 P.3d 278 (Idaho 2005) (physician has duty to obtain informed consent; hospital merely assists in documentation). Should health care institutions have a duty to disclose some types of risks? Should there be an institutional duty to ensure that patients have given their informed consent to care? If so, what should be the doctrinal source of this obligation?

7. *Informed Consent and Battery.* Why couldn't claims of this type be resolved using principles from battery cases? Plaintiffs pleading informed consent violations as battery actions have two key advantages: They do not have to prove a deviation from the standard of care and they have greater access to punitive damages awards. There are drawbacks, of course; a battery theory is difficult to apply where the medical treatment is noninvasive, and a defendant's insurance policy may exclude coverage for intentional torts.

In the typical informed consent claim, the patient has given technical consent to being "touched" by the defendant but argues that consent would not have been given if appropriate disclosures had been made. Courts generally reject battery claims because the patient has "consented" to the touching. In most jurisdictions, battery claims are reserved for those situations in which (1) the patient has not consented to any treatment at all, (2) the health care provider performs a completely different procedure than that for which consent was given, (3) the health care provider performs a procedure on the wrong area of the body, or (4) a different, unconsented-to provider performs the procedure. See, e.g., Gragg v. Calandra, 696 N.E.2d 1282 (Ill. App. Ct. 1998) (allegation that hospital conducted open heart surgery and then maintained patient on life support without patient's or family's consent addressed as medical battery); Coulter v. Thomas, 33 S.W.3d 522 (Ky. 2000) (physician's failure to remove blood pressure cuff as requested by patient addressed in battery claim, not under state informed consent statute); Annot., 39 A.L.R.4th 1034 (1985).

8. *Fraud and Misrepresentation.* Health care providers who misrepresent the risks associated with treatments could be held liable for fraud or misrepresentation. See, e.g., Annot., 42 A.L.R.4th 543 (1985).

9. *Free Speech and Informed Consent.* The First Amendment to the U.S. Constitution protects "freedom of speech." Do governmental efforts to regulate the content of physician-patient communication violate the First Amendment? The Supreme Court has upheld the constitutional validity of state laws that impose specific informed consent obligations on physicians performing abortions.

Planned Parenthood of Southeastern Pennsylvania v. Casey, 505 U.S. 833, 884, (1992). The issue is considered further at pages 470–471.

Notes: The Other Elements of a Nondisclosure Claim

1. *Elements of a Cause of Action.* Plaintiffs in informed consent claims generally will be required to prove that (1) the medical procedure carried a specific risk that was not disclosed, (2) that the physician violated the applicable standard of disclosure, (3) that the undisclosed risk materialized, and (4) that the failure to disclose the information caused the patient's injury.

2. *The Materialization of the Undisclosed Risk.* All jurisdictions require the plaintiff to show that the undisclosed risk actually materialized into harm. As a result, many failures to disclose information are never litigated. Does this make sense? Can you draw a parallel to the concept of proximate cause in traditional negligence actions? If the purpose of the informed consent doctrine is to protect individual autonomy and to encourage the transfer of information, doesn't a violation of the disclosure obligation cause a cognizable injury even without a physical harm? Several commentators have argued that individual autonomy would be better protected through the adoption of a "dignitary tort" doctrine, in which the failure to disclose information would be actionable even in the absence of any physical injury. See, e.g., Alan Meisel, A "Dignitary Tort" as a Bridge between the Idea of Informed Consent and the Law of Informed Consent, 16 L. Med. & Health Care 210, 211-214 (1988); Aaron D. Twerski & Neil B. Cohen, Informed Decision Making and the Law of Torts: The Myth of Justiciable Causation, 1988 U. Ill. L. Rev. 607, 655; Alan J. Weisbard, Informed Consent: The Law's Uneasy Compromise with Ethical Theory, 65 Neb. L. Rev. 749, 763-764 (1986).

How should damages be measured? "The damages analysis . . . involves a comparison between the condition a plaintiff would have been in had he or she been properly informed and not consented to the risk, with the plaintiff's impaired condition as a result of the risk's occurrence." Howard v. University of Medicine & Dentistry of N.J., 800 A.2d 73 (N.J. 2002). The damages calculations can be more difficult when the patient's initial condition is serious and there are no other alternative treatments.

3. *Objective Causation.* The causation issues associated with informed consent actions are somewhat complex. Most jurisdictions — including those applying the material risk standard — will require proof of objective causation. That is, a plaintiff will be required to show that a reasonable patient would not have undergone the treatment had the risk been disclosed. Does this version of the informed consent doctrine adequately protect the patient's right to the information necessary to participate in medical decision-making? Consider the range of circumstances in which the defendant will be found liable for failing to disclose information. The defendant will be held liable only where he or she suggests that a patient undergo a procedure that, had the true risks been disclosed, a reasonable patient would have refused to undergo. Why wouldn't this simply constitute ordinary malpractice?

How much of the "plaintiff's position" is the jury to consider within the limits of objective causation? See Bernard v. Char, 903 P.2d 667, 675-676 (Haw. 1995) (jury permitted to consider whether a reasonable person who was in great pain and who had no health insurance would have opted for tooth extraction or a more expensive root canal procedure); Ashe v. Radiation Oncology Associates, 9 S.W.3d 119, 123-24 (Tenn. 1999) (fact finder applying objective causation rules may take into account characteristics of plaintiff, including "idiosyncrasies, fears, age, medical condition, and religious beliefs"). At what point does the objective causation standard dissolve into a subjective standard?

4. *The Critique of Objective Causation.* Critics of the objective causation standard argue that it undercuts the goal of protecting individual autonomy. The standard is only a rough approximation or a surrogate device for the protection of individual autonomy because it works only so long as the individual is "reasonable." The Oklahoma Supreme Court has agreed:

> The *Canterbury* view certainly severely limits the protection granted an injured patient. To the extent the plaintiff, given an adequate disclosure, would have declined the proposed treatment, and a reasonable person in similar circumstances would have consented, a patient's right of self-determination is irrevocably lost. This basic right to know and decide is the reason for the full-disclosure rule. Accordingly, we decline to jeopardize this right by the imposition of the "reasonable man" standard. . . .
>
> If a plaintiff testifies he would have continued with the proposed treatment had he been adequately informed, the trial is over under either the subjective or objective approach. If he testifies he would not, then the causation problem must be resolved by examining the credibility of plaintiff's testimony. The jury must be instructed that it must find plaintiff would have refused the treatment if he is to prevail.
>
> Although it might be said this approach places a physician at the mercy of a patient's hindsight, a careful practitioner can always protect himself by insuring that he has adequately informed each patient he treats. If he does not breach this duty, a causation problem will not arise. Scott v. Bradford, 606 P.2d 554, 559 (Okla. 1979).

Oklahoma's "subjective causation" approach has not gained many adherents. But see Zalazar v. Vercimak, 633 N.E.2d 1223, 1227 (Ill. App. Ct. 1993) (severely limiting the use of objective causation and expert opinion in informed consent cases arising from cosmetic surgery). For a scholarly analysis of the causation issues in informed cases, see Aaron D. Twerski & Neil B. Cohen, Informed Decision Making and the Law of Torts: The Myth of Justiciable Causation, 1988 U. Ill. L. Rev. 607.

3. Limiting Liability for Failure to Disclose

■ RIZZO v. SCHILLER
445 S.E.2d 153 (Va. 1994)

HASSELL, Justice.

In this appeal, we consider whether the plaintiffs presented sufficient evidence to establish a prima facie case of medical malpractice against a physician who allegedly failed to obtain the mother's informed consent to use obstetrical forceps to deliver her baby.

Michael Sean Rizzo, Jr., by Pamela Rizzo, his mother and next friend, Pamela Rizzo, individually, and Michael Sean Rizzo, Sr., filed this action against Maurice Schiller, M.D. The plaintiffs alleged that Dr. Schiller, an obstetrician and gynecologist, breached the standard of care owed to them when he assisted Ms. Rizzo with the delivery of Michael. Specifically, the plaintiffs alleged that Dr. Schiller was negligent in the use of obstetrical forceps during the delivery and that he failed to obtain Ms. Rizzo's informed consent to use the forceps.

The case was tried before a jury. The trial court granted Dr. Schiller's motion to strike the plaintiffs' informed consent claim. The case proceeded to the jury on the theory that Dr. Schiller was negligent in the use of the obstetrical forceps. The jury returned a verdict in favor of Dr. Schiller, and we awarded the plaintiffs an appeal on issues related to their informed consent claim.

Pamela Rizzo was admitted to Fairfax Hospital on November 7, 1989, about 9:00 A.M. She was in active labor, and Dr. Schiller was notified of her admission. Upon admission to the hospital, Ms. Rizzo signed the following form:

Authorization for Medical and Surgical Procedures

Patient History No. /P/9456

I hereby authorize Dr. Schiller, and/or other members of the Medical Staff of The Fairfax Hospital of his choice, to perform diagnostic or therapeutic medical and surgical procedures on and to administer anesthetics to Pamela Rizzo. I further authorize The Fairfax Hospital to dispose of any removed tissue or amputated parts.

11/07/89   [Signed] *Pamela S. Rizzo*

_____   _____
(Date)   (Signature)
[Signed] *Vera Thomas*

_____   _____
(Witness)   (Relationship)

About 12 hours later, Ms. Rizzo's fetal membranes were artificially ruptured at 8:50 P.M., and about 10:00 P.M., she was "pushing with contractions." At 10:15 P.M., Dr. Schiller ordered that Ms. Rizzo be taken to the delivery room. While in the delivery room, Ms. Rizzo made a few, but unsuccessful, attempts to "push" the baby through the birth canal with her abdominal muscles. When Ms. Rizzo's attempts to "push" were unsuccessful, Dr. Schiller told her that he was going to use forceps to deliver the baby. Ms. Rizzo testified that "before I could even get my composure together, ask what they were for, why, [the forceps] were inside me. And my son's head was out, just the head."

[Michael Rizzo developed a subdural hematoma after his birth. Experts testified that the forceps injured his head, causing the hematoma and Michael's subsequently diagnosed cerebral palsy.]

Dr. Arner qualified as an expert witness on the subjects of obstetrics and gynecology and gave the following testimony. Even though Ms. Rizzo had been given certain medication, she was capable of making medical decisions. Ms. Rizzo would have been able to deliver Michael spontaneously, without the use of forceps, had Dr. Schiller simply waited. If forceps are used in "non-emergent situations," the patient should be informed about the use of the forceps and should be given the opportunity to participate in the decision regarding whether the forceps will be used. Dr. Arner opined that Dr. Schiller breached the standard of care owed to Ms. Rizzo because he failed to allow her to participate in the decision to use forceps.

The plaintiffs contend that the trial court erred by striking their evidence because they established a prima facie case that Dr. Schiller failed to obtain Ms. Rizzo's informed consent for the use of obstetrical forceps during Michael's delivery. Dr. Schiller, however, argues that the plaintiffs' evidence fails to establish a prima facie case and that the plaintiffs failed to present evidence of proximate causation. Furthermore, Dr. Schiller asserts that Ms. Rizzo was allowed to participate in the decision to use forceps because she signed the authorization form. We disagree with Dr. Schiller.

In Hunter v. Burroughs, 96 S.E. 360, 366-367 (1918), we held that "it is the duty of a physician in the exercise of ordinary care to warn a patient of the danger of possible bad consequences of using a remedy," but that the physician's failure to warn "is not per se an act of negligence." Rather, the physician owes a duty to make a reasonable disclosure to the patient of all significant facts under the circumstances. This duty is limited to those disclosures that a reasonable medical practitioner would provide under the same or similar circumstances. Bly v. Rhoads, 222 S.E.2d 783, 785-787 (1976). In most cases, expert testimony is necessary to establish those instances where the duty to disclose arises and what disclosures a reasonable medical practitioner would have made under the same or similar circumstances. Id.

We are of opinion that the plaintiffs presented sufficient evidence to establish a prima facie case that Dr. Schiller failed to obtain Ms. Rizzo's informed consent to use the obstetrical forceps. As we have already mentioned, Dr. Arner testified that the appropriate standard of care required that Dr. Schiller inform Ms. Rizzo about the use of the forceps and that she be given an opportunity to participate in the decision whether to use forceps. Ms. Rizzo testified that Dr. Schiller did not disclose any information to her about the use of the forceps and that he used the forceps without her consent.

It is true that Ms. Rizzo signed a document that purportedly is a consent form. However, this form did not inform her of any specific procedures that Dr. Schiller intended to perform; nor did it inform her of foreseeable risks associated with any procedures or risks in failing to perform any procedures. As Dr. Arner observed, the form is so general in nature that "you could also justify amputating her foot." We hold that the duty imposed upon a physician to obtain a patient's informed consent requires more than simply securing the patient's signature on a generalized consent form, similar to the form present here. The law requires informed consent, not mere consent, and the failure to obtain informed consent is tantamount to no consent.

We are also of opinion that the plaintiffs presented sufficient evidence of proximate causation as an element of their prima facie case. Here, the plaintiffs presented evidence from which the jury might have inferred that had Ms. Rizzo been informed of the possible consequences associated with the use of obstetrical forceps, she would have continued to assist in the birth process by "pushing" and that Michael would have been born spontaneously. The plaintiffs also presented evidence from which the jury could have found that but for the use of the forceps, Michael would not have suffered the brain injury.

Accordingly, we will remand this case for a trial of the plaintiffs' claims of lack of informed consent.

Notes: Limiting Liability for Failure to Disclose

1. *Informed Consent and Competence.* The patient's capacity is an important factor in informed consent cases. Physicians must secure consent from someone who has the legal capacity to give it. See Chapter 3.A.2. See generally Laura B. Dunn et al., Assessing Decisional Capacity for Clinical Research or Treatment: A Review of Instruments, 163 Am. J. Psychiatry 1323 (2006); Bruce J. Winick, Competency to Consent to Treatment: The Distinction Between Assent and Objection, 28 Hous. L. Rev. 15 (1991); Annot., 25 A.L.R.3d 1439 (1969). Consent issues are particularly acute for in the treatment of minors. See generally, Jennifer L. Rosato, Let's Get Real: Quilting a Principled Approach to Adolescent Empowerment in Health Care Decision-Making, 51 DePaul L. Rev. 769 (2002); David Vukadinovich, Minors' Consent Rights to Treatment: Navigating the Complexity of State Laws, 37 J. Health L. 6667 (2004).

Where the patient is incapable of giving consent him- or herself, alternative decisionmaking methods have been adopted by courts and legislatures. These are discussed in Chapter 3.A.3. Did Pamela Rizzo have the capacity to make intelligent health care decisions? Her medical expert testified affirmatively.

2. *The Limits of the Duty to Inform.* Courts and commentators have discussed five general limitations to the duty to disclose:

- *Common Knowledge.* There is no duty to disclose risks "of which persons of average sophistication are aware."
- *Patient Knowledge.* The patient cannot recover for the physician's failure to disclose a risk already known by the patient.
- *Emergencies.* There is no duty to disclose information in an emergency situation where the patient is not competent, immediate treatment is required to prevent more serious harm, and no substitute decision maker is available. The issue of decisionmaking for incompetent persons is considered in more detail at pages 279–292.
- *Therapeutic Privilege.* There is no duty to disclose information where the disclosure process would "foreclose rational decision" or "pose psychological damage" to the patient. The *Canterbury* court was particularly concerned about the need to circumscribe this exception lest it swallow the general rule. For academic commentary on the therapeutic exception, see, e.g., Kathleen M. Boozang, The Therapeutic Placebo: The Case for

Patient Deception, 54 Fla. L. Rev. 687 (2002); Developments in the
Law — Medical Technology and the Law, VI. The Right to Refuse Medical
Treatment, 103 Harv. L. Rev. 1643, 1676 (1990). There are few reported
applications of the rule. See, e.g., Barrai v. Betwee, 50 P.3d 946 (Haw.
2002) (psychiatrist fails to establish therapeutic privilege exception); and
Marsingill v. O'Malley, 58 P.3d 495 (Alaska 2002) (plaintiffs essentially
claim that physician should have applied the therapeutic privilege by
withholding information about the likelihood that emergency room
treatment would be painful or uncomfortable; patient allegedly suffered
injuries from her decision to delay seeking emergency medical assistance
after hearing about the nature of the likely treatment).

- *Waiver.* Although there are few court decisions on the issue, the disclosure
  doctrine's grounding in autonomy suggests that patients should be able to
  refuse information offered by the physician. See Stover v. Association of
  Thoracic & Cardiovascular Surgeons, 635 A.2d 1047, 1055-1056 (Pa.
  Super. Ct. 1993); & Mark A. Hall, A Theory of Economic Informed
  Consent, 31 Ga. L. Rev. 511 (1997).

These limitations on the duty to disclose may be announced by courts or, in
professional disclosure standard jurisdictions, may be established by the testimony
of medical experts. The defendant generally has the burden of proving that an
exception to the duty to inform is present. For a general discussion of exceptions
to the duty to disclose, see Alan Meisel, The "Exceptions" to the Informed
Consent Doctrine: Striking a Balance Between Competing Values in Medical
Decisionmaking, 1979 Wis. L. Rev. 413.

3. *The "Consent" Process, or the Use of Forms.* Critics of the informed consent
process argue that the ideal of a meaningful exchange of information between
patient and physician has been replaced with the ritual of the informed consent
form. How does the *Rizzo* court analyze the validity of the informed consent
document signed by the plaintiff? Why shouldn't a physician be entitled to rely
upon informed consent forms as a shield to liability? How was the document
defective? Who should draft informed consent documents — health care providers
or attorneys? Would a physician relying on the validity of an informed consent
form have a malpractice claim against the drafter?

Physician defendants hope that a signed consent form will foreclose any
informed consent claim. It is true that a properly completed form can establish at
least a presumption that a patient has consented to treatment. Sometimes the
presumption is established by statute. See, e.g., Ohio Rev. Code Ann. §2317.54. A
form indicating only that a patient has received information and consents is
probably not sufficient. See, e.g., Havens v. Hoffman, 902 P.2d 219, 223 (Wyo.
1995) (overturning physician's summary judgment; hospital form is an acknowledgment of the receipt of information but does not indicate the nature of the
information disclosed). Should a signed consent form bar recovery where the
patient did not read the disclosure before signing and where the physician failed
to determine whether the form had been read? Roberts v. Cox, 669 So. 2d 633,
640 (La. Ct. App. 1996) (jury determination that informed consent doctrine
satisfied not "manifestly erroneous").

4. *Informed Consent Forms in Hospitals.* Hospital employees, such as nurses, often procure patients' signatures on informed consent forms prior to surgery. Does this mean that hospitals have a duty to obtain the informed consent of patients? Courts routinely find that the answer is "no." The duty to obtain informed consent is the physician's; the hospital's involvement in the process normally is considered to be merely facilitative. Annot., 88 A.L.R.3d 1008 (1978). For a cogent critique, see Robert Gatter, The Mysterious Survival of the Policy Against Informed Consent Liability for Hospitals, 81 Notre Dame L. Rev. 1203 (2006).

5. *Forms and Assumption of Risk.* An informed consent form is essentially a written documentation of the patient's assumption of the disclosed risks, assumed in order to achieve a procedure's potential benefits. See Karp v. Cooley, 493 F.2d 408 (5th Cir. 1974) (directed verdict for the defendant affirmed; patient undergoing first attempted implantation of a mechanical heart had been given extensive information and counseling about the experimental nature of the treatment and its risks). Patients ordinarily are not permitted, however, to assume the risk that a procedure will be negligently recommended or performed; they assume only the risks that are non-negligently produced. In the typical case, then, a signed informed consent form signifies that the patient was informed of the required risks and agreed to accept those risks; a form is powerful evidence of a physician's compliance with the duty to disclose but is irrelevant to an ordinary malpractice action brought against a physician for delivering substandard care.

As is often true in legal matters, things are not quite this simple, however. Informed consent and ordinary malpractice overlap and interact in several important respects. Where there are alternative standards of care or courses of treatment, obtaining informed consent may be important to the physician's malpractice defense that the physician complied with a "respectable minority" point of view. For instance, informed consent can justify departing from customary practice in order to participate in medical research or to try out an untested procedure. Similarly, informed consent might be used to bolster an affirmative defense that the patient assumed the risk or was contributorily negligent. See, e.g., Smith v. Hull, 659 N.E.2d 185 (Ind. Ct. App. 1995) (in a case involving injuries from treatment for baldness, a contributory negligence finding "was supported by evidence that patient sought out physician and hair injection procedure, received extensive literature and discussed risks with physician, and signed consent forms prior to undergoing procedures, . . . leav[ing] us with little doubt that Smith's desire to sport a full head of hair motivated him to pursue remedies that he knowingly undertook at his own peril").

6. *Contributory Negligence.* Should patients have an obligation to truthfully disclose information to their physicians? Should the obligation arise only in response to a physician's inquiries, or should patients have a duty to affirmatively disclose matters that a reasonable patient would think might be relevant to his or her medical treatment? In Brown v. Dibbell, 595 N.W.2d 358 (Wis. 1999), the court held that

> for patients to exercise ordinary care, they must tell the truth and give complete
> and accurate information about personal, family, and medical histories to a doctor

> to the extent possible in response to the doctor's requests for information when the requested information is material to a doctor's duty as prescribed by . . . [the informed consent statute] and that a patient's breach of that duty might, under certain circumstances, constitute contributory negligence. Id. at 368-369.

The court did not consider whether patients had a duty to disclose information sua sponte.

7. *Injury and Causation.* Note that Ms. Rizzo's claim would have failed if the undisclosed risk had not materialized, that is, if the use of forceps had not resulted in her son's injuries. How did Dr. Schiller's failure to disclose the risks associated with using forceps cause Michael Rizzo's injuries? The court holds that the plaintiffs presented sufficient evidence of proximate causation for a jury to decide in their favor. A jury could have decided that Ms. Rizzo, had she been appropriately informed, might have rejected the use of forceps and continued to "push" and that Michael's brain injuries would not have occurred. Assume that you represent the defendant. What types of counter-evidence might you want to present on this issue?

8. *Alternative Treatments.* Under the professional malpractice standard, a physician must disclose treatment alternatives if the reasonable, competent physician would have done so. The existence of alternative treatments would also be considered "material" under the patient-centered standard of disclosure. Annot., 38 A.L.R.4th 900 (1985). What should be the physician's disclosure obligation where a treatment alternative is not readily available, perhaps because of cost considerations or geographic location? See, e.g., Mark Hall, A Theory of Economic Informed Consent, 31 Ga. L. Rev. 511 (1997). Should the physician be required to disclose the option of "doing nothing"? See, e.g., Wecker v. Amend, 918 P.2d 658 (Kan. Ct. App. 1996) (yes).

9. *Informed Consent and the Therapeutic Placebo.* Physicians and medical researchers have long believed in the "placebo effect," under which some patients appear to improve after the administration of spurious "treatment," although some recent research results suggest that the effect may be overstated. See Franklin G. Miller & Donald L. Rosenstein, The Nature and Power of the Placebo Effect, 59 J. Clin. Epid. 331 (2006); John C. Bailar, The Powerful Placebo and the Wizard of Oz, 344 New Eng. J. Med. 1630 (2001); Asbjorn Hrobjarsson & Peter C. Gotzsche, Is the Placebo Powerless?, 344 New Eng. J. Med. 1594 (2001); The Placebo Effect: An Interdisciplinary Exploration (Anne Harrington ed., 1997). Does the informed consent doctrine implicitly prohibit the use of placebos? Can you design a method of using placebos that would allow physicians (and patients) to gain the benefits of the placebo effect without violating the disclosure doctrine? See Kathleen M. Boozang, The Therapeutic Placebo: The Case for Patient Deception, 54 U. Fla. L. Rev. 687 (2002).

10. *Diagnostic Tests vs. Treatments.* Should the duty to disclose alternatives depend on whether a treatment or a diagnostic test is at issue? Compare McGeshick v. Choucair, 9 F.3d 1229 (7th Cir. 1993) (Wisconsin informed consent statute does not impose duty to inform patient about diagnostic alternatives), with Martin v. Richards, 531 N.W.2d 70 (Wis. 1995) (statute covers diagnostic tests as well as treatments). Under the professional malpractice standard, the answer presumably would depend on whether the competent physician would disclose the

information. *Martin* is a singularly interesting case, in which parents sued an emergency room physician for failing to disclose that a CT scan was available to examine their child and for failing to disclose that if the child had intracranial bleeding, she would have to be transferred to another facility. The child developed intracranial bleeding, which, though eventually treated, left her with partial spastic quadriplegia. The Wisconsin Supreme Court held that a physician's duty to discuss alternatives was broad enough to encompass a failure to disclose the existence of additional diagnostic techniques.

11. *Law in Books, Law in Action, and the "New" Model of Shared Decisionmaking.* Does the informed consent duty established under malpractice principles provide adequate protection for patient autonomy? Does it protect physicians from unwarranted intrusions into professional autonomy?

There have been flurries of reformist proposals over the past ten years exploiting the many weaknesses of the current legal approach to informed consent and advocating some form of "shared medical decisionmaking." Although the model has many variations, a recent description is typical:

> Shared medical decision-making is a process in which the physician shares with the patient all relevant risk and benefit information on all treatment alternatives and the patient shares with the physician all relevant personal information that might make one treatment or side effect more or less tolerable than others. Then, both parties use this information to come to a mutual medical decision. Jamie Staples King & Benjamin W. Moulton, Rethinking Informed Consent: The Case for Shared Medical Decision-Making, 32 Am. J. L. & Med. 429, 431 (2006) (citations omitted).

Does this approach seem to address the problems with the current informed consent rules? Can you identify any practical or legal issues with the implementation of shared medical decisionmaking? For a recent critique of the model, see Carl E. Schneider, Void for Vagueness, Hastings Center Rep. 10 (Jan.-Feb. 2006)

Discussion Problem: Informed Refusals?

Dr. Claude R. Thomas was Mrs. Rena Truman's personal physician from 1963 to 1969. In 1969, another physician discovered that Mrs. Truman had advanced cervical cancer. Mrs. Truman died in 1970, at the age of 30. Rena Truman's children sued Dr. Thomas for failing to perform a Pap test on Mrs. Truman between 1964 and 1969. Trial testimony indicated that (1) if the Pap smear had been performed during this time period, Mrs. Truman's condition would have been discovered at an earlier stage and she probably would have lived; (2) medical practice required physicians to inform women of the purpose of a Pap test; and (3) Dr. Thomas repeatedly advised Mrs. Truman to undergo the test but did not specifically explain the possible consequences of her refusal. Consider this case under the professional and material risk standards of disclosure. What arguments can you make on behalf of Mrs. Truman's children? What arguments or defenses might you raise on behalf of Dr. Thomas? See Truman v. Thomas, 611 P.2d 902 (Cal. 1980).

4. Fiduciary Obligations, Conflicts of Interest, and Novel Disclosure Obligations

This chapter demonstrates that courts modify pure contract and tort principles to provide special protections for patients. This is done with the implied or expressed belief that the treatment relationship is a fiduciary one, in which the physician owes heightened duties to protect the vulnerable patient's interests. This section explores the extent to which physicians have fiduciary obligations to their patients, as well as the implications of those obligations.

Fiduciary law can be thought of as a separate source of distinct legal duties or as a legal status that heightens or alters ordinary contract and tort law duties. Fiduciary principles impose a special measure of loyalty and devotion on several classes of professionals (lawyers, trustees, and general agents) by virtue of their control over important matters, the vulnerability of their clients, and the resulting potential for abuse. The materials in Chapter 1.B.3 explain why some courts have found that "the relationship of patients and physicians is a fiduciary one of the highest degree. It involves every element of trust, confidence and good faith."[1] Doctors possess a complex body of knowledge and skills that are critical to preserving the life and restoring the health of their patients. Doctors control their patients' welfare in the most vital aspects imaginable. Sick patients, by virtue of their debilitated and vulnerable state, are dependent on their physicians' judgments and actions. Accurate diagnosis requires that patients reveal the most personal details of their lives, and effective treatment often entails invasion of the most essential aspects of bodily intimacy, invading the very blood and guts of our integrated sense of self. Thus many legal decisions and commentators have recognized doctors' fiduciary status.[2] For a sampling of the literature, see Marc A. Rodwin, Medicine, Money and Morals: Physicians' Conflicts of Interest (1993); Peter D. Jacobson, Strangers in the Night: Law and Medicine in the Managed Care Era (2002); Maxwell J. Mehlman, Fiduciary Contracting: Limitations on Bargaining Between Patients and Health Care Providers, 51 U. Pitt. L. Rev. 365, 388-416 (1990); Frances H. Miller, Trusting Doctors: Tricky Business When It Comes to Clinical Research, 81 B.U. L. Rev. 423 (2001); Michelle Oberman, Mothers and Doctors' Orders: Unmasking the Doctor's Fiduciary Role in Maternal-Fetal Conflicts, 94 Nw. U. L. Rev. 451 (2000); Mark A. Hall et al., Trust in Physicians and Medical Institutions: What Is It, Can It Be Measured, and Does It Matter?, 79 Milbank Q. 613 (2001); Mark A. Hall, Law, Medicine, and Trust, 55 Stan. L. Rev. 463 (2002); Robert Gatter, Faith, Confidence and Health Care: Fostering Trust in Medicine Through Law, 39 Wake Forest L. Rev. 395, 396 (2004); and Mark A. Hall, Caring, Curing, and Trust: A Response to Gatter, 39 Wake Forest L. Rev. 447 (2004).

---

[1] Lockett v. Goodill, 430 P.2d 589, 591 (Wash. 1967).
[2] Some authorities, however, distinguish confidential relations from fiduciary relations and declare that physicians are subject only to the former. See, e.g., Restatement (Third) of Trusts §2 cmt. b(1) (2003); 1 Austin W. Scott & William F. Fratcher, The Law of Trusts §2.5, at 43 (4th ed. 1987). The primary thrust of the distinction, however, is burden of proof, not scope of obligation. The law does not assume that a position of trust exists in a confidential relation as readily as it does for a fiduciary one, but where such trust exists, the duties are essentially the same.

Depending on the jurisdiction, the informed consent doctrine has grown out of the rich soil of cases involving fiduciary law, as well as battery and malpractice. The doctrine has the potential for continued expansive growth, particularly in those jurisdictions emphasizing a physician's fiduciary obligations over the professional standard of care. In these states, the scope of informed consent is not limited by the current standard of professional conduct. As you read the following cases, consider whether the courts have gone too far or not far enough in regulating the scope of physician disclosure. Does the imposition of liability in these cases seem "just"? Do the courts' decisions seem consistent with the informed consent doctrine they purport to apply? What is the likely impact of these decisions on the nature of physician-patient communications? Are patients more likely to receive important information? What will physicians do to minimize liability?

■ AUTONOMY AND PRIVACY: PROTECTING PATIENTS FROM THEIR PHYSICIANS
Mary Anne Bobinski
55 U. Pitt. L. Rev. 291, 347-356 (1994)

. . . Jurisdictions with more generous disclosure requirements typically rely, at least in part, on fiduciary principles as a basis for the disclosure obligation. Fiduciary law thus presents a possible avenue for future growth of a more vibrant disclosure duty. Tort law and the law governing fiduciary relationships are similar in that they impose extra-contractual duties on individuals. The two regulatory schemes, however, differ in conception of those duties. Tort law most often imposes general duties irrespective of the status of the parties. The law of fiduciaries, in contrast, is based on the special character of the relationship between two parties. Courts struggling to define the scope of tort-based disclosure duties have often noted the fiducial characteristics of the doctor-patient relationship as a justification for disclosure. This linkage between ordinary tort and fiduciary principles creates the opportunity for both growth and confusion. Ordinary tort duties may be expanded or amplified because of the perceived relevance of fiduciary principles. To date, few courts have explicitly considered the implications of wholesale acceptance of the doctor-patient relationship as one subject to fiduciary law. There has been little judicial analysis of the appropriateness of applying fiduciary-based disclosure obligations to the physician-patient relationship, and virtually no judicial analysis of the special problems presented by provider-associated risk.

The first question is whether the relationship between physicians and patients is a fiduciary one. Fiduciary relationships are generally described as those in which some aspect of the relationship between the parties [such as an imbalance of power or knowledge] justifies the imposition of special obligations on one of them. Several treatises on fiduciary law name the physician-patient relationship as a fiduciary one and the courts have tended to concur.

Next, the fiduciary duties that physicians owe to patients must be determined. Generally, a fiduciary must act for the benefit of another, but the specific duties imposed on a fiduciary will vary with the scope of the relationship between the parties. The fiduciary owes a duty of loyalty, "good faith, trust, special confidence and candor" to the other party. Obviously, it is not a breach of the fiduciary relationship for the fiduciary to receive compensation for her services. However, the fiduciary can breach her duty by engaging in self-dealing, by receiving bribes or kickbacks, or by misappropriating that knowledge or property which belongs to the entrustor. The role of disclosure in fiduciary law is somewhat complicated. The fiduciary's failure to disclose information to the entrustor can constitute an independent breach of fiduciary duty when the information was gathered in the course of the fiduciary's duties. Disclosure may also help determine whether an apparent breach of fiduciary duties has been "cured" by the consent of the entrustor. The validity of the entrustor's consent will be the important question because the fiduciary's influence over the entrustor may make any consent presumptively invalid. Disclosure in these cases is of evidentiary significance; it may bolster the fiduciary's claim that the entrustor's consent to the transaction was valid. As a substantive matter, disclosure may not be sufficient where the fiduciary's influence over the entrustor makes any — even informed — consent illusory. . . .

This analysis of fiduciary principles assumes that a breach will provide some effective remedy for patients. A fiduciary is liable to the entrustor for a breach of fiduciary duties. A breach of a fiduciary obligation can be remedied by voiding a transaction, by payment by the fiduciary to the trusting party of any impermissible benefits or profits, or by payment by the fiduciary to compensate the other party for actual damages, which may include compensation for personal injury. Courts are divided on whether the entrustor is required to show some specific injury flowed from the fiduciary's breach of her duties.

The significant number of courts that have applied fiduciary principles to the physician-patient relationship can be deceiving. Most courts have failed to consider the broader policy implications of classifying the physician-patient relationship as a fiduciary one; most have also failed to analyze the range of physicians' required fiduciary duties. Some courts have responded to these problems by hedging, noting that the relationship has fiducial "qualities" or "characteristics" or finding that it is a "confidential" relationship. . . .

The . . . [most important] judicial consideration of common law economic disclosure obligations occurred in Moore v. Regents of the University of California. . . .

■ MOORE v. THE REGENTS OF THE UNIVERSITY OF CALIFORNIA
793 P.2d 479 (Cal. 1990), cert. denied, 499 U.S. 936 (1991)

PANELLI, Justice.

We granted review in this case to determine whether plaintiff has stated a cause of action against his physician and other defendants for using his cells in potentially lucrative medical research without his permission. Plaintiff alleges that his physician failed to disclose preexisting research and economic interests in the cells before obtaining consent to the medical procedures by which they were extracted. . . . We hold that the complaint states a cause of action for breach of the physician's disclosure obligations, but not for conversion.

FACTS

. . . The plaintiff is John Moore (Moore), who underwent treatment for hairy-cell leukemia at the Medical Center of the University of California at Los Angeles (UCLA Medical Center). The five defendants are: (1) Dr. David W. Golde (Golde), a physician who attended Moore at UCLA Medical Center; (2) the Regents of the University of California (Regents), who own and operate the university; (3) Shirley G. Quan, a researcher employed by the Regents; (4) Genetics Institute, Inc. (Genetics Institute); and (5) Sandoz Pharmaceuticals Corporation and related entities (collectively Sandoz).

Moore first visited UCLA Medical Center on October 5, 1976, shortly after he learned that he had hairy-cell leukemia. After hospitalizing Moore and "withdrawing extensive amounts of blood, bone marrow aspirate, and other bodily substances," Golde confirmed that diagnosis. At this time all defendants, including Golde, were aware that "certain blood products and blood components were of great value in a number of commercial and scientific efforts" and that access to a patient whose blood contained these substances would provide "competitive, commercial, and scientific advantages."

On October 8, 1976, Golde recommended that Moore's spleen be removed. Golde informed Moore "that he had reason to fear for his life, and that the proposed splenectomy operation . . . was necessary to slow down the progress of his disease." Based upon Golde's representations, Moore signed a written consent form authorizing the splenectomy.

Before the operation, Golde and Quan "formed the intent and made arrangements to obtain portions of [Moore's] spleen following its removal" and to take them to a separate research unit. Golde gave written instructions to this effect on October 18 and 19, 1976. These research activities "were not intended to have . . . any relation to [Moore's] medical . . . care." However, neither Golde nor Quan informed Moore of their plans to conduct this research or requested his permission. Surgeons at UCLA Medical Center, whom the complaint does not name as defendants, removed Moore's spleen on October 20, 1976.

Moore returned to the UCLA Medical Center several times between November 1976 and September 1983. He did so at Golde's direction and based upon representations "that such visits were necessary and required for his health and well-being, and based upon the trust inherent in and by virtue of the physician-patient relationship. . . . " On each of these visits Golde withdrew additional samples of "blood, blood serum, skin, bone marrow aspirate, and sperm." On each occasion Moore travelled to the UCLA Medical Center from his home in Seattle because he had been told that the procedures were to be performed only there and only under Golde's direction.

"In fact, [however,] throughout the period of time that [Moore] was under [Golde's] care and treatment, . . . the defendants were actively involved in a number of activities which they concealed from [Moore]. . . . " Specifically, defendants were conducting research on Moore's cells and planned to "benefit financially and competitively . . . [by exploiting the cells] and [their] exclusive access to [the cells] by virtue of [Golde's] on-going physician-patient relationship. . . . "

Sometime before August 1979, Golde established a cell line from Moore's T-lymphocytes.[2] On January 30, 1981, the Regents applied for a patent on the cell line, listing Golde and Quan as inventors. "[B]y virtue of an established policy . . . , [the] Regents, Golde, and Quan would share in any royalties or profits . . . arising out of [the] patent." The patent issued on March 20, 1984, naming Golde and Quan as the inventors of the cell line and the Regents as the assignee of the patent. The Regent's patent also covers various methods for using the cell line to produce lymphokines. Moore admits in his complaint that "the true clinical potential of each of the lymphokines . . . [is] difficult to predict, [but] . . . competing commercial firms in these relevant fields have published reports in biotechnology industry periodicals predicting a potential market of approximately $3.01 Billion Dollars by the year 1990 for a whole range of [such lymphokines]. . . . " [Golde and his associates received several hundred thousand dollars over the next three years plus shares of stock, under agreements with Genetics Institute to develop the cell line products.]

Based upon these allegations, Moore attempted to state 13 causes of action.[4] . . . [T]he superior court sustained a general demurrer to the entire complaint. . . .

DISCUSSION

A. BREACH OF FIDUCIARY DUTY AND LACK OF INFORMED CONSENT

Moore repeatedly alleges that Golde failed to disclose the extent of his research and economic interests in Moore's cells[6] before obtaining consent to the medical procedures by which the cells were extracted. These allegations, in our view, state a cause of action against Golde for invading a legally protected interest of his patient. This cause of action can properly be characterized either as the breach of a fiduciary duty to disclose facts material to the patient's consent or, alternatively, as the performance of medical procedures without first having obtained the patient's informed consent.

Our analysis begins with three well-established principles. First, "a person of adult years and in sound mind has the right, in the exercise of control over his own body, to determine whether or not to submit to lawful medical treatment." Cobbs v. Grant, 8 Cal. 3d 229, 242 (1972). Second, "the patient's consent to

---

[2] A T-lymphocyte is a type of white blood cell. T-lymphocytes produce lymphokines, or proteins that regulate the immune system. Some lymphokines have potential therapeutic value. If the genetic material responsible for producing a particular lymphokine can be identified, it can sometimes be used to manufacture large quantities of the lymphokine through the techniques of recombinant DNA. . . . Moore's T-lymphocytes were interesting to the defendants because they overproduced certain lymphokines, thus making the corresponding genetic material easier to identify. . . .

[4] (1) "Conversion"; (2) "lack of informed consent"; (3) "breach of fiduciary duty"; (4) "fraud and deceit"; (5) "unjust enrichment"; (6) "quasi-contract"; (7) "bad faith breach of the implied covenant of good faith and fair dealing"; (8) "intentional infliction of emotional distress"; (9) "negligent misrepresentation"; (10) "intentional interference with prospective advantageous economic relationships"; (11) "slander of title"; (12) "accounting"; and (13) "declaratory relief."

[6] In this opinion we use the inclusive term *cells* to describe all of the cells taken from Moore's body, including blood cells, bone marrow, spleen, etc.

treatment, to be effective, must be an informed consent." *Cobbs*, 8 Cal. 3d at 242. Third, in soliciting the patient's consent, a physician has a fiduciary duty to disclose all information material to the patient's decision.

These principles lead to the following conclusions: (1) A physician must disclose personal interests unrelated to the patient's health, whether research or economic, that may affect the physician's professional judgment; and (2) a physician's failure to disclose such interests may give rise to a cause of action for performing medical procedures without informed consent or breach of fiduciary duty. . . .

Indeed, the law already recognizes that a reasonable patient would want to know whether a physician has an economic interest that might affect the physician's professional judgment. As the Court of Appeal has said, "[c]ertainly a sick patient deserves to be free of any reasonable suspicion that his doctor's judgment is influenced by a profit motive." Magan Medical Clinic v. Cal. State Bd. of Medical Examiners, 249 Cal. App. 2d 124, 132 (1967). The desire to protect patients from possible conflicts of interest has also motivated legislative enactments. Among these is Business and Professions Code §654.2. Under that section, a physician may not charge a patient on behalf of, or refer a patient to, any organization in which the physician has a "significant beneficial interest, unless [the physician] first discloses in writing to the patient, that there is such an interest and advises the patient that the patient may choose any organization for the purposes of obtaining the services ordered or requested by [the physician]." Similarly, under Health and Safety Code §24173, a physician who plans to conduct a medical experiment on a patient must, among other things, inform the patient of "[t]he name of the sponsor or funding source, if any, . . . and the organization, if any, under whose general aegis the experiment is being conducted."

It is important to note that no law prohibits a physician from conducting research in the same area in which he practices. Progress in medicine often depends upon physicians, such as those practicing at the university hospital where Moore received treatment, who conduct research while caring for their patients.

Yet a physician who treats a patient in whom he also has a research interest has potentially conflicting loyalties. This is because medical treatment decisions are made on the basis of proportionality—weighing the benefits to the patient against the risks to the patient. As another court has said, "the determination as to whether the burdens of treatment are worth enduring for any individual patient depends upon the facts unique in each case," and "the patient's interests and desires are the key ingredients of the decision-making process." A physician who adds his own research interests to this balance may be tempted to order a scientifically useful procedure or test that offers marginal, or no, benefits to the patient.[8] The possibility that an interest extraneous to the patient's health has affected the physician's judgment is something that a reasonable patient would want to know in deciding whether to consent to a proposed course of treatment. It is material to the patient's decision and, thus, a prerequisite to informed consent. . . .

---

[8] This is, in fact, precisely what Moore has alleged with respect to the postoperative withdrawals of blood and other substances.

We acknowledge that there is a competing consideration. To require disclosure of research and economic interests may corrupt the patient's own judgment by distracting him from the requirements of his health.[9] But California law does not grant physicians unlimited discretion to decide what to disclose. . . .

Accordingly, we hold that a physician who is seeking a patient's consent for a medical procedure must, in order to satisfy his fiduciary duty[10] and to obtain the patient's informed consent, disclose personal interests unrelated to the patient's health, whether research or economic, that may affect his medical judgment.

1. Dr. Golde

We turn now to the allegations of Moore's third amended complaint to determine whether he has stated such a cause of action. . . . Moore alleges that Golde actively concealed his economic interest in Moore's cells during this time period.

> [D]uring each of these visits . . . , and even when [Moore] inquired as to whether there was any possible or potential commercial or financial value or significance of his Blood and Bodily Substances, or whether the defendants had discovered anything . . . which was or might be . . . related to any scientific activity resulting in commercial or financial benefits . . . , the defendants repeatedly and affirmatively represented to [Moore] that there was no commercial or financial value to his Blood and Bodily Substances . . . and in fact actively discouraged such inquiries.

. . . In these allegations, Moore plainly asserts that Golde concealed an economic interest in the postoperative procedures. Therefore, applying the principles already discussed, the allegations state a cause of action for breach of fiduciary duty or lack of informed consent.

We thus disagree with the superior court's ruling that Moore had not stated a cause of action . . . [because he] failed to allege that the operation lacked a therapeutic purpose or that the procedure was totally unrelated to therapeutic purposes. In our view, neither allegation is essential. Even if the splenectomy had a therapeutic purpose, it does not follow that Golde had no duty to disclose his additional research and economic interests. As we have already discussed, the existence of a motivation for a medical procedure unrelated to the patient's health is a potential conflict of interest and a fact material to the patient's decision.

---

[9] . . . [A] physician who orders a procedure partly to further a research interest unrelated to the patient's health should not be able to avoid disclosure with the argument that the patient might object to participation in research. In some cases, however, a physician's research interest might play such an insignificant role in the decision to recommend a medically indicated procedure that disclosure should not be required because the interest is not material. By analogy, we have not required disclosure of "remote" risks that "are not central to the decision to administer or reject [a] procedure." Truman v. Thomas, 27 Cal. 3d 285, 293 (1980).

[10] In some respects the term *fiduciary* is too broad. In this context the term *fiduciary* signifies only that a physician must disclose all facts material to the patient's decision. A physician is not the patient's financial adviser. As we have already discussed, the reason why a physician must disclose possible conflicts is not because he has a duty to protect his patient's financial interests, but because certain personal interests may affect professional judgment.

2. The Remaining Defendants

The Regents, Quan, Genetics Institute, and Sandoz are not physicians. In contrast to Golde, none of these defendants stood in a fiduciary relationship with Moore or had the duty to obtain Moore's informed consent to medical procedures. If any of these defendants is to be liable for breach of fiduciary duty or performing medical procedures without informed consent, it can only be on account of Golde's acts and on the basis of a recognized theory of secondary liability, such as respondeat superior. The procedural posture of this case, however, makes it unnecessary for us to address the sufficiency of Moore's secondary-liability allegations. . . .

B. CONVERSION

[The portion of the opinion rejecting Moore's attempt to characterize the invasion of his rights as a conversion is excerpted at page 393. The court reasoned that such an unprecedented extension of property law concepts is not warranted because strict liability would be too threatening to legitimate and socially useful scientific research.] For these reasons, we hold that the allegations of Moore's third amended complaint state a cause of action for breach of fiduciary duty or lack of informed consent, but not conversion.

Mosk, Justice, dissenting.
. . . I disagree with the majority's . . . conclusion that in the present context a nondisclosure cause of action is an adequate—in fact, a superior—substitute for a conversion cause of action. In my view the nondisclosure cause of action falls short on at least three grounds. First, . . . the majority's theory apparently is that the threat of [a damages action based on nondisclosure] . . . will have a prophylactic effect: It will give physician-researchers incentive to disclose any conflicts of interest before treatment, and will thereby protect their patients' right to make an informed decision about what may be done with their body parts.
The remedy is largely illusory. . . . There are two barriers to recovery. First, the patient must show that if he or she had been informed of all pertinent information, he or she would have declined to consent to the procedure in question. . . . The second barrier to recovery is still higher, and is erected on the first: It is not even enough for the plaintiff to prove that he personally would have refused consent to the proposed treatment if he had been fully informed; he must also prove that in the same circumstances no reasonably prudent person would have given such consent. . . . Few if any judges or juries are likely to believe that disclosure of . . . a possibility of research or development would dissuade a reasonably prudent person from consenting to the treatment. For example, in the case at bar no trier of fact is likely to believe that if defendants had disclosed their plans for using Moore's cells, no reasonably prudent person in Moore's position—i.e., a leukemia patient suffering from a grossly enlarged spleen—would have consented to the routine operation that saved or at least prolonged his life. Here . . . a motion for nonsuit for failure to prove proximate cause will end the matter. In this context, accordingly, the threat of suit on a nondisclosure cause of action is largely a paper tiger.

The second reason why the nondisclosure cause of action is inadequate for the task that the majority assign to it is that it fails to solve half the problem before us: It gives the patient only the right to refuse consent, i.e., the right to prohibit the commercialization of his tissue; it does not give him the right to grant consent to that commercialization on the condition that he share in its proceeds. . . . Third, the nondisclosure cause of action fails to reach a major class of potential defendants: all those who are outside the strict physician-patient relationship with the plaintiff. . . .

In sum, the nondisclosure cause of action (1) is unlikely to be successful in most cases, (2) fails to protect patients' rights to share in the proceeds of the commercial exploitation of their tissue, and (3) may allow the true exploiters to escape liability. It is thus not an adequate substitute, in my view, for the conversion cause of action. . . .

BROUSSARD, Justice, concurring and dissenting.

. . . I disagree with the suggestion in [Justice Mosk's] dissenting opinion that defendants will be able to avoid all liability under the breach-of-fiduciary-duty theory simply by showing that plaintiff would have proceeded with the surgical removal of his diseased spleen even if defendants had disclosed their research and commercial interest in his cells. . . . [I]n this context [of a breach of fiduciary duty]—unlike in the traditional "informed consent" context of *Cobbs*—a plaintiff should not be required to establish that he would not have proceeded with the medical treatment in question if his physician had made full disclosure, but only that the doctor's wrongful failure to disclose information proximately caused the plaintiff some type of compensable damage. . . . [I]n appropriate circumstances, punitive as well as compensatory damages would clearly be recoverable in such an action. Accordingly, [Justice Mosk] underestimates the potential efficacy of the breach-of-fiduciary-duty cause of action in dismissing the action as a "paper tiger."

■ HOWARD v. UNIVERSITY OF MEDICINE & DENTISTRY OF NEW JERSEY
800 A.2d 73 (N.J. 2002)

LaVECCHIA, J.

In this appeal we consider what causes of action will lie when a plaintiff contends that a physician misrepresented his credentials and experience at the time he obtained the plaintiff's consent to surgery. . . .

[The plaintiff suffered serious and progressive back injuries in an automobile accident but decided to forgo recommended surgery. The plaintiff was referred to Dr. Heary, a professor at the defendant University, after the plaintiff sustained additional back injuries in a second car accident.] Dr. Heary had two pre-operative consultations with plaintiff. In the first consultation, Dr. Heary determined that plaintiff needed surgery to correct a cervical myelopathy secondary to cervical stenosis and a significantly large C3 C4 disc herniation. Because of the serious nature of the surgery, Dr. Heary recommended that plaintiff's wife attend a second consultation. The doctor wanted to explain again the risks, benefits, and alternatives to surgery, and to answer any questions concerning the procedure.

Plaintiff returned with his wife for a second consultation, but what transpired is disputed. An "Office Note" written by Dr. Heary detailing the contents of the consultation states that "[a]ll alternatives have been discussed and patient elects at this time to undergo the surgical procedure, which has been scheduled for March 5, 1997." Dr. Heary asserts that he informed plaintiff and his wife that the surgery entailed significant risks, including the possibility of paralysis. Plaintiffs dispute that they were informed of such risks. Further, they contend that during the consultation plaintiff's wife asked Dr. Heary whether he was Board Certified and that he said he was. Plaintiffs also claim that Dr. Heary told them that he had performed approximately sixty corpectomies in each of the eleven years he had been performing such surgical procedures. According to Mrs. Howard, she was opposed to the surgery and it was only after Dr. Heary's specific claims of skill and experience that she and her husband decided to go ahead with the procedure.

Dr. Heary denies that he represented that he was Board Certified in Neurosurgery.[1] He also denies that he ever claimed to have performed sixty corpectomies per year for the eleven years he had practiced neurosurgery.

Dr. Heary performed the surgical procedure on March 5, 1997, but it was unsuccessful. A malpractice action was filed alleging that Mr. Howard was rendered quadriplegic as a result of Dr. Heary's negligence. [The plaintiffs sought leave to add a fraud claim to their complaint. The trial court rejected the motion, the appellate division reversed, and the matter was appealed to the state supreme court.]

Presently, a patient has several avenues of relief against a doctor: (1) deviation from the standard of care (medical malpractice); (2) lack of informed consent; and (3) battery. . . . Plaintiffs' motion to amend the complaint to add a fraud claim raises the question whether a patient's consent to surgery obtained through alleged misrepresentations about the physician's professional experience and credentials is properly addressed in a claim of lack of informed consent, or battery, or whether it should constitute a separate and distinct claim based on fraud.

We focus first on the distinction between lack of informed consent and battery as they are recognized in New Jersey. The doctrine of informed consent was tied initially to the tort of battery, but its evolution has firmly established it as a negligence concept. . . . By the mid-twentieth century, as courts began to use a negligence theory to analyze consent causes of action, the case law evolved from the notion of consent to *informed* consent, balancing the patient's need for sufficient information with the doctor's perception of the appropriate amount of information to impart for an informed decision. . . . The doctrine of informed consent continued to be refined. See Natanson v. Kline, 350 P.2d 1093, 1106, modified on other grounds, 354 P.2d 670 (1960) (holding that doctor's required disclosure was "limited to those disclosures which a reasonable medical practitioner would make under the same or similar circumstances," known as the "professional standard"). Eventually, the "prudent patient," or "materiality of

---

[1] Although he was Board Eligible at the time of Mr. Howard's surgery, Dr. Heary did not become Board Certified in Neurosurgery until November 1999. . . .

risk" standard was introduced. Canterbury v. Spence, 464 F.2d 772, 786-88 (D.C. Cir.1972), cert. denied, 409 U.S. 1064 (1972). That patient-centered view of informed consent stresses the patient's right to self-determination, and the fiduciary relationship between a doctor and his or her patients. . . . [New Jersey originally followed the professional standard of disclosure but later adopted the patient-centered material risk standard discussed in *Canterbury.*]

Our common law also authorizes a medical battery cause of action where a doctor performs a surgery without consent, rendering the surgery an unauthorized touching. . . . In circumstances where the surgery that was performed was authorized with arguably inadequate information, however, an action for negligence is more appropriate. . . . Thus, although a claim for battery will lie where there has been "ghost surgery"[3] or where no consent has been given for the procedure undertaken, if consent has been given for the procedure only a claim based on lack of informed consent will lie. A claim based on lack of informed consent properly will focus then on the adequacy of the disclosure, its impact on the reasonable patient's assessment of the risks, alternatives, and consequences of the surgery, and the damages caused by the occurrence of the undisclosed risk. . . .

Few jurisdictions have confronted the question of what cause of action should lie when a doctor allegedly misrepresents his credentials or experience. Research has revealed only one jurisdiction that has allowed a claim based on lack of informed consent under similar circumstances. See Johnson v. Kokomoor, 545 N.W.2d 495 (Wis. 1996) (analyzing doctor's affirmative misrepresentation as claim for lack of informed consent and finding that reasonable person would have considered information regarding doctor's relative lack of experience in performing surgery to have been material in making intelligent and informed decision). Although some suggest that a claim based in fraud may be appropriate if a doctor actively misrepresents his or her background or credentials, we are aware of no court that has so held. . . .

The thoughtful decision of the Appellate Division notwithstanding, we are not convinced that our common law should be extended to allow a novel fraud or deceit-based cause of action in this doctor-patient context that regularly would admit of the possibility of punitive damages, and that would circumvent the requirements for proof of both causation and damages imposed in a traditional informed consent setting. We are especially reluctant to do so when plaintiff's damages from this alleged "fraud" arise exclusively from the doctor-patient relationship involving plaintiff's corpectomy procedure. . . . Accordingly, we hold that a fraud or deceit-based claim is unavailable to address the wrong alleged by plaintiff. We next consider whether a claim based on lack of informed consent is the more appropriate analytical basis for the amendment to the complaint permitted by the Appellate Division. . . .

Our case law never has held that a doctor has a duty to detail his background and experience as part of the required informed consent disclosure; nor are we called on to decide that question here. . . . Courts generally have held that claims of lack of informed consent based on a failure to disclose professional-background

---

[3] ["Ghost surgery" occurs if the patient consents to a surgical procedure to be performed by Physician A but the surgery actually is performed by Physician B. — EDS.]

information are without merit. . . . Although personal credentials and experience may not be a required part of an informed consent disclosure under the current standard of care required of doctors, the question raised in this appeal is whether significant misrepresentations concerning a physician's qualifications can affect the validity of consent obtained. The answer obviously is that they can.

In certain circumstances, a serious misrepresentation concerning the quality or extent of a physician's professional experience, viewed from the perspective of the reasonably prudent patient assessing the risks attendant to a medical procedure, can be material to the grant of intelligent and informed consent to the procedure. See 1 Dan B. Dobbs, *The Law of Torts,* §251 at 660-61 (2001) (citing *Kokemoor, supra,* and discussing that some authority has begun to suggest that patient is entitled to information concerning doctor's experience in performing specific surgery). In *Kokemoor, supra,* the Supreme Court of Wisconsin reviewed a case in which the plaintiff alleged that her surgeon did not obtain her informed consent to perform a surgical procedure because he had misrepresented his experience in response to a direct question during a pre-operative consultation. 545 N.W.2d at 505. At trial, evidence was introduced suggesting that the type of surgery performed—basilar bifurcation aneurysm—was "among the most difficult in all of neurosurgery." Ibid. The court found that evidence of the defendant's lack of experience was relevant to an informed consent claim because "[a] reasonable person in the plaintiff's position would have considered such information material in making an intelligent and informed decision about the surgery." Ibid.

The allegation here is that defendant's misrepresentations concerning his credentials and experience were instrumental in overcoming plaintiff's reluctance to proceed with the surgery. The theory of the claim is not that the misrepresentation induced plaintiff to proceed with unnecessary surgery. . . . Rather, plaintiff essentially contends that he was misled about material information that he required in order to grant an intelligent and informed consent to the performance of the procedure because he did not receive accurate responses to questions concerning defendant's experience in performing corpectomies and whether he was "Board Certified." Plaintiff allegedly was warned of the risk of paralysis from the corpectomy procedure; however, he asserts that if he had known the truth about defendant's qualifications and experience, it would have affected his assessment of the risks of the procedure. Stated differently, defendant's misrepresentations induced plaintiff to consent to a surgical procedure, and its risk of paralysis, that he would not have undergone had he known the truth about defendant's qualifications. Stripped to its essentials, plaintiff's claim is founded on lack of informed consent.

As noted earlier, a patient-specific standard of what is material to a full disclosure does not apply in a claim based on lack of informed consent. Thus, plaintiff's subjective preference for a Board Certified physician, or one who had performed more corpectomies than defendant had performed, is not the actionable standard. Nonetheless, assuming the misrepresentations are proved, if an objectively reasonable person could find that physician experience was material in determining the medical risk of the corpectomy procedure to which plaintiff consented, and if a reasonably prudent person in plaintiff's position informed of the defendant's misrepresentations about his experience would not have consented, then a claim based on lack of informed consent may be maintained.

Modern advances in medicine coupled with the increased sophistication of medical consumers require an evolving notion of the reasonably prudent patient when assessing a claim based on lack of informed consent. . . . That said, most informed consent issues are unlikely to implicate a setting in which a physician's experience or credentials have been demonstrated to be a material element affecting the risk of undertaking a specific procedure. The standard requires proof on which an objectively reasonable person would base a finding that physician experience could have a causal connection to a substantial risk of the procedure. . . .

The alleged misrepresentations in this case about "physician experience" (credentials and surgical experience) provide a useful context for demonstrating the difficulty inherent in meeting the materiality standard required in order for physician experience to have a role in an informed consent case. We recognize that a misrepresentation about a physician's experience is not a perfect fit with the familiar construct of a claim based on lack of informed consent. The difficulty arises because physician experience is not information that directly relates to the procedure itself or one of the other areas of required medical disclosure concerning the procedure, its substantial risks, and alternatives that must be disclosed to avoid a claim based on lack of informed consent. But the possibility of materiality is present. If defendant's true level of experience had the capacity to enhance substantially the risk of paralysis from undergoing a corpectomy, a jury could find that a reasonably prudent patient would not have consented to that procedure had the misrepresentation been revealed. That presumes that plaintiff can prove that the actual level of experience possessed by defendant had a direct and demonstrable relationship to the harm of paralysis, a substantial risk of the procedure that was disclosed to plaintiff. Put differently, plaintiff must prove that the additional undisclosed risk posed by defendant's true level of qualifications and experience increased plaintiff's risk of paralysis from the corpectomy procedure.

The standard for causation that we envision in such an action will impose a significant gatekeeper function on the trial court to prevent insubstantial claims concerning alleged misrepresentations about a physician's experience from proceeding to a jury. We contemplate that misrepresented or exaggerated physician experience would have to significantly increase a risk of a procedure in order for it to affect the judgment of a reasonably prudent patient in an informed consent case. As this case demonstrates, the proximate cause analysis will involve a two-step inquiry.

The first inquiry should be, assuming a misrepresentation about experience, whether the more limited experience or credentials possessed by defendant could have substantially increased plaintiff's risk of paralysis from undergoing the corpectomy procedure. We envision that expert testimony would be required for such a showing. The second inquiry would be whether that substantially increased risk would cause a reasonably prudent person not to consent to undergo the procedure. If the true extent of defendant's experience could not affect materially the risk of paralysis from a corpectomy procedure, then the alleged misrepresentation could not cause a reasonably prudent patient in plaintiff's position to decline consent to the procedure. The court's gatekeeper function in respect of the first question will require a determination that a genuine issue of material fact exists requiring resolution by the factfinder in order to proceed to the second question involving an assessment by the reasonably prudent patient. Further, the trial court must conclude that there is a genuine issue of material fact concerning both questions in order to allow the claim to proceed to trial.

Finally, to satisfy the damages element in a claim based on lack of informed consent, a plaintiff typically has to show a causal connection between the inadequately disclosed risk of the procedure and the injury sustained. . . . If that risk materialized and harmed plaintiff, damages for those injuries are awarded. . . . Here, if successful in his claim based on lack of informed consent, plaintiff may receive damages for injuries caused by an inadequately disclosed risk of the corpectomy procedure. However, as noted, to be successful plaintiff must prove that defendant's allegedly misrepresented qualifications and experience can satisfy the stringent test for proximate causation that is required for physician experience to be material to the substantial risk of the procedure that occurred (paralysis) and injured plaintiff. If he can, then plaintiff may be compensated for that injury caused by the corpectomy irrespective of whether defendant deviated from the standard of care in performing the surgical procedure.

In conclusion, plaintiff's medical malpractice action will address any negligence in defendant's performance of the corpectomy procedure. We hold that in addition plaintiff may attempt to prove that defendant's alleged misrepresentation about his credentials and experience presents a claim based on lack of informed consent to the surgical procedure, consistent with the requirements and limitations that we have imposed on such a claim. . . .

Notes: Fiduciary Principles and the Disclosure of Provider-Associated Risks

1. *Do Fiduciary Principles Add Anything?* Why couldn't the *Moore* court analyze the facts solely using traditional informed consent analysis? Read the opinion to determine (1) the theory underlying the imposition of fiduciary obligations; (2) the scope of the fiduciary duty; (3) the actions that might constitute a breach of the duty; (4) the injury requirements, if any; and (5) the remedies for a breach of fiduciary duty. Do fiduciary duties expand or merely parallel the duties already created under the material risk standard in informed consent cases? What should Golde have done to avoid liability? Why doesn't the court impose disclosure duties on the other defendants? Would a conversion claim have been an easier basis of recovering damages from all of the defendants? *Moore*'s conversion claim is discussed in more detail in Chapter 4, at pages 401–403.

2. *Causation Problems in* Moore. Who has the better of the causation and damages arguments between Justice Mosk and Justice Broussard? On remand, Moore's claim was settled before going to trial, so the court never had to resolve these issues. The *Howard* court directly confronts the knotty causation questions created by provider-associated risk disclosure claims. Will Mr. Howard be able to recover on his informed consent claim without expert proof that the surgeon

violated the standard of care in the conduct of the surgery? Why or why not? See Starozytnyk v. Reich, 871 A.2d 733 (N.J. Super. 2005) (affirming dismissal of plaintiff's informed consent and fiduciary duty claims due to absence of proximate cause); Christine Grady et al., The Limits of Disclosure: What Research Subjects Want to Know About Investigator Financial Interests, 34 J.L. Med. & Ethics 592 (2006) (majority of respondents wanted to know about investigators' interest but "only a minority thought such financial information would influence their decisions about research participation in any way.").

3. *The Theoretical Application of Fiduciary Theories to Remedy Economic Conflicts of Interest.* No one supposes that doctors must disclose the distorting effects of fee-for-service reimbursement, which might result in harms from unnecessary treatment. Cf. Wright v. Jeckle, 144 P.3d 301 (Wash. 2006) (rejecting claim that physician's direct sale of anti-obesity drug constituted a violation of fiduciary duty under state anti-kickback legislation merely because physician profited from sales). Should there nonetheless be a duty to disclose incentives related to managed care? Could you argue that incentives to reduce health care expenses in managed care are "common knowledge"?

If there is a financial disclosure obligation on the part of physicians participating in managed care arrangements, how great should the financial incentive be before it is considered "material"? Should the plaintiff be required to prove that the incentive was sufficient to affect physician decision-making in individual cases? Or can we presume that managed care companies would not use financial incentives unless they worked, by affecting physician decisions at least to some extent? Managed care physicians might argue that incentives are designed only to reduce unnecessary medical care and are not large enough to induce physicians to refrain from making necessary medical referrals. Even if incentives potentially affect necessary care, isn't the threat of a malpractice claim enough to ensure that physicians will still make appropriate referrals, or a sufficient remedy when they fail to do so?

And now, a final set of issues. If there is an obligation to disclose managed care financial incentives, should it be satisfied by a global disclosure when the patient first enrolls (and perhaps once a year thereafter), or must the incentives be repeated each time the patient seeks treatment? For an argument that disclosure at enrollment satisfies the fiduciary obligation, or perhaps acts as a waiver of subsequent disclosures, see Mark A. Hall, A Theory of Economic Informed Consent, 31 Ga. L. Rev. 511 (1997).

4. *Discussing the Costs of Care.* Curiously, there is virtually no legal or ethical guidance on whether physicians should tell patients how much treatment options cost. In the distant past, this may have been because physicians followed an ethic of treat first and bill later, letting patients pay what they were able. In the more recent past, this may be because insurance usually pays for the majority of costs. In the future, however, these cost-insulating features may soon recede, under the influence of "consumer-driven" health insurance plans that expose patients to much greater cost-sharing obligations. See pages 59–60. This will likely generate disputes by patients who feel they were not adequately informed about the costs of the treatments they agreed to. Under the informed consent and fiduciary principles you have learned, should physicians have to volunteer information about costs, or only wait for patients to ask first? Does the answer differ for the

costs of the physicians' own services versus costs charged by other providers, goods, or services the physician may recommend (such as lab tests, drugs, or specialist referrals)? For preliminary discussion, see Haavi Morreim, High-Deductible Health Plans: New Twists on Old Challenges from Tort and Contract, 59 Vand. L. Rev. 1207 (2006); G. Caleb Alexander et al., Rethinking Professional Ethics in the Cost-Sharing Era, 6(4) Am. J. Bioethics W17-W22 (2006); Marshall Kapp, Patient Autonomy in the Age of Consumer-Driven Health Care: Informed Consent and Informed Choice, 28 J. Leg. Med. 91 (2007).

5. *Financial Disclosure Claims in the Courts. Moore* appeared to open the door to using informed consent and/or fiduciary theories to protect patients from the risks created by a provider's financial arrangements with third parties, such as managed care organizations. Subsequent courts have tried to push the door shut, at least on some types of claims. In Neade v. Portes, 739 N.E.2d 496 (Ill. 2000), for example, the Illinois Supreme Court rejected the use of fiduciary theories in a case involving managed care incentives. Mr. Neade was only 37 but had a number of significant risk factors for heart disease. Mr. Neade began to experience radiating chest pain and shortness of breath. Mr. Neade's primary physician, Dr. Portes, authorized Mr. Neade's hospitalization. While hospitalized, Mr. Neade underwent a battery of tests that appeared to rule out heart disease. Thereafter, Dr. Portes failed to refer Mr. Neade for more specific tests for heart disease, despite recurring symptoms. Mr. Neade had a heart attack and died. Mr. Neade's estate brought claims for breach of fiduciary duty and medical negligence against Dr. Portes and others. Dr. Portes participated in a risk-sharing agreement with the patient's HMO that arguably gave the physician an incentive to deny referrals to his patients.

Relying in part on some of the language found in the United States Supreme Court's opinion in Pegram v. Herdrich, 530 U.S. 211 (2000) (exploring fiduciary duty under federal ERISA statute) the Illinois Supreme Court rejected the breach of fiduciary duty claim. The Illinois Supreme Court held that a cause of action for breach of fiduciary duty based on a physician's failure to reveal a financial interest in a medical incentive fund essentially duplicated the underlying medical negligence claim:

> [I]t is operative facts together with the injury that we look to in order to determine whether a cause of action is duplicative. In the case at bar, the operative fact in both [the malpractice and fiduciary duty] counts is Dr. Portes' failure to order an angiogram for Mr. Neade. Plaintiff alleges in both counts that Mr. Neade's failure to receive an angiogram is the ultimate reason for his subsequent death. Plaintiff also alleges the same injury in both her medical negligence claim and her breach of fiduciary duty claim, namely, Mr. Neade's death and its effect on plaintiff and her family. We determine that plaintiff's breach of fiduciary duty claim is a re-presentment of her medical negligence claim.
>
> An examination of the elements of a medical negligence claim and breach of fiduciary duty claim illustrates the way in which a breach of fiduciary duty claim would "boil down to a malpractice claim." *Herdrich*, 530 U.S. at —, 120 S. Ct. at 2157. To sustain an action for medical negligence, plaintiff must show: (1) the standard of care in the medical community by which the physician's treatment was measured; (2) that the physician deviated from the standard of care; and (3) that a resulting injury was proximately caused by the deviation from the standard of

care. . . . Thus, the standard of care is the relevant inquiry by which we judge a physician's actions in a medical negligence case. . . .

In contrast to an action for medical negligence, in order to state a claim for breach of fiduciary duty, it must be alleged that a fiduciary duty exists, that the fiduciary duty was breached, and that such breach proximately caused the injury of which the plaintiff complains. . . .

In order to sustain a breach of fiduciary duty claim against Dr. Portes, plaintiff would have to allege, inter alia, that: (1) had she known of the Medical Incentive Fund she would have sought an opinion from another physician; (2) that the other physician would have ordered an angiogram for Mr. Neade; (3) that the angiogram would have detected Mr. Neade's heart condition; and (4) that treatment could have prevented his eventual myocardial infarction and subsequent death. In order to prove the second element, plaintiff would have been required to present expert testimony that the expert, after examining Mr. Neade and considering his history, would have ordered an angiogram. This requirement relates to the standard of care consideration— the first prong in a traditional medical negligence claim—under which a physician is held to "the reasonable skill which a physician in good standing in the community would use." That is precisely what plaintiff must prove to support her breach of fiduciary duty claim. As the Supreme Court stated in *Herdrich,* the breach of fiduciary duty claim "would boil down to a malpractice claim, and the fiduciary standard would be nothing but the malpractice standard traditionally applied in actions against physicians." *Herdrich,* 530 U.S. at —, 120 S. Ct. at 2157. Thus, we need not recognize a new cause of action for breach of fiduciary duty when a traditional medical negligence claim sufficiently addresses the same alleged misconduct. The breach of fiduciary duty claim in the case at bar would be duplicative of the medical negligence claim.

Our decision to refrain from permitting the creation of this new cause of action finds additional support in statutory law. The Illinois legislature has placed the burden of disclosing HMO incentive schemes on HMOs themselves. . . .

Moreover, the outcome that would result if we were to allow the creation of a new cause of action for breach of fiduciary duty against a physician in these circumstances may be impractical. For example, physicians often provide services for numerous patients, many of whom may be covered by different HMOs. In order to effectively disclose HMO incentives, physicians would have to remain cognizant at all times of every patient's particular HMO and that HMO's policies and procedures. See, e.g., Mark Hall, A Theory of Economic Informed Consent, 31 Ga. L. Rev. 511, 525-26 (1997). . . . If we were to recognize a breach of fiduciary duty claim in the context of the case at bar, we fear the effects of such a holding may be unworkable. Neade v. Portes, 739 N.E.2d. at 502-506.

The court also held that evidence of the physician's financial incentives could be relevant on issues relating to interest and bias, in the event that physician testified in the medical negligence trial. Id. at 506.

Chief Justice Harrison dissented:

A complaint against a lawyer for professional malpractice may be couched in either contract or tort. . . . The same rule should apply here. Although this case involves medical rather than legal malpractice, that distinction is insignificant. . . . The right to assert claims for breach of fiduciary duty and negligence in the same professional malpractice action is not unfettered. When the same operative facts support a negligence count and a count for breach of fiduciary duty based on the same injury to the client, the counts are identical and the fiduciary duty count should be dismissed as duplicative. . . . In this case, however, the negligence and breach of fiduciary duty counts asserted by plaintiff are not identical. . . . As the appellate court correctly recognized,

> It is conceivable that a trier of fact could find both that Dr. Portes was within the standard of care and therefore not negligent in relying on the thallium stress test and the EKG in deciding that an angiogram was not necessary and also that Dr. Portes did breach his fiduciary duty in not disclosing his financial incentive arrangement and, as a proximate result thereof, Neade did not obtain a second opinion, suffered a massive coronary infarction, and died.

710 N.E.2d 418. . . . Id. at 506.

Other courts have reached similar results. See Weiss v. CIGNA Healthcare, Inc., 972 F. Supp. 748, 752 (S.D.N.Y. 1997); D.A.B. v. Brown, 570 N.W.2d 168 (Minn. Ct. App. 1997). But see Darke v. Estate of Isner, 20 Mass. L. Rptr. 419 (Mass. Superior Ct. 2005) (plaintiff's deceit claims survive summary judgment motion in case involving physician's failure to disclose financial interest in research). For an unsuccessful effort to use fiduciary theories in the context of obesity drug litigation, see Wright v. Jeckle, 90 P.3d 65 (Wash. App. 2004).

6. *Institutional Disclosure Obligations under Fiduciary Law.* Under common law principles, as *Moore* holds, institutions are generally free from the disclosure duties imposed on physicians. A federal statute, the Employee Retirement Income Security Act of 1974 (ERISA), regulates health plans provided as a benefit of employment. This statute has a number of important implications for the organization and delivery of health care in the United States. For present purposes, it is enough to note that the Supreme Court's decision in *Pegram* closed the door to efforts to use ERISA's fiduciary principles as a tool for imposing disclosure obligations on managed care employee benefit plans.

7. *Other Financial Conflicts.* As *Moore* briefly indicates, statutory law sometimes requires disclosure of certain kinds of financial conflicts of interest. A prime example is when physicians have investment or ownership interests in the facilities to which they refer their patients. State and federal laws prohibit or regulate these investment interests in many circumstances. Which approach strikes you as more appropriate: disclosure or prohibition/regulation?

Different types of financial and nonfinancial conflicts of interest permeate medical relationships, as they do most human affairs. (For example, the authors of this book receive modest royalties when their own students purchase it.) How assiduous should physicians be in avoiding or disclosing them? Consider, for instance, the many tactics that drug companies have used to encourage physicians to prescribe their products. Kickbacks and direct financial incentives are illegal; other types of arrangements have elicited increasing attention. See Troyen A. Brennan et al., Health Industry Practices That Create Conflicts of Interest: A Policy Proposal for Academic Medical Centers, 295 JAMA 429 (2006); Susan L. Coyle, Physician-Industry Relations. Part I: Individual Physicians, 136 Annals Internal Med. 396 (2002); Council on Ethical and Judicial Affairs of the American Medical Association, Guidelines on Gifts to Physicians from Industry: An Update,

56 Food & Drug L.J. 27 (2001). For an article that examines financial conflict of interest between physicians and medical device companies see Reed Abelson, Hospitals See Possible Conflict on Medical Devices for Doctors, N.Y. Times, Sept. 22, 2006, at A1.

8. *Nonfinancial Provider-Associated Risks.* Should physicians have a duty to disclose risks to patients that arise from the identity of the provider rather than the type of procedure? *Howard* is part of a small new line of cases considering whether physicians have any duty to disclose provider risks, as distinguished from procedural risks.

(a) *Experience and Success Rates.* Health care organizations and purchasers are developing and collecting information about health care outcomes for individual practitioners. Should health care providers have a duty to disclose their own "scorecards" to patients? How does the *Howard* court distinguish between informed consent and misrepresentation claims in this area?

For other cases involving physician experience, see Duffy v. Flagg, 905 A.2d 15 (2006) (informed consent does not require physician to give detailed account of her past experience with a procedure when answers would not have been relevant to key informed consent issues); DeGennaro v. Tandon, 873 A.2d 191 (Conn. App. 2005) (reasonable patient would consider lack of experience in using equipment, and lack of assistance, to be material information about provider-specific risk); Wlosinski v. Cohn, 713 N.W.2d 16 (Mich. App. 2005) ("raw success rates" need not be disclosed; interesting concurring and dissenting opinions); Duttry v. Patterson, 771 A.2d 1255 (Pa. 2001) (physician's personal characteristics and experience irrelevant in informed consent claim; misrepresentation claim possible); Johnson v. Kokemoor, 545 N.W.2d 495 (Wis. 1996) (applying informed consent principles to a case involving a physician's relative lack of experience).

For commentaries on the subject, see Heyward H. Bouknight, III, Note, Between the Scalpel and the Lie: Comparing Theories of Physician Accountability for Misrepresentations of Experience and Competence, 60 Wash. & Lee L. Rev. 1515 (2003); Janet L. Dolgin, The Evolution of the "Patient": Shifts in Attitudes About Consent, Genetic Information, and Commercialization in Health Care, 34 Hofstra L. Rev. 137 (2005) (critiquing expansion of disclosure obligation in *Howard*); Milt Freudenheim, To Find a Doctor, Mine the Data, N.Y. Times, Sept. 22, 2005, at C1; Aaron D. Twerski, The Second Revolution in Informed Consent: Comparing Physicians to Each Other, 94 Nw. U. L. Rev. 1 (1999); Aaron D. Twerski & Neil B. Cohen, Comparing Medical Providers: A First Look at the New Era of Medical Statistics, 58 Brook. L. Rev. 5 (1992); Robert Weinstein et al., Infection Control Report Cards — Ensuring Patient Safety, 353 New Eng. J. Med. 225 (2005); J. Wilks et al., Surgeon with Worst Performance Figures Might Be the Best Option, 323 Brit. Med. J. 1071 (2001).

(b) *Abuse of Drug or Alcohol.* Would the reasonable patient consider a physician's cocaine addiction to be a material fact in deciding whether or not to undergo surgery? Would the professional standard of care require such a disclosure? Compare Albany Urology Clinic, P.C. v. Cleveland, 528 S.E.2d 777 (Ga. 2000) (no duty to disclose drug use under common law or state informed consent statute), with Hidding v. Williams, 578 So. 2d 1192 (La. Ct. App. 1991) (physician has duty to reveal his alcoholism; concurring opinion raises interesting causation problem).

(c) *Infection with HIV.* There has been a vigorous debate about whether a physician has or should have a duty to disclose his or her HIV status. See, e.g., Mary Anne Bobinski, Autonomy and Privacy: Protecting Patients from Their Physicians, 55 U. Pitt. L. Rev. 291 (1994). The application of the informed consent doctrine to the problem of HIV disclosure in health care is complicated by the fact that many patients are more fearful about the very low risk of HIV transmission from health care worker to patient than they are about other, larger risks. In addition, persons with HIV infection are protected from discrimination under a variety of statutes, including the Americans with Disabilities Act, unless they pose a "significant risk" to the health or safety of others. 42 U.S.C. §§12111-12113; see supra at page 118. From the perspective of the infected physician, disclosure ought not be required unless there is a significant risk of transmission. From the perspective of the patient, even a "less than significant" risk could be avoided by selecting an (apparently) uninfected health care provider. One court has resolved the conflict in favor of the patient's right to know:

> [Dr. Behringer, a surgeon] argues: (1) the risk of transmission of HIV from surgeon to patient is too remote to require informed consent, and (2) the law of informed consent does not require disclosure of the condition of the surgeon. . . . [Dr. Behringer] argues that the use of the informed consent form is tantamount to a de facto termination of surgical privileges. [Dr. Behringer] further urges that patient reaction is likely to be based more on public hysteria than on a studied assessment of the actual risk involved.
>
> The answer to these arguments is two-fold. First, it is the duty of the surgeon utilizing the informed consent procedure to explain to the patient the real risk involved. If the patient's fear is without basis, it is likewise the duty of the surgeon to allay that fear. This court recognizes that the burden imposed on the surgeon may not be surmountable absent further education of both the public and the medical community about the realities of HIV and AIDS. Second, the difficulties created by the public reaction to AIDS cannot deprive the patient of making the ultimate decision where the ultimate risk is so significant. The last word has not been spoken on the issue of transmission of HIV and AIDS. Facts accepted at one point in time are no longer accurate as more is learned about this disease and its transmission. . . .
>
> [Dr. Behringer] further argues that there is no requirement under the doctrine of informed consent that a surgeon's physical condition be revealed as a risk of the surgery itself. The informed consent cases are not so narrow as to support that argument. In [a prior New Jersey Supreme Court case] . . . the court spoke of not only an evaluation of the nature of the treatment, but of "any attendant substantial risks." . . .
>
> [Dr. Behringer] urges that these issues should be dealt with on a case-by-case basis, wherein the hospital or medical staff monitors an HIV-positive surgeon and makes a determination as to the surgeon's ability to perform a particular invasive procedure. . . . The position [Dr. Behringer] seeks to implement is replete with the "anachronistic paternalism" rejected in both Canterbury v. Spence, supra, and by the [New Jersey] Supreme Court. . . .
>
> [The court summarized the views of several commentators, one of whom had noted the fiduciary character of the physician-patient relationship.] . . . The

obligation of a surgeon performing invasive procedures, such as [Dr. Behringer], to reveal his AIDS condition, is one which requires a weighing of [Dr. Behringer's] rights against the patient's rights. New Jersey's strong policy supporting patient rights, weighed against [Dr. Behringer's] individual right to perform an invasive procedure as a part of the practice of his profession, requires the conclusion that the patient's rights must prevail. At a minimum, the physician must withdraw from performing any invasive procedure which would pose a risk to the patient. Where the ultimate harm is death, even the presence of a low risk of transmission justifies the adoption of a policy which precludes invasive procedures when there is "any" risk of transmission. In the present case, the debate raged as to whether there was "any" risk of transmission, and the informed-consent procedure was left in place. If there is to be an ultimate arbiter of whether the patient is to be treated invasively by an AIDS-positive surgeon, the arbiter will be the fully-informed patient. The ultimate risk to the patient is so absolute — so devastating — that it is untenable to argue against informed consent combined with a restriction on procedures which present "any risk" to the patient. Estate of Behringer v. Medical Center at Princeton, 592 A.2d 1251, 1279-1283 (N.J. Super. Ct. Div. 1991).

Problem: *Moore* Liability?

Consider the informed consent doctrine applicable in your state. What types of disclosures would be required in the following situations?

1. A physician recommending a surgical procedure necessary to save the patient's life will earn about $15,000 from the surgery and follow-up care. What if the surgery was for cosmetic purposes?

2. A physician recommends that a patient see a specialist for her condition. The physician is married to the specialist.

3. A physician providing care for an HMO patient earns a flat fee per month per patient. The physician is treating a patient's digestive complaints and suggests that the patient wait two months to see if the condition gets better on its own.

4. A physician providing care for an HMO patient with back pain suggests that the patient take a conservative approach to treatment, delaying expensive diagnostic tests and surgery for as long as possible. The physician's financial arrangements with the HMO include provisions that decrease the physician's income if the physician spends more than an allocated amount on diagnostic tests or hospitalization.

5. A physician describes herself as a social drinker. She only drinks during the evenings and on weekends. On average, she consumes about 21 mixed drinks per week.

6. A general internist learns that he has HIV infection.

7. A physician fails to inform a patient suffering from pancreatic cancer of the patient's low statistical life expectancy. The patient does not make the proper financial arrangements, leading to substantial real estate and tax losses. See Arato v. Avedon, 858 P.2d 598 (Cal. 1993).

5. Human Experimentation and Research

The *Moore* litigation arose because of the alleged conflicts of interest created by the research interests of the defendants. Nightly news stories regularly focus on the results of medical research, touting the next great cures for long-feared diseases (as well as informing us about cures for diseases that we never knew existed). Society clearly has a strong interest in ensuring that medical research is not stymied by excessive regulation. Researchers and biotechnology companies may have significant economic interests in the research enterprise. Statistics are difficult to obtain because medical research is conducted in a range of public and private settings, funded by public and private sources, and regulated either by different federal regulatory entities or by much more diffuse common law rules. Medical research is commonly described as a multi-billion-dollar activity, with "an estimated 20 million Americans tak[ing] part in more than 41,000 clinical trials and uncounted more federally funded experiments." Tom Abate, Experiments on Humans: Business of Clinical Trials Soars, but Risk Unknown, S.F. Chron., Aug. 4, 2002, at A1.

There are two central concerns in the research context. The first is that experimental treatment is often not done for the patient's immediate benefit. Some patients may approach medical research thinking they will receive better care because it is "state of the art," but this is usually a false impression. Instead, the treatment that is being studied may be riskier; almost certainly its risks are less well known than standard treatment. Also, patients are often "randomized" "blindly" between an "experimental arm" and a "control arm." This means that, by luck of the draw, a significant percentage will receive ordinary treatment or even, in some cases, a placebo; participants generally will not know which type of care they will receive. Moreover, the innovation in treatment may have nothing at all to offer their condition, but may be intended solely to provide an improvement for other patients. The relevant distinction is between "therapeutic" and "nontherapeutic research." Only in the former is there something that a patient might benefit from immediately, but even then, patients are often asked to undergo risks that are greater than the potential rewards in order to further the aims of science.

Fully informed patients may be more than willing to accept these arrangements out of a sense of altruism and a desire to be a part of progress. But there is a second difficulty: How well informed are they, and how freely do they make their decision? Some patients may feel pressured in subtle ways without the knowledge of their physicians. Imagine a physician who eagerly pitches her pet research project, and a patient who fears (irrationally or not?) that disappointing his doctor will jeopardize his treatment. For other patients, coercion could be more overt. The reluctance of well-informed patients to participate in risky experiments might lead researchers either to conceal the experiment or to use patients from vulnerable or socially disadvantaged groups.

These concerns are not merely speculative. The history of medical research reveals both astounding advances and disquieting practices. Scientists have sought to expand the knowledge of human biology, illness, and treatment, often at the expense of the least fortunate in society: slaves, the poor, criminals, and other institutionalized persons. Several twentieth century examples have left a legacy of fear and mistrust. Nazi scientists conducted a vigorous program of medical research on prisoners and internees during World War II. Their appalling lack of respect for human life and humane principles resulted in the Nuremberg Code. The Code's central tenet is a requirement that human research subjects give consent to participation in any research project. See Evelyn Shuster, Fifty Years Later: The Significance of the Nuremberg Code, 337 New Eng. J. Med. 1436 (1997).

Violations of human rights by researchers are not limited, however, to some distant time and distant place. Two examples of research abuses in the United States have had a profound impact. In the Tuskegee Study, which ran from the 1950s until the early 1970s, researchers studied the effects of untreated syphilis in a group of African-American men. The researchers purported to treat the men for their ailments but never disclosed to their subjects that they continued to suffer from a highly treatable, yet debilitating illness. The researchers' apparently cavalier disregard for their subjects has resulted in a legacy of distrust among minority and poor communities.

Recent revelations have been no more comforting. In the mid-1990s, the federal government revealed that hundreds of persons had been involuntarily, and in some cases unknowingly, subjected to research in which they were exposed to radiation and other harmful substances. President Clinton was forced to announce the adoption of newly strengthened protections for human subjects participating in classified research projects. Strengthened Protections for Human Subjects of Classified Research, 62 Fed. Reg. 26,367 (1997). See generally U.S. Advisory Comm. on Human Radiation Experiments, Final Report of the Advisory Committee on Human Radiation Experiments (Ruth Faden ed., 1996).

A special set of rules governs the disclosure and consent process in medical research. Federal regulations require an elaborate consent process in order for research to receive federal funding. U.S. Dep't Health & Human Servs., Protection of Human Subjects, 45 C.F.R. §§46.101-.409; U.S. Food & Drug Admin., Protection of Human Subjects, 21 C.F.R. §§50.1-.56. Entities that accept federally funded research projects also assure that they will protect human subjects in research projects funded by non-federal sources. 45 C.F.R. §46.103(b). Private foundations that fund research usually follow suit. The end result is that the federal regulations effectively govern most planned medical research in the United States. These federal rules, while influential, do not preempt state laws providing greater protection of human subjects. State regulation of research through the common law may become increasingly important.

▉ WHY INFORMED CONSENT? HUMAN EXPERIMENTATION AND THE ETHICS OF AUTONOMY
Richard W. Garnett*
36 Cath. Law. 455 (1996)

. . . Why does consent have such moral power? Accept for now that our deference to consent is — perhaps mistakenly — rooted in a commitment to

---

* Law professor at Notre Dame Law School; B.A. Duke, 1990; J.D. Yale, 1995.

human dignity, expressed through respect for autonomy. Is consent's justifying role necessarily required by this commitment to human dignity? Why have we come to think that it is? Does our dignity as persons follow from, or does it instead create and condition, our autonomy? Do we respect consent because one feature of our dignity is that we always know what is best for us? Clearly we do not. . . .

III. REGULATING HUMAN EXPERIMENTATION THROUGH CONSENT

A. THE NUREMBERG CODE AND "INFORMED CONSENT"

The Nuremberg Code and the memory of the Nazi doctors' trial animate and permeate modern thinking about regulation of human experimentation. The Code was our most morally rigorous attempt to limit human experimentation. Its most memorable command was that, in medical research, "[t]he voluntary consent of the human subject is absolutely essential."[70] But while the Code has come to stand for "informed consent," it required more. It focused as much on the experiment itself, on the welfare of the subject, and on the conduct of the researcher as it did on the need for the subject's consent. Sadly, this broad focus has received relatively short shrift, and the consent principle has eclipsed the others.

The Code stands tall in memory but its influence has never lived up to its aims. Seen by many as a product of and reaction to Nazi terror, the Code is often dismissed as a context-bound relic, no longer useful for today's researchers. Pragmatists argue that the Code is simply too demanding, that its standards are too high for necessary research to meet, and that its absolutism cannot compete with the utilitarian and impersonal ethics of modern medicine. . . .

B. REGULATING EXPERIMENTATION AFTER NUREMBERG: THE STANDARD MODEL OF INFORMED CONSENT

. . . Today, human experimentation is regulated by a crazy-quilt of hortatory codes and maxims, scattered federal laws and regulations, and most importantly, by Institutional Review Boards,[85] which provide peer review of proposed experiments. "Informed consent" is still the touchstone, but modern regulations and procedures tolerate and expect deviations from this ideal. Thus, when addressing human experimentation—and they rarely do—courts occasionally mention the [Nuremberg] Code, but generally apply and enforce the more flexible informed consent requirements of later regulations.

The legal doctrine of informed consent as it has developed is quite different from the dignity-based commitment to self-determination animating the Nuremberg Code. The most important feature of today's regulatory regime is that it focuses on the subject's state of mind more than on the experiment itself. What is referred to here as the "Standard Model" of informed consent is this

---

[70] The Nazi Doctors and the Nuremberg Code: Human Rights in Human Experimentation 2 (George J. Annas & Michael A. Grodin eds., 1992).

[85] For a complete review of the structure and function of Institutional Review Boards, see, e.g., 45 C.F.R. §§46.107-111 (1994); 21 C.F.R. §§56.101-114 (1994). "IRB approval means the determination of the IRB that the research has been reviewed and may be conducted at an institution within the constraints set forth by the IRB and by other institutional and federal requirements." 45 C.F.R. §46.102(h).

subjectively oriented informed consent in the context of peer review. In practice, research peers have proven insufficiently critical when evaluating proposed experiments. In addition, the informed consent "requirement" is viewed as a chore and a ritual, an impersonal incantation, a hurried signing of papers. We know this is true, yet we cherish the myth of informed consent, skating over its lack of real content or impact. But because the Standard Model is a subterfuge aimed more at easing our consciences than at protecting research subjects, it fails both as a necessary condition for proposed experiments and as a justification for them.

IV. THE STANDARD MODEL IN ACTION: INFORMED CONSENT IN HARD CASES

. . . The Standard Model regulates experiments by requiring the subjects' informed consent. Comparatively little attention is given to the nature of the experiment itself—apart from its riskiness—or to the researcher's goals and intentions. Under the Standard Model, concern may be triggered by some characteristic of the subject (age, health, mental capabilities) or by the experiment's location (prison, hospital, university). These characteristics and locations, however, relate less to whether the researcher's plan is itself ethical, than whether the subject's consent was really given, or was truly informed. When experiments are prohibited, it is due to the quality, or lack thereof, of the consent given, not the propriety of the experiment itself. In these situations, whatever it is that gives the subject's consent its justificatory power — the mysterious indicia of autonomy worth respecting — is deemed lacking. To illustrate this dynamic at work, I review below the operation of the Standard Model in three paradigmatically hard cases.

A. PRISONERS

Prisoners have long been conveniently immobile, docile, and hence ideal subjects for research and experimentation. . . . Accordingly, experimentation on prisoners is carefully scrutinized under the Standard Model. The Department of Health and Human Services warns that "prisoners may be under constraints because of their incarceration which could affect their ability to make a truly voluntary and uncoerced decision whether or not to participate as subjects in research." . . .

B. THE TERMINALLY ILL

. . . As with prisoners, experimentation with terminally or grievously ill patients distorts the Standard Model. Like children or the mentally handicapped, dying persons are often thought of as incapable of making informed decisions; and like prisoners, they are viewed as not "really" free, but instead, captive to the course of their disease and therefore under duress. Even when these patients are lucid, we fear their assessment of an experiment's benefits and risks may be skewed; we worry they might submit to quackery in a hopeless and desperate attempt to beat the inevitable. We also worry that the dying may, having abandoned all hope, submit to immoral experiments out of misplaced or entirely genuine altruism. Finally, we fear that we may be tempted to exploit these subjects' despair, incapacity, or altruism, and to railroad through experiments which might not otherwise pass ethical muster. . . .

C. CHILDREN

The use of children poses even thornier problems for research. We need to experiment on children; their problems and illnesses are often sui generis and can only be solved through experiments on them. However, the Standard Model assumes children cannot give adequate consent, and so it gives in to necessity, though the Nuremberg Code insisted that the subject's consent was essential. Because children cannot, by definition, give consent, we settle for less. In addition, because children are a necessary and unique research class, we are forced to face the steely utilitarian calculus that hides beneath the Standard Model's veneer of respect for persons.

The Standard Model requires someone's consent, and parents are the most obvious candidates. However, even parents might not be able to isolate and protect an individual child's safety and dignity, especially when another child is thrown into the equation. The same considerations that call into question whether a prisoner's consent was voluntary or informed might undermine a desperate parent's consent as well. . . .

■ GRIMES v. KENNEDY KRIEGER INSTITUTE, INC.
782 A.2d 807 (Md. 2001)

Opinion by CATHELL, J.

PROLOGUE

We initially note that these are cases of first impression for this Court. For that matter, precious few courts in the United States have addressed the issues presented in the cases at bar. . . .

In these present cases, a prestigious research institute, associated with Johns Hopkins University, based on this record, created a nontherapeutic research program whereby it required certain classes of homes to have only partial lead paint abatement modifications performed, and in at least some instances, including at least one of the cases at bar, arranged for the landlords to receive public funding by way of grants or loans to aid in the modifications. The research institute then encouraged, and in at least one of the cases at bar, required, the landlords to rent the premises to families with young children. In the event young children already resided in one of the study houses, it was contemplated that a child would remain in the premises, and the child was encouraged to remain, in order for his or her blood to be periodically analyzed. In other words, the continuing presence of the children that were the subjects of the study was required in order for the study to be complete. Apparently, the children and their parents involved in the[se] cases . . . were from a lower economic strata and were, at least in one case, minorities.

The purpose of the research was to determine how effective varying degrees of lead paint abatement procedures were. Success was to be determined by periodically, over a two-year period of time, measuring the extent to which lead dust remained in, or returned to, the premises after the varying levels of abatement modifications, and, as most important to our decision, by measuring the extent to which the theretofore healthy children's blood became contaminated with lead, and comparing that contamination with levels of lead dust in the houses over the same periods of time. [Some evidence suggests that families with young children were given priority in renting abated apartments.]. . . .

The same researchers had completed a prior study on abatement and partial abatement methods that indicated that lead dust remained and/or returned to abated houses over a period of time. . . . [The researchers also acknowledged that exposure to lead was "particularly hazardous for children"]. . . . After publishing this report, the researchers began the present research project in which children were encouraged to reside in households where the possibility of lead dust was known to the researcher to be likely, so that the lead dust content of their blood could be compared with the level of lead dust in the houses at periodic intervals over a two-year period.

Apparently, it was anticipated that the children, who were the human subjects in the program, would, or at least might, accumulate lead in their blood from the dust, thus helping the researchers to determine the extent to which the various partial abatement methods worked. There was no complete and clear explanation in the consent agreements signed by the parents of the children that the research to be conducted was designed, at least in significant part, to measure the success of the abatement procedures by measuring the extent to which the children's blood was being contaminated. It can be argued that the researchers intended that the children be the canaries in the mines but never clearly told the parents. . . .

The researchers and their Institutional Review Board apparently saw nothing wrong with the research protocols that anticipated the possible accumulation of lead in the blood of otherwise healthy children as a result of the experiment, or they believed that the consents of the parents of the children made the research appropriate. Institutional Review Boards (IRB) are oversight entities [that are within the organizational structure of the institution conducting the research]. In research experiments, an IRB can be required in some instances by either federal or state regulation, or sometimes by the conditions attached to governmental grants that are used to fund research projects. Generally, their primary functions are to assess the protocols of the project to determine whether the project itself is appropriate, whether the consent procedures are adequate, whether the methods to be employed meet proper standards, whether reporting requirements are sufficient, and the assessment of various other aspects of a research project. One of the most important objectives of such review is the review of the potential safety and the health hazard impact of a research project on the human subjects of the experiment, especially on vulnerable subjects such as children. Their function is not to help researchers seek funding for research projects.

In the instant case, as is suggested by some commentators as being endemic to the research community as a whole, infra, the IRB involved here, the Johns Hopkins University Joint Committee on Clinical Investigation, in part, abdicated that responsibility, instead suggesting to the researchers a way to miscast the characteristics of the study in order to avoid the responsibility inherent in nontherapeutic research involving children. . . .

While the suggestion of the IRB would not make this experiment any less nontherapeutic or, thus, less regulated, . . . [its action] shows two things: (1) that the IRB had a partial misperception of the difference between therapeutic and nontherapeutic research and the IRB's role in the process and (2) that the IRB was willing to aid researchers in getting around federal regulations designed to protect children used as subjects in nontherapeutic research. An IRB's primary role is to assure the safety of human research subjects—not help researchers avoid safety or health-related requirements. The IRB, in this case, misconceived, at least partially, its own role.

The provisions or conditions imposed by the federal funding entities, pursuant to federal regulations, are conditions attached to funding. As far as we are aware, or have been informed, there are no federal or state (Maryland) statutes that mandate that all research be subject to certain conditions. Certain international "codes" or "declarations" exist (one of which is supposedly binding but has never been so held) that, at least in theory, establish standards. We shall describe them, infra. Accordingly, we write on a clean slate in this case. We are guided, as we determine what is appropriate, by those international "codes" or "declarations," as well as by studies conducted by various governmental entities, by the treatises and other writings on the ethics of using children as research subjects, and by the duties, if any, arising out of the use of children as subjects of research.

Otherwise healthy children, in our view, should not be enticed into living in, or remaining in, potentially lead-tainted housing and intentionally subjected to a research program, which contemplates the probability, or even the possibility, of lead poisoning or even the accumulation of lower levels of lead in blood, in order for the extent of the contamination of the children's blood to be used by scientific researchers to assess the success of lead paint or lead dust abatement measures. Moreover, in our view, parents, whether improperly enticed by trinkets, food stamps, money or other items, have no more right to intentionally and unnecessarily place children in potentially hazardous nontherapeutic research surroundings, than do researchers. In such cases, parental consent, no matter how informed, is insufficient.

While the validity of the consent agreement and its nature as a contract, the existence or nonexistence of a special relationship, and whether the researchers performed their functions under that agreement pursuant to any special relationships are important issues in these cases that we will address, the very inappropriateness of the research itself cannot be overlooked. It is apparent that the protocols of research are even more important than the method of obtaining parental consent and the extent to which the parents were, or were not, informed. If the research methods, the protocols, are inappropriate then, especially when the IRB is willing to help researchers avoid compliance with applicable safety requirements for using children in nontherapeutic research, the consent of the parents, or of any consent surrogates, in our view, cannot make the research appropriate or the actions of the researchers and the Institutional Review Board proper.

The research relationship proffered to the parents of the children the researchers wanted to use as measuring tools, should never have been presented in a nontherapeutic context in the first instance. Nothing about the research was designed for treatment of the subject children. They were presumed to be healthy at the commencement of the project. As to them, the research was clearly nontherapeutic in nature. The experiment was simply a "for the greater good" project.[6] The specific children's health was put at risk, in order to develop low-cost abatement measures that would help all children, the landlords, and the general public as well. . . .

The research project at issue here, and its apparent protocols, differs in large degree from, but presents similar problems as those in the Tuskegee Syphilis Study conducted from 1932 until 1972 . . . the intentional exposure of soldiers to radiation in the 1940s and 50s . . . the tests involving the exposure of Navajo miners to radiation . . . and the secret administration of LSD to soldiers by the CIA and the Army in the 1950s and 60s. . . . [In] the Tuskegee Syphilis Study . . . patients infected with syphilis were not subsequently informed of the availability of penicillin for treatment of the illness, in order for the scientists and researchers to be able to continue research on the effects of the illness. . . . [P]erhaps [the] most notorious . . . [nontherapeutic research project was] the deliberate use of infection . . . in order to study the degree of infection and the rapidity of the course of the disease in the . . . typhus experiments at Buchenwald concentration camp during World War II. These programs were somewhat alike in the vulnerability of the subjects; uneducated African American men, debilitated patients in a charity hospital, prisoners of war, inmates of concentration camps and others falling within the custody and control of the agencies conducting or approving the experiments. In the present case, children, especially young children, living in lower economic circumstances, albeit not as vulnerable as the other examples, are nonetheless, vulnerable as well.

It is clear to this Court that the scientific and medical communities cannot be permitted to assume sole authority to determine ultimately what is right and appropriate in respect to research projects involving young children free of the limitations and consequences of the application of Maryland law. The Institutional Review Boards, IRBs, are, primarily, in-house organs. In our view, they are not designed, generally, to be sufficiently objective in the sense that they are as sufficiently concerned with the ethicality of the experiments they review as they are with the success of the experiments. . . . Here, the IRB, whose primary function was to insure safety and compliance with applicable regulations, encouraged the researchers to misrepresent the purpose of the research in order to bring the study under the label of "therapeutic" and thus under a lower safety

---

[6] The ultimate goal was to find the cost of the minimal level of effective lead paint or lead dust abatement costs so as to help landlords assess, hopefully positively, the commercial feasibility of attempting to abate lead dust in marginally profitable, lower rent-urban housing, in order to help preserve such housing in the Baltimore housing market. . . . The tenants involved, presumably, would be from a lower rent-urban class. . . . The children of middle class or rich parents apparently were not involved.

Indeed, the literature on the law and ethics of human experimentation is replete with warnings that all subjects, but especially vulnerable subjects, are at risk of abuse by inclusion [as research subjects]. Those vulnerable subjects included prisoners, who are subject to coercion, . . . children and the elderly . . . and racial minorities, ethnic minorities, and women . . . whom history shows to be the most frequent victims of abuses in human experimentations.

R. Alta Charo, Protecting Us to Death: Women, Pregnancy and Clinical Research Trials, 38 St. Louis U. L.J. 135, 135 (Fall, 1993). . . .

standard of regulation. The IRB's purpose was ethically wrong, and its understanding of the experiment's benefit incorrect.

The conflicts are inherent. This would be especially so when science and private industry collaborate in search of material gains. Moreover, the special relationship between research entities and human subjects used in the research will almost always impose duties.

In respect to examining that special relationship, we are obliged to further examine its nature and its ethical constraints. In that regard, when contested cases arise, the assessment of the legal effect of research on human subjects must always be subject to judicial evaluation. One method of making such evaluations is the initiation of appropriate actions bringing such matters to the attention of the courts, as has been done in the cases at bar. It may well be that in the end, the trial courts will determine that no damages have been incurred in the instant cases and thus the actions will fail for that reason. In that regard, we note that there are substantial factual differences in the . . . [separate cases under review]. But the actions, themselves, are not defective on the ground that no legal duty can, according to the trial courts, possibly exist. For the reasons discussed at length in the main body of the opinion, a legal duty normally exists between researcher and subject and in all probability exists in the cases at bar. Moreover, as we shall discuss, the consents of the parents in these cases under Maryland law constituted contracts creating duties. Additionally, under Maryland law, to the extent parental consent can ever be effective in research projects of this nature, the parents may not have been sufficiently informed and, therefore, the consents ineffective and, based on the information contained in the sparse records before this court, the research project . . . may have invaded the legal rights of the children subjected to it. . . .

II. Facts & Procedural Background . . .

The research study [giving rise to these cases] was sponsored jointly by the EPA and the Maryland Department of Housing and Community Development (DHCD). It was thus a joint federal and state project. The Baltimore City Health Department and Maryland Department of the Environment also collaborated in the study. It appears that, because the study was funded and sponsored in part by a federal entity, certain federal conditions were attached to the funding grants and approvals. There are certain uniform standards required in respect to federally funded or approved projects. We, however, are unaware of, and have not been directed to, any federal or state statute or regulation that imposes limits on this Court's powers to conduct its review of the issues presented. None of the parties have questioned this Court's jurisdiction in these cases. Moreover, 45 Code Federal Regulations (C.F.R.) 46.116(e) specifically provides: "The informed consent requirements in this policy are not intended to preempt any applicable federal, state, or local laws which require additional information to be disclosed in order for informed consent to be legally effective." Those various federal or state conditions, recommendations, etc., may well be relevant at a trial on the merits as to whether any breach of a contractual or other duty occurred, or whether negligence did, in fact, occur; but have no limiting effect on the issue of whether, at law, legal duties, via contract or "special relationships" are created in Maryland in experimental nontherapeutic research involving Maryland children. . . .

In summary, KKI conducted a study of five test groups of twenty-five houses each. The first three groups consisted of houses known to have lead present. The amount of repair and maintenance conducted increased from Group 1 to Group 2 to Group 3. The fourth group consisted of houses, which had at one time lead present but had since allegedly received a complete abatement of lead dust. The fifth group consisted of modern houses, which had never had the presence of lead dust. The twenty-five homes in each of the first three testing levels were then to be compared to the two control groups: the twenty-five homes in Group 4 that had previously been abated and the 25 modern homes in Group 5. The research study was specifically designed to do less than full lead dust abatement in some of the categories of houses in order to study the potential effectiveness, if any, of lesser levels of repair and maintenance.

If the children were to leave the houses upon the first manifestation of lead dust, it would be difficult, if not impossible, to test, over time, the rate of the level of lead accumulation in the blood of the children attributable to the manifestation. In other words, if the children were removed from the houses before the lead dust levels in their blood became elevated, the tests would probably fail, or at least the data that would establish the success of the test — or of the abatement results, would be of questionable use. Thus, it would benefit the accuracy of the test, and thus KKI, the compensated researcher, if children remained in the houses over the period of the study even after the presence of lead dust in the houses became evident. . . .

[The consent form for the study provided:]

Purpose of Study

As you may know, lead poisoning in children is a problem in Baltimore City and other communities across the country. Lead in paint, house dust and outside soil are major sources of lead exposure for children. Children can also be exposed to lead in drinking water and other sources. We understand that your house is going to have special repairs done in order to reduce exposure to lead in paint and dust. On a random basis, homes will receive one of two levels of repair. We are interested in finding out how well the two levels of repair work. The repairs are not intended, or expected, to completely remove exposure to lead.

We are now doing a study to learn about how well different practices work for reducing exposure to lead in paint and dust. We are asking you and over one hundred other families to allow us to test for lead in and around your homes up to 8 to 9 times over the next two years provided that your house qualifies for the full two years of study. Final eligibility will be determined after the initial testing of your home. We are also doing free blood lead testing of children aged 6 months to 7 years, up to 8 to 9 times over the next two years. We would also like you to respond to a short questionnaire every 6 months. This study is intended to monitor the effects of the repairs and is not intended to replace the regular medical care your family obtains. . . .

Benefits

To compensate you for your time answering questions and allowing us to sketch your home we will mail you a check in the amount of $5.00. In the future we would mail you a check in the amount of $15 each time the full questionnaire is completed. The dust, soil, water, and blood samples would be tested for lead at the Kennedy Krieger Institute at no charge to you. We would provide you with specific blood-lead results. We would contact you to discuss a summary of house test results and steps that you could take to reduce any risks of exposure. . . .

On appeal, appellant[s] seek[] review of the Circuit Court's decision granting KKI summary judgment. . . . [They] contend[] that KKI owed a duty of care . . . based on the nature of its relationship with [the children and parents participating in the study] . . . arising out of: (1) a contract between the parties; (2) a voluntary assumption by KKI; (3) a "special relationship" between the parties; and (4) a Federal regulation. . . . [The appellants argued that KKI was negligent in, for example, failing to notify a parent about elevated lead levels in a rental property for nine months, by which time her child had elevated blood levels of lead.]

III. Discussion

A. STANDARD OF REVIEW

We resolve these disputes in the context of the trial court's granting of the appellee's motions for summary judgment in the two distinct cases. The threshold issues before this Court are whether, in the two cases presented, appellee, KKI, was entitled to summary judgment as a matter of law on the basis that no contract existed and that there is inherently no duty owed to a research subject by a researcher. Perhaps even more important is the ancillary issue of whether a parent in Maryland, under the law of this State, can legally consent to placing a child in a nontherapeutic research study that carries with it any risk of harm to the health of the child. We shall resolve all of these primary issues. . . .

B. GENERAL DISCUSSION

Initially, we note that we know of no law, nor have we been directed to any applicable in Maryland courts, that provides that the parties to a scientific study, because it is a scientific, health-related study, cannot be held to have entered into special relationships with the subjects of the study that can create duties, including duties, the breach of which may give rise to negligence claims. We also are not aware of any general legal precept that immunizes nongovernmental "institutional volunteers" or scientific researchers from the responsibility for the breaches of duties arising in "special relationships." Moreover, we, at the very least, hold that, under the particular circumstances testified to by the parties, there are genuine disputes of material fact concerning whether a special relationship existed between KKI and . . . [the appellants]. Concerning this issue, the granting of the summary judgment motions was clearly inappropriate. When a "special relationship" can exist as a matter of law, the issue of whether, given certain facts, a special relationship does exist, when there is a dispute of material fact in that respect, is a decision for the finder of fact, not the trial judge. We shall hold initially that the very nature of nontherapeutic scientific research on human subjects can, and normally will, create special relationships out of which duties arise. Since World War II the specialness or nature of such relationships has been frequently of concern in and outside of the research community.

As a result of the atrocities performed in the name of science during the Holocaust, and other happenings in the World War II era, what is now known as The Nuremberg Code evolved. Of special interest to this Court, the Nuremberg Code, at least in significant part, was the result of legal thought and legal principles, as opposed to medical or scientific principles, and thus should be the preferred standard for assessing the legality of scientific research on human subjects. Under it, duties to research subjects arise. . . . [The court cited a work by distinguished Boston University Professor George Annas detailing the history of the Nuremberg Code and explaining the lack of U.S. case law regarding the regulation of research under the Nuremberg Code or any other source of regulation.] . . .

In arguing that a fuller disclosure should be made when consent is sought for nontherapeutic research, as opposed to therapeutic research, [ethicist Karine] Morin notes:

> Furthermore, as long as courts continue to interpret the doctrine of informed consent in experimentation as it applies in the context of treatment, the uniqueness of the protection needed for human research subjects will be overlooked. Failing to recognize that subjects who volunteer for the sake of the advancement of science are differently situated from patients who stand to benefit from treatment results in an analysis that misconceives the purpose of disclosure. Beyond informing the patient as to means available to treat him or her, a subject must become a voluntary and willing participant in an endeavor that may yield no direct benefit to him or her, or worse, that may cause harm.

[Karine Morin, The Standard of Disclosure in Human Subject Experimentation, 19 J. Legal Med. 157, 220 (1998).] . . .

[T]here is no[t] [a] complete record of the specific compensation of the researchers involved. Although the project was funded by the EPA, at the request of KKI the EPA has declined to furnish such information to the attorney for one of the parties, who requested it under the federal Freedom of Information Act. Whether the research's character as a co-sponsored state project opens the records under the Maryland Public Information Act has apparently not been considered. Neither is there in the record any development of what pressures, if any, were exerted in respect to the researchers obtaining the consents of the parents and conducting the experiment. Nor, for the same reason, is there a sufficient indication as to the extent to which the Institute has joined with commercial interests, if it has, for the purposes of profit, that might potentially impact upon the researcher's motivations and potential conflicts of interest — motivations that generally are assumed, in the cases of prestigious entities such as John Hopkins University, to be for the public good rather . . . [than] a search for profit.

We do note that the institution involved, the respondent here . . . is a highly respected entity, considered to be a leader in the development of treatments, and treatment itself, for children infected with lead poisoning. With reasonable assurance, we can note that its reputation alone might normally suggest that there was no realization or understanding on the Institute's part that the protocols of the experiment were questionable, except for the letter from the IRB requesting that the researchers mischaracterize the study.

We shall further address both the factual and legal bases for the findings of the trial courts, holding, ultimately, that the respective courts erred in both respects.

C. NEGLIGENCE

It is important for us to remember that appellants allege that KKI was negligent. Specifically, they allege that KKI, as a medical researcher, owed a duty of care to them, as subjects in the research study, based on the nature of the agreements between them and also based on the nature of the relationship between the parties. They contend specifically that KKI was negligent because KKI breached its duty to: (1) design a study that did not involve placing children at unnecessary risk; (2) inform participants in the study of results in a timely manner; and (3) to completely and accurately inform participants in the research study of all the hazards and risks involved in the study. . . .

Because this is a review of the granting of the two summary judgments based solely on the grounds that there was no legal duty to protect the children, we are primarily concerned with . . . whether KKI was under a duty to protect appellants from injury.[33] . . .

The relationship that existed between KKI and both sets of appellants in the case at bar was that of medical researcher and research study subject. Though not expressly recognized in the Maryland Code or in our prior cases as a type of relationship which creates a duty of care, evidence in the record suggests that such a relationship involving a duty or duties would ordinarily exist, and certainly could exist, based on the facts and circumstances of each of these individual cases. . . .

IV. THE SPECIAL RELATIONSHIPS

A. THE CONSENT AGREEMENT CONTRACT

Both sets of appellants signed a similar Consent Form prepared by KKI in which KKI expressly promised to: (1) financially compensate (however minimally) appellants for their participation in the study; . . . (2) collect lead dust samples from appellants' homes, analyze the samples, discuss the results with appellants, and discuss steps that could be taken, which could reduce exposure to lead; and (3) collect blood samples from children in the household and provide appellants with the results of the blood tests. In return, appellants agreed to participate in the study, by: (1) allowing KKI into appellants' homes to collect dust samples; (2) periodically filling out questionnaires; and (3) allowing the children's blood to be drawn, tested, and utilized in the study. If consent agreements contain such provisions, and the trial court did not find otherwise, we hold from our own examination of the record that such provisions were so contained, mutual assent, offer, acceptance, and consideration existed, all of which created contractual relationships imposing duties by reason of the consent agreement . . . (as well, as we discuss elsewhere, by the very nature of such relationships).

---

[33] We note that there was little suggestion of actual permanent injury to the children involved with these two cases. Our opinion is not directed to the matter of whether damages can be proven in the present cases.

By having appellants sign this Consent Form, both KKI and appellants expressly made representations, which, in our view, created a bilateral contract between the parties. At the very least, it suggests that appellants were agreeing with KKI to participate in the research study with the expectation that they would be compensated, albeit, more or less, minimally, be informed of all the information necessary for the subject to freely choose whether to participate, and continue to participate, and receive promptly any information that might bear on their willingness to continue to participate in the study. This includes full, detailed, prompt, and continuing warnings as to all the potential risks and hazards inherent in the research or that arise during the research. KKI, in return, was getting the children to move into the houses and/or to remain there over time, and was given the right to test the children's blood for lead. As consideration to KKI, it got access to the houses and to the blood of the children that had been encouraged to live in a "risk" environment. In other words, KKI received a measuring tool—the children's blood. Considerations existed, mainly money, food coupons, trinkets, bilateral promises, blood to be tested in order to measure success. "Informed consent" of the type used here, which imposes obligation and confers consideration on both researcher and subject (in these cases, the parents of the subjects) may differ from the more one-sided "informed consent" normally used in actual medical practice. Researcher/subject consent in nontherapeutic research can, and in this case did, create a contract.[35]

B. THE SUFFICIENCY OF THE CONSENT FORM

The consent form did not directly inform the parents of the fact that it was contemplated that some of the children might ingest lead dust particles, and that one of the reasons the blood of the children was to be tested was to evaluate how effective the various abatement measures were.

A reasonable parent would expect to be clearly informed that it was at least contemplated that her child would ingest lead dust particles, and that the degree to which lead dust contaminated the child's blood would be used as one of the ways in which the success of the experiment would be measured. The fact that if such information was furnished, it might be difficult to obtain human subjects for the research, does not affect the need to supply the information, or alter the ethics of failing to provide such information. A human subject is entitled to all material information. The respective parent should also have been clearly informed that in order for the measurements to be most helpful, the child needed to stay in the house until the conclusion of the study. Whether assessed by a subjective or an objective standard, the children, or their surrogates, should have been additionally informed that the researchers anticipated that, as a result of the experiment, it was possible that there might be some accumulation of lead in the blood of the children. The "informed" consent was not valid because full material information was not furnished to the subjects or their parents.

---

[35] We make no determination as to whether informed consent in a therapeutic medical context can generate contractual obligations.

C. SPECIAL RELATIONSHIP

In Case Number 128, Ms. Hughes signed a Consent Form in which KKI agreed to provide her with "specific blood-lead results" and discuss with her "a summary of house test results and steps that [she] could take to reduce any risks of exposure." She contends that this agreement between the parties gave rise to a duty owed by KKI to provide her with that information in a timely manner. She signed the Consent Form on March 10, 1993. The project began almost simultaneously. KKI collected dust samples in the Monroe Street property on March 9, 1993, August 23, 1993, March 9, 1994, September 19, 1994, April 18, 1995, and November 13, 1995. The March 9, 1993 dust testing revealed what the researchers referred to as "hot spots," where the level of lead was "higher than might be found in a completely renovated house." . . . [T]his information was not furnished to Ms. Hughes until December 16, 1993, more than nine months after the samples had been collected and not until after Ericka Grimes's blood was found to contain elevated levels of lead. She contends that not only did KKI have a duty to report such information in a timely manner but that it breached this duty by delaying to such a time that her daughter was allowed to contract lead poisoning. Looking at the relevant facts of Case Number 128, they are susceptible to inferences supporting the position of appellant, Ericka Grimes, and, moreover, that, if true, would create a "special relationship" out of which duties would be created. Therefore, for this reason alone, the grant of summary judgment was improper. . . .

[T]he trial courts appear to have held that special relationships out of which duties arise cannot be created by the relationship between researchers and the subjects of the research. While in some rare cases that may be correct, it is not correct when researchers recruit people, especially children whose consent is furnished indirectly, to participate in nontherapeutic procedures that are potentially hazardous, dangerous, or deleterious to their health. As opposed to compilation of already extant statistics for purposes of studying human health matters, the creation of study conditions or protocols or participation in the recruitment of otherwise healthy subjects to interact with already existing, or potentially existing, hazardous conditions, or both, for the purpose of creating statistics from which scientific hypotheses can be supported, would normally warrant or create such special relationships as a matter of law.

It is of little moment that an entity is an institutional volunteer in a community. If otherwise, the legitimacy of the claim to noble purpose would always depend upon the particular institution and the particular community it is serving in a given case. As we have indicated, history is replete with claims of noble purpose for institutions and institutional volunteers in a wide variety of communities.

Institutional volunteers may intend to do good or, as history has proven, even to do evil and may do evil or good depending on the institution and the community they serve. Whether an institutional volunteer[36] in a particular

---

[36] Moreover, it is not clear that KKI was a mere volunteer in any event. It received funding for developing and conducting the research. Whether it recognized a profit is unknown from the record. The "for profit" nature of some research may well increase the duties of researchers to insure the safety of research subjects, and may well increase researchers' or an institution's susceptibility for damages in respect to any injuries incurred by research subjects.

community should be granted exceptions from the application of law is a matter that should be scrutinized closely by an appropriate public policy maker. Generally, but not always, the legislative branch is appropriately the best first forum to consider exceptions to the tort laws of this State — even then it should consider all ramifications of the policy — especially considering the general vulnerability of subjects of such studies — in this case, small children. In the absence of the exercise of legislative policymaking, we hold that special relationships, out of which duties arise, the breach of which can constitute negligence, can result from the relationships between researcher and research subjects.

D. THE FEDERAL REGULATIONS

A duty may be prescribed by a statute, or a special relationship creating duties may arise from the requirement for compliance with statutory provisions. Although there is no duty of which we are aware prescribed by the Maryland Code in respect to scientific research . . . , federal regulations have been enacted that impose standards of care that attach to federally funded or sponsored research projects that use human subjects. See 45 C.F.R. Part 46 (2000). 45 C.F.R. Part 46, Subpart A, is entitled "Basic HHS Policy for Protection of Human Research Subjects" and Subpart D of the regulation is entitled "Additional Protections for Children Involved as Subjects in Research." . . . [T]his study was funded, and co-sponsored, by the EPA and presumably was therefore subject to these federal conditions. These conditions, if appropriate administrative action has been taken, require fully informed consent in any research using human subjects conducted, supported, or otherwise subject to any level of control or funding by any federal department or agency. . . .

These federal regulations, especially the requirement for adherence to sound ethical principles, strike right at the heart of KKI's defense of the granting of the Motions for Summary Judgment. Fully informed consent is lacking in these cases. The research did not comply with the regulations. There clearly was more than a minimal risk involved. Under the regulations, children should not have been used for the purpose of measuring how much lead they would accumulate in their blood while living in partially abated houses to which they were recruited initially or encouraged to remain, because of the study. . . .

Clearly, KKI, as a research institution, is required to obtain a human participant's fully informed consent, using sound ethical principles. It is clear from the wording of the applicable federal regulations that this requirement of informed consent continues during the duration of the research study and applies to new or changing risks. In this case, a special relationship out of which duties might arise might be created by reason of the federally imposed regulations. The question becomes whether this duty of informed consent created by federal regulation, as a matter of state law, translates into a duty of care arising out of the unique relationship that is researcher-subject, as opposed to doctor-patient. We answer that question in the affirmative. In this State, it may, depending on the facts, create such a duty.

Additionally, the Nuremberg Code, intended to be applied internationally, and never expressly rejected in this country, inherently and implicitly, speaks strongly to the existence of special relationships imposing ethical duties on researchers who conduct nontherapeutic experiments on human subjects. The Nuremberg Code specifically requires researchers to make known to human subjects of research "all inconveniences and hazards reasonably to be expected; and the effects upon his health or person which may possibly come from his participation in the experiment." The breach of obligations imposed on researchers by the Nuremberg Code, might well support actions sounding in negligence in cases such as those at issue here. We reiterate as well that, given the facts and circumstances of both of these cases, there were, at the very least, genuine disputes of material facts concerning the relationship and duties of the parties, and compliance with the regulations.

V. THE ETHICAL APPROPRIATENESS OF THE RESEARCH

The World Medical Association in its Declaration of Helsinki . . . included a code of ethics for investigative researchers and was an attempt by the medical community to establish its own set of rules for conducting research on human subjects. . . . [39]

The determination of whether a duty exists under Maryland law is the ultimate function of various policy considerations as adopted by either the Legislature, or, if it has not spoken, as it has not in respect to this situation, by Maryland courts. In our view, otherwise healthy children should not be the subjects of nontherapeutic experimentation or research that has the potential to be harmful to the child. It is, first and foremost, the responsibility of the researcher and the research entity to see to the harmlessness of such nontherapeutic research. Consent of parents can never relieve the researcher of this duty. We do not feel that it serves proper public policy concerns to permit children to be placed in situations of potential harm, during nontherapeutic procedures, even if parents, or other surrogates, consent. Under these types of circumstances, even where consent is given, albeit inappropriately, policy considerations suggest that there remains a special relationship between researchers and participants to the research study, which imposes a duty of care. This is entirely consistent with the principles found in the Nuremberg Code.

Researchers cannot ever be permitted to completely immunize themselves by reliance on consents, especially when the information furnished to the subject, or the party consenting, is incomplete in a material respect. A researcher's duty is not created by, or extinguished by, the consent of a research subject or by IRB approval. The duty to a vulnerable research subject is independent of consent, although the obtaining of consent is one of the duties a researcher must perform. All of this is especially so when the subjects of research are children. Such legal duties, and legal protections, might additionally be warranted because of the likely conflict of interest between the goal of the research experimenter and the health of the human subject, especially, but not exclusively, when such research is commercialized. There is always a potential substantial conflict of interest on the part of researchers as between them and the human subjects used in their

---

[39] . . . Declaration of Helsinki, World Medical Assembly (WMA) 18th Assembly (June 1964), amended by 29th WMA Tokyo, Japan (October 1975), 35th WMA Venice, Italy (October 1983) and the 41st WMA Hong Kong (September 1989).

research. If participants in the study withdraw from the research study prior to its completion, then the results of the study could be rendered meaningless. There is thus an inherent reason for not conveying information to subjects as it arises, that might cause the subjects to leave the research project. That conflict dictates a stronger reason for full and continuous disclosure. . . .

A special relationship giving rise to duties, the breach of which might constitute negligence, might also arise because, generally, the investigators are in a better position to anticipate, discover, and understand the potential risks to the health of their subjects. . . .

This duty requires the protection of the research subjects from unreasonable harm and requires the researcher to completely and promptly inform the subjects of potential hazards existing from time to time because of the profound trust that participants place in investigators, institutions, and the research enterprise as a whole to protect them from harm. . . .

While we acknowledge that foreseeability does not necessarily create a duty, we recognize that potential harm to the children participants of this study was both foreseeable and potentially extreme. A "special relationship" also exists in circumstances where such experiments are conducted.

VI. Parental Consent for Children to Be Subjects of Potentially Hazardous Nontherapeutic Research

The issue of whether a parent can consent to the participation of her or his child in a nontherapeutic health-related study that is known to be potentially hazardous to the health of the child raises serious questions with profound moral and ethical implications. What right does a parent have to knowingly expose a child not in need of therapy to health risks or otherwise knowingly place a child in danger, even if it can be argued it is for the greater good? The issue in these specific contested cases does not relate primarily to the authority of the parent, but to the procedures of KKI and similar entities that may be involved in such health-related studies. The issue of the parents' right to consent on behalf of the children has not been fully presented in either of these cases, but should be of concern not only to lawyers and judges, but to moralists, ethicists, and others. The consenting parents in the contested cases at bar were not the subjects of the experiment; the children were. Additionally, this practice presents the potential problems of children initiating actions in their own names upon reaching majority, if indeed, they have been damaged as a result of being used as guinea pigs in nontherapeutic scientific research. Children, it should be noted, are not in our society the equivalent of rats, hamsters, monkeys, and the like. Because of the overriding importance of this matter and this Court's interest in the welfare of children—we shall address the issue.

Most of the relatively few cases in the area of the ethics of protocols of various research projects involving children have merely assumed that a parent can give informed consent for the participation of their children in nontherapeutic research. . . .

It is not in the best interest of a specific child, in a nontherapeutic research project, to be placed in a research environment, which might possibly be, or which proves to be, hazardous to the health of the child . . . in order to test methods that may ultimately benefit all children. . . .

One simply does not expose otherwise healthy children, incapable of personal assent (consent), to a nontherapeutic research environment that is known at the inception of the research, might cause the children to ingest lead dust. It is especially troublesome, when a measurement of the success of the research experiment is, in significant respect, to be determined by the extent to which the blood of the children absorbs, and is contaminated by, a substance that the researcher knows can, in sufficient amounts, whether solely from the research environment or cumulative from all sources, cause serious and long term adverse health effects. Such a practice is not legally acceptable. . . .

In the[se] case[s], no impartial judicial review or oversight was sought by the researchers or by the parents. . . . Science cannot be permitted to be the sole judge of the appropriateness of such research methods on human subjects, especially in respect to children. We hold that in these contested cases, the research study protocols [presented to the court] . . . were not appropriate. . . .

VII. Conclusion

We hold that in Maryland a parent, appropriate relative, or other applicable surrogate, cannot consent to the participation of a child or other person under legal disability in nontherapeutic research or studies in which there is any risk of injury or damage to the health of the subject.

We hold that informed consent agreements in nontherapeutic research projects, under certain circumstances can constitute contracts; and that, under certain circumstances, such research agreements can, as a matter of law, constitute "special relationships" giving rise to duties, out of the breach of which negligence actions may arise. We also hold that, normally, such special relationships are created between researchers and the human subjects used by the researchers. Additionally, we hold that governmental regulations can create duties on the part of researchers towards human subjects out of which "special relationships" can arise. Likewise, such duties and relationships are consistent with the provisions of the Nuremberg Code.

The determination as to whether a "special relationship" actually exists is to be done on a case by case basis. . . . The determination as to whether a special relationship exists, if properly pled, lies with the trier of fact. We hold that there was ample evidence in the cases at bar to support a fact finder's determination of the existence of duties arising out of contract, or out of a special relationship, or out of regulations and codes, or out of all of them, in each of the cases.

We hold that on the present record, the Circuit Courts erred in their assessment of the law and of the facts as pled in granting KKI's motions for summary judgment in both cases before this Court. Accordingly, we vacate the rulings of the Circuit Court for Baltimore City and remand these cases to that court for further proceedings consistent with this opinion. . . .

Raker, J., concurring in result only:

These appeals present the narrow question of whether the Circuit Courts erred in granting summary judgments to appellee, the Kennedy Krieger Institute, a research entity, on the ground that, as a matter of law, it owed no duty to warn appellants, Ericka Grimes and Myron Higgins, et al., human subjects participating in its research study. I concur in the judgment of the Court only and join in the Court's judgment that the Circuit Courts erred in granting summary judgments to appellee. These cases should be remanded for further proceedings.

I concur in the Court's judgment because I find that appellants have alleged sufficient facts to establish that there existed a special relationship between the parties in these cases, which created a duty of care that, if breached, gives rise to an action in negligence. . . . I would hold that a special relationship giving rise to a duty of care, the breach of which would be the basis for an action in negligence, existed in these cases and would remand the cases at bar to the Circuit Courts for further proceedings. I agree with the majority that this duty includes the protection of research subjects from unreasonable harm and requires the researcher to inform research subjects completely and promptly of potential hazards resulting from participation in the study. . . . As a result of the existence of this tort duty, I find it unnecessary to reach the thorny question, not even raised by any of the parties, of whether the informed consent agreements in these cases constitute legally binding contracts. . . .

As I have indicated, this case presents a narrow question of whether a duty in tort exists between the plaintiffs and the defendants. . . . Nonetheless, the majority appears to have decided the issue of whether such duty of care was, in fact, breached as a matter of law, without a hearing or a trial on the merits.

I cannot join in the majority's sweeping factual determinations. . . .

ON MOTION FOR RECONSIDERATION

PER CURIAM.

The Court has considered the motion for reconsideration and the submissions by the various amici curiae. The motion is denied, with this explanation.

Some of the issues raised in this case, in the briefs and at oral argument, were important ones of first impression in this State, and the Court therefore attempted to address those issues in a full and exhaustive manner. The case reached us in the context of summary judgments entered by the Circuit Court, which entailed rulings that the evidence presented by the plaintiffs, for purposes of the motions, even when taken in a light most favorable to them, was insufficient as a matter of law to establish the prospect of liability. We disagreed with that determination. Although we discussed the various issues and arguments in considerable detail, the only conclusion that we reached as a matter of law was that, on the record currently before us, summary judgment was improperly granted — that sufficient evidence was presented in both cases which, if taken in a light most favorable to the plaintiffs and believed by a jury, would suffice to justify verdicts in favor of the plaintiffs. Thus, the cases were remanded for further proceedings in the Circuit Court. Every issue bearing on liability or damages remains open for further factual development, and any relevant evidence not otherwise precluded under our rules of evidence is admissible.

Much of the argument in support of and in opposition to the motion for reconsideration centered on the question of what limitations should govern a parent's authority to provide informed consent for the participation of his or her minor child in a medical study. In the Opinion, we said at one point that a parent "cannot consent to the participation of a child . . . in nontherapeutic research or studies in which there is any risk of injury or damage to the health of the subject." As we think is clear from Section VI of the Opinion, by "any risk," we meant any articulable risk beyond the minimal kind of risk that is inherent in any endeavor. The context of the statement was a non-therapeutic study that promises no medical benefit to the child whatever, so that any balance between risk and benefit is necessarily negative. As we indicated, the determination of whether the study in question offered some benefit, and therefore could be regarded as therapeutic in nature, or involved more than that minimal risk is open for further factual development on remand.

RAKER. Judge, dissenting.

I respectfully dissent from the order denying the motions for reconsideration. I adhere to the views previously expressed in my concurring opinion filed herein. . . . The majority's discussion of the ability of a parent or guardian to consent to the participation of a minor child in a nontherapeutic research study and the discussion regarding the ethics of the research conducted in these cases involve serious public policy considerations. The statements are a declaration of public policy that, in the posture of this case, are best left to the General Assembly. . . .

Notes: Conflicts of Interest and Human Subjects Research

1. *Federal Regulation.* Most of the field of clinical investigation is now very closely regulated by the federal Food and Drug Administration and by the Department of Health and Human Services Office for Human Research Protections. U.S. Dep't of Health & Human Servs., Protection of Human Subjects, 45 C.F.R. §§46.101-.409; U.S. Food & Drug Admin., Protection of Human Subjects, 21 C.F.R. §§50.1-.58. The federal regulatory structure differs from informed consent law in that the penalty for violation is not damages but disqualification from federal funding. The regulatory focus, however, mirrors the informed consent themes already introduced in our discussion of fiduciary liability.

The regulations are designed to safeguard individual autonomy from overreaching by researchers. The mechanism used to provide protection is a combination of mandatory disclosure and individual assent. The researcher is charged with a special obligation to care for his or her research subject and to protect the subject from harm. The federal regulations require prior approval of informed consent process that typically includes written disclosures and consents. These documents are reviewed by interdisciplinary ethical review committees (called "institutional review boards" or "IRBs") located in hospitals, in other medical research centers, and in universities where research is conducted using human subjects. The federal regulations governing research involving human subjects explicitly preserve from preemption foreign, state, or local laws providing additional protections. 45 C.F.R. §46.101(f), (g). The relevant federal agency may also permit federal agencies to apply equivalent or more protective internationally recognized protections for human research subjects in research conducted in foreign countries. Id. §46.101(h). For a discussion of the importance of state regulation of pharmaceutical clinical trials, see Jeffrey Gibbs, State Regulation of Pharmaceutical Clinical Trials, 59 Food & Drug L.J. 265 (2004).

2. *Basic Definitions: What Is Research?* The federal regulations establish a broad definition of *research* as "a systemic investigation, including research development, testing, and evaluation, designed to develop or contribute to generalizable knowledge." 45 C.F.R. §46.102(d). A "[h]uman subject" is "a living individual about whom the investigator (whether professional or student) conducting research obtains (1) data through intervention or interaction with the individual, or (2) identifiable private information." Id. 46.102(f). Should the collection of data about the side effects of drugs after they have been approved and sold in the marketplace be considered human subjects research? See Susan Okie, Safety in Numbers — Monitoring Risk in Approved Drugs, 352 New Eng. J. Med. 1173 (2005). Is the line between medical treatment and medical research always clear? See Lars Noah, Informed Consent and the Elusive Dichotomy Between Standard and Experimental Therapy, 28 Am. J.L. & Med. 361 (2002).

Human subjects research is generally considered to be ethical so long as the participants consent, the risks to subjects are minimized, the selection of subjects is equitable, the anticipated benefits outweigh the risk to the subjects, data is monitored to protect patient safety, and subjects' privacy is protected. See, e.g., 45 C.F.R. §46.111. Therapeutic research provides the possibility of benefit to the research subject; some risk to the subject might therefore be tolerated so long as it is outweighed by the anticipated benefit and other criteria are met. Id. Nontherapeutic research does not offer a benefit to the subject; the research therefore cannot proceed unless the risks are minimal.

The *Grimes* court characterized the lead abatement research as involving more than minimal risk and suggested that parents might not be permitted to consent to nontherapeutic research involving children that poses more than a minimal risk. What is a minimal risk? Federal regulations provide that "minimal risk means that the probability and magnitude of harm or discomfort anticipated in the research are not greater in and of themselves than those ordinarily encountered in daily life. . . . " 45 C.F.R. §46.102(i). Is this the definition used by the *Grimes* court? Why didn't the *Grimes* court consider the risk to be minimal, given that children who live in older housing frequently are exposed to the risk of lead paint?

3. *The Role of IRBs.* Under federal law, the membership of an IRB is supposed to be diverse and professionally knowledgeable about research proposals and research ethics. 45 C.F.R. §46.107. The IRB must include at least one member who is unaffiliated with the institution. IRB members may not participate in the review of a research project in which they have a conflict of interest. Id.

The *Grimes* court was skeptical about the independence of IRBs. Commentators have raised many questions about the ability of potentially overworked and conflicted IRBs to safeguard research subjects. These criticisms and various reform proposals are well summarized in Carl Coleman, Rationalizing Risk Assessment in Human Subject Research, 46 Ariz. L. Rev. 1 (2004); Barbara Noah,

Bioethical Malpractice: Risk and Responsibility in Human Research, 7 J. Health Care L. & Pol'y 175 (2004); Eve E. Slater, IRB Reform, 346 New Eng. J. Med. 1402 (2002); Robert Steinbrook, Improving Protection for Research Subjects, 346 New Eng. J. Med. 1425 (2002); Michael C. Christian et al., Central Institutional Review Board for Multi-Institutional Trials, 346 New Eng. J. Med. 1405 (2002).

4. *The Role of Informed Consent.* The federal regulations focus on the informed consent process as the major tool for protecting human subjects. The informed consent rules are much more detailed in some areas than common law rules but do not preempt those laws. 45 C.F.R. §46.116. Note that federal law prohibits research sponsors from requiring waivers of liability for negligence. Id. Examine the informed consent form excerpted in the *Grimes* decision. In what way(s) was it deficient? For an overview of the current informed consent process globally and the continuing development of the informed consent doctrine see Jennifer Couture, The Changes in Informed Consent in Experimental Procedures: The Evolution of a Concept, 1 J. Health & Biomedical L. 125 (2004); Richard S. Saver, Medical Research and Intangible Harm, U. Cin. L. Rev. 941 (2006).

5. *The Aftermath of* Grimes. There have been few lawsuits involving experimental medicine using either negligence or informed consent theories, despite the huge volume of activity involving research subjects. A few courts have considered whether clinical trial sponsors owe a fiduciary duty to participants. See, e.g., Suthers v. Amgen Inc. 441 F. Supp. 2d 478, (S.D.N.Y. 2006) (plaintiffs' complaint dismissed in case challenging drug company's decision to terminate clinical trial and deny access to experimental drug; no fiduciary duty owed); and Abney v. Amgen Inc., 443 F.3d 540 (6th Cir. 2006) (no fiduciary duty as the clinical trial sponsors were not acting primarily for the benefit of the participants). See also Paul B. Miller & Charles Weijer, Fiduciary Obligation in Clinical Research, 34 J. L. Med. & Ethics 424 (2006) (advocating the view that physician-researchers have a fiduciary relationship with their patient-subjects); E. Haavi Morreim, The Clinical Investigator as Fiduciary: Discarding a Misguided Idea, 33 J. L. Med. & Ethics 586 (2005) (critical of the application of fiduciary principles to the research context); E. Haavi Morreim, Litigation in Clinical Research: Malpractice Doctrines Versus Research Realities, 32 J. L. Med & Ethics 474 (2004) (advocating a specialized tort approach to cases involving research). See also Beth S. Rose & Vincent Lodato, Emerging Litigation Involving Human Subjects: A Future for Class Actions?, 35 The Brief 43 (Summer 2006); Carl H. Coleman, Duties to Subjects in Clinical Research, 58 Vand. L. Rev. 387 (2005).

The *Grimes* decision was understandably controversial. Imagine how medical researchers might feel about a decision that appears to compare a research study sponsored by the federal government and conducted by a leading research institution to Nazi war crimes. The *Grimes* decision sparked a number of commentaries, including Lainie Friedman Ross, In Defense of the Hopkins Lead Abatement Studies, 30 J. L. Med. & Ethics 50 (2002).

What did the court actually hold in *Grimes*? The lengthy opinion (more than seventy pages, heavily edited here) explores the broad terrain of human subjects research and appears to hold that (1) parents/surrogates cannot consent to the participation of their children/incompetents in nontherapeutic research where there is any risk of injury or damage to the health of the subject; (2) informed consent agreements in nontherapeutic research trials may create "special relationships," and violation of the agreements may be addressed in breach of contract and negligence; and (3) other sources of the "special relationship" include the researcher-subject relationship itself and governmental research regulations. How much does the court majority take back in the per curiam opinion rejecting reconsideration? The court suggests that the parties are free to present evidence on any of these issues. What evidence would you present for either side?

6. *Conflicts of Interest.* The *Grimes* court repeatedly expressed concerns about the conflicts of interest between human subjects and researchers. Researchers may have a financial interest in the subject matter of their research that puts their research subjects at risk or affects the reliability of research results. See *Moore*, supra. See, e.g., Justin E. Beckelman, Yan Li, & Cary P. Gross, Scope and Impact of Financial Conflicts of Interest in Biomedical Research: A Systemic Review, 289 JAMA 454 (2003); Roy H. Perlis et al., Industry Sponsorship and Financial Conflict of Interest in the Reporting of Clinical Trials in Psychiatry, 162 Am. J. Psychiatry 1957 (2005).

A researcher's financial interests might also create broader risks, such as when a researcher signs a confidentiality agreement or "gag clause" limiting the public disclosure of research results or when a drug company seeks to hide negative information about the safety or efficacy of a new drug. For a discussion of the use of gag clauses in clinical trials, see Robert Steinbrook, Gag Clauses in Clinical-Trial Agreements, 352 New Eng J. Med. 2160 (May 2005). For discussion of initiatives designed to ensure access to both positive and negative information about the safety and efficacy of new drugs, see Robert Steinbrook, Public Registration of Clinical Trials, 351 New Eng. J. Med. 315 (2004); Robert Steinbrook, Registration of Clinical Trials — Voluntary or Mandatory?, 351 New Eng. J. Med. 1820 (2004); and Catherine D. De Angelis et al., Is This Clinical Trial Fully Registered? — A Statement from the International Committee of Medical Journal Editors, 352 New Eng. J. Med. 2436 (2005).

A number of organizations have focused on methods of identifying and limiting conflicts of interest between researchers and research subjects. The Association of American Medical Colleges (AAMC) has issued guidelines on individual researcher conflicts and institutional conflicts. See http://www.aamc.org/research/coi/start.htm. See also DHHS's Office for Human Research Protections, Financial Relationships in Clinical Research (May 2004). See generally Robert Gatter, Walking the Talk of Trust in Human Subjects Research: The Challenge of Regulating Financial Conflicts of Interest, 52 Emory L.J. 327 (2003); Robert P. Kelch, Maintaining the Public Trust in Clinical Research, 346 New Eng. J. Med. 285 (2002); Karine Marin et al., Managing Conflicts of Interest in the Conduct of Clinical Trials, 287 JAMA 78 (2002); Michelle Mello, Brian Clarridge & David Studdert, Academic Medical Centers; Standards for Clinical-Trial Agreements with Industry, 352 New Eng. J. Med. 2202 (2005); Kevin P. Weinfurt et al., Policies of Academic Medical Center for Disclosing Financial Conflicts of Interest to Potential Research Subjects, 81 Acad. Med. 113 (2006); Kevin Williams, Managing Physician Financial Conflicts of Interest in Clinical Trials Conducted in the Private Practice Setting, 59 Food & Drug L.J. 45 (2004); Paul E. Kalb & Kristin Graham Koehler, Legal Issues in Scientific Research, 287 JAMA 85 (2002). The economic aspects of medical research may also be regulated under the federal fraud and abuse laws.

7. *The Economic Interests of Clinical Research Subjects.* Should clinical research subjects share in the economic value of discoveries? The ownership issue, famously raised in Moore v. Regents of the University of California, 793 P.2d 479 (Cal. 1990), supra at page 182, has resurfaced. In Washington University v. Catalona, a federal district court found that fully informed tissue donors retained no ownership rights to their biological materials. 437 F. Supp. 2d 985 (2006). Universities were keenly interested in this outcome due to fears that research biobanks would be severely restricted if donor-patients could control the use of their donated tissues. See Jocelyn Kaiser, Court Decides Tissue Samples Belong to University, Not Patients, 312 Science 345 (2006); Rebecca Skloot, Taking the Least of You, N.Y. Times Magazine, April 16, 2006, at p. 38.

The economic interests of research subjects have also been debated in the domain of intellectual property law. See, e.g., Greenberg v. Miami Children's Hospital Research Inst. Inc., 264 F. Supp. 2d 1064 (S.D. Fla. 2003), excerpted at page 398 (dismissing all but unjust enrichment claims brought by families whose samples had been used to develop a genetic test for Canavan's Disease). See also Eliot Marshall, Genetic Testing: Families Sue Hospital, Scientist for Control of Canavan Gene, 290 Science 1062 (2000); Charlotte H. Harrison, Neither *Moore* nor the Market: Alternative Models for Compensating Contributors of Human Tissue, 28 Am. J.L. & Med. 77 (2002). See infra at page 565.

8. *Research on Vulnerable Populations.* As Professor Richard Garnett notes, much of the controversy in human research has surrounded projects involving groups viewed as particularly vulnerable to coercion or abuse. Should it matter who or what the subject matter of the research is? Is it possible that some of the rules meant to prevent potential research subjects from feeling pressure to participate have gone too far? See David Orentlicher, Making Research a Requirement of Treatment: Why We Should Sometimes Let Doctors Pressure Patients to Participate in Research, 35 Hastings Center Rep. 20 (2005).

(a) *Children.* The use of children in research presents special problems because the only "consent" available is parental consent, and parents do not always protect their children from harm. Federal regulations provide special protections for children serving as research subjects. See 45 C.F.R. §§46.401-.409 (HHS regulations); 21 C.F.R. §§50.50-.56 (FDA regulations). See also NIH Policy Guidance on the Inclusion of Children in Research (1998). Research can be particularly controversial if it involves pregnant women, fetuses, and neonates. 45 C.F.R. §§46.201-.20.

There are conflicting objectives of scientific research involving children: (1) ensuring that children benefit from the progress in medical care made possible by such research and (2) minimizing the risks to children from their participation in scientific research. See, e.g., Marilyn Field & Richard Behrman, Ethical Conduct of Clinical Research Involving Children (2004); Carrie Fisher & Thomas Keens, Participation of Children in Research, 26 Whittier L. Rev. 823 (2005); and Lainie Friedman Ross, Children in Medical Research: Access Versus Protection (2006).

Despite the controversy, public policy makers sometimes actually seek to encourage research involving children. One example involves pediatric drug testing. Many drugs have been tested only in adults, leaving physicians to choose between denying children access to potentially useful medications or guessing about the correct dosage for pediatric use. Congress has become very involved in the issue. See, e.g., Best Pharmaceuticals for Children Act, Pub. L. No. 107-109, 115 Stat. 1408 (2002) (incentives for pediatric research on certain drugs; expires due to sunset clause in 2007, absent congressional action); Pediatric Research Equality Act, Pub. L. No. 108-155, 117 Stat. 1936 (2003) (permitting the FDA to require pediatric data in some circumstances). The FDA Web site includes a collection of material on pediatric issues, http://www.fda.gov/cder/pediatric/. See also Holly Fernandez Lynch, Give Them What They Want? The Permissibility of Pediatric Placebo-Controlled Trials Under the Best Pharmaceuticals for Children Act, 16 Annals Health L. 79 (2007).

(b) *Patients with Life-Threatening Illnesses.* Research is an important issue for persons with terminal conditions. Where the current, tested treatments are ineffective, people are often tempted to view "research" as providing the best treatment. They may be particularly vulnerable to coercion and the implicit promises and hopes offered by researchers. On the other hand, of course, research in these areas is extremely important for current and future patients. The issue is addressed again in Chapter 6's discussion of the power of the state to protect terminally ill persons from potentially harmful drugs.

(c) *Mentally Ill/Incompetent Patients.* Similar concerns exist about whether surrogates can give consent for research on mentally ill and other incompetent patients, with the additional concern about who is an appropriate surrogate. See generally Rebecca Dresser, Dementia Research: Ethics and Policy for the Twenty-first Century, 35 Ga. L. Rev. 661 (2001); Ethics in Psychiatric Research: A Resource Manual for Human Subjects Protection (Harold Alan Pincus et al. eds., 1999).

(d) *Prisoners.* Should prisoners be permitted to participate in research, even when they "consent"? HHS regulations provide special protections for prisoners. See 45 C.F.R. §§46.301-.306; OHRP Guidance on the Involvement of Prisoners in Research (2003). The special rules require, for example, that a majority of the IRB members have no other association with the prison and that one member be a prisoner or prisoner representative. Another provision requires assurance that parole boards will not take the prisoner's participation into account; prisoners must also be informed of this policy. See also Lawrence O. Gostin, Biomedical Research Involving Prisoners: Ethical Values and Legal Regulation, 297 JAMA 737 (2007) (proposals to modify rules governing research on prisoners); Barron H. Lerner, Subject or Objects? Prisoners and Human Experimentation, 356 New Eng. J. Med. 1806 (2007).

9. *Emergency Research.* Federal regulators recently carved out an exception to the norm of disclosure and consent. FDA regulations now permit research experimentation on patients who have not consented, personally or through surrogates, in certain circumstances. Under the rule, an independent physician and an IRB must agree that the clinical trial concerns a life-threatening condition and that there is no proven, available treatment; that obtaining consent is not feasible; that the research cannot be carried out in another manner; and that the risks and benefits of the experimental procedure are reasonable under the circumstances. 21 C.F.R. §50.24.

The new regulations have been somewhat controversial because they explicitly abandon the Nuremberg Code's requirement of informed consent. See Nuremberg Code, available at http://ohsr.od.nih.gov/guidelines/nuremberg. html. Some commentators also maintain that these regulations allow research that has no therapeutic benefit for the immediate patient since they include patients who are near death with no hope of recovery. For commentaries on the new guidelines, see Richard S. Saver, Critical Care Research and Informed Consent, 75 N.C. L. Rev. 205 (1996); Jeremy Sugarman, Examining Provisions for Research Without Consent in the Emergency Setting, 37(1) Hastings Center Rep. 12 (Jan.-Feb. 2007); Symposium, In Case of Emergency: No Need for Consent, 27(1) Hastings Center Rep. 7-12 (1997).

Post-9/11, the FDA extended the emergency exception to informed consent to cover the "use of investigational in vitro diagnostic devices to identify chemical, biological, radiological, or nuclear agents without informed consent in some circumstances." Medical Devices; Exception from General Requirements for Informed Consent, 71 Fed. Reg. 32827, 32827 (2006). The new rule was issued without the usual notice and comment procedures. See also Gail H. Javitt, Old Legacies and New Paradigms: Confusing "Research" and "Treatment" and Its Consequences in Responding to Emergent Health Threats, 8 J. Health Care L. & Pol'y 38 (2005).

10. *Inclusion of Women and Minorities.* The *Grimes* court focuses on the potential exploitation of the poor and members of minority groups. Commentators have also criticized the failure of medical research to include women and members of minority groups. The federal government responded in the NIH Revitalization Act of 1993, Pub. L. No. 103-43, 107 Stat. 122 (1993). See also NIH Policy and Guidelines Concerning the Inclusion of Women and Minorities as Subjects in Clinical Research (as amended October 2001), available along with other information at http://grants.nih.gov/grants/funding/women_min/ women_min.htm; Allen L. Gifford, M.D., et al., Participation in Research and Access to Experimental Treatments by HIV-Infected Patients, 346 New Eng. J. Med. 1373 (2002); T. E. King, Jr., Racial Disparities in Clinical Trials, 346 New Eng. J. Med. 1400 (2002).

11. *"Biobanks," Informed Consent, and Privacy.* Privacy concerns pervade medical research. How will medical researchers be able to identify potentially appropriate medical research subjects without having access to medical records? How confidential are the records of medical research projects? These issues are growing increasingly complex, in part due to large-scale research involving medical records, biological samples, and genetic testing. As one example, researchers in the U.K. are moving forward with plans to collect genetic and lifestyle "data from half a million middle-aged Britons over the next decade." Gretchen Vogel, U.K.'s Mass Appeal for Disease Insights, 296 Science 824 (2002); and the program Web site, http://www.ukbiobank.ac.uk/. Privacy and commercialization rules for the database have not yet been finalized. For other examples, see Jack V. Tu et al., Impracticability of Informed Consent in the Registry of the Canadian Stroke Network, 350 New Eng. J. Med. 1414 (2004); and Julie R. Ingelfinger & Jeffrey M. Drazen, Registry Research and Medical Privacy, 350 New Eng. J. Med. 1452 (2004). For academic commentaries on some of the key issues, see Ellen Wright Clayton, Informed Consent and Biobanks, 33 J.L. Med. & Ethics

(2005); Russell Korobkin, Autonomy and Informed Consent in Nontherapeutic Biomedical Research, 54 UCLA L. Rev. 605 (2007) (focusing on stem cell research); and Mark A. Rothstein, The Role of IRBs in Research Involving Commercial Biobanks, 30 J.L. Med. & Ethics 105 (2002).

The HIPAA privacy rules include provisions designed to ensure the privacy of information without creating insurmountable barriers to research. Critics nonetheless argued that the privacy rules would have unintended consequences for researchers. See, e.g., George J. Annas, Medical Privacy and Medical Research—Judging the New Federal Regulations, 346 New Eng. J. Med. 216 (2002); Jennifer Kulynynch & David Korn, The Effect of the New Federal Medical-Privacy Rules on Research, 346 New Eng. J. Med. 201 (2002).

12. *Research in Developing Countries.* It has become increasingly difficult to test drugs in Western countries because of strict regulations governing safety, difficulties with compensation, and difficulty in recruiting a statistically meaningful number of study subjects. Many research-based companies are now outsourcing some of their trials to developing countries such as India. For a discussion involving testing in India, see Samiran Nundy & Chandra Gulhati, A New Colonialism? Conducting Clinical Trials in India, 352 New Eng. J. Med. 1633 (2005). What rules should apply to research on human subjects conducted outside the United States by companies affiliated with U.S. companies or where the study results will be used to seek approval to market a drug in the United States? Informed consent issues are particularly salient in developing countries. See Roberto Rivera, Informed Consent: An International Researchers' Perspective, Am. J. Pub. Health 25 (2007) (recommendations regarding content and process for informed consent); Michael T. Krosin et al., Problems in Comprehension of Informed Consent in Rural and Peri-Urban Mali, West Africa, Clinical Trials 306 (2006).

13. *Resources and Commentaries.* HHS's Office for Human Research Protections maintains a Web site with links to key federal regulations and documents. http://www.hhs.gov/ohrp/. For influential criticisms of human subjects research, see the articles cited in *Grimes* and George J. Annas, Questing for Grails: Duplicity, Betrayal and Self-Deception in Research, 12 J. Contemp. Health L. & Pol'y 297 (1996); Jay Katz, Human Experimentation and Human Rights, 38 St. Louis U. L.J. 7 (1993). Important books on human subjects research include Baruch A. Brody, The Ethics of Biomedical Research: An International Perspective (1998); Claire Foster, The Ethics of Medical Research on Humans (2001); Jerry Menikoff and Edward P. Richards, What the Doctor Didn't Say: The Hidden Truth About Medical Research (2006).

3

The Right and "Duty" to Die

A. REFUSAL OF LIFE-SUSTAINING TREATMENT

In Chapter 2 we saw that patients enjoy a right of informed consent: Physicians may not deliver care to a patient without first informing the patient about the care and its alternatives and obtaining the patient's voluntary and competent consent to the treatment. If the patient must consent to treatment, it follows that the patient also enjoys a right to withhold consent and refuse the treatment.

Ordinarily, this corollary right to refuse treatment is not controversial. Patients with lower back pain from a slipped disk are free to choose between surgery to remove the disk and alternatives like anti-inflammatory drugs, exercise, and chiropractic manipulation. Patients with coronary artery disease may choose among coronary artery bypass surgery, coronary angioplasty, and medical therapies like antianginal drugs.

In many cases, however, a refusal of treatment will result in the patient's death. In such cases, the state (or the health care provider) may want to invoke its interest in preserving life to ensure that the patient receives the treatment necessary to sustain life. The issue, then, is how we balance the individual's right to refuse treatment with the state's or other persons' interest in preserving the patient's life.

It is useful to begin the analysis with the right to accept or refuse life-sustaining treatment when only the patient's interests are directly at stake. For example, an adult patient dying of cancer might reject additional rounds of chemotherapy on the grounds that the treatment is unlikely to provide much benefit but will likely cause significant discomfort. In such a case, the health of another person is not jeopardized by the refusal of treatment.

In later sections and chapters, we will consider whether the patient's right to make treatment decisions becomes circumscribed as we move beyond the core right. Does it matter that a pregnant woman's refusal of treatment will jeopardize the health of her fetus? Does it matter that a patient's refusal of treatment for tuberculosis would place other persons at risk? What if the patient is not refusing offered treatment but is requesting treatment that has not been offered? Does it matter, for example, that the patient is trying to take a lethal drug to end life? Similarly, does it matter that the patient is requesting treatment to sustain life that the patient's physician is unwilling to provide on the ground that the treatment provides little benefit?

Social recognition of the right to refuse life-sustaining treatment reflects the confluence of several factors. In recent decades, advances in medical technology have permitted physicians to save many lives that once were lost to disease or accident. In some cases, however, the person survives with a very poor quality of life and no hope of recovery. While medical care can maintain the person's life for weeks, months, or even years, the greatly diminished quality of life and the burdensomeness of the treatment means to some individuals that the treatment is not desired. In addition, these life-saving advances in technology have become very costly. If the life that can be saved has a very poor quality and society's limited resources could be used for other patients who would have a better quality of life and who want treatment, then it is not clear that the state has an interest in always preserving the patient's life. Finally, the law not only had recognized a right of informed consent, it also had recognized a right of pregnant women to choose an abortion. In 1973, the U.S. Supreme Court handed down its decision in Roe v. Wade. If the state's interest in preserving the life of a fetus does not overcome the woman's interest in personal autonomy, then it becomes more difficult to justify a state interest in preserving the life of a dying person against the person's will.

There is an extensive literature on the refusal of life-sustaining treatment including Allen E. Buchanan & Dan W. Brock, Deciding for Others (1989); Robert Burt, Taking Care of Strangers (1979); Margaret L. Campbell & J. Randall Curtis, eds., End-of-Life Care (2004); Norman Cantor, Legal Frontiers of Death & Dying (1987); Hastings Center, Guidelines on the Termination of Life-Sustaining Treatment (1987); Alan Meisel & Kathy L. Cerminara, The Right to Die (3d ed. 2004); National Center for State Courts, Guidelines for State Court Decision Making in Life-Sustaining Medical Treatment Cases (rev. 2d ed. 1993); President's Commission for the Study of Ethical Problems in Medicine, Deciding to Forego Life-Sustaining Treatment (1983); Paul Ramsey, Ethics at the Edges of Life (1978).

1. The Competent Patient

The right to refuse life-sustaining treatment is most straightforward when the patient possesses decisionmaking capacity and therefore is able to make informed and voluntary decisions about medical care. If the patient is incompetent, we confront an additional issue of how to decide whether the patient's right to refuse treatment is being exercised properly. While we directly consider that issue in the next section, we nevertheless begin our analysis here with cases involving incompetent patients, since it was in those cases that the courts developed the law governing treatment refusals by competent patients.

■ IN THE MATTER OF KAREN QUINLAN
355 A.2d 647 (N.J. 1976)

HUGHES, Chief Justice.

On the night of April 15, 1975, for reasons still unclear, Karen Quinlan ceased breathing for at least two 15 minute periods. She received some ineffectual mouth-to-mouth resuscitation from friends. She was taken by ambulance to Newton Memorial Hospital. There she had a temperature of 100 degrees, her pupils were unreactive and she was unresponsive even to deep pain. The history at the time of her admission to that hospital was essentially incomplete and uninformative. . . . Dr. Morse and other expert physicians who examined her characterized Karen as being in a "chronic persistent vegetative state." Dr. Fred Plum, one of such expert witnesses, defined this as a "subject who remains with the capacity to maintain the vegetative parts of neurological function but who . . . no longer has any cognitive function." . . . In this respect it was indicated by Dr. Plum that the brain works in essentially two ways, the vegetative and the sapient. He testified:

> We have an internal vegetative regulation which controls body temperature, which controls breathing, which controls to a considerable degree blood pressure, which controls to some degree heart rate, which controls chewing, swallowing and which controls sleeping and waking. We have a more highly developed brain which is uniquely human which controls our relation to the outside world, our capacity to talk, to see, to feel, to sing, to think. Brain death necessarily must mean the death of both of these functions of the brain, vegetative and the sapient. Therefore, the presence of any function which is regulated or governed or controlled by the deeper parts of the brain which in laymen's terms might be considered purely vegetative would mean that the brain is not biologically dead.

. . . The experts believe that Karen [who is 22 years old] cannot now survive without the assistance of the respirator; that exactly how long she would live without it is unknown; that the strong likelihood is that death would follow soon after its removal, and that removal would also risk further brain damage and would curtail the assistance the respirator presently provides in warding off infection. . . .

The further medical consensus was that Karen in addition to being comatose is in a chronic and persistent "vegetative" state, having no awareness of anything or anyone around her and existing at a primitive reflex level. Although she does have some brain stem function (ineffective for respiration) and has other reactions one normally associates with being alive, such as moving, reacting to light, sound and noxious stimuli, blinking her eyes, and the like, the quality of her feeling impulses is unknown. She grimaces, makes stereotyped cries and sounds and has chewing motions. Her blood pressure is normal. . . .

Karen is described as emaciated, having suffered a weight loss of at least 40 pounds, and undergoing a continuing deteriorative process. Her posture is described as fetal-like and grotesque; there is extreme flexion-rigidity of the arms, legs and related muscles and her joints are severely rigid and deformed.

. . . No form of treatment which can cure or improve that condition is known or available. As nearly as may be determined, considering the guarded area of remote uncertainties characteristic of most medical science predictions, she can *never* be restored to cognitive or sapient life. . . .

She is debilitated and moribund and although fairly stable at the time of argument before us (no new information having been filed in the meanwhile in expansion of the record), no physician risked the opinion that she could live more than a year and indeed she may die much earlier. Excellent medical and nursing care so far has been able to ward off the constant threat of infection, to which she is peculiarly susceptible because of the respirator, the tracheal tube and other incidents of care in her vulnerable condition. Her life accordingly is sustained by the respirator and tubal feeding, and removal from the respirator would cause her death soon, although the time cannot be stated with more precision. . . .

[Ms. Quinlan's father asked the superior court to appoint him the guardian of his daughter and to be given the express power to "authorize the discontinuance of all extraordinary medical procedures" sustaining his daughter's life. Ms. Quinlan's father also asked that the treating physicians and hospitals and the local prosecutor be enjoined from interfering with the discontinuation and that the local prosecutor also be enjoined from bringing a criminal prosecution after a discontinuation of treatment. The father's requests were opposed by the doctors, the hospital, the county prosecutor, the State of New Jersey, and Ms. Quinlan's guardian ad litem. The superior court denied the father's request for power to stop treatment.]

III. THE RIGHT OF PRIVACY

It is the issue of the constitutional right of privacy that has given us most concern, in the exceptional circumstances of this case. Here a loving parent, . . . seeks authorization to abandon specialized technological procedures which can only maintain for a time a body having no potential for resumption or continuance of other than a "vegetative" existence.

We have no doubt, in these unhappy circumstances, that if Karen were herself miraculously lucid for an interval (not altering the existing prognosis of the condition to which she would soon return) and perceptive of her irreversible condition, she could effectively decide upon discontinuance of the life-support apparatus, even if it meant the prospect of natural death. To this extent we may distinguish [John F. Kennedy Memorial Hospital v. Heston, 279 A.2d 670 (N.J. 1971)], which concerned a severely injured young woman (Delores Heston), whose life depended on surgery and blood transfusion; and who was in such extreme shock that she was unable to express an informed choice (although the court apparently considered the case as if the patient's own religious decision to resist transfusion were at stake), but most importantly a patient apparently salvable to long life and vibrant health; — a situation not at all like the present case.

We have no hesitancy in deciding, in the instant diametrically opposite case, that no external compelling interest of the state could compel Karen to endure the unendurable, only to vegetate a few measurable months with no realistic possibility of returning to any semblance of cognitive or sapient life. We perceive no thread of logic distinguishing between such a choice on Karen's part and a similar choice which, under the evidence in this case, could be made by a competent patient terminally ill, riddled by cancer and suffering great pain; such a patient would not be resuscitated or put on a respirator . . . , and a fortiori would not be kept *against his will* on a respirator.

Although the Constitution does not explicitly mention a right of privacy, Supreme Court decisions have recognized that a right of personal privacy exists and that certain areas of privacy are guaranteed under the Constitution. . . .

The Court in *Griswold* found the unwritten constitutional right of privacy to exist in the penumbra of specific guarantees of the Bill of Rights "formed by emanations from those guarantees that help give them life and substance." Presumably this right is broad enough to encompass a patient's decision to decline medical treatment under certain circumstances, in much the same way as it is broad enough to encompass a woman's decision to terminate pregnancy under certain conditions.

Nor is such right of privacy forgotten in the New Jersey Constitution. N.J. Const. (1947), Art. I, par. 1.

The claimed interests of the state in this case are essentially the preservation and sanctity of human life and defense of the right of the physician to administer medical treatment according to his best judgment. In this case the doctors say that removing Karen from the respirator will conflict with their professional judgment. The plaintiff answers that Karen's present treatment serves only a maintenance function; that the respirator cannot cure or improve her condition but at best can only prolong her inevitable slow deterioration and death; and that the interests of the patient, as seen by her surrogate, the guardian, must be evaluated by the court as predominant, even in the face of an opinion *contra* by the present attending physicians. Plaintiff's distinction is significant. The nature of Karen's care and the realistic chances of her recovery are quite unlike those of the patients discussed in many of the cases where treatments were ordered. In many of those cases the medical procedure required (usually a transfusion) constituted a minimal bodily invasion and the chances of recovery and return to functioning life were very good. We think that the state's interest *contra* weakens and the individual's right to privacy grows as the degree of bodily invasion increases and the prognosis dims. Ultimately there comes a point at which the individual's rights overcome the state interest. It is for that reason that we believe Karen's choice, if she were competent to make it, would be vindicated by the law. Her prognosis is extremely poor, — she will never resume cognitive life. And the bodily invasion is very great, — she requires 24 hour intensive nursing care, antibiotics, the assistance of a respirator, a catheter and feeding tube. . . .

IV. The Medical Factor

Having declared the substantive legal basis upon which plaintiff's rights as representative of Karen must be deemed predicated, we face and respond to the assertion on behalf of defendants that our premise unwarrantably offends prevailing medical standards. . . .

We glean from the record here that physicians distinguish between curing the ill and comforting and easing the dying; that they refuse to treat the curable as if they were dying or ought to die, and that they have sometimes refused to treat the hopeless and dying as if they were curable. . . . [M]any [physicians] have refused to inflict an undesired prolongation of the process of dying on a patient in irreversible condition when it is clear that such "therapy" offers neither human nor humane benefit. We think these attitudes represent a balanced implementation of a profoundly realistic perspective on the meaning of life and death and that they respect the whole Judeo-Christian tradition of regard for human life. No less would they seem consistent with the moral matrix of medicine, "to heal." . . .

Yet this balance, we feel, is particularly difficult to perceive and apply in the context of the development by advanced technology of sophisticated and artificial life-sustaining devices. For those possibly curable, such devices are of great value, and, as ordinary medical procedures, are essential. Consequently, as pointed out by Dr. Diamond, they are necessary because of the ethic of medical practice. But in light of the situation in the present case (while the record here is somewhat hazy in distinguishing between "ordinary" and "extraordinary" measures), one would have to think that the use of the same respirator or like support could be considered "ordinary" in the context of the possibly curable patient but "extraordinary" in the context of the forced sustaining by cardio-respiratory processes of an irreversibly doomed patient. . . .

The evidence in this case convinces us that the focal point of decision should be the prognosis as to the reasonable possibility of return to cognitive and sapient life, as distinguished from the forced continuance of that biological vegetative existence to which Karen seems to be doomed. [The court granted Mr. Quinlan's request, authorizing him to discontinue his daughter's life support. Surprisingly, Karen ended up living for another ten years without ventilator support.]

■ IN RE CONROY
486 A.2d 1209 (N.J. 1985)

SCHREIBER, Justice.

In 1979 Claire Conroy, who was suffering from an organic brain syndrome that manifested itself in her exhibiting periodic confusion, was adjudicated an incompetent, and plaintiff, her nephew, was appointed her guardian. . . .

During [a July 21–November 17, 1982] hospitalization, Dr. Kazemi observed that Ms. Conroy was not eating adequately, and therefore, on July 23, he inserted a nasogastric tube that extended from her nose through her esophagus to her stomach. Medicines and food were then given to her through this tube. On October 18, the tube was removed, and Ms. Conroy was fed by hand through her mouth for two weeks. However, she was unable to eat a sufficient amount in this manner, and the tube was reinserted on November 3. . . .

At the time of trial, Ms. Conroy [age 84] was no longer ambulatory and was confined to bed, unable to move from a semi-fetal position. She suffered from arteriosclerotic heart disease, hypertension, and diabetes mellitus; her left leg was gangrenous to her knee; she had several necrotic decubitus ulcers (bed sores) on her left foot, leg, and hip; an eye problem required irrigation; she had a urinary catheter in place and could not control her bowels; she could not speak; and her ability to swallow was very limited. On the other hand, she interacted with her environment in some limited ways: she could move her head, neck, hands, and arms to a minor extent; she was able to scratch herself, and had pulled at her bandages, tube, and catheter; she moaned occasionally when moved or fed through the tube, or when her bandages were changed; her eyes sometimes followed individuals in the room; her facial expressions were different when she was awake from when she was asleep; and she smiled on occasion when her hair was combed, or when she received a comforting rub. . . .

[This case arose when Ms. Conroy's guardian, who was also her nephew, petitioned the trial court for permission to discontinue Ms. Conroy's feeding tube. The guardian ad litem opposed the petition, and the trial court granted permission. The guardian ad litem appealed, and the intermediate court of appeals reversed. At issue in the case was whether Ms. Conroy's feeding tube could be withdrawn. While this case was before the intermediate court of appeals, Ms. Conroy died with her feeding tube in place. The N.J. Supreme Court nevertheless heard the case, as one involving a matter "of substantial importance and . . . capable of repetition but evad[ing] review."]

III

The starting point in analyzing whether life-sustaining treatment may be withheld or withdrawn from an incompetent patient is to determine what rights a competent patient has to accept or reject medical care. It is therefore necessary at the outset of this discussion to identify the nature and extent of a patient's rights that are implicated by such decisions.

The right of a person to control his own body is a basic societal concept, long recognized in the common law. . . .

The doctrine of informed consent is a primary means developed in the law to protect this personal interest in the integrity of one's body. "Under this doctrine, no medical procedure may be performed without a patient's consent, obtained after explanation of the nature of the treatment, substantial risks, and alternative therapies." Cantor, A Patient's Decision to Decline Life-Saving Medical Treatment: Bodily Integrity Versus the Preservation of Life, 26 Rutgers L. Rev. 228, 237 (1973). . . .

The patient's ability to control his bodily integrity through informed consent is significant only when one recognizes that this right also encompasses a right to informed refusal. Thus, a competent adult person generally has the right to decline to have any medical treatment initiated or continued.

The right to make certain decisions concerning one's body is also protected by the federal constitutional right of privacy. . . . While this right of privacy might apply in a case such as this, we need not decide that issue since the right to decline medical treatment is, in any event, embraced within the common-law right to self-determination.

Whether based on common-law doctrines or on constitutional theory, the right to decline life-sustaining medical treatment is not absolute. In some cases, it may yield to countervailing societal interests in sustaining the person's life. Courts and commentators have commonly identified four state interests that may limit a person's right to refuse medical treatment: preserving life, preventing suicide, safeguarding the integrity of the medical profession, and protecting innocent third parties.

The state's interest in preserving life is commonly considered the most significant of the four state interests. It may be seen as embracing two separate but related concerns: an interest in preserving the life of the particular patient, and an interest in preserving the sanctity of all life.

While both of these state interests in life are certainly strong, in themselves they will usually not foreclose a competent person from declining life-sustaining medical treatment for himself. This is because the life that the state is seeking to protect in such a situation is the life of the same person who has competently decided to forego the medical intervention; it is not some other actual or potential life that cannot adequately protect itself.

In cases that do not involve the protection of the actual or potential life of someone other than the decisionmaker, the state's indirect and abstract interest in preserving the life of the competent patient generally gives way to the patient's much stronger personal interest in directing the course of his own life. . . .

[As to the state interest in preventing suicide], declining life-sustaining medical treatment may not properly be viewed as an attempt to commit suicide. Refusing medical intervention merely allows the disease to take its natural course; if death were eventually to occur, it would be the result, primarily, of the underlying disease, and not the result of a self-inflicted injury. In addition, people who refuse life-sustaining medical treatment may not harbor a specific intent to die; rather, they may fervently wish to live, but to do so free of unwanted medical technology, surgery, or drugs, and without protracted suffering. . . . The difference is between self-infliction or self-destruction and self-determination. . . .

The third state interest that is frequently asserted as a limitation on a competent patient's right to refuse medical treatment is the interest in safeguarding the integrity of the medical profession. . . . Medical ethics do not require medical intervention in disease at all costs. . . . Indeed, recent surveys have suggested that a majority of practicing doctors now approve of passive euthanasia and believe that it is being practiced by members of the profession.

Moreover, even if doctors were exhorted to attempt to cure or sustain their patients under all circumstances, that moral and professional imperative, at least in cases of patients who were clearly competent, presumably would not require doctors to go beyond advising the patient of the risks of foregoing treatment and urging the patient to accept the medical intervention. If the patient rejected the doctor's advice, the onus of that decision would rest on the patient, not the doctor. . . .

The fourth asserted state interest in overriding a patient's decision about his medical treatment is the interest in protecting innocent third parties who may be harmed by the patient's treatment decision. [The court cites cases involving minor children who would be abandoned by a parent's death or involving threats to public health or prison security.] . . .

On balance, the right to self-determination ordinarily outweighs any countervailing state interests, and competent persons generally are permitted to refuse medical treatment, even at the risk of death. Most of the cases that have held otherwise, unless they involved the interest in protecting innocent third parties, have concerned the patient's competency to make a rational and considered choice of treatment. . . .

In view of the case law, we have no doubt that Ms. Conroy, if competent to make the decision and if resolute in her determination, could have chosen to have her nasogastric tube withdrawn. Her interest in freedom from nonconsensual invasion of her bodily integrity would outweigh any state interest in preserving life or in safeguarding the integrity of the medical profession. In addition, rejecting her artificial means of feeding would not constitute attempted suicide, as the decision would probably be based on a wish to be free of medical intervention rather than a specific intent to die, and her death would result, if at all, from her underlying medical condition, which included her inability to swallow. Finally, removal of her feeding tube would not create a public health or safety hazard, nor would her death leave any minor dependents without care or support.

It should be noted that if she were competent, Ms. Conroy's right to self-determination would not be affected by her medical condition or prognosis. . . . Of course, a patient's decision to accept or reject medical treatment may be influenced by his medical condition, treatment, and prognosis; nevertheless, a competent person's common-law and constitutional rights do not depend on the quality or value of his life.

[In the section on the incompetent patient, at page 263, we consider the second half of the court's opinion, which discusses how decisions about life-sustaining treatment should be made for patients like Ms. Conroy.]

CRUZAN v. DIRECTOR, MISSOURI DEPARTMENT OF HEALTH
497 U.S. 261 (1990)

REHNQUIST, Chief Justice.
. . . On the night of January 11, 1983, Nancy Cruzan lost control of her car as she traveled down Elm Road in Jasper County, Missouri. The vehicle overturned, and Cruzan was discovered lying face down in a ditch without detectable respiratory or cardiac function. Paramedics were able to restore her breathing and heartbeat at the accident site, and she was transported to a hospital in an unconscious state. An attending neurosurgeon diagnosed her as having sustained probable cerebral contusions compounded by significant anoxia (lack of oxygen). The Missouri trial court in this case found that permanent brain damage generally results after six minutes in an anoxic state; it was estimated that Cruzan was deprived of oxygen from 12 to 14 minutes. She remained in a coma for approximately three weeks and then progressed to an unconscious state in which she was able to orally ingest some nutrition. In order to ease feeding and further the recovery, surgeons implanted a gastrostomy feeding and hydration tube in Cruzan with the consent of her then husband. Subsequent rehabilitative efforts proved unavailing. [Now age 31, she] lies in a Missouri state hospital in what is commonly referred to as a persistent vegetative state: generally, a condition in which a person exhibits motor reflexes but evinces no indications of significant cognitive function. The state of Missouri is bearing the cost of her care.

After it had become apparent that Nancy Cruzan had virtually no chance of regaining her mental faculties, her parents asked hospital employees to terminate the artificial nutrition and hydration procedures. . . . The employees refused to honor the request without court approval. [Ms. Cruzan's parents then sought judicial authorization from a state trial court. The trial court granted approval, but the Missouri Supreme Court reversed that decision.] . . .

We granted certiorari to consider the question whether Cruzan has a right under the United States Constitution which would require the hospital to withdraw life-sustaining treatment from her under these circumstances.

At common law, even the touching of one person by another without consent and without legal justification was a battery. Before the turn of the century, this Court observed that "[n]o right is held more sacred, or is more carefully guarded, by the common law, than the right of every individual to the possession and control of his own person, free from all restraint or interference of others, unless by clear and unquestionable authority of law." Union Pacific R. Co. v. Botsford, 141 U.S. 250, 251 (1891). This notion of bodily integrity has been embodied in the requirement that informed consent is generally required for medical treatment. Justice Cardozo, while on the Court of Appeals of New York, aptly described this doctrine: "Every human being of adult years and sound mind has a right to determine what shall be done with his own body; and a surgeon who performs an operation without his patient's consent commits an assault, for which he is liable in damages." Schloendorff v. Society of New York Hospital, 105 N.E. 92, 93 (N.Y. 1914). The informed consent doctrine has become firmly entrenched in American tort law.

The logical corollary of the doctrine of informed consent is that the patient generally possesses the right not to consent, that is, to refuse treatment. Until about 15 years ago and the seminal decision in In re Quinlan, the number of right-to-refuse-treatment decisions was relatively few. Most of the earlier cases involved patients who refused medical treatment forbidden by their religious beliefs, thus implicating First Amendment rights as well as common law rights of self-determination. More recently, however, with the advance of medical technology capable of sustaining life well past the point where natural forces would have brought certain death in earlier times, cases involving the right to refuse life-sustaining treatment have burgeoned. . . .

As these cases demonstrate, the common law doctrine of informed consent is viewed as generally encompassing the right of a competent individual to refuse medical treatment. Beyond that, these cases demonstrate both similarity and diversity in their approaches to decision of what all agree is a perplexing question with unusually strong moral and ethical overtones. . . . This is the first case in which we have been squarely presented with the issue whether the United States Constitution grants what is in common parlance referred to as a "right to die." . . .

The Fourteenth Amendment provides that no state shall "deprive any person of life, liberty, or property, without due process of law." The principle that a competent person has a constitutionally protected liberty interest in refusing unwanted medical treatment may be inferred from our prior decisions. In Jacobson v. Massachusetts, 197 U.S. 11, 24-30 (1905), for instance, the Court balanced an individual's liberty interest in declining an unwanted smallpox vaccine against the state's interest in preventing disease. Decisions prior to the incorporation of the Fourth Amendment into the Fourteenth Amendment analyzed searches and seizures involving the body under the due process clause and were thought to implicate substantial liberty interests.

Just this Term, in the course of holding that a state's procedures for administering antipsychotic medication to prisoners were sufficient to satisfy due process concerns, we recognized that prisoners possess "a significant liberty interest in avoiding the unwanted administration of antipsychotic drugs under the due process clause of the Fourteenth Amendment." Washington v. Harper, 494 U.S. 210, 221-222 (1990). Still other cases support the recognition of a general liberty interest in refusing medical treatment. Vitek v. Jones, 445 U.S. 480, 494 (1980) (transfer to mental hospital coupled with mandatory behavior modification treatment implicated liberty interests); Parham v. J.R., 442 U.S. 584, 600 (1979) ("[A] child, in common with adults, has a substantial liberty interest in not being confined unnecessarily for medical treatment").

But determining that a person has a "liberty interest" under the due process clause does not end the inquiry; "whether respondent's constitutional rights have been violated must be determined by balancing his liberty interests against the relevant state interests." Youngberg v. Romeo, 457 U.S. 307, 321 (1982).

Petitioners insist that under the general holdings of our cases, the forced administration of life-sustaining medical treatment, and even of artificially delivered food and water essential to life, would implicate a competent person's liberty interest. Although we think the logic of the cases discussed above would embrace such a liberty interest, the dramatic consequences involved in refusal of such treatment would inform the inquiry as to whether the deprivation of that interest is constitutionally permissible. But for purposes of this case, we assume that the United States Constitution would grant a competent person a constitutionally protected right to refuse lifesaving hydration and nutrition. . . .

[While the Court assumed for purposes of the case that Nancy Cruzan had a right to refuse her treatment, it also upheld Missouri's imposition of treatment on the ground that the Missouri Supreme Court had adopted a reasonable procedural standard for deciding when an incompetent person's right to refuse treatment should be invoked. That part of the decision is considered at page 274, in the section on the incompetent patient.]

SCALIA, Justice, concurring.

. . . While I agree with the Court's analysis today, and therefore join in its opinion, I would have preferred that we announce, clearly and promptly, that the federal courts have no business in this field; that American law has always accorded the state the power to prevent, by force if necessary, suicide — including suicide by refusing to take appropriate measures necessary to preserve one's life; that the point at which life becomes "worthless," and the point at which the means necessary to preserve it become "extraordinary" or "inappropriate," are neither set forth in the Constitution nor known to the nine Justices of this Court any better than they are known to nine people picked at random from the Kansas City telephone directory; and hence that . . . [when] a patient no longer wishes certain measures to be taken to preserve his or her life, it is up to the citizens of Missouri to decide, through their elected representatives, whether that wish will be honored. It is quite impossible (because the Constitution says nothing about the matter) that those citizens will decide upon a line less lawful than the one we would choose; and it is unlikely (because we know no more about "life and death" than they do) that they will decide upon a line less reasonable. . . .

Petitioners rely on three distinctions to separate Nancy Cruzan's case from ordinary suicide: (1) that she is permanently incapacitated and in pain; (2) that she would bring on her death not by any affirmative act but by merely declining treatment that provides nourishment; and (3) that preventing her from effectuating her presumed wish to die requires violation of her bodily integrity. None of these suffices. Suicide was not excused even when committed "to avoid those ills which [persons] had not the fortitude to endure." 4 Blackstone, supra, at *189. "The life of those to whom life has become a burden — of those who are hopelessly diseased or fatally wounded — nay, even the lives of criminals condemned to death, are under the protection of the law, equally as the lives of those who are in the full tide of life's enjoyment, and anxious to continue to live." Blackburn v. State, 23 Ohio St. 146, 163 (1873). . . . "[Assisted suicide] is declared by the law to be murder, irrespective of the wishes or the condition of the party to whom the poison is administered. . . ." Blackburn, supra, at 163.

The second asserted distinction — suggested by the recent cases canvassed by the Court concerning the right to refuse treatment — relies on the dichotomy between action and inaction. Suicide, it is said, consists of an affirmative act to end one's life; refusing treatment is not an affirmative act "causing" death, but merely a passive acceptance of the natural process of dying. I readily acknowledge that the distinction between action and inaction has some bearing upon the legislative judgment of what ought to be prevented as suicide — though even there it would seem to me unreasonable to draw the line precisely between action and inaction, rather than between various forms of inaction. It would not make much sense to say that one may not kill oneself by walking into the sea, but may sit on the beach until submerged by the incoming tide; or that one may not intentionally lock oneself into a cold storage locker, but may refrain from coming indoors when the temperature drops below freezing. Even as a legislative matter, in other words, the intelligent line does not fall between action and inaction but between those forms of inaction that consist of abstaining from "ordinary" care and those that consist of abstaining from "excessive" or "heroic" measures. Unlike action versus inaction, that is not a line to be discerned by logic or legal analysis, and we should not pretend that it is.

. . . Of course the common law rejected the action-inaction distinction in other contexts involving the taking of human life as well. In the prosecution of a parent for the starvation death of her infant, it was no defense that the infant's death was "caused" by no action of the parent but by the natural process of starvation, or by the infant's natural inability to provide for itself. A physician, moreover, could be criminally liable for failure to provide care that could have extended the patient's life, even if death was immediately caused by the underlying disease that the physician failed to treat.

It is not surprising, therefore, that the early cases considering the claimed right to refuse medical treatment dismissed as specious the nice distinction between "passively submitting to death and actively seeking it. The distinction may be merely verbal, as it would be if an adult sought death by starvation instead of a drug. If the state may interrupt one mode of self-destruction, it may with equal authority interfere with the other." John F. Kennedy Memorial Hosp. v. Heston, 279 A.2d 670, 672-673 (N.J. 1971).

The third asserted basis of distinction — that frustrating Nancy Cruzan's wish to die in the present case requires interference with her bodily integrity — is likewise inadequate, because such interference is impermissible only if one begs the question whether her refusal to undergo the treatment on her own is suicide. It has always been lawful not only for the state, but even for private citizens, to interfere with bodily integrity to prevent a felony. That general rule has of course been applied to suicide. . . . The state-run hospital, I am certain, is not liable under 42 U.S.C. §1983 for violation of constitutional rights, nor the private hospital liable under general tort law, if, in a state where suicide is unlawful, it pumps out the stomach of a person who has intentionally taken an overdose of barbiturates, despite that person's wishes to the contrary. . . .

What I have said above is not meant to suggest that I would think it desirable, if we were sure that Nancy Cruzan wanted to die, to keep her alive by the means at issue here. I assert only that the Constitution has nothing to say about the subject. To raise up a constitutional right here we would have to create out of nothing (for it exists neither in text nor tradition) some constitutional principle whereby, although the state may insist that an individual come in out of the cold and eat food, it may not insist that he take medicine; and although it may pump his stomach empty of poison he has ingested, it may not fill his stomach with food he has failed to ingest. Are there, then, no reasonable and humane limits that ought not to be exceeded in requiring an individual to preserve his own life? There obviously are, but they are not set forth in the due process clause. What assures us that those limits will not be exceeded is the same constitutional guarantee that is the source of most of our protection — what protects us, for example, from being assessed a tax of 100 percent of our income above the subsistence level, from being forbidden to drive cars, or from being required to send our children to school for ten hours a day, none of which horribles are categorically prohibited by the Constitution. Our salvation is the equal protection clause, which requires the democratic majority to accept for themselves and their loved ones what they impose on you and me. This Court need not, and has no authority to, inject itself into every field of human activity where irrationality and oppression may theoretically occur, and if it tries to do so it will destroy itself.

Notes: The Individual Interest in Refusing Treatment

1. *Karen Quinlan.* Even though Karen Quinlan's family won the right to have her ventilator discontinued, her physician and the hospital administration refused to comply with the decision of the New Jersey Supreme Court. Rather than turning off the ventilator immediately, Ms. Quinlan's physician, Dr. Morse, spent the next five months "weaning" her from the ventilator so she could breathe on her own. Ms. Quinlan eventually lived for another ten years. Gregory E. Pence, Classic Cases in Medical Ethics 39 (4th ed. 2004). See also Annette E. Clark, The Right to Die: The Broken Road from *Quinlan* to *Schiavo*, 37 Loy. U. Chi. L.J. 383 (2006).

As the *Quinlan* case illustrates, physicians may incorrectly believe that a patient will be permanently dependent on a ventilator or other medical treatment. Similarly, physicians may incorrectly believe that a patient is terminally ill. People may therefore decline life-sustaining treatment on the basis of mistaken assumptions about their prognoses. How would you respond to the argument that this kind of uncertainty should preclude a patient from refusing life-sustaining treatment?

2. *Persistent Vegetative State, Coma, and Brain Death*. The persistent vegetative state of Karen Quinlan and Nancy Cruzan is often confused with coma and brain death. There is some similarity among the three conditions. With all three, the person suffers a total and sustained loss of consciousness. That is, the cerebral hemispheres, which are responsible for conscious behavior, do not function. Accordingly, the person has no thoughts, feelings, sensations, desires or emotions. There is no purposeful action, social interaction, memory, pain or suffering. The person has lost all awareness of self and environment.

Brain death, coma, and the persistent vegetative state differ in the extent to which there is function of the brain stem, the part of the brain that controls unconscious activity. In brain death, there is a nearly complete and an irreversible loss of brain stem function (as well as a complete and irreversible loss of cerebral hemisphere function). As a result, the brain is no longer able to regulate what are known as the body's "vegetative" functions, which include the functions of the heart, lungs, kidneys, intestinal tract, and certain reflex actions. Brain-dead persons appear to be in a deep coma in which they generally do not engage in any spontaneous movement. Moreover, they do not respond to stimuli such as pain, touch, sound, or light. Mechanical measures and other artificial support can maintain a brain-dead person's heartbeat, breathing, and other vegetative functions temporarily, but usually only for a few days or weeks after brain death occurs. As discussed at the end of this chapter, a patient who is brain dead is legally, not just figuratively, dead. As a consequence, patients and families have no choice over "life support"; treatment *must* be withdrawn, not as a matter of the patient's rights, but simply as a matter of medical routine and out of proper respect for the deceased. The one important qualification is when the patient and family have authorized organ donation, in which case "life support" may be continued for a brief time even though the patient is dead in order to keep the organs from deteriorating before "harvesting." See pages 367-373 for further discussion of brain death and its role in organ transplantation.

In contrast to brain-dead persons, patients in a persistent vegetative state are still alive. Because they maintain relatively normal brain stem function, they can usually breathe air, digest food, and produce urine without any assistance. They experience cycles of sleeping, in which their eyes are closed, and waking, in which their eyes are open. They may smile, utter unintelligible sounds, or move their eyes, arms, and legs sporadically. Vegetative state patients also manifest a range of reflex reactions to different stimuli; they will grimace, cough, gag, and move their arms and legs. While all of this activity gives the appearance of consciousness, there is none.

Coma may be viewed as a condition intermediate between brain death and the vegetative state. The brain stem retains some function, but not the range of activity seen in the vegetative state. For example, coma is a sleep-like state in which the eyes remain closed. The patient's breathing is impaired, and many reflexes are absent. Coma and the vegetative state also differ in their duration. Comas rarely last more than two to four weeks, by which time the patient either dies, enters a vegetative state, or regains some degree of consciousness. The duration of the vegetative state, on the other hand, frequently lasts for more than a few weeks. Once it has existed for several months, it is characterized as a persistent vegetative state. Patients can survive for years, even decades, in a persistent vegetative state. In rare cases, patients have regained consciousness from a persistent vegetative state, but these patients usually remain severely disabled neurologically. The Multi-Society Task Force on PVS, Medical Aspects of the Persistent Vegetative State (Second of Two Parts), 330 New Eng. J. Med. 1572 (1994).

3. *Sources of a Right to Refuse Life-Sustaining Treatment.* In the early cases that recognized a right to refuse treatment, courts rested the right on two individual interests: the common law right to be free of nonconsensual bodily invasion (i.e., the right to informed consent) and the substantive due process right to make decisions of critical importance to one's destiny (i.e., the right to privacy). As the U.S. Supreme Court began to narrow the reach of the right to privacy, state courts relied more heavily on common law principles of informed consent to find a right to refuse life-sustaining treatment. This trend is reflected in the excerpts printed above from the *Quinlan* and *Conroy* decisions of the New Jersey Supreme Court. After the *Cruzan* decision, however, courts are again relying on the substantive due process right, although now framed as a liberty interest rather than a privacy right. It is true that the *Cruzan* majority only assumed for purposes of the case that individuals enjoy a constitutional right to refuse life-sustaining treatment. Nevertheless, the decision has been read by courts and commentators as establishing such a right. See, e.g., State v. Pelham, 824 A.2d 1082, 1087 (N.J. 2003) (observing that "[s]ince the 1976 decision in *Quinlan,* numerous other courts, including the United States Supreme Court, have recognized the so-called 'right to die' "); Browning v. Herbert, 568 So. 2d 4, 10 (Fla. 1990) ("A competent individual has the constitutional right to refuse medical treatment regardless of his or her medical condition," citing *Cruzan*); John A. Robertson, *Cruzan* and the Constitutional Status of Nontreatment Decisions for Incompetent Patients, 25 Ga. L. Rev. 1139 (1991); Mara Silver, Note, Testing Cruzan: Prisoners and the Constitutional Question of Self-Starvation, 58 Stan. L. Rev. 631 (2005).

Although we can easily view the informed consent right and the substantive due process right as independent rights — the first, a right to be free of unwanted bodily invasion; the second, a right to make important personal decisions — the *Cruzan* Court collapsed the two. There, as we saw, the Court turned to common law principles of informed consent as the basis for finding a constitutional liberty interest in refusing life-sustaining treatment. Yet, in terms of underlying principles, it arguably makes more sense to collapse the rights in the other direction. Do you see how the right to informed consent ultimately comes down to a notion of privacy or liberty in making important personal decisions? See, e.g., Schloendorff v. Society of New York Hospital, 105 N.E. 92, 93 (N.Y. 1914) (Cardozo, J.) (holding that surgery without consent is an unlawful assault because "[e]very human being of adult years and sound mind has a right to determine what shall be done with his own body"). In terms of future implications, why do you think the *Cruzan* Court preferred to rest its constitutional right on principles of informed consent rather than on the kind of privacy analysis employed in its abortion cases, Roe v. Wade or Planned Parenthood of Southeastern Pennsylvania v. Casey?

4. *State Action.* In *Cruzan,* the patient was being treated in a state rehabilitation facility, so the Supreme Court did not need to worry whether the state action requirement of the Fourteenth Amendment was satisfied (i.e., the

Fourteenth Amendment protects against government, not private, action). Yet, in many cases, it is a private physician or hospital refusing to discontinue life-sustaining treatment. In those cases, it is not clear how the patients could invoke their federal constitutional right to refuse treatment. See Blum v. Yaretsky, 457 U.S. 991, 1004 (1982) (no state action implicated by a private nursing home's decision to transfer a patient despite a reduction in the patient's Medicaid benefits by the state in response to the transfer; "a state normally can be held responsible for a private decision only when it has exercised [such] coercive power . . . that the choice must in law be deemed to be that of the state"). Most likely, state action has not been viewed as an issue in treatment withdrawal cases both because state common law grounds are available to justify withdrawal and because the courts recognize that the state is doing more than refusing to intervene but is also using the threat of criminal liability to effectively force the physician or hospital to treat. See, e.g., In re Colyer, 660 P.2d 738, 742 (Wash. 1983) (finding state action in part because of the state's "capability of imposing criminal sanctions on the hospital and its staff"). In some cases, a court's finding of state action is difficult to reconcile with the U.S. Supreme Court's state action decisions. See, e.g., Rasmussen v. Fleming, 741 P.2d 674, 682 n.9 (Ariz. 1987) (finding state action on the basis of the state's regulation and licensing of hospitals and physicians and the state's supervisory authority over the guardianship of incapacitated persons).

5. *Withdrawing vs. Withholding.* The *Quinlan* opinion suggests that, if the issue had been whether to put Karen Quinlan on a ventilator, she clearly would have enjoyed a right to have the ventilator withheld. At one time, some commentators argued that it was permissible to withhold life-sustaining treatment but not to withdraw such treatment, just as there is no obligation to come to someone's rescue, but there is an obligation not to abandon a rescue. Over time, however, in both ethics and the law, the distinction between withdrawing and withholding was rejected. Indeed, as many commentators have observed, it is arguably worse to withhold than to withdraw. If treatment is withheld, then an opportunity is lost to see if the treatment would provide unexpected benefit. Withdrawal presumably occurs only after it becomes clear that the treatment provides insufficient benefit. Moreover, as suggested by Justice Brennan in his dissent in *Cruzan*, 497 U.S. at 314, if we did not recognize a right to refuse treatment, many people might not seek care in the first place because they would be afraid of not being able to stop treatment once it was started. If the treatment ended up not working and causing greater suffering, the person would be stuck. Do you agree with this latter argument? Is it likely that people would hesitate to seek potentially life-saving care because they might not be able to stop the care at some later time?

Despite years of ethicists and courts rejecting the distinction between withholding and withdrawing, health care providers feel very differently about the two acts. Many physicians believe it is ethically and legally less acceptable to withdraw care than to withhold it. See, e.g., Neil J. Farber et al., Physicians' Decisions to Withhold and Withdraw Life-Sustaining Treatment, 166 Arch. Intern. Med. 560 (2006); Terri R. Fried et al., Limits of Patient Autonomy: Physician Attitudes and Practices Regarding Life-Sustaining Treatments and Euthanasia, 153 Arch. Intern. Med. 722, 723-724 (1993); Philip G. Peters Jr. et al., Physician Willingness to Withhold Tube Feeding After *Cruzan*: An Empirical Study, 57 Mo. L. Rev. 831, 838-839 (1992).

These feelings are not surprising. It is hard not to feel responsible for a patient's death when you turn off a ventilator and the patient dies within minutes. Two ethics consultants wrote about their experience in discontinuing a ventilator from a competent, 67-year-old patient, Mr. Larson, who was irreversibly dependent on the ventilator because of "post-polio syndrome."

> Although we received grateful hugs from the family and thanks from the health care team, we were struck by the gravity of what we had done. Doubts kept creeping into our minds. We each experienced a wave of disquieting emotion, feelings that we had killed this patient who would have otherwise continued to live connected to the ventilator. We knew intellectually that he had the legal and ethical right to refuse this medical treatment, but the gravity of the decision and our participation haunted us. We returned to our immediate commitments of caring for other patients, one of us responding next to the need of a patient who wanted medical help for a pulmonary problem to prolong his life. Both of us remained preoccupied throughout the afternoon thinking about Mr. Larson and what we had done. Our respective medical careers have generally been devoted to responding to patient wishes to postpone death and to prolong life. We've seen our patients die of their various diseases, but now our acquiescence in allowing his death caused us much anguish. This anguish continued in both of us for several days. One of us sought counsel from a psychiatrist who reinforced our belief that we did the right thing, counteracting those deep feelings that somehow we had killed this patient. Gradually we came to terms with what had happened. . . . Our consciences were clear, but we were left feeling very impressed with how difficult it had been to honor this man's request. Miles J. Edwards & Susan W. Tolle, Disconnecting a Ventilator at the Request of a Patient Who Knows He Will Then Die: The Doctor's Anguish, 117 Ann. Intern. Med. 254, 256 (1992).

How should the law take account of these feelings?

6. *Type of Treatment at Stake.* As the *Quinlan* and *Cruzan* cases suggest, it was once unclear legally whether artificial ventilation or artificial nutrition and hydration could be discontinued, and there were many commentators opposed to withdrawal of feeding tubes. See, e.g., Daniel Callahan, On Feeding the Dying, 13(5) Hastings Center Rep. 22 (1983); Mark Siegler & Alan J. Weisbard, Against the Emerging Stream: Should Fluids and Nutritional Support Be Discontinued?, 145 Arch. Intern. Med. 129 (1985). The *Cruzan* case essentially resolved the debate in terms of the law, and now it is widely accepted that patients can refuse any medical treatment. Nevertheless, many physicians are still slow to withdraw feeding tubes because of their personal moral concerns. Cf. Heikki Hinkka et al., Factors Affecting Physicians' Decisions to Forgo Life-Sustaining Treatments in Terminal Care, 28 J. Med. Ethics 109 (2002) (finding that physicians in Finland were much more willing to withhold a ventilator than a feeding tube); Jeffrey S. Rubenstein, Pediatric Resident Attitudes About Technologic Support of Vegetative Patients and the Effects of Parental Input—A Longitudinal Study, 94 Pediatrics 8 (1994) (finding that pediatric residents expressed a much greater willingness to withdraw a ventilator than artificial nutrition and hydration from a child in a persistent vegetative state).

Not all treatment decisions have been so controversial. In particular, do-not-resuscitate (DNR) orders have been accepted medical practice for decades. Such orders, often called DNAR (do-not-attempt-resuscitation) orders, were developed because dying patients do not always want physicians to try to restart their heartbeat when their illness results in the terminal event of cardiac arrest. A DNR order means that cardiopulmonary resuscitation (CPR) will be withheld from the patient. The acceptance of DNR orders is reflected in the hospital accreditation standards of the Joint Commission for the Accreditation of Healthcare Organizations, which *require* hospitals to maintain a specific policy for DNR orders. What is controversial about DNR orders is whether physicians may write them over the objection of the patient or the patient's family, on the ground that CPR serves no useful purpose. This issue will be discussed in greater depth in the section on futility, pages 338-353.

7. *Costs of Care*. While the right to refuse treatment coincides with a trend toward greater recognition of patient's rights, it also coincides, as mentioned in the introduction to this section, with concerns about the high cost of medical care. When the *Cruzan* case was working its way through the courts, it was common to hear people justify withdrawal of care on the ground that it was costing more than $100,000 a year to keep her alive and that money could be better spent on other kinds of medical care. Does the right to refuse treatment simply reflect the economic cost to society of enforcing a duty to receive life-sustaining treatment?

Much has been made about the high percentage of health care costs that are consumed in the last six or twelve months of people's lives. However, there is a good deal of misunderstanding about those costs. First, while 26 percent of Medicare expenditures are consumed in the last twelve months of life, Donald R. Hoover et al., Medical Expenditures During the Last Year of Life: Findings from the 1992–1996 Medicare Current Beneficiary Study, 37 Health Serv. Res. 1625 (2002), only 10 to 12 percent of all health care costs go for such care, Ezekiel J. Emanuel & Linda L. Emanuel, The Economics of Dying: The Illusion of Cost Savings at the End of Life, 330 New Eng. J. Med. 540 (1994). Second, physicians tend to treat people aggressively during the last six or twelve months of life when it appears that the patient has a reasonable chance of a good recovery. For patients with dismal prognoses, most of the costs of care go to cover nursing home and home health care, in other words, basic supportive care. Anne A. Scitovsky, Medical Care in the Last Twelve Months of Life: The Relation between Age, Functional Status, and Medical Care Expenditures, 66 Milbank Q. 640 (1988). See also Samuel S. Richardson et al., Use of Aggressive Medical Treatments Near the End of Life: Differences Between Patients with and Without Dementia, 42 Health Serv. Res. 183 (2007) (concluding that "during the final 30 days of life, acute care patients with dementia are treated substantially less aggressively than patients without dementia"). For further discussion, see Berhanu Alemayehu & Kenneth E. Warner, The Lifetime Distribution of Health Care Costs, 39 Health Serv. Res. 627 (2004) (finding that nearly half of the lifetime spending for health care occurs after age 65 for the average person and for those who live at least 85 years, more than a third of their spending occurs after age 85).

Notes: The State's Interest in Preserving Life

1. *The State's Interest.* In *Conroy*, the New Jersey Supreme Court essentially argues that the state interest in preserving patients' lives is sufficient to justify the imposition of medical treatment only when patients want their lives preserved. The state's primary interest is to protect patients from having their lives taken involuntarily. Similarly, in his dissent in *Cruzan*, Justice Brennan wrote:

> The only state interest asserted here is a general interest in the preservation of life. But the state has no legitimate general interest in someone's life, completely abstracted from the interest of the person living that life, that could outweigh the person's choice to avoid medical treatment. . . . [T]he state's general interest in life must accede to Nancy Cruzan's particularized and intense interest in self-determination in her choice of medical treatment. There is simply nothing legitimately within the state's purview to be gained by superseding her decision. *Cruzan*, 497 U.S. at 313-314 (Brennan, J., with Marshall, J., and Blackmun, J., dissenting).

David Blake argues that such a view conflates the value of life with the ability to exercise individual autonomy. Self-determination surely is a critical value, he observes, but there is intrinsic value to a person's life above and beyond the value recognized by that person. David Blake, State Interests in Terminating Medical Treatment, 19(3) Hastings Center Rep. 5 (1989). Why might the state have interests in preserving life even when a competent adult rejects continued life? Consider concerns about preserving the moral worth of society (if patients are allowed to die when they consent, people may have less respect for life and be less troubled when death comes about involuntarily); about preserving freedom of choice in areas of profound consequence to happiness (we do not permit people to become slaves or renounce their right to a divorce); and about avoiding the domination of one group by another (here, preventing the victimization of severely disabled persons). David Orentlicher, Physician-Assisted Dying: The Conflict with Fundamental Principles of American Law, *in* Medicine Unbound: The Human Body and the Limits of Medical Intervention 256 (Blank & Bonnicksen eds., 1994).

2. *Balancing the Individual and State Interests.* If the state's interest in preserving a patient's life exists only insofar as the patient wishes to continue living, then there is no need to balance the state's interest against the individual interest. If the state's interest has some content that is independent of the individual's interest, then that raises the question of how we should balance the state's interest in preserving life with the individual's interest in being able to refuse treatment. Should the right to refuse life-sustaining treatment be unlimited or should it be restricted according to the type of treatment at issue (e.g., a ventilator vs. antibiotics) or the patient's medical condition (e.g., end-stage AIDS vs. pneumonia in an otherwise healthy person)? Do you agree with the *Quinlan* court's view that the right to refuse life-sustaining treatment should grow as the degree of bodily invasion increases and the prognosis dims? Should it matter whether the patient is terminally ill or might be able to live for many years?

As the case law has developed, courts have seemingly abandoned any effort to balance the individual's right to refuse treatment with the state's interest in preserving life, almost without exception permitting competent patients to refuse life-sustaining treatment. In the early cases, including *Quinlan*, the courts had suggested that the right to refuse life-sustaining treatment was a right that existed when life could be prolonged for only a short time, with a poor quality of life and at considerable cost to the patient (with cost being measured in terms of pain, other suffering, and economic burden). However, recent cases have not so limited the right.

As we saw, the New Jersey Supreme Court in *Conroy* concluded that:

> the right to self-determination ordinarily outweighs any countervailing state interests, and competent persons generally are permitted to refuse medical treatment, even at the risk of death. . . . Ms. Conroy's right to self-determination would not be affected by her medical condition or prognosis. . . . [A] competent person's common-law and constitutional rights do not depend on the quality or value of his life. 486 A.2d at 1225-1226.

Two years later, in In re Peter, 529 A.2d 419 (N.J. 1987), involving the removal of a feeding tube from a patient in a persistent vegetative state, the same court wrote:

> Medical choices . . . are not to be decided by societal standards of reasonableness or normalcy. Rather, it is the patient's preferences — formed by his or her unique personal experiences — that should control.
>
> The privacy that we accord medical decisions does not vary with the patient's condition or prognosis. The patient's medical condition is generally relevant only to determine whether the patient is or is not competent. . . . [529 A.2d at 423.]

Other courts have taken the same view of the state's interest in preserving life. In the case of Elizabeth Bouvia, an intermediate appeals court permitted a 28-year-old college graduate who retained her full intellectual capacity to refuse a feeding tube. Because of severe cerebral palsy, Ms. Bouvia was quadriplegic, confined to bed, and dependent on others for all of her needs. She also was in continual pain from severe arthritis. She had suffered a series of emotional setbacks when her husband left her and her physical deterioration forced her to drop out of school and become dependent on others. Despondent, she admitted herself to a public hospital as a psychiatric patient, with the apparent intent of starving herself to death using the assistance of pain relief and other comfort care provided by the hospital. After a trial court denied her judicial assistance, she abandoned that effort and lived at several different facilities before seeking permission from a trial court to have her feeding tube withdrawn. In addressing the fact that Ms. Bouvia was not terminally ill, the appellate court wrote,

> All decisions permitting cessation of medical treatment or life-support procedures to some degree hastened the arrival of death. In part, at least, this was permitted because the quality of life during the time remaining in those cases had been terribly diminished. In Elizabeth Bouvia's view, the quality of her life has been

diminished to the point of hopelessness, uselessness, unenjoyability and frustration. She, as the patient, lying helplessly in bed, unable to care for herself, may consider her existence meaningless. She cannot be faulted for so concluding. If her right to choose may not be exercised because there remains to her, in the opinion of the court, a physician or some committee, a certain arbitrary number of years, months, or days, her right will have lost its value and meaning. Who shall say what the minimum amount of available life must be? Does it matter if it be 15 to 20 years, 15 to 20 months, or 15 to 20 days, if such life has been physically destroyed and its quality, dignity and purpose be gone? As in all matters lines must be drawn at some point, somewhere, but that decision must ultimately belong to the one whose life is in issue. Here Elizabeth Bouvia's decision to forego medical treatment or life-support through a mechanical means belongs to her. It is not a medical decision for her physicians to make. Neither is it a legal question whose soundness is to be resolved by lawyers or judges. It is not a conditional right subject to approval by ethics committees or courts of law. It is a moral and philosophical decision that, being a competent adult, is hers alone. Bouvia v. Superior Court, 225 Cal. Rptr. 297, 304-305 (Cal. Ct. App. 1986).

According to the *Bouvia* court, a competent adult "has the right to refuse *any* medical treatment, even that which may save or prolong her life." 225 Cal. Rptr. at 300 (emphasis in original). Despite winning her case, Ms. Bouvia did not exercise her right to refuse life-sustaining treatment and is still alive.

The Nevada Supreme Court also has given little weight to the state's interest in preserving life. In McKay v. Bergstedt, 801 P.2d 617 (Nev. 1990), a 31-year-old man, Kenneth Bergstedt, sought permission to discontinue a ventilator. Mr. Bergstedt had been quadriplegic, and therefore ventilator-dependent, since a swimming accident at age 10. He was able to read, watch television, write poetry by orally operating a computer, and move around in a wheelchair. His quadriplegia was irreversible, but he was not terminally ill. When the death of his father appeared imminent, Mr. Bergstedt wanted to end his life because "he despaired over the prospect of life without the attentive care, companionship and love of his devoted father." Id. at 620. His mother had died several years earlier. The court observed that Mr. Bergstedt's desire to end his life was driven primarily by "[f]ear of the unknown," that he was preoccupied with concern "over the quality of his life after the death of his father." Id. at 624. In concluding that Mr. Bergstedt's right to refuse treatment overrode the state's interest in preserving life, the court "attach[ed] great significance to the quality of Kenneth's life as he perceived it under the particular circumstances that were afflicting him." Id. at 625.[1] Like many of the decisions in this area, the Nevada Supreme Court's opinion came down after Mr. Bergstedt died. About a month before the decision, and a week before his father died, Mr. Bergstedt's father disconnected his son's ventilator. Father Succumbs to Cancer After Fulfilling Son's Death Wish, San Diego Union-Tribune, October 12, 1990, at A15.

---

[1] The *Bergstedt* court also recognized a fifth state interest beyond the four generally relied on by courts. According to the court, there is an interest "in encouraging the charitable and humane care of afflicted persons." 801 P.2d at 628. Patients contemplating refusal of life-sustaining treatment therefore must be fully informed of the care alternatives that would be available to them if they remained alive. Id.

Although there are some early cases to the contrary,[2] courts have approved refusals of treatments necessary to sustain life even when the treatment is simple and minimally invasive, and the person could readily be restored to good health. In Fosmire v. Nicoleau, 551 N.E.2d 77 (N.Y. 1990), the court recognized the right of a 36-year-old adult to refuse blood transfusions that could restore her to good health following blood loss during a cesarean section. The patient refused the transfusions both because she was a Jehovah's Witness and because she feared that a transfusion would transmit HIV or other infectious organisms. In Stamford Hospital v. Vega, 674 A.2d 821, 824-825 (Conn. 1996), the court also recognized a patient's right to refuse blood transfusions after she had lost a good deal of blood during the vaginal delivery of her child. The patient refused the transfusions because she was a Jehovah's Witness.[3] It is important to recognize that, while a blood transfusion does not have the intrusiveness of a ventilator, Jehovah's Witnesses are expressing a central tenet of their religion when they refuse transfusions. See Dena S. Davis, Does "No" Mean "Yes"? The Continuing Problem of Jehovah's Witnesses and Refusal of Blood Products, 19(3) Second Opinion 34 (1994); Richard Singelenberg, The Blood Transfusion Taboo of Jehovah's Witnesses: Origin, Development and Function of a Controversial Doctrine, 31 Soc. Sci. Med. 515 (1990).

Prisoner cases are an area in which courts will require continuation of treatment.[4] In In re Caulk, 480 A.2d 93 (N.H. 1984), a 36-year-old prisoner in good health stopped eating with the intent to end his life because he was serving a fifteen- to thirty-year sentence and was facing additional charges that could ultimately add up to a sentence of life without parole. The court permitted the state to forcibly feed Mr. Caulk, citing concerns about institutional order and the fact that Mr. Caulk was not suffering from any illness. The court also observed that Mr. Caulk's attempt at starvation was frustrating the criminal justice system. Because of his condition, two states that had pending indictments against Mr. Caulk were forced to postpone his trials. As a result, the two states could not meet their duty "to bring to finality pending investigations in such a way that the public knows that the criminal justice system has successfully responded to accusations of criminal behavior." 480 A.2d at 96. See also Polk County Sheriff v. Iowa District Court, 594 N.W.2d 421 (Iowa 1999) (rejecting a pretrial detainee's request to discontinue chronic dialysis); Laurie v. Senecal, 666 A.2d 806 (R.I. 1995) (rejecting healthy prisoner's request to die by refusing food and water). Note that courts have upheld the right of prisoners to refuse life-sustaining treatment when they are doing so for reasons similar to nonincarcerated persons. For example, in Thor v. Superior Court, 855 P.2d 375 (Cal. 1993), the California

---

[2] See, e.g., Application of President & Directors of Georgetown College, Inc., 331 F.2d 1000 (D.C. Cir.), cert. denied, 377 U.S. 968 (1964) (25-year-old required to accept a blood transfusion to treat severe blood loss from a perforated ulcer); John F. Kennedy Memorial Hospital v. Heston, 279 A.2d 670 (N.J. 1971) (22-year-old required to accept a blood transfusion during surgery that was performed because her spleen was ruptured in an automobile accident).

[3] In both Fasmire and Stamford Hospital, the patient had received transfusions by virtue of a lower court's order before winning on appeal.

[4] As discussed in Chapters 5 and 6, courts have also been much more willing to impose treatment when a third party's interest is at stake, for example, when a woman is pregnant or there is a threat to public health.

Supreme Court held that a prisoner who was quadriplegic from a neck fracture had a right to refuse a feeding tube.

3. *Burdensome Treatment vs. Burdensome Life.* The nearly unlimited recognition of a right to refuse life-sustaining treatment means that courts have not distinguished between patients who refuse treatment because the treatment itself is not desired and patients who refuse treatment because their life with treatment has become undesirable. The former category includes Jehovah's Witnesses who reject a blood transfusion or a patient with end-stage cancer who rejects an experimental drug with severe side effects. The latter category includes patients like Elizabeth Bouvia and Kenneth Bergstedt. Does it make sense to distinguish between patients who reject treatment and patients who reject life? When a person with kidney failure who is dependent on dialysis becomes tired of the dependency and decides to stop receiving dialysis treatments, is the person rejecting the treatment or life? Even if we could distinguish between rejecting treatment and rejecting life, why does that distinction matter if the right to refuse treatment is based on principles of self-determination and concerns about avoiding suffering?

4. *Practice vs. the Law.* Despite the fairly clear message from appellate courts that competent patients have the right to refuse life-sustaining treatment, irrespective of the prognosis or the type of treatment, actual practices by physicians and lower court judges retain some of the *Quinlan* kind of balancing. For example, as discussed in more detail in the note on innocent third parties, pages 255-256, some trial court judges will order blood transfusions for Jehovah's Witnesses despite the religiously based refusal of the patient, only to have the decision reversed on appeal after it is impossible to undo the transfusion. See, e.g., In re Duran, 769 A.2d 497 (Pa. Super. Ct. 2001) (patient received blood transfusion following liver transplant surgery despite written statement before surgery refusing any transfusions). Similarly, in a leading medical ethics guide for practicing physicians, the authors present the following case and analysis:

> Mr. CURE, a 24-year-old white male has been brought to the emergency room by a friend. Previously in good health, he is complaining of a severe headache and a stiff neck. . . . [Based on physical examination and laboratory tests, a] diagnosis of pneumococcal pneumonia and pneumococcal meningitis is reached. . . .
>
> [Mr. CURE] is informed that he needs immediate hospitalization and administration of antibiotics. He refuses treatment and says he wants to go home. The physician explains the extreme dangers of going untreated and the minimal risks of treatment. [Without treatment, there is a likelihood of death of 60 to 80 percent, with survivors generally having major and permanent neurologic damage. With treatment, there is a greater than 90 percent chance of full recovery.] The young man persists in his refusal. Apart from this strange adamancy, he exhibits no evidence of mental derangement or altered mental status. . . .
>
> This patient's refusal is truly enigmatic. There is no evidence of incapacity to choose due to altered mental state (although the patient's high fever might lead the physician to suspect some incapacitation). Further, there is no expression of an "unusual belief," for example, a religious objection to antibiotics. The patient simply refuses and will provide no reason for the refusal. Given both this enigmatic refusal and the urgent, serious need for treatment, the patient should be treated, even against his will. Should there be time, legal authorization should

be sought. In offering this counsel, we reluctantly favor paternalistic intervention at the expense of personal autonomy. Our reluctance stems from the unwilling-ness to violate the liberty of another. It is overcome by the consideration that something essential is missing in this case. It is difficult to believe that this young man wishes to die. Albert R. Jonsen, Mark Siegler & William J. Winslade, Clinical Ethics: A Practical Approach to Ethical Decisions in Clinical Medicine 15, 47, 62 (3d ed. 1992).

How should we view the willingness of physicians and courts to override treatment refusals by persons who easily could be restored to good health? Is this a reasonable safeguard against taking too far the important ethical and legal principle of patient autonomy? Or should we worry about physicians and courts going too far the other way in frustrating patient autonomy? In explaining their willingness to override Mr. CURE's refusal of treatment, Jonsen et al. give a reason that is perfectly consistent with respect for patient autonomy. How do they justify their action in terms of individual self-determination? For a similar argument, see Richard A. Epstein, Moral Peril: Our Inalienable Right to Health Care?, 300-305 (1997).

Notes: The State's Interest in Preventing Suicide

While we will save most of our analysis of the relationship between withdrawal of life-sustaining treatment and suicide for the section on physician aid in dying, at pages 308-336, it is worth thinking about the distinction now:

1. *The State's Interest in Preventing Suicide.* In discussing the state's interest in preventing suicide, the courts almost summarily dismiss this objection to the withdrawal of life-sustaining treatment. In the *Saikewicz* case, the Massachusetts Supreme Court relegated the concern about suicide to a footnote, began its analysis in the footnote by stating that "[t]he interest in protecting against suicide seems to require little if any discussion," and completed its analysis by stating, "[t]here is no connection between the conduct here in issue and any state concern to prevent suicide." Superintendent of Belchertown State School v. Saikewicz, 370 N.E.2d 417, 426 n.11 (Mass. 1977). Yet, under a dictionary definition of suicide, would it not be suicide if a patient on a ventilator flipped a switch that turned off the ventilator? (According to Merriam-Webster's Collegiate Dictionary 1177 (11th ed. 2003), suicide is "the act or an instance of taking one's own life voluntarily and intentionally esp. by a person of years of discretion and of sound mind.")

The *Saikewicz* court and the *Conroy* court emphasized that, with withdrawal, the cause of death is natural and the patient has no intent to die. In addition, the *Saikewicz* court observed that "the underlying state interest in this area lies in the prevention of irrational self-destruction." Note that this "irrational self-destruction" argument is a different kind of argument than the "natural cause" and "intent" arguments. Which of these three arguments do you find persuasive? Do you see how the three arguments might play out differently on the question of permitting physician aid in dying? (As discussed in the section on physician aid in dying, this text prefers that term to physician-assisted suicide.)

2. *Distinguishing Treatment Withdrawal from Aid in Dying.* In contrast to the usual judicial analysis, Justice Scalia in his dissent in *Cruzan* saw no distinction between the refusal of life-sustaining treatment and suicide. Indeed, in his view, refusing life-sustaining treatment is a form of suicide. He seems to be saying that the categories of treatment refusal and suicide are not self-defining but are labels we apply once we have decided whether a particular life-ending act should be permitted. If we do not approve of a life-ending act, we characterize it as suicide or euthanasia; if we approve of a life-ending act, we find some other term to describe it, for example, the withdrawal of life-sustaining treatment. Indeed, at one time, when its propriety was still in question, the withdrawal of life-sustaining treatment was commonly characterized as "passive euthanasia." John A. Robertson, Involuntary Euthanasia of Defective Newborns, 27 Stan. L. Rev. 213, 214-215 & n.16 (1975). Can we find any content to the concept of suicide, or is it simply a way to express a moral conclusion that we have reached on other grounds? One way to answer this question would be to consider two other questions: Do you think that Kenneth Bergstedt was suicidal when he sought discontinuation of his ventilator? Why wouldn't a physician who discontinued Mr. Bergstedt's ventilator be guilty of active euthanasia?

Notes: The Ethical Integrity of the Medical Profession

1. *Professional Objection to Withdrawal.* The state's interest in preserving the ethical integrity of the medical profession has rarely been invoked to prevent the withdrawal of life-sustaining treatment. Courts either conclude that withdrawing treatment is consistent with the ethics of the medical profession (as in *Quinlan* and *Conroy*) and/or indicate that the weight of the interest in professional integrity is not sufficient to override the individual interest in refusing life-sustaining treatment (as in *Conroy*).

Still, there may be cases in which the physician has a personal, moral objection to discontinuing life-sustaining treatment. If the patient's right to refuse treatment rests on a principle of individual autonomy, how do we resolve the conflict when the physician invokes the same principle of individual autonomy to resist participation in the patient's death? We might say that the physician's rights are not violated since the physician need only refrain from acting, but is that an answer to the physician who is morally opposed to helping cause a patient's death? There may also be situations in which the hospital or nursing home has an institutional policy against withdrawing life-sustaining treatment. How should these cases be handled?

Courts have responded to this problem in different ways. In Brophy v. New England Sinai Hospital, 497 N.E.2d 626, 639 (Mass. 1986), the court wrote:

> There is nothing in *Saikewicz* and its progeny which would justify compelling medical professionals, in a case such as this, to take active measures which are contrary to their view of their ethical duty toward their patients. There is substantial disagreement in the medical community over the appropriate medical action. It would be particularly inappropriate to force the hospital, which is willing to assist in a transfer of the patient, to take affirmative steps to end the provision

of nutrition and hydration to him. A patient's right to refuse medical treatment does not warrant such an unnecessary intrusion upon the hospital's ethical integrity in this case.

Similarly, in Gray v. Romeo, 697 F. Supp. 580 (D.R.I. 1988), the court allowed the hospital to arrange for a transfer of the patient but held that the hospital must accede to the patient's refusal of artificial nutrition and hydration if the patient could not be "promptly transferred to a health care facility that will respect her wishes." Id. at 591.

Two New Jersey courts have refused to permit a transfer of the patient even though a transfer might have been feasible. In both cases, there was no warning of the hospital's policy when the patient was admitted for care, the policy was not formalized until the request was made to stop treatment and the patient had been hospitalized for some time. According to the court in In re Jobes, 529 A.2d 434, 450 (N.J. 1987):

> Mrs. Jobes' family had no reason to believe they were surrendering the right to choose among medical alternatives when they placed her in the nursing home [in 1980]. The nursing home apparently did not inform Mrs. Jobes' family about its policy toward artificial feeding until May of 1985 when they requested that [her feeding tube] be withdrawn. In fact there is no indication that this policy has ever been formalized. Under these circumstances Mrs. Jobes and her family were entitled to rely on the nursing home's willingness to defer to their choice among courses of medical treatment.
>
> We do not decide the case in which a nursing home gave notice of its policy not to participate in the withdrawal or withholding of artificial feeding at the time of a patient's admission. Thus, we do not hold that such a policy is never enforceable. But we are confident in this case that it would be wrong to allow the nursing home to discharge Mrs. Jobes. . . . [Id. at 450.]

Accord In re Requena, 517 A.2d 886 (N.J. Super. Ct. Ch. Div.), *aff'd*, 517 A.2d 869 (N.J. Super. Ct. App. Div. 1986) (patient had been in the hospital for 17 months and was admitted before the hospital merged with a Catholic hospital).

This issue is also addressed in advance directive statutes. Typically, the statutes direct the physician to arrange for transfer of the patient's care to another physician, without speaking to situations in which a transfer cannot be arranged. Those statutes that do address that situation generally require the physician to comply with the patient's request or bring the case before a court. But see Ind. Code Ann. §16-36-4-13(f) ("If the attending physician, after reasonable investigation, finds no other physician willing to honor the patient's declaration, the attending physician may refuse to withhold or withdraw life prolonging procedures.").

For further discussion of this issue, see George Annas, When Suicide Prevention Becomes Brutality: The Case of Elizabeth Bouvia, 14(2) Hastings Center Rep. 20 (1984); John K. Davis, Conscientious Refusal and a Doctor's Right to Quit, 29 J. Med. Phil. 75 (2004); Anne M. Dellinger & Ann Morgan Vickery, When Staff Object to Participating in Care, 28 J. Health & Hosp. L. 269 (1995); Brian C. Kalt, Death, Ethics, and the State, 23 Harv. J.L. & Pub. Pol'y 487 (2000); Note, Life-Sustaining Treatment Law, 47 B.C. L. Rev. 815 (2006); page 474.

2. *Legal Liability*. In addition to moral considerations, provider objection to treatment withdrawal may reflect legal concerns. Although the right to refuse life-sustaining treatment is now well established, in 1983, prosecutors brought criminal charges against two physicians for withdrawing life-sustaining treatment at the behest of the patient's family. Barber v. Superior Court, 195 Cal. Rptr. 478 (Cal. Ct. App. 1983). The patient, Clarence Herbert, had suffered a cardiac arrest after intestinal surgery, causing "severe brain damage" and leaving him "in a vegetative state, which was likely to be permanent." Three days later, the family requested that all life-sustaining "machines" be discontinued. The physicians immediately withdrew Mr. Herbert's ventilator, and, two days later, after further consultation with the family, they withdrew Mr. Herbert's feeding tube. After Mr. Herbert died, prosecutors brought murder charges against Mr. Herbert's surgeon and internist. The court recognized the authority of Mr. Herbert's family to refuse life-sustaining treatment on his behalf and therefore concluded that "the [physicians'] omission to continue treatment under the circumstances, though intentional and with knowledge that the patient would die, was not an unlawful failure to perform a legal duty." Id. at 493.

Although no physician has suffered civil or criminal liability for withdrawing life-sustaining treatment at the request of a patient or the patient's family, physicians often express concerns about the risks of legal liability when faced with a request to withdraw treatment. Mildred Z. Solomon et al., Decisions Near the End of Life: Professional Views on Life-Sustaining Treatments, 83 Am. J. Pub. Health 14, 19 (1993). Part of this concern may reflect the fact that, in *Barber*, Mr. Herbert's physicians were in fact prosecuted, but consider whether physicians may rebuff a request to discontinue treatment by pointing to legal concerns as a camouflage, conscious or not, of their moral disagreement with the request. In other words, physicians who think it is morally wrong to discontinue treatment may find it easier — and more persuasive — to say that they cannot stop treatment rather than to acknowledge that they can, but do not want to do so.

Notes: The Protection of Innocent Third Parties

1. *Protecting the Interests of Third Parties*. Courts regularly cite the state's interest in protecting the interests of innocent third parties when a patient wants to refuse life-sustaining medical treatment, particularly when the patient has minor children who would arguably suffer from the loss of a parent. At one time, courts would invoke the interest in innocent third parties to impose treatment. For example, in Application of the President and Directors of Georgetown College, 331 F.2d 1000 (D.C. Cir. 1964), the court ordered blood transfusions for Mrs. Jesse E. Jones, a 25-year-old married woman who was the mother of a 7-month-old child. Mrs. Jones had "lost two thirds of her body's blood supply from a ruptured ulcer" and was refusing transfusion because of her religious beliefs as a Jehovah's Witness. Id. at 1006. The court justified its order on several grounds, including the fact that "Mrs. Jones was *in extremis* and hardly *compos mentis* at the time in question," the state had an interest in preventing the abandonment of her child, Mrs. Jones did not want to die even if she did not want a blood transfusion, and "a life hung in the balance." Id. at 1008-1009.

In more recent cases, courts have generally recognized a parent's right to refuse life-sustaining treatment even though the parent has young children. In In re Debreuil, 629 So. 2d 819 (Fla. 1993), Patricia Debreuil, an otherwise healthy woman, suffered life-threatening bleeding after delivering her fourth child by cesarean section. The trial court ordered transfusions, which were administered, but, on appeal, the Florida Supreme Court held that the trial court erred. According to the court, concerns about the children, who were newborn, 4, 6, and 12 years of age, did not justify the transfusions since the children could be cared for by their father. However, the court "decline[d] at this time to rule out the possibility that some case not yet before us may present a compelling interest to prevent abandonment." Id. at 827. In a similar case, Fosmire v. Nicoleau, 551 N.E.2d 77 (N.Y. 1990), the New York court of appeals also held that the parent had the right to refuse life-sustaining treatment. In that case, Denise Nicoleau had lost a substantial amount of blood after delivering a baby boy via cesarean section. Ms. Nicoleau was married and otherwise in good health. She refused transfusions because of both her religious beliefs as a Jehovah's Witness and her fear of contracting AIDS or other communicable diseases. After the hospital obtained a court order, Ms. Nicoleau received two blood transfusions. The court of appeals held that the trial court erred in ordering the transfusions. Moreover, the court suggested in its dicta that its holding would have been the same even if she had been the only parent available to care for her child: "The state does not prohibit parents from engaging in dangerous activities because there is a risk that their children will be left orphans." Id. at 84. See also Stamford Hospital v. Vega, 674 A.2d 821 (Conn. 1996) (Jehovah's Witness had the right to refuse a blood transfusion needed after she delivered a child although, again, she won on appeal after receiving blood transfusions ordered by the trial court). Still, courts have not yet faced the issue whether a parent would have to receive life-sustaining treatment if the parent's death would leave a minor child as an orphan.

How should courts respond to a single parent's refusal of life-sustaining treatment when the parent has young children? Would it depend on whether the treatment would restore the parent to good health or would only maintain the parent in a severely disabled condition? What if the parent has arranged for a grandparent, aunt and/or uncle to take care of the children? Is the refusal of life-sustaining treatment by a single parent any different from single parents who engage in risky vocations or avocations? Should we prohibit single parents from being soldiers, police, firefighters, or coal miners? Should exercising your right to procreate require you to forfeit your right to refuse life-sustaining treatment?

2. *Law on the Books vs. Law in Practice*. While appellate courts in recent years have consistently upheld the right of healthy people to refuse blood transfusions, the courts typically do so only after the person has received the transfusion because of an order by a lower court. See, e.g., *Fosmire*, 551 N.E.2d at 79; *Vega*, 674 A.2d at 826; *Dubreuil*, 629 So. 2d at 821. The *Dubreuil* case is particularly striking because the Florida Supreme Court had previously held that a young woman could refuse blood transfusions even though she had minor children. Wons v. Public Health Trust, 541 So. 2d 96 (Fla. 1989). The only apparent difference between the *Dubreuil* and *Wons* cases was that Ms. Dubreuil was estranged from her husband while Ms. Wons was apparently living amicably with her husband. *Dubreuil*, 629 So. 2d at 826. On the other hand, the Florida Supreme Court stated in *Wons* that "these cases demand

individual attention. No blanket rule is feasible which could sufficiently cover all occasions in which this situation will arise." 541 So. 2d at 98.

What should we make of the fact that the appellate courts consistently recognize a right of healthy persons to refuse blood transfusions while some trial courts order the blood transfusions? If you were a hospital lawyer, and a physician in your hospital wanted to obtain a court order to transfuse a parent of young children against the parent's wishes, what action would you pursue?

2. The Patient Whose Competence Is Uncertain

In the vast majority of cases, it is clear whether the patient is competent. Most patients either clearly possess decisionmaking capacity or they clearly do not. In some cases, however, whether the patient can competently consent to or refuse treatment is not so easily decided. While patient competence has been a long-standing issue, physicians, lawyers, and other professionals have not yet developed a readily applied standard for assessing competence, perhaps because of its elusive nature. Several different tests have been used for competency: (1) whether the patient expresses a preference for or against treatment, (2) whether the patient's decision is a "reasonable" one, (3) whether the patient's decision is based on "rational" reasons, and (4) whether the patient has the ability to understand or has demonstrated actual understanding. Loren H. Roth, Alan Meisel & Charles W. Lidz, Tests of Competency to Consent to Treatment, 134 Am. J. Psychiatry 279 (1977). The latter two of the four tests have emerged as the predominant ones. For example, the New Jersey Supreme Court has written that "[a] competent patient has a clear understanding of the nature of his or her illness and prognosis, and of the risks and benefits of the proposed treatment, and has the capacity to reason and make judgments about that information." In re Farrell, 529 A.2d 404, 413 n.7 (N.J. 1987). Even so, it is not a simple matter to assess a person's capacity for reasoning and understanding nor is it clear what level of understanding a person must be able to exercise to be considered competent. Note also that the tests are not necessarily exclusive. Whether a person exhibits understanding will be judged in part on the rationality of the person's reasoning. For further discussion, see George Annas & Jean E. Densberger, Competence to Refuse Medical Treatment: "Autonomy vs. Paternalism," 15 U. Tol. L. Rev. 561 (1984); Jessica Wilen Berg, Paul S. Appelbaum & Thomas Grisso, Constructing Competence: Formulating Standards of Legal Competence to Make Medical Decisions, 48 Rutgers L. Rev. 345 (1996); Daniel Marson & Kellie Ingram, Competency to Consent to Treatment: A Growing Field of Research, 2 J. Ethics L. & Aging 59 (1996).

■ LANE v. CANDURA
376 N.E.2d 1232 (Mass. App. Ct. 1978)

Per Curiam.

[Ms. Rosaria Candura was a 77-year-old woman with gangrene in her right foot and lower leg. Her physicians recommended amputation without delay, but Ms. Candura refused after originally agreeing to the surgery. She already had undergone two amputative operations on her right foot, losing a toe in one and part of her foot in the other. In explaining her reasons for refusing a third amputative surgery, she said] that she has been unhappy since the death of her husband [two years earlier]; that she does not wish to be a burden to her children; that she does not believe that the operation will cure her; that she does not wish to live as an invalid or in a nursing home; and that she does not fear death but welcomes it. . . .

[The court further found that Ms. Candura] is discouraged by the failure of the earlier operations to arrest the advance of the gangrene. She tends to be stubborn and somewhat irrascible [sic] . . . [S]he expressed a desire to get well but indicated that she was resigned to death and was adamantly against the operation. . . . [S]he is lucid on some matters and confused on others. Her train of thought sometimes wanders. Her conception of time is distorted. She is hostile to certain doctors. She is on occasion defensive and sometimes combative in her responses to questioning. But she has exhibited a high degree of awareness and acuity. . . . [One psychiatrist testified that Ms. Candura lacked decisionmaking capacity, in part because she would not discuss her reasons for refusal with him and because he thought her gangrene might be compromising her thinking. Another psychiatrist, who was able to elicit Ms. Candura's reasons for refusing treatment, testified that she possessed decisionmaking capacity.]

[The court held that Ms. Candura was competent to refuse treatment, noting that her competence had not been questioned until she withdrew her original consent to the surgery; that she had a right to make her own decisions about medical treatment, even if the decisions seemed unwise; that, while she might have symptoms of senility, there was no evidence that her confusion or forgetfulness was interfering with her ability to decide about the surgery; and that her case did not involve] the uninformed decision of a person incapable of appreciating the nature and consequences of her act. . . .

■ DEPARTMENT OF HUMAN SERVICES v. NORTHERN
563 S.W.2d 197 (Tenn. Ct. App. 1978)

TODD, Judge.

[Ms. Mary Northern was a 72-year-old woman with gangrene of both feet who refused her physicians' recommendation of amputative surgery of the feet to prevent her death. A physician reported that] he found the patient to be generally lucid and sane, . . . [but that] she is functioning on a psychotic level with respect to her gangrenous feet. She tends to believe that her feet are black because of soot or dirt. . . . There is an adamant belief that her feet will heal without surgery. . . . There is no desire to die, yet her judgment concerning recovery is markedly impaired. If she appreciated the seriousness of her condition, heard her physicians' opinions, and concluded against an operation, then I would believe she understood and could decide for herself. But my impression is that she does not appreciate the dangers to her life. . . .

[The court found Ms. Northern incompetent to decide about the surgery, basing its decision on her failure to appreciate the nature of her medical condition and her refusal to make a choice between living and keeping her feet. In the view of the court, Ms. Northern was resorting to the "device of denying" her medical condition to avoid having to choose between losing her life and losing her feet.] If, as repeatedly stated, this patient could and would give evidence of a comprehension of the facts of her condition and could and would express her unequivocal desire in the face of such comprehended facts, then her decision, however unreasonable to others, would be accepted and honored by the courts and her doctors. The difficulty is that she cannot or will not comprehend the facts. . . .

Notes: Assessing Competence

1. *Applying the Tests for Competence*. It makes good sense to consider a patient's degree of understanding and rationality of reasoning, but how should we respond to patients who do not want to explain their decision? What if the patient says, "I don't want the surgery, and it's none of your business why"? The court in *Northern* makes much of Ms. Northern's misunderstanding of what was going on with her feet, but what if she appreciated that her feet were gangrenous but misunderstood other issues? What if she had said that she understood that her feet were gangrenous but that they became that way because she had sinned and that the good Lord would heal them for her now that she was repenting? Would that constitute an incompetent refusal of surgery? For an interesting discussion of religious beliefs and decisionmaking capacity, see Adrienne M. Martin, Tales Publicly Allowed: Competence, Capacity, and Religious Beliefs, 37(1) Hastings Center Rep. 33 (2007) (arguing that religious beliefs that interfere with understanding may make the patient incapacitated but that respect for the patient's religious values may lead us to accept the patient's decision).

2. *Adolescents*. Issues of competence also arise for adolescents. There are two separate questions that must be answered: (1) Do minors have capacity to decide for themselves? (2) If not, is the decision one that parents can make for them? In general, the answer to (1) is "no" and to (2) is "yes": Minors usually are held to lack decisionmaking capacity, and parents usually have authority to make decisions on their behalf. Both rules have important exceptions, however. The exceptions to the second rule are discussed infra at pages 301-303, where we learn that courts often deny parents authority to refuse life-sustaining treatment for their children. These notes discuss exceptions to the first rule, that is, situations where minors may make important medical decisions for themselves.

While minors generally lack decisionmaking capacity, "mature minors" may be accorded decisionmaking authority if they can show decisionmaking capacity despite their age. For example, in a medical malpractice case, Caldwell v. Bechtol, 724 S.W.2d 739 (Tenn. 1987), the Tennessee Supreme Court considered whether a woman five months shy of her eighteenth birthday could give consent to treatment by an osteopathic physician for her lower back pain. The court stated:

> Several relevant principles from these cases may be stated for this case. Whether a minor has the capacity to consent to medical treatment depends upon the age, ability, experience, education, training, and degree of maturity or judgment obtained by the minor, as well as upon the conduct and demeanor of the minor at

the time of the incident involved. Moreover, the totality of the circumstances, the nature of the treatment and its risks or probable consequences, and the minor's ability to appreciate the risks and consequences are to be considered. Guided by the presumptions in the Rule of Sevens, these are questions of fact for the jury to decide. [Id. at 748.]

The Rule of Sevens holds that "under the age of seven, no capacity; between seven and fourteen, a rebuttable presumption of no capacity; between fourteen and twenty-one, a rebuttable presumption of capacity." Id. at 745.

The Supreme Court of Appeals of West Virginia adopted a test very similar to that of the *Caldwell* court in the context of a life-sustaining treatment decision. In Belcher v. Charleston Area Medical Center, 422 S.E.2d 827 (W. Va. 1992), Larry Belcher, a minor of 17 years and 8 months, suffered from muscular dystrophy, and it appeared that he would become ventilator dependent imminently. His physician and parents decided that Mr. Belcher would not be ventilated or resuscitated in the event of a respiratory arrest, and Mr. Belcher died the following day from a respiratory arrest. An issue before the court was whether his physician should have consulted Mr. Belcher before a decision was made about ventilation and resuscitation. The court wrote:

> Whether the child has the capacity to consent depends upon the age, ability, experience, education, training, and degree of maturity or judgment obtained by the child, as well as upon the conduct and demeanor of the child at the time of the procedure or treatment. The factual determination would also involve whether the minor has the capacity to appreciate the nature, risks, and consequences of the medical procedure to be performed, or the treatment to be administered or withheld. Where there is a conflict between the intentions of one or both parents and the minor, the physician's good faith assessment of the minor's maturity level would immunize him or her from liability for the failure to obtain parental consent. [Id. At 838.]

In In re Swan, 569 A.2d 1202 (Me. 1990), the Maine Supreme Court relied on the statements of a minor, Chad Swan, to permit the withholding of a feeding tube. Mr. Swan was 18 years old at the time of the decision but had become permanently unconscious from an automobile accident at age 17. In permitting the withholding, the court relied on statements that Mr. Swan had made about his wishes regarding life-sustaining treatment. At age 16 he had spoken to his mother about a highly publicized local case in which the patient had also become permanently unconscious from a motor vehicle accident and said, "If I can't be myself . . . no way . . . let me go to sleep." In addition, eight days before his accident, after visiting a comatose friend in the hospital, Mr. Swan told his brother, "I don't ever want to get like that. . . . I would want somebody to let me leave—to go in peace." Id. at 1205. According to the court,

> The fact that Chad made these declarations as to medical treatment before he reached the age of eighteen is at most a factor to be considered by the fact finder in assessing the seriousness and deliberativeness with which his declarations were made. . . . Capacity exists when the minor has the ability of the average person to understand and weigh the risks and benefits. [Id.]

Another leading case discussing the mature minor doctrine in the context of life-sustaining treatment is In re E.G., 549 N.E.2d 322 (Ill. 1989). In that case, a 17-year-old woman with an acute leukemia consented to treatment for her leukemia except for blood transfusions. Her refusal was based on her religious beliefs as a Jehovah's Witness. Her physician testified that, without blood transfusions, E.G. would likely die within a month. With blood transfusions, her chemotherapy had an 80 percent chance of achieving a remission of her leukemia but only a 20 to 25 percent chance of giving E.G. a long-term survival. After the trial court appointed one of the hospital's counsel as E.G.'s temporary guardian, blood transfusions were administered. On appeal, the Illinois Supreme Court held that mature minors enjoy a right to refuse life-sustaining medical treatment. In deciding when that right can be exercised, the court first concluded that "[w]hen a minor's health and life are at stake," proof of a minor's maturity must be made "by clear and convincing evidence." Id. at 327. In addition, the state's interest in protecting the minor's health "will vary depending upon the nature of the medical treatment involved. Where the health care issues are potentially life threatening, the state's *parens patriae* interest is greater than if the health care matter is less consequential." Id. Minors should be considered mature enough to make their own life-sustaining treatment decisions "[i]f the evidence is clear and convincing that the minor is mature enough to appreciate the consequences of her actions, and . . . the minor is mature enough to exercise the judgment of an adult." Invoking the state's interest in protecting the interests of third parties, the court also wrote that "[i]f a parent or guardian opposes an unemancipated mature minor's refusal to consent to treatment for a life-threatening health problem, this opposition would weigh heavily against the minor's right to refuse." Id. at 328. Since E.G.'s mother agreed with her decision, the court did not indicate how the balance between the minor's right to decide and the state's interest in third parties would play out. In addition, since E.G. had become an adult by the time the decision was issued, the court did not remand the case for determination of her maturity.

Do you agree with the *E.G.* court that the minor's right should depend on the "nature of the medical treatment involved"? Note that this standard would result in mature minors essentially being governed by the *Quinlan* substantive standard ("the state's interest *contra* weakens and the individual's right to privacy grows as the degree of bodily invasion increases and the prognosis dims," *Quinlan*, 355 A.2d at 664) and adults by the *Conroy* substantive standard (a competent patient's right to refuse life-sustaining treatment "would not be affected by her medical condition or prognosis," *Conroy*, 486 A.2d at 1226).

Which court do you think has the better approach on the issue of parental disagreement with the child, *E.G.* or *Belcher*?

Not all states recognize a mature minor doctrine. For example, a federal district court in Georgia concluded that Georgia state law grants decisionmaking capacity only in certain statutorily specified situations (e.g., minors who are married, pregnant, or have children) but does not include a mature minor doctrine. Novak v. Cobb County-Kennestone Hosp. Auth., 849 F. Supp. 1559 (N.D. Ga. 1994). Other states have not decided one way or another whether maturity serves as the basis for decisionmaking capacity for a minor. In re Conner, 140 P.3d 1167 (Or. Ct. App. 2006)

For further discussion of these issues, see Rhonda Gay Hartman, Adolescent Decisional Autonomy for Medical Care: Physician Perceptions and Practices, 8 U. Chi. L. Sch. Roundtable 87 (2001); Angela Holder, Minors' Rights to Consent to Medical Care, 257 JAMA 3400 (1987); Kimberly M. Mutcherson, Whose Body Is It Anyway? An Updated Model of Healthcare Decision-Making Rights for Adolescents, 14 Cornell J.L. & Pub. Pol'y 251 (2005); Michelle Oberman, Minor Rights and Wrongs, 24 J.L. Med. & Ethics 127 (1996); Jessica A. Penkower, Comment, The Potential Right of Chronically Ill Adolescents to Refuse Life Saving Medical Treatment — Fatal Misuse of the Mature Minor Doctrine, 45 DePaul L. Rev. 1165 (1996); Jennifer L. Rosato, Let's Get Real: Quilting a Principled Approach to Adolescent Empowerment in Health Care Decision-Making, 51 DePaul L. Rev. 769 (2002); Elizabeth S. Scott, Judgment and Reasoning in Adolescent Decisionmaking, 37 Vill. L. Rev. 1607 (1992); 93 A.L.R.3d 67 (1979).

3. *Reliability of Patient Decisions*. While a patient may be competent to decide, there still is the question whether the patient has in fact reached a firm and settled decision. We might expect patients to express a good deal of ambivalence when making life-sustaining treatment decisions. When faced with a patient who has come to a decision with some difficulty and gone back and forth on the matter, should we require some kind of waiting period to ensure that the decision really is a reliable one? As discussed in the section on physician aid in dying at page 308, when Oregon adopted its physician aid in dying law, it included a requirement that patients wait at least fifteen days from the time they request physician assistance until they can obtain a prescription for a lethal dose of a drug. Should there be a similar waiting period for refusals of life-sustaining treatment? Recall that Kenneth Bergstedt sought and received permission to disconnect his ventilator because he feared what his life would be like after his father died. In that case, Mr. Bergstedt died one week before his father died and one month before the court issued its ruling, apparently because his father disconnected the ventilator. If Mr. Bergstedt had been alive when the court decided the case, should the court have required that Mr. Bergstedt see what his life was like after his father died before deciding whether to refuse the ventilator? How long a trial of living without his father would be sufficient?

There are studies that have considered whether patients' treatment preferences are stable over time. In these studies, researchers questioned individuals in three categories: people who were healthy; people who had mild health problems; and people who had serious illnesses. The individuals gave their treatment preferences at the outset of the studies, six months later, and one year later. In general, the treatment preferences were stable over the course of a year. Linda L. Emanuel et al., Advance Directives: Stability of Patients' Treatment Choices, 154 Arch. Intern. Med. 209 (1994); Lawrence J. Schneiderman et al., Relationship of General Advance Directive Instructions to Specific Life-Sustaining Treatment Preferences in Patients with Serious Illness, 152 Arch. Intern. Med. 2114 (1992). See also Peter H. Ditto et al., Stability of Older Adults' Preferences for Life-Sustaining Medical Treatment, 22 Health Psych. 605 (2003) (finding moderate stability in treatment preferences over two-year time period). For patients whose health status changes, however, their treatment preferences also may change. As health status worsens and patients see that their quality of life is better than they had thought it would be, patients become more accepting of treatments that provide lower levels of benefit or impose greater levels of discomfort. Terri R. Fried et al., Prospective Study of Health Status Preferences and Changes in Preferences Over Time in Older Adults, 166 Arch. Intern. Med. 890 (2006).

3. The Incompetent Patient

When a patient is incompetent, as is common when decisions about life-sustaining treatment are made, a few questions arise: Does the right to refuse life-sustaining treatment survive incompetence? If it does, is the right the same? How is the right invoked on behalf of the patient? You should pay particular attention to the procedural safeguards that the courts have adopted to govern life-sustaining treatment decisions for incompetent patients.

We will begin with two cases from the New Jersey Supreme Court. By way of background, the New Jersey Supreme Court has also adopted procedural safeguards for withdrawal decisions involving competent patients. It is useful to consider how these safeguards change when we move from the competent to the incompetent patient. New Jersey's safeguards for competent patients were developed in In re Farrell, 529 A.2d 404 (N.J. 1987). That case involved a woman, Kathleen Farrell, who became ventilator dependent from amyotrophic lateral sclerosis (ALS, or Lou Gehrig's disease). ALS is a disorder of the nervous system that results in degeneration of the nerves controlling voluntary muscle movements. The disease, whose cause is unknown, gradually leaves people unable to move their muscles. Ultimately, this means that they cannot move their arms or legs, swallow, speak intelligibly, or breathe. At the time of Ms. Farrell's diagnosis, a victim's life expectancy even with life-sustaining treatment was usually one to three years. For "competent patients who are living at home" and "who request the discontinuance of life-sustaining medical treatment," the *Farrell* court adopted the following procedural safeguards:

> First, it must be determined that the patient is competent and properly informed about his or her prognosis, the alternative treatments available, and the risk involved in the withdrawal of the life-sustaining treatment. Then it must be determined that the patient made his or her choice voluntarily and without coercion. . . . These issues are more easily resolved when the patient is in a hospital, nursing home, or other institution, because in those settings the patient is observed by more people. To protect the patient who is at home, we require that two non-attending physicians examine the patient to confirm that he or she is competent and is fully informed about his or her prognosis, the medical alternatives available, the risks involved, and the likely outcome if medical treatment is disconnected.[8] . . . The two independent confirmations of competency that we require should satisfy any questions that might later arise about the propriety of the withholding or withdrawal of treatment. Additionally,

---

[8] The procedure we hereby establish for determining the competency of a patient at home who has decided to forgo life-sustaining treatment is likewise applicable to patients in hospitals and nursing homes.

this procedural requirement should serve to forestall hasty medical decisions made while a patient is in an emotionally disturbed state because of a sudden illness or major catastrophe.

529 A.2d at 413-415. The *Farrell* court also held that there is no need to seek court approval before treatment is withdrawn.

■ IN RE CONROY
486 A.2d 1209 (N.J. 1985)

SCHREIBER, Justice.

Plaintiff, Thomas C. Whittemore, nephew and guardian of Claire Conroy, an incompetent, sought permission to remove a nasogastric feeding tube, the primary conduit for nutrients, from his ward, an eighty-four-year-old bedridden woman with serious and irreversible physical and mental impairments who resided in a nursing home. [Additional medical facts for this case are presented in the case excerpt at pages 234-236 in the section on the competent patient. As mentioned there, Ms. Conroy died while her case was before the intermediate court of appeals, but the New Jersey Supreme Court still heard the case as one involving a matter "of substantial importance and . . . capable of repetition but evad[ing] review."]

. . . Ms. Conroy had lived a rather cloistered life. She had been employed by a cosmetics company from her teens until her retirement at age 62 or 63. She had lived in the same home from her childhood until she was placed in the nursing home, had never married, and had very few friends. She had been very close to her three sisters, all of whom had died. . . .

Mr. Whittemore testified that Ms. Conroy feared and avoided doctors and that, to the best of his knowledge, she had never visited a doctor until she became incompetent in 1979. He said that on the couple of occasions that Ms. Conroy had pneumonia, "[y]ou couldn't bring a doctor in," and his wife, a registered nurse, would "try to get her through whatever she had." He added that once, when his wife took Ms. Conroy to the hospital emergency room, "as foggy as she was she snapped out of it, she would not sign herself in and she would have signed herself out immediately." According to the nephew, "[a]ll [Ms. Conroy and her sisters] wanted was to . . . have their bills paid and die in their own house." He also stated that he had refused to consent to the amputation of her gangrenous leg in 1982 and that he now sought removal of the nasogastric tube because, in his opinion, she would have refused the amputation and "would not have allowed [the nasogastric tube] to be inserted in the first place."

Ms. Conroy was a Roman Catholic. The Rev. Joseph Kukura, a Roman Catholic priest and an associate professor of Christian Ethics at the Immaculate Conception Seminary in Mahwah, New Jersey, testified that acceptable church teaching could be found in a document entitled "Declaration of Euthanasia" published by the Vatican Congregation for the Doctrine of the Faith, dated June 26, 1980. The test that this document espoused required a weighing of the burdens and the benefits to the patient of remaining alive with the aid of extraordinary life-sustaining medical treatment. Father Kukura said that life-sustaining procedures could be withdrawn if they were extraordinary, which he defined to embrace "all procedures, operations or other interventions which are excessively expensive, burdensome or inconvenient or which offer no hope of benefit to a patient." Here, he said, the hope of recovery and of returning to cognitive life, even with the nasogastric feeding, was not a reasonable possibility. The means of care were not adding to the value of her life, which was outweighed by the burdens of that life. He therefore considered the use of the nasogastric tube extraordinary. It was his judgment that removal of the tube would be ethical and moral, even though the ensuing period until her death would be painful. . . .

II

This case requires us to determine the circumstances under which life-sustaining treatment may be withheld or withdrawn from an elderly nursing-home resident who is suffering from serious and permanent mental and physical impairments, who will probably die within approximately one year even with the treatment, and who, though formerly competent, is now incompetent to make decisions about her life-sustaining treatment and is unlikely to regain such competence. Subsumed within this question are two corollary issues: what substantive guidelines are appropriate for making these treatment decisions for incompetent patients, and what procedures should be followed in making them. . . .

The *Quinlan* decision dealt with a special category of patients: those in a chronic, persistent vegetative or comatose state. In a footnote, the opinion left open the question whether the principles it enunciated might be applicable to incompetent patients in "other types of terminal medical situations . . . , not necessarily involving the hopeless loss of cognitive or sapient life." 355 A.2d at 671 n.10. We now are faced with one such situation: that of elderly, formerly competent nursing-home residents who, unlike Karen Quinlan, are awake and conscious and can interact with their environment to a limited extent, but whose mental and physical functioning is severely and permanently impaired and whose life expectancy, even with the treatment, is relatively short. The capacities of such people, while significantly diminished, are not as limited as those of irreversibly comatose persons, and their deaths, while no longer distant, may not be imminent. Large numbers of aged, chronically ill, institutionalized persons fall within this general category.

Such people . . . are unable to speak for themselves on life-and-death issues concerning their medical care. This does not mean, however, that they lack a right to self-determination. The right of an adult who, like Claire Conroy, was once competent, to determine the course of her medical treatment remains intact even when she is no longer able to assert that right or to appreciate its effectuation. As one commentator has noted:

> Even if the patient becomes too insensate to appreciate the honoring of his or her choice, self-determination is important. After all, law respects testamentary dispositions even if the testator never views his gift being bestowed. [Cantor, supra, 30 Rutgers L. Rev. at 259.]

Any other view would permit obliteration of an incompetent's panoply of rights merely because the patient could no longer sense the violation of those rights. [Id. at 252.]

Since the condition of an incompetent patient makes it impossible to ascertain definitively his present desires, a third party acting on the patient's behalf often cannot say with confidence that his treatment decision for the patient will further rather than frustrate the patient's right to control his own body. Nevertheless, the goal of decisionmaking for incompetent patients should be to determine and effectuate, insofar as possible, the decision that the patient would have made if competent. Ideally, both aspects of the patient's right to bodily integrity — the right to consent to medical intervention and the right to refuse it — should be respected.

In light of these rights and concerns, we hold that life-sustaining treatment may be withheld or withdrawn from an incompetent patient when it is clear that the particular patient would have refused the treatment under the circumstances involved. The standard we are enunciating is a subjective one, consistent with the notion that the right that we are seeking to effectuate is a very personal right to control one's own life. The question is not what a reasonable or average person would have chosen to do under the circumstances but what the particular patient would have done if able to choose for himself.

The patient may have expressed, in one or more ways, an intent not to have life-sustaining medical intervention. Such an intent might be embodied in a written document, or "living will," stating the person's desire not to have certain types of life-sustaining treatment administered under certain circumstances. It might also be evidenced in an oral directive that the patient gave to a family member, friend, or health care provider. It might consist of a durable power of attorney or appointment of a proxy authorizing a particular person to make the decisions on the patient's behalf if he is no longer capable of making them for himself. It might take the form of reactions that the patient voiced regarding medical treatment administered to others. It might also be deduced from a person's religious beliefs and the tenets of that religion, or from the patient's consistent pattern of conduct with respect to prior decisions about his own medical care. Of course, dealing with the matter in advance in some sort of thoughtful and explicit way is best for all concerned.

Any of the above types of evidence, and any other information bearing on the person's intent, may be appropriate aids in determining what course of treatment the patient would have wished to pursue. . . .

Although all evidence tending to demonstrate a person's intent with respect to medical treatment should properly be considered by surrogate decision-makers, . . . the probative value of such evidence may vary depending on the remoteness, consistency, and thoughtfulness of the prior statements or actions and the maturity of the person at the time of the statements or acts. Thus, for example, an offhand remark about not wanting to live under certain circumstances made by a person when young and in the peak of health would not in itself constitute clear proof 20 years later that he would want life-sustaining treatment withheld under those circumstances. In contrast, a carefully considered position, especially if written, that a person had maintained over a number of years or that he had acted upon in comparable circumstances might be clear evidence of his intent.

Another factor that would affect the probative value of a person's prior statements of intent would be their specificity. Of course, no one can predict with accuracy the precise circumstances with which he ultimately might be faced. Nevertheless, any details about the level of impaired functioning and the forms of medical treatment that one would find tolerable should be incorporated into advance directives to enhance their later usefulness as evidence.

Medical evidence bearing on the patient's condition, treatment, and prognosis, like evidence of the patient's wishes, is an essential prerequisite to decisionmaking under the subjective test. . . . [S]ince the goal is to effectuate the patient's right of informed consent, the surrogate decisionmaker must have at least as much medical information upon which to base his decision about what the patient would have chosen as one would expect a competent patient to have before consenting to or rejecting treatment. . . . Particular care should be taken not to base a decision on a premature diagnosis or prognosis.

We recognize that for some incompetent patients it might be impossible to be clearly satisfied as to the patient's intent either to accept or reject the life-sustaining treatment. Many people may have spoken of their desires in general or casual terms, or, indeed, never considered or resolved the issue at all. In such cases, a surrogate decisionmaker cannot presume that treatment decisions made by a third party on the patient's behalf will further the patient's right to self-determination, since effectuating another person's right to self-determination presupposes that the substitute decisionmaker knows what the person would have wanted. Thus, in the absence of adequate proof of the patient's wishes, it is naive to pretend that the right to self-determination serves as the basis for substituted decisionmaking.

We hesitate, however, to foreclose the possibility of humane actions, which may involve termination of life-sustaining treatment, for persons who never clearly expressed their desires about life-sustaining treatment but who are now suffering a prolonged and painful death. An incompetent, like a minor child, is a ward of the state, and the state's *parens patriae* power supports the authority of its courts to allow decisions to be made for an incompetent that serve the incompetent's best interests, even if the person's wishes cannot be clearly established. . . . We therefore hold that life-sustaining treatment may also be withheld or withdrawn from a patient in Claire Conroy's situation if either of two "best interests" tests — a limited-objective or a pure-objective test — is satisfied.

Under the limited-objective test, life-sustaining treatment may be withheld or withdrawn from a patient in Claire Conroy's situation when there is some trustworthy evidence that the patient would have refused the treatment, and the decisionmaker is satisfied that it is clear that the burdens of the patient's continued life with the treatment outweigh the benefits of that life for him. By this we mean that the patient is suffering, and will continue to suffer throughout the expected duration of his life, unavoidable pain, and that the net burdens of his prolonged life (the pain and suffering of his life with the treatment less the amount and duration of pain that the patient would likely experience if the treatment were withdrawn) markedly outweigh any physical pleasure, emotional enjoyment, or intellectual satisfaction that the patient may still be able to derive from life. . . .

In the absence of trustworthy evidence, or indeed any evidence at all, that the patient would have declined the treatment, life-sustaining treatment may still be withheld or withdrawn from a formerly competent person like Claire Conroy if a third, pure-objective test is satisfied. Under that test, as under the limited-objective test, the net burdens of the patient's life with the treatment should clearly and markedly outweigh the benefits that the patient derives from life. Further, the recurring, unavoidable and severe pain of the patient's life with the treatment should be such that the effect of administering life-sustaining treatment would be inhumane. Subjective evidence that the patient would not have wanted the treatment is not necessary under this pure-objective standard. Nevertheless, even in the context of severe pain, life-sustaining treatment should not be withdrawn from an incompetent patient who had previously expressed a wish to be kept alive in spite of any pain that he might experience. . . .

We are aware that it will frequently be difficult to conclude that the evidence is sufficient to justify termination of treatment under either of the "best interests" tests that we have described. Often, it is unclear whether and to what extent a patient such as Claire Conroy is capable of, or is in fact, experiencing pain. Similarly, medical experts are often unable to determine with any degree of certainty the extent of a nonverbal person's intellectual functioning or the depth of his emotional life. When the evidence is insufficient to satisfy either the limited-objective or pure-objective standard, however, we cannot justify the termination of life-sustaining treatment as clearly furthering the best interests of a patient like Ms. Conroy. . . .

The decisionmaking procedure for comatose, vegetative patients suggested in *Quinlan*, namely, the concurrence of the guardian, family, attending physician, and hospital prognosis committee, is not entirely appropriate for patients such as Claire Conroy, who are confined to nursing homes. There are significant differences in the patients, the health-care providers, and the institutional structures of nursing homes and hospitals. . . .

[The court went on to discuss special concerns with treatment withdrawal in nursing homes, including the vulnerability of nursing home residents, the fact that residents are often without any surviving family, the limited role that physicians play in nursing home care, and the occurrence of neglectful and abusive care in nursing homes. Because of these concerns, the court required the involvement of New Jersey's Office of the Ombudsman before the discontinuation of life-sustaining treatment from a patient like Claire Conroy. In addition, two physicians, unaffiliated with the nursing home or with the attending physician, would have to have confirmed the patient's medical condition and prognosis.]

Provided that the two physicians supply the necessary medical foundation, the guardian, with the concurrence of the attending physician, may withhold or withdraw life-sustaining treatment if he believes in good faith, based on the medical evidence and any evidence of the patient's wishes, that it is clear that the subjective, limited-objective or pure-objective test is satisfied. In addition, the ombudsman must concur in that decision. . . . Finally, if the limited-objective or pure-objective test is being used, the family — that is, the patient's spouse, parents, and children, or in their absence, the patient's next of kin, if any — must also concur in the decision to withhold or withdraw life-sustaining treatment. . . .

[The court then concluded that the evidence about Ms. Conroy's condition was insufficient to find that any of these three tests was met in this case. The court did not believe that it was sufficiently clear what decision she personally would have made, nor was it satisfied by the available information about the extent of pleasure or pain she was experiencing before she died. Therefore, were she still alive, the court would have instructed her guardian to find out more about her prior preferences and the benefits and burdens of her life before deciding whether any of the three standards for withdrawing treatment were satisfied.]

■ IN RE JOBES
529 A.2d 434 (N.J. 1987)

GARIBALDI, Justice.

. . . This appeal requires us to develop the guidelines and procedures under which life-sustaining medical treatment may be withdrawn from a non-elderly nursing home patient in a persistent vegetative state who, prior to her incompetency, failed to express adequately her attitude toward such treatment. . . .

[The case arose when the patient's husband and parents asked the nursing home to withdraw the patient's feeding tube. The nursing home refused on moral grounds, and the husband sought judicial authorization of the withdrawal.]

II

Nancy Ellen Jobes is thirty-one years old. . . . Prior to March of 1980, Mrs. Jobes had no significant mental or physical handicap. She was employed as a certified laboratory technologist, and was four and one-half months pregnant with her first child.

On March 11, 1980, Mrs. Jobes was admitted to Riverside Hospital for treatment of injuries sustained in an automobile accident. Doctors soon determined that her fetus had been killed. During the course of an operation to remove the dead fetus, she sustained a severe loss of oxygen and blood flow to her brain. She suffered massive and irreversible damage to the part of her brain that controls thought and movement. She has never regained consciousness. . . .

She cannot swallow. Originally she was fed and hydrated intravenously, then through a nasogastric tube, then a gastrotomy tube. In June 1985, complications with the gastrotomy tube necessitated an even more direct approach. Since then, Mrs. Jobes has been fed through a j-tube inserted — through a hole cut into her abdominal cavity — into the jejunum of her small intestine. Water and a synthetic, pre-digested formula of various amino acids are pumped through the j-tube continuously. . . .

IV

Mrs. Jobes' closest friends, her cousin, her clergyman, and her husband offered testimony that was intended to prove that if she were competent, Mrs. Jobes would refuse to be sustained by the j-tube. Deborah Holdsworth, a registered nurse and life-long friend of Mrs. Jobes, recalled a conversation in 1971 in which Mrs. Jobes stated that if she were ever crippled like the children with multiple sclerosis and muscular dystrophy that Ms. Holdsworth cared for, she would not want to live. Ms. Holdsworth also recalled telling Mrs. Jobes on numerous occasions that she, Holdsworth, would not want to live like Karen Quinlan did after the removal of her respirator. She recalled that Mrs. Jobes had not disagreed with her, but could not recall Mrs. Jobes' position any more clearly than that. Finally Holdsworth recalled that in late 1979 Mrs. Jobes specifically stated that she would not want to be kept alive on a respirator like a patient suffering from amyotrophic lateral sclerosis whom Ms. Holdsworth had described to her.

Another friend of Mrs. Jobes' since childhood, Donna DeChristofaro, testified that in Autumn 1979 Mrs. Jobes had told her that "it was a shame that [Karen Quinlan] hadn't died when they removed the respirator; that that wasn't living, it was existing; that she had wished that God had taken her then. . . ."

Mrs. Jobes' first cousin, Dr. Cleve Laird, recalled a discussion he had with her in the summer of 1975 about a victim of an automobile accident who was being kept alive by a cardiac stimulator:

> She said that she wouldn't want those measures taken in her case and that she certainly wouldn't want to live that way. I said, well, they wouldn't do that to me because I carried and still carry a form of identification that says that I do not wish to have any heroic measures taken in case of massive injury.
>
> Subsequent to that she became interested in where I had gotten that and I told her that it was pretty common both at Baylor where I had taught prior to going up to Massachusetts and also at Harvard. I said that I would send her a card. My wife was there and I turned around to her and told her why didn't she send one. Then we moved on into discussion of other technical things.

Dr. Laird testified that his wife had sent the card to Mrs. Jobes, and that Mrs. Jobes thanked them for it in a note she sent them at Christmas. The card has not been found.

John Jobes testified that if his wife were competent, she would "definitely" choose to terminate the artificial feeding that sustains her in her present condition. He generally recalled her having stated that she would not want to be kept alive under Karen Quinlan's circumstances. She did this frequently when the *Quinlan* case was in the news, mostly during 1976-1977.

The Reverend George A. Vorsheim, minister of the Morris Plains Presbyterian Church, testified that he had married the Jobes, and that he was familiar with them and with Mrs. Jobes' parents. They are all members of the Presbyterian Church (U.S.A.). The Reverend Mr. Vorsheim testified that Mrs. Jobes was raised in the Presbyterian Faith, and that in the Presbyterian Faith there is no religious requirement to perpetuate life by artificial means nor is there any doctrine prohibiting life-sustaining medical treatment. The Presbyterian Church leaves decisions like the one at issue here to the individual conscience. . . .

V

In *Conroy* and *Peter* we have described the type of evidence that can establish a person's medical preferences under the "subjective test." We have explained that the probative value of prior statements offered to prove a patient's inclination for or against medical treatment depends on their specificity, their "remoteness, consistency and thoughtfulness . . . [,] and the maturity of the person at the time of the statements. . . ." *Conroy*, 486 A.2d at 1230. All of the statements about life-support that were attributed to Mrs. Jobes were remote, general, spontaneous, and made in casual circumstances. Indeed, they closely track the examples of evidence that we have explicitly characterized as unreliable.

Other than her prior statements, the only evidence of Mrs. Jobes' intent that the trial court relied on was her membership in the Presbyterian Church. There is no specific evidence of her personal belief in the tenets of that Church; nevertheless, we have consistently recognized that "a person's religious affiliation and the tenets of that religion may furnish evidence of his or her intent with regard to medical decisions." *Conroy*, supra, 98 N.J. at 362. In this case, however, Mrs. Jobes' minister testified that her religion neither requires nor forbids medical treatment like that at issue here. Therefore, Mrs. Jobes' religious affiliation does not offer much guidance in determining what her preference would be in this situation.

Thus, we conclude that although there is some "trustworthy" evidence that Mrs. Jobes, if competent, would want the j-tube withdrawn, it is not sufficiently "clear and convincing" to satisfy the subjective test. Therefore, we must determine the guidelines and procedures under which life-sustaining medical treatment may be withdrawn from a patient like Mrs. Jobes when there is no clear and convincing proof of her attitude toward such treatment.

VI

Because of the unique problems involved in decisionmaking for any patient in the persistent vegetative state, we necessarily distinguish their cases from cases involving other patients. Accordingly, in *Peter* we held that neither the life-expectancy test nor the balancing tests set forth in *Conroy* are appropriate in the case of a persistently vegetative patient. Those holdings are equally relevant in this case. In any case involving a patient in the persistent vegetative state, "we look instead primarily to *Quinlan* for guidance." *Peter*, 529 A.2d at 425 [observing that "[w]hile a benefits-burdens analysis is difficult with marginally cognitive patients like Claire Conroy, it is essentially impossible with patients in a persistent vegetative state. By definition such patients, like Ms. Peter, do not experience any of the benefits or burdens that the *Conroy* balancing tests are intended or able to appraise"]. . . .

In light of Karen Quinlan's inability to assert her right to decline continued artificial respiration, we determined that "[t]he only practical way to prevent destruction of the right [was] to permit the guardian and family of Karen to render their best judgment, subject to the qualifications [t]hereinafter stated, as to whether she would exercise it in [her] circumstances." 355 A.2d at 664. The term *substituted judgment* is commonly used to describe our approach in *Quinlan*. This approach is intended to ensure that the surrogate decisionmaker effectuates as much as possible the decision that the incompetent patient would make if he or she were competent. Under the substituted judgment doctrine, where an incompetent's wishes are not clearly expressed, a surrogate decisionmaker considers the patient's personal value system for guidance. The surrogate considers the patient's prior statements about and reactions to medical issues, and all the facets of the patient's personality that the surrogate is familiar with — with, of course, particular reference to his or her relevant philosophical, theological, and ethical values — in order to extrapolate what course of medical treatment the patient would choose.

In *Quinlan* we held that the patient's family members were the proper parties to make a substituted medical judgment on her behalf. We make the same determination today. Almost invariably the patient's family has an intimate understanding of the patient's medical attitudes and general world view and therefore is in the best position to know the motives and considerations that would control the patient's medical decisions. . . .

Family members are best qualified to make substituted judgments for incompetent patients not only because of their peculiar grasp of the patient's approach to life, but also because of their special bonds with him or her. Our common human experience informs us that family members are generally most concerned with the welfare of a patient. It is they who provide for the patient's comfort, care, and best interests, and they who treat the patient as a person, rather than a symbol of a cause. Where strong and emotional opinions and proponents exist on an issue involving the treatment of an incompetent, extreme care must be exercised in determining who will act as his or her surrogate decisionmaker. We believe that a family member is generally the best choice.

As we stated in *Farrell*:

> Our common human experience teaches us that family and close friends care most and best for a patient. They offer love and support and concern, and have the best interest of the patient at heart. The importance of the family in medical treatment decisions is axiomatic.
>
>> [F]amilies commonly exhibit the greatest degree of concern about the welfare of ailing family members. It is they who come to the hospital and involve themselves in the sick person's care and comfort. Competent patients usually actively solicit the advice and counsel of family members in decisionmaking. Family members routinely ask questions of the medical staff about the patient's condition and prognosis; one study found they frequently asked more questions than patients themselves did. Family members, in fact, commonly act as advocates for patients in the hospital, looking out for their comfort, care, and best interests. . . . [Newman, Treatment Refusals for the Critically Ill: Proposed Rules for Family, the Physician and the State, III N.Y. L. Sch. Human Rights Annual 35 (1985).]
>
> The law has traditionally respected the private realm of family life which the state cannot enter. . . . We believe that this tradition of respect for and confidence in the family should ground our approach to the treatment of the sick. [Farrell, 529 A.2d at 414. . . .]

Normally those family members close enough to make a substituted judgment would be a spouse, parents, adult children, or siblings. Generally in the absence of such a close degree of kinship, we would not countenance health care professionals deferring to the relatives of a patient, and a guardian would have to be appointed. However, if the attending health care professionals determine that another relative, e.g., a cousin, aunt, uncle, niece, or nephew, functions in the role of the patient's nuclear family, then that relative can and should be treated as a close and caring family member.

There will, of course, be some unfortunate situations in which family members will not act to protect a patient. We anticipate that such cases will be exceptional. Whenever a health-care professional becomes uncertain about whether family members are properly protecting a patient's interests, termination of life-sustaining treatment should not occur without the appointment of a guardian. . . .

Mrs. Jobes is blessed with warm, close, and loving family members. It is entirely proper to assume that they are best qualified to determine the medical decisions she would make. Moreover, there is some trustworthy evidence that supports their judgment of Mrs. Jobes' personal inclinations. Therefore, we will not presume to disturb their decision.

Thus, we hold that the right of a patient in an irreversibly vegetative state to determine whether to refuse life-sustaining medical treatment may be exercised by the patient's family or close friend. If there are close and caring family members who are willing to make this decision there is no need to have a guardian appointed. We require merely that the responsible relatives comply with the medical confirmation procedures that we henceforth establish. . . .

VII

. . . For non-elderly non-hospitalized patients in a persistent vegetative state who, like Mrs. Jobes, have a caring family or close friend, or a court-appointed guardian in attendance, we hold that the surrogate decisionmaker who declines life-sustaining medical treatment must secure statements from at least two independent physicians knowledgeable in neurology that the patient is in a persistent vegetative state and that there is no reasonable possibility that the patient will ever recover to a cognitive, sapient state. If the patient has an attending physician, then that physician likewise must submit such a statement. These independent neurological confirmations will substitute for the concurrence of the prognosis committee for patients who are not in a hospital setting and thereby prevent inappropriate withdrawal of treatment. In a proper case, however, they should not be difficult to obtain, and this requirement should not subject the patient to undesired treatment.

As long as the guidelines we hereby establish are followed in good faith, no criminal or civil liability will attach to anyone involved in the implementation of a surrogate decision to decline medical treatment. Accordingly, judicial review of such decisions is not necessary or appropriate. . . .

IX

. . . If a disagreement arises among the patient, family, guardian, or doctors, or if there is evidence of improper motives or malpractice, judicial intervention will be required. We expect, however, that disagreements will be rare and that intervention seldom will be necessary. We emphasize that even in those few cases in which the courts may have to intervene, they will not be making the ultimate decision whether to terminate medical treatment. Rather, they will be acting to insure that all the guidelines and procedures that we have set forth are properly followed. . . .

■ CRUZAN v. DIRECTOR, MISSOURI DEPARTMENT OF HEALTH
497 U.S. 261 (1990)

REHNQUIST, Chief Justice.

[The facts of this case and the Court's discussion of the existence of a right to refuse treatment are excerpted at pages 237-240 in the section on the competent patient. Ms. Cruzan suffered severe brain damage from an automobile accident that left her in a persistent vegetative state. A few years later, when her parents sought to have Ms. Cruzan's feeding tube discontinued, the Missouri Supreme Court found there to be insufficient evidence that Ms. Cruzan would want the treatment withdrawn. The primary evidence of her wishes were thoughts expressed about a year before the accident "in somewhat serious conversation with a housemate friend that if sick or injured she would not wish to continue her life unless she could live at least halfway normally."]

. . . Petitioners go on to assert that an incompetent person should possess the same right in this respect as is possessed by a competent person. . . .

The difficulty with petitioners' claim is that in a sense it begs the question: An incompetent person is not able to make an informed and voluntary choice to exercise a hypothetical right to refuse treatment or any other right. Such a "right" must be exercised for her, if at all, by some sort of surrogate. Here, Missouri has in effect recognized that under certain circumstances a surrogate may act for the patient in electing to have hydration and nutrition withdrawn in such a way as to cause death, but it has established a procedural safeguard to assure that the action of the surrogate conforms as best it may to the wishes expressed by the patient while competent. Missouri requires that evidence of the incompetent's wishes as to the withdrawal of treatment be proved by clear and convincing evidence. The question, then, is whether the United States Constitution forbids the establishment of this procedural requirement by the state. We hold that it does not.

Whether or not Missouri's clear and convincing evidence requirement comports with the United States Constitution depends in part on what interests the state may properly seek to protect in this situation. Missouri relies on its interest in the protection and preservation of human life, and there can be no gainsaying this interest. As a general matter, the states — indeed, all civilized nations — demonstrate their commitment to life by treating homicide as a serious crime. Moreover, the majority of states in this country have laws imposing criminal penalties on one who assists another to commit suicide. We do not think a state is required to remain neutral in the face of an informed and voluntary decision by a physically able adult to starve to death.

But in the context presented here, a state has more particular interests at stake. The choice between life and death is a deeply personal decision of obvious and overwhelming finality. We believe Missouri may legitimately seek to safeguard the personal element of this choice through the imposition of heightened evidentiary requirements. It cannot be disputed that the due process clause protects an interest in life as well as an interest in refusing life-sustaining medical treatment. Not all incompetent patients will have loved ones available to serve as surrogate decisionmakers. And even where family members are present, "[t]here will, of course, be some unfortunate situations in which family members will not act to protect a patient." In re Jobes, 529 A.2d 434, 447 (N.J. 1987). A state is entitled to guard against potential abuses in such situations. . . . Finally, we think a state may properly decline to make judgments about the "quality" of life that a particular individual may enjoy, and simply assert an unqualified interest in the preservation of human life to be weighed against the constitutionally protected interests of the individual.

In our view, Missouri has permissibly sought to advance these interests through the adoption of a "clear and convincing" standard of proof to govern such proceedings. . . . "This Court has mandated an intermediate standard of proof — 'clear and convincing evidence' — when the individual interests at stake in a state proceeding are both 'particularly important' and 'more substantial than mere loss of money.' " Santosky v. Kramer, 455 U.S. 745, 756 (1982) (quoting *Addington*, supra, [441 U.S.] at 424). Thus, such a standard has been required in deportation proceedings, in denaturalization proceedings, in civil commitment proceedings, and in proceedings for the termination of parental rights. . . .

We think it self-evident that the interests at stake in the instant proceedings are more substantial, both on an individual and societal level, than those involved in a run-of-the-mine civil dispute. But not only does the standard of proof reflect the importance of a particular adjudication, it also serves as "a societal judgment about how the risk of error should be distributed between the litigants." *Santosky*, 455 U.S., at 755. The more stringent the burden of proof a party must bear, the more that party bears the risk of an erroneous decision. We believe that Missouri may permissibly place an increased risk of an erroneous decision on those seeking to terminate an incompetent individual's life-sustaining treatment. An erroneous decision not to terminate results in a maintenance of the status quo; the possibility of subsequent developments such as advancements in medical science, the discovery of new evidence regarding the patient's intent, changes in the law, or simply the unexpected death of the patient despite the administration of life-sustaining treatment at least create the potential that a wrong decision will eventually be corrected or its impact mitigated. An erroneous decision to withdraw life-sustaining treatment, however, is not susceptible of correction.

It is also worth noting that most, if not all, states simply forbid oral testimony entirely in determining the wishes of parties in transactions which, while important, simply do not have the consequences that a decision to terminate a person's life does. . . . There is no doubt that statutes requiring wills to be in writing, and statutes of frauds which require that a contract to make a will be in writing, on occasion frustrate the effectuation of the intent of a particular decedent, just as Missouri's requirement of proof in this case may have frustrated the effectuation of the not fully-expressed desires of Nancy Cruzan. But the Constitution does not require general rules to work faultlessly; no general rule can.

In sum, we conclude that a state may apply a clear and convincing evidence standard in proceedings where a guardian seeks to discontinue nutrition and hydration of a person diagnosed to be in a persistent vegetative state.

Petitioners alternatively contend that Missouri must accept the "substituted judgment" of close family members even in the absence of substantial proof that their views reflect the views of the patient. . . .

No doubt is engendered by anything in this record but that Nancy Cruzan's mother and father are loving and caring parents. If the state were required by the United States Constitution to repose a right of "substituted judgment" with anyone, the Cruzans would surely qualify. But we do not think the due process clause requires the state to repose judgment on these matters with anyone but the patient herself. Close family members may have a strong feeling — a feeling not at all ignoble or unworthy, but not entirely disinterested, either — that they do not wish to witness the continuation of the life of a loved one which they regard as hopeless, meaningless, and even degrading. But there is no automatic assurance that the view of close family members will necessarily be the same as the patient's would have been had she been confronted with the prospect of her situation while competent. All of the reasons previously discussed for allowing Missouri to require clear and convincing evidence of the patient's wishes lead us to conclude that the State may choose to defer only to those wishes, rather than confide the decision to close family members.

O'CONNOR, Justice, concurring.

[In her concurrence, Justice O'Connor suggested that the Constitution gives individuals the right to have their life-sustaining treatment decisions made by a formally appointed surrogate decisionmaker (e.g., through a durable power of attorney).]

BRENNAN, Justice, with whom MARSHALL, Justice, and BLACKMUN, Justice, join, dissenting.

. . . As the majority recognizes, Missouri has a *parens patriae* interest in providing Nancy Cruzan, now incompetent, with as accurate as possible a determination of how she would exercise her rights under these circumstances. Second, if and when it is determined that Nancy Cruzan would want to continue treatment, the state may legitimately assert an interest in providing that treatment. But until Nancy's wishes have been determined, the only state interest that may be asserted is an interest in safeguarding the accuracy of that determination.

Accuracy, therefore, must be our touchstone. Missouri may constitutionally impose only those procedural requirements that serve to enhance the accuracy of a determination of Nancy Cruzan's wishes or are at least consistent with an accurate determination. The Missouri "safeguard" that the Court upholds today does not meet that standard. The determination needed in this context is whether the incompetent person would choose to live in a persistent vegetative state on life support or to avoid this medical treatment. Missouri's rule of decision imposes a markedly asymmetrical evidentiary burden. Only evidence of specific statements of treatment choice made by the patient when competent is admissible to support a finding that the patient, now in a persistent vegetative state, would wish to avoid further medical treatment. Moreover, this evidence must be clear and convincing. No proof is required to support a finding that the incompetent person would wish to continue treatment.

A

The majority offers several justifications for Missouri's heightened evidentiary standard. First, the majority explains that the state may constitutionally adopt this rule to govern determinations of an incompetent's wishes in order to advance the state's substantive interests, including its unqualified interest in the preservation of human life. Missouri's evidentiary standard, however, cannot rest on the state's own interest in a particular substantive result. To be sure, courts have long erected clear and convincing evidence standards to place the greater risk of erroneous decisions on those bringing disfavored claims. In such cases, however, the choice to discourage certain claims was a legitimate, constitutional policy choice. In contrast, Missouri has no such power to disfavor a choice by Nancy Cruzan to avoid medical treatment, because Missouri has no legitimate interest in providing Nancy with treatment until it is established that this represents her choice. Just as a state may not override Nancy's choice directly, it may not do so indirectly through the imposition of a procedural rule. . . .

The majority claims that the allocation of the risk of error is justified because it is more important not to terminate life support for someone who would wish it continued than to honor the wishes of someone who would not. An erroneous decision to terminate life support is irrevocable, says the majority, while an erroneous decision not to terminate "results in a maintenance of the status quo." But, from the point of view of the patient, an erroneous decision in either direction is irrevocable. An erroneous decision to terminate artificial nutrition and hydration, to be sure, will lead to failure of that last remnant of physiological life, the brain stem, and result in complete brain death. An erroneous decision not to terminate life support, however, robs a patient of the very qualities protected by the right to avoid unwanted medical treatment. His own degraded existence is perpetuated; his family's suffering is protracted; the memory he leaves behind becomes more and more distorted.

Even a later decision to grant him his wish cannot undo the intervening harm. But a later decision is unlikely in any event. "[T]he discovery of new evidence," to which the majority refers, is more hypothetical than plausible. The majority also misconceives the relevance of the possibility of "advancements in medical science," by treating it as a reason to force someone to continue medical treatment against his will. The possibility of a medical miracle is indeed part of the calculus, but it is a part of the patient's calculus. If current research suggests that some hope for cure or even moderate improvement is possible within the lifespan projected, this is a factor that should be and would be accorded significant weight in assessing what the patient himself would choose.[18]

B

Even more than its heightened evidentiary standard, the Missouri court's categorical exclusion of relevant evidence dispenses with any semblance of accurate factfinding. The court adverted to no evidence supporting its decision, but held that no clear and convincing, inherently reliable evidence had been presented to show

---

[18] For Nancy Cruzan, no such cure or improvement is in view. So much of her brain has deteriorated and been replaced by fluid, see App. to Pet. for Cert. A94, that apparently the only medical advance that could restore consciousness to her body would be a brain transplant.

that Nancy would want to avoid further treatment. In doing so, the court failed to consider statements Nancy had made to family members and a close friend. The court also failed to consider testimony from Nancy's mother and sister that they were certain that Nancy would want to discontinue artificial nutrition and hydration, even after the court found that Nancy's family was loving and without malignant motive. The court also failed to consider the conclusions of the guardian ad litem, appointed by the trial court, that there was clear and convincing evidence that Nancy would want to discontinue medical treatment and that this was in her best interests. The court did not specifically define what kind of evidence it would consider clear and convincing, but its general discussion suggests that only a living will or equivalently formal directive from the patient when competent would meet this standard.

Too few people execute living wills or equivalently formal directives for such an evidentiary rule to ensure adequately that the wishes of incompetent persons will be honored. While it might be a wise social policy to encourage people to furnish such instructions, no general conclusion about a patient's choice can be drawn from the absence of formalities. The probability of becoming irreversibly vegetative is so low that many people may not feel an urgency to marshal formal evidence of their preferences. Some may not wish to dwell on their own physical deterioration and mortality. Even someone with a resolute determination to avoid life support under circumstances such as Nancy's would still need to know that such things as living wills exist and how to execute one. Often legal help would be necessary, especially given the majority's apparent willingness to permit states to insist that a person's wishes are not truly known unless the particular medical treatment is specified.

. . . When Missouri enacted a living will statute, it specifically provided that the absence of a living will does not warrant a presumption that a patient wishes continued medical treatment. Thus, apparently not even Missouri's own legislature believes that a person who does not execute a living will fails to do so because he wishes continuous medical treatment under all circumstances.

The testimony of close friends and family members, on the other hand, may often be the best evidence available of what the patient's choice would be. It is they with whom the patient most likely will have discussed such questions and they who know the patient best. . . .

. . . The rules by which an incompetent person's wishes are determined must represent every effort to determine those wishes. The rule that the Missouri court adopted and that this Court upholds, however, skews the result away from a determination that as accurately as possible reflects the individual's own preferences and beliefs. It is a rule that transforms human beings into passive subjects of medical technology. . . .

D

Finally, I cannot agree with the majority that where it is not possible to determine what choice an incompetent patient would make, a state's role as *parens patriae* permits the state automatically to make that choice itself. Under fair rules of evidence, it is improbable that a court could not determine what the patient's choice would be. Under the rule of decision adopted by Missouri and upheld today by this Court, such occasions might be numerous. But in neither case does it follow that it is constitutionally acceptable for the state invariably to assume the role of deciding for the patient. A state's legitimate interest in safeguarding a patient's choice cannot be furthered by simply appropriating it.

The majority justifies its position by arguing that, while close family members may have a strong feeling about the question, "there is no automatic assurance that the view of close family members will necessarily be the same as the patient's would have been had she been confronted with the prospect of her situation while competent." I cannot quarrel with this observation. But it leads only to another question: Is there any reason to suppose that a state is more likely to make the choice that the patient would have made than someone who knew the patient intimately? To ask this is to answer it. . . .

. . . A state may ensure that the person who makes the decision on the patient's behalf is the one whom the patient himself would have selected to make that choice for him. And a state may exclude from consideration anyone having improper motives. But a state generally must either repose the choice with the person whom the patient himself would most likely have chosen as proxy or leave the decision to the patient's family.

Notes: Deciding for the Incompetent Patient

1. *Nancy Cruzan*. After the U.S. Supreme Court upheld the Missouri Supreme Court's holding that there was not sufficient evidence to show that Nancy Cruzan would want her feeding tube withdrawn, Ms. Cruzan's family returned to a state trial court with new evidence of her wishes. Because of wide publicity about her case, friends who had discussed end-of-life decisionmaking with Ms. Cruzan came forward with additional testimony about her wishes. These friends had not come forward sooner because they knew Ms. Cruzan under her married name, Nancy Davis, and she had taken her maiden name back when she divorced her husband shortly before her accident. The state did not oppose withdrawal of the feeding tube, and the court ruled in favor of the family. The feeding tube was withdrawn, and Ms. Cruzan died shortly thereafter, five months after the U.S. Supreme Court's decision. Gregory E. Pence, Classic Cases in Medical Ethics 43 (4th ed. 2004). For additional discussion of the *Cruzan* case, see Yale Kamisar, When Is There a Constitutional "Right to Die"? When Is There No Constitutional "Right to Live"?, 25 Ga. L. Rev. 1203 (1991); Thomas W. Mayo, Constitutionalizing the "Right to Die," 49 Md. L. Rev. 103 (1990).

2. *The Right of Incompetent Patients*. In *Conroy*, the court held that a competent adult's right to refuse life-sustaining medical treatment remains intact when the person loses competence. Similarly, the *Saikewicz* court wrote that "[t]he recognition of that right must extend to the case of an incompetent, as well as a competent, patient because the value of human dignity extends to both." Superintendent of Belchertown State School v. Saikewicz, 370 N.E.2d 417, 427 (Mass. 1977). Is it so clear that the right to refuse life-sustaining treatment should survive incompetence? If the right is justified by principles of self-determination, why should the right exist for individuals who can no longer express their preferences?

Consider the following explanations for a right to refuse life-sustaining treatment for incompetent persons:

(a) We can justify the extension of the right to refuse treatment by analogy to a person's right to dispose of property at death through a will. By letting people pass their wealth on to their family or other chosen beneficiaries, we do not discourage people from engaging in socially desirable activities while they are alive (e.g., wealth-generating activities.) In addition, we want people to be able to ensure the financial security of their loved ones. Both justifications arguably apply to treatment withdrawals. Do you see how this is so?

(b) To properly understand the right to refuse treatment, we need to consider not only who gets to make the treatment decision but also who does *not* get to make the decision. When individuals enjoy a right to refuse treatment, they gain personal control over an important aspect of their lives, and they also are freed from government control over that important aspect. This anti-totalitarian justification for the right to refuse treatment is still very much present for incompetent persons. Giles Scofield, The Calculus of Consent, 20(1) Hastings Center Rep. 44 (1990); Jed Rubenfeld, The Right of Privacy, 102 Harv. L. Rev. 737 (1989).

(c) Incompetent persons may not have any interests in self-determination, but they do have interests in being spared from suffering and in being treated with dignity. A right to refuse treatment is essential to ensure that incompetent persons do not undergo unjustified suffering from the imposition of medical treatment. It is also essential to ensure that incompetent persons are not robbed of their dignity.

Which of these statements do you think explain(s) or should explain the right to refuse treatment for incompetent persons? Would the nature of the right vary depending on which of the explanations actually is at work? That is, do any of the explanations justify a broader right than the other explanations? Would explanation (c) justify withdrawal of Nancy Jobes' or Nancy Cruzan's feeding tube?

In thinking about why we permit the right to refuse treatment to survive incompetence, does your explanation account for why we do not permit the right to vote to survive incompetence? Suppose a person had voted consistently as a Democrat and explained such voting on the basis that Democrats were more likely to provide adequate funding for nursing homes and other long term care. Should that person's ballot be cast for Democratic candidates even after the person becomes incompetent?

3. *Variation in Procedural Rules.* The recognition of a right to refuse treatment for incompetent persons still leaves the question as to how the right should be implemented. In *Cruzan*, the U.S. Supreme Court gave states broad leeway to adopt procedural rules for deciding when life-sustaining treatment can be withdrawn from incompetent persons.

In general, states will permit withdrawal of treatment if there is clear and convincing evidence of the patient's treatment preferences from written or oral statements made by the patient before losing competence. Evidence of the patient's wishes is clear and convincing when it is "sufficient to persuade the trier of fact that the patient had a firm and settled commitment" to decline treatment. In re Westchester County (O'Connor), 531 N.E.2d 607, 613 (N.Y. 1988). If clear and convincing evidence does not exist, there is considerable variation from state to state as to whether treatment may be discontinued.

As we have seen, New Jersey has adopted different standards for patients in different conditions. For patients who are permanently unconscious and who did not leave clear and convincing evidence of their wishes, family members may decide on the patient's behalf under a "substituted judgment" standard in which the family members draw on their knowledge of the patient to reach "as much as possible the decision that the incompetent patient would make if he or she were competent." *Jobes*, 529 A.2d at 444. For patients who have some degree of consciousness and have a short life expectancy (but are not expected to die imminently), treatment withdrawals must be justified either by clear and convincing evidence that this is what the patient would have wanted (*Conroy*'s "subjective" standard) or by a demonstration that the pain and suffering of continued treatment markedly outweigh the benefits of continued treatment (*Conroy*'s two "objective" or "best interests" standards).

Other states have adopted a single standard for all incompetent patients. At one end of the spectrum is New York. In the *O'Connor* case, New York state's highest court adopted essentially the same standard for all patients that Missouri adopted for cases like the *Cruzan* case—a strict version of *Conroy*'s subjective standard. The New York court of appeals not only required clear and convincing evidence of the patient's wishes, as in *Conroy*, but also adopted a strict view of clear and convincing evidence, requiring

> proof sufficient to persuade the trier of fact that the patient held a firm and settled commitment to the termination of life supports *under the circumstances like those presented*. As a threshold matter, the trier of fact must be convinced, as far as is humanly possible, that the strength of the individual's beliefs and the durability of the individual's commitment to those beliefs makes a recent change of heart unlikely. The persistence of the individual's statements, the seriousness with which those statements were made and the inferences, if any, that may be drawn from the surrounding circumstances are among the factors which should be considered. *O'Connor*, 531 N.E.2d at 613 (emphasis added).

While Ms. O'Connor had stated "on several occasions that if she became ill and was unable to care for herself she would not want her life to be sustained artificially," id. at 611, the court found these statements insufficient evidence of a desire to have her feeding tube discontinued:

> Her comments—that she would never want to lose her dignity before she passed away, that nature should be permitted to take its course, that it is "monstrous" to use life-support machinery—are, in fact, no different than those that many of us might make after witnessing an agonizing death. Similarly, her statements to the effect that she would not want to be a burden to anyone are the type of statements that older people frequently, almost invariably make. If such statements were routinely held to be clear and convincing proof of a general intent to decline all medical treatment once incompetency sets in, few nursing home patients would ever receive life-sustaining medical treatment in the future. . . . Her statements with respect to declining artificial means of life support were generally prompted by her experiences with persons suffering from terminal illnesses, particularly cancer. However, Mrs. O'Connor does not have a terminal illness, except in the sense that she is aged and infirm. Neither is she in a coma nor vegetative state.

She is awake and conscious; she can feel pain, responds to simple commands, can carry on limited conversations, and is not experiencing any pain. She is simply an elderly person who as a result of several strokes suffers certain disabilities, including an inability to feed herself or eat in a normal manner. . . . It is true, of course, that in her present condition she cannot care for herself or survive without medical assistance and that she has stated that she never wanted to be a burden and would not want to live, or be kept alive "artificially" if she could not care for herself. But no one contends, and it should not be assumed, that she contemplated declining medical assistance when her prognosis was uncertain. Here both medical experts agreed that she will never regain sufficient mental ability to care for herself, but it is not clear from the record that the loss of her gag reflex is permanent and that she will never be able to obtain food and drink without medical assistance. [Id. at 614-615.]

At the other end of the spectrum are states that permit family members or guardians to employ a *Jobes*-like substituted judgment standard for all incompetent patients. Brophy v. New England Sinai Hospital, Inc., 497 N.E.2d 626, 634-635 (1986); In re Tavel, 661 A.2d 1061, 1068-1069 (Del. 1995). As the Indiana Supreme Court wrote:

Respect for patient autonomy does not end when the patient becomes incompetent. In our society, health care decisionmaking for patients typically transfers upon incompetence to the patient's family. . . . Even when they have not left formal advance directives or expressed particular opinions about life-sustaining medical treatment, most Americans want the decisions about their care, upon their incapacity, to be made for them by family and physician, rather than by strangers or by government. [In re Lawrance, 579 N.E.2d 32, 39 (Ind. 1991).]

Illinois also relies on family decisionmaking, although not for all patients. The Illinois Supreme Court struggled with the question of treatment withdrawal in In re Estate of Longeway, 549 N.E.2d 292 (Ill. 1989), and In re Greenspan, 558 N.E.2d 1194 (Ill. 1990), and Rudy Linares highlighted the need for better legal guidance when he discontinued a ventilator from his 15-month-old child while holding medical staff at bay with a gun. John D. Lantos, Steven H. Miles & Christine K. Cassel, The Linares Affair, 17 L. Med. & Health Care 308 (1989). In response, the Illinois legislature passed its Health Care Surrogate Act. 755 Ill. Comp. Stat. 40. The Act applies to incompetent patients who have not executed a living will or durable power of attorney for health care and who either are terminally ill, are permanently unconscious, or have some other incurable or irreversible condition "that imposes severe pain or otherwise imposes an inhumane burden on the patient," and for which life-sustaining medical treatment "provides only minimal medical benefit." 755 Ill. Comp. Stat. 40/10. For persons covered by the Act, life-sustaining treatment decisions are to be made by family members or close friends. The Act instructs surrogate decisionmakers to decide first on the basis of how they believe the patient would have decided. Essentially, then, surrogates are governed first by New Jersey's "subjective" and "substituted judgment" standards. If surrogates are unable to figure out what the patient would have wanted, decisions for the patient "shall be made on the basis of the patient's best interests *as determined by the surrogate decision maker*." 755 Ill. Comp. Stat.

40/20(b)(1) (emphasis added). The best interests judgment is to be made by weighing the benefits to and burdens on the patient from treatment against the benefits and burdens of the treatment itself.

Most states now have statutes authorizing surrogate decisionmaking in the event that the patient did not execute an advance directive. Like Illinois, they tend to restrict the surrogate's authority in terms of the patient's condition. For example, in Maryland, the patient must be terminally ill or permanently unconscious, or must have an "end-stage condition," defined as an "advanced, progressive, irreversible condition . . . [t]hat has caused severe and permanent deterioration indicated by incompetency and complete physical dependency." Md. Code Ann., Health Gen. §5-601(i). Still, the Uniform Health Care Decisions Act and surrogate statutes in some states recognize the authority of surrogates to make life-sustaining treatment decisions without qualification in terms of the patient's condition. See, e.g., Uniform Health Care Decisions Act §5(a) (1993); D.C. Code Ann. §21-2210; Va. Code Ann. §54.1-2986. For further discussion, see Diane E. Hoffmann, The Maryland Health Care Decisions Act: Achieving the Right Balance?, 53 Md. L. Rev. 1064 (1994); Aaron N. Krupp, Health Care Surrogate Statutes: Ethics Pitfalls Threaten the Interests of Incompetent Patients, 101 W. Va. L. Rev. 99 (1998); Jerry A. Menikoff, Greg A. Sachs & Mark Siegler, Beyond Advance Directives—Health Care Surrogate Laws, 327 New Eng. J. Med. 1165 (1992); Charles P. Sabatino, The New Uniform Health Care Decisions Act: Paving a Health Care Decisions Superhighway?, 53 Md. L. Rev. 1238 (1994); Marah Stith, The Semblance of Autonomy: Treatment of Persons with Disabilities Under the Uniform Health-Care Decisions Act, 22 Issues L. & Med. 39 (2006).

Some courts have adopted a simple best interests standard for cases in which the patient's preferences cannot be established. See, e.g., Rasmussen v. Fleming, 741 P.2d 674, 689 (Ariz. 1987) (observing that "[w]here no reliable evidence of a patient's intent exists, as here, the substituted judgment standard provides little, if any, guidance to the surrogate decisionmaker and should be abandoned in favor of the 'best interests' standard"); In re Torres, 357 N.W.2d 332, 338-339 (Minn. 1984).

A good illustration of the best interests standard is the court's discussion in *Saikewicz*. Although the court stated that it was employing a substituted judgment approach, it actually was employing a best interests approach. Indeed, inasmuch as Mr. Saikewicz had never been competent, it made no sense to employ a substituted judgment, or, as one expert testified in a case involving a profoundly retarded patient, it "would be similar to asking whether 'if it snowed all summer would it then be winter?'" In re Storar, 420 N.E.2d 64, 72-73 (N.Y. 1981). The analysis of the *Saikewicz* court follows:

> . . . In short, the decision in cases such as this should be that which would be made by the incompetent person, if that person were competent, but taking into account the present and future incompetency of the individual as one of the factors which would necessarily enter into the decisionmaking process of the competent person. . . .
>
> The two factors considered by the probate judge to weigh in favor of administering chemotherapy were: (1) the fact that most people elect chemotherapy and (2) the chance of a longer life. Both are appropriate indicators of what

Saikewicz himself would have wanted, provided that due allowance is taken for this individual's present and future incompetency. . . . With regard to the second factor, the chance of a longer life carries the same weight for Saikewicz as for any other person, the value of life under the law having no relation to intelligence or social position. Intertwined with this consideration is the hope that a cure, temporary or permanent, will be discovered during the period of extra weeks or months potentially made available by chemotherapy. The guardian ad litem investigated this possibility and found no reason to hope for a dramatic breakthrough in the time frame relevant to the decision.

The probate judge identified six factors weighing against administration of chemotherapy. Four of these — Saikewicz's age,[17] the probable side effects of treatment, the low chance of producing remission, and the certainty that treatment will cause immediate suffering — were clearly established by the medical testimony to be considerations that any individual would weigh carefully. A fifth factor — Saikewicz's inability to cooperate with the treatment — introduces those considerations that are unique to this individual and which therefore are essential to the proper exercise of substituted judgment. The judge heard testimony that Saikewicz would have no comprehension of the reasons for the severe disruption of his formerly secure and stable environment occasioned by the chemotherapy. He therefore would experience fear without the understanding from which other patients draw strength. The inability to anticipate and prepare for the severe side effects of the drugs leaves room only for confusion and disorientation. The possibility that such a naturally uncooperative patient would have to be physically restrained to allow the slow intravenous administration of drugs could only compound his pain and fear, as well as possibly jeopardize the ability of his body to withstand the toxic effects of the drugs.

The sixth factor identified by the judge as weighing against chemotherapy was "the quality of life possible for him even if the treatment does bring about remission." To the extent that this formulation equates the value of life with any measure of the quality of life, we firmly reject it. A reading of the entire record clearly reveals, however, the judge's concern that special care be taken to respect the dignity and worth of Saikewicz's life precisely because of his vulnerable position. The judge, as well as all the parties, was keenly aware that the supposed inability of Saikewicz, by virtue of his mental retardation, to appreciate or experience life had no place in the decision before them. Rather than reading the judge's formulation in a manner that demeans the value of the life of one who is mentally retarded, the vague, and perhaps ill-chosen, term "quality of life" should be understood as a reference to the continuing state of pain and disorientation precipitated by the chemotherapy treatment. Viewing the term in this manner, together with the other factors properly considered by the judge, we are satisfied that the decision to withhold treatment from Saikewicz was based on a regard for his actual interests and preferences and that the facts supported this decision. Superintendent of Belchertown State School v. Saikewicz, 370 N.E.2d 417, 431-432 (Mass. 1977).

---

[17] This factor is relevant because of the medical evidence in the record that people of Saikewicz's age do not tolerate the chemotherapy as well as younger people and that the chance of remission is decreased. Age is irrelevant, of course, to the question of the value or quality of life.

Which of the different approaches for deciding about end-of-life care for incompetent persons make the most sense to you? Or is it better, in a pluralistic society, to have different approaches in different states?

4. *General Trends in Procedural Rules.* Despite the state-to-state variation, some patterns do emerge. In particular, states tend to adopt stricter procedural rules when the incompetent patient is neither terminally ill nor permanently unconscious. In such cases, the patient has some degree of consciousness and may live for a year or more. The *Conroy* case falls into this category, and the New Jersey Supreme Court adopted a stricter standard than it did in the *Jobes* case for patients who are permanently unconscious. The California Supreme Court also has adopted strict standards for patients who are neither terminally ill nor permanently unconscious. In *Wendland*, the court required clear and convincing evidence that patients would have refused treatment under the circumstances in which they now find themselves, or clear and convincing evidence that withdrawal of treatment would be in the patient's best interests. Conservatorship of Wendland, 28 P.3d 151 (Cal. 2001). (The court did not "attempt to define the extreme factual predicates that, if proved by clear and convincing evidence, might support a [surrogate's] decisions that withdrawing life support would be in the best interest of a conscious [patient]." Id. at 174. The court did observe that a surrogate's "own subjective judgment that the [patient] d[oes] not enjoy a satisfactory quality of life" is insufficient. Id.) Other courts have adopted the strict subjective standard of *Conroy* and *Wendland* but have not included an alternative objective standard. For example, in the *Martin* case, the Michigan Supreme Court adopted a purely subjective standard for patients who are neither terminally ill nor permanently unconscious, a standard similar to New York's *O'Connor* standard. For such patients in Michigan, in the absence of a written directive expressing the patient's preferences, prior oral statements will be sufficient to justify withdrawal of treatment "[o]nly when the patient's prior statements clearly illustrate a serious, well thought out, consistent decision to refuse treatment under these exact circumstances or circumstances highly similar to the current situation." In re Martin, 538 N.W.2d 399, 411 (Mich. 1995).

In Michael Martin's case, this test was not satisfied despite considerable testimony suggesting he would not want treatment provided. Mr. Martin had suffered serious injuries, including a head injury, from an automobile accident that left him "unable to walk or talk, and rendered him dependent on a colostomy for defecation and a gastrostomy tube for nutrition." He was able to understand "only very short and very simple questions." He could not "accurately comprehend questions that are lengthy, verbose, or that require the retention of multiple thoughts." In particular, he could not understand "his physical capabilities and medical condition." Id. at 402-404. Mr. Martin's wife testified to eight years of discussions regarding his wishes in the event of a serious accident or disabling illness, the most recent discussion occurring one month before his accident. These discussions took place after the Martins watched movies about people who could no longer take care of themselves because of an accident or illness.

> Mike stated to me on several occasions: "That's bullshit. I would never want to live like that." He also said to me, "Please don't ever let me exist that way because those people don't even have their dignity." . . . [Regarding a movie about a football

player with a terminal illness,] Mike said to me after we saw it together: "If I ever get sick don't put me on any machines to keep me going if there is no hope of getting better." He also said that if I ever put him on machines to keep him alive: "I'll always haunt you, Mary." Then he would say, "Do you understand?" I always said "Yes." We watched this movie at least two or three times and had virtually the same discussion each time. . . . Mike was an avid hunter and frequently expressed concerned [sic] about a hunting accident. Mike frequently told me that if he ever had an accident from which he would "not recover" and "could not be the same person," he did "not want to live that way." He would say, "Mary, promise me you wouldn't let me live like that if I can't be the person I am right now, because if you do, believe me I'll haunt you every day of your life." [Id. at 412.]

The Michigan court found that this testimony did not represent clear and convincing evidence of Mr. Martin's wishes. Two of his co-workers stated that, while Mr. Martin had indicated his desire not to be kept alive if in a vegetative state, Mr. Martin's present condition was not "the type referred to in conversations with them before his injury." In addition, several witnesses testified that, after his accident, Mr. Martin would shake his head no "when asked if he ever felt that he did not want to continue living." Id. at 412-413. For discussion of the *Martin* case, see the articles by Andrew J. Broder and Ronald E. Cranford, and by Thomas J. Marzen and Daniel Avila in Symposium Issue: Assisted Suicide, Health Care and Medical Treatment Choices, 72 U. Det. Mercy L. Rev. 719 (1995). For another case requiring clear evidence of the patient's wishes before removing a life-sustaining treatment from a patient who is neither terminally ill nor permanently unconscious, see Spahn v. Eisenberg, 563 N.W.2d 485 (Wis. 1997).

Does it make sense to vary the procedural rules depending on the patient's medical condition? If we have a different procedural standard for patients like Mr. Martin or Ms. Conroy than we do for patients like Ms. Jobes, have we maintained the principle that the substantive right to refuse life-sustaining treatment is not altered by incompetence? Should we be concerned about the fact that stricter procedural standards are likely to affect people differently depending on their socioeconomic status?

Although it is controversial whether clear and convincing evidence of the patient's wishes should be required before discontinuing life-sustaining treatment, it is less controversial when courts impose strict standards for establishing the patient's prognosis. If life-sustaining treatment is withdrawn because the patient is terminally ill or permanently unconscious, for example, we would want to be reasonably sure that the patient really is terminally ill or permanently unconscious. The Alabama Supreme Court came to that conclusion when it adopted a clear and convincing evidence standard for deciding that a patient is permanently unconscious for purposes of carrying out the patient's advance directive in the event of permanent unconsciousness. Knight v. Beverly Health Care Bay Manor Health Care Center, 820 So. 2d 92, 102 (Ala. 2001).

5. *The Patient's Best Interests*. While most courts and commentators believe that decisions for incompetent patients should reflect a judgment of what the patient would have wanted based on the patient's statements and values while competent, others disagree. Rebecca Dresser and John Robertson contend that medical decisions for incompetent persons should be based on an assessment of

the patient's current best interests, that the incompetent person is very different from the person's previously competent self:

> It is wrong to assume that the incompetent patient's prior competent preferences are the best indicator of the patient's current interests. If we could determine the choice that these patients would make if suddenly able to speak—if they could tell us what their interests in their compromised states are—such choices would reflect their current and future interests as incompetent individuals, not their past preferences. . . . When people become incompetent and seriously ill, . . . their interests may radically change. With their reduced mental and physical capacities, what was once of extreme importance to them no longer matters, while things that were previously of little moment assume much greater significance. An existence that seems demeaning and unacceptable to the competent person may still be of value to the incompetent patient, whose abilities, desires and interests have greatly narrowed. Rebecca S. Dresser & John A. Robertson, Quality of Life and Non-Treatment Decisions for Incompetent Patients: A Critique of the Orthodox Approach, 17 Med. L. & Health Care 234 (1989).

Some support for this view comes from the empirical literature. Studies consistently indicate that healthy persons underestimate the quality of life of disabled persons. That is, when healthy persons are asked to estimate the quality of life of disabled persons, they give a lower quality of life than that given by the disabled persons about their own quality of life. David Orentlicher, Destructuring Disability: Rationing of Health Care and Unfair Discrimination Against the Sick, 31 Harv. C.R.-C.L. L. Rev. 49, 69 (1996). In addition, people who become disabled find that they have a higher quality of life than they thought they would. Norman F. Boyd et al., Whose Utilities for Decision Analysis?, 10 Med. Decis. Making 58 (1990). See also Terri R. Fried, 166 Arch. Intern. Med. 890 (2006) (finding that patients more accepting of diminished health states as their own health declines); Peter A. Ubel et al., Mismanaging the Unimaginable: The Disability Paradox and Health Care Decision Making, 24(4) Health Psych. S57 (2005).

Which approach do you prefer, a "subjective" and/or "substituted judgment" approach based on the patient's statements and values while competent, or an "objective" approach based on the patient's current best interests?

In a study of patients on dialysis because of kidney failure, the patients were asked to consider whether they would want dialysis continued if they developed advanced Alzheimer's disease. They were then asked how much leeway they would want their family and physician to have in terms of overriding their wishes if overriding would be in their best interests. The researchers found that 39 percent of the patients would want their family and physicians to have "no leeway" in overriding their wishes, 31 percent of the patients would want their family and physicians to have "complete leeway" in overriding their wishes, and the remaining 30 percent of patients would want their family and physician to have some leeway (19 percent a "little leeway" and 11 percent a "lot of leeway"). Ashwini Sehgal et al., How Strictly Do Dialysis Patients Want Their Advance Directives Followed?, 267 JAMA 59 (1992). In another study of patients who were either seriously ill or at least 80 years old, researchers asked the patients about their wishes for CPR in the event of cardiac arrest. They then asked the patients whether their wishes about CPR should be followed if they lost decisionmaking capacity, or whether the CPR decision should be made by their family and physician. More than 70 percent of the patients preferred that their family and physician decide about CPR. Christina M. Puchalski, Patients Who Want Their Family and Physician to Make Resuscitation Decisions for Them: Observations from SUPPORT and HELP, 48(5) J. Am. Geriatrics Soc'y S84 (2000). How do these studies affect your feelings about a subjective vs. objective standard?

For further discussion, see Norman L. Cantor, Discarding Substituted Judgment and Best Interests: Toward a Constructive Preference Standard for Dying, Previously Competent Patients without Advance Directives, 48 Rutgers L. Rev. 1193 (1996); Rebecca Dresser, Missing Persons: Legal Perceptions of Incompetent Persons, 46 Rutgers L. Rev. 609 (1994).

6. *Family Decisionmaking.* For an argument in favor of family decisionmaking in all cases of incompetent persons, see Nancy K. Rhoden, Litigating Life and Death, 102 Harv. L. Rev. 375, 438-439 (1988) (emphasis in original):

> Families have historically exercised and continue to exercise a great deal of autonomy over decisions about procreation, education, and the upbringing of children. Family members have likewise attended to other members during their illnesses and have helped make their treatment choices for them. Not surprisingly, polls repeatedly show that patients, and members of society in general, believe that family members should function as surrogate decision-makers. In short, there is a deep-rooted and almost instinctual sense that a close family member should make decisions. Most readers will understand this if they consider whom they would want to make treatment decisions for themselves — their families or physicians and hospital administrators.
>
> Moreover, because of the nature of the family as an association, its members are in the best position to reproduce preferences of an incompetent patient. . . . Not only are family members most likely to be privy to any relevant statements that patients have made on the topics of treatment or its termination, but they also have longstanding knowledge of the patient's character traits. Although evidence of character traits may seem inconclusive to third parties, closely related persons may, quite legitimately, "just know" what the patient would want in a way that transcends purely logical evidence. . . . Family members also *care* most: . . . humans naturally care most for those closest to them.
>
> Moreover, no patient is an island. The family is the context within which a person first develops her powers of autonomous choice, and the values she brings to these choices spring from, and are intertwined with, the family's values. A parent may understand a child's values because she helped to form them, a child may grasp a parent's values because the parent imparted them to her, and a couple may have developed and refined their views in tandem.

Rhoden recommends a presumption in favor of the family's choice, except that when "the patient recognizes caretakers and can interact with her environment in some way — even if she is completely nonverbal — then the patient has an interest in living, and foregoing treatment, unless it is excessively burdensome, is not a reasonable choice." Id. at 442.

Interestingly, Rhoden's approach and the best interests approach of Dresser and Robertson may not be that different in the end in terms of the kinds of decisions that would be made for incompetent persons. Dresser and Robertson generally would respect families' judgments as to whether treatment is in the patient's best interests except that it would not be acceptable for a family to decline treatment when the patient is a conscious, incompetent person "who can experience enjoyment and pleasure, and whose conditions and necessary treatment interventions impose on them small or moderate burdens." Dresser & Robertson, 17 L. Med. & Health Care at 242. In other words, Dresser and Robertson defer to the family as a general matter, as does Rhoden, and they limit the family's authority in essentially the same situations.

In thinking about family decisionmaking as an approach, consider the following results from the empirical literature:

> Several studies have examined the accuracy of surrogate decisionmakers by presenting individuals with hypothetical scenarios and asking them to indicate their treatment preferences for each scenario. Potential surrogates are simultaneously asked to predict the preferences of the individuals. These studies consistently demonstrate that the potential surrogates' predictions do not reach a statistically significant degree of agreement with the choices of the individuals. This holds true even when individuals chose people that they would feel most comfortable with as surrogate decisionmakers. David Orentlicher, The Limitations of Legislation, 53 Md. L. Rev. 1255, 1278 (1994).

Do these results affect your view as the appropriate role of family decisionmaking? How do you respond to the concern of the *Cruzan* majority that family members are not disinterested parties to the decision? How might a patient's children react to the prospects of several more months or years of hospital or nursing home costs for the patient?

Note that family decisionmaking and substituted judgment approaches overlap substantially. In *Jobes,* for example, the court approved substituted judgments by families, and other courts or statutes also authorize family members to make substituted judgments for incompetent patients.

For further discussion, see Kathleen M. Boozang, An Intimate Passing: Restoring the Role of Family and Religion in Dying, 58 U. Pitt. L. Rev. 549 (1997); Allen E. Buchanan, The Limits of Proxy Decisionmaking for Incompetents, 29 UCLA L. Rev. 386 (1981); Jacqueline J. Glover, Should Families Make Health Care Decisions?, 53 Md. L. Rev. 1158 (1994); John Hardwig, What About the Family?, 20(2) Hastings Center Rep. 5 (1990); Nancy S. Jecker, The Role of Intimate Others in Medical Decision Making, 30 Gerontologist 65 (1990); James L. Nelson, Taking Families Seriously, 22(4) Hastings Center Rep. 6 (1992); David I. Shalowitz et al., The Accuracy of Surrogate Decision Makers, 166 Arch. Intern. Med. 493 (2006).

7. *Disagreements Among Family Members.* An important concern with family decisionmaking is how to resolve disagreements among family members. To some extent, this issue is addressed by state statutes governing surrogate decisionmaking. Typically, these statutes establish a hierarchy of family members according to their authority to make decisions on behalf of the patient. See, e.g., Md. Code

Ann., Health-Gen. §5-605(a)(2) (establishing a hierarchy of legal guardian (if one has been appointed), spouse, adult child, parent, adult brother or sister, other close relative or friend). However, not all states have such statutes, and even when they exist, physicians may be reluctant to implement a request by some family members to discontinue treatment over the objections of other family members.

Courts also are reluctant to permit withdrawal of treatment in the presence of a disagreement among family members. Indeed, the reluctance to order withdrawal of treatment in the midst of a family dispute may explain many of the court decisions that seem most at odds with the ethical and legal principles underlying the law in this area. For example, in the *Martin* case, supra pages 285-286, in which Mr. Martin's wife seemed to be acting on repeatedly expressed wishes of her husband when she asked that treatment be discontinued, the court's decision to require treatment may have reflected the opposition of Mr. Martin's parents to withdrawal as much it reflected a desire for stricter standards for patients who are neither terminally ill nor permanently unconscious. Similarly in *Spahn*, supra page 286, there was a disagreement between the patient's sister and niece. Even more problematic is the court's decision in Couture v. Couture, 549 N.E.2d 571, 576 (Ohio Ct. App. 1989). In that case, a patient's divorced parents disagreed as to whether his artificial nutrition and hydration should be discontinued. The patient was in a persistent vegetative state, and the appellate court upheld the lower court's finding of clear and convincing evidence that Mr. Couture would want the treatment discontinued. Nevertheless, the court ordered that the treatment be continued.

Perhaps the most extreme family dispute occurred in the case of Terri Schiavo in Florida. A dispute between Ms. Schiavo's husband and parents resulted in nearly seven years of litigation with more than a dozen state and federal court decisions, statutes by the Florida Legislature and Congress, and intervention by Governor Jeb Bush and President George W. Bush. Ms Schiavo's husband requested the withdrawal of her feeding tube after she had been in a persistent vegetative state for several years. After reviewing the testimony, the trial court judge concluded that there was clear and convincing evidence that Terri would not want a feeding tube, based on her prior oral statements to family members. In re Schiavo, 780 So. 2d 176, 179-180 (Fla. Ct. App. 2001). Ms. Schiavo's parents petitioned successfully for reinsertion of the feeding tube, and after a second removal and reinsertion in 2003, Ms. Schiavo's feeding tube was finally removed in March 2005. Her death ensued 13 days later. For further discussion, see symposia at 22 Const. Comment. 383 (2005) and 35 Stetson L. Rev. 1 (2005); Barbara A. Noah, Politicizing the End of Life: Lessons from the Schiavo Controversy, 59 U. Miami L. Rev. 107 (2004); Lois Shepherd, Shattering the Neutral Surrogate Myth in End-of-Life Decisionmaking: Terri Schiavo and Her Family, 35 Cumb. L. Rev. 575 (2004/2005). For a timeline of the case and links to key documents, see the University of Miami Bioethics Program's Web site (www6. miami.edu/ethics/schiavo/terri_schiavo_timeline.html).

For discussions of the role of mediation and alternative dispute resolution more generally in resolving disagreements, see I. Glenn Cohen, Negotiating Death: ADR and End of Life Decision-Making, 9 Harv. Negot. L. Rev. 253 (2004); Nancy Neveloff Dubler & Carol B. Liebman, Bioethics Mediation: A Guide to Shaping Shared Solutions (2004); Robert Gatter, Unnecessary Adversaries at the

End of Life: Mediating End-of-Life Treatment Disputes to Prevent Erosion of Physician-Patient Relationships, 79 B.U. L. Rev. 1091 (1999); Diane E. Hoffmann, Mediating Life and Death Decisions, 36 Ariz. L. Rev. 821 (1994).

8. *Ethics Committees and Consultants.* Many commentators and courts have encouraged resort to ethics committees and/or ethics consultants to help resolve disagreements among patients, family members, and health care providers. Indeed, the *Quinlan* court suggested that physicians might routinely turn to a hospital ethics committee for guidance when faced with requests by a patient or family to discontinue life-sustaining treatment. *Quinlan*, 355 A.2d at 668-669 (citing Karen Teel, The Physician's Dilemma: A Doctor's View: What the Law Should Be, 27 Baylor L. Rev. 6 (1975)). There are two basic types of committees, with many variations. "Prognosis committees" are composed primarily of medical personnel and their principal role is to help clinicians resolve questions about the patient's medical condition and likely outcomes of treatment. Full-fledged "ethics committees" include physicians, nurses, social workers, ethicists, lawyers, clergy and others, including community representatives, and they serve as an interface between clinicians and families. Whereas ethics committees tend to be ongoing, standing committees, prognosis committees may be ad hoc committees constituted as particular cases arise. In re Colyer, 660 P.2d 738, 749 & n.7 (Wash. 1983). Note too that courts in some cases require or recommend confirmation of prognosis by independent consulting physicians rather than a committee. In re Conroy, 486 A.2d 1209, 1242 (N.J. 1985).

Prodded partly by accreditation requirements, hospitals are increasingly likely to have the full-fledged ethics committees that are available to consider ethical questions that arise in the hospital, and to serve in an advisory role to the patients and physicians involved. In their advisory role, they make no formal decisions and issue nothing of binding force. Ethics committees may, however, develop binding hospital policies and protocols for dealing with specific recurring ethical issues. They also provide ethics education to clinicians. Committee on Bioethics, Institutional Ethics Committees, 107 Pediatrics 205 (2001). It is also becoming more common for hospitals to have ethics consultants, who are physician or nonphysician ethicists whom treating physicians can call on for advice, much as they call on medical specialists for consultation.

An important question is what the goals of the ethics committee or consultant should be. Is it to reach the ethically "correct" result, or is it to guide the involved parties to a result that all can accept? While these two goals may be compatible, they may also be in conflict, and there is often a tendency to view compromise as a desirable goal. The issue whether to aim for the right result or an amicable outcome raises the further question as to whether ethics can lead us to a correct answer or only provide analytic tools to better understand the issues at stake. There are also important legal issues, including whether committee proceedings are confidential and whether committee members are subject to tort liability for their decisions.

For further discussion, see Alan Meisel & Kathy L. Cerminara, The Right to Die §3.25 (3d ed. 2004); Judith Wilson Ross et al., Health Care Ethics Committees: The Next Generation (1993); David C. Blake, The Hospital Ethics Committee: Health Care's Moral Conscience or White Elephant?, 22(1) Hastings Center Rep. 5 (1992); John C. Fletcher & Mark Siegler, What Are the Goals of

Ethics Consultation? A Consensus Statement, 7 J. Clin. Ethics 122 (1996); Diane Hoffman, Evaluating Ethics Committees: A View from the Outside, 71 Milbank Q. 667 (1993); Bethany Spielman, Has Faith in Health Care Ethics Consultants Gone Too Far? Risks of an Unregulated Practice and a Model Act to Contain Them, 85 Marq. L. Rev. 161 (2001); Robin Wilson, Hospital Ethics Committees as the Forum of Last Resort: An Idea Whose Time Has Not Come, 76 N.C. L. Rev. 353 (1998); Symposium: Hospital Ethics Committees and the Law, 50 Md. L. Rev. 742 (1991).

For an interesting historical perspective on hospital ethics committees, including discussion of their use to approve abortions, allocate limited kidney dialysis slots, and review decisions to withdraw life-sustaining treatment from seriously disabled newborns, see George J. Annas, Ethics Committees: From Ethical Comfort to Ethical Cover, 21(3) Hastings Center Rep. 18 (1991).

9. *Resort to the Courts.* Courts routinely discourage judicial intervention into end-of-life cases, on the basis either that these are matters for legislatures to work out or that these are matters that are best resolved by patients, families, and physicians. Two typical statements follow:

> . . . Because the issue with all its ramifications is fraught with complexity and encompasses the interests of the law, both civil and criminal, medical ethics and social morality, it is not one which is well-suited for resolution in an adversary judicial proceeding. It is the type [of] issue which is more suitably addressed in the legislative forum, where fact finding can be less confined and the viewpoints of all interested institutions and disciplines can be presented and synthesized. In this manner only can the subject be dealt with comprehensively and the interests of all institutions and individuals be properly accommodated. [Satz v. Perlmutter, 379 So. 2d 359, 260 (Fla. 1980).]
>
> . . . [J]udicial review of a competent patient's refusal of life-sustaining medical treatment is generally not appropriate. Only unusual circumstances, such as a conflict among the physicians, or among the family members, or between the physicians and the family or other health care professionals, would necessitate judicial intervention. . . .
>
> No matter how expedited, judicial intervention in this complex and sensitive area may take too long. Thus, it could infringe the very rights that we want to protect. The mere prospect of a cumbersome, intrusive, and expensive court proceeding during such an emotional and upsetting period in the lives of a patient and his or her loved ones would undoubtedly deter many persons from deciding to discontinue treatment. And even if the patient or the family were willing to submit to such a proceeding, it is likely that the patient's rights would nevertheless be frustrated by judicial deliberation. Too many patients have died before their right to reject treatment was vindicated in court. Even in this case—where the judicial system acted in an extremely prompt and efficient manner (only 14 days elapsed between the filing of the complaint and the grant of the petition for certification)—we were unable to act in time. Mrs. Farrell died shackled to the respirator. [In re Farrell, 529 A.2d 404, 415 (N.J. 1987).]

Other concerns with judicial involvement include the consequence of forcing the family and physicians into an adversarial posture and the requirement that the court issue its decision based on the state of affairs that existed at the time the record was made despite the possibility of rapidly changing facts. See In re

L.H.R., 321 S.E.2d 716, 720-721 (Ga. 1984); William J. Curran, The *Saikewicz* Decision, 298 New Eng. J. Med. 499 (1978).

Nevertheless, some courts have required judicial review of treatment withdrawal cases, requirements that have proven to be short-lived. The Massachusetts Supreme Court, in the *Saikewicz* case, required probate court approval before life-sustaining treatment could be withdrawn from incompetent persons. *Saikewicz*, 370 N.E.2d at 433-434. Not surprisingly, medical reaction to the *Saikewicz* court's requirement of judicial involvement was immediate and overwhelmingly disapproving. Hospital attorneys were also generally opposed to the decision. Civil rights groups and many academic lawyers, on the other hand, supported the court's holding. Impassioned debate took up many pages of volumes 4 and 5 of the American Journal of Law & Medicine (1978-1979). Ultimately, the issue was dissipated two years later by a subsequent Massachusetts Supreme Court decision in which the court wrote that "our opinions should not be taken to establish any requirement of prior judicial approval that would not otherwise exist." In re Spring, 405 N.E.2d 115, 120 (Mass. 1980).

In 1989, the Illinois Supreme Court also imposed a requirement of a court order for cases in which family members or other surrogate decisionmakers seek to discontinue artificial nutrition and hydration from an incompetent person. In re Longeway, 549 N.E.2d 292, 300-301 (Ill. 1989). Despite the court's holding, there was no surge in petitions for court orders to withdraw feeding tubes. Some hospitals and nursing homes continued to stop artificial nutrition and hydration without seeking judicial approval; others may have simply continued to provide artificial nutrition and hydration. In 1991, the Illinois legislature eliminated the need for judicial approval when it passed the state's Health Care Surrogate Act. 755 Ill. Comp. Stat. 40.

Notes: Advance Planning

As the court opinions regularly observe, people can avoid many of the problems with end-of-life decisionmaking by executing a living will, durable power of attorney for health care, or other advance directive while competent. All states have either a living will or power of attorney statute and almost all states have both. Alan Meisel & Kathy L. Cerminara, The Right to Die §§7.01, 7.13 (3d ed. Supp. 2007). The statutes typically state that the rights granted therein are cumulative with other rights individuals might have with respect to end-of-life medical decisions.

1. *Living Wills.* The first living will statute was enacted in California in 1976; the document is called a "living" will because it takes effect while the testator is still alive. With a living will, also called a treatment directive, a person describes the circumstances under which treatment would not be desired. A person also might use a living will to indicate a desire that treatment *not* be withheld as long as life can be prolonged. Indeed, Indiana's living will statute includes two forms, one a typical "living will declaration" to express a desire that treatment be withheld, the other a "life prolonging procedures declaration" to express a desire that treatment be provided. Ind. Stat. Ann. §§16-36-4-10 and 16-36-4-11. The Indiana statute also states that a life prolonging procedures declaration has

conclusive weight while a living will declaration has "great weight." Ind. Stat. Ann. §16-36-4-8 (f)-(g).

Living wills have several drawbacks. If a person gives specific instructions, the document will not provide guidance in unanticipated situations. If a person instead tries to give general guidance that can be applied to any particular situation, then there will likely be a good deal of ambiguity in the living will, ambiguity that may lead different people to different interpretations of the person's wishes. Some statutes apply only to patients with terminal illnesses and persistent vegetative states, and some statutes restrict the circumstances under which artificial nutrition and hydration may be withdrawn. People can avoid such limitations by attaching addenda or using one of the model forms available from national organizations, although most people are likely to use the statutory form out of either convenience or unawareness of the alternatives. David Orentlicher, Advance Medical Directives, 263 JAMA 2365 (1990). See also Leslie Francis, The Evanescence of Living Wills, 14 J. Contemp. L. 27 (1988); Symposium, Advance Directive Instruments for End-of-Life and Health Care Decision Making, 4 Psych. Pub. Pol'y & L. 579 (1998); Katherine Taylor, Compelling Pregnancy at Death's Door, 7 Colum. J. Gender & L. 85 (1997).

For a case illustrating the problems that patients can experience with having their living wills followed, see Wright v. Johns Hopkins Health Systems Corp., 728 A.2d 166 (Md. 1999) (discussed infra at page 298).

2. *Proxy Appointments.* Rather than giving treatment instructions, a person might choose to appoint a proxy or surrogate decisionmaker by executing a durable power of attorney for health care. By doing so, the individual can transfer authority to make medical decisions to someone else. Durable powers of attorney were created because under the common law, all agency power ceases when the principal becomes incompetent. With a "durable" power of attorney, the proxy's agency authority survives the incompetence of the patient. Technically, durable powers of attorney for health care are actually "springing" powers of attorney. In other words, strictly speaking, a durable power of attorney takes effect while the principal is still competent and continues to have effect if the principal becomes incompetent. A springing power of attorney, on the other hand, does not take effect until the principal becomes incompetent. Despite the inaccuracy of the term, powers of attorney for health care are universally characterized as durable powers of attorney.

With a power of attorney, a person can avoid many of the problems with living wills. Power of attorney statutes generally apply to patients in any condition and with regard to any treatment. It is unusual for them to qualify the surrogate's authority to situations in which the patient is terminally ill or to restrict the surrogate's authority to decline artificial nutrition and hydration. Accordingly, people can provide for the exercise of their right to refuse treatment in all circumstances. Since proxies have broad authority, they are able to make decisions even when patients have not expressed their wishes or expressed them in too vague a way to be sure what the patient intended. Of course, some people may not have anyone whom they trust enough to appoint as a proxy.

Some people choose to combine a treatment directive with a power of attorney, giving some instructions and leaving authority to the surrogate for situations not covered by their instructions. What do you see as the problem with this approach?

3. *Statutory Forms*. Advance directive laws typically include a statutory form but generally state that individuals need not use the statutory form. However, in a few states, the statutes require compliance with the statutory form. See, e.g., Texas Medical Power of Attorney, Tex. Health & Safety Code §§166.163, 166.164. What would be the legal significance of a handwritten living will that does not follow the statutory format?

4. *Limitations of Advance Directives*. For all of their usefulness, advance directives have been disappointing in practice. Most people do not fill them out, even when encouraged to do so by physicians. Moreover, as indicated, when living wills are executed, they are often too vague to give sufficient guidance. Most troubling is the fact that, even when living wills give sufficient guidance, they are often overridden by physicians.

Although courts have clearly and emphatically recognized that end-of-life-decisions should be based on patient preferences and values, empirical studies indicate that it is the physician's preferences and values that seem to drive decisions regarding the withdrawal of life-sustaining medical treatment. David Orentlicher, The Limitations of Legislation, 53 Md. L. Rev. 1255, 1280-1288 (1994). In one study, after nursing home residents completed living wills, researchers followed the residents to determine whether subsequent medical decisions were consistent with them. The researchers found that physicians overrode the living wills 25 percent of the time. Marion Danis et al., A Prospective Study of Advance Directives for Life-Sustaining Care, 324 New Eng. J. Med. 882 (1991). While a 75 percent agreement may seem good, the study suggests that physicians overrode the patient's preferences the majority of the time when there was a disagreement between the patient's choice and the physician's preferences:

> [I]n most end-of-life situations, physicians and patients probably agree on whether treatment should be provided, and much of the 75 percent consistency between the living wills and the physicians' decisions can be explained by a sharing of values between patients and physicians. When there is disagreement between physicians and patients, however, it follows that the physicians' preferences generally prevail. Assuming that there is a 60 percent agreement rate and a 40 percent disagreement rate between patients and physicians, then a 25 percent override rate means that physicians prevail in 62.5 percent of the disagreements (25 percent/40 percent). Orentlicher, the Limitations of Legislation, at 1282.

This predominance of physicians' values also can be found in situations involving competent patients or in which family members have decisionmaking authority. David Orentlicher, The Illusion of Patient Choice in End-of-Life Decisions, 267 JAMA 2101, 2101-2102 (1992). See also Susan Adler Channick, The Myth of Autonomy at the End-of-Life: Questioning the Paradigm of Rights, 44 Vill. L. Rev. 577 (1999); Kenneth E. Covinsky et al., Communication and Decision-Making in Seriously Ill Patients: Findings of the SUPPORT Project, 48(5) J. Am. Geriatrics Soc'y S187 (2000) (reporting that physicians wrote DNR orders for only 52 percent of patients who said they did not want CPR and that physicians frequently misjudged patient willingness to live in a nursing home).

Moreover, physicians' personal values often diverge from the principles that have become widely recognized in ethics and the law. Even though patients are as free to have treatment withdrawn as to have it withheld, many physicians believe it is ethically and legally less acceptable to withdraw care than to withhold it, as discussed at pages 244-245 in the section on the competent patient. Similarly, even though the patient's right to refuse treatment applies to all medical treatments, whether the decision to withhold or withdraw involves a ventilator, CPR, or a feeding tube, physicians often express a greater reluctance to withdraw some treatments than others, particularly feeding tubes. See, e.g., Heikki Hinkka et al., Factors Affecting Physicians' Decisions to Forgo Life-Sustaining Treatments in Terminal Care, 28 J. Med. Ethics 109 (2002); William R. Mower & Larry J. Baraff, Advance Directives: Effect of Type of Directive on Physicians' Therapeutic Decisions, 153 Arch. Intern. Med. 375, 380 Table 3 (1993); Mildred S. Solomon et al., Decisions Near the End of Life: Professional Views on Life-Sustaining Treatments, 83 Am. J. Pub. Health 14, 18 Table 4 (1993). See also David A. Asch et al., The Sequence of Withdrawing Life-Sustaining Treatment from Patients, 107 Am. J. Med. 153 (1999) (finding that when life-sustaining treatment is withdrawn from patients, intravenous fluids and tube feedings are the last treatments to be withdrawn); David A. Asch & Nicholas A. Christakis, Why Do Physicians Prefer to Withdraw Some Forms of Life Support over Others?, 34 Med. Care 103 (1996) (finding that physicians prefer to withdraw treatments that are scarce, expensive, emotionally taxing, high technology, and rapidly fatal when withdrawn).

It is not only physicians who view feeding tubes differently than dialysis, ventilators or other treatments. Statutory treatment of end-of-life decisions indicates that this view is shared more widely. In one study, researchers found that twenty states set more stringent standards for withdrawal of artificial nutrition and hydration than for withdrawal of other treatments. Carol E. Sieger et al., Refusing Artificial Nutrition and Hydration: Does Statutory Law Send the Wrong Message?, 50 J. Am. Geriatrics Soc'y 544 (2002). Not all of those standards are constitutionally valid. According to an opinion by the Oklahoma Attorney General, Oklahoma's advance directive statute is unconstitutional when it limits the withholding of artificial nutrition and hydration to patients who are terminally ill or persistently unconscious. Okla. Att'y Gen. Op., No. 06-7 (Apr. 6, 2006).

Knowing that physicians may not follow instructions in an advance directive and that they may also impose their views on surrogate decisionmakers, what advice might you give to clients who want to ensure that their wishes are carried out?

For an interesting study of efforts to ensure that patients have advance directives or surrogates, see Daniel P. Kessler & Mark B. McClellan, Advance Directives and Medical Treatment at the End of Life, 23 J. Health Econ. 111 (2004) (finding that state laws with incentives for physicians or hospitals to comply with advance directives reduce the probability of patients dying in an acute care hospital; that laws requiring the appointment of a surrogate in the absence of an advance directive increase the probability of receiving acute care in the last month of life, but decrease the probability of receiving non-acute care; and that neither type of law leads to any savings in medical expenditures).

5. *Patient Self-Determination Act.* The federal government has tried to facilitate advance planning with the enactment of the Patient Self-Determination Act. The Act applies to health care institutions that receive Medicare or Medicaid funds.

Under the Act, people must be informed of their rights regarding medical decisionmaking, including the right to refuse life-sustaining treatment, when they are admitted to a hospital or nursing home, come under the care of a home health agency or hospice, or enroll in a health maintenance organization (HMO). These institutions must also inquire as to whether patients have an advance directive and document any directive in the patient's medical record. The institutions must ensure that they are in compliance with state law regarding advance directives and must not condition their provision of care on whether a patient has an advance directive. John La Puma, David Orentlicher & Robert J. Moss, Advance Directives on Admission: Clinical Implications and Analysis of the Patient Self-Determination Act of 1990, 266 JAMA 402 (1991); Susan M. Wolf et al., Sources of Concern About the Patient Self-Determination Act, 325 N. Eng. J. Med. 1666 (1991).

A government study of the implementation of the Act found that facilities failed to document whether the patient had completed an advance directive in 20 percent of cases. In addition, for 40 percent of the individuals with advance directives, there was no copy of the directive in the person's medical record. Office of Inspector General, Department of Health and Human Services, Patient Advance Directives: Facility and Patient Responses (August 1993).

Other studies have found little evidence that the Act has affected the use of advance directives or do-not-resuscitate orders. David W. Baker et al., Changes in the Use of Do-Not-Resuscitate Orders After Implementation of the Patient Self-Determination Act, 18 J. Gen. Intern. Med. 353 (2003) (but finding a small shift toward addressing resuscitation status earlier in a patient's hospital stay); Eric D. Morrell, The Do-Not-Resuscitate (DNR) Order: Associations with Advance Directives, Physician Specialty, and Documentation of Discussion 15 Years After the Patient Self-Determination Act (in press); Joan Teno et al., Advance Directives for Seriously Ill Hospitalized Patients: Effectiveness with the Patient Self-Determination Act and the SUPPORT Intervention, 45 J. Am. Geriatrics Soc'y 500 (1997) (but finding greater likelihood of documentation of existing advance directives). See also Edward J. Larson & Thomas A. Eaton, The Limits of Advance Directives: A History and Assessment of the Patient Self-Determination Act, 32 Wake Forest L. Rev. 249 (1997). But see Nicholas G. Castle & Victor Mor, Advance Care Planning in Nursing Homes: Pre- and Post-Patient Self-Determination Act, 33 Health Services Res. 101 (1998) (finding evidence that the PSDA has promoted advance planning).

6. *Enforcement of the Legal Standards.* As discussed at pages 295 and 299, in the section on the incompetent patient, end-of-life decisions may be driven more by the physician's views or the hospital's legal defensiveness than by the patient's preferences. One way to address the failure to follow patients' wishes is to hold physicians and institutions liable in tort suits when they ignore the patient's preferences. Individuals or their families have sued providers for administering unwanted life-sustaining treatment, but courts have generally refused to impose liability.

In an Ohio case, for example, the patient, a Mr. Winter, had stated his desire not to be resuscitated in the event of cardiac arrest. He wanted to avoid the fate of his wife, whose health seriously deteriorated after she received cardiopulmonary resuscitation (CPR). Mr. Winter's physician wrote a do-not-resuscitate (DNR) order in the medical chart, but Mr. Winter was resuscitated nevertheless. Two days later, Mr. Winter suffered a stroke, and he required nursing home care until his death two years later. The court permitted nominal damages only for the battery of receiving unwanted CPR, holding that the stroke was not a direct result of the CPR. Anderson v. St. Francis-St. George Hospital, 671 N.E.2d 225 (Ohio 1996).

Maryland's supreme court also rejected a claim based on wrongful administration of life-sustaining care. In Wright v. Johns Hopkins Health Systems Corp., 728 A.2d 166 (Md. 1999), a man with HIV disease, Robert Lee Wright, Jr., had executed a living will declining life-sustaining care, and he had also requested a DNR order on the hospital's HIV Case Management Plan of Care. More than a year later, when he was terminally ill with AIDS, Mr. Wright received a blood transfusion on what was supposed to be the final day of a three-day hospitalization for treatment of his AIDS. Immediately following the transfusion, Wright suffered a cardiac arrest and was resuscitated despite his advance planning. The cardiac arrest left him with severe brain damage, and he died ten days later, still in the hospital. The court upheld summary judgment in favor of the hospital on two grounds. First, by its language, the living will took effect when Wright had been "certified [to have] a terminal condition by two (2) physicians," and that certification had not occurred. Id. at 175. Second, although Wright had requested a DNR order, hospital policy set forth the physician's responsibility to discuss the withholding of CPR when patients had an irreversible disease and death was imminent or there was a high probability of cardiac arrest during the current hospitalization. Although Wright's life expectancy was less than six months, his death was not imminent. Id. at 177.

Other cases rejecting damages include Duarte v. Chino Community Hospital, 85 Cal. Rptr. 2d 521 (Ct. App. 1999); Taylor v. Muncie Medical Investors, 727 N.E.2d 466, 471 (Ind. Ct. App. 2000). For a case rejecting a lawsuit by parents for the undesired resuscitation of a premature infant, see Miller v. HCA, Inc., 118 S.W.3d 758 (Tex. 2003).

For a decision recognizing a cause of action and remanding for trial, see Gragg v. Calandra, 696 N.E.2d 1282 (Ill. Ct. App. 1998). In addition, there have been some jury verdicts and settlements in which damages were recovered. Rose Gasner, Financial Penalties for Failing to Honor Patient Wishes to Refuse Treatment, 11 St. Louis U. Pub. L. Rev. 499 (1992). In one case, a jury awarded $16.5 million after a hospital continued life-sustaining treatment over the apparent objections of the patient's family members. Andrew J. Broder, "She Don't Want No Life Support," 75 U. Det. Mercy L. Rev. 595 (1998). In that case, the hospital claimed at trial that family members agreed to the provision of treatment. The trial judge reduced the verdict to $1.43 million, and a settlement was reached while the appeal was pending.

Courts have not only been reluctant to authorize damages for the imposition of unwanted life-sustaining treatment, they have sometimes required families to pay hospital bills that accrued during the time between the family's request that treatment be stopped and the issuance of a court order upholding the family's request. Grace Plaza of Great Neck, Inc. v. Elbaum, 623 N.E.2d 513 (N.Y. 1993); First Healthcare Corp. v. Rettinger, 467 S.E.2d 243 (N.C. 1996).

Since some of the courts' reluctance to award damages reflects a sense that the law regarding withdrawal of treatment was not well established when the cases arose, courts in the future may be more willing to assess damages for the unwanted imposition of treatment. But even then tort law principles may yield low levels of damages. Alan Meisel & Kathy L. Cerminara, The Right to Die §11.01[A] (3d ed. 2005 and 2007 Supp.).

Why do you suppose that courts are so reluctant to impose damages in these cases?

The reluctance of courts to award damages for unwanted life-sustaining treatment may explain in part why hospitals often will not honor a patient's request to discontinue treatment in the absence of a court order. Court cases arise even when the patient's wishes and the law clearly support withdrawal. See, e.g., Bartling v. Superior Court, 209 Cal. Rptr. 220 (Ct. App. 1984) (hospital refused to remove ventilator upon request of competent adult patient). To some extent, the hospitals are likely acting on the basis of religious or other moral scruples. It may also be the case that the hospital's attorneys view the legal risks, however minimal, as existing primarily on the side of withdrawing treatment. As discussed at page 255, regarding the ethical integrity of the medical profession, even though no physician or hospital has been held civilly or criminally liable for withdrawing life-sustaining treatment at the behest of the patient or family, criminal charges were lodged against two physicians in Barber v. Superior Court, 195 Cal. Rptr. 478 (Ct. App. 1983). Moreover, most lawyers would probably prefer to explain to a jury why they kept someone alive too long than why they let someone die prematurely.

For further discussion, see Adam A. Milani, Better Off Dead than Disabled?: Should Courts Recognize a "Wrongful Living" Cause of Action When Doctors Fail to Honor Patients' Advance Directives?, 54 Wash. & Lee L. Rev. 149 (1997); A. Samuel Oddi, The Tort of Interference with the Right to Die: The Wrongful Living Cause of Action, 75 Geo. L.J. 625 (1986); Philip G. Peters, Jr., The Illusion of Autonomy at the End of Life: Unconsented Life Support and the Wrongful Life Analogy, 45 UCLA L. Rev. 673 (1998); Annotation, Tortious Maintenance or Removal of Life Supports, 58 A.L.R.4th 222 (1987). For a related issue, consider "wrongful life" and "wrongful birth" causes of action when a child is born with a disability that could have been detected with prenatal screening.

7. *Further Reading*. Good discussions of advance directives and/or the Patient-Self Determination Act can be found in Norman L. Cantor, Advance Directives and the Pursuit of Death with Dignity (1993); Rebecca Dresser, Precommitment: A Misguided Strategy for Securing Death with Dignity, 81 Tex. L. Rev. 1823 (2003); Angela Fagerlin & Carl E. Schneider, Enough: The Failure of the Living Will, 34(2) Hastings Center Rep. 30 (2004); Pam Lambert, Joan McIver Gibson & Paul Nathanson, The Values History: An Innovation in Surrogate Medical Decision-Making, 18 L. Med. & Health Care 202 (1990); Bernard Lo & Robert Steinbrook, Resuscitating Advance Directives, 164 Arch. Intern. Med. 1501 (2004); Practicing the PSDA: A Hastings Center Report Special Supplement, 21(5) Hastings Center Rep. S1-S16 (1991); Joan M. Teno et al., Association Between Advance Directives and Quality of End-of-Life Care: A National Study, 55 J. Am. Geriatrics Soc'y 189 (2007).

Problems: Interpreting and Drafting Advance Directives

1. Karen Thomas was a 65-year-old woman with a severe narrowing of her left carotid artery (one of the two main arteries that carry blood to the brain).

Because of the high risk of a disabling stroke, her physician recommended surgery to correct the narrowing. When he explained that there was a small risk that the surgery itself would precipitate a stroke or heart attack, Ms. Thomas told her physician about her living will. Four years earlier, after her husband had died of a prolonged illness, Ms. Thomas had executed the will, and she told her surgeon that she wished her will to be carried out in the event that she became incapacitated as a result of the surgery. She also told the surgeon that she considered life to be worth living only if she could live independently. Her living will included the following passage:

> If a situation should arise in which there is no reasonable expectation of my recovery from physical or mental disability, I request that I be allowed to die and not be kept alive by artificial means or heroic measures. I do not fear death itself as much as the indignities of deterioration, dependence, and hopeless pain. I therefore ask that medications be mercifully administered to me to alleviate suffering, even though this may hasten the moment of death. This request is made after careful consideration. I hope that you who care for me will feel morally bound to follow its mandate.

Ms. Thomas' surgery went well, and she awoke with full neurological function. However, shortly thereafter, she began to experience progressively worsening weakness on her right side and other abnormalities consistent with a serious stroke on the left side of her brain. She was taken back to the operating room, and her surgeons removed a large clot in a main artery that delivers blood to the left side of the brain. Nevertheless, Ms. Thomas continued to manifest signs of a severe stroke, with paralysis of her right side and loss of consciousness with responsiveness only to painful stimuli. Over the next week, Ms. Thomas showed no improvement in her condition, and, because of a pneumonia, needed a ventilator to ensure adequate oxygenation. Ms. Thomas' brother reminded the hospital of her living will and requested that the ventilator be discontinued. Her physician asked for a neurology consult, and the neurologists indicated that it could take several months before her ultimate prognosis became clear. They felt there was a 10 percent chance that she could recover most of her mental and physical capacity, although she might always need a wheelchair, a 30 percent chance that she would die without recovering consciousness, and a 60 percent chance that she would be seriously and permanently disabled. If you were the hospital's attorney, and Ms. Thomas' physician asked for your guidance, what would you say and/or do? (This case is a modified version of a case presented in Stuart J. Eisendrath & Albert R. Jonsen, The Living Will: Help or Hindrance?, 249 JAMA 2054 (1983).)

2. As an exercise to promote understanding of advance directives, you will serve as the "attorney" of a layperson you know and assist your "client" in filling out an advance directive. The exercise also requires you to write a one-page, single-spaced report about the reasoning behind the choices made and your impressions of the process. Your responsibility is to help your client understand the advance directive process and reach some resolution of the necessary decisions (e.g., whom to appoint as an agent, in what circumstances treatment may be withdrawn). If the person you approach is willing to discuss these decisions with you but unwilling to commit to any definitive answers, that is all right. Just leave

the form blank and explain the client's reasoning in your report. It is your responsibility to select an advance directive form to be used. You may want to use the statutory form for your state, which you can find in your state's statutory code, or you may want to use a generic form. You can find several generic forms at the Web site for the University of Buffalo Center for Clinical Ethics, http://wings.buffalo.edu/faculty/research/bioethics/adv-dir.html. You may also use an advance directive form that you find elsewhere. The Web site for this book also has a list of discussion questions you may want to use with your client. After your completed advance directive and one-page report are due, you will be given a patient scenario. You should then write down what would be the effect of your client's advance directive and ask your client whether that effect is consistent with what the client would want done if the client were ever in the condition described in the scenario. If it is unclear what outcome would result from the advance directive, or if the result would depend on information not available, then you should indicate that such is the case.

Notes: Young Children and Adolescents (Not Competent)

1. *Presumption of Parental Authority.* As mentioned at page 279, parents generally have authority to make medical decisions, including decisions about life-sustaining medical treatment on behalf of their children. The usual standard for parental decisionmaking is a best interests standard. Alan Meisel & Kathy L. Cerminara, The Right to Die §9.05[A] (3d ed. 2007 Supp.). The child's lack of decisionmaking capacity precludes the adoption of a standard based solely on the child's wishes. Still, one can consider the child's desires even if they are not determinative. Two descriptions of the best interests standard for children follow:

> The state should examine the seriousness of the harm the child is suffering or the substantial likelihood that he will suffer serious harm; the evaluation for the treatment by the medical profession; the risks involved in medically treating the child; and the expressed preferences of the child. [In re Phillip B., 156 Cal. Rptr. 48, 51 (Cal. Ct. App. 1979).]
>
> The court must first consider the effectiveness of the treatment and determine the child's chances of survival with and without medical care. The court must then consider the nature of the treatments and their effect on the child. [Newmark v. Williams, 588 A. 2d 1108, 1117 (Del. 1991).]

As the best interests standard suggests, parents will be denied authority to refuse life-sustaining treatment in some situations. The classic cases are those involving families of Jehovah's Witnesses where the children need blood transfusions and their parents decline the transfusions on religious grounds. In those cases, the courts have held that the children must be given the transfusions. See, e.g., In re McCauley, 565 N.E.2d 411 (Mass. 1991) (8-year-old child needed blood transfusion as part of treatment for an acute leukemia); In re Cabrera, 552 A.2d 1114 (Pa. Super. Ct. 1989) (6-year-old child with sickle cell anemia who had already suffered two strokes needed weekly blood transfusions over at least a year's time to reduce the risk of a recurrence of her strokes from 70 percent to

10 percent). In ordering treatment, the courts typically cite Prince v. Massachusetts, 321 U.S. 158, 170 (1944), where the Court wrote:

> Parents may be free to become martyrs themselves. But it does not follow they are free, in identical circumstances, to make martyrs of their children before they have reached the age of full and legal discretion when they can make that choice for themselves.

As the *Prince* excerpt indicates, the theory of these cases is that the children must be given an opportunity to reach adulthood to decide for themselves which religious tenets they will follow. What is the problem with this theory?

2. *Applying the Best Interests Standard to Children*. The hard question in this area is where the limits of parental authority end, and when a refusal of treatment becomes child neglect or abuse. At either end of the spectrum, the law is fairly clear. Courts have had no trouble holding that, when a child can readily be restored to good health or when treatment poses little risk, parents may *not* refuse a life-sustaining treatment, such as a blood transfusion (*McCauley* and *Cabrera*, supra, In re L.S., 87 P.3d 521 (Nev. 2004)), antibiotics (Walker v. Superior Court, 763 P.2d 852 (Cal. 1988) (upholding conviction of Christian Science parents of involuntary manslaughter for withholding treatment for meningitis from 9-month-old child)), or abdominal surgery (Commonwealth v. Twitchell, 617 N.E.2d 609 (Mass. 1993) (finding that Christian Science parents were not entitled to withhold intestinal surgery from their 2½-year-old child, but overturning their conviction for involuntary manslaughter on grounds that they were prevented from presenting the affirmative defense that they were misled as to their risk of prosecution by an opinion of the state's Attorney General)). Similarly, courts have had no trouble holding that parents *may* refuse life-sustaining ventilators or feeding tubes when the child is irreversibly unconscious. See, e.g., In re L.H.R., 321 S.E.2d 716 (Ga. 1984) (permitting the removal of a ventilator from a several-month-old child in an irreversible coma); In re P.V.W., 424 So. 2d 1015 (La. 1982) (permitting the removal of artificial life supports from an infant who had been irreversibly comatose since birth); In re Guardianship of Crum, 580 N.E.2d 876 (Ohio Prob. Ct. 1991) (permitting the removal of a feeding tube from a 17-year-old who was irreversibly unconscious); In re Guardianship of Myers, 610 N.E.2d 663 (Ohio Prob. Ct. 1993) (permitting the removal of a feeding tube from a minor, apparently an adolescent, who was irreversibly unconscious).

Other decisions, however, are not so clear. Some treatments will have a low likelihood of success and may carry substantial risks. As the following cases indicate, the courts have not come to a consensus on the extent of parental discretion:

Newmark v. Williams, 588 A.2d 1108 (Del. 1991). A 3-year-old boy was diagnosed as having an aggressive malignancy of the immune system, Burkitt's lymphoma. By the time a diagnosis was made during surgery for an intestinal obstruction, the cancer had spread elsewhere in the boy's body. His physician recommended that he be treated with a heavy regimen of chemotherapy. According to the medical testimony, there was a 40 percent chance of a "cure." Without treatment, he would likely die within six to eight months. Medical testimony also indicated that the treatment itself was quite toxic and might prove fatal. The boy's parents declined the chemotherapy in favor of care from a Christian Science practitioner. Given the substantial risks of treatment and the less than 50 percent chance of success, the court upheld the parental refusal of treatment.

In re Hamilton, 657 S.W.2d 425 (Tenn. Ct. App. 1983). A 12-year-old girl was diagnosed with Ewing's sarcoma, a bone cancer for which the girl had a 25 to 50 percent chance of long-term remission with treatment. Without treatment, she would likely die within six to nine months. Her father, a lay minister of the Church of God of the Union Assembly, refused treatment on religious grounds. Given the apparent certainty of death without treatment, and the reasonable possibility of long-term success with treatment, the court overrode the parental refusal of treatment. The court seemed to consider the fact that the family's religious sect did not refuse all kinds of medical treatment.

In re Hofbauer, 393 N.E.2d 1009 (N.Y. 1979). A 7-year-old boy developed Hodgkin's lymphoma, and his parents rejected conventional radiation and chemotherapy in favor of metabolic therapy, which included injections of laetrile. The parents explained that they were concerned about the side effects of conventional treatment and that they would agree to conventional therapy if the boy's physician, who was a proponent of metabolic therapy, so advised. The physician testified that the boy was responding well to the metabolic therapy and indicated that he would use conventional treatment if there was a significant deterioration in the boy's condition. The court found that, given these considerations, the family was acting reasonably.

Custody of a Minor, 393 N.E.2d 836 (Mass. 1979). A 3-year-old boy was being treated with conventional medical therapy for an acute leukemia, and the leukemia was in remission with a chance of cure as high as 80 percent. However, the boy's parents decided to discontinue his chemotherapy and substitute metabolic therapy, involving the daily taking of enzymes, laetrile and megadoses of vitamins. The child's leukemia reappeared, and the trial court ordered resumption of conventional chemotherapy, whereupon the leukemia went back into remission, albeit with the chance of cure now at 50 percent. The parents agreed to continue with conventional chemotherapy but also wanted to continue with the metabolic therapy. The trial court ordered the parents to stop the metabolic therapy. The state supreme court affirmed the trial court's order, observing that the metabolic therapy was not only ineffective in treating the leukemia but also posed significant risks of toxicity from the megadoses of vitamins and from the laetrile. In particular, noted the court, laetrile can be broken down in the body to cyanide, leading to chronic cyanide poisoning and eventually to blindness, deafness, and an inability to walk.

In re Phillip B., 156 Cal. Rptr. 48 (Cal. Ct. App. 1979). A 12-year-old boy with Down syndrome suffered from a congenital heart defect that, without surgical correction, would result in gradually worsening incapacity and, ultimately, an early death. The parents opposed surgery. Because of the child's Down syndrome and the fact that his heart defect had caused changes in his lung's blood vessels over time, his risk of death from the surgery—5 to 10 percent—was higher than usual, and he had a higher than usual risk of postoperative complications. Because of the child's elevated risks from surgery, the court upheld the parent's decision to refuse surgery. (Subsequently, volunteers at a facility where Phillip B. resided successfully petitioned to become his guardians and for authorization for medical testing, Guardianship of Phillip B., 188 Cal. Rptr. 781 (Cal. Ct. App. 1983)).)

Which of these court decisions do you think are correctly decided?

For other interesting cases, see In re Nicholas E., 720 A.2d 562 (Me. 1998) (permitting mother to refuse aggressive antiviral drug therapy to treat HIV infection in her 4-year-old son); In re Martin F. v. D.L., 820 N.Y.S.2d 759 (N.Y. Sup. Ct. 2006) (deferring to parent's refusal of antipsychotic drug for 3-year-old child).

3. *Bibliography*. Good discussions of this topic include Joseph Goldstein, Medical Care for the Child at Risk: On State Supervention of Parental Autonomy, 86 Yale L.J. 645 (1977); Martin T. Harvey, Adolescent Competency and the Refusal of Medical Treatment, 13 Health Matrix 297 (2003); Jennifer L. Rosato, Using Bioethics Discourse to Determine When Parents Should Make Health Care Decisions for Their Children: Is Deference Justified?, 73 Temp. L. Rev. 1 (2000); Lainie Ross, Children, Families, and Health Care Decision Making (1998); Walter Wadlington, Medical Decision Making for and by Children: Tensions Between Parent, State, and Child, 1994 U. Ill. L. Rev. 311; Annotation, Physician's Treatment of Child Without Parental Consent, 67 A.L.R.4th (1989).

Notes: Severely Disabled Newborns

1. *Historical Background and Congressional Action*. Treatment of severely disabled newborns generated considerable debate in the 1980s in conjunction with several celebrated cases in which parents sought to withhold life-sustaining treatment from children born with Down syndrome or other, more serious conditions. One case involved the death in 1982 of a Bloomington, Indiana, infant with Down syndrome. The child suffered from several congenital abnormalities associated with Down syndrome, including an esophageal obstruction that prevented oral feeding but that could have been corrected by surgery. The parents declined surgery, and the child died after a trial court and the local Child Protection Committee upheld the parents' decision. In response to the case, the U.S. Department of Health and Human Services adopted rules under the Rehabilitation Act of 1973 to regulate treatment decisions for severely disabled newborns, but the Supreme Court invalidated the rules as not justified by any evidence that such persons were being discriminated against in the provision of health care. Bowen v. American Hospital Association, 476 U.S. 610 (1986).

Also in response to the controversy generated by the Bloomington case, Congress enacted provisions of the Child Abuse Amendments of 1984 to address concerns about the "withholding of medically indicated treatment from disabled infants with life-threatening conditions." 42 U.S.C.A. §5106a(b)(10) (West 1995) (now §5106a(b)(2)(B). Regulations adopted under this legislation are in effect; the regulations condition federal grants for child abuse prevention on whether states establish programs or procedures to respond to cases of alleged "medical neglect." 45 C.F.R. §1340.15). Only two states, Indiana and Pennsylvania, have decided to forgo funding and not comply with the regulations (the noncompliance is only in part related to the medical neglect provisions of the child abuse regulations). As to the definition of medical neglect,

The term "medical neglect" includes, but is not limited to, the withholding of medically indicated treatment from a disabled infant with a life-threatening condition.

The term "withholding of medically indicated treatment" means the failure to respond to the infant's life-threatening conditions by providing treatment . . . which, in the treating physician's . . . reasonable medical judgment, will be most likely to be effective in ameliorating or correcting all such conditions, except that the term does not include the failure to provide treatment (other than appropriate nutrition, hydration, or medication) to an infant when, in the treating physician's . . . reasonable medical judgment any of the following circumstances apply:

(i) The infant is chronically and irreversibly comatose;

(ii) The provision of such treatment would merely prolong dying, not be effective in ameliorating or correcting all of the infant's life-threatening conditions, or otherwise be futile in terms of the survival of the infant; or

(iii) The provision of such treatment would be virtually futile in terms of the survival of the infant and the treatment itself under such circumstances would be inhumane.

[45 C.F.R. §1340.15(b).]

In the interpretive guidelines to these regulations, the Department of Health and Human Services observed that the "third key feature" of the definition of "withholding of medically indicated treatment" is "that even when one of [the] three circumstances is present, and thus failure to provide treatment is not a 'withholding of medically indicated treatment,' the infant must nonetheless be provided with appropriate nutrition, hydration, and medication." 45 C.F.R. pt. 1340, app. While the interpretive guidelines suggest that nutrition and hydration may never be withheld from a newborn, some commentators have argued that there is ambiguity in the qualifying use of "appropriate" before "nutrition, hydration, and medication." One could interpret the term as meaning that nutrition and hydration must be provided and that the way in which it is provided must be appropriate for the child (e.g., the composition of the feedings must meet the dietary needs of the child or the method of feeding, by oral feeding or a feeding tube, must be tailored to the child's condition). Alternatively, one could interpret "appropriate" as meaning that nutrition and hydration must be provided only when it is appropriate given the child's overall medical condition and that, for some newborns, parents may reasonably conclude that artificial nutrition and hydration should be withdrawn. Lawrence J. Nelson et al., Forgoing Medically Provided Nutrition and Hydration in Pediatric Patients, 23 J.L. Med. & Ethics 33, 40-41 (1995).

The reach of the federal regulations is limited because it is a condition for grants, not a substantive standard directly applicable to parents, physicians, or hospitals. Indeed, as indicated in the previous notes section, courts do permit parents to decline artificial nutrition and hydration for their irreversibly unconscious children. Moreover, while there have been cases in which the regulations were at issue, the courts ultimately concluded that the parents could proceed with their decision to decline treatment. Mary A. Crossley, Of Diagnoses and Discrimination: Discriminatory Nontreatment of Infants with HIV Infection, 93 Colum. L. Rev. 1581, 1613-1614 n.134 (1993) (describing a case in which parents could decline CPR for a child who was irreversibly unconscious and a case in which parents could decline ventilation for a terminally ill child with severe mental and physical disabilities); Carol R. Leicher & Francis J. DiMario, Termination of Nutrition and Hydration in a Child with Vegetative State, 148 Arch. Pediat. & Adolescent Med. 87 (1994) (describing a case in which parents could decline artificial nutrition and hydration for a permanently unconscious child).

Nevertheless, parental wishes may be frustrated by the unwillingness of physicians to withdraw or withhold care, either out of personal conviction or because of a belief that the federal regulations mandate care. In a survey of pediatric neurologists, researchers found that 75 percent of the responders stated that "they 'never' recommend the withholding of fluids and nutrition." Stephen Ashwal et al., The Persistent Vegetative State in Children: Report of The Child Neurology Society Ethics Committee, 32 Ann. Neurol. 570, 573 (1992). In a survey in which neonatologists were asked to consider cases of infants with a short life expectancy and severe neurologic disabilities, many responders reported that the federal regulations required the provision of treatment that was not in the best interests of the child. Many also reported that the regulations had led them to change their practices. Loretta M. Kopelman, Thomas G. Irons & Arthur E. Kopelman, Neonatologists Judge the "Baby Doe" Regulations, 318 New Eng. J. Med. 677 (1988). For further discussion, see Dianne Koller Fine, Government as God: An Update on Federal Intervention in the Treatment of Critically Ill Newborns, 37 New Eng. L. Rev. 343 (2000).

2. *Rehabilitation Act and Americans with Disabilities Act.* While there has not been much litigation over the regulations implementing the Child Abuse Amendments of 1984, there has been some important litigation of treatment decisions for severely disabled newborns under §504 of the Rehabilitation Act of 1973. Section 504 prohibits recipients of federal funds from discriminating against "otherwise qualified" disabled persons solely on the basis of their disability. 29 U.S.C. §794. The Americans with Disabilities Act of 1990 extends the protections of §504 to virtually all health care settings. In the §504 cases, the claim is that denying treatment to the newborn is an unlawful act of discrimination. In these cases, the courts have permitted the withholding of treatment. For example, in United States v. University Hospital, 729 F.2d 144 (2d Cir. 1984), the issue was whether surgery could be withheld from an infant with spina bifida, a condition of variable severity in which there is incomplete closure of the tissues surrounding the spinal cord. In this case, the infant had serious physical problems like impaired bowel and bladder function and was thought to have such compromised mental function that she would "never interact with her environment or other people." Id. at 146. The surgery, which would have closed the opening in her spine and implanted a shunt to drain excessive fluid build-up in her brain, was likely to prolong the infant's life but not do anything to treat her disabilities. A state appellate court had refused to intervene, noting that, while the surgery would enhance the infant's chances of living, it also might aggravate her disabilities. In also refusing to intervene, the Second Circuit wrote:

> *Doe* [v. New York University, 666 F.2d 761 (2d Cir. 1981),] establishes that §504 prohibits discrimination against a handicapped individual only where the individual's handicap is unrelated to, and thus improper to consideration of,

the services in question. As defendants here point out, however, where medical treatment is at issue, it is typically the handicap itself that gives rise to, or at least contributes to, the need for services. Defendants thus argue, and with some force, that the "otherwise qualified" criterion of §504 cannot be meaningfully applied to a medical treatment decision. Similarly, defendants argue that it would be pointless to inquire whether a patient who was affected by a medical treatment decision, was "solely by reason of his handicap . . . subjected to discrimination."

. . . Where the handicapping condition is related to the condition(s) to be treated, it will rarely, if ever, be possible to say with certainty that a particular decision was "discriminatory." 729 F.2d at 156-157.

See also Johnson v. Thompson, 971 F.2d 1487 (10th Cir. 1992) (finding no violation of §504 when surgery was withheld from children with spina bifida).

In the end, the parents in *University Hospital* agreed to have a shunt implanted to drain the fluid in their daughter's brain, although the surgery was delayed because of an infection that was likely related to the opening in her spine. The child, Keri-Lynn, has done much better than predicted. She is confined to a wheelchair, but she not only can talk, she also attends a school for developmentally disabled children. At age 20, she had attained a first or second grade level of scholastic achievement. Experts continued to disagree as to whether surgery to close Keri-Lynn's spine would have improved her outcome. Jamie Talan, A Fighter's Spirit; 20-Year-Old Keri-Lynn—Baby Jane Doe—Beat Steep Odds, Newsday, October 13, 2003, at A3; B. D. Colen, What Ever Happened to Baby Jane Doe?, 24(3) Hastings Center Rep. 2, 2 (1994); Kathleen Kerr, Proving Their Prognosis Wrong; Baby Jane Doe Busy Learning, Laughing, Newsday, Sep. 2, 1990, at 7. The *University Hospital* decision is excerpted on pages 118-124 and discussed on pages 128-130. The ADA is discussed further in Chapter 2.A.3.

3. *The Role of Physicians*. There have been important changes with respect to parental discretion over the past two decades because of changes in physicians' views as to what constitutes appropriate care for seriously disabled newborns. Partly because advances in medical care are resulting in better outcomes and partly because of changing social attitudes about disabled infants, physicians are becoming more aggressive in recommending treatment. For example, while many physicians once believed it reasonable to withhold surgery to correct an intestinal obstruction in a child with Down syndrome and allow the child to die, it would probably be very difficult today to find a physician taking that position. Sarah Glazer, Born Too Soon, Too Small, Too Sick; Whatever Happened to Baby Doe?, Washington Post, Apr. 2, 1991, at Z8; Betty Wolder Levin, John M. Driscoll, Jr. & Alan R. Fleischman, Treatment Choice for Infants in the Neonatal Intensive Care Unit at Risk for AIDS, 265 JAMA 2976, 2978 Table 3 (1991). Since courts are likely to defer to physicians as to whether treatment is necessary, the range of parental discretion has been narrowing. Indeed, it is not clear that the *Phillip B.* case discussed at pages 303-304 would come out the same way if it were decided today.

4. *Additional Readings*. For further discussion of this topic, see Robert F. Weir, Selective Nontreatment of Handicapped Newborns: Moral Dilemmas in Neonatal Medicine (1984); Legislative Workshop, Baby Doe: Problems and Legislative Proposals, 1984 Ariz. St. L.J. 601; Benjamin H. Levi, Withdrawing Nutrition and Hydration from Children: Legal, Ethical, and Professional Issues, 42 Clin. Pediat.

139 (2003); Martha Minow, Beyond State Intervention in the Family: For Baby Jane Doe, 18 U. Mich. J.L. Reform 933 (1985); Nancy K. Rhoden, Treatment Dilemmas for Imperiled Newborns: Why Quality of Life Counts, 58 S. Cal. L. Rev. 1283 (1985); Carl E. Schneider, Rights Discourse and Neonatal Euthanasia, 76 Cal. L. Rev. 151 (1988); George P. Smith, II, Murder, She Wrote or Was It Merely Selective Nontreatment?, 8 J. Contemp. Health L. & Pol'y 49 (1992).

B. PHYSICIAN AID IN DYING

We have seen that the competent patient has an almost unlimited right to refuse medical treatment even though death might result. An important question is whether this strong right should be extended to permit a patient to hasten death by taking a lethal dose of a drug.

As a preliminary matter, it is worth considering the different descriptive terms used for this topic. Although courts commonly talk about "physician-assisted suicide," others prefer "physician aid in dying," "death with dignity," or similar terms. Choice of terms depends a good deal on whether one views decisions by dying persons to manage their deaths with self-administered medications as "suicides" or more like decisions to refuse life-sustaining medical treatment. Following the recommendation of the American Public Health Association, this text will use the term "physician aid in dying."

■ WASHINGTON v. GLUCKSBERG
521 U.S. 702 (1997)

REHNQUIST, Chief Justice.

The question presented in this case is whether Washington's prohibition against "causing" or "aiding" a suicide offends the Fourteenth Amendment to the United States Constitution. We hold that it does not.

It has always been a crime to assist a suicide in the state of Washington. In 1854, Washington's first Territorial Legislature outlawed "assisting another in the commission of self-murder." Today, Washington law provides: "A person is guilty of promoting a suicide attempt when he knowingly causes or aids another person to attempt suicide." Wash. Rev. Code §9A.36.060(1) (1994). "Promoting a suicide attempt" is a felony, punishable by up to five years' imprisonment and up to a $10,000 fine. . . .

Petitioners in this case are the state of Washington and its Attorney General. Respondents Harold Glucksberg, M.D., Abigail Halperin, M.D., Thomas A. Preston, M.D., and Peter Shalit, M.D., are physicians who practice in Washington. These doctors occasionally treat terminally ill, suffering patients, and declare that they would assist these patients in ending their lives if not for Washington's assisted-suicide ban. In January 1994, respondents, along with three gravely ill, pseudonymous plaintiffs who have since died and Compassion in Dying, a nonprofit organization that counsels people considering physician-assisted suicide, sued in the United States district court, seeking a declaration that Wash. Rev. Code §9A.36.060(1) (1994) is, on its face, unconstitutional.

The plaintiffs asserted "the existence of a liberty interest protected by the Fourteenth Amendment which extends to a personal choice by a mentally competent, terminally ill adult to commit physician-assisted suicide." . . . [T]he district court agreed and concluded that Washington's assisted-suicide ban is unconstitutional because it "places an undue burden on the exercise of [that] constitutionally protected liberty interest." . . .

A panel of the court of appeals for the Ninth Circuit reversed. . . . Compassion in Dying v. Washington, 49 F.3d 586, 591 (1995). The Ninth Circuit reheard the case en banc, reversed the panel's decision, and affirmed the district court. Compassion in Dying v. Washington, 79 F.3d 790, 798 (1996). . . . The court . . . concluded that "the Constitution encompasses a due process liberty interest in controlling the time and manner of one's death . . ." [and] that the state's assisted-suicide ban was unconstitutional "as applied to terminally ill competent adults who wish to hasten their deaths with medication prescribed by their physicians." . . . We granted certiorari and now reverse.

I

We begin, as we do in all due-process cases, by examining our nation's history, legal traditions, and practices. In almost every state — indeed, in almost every Western democracy — it is a crime to assist a suicide. The states' assisted-suicide bans are not innovations. Rather, they are longstanding expressions of the states' commitment to the protection and preservation of all human life. . . .

More specifically, for over 700 years, the Anglo-American common-law tradition has punished or otherwise disapproved of both suicide and assisting suicide. [The court continues by noting that English law initially treated suicide as a form of murder, with the person's real and personal property being forfeited to the king. Only the personal property was forfeited, however, if the suicide was motivated by serious illness. Beginning in 1701, the colonies, and later the states, rescinded their laws criminalizing suicide because of the unfairness to the decedent's family, rather than out of any acceptance of suicide.]

That suicide remained a grievous, though nonfelonious, wrong is confirmed by the fact that colonial and early state legislatures and courts did not retreat from prohibiting assisting suicide. . . . And the prohibitions against assisting suicide never contained exceptions for those who were near death. . . . By the time the Fourteenth Amendment was ratified, it was a crime in most states to assist a suicide. . . . In this century, the Model Penal Code also prohibited "aiding" suicide, prompting many states to enact or revise their assisted-suicide bans. . . .

The Washington statute at issue in this case, Wash. Rev. Code §9A.36.060 (1994), was enacted in 1975 as part of a revision of that state's criminal code. . . . In 1991, Washington voters rejected a ballot initiative which, had it passed, would have permitted a form of physician-assisted suicide. . . .

California voters rejected an assisted-suicide initiative similar to Washington's in 1993. On the other hand, in 1994, voters in Oregon enacted, also through ballot initiative, that state's "Death With Dignity Act," which legalized physician-assisted suicide for competent, terminally ill adults. Since the Oregon vote, many proposals to legalize assisted-suicide have been and continue to be introduced in the states' legislatures, but none has been enacted. And just last year, Iowa and Rhode Island joined the overwhelming majority of states explicitly prohibiting assisted suicide. . . .

Attitudes toward suicide itself have changed since [the thirteenth century], but our laws have consistently condemned, and continue to prohibit, assisting suicide. . . . Against this backdrop of history, tradition, and practice, we now turn to respondents' constitutional claim.

II

The due process clause guarantees more than fair process, and the "liberty" it protects includes more than the absence of physical restraint. The clause also provides heightened protection against government interference with certain fundamental rights and liberty interests. In a long line of cases, we have held that, in addition to the specific freedoms protected by the Bill of Rights, the "liberty" specially protected by the due process clause includes the rights to marry, to have children, to direct the education and upbringing of one's children, to marital privacy, to use contraception, to bodily integrity, and to abortion. We have also assumed, and strongly suggested, that the due process clause protects the traditional right to refuse unwanted lifesaving medical treatment. *Cruzan*, 497 U.S., at 278-279.

But we "have always been reluctant to expand the concept of substantive due process because guideposts for responsible decisionmaking in this unchartered area are scarce and open-ended." *Collins*, 503 U.S., at 125. By extending constitutional protection to an asserted right or liberty interest, we, to a great extent, place the matter outside the arena of public debate and legislative action. We must therefore "exercise the utmost care whenever we are asked to break new ground in this field," ibid., lest the liberty protected by the due process clause be subtly transformed into the policy preferences of the members of this Court.

Our established method of substantive-due-process analysis has two primary features: First, we have regularly observed that the due process clause specially protects those fundamental rights and liberties which are, objectively, "deeply rooted in this nation's history and tradition," *Moore*, 431 U.S. at 503 (plurality opinion), and "implicit in the concept of ordered liberty," such that "neither liberty nor justice would exist if they were sacrificed," Palko v. Connecticut, 302 U.S. 319, 325, 326 (1937). Second, we have required in substantive-due-process cases a "careful description" of the asserted fundamental liberty interest. *Flores*, 507 U.S. at 302. . . .

Turning to the claim at issue here, the court of appeals stated that "properly analyzed, the first issue to be resolved is whether there is a liberty interest in determining the time and manner of one's death," or, in other words, "is there a right to die?" Similarly, respondents assert a "liberty to choose how to die" and a right to "control of one's final days," and describe the asserted liberty as "the right to choose a humane, dignified death," and "the liberty to shape death." . . .

Respondents contend that in *Cruzan* we "acknowledged that competent, dying persons have the right to direct the removal of life-sustaining medical treatment and thus hasten death" and that "the constitutional principle behind recognizing the patient's liberty to direct the withdrawal of artificial life support applies at least as strongly to the choice to hasten impending death by consuming lethal medication." . . .

The right assumed in *Cruzan*, however, was not simply deduced from abstract concepts of personal autonomy. Given the common-law rule that forced medication was a battery, and the long legal tradition protecting the decision to refuse unwanted medical treatment, our assumption was entirely consistent with this nation's history and constitutional traditions. The decision to commit suicide with the assistance of another may be just as personal and profound as the decision to refuse unwanted medical treatment, but it has never enjoyed similar legal protection. Indeed, the two acts are widely and reasonably regarded as quite distinct. In *Cruzan* itself, we recognized that most states outlawed assisted suicide—and even more do today—and we certainly gave no intimation that the right to refuse unwanted medical treatment could be somehow transmuted into a right to assistance in committing suicide.

Respondents also rely on *Casey*. There, the Court's opinion concluded that "the essential holding of Roe v. Wade should be retained and once again reaffirmed." *Casey*, 505 U.S., at 846. . . . In reaching this conclusion, the opinion discussed in some detail this Court's substantive-due-process tradition of interpreting the due process clause to protect certain fundamental rights and "personal decisions relating to marriage, procreation, contraception, family relationships, child rearing, and education," and noted that many of those rights and liberties "involve the most intimate and personal choices a person may make in a lifetime."

The court of appeals, like the district court, found *Casey* "highly instructive" and "almost prescriptive" for determining "what liberty interest may inhere in a terminally ill person's choice to commit suicide":

> "Like the decision of whether or not to have an abortion, the decision how and when to die is one of 'the most intimate and personal choices a person may make in a lifetime,' a choice 'central to personal dignity and autonomy.'" [79 F.3d, at 813-814.]

Similarly, respondents emphasize the statement in *Casey* that:

> "At the heart of liberty is the right to define one's own concept of existence, of meaning, of the universe, and of the mystery of human life. Beliefs about these matters could not define the attributes of personhood were they formed under compulsion of the State." [*Casey*, 505 U.S., at 851.]

By choosing this language, the Court's opinion in *Casey* described, in a general way and in light of our prior cases, those personal activities and decisions that this Court has identified as so deeply rooted in our history and traditions, or so fundamental to our concept of constitutionally ordered liberty, that they are protected by the Fourteenth Amendment. The opinion moved from the recognition that liberty necessarily includes freedom of conscience and belief about ultimate considerations to the observation that "though the abortion decision may originate within the zone of conscience and belief, it is more than a philosophic exercise." *Casey*, 505 U.S., at 852. That many of the rights and liberties protected by the due process clause sound in personal autonomy does not warrant the sweeping conclusion that any and all important, intimate, and personal decisions are so protected, and *Casey* did not suggest otherwise.

The history of the law's treatment of assisted suicide in this country has been and continues to be one of the rejection of nearly all efforts to permit it. That being the case, our decisions lead us to conclude that the asserted "right" to assistance in committing suicide is not a fundamental liberty interest protected by the due process clause. The Constitution also requires, however, that Washington's assisted-suicide ban be rationally related to legitimate government interests. This requirement is unquestionably met here. As the court below recognized, Washington's assisted-suicide ban implicates a number of state interests.

First, Washington has an "unqualified interest in the preservation of human life." The state's prohibition on assisted suicide, like all homicide laws, both reflects and advances its commitment to this interest. . . .

. . . The court of appeals also recognized Washington's interest in protecting life, but held that the "weight" of this interest depends on the "medical condition and the wishes of the person whose life is at stake." Washington, however, has rejected this sliding-scale approach and, through its assisted-suicide ban, insists that all persons' lives, from beginning to end, regardless of physical or mental condition, are under the full protection of the law. As we have previously affirmed, the states "may properly decline to make judgments about the 'quality' of life that a particular individual may enjoy," *Cruzan*, 497 U.S., at 282. This remains true, as *Cruzan* makes clear, even for those who are near death.

Relatedly, all admit that suicide is a serious public-health problem, especially among persons in otherwise vulnerable groups. . . . The state has an interest in preventing suicide, and in studying, identifying, and treating its causes.

Those who attempt suicide — terminally ill or not — often suffer from depression or other mental disorders. Research indicates, however, that many people who request physician-assisted suicide withdraw that request if their depression and pain are treated. The New York Task Force, however, expressed its concern that, because depression is difficult to diagnose, physicians and medical professionals often fail to respond adequately to seriously ill patients' needs. Thus, legal physician-assisted suicide could make it more difficult for the state to protect depressed or mentally ill persons, or those who are suffering from untreated pain, from suicidal impulses.

The state also has an interest in protecting the integrity and ethics of the medical profession. In contrast to the court of appeals' conclusion that "the integrity of the medical profession would [not] be threatened in any way by [physician-assisted suicide]," the American Medical Association, like many other medical and physicians' groups, has concluded that "physician-assisted suicide is fundamentally incompatible with the physician's role as healer." American Medical Association, Code of Ethics §2.211 (1994). And physician-assisted suicide could, it is argued, undermine the trust that is essential to the doctor-patient relationship by blurring the time-honored line between healing and harming.

Next, the state has an interest in protecting vulnerable groups—including the poor, the elderly, and disabled persons—from abuse, neglect, and mistakes. . . . We have recognized [in *Cruzan*] . . . the real risk of subtle coercion and undue influence in end-of-life situations. . . . If physician-assisted suicide were permitted, many might resort to it to spare their families the substantial financial burden of end-of-life health-care costs.

The state's interest here goes beyond protecting the vulnerable from coercion; it extends to protecting disabled and terminally ill people from prejudice, negative and inaccurate stereotypes, and "societal indifference." The state's assisted-suicide ban reflects and reinforces its policy that the lives of terminally ill, disabled, and elderly people must be no less valued than the lives of the young and healthy, and that a seriously disabled person's suicidal impulses should be interpreted and treated the same way as anyone else's.

Finally, the state may fear that permitting assisted suicide will start it down the path to voluntary and perhaps even involuntary euthanasia. The court of appeals struck down Washington's assisted-suicide ban only "as applied to competent, terminally ill adults who wish to hasten their deaths by obtaining medication prescribed by their doctors." Washington insists, however, that the impact of the court's decision will not and cannot be so limited. . . . The court of appeals' decision, and its expansive reasoning, provide ample support for the state's concerns. The court noted, for example, that the "decision of a duly appointed surrogate decision maker is for all legal purposes the decision of the patient himself," that "in some instances, the patient may be unable to self-administer the drugs and . . . administration by the physician . . . may be the only way the patient may be able to receive them,'" and that not only physicians, but also family members and loved ones, will inevitably participate in assisting suicide. Thus, it turns out that what is couched as a limited right to "physician-assisted suicide" is likely, in effect, a much broader license, which could prove extremely difficult to police and contain.

This concern is further supported by evidence about the practice of euthanasia in the Netherlands. The Dutch government's own study revealed that in 1990, there were 2,300 cases of voluntary euthanasia (defined as "the deliberate termination of another's life at his request"), 400 cases of assisted suicide, and more than 1,000 cases of euthanasia without an explicit request. In addition to these latter 1,000 cases, the study found an additional 4,941 cases where physicians administered lethal morphine overdoses without the patients' explicit consent. This study suggests that, despite the existence of various reporting procedures, euthanasia in the Netherlands has not been limited to competent, terminally ill adults who are enduring physical suffering, and that regulation of the practice may not have prevented abuses in cases involving vulnerable persons, including severely disabled neonates and elderly persons suffering from dementia. . . . Washington, like most other states, reasonably ensures against this risk by banning, rather than regulating, assisting suicide.

We need not weigh exactly the relative strengths of these various interests. They are unquestionably important and legitimate, and Washington's ban on assisted suicide is at least reasonably related to their promotion and protection. We therefore hold that Wash. Rev. Code §9A.36.060(1) (1994) does not violate the Fourteenth Amendment, either on its face or "as applied to competent, terminally ill adults who wish to hasten their deaths by obtaining medication prescribed by their doctors." 79 F.3d, at 838.[24]

. . . Throughout the nation, Americans are engaged in an earnest and profound debate about the morality, legality, and practicality of physician-assisted suicide. Our holding permits this debate to continue, as it should in a democratic society. The decision of the en banc court of appeals is reversed, and the case is remanded for further proceedings consistent with this opinion. . . .

■ VACCO v. QUILL
521 U.S. 793 (1997)

REHNQUIST, Chief Justice.

In New York, as in most states, it is a crime to aid another to commit or attempt suicide, but patients may refuse even lifesaving medical treatment. The question presented by this case is whether New York's prohibition on assisting suicide therefore violates the equal protection clause of the Fourteenth Amendment. We hold that it does not.

Petitioners are various New York public officials. Respondents Timothy E. Quill, Samuel C. Klagsbrun, and Howard A. Grossman are physicians who practice in New York. They assert that although it would be "consistent with the standards of [their] medical practices" to prescribe lethal medication for "mentally competent, terminally ill patients" who are suffering great pain and desire a doctor's help in taking their own lives, they are deterred from doing so by New York's ban on assisting suicide. Respondents, and three gravely ill patients who have since died, sued the state's Attorney General in the United States district court. They urged that because New York permits a competent person to refuse life-sustaining medical treatment, and because the refusal of such treatment is "essentially the same thing" as physician-assisted suicide, New York's assisted-suicide ban violates the equal protection clause.

The district court disagreed: "It is hardly unreasonable or irrational for the state to recognize a difference between allowing nature to take its course, even in the most severe situations, and intentionally using an artificial death-producing device." . . .

The court of appeals for the Second Circuit reversed. The court determined that, despite the assisted-suicide ban's apparent general applicability, "New York law does not treat equally all competent persons who are in the final stages of fatal illness and wish to hasten their deaths," because "those in the final stages of

---

[24] . . . We emphasize that we today reject the court of appeals' specific holding that the statute is unconstitutional "as applied" to a particular class. Justice Stevens agrees with this holding, but would not "foreclose the possibility that an individual plaintiff seeking to hasten her death, or a doctor whose assistance was sought, could prevail in a more particularized challenge." Our opinion does not absolutely foreclose such a claim. However, given our holding that the due process clause of the Fourteenth Amendment does not provide heightened protection to the asserted liberty interest in ending one's life with a physician's assistance, such a claim would have to be quite different from the ones advanced by respondents here.

terminal illness who are on life-support systems are allowed to hasten their deaths by directing the removal of such systems; but those who are similarly situated, except for the previous attachment of life-sustaining equipment, are not allowed to hasten death by self-administering prescribed drugs." . . . We granted certiorari and now reverse.

The equal protection clause commands that no state shall "deny to any person within its jurisdiction the equal protection of the laws." This provision creates no substantive rights. Instead, it embodies a general rule that states must treat like cases alike but may treat unlike cases accordingly. If a legislative classification or distinction "neither burdens a fundamental right nor targets a suspect class, we will uphold [it] so long as it bears a rational relation to some legitimate end." Romer v. Evans, 517 U.S. (slip op., at 10) (1996).

New York's statutes outlawing assisting suicide affect and address matters of profound significance to all New Yorkers alike. They neither infringe fundamental rights nor involve suspect classifications. These laws are therefore entitled to a "strong presumption of validity." Heller v. Doe, 509 U.S. 312, 319 (1993).

On their faces, neither New York's ban on assisting suicide nor its statutes permitting patients to refuse medical treatment treat anyone differently than anyone else or draw any distinctions between persons. Everyone, regardless of physical condition, is entitled, if competent, to refuse unwanted lifesaving medical treatment; no one is permitted to assist a suicide. Generally speaking, laws that apply evenhandedly to all "unquestionably comply" with the equal protection clause. New York City Transit Authority v. Beazer, 440 U.S. 568, 587 (1979).

The court of appeals, however, concluded that some terminally ill people — those who are on life-support systems — are treated differently than those who are not, in that the former may "hasten death" by ending treatment, but the latter may not "hasten death" through physician-assisted suicide. This conclusion depends on the submission that ending or refusing lifesaving medical treatment "is nothing more nor less than assisted suicide." Unlike the court of appeals, we think the distinction between assisting suicide and withdrawing life-sustaining treatment, a distinction widely recognized and endorsed in the medical profession and in our legal traditions, is both important and logical; it is certainly rational.

The distinction comports with fundamental legal principles of causation and intent. First, when a patient refuses life-sustaining medical treatment, he dies from an underlying fatal disease or pathology; but if a patient ingests lethal medication prescribed by a physician, he is killed by that medication.

Furthermore, a physician who withdraws, or honors a patient's refusal to begin, life-sustaining medical treatment purposefully intends, or may so intend, only to respect his patient's wishes and "to cease doing useless and futile or degrading things to the patient when [the patient] no longer stands to benefit from them." Assisted Suicide in the United States, Hearing before the Subcommittee on the Constitution of the House Committee on the Judiciary, 104th Cong., 2d Sess., 368 (1996) (testimony of Dr. Leon R. Kass). The same is true when a doctor provides aggressive palliative care; in some cases, painkilling drugs may hasten a patient's death, but the physician's purpose and intent is, or may be, only to ease his patient's pain. A doctor who assists a suicide, however, "must, necessarily and indubitably, intend primarily that the patient be made dead." Id. at 367. Similarly, a patient who commits suicide with a doctor's aid necessarily has the specific intent to end his or her own life, while a patient who refuses or discontinues treatment might not.

The law has long used actors' intent or purpose to distinguish between two acts that may have the same result. Put differently, the law distinguishes actions taken "because of" a given end from actions taken "in spite of" their unintended but foreseen consequences. . . .

Given these general principles, it is not surprising that many courts, including New York courts, have carefully distinguished refusing life-sustaining treatment from suicide. . . . Similarly, the overwhelming majority of state legislatures have drawn a clear line between assisting suicide and withdrawing or permitting the refusal of unwanted lifesaving medical treatment by prohibiting the former and permitting the latter. . . .

For all these reasons, we disagree with respondents' claim that the distinction between refusing lifesaving medical treatment and assisted suicide is "arbitrary" and "irrational." Granted, in some cases, the line between the two may not be clear, but certainty is not required, even were it possible. Logic and contemporary practice support New York's judgment that the two acts are different, and New York may therefore, consistent with the Constitution, treat them differently. By permitting everyone to refuse unwanted medical treatment while prohibiting anyone from assisting a suicide, New York law follows a longstanding and rational distinction.

New York's reasons for recognizing and acting on this distinction — including prohibiting intentional killing and preserving life; preventing suicide; maintaining physicians' role as their patients' healers; protecting vulnerable people from indifference, prejudice, and psychological and financial pressure to end their lives; and avoiding a possible slide towards euthanasia — are discussed in greater detail in our opinion in *Glucksberg*. These valid and important public interests easily satisfy the constitutional requirement that a legislative classification bear a rational relation to some legitimate end.

The judgment of the court of appeals is reversed. . . .

O'CONNOR, Justice concurring.*

Death will be different for each of us. For many, the last days will be spent in physical pain and perhaps the despair that accompanies physical deterioration and a loss of control of basic bodily and mental functions. Some will seek medication to alleviate that pain and other symptoms.

The Court frames the issue in this case as whether the due process clause of the Constitution protects a "right to commit suicide which itself includes a right to assistance in doing so," and concludes that our nation's history, legal traditions, and practices do not support the existence of such a right. I join the Court's opinions because I agree that there is no generalized right to "commit suicide." But respondents urge us to address the narrower question whether a mentally competent person who is experiencing great suffering has a constitutionally cognizable interest in controlling the circumstances of his or her imminent death. I see no need to reach that question in the context of the facial challenges to the

---

* Justice Ginsburg concurs in the Court's judgments substantially for the reasons stated in this opinion. Justice Breyer joins this opinion except insofar as it joins the opinions of the Court.

New York and Washington laws at issue here. The parties and amici agree that in these states a patient who is suffering from a terminal illness and who is experiencing great pain has no legal barriers to obtaining medication, from qualified physicians, to alleviate that suffering, even to the point of causing unconsciousness and hastening death. In this light, even assuming that we would recognize such an interest, I agree that the state's interests in protecting those who are not truly competent or facing imminent death, or those whose decisions to hasten death would not truly be voluntary, are sufficiently weighty to justify a prohibition against physician-assisted suicide.

Every one of us at some point may be affected by our own or a family member's terminal illness. There is no reason to think the democratic process will not strike the proper balance between the interests of terminally ill, mentally competent individuals who would seek to end their suffering and the state's interests in protecting those who might seek to end life mistakenly or under pressure. As the Court recognizes, states are presently undertaking extensive and serious evaluation of physician-assisted suicide and other related issues. In such circumstances, "the . . . challenging task of crafting appropriate procedures for safeguarding . . . liberty interests is entrusted to the 'laboratory' of the states . . . in the first instance." Cruzan v. Director, Missouri Department of Health, 497 U.S. 261, 292 (1990) (O'Connor, J., concurring) (citing New State Ice Co. v. Liebmann, 285 U.S. 262, 311 (1932)). . . .

STEVENS Justice, concurring in the judgments.

The Court ends its opinion with the important observation that our holding today is fully consistent with a continuation of the vigorous debate about the "morality, legality, and practicality of physician-assisted suicide" in a democratic society. I write separately to make it clear that there is also room for further debate about the limits that the Constitution places on the power of the states to punish the practice.

I

The morality, legality, and practicality of capital punishment have been the subject of debate for many years. In 1976, this Court upheld the constitutionality of the practice in cases coming to us from Georgia, Florida, and Texas. In those cases we concluded that a state does have the power to place a lesser value on some lives than on others; there is no absolute requirement that a state treat all human life as having an equal right to preservation. Because the state legislatures had sufficiently narrowed the category of lives that the state could terminate, and had enacted special procedures to ensure that the defendant belonged in that limited category, we concluded that the statutes were not unconstitutional on their face. In later cases coming to us from each of those states, however, we found that some applications of the statutes were unconstitutional.

Today, the Court decides that Washington's statute prohibiting assisted suicide is not invalid "on its face," that is to say, in all or most cases in which it might be applied. That holding, however, does not foreclose the possibility that some applications of the statute might well be invalid. . . .

History and tradition provide ample support for refusing to recognize an open-ended constitutional right to commit suicide. Much more than the state's

paternalistic interest in protecting the individual from the irrevocable consequences of an ill-advised decision motivated by temporary concerns is at stake.
There is truth in John Donne's observation that "No man is an island." The state
has an interest in preserving and fostering the benefits that every human being
may provide to the community—a community that thrives on the exchange of
ideas, expressions of affection, shared memories and humorous incidents as well
as on the material contributions that its members create and support. . . .

But just as our conclusion that capital punishment is not always unconstitutional did not preclude later decisions holding that it is sometimes impermissibly
cruel, so is it equally clear that a decision upholding a general statutory
prohibition of assisted suicide does not mean that every possible application of the
statute would be valid. . . .

III

. . . Although as a general matter the state's interest in the contributions each
person may make to society outweighs the person's interest in ending her life, this
interest does not have the same force for a terminally ill patient faced not with the
choice of whether to live, only of how to die. Allowing the individual, rather than
the state, to make judgments "about the 'quality' of life that a particular individual
may enjoy," does not mean that the lives of terminally-ill, disabled people have
less value than the lives of those who are healthy. Rather, it gives proper
recognition to the individual's interest in choosing a final chapter that accords
with her life story, rather than one that demeans her values and poisons memories
of her.

Similarly, the state's legitimate interests in preventing suicide, protecting the
vulnerable from coercion and abuse, and preventing euthanasia are less
significant in this context. I agree that the state has a compelling interest in
preventing persons from committing suicide because of depression, or coercion
by third parties. But the state's legitimate interest in preventing abuse does not
apply to an individual who is not victimized by abuse, who is not suffering from
depression, and who makes a rational and voluntary decision to seek assistance in
dying. . . .

Relatedly, the state and amici express the concern that patients whose
physical pain is inadequately treated will be more likely to request assisted suicide.
Encouraging the development and ensuring the availability of adequate pain
treatment is of utmost importance; palliative care, however, cannot alleviate all
pain and suffering. See Orentlicher, Legalization of Physician Assisted Suicide: A
Very Modest Revolution, 38 Boston College L. Rev. 443, 454 (1997) ("Greater use
of palliative care would reduce the demand for assisted suicide, but it will not
eliminate [it]"). An individual adequately informed of the care alternatives thus
might make a rational choice for assisted suicide. For such an individual, the
state's interest in preventing potential abuse and mistake is only minimally
implicated.

The final major interest asserted by the state is its interest in preserving the
traditional integrity of the medical profession. The fear is that a rule permitting
physicians to assist in suicide is inconsistent with the perception that they serve
their patients solely as healers. But for some patients, it would be a physician's

refusal to dispense medication to ease their suffering and make their death tolerable and dignified that would be inconsistent with the healing role. For doctors who have long-standing relationships with their patients, who have given their patients advice on alternative treatments, who are attentive to their patient's individualized needs, and who are knowledgeable about pain symptom management and palliative care options, heeding a patient's desire to assist in her suicide would not serve to harm the physician-patient relationship. Furthermore, because physicians are already involved in making decisions that hasten the death of terminally ill patients — through termination of life support, withholding of medical treatment, and terminal sedation — there is in fact significant tension between the traditional view of the physician's role and the actual practice in a growing number of cases.

As the New York State Task Force on Life and the Law recognized, a state's prohibition of assisted suicide is justified by the fact that the "ideal" case in which "patients would be screened for depression and offered treatment, effective pain medication would be available, and all patients would have a supportive committed family and doctor" is not the usual case. New York State Task Force on Life and the Law, When Death Is Sought: Assisted Suicide and Euthanasia in the Medical Context 120 (May 1994). Although, as the Court concludes today, these potential harms are sufficient to support the state's general public policy against assisted suicide, they will not always outweigh the individual liberty interest of a particular patient. Unlike the court of appeals, I would not say as a categorical matter that these state interests are invalid as to the entire class of terminally ill, mentally competent patients. I do not, however, foreclose the possibility that an individual plaintiff seeking to hasten her death, or a doctor whose assistance was sought, could prevail in a more particularized challenge. Future cases will determine whether such a challenge may succeed. . . .

Notes: Physician Aid in Dying

1. *Factual Background.* The debate over physician aid in dying was sparked anew in March 1989, when a distinguished group of physicians argued in favor of physician aid in dying as a last resort for relieving patient suffering, Sidney H. Wanzer et al., The Physician's Responsibility Toward Hopelessly Ill Patients: A Second Look, 320 New Eng. J. Med. 844 (1989), and in June 1990, when Dr. Jack Kevorkian, a retired pathologist living in Michigan, assisted the dying of Janet Adkins. Ms. Adkins was a 54-year-old woman in the early stages of Alzheimer's disease who decided to end her life before she became even more affected. Lisa Belkin, Doctor Tells of First Death Using His Suicide Device, N.Y. Times, June 6, 1990, at A1.

While Kevorkian's license to practice medicine was revoked, he continued to aid patient dying. By December 1997, he had disclosed his assistance in more than fifty deaths, and his attorney indicated that he had assisted in the range of 100 deaths.

Kevorkian lost his constitutional challenge to Michigan's prohibition of physician aid in dying, People v. Kevorkian, 527 N.W.2d 714 (Mich. 1994), and was prosecuted four different times, but juries acquitted him in three trials and a mistrial was declared in the fourth prosecution. When he crossed the line from aid in dying to euthanasia, however, Kevorkian was convicted. On March 26, 1999, a jury found him guilty of second-degree murder for administering a fatal injection to Thomas Youk, a 52-year-old man suffering from amyotrophic lateral sclerosis (ALS or Lou Gehrig's disease). Pam Belluck, Dr. Kevorkian Is a Murderer, The Jury Finds, N.Y. Times, Mar. 27, 1999, at A1. This was the case in which Kevorkian taped the patient's death, and the tape was televised by *60 Minutes* in November 1998. On April 13, 1999, the trial court judge sentenced Kevorkian to 10 to 25 years in prison. Dirk Johnson, Kevorkian Sentenced to 10 to 25 Years in Prison, N.Y. Times, Apr. 14, 1999, at A1. Eight years later, Kevorkian was released from prison on parole. Monica Davey, Kevorkian Freed After Years in Prison for Aiding Suicide, N.Y. Times, June 2, 2007, at A3.

The fact that Kevorkian was convicted despite his earlier escapes from punishment can be attributed to a few factors: (1) this was a case of euthanasia rather than aid in dying; (2) during his interview on *60 Minutes,* Kevorkian indicated that he chose euthanasia rather than aid in dying to advance his agenda rather than to serve the patient's needs (and Youk could have chosen aid in dying); (3) Kevorkian was aggressively flouting the law with the televising of Youk's death; and (4) Kevorkian defended himself rather than relying on a lawyer to make his case.

Dr. Timothy Quill also focused discussion on physician aid in dying by disclosing in 1991 that he prescribed a lethal dose of barbiturates for a cancer patient who was terminally ill. Timothy E. Quill, Death and Dignity: A Case of Individualized Decision Making, 324 New Eng. J. Med. 691 (1991). In Quill's case, prosecutors were unable to persuade a grand jury to bring an indictment. Lawrence K. Altman, Jury Declines to Indict a Doctor Who Said He Aided in a Suicide, N.Y. Times, July 27, 1991, at A1.

The absence of a conviction for either Kevorkian or Quill for aid in dying did not reflect a gap in the law. In both Michigan and New York, the law prohibited aid in dying. However, juries are generally unwilling to convict physicians who help dying patients self-administer a lethal dose of drugs. Prosecutions of a physician for either aid in dying or euthanasia are rare. Convictions are almost unheard of, with only one case reported in the literature before Kevorkian's, a case in which a physician injected his mother-in-law with a fatal dose of Demerol. The mother-in-law suffered from advanced Alzheimer's disease, and the physician pled guilty to a charge of manslaughter and was sentenced to two years' probation after a plea-bargain. Maria T. CeloCruz, Aid-in-Dying: Should We Decriminalize Physician-Assisted Suicide and Physician-Committed Euthanasia?, 18 Am. J.L. & Med. 369, 377-383 (1992); Leonard Glantz, Withholding and Withdrawing Treatment: The Role of the Criminal Law, 15 L. Med. & Health Care 231, 232 (1987). For a case in which a physician was acquitted of charges of performing euthanasia, on grounds that his treatment fell within the standard of care for palliative care, see State v. Naramore, 965 P.2d 211 (Kan. 1998).

The legal system is also sympathetic to cases of aid in dying and euthanasia involving family members or close friends of the patient, but to a lesser extent than with physicians. Family members have been convicted of criminal charges, but they are likely to be sentenced leniently.

2. *Legalized Aid in Dying in Oregon.* In November 1994, Oregon voters approved by referendum the Oregon Death with Dignity Act, a law that permits mentally competent, terminally ill persons to obtain a prescription from their physicians for a lethal dose of a drug. The statute requires patients to make their request for aid in dying orally and in writing and to reiterate their request orally at least fifteen days after the initial request. The physician is required to inform the patient of the medical diagnosis, prognosis, and alternatives to aid in dying, and must refer the patient to a consulting physician to confirm both the diagnosis and that the patient is competent and making a voluntary and informed decision. If either physician believes that the patient suffers from a psychiatric disorder or from a depression that impairs judgment, the patient must be referred for counseling. Or. Rev. Stat. §§127.800-.897 (2001).

A constitutional challenge to the statute was brought, and the district court judge enjoined the law. According to the court, terminally ill persons were denied equal protection by the statute because the state did not employ the same safeguards to protect terminally ill persons from impaired judgment or abuse as used to protect non-terminally ill persons. Lee v. Oregon, 891 F. Supp. 1429 (D. Or. 1995). On appeal, the Ninth Circuit held that the plaintiffs did not have standing to challenge the Oregon statute and so vacated the district court judgment and remanded with instructions to dismiss for lack of jurisdiction. Lee v. Oregon, 107 F.3d 1382, 1392 (9th Cir. 1997). After the Ninth Circuit's decision, the Oregon legislature voted to send the Death with Dignity Act back to the electorate for a second vote by referendum in November 1997. Oregon's voters reaffirmed their earlier approval, this time by a larger margin, 60 to 40 percent versus 51 to 49 percent in 1994.

The first public report of a death under Oregon's aid in dying law came on March 25, 1998. Timothy Egan, First Death under an Assisted-Suicide Law, N.Y. Times, Mar. 26, 1998, at A14. After the report, it was disclosed that the law had been invoked earlier by another patient. On August 18, 1998, the Oregon Department of Human Resources (now Human Services) released data on the first ten patients who exercised their rights under the Death with Dignity Act, and since then the Department has issued annual reports describing Oregon's experience with aid in dying. The full reports are available at the Web site of the Department (http://oregon.gov/DHS/ph/pas); summaries have been published for the earlier years in the New England Journal of Medicine.

Through December 31, 2006, physicians had written 456 prescriptions under the Death with Dignity Act, and 292 patients had taken the lethal medication (with the other 36 percent either still alive or having died of their illness). Oregon Department of Human Services, Summary of Oregon's Death with Dignity Act (March 2007). Somewhat more than a tenth of 1 percent of deaths in Oregon are by aid in dying. The most common diagnosis has been cancer, and the patients have been similar to other dying patients with regard to sex, race, urban or rural residence, health insurance coverage, and hospice enrollment. The level of education has been higher for patients who choose aid in dying. The most common concerns of patients choosing aid in dying have been loss of autonomy, decreased ability to participate in enjoyable activities, and loss of dignity.

In the 2006 report, three pieces of data suggest the possibility of potential problems. During 2006, 76 percent of patients who took their medication were enrolled in some form of hospice care before they died, a decrease from the first eight years of the Act, when 87 percent of patients received hospice care. There also was an increase in the number of patients concerned about inadequate pain control, rising from an eight-year average of 22 percent to a 2006 level of 48 percent. Finally, referrals were made in 10 cases to the Board of Medical Examiners for incorrect completing of reporting forms. On the other hand, in none of those cases did the Board conclude that a physician failed to act in good faith compliance with the Act, and the Board did not cite any of the physicians for unprofessional conduct.

Researchers studying patients' reasons for aid in dying have found similar results to those of the Department of Human Services. According to one study, loss of autonomy and a desire to control the circumstances of death are leading reasons for patients to invoke the Death with Dignity Act. Linda Ganzini et al., Experiences of Oregon Nurses and Social Workers with Hospice Patients Who Requested Assistance with Suicide, 347 New Eng. J. Med. 582 (2002). Another study found that reasons for pursuing aid in dying included loss of function and other physical consequences of illness, loss of sense of self and a desire for control, and fears about the future. Depression was not a significant factor. Robert A. Pearlman et al., Motivations for Physician-assisted Suicide, 20 J. Gen. Intern. Med. 234 (2005).

Researchers have also looked at physicians' responses to requests under the Oregon Act. A study found that physicians in Oregon grant roughly one in six requests for a lethal prescription and that one in ten requests actually result in aid in dying. Physicians did not provide a prescription in 82 percent of cases because the physician was not willing to aid in dying ever (29 percent), the physician was not willing to assist in the particular case (24 percent), the patient died before meeting Oregon's legal requirements or before receiving a prescription (22 percent), the patient had a change of mind before meeting Oregon's legal requirements or before receiving a prescription (17 percent), or the patient did not meet Oregon's legal requirements (15 percent). While 20 percent of requests came from patients with depression, none of their requests were granted. Linda Ganzini et al., Physicians' Experiences with the Oregon Death with Dignity Act, 342 New Eng. J. Med. 557 (2000). Data from the Netherlands suggest that physicians there are more likely to grant a patient's request for physician aid in dying or euthanasia. Jansen-van der Weide et al., Granted, Undecided, Withdrawn, and Refused Requests for Euthanasia and Physician-Assisted Suicide, 165 Arch. Intern. Med. 1698 (2005) (finding in a physician survey that 44 percent of explicit requests for physician aid in dying or euthanasia were granted).

For more discussion of the Oregon experience, see Susan Okie, Physician-Assisted Suicide—Oregon and Beyond, 352 New Eng. J. Med. 1627 (2005); Robert Steinbrook, Physician-Assisted Suicide in Oregon—An Uncertain Future, 346 New Eng. J. Med. 460 (2002).

The Task Force to Improve the Care of Terminally Ill Oregonians has published a 91-page guidebook on the Oregon law, Oregon's Death with Dignity Act: A Guidebook for Health Care Providers. The Task Force represents twenty-five health care professional organizations, state agencies, and health care systems. You can find the Guidebook at the Web site of the Center for Ethics in Health Care at Oregon Health Sciences University (www.ohsu.edu/ethics/docs/guide1.htm). For an article observing that efforts to address patients' concerns can diminish the desire for physician aid in dying, see Paul B. Bascom & Susan W. Tolle, Responding to Requests for Physician-Assisted Suicide: "These Are Uncharted Waters for Both of Us. . . . ," 288 JAMA 91 (2002).

3. *States' Rights and the Right to Die.* As controversial end-of-life decisions have worked their way through state courts and legislatures, federal government officials have sometimes tried to intervene. Earlier, on page 290, the *Schiavo* discussion referenced congressional and presidential involvement. Federal intervention has been even more active with respect to Oregon's Death with Dignity Act.

In November 2001, Attorney General John Ashcroft tried to reverse the federal government's policy on physician aid in dying in Oregon. Under a June 1998 declaration by Ashcroft's predecessor, Janet Reno, the Drug Enforcement Administration (DEA) did not intervene when physicians used federally controlled prescription drugs to assist a patient's death under Oregon law. Ashcroft's directive to the DEA specifically allowed for the revocation of drug prescription licenses of doctors who participated in aid in dying using federally controlled substances. His directive did not speak to criminal prosecution of the doctors, but they would have been subjected to severe prison sentences under the Controlled Substances Act.

The U.S. Court of Appeals for the Ninth Circuit rejected Attorney General Ashcroft's effort to override Oregon's law, holding that he lacked authority under the Controlled Substances Act to intervene. Oregon v. Ashcroft, 368 F.3d 1118 (9th Cir. 2004). In January 2006, the Supreme Court affirmed the Ninth Circuit, concluding that the Controlled Substances Act does not give the Attorney General authority to declare "illegitimate a medical standard for care and treatment of patients that is specifically authorized under state law." Gonzales v. Oregon, 546 U.S. 243 (2006).

Previously, members of Congress were unsuccessful in their efforts to override Oregon's law. Companion bills were introduced in the U.S. House and Senate that would have permitted the DEA to revoke a physician's registration to prescribe federally controlled substances if the physician prescribed a lethal dose of drugs under Oregon's law. Neither bill was passed, and Congress considered a new bill, the Pain Relief Promotion Act, during 1999 and 2000, that would have overridden Oregon's law by stating that no drugs regulated as controlled substances by the federal government could be used to aid in dying. For a discussion of the Act, see David Orentlicher & Arthur Caplan, The Pain Relief Promotion Act of 1999: A Serious Threat to Palliative Care, 283 JAMA 255 (2000).

Many commentators have criticized federal involvement in end-of-life decisions as being politically motivated; others see value in the federal oversight. For further discussion, see Brian Bix, Physician-Assisted Suicide and Federalism, 17 Notre Dame J.L. Ethics & Pub Pol'y 53 (2003); Steven G. Calabresi, The Terri Schiavo Case: In Defense of the Special Law Enacted by Congress and President Bush, 100 Nw. U. L. Rev. 151 (2006); Lars Noah, Ambivalent Commitments to Federalism in Controlling the Practice of Medicine, 53 U. Kan. L. Rev. 149 (2004); Adam M. Samaha, Undue Process: Congressional Referral and Judicial

Resistance in the Schiavo Controversy, 22 Const. Comment. 505 (2005); Marc Spindelman, A Dissent from the Many Dissents from Attorney General Ashcroft's Interpretation of the Controlled Substances Act, 19 Issues L. & Med. 3 (2003). Similar issues arise with federal intrusion into state decisions to allow marijuana use for medical purposes. See page 621.

4. *Aid in Dying in Other States.* Even before Oregon legalized aid in dying, studies suggested that physician aid in dying and physician-caused euthanasia occur on a regular, albeit infrequent, basis in the United States. Anthony L. Back et al., Physician-Assisted Suicide and Euthanasia in Washington State: Patient Requests and Physician Responses, 275 JAMA 919 (1996); Ezekiel J. Emanuel et al., The Practice of Euthanasia and Physician-Assisted Suicide in the United States, 280 JAMA 506 (1998); Diane E. Meier et al., A National Survey of Physician-Assisted Suicide and Euthanasia in the United States, 338 New Eng. J. Med. 1193 (1998).

In a national survey regarding requests for physician aid in dying or euthanasia, physicians reported that patients receiving aid in dying had a "substantial burden of physical pain and distress," and were "expected to die of their illness within a short time." For euthanasia, physicians reported that the patients were "imminently dying, bedridden, and severely uncomfortable." About twenty to thirty patients who died by aid in dying or euthanasia were reported to be depressed, but patients with depression were significantly less likely to have their requests granted. Diane E. Meier et al., Characteristics of Patients Requesting and Receiving Physician-Assisted Death, 163 Arch. Intern. Med. 1537 (2003).

5. *The Patient-Plaintiffs in* Glucksberg. The Supreme Court provided little information about the patients who claimed a constitutional right to aid in dying in the *Glucksberg* case. In contrast, when the Ninth Circuit found such a right, it provided the following descriptions:

> Jane Roe is a 69-year-old retired pediatrician who has suffered since 1988 from cancer which has now metastasized throughout her skeleton. Although she tried and benefitted temporarily from various treatments including chemotherapy and radiation, she is now in the terminal phase of her disease. In November 1993, her doctor referred her to hospice care. Only patients with a life expectancy of less than six months are eligible for such care.
>
> Jane Roe has been almost completely bedridden since June of 1993 and experiences constant pain, which becomes especially sharp and severe when she moves. The only medical treatment available to her at this time is medication, which cannot fully alleviate her pain. In addition, she suffers from swollen legs, bed sores, poor appetite, nausea and vomiting, impaired vision, incontinence of bowel, and general weakness. . . .
>
> John Doe is a 44-year-old artist dying of AIDS. Since his diagnosis in 1991, he has experienced two bouts of pneumonia, chronic, severe skin and sinus infections, grand mal seizures and extreme fatigue. He has already lost 70 percent of his vision to cytomegalovirus retinitis, a degenerative disease which will result in blindness and rob him of his ability to paint. His doctor has indicated that he is in the terminal phase of his illness.
>
> John Doe is especially cognizant of the suffering imposed by a lingering terminal illness because he was the primary caregiver for his long-term

companion who died of AIDS in June of 1991. He also observed his grandfather's death from diabetes preceded by multiple amputations as well as loss of vision and hearing. Mr. Doe is mentally competent, understands there is no cure for AIDS and wants his physician to prescribe drugs which he can use to hasten his death.

James Poe is a 69-year-old retired sales representative who suffers from emphysema, which causes him a constant sensation of suffocating. He is connected to an oxygen tank at all times, and takes morphine regularly to calm the panic reaction associated with his feeling of suffocation. Mr. Poe also suffers from heart failure related to his pulmonary disease which obstructs the flow of blood to his extremities and causes severe leg pain. There are no cures for his pulmonary and cardiac conditions, and he is in the terminal phase of his illness. Mr. Poe is mentally competent and wishes to commit suicide by taking physician-prescribed drugs. Compassion in Dying v. Washington, 79 F.3d 790, 794-795 (9th Cir. 1996).

6. *Substantive Due Process.* As discussed in the Court's opinions, a right to aid in dying can be analogized to the right to refuse unwanted medical treatment and the right to abortion.

The right to refuse treatment: The Supreme Court had no trouble upholding the traditional distinction between the withdrawal of life-sustaining treatment and physician aid in dying. The Ninth and Second Circuits in *Glucksberg* and *Quill*, however, found the distinction to be unconstitutional, at least for persons who are terminally ill. Consider the following arguments for the distinction. Do they really explain why treatment withdrawal and aid in dying should be treated differently?

(a) "[D]eclining life-sustaining medical treatment may not properly be viewed as an attempt to commit suicide. Refusing medical intervention merely allows the disease to take its natural course; if death were eventually to occur, it would be the result, primarily, of the underlying disease, and not the result of a self-inflicted injury." In re Conroy, 486 A.2d 1209, 1224 (N.J. 1985).

(b) "[P]eople who refuse life-sustaining medical treatment may not harbor a specific intent to die; rather, they may fervently wish to live, but to do so free of unwanted medical technology, surgery, or drugs, and without protracted suffering." In re Conroy, 486 A.2d 1209, 1224 (N.J. 1985).

(c) The right to die is only a right to refuse unwanted bodily invasion. As the Massachusetts Supreme Court wrote in the *Saikewicz* case, "[A] person has a strong interest in being free from nonconsensual invasion of his bodily integrity." Superintendant of Belchertown v. Saikewicz, 370 N.E.2d 417, 424 (Mass. 1977). Similarly, the right to abortion is essentially the right to avoid an unwanted invasion of the body by a fetus. Aid in dying in contrast is a right to demand a bodily invasion, and there is no tradition in the law of such a right.

(d) If physicians began to dispense death-causing agents, patients would develop a profound distrust of the medical profession. "[I]f physicians become killers or are even merely licensed to kill, the profession—and, therewith, each physician—will never again be worthy of trust and respect as healer and comforter and protector of life in all its frailty." Willard Gaylin et al., Doctors Must Not Kill, 259 JAMA 2140, 2141 (1988).

(e) "How easily will [physicians] be able to care wholeheartedly for patients when it is always possible to think of killing them as a 'therapeutic option'? Shall it be penicillin and a respirator one more time, or perhaps just an overdose of morphine this time? Physicians get tired of treating patients who are hard to cure, who resist their best efforts, who are on their way down — 'gorks,' 'gomers,' and 'vegetables' are only some of the less than affectionate names they receive from the house officers. Won't it be tempting to think that death is the best treatment for the little old lady 'dumped' again on the emergency room by the nearby nursing home?" Leon Kass, Neither for Love nor Money: Why Doctors Must Not Kill, 94 Pub. Int. 25, 35 (Winter 1989).

(f) Many physicians are poorly trained in the relief of pain and other symptoms of suffering, and studies indicate that half of terminally ill patients receive inadequate pain control during their hospitalizations. Joanne Lynn et al., Perceptions by Family Members of the Dying Experience of Older and Seriously Ill Patients, 126 Annals Intern. Med. 97 (1997). It would be dangerous to legalize aid in dying before we ensure that physicians are providing appropriate palliative care to their patients.

(g) "Two strong movements have each begun to enlist many enthusiastic adherents throughout the nation: a movement toward managed care as a means of cost control and a movement toward managed death through euthanasia and assisted suicide. . . . In managed care, . . . [physicians] are usually given financial incentives to control costs while maintaining quality. . . . As providers of managed care, many physicians will be motivated by concern for quality, but concerns about cost will also be significant. Their concern for quality will probably be made explicit, but their concern for cost will generally be left unspoken. As providers of managed death, many physicians will be sincerely motivated by respect for patient autonomy, but the cost factor will always lurk silently in the background. This will be especially true if they are providing managed death in a setting of managed care." Daniel P. Sulmasy, Managed Care and Managed Death, 155 Arch. Intern. Med. 133, 133, 134 (1995).

(h) "Is this the kind of choice, assuming that it can be made in a fixed and rational manner, that we want to offer a gravely ill person? Will we not sweep up, in the process, some who are not really tired of life, but think others are tired of them; some who do not really want to die, but who feel they should not live on, . . . ? Will not some feel an obligation to have themselves 'eliminated' in order that funds allocated for their terminal care might be better used by their families or, financial worries aside, in order to relieve their families of the emotional strain involved?" Yale Kamisar, Some Non-religious Views Against Proposed "Mercy-killing" Legislation, 42 Minn. L. Rev. 669, 690 (1958).

(i) "Studies of suicide have found that 90 to 100 percent of the victims die while they have a diagnosable psychiatric illness, an observation that is equally true in suicides among the elderly. The elderly appear to be more prone than younger victims to take their lives during the type of acute depressive episode that responds most effectively to available, modern treatments. . . . One study showed that of 44 patients in the later stages of cancer, only 3 had considered suicide, and each of them had a severe clinical depression. . . . [T]he medical literature is replete with studies demonstrating that primary care physicians often fail to recognize treatable depression in their patients, particularly the elderly. . . . Our data on suicides among the elderly show that 75 percent of those who took their lives had seen a primary care physician during the month before death, yet their psychiatric disturbances usually went undetected or were inadequately treated." Yeates Conwell & Eric D. Caine, Rational Suicide and the Right to Die: Reality and Myth, 325 New Eng. J. Med. 1100, 1101-1102 (1991).

(j) "Slavery was long ago outlawed on the ground that one person should not have the right to own another, even with the other's permission. Why? Because it is a fundamental moral wrong for one person to give over his life and fate to another, whatever the good consequences, and no less a wrong for another person to have that kind of total, final power. Like slavery, dueling was long ago banned on similar grounds: even free, competent individuals should not have the power to kill each other, whatever their motives, whatever the circumstances. Consenting adult killing, like consenting adult slavery or degradation, is a strange route to human dignity." Daniel Callahan, When Self-Determination Runs Amok, 22(2) Hastings Center Rep. 52, 52 (1992).

(k) "It is not medicine's place to determine when lives are not worth living or when the burden of life is too great to be borne. Doctors have no conceivable way of evaluating such claims on the part of patients, and they should have no right to act in response to them. Medicine should try to relieve human suffering, but only that suffering which is brought on by illness and dying as biological phenomena, not that suffering which comes from anguish or despair at the human condition." Daniel Callahan, When Self-Determination Runs Amok, 22(2) Hastings Center Rep. 52, 55 (1992).

The right to abortion: In some ways, a right to aid in dying seems more defensible than a right to abortion. The life being ended is the life of the person making the decision rather than the life of a third party. Moreover, what is being taken away is a short period of great suffering rather than a potential for a full span of a healthy and productive life. In other ways, the right to aid in dying is the harder case. In particular, the life of a person rather than a pre-viable fetus is being taken.

How well the analogy works depends on which theory you accept for the right to abortion. Consider the following arguments for a right to abortion. How well do they support a right to aid in dying?

(a) "Our law affords constitutional protection to personal decisions relating to marriage, procreation, contraception, family relationships, child rearing and education. [These] matters, involving the most intimate and personal choices a person may make in a lifetime, choices central to personal dignity and autonomy, are central to the liberty protected by the Fourteenth Amendment. At the heart of liberty is the right to define one's own concept of existence, of meaning, of the universe, and of the mystery of human life. Beliefs about these matters could not define the attributes of personhood were they formed under compulsion of the state." Planned Parenthood of Southeastern Pennsylvania v. Casey, 505 U.S. 833, 851 (1992).

(b) "It is a deeply rooted principle of American law that an individual is ordinarily not required to volunteer aid to another individual who is in danger or in need of assistance. In brief, our law does not require people to be Good Samaritans. . . . [I]f we require a pregnant woman to carry the fetus to term and deliver it — if we forbid abortion, in other words — we are compelling her to be a Good Samaritan. . . . [I]f we consider the generally very limited scope of obligations of samaritanism under our law, and if we consider the special nature of the burdens imposed on pregnant women by laws forbidding abortion, we must eventually conclude that the equal protection clause forbids imposition of these burdens on pregnant women." Donald H. Regan, Rewriting Roe v. Wade, 77 Mich. L. Rev. 1569, 1569 (1979).

(c) "The distinctive and singular characteristic of the laws against which the right to privacy has been applied lies in their *productive or affirmative* consequences. There are perhaps no legal proscriptions with more profound, more extensive, or more persistent affirmative effects on individual lives than the laws struck down as violations of the right to privacy. Anti-abortion laws . . . involve the forcing of lives into well-defined and highly confined institutional layers. . . . They affirmatively and very substantially shape a person's life; they direct a life's development along a particular avenue. These laws do not simply proscribe one act or remove one liberty; they inform the totality of a person's life. . . . Anti-abortion laws produce motherhood: They take diverse women with every variety of career, life-plan, and so on, and make mothers of them all. . . . For a period of months and quite possibly years, forced motherhood shapes women's occupations and preoccupations in the minutest detail; it creates a perceived identity for women and confines them to it. . . ." Jed Rubenfeld, The Right of Privacy, 102 Harv. L. Rev. 737, 784, 788 (1989).

7. *The Patient's Condition.* An important question in determining due process rights in end-of-life care is whether the critical issue is the physician's action or the patient's condition. We have seen that the courts permit withdrawal of treatment regardless of the patient's condition but are generally unwilling to recognize a right to aid in dying (or euthanasia), also regardless of the patient's condition. In contrast, when the Ninth and Second Circuits in *Glucksberg* and *Quill* recognized a right to aid in dying, the courts suggested that the critical question is not the nature of the physician's action but the condition of the patient. That is, the critical issue is whether the patient has an irreversible and fatal medical problem, not whether there is a withdrawal of treatment or aid in dying. Consider the following perspectives:

> Suppose the doctor agrees to withhold treatment [from a dying patient], as the conventional doctrine says he may. The justification for his doing so is that the patient is in terrible agony, and since he is going to die anyway, it would be wrong to prolong his suffering needlessly. But now notice this. If one simply withholds treatment, it may take the patient longer to die, and so he may suffer more than he would if more direct action were taken and a lethal injection given. This fact provides strong reason for thinking that, once the initial decision not to prolong his agony has been made, active euthanasia is actually preferable to passive euthanasia, rather than the reverse. To say otherwise is to endorse the option that leads to more suffering rather than less, and is contrary to the humanitarian impulse that prompts the decision not to prolong his life in the first place. [James Rachels, Active and Passive Euthanasia, 292 New Eng. J. Med. 78, 78 (1975).]
>
> There are two individuals, one of whom is twenty-eight years old, is despondent from a recent romantic breakup and, because of an acute asthma attack, is temporarily ventilator dependent. Other than the asthma, this person is in good health. The other individual is eighty-two years old, is wracked with pain from widely metastatic cancer and has no more than a few weeks to live. Assume that both of these individuals wish to end their lives, the twenty-eight-year-old by

refusing the ventilator and the eighty-two-year-old by suicide. Under current law, the twenty-eight-year-old may have the ventilator discontinued while the eighty-two-year-old generally lacks a right to suicide assistance.

Yet, in terms of the reasons why we recognize a right to refuse life-sustaining treatment, it would be more justifiable for a physician to assist the eighty-two-year-old's suicide than to accede to the twenty-eight-year-old's refusal of the ventilator. . . . [T]he right to refuse life-sustaining treatment arose out of a sense that hopelessly ill patients should be able to refuse treatment that provides little, if any, benefit and merely prolongs the dying process. Society's interest in preserving a patient's life becomes attenuated when there is little life left to save, and treatment becomes burdensome rather than beneficial. In the same way, society's interest in preserving the life of the eighty-two-year-old becomes attenuated—the patient's remaining life is very short and overcome by severe suffering. Conversely, imposing a ventilator on the twenty-eight-year-old would not result in the brief prolongation of a dying process but the long extension of a life that likely would become very much valued by the patient. If we were to decide these cases strictly on their own merits, we would probably permit physicians to assist the suicide of the eighty-two-year-old but not permit them to withdraw the ventilator from the twenty-eight-year-old. [David Orentlicher, The Legalization of Physician-Assisted Suicide: A Very Modest Revolution, 38 B.C. L. Rev. 443, 462-463 (1997).]

If the patient's condition is more critical than the nature of the physician's act, does this imply that the appropriate standard for both the right to refuse life-sustaining treatment and a right to aid in dying is the standard of the *Quinlan* court, that the individual's right should "grow [] as the degree of bodily invasion increases and the prognosis dims. Ultimately there comes a point at which the individual's rights overcome the state interest. . . ." *Quinlan*, 355 A.2d at 664.

8. *Equal Protection.* The *Quill* court addressed the question whether a right to refuse life-sustaining treatment implies a right to physician aid in dying under the equal protection clause. In the lawsuit over Oregon's statute legalizing physician aid in dying, on the other hand, the federal district court used the equal protection clause to limit the ability of states to permit aid in dying. See supra at page 323.

If the Second Circuit in *Quill* used the equal protection clause to strike down a prohibition on aid in dying, and the district court in *Lee* used the equal protection clause to strike down a statute permitting aid in dying, do the two opinions simply demonstrate that the equal protection clause is hopelessly indeterminate, or is there a way to reconcile the two rulings?

If we accept the logic of the *Lee* court, must we require the same safeguards for withdrawal of life-sustaining treatment that we require for aid in dying? Aren't patients on life-sustaining treatment given less protection from abuse or impaired judgment than persons who are not being sustained by medical treatment but who want to die? Isn't it easier for a patient like Kenneth Bergstedt, at pages 249-250, to end his life involuntarily than for a person who isn't dependent on a ventilator?

9. *Limiting a Right to Aid in Dying.* In *Glucksberg* and *Quill*, the Supreme Court echoed concerns from many commentators that a right to aid in dying cannot be easily cabined. As one scholar has observed,

If personal autonomy and the termination of suffering are supposed to be the touchstones for physician-assisted suicide, why exclude those with nonterminal illnesses or disabilities who might have to endure greater pain and suffering *for much longer periods of time* than those who are expected to die in the next few weeks or months? If the terminally ill do have a right to assisted suicide, doesn't someone who must continue to live what *she considers* an intolerable or unacceptable existence *for many years* have an equal — or even greater — right to assisted suicide? . . . [I]f, as proponents of assisted suicide maintain, there is no significant difference between the right to assisted suicide and the right to reject unwanted life-saving treatment, it is fairly clear that, once established, the right to assisted suicide would not be limited to the terminally ill. For the right of a person to reject life-sustaining medical treatment *has not been so limited*. Yale Kamisar, Against Assisted Suicide — Even a Very Limited Form, 72 U. Det. Mercy L. Rev. 735, 740-741 (1995) (emphasis in original).

Is the Court's observation in *Glucksberg* correct that, if we permit physician aid in dying for terminally ill persons, we must also permit euthanasia for terminally ill persons who lack the physical ability to self-administer a lethal dose of medication? Is the Court also correct that we must honor the living will of a patient who requested euthanasia in the event of terminal illness? Must we permit aid in dying for patients who are not terminally ill but who have an incurable and irreversible illness and are suffering greatly?

For an argument that a right to aid in dying is not readily susceptible to expansion, see David Orentlicher & Christopher M. Callahan, Feeding Tubes, Slippery Slopes, and Physician-Assisted Suicide, 25 J. Leg. Med. 389 (2004).

10. *Palliative Sedation.* In her concurring opinion, Justice O'Connor suggested that dying patients have a constitutional right to alleviate their suffering, but that such a right would not imply a right to aid in dying since patients are able to obtain medications to relieve their suffering "even to the point of causing unconsciousness and hastening death."

It is well accepted in ethics and law that physicians can administer medications to relieve pain or other suffering even if doing so poses some increased risk of death for the patient. Under this principle of "double effect," the risk of death is acceptable as long as the medication is used in a reasonable effort to treat the patient's suffering. By way of analogy, we permit physicians to perform open heart surgery, despite the risk of patient death, because the primary purpose of the surgery is to treat the patient's heart disease, and the benefits of the surgery are reasonable when compared with the risks.

In some cases, as Justice O'Connor noted, the patient must be sedated into unconsciousness to relieve the suffering. In these cases, the patient is sedated into a coma from which the patient usually dies in a few days, either because the patient is at the end stage of the underlying illness or because food and water are withheld.

Is there a good reason to permit palliative sedation (once, and at the time of *Glucksberg* and *Quill*, called "terminal sedation") but not to permit aid in dying? From the patient's perspective, which is the more desirable approach? Do you see how palliative sedation could be viewed as a form of euthanasia? See David Orentlicher, The Supreme Court and Physician-Assisted Suicide: Rejecting

Assisted Suicide but Embracing Euthanasia, 337 New Eng. J. Med. 1236 (1997) (and a fuller version of the argument in 24 Hastings Const. L.Q. 947 (1997)). In the Netherlands, where both practices are permitted, one study found that palliative sedation is "typically used to address severe physical and psychological suffering in dying patients, whereas perceived loss of dignity during the last phase of life is a major problem for patients requesting euthanasia." Judith A. C. Rietjens, Terminal Sedation and Euthanasia, 166 Arch. Intern. Med. 749 (2006). But see Jean-Jacques Georges et al., Differences Between Terminally Ill Cancer Patients Who Died After Euthanasia Had Been Performed and Terminally Ill Cancer Patients Who Did Not Request Euthanasia, 19 Palliative Med. 578 (2005) (finding that patients choosing euthanasia had much higher levels of severe pain, vomiting, and nausea than patients who did not choose euthanasia).

If there is a right to receive medications to alleviate the symptoms of disease, is there also a right to receive medications to treat the disease itself? In a surprising decision in favor of patients' rights based on *Cruzan* and *Glucksberg*, a panel of the D.C. Circuit initially found a limited constitutional right of terminally ill persons to receive experimental cancer chemotherapy or other potentially therapeutic drugs without Food and Drug Administration (FDA) approval, when there are no other therapeutic options left. Abigail Alliance v. Eschenbach, 445 F.3d 470 (D.C. Cir. 2006). This decision was reversed by the en banc court, however, 495 F.3d 695 (D.C. Cir. 2007), which reasoned that such a right is not deeply rooted in the nation's history and tradition, considering the long history of the regulation of pharmacists and pharmaceuticals. During the litigation, the FDA proposed a new rule to give terminally ill patients greater access to experimental drugs. 71 Fed. Reg. 75147 (2006). For further discussion of *Abigail Alliance* see Chapter 6.C.1.

For discussion of the medical and ethical aspects of palliative sedation, see Nathan I. Cherny & Russell K. Portenoy, Sedation in the Management of Refractory Symptoms: Guidelines for Evaluation and Treatment, 10(2) J. Palliative Care 31 (1994); National Ethics Committee, Veterans Health Administration, The Ethics of Palliative Sedation as a Therapy of Last Resort, 23 Am. J. Hospice Palliative Care 483 (2007); Bernard Lo & Gordon Rubenfeld, Palliative Sedation in Dying Patients, 294 JAMA (2005); Timothy E. Quill & Robert V. Brody, "You Promised Me I Wouldn't Die Like This!": A Bad Death as a Medical Emergency, 155 Arch. Intern. Med. 1250 (1995); Robert D. Truog et al., Barbiturates in the Care of the Terminally Ill, 327 New Eng. J. Med. 1678 (1992).

11. *Predicting Patient Outcome.* An important concern about a right of terminally ill persons to aid in dying is the reliability of a physician's prediction that a patient will die soon (e.g., within six months). For many patients, it is difficult to predict when they will die. Certainty varies not only from patient to patient but also from disease to disease—while predictions are fairly reliable for patients with cancers, they are rather unreliable for patients with emphysema or congestive heart failure. Ellen Fox et al., Evaluation of Prognostic Criteria for Determining Hospice Eligibility in Patients with Advanced Lung, Heart, or Liver Disease, 282 JAMA 1638 (1999); Joanne Lynn et al., Defining the "Terminally Ill": Insights from SUPPORT, 35 Duq. L. Rev. 311 (1996). Still, among all patients certified as likely to die within six months for purposes of hospice benefits under Medicare, 85 percent died within six months. Nicholas A. Christakis & Jose J.

Escarce, Survival of Medicare Patients After Enrollment in Hospice Programs, 335 New Eng. J. Med. 172, 174 (1996).

If we reject a right to aid in dying for the terminally ill because of uncertainties as to when a patient is terminally ill, does it follow that we should reject a right to refuse life-sustaining treatment because patients might refuse treatment on the mistaken assumption either that they are terminally ill or that, while not terminally ill, they will be permanently dependent on a ventilator or other treatment?

12. *Refusing Food and Water*. Some commentators have argued that patients who are not dependent upon life-sustaining treatment but who desire aid in dying can always end their lives by refraining from eating and drinking. James L. Bernat, Bernard Gert & R. Peter Mogielnicki, Patient Refusal of Hydration and Nutrition: An Alternative to Physician-Assisted Suicide or Voluntary Active Euthanasia, 153 Arch. Intern. Med. 2723 (1993). While some courts and commentators have suggested that death by starvation is painful, Brophy v. New England Sinai Hospital, 497 N.E.2d 626, 641 n.2 (Mass. 1986) (Lynch, J., dissenting), there actually seems to be little discomfort from dying by withdrawal of nutrition and hydration, and the discomfort can easily be relieved with appropriate care. Robert J. Sullivan, Accepting Death without Artificial Nutrition or Hydration, 8 J. Gen. Intern. Med. 220, 221 (1993). In most cases, death will occur within a few days. If people can end their lives by starvation, or, for that matter, by a number of ways described in Derek Humphrey, Final Exit: The Practicalities of Self-Deliverance and Assisted Suicide for the Dying (1991), why do patients request aid in dying? Note that, even with cessation of eating and drinking, it still may take several weeks in rare cases for the patient to die. Sullivan, supra, at 221-222.

13. *Conscientious Objection*. Living will statutes routinely recognize a conscientious objection on the part of physicians who are unwilling to participate in a withdrawal of life-sustaining treatment. Cal. Prob. Code §4734; Ohio Rev. Code Ann. §2133.10(A); Pa. Cons. Stat. tit. 20, §5424(a). If the physician believes that it is morally wrong to discontinue life-sustaining treatment, then the physician may withdraw from the case and arrange for another physician to carry out the patient's request. To the physician with a conscientious objection of this sort, withdrawal of treatment is understood to cause the patient's death; it does not matter that the physician is doing so by omission or "inaction." To the conscientious objector, withdrawing treatment is just as much an action as aiding in dying. If the physician who opposes withdrawal of treatment may equate it to aid in dying, does it follow that the physician who supports aid in dying may equate it to withdrawal of treatment?

14. *Euthanasia*. While most of the legal activity surrounding this issue in the United States has focused on aid in dying, some statutory proposals and cases seek a right to euthanasia. As mentioned, the California and Washington legislative initiatives that were defeated would have granted a right to both aid in dying and euthanasia. Also, a California man sought a declaratory judgment permitting him to have his body preserved cryogenically before he died in the hope that physicians could reanimate his body once a cure was found for his brain cancer. Since the "freezing" process would result in the man's death, his claim rested on the existence of a constitutional right to euthanasia, but the court held that no

such right exists. Donaldson v. Van de Kamp, 4 Cal. Rptr. 2d 59 (Cal. Ct. App. 1992). (Normally, cryopreservation takes place after the person dies.)

15. *Other Countries.* Australia's Northern Territory became the first jurisdiction to legalize euthanasia when it enacted the Rights of the Terminally Ill Act in May 1996. The legislation took effect on July 1, 1996, and the first reported death under the Act occurred on September 22, 1996. The law permitted euthanasia and aid in dying for terminally ill persons after evaluation by two physicians, including a psychiatrist, and after a nine-day waiting period. Robert L. Schwartz, Rights of the Terminally Ill Act of the Australian Northern Territory, 5 Cambridge Q. Healthcare Ethics 157 (1996). In March 1997, after four persons had invoked the law, the Australian Parliament repealed the legislation. Reuters, Euthanasia Law Struck Down in Australia, N.Y. Times, March 27, 1997, at A15.

In the Netherlands, euthanasia and aid in dying were treated as criminal acts, but they were not prosecuted if performed under guidelines that were developed between 1973 and 1984 by the legal system and the medical profession. In 2001, legislation formally legalized aid in dying and euthanasia in accordance with existing practices, with some extension of those practices. The legislation took effect in April 2002.

Under existing practices, the patient must be competent and have made a consistent, persistent, and voluntary request for euthanasia or aid in dying. The patient need not be terminally ill but must be incurably ill and experiencing unbearable suffering that cannot be relieved. The patient's physician must consult with an experienced colleague before acceding to the patient's request. Maurice A. M. Wachter, Active Euthanasia in the Netherlands, 262 JAMA 3316 (1989). In 1995, the deaths of about 4,600 persons in the Netherlands were ascribed to euthanasia or aid in dying. Paul J. van der Maas et al., Euthanasia, Physician-Assisted Suicide, and Other Medical Practices Involving the End of Life in the Netherlands, 1990-1995, 335 New Eng. J. Med. 1699, 1701 (1996). In more than 90 percent of cases, the patient was expected to live no more than a month longer. Id. at 1704.

As discussed in *Glucksberg*, there is evidence that the guidelines for euthanasia and aid in dying were not rigorously followed in a substantial number of cases before 2002. Empirical data indicate that in about one-fourth of cases of euthanasia or aid in dying, physicians do not observe the strict criteria for those procedures. In these cases, the patient "had in a previous phase of his or her illness expressed a wish for euthanasia should suffering become unbearable," the patient was "near to death and clearly suffering grievously, yet verbal contact had become impossible," or the decision had been discussed with the patient but the patient's wishes had not been expressed explicitly and persistently. Paul J. van der Maas et al., Euthanasia and Other Medical Decisions Concerning the End of Life, 338 Lancet 669, 672 (1991); van der Maas et al., Euthanasia, supra, 335 New Eng. J. Med. at 1701. In response to this evidence, the Royal Dutch Medical Association issued new guidelines in August 1995 that emphasized that existing rules needed to be followed and that stated that euthanasia should not be performed unless aid in dying is not an option (e.g., because the patient is too sick to swallow the lethal drug) and that the consulting physician may not have a professional or family relationship with the patient or physician. M. Simons, Dutch Doctors to Tighten

Rules on Mercy Killings, N.Y. Times, Sept. 11, 1995, at A3. A subsequent study found that rates of aid in dying and euthanasia had stabilized between 1995 and 2001, with physicians becoming somewhat more reluctant to engage in the two practices. Bregje D. Onwuteaka-Philipsen, Euthanasia and Other End-of-Life Decisions in the Netherlands in 1990, 1995, and 2001, 362 Lancet 395 (2003).

After the 2002 legalization of euthanasia and aid in dying, it appears that physicians have become less reluctant to employ those practices. A survey of Dutch physicians in 2005 found a significant decrease in the use of aid in dying and euthanasia, accompanied by greater use of palliative sedation. For example, the euthanasia rate in 2005 was 1.7 percent of all deaths, down from 2.6 percent in 2001 and equal to the rate in 1990. In addition the rate of life-ending acts without a current explicit request from the patient dropped from 0.7 percent in 2001 to 0.4 percent in 2005. The researchers observed that the reduction in aid in dying and euthanasia may have reflected a substitution of palliative sedation for the two practices and/or a decline in the likelihood that physicians would attribute patient death to the effects of opioid administration. As to the latter, it is possible that physicians were less likely in 2005 than in previous years to mistakenly believe that their use of opioids to treat patient suffering had hastened patient deaths. Agnes van der Heide et al., End-of-Life Practices in the Netherlands under the Euthanasia Act, 356 New Eng. J. Med. 1957 (2007).

In addition to legalizing existing rules for non-prosecuted euthanasia and aid in dying for competent persons, the 2002 law also permits euthanasia by advance directive. In a survey of physicians asking about euthanasia by advance directive in 2000-2001, before its recognition under the law, researchers found that 29 percent of the physicians had treated demented patients with a euthanasia advance directive, but only 3 percent of the physicians complied with such a directive, and 54 percent reported that they never would comply with such a directive. Mette L. Rurup et al., Physicians' Experiences with Demented Patients with Advance Euthanasia Directives in the Netherlands, 53 J. Am. Geriatrics Soc'y 1138 (2005).

For more information about euthanasia in the Netherlands, see the Dutch Ministry of Justice's Web site (http://english.justitie.nl/themes/euthanasia/). For a comprehensive discussion of euthanasia and aid in dying in the Netherlands before legalization, see John Griffiths et al., Euthanasia & Law in the Netherlands (Amsterdam Univ. Press 1998).

In Belgium, final approval was given in 2002 to legislation permitting euthanasia under rules like those in the Netherlands. In Germany, euthanasia is prohibited by law, but aid in dying is not. However, physicians are legally obligated to try to resuscitate persons who have attempted suicide. Consequently, while aid in dying is practiced in Germany, the assistance is usually provided by family members or friends rather than physicians. The Germane Society for Humane Dying is a large, private, nonmedical organization that provides advice to members about aid in dying after they have been members for at least a year. Margaret P. Battin, Assisted Suicide: Can We Learn from Germany?, 22(2) Hastings Center Rep. 44 (1992). Switzerland permits aid in dying without the involvement of a physician; there too lay assistance is common. Samia A. Hurst & Alex Mauron, Assisted Suicide and Euthanasia in Switzerland: Allowing a Role for Non-Physicians, 326 Brit. Med. J. 271 (2003).

16. *Additional Arguments.* Consider the following additional arguments regarding aid in dying (or euthanasia):

> The common concern that assisted suicide will shorten life may be mistaken. Seriously ill patients often face an option of treatment that has a small but still significant chance of prolonging life. At the same time, there may be a substantial risk that the treatment will fail and only cause painful and debilitating side effects. The prospect of the treatment failure and the side effects will discourage many patients from accepting the treatment. A small chance of success may not be enough to overcome a high risk of great suffering. If a right to assisted suicide existed, however, those same patients would be more likely to accept the treatment. The patients would know that, if the treatment did not work, they would always have the option of ending their suffering through physician assisted suicide. The patients would not have to fear the consequences of treatment failure. They also would know that, with their physician's guidance, their suicide attempt would be more dignified, less painful and less likely to fail and leave the patient in a condition of even greater suffering. [David Orentlicher, The Legalization of Physician-Assisted Suicide: A Very Modest Revolution, 38 B.C. L. Rev. 443, 452-453 (1997).]
>
> [P]hysician assisted suicide has been prohibited not because it is meaningfully different from withdrawal of life-sustaining treatment, but because the distinction between suicide assistance and treatment withdrawal served as a useful proxy for distinguishing between morally acceptable and morally unacceptable decisions by patients to end their lives. Society commonly implements its principles through generally valid rules rather than through case-by-case determinations, recognizing that the rules will not fit every case perfectly but also recognizing the infeasibility of case-by-case determinations. The distinction between suicide assistance and treatment withdrawal is an example of rule-based lawmaking that, in the view of the public and the courts, was an effective way to ensure that patients could end their lives only when they were morally justified in doing so.
>
> Now, however, the distinction between physician assisted suicide and withdrawal of life-sustaining treatment has lost its utility as a moral proxy. . . . [T]here are many patients desiring assisted suicide whose wishes to end their lives are morally justified — in society's view. The distinction between assisted suicide and withdrawal of treatment no longer does a good job of sorting morally valid from morally invalid requests by patients to end their lives. Accordingly, the distinction is being replaced — and may continue to be replaced — by new proxy distinctions that allow for physician assisted suicide in limited situations. [Id. at 445.]

See also David Orentlicher, Matters of Life and Death: Making Moral Theory Work in Medical Ethics and the Law 16-23 (2001).

17. *State Law Activity Outside of Oregon.* The Supreme Court's rejection of a federal constitutional right has shifted the aid in dying debate back to the state courts and legislatures. As the Court observed, legislative initiatives to legalize aid in dying and euthanasia were defeated in Washington in 1991 and California in 1993, both by 54 percent to 46 percent votes. Voters in Maine rejected aid in dying by referendum in 2000 on a 51.5 percent to 48.5 percent vote, and an aid in dying referendum lost by 71 percent to 29 percent in Michigan in 1998. The Oregon statute was adopted in 1994 by a 51 percent to 49 percent margin,

and, as mentioned, was reaffirmed by a 60 percent to 40 percent margin in November 1997. Bills to legalize aid in dying have been introduced in other state legislatures, and several states have enacted or reaffirmed their prohibitions of aid in dying in recent years. For updates on legislative activity, see the Death with Dignity National Center Web site, at www.deathwithdignity.org/news/statenews.asp.

Seriously ill persons also have gone to state court for relief, arguing unsuccessfully so far for a right to aid in dying under state constitutional law. See Sampson v. Alaska, 31 P.3d 88 (Alaska 2001); Krischer v. McIver, 697 So. 2d 97 (Fla. 1997).

For an interesting argument that physician aid in dying should not be legalized but that there should be an affirmative defense to charges of aid in dying when the patient is competent, terminally ill, and suffering, see James A. Tulsky, Ann Alpers & Bernard Lo, A Middle Ground on Physician-Assisted Suicide, 5 Cambridge Q. Healthcare Ethics 33 (1996).

18. *Further Readings.* For additional discussions of physician aid in dying, see Daniel Callahan & Margot White, The Legalization of Physician-Assisted Suicide: Creating a Regulatory Potemkin Village, 30 U. Rich. L. Rev. 1 (1996); Ronald Dworkin, Life's Dominion: An Argument About Abortion, Euthanasia, and Individual Freedom (1993); Leonard M. Fleck, Just Caring: Assisted Suicide and Health Care Rationing, 72 U. Det. Mercy L. Rev. 873 (1995); Sylvia A. Law, Physician-Assisted Death: An Essay on Constitutional Rights and Remedies, 55 Md. L. Rev. 292 (1996); Thomas Marzen, "Out, Out Brief Candle": Constitutionally Prescribed Suicide for the Terminally Ill, 21 Hastings Const. L.Q. 799 (1994); Physician-Assisted Suicide: Expanding the Debate (Margaret P. Battin et al. eds., 1998); Robert A. Sedler, Constitutional Challenges to Bans on "Assisted Suicide": The View from Without and Within, 21 Hastings Const. L.Q. 777 (1994); Symposium: Physician-Assisted Suicide, 82 Minn L. Rev. 885 (1998); Symposium: Visions of Death and Dying, 24 Hastings Const. L.Q. 833 (1997); Symposium, Physician-Assisted Suicide, 35 Duq. L. Rev. 1 (1996).

Problem: Is It Aid in Dying or Is It Withdrawal of Treatment?*

Laura is a chronically depressed woman in her late 60s who has very symptomatic arthritis and is seriously overweight. The arthritis causes her chronic pain, which in turn has led her to become addicted to pain medications. Her arthritis and obesity have also caused her to be nonambulatory. Four days ago, Robert, Laura's husband, came into the room at home where Laura appeared injured. Robert called the paramedics, and Laura was brought to the hospital. Robert says that, at the time he called the paramedics, he had not realized that Laura had shot herself with a pistol to the head (actually under her chin with an exit wound in the forehead). He says if he had known, he would not have called them. What happened next was that Laura was taken to surgery and found to have sustained considerable

---

* This problem was adapted from a case originally presented by Maurice Bernstein, M.D., University of Southern California School of Medicine, and Scott Rae, Ph.D., Talbot School of Theology, Biola University (California).

damage to her head but not much damage to the brain except some to the frontal lobes. The surgeons indicate that although the patient is intubated and ventilator-dependent, it is because of the mechanical damage and edema in her neck, and they feel they will be able to take her off the ventilator shortly. Because her brain damage is minimal and involving only the frontal lobes, without the development of meningitis, she is not expected to have any loss of movement or sensation. [Injuries to the frontal lobes can cause a number of personality changes. People with such injuries may become indifferent to the problems of others, give little thought to the effects of their conduct on others, exhibit socially inappropriate behavior like telling silly or tasteless jokes, and become distractible and given to euphoria and emotional outbursts. There also is often a reduction in worry, anxiety, depression, and sensitivity to stressful stimuli, and patients who suffer from chronic pain often complain less of the pain after a frontal lobe injury. There may be compromise of memory or intellectual skills, including problem solving ability, or there may be very little effect on memory and intellect.]

Shortly after Laura's arrival to the hospital, Robert brought a copy of the state's standard Durable Power of Attorney for Health Care (DPAHC) form which was signed by Laura, duly witnessed and dated three months before the date of her gunshot wound. Laura had designated Robert as her DPAHC agent. Robert told the hospital doctors and staff that he and his family were aware of the emotional and physical pain and suffering that Laura had experienced over the years and understood that she was depressed (indeed, she had attempted suicide in the 1970s with pills), but she really did not want to live and suffer from her infirmities any longer and she wanted to end the suffering, and, as her agent, he wanted them to stop the emergency treatment and let her die.

Emergency treatment was continued despite the protestations of Robert and the family, who wanted to let Laura die. Currently, Laura is under morphine pain management in the intensive care unit, still ventilator-dependent and unable to communicate, is not deteriorating and indeed her doctors are optimistic about a possible recovery. "A recovery . . . , but to what?," Robert and family say. "A return to the misery of her life before she shot herself and possibly with some additional impairments?" What Robert and the family want the medical staff to do is take Laura off the ventilator and let her die.

You work in the office of the hospital's legal counsel, who receives a call from the physicians taking care of Laura asking for legal advice. They want to know whether the law permits, requires, or forbids them to comply with the family's request to discontinue the ventilator. The legal counsel asks you for a memo analyzing the legal issues raised by this case. What would you write in the memo? In considering whether discontinuation of the ventilator would constitute withdrawal of life-sustaining treatment or aid in dying, do you see how the answer depends on your theory as to why aid in dying is different from withdrawal of treatment?

C. FUTILITY

While cases about life-sustaining medical treatment have generally involved situations in which the patient or patient's proxy wanted to stop treatment over the objection of physicians or the hospital, cases are also arising in which the positions are reversed: the patient or proxy wants to continue with treatment, but the physicians or hospital want to stop providing care. In such cases, the patient or family asserts the patient's right to make medical decisions; the physicians or hospital argue that the treatment is medically "futile," that it does not provide sufficient — or any — medical benefit and therefore ought not to be offered to the patient.

■ IN RE BABY K
16 F.3d 590 (4th Cir. 1994)

WILKINS, Circuit Judge.

The Hospital instituted this action against Ms. H, Mr. K, and Baby K, seeking a declaratory judgment that it is not required under the Emergency Medical Treatment and Active Labor Act (EMTALA), 42 U.S.C.A. §1395dd (West 1992),[2] to provide treatment other than warmth, nutrition, and hydration to Baby K, an anencephalic infant. Because we agree with the district court that EMTALA gives rise to a duty on the part of the Hospital to provide respiratory support to Baby K when she is presented at the Hospital in respiratory distress and treatment is requested for her, we affirm.

I

Baby K was born at the Hospital in October of 1992 with anencephaly, a congenital malformation in which a major portion of the brain, skull, and scalp are missing. While the presence of a brain stem does support her autonomic functions and reflex actions, because Baby K lacks a cerebrum, she is permanently unconscious. Thus, she has no cognitive abilities or awareness. She cannot see, hear, or otherwise interact with her environment.

When Baby K had difficulty breathing on her own at birth, Hospital physicians placed her on a mechanical ventilator. This respiratory support allowed the doctors to confirm the diagnosis and gave Ms. H, the mother, an opportunity to fully understand the diagnosis and prognosis of Baby K's condition. The physicians explained to Ms. H that most anencephalic infants die within a few days of birth due to breathing difficulties and other complications. Because aggressive treatment would serve no therapeutic or palliative purpose, they recommended that Baby K only be provided with supportive care in the form

---

[2] The Hospital also sought declaratory relief under §504 of the Rehabilitation Act of 1973 (Rehabilitation Act), 29 U.S.C.A. §794 (West Supp. 1993); the Americans with Disabilities Act of 1990 (ADA), 42 U.S.C.A. §§12101 et seq. (West 1993); the Child Abuse Prevention and Treatment Act (Child Abuse Act), 42 U.S.C.A. §§5101-5106h (West Supp. 1993); and the statutes and common law of Virginia. In addressing these provisions, the district court concluded that a failure to provide respiratory support to Baby K because of her condition of anencephaly would constitute discrimination in violation of the ADA and the Rehabilitation Act but declined to rule on the application of the Child Abuse Act or Virginia law. Because we conclude that the Hospital has a duty to render stabilizing treatment under EMTALA, we need not address its obligations under the remaining federal statutes or the laws of Virginia.

of nutrition, hydration, and warmth. Physicians at the Hospital also discussed with Ms. H the possibility of a "Do Not Resuscitate Order" that would provide for the withholding of lifesaving measures in the future.

The treating physicians and Ms. H failed to reach an agreement as to the appropriate care. Ms. H insisted that Baby K be provided with mechanical breathing assistance whenever the infant developed difficulty breathing on her own, while the physicians maintained that such care was inappropriate. As a result of this impasse, the Hospital sought to transfer Baby K to another hospital. This attempt failed when all of the hospitals in the area with pediatric intensive care units declined to accept the infant. In November of 1992, when Baby K no longer needed the services of an acute-care hospital, she was transferred to a nearby nursing home.

Since being transferred to the nursing home, Baby K has been readmitted to the Hospital three times due to breathing difficulties. Each time she has been provided with breathing assistance and, after stabilization, has been discharged to the nursing home. Following Baby K's second admission, the Hospital filed this action to resolve the issue of whether it is obligated to provide emergency medical treatment to Baby K that it deems medically and ethically inappropriate. Baby K's guardian ad litem and her father, Mr. K, joined in the Hospital's request for a declaration that the Hospital is not required to provide respiratory support or other aggressive treatments. . . .

II

Congress enacted EMTALA in response to its "concern that hospitals were 'dumping' patients [who were] unable to pay, by either refusing to provide emergency medical treatment or transferring patients before their emergency conditions were stabilized." Brooks v. Maryland General Hospital Inc., 996 F.2d 708, 710 (4th Cir. 1993). Through EMTALA, Congress sought "to provide an 'adequate first response to a medical crisis' for all patients," Baber v. Hospital Corp. of America, 977 F.2d 872, 880 (4th Cir. 1992), by imposing two duties on hospitals that have entered into Medicare provider agreements.

First, those hospitals with an emergency medical department must provide an appropriate medical screening to determine whether an emergency medical condition exists for any individual who comes to the emergency medical department requesting treatment. A hospital fulfills this duty if it utilizes identical screening procedures for all patients complaining of the same condition or exhibiting the same symptoms.

An additional duty arises if an emergency medical condition is discovered during the screening process. EMTALA defines an "emergency medical condition" as including:

> a medical condition manifesting itself by acute symptoms of sufficient severity (including severe pain) such that the absence of immediate medical attention could reasonably be expected to result in—
>
> (i) placing the health of the individual . . . in serious jeopardy,
> (ii) serious impairment to bodily functions, or
> (iii) serious dysfunction of any bodily organ or part.

[42 U.S.C.A. §1395dd(e)(1)(A).]

When an individual is diagnosed as presenting an emergency medical condition:

the hospital must provide either —

(A) within the staff and facilities available at the hospital, for such further medical examination and such treatment as may be required to stabilize the medical condition, or
(B) for the transfer of the individual to another medical facility in accordance with subsection (c) of this section.

[42 U.S.C.A. §1395dd(b)(1).]

The treatment required "to stabilize" an individual is that treatment "necessary to assure, within reasonable medical probability, that no material deterioration of the condition is likely to result from or occur during the transfer of the individual from a facility." 42 U.S.C.A. §1395dd(e)(3)(A). Therefore, once an individual has been diagnosed as presenting an emergency medical condition, the hospital must provide that treatment necessary to prevent the material deterioration of the individual's condition or provide for an appropriate transfer to another facility.

In the application of these provisions to Baby K, the Hospital concedes that when Baby K is presented in respiratory distress a failure to provide "immediate medical attention" would reasonably be expected to cause serious impairment of her bodily functions. Thus, her breathing difficulty qualifies as an emergency medical condition, and the diagnosis of this emergency medical condition triggers the duty of the hospital to provide Baby K with stabilizing treatment or to transfer her in accordance with the provisions of EMTALA. Since transfer is not an option available to the Hospital at this juncture,[5] the Hospital must stabilize Baby K's condition. . . .

III

. . . As the Hospital acknowledged during oral argument, Baby K resides at the nursing home for months at a time without requiring emergency medical attention. Only when she has experienced episodes of bradypnea or apnea[9] has

---

[5] In order for a hospital to transfer a patient prior to stabilization, EMTALA requires: (1) the patient or a person acting on the patient's behalf to request a transfer in writing after being informed of the risks involved and the obligations of the hospital under EMTALA; or (2) a proper certification that the medical benefits expected from the transfer outweigh the risks involved. 42 U.S.C.A. §1395dd (c)(1). In addition, the transfer must meet the criteria for an appropriate transfer which include the requirement that a qualified receiving facility agree to accept the patient and to provide appropriate medical treatment. 42 U.S.C.A. §1395dd(c)(1)(B), (c)(2). Since Ms. H objects to the transfer of Baby K, since the Hospital has not obtained a certificate that the benefits of a transfer would outweigh the medical risks involved, and since no qualified medical facility has agreed to accept Baby K, the requirements for transfer prior to stabilization have not been met. If Ms. H requests a transfer or the Hospital obtains a certification that the benefits of a transfer would outweigh the risks involved, and all of the requirements for an appropriate transfer are met, then the Hospital could, of course, transfer Baby K to another qualified medical facility prior to stabilization.

[9] Bradypnea is an "abnormal slowness of breathing." Dorland's Illustrated Medical Dictionary 230 (27th ed. 1988). In an infant who has established and sustained spontaneous breathing, apnea describes the cessation of respiration for more than sixty seconds. Id. at 112.

Baby K required respiratory support to prevent serious impairment of her bodily functions. It is bradypnea or apnea, not anencephaly, that is the emergency medical condition that brings Baby K to the Hospital for treatment. . . . The Hospital does not allege that it would refuse to provide respiratory support to infants experiencing bradypnea or apnea who do not have anencephaly. Indeed, a refusal to provide such treatment would likely be considered as providing no emergency medical treatment. . . .

[The Hospital argues] that, in redressing the problem of disparate emergency medical treatment, Congress did not intend to require physicians to provide medical treatment outside the prevailing standard of medical care. The Hospital asserts that, because of their extremely limited life expectancy and because any treatment of their condition is futile, the prevailing standard of medical care for infants with anencephaly is to provide only warmth, nutrition, and hydration. Thus, it maintains that a requirement to provide respiratory assistance would exceed the prevailing standard of medical care. However, the plain language of EMTALA requires stabilizing treatment for any individual who comes to a participating hospital, is diagnosed as having an emergency medical condition, and cannot be transferred. . . . The Hospital has been unable to identify, nor has our research revealed, any statutory language or legislative history evincing a congressional intent to create an exception to the duty to provide stabilizing treatment when the required treatment would exceed the prevailing standard of medical care. We recognize the dilemma facing physicians who are requested to provide treatment they consider morally and ethically inappropriate, but we cannot ignore the plain language of the statute because "to do so would 'transcend our judicial function.'" *Baber*, 977 F.2d at 884. The appropriate branch to redress the policy concerns of the Hospital is Congress. . . .

IV

It is beyond the limits of our judicial function to address the moral or ethical propriety of providing emergency stabilizing medical treatment to anencephalic infants. We are bound to interpret federal statutes in accordance with their plain language and any expressed congressional intent. Congress rejected a case-by-case approach to determining what emergency medical treatment hospitals and physicians must provide and to whom they must provide it; instead, it required hospitals and physicians to provide stabilizing care to any individual presenting an emergency medical condition. EMTALA does not carve out an exception for anencephalic infants in respiratory distress any more than it carves out an exception for comatose patients, those with lung cancer, or those with muscular dystrophy — all of whom may repeatedly seek emergency stabilizing treatment for respiratory distress and also possess an underlying medical condition that severely affects their quality of life and ultimately may result in their death. Because EMTALA does not provide for such an exception, the judgment of the district court is affirmed.

▮ **CAUSEY v. ST. FRANCIS MEDICAL CENTER**
719 So. 2d 1072 (La. Ct. App. 1998)

BROWN, J.,

The facts of this end of life drama are not materially disputed. Believing it medically and ethically inappropriate, a physician and hospital withdrew life-sustaining care to a 31-year-old, quadriplegic, end-stage renal failure, comatose patient over the strongly expressed objections of the patient's family. . . .

FACTS

Having suffered cardiorespiratory arrest, Sonya Causey was transferred to St. Francis Medical Center (SFMC) from a nursing home. She was comatose, quadriplegic and in end-stage renal failure. Her treating physician, Dr. Herschel R. Harter, believed that continuing dialysis would have no benefit. Although Dr. Harter agreed that with dialysis and a ventilator Mrs. Causey could live for another two years, he believed that she would have only a slight (1% to 5%) chance of regaining consciousness. Because Mrs. Causey's family demanded aggressive life-sustaining care, Dr. Harter sought unsuccessfully to transfer her to another medical facility willing to provide this care.

Dr. Harter enlisted support from SFMC's Morals and Ethics Board. The Board agreed with Dr. Harter's opinion to discontinue dialysis, life-support procedures, and to enter a "no-code" status (do not resuscitate). Mrs. Causey was taken off a feeding tube and other similar devices. The day the ventilator was removed, Mrs. Causey died of respiratory and cardiac failure.

Plaintiffs, the husband, father and mother of Sonya Causey, brought this petition for damages against SFMC and Dr. Harter. Defendants filed an exception of prematurity asserting that this action was covered under Louisiana's Medical Malpractice Act, which requires that malpractice claims be first submitted to a medical review panel before any action can be filed. . . .

DISCUSSION

Patient participation in medical decision-making is now well-established. Recognizing individual autonomy and the right to self-determination, our state legislature enacted a statute granting a competent, terminally ill person the right to *refuse* medical treatment.

In the *Karen Quinlan* case the court rejected a physician's adamant stand that he had a moral duty to treat to the last gasp. In that case, the father, not the physician, was given the power to decide whether his comatose daughter's life-prolonging care was beneficial. . . .

Now the roles are reversed. Patients or, if incompetent, their surrogate decision-makers, are demanding life-sustaining treatment regardless of its perceived futility, while physicians are objecting to being compelled to prolong life with procedures they consider futile. . . .

The problem is not with care that the physician believes is harmful or literally has no effect. For example, radiation treatment for Mrs. Causey's condition would not have been appropriate. This is arguably based on medical science. Rather, the problem is with care that has an effect on the dying process, but which the physician believes has no benefit. Such life-prolonging care is grounded in beliefs and values about which people disagree. Strictly speaking, if a physician can keep the patient alive, such care is not medically or physiologically "futile;" however, it may be "futile" on philosophical, religious or practical grounds.

Placement of statistical cut-off points for futile treatment involves subjective value judgments. The difference in opinion as to whether a 2% or 9% probability of success is the critical point for determining futility can be explained in terms of personal values, not in terms of medical science. When the medical professional and the patient, through a surrogate, disagree on the worth of pursuing life, this is a conflict over values, i.e., whether extra days obtained through medical intervention are worth the burden and costs.

SFMC had in place a Futile Care Policy which allowed for the discontinuance of medical care over and above that necessary for comfort and support if the probability of improving the patient's condition was slight and would serve only to prolong life in that condition. The inclusion of non-medical persons on the Morals and Ethics Board signals that this is not strictly a physiological or medical futility policy, but a policy asserting values and beliefs on the worth of sustaining life, even in a vegetative condition.

Futility is a subjective and nebulous concept which, except in the strictest physiological sense, incorporates value judgments. Obviously, in this case, subjective personal values of the benefit of prolonging life with only a slight possibility of improvement dictated SFMC's and Dr. Harter's decision.

To focus on a definition of "futility" is confusing and generates polemical discussions. We turn instead to an approach emphasizing the standard of medical care.

Physicians are professionals and occupy a special place in our community. They are licensed by society to perform this special role. No one else is permitted to use life-prolonging technology, which is considered by many as "fundamental" health care. The physician has an obligation to present all medically acceptable treatment options for the patient or her surrogate to consider and either choose or reject; however, this does not compel a physician to provide interventions that in his view would be harmful, without effect or "medically inappropriate." In recognizing a terminal patient's right to refuse care, La. R.S. 40:1299.58.1(a)(4) states that the statute is not to be construed "to require the application of *medically inappropriate* treatment or life-sustaining procedures to any patient or to interfere with *medical judgment* with respect to the application of medical treatment or life-sustaining procedures." (Emphasis added). Unfortunately, "medically inappropriate" and "medical judgment" are not defined. . . .

Standards of medical malpractice require a physician to act with the degree of skill and care ordinarily possessed by those in that same medical specialty acting under the same or similar circumstances. Departure from this prevailing standard of care, coupled with harm, may result in professional malpractice liability. A finding that treatment is "medically inappropriate" by a consensus of physicians practicing in that specialty translates into a standard of care. Thus, in this case, whether Dr. Harter and SFMC met the standard of care concerning the withdrawal of dialysis, life-support procedures and the entering of a "no code" status must be determined. . . . [T]he Medical Malpractice Act is applicable and the matter should first be submitted to a medical review panel. [Although multiple experts supported the withdrawal of care in their testimony to the medical review panel, the *Causey* case was settled before trial on remand.]

Notes: Medical Futility

1. *Baby K.* Additional facts about the *Baby K* case and questions for consideration are presented in Chapter 1, at pages 2-3. You should read those notes now.

As the notes indicate, an important issue raised by the *Baby K* case is whether a denial of treatment would violate the Americans with Disabilities Act (and the Rehabilitation Act). Although the Fourth Circuit declined to decide this issue, supra page 338 n.2, the court did allude to the issue in its opinion, supra page 341. There, the Court observes that the hospital would provide ventilator support to infants in respiratory distress who were not anencephalic. This argument is analogous to the argument raised in the *University Hospital* case, reprinted at pages 118-124 and discussed at pages 128-130. In *University Hospital*, there were charges of discrimination when potentially life-prolonging treatments were withheld from a seriously disabled infant. The crux of the argument is as follows: Anti-discrimination law requires similarly situated persons to be treated alike. Is *Baby K* similarly situated to other infants needing ventilator treatment because she is also in respiratory distress, or is she not similarly situated because her respiratory distress is related to her anencephaly rather than to a condition that is more responsive to medical treatment? A major concern in these cases is whether scarce resources can be allocated. For a relevant discussion of this concern in the context of allocating organs for transplantation, see pages 403-420. For further discussion of the Americans with Disabilities Act, see Chapter 2.A.3.

The implications of *Baby K* for hospitals trying to limit health care costs are serious. Perhaps in recognition of that fact, the Fourth Circuit cabined the holding of *Baby K* two years later in Bryan v. Rectors and Visitors of the University of Virginia, 95 F.3d 349 (4th Cir. 1996) (discussed at pages 3-4). In *Bryan*, the court rejected the family's claim when physicians withheld resuscitative treatment from a hopelessly ill patient who died of a heart attack 20 days after her hospital admission.

2. *Literature on Futility.* While there are a relatively small number of court cases involving "futility," there is already an extensive literature on the topic of medical futility. Useful readings on the issue include Paul R. Helft et al., The Rise and Fall of the Futility Movement, 343 New Eng. J. Med. 293 (2000); Jerry Menikoff, Demanded Medical Care, 30 Ariz. St. L.J. 1091 (1998); Leslie Blackhall, Must We Always Use CPR?, 317 New Eng. J. Med. 1281 (1987); Allen S. Brett & Laurence B. McCullough, When Patients Request Specific Interventions: Defining the Limits of the Physician's Obligation, 315 New Eng. J. Med. 1347 (1986); Council on Ethical and Judicial Affairs, Guidelines for the Appropriate Use of Do-Not-Resuscitate Orders, 265 JAMA 1868 (1991); David Orentlicher, Matters of Life and Death, 123-166 (2002); Tom Tomlinson & Howard Brody, Futility and

the Ethics of Resuscitation, 264 JAMA 1276 (1990); Robert D. Truog et al., The Problem with Futility, 326 New Eng. J. Med. 1560 (1992).

Other useful articles include contributions to a Symposium on Medical Futility, 25 Seton Hall L. Rev. 873-1026 (1995); Mary A. Crossley, Medical Futility and Disability Discrimination, 81 Iowa L. Rev. 179 (1995); Philip G. Peters, Jr., When Physicians Balk at Futile Care: Implications of the Disability Rights Laws, 91 Nw. U. L. Rev. 798 (1997); and Lance K. Stell, Stopping Treatment on Grounds of Futility: A Role for Institutional Policy, 11 St. Louis U. Pub. L. Rev. 481 (1992).

3. *Defining Futility.* Futility is generally analyzed under two rubrics: qualitative and quantitative futility. Under qualitative futility, the claim is that medical treatment cannot provide a sufficient benefit to justify its use. Some commentators argue that there is qualitative futility when the patient would not recover enough to go home from the hospital, some find qualitative futility when the patient is permanently unconsciousness, and others believe there is futility only when treatment cannot provide a physiological benefit. In this third view, treatment is not futile as long as it can prolong life or affect the quality of life in any way.

Under quantitative futility, the claim is that there is too low a likelihood that medical treatment will have its desired effect. Here, too, there is disagreement as to when futility exists. Some would find futility when a particular treatment has been consistently unsuccessful for at least 100 tries. Lawrence J. Schneiderman, Nancy S. Jecker & Albert R. Jonsen, Medical Futility: Its Meaning and Ethical Implications, 112 Ann. Intern. Med. 949 (1990). Others would place it at different likelihoods of success. In one study, researchers discussed with internal medicine residents the reasons why the residents wrote do-not-resuscitate (DNR) orders for their patients. In two-thirds of the cases in which quantitative futility was a contributing factor to the DNR order, the likelihood that the patient would be resuscitated and be able to go home from the hospital was 1 percent or less. In 9 percent of cases, on the other hand, the likelihood of success was 20 percent or more. J. Randall Curtis et al., Use of the Medical Futility Rationale in Do-Not-Attempt-Resuscitation Orders, 273 JAMA 124, 126-127 (1995). Of course, one's view about quantitative futility depends on the qualitative benefit to be gained. The greater the potential qualitative benefit, the lower the likelihood of benefit before a treatment would be considered futile.

4. *Comparison with* Quinlan. In 1991, doctors at Hennepin County Medical Center unsuccessfully invoked futility to discontinue a ventilator from a patient in a persistent vegetative state. In re Wanglie, No. PX-91-283 (Hennepin County Prob. Ct. Minn. July 1, 1991), discussed in Steven H. Miles, Informed Demand for "Non-beneficial" Medical Treatment, 325 New Eng. J. Med. 512 (1991).

The *Wanglie* case is exactly the reverse of the *Quinlan* case. Both cases involved a patient who was permanently unconscious and thought to be ventilator dependent. In *Quinlan*, the family was in court trying to have the ventilator stopped. In *Wanglie*, the family was in court trying to have the ventilator continued. If ventilator treatment for Mrs. Wanglie was futile, how could it not have been futile for Ms. Quinlan? Why do you suppose the hospital in *Wanglie* asked the court to appoint a conservator for Mrs. Wanglie rather than simply to authorize discontinuation of her ventilator?

5. *Other Futility Cases*. In futility cases, courts so far have split between siding with the patient or the patient's family and siding with the physicians and hospital.

For cases rejecting futility, in addition to *Baby K* and *Wanglie*, there is In re Jane Doe, 418 S.E.2d 3 (Ga. 1992). In that case, an adolescent suffered from a severe and degenerative neurological disease that left her comatose or nearly comatose. Jane Doe's physicians and hospital wanted to deescalate life support and enter a DNR order, and her parents split on the issue. Although the case was brought at least in part as a futility case, the positions of the parties changed during the judicial proceedings such that the Georgia Supreme Court ended up deciding the case on the issue of resolving parental disagreements over CPR. The court held that a DNR order could not be written without the consent of both parents.

In another unreported case, In re Ryan N. Nguyen, #94206074-5 (Wash. Super. Ct., Spokane County, Nov. 22, 1994), the futility argument also was rejected. Ryan Nguyen was born six weeks early and was diagnosed with severe brain damage, an intestinal blockage, and malfunctioning kidneys. The hospital where he was being treated could not provide the necessary dialysis, and two academic medical centers refused to accept a referral, in at least one case on the ground that the child had such a dismal prognosis. The family obtained a court order for treatment, and the publicity resulted in a hospital offering to provide care. Ultimately, Ryan's intestinal blockage was cleared, his kidney problems resolved, and it turned out that he had not suffered any irreversible brain injury. Alexander Morgan Capron, Baby Ryan and Virtual Futility, 25(2) Hastings Center Rep. 20 (1995).

For a case accepting futility in addition to *Bryan* and *Causey*, consider the *Gilgunn* case. Gilgunn v. Massachusetts General Hospital, No. 92-4820 (Mass. Super. Ct. Suffolk Cty., April 22, 1995). In that case, Catherine Gilgunn became comatose and terminally ill at age 71, and her physicians decided to write a do-not-resuscitate order and discontinue her ventilator over the objections of one of her children. Alexander Morgan Capron, Abandoning a Waning Life, 25(4) Hastings Center Rep. 24 (1995). After Mrs. Gilgunn died, her daughter sued the hospital and physician, and the jury decided in favor of the defendants. This case, however, may not tell us very much about the law on futility since the verdict was not appealed, and the jury may have sided with the hospital and physicians on any of several theories. Capron, supra, at 25-26.

Nearly a decade after the *Gilgunn* case, Massachusetts General Hospital sought judicial permission to discontinue aggressive treatment of a patient severely disabled by ALS (Lou Gehrig's disease), over the objections of the patient's daughter. For the most part in this case, the hospital did not succeed with its futility argument. The trial court upheld the patient's appointment of her daughter as health care proxy and also ordered the writing of a do-not-resuscitate order (which by the time of the decision had been agreed to by the daughter) on the grounds that CPR would be both "inappropriate and harmful." The court also instructed the daughter to make future medical decisions based on the daughter's assessment of the patient's best interests. The court felt that the patient's condition had deteriorated in ways unanticipated by the patient and that the patient's wishes were no longer ascertainable. (In the appointment, the patient directed her daughter to decide on the basis of her wishes unless her wishes were unknown, in which case her daughter was supposed to decide on the basis of an assessment of best interests.) In re Barbara Howe, No. 03 P 1255 (Mass. Prob. & Fam. Ct., Suffolk Div., March 22, 2004). A year later, the daughter and hospital were back in court and settled the dispute with an agreement that the hospital would maintain ventilator support for three more months and then be free to discontinue treatment. Ms. Howe died 26 days before the expiration of the three month period. John J. Paris et al., *Howe v. MGH* and *Hudson v. Texas Children's Hospital*: Two Approaches to Resolving Family-Physician Disputes in End-of-Life Care, 26 J. Perinatology 726 (2006).

6. *Futility Statutes.* As in Louisiana, some states have addressed futility by statute. See Cal. Prob. Code §§4735-4736 (modifying Section 7(f) of the Uniform Health Care Decisions Act (1993)); Md. Code Ann., Health—General §5-611; Tex. Health & Safety Code Ann. §166.046; Va. Code Ann. §54.1-2990.

The Texas statute is notable for the procedures it sets out to invoke futility. In Texas, a physician's refusal to honor a request for treatment requires review by an ethics or medical committee, and the patient or surrogate decisionmaker is entitled to attend the committee's meeting and receive a written explanation for the committee's decision. If the patient or family disagrees with a committee's decision affirming the refusal, the physician must make a reasonable effort to transfer the patient to a physician who will provide the desired treatment. Although treatment must be provided pending transfer, there is no obligation to provide treatment beyond the 10th day after a committee decision in favor of refusing treatment.

While some view the Texas approach as a model, Paris et al., *Howe v. MGH*, supra, it has provoked considerable controversy in some cases when doctors and hospitals have invoked it, and family members have been able to delay the withdrawal of treatment through court challenges. The Texas Senate passed legislation in 2007 that would have amended the statute, but the bill died in the House. Michael Grabell, Boy at Center of Ethics Case Dies, Dallas Morning News (Central Edition), May 31, 2007, at 1B.

7. *Futility in Practice.* What do you make of the fact that the physicians in *Baby K* were willing to provide the child with nutrition and hydration but not a ventilator to ensure adequate oxygenation? If a ventilator is futile because the child is anencephalic, then why isn't a feeding tube futile? Conversely, if we say that Mrs. Wanglie is entitled to a ventilator because it could maintain her life, would we also say she is entitled to a heart valve replacement if one were needed to maintain her life?

Is there some difference between *Bryan, Causey,* and *Gilgunn,* on one hand, and many of the other cases presented (e.g., *Baby K, Howe, Jane Doe, Wanglie,* and *Ryan Nguyen*) that might explain why the two groups of cases came out differently?

8. *Additional Views.* Consider the following perspectives on futility:

   (a) "In the event that the patient or surrogate requests a treatment that the responsible health care professional regards as clearly futile in achieving its physiological objective and so offering no physiological benefit to the patient, the professional has no obligation to provide it. However, the health care professional's value judgment that although a treatment will produce physiological benefit, the benefit is not sufficient to warrant the treatment, should not be used as a basis for determining a treatment to be futile." Guidelines on the

Termination of Life-Sustaining Treatment and the Care of the Dying: A Report of the Hastings Center 32 (1987).

(b) "The argument that physician judgments about the futility of CPR are improper simply because they incorporate value judgments relies on a principle that has implausible implications for the rest of medical practice. . . . If the physician cannot refuse because, as a matter of principle, he or she is forbidden to employ 'value judgments,' then no justification can remain for refusal to provide a computed tomographic scan for the anxious patient with a headache, who also may have attached symbolic importance to the procedure, and no justification is available for resisting a family's demand that even 'physiologically futile' resuscitation efforts must continue indefinitely. . . . The real question can no longer be *whether* value judgments can be made concerning the provision of CPR or other medical techniques; rather, the question is *which* value judgments physicians may use in deciding whether to meet patients' demands." Tom Tomlinson & Howard Brody, Futility and the Ethics of Resuscitation, 264 JAMA 1276, 1277-1278 (1990)

(c) Claims that a particular treatment is "futile" are really claims that the treatment is too expensive at a time when health care resources are severely strained. Physicians prefer to characterize a treatment as futile rather than as too costly for the same reason that judges prefer to justify a decision on the ground that it is compelled by precedent rather than to acknowledge the indeterminacy in the law and concede that they are deciding on the basis of personal philosophy. By characterizing a treatment as medically futile and therefore of no purpose, physicians can hide the fact that they are rationing care, and thereby avoid patient challenges to their rationing decisions. It is much easier for a patient to challenge a rationing decision than a "medical" decision. Calling a treatment futile serves another purpose. It permits physicians to regain some of the authority they have lost since the mid-1960s when medical ethics and the law began to give greater recognition to patient autonomy. If a treatment decision is viewed as a medical decision rather than a value judgment, then physicians can colorably claim that the decision is exclusively for them to make.

Note: Brain Death

Although futility has been debated seriously as an issue only since the late 1980s, the development of the concept of brain death in the late 1960s and early 1970s can be seen as an early manifestation of the futility concern.

1. *Medical Background.* Traditionally, death was pronounced based on the cessation of the beating of the heart and the breathing of the lungs. In other words, death was determined on the basis of "cardiopulmonary" criteria. Typically at death, a person's heart stops functioning because of injury or illness. The person's lungs and brain also stop functioning because they are deprived of their blood flow. Since it is a much simpler matter to detect loss of heart and lung function than to detect loss of brain function, cardiopulmonary criteria for death were adopted. In some cases, injury or illness causes loss of brain function first, and without the regulation of the brain, the lungs also stop functioning (i.e., the

breathing of the lungs is controlled by the brain stem — the beating of the heart is also regulated by the brain stem, but the heart can pump an adequate amount of blood in the absence of brain stem function). When the lungs stop, the heart is deprived of oxygen, and it then ceases beating. Historically, loss of lung and heart function followed within minutes of the loss of brain function, and patients who had lost brain function satisfied cardiopulmonary criteria for death.

With advances in medical technology, however, it became possible to support a person's heart and lungs with mechanical ventilation even after cessation of brain function. According to cardiopulmonary criteria, these persons were not dead, but to many observers, they seemed to have lost their vitality. Patients who have lost all brain function appear to be in a very deep coma. (Interestingly, spontaneous movements are more common in brain-dead patients than once thought. In a study, researchers found that 39 percent of their brain-dead patients exhibited spontaneous movements of their fingers, toes, and arms. These movements are believed to reflect spinal cord reflexes, and, in fact, no brain activity was seen on EEGs during the movements. Gustavo Saposnik et al., Spontaneous and Reflex Movements in Brain Death, 54 Neurology 221 (2000).) Mechanical measures and other artificial support can maintain brain-dead patients' heartbeat and breathing temporarily, but usually only for a few weeks or months, after cessation of brain function. But see D. Alan Shewmon, Chronic "Brain Death": Meta-analysis and Conceptual Consequences, 51 Neurology 1538 (1998) (describing the maintenance of a heartbeat in brain-dead patients for more than a year, including one patient for more than fourteen years). Because of the profound loss of functioning, the permanence of the condition, and the inability to prolong the state for very long, many observers questioned whether it made sense to provide treatment to these patients.

Ordinarily, such questioning might lead to a right to have medical treatment withdrawn when a person's brain stops functioning, just as Karen Quinlan's persistent vegetative state led the New Jersey Supreme Court to recognize her right to have her ventilator withdrawn. Instead, "brain" criteria for death were developed. In a report that was highly influential in leading to the acceptance of "brain death," the authors wrote:

> Our primary purpose is to define irreversible coma as a new criterion for death. There are two reasons why there is need for a definition: (1) Improvements in resuscitative and supportive measures have led to increased efforts to save those who are desperately injured. Sometimes these efforts have only partial success so that the result is an individual whose heart continues to beat but whose brain is irreversibly damaged. The burden is great on patients who suffer permanent loss of intellect, on their families, on the hospitals, and on those in need of hospital beds already occupied by these comatose patients. (2) Obsolete criteria for the definition of death can lead to controversy in obtaining organs for transplantation. Report of the Ad Hoc Committee of the Harvard Medical School to Examine the Definition of Brain Death, A Definition of Irreversible Coma, 205 JAMA 85, 85 (1968).

As this excerpt suggests, the adoption of brain criteria for death may have been motivated primarily by futility-type concerns — the high burdens and low benefits of treatment—as well as by concerns about the shortage of organs for transplantation. Philosophical considerations about the meaning of life seemingly played little role in the change.

In the next chapter, we take up the issues of organ transplantation related to brain death. Here, we consider the implications for patient autonomy of brain criteria for death. By defining patients as dead when they lose brain function, it would seem to follow that one could not choose for oneself or one's family member to have mechanical ventilation continued after cessation of brain function. That implication has been confirmed by the law.

2. *Adoption of Brain Criteria for Death.* Kansas was the first state to adopt a brain death statute, and its constitutionality was upheld in State v. Schaffer, 574 P.2d 205 (1977). It did so in the context of a murder prosecution, where the defendant had argued that the doctors who removed life support, and not himself, caused the death of the victim. A later case adopting the brain death definition as a matter of common law provides a particularly thorough explanation of the relationship between the definition of death and homicide statutes. People v. Eulo, 472 N.E.2d 286 (N.Y. 1984). Death by brain criteria is accepted in every state as well as the District of Columbia. Alan Meisel & Kathy L. Cerminara, The Right to Die §6.04[A] (3d ed. 2007 Supp.). The Uniform Determination of Death Act has been enacted by statute in a majority of states. Several states, like Washington, have adopted brain death by court decision, and the remainder of the states have enacted brain death legislation without relying on the uniform law.

In re Bowman, 617 P.2d 731 (Wash. 1980) (en banc), provides a good discussion of the principles undergirding brain death. According to the court,

> Death is both a legal and medical question. Traditionally, the law has regarded the question of at what moment a person died as a question of fact to be determined by expert medical testimony. However, recognizing that the law has independent interests in defining death which may be lost when deference to medicine is complete, courts have established standards which, although based on medical knowledge, define death as a matter of law. Thus, the law has adopted standards of death but has turned to physicians for the criteria by which a particular standard is met. [Id. at 734.]

3. *The Meaning of Adopting Brain Criteria for Death.* It is not clear what the significance has been of changing the definition of death to include cessation of brain function. We could characterize the change as substituting brain death for cardiopulmonary death. Under this view, the essence of personhood is found in the functioning of the mind rather than the body, so that death occurs when the brain stops functioning. We can identify brain death either directly, by showing the absence of brain function, or indirectly, by showing the absence of cardiac function (i.e., once the heart stops pumping blood to the brain, the brain cells die). According to another view, life requires the presence of both brain and cardiopulmonary function. Once one of the two functions is lost, the person is dead.

A third view, and the one given by most commentators to explain the development of neurological criteria for death, is that death has always meant loss of the body's integrative capacity. Under this view, death occurs when the body loses its ability to function as an integrated whole rather than as a collection of independently functioning cells or tissues. President's Commission for the Study of Ethical Problems in Medicine and Biomedical and Behavioral Research, Defining Death: A Report on the Medical, Legal, and Ethical Issues in the Determination of Death 32-38 (1981); Alexander M. Capron & Leon Kass, A Statutory Definition of the Standards for Determining Human Death: An Appraisal and a Proposal, 121 U. Pa. L. Rev. 87, 102 (1972). After all, a person's cells can be maintained indefinitely in the laboratory, but we would not therefore say that the person is still alive. The body retains some ability to integrate bodily functions as long as there is some brain function, but once the brain ceases all function, the body has lost its integrative capacity. Again, we can measure loss of integrative function either directly, by establishing loss of brain function, or indirectly, by establishing loss of cardiopulmonary function. According to this view, we always thought of death as the loss of integrative capacity, but, until recently, we were able to determine its existence only when the heart stopped beating. Once we were able to support cardiopulmonary function artificially even after loss of brain function, we were able to have different ways to measure death. Under the integrative capacity view, the definition of death did not change; rather, we have only changed the criteria for ascertaining death.

4. *Loss of Integrative Capacity.* While the President's Commission and others accept integrative capacity as the basis for life, there are serious problems with this theory. First, it turns out that people who are dead according to neurological criteria still maintain some integrative capacity. For example, their brains still regulate water retention by the kidneys to ensure the appropriate balance among water, blood cells, and other components of blood in the body's bloodstream. In addition, many patients who are dead by brain criteria have some electrical activity on their electroencephalograms (EEGs), and they "frequently respond to surgical incision at the time of organ procurement with a significant rise in both heart rate and blood pressure." Robert D. Truog, Is It Time to Abandon Brain Death?, 27(1) Hastings Center Rep. 29, 29-30 (1997). Proponents of the integrative capacity theory respond that death occurs when there is loss of all critical or essential bodily functions, James L. Bernat, Brain Death: Occurs Only With Destruction of the Cerebral Hemispheres and the Brain Stem, 49 Arch. Neurol. 569, 569 (1992), but that begs the question of what bodily functions are critical.

A second problem with the integrative capacity theory is that it does not seem to explain how people think about death. The fact that we still use the term "brain death" and speak of keeping "brain-dead" patients on "life support" suggests that people think of death by neurological criteria differently than death by cardiopulmonary criteria. Indeed, in one study, physicians and nurses likely to be involved in organ procurement for transplantation were asked to explain why they thought a person was dead when the brain stopped functioning. While 25 percent of the physicians and nurses gave loss of integrative capacity as their reason, 36 percent spoke in terms of loss of consciousness and 32 percent indicated that they really did not believe the patient was dead, explaining that the patient would die soon no matter what was done or that the patient's quality of life was unacceptable. Stuart J. Youngner, Defining Death: A Superficial and Fragile Consensus, 49 Arch. Neurol. 570, 571 (1992). See also Richard Willing,

Brain-Dead Woman Dies After Baby Born, USA Today, Aug. 4, 2005, at 3A (marking woman's death when ventilator was discontinued nearly three months after declaration of death by brain criteria).

5. *Choosing a Definition of Death.* How should we define death? How do we choose among cardiopulmonary death, brain death, and upper brain death (i.e., loss of consciousness)? What is the moral, philosophical, or legal principle that helps us decide what it means to be dead? If the issue is whether the person has the essential characteristics of a human being, why not require only permanent loss of consciousness before declaring someone dead? Is it because unconscious persons do things that make them appear to be conscious (e.g., random or reflexive movements of the eyes, arms, or legs)? Or is it that we cannot be sure they are really unconscious and therefore those things that look like conscious activity may really reflect conscious activity? For useful readings on these issues, see Alexander Morgan Capron, Brain Death — Well Settled Yet Still Unresolved, 344 New Eng. J. Med. 1244 (2001); Michael B. Green & Daniel Wikler, Brain Death and Personal Identity, 9 Phil. Pub. Aff. 105 (1980); President's Commission for the Study of Ethical Problems in Medicine and Biomedical and Behavioral Research, Defining Death (1981); Tom Stacy, Death, Privacy, and the Free Exercise of Religion, 77 Cornell L. Rev. 490 (1992); Robert M. Veatch, The Whole-Brain-Oriented Concept of Death. An Outmoded Philosophical Formulation, 3 J. Thanatology 13 (1975); Stuart J. Youngner et al., eds., The Definition of Death: Contemporary Controversies (1999).

6. *Lack of Patient or Family Choice.* When a person has been declared dead, that person's legal representative (in this case the guardian ad litem) cannot insist that the patient be maintained on a ventilator. Indeed, in In re Bowman, the court automatically assumed that the declaration of death by brain criteria foreclosed a choice of continued treatment. 617 P.2d at 420-421. Although *Bowman* involved child abuse and a guardian ad litem, the same result has been reached when foul play was not involved and the parents had religious reasons for wanting to continue ventilation of their child. In re Long Island Jewish Medical Center, 641 N.Y.S.2d 989 (N.Y. Sup. Ct. 1996).

Does it necessarily follow from the fact that a person is dead that we do not respect the person's or the family's wishes for ventilation to be continued until the heart stops beating? We can point to public health concerns to explain why a person must be buried or cremated after cardiopulmonary death, but what is the justification for insisting that a ventilator be discontinued after brain death? Would it matter if the person could pay for the costs of the continued treatment, through either an insurance policy or personal wealth?

7. *Single or Multiple Definitions.* Must we have a standard definition of death to which everyone subscribes? In New Jersey, under the determination of death statute, people are dead when either their heart and lungs or their brain stop functioning. However,

> [t]he death of an individual shall not be declared upon the basis of neurological criteria . . . when the licensed physician authorized to declare death, has reason to believe, on the basis of information in the individual's available medical records, or information provided by a member of the individual's family or any other person knowledgeable about the individual's personal religious beliefs that such a

declaration would violate the personal religious beliefs of the individual. In these cases, death shall be declared, and the time of death fixed, solely upon the basis of cardio-respiratory criteria. . . . [N.J. Stat. Ann. 26:6A-5.]

In New York, a New York State Department of Health Regulation provides that hospitals shall establish "a procedure for the reasonable accommodation of the individual's religious or moral objection to the determination" of death by neurological criteria. N.Y. Comp. Codes R. & Regs. tit. 10, §400.16(e)(3). New York physicians and hospitals vary in the extent to which they will continue treatment of a brain-dead person under that provision, but the regulation's requirement of reasonable accommodation does not mandate the continuation of treatment beyond the time necessary for the family to obtain an independent medical opinion and try to arrange for transfer of the patient to another facility. *Long Island Jewish*, 641 N.Y.S.2d at 992.

Could we permit all persons to decide when they are dead, as long as their definition of death falls within a reasonable range, say as long as the definition is permanent unconsciousness, brain death, or cardiac death? Would this be any different from the current status of abortion law, which essentially allows women to decide when their fetus becomes a person, as long as the woman chooses some point between conception and viability? For an argument that the free exercise clause of the First Amendment gives patients and their families a right to determine when death occurs, see Stacy, supra page 352.

We might also want to have different definitions of death depending on the reasons for wanting to know whether the patient is still alive. In this regard, see Roger Dworkin, Death in Context, 48 Ind. L.J. 623 (1975). Dworkin argues that "the effort devoted to defining death is wasted at best, counterproductive at worst," because of the variety of contexts in which the issue is relevant, namely: (1) procedural issues such as when the statutes of limitations begin to run for wrongful death actions and murder prosecutions; (2) numerous property and wealth devolution issues such as who died first for purposes of probating the wills of two people with interests in each others' estates; and (3) status relationships such as when remarriage is valid. Consider, for instance, that one accepted departure from the uniform definition of death is the presumption in many states that a person is dead who is missing for more than seven years.

8. *Criteria for Brain Death*. Guidelines for determining brain death have been published by medical specialty societies. Guidelines and discussion of brain death in adults can be found at Eelco F. M. Wijdicks, The Diagnosis of Brain Death, 344 New Eng. J. Med. 1215 (2001); Report of the Quality Standards Subcommittee of the American Academy of Neurology, Practice Parameters for Determining Brain Death in Adults, 45 Neurology 1012 (1995); Eelco F. M. Wijdicks, Determining Brain Death in Adults, 45 Neurology 1003 (1995). Guidelines and discussion of brain death in children can be found at American Academy of Pediatrics, Report of Special Task Force: Guidelines for the Determination of Brain Death in Children, 80 Pediatrics 298 (1987); Joan Lynch & Maher K. Eldadah, Brain-Death Criteria Currently Used by Pediatric Intensivists, 31 Clin. Pediat. 457 (1992). See also Eelco F. M. Wijdicks, ed., Brain Death (2001).

Perhaps in part because of disagreement over the validity of the guidelines for determining brain death in children, one study demonstrated considerable deviation from the guidelines by pediatric intensive care specialists. Rodrigo E. Mejia & Murray M. Pollack, Variability in Brain Death Determination Practices in Children, 274 JAMA 550 (1995). Similarly, the guidelines for determining brain death in adults were issued in part because of variation in practice among neurologists diagnosing death by brain criteria. Wijdicks, supra, 45 Neurology at 1003. See also Stuart J. Youngner et al., "Brain Death" and Organ Retrieval: A Cross-Sectional Survey of Knowledge and Concepts Among Health Professionals, 261 JAMA 2205 (1989) (finding in a survey of 39 medical personnel responsible for identifying brain-dead patients that one-third were unable to identify the correct legal and medical criteria for death and apply them to two simple cases).

4

■

Organ Transplantation: The Control, Use, and Allocation of Body Parts

This chapter explores another dimension of personal control over medical decisions: the supply and distribution of lifesaving organs for transplantation. Because of the serious shortage of transplantable organs, this is a topic that sparks much debate: Can financial payments to organ donors be used to increase the supply of organs? Can organs or other tissues be taken without permission? When organs are in short supply and lives of those who need them are at stake, who gets them first and who decides? These questions range broadly among issues and themes that are addressed elsewhere in this book, but they are more compelling here because the stakes are so clearly life-and-death, and because the use of body parts is so infused with moral and emotional value.

We start by focusing on who controls the decision for organ donation. We have seen that patients may refuse unwanted offers of medical treatment even if doing so results in death. Courts have concluded that the state has a weaker interest than the patient in deciding how to balance concerns about bodily integrity with concerns about the preservation of the patient's own life. What if, on the other hand, there are other lives at stake? Does the state have a greater interest than the patient in making medical decisions when the issue is balancing the individual's concerns with the needs of other persons? That question extends beyond this chapter since an individual's medical decisions can implicate the interests of other persons in a number of ways. In Chapter 3, we considered situations in which a person's death would leave minor children without one of their parents. In Chapters 5 and 6, we consider situations in which a fetus' health is at stake or in which a person's illness poses a public health threat to other persons.

In this chapter, the question is how the balance of affected interests is struck with respect to bodily organs and other tissues. The state may perceive an interest in overriding a person's desire to maintain bodily integrity after death by taking kidneys or other tissues from cadavers for persons who have a greater need for the tissues. Or the state may perceive an interest in protecting individuals from unwise decisions to give up their organs while they are still alive. In some cases, then, the question is whether the state can require a transfer of tissue (e.g., remove corneas from cadavers for transplantation); in other cases, the question is whether the state can make it harder for people to give up their tissues (e.g., prohibit sales of kidneys). Should the balance be struck by individuals since it is their body, or by the state since it has a longer and broader range view of both individual and collective interests, or should there be a division of responsibility? As we will see, much of the law in this area has developed in response to the shortage of organs for transplantation, so before we begin, it is helpful to understand more about the need for organ donation and the existing sources of supply.

Good background readings include Michelle Goodwin, Black Markets: The Supply and Demand of Body Parts (2006); Organ Substitution Technology: Ethical, Legal, and Public Policy Issues (Deborah Matheiu ed., 1988); The Ethics of Organ Transplantation (Wayne Shelton & John Balint eds., 2001); Organ Donation: Legal, Ethical, and Policy Issues (Bethany Spielman ed., 1996); Robert M. Veatch, Transplantation Ethics (2000); Organ Transplantation: Meanings and Realities (Stuart J. Youngner, Renée C. Fox & Laurence J. O'Connell eds., 1996).

Note: The Shortage of Organs for Transplantation

The shortage of organs for transplantation is substantial. In June 2007, there were more than 103,000 registrations, and more than 96,000 people on waiting lists for transplantation of a kidney, liver, heart, lung, intestine, or pancreas. (The number of registrations exceeds the number of people waiting since individuals may register on the waiting lists of more than one transplant center.) Moreover, more than 6,000 people die each year waiting for an organ to become available, and more than 1,500 people are removed from the waiting list because they become too sick to receive a transplant. Even these statistics understate the problem. Given the serious shortage of organs for transplantation, many individuals never make it onto a waiting list since it is clear that they will not have sufficient priority to receive a transplant. (Current and historical data on organ transplantation can be found on the Internet at www.unos.org, the Web site of the United Network for Organ Sharing (UNOS)).

The gap between need and supply reflects a number of considerations. First, in a substantial percentage of cases in which a person dies and the person's organs could be transplanted, there is no transplantation. Physicians may neglect to ask for permission, or family members may refuse to donate the decedent's organs. Physicians are often uncomfortable raising the issue of transplantation, fearing that it will only aggravate the family's grief. Families may deny permission for transplantation because they have religious or other objection to the removal of a body's organs after death. Deborah Matheiu, Introduction, *in* Organ Substitution Technology: Ethical, Legal, and Public Policy Issues 33, 34-35 (Deborah Matheiu ed., 1988). Efforts have been made to encourage the use of organ donor cards, but most people do not fill them out, sometimes because of fears that their physicians will hasten their death, sometimes because of unwillingness to consider their mortality, sometimes because of religious conviction or a desire for an intact body. But even when people do fill out organ donor cards and physicians know that they have done so, the cards may not ensure organ retrieval unless family consent can be obtained. Many physicians will not remove a deceased person's organs without family consent despite the fact that ethics and the law give priority to the decedent's previously expressed wishes. Indeed, according to the Revised Uniform Anatomical Gift Act, if a person does not revoke a decision to donate before dying, other persons are generally barred from amending or revoking the decedent's consent to donate. Rev. Unif. Anatomical Gift Act §8(a) (2006). This provision is designed to strengthen a similar provision in the previous Uniform Act, according to which a decedent's decision to donate is "irrevocable and does not require the consent or concurrence of any person after the donor's death." Unif. Anatomical Gift Act §2(h) (1987). Even before the 2006 revision a number of states enacted legislation to firmly indicate that the decedent's wishes control. See, e.g., Ind. Code §29-2-16-2.5. For further discussion, see James R. Rodrigue et al., Organ Donation Decision: Comparison of Donor and Nondonor Families, 6 Am. J. Transplant. 190 (2006); Laura A. Siminoff et al., Factors Influencing Families' Consent for Donation of Solid Organs for Transplantation, 286 JAMA 71 (2001); Dave Wendler & Neal Dickert, The Consent Process for Cadaveric Organ Procurement: How Does It Work? How Can It Be Improved?, 285 JAMA 329 (2001).

The gap between need and supply of organs also reflects the fact that, while the number of transplants each year has been increasing, the number of waiting list registrations has been growing twice as fast. The number of waiting list registrations rose from 16,000 to more than 101,000 between 1988 and 2006, but the number of transplants rose from about 13,000 to 29,000. This continually growing gap between candidates for transplant and available organs reflects several factors. The number of persons who die in a way that leaves their organs suitable for transplantation is being reduced by the enactment of laws requiring seat belts or motorcycle helmets, the use of air bags in automobiles, gun control legislation, and the stricter enforcement of laws that prohibit driving under the influence of alcohol. At the same time, progress in medicine is increasing the number of persons who could benefit from a transplant.

A. ORGAN DONATION

1. Competent Organ Donors

Traditionally, organ donation has been governed by state law. The National Organ Transplant Act of 1984 added a good deal of federal regulation. The Act created the Organ Procurement and Transportation Network as a private, nonprofit entity to determine standards for organ allocation and to establish a system for matching organ donors with recipients. 42 U.S.C. §274(b). The Act also imposed a ban on the sale of organs or other tissues used in transplantation. 42 U.S.C. §274e. However, the ban does not apply to blood, sperm, or ova.

When patients are alive, they are free to donate renewable tissues (e.g., blood and semen) and tissues that are not necessary to maintain health (e.g., ova). They may also sell these tissues (though there is controversy about the selling of ova). On the other hand, people may not donate or sell life-necessary organs (e.g., hearts). In between these two extremes are donations — but not sales — of organs or parts of organs where there may be a significant health risk to the donor. For example, a person might want to donate a kidney to a family member. Since people typically have two kidneys, the donor ordinarily would function reasonably well without the second kidney. As with any major surgery, however, there are some risks from the donation — the chance of dying is less than 0.1 percent. Jürgen Weitz et al., Living-Donor Kidney Transplantation: Risks of the Donor — Benefits of the Recipient, 20 (s17) Clin. Transplant. 13 (2006). In addition, if something happened to the remaining kidney, there would be no backup. The long-term consequences for a kidney donor are not definitively known, but they appear to be minimal. To date, studies of kidney donors have not found any long-term medical problems related to the donation. Dicken S. C. Ko & A. Benedict Cosimi, The Donor and Donor Nephrectomy, in Kidney Transplantation: Principles and Practice 89, 95 (Peter J. Morris ed., 5th ed. 2001). See also Aaron Spital & Tomoko Kokmen, Health Insurance for Kidney Donors: How Easy Is It to Obtain?, 62 Transplantation 1356 (1996) (finding in a survey of health insurers that "healthy kidney donors should be able to obtain and maintain health insurance at standard rates"); Aaron Spital & Cheryl Jacobs, Life Insurance for Kidney Donors: Another Update, 74 Transplantation 972 (2002) (finding in a survey of life insurers that healthy kidney donors are generally able to purchase life insurance at standard rates).

It may be that the absence of problems reflects in part a screening process for donation that selects individuals who are healthier than the average person. Also, even if kidney donation does not raise the risk of hypertension, kidney donors who develop hypertension for other reasons might be more vulnerable to kidney damage from the high blood pressure. Ingela Fehrman-Ekholm & Gilbert T. Thiel, Long-Term Risks After Kidney Donation, in Living Donor Kidney Transplantation 99, 106-107, 110 (Robert S. Gaston & Jonas Wadström eds. 2005).

Because of the risks to the donor — even if small — and concerns about donor motivation, donation of kidneys by living persons still provokes some controversy. When the donation occurs within the family, there are concerns about coercion; when the donation is extra-familial, there are concerns about hidden payments or psychological stability of the donor. Nevertheless, transplant centers generally welcome donation of kidneys within families. When there is no close relationship between the donor and recipient, however, transplant centers are decidedly less enthusiastic about donations from living persons. Megan Crowley-Matoka & Galen Switzer, Nondirected Living Donation: A Survey of Current Trends and Practices, 79 Transplantation 515 (2005). Still, such donations are becoming more common, and studies suggest that transplant centers can screen potential donors to ensure that their desire to donate does not reflect psychopathology. Martin D. Jendrisak et al., Altruistic Living Donors: Evaluation for Nondirected Kidney or Liver Donation, 6 Am. J. Transplant. 115 (2006); Paul

E. Morrissey et al., Good Samaritan Kidney Donation, 27 Transplantation 1369 (2005). See also M. A. Dew et al., Guidelines for the Psychosocial Evaluation of Living Unrelated Kidney Donors in the United States, 7 Am. J. Transplant. 1047 (2007).

Similar issues are raised with regard to donations of a partial liver, lung, or pancreas. In those cases, the concerns are accentuated since the risks to the donor are greater and the procedures are still being developed. Consequently, these transplants are largely limited to circumstances in which the donor has a close relationship to the recipient. For discussion of concerns regarding partial-liver transplants, see Mark W. Russo & Robert S. Brown, Jr., Adult Living Donor Liver Transplantation, 4 Am. J. Transplant. 458 (2004); David C. Cronin II et al., Transplantation of Liver Grafts from Living Donors into Adults — Too Much, Too Soon, 344 New Eng. J. Med. 1633 (2001); James F. Trotter et al., Adult-to-Adult Transplantation of the Right Hepatic Lobe from a Living Donor, 346 New Eng. J. Med. 1074 (2002). See also Kim M. Olthoff, Outcomes of 385 Adult-to-Adult Living Donor Liver Transplant: A Report from the A2ALL Consortium, 242 Annals Surgery 314 (2005) (concluding that partial-liver transplants offer a good option to patients with liver failure, but that complications from the procedure are a significant problem).

People may also agree while competent to have their organs (and other tissues) taken for transplantation after they die. These donations are governed by the relevant state's version of the Revised Uniform Anatomical Gift Act, 8A U.L.A. 1 (Supp. 2007), or the Uniform Anatomical Gift Act, 8A U.L.A. 3 or 69 (2003). Some version of the 1968 Act was adopted by every state and the District of Columbia within four years of the Act's issuance. By the time the 1987 Act was issued, some states had already adopted at least one of the new provisions, and by 1992, forty-six states and the District of Columbia had done so. Fred H. Cate, Human Organ Transplantation: The Role of Law, 20 Iowa J. Corp. L. 69, 71-74 (1994). The 2006 Revised Act quickly elicited interest. By June 2007, fourteen states had adopted the Act, and legislators in another fourteen states had introduced legislation based on the Act.

Under all versions of the Act, competent adults may make a gift of their organs, with the gift to take effect upon their deaths. The gift may be for education, research, transplantation, or other therapy. For individuals who have not made a gift and who have not expressed opposition to the use of their organs, family members may authorize the taking of their organs. The 1987 Act added a few new provisions: hospitals must ask adult patients whether they want to be organ donors after death (routine inquiry); hospitals must discuss with family members their authority to authorize the taking of organs from deceased patients (routine request); medical examiners may authorize the taking of organs after autopsy if they do not find any objection after reasonable efforts to ascertain the person's or family's wishes; and, as with federal law, sales are prohibited. There is also duplication of federal law with respect to routine requests. That step is required of hospitals as a condition of receiving Medicare and Medicaid reimbursement. 42 U.S.C. §1320b-8. The 2006 Revised Act eliminated the ability of medical examiners to authorize organ retrieval in the absence of consent, in light of case law questioning that authority (discussed in section B.1, infra). Rev. Unif. Anatomical Gift Act §23 (2006). It also expanded the list of persons who may consent to organ donation after a person's death to include adult grandchildren, adults who "exhibited special care and concern for the decedent," and health care agents. Id. at §9(a)

2. Incompetent Organ "Donors"

An important issue is whether the right of a competent person to donate organs survives incompetence. Is the issue analogous to whether the right to refuse life-sustaining treatment survives incompetence? We worry about abuse with organ transplantation — society might be too willing to take organs from incompetent persons to give the organs to competent persons — but is that concern any different than for withdrawal of treatment?

■ STRUNK v. STRUNK
445 S.W.2d 145 (Ky. Ct. App. 1969)

OSBORNE, Judge.

The specific question involved upon this appeal is: Does a court of equity have the power to permit a kidney to be removed from an incompetent ward of the state upon petition of his . . . mother, for the purpose of being transplanted into the body of his brother, who is dying of a fatal kidney disease? We are of the opinion it does.

The facts of the case are as follows: Arthur L. Strunk, 54 years of age, and Ava Strunk, 52 years of age, of Williamstown, Kentucky, are the parents of two sons. Tommy Strunk is 28 years of age, married, an employee of the Penn State Railroad and a part-time student at the University of Cincinnati. Tommy is now suffering from chronic glomerulus nephritis, a fatal kidney disease. He is now being kept alive by frequent treatment on an artificial kidney, a procedure which cannot be continued much longer.

Jerry Strunk is 27 years of age, incompetent, and through proper legal proceedings has been committed to the Frankfort State Hospital and School, which is a state institution maintained for the feebleminded. He has an I.Q. of approximately 35, which corresponds with the mental age of approximately six years. He is further handicapped by a speech defect, which makes it difficult for him to communicate with persons who are not well acquainted with him. When it was determined that Tommy, in order to survive, would have to have a kidney the doctors considered the possibility of using a kidney from a cadaver if and when one became available or one from a live donor if this could be made available. The entire family, his mother, father and a number of collateral relatives were tested. Because of incompatibility of blood type or tissue none were medically acceptable as live donors. As a last resort, Jerry was tested and found to be highly acceptable. . . . The mother . . . petitioned the county court for authority to proceed with the operation. The court found that the operation was necessary, that under the peculiar circumstances of this case it would not only be beneficial to Tommy but also beneficial to Jerry because Jerry was greatly dependent upon Tommy, emotionally and psychologically, and that his well-being would be jeopardized more severely by the loss of his brother than by the removal of a kidney. . . .

A psychiatrist, in attendance to Jerry, who testified in the case, stated in his opinion the death of Tommy under these circumstances would have "an extremely traumatic effect upon him" (Jerry).

The Department of Mental Health of this Commonwealth has entered the case as amicus curiae and on the basis of its evaluation of the seriousness of the operation as opposed to the traumatic effect upon Jerry as a result of the loss of Tommy, recommended to the court that Jerry be permitted to undergo the surgery. Its recommendations are as follows:

> . . . Jerry Strunk, a mental defective, has emotions and reactions on a scale comparable to that of normal person. He identifies with his brother Tom; Tom is his model, his tie with his family. Tom's life is vital to the continuity of Jerry's improvement at Frankfort State Hospital and School. The testimony of the hospital representative reflected the importance to Jerry of his visits with his family and the constant inquiries Jerry made about Tom's coming to see him. Jerry is aware he plays a role in the relief of this tension. We the Department of Mental Health must take all possible steps to prevent the occurrence of any guilt feelings Jerry would have if Tom were to die.
>
> The necessity of Tom's life to Jerry's treatment and eventual rehabilitation is clearer in view of the fact that Tom is his only living sibling and at the death of their parents, now in their fifties, Jerry will have no concerned, intimate communication so necessary to his stability and optimal functioning.
>
> The evidence shows that at the present level of medical knowledge, it is quite remote that Tom would be able to survive several cadaver transplants. Tom has a much better chance of survival if the kidney transplant from Jerry takes place.

Upon this appeal we are faced with the fact that all members of the immediate family have recommended the transplant. The Department of Mental Health has likewise made its recommendation. The county court has given its approval. The circuit court has found that it would be to the best interest of the ward of the state that the procedure be carried out. Throughout the legal proceedings, Jerry has been represented by a guardian ad litem, who has continually questioned the power of the state to authorize the removal of an organ from the body of any incompetent who is a ward of the state. . . .

The renal transplant is becoming the most common of the organ transplants. This is because the normal body has two functioning kidneys, one of which it can reasonably do without, thereby making it possible for one person to donate a kidney to another. Testimony in this record shows that there have been over 2,500 kidney transplants performed in the United States up to this date. The process can be effected under present techniques with minimal danger to both the donor and the donee. Doctors Hamburger and Crosneir describe the risk to the donor as follows:

> This discussion is limited to renal transplantation, since it is inconceivable that any vital organ other than the kidney might ever be removed from a healthy living donor for transplantation purposes. The immediate operative risk of unilateral nephrectomy in a healthy subject has been calculated as approximately 0.05 percent. The long-term risk is more difficult to estimate, since the various types of renal disease do not appear to be more frequent or more severe in

individuals with solitary kidneys than in normal subjects. On the other hand, the development of surgical problems, trauma, or neoplasms, with the possible necessity of nephrectomy, do increase the long-term risks in living donors; the long-term risk, on this basis, has been estimated at 0.07 percent. These data must, however, be considered in the light of statistical life expectancy which, in a healthy 35-year-old adult, goes from 99.3 percent to 99.1 percent during the next five succeeding years; this is an increase in risk equal to that incurred by driving a car for 16 miles every working day. The risks incurred by the donor are therefore very limited, but they are a reality, even if, until now, there have been no reports of complications endangering the life of a donor anywhere in the world. Unfortunately, there is no doubt that, as the number of renal transplants increases, such an incident will inevitably be recorded. Hamburger and Crosneir, Moral and Ethical Problems in Transplantation, *in* Human Transplantation 37 (Rapaport and Dausset ed. 1968). . . .

We are of the opinion that a chancery court does have sufficient inherent power to authorize the operation. The circuit court having found that the operative procedures in this instance are to the best interest of Jerry Strunk and this finding having been based upon substantial evidence, we are of the opinion the judgment should be affirmed. . . .

STEINFELD, Judge, dissenting.

Apparently because of my indelible recollection of a government which, to the everlasting shame of its citizens, embarked on a program of genocide and experimentation with human bodies I have been more troubled in reaching a decision in this case than in any other. My sympathies and emotions are torn between a compassion to aid an ailing young man and a duty to fully protect unfortunate members of society. . . .

The majority opinion is predicated upon the finding of the circuit court that there will be psychological benefits to the ward but points out that the incompetent has the mentality of a six-year-old child. It is common knowledge beyond dispute that the loss of a close relative or a friend to a six-year-old child is not of major impact. Opinions concerning psychological trauma are at best most nebulous. Furthermore, there are no guarantees that the transplant will become a surgical success, it being well known that body rejection of transplanted organs is frequent. The life of the incompetent is not in danger, but the surgical procedure advocated creates some peril. . . .

Unquestionably the attitudes and attempts of the . . . members of the family of the two young men whose critical problems now confront us are commendable, natural and beyond reproach. However, they refer us to nothing indicating that they are privileged to authorize the removal of one of the kidneys of the incompetent for the purpose of donation, and they cite no statutory or other authority vesting such right in the courts. The proof shows that less compatible donors are available and that the kidney of a cadaver could be used, although the odds of operational success are not as great in such case as they would be with the fully compatible donor brother.

I am unwilling to hold that the gates should be open to permit the removal of an organ from an incompetent for transplant, at least until such time as it is conclusively demonstrated that it will be of significant benefit to the incompetent. The evidence here does not rise to that pinnacle. To hold that . . . guardians or courts have such awesome power even in the persuasive case before us, could establish legal precedent, the dire result of which we cannot fathom. Regretfully I must say no.

◼ IN RE PESCINSKI
226 N.W.2d 180 (Wis. 1975)

WILKIE, Chief Justice.

Does a county court have the power to order an operation to be performed to remove a kidney of an incompetent ward, under guardianship of the person, and transfer it to a sister where the dire need of the transfer is established but where no consent has been given by the incompetent or his guardian ad litem, nor has any benefit to the ward been shown?

That is the issue presented on appeal here. The trial court held that it did not have that power and we agree. The appellant, Janice Pescinski Lausier, on her own petition, was appointed guardian of the person of her brother, the respondent, Richard Pescinski. In 1958, Richard was declared incompetent and was committed to Winnebago State Hospital. He has been a committed mental patient since that date, classified as a schizophrenic, chronic, catatonic type.

On January 31, 1974, Janice Pescinski Lausier petitioned for permission to Dr. H. M. Kauffman to conduct tests to determine whether Richard Pescinski was a suitable donor for a kidney transplant for the benefit of his sister, Elaine Jeske. Elaine had both kidneys surgically removed in 1970, because she was suffering from kidney failure diagnosed as chronic glomerulonephritis. In order to sustain her life, she was put on a dialysis machine, which functions as an artificial kidney. Because of the deterioration of Elaine, the petition contended that a kidney transplant was needed. Subsequent tests were completed establishing that Richard was a suitable donor, and a hearing was then held on the subject of whether permission should be granted to perform the transplant. The guardian ad litem would not give consent to the transplant and the county court held that it did not have the power to give consent for the operation.

At the time of the hearing Elaine was 38 and her brother Richard was 39. Evidence was produced at the hearing that the other members of the Pescinski family had been ruled out as possible donors on the basis of either age or health. The father, aged 70, and the mother, aged 67, were eliminated as possible donors by Dr. Kauffman because, as a matter of principle, he would not perform the operation on a donor over 60. A similar rationale was applied by Dr. Kauffman as to all of the six minor children of Elaine, the doctor concluding that he "would not personally use their kidneys" as a matter of his "own moral conviction." Mrs. Jeske's sister, Mrs. Lausier, was excluded as a donor because she has diabetes. Another brother, Ralph Pescinski, testified that he was 43 years old, had been married 20 years and had 10 children, 9 of whom remained at home. He is a dairy farmer and did not care to be a donor because there would be nobody to take over his farm and he felt he had a duty to his family to refuse. He further testified that he had a stomach disorder which required a special diet and had a rupture on his left side. He had been to see Dr. Capati at the Neillsville Clinic, who told him he should not get involved and that his family should come first.

The testimony showed that Richard was suffering from schizophrenia—catatonic type, and that while he was in contact with his environment there was marked indifference in his behavior. Dr. Hoffman, the medical director at the Good Samaritan Home, West Bend, Wisconsin, testified that in layman's terms Richard's mental disease was a flight from reality. He estimated Richard's mental capacity to be age 12. No evidence in the record indicates that Richard consented to the transplant. Absent that consent, there is no question that the trial court's conclusion that it had no power to approve the operation must be sustained.

"A guardian of the person has the care of the ward's person and must look to the latter's health, education, and support." 39 Am. Jur. 2d, Guardian and Ward, p.60, §68. The guardian must act, if at all, "loyally in the best interests of his ward." Guardianship of Nelson, 123 N.W.2d 505, 509 (Wis. 1963). There is absolutely no evidence here that any interests of the ward will be served by the transplant.

. . . We decline to adopt the concept of "substituted judgment" which was specifically approved by the Kentucky Court of Appeals in Strunk v. Strunk. . . .

As the dissenting opinion in Strunk v. Strunk points out, "substituted judgment" is nothing more than an application of the maxim that equity will speak for one who cannot speak for himself. Historically, the substituted judgment doctrine was used to allow gifts of the property of an incompetent. If applied literally, it would allow a trial court, or this court, to change the designation on a life insurance policy or make an election for an incompetent widow, without the requirement of a statute authorizing these acts and contrary to prior decisions of this court.

We conclude that the doctrine should not be adopted in this state.

We, therefore, must affirm the lower court's decision that it was without power to approve the operation, and we further decide that there is no such power in this court. An incompetent particularly should have his own interests protected. Certainly no advantage should be taken of him. In the absence of real consent on his part, and in a situation where no benefit to him has been established, we fail to find any authority for the county court, or this court, to approve this operation. . . .

DAY, Justice, dissenting. . . .

. . . The guardian ad litem for the incompetent in this case has interposed strong objection to the transplant from Richard Pescinski to his sister, who . . . has now deteriorated to the point of confinement in a wheelchair. We were advised that without a kidney transplant death for her is quite imminent. The brother, on the other hand, the incompetent, is in good health. The medical testimony is that the removal of one of his kidneys would be of minimal risk to him and that he would function normally on one kidney for the rest of his natural life, as do thousands of others in similar circumstances. . . . To avoid the concerns expressed by the guardian ad litem, there are certain definite standards which could and should be imposed. First of all, a strong showing should be made that without the kidney transplant the proposed donee or recipient stands to suffer death. This is certainly the evidence here. Secondly, that reasonable steps have been taken to try and acquire a kidney from other sources and the record is clear that such attempt was made here. Because of the fact that the donee has had six children, she has built up certain chemical resistance to the receipt of foreign tissue into her body which can be overcome only by a transplant from one close to her by blood such as a brother or sister. The testimony showed the impracticality of acquiring a kidney from either her other brother or her sister. No suitable kidney from a cadaver has been found since her kidneys were removed in 1970. The next showing that should be made is that the incompetent proposed donor is closely related by blood to the proposed donee, such as a brother or sister, which of course is the case here. Showing should be made that the donor, if competent, would most probably consent because of the normal ties of family. Here, the trial court specifically found ". . . the conclusion would appear to be inescapable that the ward [the incompetent proposed donor] would so consent and that such authorization should be granted." Another showing should be that the proposed incompetent donor is in good health and that was shown here. And lastly, that the operation is one of minimal risk to the donor and that the donor could function normally on one kidney following such operation. The medical testimony is all to the effect that the donor would undergo minimal risk and would be able to function normally on one kidney. In fact, the testimony is that a person can function on as little as one tenth of one normal kidney.

With these guidelines the fear expressed that institutions for the mentally ill will merely become storehouses for spare parts for people on the outside is completely unjustified. I agree with the trial court that if the brother here were competent in all probability he would be willing to consent to the transplant to save his sister's life. For him it would be a short period of discomfort which would not affect his ability either to enjoy life or his longevity. . . .

Notes: The Incompetent Organ Donor

1. *The Appropriate Legal Standard*. Which decision do you prefer, *Strunk* or *Pescinski*? Consider the following perspective:

> Despite widespread acceptance in the United States, few other nations allow routine use of minors or mentally incompetent persons as organ donors. Judicial decisions of United States courts seem to be without parallel in any other country. . . . By legislation, Mexico and British Columbia prohibit organ donation by minors and incompetent persons. Restrictions on such donations have been enacted by France and Australia. The Council of Europe has recommended that organ donation from wards be forbidden except when the donor, having capacity of understanding, has given consent. . . . Rodney K. Adams, Live Organ Donors and Informed Consent: A Difficult Minuet, 8 J. Leg. Med. 555, 572 (1987).

(The Council of Europe does condone removal of regenerative tissue like bone marrow from persons lacking capacity to consent in limited circumstances (e.g., the recipient must be a sibling of the donor). Council of Europe, Additional Protocol to the Convention on Human Rights and Biomedicine, on Transplantation of Organs and Tissues of Human Origin (January 24, 2002).) For cases in agreement with *Strunk*, see Hart v. Brown, 289 A.2d 386 (Conn. Super. Ct. 1972); In re Doe, 481 N.Y.S.2d 932 (App. Div. 1981); Little v. Little, 576 S.W.2d 493 (Tex. Ct. App. 1979). For a case in agreement with *Pescinski*, see In re Richardson, 284 So. 2d 185 (La. Ct. App. 1973).

Are these two decisions consistent with each other? Is the dissent in *Strunk* correct that we should not base the decision on supposed psychological benefit to Jerry Strunk inasmuch as such benefit is highly speculative? What about having Strunk's brother not visit him for a couple of weeks to see if he is adversely affected by his brother's absence? Were the outcomes different in *Strunk* and *Pescinski* because Strunk could relate to his sibling while Pescinski could not? Or because the recipient in *Strunk* would have been a man, and the recipient in *Pescinski* a woman? What incentives do you think the court in *Pescinski* might have been trying to avoid? After the Wisconsin Supreme Court denied her request for organ transplantation, Elaine Jeske died of kidney failure.

Which of the following factors should a court consider in deciding whether to order a transplantation from an incompetent person, and how should they be weighed: benefit to the recipient of the organ; risk to the donor; the relationship between the donor and recipient; the availability of alternative donors; and the feelings of the donor about the procedure? Do you agree with Justice Day's dissent in *Pescinski* on this question? Why do you suppose he believed that Richard Pescinski, if competent, would agree to be a donor when the other brother, Ralph Pescinski, did not agree to be a donor?

2. *Additional Readings.* For further discussion of these issues, see Charles Baron et al., Live Organ and Tissue Transplants from Minor Donors in Massachusetts, 55 B.U. L. Rev. 159 (1975); Cara Cheyette, Note, Organ Harvests from the Legally Incompetent: An Argument against Compelled Altruism, 41 B.C. L. Rev. 465 (2000); Michael T. Marley, Note, Proxy Consent to Organ Donation by Incompetents, 111 Yale L.J. 1215 (2002); Sara Lind Nygren, Note, Organ Donation by Incompetent Patients: A Hybrid Approach, 2006 U. Chi. Legal F. 471; Jennifer K. Robbennolt et al., Advancing the Rights of Children and Adolescents to Be Altruistic: Bone Marrow Donation by Minors, 9 J.L. & Health 213 (1994); John Robertson, Organ Donations by Incompetents and the Substituted Judgment Doctrine, 76 Colum. L. Rev. 48 (1976).

Problem: Conceiving a Child to Make Tissue Available for Transplantation

A couple, John and Joanne, have a 10-year-old daughter with leukemia who will almost certainly die within five years without a stem cell transplant. (Historically, stem cells for transplantation were taken from the donor's bone marrow, but now stem cells can often be retrieved as well from a donor's circulating blood or a newborn's umbilical cord blood.) With a transplant, there is a 70 percent chance of a long-term survival. Family members and friends have been tested to see if their stem cells are compatible, but none are candidates for transplantation. Despite a nationwide search to find a compatible donor, none has been found. John and Joanne decide to conceive another child in the hope that this child's stem cells will be suitable for transplantation in their daughter. There is a 25 percent chance that a new child will have compatible cells, but the odds can be improved to 100 percent with preimplantation genetic screening. With this approach, a couple can create embryos through in vitro fertilization. The embryos can then be tested to see if the new child's stem cells will be compatible with the existing child. Yury Verlinsky et al., Preimplantation HLA Testing, 291 JAMA 2079 (2004). If John and Joanne bear a child, and the child's cells are compatible, then physicians would perform a transplant with stem cells from umbilical cord blood after birth or other stem cells when the new child is older. There is no risk to the child from using its umbilical cord blood; the risk that the child would die from a surgery to remove her marrow is unknown, but probably in the range of 1/25,000 to 1/100,000. The risk of serious complications from using stem cells from circulating blood is also very low. Should John and Joanne be able to conceive the child and consent to the transplantation? [This problem is based on the Ayala case, in which a couple conceived a child to serve as a bone marrow donor for their daughter. Diane M. Gianelli, Bearing a Donor? Ethical Concerns Raised Over Having a Baby for Marrow Match, American Medical News, Mar. 2, 1990, at 3. For further discussion, see Katrien Devolder, Preimplantation HLA Typing: Having Children to Save Our Loved Ones, 31 J. Med. Ethics 582 (2005); Susan M. Wolf et al., Using Preimplantation Genetic Diagnosis to Create a Stem Cell Donor: Issues, Guidelines & Limits, 31 J.L. Med. & Ethics 327 (2003).]

3. Redefining Death

According to the law of every state, organs necessary for life (e.g., the heart or an entire liver) cannot be removed from a person for transplantation unless the person is dead (the "dead donor" rule). See, e.g., Ind. Code Ann. §29-2-16-2. Moreover, even with kidneys, which can be donated while the person is alive, more than half of organs for transplantation come from cadavers. This is both because two kidneys can be taken from dead persons and only one kidney from a living person, and also because persons are more reluctant to donate a kidney while alive than once dead. Most kidney transplants from a live donor go to a family member.

Almost all organs taken from dead persons come from patients whose death is diagnosed by cessation of brain function ("brain death") rather than from patients whose death is diagnosed by cessation of cardiopulmonary function (loss of heart and lung function). This is because the blood flow of brain-dead patients can be maintained with the provision of artificial life supports until the organs are removed for transplantation. Without continued blood supply, organs in the body deteriorate and quickly become unavailable for transplantation.[1]

---

[1] Efforts are being made to increase the number of organs taken from persons who die from cessation of cardiopulmonary function. One approach is to infuse cold fluids into the cadaver to rapidly cool the organs and prevent their deterioration. Another approach, for patients whose ventilators are being withdrawn, is to withdraw the ventilator in an operating room. That way, once the ventilator is withdrawn and the patient dies, action can be taken quickly to maintain the vitality of the organs before they are removed for transplantation. Procuring Organs for Transplant: The Debate over Non-Heart-Beating Cadaver Protocols (Robert M. Arnold, Stuart J. Youngner, Renie Shapiro & Carol Mason Spicer eds., 1995). See also Mona D. Doshi & Lawrence G. Hunsicker, Short- and Long-Term Outcomes with the Use of Kidneys and Livers Donated after Cardiac Death, 7 Am. J. Transplantation 122 (2007); Ethics Committee, American College of Critical Care Medicine, Society of Critical Care Medicine, Recommendations for Nonheartbeating Organ Donation, 29 Crit. Care Med. 1826 (2001); Markus Weber et al., Kidney Transplantation from Donors without a Heartbeat, 347 New Eng. J. Med. 248 (2002).

As discussed in Chapter 3, when a person is brain dead, the heart and lungs will ordinarily also stop working unless the person is maintained on a ventilator. Artificial ventilation and other medical support can maintain a brain-dead person's heartbeat and breathing for days to months but not indefinitely. Pregnant women have been maintained in brain death until their fetuses mature enough to be delivered by cesarean section. David R. Field et al., Maternal Brain Death During Pregnancy: Medical and Ethical Issues, 260 JAMA 816 (1988) (describing a case in which a brain-dead, pregnant woman was maintained on a ventilator for nine weeks). There is some question whether cessation of heartbeat and respiration are really inevitable after brain death. While it appears that most brain-dead patients cannot be maintained more than two or three months, some have been maintained for more than a year, including one patient for more than fourteen years. D. Alan Shewmon, Chronic "Brain Death": Meta-Analysis and Conceptual Consequences, 51 Neurology 1538 (1998).

Some commentators have proposed that death be redefined so that more persons would be candidates for organ transplantation. In particular, it has been argued that brain death should be defined by whether there is brain function sufficient to achieve consciousness, not by whether there is brain function at all.[2] If brain death were defined by the absence of consciousness, then anencephalic children and permanently unconscious persons would be dead, and their organs could be removed for transplantation. Other commentators have suggested that we no longer use death as the sole criterion for removing life-necessary organs but permit removal of life-necessary organs from living persons in limited situations. See, e.g., Robert D. Truog, Is It Time to Abandon Brain Death?, 29(1) Hastings Center Rep. 29, 34 (1997) (suggesting a focus on the ethical concerns of consent and harm, which would allow a person to give consent to organ retrieval if the person became permanently unconscious in the future).

The question, then, for this section is whether the need for more organs is sufficient reason for the state to either change the definition of death or permit individuals to donate their own organs or the organs of family members before death occurs. Does the individual's right to control bodily integrity and to make decisions about important personal matters include a right to decide when life-necessary organs may be given to others?

■ IN RE T.A.C.P.
609 So. 2d 588 (Fla. 1992)

KOGAN, Justice.

We have for review an order of the trial court certified by the Fourth District Court of Appeal as touching on a matter of great public importance requiring immediate resolution by this court. We frame the issue as follows: Is an anencephalic newborn considered "dead" for purposes of organ donation solely by reason of its congenital deformity? We have jurisdiction.

---

[2] To be sure, not all persons who support a change in the definition of death do so because such a change will increase the organ supply.

I. Facts

At or about the eighth month of pregnancy, the parents of the child T.A.C.P. were informed that she would be born with anencephaly. This is a birth defect invariably fatal, in which the child typically is born with only a "brain stem" but otherwise lacks a human brain. In T.A.C.P.'s case, the back of the skull was entirely missing and the brain stem was exposed to the air, except for medical bandaging. The risk of infection to the brain stem was considered very high. Anencephalic infants sometimes can survive several days after birth because the brain stem has a limited capacity to maintain autonomic bodily functions such as breathing and heartbeat. This ability soon ceases, however, in the absence of regulation from the missing brain.

In this case, T.A.C.P. actually survived only a few days after birth. . . .

On the advice of physicians, the parents continued the pregnancy to term and agreed that the mother would undergo cesarean section during birth. The parents agreed to the cesarean procedure with the express hope that the infant's organs would be less damaged and could be used for transplant in other sick children. Although T.A.C.P. had no hope of life herself, the parents both testified in court that they wanted to use this opportunity to give life to others. However, when the parents requested that T.A.C.P. be declared legally dead for this purpose, her health care providers refused out of concern that they thereby might incur civil or criminal liability.

The parents then filed a petition in the circuit court asking for a judicial determination. After hearing testimony and argument, the trial court denied the request on grounds that §382.009(1), Florida Statutes (1991), would not permit a determination of legal death so long as the child's brain stem continued to function. On appeal, the Fourth District summarily affirmed but then certified the trial court's order to this court for immediate resolution of the issue. We have accepted jurisdiction to resolve this case of first impression.

II. The Medical Nature of Anencephaly

Although appellate courts appear never to have confronted the issues there already is an impressive body of published medical scholarship on anencephaly. From our review of this material, we find that anencephaly is a variable but fairly well defined medical condition. Experts in the field have written that anencephaly is the most common severe birth defect of the central nervous system seen in the United States, although it apparently has existed throughout human history.

A statement by the Medical Task Force on Anencephaly ("Task Force") printed in the New England Journal of Medicine[3] generally described "anencephaly" as "a congenital absence of major portions of the brain, skull, and scalp, with its genesis in the first month of gestation" David A. Stumpf et al., The Infant with Anencephaly, 322 New Eng. J. Med. 669, 669 (1990). The large opening in the skull accompanied by the absence or severe congenital disruption of the cerebral hemispheres is the characteristic feature of the condition.

---

[3] The statement also was approved by the American Academy of Pediatrics, the American Academy of Neurology, the American College of Obstetricians and Gynecologists, the American Neurological Association, and the Child Neurology Society.

The Task Force defined anencephaly as diagnosable only when all of the following four criteria are present:

(1) A large portion of the skull is absent. (2) The scalp, which extends to the margin of the bone, is absent over the skull defect. (3) Hemorrhagic, fibrotic tissue is exposed because of defects in the skull and scalp. (4) Recognizable cerebral hemispheres are absent. [Id. at 670.]

Anencephaly is often, though not always, accompanied by defects in various other body organs and systems, some of which may render the child unsuitable for organ transplantation. . . .

The Task Force stated that most reported anencephalic children die within the first few days after birth, with survival any longer being rare. After reviewing all available medical literature, the Task Force found no study in which survival beyond a week exceeded 9 percent of children meeting the four criteria. Two months was the longest confirmed survival of an anencephalic, although there are unconfirmed reports of one surviving three months and another surviving fourteen months. [This decision preceded the *Baby K* case, page 338, involving an anencephalic child who lived for 2½ years.] The Task Force reported, however, that these survival rates are confounded somewhat by the variable degrees of medical care afforded to anencephalics. Some such infants may be given considerable life support while others may be given much less care.

The Task Force reported that the medical consequences of anencephaly can be established with some certainty. All anencephalics by definition are permanently unconscious because they lack the cerebral cortex necessary for conscious thought. Their condition thus is quite similar to that of persons in a persistent vegetative state. Where the brain stem is functioning, as it was here, spontaneous breathing and heartbeat can occur. In addition, such infants may show spontaneous movements of the extremities, "startle" reflexes, and pupils that respond to light. Some may show feeding reflexes, may cough, hiccup, or exhibit eye movements, and may produce facial expressions.

The question of whether such infants actually suffer from pain is somewhat more complex. It involves a distinction between "pain" and "suffering." The Task Force indicated that anencephaly in some ways is analogous to persons with cerebral brain lesions. Such lesions may not actually eliminate the reflexive response to a painful condition, but they can eliminate any capacity to "suffer" as a result of the condition. Likewise, anencephalic infants may reflexively avoid painful stimuli where the brain stem is functioning and thus is able to command an innate, unconscious withdrawal response; but the infants presumably lack the capacity to suffer. It is clear, however, that this incapacity to suffer has not been established beyond all doubt. . . .

There appears to be general agreement that anencephalics usually have ceased to be suitable organ donors by the time they meet all the criteria for "whole brain death," i.e., the complete absence of brain-stem function. There also is no doubt that a need exists for infant organs for transplantation. Nationally, between 30 and 50 percent of children under two years of age who need transplants die while waiting for organs to become available.

III. Legal Definitions of "Death" & "Life"

[The court discussed the history of the cardiopulmonary definition of death and the development of a definition of death based on cessation of brain function. The court then discusses Florida's approach to defining death.]

Indeed, Florida appears to have struck out on its own. The statute cited as controlling by the trial court does not actually address itself to the problem of anencephalic infants, nor indeed to any situation other than patients actually being sustained by artificial life support. The statute provides:

> For legal and medical purposes, *where respiratory and circulatory functions are maintained by artificial means of support* so as to preclude a determination that these functions have ceased, the occurrence of death *may* be determined where there is the irreversible cessation of the functioning of the entire brain, including the brain stem, determined in accordance with this section.

§382.009(1), Fla. Stat. (1991) (emphasis added). A later subsection goes on to declare:

> Except for a diagnosis of brain death, the standard set forth in this section is not the exclusive standard for determining death or for the withdrawal of life-support systems.

§382.009(4), Fla. Stat. (1991). This language is highly significant for two reasons.

First, the statute does not purport to codify the common law standard applied in some other jurisdictions, as does the uniform act. The use of the permissive word *may* in the statute in tandem with the savings clause of §382.009(4) buttresses the conclusion that the legislature envisioned other ways of defining "death." Second, the statutory framers clearly did not intend to apply the statute's language to the anencephalic infant not being kept alive by life support. To the contrary, the framers expressly limited the statute to that situation in which "respiratory and circulatory functions are maintained by artificial means of support." . . .

The parties have cited to no authorities directly dealing with the question of whether anencephalics are "alive" or "dead." Our own research has disclosed no other federal or Florida law or precedent arguably on point or applicable by analogy. We thus are led to the conclusion that no legal authority binding upon this court has decided whether an anencephalic child is alive for purposes of organ donation. In the absence of applicable legal authority, this court must weigh and consider the public policy considerations at stake here.

IV. Common Law & Policy

Initially, we must start by recognizing that §382.009, Florida Statutes (1991), provides a method for determining death in those cases in which a person's respiratory and circulatory functions are maintained artificially. §382.009(4), Fla. Stat. (1991). Likewise, we agree that a cardiopulmonary definition of death must be accepted in Florida as a matter of our common law, applicable whenever §382.009 does not govern. Thus, if cardiopulmonary function is not being maintained artificially as stated in §382.009, a person is dead who has sustained irreversible cessation of circulatory and respiratory functions as determined in accordance with accepted medical standards. We have found no credible authority arguing that this definition is inconsistent with the existence of death, and we therefore need not labor the point further.

The question remaining is whether there is good reason in public policy for this court to create an additional common law standard applicable to anencephalics. Alterations of the common law, while rarely entertained or allowed, are within this court's prerogative. However, the rule we follow is that the common law will not be altered or expanded unless demanded by public necessity, or where required to vindicate fundamental rights. We believe, for example, that our adoption of the cardiopulmonary definition of death today is required by public necessity and, in any event, merely formalizes what has been the common practice in this state for well over a century.

Such is not the case with petitioners' request. Our review of the medical, ethical, and legal literature on anencephaly discloses absolutely no consensus that public necessity or fundamental rights will be better served by granting this request. . . .

There is an unquestioned need for transplantable infant organs. Yet some medical commentators suggest that the organs of anencephalics are seldom usable, for a variety of reasons, and that so few organ transplants will be possible from anencephalics as to render the enterprise questionable in light of the ethical problems at stake — even if legal restrictions were lifted.

Others note that prenatal screening now is substantially reducing the number of anencephalics born each year in the United States and that, consequently, anencephalics are unlikely to be a significant source of organs as time passes. And still others have frankly acknowledged that there is no consensus and that redefinition of death in this context should await the emergence of a consensus.

A presidential commission in 1981 urged strict adherence to the Uniform Determination of Death Act's definition, which would preclude equating anencephaly with death. President's Commission for the Study of Ethical Problems, Biomedical, and Behavioral Research, Defining Death: Medical, Legal and Ethical Issues in the Determination of Death 2 (1981). Several sections of the American Bar Association have reached much the same conclusion. National Conference on Birth, Death, and Law, Report on Conference, 29 Jurimetrics J. 403, 421 (Lori B. Andrews et al. eds., 1989).

Some legal commentators have urged that treating anencephalics as dead equates them with "nonpersons," presenting a "slippery slope" problem with regard to all other persons who lack cognition for whatever reason. Others have quoted physicians involved in infant-organ transplants as stating, "The slippery slope is real," because some physicians have proposed transplants from infants with defects less severe than anencephaly.

We express no opinion today about who is right and who is wrong on these issues — if any "right" or "wrong" can be found here. The salient point is that no consensus exists as to: (a) the utility of organ transplants of the type at issue here; (b) the ethical issues involved; or (c) the legal and constitutional problems implicated.

V. CONCLUSIONS

Accordingly, we find no basis to expand the common law to equate anencephaly with death. We acknowledge the possibility that some infants' lives might be saved by using organs from anencephalics who do not meet the traditional definition of "death" we reaffirm today. But weighed against this is the utter lack of consensus, and the questions about the overall utility of such organ donations. The scales clearly tip in favor of not extending the common law in this instance. . . .

Notes: Redefining Death

1. *The T.A.C.P. Decision.* At the end of Section III of the opinion, the court observed that there was no binding legal authority on the issue of whether an anencephalic child is alive for purposes of organ donation. Accordingly, said the court, it was an issue for the court to decide after weighing the public policy considerations at stake. What standard did the court employ for deciding whether to expand the common law in this case? Is it so clear that organ retrieval from anencephalic infants did not satisfy the court's standard? Why isn't the desire to avoid needless deaths a sufficiently strong basis for changing the common law? Were the justifications behind the court's adoption of the cardiopulmonary definition of death any more compelling? The court points to the lack of consensus on the issue, but doesn't the lack of consensus cut both ways (i.e., how should the court decide when there is no consensus for either position)? Should the court feel bound by its perception of academic opinion?

2. *The Role of Utilitarian Justifications.* Although it may seem too utilitarian to change the definition of death in order to facilitate organ transplantation, we saw in Chapter 3 that utilitarian concerns essentially were responsible when the definition of death was changed to include the cessation of brain function. In justifying a change in the definition of death, the influential Harvard Medical School report cited the burdens of treating brain-dead persons, including the diversion of resources from other patients, and the difficulty in obtaining organs for transplantation. Report of the Ad Hoc Committee of the Harvard Medical School to Examine the Definition of Brain Death, A Definition of Irreversible Coma, 205 JAMA 85, 85 (1968), excerpted at page 349. In other words, there are two important questions here. First, is there a principled difference between permitting organ retrieval from anencephalic infants now and permitting organ retrieval from brain-dead persons twenty-five years ago? Or is the real difference the fact that many more organs can be retrieved from brain-dead persons than from anencephalic infants? Second, even if there is no principled difference, might we still want to say that it would be wrong to retrieve organs from anencephalic infants? For further discussion, see Margaret Lock, Twice Dead: Organ Transplants and the Reinvention of Death (2002); Jay A. Friedman, Taking the Camel by the Nose: The Anencephalic as a Source for Pediatric Organ Transplants, 90 Colum. L. Rev. 917 (1990); D. Alan Shewmon et al., The Use of Anencephalic Infants as Organ Sources, 261 JAMA 1773 (1989).

3. *Modifying the "Dead Donor" Rule.* Some commentators have proposed that, rather than change the definition of death to facilitate organ donation, we should modify the dead donor rule. Instead of insisting that people be dead before taking their heart, liver, lungs, and kidneys for transplantation, we would permit organ donation before death, in limited circumstances. For example, people could direct in a living will that, in the event of a condition of permanent unconsciousness, they want their organs taken for transplantation. Or parents of anencephalic children could be given the opportunity to choose among continuing treatment, stopping treatment, or donating their child's organs before the child dies. Robert M. Arnold & Stuart J. Youngner, The Dead Donor Rule: Should We Stretch It, Bend It, or Abandon It?, 2 Kennedy Inst. Ethics J. 263 (1993); Council on Ethical and Judicial Affairs, American Medical Association, The Use of Anencephalic Neonates as Organ Donors, 273 JAMA 1614 (1995) (position reversed in Charles W. Plows, Reconsideration of AMA Opinion on Anencephalic Neonates as Organ Donors, 275 JAMA 443 (1996)); Sheldon F. Kurtz & Michael J. Saks, Living Organ Donor Act, 18 Iowa J. Corp. L. 523, 561 (1993).

Would this approach be more acceptable than changing the definition of death? Do you think that the reasons for having the dead donor rule apply when a person is permanently unconscious? Can we distinguish the removal of organs from permanently unconscious persons from other actions that we already permit? For example, can we really distinguish taking a ventilator away from a permanently unconscious person, because the ventilator could be better used by someone else, from taking the lungs from a permanently unconscious person, because the lungs could be better used by someone else? Indeed, if we had consent to take the lungs from the person's advance directive, would it be less troublesome than taking away a ventilator when doing so would be over the objections of the family and in disregard of the patient's advance directive?

B. OWNERSHIP AND CONTROL OF THE BODY

1. Mandates or Incentives for Organ Donation

In accordance with §4 of the 1987 Uniform Anatomical Gift Act, many states enacted statutes permitting the removal of corneas and other tissues or organs from persons who have died and are undergoing an autopsy by a coroner or medical examiner. In such cases, the legislatures probably reasoned, the body is being cut open and some tissue permanently removed anyway as part of the autopsy. If additional tissue can be used to improve the health of a living person, particularly if the tissue is the cornea whose absence would not be detectable by looking at the corpse, then should we not give preference to the living person over the dead person? Is there any reason to limit mandatory "donation" to cadavers undergoing an autopsy? Why not take organs and tissues from every cadaver? Why not require living persons to give up renewable tissues, like bone marrow, for transplantation? To the extent that takings of organs or tissues raise concerns about people being deprived of their body parts without their consent and without compensation, can we answer those concerns by offering financial incentives for organ donation?

■ STATE v. POWELL
497 So. 2d 1188 (Fla. 1986)

OVERTON, Justice.

This is a petition to review a circuit court order finding unconstitutional §732.9185, Florida Statutes (1983), which authorizes medical examiners to remove corneal tissue from decedents during statutorily required autopsies when such tissue is needed for transplantation. The statute prohibits the removal of the corneal tissue if the next of kin objects, but does not require that the decedent's next of kin be notified of the procedure. The Fifth District Court of Appeal certified that this case presents a question of great public importance requiring immediate resolution by this court. We accept jurisdiction . . . , and, for the reasons expressed below, find that the statute is constitutional.

The challenged statute provides:

Corneal removal by medical examiners. —

(1) In any case in which a patient is in need of corneal tissue for a transplant, a district medical examiner or an appropriately qualified designee with training in ophthalmologic techniques may, upon request of any eye bank authorized under s. 732.918, provide the cornea of a decedent whenever all of the following conditions are met:

(a) A decedent who may provide a suitable cornea for the transplant is under the jurisdiction of the medical examiner and an autopsy is required in accordance with s. 406.11.

(b) No objection by the next of kin of the decedent is known by the medical examiner.

(c) The removal of the cornea will not interfere with the subsequent course of an investigation or autopsy.

(2) Neither the district medical examiner nor his appropriately qualified designee nor any eye bank authorized under s. 732.918 may be held liable in any civil or criminal action for failure to obtain consent of the next of kin.

The trial court decided this case by summary judgment. The facts are not in dispute. On June 15, 1983, James White drowned while swimming at the city beach in Dunellon, Florida. Associate Medical Examiner Dr. Thomas Techman, who is an appellant in this cause, performed an autopsy on James' body at Leesburg Community Hospital. On July 11, 1983, Anthony Powell died in a motor vehicle accident in Marion County. Medical Examiner Dr. William H. Shutze, who is also an appellant in this cause, performed an autopsy on Anthony's body. In each instance, under the authority of §732.9185, the medical examiner removed corneal tissue from the decedent without giving notice to or obtaining consent from the parents of the decedent.

James' and Anthony's parents, who are the appellees in this case, each brought an action claiming damages for the alleged wrongful removal of their sons' corneas and seeking a judgment declaring §732.9185 unconstitutional. . . .

In addressing the issue of the statute's constitutionality, we begin with the premise that a person's constitutional rights terminate at death. If any rights exist, they belong to the decedent's next of kin.

Next, we recognize that a legislative act carries with it the presumption of validity and the party challenging a statute's constitutionality must carry the burden of establishing that the statute bears no reasonable relation to a permissible legislative objective. In determining whether a permissible legislative objective exists, we must review the evidence arising from the record in this case.

The unrebutted evidence in this record establishes that the state of Florida spends approximately $138 million each year to provide its blind with the basic necessities of life. At present, approximately 10 percent of Florida's blind citizens are candidates for cornea transplantation, which has become a highly effective procedure for restoring sight to the functionally blind. As advances are made in the field, the number of surgical candidates will increase, thereby raising the demand for suitable corneal tissue. The increasing number of elderly persons in our population has also created a great demand for corneas because corneal blindness often is age-related. Further, an affidavit in the record states:

> Corneal transplants are particularly important in newborns. The brain does not learn to see if the cornea is not clear. There is a critical period in the first few months of life when the brain "learns to see." If the cornea is not clear, the brain not only does not "learn to see," but the brain loses its ability to "learn to see." Hence, corneal transplant in children must be made as soon as practicable after the problem is discovered. Without the medical examiner legislation, there would be virtually no corneal tissue available for infants and these children would remain forever blind.

The record reflects that the key to successful corneal transplantation is the availability of high-quality corneal tissue and that corneal tissue removed more than ten hours after death is generally unsuitable for transplantation. The implementation of §732.9185 in 1977 has, indisputably, increased both the supply and quality of tissue available for transplantation. Statistics show that, in 1976, only 500 corneas were obtained in Florida for transplantation while, in 1985, more than 3,000 persons in Florida had their sight restored through corneal transplantation surgery.

The record also demonstrates that a qualitative difference exists between corneal tissue obtained through outright donation and tissue obtained pursuant to §732.9185. In contrast to the tissue donated by individuals, which is largely unusable because of the advanced age of the donor at death, approximately 80 to 85 percent of tissue obtained through medical examiners is suitable for transplantation. The evidence establishes that this increase in the quantity and quality of available corneal tissue was brought about by passage of the statute and is, in large part, attributable to the fact that §732.9185 does not place a duty upon medical examiners to seek out the next of kin to obtain consent for cornea removal. An affidavit in the record reveals that, before legislation authorized medical examiners in California to remove corneas without the consent of the next of kin, the majority of the families asked by the Los Angeles medical examiner's office responded positively; however, approximately 80 percent of the families could not be located in sufficient time for medical examiners to remove usable corneal tissue from the decedents.

An autopsy is a surgical dissection of the body; it necessarily results in a massive intrusion into the decedent. This record reflects that cornea removal, by comparison, requires an infinitesimally small intrusion which does not affect the decedent's appearance. With or without cornea removal, the decedent's eyes must be capped to maintain a normal appearance.

Our review of §732.9185 reveals certain safeguards which are apparently designed to limit cornea removal to instances in which the public's interest is greatest and the impact on the next of kin the least: corneas may be removed only if the decedent is under the jurisdiction of the medical examiner; an autopsy is mandated by Florida law; and the removal will not interfere with the autopsy or an investigation of the death. Further, medical examiners may not automatically remove tissue from all decedents subject to autopsy; rather, a request must be made by an eye bank based on a present need for the tissue.

We conclude that this record clearly establishes that this statute reasonably achieves the permissible legislative objective of providing sight to many of Florida's blind citizens.

We next address the trial court's finding that §732.9185 deprives appellees of a fundamental property right. All authorities generally agree that the next of kin have no property right in the remains of a decedent. Although, in Dunahoo v. Bess, 200 So. 541, 542 (1941), this court held that a surviving husband had a "property right" in his wife's body which would sustain a claim for negligent embalming, . . . [m]ore recently, we affirmed the district court's determination that the next of kin's right in a decedent's remains is based upon "the personal right of the decedent's next of kin to bury the body rather than any property right in the body itself." Jackson v. Rupp, 228 So. 2d 916, 918 (Fla. 4th DCA 1969), *affirmed*, 238 So. 2d 86 (Fla. 1970). The view that the next of kin has no property right but merely a limited right to possess the body for burial purposes is universally accepted by courts and commentators. Prosser states:

> A number of decisions have involved the mishandling of dead bodies. . . . In these cases the courts have talked of a somewhat dubious "property right" to the body, usually in the next of kin, which did not exist while the decedent was living, cannot be conveyed, can be used only for the one purpose of burial, and not only has no pecuniary value but is a source of liability for funeral expenses. It seems reasonably obvious that such "property" is something evolved out of thin air to meet the occasion, and that it is in reality the personal feelings of the survivors which are being protected, under a fiction likely to deceive no one but a lawyer.

W. Prosser, The Law of Torts, 43-44 (2d ed. 1955). . . .

Under the facts and circumstances of these cases, we find no taking of private property by state action for a non-public purpose in violation of article X, §6, of the Florida Constitution. We note that the right to bring an action in tort does not necessarily invoke constitutional protections. Decisions of the United States Supreme Court have clearly established that the loss of a common law right by legislative act does not automatically operate as a deprivation of substantive due process. Tort actions may be restricted when necessary to obtain a permissible legislative objective.

Appellees also assert that their right to control the disposition of their decedents' remains is a fundamental right of personal liberty protected against unreasonable governmental intrusion by the due process clause. Appellees argue that, because the statute permits the removal of a decedent's corneas without reference to his family's preferences, it infringes upon a right, characterized as one of religion, family, or privacy, which is fundamental and must be subjected to strict scrutiny. . . .

We reject appellees' argument. The cases cited recognize only freedom of choice concerning personal matters involved in existing, ongoing relationships among living persons as fundamental or essential to the pursuit of happiness by free persons. We find that the right of the next of kin to a tort claim for interference with burial, established by this court in *Dunahoo*, does not rise to the constitutional dimension of a fundamental right traditionally protected under either the United States or Florida Constitution. Neither federal nor state privacy provisions protect an individual from every governmental intrusion into one's private life, especially when a statute addresses public health interests.

The record contains no evidence that the appellees' objections to the removal of corneal tissues for human transplants are based on any "fundamental tenets of their religious beliefs." Wisconsin v. Yoder, 406 U.S. at 218. . . .

In conclusion, we hold that §732.9185 is constitutional because it rationally promotes the permissible state objective of restoring sight to the blind.[4] In so holding, we note that laws regarding the removal of human tissues for transplantation implicate moral, ethical, theological, philosophical, and economic concerns which do not readily lend themselves to analysis within a traditional legal framework. Applying constitutional standards of review to §732.9185 obscures the fact that at the heart of the issue lies a policy question which calls for a delicate balancing of societal needs and individual concerns more appropriately accomplished by the legislature. . . .

■ BROTHERTON v. CLEVELAND
923 F.2d 477 (6th Cir. 1991)

Martin, Circuit Judge.

Deborah S. Brotherton, the wife of decedent Steven Brotherton, appeals the dismissal of her §1983 claim for wrongful removal of her deceased husband's corneas. Because we find that Deborah Brotherton has a protected property interest in her husband's corneas and that the removal of those corneas was caused by established state procedures, we reverse.

On February 15, 1988, Steven Brotherton was found "pulseless" in an automobile and was taken to Bethesda North Hospital in Cincinnati, Ohio. He was pronounced dead on arrival. The hospital asked Deborah Brotherton to consider making an anatomical gift; she declined, based on her husband's aversion to such a gift, and her refusal was documented in the hospital's "Report of Death."

---

[4] Courts in Georgia and Michigan have upheld the constitutionality of cornea removal statutes similar to Florida's. See Georgia Lions Eye Bank, Inc. v. Lavant, 335 S.E.2d 127 (Ga. 1985), *cert. denied*, 475 U.S. 1084 (1986); Tillman v. Detroit Receiving Hospital, 360 N.W.2d 275 (Mich. Ct. App. 1984).

Because Steven Brotherton's death was considered a possible suicide, his body was taken to the Hamilton County coroner's office. An autopsy of Steven Brotherton's body was performed on February 16, 1988; after the autopsy, the coroner permitted Steven Brotherton's corneas to be removed and used as anatomical gifts. The coroner's office had called the Cincinnati Eye Bank, which sent the technician who removed the corneas. Deborah Brotherton did not learn that her husband's corneas had been removed until she read the autopsy report.

Bethesda North Hospital made no attempt to inform the coroner's office of Deborah Brotherton's objection to making an anatomical gift, and the coroner's office did not inquire into whether there was an objection. Ohio Rev. Code §2108.60 permits a coroner to remove the corneas of autopsy subjects without consent, provided that the coroner has no knowledge of an objection by the decedent, the decedent's spouse, or, if there is no spouse, the next of kin, the guardian, or the person authorized to dispose of the body. The custom and policy of the Hamilton County coroner's office is not to obtain a next of kin's consent or to inspect the medical records or hospital documents before removing corneas. [Indeed, when personnel at the eye bank started asking about the existence of objections to removals, the coroner instructed his staff to withhold information about next of kin. Brotherton v. Cleveland, 173 F.3d 552, 556 (6th Cir. 1999).]

Deborah Brotherton, on her own behalf and on behalf of her children, as well as a purported class of similarly situated plaintiffs, filed this case under 42 U.S.C. §1983, alleging that her husband's corneas were removed without due process of law and in violation of the equal protection clause. She also asserted pendent state law claims for emotional distress. . . .

A majority of the courts confronted with the issue of whether a property interest can exist in a dead body have found that a property right of some kind does exist and often refer to it as a "quasi-property right." . . . However, two Ohio appellate courts which have been confronted with determining the nature of the right have avoided characterizing it in this manner.

In *Carney*, an appellate court ruled on who has standing to bring a claim for mishandling a dead body. The court stated that calling the right to control the dead body of a relative a "quasi-property right" would create a legal fiction and concluded:

> This court rejects the theory that a surviving custodian has quasi-property rights in the body of the deceased, and acknowledges the cause of action for mishandling of a dead body as a subspecies of the tort of infliction of emotional distress. *Carney*, 33 Ohio App. 3d at 37. . . .

In *Everman*, an appellate court rejected the argument that a husband's right to possession of his deceased wife's body for purposes of preparation, mourning, and burial is protected against unreasonable search or seizure. In so ruling, the court stated:

> There is no issue in this case of the possessory right of a spouse or other appropriate member of the family of a deceased for the purposes of preparation, mourning and burial. This right is recognized by law and by the decisions. This is not the [sic] say that a person has a property right in the body of another, living or dead, or that a corpse may not be temporarily held for investigation as to the true cause of death. *Everman*, 54 Ohio App. 3d at 122.

Evading the question of whether to call the spouse's interest "property," the *Everman* court recognized that Ohio does grant that right which resides at the very core of a property interest: the right to possess.

The concept of "property" in the law is extremely broad and abstract. The legal definition of "property" most often refers not to a particular physical object, but rather to the legal bundle of rights recognized in that object. Thus, "property" is often conceptualized as a "bundle of rights." The "bundle of rights" which have been associated with property include the rights to possess, to use, to exclude, to profit, and to dispose. . . .

Though some early American cases adopted the English common-law rule that there was no property right in a dead body, other cases held that the rule was unsound in light of the rights of next of kin with regard to burial. The tendency to classify the bundle of rights granted by states as a property interest of some type was a direct function of the increased significance of those underlying rights. The prevailing view of both English and American courts eventually became that next of kin have a "quasi-property" right in the decedent's body for purposes of burial or other lawful disposition.

The importance of establishing rights in a dead body has been, and will continue to be, magnified by scientific advancements. The recent explosion of research and information concerning biotechnology has created a market place in which human tissues are routinely sold to and by scientists, physicians and others. The human body is a valuable resource. As biotechnology continues to develop, so will the capacity to cultivate the resources in a dead body. A future in which hearts, kidneys, and other valuable organs could be maintained for expanded periods outside a live body is far from inconceivable.

Thankfully, we do not need to determine whether the Supreme Court of Ohio would categorize the interest in the dead body granted to the spouse as property, quasi-property or not property. Although the existence of an interest may be a matter of state law, whether that interest rises to the level of a "legitimate claim of entitlement" protected by the due process clause is determined by federal law. This determination does not rest on the label attached to a right granted by the state but rather on the substance of that right.

Ohio Rev. Code §2108.02(B), as part of the Uniform Anatomical Gift Act governing gifts of organs and tissues for research or transplants, expressly grants a right to Deborah Brotherton to control the disposal of Steven Brotherton's body. *Everman* expresses the recognition that Deborah Brotherton has a possessory right to his body. *Carney* allows a claim for disturbance of his body. Although extremely regulated, in sum, these rights form a substantial interest in the dead body, regardless of Ohio's classification of that interest. We hold the aggregate of rights granted by the state of Ohio to Deborah Brotherton rises to the level of a "legitimate claim of entitlement" in Steven Brotherton's body, including his corneas, protected by the due process clause of the Fourteenth Amendment.

We also hold the removal of Steven Brotherton's corneas were caused by established state procedures and that Ohio failed to provide the necessary predeprivation process. The Supreme Court has often reiterated that a property interest may not be destroyed without a hearing. See, e.g., Logan v. Zimmerman Brush Co., 455 U.S. 422, 434 (1982). In *Logan*, the Supreme Court ruled that the timing of a hearing depends upon the accommodation of competing interests involved, which include: the importance of the private interests, the length and finality of deprivation, and the magnitude of governmental interest. The Court added that deprivation of property resulting from an established state procedure can only satisfy due process if there is a predeprivation hearing. . . .

It is the policy and custom of the Hamilton County coroner's office not to review medical records or paperwork pertaining to a corpse prior to the removal of corneas. This intentional ignorance is induced by Ohio Rev. Code §2108.60 which allows the office to take corneas from the bodies of deceased without considering the interest of any other parties, as long as they have no knowledge of any objection to such a removal. After the cornea is removed, it is not returned and the corpse is permanently diminished. The only governmental interest enhanced by the removal of the corneas is the interest in implementing the organ/tissue donation program; this interest is not substantial enough to allow the state to consciously disregard those property rights which it has granted. Moreover, predeprivation process undertaken by the state would be a minimal burden to this interest. This court does not at this time need to establish the type or extent of predeprivation process required by the due process clause; we merely hold that the policy and custom of the Hamilton County coroner's office is an established state procedure necessitating predeprivation process. . . . [The litigation in *Brotherton* was finally settled ten years after this decision with a change in policy at the coroner's office and the payment of $5.25 million into a settlement fund to compensate the class of people harmed by the coroner's practices. Brotherton v. Cleveland, 141 F. Supp. 2d 894 (S.D. Ohio 2001).]

◼ McFALL v. SHIMP
10 Pa. D. & C.3d 90 (Allegheny County 1978)

FLAHERTY, Judge.

Plaintiff, Robert McFall, suffers from a rare bone marrow disease and the prognosis for his survival is very dim, unless he receives a bone marrow transplant from a compatible donor. Finding a compatible donor is a very difficult task and limited to a selection among close relatives. After a search and certain tests, it has been determined that only defendant [David Shimp] is suitable as a donor. Defendant refuses to submit to the necessary transplant, and before the court is a request for a preliminary injunction which seeks to compel defendant to submit to further tests, and, eventually, the bone marrow transplant. [McFall had aplastic anemia, and Shimp was his first cousin.]

Although a diligent search has produced no authority, plaintiff cites the ancient statute of King Edward I, 811 Westminster 2, 13 Ed. I, c.24, pointing out, as is the case, that this court is a successor to the English courts of Chancery and derives power from this statute, almost 700 years old. The question posed by plaintiff is that, in order to save the life of one of its members by the only means available, may society infringe upon one's absolute right to his "bodily security"?

The common law has consistently held to a rule which provides that one human being is under no legal compulsion to give aid or to take action to save another human being or to rescue. A great deal has been written regarding this rule which, on the surface, appears to be revolting in a moral sense. Introspection, however, will demonstrate that the rule is founded upon the very essence of our free society. It is noteworthy that counsel for plaintiff has cited authority which has developed in other societies in support of plaintiff's request in this instance. Our society, contrary to many others, has as its first principle, the respect for the individual, and that society and government exist to protect the individual from being invaded and hurt by another. Many societies adopt a contrary view which has the individual existing to serve the society as a whole. In preserving such a society as we have, it is bound to happen that great moral conflicts will arise and will appear harsh in a given instance. In this case, the chancellor is being asked to force one member of society to undergo a medical procedure which would provide that part of that individual's body would be removed from him and given to another so that the other could live. Morally, this decision rests with defendant, and, in the view of the court, the refusal of defendant is morally indefensible. For our law to *compel* defendant to submit to an intrusion of his body would change every concept and principle upon which our society is founded. To do so would defeat the sanctity of the individual, and would impose a rule which would know no limits, and one could not imagine where the line would be drawn.

This request is not to be compared with an action at law for damages, but rather is an action in equity before a chancellor, which, in the ultimate, if granted, would require the forceable submission to the medical procedure. For a society which respects the rights of *one* individual, to sink its teeth into the jugular vein or neck of one of its members and suck from it sustenance for *another* member, is revolting to our hard-wrought concepts of jurisprudence. Forceable extraction of living body tissue causes revulsion to the judicial mind. Such would raise the spectre of the swastika and the Inquisition, reminiscent of the horrors this portends.

This court makes no comment on the law regarding plaintiff's rights in an action at law for damages, but has no alternative but to deny the requested equitable relief. An order will be entered denying the request for a preliminary injunction. . . .

[Mr. McFall died two weeks after the court's opinion was issued. For details about the case, see Fordham E. Huffman, Comment, Coerced Donation of Body Tissues: Can We Live with *McFall v. Shimp*?, 40 Ohio St. L.J. 409 (1979); Alan Meisel & Loren H. Roth, Must a Man Be His Cousin's Keeper?, 8(5) Hastings Center Rep. 5 (1978) (observing that newspaper accounts reported strong pressures from Shimp's wife and mother for him not to donate and that Shimp explained his refusal in terms of the risks of anesthesia, concerns that the procedure would aggravate existing aches and pains, and the possibility that his job-related exposure to chemicals might interfere with the regeneration of his bone marrow).]

Notes: Obligations to Give Up Organs
and Tissues; Autopsies

1. *The Family's Property Rights.* Which of the two courts, *Powell* or *Brotherton*, has the better analysis on the issue of whether the family has a property right? If the family can choose whether or not to donate the organs of a person who has just

died, doesn't that make it clear that the family possesses a property right in the decedent's organs?

2. *Authority for Autopsies.* As the first two cases illustrate, state law gives broad authority for coroners or medical examiners to perform autopsies in cases of unnatural death or for public health reasons, despite any objection by the family. In a full autopsy, internal organs are removed, examined, and placed back in the body, but not necessarily reattached with any care or precision. These statutes are widely regarded as constitutional and are rarely challenged. See, e.g., Rielly v. City of New York, 1992 WL 368082 (E.D.N.Y. 1992) (autopsy statute that permits performance of procedure without consent of relatives when part of a criminal homicide investigation is "plainly" constitutional). The reasoning is both that important public health and law enforcement objectives outweigh any private interests, and also that opening and examining a corpse does not clearly infringe any constitutionally protected interest. An autopsy may not constitute a deprivation of "property" at all since, after the body is examined, it is returned to the family more or less intact. The constitutionality of autopsy statutes is buttressed by the fact that they frequently allow the family to object for religious reasons.

While there is no constitutional obstacle to performing autopsies in the proper manner, if this authority is abused, courts do recognize that families have protected interests in the nature of a quasi-property right to respectful treatment and to exercise some control over the disposition of the decedent's body. In one case, a court allowed a constitutional tort action against a part-time coroner who also ran an eye bank and was allegedly caught stealing eyeballs from corpses before sewing the eyelids shut. Whaley v. County of Tuscola, 58 F.3d 1111 (6th Cir. 1995). See also Whitehair v. Highland Memory Gardens, 327 S.E.2d 438 (W. Va. 1985) (tort suit allowed for mishandling of corpse during internment process). But see Hinkle v. City of Clarksburg, 81 F.3d 416 (4th Cir. 1996) (medical examiners entitled to qualified immunity on claim that they improperly disposed of decedent's internal organs); Arnaud v. Odom, 870 F.2d 304, 309 (5th Cir. 1989) (no §1983 due process claim against physician for performing unauthorized experiments on decedent during autopsy because state law provided adequate postdeprivation remedy of action for tampering with a corpse).

3. *The Process Due the Family.* Powell, Brotherton, and other cases have clearly established the state's right to take corneas for transplantation from bodies that are undergoing an autopsy by the state (in the absence of an objection). See Erik S. Jaffee, Note, "She's Got Bette Davis['s] Eyes": Assessing the Nonconsensual Removal of Cadaver Organs Under the Takings and Due Process Clauses, 90 Colum. L. Rev. 528 (1990); Annot., 54 A.L.R. 4th 1214 (1987). *Brotherton,* however, requires some kind of process before the corneas can be taken. What kind of process do you think *Brotherton* requires? Would it have been sufficient if the coroner had reviewed Mr. Brotherton's medical records to see if an objection to tissue removal had been registered? Should the coroner have to contact the family to ascertain their wishes before taking any corneas? What if, after reasonable efforts to contact family members, they cannot be reached before the autopsy? (Perhaps family members are out-of-town or overseas and are not responding to messages left on their telephone answering machine.)

For a case with a result similar to that in *Brotherton*, see Newman v. Sathyavaglswaran, 287 F.3d 786 (9th Cir. 2002) (expressing great concern with the absence of a pre-removal process before removal of corneas, but leaving for future proceedings exactly what process is due). Before the *Newman* litigation commenced, and in response to an article in the *Los Angeles Times* about alleged trafficking in corneas by the Los Angeles County Coroner's Office, California amended its cornea removal statute to require consent by the decedent or a surrogate decisionmaker. 1998 Cal. Adv. Legis. Serv. 887. The current statute can be found at Cal. Gov't Code §27491.47. (Mr. Newman had been under the custody of the Los Angeles County Coroner's Office when his corneas were taken.) But California still permits retrieval of organs and other tissues in coroners' or medical examiners' cases in the absence of consent if there is no known objection. Cal. Health & Safety Code §7151.5.

In response to *Brotherton* and *Newman*, the Revised Uniform Anatomical Gift Act §23 (2006) removes the authority of coroners to release corneas (or other tissues or organs) in the absence of consent. For more background, see the discussion of Sections 22 and 23 of the Revised Act in the "Summary of the Changes in the Revised Act." The Revised Act may substantially curtail the already limited use of presumed consent in the United States. Indeed, in 2007, Minnesota, New Mexico and North Dakota followed the Revised Act in revoking its grant of authority to coroners and medical examiners. 2007 Minn. Laws 120 (repealing Minn. Stat. §525.9213 (2006)); 2007 N.M. Laws 323 (repealing N.M. Stat. Ann. §24-6A-4 (2006)); 2007 N.D. Laws 237 (repealing N.D. Cent. Code, §23-06.2-04 (2006)).

4. *Retrieving Visceral Organs in Medical Examiners' Cases.* A number of states have gone even further than Florida and Ohio and enacted a statute allowing coroners or medical examiners to remove hearts, lungs, kidneys, hearts, livers, and other visceral organs for transplantation if there has been no objection by the decedent while alive or the family members either before or after the decedent's death, and efforts to contact the family have not been successful. See, e.g., Code of Ala. §22-19-54; Cal. Health & Safety Code §7151.5; Md. Code Ann., Est. & Trusts §4-509; Mont. Code Ann. §72-17-215; Tex. Health & Safety Code §§693. 002-.003; W. Va. Code §16-19-4. Such statutes do not necessarily result in the retrieval of organs. Coroners and medical examiners are reluctant to remove visceral organs for transplantation without the family's permission, and the organs may have lost their vitality by the time the body is found. In Texas, in the first year after medical examiners were given authority to remove visceral organs without consent, that authority was used only twice. Medical examiners are not the only persons reluctant to remove organs without family consent. Even in cases in which a person has completed an organ donor card, transplant surgeons often will not remove the person's organs without the family's permission. David Orentlicher, Organ Donation — The Willing Donor, *in* Ethics in Emergency Medicine 214, 217 (Kenneth V. Iserson et al. eds., 2d ed. 1995).

As with removal of corneas, the Revised Uniform Anatomical Gift Act may lead states to revoke the authority of coroners or medical examiners to remove other tissues and organs in the absence of consent. Minnesota, New Mexico and North Dakota all did so in 2007. Indiana revoked authority for coroners to retrieve organs, 2007 Ind. Acts 147, but retained authority for coroners to retrieve corneas, Ind. Code §36-2-14-19. Interestingly, in Montana, the legislature followed the provisions of the Revised Uniform Anatomical Gift Act on coroners and medical examiners, but also retained its statutory provision granting authority to retrieve organs and tissues in the absence of consent. 2007 Mont. Laws 345.

Presumed consent is not limited to coroner or medical examiner cases. California will allow removal of organs in the absence of objection or consent when someone dies in the hospital and the hospital is unable to locate a family member, guardian, or health care agent, as long as the hospital has made a reasonable effort for at least twelve hours to locate a representative of the decedent. Cal. Health & Safety Code §7151.5(b). States that allow organ retrieval in the absence of objection or consent for decedents under the custody of coroners or medical examiners often also allow organ retrieval in the absence of objection or consent for decedents under the custody of public health officers. See, e.g., Cal. Health & Safety Code §7151.5(c); Hawaii Rev. Stat. §327-4(b); Mont. Code Ann. §72-17-215(2); W. Va. Code §16-19-4(b).

5. *Presumed Consent More Broadly.* A number of commentators have argued that retrieval of organs should not be limited to medical examiner (or public health official) cases but should become a routine practice for all deceased persons. Under this "presumed consent" approach, the law would shift the presumption that people do not want to donate their organs in the absence of explicit consent to a presumption that people do want to donate their organs in the absence of an explicit refusal. See Paul T. Menzel, Strong Medicine (1990); Jesse Dukeminier & David Sanders, Organ Transplantation: A Proposal for Routine Salvaging of Cadaver Organs, 279 New Eng. J. Med. 413 (1968); Arthur J. Matas et al., A Proposal for Cadaver Organ Procurement: Routine Removal with Right of Informed Refusal, 10 J. Health Pol. Pol'y & L. 231 (1985); Theodore Silver, The Case for a Post-Mortem Organ Draft and a Proposed Model Organ Draft Act, 68 B.U. L. Rev. 681 (1988). For a dissenting view, see Robert M. Veatch & J. B. Pitt, The Myth of Presumed Consent: Ethical Problems in New Organ Procurement Strategies, 27 Transplant. Proc. 1888 (1995).

Presumed consent has been enacted in several European countries, in part as a response to a recommendation of the Council of Europe in 1978, but, even in countries with presumed consent, physicians still typically ask the family for consent to take the organs. Austria, and to some extent Belgium, are apparently the only European countries with a true presumed consent system, and there is some evidence that presumed consent has meaningfully increased the rate of organ retrieval. Hakan Gabel, How Presumed Is Presumed Consent?, 28 Transplant. Proc. 27 (1996); Maxwell J. Mehlman, Presumed Consent to Organ Donation: A Reevaluation, 1 Health Matrix 31 (1991); Paul Michielsen, Presumed consent to organ donation: 10 years' experience in Belgium, 89 J. Royal Soc. Med. 663 (1996). Perhaps because family consent is typically sought in most presumed consent countries, studies generally do not find higher rates for organ donation in those countries. Chris Rudge, Organ Donation and the Law, 82 Transplantation 1140 (2006). However, in a recent study controlling for other variables that influence organ donation, researchers found organ donation rates 25 to 30 percent higher in presumed consent countries. The authors suggested that the legislative presumption of consent may affect family decisionmaking, such that families are more likely to consent to organ donation when the law authorizes presumed consent. Alberto Abadie & Sebastien Gay, The Impact of Presumed Consent Legislation on Cadaveric Organ Donation: A Cross-Country Study, 25 J. Health Economics 599 (2006). For a review of the law and practice in European countries with presumed consent, see Anke Janssen & Sjef Gevers, Explicit or Presumed Consent and Organ Donation Post-Mortem: Does It Matter?, 24 Med. Law 575 (2005).

If we allow states to conduct autopsies without permission in criminal cases, does it follow that we should allow removal of organs from all dead persons for transplantation? Would a presumed consent law be constitutional assuming an adequate option to register objection? If the relevant issues are the violation of the person's bodily integrity and the benefit to society, how does an autopsy to solve a crime compare with a removal of organs to save a life or to improve someone's health? How does being subject to organ removal after death compare to being subject to a military draft while alive?

Assuming policy and constitutional objections to presumed consent laws could be overcome, it is not clear how great an impact they would have. As mentioned in the previous note, the laws permitting medical examiners to remove organs do not seem to have been employed very much for visceral organs despite their widespread use for removal of corneas. In this regard, it is instructive that the two countries in which the practical impact of presumed consent laws has been greatest—Austria and Belgium—are countries with a tradition of routine autopsies in the absence of consent. Michielsen, supra, at 663. In addition, it appears that presumed consent laws may succeed in part because they are combined with other measures to increase the organ supply. M.F.X. Gnant et al., The Impact of the Presumed Consent Law and a Decentralized Organ Procurement System on Organ Donation: Quadruplication in the Number of Organ Donors, 23 Transplant. Proc. 2685 (1991); Kieran Healy, Do Presumed-Consent Laws Raise Organ Procurement Rates?, 55 DePaul L. Rev. 1017 (2006).

6. *Required Request and Mandated Choice.* States have tried to increase organ donation through the adoption of "required request" laws. These laws, which almost all states have, require hospitals to ensure that families are asked for permission to retrieve organs from patients who die. Required request is also a condition for hospitals to receive Medicare and Medicaid reimbursement. 42 U.S.C. §1320b-8. Required request was designed to overcome the reluctance of physicians to raise the issue of organ donation with families, but the laws have not had much impact. In a study to ascertain why required request was not working, researchers found that families were generally asked about organ donation, but family members frequently refused consent. Laura A. Siminoff et al., Public Policy Governing Organ and Tissue Procurement in the United States: Results from the National Organ and Tissue Procurement Study, 123 Ann. Intern. Med. 10 (1995). See also Ellen Sheehy et al., Estimating the Number of Potential Organ Donors in the United States, 349 New Eng. J. Med. 667 (2003) (finding that "[l]ack of consent to a request for donation was the primary cause of the gap between the number of potential donors and the number of actual donors").

A number of commentators have urged the adoption of "mandated choice" laws, under which all competent adults would have to explicitly state whether or not they wish to be organ donors after they die. The choice might be required at the time of obtaining a driver's license or filing a tax return. Supporters of mandated choice observe that it would place the decision in the hands of the individual rather than in the hands of family members, and they suggest that people might be more willing to agree to a donation while alive than are their family members who are asked when the person has just died. Council on Ethical and Judicial Affairs, American Medical Association, Strategies for Cadaveric Organ Procurement: Mandated Choice and Presumed Consent, 272 JAMA 809 (1994); Sheldon F. Kurtz & Michael J. Saks, Cadaveric Organ Donor Act, 18 Iowa J. Corp. L. 523, 527 (1993); Aaron Spital, Mandated Choice for Organ Donation: Time to Give It a Try, 125 Ann. Intern. Med. 66 (1996).

However, since mandated choice is likely to be implemented without the prospective donor receiving much information, refusals may be common. Some early data from a Texas routine request program were consistent with this fear. In Texas (as in other states), driver's license applicants have automatically been asked whether they want to be organ donors, and the refusal rate has been as high as 80 percent. Siminoff et al., supra, at 16.

7. *Taking Tissue from Living Persons.* The *McFall* case may have come from a local Pennsylvania court, but it nevertheless represents the state of the law. There is no case that has required one person to give up tissue for the benefit of another person over the first person's objection. A subsequent case goes even further and denies access to the name of a potential donor, whom the dying person wants to contact and try to persuade to serve as a donor. In Head v. Colloton, 331 N.W.2d 870 (Iowa 1983), William Held, who was living in Texas, needed a bone marrow transplant to treat his leukemia. He had heard that the University of Iowa maintained a registry of potential bone marrow donors, and, through conversations with a staff member, discovered that a woman in the registry might have compatible tissue for donation. The woman had been entered into the registry without her knowledge — she had been tested at one time to see if she could be a blood platelet donor to a family member — and the registry's practice was to ask potential donors whether they were willing as a general matter to participate in bone marrow transplants. When this woman was contacted, she indicated that she would consider donation but only for a family member. Mr. Head then filed suit, seeking disclosure of the woman's name to the court or his attorney so the woman could be informed about Mr. Head's situation and asked if she would consider donation in this particular case. The court held that, while the bone marrow registry was a public record under Iowa law, it was a confidential record to which public access must be denied.

If we consider just the case itself, the result in *Head* may seem problematic. However, from a broader perspective, why do you think the court felt it had to preserve the confidentiality of the woman's name? Does your answer explain why the court was not even willing to require the bone marrow registry to send the woman a letter about Mr. Head without disclosing the woman's name to Mr. Head?

8. *The Other Side of the Argument.* Is it so obvious that *McFall* and *Head* are correctly decided? Most persons share the *McFall* court's abhorrence at the idea of an involuntary taking of a person's tissue for use by another person. Yet, our society already condones behavior that is arguably more coercive. If given the choice between paying taxes and donating blood every three months, which would

you choose? Even bone marrow donation is not as onerous as you might think. Researchers have examined the risks to bone marrow donors by reviewing the experiences of 493 persons who donated marrow through the National Marrow Donor Program. No donor died or suffered any serious permanent consequences of the procedure. Most donors experienced tiredness, pain at the donation site (i.e., the upper part of the pelvic bone), and low back pain. On average, donors recovered within two weeks, but 10 percent took more than a month to recover fully. David F. Stroncek et al., Experiences of the First 493 Unrelated Marrow Donors in the National Marrow Donor Program, 81 Blood 1940 (1993). Consider also the following argument:

> [I]f you are talking about fairness, I really do not understand why the fact that I have inherited good kidneys, or good bone marrow, . . . or indeed inherited a good environment, gives me more rights than the person who has inherited bad ones. I am not sure that a person deserves inherited desirable body parts any more than he or she deserves inherited wealth. . . . Consider this situation from a Rawlsian point of view. If one did not know whether or not one would have good marrow or kidneys, then what would one say if asked whether one preferred the right to obtain somebody else's bone marrow or kidneys or the right to retain one's own? In the real world, where there are more people who have good kidneys than there are people who need them, it is all too easy to vote against a law which mandates donation. But what about voting behind a Rawlsian veil, where we would not know whether we were the needy or the well-endowed? Guido Calabresi, Do We Own Our Bodies?, 1 Health Matrix 5, 16 (1991).

Calabresi observes that laws requiring organ or tissue donation might only be passed by the majority if the potential donors were relative weak politically and the potential recipients were relatively powerful politically, and that such laws would therefore "have to be constitutionally suspect." Id. at 11-12. But what if discrimination were not an issue?

> Now consider a communitarian-based law under which . . . *everyone* would have to be donors because we wanted to show that we are *all* willing to take on the burden. . . . Of course, it is unlikely that a legislature would actually do this, which again says something about whether or not we as a society are sufficiently concerned about "life" to be *nondiscriminating* communitarians. If we were, then I would argue the law might well be constitutional.

Advances in medicine have resulted in a procedure that replaces bone marrow transplants in most cases. Rather than harvesting adult blood stem cells from bone marrow for transplantation in cases like *McFall*, doctors can retrieve stem cells from the patient's circulating blood after giving the patient a drug to stimulate stem cell production. Like bone marrow donation, circulating blood stem cell donation is generally safe, although rare serious complications can occur with either procedure. In one international study, two deaths were found among more than 7,800 bone marrow donors. No deaths have been reported from circulating blood donors, but a small number of patients have suffered a ruptured spleen or other serious complication. Because it is less invasive to retrieve stem cells from circulating blood, recovery time is generally shorter. It is unknown whether there are long-term side effects from the drugs used to stimulate stem cell production for the procedure using circulating blood. Paolo Anderlini et al., Peripheral Blood Stem Cell Donation: An Analysis from the International Bone Marrow Transplant Registry (IBMTR) and European Group for Blood and Marrow Transplant (EBMT) Databases, 27 Bone Marrow Transplantation 689 (2001); Martin Körbling & Paolo Anderlini, Peripheral Blood Stem Cell Versus Bone Marrow Allotransplantation: Does the Source of Hematopoietic Stem Cells Matter?, 98 Blood 2900 (2001).

9. *The "Trolley Problem."* Moral theorists have posed the following dilemma: If a trolley conductor is steering a runaway car through a crowded city and must choose between two tracks, it is morally permissible, and perhaps mandatory, to choose the track that will result in harm to fewer people, even if in doing so the conductor will purposefully kill someone. That being the case, why can't a physician take five life-necessary organs from one person in order to save the lives of five other persons, or even take tissue from a person for whom it is not life-necessary to give it to another person for whom it would be life-sustaining? The possible answers turn out to be more complicated than you would first think, and lead to fascinating extrapolations. For a discussion, see Michael J. Costa, The Trolley Problem Revisited, 24 S.J. Phil. 437 (1986); Frances M. Kamm, Harming Some to Save Others, 57 Phil. Stud. 227 (1989); James A. Montmarquet, On Doing Good: The Right and the Wrong Way, 79 J. Phil. 439 (1982); Eric Rakowski, Taking and Saving Lives, 93 Colum. L. Rev. 1063 (1993); Judith Jarvis Thomson, The Trolley Problem, 94 Yale L.J. 1395 (1985); Judith Jarvis Thomson, The Realm of Rights 176-202 (1990).

Problem: Obligatory Stem Cell Donation

Suppose a legislature, concerned about the shortage of stem cell donors for transplants, passed a law requiring that all persons be included in a national stem cell registry. People would automatically be registered at birth by having a small amount of additional blood taken at the time that blood was taken for routine newborn medical testing. Other persons would have to bring a certificate showing that they had registered before they could obtain or renew a driver's license or begin a new academic year in school. When someone needed a stem cell transplant (either from bone marrow or circulating blood), the person's physician could check with the registry for a match. If a match was found, the person who matched would have to donate stem cells for a transplant. People could be excused from having to donate if they had religious objections or had a medical reason that disqualified them as a donor (just as the military excuses conscientious objectors and those with health problems from the draft). Should this law be constitutional? If constitutional, is it good policy? Would it matter whether the state paid some compensation to the donors as it does with military or jury duty? Would any constitutional concerns be eliminated if the law simply required automatic registration, leaving with the individual the decision whether to donate stem cells if a match occurred?

Consider the following variation on the facts: A Chernobyl-like disaster occurs in the United States, and, because of the nuclear fallout, tens or hundreds of thousands of persons need stem cell transplants. In response to the disaster, Congress passes a law requiring all healthy adults to register as potential stem cell donors. Do your answers to the previous questions come out any differently?

Notes: Financial Incentives for Organ Donation

1. *Proposals for Financial Incentives.* Another obvious way to increase the supply of transplantable organs is with financial inducement. A number of commentators have criticized the federal law that prohibits payment for organs. 42 U.S.C. §274e. They propose that people should be able either to sell their tissues and body parts that are not essential for life, as they now do with blood products, or to receive payment now for a promise to give up their organs when they die. T Randolph Beard & David L. Kaserman, On the Ethics of Paying Organ Donors: An Economics Perspective, 55 DePaul L. Rev. 827 (2006); Richard A. Epstein, Mortal Peril: Our Inalienable Right to Health Care? 249-261 (1997); Henry Hansmann, The Economics and Ethics of Markets for Human Organs, 14 J. Health Pol. Pol'y & L. 57 (1989); Richard Schwindt & Aidan R. Vining, Proposal for a Future Delivery Market for Transplant Organs, 11 J. Health Pol. Pol'y & L. 483 (1986); James S. Taylor, Stakes and Kidneys: Why Markets in Human Body Parts Are Morally Imperative (2005); Note, The Sale of Human Body Parts, 72 Mich. L. Rev. 1182 (1974).

In 2000, Pennsylvania enacted a statute authorizing payments of $3,000 to families for medical or funeral expenses of the decedent. 20 Pa. Cons. Stat. Ann. §8622. The federal prohibition against sales of organs has prevented the statute from taking effect. In June 2002, the American Medical Association called for pilot studies of financial incentives for organ donation. Deborah Josefson, AMA Considers Whether to Pay for Donation of Organs, 324 Brit. Med. J. 1541 (2002).

In January 2004, Wisconsin enacted a state tax deduction for live organ donors that passes muster under federal law. Organ donors can deduct up to $10,000 from adjusted gross income for travel expenses, lodging expenses, or lost wages that are not reimbursed (a donor can claim the deduction only once). Wis. Stat. §71.05 (10) (i). Under federal law, "valuable consideration" may not be paid for a human organ, but valuable consideration does not include "the expenses of travel, housing, and lost wages incurred by the donor of a human organ in connection with the donation of the organ." 42 U.S.C. §274e(c)(2). Since Wisconsin's enactment, several states have passed similar statutes. With regard to the concern that payments will have a coercive effect on poor people, why is Wisconsin's approach particularly good?

Such incentives would increase the organ supply, it is argued. But see Jeffrey M. Prottas, Buying Human Organs — Evidence that Money Doesn't Buy Everything, 53 Transplantation 1371 (1992). In addition, considerations of justice also can support payments to donors. Noting that transplant surgeons, organ recipients, and others involved in transplantation benefit, commentators argue that donors also ought to benefit. A third argument in favor of some kind of payment is that we may have fewer problems with donors or their families wanting to be involved with recipients or feeling that the recipient owes them something. Thomas Murray has observed that gift giving, unlike business dealings, can result in open-ended human relationships:

> In short, gifts create moral relationships that are much more open-ended, less specifiable, and less contained than contracts. Contracts are well suited to the marketplace where a strictly limited relationship for a narrow purpose — trading

goods or services — is desired. Gifts are better for initiating and sustaining more rounded human relationships, where future expectations are unknown, and where the exchange of goods is secondary in importance to the relationship itself. Thomas H. Murray, Gifts of the Body and the Needs of Strangers, 17(2) Hastings Center Rep. 30, 31 (1987) (but preferring a system of donation for organs because of the important social values that it promotes).

After studying the relations between organ recipients and the donor or the donor's family, Renée Fox and Judith Swazey concluded that

> [W]hat recipients believe they owe to donors and the sense of obligation they feel about repaying "their" donor for what has been given, weigh heavily on them. This psychological and moral burden is especially onerous because the gift the recipient has received from the donor is so extraordinary that it is inherently unreciprocal. It has no physical or symbolic equivalent. As a consequence, the giver, the receiver, and their families may find themselves locked in a creditor-debtor vise that binds them one to another in a mutually fettering way. We have called these aspects of the gift-exchange dimensions of transplantation, "the tyranny of the gift." . . . In the case of a live kidney donation, for example, the donor may exhibit a great deal of "proprietary interest" in the health, work, and private life of the close relative who has received his or her organ. . . . Recipients of cadaveric organ transplants also suffer from the magnitude of the gift they have received and from its unrequitable nature. . . . [T]he import of what has been given may not only drive close relatives of a cadaver donor to seek out the recipient but also, especially with heart transplants, to relate to this person as if he or she embodied the living spirit of the donor. However painful it may be for the recipients and their families to be united with their organ donors' kin, they are likely to feel obligated to yield to them because of their ineffable sense of indebtedness. . . . Renée C. Fox & Judith P. Swazey, Spare Parts: Organ Replacement in American Society 40-41 (1992).

Do we want open-ended relationships between organ donors and recipients?

2. *Concerns with Financial Incentives.* Opponents of organ sales claim that it will undermine altruistic sentiments in society. Proponents counter that we do not lose altruism by using tax deductions to encourage charitable contributions and that, in any event, altruism in society is not based on what kind of organ donation system we have. Opponents also worry that organ sales "commodify" the body (i.e., turn the body into a commodity). Proponents respond that society already permits a great deal of commodification when it permits people to work for a wage. Should we be more worried about commodifying people by buying their organs than commodifying people when we pay them for the fruits of their minds? There is also a concern about desperate persons taking unacceptable risks for pay. In response to this concern, there have been proposals to pay people for their organs, but only if the organs are taken after death, with payment to the person's heirs:

> My proposed solution is a futures market in which healthy individuals would be given the opportunity to contract for the sale of their body tissue for delivery after their death. If the vendor's organs are harvested and transplanted, a payment in the range of $5,000 for each major organ and lesser amounts for minor tissue

would be made to his estate or designee. The hospital in which the vendor dies, as any bailee entrusted with valuable property, would have the legal duty to preserve his cadaver in a manner suitable for organ harvesting and to notify the purchasing agency of the decedent's condition so that it may harvest his organs. The proposal speaks only to increasing the supply of organs, not to allocating them. . . . The futures market I propose avoids three potential ethical and political pitfalls. First, because there will be no acquisition of organs from live donors, it does not raise the spectre of exploiting the poor. Second, because the market need not be used to allocate the harvested organs, the rich need have no greater access than the poor. Finally, because people will be selling their own organs, their next of kin will not be required to traffic in the decedents' remains. Lloyd R. Cohen, Increasing the Supply of Transplant Organs: The Virtues of a Futures Market, 58 Geo. Wash. L. Rev. 1, 2 (1989).

Are there in fact good reasons for denying a person the freedom to sell a kidney? We might be concerned about a system in which the wealthy are able to obtain kidneys more easily than the poor, but suppose we permit sales of organs only if the organ is sold to the United Network for Organ Sharing (UNOS), which in turn would allocate the organ according to its customary criteria? Organ selling seems ghoulish, but is there more than an aesthetic preference that underlies the opposition to sales? Are the reasons for opposing sales sufficient to deny poor persons the means to purchase basic necessities for their families? Might the prohibition on sales exist so that we can, as a society, avoid having to deal with the reality of people being so desperately poor as to want to sell a kidney?

For empirical evidence on organ selling by living persons in a country where the practice is prohibited by law, see Madhav Goyal et al., Economic and Health Consequences of Selling a Kidney in India, 288 JAMA 1589 (2002) (finding that the sale of a kidney "does not lead to a long-term economic benefit and may be associated with a decline in health").

For further discussion of the concerns raised by organ selling, see Robert Arnold et al., Financial Incentives for Cadaver Organ Donation: An Ethical Reappraisal, 73 Transplantation 1361 (2002) (representing the ethics committee of the American Society of Transplant Surgeons); Margaret Jane Radin, Market-Inalienability, 100 Harv. L. Rev. 1849 (1987) (arguing that we should prevent commodification when doing so is necessary to foster personhood and human flourishing).

3. *Costs of Financial Incentives.* In considering the option of financial incentives, you may be concerned about the added cost to organ transplantation from the need to pay donors. But why is that a problem if a life is saved? Is it clear that the cost of transplantation will go up? Finally, consider the fact that educational campaigns to increase organ donation are also costly.

2. Ownership of Human Tissue

Whether organs and other tissues can be taken involuntarily or can be willingly sold depends in part on whether we think people have a property interest in their body. That issue is explored in the following case, but in a somewhat different context: using human tissue for research purposes rather than for transplantation. As you read this case, consider whether the court's answer to the ownership question can be generalized to other contexts, or whether the court creates a special rule just for medical research.

■ MOORE v. THE REGENTS OF THE UNIVERSITY OF CALIFORNIA
793 P.2d 479 (Cal. 1990)

PANELLI, Justice.

[The facts of this case are presented at page 182. After holding that people have a right of informed consent when a researcher profits from studying and using their cells, the court considered whether use of a person's cells without permission violates the person's property rights.]

. . . Moore also attempts to characterize the invasion of his rights as a conversion—a tort that protects against interference with possessory and ownership interests in personal property. He theorizes that he continued to own his cells following their removal from his body, at least for the purpose of directing their use, and that he never consented to their use in potentially lucrative medical research. . . .

No court, however, has ever in a reported decision imposed conversion liability for the use of human cells in medical research. While that fact does not end our inquiry, it raises a flag of caution. In effect, what Moore is asking us to do is to impose a tort duty on scientists . . . [that] would affect medical research of importance to all of society, implicat[ing] policy concerns far removed from the traditional, two-party ownership disputes in which the law of conversion arose. . . .

"To establish a conversion, plaintiff must establish an actual interference with his *ownership or right of possession*. . . . Where plaintiff neither has title to the property alleged to have been converted, nor possession thereof, he cannot maintain an action for conversion." (Del E. Webb Corp. v. Structural Materials Co., 123 Cal. App. 3d 593, 610-611 (1981)) (emphasis added). . . .

Moore . . . argues that "[i]f the courts have found a sufficient proprietary interest in one's persona, how could one not have a right in one's own genetic material, something far more profoundly the essence of one's human uniqueness than a name or a face?" However, . . . the goal and result of defendants' efforts has been to manufacture lymphokines. Lymphokines, unlike a name or a face, have the same molecular structure in every human being and the same important functions in every human being's immune system. Moreover, the particular genetic material which is responsible for the natural production of lymphokines, and which defendants use to manufacture lymphokines in the laboratory, is also the same in every person; it is no more unique to Moore than the number of vertebrae in the spine or the chemical formula of hemoglobin.

. . . [T]he Court of Appeal in this case concluded that "[a] patient must have the ultimate power to control what becomes of his or her tissues. To hold otherwise would open the door to a massive invasion of human privacy and dignity in the name of medical progress." Yet one may earnestly wish to protect privacy and dignity without accepting the extremely problematic conclusion that interference with those interests amounts to a conversion of personal property. Nor is it necessary to force the round pegs of "privacy" and "dignity" into the square hole of "property" in order to protect the patient, since the fiduciary-duty and informed-consent theories protect these interests directly by requiring full disclosure. . . .

Finally, the subject matter of the Regents' patent—the patented cell line and the products derived from it—cannot be Moore's property. This is because the patented cell line is both factually and legally distinct from the cells taken from Moore's body. Federal law permits the patenting of organisms that represent the product of "human ingenuity," but not naturally occurring organisms. Human cell lines are patentable because "[l]ong-term adaptation and growth of human tissues and cells in culture is difficult—often considered an art . . . ," and the probability of success is low. U.S. Congress, Office of Technology Assessment, New Developments in Biotechnology: Ownership of Human Tissues and Cells 33 (1987). It is this *inventive effort* that patent law rewards, not the discovery of naturally occurring raw materials. . . .

Of the relevant policy considerations, two are of overriding importance. The first is protection of a competent patient's right to make autonomous medical decisions. . . . This policy weighs in favor of providing a remedy to patients when physicians act with undisclosed motives that may affect their professional judgment. The second important policy consideration is that we not threaten with disabling civil liability innocent parties who are engaged in socially useful activities, such as researchers who have no reason to believe that their use of a particular cell sample is, or may be, against a donor's wishes. . . .

We need not, however, make an arbitrary choice between liability and nonliability. Instead, an examination of the relevant policy considerations suggests an appropriate balance: Liability based upon existing disclosure obligations, rather than an unprecedented extension of the conversion theory, protects patients' rights of privacy and autonomy without unnecessarily hindering research. . . .

Research on human cells plays a critical role in medical research. This is so because researchers are increasingly able to isolate naturally occurring, medically useful biological substances and to produce useful quantities of such substances through genetic engineering. These efforts are beginning to bear fruit. Products developed through biotechnology that have already been approved for marketing in this country include treatments and tests for leukemia, cancer, diabetes, dwarfism, hepatitis-B, kidney transplant rejection, emphysema, osteoporosis, ulcers, anemia, infertility, and gynecological tumors, to name but a few.

The extension of conversion law into this area will hinder research by restricting access to the necessary raw materials. Thousands of human cell lines already exist in tissue repositories. . . . These repositories respond to tens of thousands of requests for samples annually. Since the patent office requires the holders of patents on cell lines to make samples available to anyone, many patent holders place their cell lines in repositories to avoid the administrative burden of responding to requests. At present, human cell lines are routinely copied and distributed to other researchers for experimental purposes, usually free of charge. This exchange of scientific materials, which still is relatively free and efficient, will surely be compromised if each cell sample becomes the potential subject matter of a lawsuit. . . .

[T]he theory of liability that Moore urges us to endorse threatens to destroy the economic incentive to conduct important medical research. If the use of cells in research is a conversion, then with every cell sample a researcher purchases a ticket in a litigation lottery. Because liability for conversion is predicated on a continuing ownership interest, "companies are unlikely to invest heavily in developing, manufacturing, or marketing a product when uncertainty about clear title exists." (OTA Rep., supra, at p. 27.) . . .

BROUSSARD, Justice, concurring and dissenting.

. . . If this were a typical case in which a patient consented to the use of his removed organ for general research purposes and the patient's doctor had no prior knowledge of the scientific or commercial value of the patient's organ or cells, I would agree that the patient could not maintain a conversion action. In that common scenario, the patient has abandoned any interest in the removed organ and is not entitled to demand compensation if it should later be discovered that the organ or cells have some unanticipated value. I cannot agree, however, with the majority that a patient may never maintain a conversion action for the unauthorized use of his excised organ or cells, even against a party who knew of the value of the organ or cells before they were removed and breached a duty to disclose that value to the patient. . . .

Although the majority opinion, at several points, appears to suggest that a removed body part, by its nature, may never constitute "property" for purposes of a conversion action, there is no reason to think that the majority opinion actually intends to embrace such a broad or dubious proposition. If, for example, another medical center or drug company had stolen all of the cells in question from the UCLA Medical Center laboratory and had used them for its own benefit, there would be no question but that a cause of action for conversion would properly lie against the thief, and the majority opinion does not suggest otherwise. Thus, the majority's analysis cannot rest on the broad proposition that a removed body part is not property, but rather rests on the proposition that a *patient* retains no ownership interest in a body part once the body part has been removed from his or her body. . . .

MOSK, Justice, dissenting.

. . . The majority's third and last reason for their conclusion that Moore has no cause of action for conversion under existing law is that "the subject matter of the Regents' patent—the patented cell line and the products derived from it—cannot be Moore's property." The majority then offer a dual explanation: "This is because the patented cell line is both *factually* and *legally* distinct from the cells taken from Moore's body" (emphasis added). Neither branch of the explanation withstands analysis.

. . . For present purposes no distinction can be drawn between Moore's cells and the Mo cell line. It appears that the principal reason for establishing a cell line is not to "improve" the quality of the parent cells but simply to extend their life indefinitely, in order to permit long-term study and/or exploitation of the qualities already present in such cells. The complaint alleges that Moore's cells naturally produced certain valuable proteins in larger than normal quantities; indeed, that was why defendants were eager to culture them in the first place. Defendants do not claim that the cells of the Mo cell line are in any degree more productive of such proteins than were Moore's own cells. . . .

I do not question that the cell line is primarily the product of defendants' inventive effort. Yet likewise no one can question Moore's crucial contribution to the invention—an invention named, ironically, after him: But for the cells of Moore's body taken by defendants, there would have been no Mo cell line. Thus the complaint alleges that Moore's "Blood and Bodily Substances were absolutely essential to defendants' research and commercial activities . . . and that defendants could not have applied for and had issued to them the Mo cell-line patent and other patents described herein without obtaining and culturing specimens of plaintiff's Blood and Bodily Substances." . . . Defendants admit this allegation by their demurrers, as well they should: For all their expertise, defendants do not claim they could have extracted the Mo cell line out of thin air.

Nevertheless the majority conclude that the patent somehow cut off all Moore's rights—past, present, and future—to share in the proceeds of defendants' commercial exploitation of the cell line derived from his own body tissue. The majority cite no authority for this unfair result, and I cannot believe it is compelled by the general law of patents: A patent is not a license to defraud. Perhaps the answer lies in an analogy to the concept of "joint inventor." . . .

> Although a patient who donates cells does not fit squarely within the definition of a "joint inventor," the policy reasons that inform joint inventor patents should also apply to cell donors. Neither John Moore nor any other patient whose cells become the basis for a patentable cell line qualifies as a "joint inventor" because he or she did not further the development of the product in any intellectual or conceptual sense. Nor does the status of patients as sole owners of a component part make them deserving of joint inventorship status. What the patients did do, knowingly or unknowingly, is collaborate with the researchers by donating their body tissue. . . . By providing the researchers with unique raw materials, without which the resulting product could not exist, the donors become necessary contributors to the product. Concededly, the patent is not granted for the cell as it is found in nature, but for the modified biogenetic product. However, the uniqueness of the product that gives rise to its patentability stems from the uniqueness of the original cell. *A patient's claim to share in the profits flowing from a patent would be analogous to that of an inventor whose collaboration was essential to the success of a resulting product. The patient was not a coequal, but was a necessary contributor to the cell line.* (Danforth, Cells, Sales, & Royalties: The Patient's Right to a Portion of the Profits, 6 Yale L. & Pol'y Rev. 179, 197 (1988) (emphasis added).) . . .

The majority begin their analysis by stressing the obvious facts that research on human cells plays an increasingly important role in the progress of medicine, and that the manipulation of those cells by the methods of biotechnology has resulted in numerous beneficial products and treatments. Yet it does not necessarily follow that, as the majority claim, application of the law of conversion to this area "will hinder research by restricting access to the necessary raw materials," i.e., to cells, cell cultures, and cell lines. . . .

To begin with, if the relevant exchange of scientific materials was ever "free and efficient," it is much less so today. Since biological products of genetic engineering became patentable in 1980, human cell lines have been amenable to patent protection and, as the court of appeal observed in its opinion below, "The rush to patent for exclusive use has been rampant." Among those who have taken advantage of this development, of course, are the defendants herein. . . . With such patentability has come a drastic reduction in the formerly free access of researchers to new cell lines and their products: The "novelty" requirement for patentability prohibits public disclosure of the invention at all times up to one year before the filing of the patent application. Thus defendants herein recited in their patent specification, "At no time has the Mo cell line been available to other than the investigators involved with its initial discovery." . . .

Secondly, to the extent that cell cultures and cell lines may still be "freely exchanged," e.g., for purely research purposes, it does not follow that the researcher who obtains such material must necessarily remain ignorant of any limitations on its use: By means of appropriate recordkeeping, the researcher can be assured that the source of the material has consented to his proposed use of it, and hence that such use is not a conversion. . . . "Record keeping would not be overly burdensome because researchers generally keep accurate records of tissue sources for other reasons: to trace anomalies to the medical history of the patient, to maintain title for other researchers and for themselves, and to insure reproducibility of the experiment." Toward the Right of Commerciality, 34 UCLA L. Rev. at 241. As the court of appeal correctly observed, any claim to the contrary "is dubious in light of the meticulous care and planning necessary in serious modern medical research." . . .

A second policy consideration adds notions of equity to those of ethics. Our society values fundamental fairness in dealings between its members, and condemns the unjust enrichment of any member at the expense of another. This is particularly true when, as here, the parties are not in equal bargaining positions. We are repeatedly told that the commercial products of the biotechnological revolution "hold the promise of tremendous profit." Toward the Right of Commerciality, 34 UCLA L. Rev. at 211. In the case at bar, for example, the complaint alleges that the market for the kinds of proteins produced by the Mo cell line was predicted to exceed $3 billion by 1990. . . .

There is, however, a third party to the biotechnology enterprise — the patient who is the source of the blood or tissue from which all these profits are derived. While he may be a silent partner, his contribution to the venture is absolutely crucial. . . . Yet defendants deny that Moore is entitled to any share whatever in the proceeds of this cell line. This is both inequitable and immoral. . . .

The majority's final reason for refusing to recognize a conversion cause of action on these facts is that "there is no pressing need" to do so because the complaint also states another cause of action that is assertedly adequate to the task [— the nondisclosure cause of action]. . . .

I disagree . . . with the majority's . . . conclusion that in the present context a nondisclosure cause of action is an adequate — in fact, a superior — substitute for a conversion cause of action. [Justice Mosk then goes on to point out how difficult it is for patients to win damages in informed consent cases. He also points out that an informed consent claim would be good only against the patient's physician, in this case Dr. Golde, but not against other persons or institutions outside the patient-physician relationship who benefited from the patient's cells.]

■ GREENBERG v. MIAMI CHILDREN'S HOSPITAL RESEARCH INSTITUTE, INC.
264 F. Supp. 2d 1064 (S.D. Fla. 2003)

MORENO, Judge ...

I. BACKGROUND ...

The Complaint alleges a tale of a successful research collaboration gone sour. In 1987, Canavan disease still remained a mystery—there was no way to identify who was a carrier of the disease, nor was there a way to identify a fetus with Canavan disease. Plaintiff Greenberg approached Dr. Matalon, a research physician ... for assistance. Greenberg requested Matalon's involvement in discovering the genes that were ostensibly responsible for this fatal disease, so that tests could be administered to determine carriers and allow for prenatal testing for the disease. [Canavan disease is a genetic disorder of the neurologic system that usually causes death by age 4 and is more common among Jews from Eastern Europe and among Saudi Arabians. If both parents carry the gene for Canavan disease, their children face a 25 percent chance of developing the disease.]

At the outset of the collaboration, Greenberg and the Chicago Chapter of the National Tay-Sachs and Allied Disease Association, Inc. ("NTSAD") located other Canavan families and convinced them to provide tissue (such as blood, urine, and autopsy samples), financial support, and aid in identifying the location of Canavan families internationally. The other individual Plaintiffs began supplying Matalon with the same types of information and samples beginning in the late 1980s. ...

The individual Plaintiffs allege that they provided Matalon with these samples and confidential information "with the understanding and expectations that such samples and information would be used for the specific purpose of researching Canavan disease and identifying mutations in the Canavan disease which could lead to carrier detection within their families and benefit the population at large." Plaintiffs further allege that it was their "understanding that any carrier and prenatal testing developed in connection with the research for which they were providing essential support would be provided on an affordable and accessible basis, and that Matalon's research would remain in the public domain to promote the discovery of more effective prevention techniques and treatments and, eventually, to effectuate a cure for Canavan disease." This understanding stemmed from their "experience in community testing for Tay-Sachs disease, another deadly genetic disease that occurs most frequently in families of Ashkenazi Jewish descent."

There was a breakthrough in the research in 1993. Using Plaintiffs' blood and tissue samples, familial pedigree information, contacts, and financial support,

Matalon and his research team successfully isolated the gene responsible for Canavan disease. After this key advancement, Plaintiffs allege that they continued to provide Matalon with more tissue and blood in order to learn more about the disease and its precursor gene.

In September 1994, unbeknownst to Plaintiffs, a patent application was submitted for the genetic sequence that Defendants had identified. This application was granted in October 1997, and Dr. Matalon was listed as an inventor on the gene patent and related applications for the Canavan disease, Patent No. 5,679,635 (the "Patent"). Through patenting, Defendants acquired the ability to restrict any activity related to the Canavan disease gene, including without limitation: carrier and prenatal testing, gene therapy and other treatments for Canavan disease and research involving the gene and its mutations.

Although the Patent was issued in October 1997, Plaintiffs allege that they did not learn of it until November 1998, when MCH revealed their intention to limit Canavan disease testing through a campaign of restrictive licensing of the Patent. . . . Defendant MCH also began restricting public accessibility through negotiating exclusive licensing agreements and charging royalty fees. . . .

. . . Plaintiffs generally seek a permanent injunction restraining Defendants from enforcing their patent rights, damages in the form of all royalties Defendants have received on the Patent as well as all financial contributions Plaintiffs made to benefit Defendants' research. Plaintiffs allege that Defendants have earned significant royalties from Canavan disease testing in excess of $75,000 through enforcement of their gene patent, and that Dr. Matalon has personally profited by receiving a recent substantial federal grant to undertake further research on the gene patent. . . .

III. ANALYSIS . . .

A. LACK OF INFORMED CONSENT

[The court rejected a duty for researchers to disclose their economic interests, distinguishing Moore v. Regents of the University of California on the ground that the researcher in that case also provided care to Mr. Moore, while Dr. Matalon did not provide care to any of the plaintiffs.] . . .

C. UNJUST ENRICHMENT

In Count III of the Complaint, Plaintiffs allege that MCH is being unjustly enriched by collecting license fees under the Patent. Under Florida law, the elements of a claim for unjust enrichment are (1) the plaintiff conferred a benefit on the defendant, who had knowledge of the benefit; (2) the defendant voluntarily accepted and retained the benefit; and (3) under the circumstances it would be inequitable for the defendant to retain the benefit without paying for it. The Court finds that Plaintiffs have sufficiently alleged the elements of a claim for unjust enrichment to survive Defendants' motion to dismiss.

While the parties do not contest that Plaintiffs have conferred a benefit to Defendants, including, among other things, blood and tissue samples and soliciting financial contributions, Defendants contend that Plaintiffs have not suffered any detriment, and note that no Plaintiff has been denied access to

Canavan testing. Furthermore, the Plaintiffs received what they sought — the successful isolation of the Canavan gene and the development of a screening test. Plaintiffs argue, however, that when Defendants applied the benefits for unauthorized purposes, they suffered a detriment. Had Plaintiffs known that Defendants intended to commercialize their genetic material through patenting and restrictive licensing, Plaintiffs would not have provided these benefits to Defendants under those terms.

Naturally, Plaintiffs allege that the retention of benefits violates the fundamental principles of justice, equity, and good conscience. While Defendants claim that they have invested significant amounts of time and money in research, with no guarantee of success and are thus entitled to seek reimbursement, the same can be said of Plaintiffs. Moreover, Defendants' attempt to seek refuge in the endorsement of the U.S. Patent system, which gives an inventor rights to prosecute patents and negotiate licenses for their intellectual property fails, as obtaining a patent does not preclude the Defendants from being unjustly enriched. The Complaint has alleged more than just a donor-donee relationship for the purposes of an unjust enrichment claim. Rather, the facts paint a picture of a continuing research collaboration that involved Plaintiffs also investing time and significant resources in the race to isolate the Canavan gene. Therefore, given the facts as alleged, the Court finds that Plaintiffs have sufficiently pled the requisite elements of an unjust enrichment claim and the motion to dismiss for failure to state a claim is DENIED as to this count. . . .

E. CONVERSION

The Plaintiffs allege in Count V of their Complaint that they had a property interest in their body tissue and genetic information, and that they owned the Canavan registry in Illinois which contained contact information, pedigree information and family information for Canavan families worldwide. They claim that MCH and Matalon converted the names on the register and the genetic information by utilizing them for the hospitals' "exclusive economic benefit." The Court disagrees and declines to find a property interest for the body tissue and genetic information voluntarily given to Defendants. These were donations to research without any contemporaneous expectations of return of the body tissue and genetic samples, and thus conversion does not lie as a cause of action.

In Florida, the tort of "conversion is an unauthorized act which deprives another of his property permanently or for an indefinite time." Using property given for one purpose for another purpose constitutes conversion.

First, Plaintiffs have no cognizable property interest in body tissue and genetic matter donated for research under a theory of conversion. This case is similar to *Moore v. Regents of the University of California*, where the Court declined to extend liability under a theory of conversion to misuse of a person's excised biological materials. The plaintiff in *Moore* alleged that he had retained a property right in excised bodily material used in research, and therefore retained some control over the results of that research. The California Supreme Court, however, disagreed and held that the use of the results of medical research inconsistent with the wishes of the donor was not conversion, because the donor had no property interest at stake after the donation was made. . . .

Second, limits to the property rights that attach to body tissue have been recognized in Florida state courts. For example, *in State v. Powell, 497 So. 2d 1188, 1192 (Fla. 1986),* the Florida Supreme Court refused to recognize a property right in the body of another after death. Similarly, the property right in blood and tissue samples also evaporates once the sample is voluntarily given to a third party.

. . . Plaintiffs cite a litany of cases in other jurisdictions that have recognized that body tissue can be property in some circumstances. *See, e.g., Brotherton v. Cleveland, 923 F.2d 477, 482 (6th Cir. 1991)* (aggregate of rights existing in body tissue is similar to property rights); *York v. Jones, 717 F. Supp. 421, 425 (E.D. Va. 1989)* (couple granted property rights in their frozen embryos). These cases, however, do not involve voluntary donations to medical research. . . .

Finally, although the Complaint sets out that Plaintiff Greenberg owned the Canavan Registry, the facts alleged do not sufficiently allege the elements of a *prima facie* case of conversion, as the Plaintiffs have not alleged how the Defendants' use of the Registry in their research was an expressly unauthorized act. The Complaint only alleges that the Defendants "utilized the information and contacts for their exclusive economic benefit." There [are] no further allegations of the circumstances or conditions that were attached to the Defendants' use of the Canavan Registry. Nor are there any allegations about any of the Plaintiffs' entitlement to possess the Registry.

The Court finds that Florida . . . law do[es] not provide a remedy for Plaintiffs' donations of body tissue and blood samples under a theory of conversion liability. Indeed, the Complaint does not allege that the Defendants used the genetic material for any purpose but medical research. Plaintiffs claim that the *fruits* of the research, namely the patented material, was commercialized. This is an important distinction and another step in the chain of attenuation that renders conversion liability inapplicable to the facts as alleged. If adopted, the expansive theory championed by Plaintiffs would cripple medical research as it would bestow a continuing right for donors to possess the results of any research conducted by the hospital. At the core, these were donations to research without any contemporaneous expectations of return. Consequently, the Plaintiffs have failed to state a claim upon which relief may be granted on this issue. Accordingly, this claim is DISMISSED. . . .

Notes: Human Tissue in Research

1. *Subsequent Developments.* When the *Moore* case went back to the trial court on remand, the parties settled for an undisclosed amount of money. Ultimately, researchers figured out how to produce large amounts of lymphokines without using Mr. Moore's cell line. The *Greenberg* case also was settled, with Miami Children's Hospital permitted to license and collect royalty fees for the laboratory test for the Canavan gene, but obligated to allow license-free use of the Canavan gene in research to cure Canavan disease. Note, 93 Geo. L.J. 365, 376 (2004).

2. *Wash. Univ. v. Catalona.* While *Moore* and *Greenberg* involved disputes between patients and researchers, disputes also may arise between researchers and their institutions. When a highly respected researcher of prostate cancer,

Dr. William Catalona, moved from Washington University, St. Louis, to Northwestern University, he wanted to take a repository of prostate tissue, blood, and DNA samples that he had collected from patients and that he used in his research. On summary judgment, a federal trial court concluded that the patients had donated their tissue samples to Washington University, which enjoyed ownership rights over those samples. The court therefore held that neither the patients nor Dr. Catalona could insist that Washington University transfer the samples to Northwestern University. Wash. Univ. v. Catalona, 437 F. Supp. 2d 985 (E.D. Mo. 2006). For further discussion of this case, see Lori Andrews, Who Owns Your Body? A Patient's Perspective on Washington University v. Catalona. 34 J.L. Med. & Ethics 398 (2006).

2. *Reconciling* Moore *and* Greenberg *with* McFall. Are the results in *Moore* and *Greenberg* consistent with the result in McFall v. Shimp, supra page 381? If the state cannot force Mr. Shimp to give up his bone marrow for the greater good of society, why can it force Mr. Moore and others to relinquish control over their cells for the same reason? Does Shimp win and the others lose only because the cells were already outside their bodies, and they therefore suffered no invasion of their bodily integrity? But didn't Moore consent to subsequent invasions of his bodily integrity after the surgery only because of Dr. Golde's deception? Does the *Moore* case simply prove Judge Calabresi's point at page 388 that we see ourselves as the Shimps and users of lymphokines of society, but not as the McFalls or Moores of society?

3. *Frozen Embryos*. In Davis v. Davis, 842 S.W.2d 588 (Tenn. 1992), the Tennessee Supreme Court held that frozen embryos could not be used for procreation without the consent of both the woman and man who contributed the egg and sperm, respectively. If Moore and Greenberg lost in their cases because there was no bodily invasion, then how do we reconcile the *Davis* case with the *Moore* and *Greenberg* cases?

4. *Researchers Profiting from Mr. Moore's Cells*. Why should everyone but Moore be able to benefit financially from the use of his cells? We might argue that the difference between paying researchers and paying patients is the fact that we worry about patients assuming undue health risks for pay, but we do not have to worry about researchers putting themselves at risk of personal harm if they benefit financially from their work. What is the counter to this argument?

Does *Greenberg*'s theory of unjust enrichment provide adequate protection for patients?

Just as researchers can earn substantial sums by manipulating a person's cells in research, so can companies realize large profits by processing a cadaver's tissues for transplantation. Although federal law prohibits payments to the decedent's family for skin, tendons, bone, heart valves, and other tissues, 42 U.S.C. §274e, tissue banks can receive reasonable payments for their retrieval and storage costs, and tissue processors can charge what the market will bear for tissues used in transplants. In contrast to the substantial regulation of the organ transplant system, the law provides considerably less oversight of the tissue processing and transplant industry. For more discussion, see Robert A. Katz, The Re-Gift of Life: Can Charity Law Prevent For-Profit Firms from Exploiting Donated Tissue and Nonprofit Tissue Banks?, 55 DePaul L. Rev. 943 (2006); Michelle Oberman,

When the Truth Is Not Enough: Tissue Donation, Altruism, and the Market, 55 DePaul L. Rev. 903 (2006).

    5. *Additional Readings.* In addition to the articles cited in *Moore*, readings on this topic include Lori B. Andrews, My Body, My Property, 16(5) Hastings Center Rep. 28 (1986); George J. Annas, Outrageous Fortune: Selling Other People's Cells, 20(6) Hastings Center Rep. 36 (1990); R. Alta Charo, Body of Research — Ownership and Use of Human Tissue, 355 New Eng. J. Med. 1517 (2006); Bernard M. Dickens, The Control of Living Body Materials, 27 U. Toronto L.J. 142 (1977); Donna M. Gitter, Ownership of Human Tissue: A Proposal for Federal Recognition of Human Research Participants' Property Rights in Their Biological Material, 61 Wash. & Lee L. Rev. 257 (2004); Sharon Nan Perley, Note, From Control Over One's Body to Control Over One's Body Parts: Extending the Doctrine of Informed Consent, 67 N.Y.U. L. Rev. 335 (1992).

C. ALLOCATION OF ORGANS

    So far, we have been discussing issues about organ procurement and proposals to increase the supply of organs. Another critical issue is organ allocation: among those in need of an organ transplant, to whom will an available organ be given? The important law for this issue is the National Transplant Act of 1984. As mentioned above, the Act created the Organ Procurement and Transportation Network (OPTN) as a private, nonprofit entity to oversee the retrieval and allocation of organs for transplantation. Since 1986, the Secretary of Health and Human Services has awarded successive contracts to the United Network for Organ Sharing (UNOS) to operate the OPTN. UNOS is a membership organization that includes the 58 organ procurement organizations throughout the country, as well as more than 250 transplant surgery centers, medical laboratories that perform tests for organ matching, volunteer and advocacy groups, and members of the general public. The organ procurement organizations are responsible for procuring organs in their geographic area and allocating the organs to patients in need. UNOS issues allocation guidelines for the procurement organizations to follow, and, while the guidelines differ for hearts, livers, kidneys, and other organs, they generally rely on criteria such as the likelihood of a successful transplant, time spent on the waiting list, and medical urgency (i.e., whether the person is likely to die or suffer irreparable injury if a transplant is not performed soon). A person's place of residence may also play a critical role. Preference for a transplant is given to people on the local waiting list, and people tend to appear only on the waiting list for their area. Often the different criteria come into conflict. A patient may gain priority because of an urgent need for a liver transplant, but then have the priority offset by a short life expectancy even with a transplant.

    While UNOS guidelines govern the allocation of organs for persons who are on a waiting list for a transplant, there are no standard rules for deciding when a person is added to a waiting list. Accordingly, while transplant centers exhibit considerable agreement in their policies, they also vary in their approaches. In deciding whom to place on the wait list, transplant centers tend to consider several factors: the likelihood that the transplant surgery will go well, the length of time that the recipient will benefit from the transplant before either the transplant is "rejected" by the patient or the patient dies, and the quality of life that the recipient will experience with the transplant. For indirect measures of these factors, transplant centers look at the severity and cause of organ failure, the presence in the recipient of other illnesses that affect either life expectancy or the ability to tolerate major surgery, the patient's age, and psychosocial criteria (e.g., alcohol or other drug abuse, psychiatric illness, mental retardation, and lack of compliance with treatment regimens in the past).

With liver transplantation, for example, a number of unofficial policies have developed. Patients with liver cancer generally do not do well with a transplant because of recurrence of the cancer, and transplant centers typically limit transplants to liver cancer patients whose cancers are found early and have not yet spread. Maria Varela et al., Hepatoma, *in* Medical Care of the Liver Transplant Patient 119, 120 (Paul G. Killenberg & Pierre-Alain Clavien eds., 2006). Other patients who are denied liver transplants are those who currently engage in drug abuse, have AIDS or other severe infections, have a non-liver, non-skin cancer, have suffered irreversible brain injury from their liver failure, or have advanced heart or lung disease. Don C. Rockey, Selection and Evaluation of the Recipient (including Retransplantation), *in* Medical Care of the Liver Transplant Patient 3, 6-10 (Paul G. Killenberg & Pierre-Alain Clavien eds., 2006) Transplantation for patients with liver failure from alcohol abuse is common, but there is variation among centers in deciding which persons with alcoholic liver disease should be considered for transplantation. Factors that are used to select candidates include documented abstinence from alcohol (typically at least six months), evidence of social stability (e.g., employment, permanent residence, and marriage), presence of a good family or social support system, absence of illicit substance use, absence of psychiatric illness, and compliance with recommendations by the patient's treating physicians. See Sheila Jowsey & Terry Schneekloth, Psychosocial Assessment of Adult Liver Transplant Recipients, *in* Transplantation of the Liver 395, 401 (Ronald W. Busuttil & Goran K. Klintmalm eds., 2d ed. 2005); see also Seonaid McCallum & George Masterton, Liver Transplantation for Alcoholic Liver Disease: A Systematic Review of Psychosocial Selection Criteria, 41 Alcohol & Alcoholism 358 (2006) (finding that social stability, past compliance with medical care and other variables, but not duration of pre-transplant abstinence from alcohol use, are good predictors of post-transplant success). Some transplant centers are now performing transplants for some patients with HIV infection. Michelle E. Roland & Peter G. Stock, Liver Transplantation in HIV-Infected Recipients, 26 Seminars Liver Disease 273 (2006).

Ability to pay is also an obstacle for many potential organ transplant recipients. Medicare pays for kidney transplants, but not for all of the associated costs (e.g., coverage is temporary for drugs to prevent rejection of the transplanted organ by the recipient's immune system that have to be taken as long as the organ is still functioning). Medicare also pays for heart, lung and liver transplants, but restricts the pool of potential recipients by requiring them to meet certain medical criteria and to qualify for Social Security disability benefits. In addition, with these organs, Medicare also does not pay all of the associated medical costs. Some recipients can rely on private insurance or Medicaid, but those patients too may receive only partial reimbursement for the costs of the transplant and its follow-up care. Accordingly, for some people, the costs of a transplant may preclude its availability. Even for people who receive a transplant, financial considerations may compromise the long-term success of the procedure. Data suggest that an important reason for failure of organs a few years after transplantation is the unaffordability of the drugs to suppress the recipient's immune system. Lisa M. Willoughby et al., Health Insurance Considerations for Adolescent Transplant Recipients as They Transition to Adulthood, 11 Pediat. Transplant. 127 (2007).

Finally, cases involving celebrities suggest that social value considerations may affect allocation decisions (e.g., the liver transplant for Mickey Mantle in June 1995).

■ UNOS POLICY FOR ORGAN DISTRIBUTION

UNOS prescribes policies for allocation of each type of organ. Below you will find an excerpt from the liver allocation policy. The excerpt reflects UNOS policy for ranking adults waiting for liver transplants. There are additional provisions for children waiting for transplants that can be found at the UNOS Web site (www.unos.org).

UNOS Policy 3.6 — December 14, 2006

3.6 *ALLOCATION OF LIVERS.* Unless otherwise approved according to [other UNOS policies], the allocation of livers according to the following point system is mandatory. For the purpose of enabling physicians to apply their consensus medical judgment for the benefit of liver transplant candidates as a group, each patient will be assigned [either] a status code or [a] probability of pre-transplant death derived from a mortality risk score corresponding to the degree of medical urgency as described in Policy 3.6.4 below. Mortality risk scores shall be determined by the prognostic factors specified in Table[] 1 . . . and calculated in accordance with the Model for End-Stage Liver Disease (MELD) Scoring System . . . described in Policy 3.6.4.1. . . . Candidates will be stratified within MELD . . . score by blood type similarity as described in Policy 3.6.2. No individual or property rights are conferred by this system of liver allocation.

Livers will be offered to candidates with an assigned Status of 1A . . . in descending point sequence with the candidate having the highest number of points receiving the highest priority before being offered for candidates listed in other categories. . . . Following Status 1, livers will be offered to candidates based upon their probability of candidate death derived from assigned MELD . . . scores, as applicable, in descending point sequence with the candidate having the highest probability ranking receiving the highest priority before being offered to candidates having lower probability rankings. . . .

[Priority Ranking for Adults on the Liver Wait List]

Local
1. Status 1A candidates in descending point order

Regional
2. Status 1A candidates in descending point order. . . .

Local
[3]. Candidates with [MELD] Scores ≥ 15 in descending order of mortality risk scores (probability of candidate death)

Regional

[4]. Candidates with [MELD] Scores ≥ 15 in descending order of mortality risk scores (probability of candidate death)

Local

[5]. Candidates with [MELD] Scores < 15 in descending order of mortality risk scores (probability of candidate death)

Regional

[6]. Candidates with [MELD] Scores < 15 in descending order of mortality risk scores (probability of candidate death)

National

[7]. Status 1A candidates in descending point order. . . .

[8]. All other candidates in descending order of mortality risk scores (probability of candidate death). . . .

The liver must be transplanted into the original designee or be released back to the Host OPO or to the Organ Center for distribution. . . . The final decision whether to use the liver will remain the prerogative of the transplant surgeon and/ or physician responsible for the care of that candidate. This will allow physicians and surgeons to exercise judgment about the suitability of the liver being offered for their specific candidate; to be faithful to their personal and programmatic philosophy about such controversial matters as the importance of cold ischemia and anatomic anomalies; and to give their best assessment of the prospective recipient's medical condition at the moment. If a liver is declined for a candidate, a notation of the reason for the decision not to accept the liver for that candidate must be made on the appropriate form and promptly submitted. . . .

3.6.1 Preliminary Stratification. For every potential liver recipient, the acceptable donor size must be determined by the responsible surgeon. The Match System will consider only potential liver recipients who are an acceptable size for that particular donor liver.

3.6.2 Blood Type Similarity Stratification/Points. For Status 1A . . . transplant candidates, those with the same ABO type as the liver donor shall receive 10 points. Candidates with compatible but not identical ABO types shall receive 5 points, and candidates with incompatible types shall receive 0 points. . . . Within each [MELD] score, donor livers shall be offered to transplant candidates who are ABO-identical with the donor first, then to candidates who are ABO-compatible, followed by candidates who are ABO-incompatible with the donor.

3.6.2.1 Allocation of Blood Type O Donors. With the Exception of Status 1A . . . candidates, blood type O donors may only be allocated to blood type O candidates, or B candidates with a MELD . . . score greater than or equal to 30. . . .

3.6.2.2 Liver Allocation to Candidates Willing to Accept an Incompatible Blood Type. For Status 1A . . . candidates or candidates with a match MELD . . . score of 30 and greater, centers may specify on the Waiting List those candidates who will accept a liver from a donor of any blood type.

3.6.3 Time Waiting. Transplant candidates on the Waiting List shall accrue waiting time within Status 1A . . . or any assigned MELD . . . score; however, waiting time accrued while listed at a lower [MELD] score will not be counted toward liver allocation if the candidate is upgraded to a higher [MELD] score. . . . For example, if there are 2 persons with a MELD score of 30 who were both of identical blood types with the donor, the candidate with the longest accrued waiting time in MELD score 30 or higher would receive the first offer. Waiting time will not be accrued by candidates awaiting a liver transplant while they are registered on the Waiting List as inactive.

Candidates in Status 1A . . . will receive waiting time points based on their waiting time in that Status. Ten points will be accrued by the candidate waiting for the longest period for a liver transplant and proportionately fewer points will be accrued by those candidates with shorter tenure. For example, if there were 75 persons of O blood type waiting who were of a size compatible with a blood group O donor, the person waiting the longest would accrue 10 points ($75/75 \times 10$). A person whose rank order was 60 would accrue 2 points. (($75 - 60)/75 \times 10 = 2$).

3.6.4 Degree of Medical Urgency. Each candidate is assigned a status code or mortality risk score (probability of candidate death) which corresponds to how medically urgent it is that the candidate receive a transplant.

3.6.4.1 Adult Candidate Status. Medical urgency is assigned to an adult liver transplant candidate (greater than or equal to 18 years of age) based on either the criteria defined below for Status 1A, or the candidate's mortality risk score as determined by the prognostic factors specified in Table 1 and calculated in accordance with the MELD Scoring System. A candidate who does not have a MELD score that, in the judgment of the candidate's transplant physician, appropriately reflects the candidate's medical urgency, may nevertheless be assigned a higher MELD score upon application by his/her transplant physician(s) and justification to the applicable Regional Review Board that the candidate is considered, by consensus medical judgment, using accepted medical criteria, to have an urgency and potential for benefit comparable to that of other candidates having the higher MELD score. The justification must include a rationale for incorporating the exceptional case as part of MELD calculation. . . .

Status	Definition
7	A candidate listed as Status 7 is temporarily inactive. Candidates who are considered to be temporarily unsuitable transplant candidates are listed as Status 7, temporarily inactive.
1A	A candidate greater than or equal to 18 years of age listed as Status 1A has fulminant liver failure with a life expectancy without a liver transplant of less than 7 days. For the purpose of Policy 3.6, fulminant liver failure shall be defined as described in (i)-(iv). . . . (i) fulminant hepatic failure defined as the onset of hepatic encephalopathy within 8 weeks of the first symptoms of liver disease. The absence of pre-existing liver disease is critical to the diagnosis. . . . or

Status	*Definition*
	(ii) primary non-function of a transplanted liver within 7 days of implantation [primary non-function is to be distinguished from secondary non-function, or loss of function from problems external to the liver, like heart disease]; . . . or
	(iii) hepatic artery thrombosis in a transplanted liver within 7 days of implantation, with evidence of severe liver injury, . . . or
	(iv) acute decompensated Wilson's disease [a rare, inherited disease that results in damage to the liver and the brain]. . . .
	Candidates who are listed as a Status 1A automatically revert back to their most recent MELD Score after 7 days unless these candidates are relisted as Status 1A by an attending physician. . . .
	All other adult liver transplant candidates on the Waiting List shall be assigned a mortality risk score calculated in accordance with the MELD scoring system. . . .

[For pediatric liver allocation, there is a status 1B as well as 1A.]

[The MELD scoring system is based on three laboratory values, with a maximum score of 40. The three laboratory values are serum bilirubin (a measure of liver function), INR (a measure of blood-clotting ability that reflects liver function), and serum creatinine (a measure of kidney function).]

3.6.4.1.1 Adult Candidate Reassessment and Recertification Schedule. The appropriateness of the MELD score assigned to each candidate listing shall be re-assessed and recertified by the listing transplant center to the OPTN Contractor in accordance with the following schedule:

Adult Candidate Reassessment and Recertification Schedule

Status 1A	Status recertification every 7 days.	Laboratory values must be no older than 48 hours.
MELD Score 25 or greater	Status recertification every 7 days.	Laboratory values must be no older than 48 hours.
Score ≤ 24 but > 18	Status recertification every 1 month.	Laboratory values must be no older than 7 days.
Score ≤ 18 but ≥11	Status recertification every 3 months.	Laboratory values must be no older than 14 days.
Score ≤ 10 but > 0	Status recertification every 12 months.	Laboratory values must be no older than 30 days.

Notes: Criteria for Rationing Organs

1. *Local vs. National Standards for Listing.* As we have seen, UNOS guidelines kick in only after patients have been selected for the waiting list. Getting on the waiting list can be a much more important step, and transplant centers are free to develop their own policies. Is that appropriate, or should UNOS issue national guidelines for determining when a patient will be added to the waiting list?

In the past, UNOS has suggested it would develop standard criteria for deciding when a person should be placed on the waiting list for either a kidney or liver. Such criteria would help address the problem of some transplant centers being too quick to place a patient on a waiting list (sometimes doing so on the theory that, by the time the patient reaches the top of the list, the patient will be ready for a transplant).

Note that to some extent, the allocation guidelines also give guidance for adding people to the waiting list. For example, if a patient's liver disease is severe enough for the patient to qualify for Status 1 once listed or the patient has a high MELD score, the disease is also severe enough that the patient should be listed.

For an example of professional guidelines for listing candidates for organ transplantation, see Michael R. Lucey et al., Minimal Criteria for Placement of Adults on the Liver Transplant Waiting List: A Report of the National Conference Organized by the American Society of Transplant Physicians and the American Association for the Study of Liver Diseases, 3 Liver Transplant. 628 (1997); Mandeep R. Mehra et al., Listing Criteria for Heart Transplantation: International Society for Heart and Lung Transplantation Guidelines for the Care of Cardiac Transplant Candidates—2006, 25 J. Heart & Lung Transplant. 1024 (2006).

For a discussion of the inequities in listing, see Michele Goodwin, Altruism's Limits: Law, Capacity, and Organ Commodification, 56 Rutgers L. Rev. 305, 330-339 (2004).

2. *Relative Weights of Different Criteria.* Under the UNOS policy for liver transplantation, the greatest weights are given to medical urgency and the length of time that the recipient will benefit from the transplant. Medical urgency comes into play through the criteria for Status 1A and the MELD score ranking. Patients do not qualify for Status 1A unless their life expectancy without a transplant is less than seven days, and sicker patients have higher MELD scores.

The length of time that the recipient will benefit from the transplant is reflected in two ways. First, and more importantly, there is consideration of the patient's life expectancy with a transplant. Adult patients qualify for Status 1A only if they suffer from "fulminant" liver failure. These patients, whose liver failure has usually come on suddenly, typically live longer with a liver transplant than patients with "chronic" or long-standing liver failure. If the liver failure has existed for only a short time, then almost all of its harm to the body can be reversed with a liver transplant. When the liver failure has been long-lived, then much of its damage to the body is permanent and cannot be reversed. As a result, the patient might die even though the new liver is functioning well. (Note that some patients qualify for Status 1A if they've experienced unsuccessful liver transplant surgery. These patients might have developed their initial need for a transplant after chronic liver failure.)

Length of benefit from the transplant is also reflected in consideration of the likelihood that the liver will be rejected by the recipient's immune system. Under Policy 3.6.2, points are given for blood type similarity (maximum of ten points) since rejection of the transplant is less likely when blood types are compatible.

Some consideration in the UNOS liver policy is given to concerns of equity in access; this is done in the awarding of points for time on the waiting list and for blood type similarity. The relationship between equity and points for blood type similarity is somewhat complicated. First, Policy 3.6.2.1 has special rules for blood type O patients. Second, if the donor and recipient have *identical* blood types, ten points are given. Five points are given for *compatible* blood types. These two policies exist because patients with blood type O would be disadvantaged if livers were allocated only on the basis of blood type compatibility. Livers from type O donors are good transplants for recipients of any blood type (i.e., type O people are "universal" donors), but type O recipients must rely almost exclusively on livers from type O donors. If only compatibility mattered, livers from type O donors would be scattered among recipients of all blood types, thereby decreasing the pool of "good" livers for blood type O patients and increasing the pool of "good" livers for patients of other blood types.

For suggestions to improve the use of MELD scores, see Scott W. Biggins & Kiran Bambha, MELD-Based Liver Allocation: Who Is Underserved, 26 Seminars Liver Disease 211 (2006)

For allocation of kidneys, UNOS assigns different relative weights. The most important difference is the unimportance of medical urgency in kidney allocation. Urgency rarely affects kidney allocation decisions since patients on the waiting list usually can be maintained on dialysis while awaiting a transplant. The greatest weight for kidney transplants is given to the length of time in which the recipient will benefit from the transplant. Most of the points for ranking potential recipients come from measuring the likelihood that the transplanted organ will be rejected, as reflected in the compatibility of tissue matching between the donor and recipient. Tissue compatibility is associated with a greater length of time in which the kidney functions in the recipient. Significant consideration under the UNOS policy is also given to the fact that some potential recipients are highly "sensitized" to foreign tissues (i.e., tissues from other persons) and are therefore much less likely to find a kidney that they would not reject immediately. Common causes of tissue sensitization are blood transfusions, pregnancy, and receipt of an organ transplant previously (i.e., situations in which the patient has been exposed to tissue from another person). Tissue compatibility is given greater weight with kidneys than livers because rejection of the transplanted organ is more frequently a problem with kidney transplants.

Although length of benefit is very important with kidney allocation, it is measured only in terms of the likelihood that the kidney will be rejected, without consideration of the patient's life expectancy with a functioning transplant. That is, there is nothing analogous for kidney allocation to the distinction in liver allocation between fulminant and chronic liver failure. This may simply reflect the fact that the distinction between fulminant and chronic liver failure dates only to November 1996. Why else might life expectancy with a transplant be more important with a liver transplant? (Life expectancy with a kidney transplant may not show up in the UNOS policy, but it undoubtedly is considered by physicians when they decide whether to place a patient with kidney failure on the transplant waiting list.) Life expectancy may become part of the UNOS kidney allocation policy soon. See Laura Meckler, More Kidneys for Transplants May Go to Young, Wall St. J., March 10-11, 2007, at A1.

3. *The Controversial Nature of Allocation Criteria.* Since the allocation of organs may have life-and-death consequences, there is often considerable controversy over the selection criteria, as occurred in November 1996 when UNOS proposed an amendment of the criteria for allocation of livers. The proposed policy gave greater weight to the patient's life expectancy with a transplant and less weight to the patient's medical urgency. Under the pre-proposal policy, urgency was the dominant consideration. Patients were classified as Status 1 if they were expected to die within seven days without a transplant, regardless of whether they suffered from fulminant or chronic liver failure. To give greater weight to expected benefit, the proposed policy limited Status 1 to patients whose need for a transplant was urgent *and* who were suffering from fulminant liver failure. Patients with chronic liver failure could not qualify for Status 1 even if their need for a liver was urgent. When the 1996 proposal was announced, there were charges of discrimination against alcoholics since alcohol abuse is one of the most common causes of chronic liver failure.

Because of the public outcry, the liver allocation rules underwent multiple modifications between 1996 and 2002. The U.S. Department of Health and Human Services provided guidance through amendment of its regulations governing organ transplantation at 42 C.F.R. 6 §§121.1 et seq. (2002). For discussion of the controversy, see Dulcinea A. Grantham, Transforming Transplantation: The Effect of the Health and Human Services Final Rules on the Organ Allocation System, 35 U.S.F. L. Rev. 751 (2001).

4. *Legal Rights to a Transplant.* Does a potential recipient of an organ ever enjoy a legal right to the organ? Recall from the liver allocation policy that UNOS has tried to foreclose that possibility. According to the policy, "[n]o individual or property rights are conferred by this system of liver allocation." Allocation policies for other organs, however, do not contain a similar statement.

The rights of a potential recipient were explored to some extent in Colavito v. New York Organ Donor Network, Inc., 860 N.E.2d 713 (N.Y. 2006) and — F.3d — (2d Cir. May 21, 2007). That case arose after a widow tried to donate a kidney from her deceased husband to the husband's longtime friend. One of the kidneys was sent to the friend's hospital, but anatomical abnormalities (renal artery aneurysms) made the kidney unsuitable for transplantation. When the friend's surgeon asked for the second kidney, he was told that it had already been transplanted into another person. The widow argued that she intended for any donation to be limited to the longtime friend, and there were questions whether the second kidney had in fact been transplanted when the call came from the friend's doctor. As it turned out, immunological testing demonstrated that the kidneys were not compatible with the friend and could not have been transplanted into him. For that reason, the New York Court of Appeals did not decide whether a disappointed transplant recipient might have a cause of action under New York public health law for failure to receive the transplant. The court did conclude that a disappointed transplant recipient is not able to bring a cause of action for conversion.

Whether or not potential recipients enjoy legal rights to a transplant, they may have a valid claim if they lose an opportunity for an organ because of a transplant program's malfeasance. Litigation against the liver transplant program at University of California–Irvine precipitated a shutting down of the program by the federal government. A patient sued the program, claiming that it wrongfully gave preference to other persons waiting for a transplant over a four-year period. In supporting her claim, the patient cited a UNOS document indicating that the transplant program had declined organs offered by UNOS for the woman approximately forty times. Irvine v. Regents of the University of California, 57 Cal. Rptr. 3d 500 (Ct. App. 2007) (reinstating claim and remanding for consideration by the trial court). During its investigation of the program, Medicare found that the program lacked adequate staffing, resulting in a very high level of deaths among patients on the waiting list. Charles Ornstein & Alan Zarembo, Hospital Halts Liver Transplant Program, L.A. Times, Nov. 11, 2005, at A1.

4. *Local vs. National Waiting Lists.* Another controversial issue has been the use of local, regional, and national waiting lists rather than a single national list. As the liver allocation policy indicates, first priority for a transplant is given to people on the local waiting list, then the regional waiting list, and finally the national waiting list. Some people are listed on multiple local waiting lists, and some health care plans require their members to be listed on the local waiting list for transplant "centers of excellence," but most people are listed only on the local waiting list where they reside.

As a result of the emphasis on local lists, patients in some parts of the country may wait only a few days for a new organ while patients in other parts of the country may wait a few months or longer, or die while waiting. This disparity explains in part why former baseball star Mickey Mantle received a liver two days after going on the waiting list. In the region for his organ procurement agency, there was a waiting list at the time of only 3.3 days for someone with Mantle's severity of illness, while the national average was 78 days. For all liver transplants, regardless of severity of illness, the average wait varied across the country from 18 to 443 days.

The use of local waiting lists also means that persons with a relatively low priority for an organ transplant will receive organs before persons with a higher priority who live in other parts of the country. At one time, local waiting lists primarily reflected the inability to transport an organ from one part of the country to another before the organ deteriorated, but currently, kidneys and livers generally can be retrieved from a deceased person in one region and flown to a recipient in another region. Why do you suppose, then, that priority is given to people in the local area or region?

5. *Social Worth.* When kidney dialysis first became available, there were not enough dialysis machines for all those who needed treatment. Hospitals therefore established committees to decide who would receive dialysis. One member of such a committee was quoted as follows:

> The choices were hard. . . . I remember voting against a young woman who was a known prostitute. I found I couldn't vote for her, rather than another candidate, a young wife and mother. I also voted against a young man who, until he learned he had renal failure, had been a ne'er do-well, a real playboy. He promised he would

reform his character, go back to school, and so on, if only he were selected for treatment. But I felt I'd lived enough to know that a person like that won't really do what he was promising at the time. Renée C. Fox & Judith P. Swazey, The Courage to Fail 232 (1974).

Discomfort with the selection process led Congress in 1972 to provide Medicare coverage for any person with kidney failure who needed dialysis. Roger W. Evans et al., Implications for Health Care Policy: A Social and Demographic Profile of Hemodialysis Patients in the United States, 245 JAMA 487 (1981).

Most commentators reject social worth as a criterion for organ allocation. Some of the reasons are presented in the following passage:

> A patient's contribution to society—or social worth—should not be a factor in allocation decisions. Such judgments are usually defended as attempts to maximize the return on society's investment in medical resources. One common use is to justify the denial of care to the elderly, who some argue no longer make a positive contribution to the social good. . . .
>
> A social worth criterion can also be used to justify discrimination against the young and virtually any other group not actively involved in the economic productivity of society, on the grounds that those who have put the most into society are entitled to get the most back out of it. Distinctions can be made among economic contributions as well; for instance, white collar workers with higher salaries may be favored over blue collar workers or the working poor. Social worth can also be measured by noneconomic criteria. Artists, writers, musicians, and other cultural elite may be favored over average citizens, and people with dependents may be preferred over those without families.
>
> Because of the pluralistic values of society, any single definition of social contribution or social worth is inherently suspect. Social worth judgments often reflect the preferences and values of individual decision makers rather than any objective criteria. In addition, by assuming that members of a certain group make greater social contributions than others, a social worth criterion ignores diversity and the value of each individual. Council on Ethical and Judicial Affairs, American Medical Association, Ethical Considerations in the Allocation of Organs and Other Scarce Medical Resources Among Patients, 155 Arch. Intern. Med. 29 (1995).

While social worth criteria may generally be inappropriate, might there be some circumstances when they are relevant? Consider the following perspective:

> Yet Dr. [Mark] Siegler said he would exempt Mickey Mantle from his rule [that people with liver failure from alcoholism should go to the bottom of the transplant waiting list] because the baseball legend is "a real American hero." He said Mr. Mantle, "who captured the imagination of a generation through his skill and ability and personality," should not be lumped in with the rest of the population. . . . "I think we have to give deference to the rare heroes in American life," he added. "We don't have enough of these people in America, and when one comes along, we have got to take them with all their warts and failures and treat them differently." Gina Kolata, Transplants, Morality and Mickey, N.Y. Times, June 11, 1995, §4, at 5.

Is Dr. Siegler's proposal any different from our country's practice of spending millions of dollars more to protect the President from assassination than to protect the lives of citizens living in high-crime areas? Or what if you were a hospital attorney and you received a call from the transplant service because a liver was available for transplantation but the person at the top of the waiting list was someone who had been convicted multiple times for child sex abuse? Would it matter if the person was still in prison? Would it matter if the person was serving a life sentence without parole?

Is it consistent to consider costs when rationing care but not to consider social value? For example, assume we would deny someone care because the costs of the care are very high (e.g., $500,000) and the benefits of care seem very low (e.g., an extra few months of life in a permanently unconscious state). If the costs to society of the person's medical treatment matter, then why doesn't it matter whether the person will recover with treatment, return to work, and benefit society?

As mentioned, commentators generally reject social worth as a legitimate criterion. Nevertheless, it is still an unwritten consideration employed by physicians who refer patients for transplants or by transplant surgeons who accept patients on referral.

6. *Individual Responsibility.* Should we take into account the extent to which people are "responsible" for their need for an organ transplant? For example, should people who need a liver because of alcoholic liver disease be given lower priority than people who need a transplant because of a congenital liver defect? Consider the following affirmative response to this question:

> We suggest that patients who develop ESLD [end-stage liver disease] through no fault of their own (e.g., those with congenital biliary atresia or primary biliary cirrhosis) should have a higher priority in receiving a liver transplant than those whose liver disease results from failure to obtain treatment for alcoholism. . . . Although alcoholics cannot be held responsible for their disease, once their condition has been diagnosed they can be held responsible for seeking treatment and preventing the complication of ARESLD [alcohol-related end-stage liver disease]. . . . We are not suggesting that some lives and behaviors have greater value than others. . . . But we are holding people responsible for their personal effort. . . .
>
> Much of the initial success in securing public and political approval for liver transplantation was achieved by focusing media and political attention not on adults but on children dying of ESLD. The public may not support transplantation for patients with ARESLD in the same way that they have endorsed this procedure for babies born with biliary atresia. . . . Just because a majority of the public holds these views does not mean they are right, but the moral intuition of the public . . . reflects community values that must be seriously considered. Alvin H. Moss & Mark Siegler, Should Alcoholics Compete Equally for Liver Transplantation?, 265 JAMA 1296-1297 (1991).

In response to the argument that persons with alcohol-related liver failure are being singled out when other persons become sick as a result of voluntary behavior, including smokers with chronic lung disease, athletes who sustain injuries, and people who develop coronary artery disease from poor diet and insufficient exercise, Moss and Siegler respond,

[t]he critical distinguishing factor for treatment of ARESLD is the scarcity of the resource needed to treat it. The resources needed to treat most of these other conditions are only moderately or relatively scarce, and patients with these diseases or injuries can receive a share of the resources . . . roughly equivalent to their need. [Id. at 1296.]

In a companion article a different perspective was presented:

We could rightly preclude alcoholics from transplantation only if we assume that qualification for a new organ requires some level of moral virtue or is canceled by some level of moral vice. But there is absolutely no agreement—and there is likely to be none—about what constitutes moral virtue and vice and what rewards and penalties they deserve. The assumption that undergirds the moral argument for precluding alcoholics is thus unacceptable. Moreover, even if we could agree . . . upon the kind of misconduct we would be looking for, the fair weighting of such a consideration would entail highly intrusive investigations into patients' moral habits—investigations universally thought repugnant. . . . We do not seek to determine whether a particular transplant candidate is an abusive parent or a dutiful daughter, whether candidates cheat on their income taxes or their spouses, or whether potential recipients pay their parking tickets or routinely lie when they think it is in their best interests. We refrain from considering such judgments for several good reasons: (1) We have genuine and well-grounded doubts about comparative degrees of voluntariness and, therefore, *cannot pass judgment fairly*. (2) Even if we could assess degrees of voluntariness reliably, we *cannot know what penalties different degrees of misconduct deserve*. (3) *Judgments of this kind could not be made consistently in our medical system*—and a fundamental requirement of a fair system in allocating scarce resources is that it treat all in need of certain goods on the same standard, without unfair discrimination by group. Carl Cohen et al., Alcoholics and Liver Transplantation, 265 JAMA 1299, 1299-1300 (1991) (emphasis in original).

7. *Quality of Life*. The UNOS guidelines do not include a criterion of quality of life, perhaps because persons with a permanently low quality of life never make it on to a waiting list. Indeed, in a survey of psychosocial criteria used by transplant centers, researchers found that over 70 percent of transplant centers would automatically deny a heart transplant to persons who suffered from dementia or severe mental retardation (i.e., IQ < 50). James L. Levenson & Mary Ellen Olbrisch, Psychosocial Evaluation of Organ Transplant Candidates: A Comparative Survey of Process, Criteria, and Outcomes in Heart, Liver, and Kidney Transplantation, 34 Psychosomatics 314 (1993). But see Marilee A. Martens et al., Organ Transplantation, Organ Donation and Mental Retardation, 10 Pediat. Transplant. 658, 660-661 (2006) (reporting good, albeit limited, outcomes data for kidney transplantation in person with mental retardation).
    Should quality of life matter?

. . . If for example some people were given life-saving treatment in preference to others because they had a better quality of life than those others, or more dependents and friends, or because they were considered more useful, this would amount to regarding such people as more valuable than others on that account.

Indeed it would be tantamount, literally, to sacrificing the lives of others so that they might continue to live.

Because my own life would be better and even of more value to me if I were healthier, fitter, had more money, more friends, more lovers, more children, more life expectancy, more everything I want, it does not follow that others are entitled to decide that because I lack some or all of these things I am less entitled to health care resources, or less worthy to receive those resources, than others, or that those resources would somehow be wasted on me. John Harris, QALYfying the Value of Life, 13 J. Med. Ethics 117, 121 (1987).

The appeal of considering [duration and quality of life] can be brought out by a contrast with an alternative position, namely that what is valuable are lives, not life-years or their quality. From this point of view society should aim purely and simply to keep the number of deaths to a minimum. It would follow that one should strive to save a baby who can only live another hour of acute suffering just as much as one who will have a happy and fruitful existence for three score years and ten. The two individuals are both human and subjects of consciousness; and surely at least some of the significance that is attributed to these characteristics is adventitious. An evaluation of life and lives without regard to actual or potential [length and quality of life] seems very incomplete. . . . Surely health is a *sine qua non* for the whole gamut of activities, experiences, aspirations and attainment of goals which make our lives valuable to us. John Cubbon, The Principle of QALY Maximisation as the Basis for Allocating Health Care Resources, 17 J. Med. Ethics 181, 182 (1991).

8. *The Tension Between Social Utility and Equality.* As the previous notes suggest, in choosing criteria for allocating organs, a critical concern is the tension between maximizing social utility and treating all persons equitably. The local guidelines used by transplant programs to decide whether a patient should be placed on the waiting list tend to emphasize utilitarian criteria, including likelihood that the transplant surgery will go well and expected duration of benefit for the recipient. The UNOS guidelines for ranking persons on the waiting list give more weight to equitable considerations like time spent waiting for an organ. How do you think the balance should be drawn? In that regard, consider the following perspectives:

. . . The fundamental ethical conflict in the distribution of scarce resources is between doing the most good with a scarce resource and ensuring that it is distributed fairly. How these values should be traded off, particularly when the good in question is needed for life itself, is controversial among not only moral philosophers but also the general public. As a result, there is a strong temptation to seek to avoid or obscure the ethical or value judgments in selection of recipients, and the principal means of doing so is by appeals . . . to medical criteria for selecting recipients. . . .

It is important to emphasize that there are *no* value-neutral selection criteria that could permit bypassing the need to make ethical judgments in the recipient selection process. Notions of medical criteria, medical eligibility, or medical need for treatment, so common in medical practice generally, implicitly embody value judgments when used in determining how a scarce resource like organ transplantation will be distributed. . . .

I believe the crux of the fairness issue is whether it requires some form of random selection among all those in need . . . or whether it merely requires that irrelevant grounds such as racial or other prejudices not be allowed to influence the selection process. These two interpretations of what fairness requires — the equal chance or lottery interpretation and the no-irrelevant-distinctions interpretation — have dramatically different implications. If fairness requires that all in need have equal chances of being selected, then that interpretation will be in strong conflict with the various factors [e.g., length of life and quality of life gained from a transplant] . . . that are relevant in doing the most good possible with these scarce resources. . . . A simple lottery selection process among all who want and might receive any benefit from transplantation would require random selection between [a 25-year-old person in otherwise good health and a 70-year-old person for whom the transplant is unlikely to be successful and who is expected even with a transplant to die from an unrelated medical condition within one or two years after transplantation]. Even the hardiest of egalitarians and the strongest proponents of fairness are very unlikely to be willing to support a random selection process between these two patients.

However, it also seems unacceptable to let very small differences in the expected good to be produced determine whether one gives the transplant to one rather than another patient, at least if doing so means ignoring the requirement of fairness that all in need be given an equal chance to be selected. . . .

What is the alternative interpretation of the requirement of equity or fairness in the selection of recipients? I have already indicated one aspect of this interpretation, that no irrelevant bases such as race or gender influence the selection process; fairness will thus exclude some factors from influencing the selection process. With this alternative interpretation, how do we respond to the idea that none morally deserves the benefit more than another and so each should be given an equal chance to be selected? There are at least two possible lines of argument in this case that are not themselves incompatible.

The first holds that what fairness requires is that all members of society must have a roughly equal input into the decision process that will determine what criteria are to be employed for selection of recipients. Moreover, that decision process should be one that imposes some condition of impartiality on those taking part in it, so that participants do not simply tailor their proposals to suit their own known interests. . . .

The second line of argument . . . offers an alternative substantive interpretation. . . . According to this argument, which persons happen to become diseased and in need of an organ for transplant, which properties particular patients happen to have that influence their relative desirability or undesirability for transplant within a system that attempts to do the most good with scarce organs . . . are all essentially random matters. They are all outcomes of a biological and social lottery. In this argument, the randomization that fairness requires is not to be imposed by a deliberate lottery after all the facts are known about how each particular individual will fare under the system. Instead, fairness is achieved by randomization at an earlier stage, in the interplay of forces that determine who will and who will not be favored by a system that distributes organs according to the criterion that benefit is to be maximized. . . . Dan W. Brock, Ethical Issues in Recipient Selection for Organ Transplantation, *in* Organ Substitution Technology: Ethical, Legal, and Public Policy Issues 86, 87-95 (Deborah Matheiu ed., 1988).

Brock goes on to describe three methods for choosing organ recipients from a waiting list of persons who are candidates for organ transplantation: a simple random lottery, use of medical criteria to rank candidates in terms of the benefit they will likely receive from a transplant, and a weighted lottery in which a candidate's chance of being picked for an organ transplant would depend on the medical benefit expected from an organ transplant. With a weighted lottery, anyone on the waiting list would have a shot at a new organ, but persons with a relatively low expected benefit would have a low likelihood of being chosen to receive the organ. Id. at 96-97. For example, he suggests placing patients into categories of low, medium, and high expected benefit with the medium patients having twice the likelihood of receiving an organ as the low patients, and the high patients having thrice the likelihood of receiving an organ as the low patients.

Brock suggests that there may be no unfairness when medical criteria are used since the winners and losers are ultimately determined by a "biological and social lottery." In that regard, consider the following argument:

> . . . [T]he environment is shaped not simply by natural, inevitable forces but also has been shaped to serve the interests of some segments of society at the expense of others. The socio-political environment cannot always be justified by the operation of neutral or objective principles or by principles that are otherwise morally valid.
>
> . . . Social norms develop not because they are pre-ordained, but because they serve the needs of social groups that are dominant either in numbers or power. . . .
>
> Social forces cause disability by commission when environmental pollution leads to lung diseases or cancers, when lead-based paint damages the neurological systems of children, or when unchecked violence results in traumatic injury.
>
> Social organization causes disability by omission when priorities are established for medical research and treatment. Some illnesses, such as heart disease and cancer, are the subject of vast research expenditures, while other illnesses receive disproportionately little federal research funding. Patients with intensively studied diseases are much more likely to be saved from disabling symptoms than patients with neglected diseases. . . . Moreover, when treatments are developed for a particular disease, they are often based on the norm of a patient without any coexisting illnesses. As a result, patients with multiple illnesses are less able to benefit from treatment. For example, persons with chronic lung disease are less likely to be viewed as appropriate candidates for coronary artery surgery. . . .
>
> All of the[se] disadvantaging aspects of social structure . . . may act to limit a disabled person's access to organ transplants. If there had been more aggressive efforts in the past to treat disabling conditions targeted by eligibility criteria for transplantation, they would not now have as much effect as they do on organ transplant success. Unfortunately, much of the neglect of certain diseases reflects the invidious prejudices that people have about those diseases. Psychiatric illnesses have not often been viewed as real illnesses, for example; other diseases, like obesity, have been ignored because they have been viewed as self-inflicted. David Orentlicher, Destructuring Disability: Rationing of Health Care and Unfair Discrimination Against the Sick, 31 Harv. C.R.-C.L. L. Rev. 49, 66-71 (1996).

While it is useful to frame the debate in terms of the trade-off between social utility and social equality, it is also important to understand how unhelpful this framing can be. It is not clear what content exists in the idea that people need to be treated as equals. Peter Westen, The Empty Idea of Equality, 95 Harv. L. Rev. 537 (1982). We can all agree that equal treatment is a moral imperative, but we can also agree that we do not want to treat everyone in the same way. People are different, and those differences need to be recognized. For example, we require all children to attend school (or be schooled at home), but we do not impose the same requirement on adults. Accordingly, we need to decide when people are the same for purposes of organ transplantation and when they are different. In this regard, it is not clear whether differences in expected length of life or expected quality of life mean that people should be treated differently for purposes of kidney transplantation or whether length and quality of life are irrelevant to organ allocation decisions.

9. *Racial Inequity.* One important area of concern in terms of equity is the evidence that African Americans are seriously disadvantaged when it comes to receiving kidney transplants. Despite the fact that African Americans are more likely than whites to need a kidney transplant, they are much less likely to receive a transplant. The disparity in access to kidney transplants remains even after researchers control for confounding variables like cause of the kidney failure, age, and family income. Much of the difference may reflect the fact that white persons waiting for a kidney are more likely to have a good tissue match with an available organ since most organs come from whites. Important questions are whether the effects of poorer tissue matching can be overcome by immunosuppressive drugs and whether achieving more successful transplants is sufficient reason to disadvantage a racial group that is already disadvantaged in the health care system. See Ian Ayres et al., Unequal Racial Access to Kidney Transplantation, 46 Vand. L. Rev. 805 (1993); Council on Ethical and Judicial Affairs, Black-White Disparities in Health Care, 263 JAMA 2344 (1990); Arnold M. Epstein et al., Racial Disparities in Access to Renal Transplantation, 343 New Eng. J. Med. 1537 (2000); Sankar D. Navaneethan & Sonal Singh, A Systematic Review of Barriers in Access to Renal Transplantation Among African Americans in the United States, 20 Clin. Transplant. 769 (2006).

The inequities in allocation may reflect and/or contribute to a lower trust in the organ retrieval and allocation systems and a lower willingness to donate organs among African Americans. Laura A. Siminoff et al., Racial Disparities in Preferences and Perceptions Regarding Organ Donation, 21 J. Gen. Intern. Med. 995 (2006). These issues are compounded by organ procurement organization staff being less likely to discuss organ donation or to discuss the details of organ donation with African American family members. Laura A. Siminoff et al., Comparison of Black and White Families' Experiences and Perceptions Regarding Organ Donation Requests, 31 Crit. Care Med. 146 (2003).

In response to the concerns about racial disparities in kidney transplantation, UNOS amended its allocation policy in November 2002 to increase minority access to kidney transplants. Recent studies had indicated that UNOS could reduce its emphasis on tissue matching while still maintaining a high rate of long-term success. Accordingly under the new policy, tissue matching is relevant only in a few areas (i.e., when the donor and recipient match perfectly or when there is matching at the "DR locus"). See also Andrea A. Zachary et al., Local Impact of 1995 Changes in the Renal Transplant Allocation System, 63 Transplantation, 669 (1997).

10. *The Americans with Disabilities Act.* The Americans with Disabilities Act (ADA), 42 U.S.C. §§12101-12213, prohibits discrimination against persons with disabilities in employment, education, housing, health care, and other services on account of their disabilities, unless the disabilities are relevant to the decision being made. Thus, for example, a construction company could refuse to hire someone confined to a wheelchair as a roofer but could not refuse to hire that person as a desk clerk. Similarly, an organ transplant program could not deny a kidney transplant to a blind person simply because the person is blind. Discrimination is also prohibited when it results from more "neutral" criteria that have a disproportionate effect (disparate impact) on persons with disabilities. For example, it might violate the ADA to deny an organ transplant to persons without a driver's license since a requirement to have a driver's license disadvantages blind persons. Which of the criteria for organ allocation discussed above potentially implicate the ADA? So far, no cases have been decided on this question.

Even if the person's disability is relevant to the decision being made, the person may not be denied the benefit if "reasonable accommodations" would overcome the effects of the disability. In some cases, a person's psychiatric condition might interfere with the success of an organ transplant. If psychiatric counseling would keep the condition under control, the organ transplant program might have to provide the counseling as part of its treatment program.

Another important question is whether the ADA limits the ability of transplant programs to take into account unrelated medical considerations that affect a person's likelihood of benefiting from a new organ. For example, would it violate the ADA if a transplant candidate is denied a kidney because the candidate has lung disease in addition to kidney failure, and the lung disease will shorten the person's life expectancy? Most likely, the lung disease would be considered a "relevant" difference under the ADA, but other criteria used by transplant programs (e.g., lack of mental retardation) are suspect under the ADA.

For further discussion, see David Orentlicher, Psychosocial Assessment of Organ Transplant Candidates and the Americans with Disabilities Act, 18 Gen. Hosp. Psych. 5S (1996); David Orentlicher, Destructuring Disability: Rationing of Health Care and Unfair Discrimination Against the Sick, 31 Harv. C.R.-C.L. L. Rev. 49 (1996). The role of the ADA in governing other kinds of rationing decisions is also taken up in Chapter 2.A.3.

11. *Absolute vs. Relative Scarcity.* Organ allocation presents a compelling case to consider criteria for rationing limited medical resources because the short supply of organs creates a situation of absolute scarcity: We know that giving an organ to one person rather than others means some people will die. Financial resources are also scarce, and affect organ transplantation as well as other life-saving medical procedures, but they are not scarce in the same absolute sense. Instead, we must decide in more relative terms which medical conditions or procedures deserve more funding than others, and whether medical needs are more demanding than other social needs. Resource allocation issues at this broader level are debated in many of the same moral terms as have been

introduced here, but the legal context is framed in terms of the right to payment under public and private insurance, and in terms of disability discrimination.

12. *Additional Reading.* For additional discussion of organ allocation issues, see Douglas J. Besharov & Jessica Dunsay Silver, Rationing Access to Advanced Medical Techniques, 8 J. Leg. Med. 507 (1987); Einer Elhauge, Allocating Health Care Morally, Cal. L. Rev. (1995); Richard A. Epstein, Mortal Peril: Our Inalienable Right to Health Care? 263-282 (1997); John F. Kilner, Who Lives? Who Dies? Ethical Criteria in Patient Selection (1990); Philip G. Peters, Jr., Health Care Rationing and Disability Rights, 70 Ind. L.J. 491 (1995).

5

Reproductive Rights and Genetic Technologies

This chapter examines both the state's right to regulate individual reproductive capacity and the use of genetic technologies. We treat reproduction as a discrete subject area, separate from the state's ability to control other sorts of human behavior, because human reproduction raises especially controversial moral, ethical, and legal issues. Reproduction is not just another bodily function; the creation of human life implicates profound moral and religious issues not encountered in other medical arenas. Therefore, many special constitutional, statutory, and common law rules have been developed to resolve disputes arising from human reproductive capacity. As you study this chapter, consider whether the rules adopted differ significantly from the rules used in other, similar disputes and whether these differences are warranted from a public policy or legal standpoint. Reproduction is at least partly a question of genetics, but advances in genetics have profound implications beyond reproduction. The final section of this chapter will focus on the legal implications of advances in genetics outside of reproduction.

This chapter will focus initially on four broad aspects of reproductive health law. The first two sections of the chapter explore the conflict between state and individual interests in controlling reproductive capacity. Do people have a constitutionally protected interest in either procreating or in refraining from procreation? Do states have the power to control or to influence personal reproductive decisions? The third section explores the legal recognition of fetal interests as distinguishable from and sometimes conflicting with those of parents. Should pregnant women be subjected to criminal or civil sanctions where their behavior presents risks of fetal injury? The fourth section focuses on the moral, ethical, and legal implications of new reproductive technologies. Who should be considered to be the legal parents of a child who is conceived from donor sperm and egg and gestated by a willing surrogate? The fifth and final section of the chapter explores the legal implications of advances in genetics and the regulation of genetic technologies. Should cloning and related procedures be allowed for reproductive, research, or therapeutic purposes? Should scientists be permitted to patent life forms and genes?

Note: Many Streams or One River: Reproductive Rights and Substantive Due Process

We all have an interest in controlling our own reproductive capacity. Through reproduction, we transmit our individual genetic heritage to a new generation, and in the process are likely to experience the rewards and pains of parenting. Biological reproduction is also associated with cultural reproduction: the ability to pass along values, religious beliefs, and one's cultural heritage. The burdens of reproduction are well known. For women, pregnancy and delivery present certain health risks. For both women and men, unwanted parenthood can be emotionally and financially burdensome. Techniques for avoiding reproduction, such as abstinence, condoms, and oral contraceptives, each have their drawbacks.

Government entities can also have an interest in controlling the reproductive capacity of certain individuals or groups. In societies struggling with overpopulation, the government may have an interest in discouraging reproduction. What is more, historically many governments have expressed an interest in *preventing* reproduction by some individuals, such as persons with disabilities or members of disfavored ethnic or racial minorities. Other societies, on the other hand, may wish to encourage stable or increasing rates of reproduction. This can be accomplished by restricting access to technologies designed to prevent reproduction. Additionally, many societies have sought to protect the new life created through procreation, sometimes at the very earliest stages of its existence within a woman's body. Finally, legislation in these areas often reflects moral and religious perspectives on sexuality, procreation, and fetal interests.

It is therefore not surprising that courts and legislatures have been occupied with the task of balancing these often conflicting individual and social interests. What is the nature of a person's interest in controlling reproduction? Do we have a constitutional right to control procreative capacity that is distinguishable from the right to control medical treatment? Is the right to procreate the mirror image of the right not to procreate? When may the state intrude on personal procreative choice, by either attempting to prevent or to encourage procreation?

Judicial review of state policies under the Constitution's Fourteenth Amendment due process clause raises some troubling constitutional history. You will recall from basic constitutional law that, in the early part of the last century, the Supreme Court took an "activist" approach to reviewing the constitutional validity of state economic regulation under the due process clause. In Lochner v. New York, 198 U.S. 45 (1905), the Court struck down a state's regulation of maximum work hours as a violation of the fundamental right to contract. However, the onslaught of programs in the late 1930s designed to ameliorate the Depression caused the Court to retreat by substituting a more deferential, rational basis, standard of review of state economic regulation. Thereafter, the *Lochner* era of "substantive due process" was thoroughly repudiated as a valid form of judicial review for economic regulation. See Ferguson v. Skrupa, 372 U.S. 726 (1963). It survived only for legislation that affects special categories of "fundamental" interests or liberties, and even then remains under suspicion and sometimes even under attack.

Courts attempting to define the nature of individual interests in procreation and to mark the permissible scope of state regulation have struggled in the shadow of the *Lochner* era. Judges have been forced to confront three important issues. What is the constitutional source of the right to procreate? What are the permissible limits of state regulation? Will the judiciary be able to avoid another *Lochner* debacle in which there is widespread criticism of its fundamental authority to engage in searching substantive due process review?

A. RIGHT TO PROCREATE?

■ BUCK v. BELL
274 U.S. 200 (1927)

HOLMES, Justice.

This is a writ of error to review a judgment of the Supreme Court of Appeals of the State of Virginia, affirming a judgment of the Circuit Court of Amherst County, by which the defendant in error, the superintendent of the State Colony for Epileptics and Feeble Minded, was ordered to perform the operation of salpingectomy upon Carrie Buck, the plaintiff in error, for the purpose of making her sterile. 130 S.E. 516. The case comes here upon the contention that the statute authorizing the judgment is void under the Fourteenth Amendment as denying to the plaintiff in error due process of law and the equal protection of the laws.

Carrie Buck is a feeble-minded white woman who was committed to the State Colony above mentioned in due form. She is the daughter of a feeble-minded mother in the same institution, and the mother of an illegitimate feeble-minded child. She was 18 years old at the time of the trial of her case in the Circuit Court in the latter part of 1924. An Act of Virginia approved March 20, 1924 recites that the health of the patient and the welfare of society may be promoted in certain cases by the sterilization of mental defectives, under careful safeguard, etc.; that the sterilization may be effected in males by vasectomy and in females by salpingectomy, without serious pain or substantial danger to life; that the Commonwealth is supporting in various institutions many defective persons who if now discharged would become a menace but if incapable of procreating might be discharged with safety and become self-supporting with benefit to themselves and to society; and that experience has shown that heredity plays an important part in the transmission of insanity, imbecility, etc. The statute then enacts that whenever the superintendent of certain institutions including the above named State Colony shall be of opinion that it is for the best interest of the patients and of society that an inmate under his care should be sexually sterilized, he may have the operation performed upon any patient afflicted with hereditary forms of insanity, imbecility, etc., on complying with the very careful provisions by which the act protects the patients from possible abuse.

The superintendent first presents a petition to the special board of directors of his hospital or colony, stating the facts and the grounds for his opinion, verified by affidavit. Notice of the petition and of the time and place of the hearing in the institution is to be served upon the inmate, and also upon his guardian, and if there is no guardian the superintendent is to apply to the Circuit Court of the County to appoint one. If the inmate is a minor notice also is to be given to his parents, if any, with a copy of the petition. The board is to see to it that the inmate may attend the hearings if desired by him or his guardian. The evidence is all to be reduced to writing, and after the board has made its order for or against the operation, the superintendent, or the inmate, or his guardian, may appeal to the Circuit Court of the County. The Circuit Court may consider the record of the board and the evidence before it and such other admissible evidence as may be offered, and may affirm, revise, or reverse the order of the board and enter such order as it deems just. Finally any party may apply to the Supreme Court of Appeals, which, if it grants the appeal, is to hear the case upon the record of the trial in the Circuit Court and may enter such order as it thinks the Circuit Court should have entered. There can be no doubt that so far as procedure is concerned the rights of the patient are most carefully considered, and as every step in this case was taken in scrupulous compliance with the statute and after months of observation, there is no doubt that in that respect the plaintiff in error has had due process at law.

The attack is not upon the procedure but upon the substantive law. It seems to be contended that in no circumstances could such an order be justified. It certainly is contended that the order cannot be justified upon the existing grounds. The judgment finds the facts that have been recited and that Carrie Buck "is the probable potential parent of socially inadequate offspring, likewise afflicted, that she may be sexually sterilized without detriment to her general health and that her welfare and that of society will be promoted by her sterilization," and thereupon makes the order. In view of the general declarations of the Legislature and the specific findings of the Court obviously we cannot say as matter of law that the grounds do not exist, and if they exist they justify the result. We have seen more than once that the public welfare may call upon the best citizens for their lives. It would be strange if it could not call upon those who already sap the strength of the state for these lesser sacrifices, often not felt to be such by those concerned, in order to prevent our being swamped with incompetence. It is better for all the world, if instead of waiting to execute degenerate offspring for crime, or to let them starve for their imbecility, society can prevent those who are manifestly unfit from continuing their kind. The principle that sustains compulsory vaccination is broad enough to cover cutting the Fallopian tubes. Jacobson v. Massachusetts, 197 U.S. 11. Three generations of imbeciles are enough.

But, it is said, however it might be if this reasoning were applied generally, it fails when it is confined to the small number who are in the institutions named and is not applied to the multitudes outside. It is the usual last resort of constitutional arguments to point out shortcomings of this sort. But the answer is that the law does all that is needed when it does all that it can, indicates a policy, applies it to all within the lines, and seeks to bring within the lines all similarly situated so far and so fast as its means allow. Of course so far as the operations enable those who otherwise must be kept confined to be returned to the world, and thus open the asylum to others, the equality aimed at will be more nearly reached.

Judgment affirmed.

■ SKINNER v. OKLAHOMA
316 U.S. 535 (1942)

DOUGLAS, Justice.

This case touches a sensitive and important area of human rights. Oklahoma deprives certain individuals of a right which is basic to the perpetuation of a race — the right to have offspring. Oklahoma has decreed the enforcement of its law against petitioner, overruling his claim that it violated the Fourteenth Amendment. Because that decision raised grave and substantial constitutional questions, we granted the petition for certiorari.

The statute involved is Oklahoma's Habitual Criminal Sterilization Act. Okla. Stat. Ann. tit. 57, §171, et seq. That Act defines an "habitual criminal" as a person who, having been convicted two or more times for crimes "amounting to felonies involving moral turpitude" either in an Oklahoma court or in a court of any other state, is thereafter convicted of such a felony in Oklahoma and is sentenced to a term of imprisonment in an Oklahoma penal institution. Machinery is provided for the institution by the Attorney General of a proceeding against such a person in the Oklahoma courts for a judgment that such person shall be rendered sexually sterile. Notice, an opportunity to be heard, and the right to a jury trial are provided. The issues triable in such a proceeding are narrow and confined. If the court or jury finds that the defendant is an "habitual criminal" and that he "may be rendered sexually sterile without detriment to his or her general health," then the court "shall render judgment to the effect that said defendant be rendered sexually sterile," by the operation of vasectomy in case of a male and of salpingectomy in case of a female. Only one other provision of the Act is material here and that is [the section] which provides that "offenses arising out of the violation of the prohibitory laws, revenue acts, embezzlement, or political offenses, shall not come or be considered within the terms of this Act."

Petitioner was convicted in 1926 of the crime of stealing chickens and was sentenced to the Oklahoma State Reformatory. In 1929 he was convicted of the crime of robbery with fire arms and was sentenced to the reformatory. In 1934 he was convicted again of robbery with firearms and was sentenced to the penitentiary. He was confined there in 1935 when the Act was passed. In 1936 the Attorney General instituted proceedings against him. Petitioner in his answer challenged the Act as unconstitutional by reason of the Fourteenth Amendment. A jury trial was had. The court instructed the jury that the crimes of which petitioner had been convicted were felonies involving moral turpitude and that the only question for the jury was whether the operation of vasectomy could be performed on petitioner without detriment to his general health. The jury found that it could be. A judgment directing that the operation of vasectomy be performed on petitioner was affirmed by the Supreme Court of Oklahoma by a 5-4 decision. 115 P.2d 123.

Several objections to the constitutionality of the Act have been pressed upon us. It is urged that the Act cannot be sustained as an exercise of the police power in view of the state of scientific authorities respecting inheritability of criminal traits. It is argued that due process is lacking because under this Act, unlike the act upheld in Buck v. Bell, 274 U.S. 200, the defendant is given no opportunity to be heard on the issue as to whether he is the probable potential parent of socially undesirable offspring. It is also suggested that the Act is penal in character and that the sterilization provided for is cruel and unusual punishment and vocative of the Fourteenth Amendment. We pass those points without intimating an opinion on them, for there is a feature of the Act which clearly condemns it. That is its failure to meet the requirements of the equal protection clause of the Fourteenth Amendment.

We do not stop to point out all of the inequalities in this Act. A few examples will suffice. In Oklahoma grand larceny is a felony. Larceny is grand larceny when the property taken exceeds $20 in value. Embezzlement is punishable "in the manner prescribed for feloniously stealing property of the value of that embezzled." Hence he who embezzles property worth more than $20 is guilty of a felony. A clerk who appropriates over $20 from his employer's till and a stranger who steals the same amount are thus both guilty of felonies. If the latter repeats his act and is convicted three times, he may be sterilized. But the clerk is not subject to the pains and penalties of the Act no matter how large his embezzlements nor how frequent his convictions. A person who enters a chicken coop and steals chickens commits a felony; and he may be sterilized if he is thrice convicted. If, however, he is a bailee of the property and fraudulently appropriates it, he is an embezzler. Hence no matter how habitual his proclivities for embezzlement are and no matter how often his conviction, he may not be sterilized. Thus the nature of the two crimes is intrinsically the same and they are punishable in the same manner. Furthermore, the line between them follows close distinctions. . . . Whether a particular act is larceny by fraud or embezzlement turns not on the intrinsic quality of the act but on when the felonious intent arose. . . .

It was stated in Buck v. Bell, supra, that the claim that state legislation violates the equal protection clause of the Fourteenth Amendment is "the usual last resort of constitutional arguments." Under our constitutional system the states in determining the reach and scope of particular legislation need not provide "abstract symmetry." They may mark and set apart the classes and types of problems according to the needs and as dictated or suggested by experience. . . . Thus, if we had here only a question as to a state's classification of crimes, such as embezzlement or larceny, no substantial federal question would be raised. For a state is not constrained in the exercise of its police power to ignore experience which marks a class of offenders or a family of offenses for special treatment. Nor is it prevented by the equal protection clause from confining "its restrictions to those classes of cases where the need is deemed to be clearest." . . .

But the instant legislation runs afoul of the equal protection clause, though we give Oklahoma that large deference which the rule of the foregoing cases requires. We are dealing here with legislation which involves one of the basic civil rights of man. Marriage and procreation are fundamental to the very existence and survival of the race. The power to sterilize, if exercised, may have subtle, far reaching and devastating effects. In evil or reckless hands it can cause races or types which are inimical to the dominant group to wither and disappear. There is no redemption for the individual whom the law touches. Any experiment which the state conducts is to his irreparable injury. He is forever deprived of a basic liberty. We mention these matters not to reexamine the scope of the police power of the states. We advert to them merely in emphasis of our view that strict scrutiny of the classification which a state makes in a sterilization law is essential, lest unwittingly or otherwise invidious discriminations are made against groups or types of individuals in violation of the constitutional guaranty of just and equal laws. The guaranty of "equal protection of the laws is a pledge of the protection of equal laws." Yick Wo v. Hopkins, 118 U.S. 356, 369. When the law lays an unequal hand on those who have committed intrinsically the same quality of offense and sterilizes one and not the other, it has made as invidious a discrimination as if it had selected a particular race or nationality for oppressive treatment. Sterilization of those who have thrice committed grand larceny with immunity for those who are embezzlers is a clear, pointed, unmistakable discrimination. Oklahoma makes no attempt to say that he who commits larceny by trespass or trick or fraud has biologically inheritable traits which he who commits embezzlement lacks. Oklahoma's line between larceny by fraud and embezzlement is determined, as we have noted, "with reference to the time when the fraudulent intent to convert the property to the taker's own use" arises. We have not the slightest basis for inferring that that line has any significance in eugenics nor that the inheritability of criminal traits follows the neat legal distinctions which the law has marked between those two offenses. In terms of fines and imprisonment the crimes of larceny and embezzlement rate the same under the Oklahoma code. Only when it comes to sterilization are the pains and penalties of the law different. The equal protection clause would indeed be a formula of empty words if such conspicuously artificial lines could be drawn. In Buck v. Bell, supra, the Virginia statute was upheld though it applied only to feebleminded persons in institutions of the state. But it was pointed out that "so far as the operations enable those who otherwise must be kept confined to be returned to the world, and thus open the asylum to others, the equality aimed at will be more nearly reached." Here there is no such saving feature. Embezzlers are forever free. Those who steal or take in other ways are not. If such a classification were permitted, distinctions which are "very largely dependent upon history for explanation" could readily become a rule of human genetics.

Reversed.

STONE, Chief Justice, concurring.

I concur in the result, but I am not persuaded that we are aided in reaching it by recourse to the equal protection clause.

If Oklahoma may resort generally to the sterilization of criminals on the assumption that their propensities are transmissible to future generations by inheritance, I seriously doubt that the equal protection clause requires it to apply the measure to all criminals in the first instance, or to none.

Moreover, if we must presume that the legislature knows—what science has been unable to ascertain—that the criminal tendencies of any class of habitual offenders are transmissible regardless of the varying mental characteristics of its individuals, I should suppose that we must likewise presume that the legislature, in its wisdom, knows that the criminal tendencies of some classes of offenders are more likely to be transmitted than those of others. And so I think the real question we have to consider is not one of equal protection, but whether the wholesale condemnation of a class to such an invasion of personal liberty, without opportunity to any individual to show that his is not the type of case which would justify resort to it, satisfies the demands of due process. . . .

Science has found and the law has recognized that there are certain types of mental deficiency associated with delinquency which are inheritable. But the state does not contend—nor can there be any pretense—that either common knowledge or experience, or scientific investigation, has given assurance that the criminal tendencies of any class of habitual offenders are universally or even generally inheritable. In such circumstances, inquiry whether such is the fact in the case of any particular individual cannot rightly be dispensed with. Whether the procedure by which a statute carries its mandate into execution satisfies due process is a matter of judicial cognizance. A law which condemns, without hearing, all the individuals of a class to so harsh a measure as the present because some or even many merit condemnation, is lacking in the first principles of due process. . . .

[Justice Jackson's concurring opinion is omitted.]

Notes: The Right to Procreate

1. *The Right to Procreate*. Did Justice Holmes suggest that there was a "fundamental" right to procreate? What standard of review did the *Buck* court apply to its review of the Virginia sterilization statute? The Court cites Jacobson v. Massachusetts, 197 U.S. 11 (1904), for the proposition that the state's interest in protecting public health was sufficient to support a program of compulsory vaccination. Are there any significant differences between the intrusions to individual liberty created by vaccination as opposed to sterilization? Note that the historical record suggests that Carrie Buck and her family did not actually suffer from "feeble-mindedness." See University of Virginia, Eugenics Historical Materials, available at http://www.healthsystem.virginia.edu/internet/library/historical/eugenics/. See also Paul A. Lombardo, Medicine, Eugenics, and the Supreme Court: From Coercive Sterilization to Reproductive Freedom, 13 J. Contemp. Health L. & Pol'y 1 (1996).

The *Skinner* decision is often thought to have overruled Buck v. Bell. Is this so? Does Justice Douglas identify the right to procreate as "fundamental"? Of what significance is the fact that *Skinner* is decided as an equal protection case rather than a substantive due process case? What was the flaw in the Oklahoma statute? Does the Court's analysis suggest that mandatory sterilization statutes could be upheld if they were supported by sufficiently rigorous scientific evidence about the heritability of a socially costly trait? There was no evidence of a hereditable condition in Jack Skinner's case. He had lost a foot in an accident and had difficulty finding work to support himself and his wife. See Lombardo, supra.

2. *Eugenics*. *Buck* and *Skinner* arose from what might be called the first wave of the genetic revolution. Public interest in genetics and Darwinism was high during the early 1900s. Leading commentators suggested that individuals and society should consider whether patterns of reproductive behavior were likely to "improve" or lead to the "deterioration" of the human stock. These eugenic theories were combined with fears about the "quality" of immigrants and other disfavored members of society, whose reproductive tendencies were viewed as a potential assault upon society. The sterilization statutes at issue in *Buck* and *Skinner* were the legislative outgrowth of these popular concerns.

During and after World War II, eugenic theories became closely associated with Nazi atrocities, which included forced sterilizations and the extermination of those deemed to sap the strength of the "Aryan race." The scientific and moral flaws of early eugenic theories were exposed and publicized. Public reaction against state-organized eugenic policies became quite strong. Despite this change in public attitudes, some social programs designed to "encourage" sterilization among poor persons or those with mental disabilities continued well into the 1960s. See, e.g., Genes and Human Self-Knowledge: Historical and Philosophical Reflections on Modern Genetics (Robert F. Weir et al. eds., 1994); Note, 72 Geo. Wash. L. Rev. 862 (2004).

The second wave of the genetic revolution is occurring now. At the turn of the century, scientists in the United States and elsewhere joined together to identify and map the human "genome," the sequence of genes found in human beings. The "working draft" was completed in 2000, but the process of identifying, understanding, and exploiting knowledge about specific human genes is still in the early stages. The federal government's Human Genome Web site offers a number of useful resources. See http://genomics.energy.gov/.

Genetic research will produce information that can be used, for good or for ill, by individuals, employers, insurance companies, health care providers, and government entities. See, e.g., Symposium, Genetic Testing and Disability Insurance, J.L. Med. & Ethics 5-89 (2007); Thomas H. Murray, Mark A. Rothstein & Robert F. Murray, Jr., The Human Genome Project and the Future of Health Care (1996). Many ethicists argue that advances in genetics will be of great benefit because people will be given better information to use in making decisions about whether and how to reproduce. Does it matter, from an ethical or legal standpoint, whether efforts to avoid the reproduction of certain "traits" arise from public or private action? Should it matter whether advances in genetics are used to avoid traits considered to be harmful or to acquire traits considered to be desirable? See, e.g., Bernard G. Prusak, Rethinking "Liberal Eugenics": Reflections and Questions on Habermas on Bioethics, Hastings Center Rep. 31 (Nov.-Dec. 2005). It remains to be seen whether the advances in knowledge about human genetics will be used for the benefit of individuals or for the reintroduction of social eugenic policies.

3. *Sterilization of Incompetent Persons*. *Buck* explored the state's ability to impose sterilization upon the mentally incompetent. The issue still arises. See Vaughn v. Ruoff, 253 F.3d 1124 (8th Cir. 2001) (government social worker not entitled to qualified immunity on claim that she violated constitutional rights of

mildly retarded woman by threatening loss of children if woman refused to consent to sterilization). The modern debate has centered on the ability of courts to authorize sterilizations when sought by the family or guardian of an incompetent person. In these cases, the "state" is involved only in the sense that the guardians seek judicial authorization of the sterilization procedure. Courts have been confronted with two separate issues: (1) Does this court have jurisdiction over the subject matter of the dispute? (2) What substantive and procedural rules should be applied to resolve the dispute? The resolution of the second issue is particularly difficult because of the potential conflict between the incompetent's rights to procreate and to refrain from procreation. See, e.g., In re Hayes, 608 P.2d 635 (Wash. 1980).

In *Hayes*, the mother of a girl with severe mental retardation sought a court order specifically authorizing her daughter's sterilization. The trial court held that it did not have the authority to authorize the sterilization. On appeal, the Washington Supreme Court held that the lower court did have jurisdiction over the question and that a petition for sterilization could be granted "in the rare and unusual case that sterilization is in the best interest of the retarded person." 608 P.2d at 637. The court established a framework of procedural and substantive protections designed to ensure that sterilization was necessary to serve the best interests of the individual rather than for the convenience of her caretakers. See also In re Valerie N., 707 P.2d 760 (Cal. 1985) (en banc) (ban on sterilization of incompetent persons violates their constitutionally protected liberty interests); In re Wirsing, 573 N.W.2d 51 (Mich. 1998) (probate court had jurisdiction to authorize guardian's consent to sterilization; clear and convincing evidence not required). Note that the vast majority of these sterilizations are performed on women. Does this present any ethical or legal concerns? Do statutes prohibiting disability-based discrimination affect the legality of these sterilizations? See James C. Dugan, Note, The Conflict Between "Disabling" and "Enabling" Paradigms in Law: Sterilization, the Developmentally Disabled, and the Americans with Disabilities Act, 78 Cornell L. Rev. 510 (1993).

Title II of the Americans with Disabilities Act prohibits disability-based discrimination in the provision of public services. 42 U.S.C.A. §§12131-12165. Some rulings by the U.S. Supreme Court have raised doubts about whether Title II could be applied to secure monetary damages from states without running afoul of the sovereign immunity provisions of the Eleventh Amendment to the U.S. Constitution. In Tennessee v. Lane, 124 S. Ct. 1978 (2004), the Court held that Title II could be applied in cases involving a valid exercise of Congressional power to enforce the Fourteenth Amendment. The Title II claim was upheld in *Lane* because the contested state action affected the fundamental right of access to the courts. The reasoning suggests that claimants might be able to use Title II of the ADA to contest state efforts to bar reproduction by persons with disabilities because these policies might be viewed as impairing the fundamental right to procreate. Cf. *Lane*, 125 S. Ct. at 1989 n.8 (noting that state policies preventing marriage of persons with disabilities provided part of basis for enactment of Title II).

4. *"Temporary Mandatory Sterilization" or Mandatory Birth Control.* Is the state also precluded from mandating birth control? Most cases have arisen when judges have ordered defendants to refrain from reproducing or have ordered defendants to use long-acting contraceptives as a condition of probation. See, e.g., Trammell

v. State, 751 N.E.2d 283 (Ind. Ct. App. 2001) (invalidating condition); and State v. Okaley, 629 N.W.2d 200 (Wis. 2001) (upholding probation condition that defendant avoid having another child absent showing his willingness to provide financial support for children). See also A. Felecia Epps, Unacceptable Collateral Damage: The Danger of Probation Conditions Restricting the Right to Have Children, 38 Creighton L. Rev. 611 (2005); Symposium, Long Term Contraception, Hastings Center Rep. S1-S33 (Jan.-Feb. 1995). Women are much more likely to be the targets of reproductive restrictions than men. See Rachel Roth, "No New Babies?" Gender Inequality and Reproductive Control in the Criminal Justice and Prison Systems, 12 Am. U. J. Gender Soc. Pol'y & L. 391 (2004). But see Smith v. Superior Court, 725 P.2d 1101 (Ariz. 1986).

5. *Governmental Encouragement.* More subtle problems are raised when governmental action is not overtly coercive, but merely seeks to encourage reproductive restraint by structuring government benefit or taxation programs to discriminate against large families. In Dandridge v. Williams, 397 U.S. 471 (1970), the Supreme Court upheld a Maryland regulation limiting payments under the state's Aid for Dependent Children program (AFDC) to no more than $240 or $250 per family. As a result of the regulation, AFDC payments equaling a calculated subsistence standard went only to families with fewer than five or six children. 397 U.S. at 509-510 n.2 (Marshall, J., dissenting). The Court did not answer plaintiffs' contentions that the regulation infringed parents' rights "to freedom of choice concerning procreation and reproduction and to marital privacy." Brief for Appellees at 31. See Yvette Barksdale, And the Poor Have Children: A Harm-Based Analysis of Family Caps and the Hollow Procreative Rights of Welfare Beneficiaries, 14 Law & Ineq. 1 (1995); Note, Legal Analysis and Population Control: The Problem of Coercion, 84 Harv. L. Rev. 1856, 1856-1858 (1971).

6. *"Private" Coercion.* In Walker v. Pierce, 560 F.2d 609 (4th Cir. 1977), *cert. denied*, 434 U.S. 1075 (1978) two African-American women claimed that the defendant, obstetrician Pierce, had sterilized or threatened to sterilize them because of their race, number of children, and status as recipients of publicly funded Medicaid benefits. Dr. Pierce's policy was to refuse to provide obstetrical services to poor women with more than two children unless the women agreed to undergo sterilization after delivery of their third child. The plaintiffs argued that Dr. Pierce had acted "under the color of state law" and that this policy violated their constitutional rights to privacy, due process, and equal protection. The court rejected the claims, in part because it found that Dr. Pierce's connection to the state Medicaid program and a hospital that had received federal funds was not sufficient to make him a state actor subject to liability for the violation of constitutional rights under 42 U.S.C. §1983. The court noted:

> We perceive no reason why Dr. Pierce could not establish and pursue the policy he has publicly and freely announced. Nor are we cited to judicial precedent or statute inhibiting this personal economic philosophy. Particularly is this so when all persons coming to him as patients are seasonably made fully aware of his professional attitude toward the increase in offspring and his determination to see it prevail. At no time is he shown to have forced his view upon any mother. Indeed, quite the opposite appears. In the single occasion in this case of a

sterilization by this doctor, not just one but three formal written consents were obtained, the first before delivery of the fourth child and two afterwards. 560 F.2d at 613.

Federal regulations now require specific informed consent and other procedures to reduce the risk of coerced sterilizations in programs supported by federal funds. 42 C.F.R. §§50.201-210.

   7. *Tort Implications of Voluntary Sterilization*. Improper sterilization can give rise to wrongful conception claims brought by parents when a negligently performed sterilization results in the birth of a healthy child. The primary conceptual difficulty in these cases is measuring the extent of damages to the unwilling parents.

Problem: Sterilization and Advances in Genetics

   Scientists completed the map of the human genome sequence — part of the billion-dollar Human Genome Project — in 2000. The completion of the genome map means the acceleration of research efforts to understand the operational significance of genes, to identify the structure and function of the thousands of proteins manufactured according to genetic instructions, and to explore the implications for the human condition. Scientific advances are likely to create more uncertainty in the short term. News stories frequently report the discovery of genes "associated with" certain human traits or diseases, but an association may be strong or weak and the mechanism may be simple or complex to understand. Therapies for genetic conditions are extremely rare. The behavioral implications of genetics are particularly controversial. See Behavioral Genetics: The Clash of Culture and Biology (Ronald A. Carson et al. eds., 1999).

   Suppose that scientists identify genetic tests for the following conditions:

1. Gene A is a "dominant" trait. Because we ordinarily carry two copies of each gene, only one of which is passed to our offspring, a child of someone who carries one of these genes has a 50 percent chance of receiving this gene and of experiencing its bad effects. Gene "A" is connected to a late-onset genetic disorder. Persons with the defective gene will develop Alzheimer's disease in their early 60s.
2. Gene B is a recessive trait and will be expressed only if a child receives the "defective" gene from each parent. Statistically speaking, for two parents who each carry one of these genes, there is a 25 percent chance of their passing two defective genes to their offspring. Children with two B genes develop a painful disorder that leads to death, usually by the age of five.
3. Genetic trait C is caused by a large number of different genetic mutations. Scientists have developed a test that will identify 75 percent of these mutations, but trait C is not always expressed in persons who have these mutations, and it is also found in persons who do not have these mutations. Persons with gene C have shortened life spans; with proper medical care they may live into their 20s or beyond.
4. Genetic trait D is associated with higher rates of criminal conduct. Persons who inherit one copy of the gene are 10 percent more likely to be

convicted of a violent crime than the general population. Persons with two copies of the gene are 30 percent more likely to be convicted of a violent crime. Although geneticists cannot completely explain the correlation between this gene and criminal conduct, they do believe that the gene is associated with greater risk taking and lower social empathy.

Is there any basis for restricting the reproduction of any of these persons? Could the risks of reproduction be used to justify premarital screening for one or more of these conditions? See page 634. Could a state require individuals who carry one or more of these genes to be counseled about the possible reproductive consequences? The ethical norms governing genetic counselors typically require "nondirective counseling," in which participants are given information about genetic risks but are not pressured to pursue any particular remedy. See Robert Wachbroit & David Wasserman, Patient Autonomy and Value—Neutrality in Nondirective Genetic Counseling, 6 Stan. L. & Pol'y Rev. 103 (1995).

Could a state prohibit reproduction for persons who carry two copies of the gene associated with trait D? How about one copy? Does *Skinner* stand for the proposition that the state can never prohibit reproduction? Or must the state merely have an adequate scientific basis and apply its standard uniformly? Could the state argue that it has a compelling interest in protecting the child from being born? See Mary Anne Bobinski, Genetics and Reproductive Decision Making, *in* The Human Genome Project and the Future of Health Care 79-107 (1996); Lois Shepherd, Protecting Parents' Freedom to Have Children with Genetic Differences, 1995 U. Ill. L. Rev. 761.

Useful background readings include Allen Buchanan et al., From Chance to Choice: Genetics and Justice (2002); Genetics and Public Health in the 21st Century (Muin J. Khoury et al. eds., 2000); Genetics: Ethics, Law & Policy (Mark Rothstein et al. eds., 2002); and The Ethics of Genetics in Human Procreation (Hille Haker & Deryck Beyleveld eds., 2000). Genetic progress may not provide benefits to all groups in society. See Mary Briody Mahowald, Genes, Women, Equality (1999); Symposium, Communities of Color and Genetic Testing: Purpose, Voice & Values, 27 Seton Hall L. Rev. 887 (1997).

Problem: Chemical or Surgical Castration
of Male Sex Offenders

Should the government's purpose matter in sterilization cases? In most of the cases discussed above, the state intended to restrict a person's ability to procreate, either because of eugenic ideology or because of a judgment that the individual would not provide properly for a child. Consider the movement in the 1990s to require male sex offenders to undergo "chemical castration" as a condition of probation. See, e.g., Daniel L. Icenogle, Sentencing Male Sex Offenders to the Use of Biological Treatments, 15 J. Leg. Med. 279 (1994). Courts and legislatures hoped to reduce recidivism rates by reducing the offender's sexual drive; the effect on reproduction, therefore, was merely incidental. Appellate courts struck down early efforts to impose chemical castration in the criminal context. See, e.g., People v. Gauntlett, 352 N.W.2d 310 (Mich. Ct. App.), modified on other grounds, 353 N.W.2d 463 (Mich. 1984) (unlawful condition of probation). Legislatures responded by explicitly authorizing the use of chemical castration as a condition of probation for certain sex offenders. See, e.g., Cal. Penal Code §645 (authorizing chemical castration). Should prisoners be entitled to voluntarily consent to castration? See Tex. Gov't Code Ann. §§501.061-.062 (repeat sex offenders authorized to voluntarily undergo orchiectomy, also known as surgical castration). Could a physician ethically perform an orchiectomy on a physically healthy male? If so, under what circumstances? Compare your views with the provisions of the Texas law. For a discussion on the efficacy of treatments for sexual offenders see Abby Goodnough & Monica Davey, For Sex Offenders, Dispute on Therapy's Benefits, N.Y. Times, March 6, 2007, at A1.

Assume that your client, Greg Aya, has been convicted of child molestation on three different occasions. His female victims were all less than 13 years old. Under the applicable California statute, chemical castration must be imposed as a condition of probation. The procedure will require Greg to receive regular shots of a drug that will reduce his sex drive and will likely impair his sexual functioning. The treatment is to continue until the state's experts certify that it is "no longer necessary." Can you devise a challenge to the California statute and its application to Greg? Will cases such as *Skinner* be useful? Should it matter whether Greg will have an opportunity to "bank" frozen sperm for possible future procreation? Are there any other sources of relevant law? Will you be successful? See People v. Foster, 124 Cal. Rptr. 2d 22 (Cal. App. 4 Dist. 2002). See also Houston v. State, 852 So. 2d 425 (Fla. App. 2003) (trial court failed to follow requirements of chemical castration statute); Bruno v. State, 837 So. 2d 521 (Fla. App. 2003) (surgical castration not authorized for violation of statute at issue in case; illegal sentence resulting from negotiated plea agreement must be set aside).

B. A RIGHT TO AVOID PROCREATION?

Court decisions identifying a constitutionally protected interest in being able to procreate without impermissible state interference are relatively uncontroversial since state efforts to limit procreation are quite intrusive. The procedure at issue in *Skinner* involved surgery and the permanent alteration of reproductive capacity. In contrast, state restrictions on access to contraception implicate individual interests in a fashion that is arguably less intrusive. Do individuals have a right to *avoid* reproduction that includes the right to use contraceptive technology? Does the right extend to post-conception techniques of avoiding reproduction, such as abortion? The next set of cases considers the constitutional validity of state efforts to restrict access to contraception and abortion. As you read these cases, try to identify the source and scope of an individual's right to avoid procreation. What types of state regulation are permissible? Does the validity of state regulation depend on its purpose or effect?

1. *Contraception*

■ GRISWOLD v. CONNECTICUT
381 U.S. 479 (1965)

DOUGLAS, Justice.

. . . The statutes whose constitutionality is involved in this appeal are §§53-32 and 54-196 of the General Statutes of Connecticut (1958 rev.). The former provides: "Any person who uses any drug, medicinal article or instrument for the purpose of preventing conception shall be fined not less than fifty dollars or imprisoned not less than sixty days nor more than one year or be both fined and imprisoned." Section 54-196 provides: "Any person who assists, abets, counsels, causes, hires or commands another to commit any offense may be prosecuted and punished as if he were the principal offender."

The appellants[, physicians who prescribed contraceptives to married persons,] were found guilty as accessories and fined $100 each, against the claim that the accessory statute as so applied violated the Fourteenth Amendment. . . .

[W]e are met with a wide range of questions that implicate the due process clause of the Fourteenth Amendment. Overtones of some arguments suggest that Lochner v. State of New York, 198 U.S. 45, should be our guide. But we decline that invitation. . . . We do not sit as a super-legislature to determine the wisdom, need, and propriety of laws that touch economic problems, business affairs, or social conditions. This law, however, operates directly on an intimate relation of husband and wife and their physician's role in one aspect of that relation.

The association of people is not mentioned in the Constitution nor in the Bill of Rights. The right to educate a child in a school of the parents' choice—whether public or private or parochial—is also not mentioned. Nor is the right to study any particular subject or any foreign language. Yet the First Amendment has been construed to include certain of those rights.

By Pierce v. Society of Sisters, 268 U.S. 510, the right to educate one's children as one chooses is made applicable to the states by the force of the First and Fourteenth Amendments. By Meyer v. State of Nebraska, 262 U.S. 390, the same dignity is given the right to study the German language in a private school. In other words, the state may not, consistently with the spirit of the First Amendment, contract the spectrum of available knowledge. The right of freedom of speech and press includes not only the right to utter or to print, but the right to distribute, the right to receive, the right to read. . . . Without those peripheral rights the specific rights would be less secure. . . .

The foregoing cases suggest that specific guarantees in the Bill of Rights have penumbras, formed by emanations from those guarantees that help give them life and substance. Various guarantees create zones of privacy. The right of association contained in the penumbra of the First Amendment is one, as we have seen. The Third Amendment in its prohibition against the quartering of soldiers "in any house" in time of peace without the consent of the owner is another facet of that privacy. The Fourth Amendment explicitly affirms the "right of the people to be secure in their persons, houses, papers, and effects, against unreasonable searches and seizures." The Fifth Amendment in its self-incrimination clause enables the citizen to create a zone of privacy which government may not force him to surrender to his detriment. The Ninth Amendment provides: "The enumeration in the Constitution, of certain rights, shall not be construed to deny or disparage others retained by the people." The Fourth and Fifth Amendments were described in Boyd v. United States, 116 U.S. 616, 630, as protection against all governmental invasions "of the sanctity of a man's home and the privacies of life." We have had many controversies over these penumbral rights of "privacy and repose." These cases bear witness that the right of privacy which presses for recognition here is a legitimate one.

The present case, then, concerns a relationship lying within the zone of privacy created by several fundamental constitutional guarantees. And it concerns a law which, in forbidding the use of contraceptives rather than regulating their manufacture or sale, seeks to achieve its goals by means having a maximum destructive impact upon that relationship. Such a law cannot stand in light of the familiar principle, so often applied by this Court, that a "governmental purpose to control or prevent activities constitutionally subject to state regulation may not be achieved by means which sweep unnecessarily broadly and thereby invade the area of protected freedoms." NAACP v. Alabama, 377 U.S. 288, 307. Would we allow the police to search the sacred precincts of marital bedrooms for telltale signs of the use of contraceptives? The very idea is repulsive to the notions of privacy surrounding the marriage relationship.

We deal with a right of privacy older than the Bill of Rights — older than our political parties, older than our school system. Marriage is a coming together for better or for worse, hopefully enduring, and intimate to the degree of being sacred. It is an association that promotes a way of life, not causes; a harmony in living, not political faiths; a bilateral loyalty, not commercial or social projects. Yet it is an association for as noble a purpose as any involved in our prior decisions.

Reversed.

GOLDBERG, Justice, whom the Chief Justice and BRENNAN, Justice, join, concurring.

I agree with the Court that Connecticut's birth-control law unconstitutionally intrudes upon the right of marital privacy, and I join in its opinion and judgment. . . . I do agree that the concept of liberty protects those personal rights that are fundamental, and is not confined to the specific terms of the Bill of Rights. My conclusion that the concept of liberty is not so restricted and that it embraces the right of marital privacy though that right is not mentioned explicitly in the Constitution is supported both by numerous decisions of this Court, referred to in the Court's opinion, and by the language and history of the Ninth Amendment. . . .

[I]t should be said of the Court's holding today that it in no way interferes with a state's proper regulation of sexual promiscuity or misconduct [such as "adultery, homosexuality, and the like"]. . . .

HARLAN, Justice, concurring.

. . . In my view, the proper constitutional inquiry in this case is whether this Connecticut statute infringes the due process clause of the Fourteenth

Amendment because the enactment violates basic values "implicit in the concept of ordered liberty," Palko v. State of Connecticut, 302 U.S. 319, 325. . . . I believe that it does. While the relevant inquiry may be aided by resort to one or more of the provisions of the Bill of Rights, it is not dependent on them or any of their radiations. The due process clause of the Fourteenth Amendment stands, in my opinion, on its own bottom.

WHITE, Justice, concurring.

In my view this Connecticut law as applied to married couples deprives them of "liberty" without due process of law, as that concept is used in the Fourteenth Amendment. I therefore concur in the judgment of the Court reversing these convictions under Connecticut's aiding and abetting statute. . . .

In these circumstances one is rather hard pressed to explain how the ban on use by married persons in any way prevents use of such devices by persons engaging in illicit sexual relations and thereby contributes to the state's policy against such relationships. . . . I find nothing in this record justifying the sweeping scope of this statute, with its telling effect on the freedoms of married persons, and therefore conclude that it deprives such persons of liberty without due process of law.

STEWART, Justice, whom BLACK, Justice, joins, dissenting.

Since 1879 Connecticut has had on its books a law which forbids the use of contraceptives by anyone. I think this is an uncommonly silly law. As a practical matter, the law is obviously unenforceable, except in the oblique context of the present case. As a philosophical matter, I believe the use of contraceptives in the relationship of marriage should be left to personal and private choice, based upon each individual's moral, ethical, and religious beliefs. As a matter of social policy, I think professional counsel about methods of birth control should be available to all, so that each individual's choice can be meaningfully made. But we are not asked in this case to say whether we think this law is unwise, or even asinine. We are asked to hold that it violates the United States Constitution. And that I cannot do.

In the course of its opinion the Court refers to no less than six Amendments to the Constitution: the First, the Third, the Fourth, the Fifth, the Ninth, and the Fourteenth. But the Court does not say which of these Amendments, if any, it thinks is infringed by this Connecticut law.

We are told that the due process clause of the Fourteenth Amendment is not, as such, the "guide" in this case. With that much I agree. There is no claim that this law, duly enacted by the Connecticut legislature, is unconstitutionally vague. There is no claim that the appellants were denied any of the elements of procedural due process at their trial, so as to make their convictions constitutionally invalid. And, as the Court says, the day has long passed since the due process clause was regarded as a proper instrument for determining "the wisdom, need, and propriety" of state laws. *Compare* Lochner v. State of New York, 198 U.S. 45, *with* Ferguson v. Skrupa, 372 U.S. 726. . . .

As to the First, Third, Fourth, and Fifth Amendments, I can find nothing in any of them to invalidate this Connecticut law. . . . [Moreover] the Ninth Amendment . . . was . . . adopted by the states simply to make clear that the adoption of the Bill of Rights did not alter the plan that the Federal Government was to be a government of express and limited powers, and that all rights and powers not delegated to it were retained by the people and the individual states. . . .

What provision of the Constitution, then, does make this state law invalid? The Court says it is the right of privacy "created by several fundamental constitutional guarantees." With all deference, I can find no such general right of privacy in the Bill of Rights, in any other part of the Constitution, or in any case ever before decided by this Court.

At the oral argument in this case we were told that the Connecticut law does not "conform to current community standards." But it is not the function of this Court to decide cases on the basis of community standards. We are here to decide cases "agreeably to the Constitution and laws of the United States." It is the essence of judicial duty to subordinate our own personal views, our own ideas of what legislation is wise and what is not. If, as I should surely hope, the law before us does not reflect the standards of the people of Connecticut, the people of Connecticut can freely exercise their true Ninth and Tenth Amendment rights to persuade their elected representatives to repeal it. That is the constitutional way to take this law off the books.

Notes: A Right to Avoid Procreation

1. *Another Constitutional Right?* Does the Court settle on the source of a constitutional right to avoid procreation in *Griswold*? Justice Douglas reviews a number of different parts of the Bill of Rights before concluding that their "penumbra" was sufficiently broad to encompass the right of married couples to use contraceptives. Is Douglas's attempt to find textual support for this right persuasive? Note that Justices Goldberg and White were dissatisfied with Douglas's analysis, preferring to rest the decision on the Ninth Amendment and "liberty" clause of the Fourteenth Amendment, respectively. Justice Stewart raises the specter of *Lochner* in his dissent, arguing that the majority is substituting its own judgment for the will of the people of Connecticut, as delivered by their elected representatives.

2. *Individuals or Married Couples.* Left unresolved in *Griswold* was the question whether the right to use contraceptives belonged to the individual or was instead some protected aspect of the marital relationship. In Eisenstadt v. Baird, 405 U.S. 438 (1972), Baird was convicted for "exhibiting contraceptives in the course of delivering a lecture on contraception to . . . students at Boston University" and "for giving a young woman a package of [contraceptive] foam at the end of his address." The Massachusetts statute at issue imposed a maximum five-year prison term for distribution of contraceptives unless certain statutory requirements were met. The statute permitted a physician to prescribe contraceptives to married persons to prevent pregnancy. Single persons were denied access to contraceptives to prevent pregnancy; however, any adult could obtain contraceptives to prevent the spread of disease. The Court struck down the statutory scheme under a rational basis, equal protection standard. The Court's holding suggested, without explicitly deciding, that individuals might have a fundamental liberty interest in decisions to avoid procreation:

[W]hatever the rights of the individual to access to contraceptives may be, the rights must be the same for the unmarried and the married alike. If under Griswold [v. Connecticut, 381 U.S. 479 (1965)] the distribution of contraceptives to married persons cannot be prohibited, a ban on distribution to unmarried persons would be equally impermissible. It is true that in *Griswold* the right of privacy in question inhered in the marital relationship. Yet the marital couple is not an independent entity with a mind and heart of its own, but an association of two individuals each with a separate intellectual and emotional makeup. If the right of privacy means anything, it is the right of the individual, married or single, to be free from unwarranted governmental intrusion into matters so fundamentally affecting a person as the decision whether to bear or beget a child. On the other hand, if *Griswold* is no bar to a prohibition on the distribution of contraceptives, the state could not, consistently with the equal protection clause, outlaw distribution to unmarried but not to married persons. In each case the evil, as perceived by the state, would be identical, and the underinclusion would be invidious. . . . We hold that by providing dissimilar treatment for married and unmarried persons who are similarly situated, Massachusetts General Laws Ann., c. 272, §§21 and 21A, violate the equal protection clause. [Id. at 453-455.]

3. *Judicial Review of Social Legislation.* According to some, the Supreme Court is essentially an antidemocratic institution in which life-tenured political appointees wield the potential power to reverse the will of the democratically elected representatives of the majority. Are you troubled by the Court's lack of deference to the will of the people as embodied in their statutes? What limits, if any, does the Court place upon itself? Are those limits meaningful? Does the very process of judicial review of social legislation betray our society's ultimate discomfort with democracy?

4. *Minors and Contraception.* The next dispute, inevitably, involved the ability of the state to regulate access to contraceptives for minors. In Carey v. Population Services, 431 U.S. 678 (1977), the Court struck down a New York statute that criminalized distribution of condoms to persons under 16 years of age and that provided condoms could be distributed only by licensed pharmacists to persons over 16. Justice Brennan, writing for the plurality, found that minors had a limited constitutional right of access to contraceptives and that the state had failed to show that its regulation served a "significant state interest." Justices White and Powell would have invalidated the statute as irrational without finding that minors had a protected constitutional interest. Justice Rehnquist authored a spirited dissent. The Court's doctrinal difficulties in this case mirror its fractured decisionmaking in abortion cases involving minors; see page 471.

Do parents have a constitutional right to be consulted (or informed) when professional clinics offer contraceptive advice or services to minor children living with parents? In Doe v. Irwin, 615 F.2d 1162 (6th Cir. 1980), the court held that there was no such parental right and reversed the district court's finding that a state-funded family planning center's practice of distributing contraceptives to unemancipated minors without parental notice or consultation violated the parent's constitutional right to oversee the care, custody, and nurturing of their children. See also Abigail English & Madlyn Morreale, A Legal and Policy Framework for Adolescent Health Care: Past, Present, and Future, 1 Hous. J. Health L. & Pol'y 63 (2001). Do parents have a constitutional right to prevent schools from distributing condoms to their children? See Parents United for Better Schools, Inc. v. Board of Education, 148 F.3d 260 (3d Cir. 1998) (voluntary high school condom distribution program does not violate parent's fundamental rights where parents could refuse to let children participate); Curtis v. School Committee of Falmouth, 652 N.E.2d 580 (Mass. 1995) (upholding voluntary, noncoercive program), *cert. denied*, 116 S. Ct. 753 (1996). Should schools learning that a minor is pregnant be required to notify the minor's parents? Melissa Prober, The Validity of School Policies Mandating Parental Notification of a Student's Pregnancy, 71 Brook. L. Rev. 557 (2005).

Family planning counseling for minors may raise special problems of medical ethics for physicians and other health care personnel. The New Morality, 335 Lancet 1041 (1990); M. A. Schuster et al., Communication Between Adolescents and Physicians about Sexual Behavior and Risk Prevention, 150 Arch. Pediatr. Adolesc. Med. 906 (1996). Should a physician who discovers that a minor is engaged in sexual activity have a duty to report the situation as a case of potential child abuse? See Jodi Rudoren, Judge Blocks Law to Report Sex Under 16, N.Y. Times, April 19, 2006, at A16.

The Supreme Court's jurisprudence governing access to abortion for minors has also influenced some legislatures to impose restrictions on minors' access to contraception. Congress and a significant number of states have considered requiring evidence of parental consent, approval by a court, or parental notification before minors can be given access to prescription contraceptives. At least some research suggests that these proposals might cause minors to turn to other, potentially less effective methods of avoiding pregnancy. Rachel K. Jones et al., Adolescents' Reports of Parental Knowledge of Adolescents' Use of Sexual Health Services and Their Reactions to Mandated Parental Notification for Prescription Contraception, 293 JAMA 340 (2005); Diane M. Reddy et al., Effect of Mandatory Parental Notification on Adolescent Girls' Use of Sexual Health Care Services, 288 JAMA 710 (2002); Madeline Zavodny, Fertility and Parental Consent for Minors to Receive Contraceptives, 94 Am. J. Public Health 1347 (2004).

5. *Paying for Contraceptives*. Contraceptives remain controversial, largely due to religious and moral views regarding the procreative purpose of sexual activity. See, e.g., Russell Shorto, Contra-Contraception, N.Y. Times Magazine, May 7, 2006, at 48. Should public and private insurers provide coverage for contraceptives? Is this a policy argument or could a failure to provide contraceptive coverage be considered impermissible sex discrimination? See Sylvia A. Law, Sex Discrimination and Insurance for Contraception, 73 Wash. L. Rev. 363 (1998). State and federal legislative initiatives in this area are summarized in the National Conference of State Legislatures, Health Insurance Coverage for Contraceptives (available on NCSL Web site). Courts have also been asked to determine whether the failure to pay for prescription contraceptives under various health plans violates federal or state law. See, e.g., Catholic Charities of Sacramento, Inc. v. Superior Court, 85 P.3d 67 (Cal.), *cert. denied*, 125 S. Ct. 53 (2004) (upholding state Women's Contraceptive Equity Act in constitutional challenge brought by employer which opposed contraceptives on religious grounds); Standridge v. Union Pac. R.R. Co. (In re Union Pac. R.R. Empl. Practices Litigation), 2007 U.S. App. LEXIS 5914 (8th Cir. Neb. Mar. 15, 2007) (finding employer did not violate

Title VII by failing to cover prescription contraception for women); Glaubach v. Regence Blueshield, 74 P.3rd 115 (Wash. 2003) (court finds that two state statutes do not require insurance coverage for contraceptives).

6. *Emergency Contraception.* Emergency contraception, also known as the "morning-after pill," generally must be taken within 72 hours of unprotected intercourse to prevent conception or the implantation of a fertilized egg in a woman's uterus. Commentators disagree about whether the drug should be treated as a method of contraception or as a drug promoting very early abortion. Those who believe that human life begins at the fertilization of an ovum view the drug as an abortifacient because it prevents the implantation of a fertilized egg. The drug is viewed as a contraceptive by those who mark the beginning of human life at implantation.

Reproductive rights advocates are concerned about the limited availability of the drug. Several states have enacted legislation related to emergency contraception, including laws authorizing specially trained pharmacists to dispense the drugs. Some states also have laws that protect pharmacists who refuse to dispense if doing so is against personal moral or religious beliefs. See the National Conference of State Legislatures, 50 State Summary of Emergency Contraception Laws (available at NCSL Web site). See also Julie Cantor & Ken Baum, The Limits of Conscientious Objection — May Pharmacists Refuse to Fill Prescriptions for Emergency Contraception? 351 New Eng. J. Med. 2008 (2004).

Advocates have sought to make the drug available "over the counter" (without a prescription). See Megan L. Ranney, Erin M. Gee & Roland C. Merchant, 47 Annals Emerg. Med. 461 (2006). The controversy spilled over to the FDA when the agency initially ignored the advice of its own expert review panel in deciding to reject over the counter access to emergency contraception. See Brian Vastag, Plan B for "Plan B": FTC Denies OTC Sales of Emergency Contraceptive, 291 JAMA 2805 (2004). The FDA reversed course and approved the drug for over-the-counter distribution in 2006. See http://www.fda.gov/cder/drug/infopage/planB/planBQandA20060824.htm; and Frank Davidoff & James Trussell, Plan B and the Politics of Doubt, 296 JAMA 1771 (2006).

Problem: Incompetent Persons and Long-Term Contraception

Grace and Tony Jones have a daughter, Alice, who is 17 years old. Alice has a low IQ. She attends school along with other children in the neighborhood but takes part in special classes designed to meet her intellectual and emotional needs. Alice is a friendly person who takes a great interest in others and in animals. She has an ordinary interest in sexual activity and often talks about looking forward to having her own child. On the other hand, she is not fond of going to her physician and has a low tolerance for pain. She is easily distractible and must be reminded by others to bathe and eat. Alice's parents are concerned about her future, particularly because they are entering their 50s and can foresee a period of declining health. They want to ensure that Alice is not "burdened by the trauma and responsibility of childrearing and/or the loss of a child by adoption." They have heard that forced sterilization of minors and incompetents is very controversial. (See discussion at page 430.) As an alternative, they have approached Alice's physician to have Alice undergo insertion of an IUD contraceptive, which could prevent against pregnancy for several years. If this is not possible, they want Alice to be given a birth control pill prescription. How would you advise Alice's physician? Are there any potential sources of liability? In what ways is this situation similar to the sterilization cases? In what ways is it different? Are the differences legally significant? What sources of law would you examine to determine the physician's obligations? Could the Americans with Disabilities Act (ADA) be relevant? Would you seek a court order, and if so, of what type?

2. Abortion

■ ROE v. WADE
410 U.S. 113 (1973)

BLACKMUN, Justice.

[Roe challenged the constitutional validity of a Texas statute that made it a crime to procure an abortion, except where necessary to save the life of the pregnant woman. The Court held that the statute violated the Fourteenth Amendment's due process clause. Justice Blackmun recognized that states had two separate interests in regulating abortion: (1) an interest in protecting the health and safety of women; and (2) an interest in protecting fetal life. These interests had to be weighed against the rights of the woman and her fetus. The Court first held that women had a protected "privacy" interest in the abortion decision:]

This right of privacy, whether it be founded in the Fourteenth Amendment's concept of personal liberty and restrictions upon state action, as we feel it is, . . . is broad enough to encompass a woman's decision whether or not to terminate her pregnancy. The detriment that the state would impose upon the pregnant woman by denying this choice altogether is apparent. Specific and direct harm medically diagnosable even in early pregnancy may be involved. Maternity, or additional offspring, may force upon the woman a distressful life and future. Psychological harm may be imminent. Mental and physical health may be taxed by child care. There is also the distress, for all concerned, associated with the unwanted child, and there is the problem of bringing a child into a family already unable, psychologically and otherwise, to care for it. In other cases, as in this one, the additional difficulties and continuing stigma of unwed motherhood may be involved. All these are factors the woman and her responsible physician necessarily will consider in consultation. . . .

[A] state may properly assert important interests in safeguarding health, in maintaining medical standards, and in protecting potential life. At some point in pregnancy, these respective interests become sufficiently compelling to sustain regulation of the factors that govern the abortion decision. The privacy right involved, therefore, cannot be said to be absolute. In fact, it is not clear to us that the claim asserted by some amici that one has an unlimited right to do with one's body as one pleases bears a close relationship to the right of privacy previously articulated in the Court's decisions. The Court has refused to recognize an unlimited right of this kind in the past. Jacobson v. Massachusetts, 197 U.S. 11

(1905) (vaccination); Buck v. Bell, 274 U.S. 200 (1927) (sterilization). [See also the assisted suicide cases in Chapter 3.]

We, therefore, conclude that the right of personal privacy includes the abortion decision, but that this right is not unqualified and must be considered against important state interests in regulation. . . .

Where certain "fundamental rights" are involved, the Court has held that regulation limiting these rights may be justified only by a "compelling state interest," and that legislative enactments must be narrowly drawn to express only the legitimate state interests at stake. . . .

The appellee and certain amici argue that the fetus is a "person" within the language and meaning of the Fourteenth Amendment. . . . If this suggestion of personhood is established, the appellant's case, of course, collapses, for the fetus' right to life would then be guaranteed specifically by the Amendment. . . . [The Court rejects this claim, noting that "person" in the Constitution is never used in a way that suggests it could have any prenatal application.] . . .

The pregnant woman cannot be isolated in her privacy. She carries an embryo and, later, a fetus, if one accepts the medical definitions of the developing young in the human uterus. The situation therefore is inherently different from [prior cases]. . . .

[W]e do not agree that, by adopting one theory of life, Texas may override the rights of the pregnant woman that are at stake. We repeat, however, that the state does have an important and legitimate interest in preserving and protecting the health of the pregnant woman . . . and that it has still another important and legitimate interest in protecting the potentiality of human life. These interests are separate and distinct. Each grows in substantiality as the woman approaches term and, at a point during pregnancy, each becomes "compelling."

With respect to the state's important and legitimate interest in the health of the mother, the "compelling" point, in the light of present medical knowledge, is at approximately the end of the first trimester. This is so because of the now-established medical fact that until the end of the first trimester mortality in abortion may be less than mortality in normal childbirth. It follows that, from and after this point, a state may regulate the abortion procedure to the extent that the regulation reasonably relates to the preservation and protection of maternal health. . . .

This means, on the other hand, that, for the period of pregnancy prior to this "compelling" point, the attending physician, in consultation with his patient, is free to determine, without regulation by the state, that, in his medical judgment, the patient's pregnancy should be terminated. If that decision is reached, the judgment may be effectuated by an abortion free of interference by the state.

With respect to the state's important and legitimate interest in potential life, the "compelling" point is at viability. This is so because the fetus then presumably has the capability of meaningful life outside the mother's womb. State regulation protective of fetal life after viability thus has both logical and biological justifications. If the state is interested in protecting fetal life after viability, it may go so far as to proscribe abortion during that period, except when it is necessary to preserve the life or health of the mother. . . .

[The Court then applied these standards to invalidate the Texas abortion statute.]

Affirmed in part and reversed in part.

REHNQUIST, Justice, dissenting.

The Court's opinion brings to the decision of this troubling question both extensive historical fact and a wealth of legal scholarship. While the opinion thus commands my respect, I find myself nonetheless in fundamental disagreement with those parts of it that invalidate the Texas statute in question, and therefore dissent. . . .

I would reach a conclusion opposite to that reached by the Court. I have difficulty in concluding, as the Court does, that the right of "privacy" is involved in this case. . . . If the Court means by the term *privacy* no more than that the claim of a person to be free from unwanted state regulation of consensual transactions may be a form of "liberty" protected by the Fourteenth Amendment, there is no doubt that similar claims have been upheld in our earlier decisions on the basis of that liberty. . . . The test traditionally applied in the area of social and economic legislation is whether or not a law such as that challenged has a rational relation to a valid state objective. Williamson v. Lee Optical Co., 348 U.S. 483, 491 (1955). The due process clause of the Fourteenth Amendment undoubtedly does place a limit, albeit a broad one, on legislative power to enact laws such as this. If the Texas statute were to prohibit an abortion even where the mother's life is in jeopardy, I have little doubt that such a statute would lack a rational relation to a valid state objective under the test stated in *Williamson,* supra. But the Court's sweeping invalidation of any restrictions on abortion during the first trimester is impossible to justify under that standard, and the conscious weighing of competing factors that the Court's opinion apparently substitutes for the established test is far more appropriate to a legislative judgment than to a judicial one. . . .

While the Court's opinion quotes from the dissent of Mr. Justice Holmes in Lochner v. New York, 198 U.S. 45, 74 (1905), the result it reaches is more closely attuned to the majority opinion of Mr. Justice Peckham in that case. As in *Lochner* and similar cases applying substantive due process standards to economic and social welfare legislation, the adoption of the compelling state interest standard will inevitably require this Court to examine the legislative policies and pass on the wisdom of these policies in the very process of deciding whether a particular state interest put forward may or may not be "compelling." The decision here to break pregnancy into three distinct terms and to outline the permissible restrictions the state may impose in each one, for example, partakes more of judicial legislation than it does of a determination of the intent of the drafters of the Fourteenth Amendment. . . .

To reach its result, the Court necessarily has had to find within the scope of the Fourteenth Amendment a right that was apparently completely unknown to the drafters of the Amendment. . . .

There apparently was no question concerning the validity of this provision or of any of the other state statutes when the Fourteenth Amendment was adopted. The only conclusion possible from this history is that the drafters did not intend to have the Fourteenth Amendment withdraw from the states the power to legislate with respect to this matter.

For all of the foregoing reasons, I respectfully dissent.

Notes: Roe v. Wade

1. *Abortion Statistics.* Abortion is a relatively common medical procedure in the United States. According to federal government statistics, there were "848,163 legal induced abortions . . . reported in the United States for 2003 from 47 states, D.C. and N.Y.C." Lilo T. Strauss et al., Abortion Surveillance—United States, 2003, 55 MMWR 1, 6 (Nov. 24, 2006) (No. SS-11). The number of abortions rose in the decades after the Court's decision in Roe v. Wade, but began to decline in the 1990s due to a number of factors. Id. For an overall review of the topic from a public health perspective, see Cynthia C. Harper, Jillian T. Henderson & Philip D. Darney, Abortion in the United States, 26 Ann. Rev. Pub. Health 501 (2005).

2. *Fetal Personhood.* The "personhood" of the fetus is an area of significant religious and philosophical debate. It is clear that many major religions treat an unborn child as a person from the moment of conception. Philosophers and bioethicists have also argued for the special, human nature of the fetus. Is it possible to argue that fetuses are "persons" for constitutional purposes? If a fetus is a constitutional person then it would be protected under the due process and equal protection clauses. How does the Court deal with this issue? Did the Texas criminal abortion statute indicate that Texas believed that fetuses were persons? See also Philip G. Peters, The Ambiguous Meaning of Human Conception, 40 U.C. Davis L. Rev. 199 (2006); Note, What We Talk About When We Talk About Persons: The Language of a Legal Fiction, 114 Harv. L. Rev. 1745 (2001). Would a fetus's status as a person automatically mean that abortion would be prohibited by the constitution? In DeShaney v. Winnebago County Dept. of Social Services, 489 U.S. 189 (1989), the Supreme Court held that the state did not owe any affirmative duty to protect a child from private violence inflicted by his father. What are the implications of this in the abortion context? Would *DeShaney* be relevant if a plaintiff argued that the state's failure to criminalize abortion while criminalizing other types of homicide violated the EPC clause? See Lee v. Oregon, 107 F.3d 182 (9th Cir. 1997) (holding plaintiffs did not have standing to bring equal protection challenge to Oregon's assisted suicide statute), *cert. denied* sub nom. Lee v. Harcleroad, 522 U.S. 927 (1997).

3. *Sources of Authority in Constitutional Interpretation.* In the full opinion, Justice Blackmun engages in a painstaking analysis of historical, legal, medical, and religious attitudes toward abortion. By what theory is this discussion constitutionally relevant? Is this an argument that the framers of the Fourteenth Amendment considered procreative liberty to be fundamental? Even if this doubtful proposition were accurate, should it be determinative? In other contexts, some have argued that the Constitution should evolve over time; could not the controversy over abortion indicate heightened sensitivity to the rights of others that should be incorporated into the Constitution? If the Constitution can grow to recognize a woman's right to choose, can it also grow to recognize fetal rights? In the unedited opinion, Justice Blackmun also details the opinions of various medical organizations. Should the medical profession have special influence on the establishment of constitutional norms where they concern biological processes?

4. *The "Right to Privacy."* What is the nature of the right to privacy? Does Justice Blackmun succeed in adequately describing its source, scope, and limits? Note that the Court adopts the theory that the source of the right is the liberty

clause of the Fourteenth Amendment. How would Justice Rehnquist determine whether the right to choose abortion is "fundamental"? Does his charge of "*Lochner*-ism" seem valid?

5. *The State's Interest.* Justice Blackmun contends that the interests of the pregnant woman and the state can be weighed and evaluated through the use of the trimester framework. Does he adequately explain what the state's interest is in the first trimester? What types of state regulation would be supported by this interest? Is Justice Blackmun's discussion of the importance of viability convincing? Or does it constitute *ipse dixit*?

6. *Additional Ethical or Moral Aspects of Abortion.* Abortion implicates our definition of personhood, the value of potential human life, and the obligations of health professionals to "do no harm" and to serve patients' medical needs. The law on abortion does not differentiate among the various possible non-therapeutic reasons underlying a woman's decision to end a pregnancy, but ethicists, philosophers, and religious groups often make these distinctions. Consider the following rationales for abortion:

   a. Should abortion be used explicitly as a means of after-the-fact birth control? See Judith Jarvis Thomson, A Defense of Abortion, 1 Phil. & Pub. Aff. 47 (1971) (mounting a defense of abortion, but suggesting that abortion merely as birth control exceeds ethical bounds). The issue is of great importance to those who fear that the increasing availability of pharmaceutical abortions might increase use of abortion as a method of family planning. The FDA approved RU-486 for the termination of early pregnancy in 2000. See also Lars Noah, A Miscarriage in the Drug Approval Process?, 36 Wake Forest L. Rev. 571 (2001).

   b. Should abortion be used to eliminate multiple births? Pregnancies with multiple fetuses carry health risks for the fetuses and for the expectant mother. Obstetricians have the ability to selectively reduce the number of fetuses in multi-fetal pregnancies. Is there an ethical basis justifying selection reduction from triplets to twins that would not apply to the reduction of twins to a singleton fetus? For a discussion of the clinical and ethical issues, see Judith F. Daar, Selective Reduction of Multiple Pregnancy: Lifeboat Ethics in the Womb, 25 U.C. Davis L. Rev. 773 (1992); Mark Evans et al., Update on Selective Reduction, 25 Prenatal Diag. 807 (2005); L. Purdy, Women's Reproductive Autonomy: Medicalisation and Beyond, 32 J. Med. Ethics 287 (2006).

   c. Should abortion be used to avoid the birth of a child with birth defects? If so, which defects? Why shouldn't this be considered an impermissible form of disability-based discrimination or eugenics? Genetic screening is already used to identify the sex of the fetus, sometimes to avoid a sex-linked genetic disorder but other times to ensure parental control over gender. Should parents be able to use genetic screening to identify the sex of a child so that they can abort a child of the "wrong" gender? See Susannah Baruch et al., Genetic Testing of Embryos: Practices and Perspectives of U.S. IVF Clinics, Fertility and Sterility (July 10, 2007); Denise Grady, Girl or Boy? As Fertility Technology Advances, So Does Ethical Debate, N.Y. Times, Feb. 6, 2007, at F5; David Stoller, Prenatal

Genetic Screening: The Enigma of Selective Abortion, 12 J.L. & Health 121 (1998); Stanford Symposium on Preimplantation Genetic Diagnosis, 85 Fertility & Sterility 1631-1660 (2006).

d. What about using abortion to "deselect" other characteristics, such as size, hair color, or personality, at a time when genetic science has progressed to make this possible? As genetic technology advances, prospective parents may be able to create even more detailed shopping lists. Is there anything ethically or legally wrong with permitting parents to abort pregnancies until they conceive a fetus with a projected IQ greater than 125? See Owen D. Jones, Reproductive Autonomy and Evolutionary Biology: A Regulatory Framework for Trait-Selection Technologies, 19 Am. J.L. & Med. 187 (1993); Maxwell J. Mehlman, The Law of Above Averages: Leveling the New Genetic Enhancement Playing Field, 85 Iowa L. Rev. 517 (2000); John A. Robertson, Genetic Selection of Offspring Characteristics, 76 B.U. L. Rev. 421 (1996); Stanford Symposium on Preimplantation Genetic Diagnosis, supra.

7. *Abortion Politics.* Those who hoped that a Supreme Court decision in this area would resolve the issue have been greatly disappointed. The *Roe* decision helped to fuel another 35 years of debate about abortion, the Constitution, and state regulation. "Pro-life" or "anti-choice" advocates were not vanquished, but in fact seemed invigorated by the Court's rejection of most types of state abortion regulation. Abortion continued to be a political issue; federal, state, and local political candidates announced their positions even in races where the controversy was largely irrelevant given the nature of the office being elected. A vibrant "Right to Life" political party endorsed and ran its own candidates in many states. Activists worked for a constitutional amendment. State legislatures continued to regulate abortion, sending test case after test case to the courts. "Pro-choice" or "pro-abortion" advocates fought to preserve *Roe*'s protections in the courts and the legislatures. While it would be naive to imagine that the judicial selection process before *Roe* was apolitical, it is clear that the abortion debate produced a new "litmus test" for potential state and federal judicial nominees. The cases and notes in the remainder of this section will summarize the judicial response to changes in the political battle lines.

8. *Supreme Court Abortion Jurisprudence Between* Roe *and* Casey. For a summary of some of the important post-*Roe* cases, see Rachael K. Pirner & Laurie B. Williams, *Roe* to *Casey*: A Survey of Abortion Law, 32 Washburn L.J. 166 (1993).

◼ PLANNED PARENTHOOD OF SOUTHEASTERN PENNSYLVANIA v. CASEY
505 U.S. 833 (1992)

O'CONNOR, KENNEDY, and SOUTER, Justices.

I

Liberty finds no refuge in a jurisprudence of doubt. Yet 19 years after our holding that the Constitution protects a woman's right to terminate her pregnancy in its early stages, Roe v. Wade, 410 U.S. 113 (1973), that definition of liberty is still questioned. Joining the respondents as amicus curiae, the United States, as it has done in five other cases in the last decade, again asks us to overrule *Roe*.

At issue in these cases are five provisions of the Pennsylvania Abortion Control Act of 1982 as amended in 1988 and 1989. 18 Pa. Cons. Stat. §§3203-3220 (1990). The Act requires that a woman seeking an abortion give her informed consent prior to the abortion procedure, and specifies that she be provided with certain information at least 24 hours before the abortion is performed. For a minor to obtain an abortion, the Act requires the informed consent of one of her parents, but provides for a judicial bypass option if the minor does not wish to or cannot obtain a parent's consent. Another provision of the Act requires that, unless certain exceptions apply, a married woman seeking an abortion must sign a statement indicating that she has notified her husband of her intended abortion. The Act exempts compliance with these three requirements in the event of a "medical emergency." In addition to the above provisions regulating the performance of abortions, the Act imposes certain reporting requirements on facilities that provide abortion services. . . .

After considering the fundamental constitutional questions resolved by *Roe*, principles of institutional integrity, and the rule of stare decisis, we are led to conclude this: The essential holding of Roe v. Wade should be retained and once again reaffirmed. . . .

II

Constitutional protection of the woman's decision to terminate her pregnancy derives from the due process clause of the Fourteenth Amendment. . . .

Our law affords constitutional protection to [certain] personal decisions relating to marriage, procreation, contraception, family relationships, child rearing, and education. . . . These matters, involving the most intimate and personal choices a person may make in a lifetime, choices central to personal dignity and autonomy, are central to the liberty protected by the Fourteenth Amendment. At the heart of liberty is the right to define one's own concept of existence, of meaning, of the universe, and of the mystery of human life. Beliefs about these matters could not define the attributes of personhood were they formed under compulsion of the state.

These considerations begin our analysis of the woman's interest in terminating her pregnancy but cannot end it, for this reason: Though the abortion decision may originate within the zone of conscience and belief, it is more than a philosophic exercise. Abortion is a unique act. It is an act fraught with consequences for others: for the woman who must live with the implications of her decision; for the persons who perform and assist in the procedure; for the spouse, family, and society which must confront the knowledge that these procedures exist, procedures some deem nothing short of an act of violence against innocent human life; and, depending on one's beliefs, for the life or potential life that is aborted. Though abortion is conduct, it does not follow that the state is entitled to proscribe it in all instances. That is because the liberty of the woman is at stake in a sense unique to the human condition and so unique to the law. The mother who carries a child to full term is subject to anxieties, to physical constraints, to pain that only she must bear. That these sacrifices have from the beginning of the human race been endured by woman with a pride that ennobles her in the eyes of others and gives to the infant a bond of love cannot alone be grounds for the state to insist she make the sacrifice. Her suffering is too intimate and personal for the state to insist, without more, upon its own vision of the woman's role, however dominant that vision has been in the course of our history and our culture. The destiny of the woman must be shaped to a large extent on her own conception of her spiritual imperatives and her place in society.

It should be recognized, moreover, that in some critical respects the abortion decision is of the same character as the decision to use contraception, to which Griswold v. Connecticut, Eisenstadt v. Baird, and Carey v. Population Services International, afford constitutional protection. We have no doubt as to the correctness of those decisions. . . .

While we appreciate the weight of the arguments made on behalf of the state in the case before us, arguments which in their ultimate formulation conclude that *Roe* should be overruled, the reservations any of us may have in reaffirming the central holding of *Roe* are outweighed by the explication of individual liberty we have given combined with the force of stare decisis. We turn now to that doctrine.

[In Part III, the Court reviewed the importance of *stare decisis* in constitutional cases, and concluded that *Roe* should not be overruled.]

IV

From what we have said so far it follows that it is a constitutional liberty of the woman to have some freedom to terminate her pregnancy. We conclude that the basic decision in *Roe* was based on a constitutional analysis which we cannot now repudiate. The woman's liberty is not so unlimited, however, that from the outset the state cannot show its concern for the life of the unborn, and at a later point in fetal development the state's interest in life has sufficient force so that the right of the woman to terminate the pregnancy can be restricted. . . .

We conclude the line should be drawn at *viability*, so that before that time the woman has a right to choose to terminate her pregnancy. We adhere to this principle for two reasons. First, as we have said, is the doctrine of *stare decisis*. Any judicial act of line-drawing may seem somewhat arbitrary, but *Roe* was a reasoned statement, elaborated with great care. We have twice reaffirmed it in the face of great opposition. . . .

The second reason is that the concept of viability, as we noted in *Roe*, is the time at which there is a realistic possibility of maintaining and nourishing a life outside the womb, so that the independent existence of the second life can in reason and all fairness be the object of state protection that now overrides the rights of the woman. See Roe v. Wade, 410 U.S., at 163. . . . [T]here may be some medical developments that affect the precise point of viability, but this is an imprecision within tolerable limits. . . . The viability line also has, as a practical matter, an element of fairness. In some broad sense it might be said that a woman who fails to act before viability has consented to the state's intervention on behalf of the developing child.

The woman's right to terminate her pregnancy before viability is the most central principle of Roe v. Wade. It is a rule of law and a component of liberty we cannot renounce. . . . On the other side of the equation is the interest of the state in the protection of potential life. The *Roe* Court recognized the state's "important and legitimate interest in protecting the potentiality of human life." The weight to be given this state interest, not the strength of the woman's interest, was the difficult question faced in *Roe*. . . . [W]e have concluded that the essential holding of *Roe* should be reaffirmed.

Yet it must be remembered that Roe v. Wade speaks with clarity in establishing not only the woman's liberty but also the state's "important and legitimate interest in potential life." That portion of the decision in *Roe* has been given too little acknowledgment and implementation by the Court in its subsequent cases. Those cases decided that any regulation touching upon the abortion decision must survive strict scrutiny, to be sustained only if drawn in narrow terms to further a compelling state interest. Not all of the cases decided under that formulation can be reconciled with the holding in *Roe* itself that the state has legitimate interests in the health of the woman and in protecting the potential life within her. In resolving this tension, we choose to rely upon *Roe*, as against the later cases. . . . Most of our cases since *Roe* have involved the application of rules derived from the trimester framework. . . .

We reject the trimester framework, which we do not consider to be part of the essential holding of *Roe*. Measures aimed at ensuring that a woman's choice contemplates the consequences for the fetus do not necessarily interfere with the right recognized in *Roe*, although those measures have been found to be inconsistent with the rigid trimester framework announced in that case. A logical reading of the central holding in *Roe* itself, and a necessary reconciliation of the liberty of the woman and the interest of the state in promoting prenatal life, require, in our view, that we abandon the trimester framework as a rigid prohibition on all provability regulation aimed at the protection of fetal life. The trimester framework suffers from these basic flaws: In its formulation it misconceives the nature of the pregnant woman's interest; and in practice it undervalues the state's interest in potential life, as recognized in *Roe*. . . .

The very notion that the state has a substantial interest in potential life leads to the conclusion that not all regulations must be deemed unwarranted. Not all burdens on the right to decide whether to terminate a pregnancy will be undue. In our view, the undue burden standard is the appropriate means of reconciling the state's interest with the woman's constitutionally protected liberty. . . . Because we set forth a standard of general application to which we intend to adhere, it is important to clarify what is meant by an undue burden.

A finding of an undue burden is a shorthand for the conclusion that a state regulation has the purpose or effect of placing a substantial obstacle in the path of a woman seeking an abortion of a nonviable fetus. A statute with this purpose is invalid because the means chosen by the state to further the interest in potential life must be calculated to inform the woman's free choice, not hinder it. And a statute which, while furthering the interest in potential life or some other valid state interest, has the effect of placing a substantial obstacle in the path of a woman's choice cannot be considered a permissible means of serving its legitimate ends. . . . Understood another way, we answer the question, left open in previous opinions discussing the undue burden formulation, whether a law designed to further the state's interest in fetal life which imposes an undue burden on the woman's decision before fetal viability could be constitutional. The answer is no.

Some guiding principles should emerge. What is at stake is the woman's right to make the ultimate decision, not a right to be insulated from all others in doing so. Regulations which do no more than create a structural mechanism by which the state, or the parent or guardian of a minor, may express profound respect for the life of the unborn are permitted, if they are not a substantial obstacle to the woman's exercise of the right to choose. Unless it has that effect on her right of choice, a state measure designed to persuade her to choose childbirth over abortion will be upheld if reasonably related to that goal. Regulations designed to foster the health of a woman seeking an abortion are valid if they do not constitute an undue burden. . . .

We give this summary:

(a) To protect the central right recognized by Roe v. Wade while at the same time accommodating the state's profound interest in potential life, we will employ the undue burden analysis as explained in this opinion. An undue burden exists, and therefore a provision of law is invalid, if its purpose or effect is to place a substantial obstacle in the path of a woman seeking an abortion before the fetus attains viability.

(b) We reject the rigid trimester framework of Roe v. Wade. To promote the state's profound interest in potential life, throughout pregnancy the state may take measures to ensure that the woman's choice is informed, and measures designed to advance this interest will not be invalidated as long as their purpose is to persuade the woman to choose childbirth over abortion. These measures must not be an undue burden on the right.

(c) As with any medical procedure, the state may enact regulations to further the health or safety of a woman seeking an abortion. Unnecessary health regulations that have the purpose or effect of presenting a substantial obstacle to a woman seeking an abortion impose an undue burden on the right.

(d) Our adoption of the undue burden analysis does not disturb the central holding of Roe v. Wade, and we reaffirm that holding. Regardless of whether exceptions are made for particular circumstances, a state may not prohibit any woman from making the ultimate decision to terminate her pregnancy before viability.

(e) We also reaffirm *Roe*'s holding that "subsequent to viability, the state in promoting its interest in the potentiality of human life may, if it chooses, regulate, and even proscribe, abortion except where it is necessary, in appropriate medical judgment, for the preservation of the life or health of the mother." Roe v. Wade, 410 U.S., at 164-165.

These principles control our assessment of the Pennsylvania statute, and we now turn to the issue of the validity of its challenged provisions.

V

A

Because it is central to the operation of various other requirements, we begin with the statute's definition of medical emergency. . . . [T]he court of appeals construed the phrase "serious risk" to include those circumstances. It stated: "we read the medical emergency exception as intended by the Pennsylvania legislature to assure that compliance with its abortion regulations would not in any way pose a significant threat to the life or health of a woman." . . . We adhere to that course today, and conclude that, as construed by the court of appeals, the medical emergency definition imposes no undue burden on a woman's abortion right.

B

We next consider the informed consent requirement. Except in a medical emergency, the statute requires that at least 24 hours before performing an abortion a physician inform the woman of the nature of the procedure, the health risks of the abortion and of childbirth, and the "probable gestational age of the unborn child." The physician or a qualified nonphysician must inform the woman of the availability of printed materials published by the state describing the fetus and providing information about medical assistance for childbirth, information about child support from the father, and a list of agencies which provide adoption and other services as alternatives to abortion. An abortion may not be performed unless the woman certifies in writing that she has been informed of the availability of these printed materials and has been provided them if she chooses to view them.

Our prior decisions establish that as with any medical procedure, the state may require a woman to give her written informed consent to an abortion. In this respect, the statute is unexceptional. Petitioners challenge the statute's definition of informed consent because it includes the provision of specific information by the doctor and the mandatory 24-hour waiting period. The conclusions reached by a majority of the Justices in the separate opinions filed today and the undue burden standard adopted in this opinion require us to overrule in part some of the Court's past decisions, decisions driven by the trimester framework's prohibition of all previability regulations designed to further the state's interest in fetal life. . . .

To the extent [that our prior decisions] find a constitutional violation when the government requires, as it does here, the giving of truthful, nonmisleading information about the nature of the procedure, the attendant health risks and those of childbirth, and the "probable gestational age" of the fetus, those cases go too far, are inconsistent with *Roe*'s acknowledgment of an important interest in potential life, and are overruled. . . .

Whether the mandatory 24-hour waiting period is . . . invalid because in practice it is a substantial obstacle to a woman's choice to terminate her pregnancy is a close question. The findings of fact by the district court indicate that because of the distances many women must travel to reach an abortion provider, the practical effect will often be a delay of much more than a day because the waiting period requires that a woman seeking an abortion make at least two visits to the doctor. The district court also found that in many instances this will increase the exposure of women seeking abortions to "the harassment and hostility of anti-abortion protestors demonstrating outside a clinic." As a result, the district court found that for those women who have the fewest financial resources, those who must travel long distances, and those who have difficulty explaining their whereabouts to husbands, employers, or others, the 24-hour waiting period will be "particularly burdensome."

These findings are troubling in some respects, but they do not demonstrate that the waiting period constitutes an undue burden. We do not doubt that, as the district court held, the waiting period has the effect of "increasing the cost and risk of delay of abortions," but the district court did not conclude that the increased costs and potential delays amount to substantial obstacles. . . .

We also disagree with the district court's conclusion that the "particularly burdensome" effects of the waiting period on some women require its invalidation. A particular burden is not of necessity a substantial obstacle. Whether a burden falls on a particular group is a distinct inquiry from whether it is a substantial obstacle even as to the women in that group. And the district court did not conclude that the waiting period is such an obstacle even for the women who are most burdened by it. Hence, on the record before us, and in the context of this facial challenge, we are not convinced that the 24-hour waiting period constitutes an undue burden. . . .

c

Pennsylvania's abortion law provides, except in cases of medical emergency, that no physician shall perform an abortion on a married woman without receiving a signed statement from the woman that she has notified her spouse that she is about to undergo an abortion. The woman has the option of providing an alternative signed statement certifying that her husband is not the man who impregnated her; that her husband could not be located; that the pregnancy is the result of spousal sexual assault which she has reported; or that the woman believes that notifying her husband will cause him or someone else to inflict bodily injury upon her. A physician who performs an abortion on a married woman without receiving the appropriate signed statement will have his or her license revoked, and is liable to the husband for damages. . . .

The spousal notification requirement is thus likely to prevent a significant number of women from obtaining an abortion. It does not merely make abortions a little more difficult or expensive to obtain; for many women, it will impose a substantial obstacle. We must not blind ourselves to the fact that the significant number of women who fear for their safety and the safety of their children are likely to be deterred from procuring an abortion as surely as if the Commonwealth had outlawed abortion in all cases. . . .

The husband's interest in the life of the child his wife is carrying does not permit the state to empower him with this troubling degree of authority over his wife. The contrary view leads to consequences reminiscent of the common law. A husband has no enforceable right to require a wife to advise him before she exercises her personal choices. If a husband's interest in the potential life of the child outweighs a wife's liberty, the state could require a married woman to notify her husband before she uses a postfertilization contraceptive. Perhaps next in line would be a statute requiring pregnant married women to notify their husbands before engaging in conduct causing risks to the fetus. After all, if the husband's interest in the fetus' safety is a sufficient predicate for state regulation, the state could reasonably conclude that pregnant wives should notify their husbands before drinking alcohol or smoking. Perhaps married women should notify their husbands before using contraceptives or before undergoing any type of surgery that may have complications affecting the husband's interest in his wife's reproductive organs. And if a husband's interest justifies notice in any of these cases, one might reasonably argue that it justifies exactly what the *Danforth* Court held it did not justify — a requirement of the husband's consent as well. A state may not give to a man the kind of dominion over his wife that parents exercise over their children.

[The statute] embodies a view of marriage consonant with the common-law status of married women but repugnant to our present understanding of marriage and of the nature of the rights secured by the Constitution. Women do not lose their constitutionally protected liberty when they marry. The Constitution protects all individuals, male or female, married or unmarried, from the abuse of governmental power, even where that power is employed for the supposed benefit of a member of the individual's family. These considerations confirm our conclusion that [the spousal notification provision] is invalid.

D

We next consider the parental consent provision. Except in a medical emergency, an unemancipated young woman under 18 may not obtain an abortion unless she and one of her parents (or guardian) provides informed consent as defined above. If neither a parent nor a guardian provides consent, a court may authorize the performance of an abortion upon a determination that the young woman is mature and capable of giving informed consent and has in fact given her informed consent, or that an abortion would be in her best interests.

We have been over most of this ground before. Our cases establish, and we reaffirm today, that a state may require a minor seeking an abortion to obtain the consent of a parent or guardian, provided that there is an adequate judicial bypass procedure. Under these precedents, in our view, the one-parent consent requirement and judicial bypass procedure are constitutional. . . .

VI

Our Constitution is a covenant running from the first generation of Americans to us and then to future generations. It is a coherent succession. Each generation must learn anew that the Constitution's written terms embody ideas and aspirations that must survive more ages than one. We accept our responsibility not to retreat from interpreting the full meaning of the covenant in light of all of our precedents. We invoke it once again to define the freedom guaranteed by the Constitution's own promise, the promise of liberty. . . .

BLACKMUN, Justice, concurring in part, concurring in the judgment in part, and dissenting in part.

Three years ago, in Webster v. Reproductive Health Serv., 492 U.S. 490 (1989), four Members of this Court appeared poised to "cas[t] into darkness the hopes and visions of every woman in this country" who had come to believe that the Constitution guaranteed her the right to reproductive choice. All that remained between the promise of *Roe* and the darkness of the plurality was a single, flickering flame. Decisions since *Webster* gave little reason to hope that this flame would cast much light. . . . But now, just when so many expected the darkness to fall, the flame has grown bright.

I do not underestimate the significance of today's joint opinion. Yet I remain steadfast in my belief that the right to reproductive choice is entitled to the full protection afforded by this Court before *Webster*. And I fear for the darkness as four Justices anxiously await the single vote necessary to extinguish the light. . . .

Make no mistake, the joint opinion of Justices O'Connor, Kennedy, and Souter is an act of personal courage and constitutional principle. . . .

Today, no less than yesterday, the Constitution and decisions of this Court require that a state's abortion restrictions be subjected to the strictest of judicial scrutiny. Our precedents and the joint opinion's principles require us to subject all non-de minimis abortion regulations to strict scrutiny. Under this standard, the Pennsylvania statute's provisions requiring content-based counseling, a 24-hour delay, informed parental consent, and reporting of abortion-related information must be invalidated. . . .

In one sense, the Court's approach is worlds apart from that of The Chief Justice and Justice Scalia. And yet, in another sense, the distance between the two approaches is short—the distance is but a single vote.

I am 83 years old. I cannot remain on this Court forever, and when I do step down, the confirmation process for my successor well may focus on the issue before us today. That, I regret, may be exactly where the choice between the two worlds will be made.

REHNQUIST, Chief Justice, with whom WHITE, SCALIA, and THOMAS, Justices, join, concurring in the judgment in part and dissenting in part.

The joint opinion, following its newly-minted variation on *stare decisis*, retains the outer shell of Roe v. Wade, but beats a wholesale retreat from the substance of that case. We believe that *Roe* was wrongly decided, and that it can and should be overruled consistently with our traditional approach to *stare decisis* in constitutional cases. We would adopt the approach of the plurality in Webster v. Reproductive Health Services, 492 U.S. 490 (1989), and uphold the challenged provisions of the Pennsylvania statute in their entirety. . . .

In construing the phrase *liberty* incorporated in the due process clause of the Fourteenth Amendment, we have recognized that its meaning extends beyond freedom from physical restraint. In Pierce v. Society of Sisters, 268 U.S. 510 (1925), we held that it included a parent's right to send a child to private school; in Meyer v. Nebraska, 262 U.S. 390 (1923), we held that it included a right to teach a foreign language in a parochial school. Building on these cases, we have held that the term *liberty* includes a right to marry, Loving v. Virginia, 388 U.S. 1 (1967); a right to procreate, Skinner v. Oklahoma ex rel. Williamson, 316 U.S. 535 (1942); and a right to use contraceptives. Griswold v. Connecticut, 381 U.S. 479 (1965); Eisenstadt v. Baird, 405 U.S. 438 (1972). But a reading of these opinions makes clear that they do not endorse any all-encompassing "right of privacy.". . .

Nor do the historical traditions of the American people support the view that the right to terminate one's pregnancy is "fundamental.". . .

We think, therefore, both in view of this history and of our decided cases dealing with substantive liberty under the due process clause, that the Court was mistaken in *Roe* when it classified a woman's decision to terminate her pregnancy as a "fundamental right" that could be abridged only in a manner which withstood "strict scrutiny." . . .

The joint opinion of Justices O'Connor, Kennedy, and Souter cannot bring itself to say that *Roe* was correct as an original matter, but the authors are of the view that "the immediate question is not the soundness of *Roe's* resolution of the issue, but the precedential force that must be accorded to its holding." Instead of claiming that *Roe* was correct as a matter of original constitutional interpretation, the opinion therefore contains an elaborate discussion of *stare decisis*. This discussion of the principle of *stare decisis* appears to be almost entirely dicta, because the joint opinion does not apply that principle in dealing with *Roe. Roe* decided that a woman had a fundamental right to an abortion. The joint opinion rejects that view. *Roe* decided that abortion regulations were to be subjected to "strict scrutiny" and could be justified only in the light of "compelling state interests." The joint opinion rejects that view. *Roe* analyzed abortion regulation under a rigid trimester framework, a framework which has guided this Court's decisionmaking for 19 years. The joint opinion rejects that framework.

The sum of the joint opinion's labors in the name of *stare decisis* and "legitimacy" is this: Roe v. Wade stands as a sort of judicial Potemkin Village, which may be pointed out to passers by as a monument to the importance of adhering to precedent. But behind the facade, an entirely new method of analysis, without any roots in constitutional law, is imported to decide the constitutionality of state laws regulating abortion. Neither *stare decisis* nor "legitimacy" are truly served by such an effort.

We have stated above our belief that the Constitution does not subject state abortion regulations to heightened scrutiny. Accordingly, we think that the correct analysis is that set forth by the plurality opinion in *Webster*. A woman's interest in having an abortion is a form of liberty protected by the due process clause, but states may regulate abortion procedures in ways rationally related to a legitimate state interest. . . .

We therefore would hold that each of the challenged provisions of the Pennsylvania statute is consistent with the Constitution. It bears emphasis that our conclusion in this regard does not carry with it any necessary approval of these regulations. Our task is, as always, to decide only whether the challenged provisions of a law comport with the United States Constitution. If, as we believe, these do, their wisdom as a matter of public policy is for the people of Pennsylvania to decide.

■ GONZALES V. CARHART
550 U.S. 321 (2007)

KENNEDY, J.

These cases require us to consider the validity of the Partial-Birth Abortion Ban Act of 2003 (Act), 18 U.S.C. § 1531, a federal statute regulating abortion procedures. In recitations preceding its operative provisions the Act refers to the Court's opinion in Stenberg v. Carhart, 530 U.S. 914 (2000), which [struck down

Nebraska's restriction on] abortion procedures used in the later stages of pregnancy. Compared to the state statute at issue in *Stenberg*, the Act is more specific concerning the instances to which it applies and in this respect more precise in its coverage. We conclude the Act should be sustained against the objections lodged by the broad, facial attack brought against it. . . .

I

A

The Act proscribes a particular manner of ending fetal life, so it is necessary here, as it was in *Stenberg*, to discuss abortion procedures in some detail. . . . [1] Abortion methods vary depending to some extent on the preferences of the physician and, of course, on the term of the pregnancy and the resulting stage of the unborn child's development. Between 85 and 90 percent of the approximately 1.3 million abortions performed each year in the United States take place in the first three months of pregnancy, which is to say in the first trimester. . . . The Act does not regulate these procedures.

Of the remaining abortions that take place each year, most occur in the second trimester. The surgical procedure referred to as "dilation and evacuation" or "D & E" is the usual abortion method in this trimester. . . . Although individual techniques for performing D & E differ, the general steps are the same. . . . A doctor must first dilate the cervix at least to the extent needed to insert surgical instruments into the uterus and to maneuver them to evacuate the fetus. . . .

The abortion procedure that was the impetus for the numerous bans on "partial-birth abortion," including the Act, is a variation of this standard. . . . The medical community has not reached unanimity on the appropriate name for this D & E variation. It has been referred to as "intact D & E," "dilation and extraction" (D & X), and "intact D & X." . . . For discussion purposes this D & E variation will be referred to as intact D & E. The main difference between the two procedures is that in intact D & E a doctor extracts the fetus intact or largely intact with only a few passes [through the cervix, instead of extracting it in pieces]. . . . Intact D & E gained public notoriety when, in 1992, Dr. Martin Haskell gave a presentation describing his method of performing the operation. . . .

D & E and intact D & E are not the only second-trimester abortion methods. Doctors also may abort a fetus through medical induction. The doctor medicates the woman to induce labor, and contractions occur to deliver the fetus. Induction, which unlike D & E should occur in a hospital, can last as little as 6 hours but can take longer than 48. It accounts for about 5 percent of second-trimester abortions before 20 weeks of gestation and 15 percent of those after 20 weeks. Doctors turn to two other methods of second-trimester abortion, hysterotomy [removal of the fetus via an incision in the abdomen and uterine wall] and hysterectomy [removal of the uterus], only in emergency situations because they carry increased risk of complications. . . .

---

[1] Ed. Note: Justice Kennedy's opinion includes graphic descriptions of various second-term abortion procedures that have been shortened and summarized in this edited version of the opinion.

B

After Dr. Haskell's procedure received public attention, with ensuing and increasing public concern, bans on "partial birth abortion" proliferated. By the time of the *Stenberg* decision, about 30 States had enacted bans designed to prohibit the procedure. . . . In 1996, Congress also acted to ban partial-birth abortion. President Clinton vetoed the congressional legislation, and the Senate failed to override the veto. Congress approved another bill banning the procedure in 1997, but President Clinton again vetoed it. In 2003, after this Court's [5-4] decision in *Stenberg* [striking down Nebraska's ban], Congress passed [and President Bush signed] the Act at issue here. . . .

The Act responded to *Stenberg* in two ways. First, Congress made factual findings. Congress determined that this Court in *Stenberg* "was required to accept the very questionable findings issued by the district court judge," . . . but that Congress was "not bound to accept the same factual findings." Congress found, among other things, that "[a] moral, medical, and ethical consensus exists that the practice of performing a partial-birth abortion . . . is a gruesome and inhumane procedure that is never medically necessary and should be prohibited." . . . Second, and more relevant here, the Act's language differs from that of the Nebraska statute struck down in *Stenberg*. . . . [The court then summarized the provisions of the Act.]

II

The principles set forth in the joint opinion in [Planned Parenthood of Southeastern Pa. v. Casey, supra at page 449] did not find support from all those who join the instant opinion. . . . Whatever one's views concerning the *Casey* joint opinion, it is evident a premise central to its conclusion—that the government has a legitimate and substantial interest in preserving and promoting fetal life—would be repudiated were the Court now to affirm the judgments of the Courts of Appeals.

[Applying the principles of *Casey*] . . . we must determine whether the Act furthers the legitimate interest of the Government in protecting the life of the fetus that may become a child. . . . We assume the following principles for the purposes of this opinion. Before viability, a State "may not prohibit any woman from making the ultimate decision to terminate her pregnancy." [*Casey*, 505 U.S. at 879 (plurality opinion)] It also may not impose upon this right an undue burden, which exists if a regulation's "purpose or effect is to place a substantial obstacle in the path of a woman seeking an abortion before the fetus attains viability." . . . On the other hand, "[r]egulations which do no more than create a structural mechanism by which the State, or the parent or guardian of a minor, may express profound respect for the life of the unborn are permitted, if they are not a substantial obstacle to the woman's exercise of the right to choose." . . . *Casey*, in short, struck a balance. The balance was central to its holding. We now apply its standard to the cases at bar. . . .

[The Act] regulates and proscribes, with exceptions or qualifications to be discussed, performing the intact D & E procedure. Respondents agree the Act encompasses intact D & E, but they contend its additional reach is both unclear and excessive. Respondents assert that, at the least, the Act is void for vagueness because its scope is indefinite. In the alternative, respondents argue the Act's text proscribes all D & Es. Because D & E is the most common second-trimester abortion method, respondents suggest the Act imposes an undue burden. In this litigation the Attorney General does not dispute that the Act would impose an undue burden if it covered standard D & E.

We conclude that the Act is not void for vagueness, does not impose an undue burden from any overbreadth, and is not invalid on its face.

The Act punishes "knowingly perform[ing]" a "partial-birth abortion." §1531(a). It defines the unlawful abortion in explicit terms. . . . "As generally stated, the void-for-vagueness doctrine requires that a penal statute define the criminal offense with sufficient definiteness that ordinary people can understand what conduct is prohibited and in a manner that does not encourage arbitrary and discriminatory enforcement." . . . The Act satisfies both requirements. . . .

Unlike the statutory language in *Stenberg* that prohibited the delivery of a "'substantial portion'" of the fetus—where a doctor might question how much of the fetus is a substantial portion—the Act defines the line between potentially criminal conduct on the one hand and lawful abortion on the other. . . . Doctors performing D & E will know that if they do not deliver a living fetus to an anatomical landmark [referring to the delivery of the fetus to a certain point as specified in the statute] they will not face criminal liability. This conclusion is buttressed by the intent that must be proved to impose liability. The Court has made clear that scienter requirements alleviate vagueness concerns. . . .

We next determine whether the Act imposes an undue burden, as a facial matter, because its restrictions on second-trimester abortions are too broad. A review of the statutory text discloses the limits of its reach. The Act prohibits intact D & E; and, notwithstanding respondents' arguments, it does not prohibit the D & E procedure in which the fetus is removed in parts. . . .

IV

. . . The abortions affected by the Act's regulations take place both previability and postviability. . . . Under the principles accepted as controlling here, . . . the question is whether the Act, measured by its text in this facial attack, imposes a substantial obstacle to late-term, but previability, abortions. The Act does not on its face impose a substantial obstacle, and we reject this further facial challenge to its validity.

A

The Act's purposes are set forth in recitals preceding its operative provisions. A description of the prohibited abortion procedure demonstrates the rationale for the congressional enactment. The Act proscribes a method of abortion in which a fetus is killed just inches before completion of the birth process. Congress stated as follows: "Implicitly approving such a brutal and inhumane procedure by choosing not to prohibit it will further coarsen society to the humanity of not only newborns, but all vulnerable and innocent human life, making it increasingly difficult to protect such life." The Act expresses respect for the dignity of human life.

Congress was concerned, furthermore, with the effects on the medical community and on its reputation caused by the practice of partial-birth abortion. The findings in the Act explain: "Partial-birth abortion . . . confuses the medical, legal, and ethical duties of physicians to preserve and promote life, as the physician acts directly against the physical life of a child, whom he or she had just delivered, all but the head, out of the womb, in order to end that life." There can be no doubt the government "has an interest in protecting the integrity and ethics of the medical profession." Washington v. Glucksberg, 521 U.S. 702 (1997). . . .

Casey reaffirmed these governmental objectives. The government may use its voice and its regulatory authority to show its profound respect for the life within the woman. A central premise of the opinion was that the Court's precedents after *Roe* had "undervalue[d] the State's interest in potential life." 505 U.S. at 873 (plurality opinion). . . . The plurality opinion indicated "[t]he fact that a law which serves a valid purpose, one not designed to strike at the right itself, has the incidental effect of making it more difficult or more expensive to procure an abortion cannot be enough to invalidate it." *Id.* at 874. This was not an idle assertion. The three premises of *Casey* must coexist. . . . The third premise, that the State, from the inception of the pregnancy, maintains its own regulatory interest in protecting the life of the fetus that may become a child, cannot be set at naught by interpreting *Casey*'s requirement of a health exception so it becomes tantamount to allowing a doctor to choose the abortion method he or she might prefer. Where it has a rational basis to act, and it does not impose an undue burden, the State may use its regulatory power to bar certain procedures and substitute others, all in furtherance of its legitimate interests in regulating the medical profession in order to promote respect for life, including life of the unborn.

The Act's ban on abortions that involve partial delivery of a living fetus furthers the Government's objectives. No one would dispute that, for many, D & E is a procedure itself laden with the power to devalue human life. Congress could nonetheless conclude that the type of abortion proscribed by the Act requires specific regulation because it implicates additional ethical and moral concerns that justify a special prohibition. Congress determined that the abortion methods it proscribed had a "disturbing similarity to the killing of a newborn infant,". . . and thus it was concerned with "draw[ing] a bright line that clearly distinguishes abortion and infanticide.". . . The Court has in the past confirmed the validity of drawing boundaries to prevent certain practices that extinguish life and are close to actions that are condemned. *Glucksberg* found reasonable the State's "fear that permitting assisted suicide will start it down the path to voluntary and perhaps even involuntary euthanasia." 521 U.S. at 732-35. . . .

Respect for human life finds an ultimate expression in the bond of love the mother has for her child. The Act recognizes this reality as well. Whether to have an abortion requires a difficult and painful moral decision. . . . While we find no reliable data to measure the phenomenon, it seems unexceptionable to conclude some women come to regret their choice to abort the infant life they once created and sustained. Severe depression and loss of esteem can follow. . . .

In a decision so fraught with emotional consequence some doctors may prefer not to disclose precise details of the means that will be used, confining themselves to the required statement of risks the procedure entails. From one standpoint this ought not to be surprising. Any number of patients facing imminent surgical procedures would prefer not to hear all details, lest the usual anxiety preceding invasive medical procedures become the more intense. This is likely the case with the abortion procedures here in issue. . . .

It is, however, precisely this lack of information concerning the way in which the fetus will be killed that is of legitimate concern to the State. *Casey*, 505 U.S. at 873 (plurality opinion) ("States are free to enact laws to provide a reasonable framework for a woman to make a decision that has such profound and lasting meaning"). The State has an interest in ensuring so grave a choice is well informed. It is self-evident that a mother who comes to regret her choice to abort must struggle with grief more anguished and sorrow more profound when she learns, only after the event, what she once did not know . . . [about how the procedure is performed].

It is a reasonable inference that a necessary effect of the regulation and the knowledge it conveys will be to encourage some women to carry the infant to full term, thus reducing the absolute number of late-term abortions. The medical profession, furthermore, may find different and less shocking methods to abort the fetus in the second trimester, thereby accommodating legislative demand. The State's interest in respect for life is advanced by the dialogue that better informs the political and legal systems, the medical profession, expectant mothers, and society as a whole of the consequences that follow from a decision to elect a late-term abortion. . . . In sum, we reject the contention that the congressional purpose of the Act was "to place a substantial obstacle in the path of a woman seeking an abortion." 505 U.S. at 878 (plurality opinion).

B

The Act's furtherance of legitimate government interests bears upon, but does not resolve, the next question: whether the Act has the effect of imposing an unconstitutional burden on the abortion right because it does not allow use of the barred procedure where " 'necessary, in appropriate medical judgment, for [the] preservation of the . . . health of the mother.' " [citing Ayotte v. Planned Parenthood of Northern New Eng., 546 U.S. 320] . . . The prohibition in the Act would be unconstitutional, under precedents we here assume to be controlling, if it "subject[ed] [women] to significant health risks." [*Id.* at 328] . . . In *Ayotte* the parties agreed a health exception to the challenged parental-involvement statute was necessary "to avert serious and often irreversible damage to [a pregnant minor's] health." . . . Here, by contrast, whether the Act creates significant health risks for women has been a contested factual question. The evidence presented in the trial courts and before Congress demonstrates both sides have medical support for their position. . . .

The question becomes whether the Act can stand when this medical uncertainty persists. The Court's precedents instruct that the Act can survive this facial attack. The Court has given state and federal legislatures wide discretion to pass legislation in areas where there is medical and scientific uncertainty. [The Court cites, among other cases, Jacobson v. Massachusetts, 197 U.S. 11 (1905), discussed in Chapter 6 at page 449.] . . . Physicians are not entitled to ignore regulations that direct them to use reasonable alternative procedures. The law need not give abortion doctors unfettered choice in the course of their medical practice, nor should it elevate their status above other physicians in the medical community. . . . Medical uncertainty does not foreclose the exercise of legislative power in the abortion context any more than it does in other contexts. . . . The medical uncertainty over whether the Act's prohibition creates significant health risks provides a sufficient basis to conclude in this facial attack that the Act does not impose an undue burden. . . .

In reaching the conclusion the Act does not require a health exception we reject certain arguments made by the parties on both sides of these cases. On the one hand, the Attorney General urges us to uphold the Act on the basis of the congressional findings alone. Although we review congressional factfinding under a deferential standard, we do not in the circumstances here place dispositive weight on Congress' findings. The Court retains an independent constitutional duty to review factual findings where constitutional rights are at stake. . . . As respondents have noted, and the District Courts recognized, some recitations in the Act are factually incorrect. . . .

On the other hand, relying on the Court's opinion in *Stenberg,* respondents contend that an abortion regulation must contain a health exception "if 'substantial medical authority supports the proposition that banning a particular procedure could endanger women's health.'" . . . As illustrated by respondents' arguments and the decisions of the Courts of Appeals, *Stenberg* has been interpreted to leave no margin of error for legislatures to act in the face of medical uncertainty. . . . A zero tolerance policy would strike down legitimate abortion regulations, like the present one, if some part of the medical community were disinclined to follow the proscription. This is too exacting a standard to impose on the legislative power, exercised in this instance under the Commerce Clause, to regulate the medical profession. Considerations of marginal safety, including the balance of risks, are within the legislative competence when the regulation is rational and in pursuit of legitimate ends. When standard medical options are available, mere convenience does not suffice to displace them; and if some procedures have different risks than others, it does not follow that the State is altogether barred from imposing reasonable regulations. The Act is not invalid on its face where there is uncertainty over whether the barred procedure is ever necessary to preserve a woman's health, given the availability of other abortion procedures that are considered to be safe alternatives. . . .

In these circumstances the proper means to consider exceptions is by as-applied challenge. . . . This is the proper manner to protect the health of the woman if it can be shown that in discrete and well-defined instances a particular condition has or is likely to occur in which the procedure prohibited by the Act must be used. In an as-applied challenge the nature of the medical risk can be better quantified and balanced than in a facial attack. . . .

Respondents have not demonstrated that the Act, as a facial matter, is void for vagueness, or that it imposes an undue burden on a woman's right to abortion based on its overbreadth or lack of a health exception. For these reasons the judgments of the Courts of Appeals for the Eighth and Ninth Circuits are reversed. . . .

[Justices Roberts, Scalia, Thomas, and Alito joined the majority opinion. Justice Thomas wrote a concurring opinion, joined by Justice Scalia, "reiterat[ing] my view that the Court's abortion jurisprudence . . . has no basis in the Constitution."]

Ginsberg, J., dissenting. . . .

Seven years ago, in *Stenberg*, . . . the Court invalidated a Nebraska statute criminalizing the performance of a medical procedure that, in the political arena, has been dubbed "partial-birth abortion." . . . [T]he Court held the Nebraska statute unconstitutional in part because it lacked the requisite protection for the preservation of a woman's health. . . .

Today's decision is alarming. It refuses to take *Casey* and *Stenberg* seriously. It tolerates, indeed applauds, federal intervention to ban nationwide a procedure found necessary and proper in certain cases by the American College of Obstetricians and Gynecologists (ACOG). It blurs the line, firmly drawn in *Casey* between previability and postviability abortions. And, for the first time since *Roe*, the Court blesses a prohibition with no exception safeguarding a woman's health.

I dissent from the Court's disposition. Retreating from prior rulings that abortion restrictions cannot be imposed absent an exception safeguarding a woman's health, the Court upholds an Act that surely would not survive under the close scrutiny that previously attended state-decreed limitations on a woman's reproductive choices.

I

As *Casey* comprehended, at stake in cases challenging abortion restrictions is a woman's "control over her [own] destiny." . . . Women, it is now acknowledged, have the talent, capacity, and right "to participate equally in the economic and social life of the Nation." . . . Their ability to realize their full potential, the Court recognized, is intimately connected to "their ability to control their reproductive lives." . . . Thus, legal challenges to undue restrictions on abortion procedures do not seek to vindicate some generalized notion of privacy; rather, they center on a woman's autonomy to determine her life's course, and thus to enjoy equal citizenship stature. See, e.g., Siegel, Reasoning from the Body: A Historical Perspective on Abortion Regulation and Questions of Equal Protection, 44 Stan. L. Rev. 261 (1992); Law, Rethinking Sex and the Constitution, 132 U. Pa. L. Rev. 955 (1984).

In keeping with this comprehension of the right to reproductive choice, the Court has consistently required that laws regulating abortion, at any stage of pregnancy and in all cases, safeguard a woman's health. . . . We have thus ruled that a State must avoid subjecting women to health risks not only where the pregnancy itself creates danger, but also where state regulation forces women to resort to less safe methods of abortion. . . .

[The courts below] made findings after full trials at which all parties had the opportunity to present their best evidence. . . . . According to the expert testimony plaintiffs introduced, the safety advantages of intact D & E are marked for women with certain medical conditions, for example, uterine scarring, bleeding disorders, heart disease, or compromised immune systems. . . . Further, plaintiffs' experts testified that intact D & E is significantly safer for women with certain pregnancy-related conditions, such as placenta previa and accreta and for women carrying fetuses with certain abnormalities, such as severe hydrocephalus. . . . Based on thoroughgoing review of the trial evidence and the congressional record, each of the District Courts to consider the issue rejected Congress' findings as unreasonable and not supported by the evidence. . . . The District Courts' findings merit this Court's respect. . . .

II

The Court offers flimsy and transparent justifications for upholding a nationwide ban on intact D & E. . . . The law saves not a single fetus from destruction, for it targets only a *method* of performing abortion. . . . And surely the statute was not designed to protect the lives or health of pregnant women. . . . In short, the Court upholds a law that, while doing nothing to "preserv[e] . . . fetal life," . . . bars a woman from choosing intact D & E although her doctor "reasonably believes [that procedure] will best protect [her]." . . .

Ultimately, the Court admits that "moral concerns" are at work, concerns that could yield prohibitions on any abortion. . . . Notably, the concerns expressed are untethered to any ground genuinely serving the Government's interest in preserving life. By allowing such concerns to carry the day and case, overriding fundamental rights, the Court dishonors our precedent. . . . .

Revealing in this regard, the Court invokes an antiabortion shibboleth for which it concededly has no reliable evidence: Women who have abortions come to regret their choices, and consequently suffer from "[s]evere depression and loss of esteem." . . . [7] Because of women's fragile emotional state and because of the "bond of love the mother has for her child," the Court worries, doctors may withhold information about the nature of the intact D & E procedure. . . . The solution the Court approves, then, is *not* to require doctors to inform women, accurately and adequately, of the different procedures and their attendant risks. . . . Instead, the Court deprives women of the right to make an autonomous choice, even at the expense of their safety. . . . This way of thinking reflects ancient notions about women's place in the family and under the Constitution — ideas that have long since been discredited. . . .

One wonders how long a line that saves no fetus from destruction will hold in face of the Court's "moral concerns." . . . The Court's hostility to the right *Roe* and *Casey* secured is not concealed. Throughout, the opinion refers to obstetrician-gynecologists and surgeons who perform abortions not by the titles of their medical specialties, but by the pejorative label "abortion doctor." . . . A fetus is described as an "unborn child," and as a "baby," . . . second-trimester, previability abortions are referred to as "late-term," . . . ; and the reasoned medical judgments of highly trained doctors are dismissed as "preferences" motivated by "mere convenience." . . . Instead of the heightened scrutiny we have previously applied, the Court determines that a "rational" ground is enough to uphold the Act. . . . And, most troubling, *Casey*'s principles, confirming the continuing vitality of "the essential holding of *Roe*" are merely "assume[d]" for the moment, . . . rather than "retained" or "reaffirmed." . . .

---

[7] The Court is surely correct that, for most women, abortion is a painfully difficult decision. . . . But "neither the weight of the scientific evidence to date nor the observable reality of 33 years of legal abortion in the United States comports with the idea that having an abortion is any more dangerous to a woman's long-term mental health than delivering and parenting a child that she did not intend to have. . . . " Cohen, Abortion and Mental Health: Myths and Realities, 9 Guttmacher Policy Rev. 8 (2006). . . .

Though today's opinion does not go so far as to discard *Roe* or *Casey*, the Court, differently composed than it was when we last considered a restrictive abortion regulation, is hardly faithful to our earlier invocations of "the rule of law" and the "principles of *stare decisis*." . . . In candor, the Act, and the Court's defense of it, cannot be understood as anything other than an effort to chip away at a right declared again and again by this Court. . . .

[This dissent was joined by Justices Stevens, Souter, and Breyer.]

Notes: The Post-*Casey* Landscape and the Implications of *Gonzales*

1. *Stare Decisis.* Did *Casey* overturn *Roe*? Does the Court's discussion of *stare decisis* in the abortion cases seem persuasive? What does it mean to reaffirm Roe v. Wade while overturning the trimester framework, as the Court did in *Casey*? What types of cases are now likely to have different results?

The *Gonzales* Court clearly was forced to wrestle with the significance of *stare decisis* given the Court's invalidation of a similar statute in *Stenberg*. In *Stenberg*, the majority seemed to constrain the state's ability to prohibit abortion procedures:

> In sum, Nebraska has not convinced us that a health exception is "never necessary to preserve the health of women." . . . Rather, a statute that altogether forbids D & X [referred to as an "intact D & E" in *Gonzales*] creates a significant health risk. The statute consequently must contain a health exception. This is not to say . . . that a State is prohibited from proscribing an abortion procedure whenever a particular physician deems the procedure preferable. . . . But where substantial medical authority supports the proposition that banning a particular abortion procedure could endanger women's health, *Casey* requires the statute to include a health exception when the procedure is "'necessary, in appropriate medical judgment, for the preservation of the life or health of the mother.'" 530 U.S. at 937-938.

Does the *Gonzales* majority overturn *Stenberg*?

The *Gonzales* case gave the newly constituted Supreme Court — with Justices Alito and Roberts and without Justices Rehnquist and O'Connor — an opportunity to revisit its approach to the jurisprudence of abortion. Justice Kennedy held the pivotal swing vote in a classic 5-4 split, a position often previously occupied by Justice Sandra Day O'Connor. Justice Kennedy's dissent in *Stenberg* argued that the Court's invalidation of Nebraska's ban on the abortion procedure was inconsistent with *Casey*'s stated deference to a state's legitimate interest in "promot[ing] the life of the unborn and to ensure respect for all human life and its potential." His majority decision in *Gonzales* emphasizes and relies upon this portion of *Casey*.

What does *Gonzales* suggest about the future of abortion jurisprudence? With the current Court composition, it would appear at the very least that governments will be given more latitude to regulate abortion to protect "moral values" and women's interests (as defined by the *Gonzales* majority rather than by Justice Ginsberg). For the moment, it does not seem that there are enough votes to overturn *Roe* and *Casey* completely. Justice Ginsberg explicitly discusses the impact of the changes in the Court's membership since *Casey* and *Stenberg* in her dissent and expresses concern about the future of the abortion right. See R. Alta Charo, The Partial Death of Abortion Rights, 356 New Eng. J. Med. 2125 (2007).

2. *A Fundamental Right?* Is a woman's right to choose whether or not to have an abortion still a "fundamental right"? What is a "liberty interest"? The composition of the Court changed between *Casey, Stenberg,* and *Gonzales.* How many Justices today actually support the use of the "undue burden" test? *Gonzales* suggests that there may be at least five, as Justice Kennedy seemed not yet willing to abandon *Casey.* The views of Chief Justice Roberts and Justice Alito are not completely clear, as they joined Justice Kennedy's majority decision "assuming" that the principles of *Casey* applied. Neither joined in Justice Thomas's dissent repudiating *Roe* and its progeny. What types of proof might be relevant to determining whether a state regulation poses an "undue burden" on a woman's abortion right post-*Casey* and post-*Gonzales?*

3. *A New Court and New Legislative Challenges.* Changes in the political climate and the composition of the United States Supreme Court have resulted in the enactment of state legislation directly challenging Roe v. Wade. South Dakota enacted legislation banning abortions, intentionally provoking a legal challenge to Roe v. Wade, but the effort was stalled by a voter referendum rejecting the ban. Monica Davey, South Dakotans Reject Sweeping Abortion Ban, N.Y. Times, Nov. 8, 2006, at P8. Louisiana enacted legislation that would ban abortion if Roe v. Wade is overturned. La. R.S. 40:1299.30 (2007); and Jeremy Alford, Louisiana's Governor Plans to Sign Anti-Abortion Law, N.Y. Times, June 7, 2006, at A18.

4. *Abortion and Equal Protection.* Some commentators have argued that restrictions on abortion ought to be challenged under equal protection grounds. Justice Ginsberg's dissent in *Gonzales* begins with a description of the abortion right as necessary to ensure women's liberty and equality. Is there any other support for this view in the Court's recent decisions? See Samuel R. Bagenstos, Disability, Life, Death, and Choice, 29 Harv. J.L. & Gender 425, 453-457 (2006). But see Charles I. Lugosi, Conforming to the Rule of Law: When Person and Human Being Finally Mean the Same Thing in Fourteenth Amendment Jurisprudence, 22 Issues L. & Med. 119 (2006) (arguing that the U.S. Supreme Court should reconsider its failure to find fetuses protected under the equal protection clause).

5. *The Undue Burden Standard Applied.* As might be expected, *Casey* has been cited nearly 1,000 times by federal and state courts since its publication. It has been used to uphold some state abortion regulations, see, e.g., Barnes v. Moore, 970 F.2d 12 (5th Cir. 1992), and to strike down others, see, e.g., Stenberg v. Carhart, supra. Litigants have sought to use *Casey* in other socially controversial areas. See, e.g., Washington v. Glucksberg, 521 U.S. 702 (1997) (Court rejects view that *Casey* supports a constitutional right to assisted suicide). Will the Court's decision in *Gonzales* have a ripple effect in other areas?

6. *Second Trimester.* Second-trimester abortions are relatively rare. See, e.g., Lilo T. Strauss et al., Abortion Surveillance — United States, 2003, 55 MMWR 1, 15 (Nov. 24, 2006) (No. SS-11) (4.2 percent of reported abortions occurred at 16 to 21 weeks of gestation, only 1.4 percent occurred at 21 weeks or greater). A majority of states have enacted severe restrictions on "intact D & E" abortions or related procedures. What explains the significant legislative activity in this area,

given the relative rarity of these procedures? The *Stenberg* decision arguably presented a blueprint for states interested in enacting limits on late-term abortions, yet most legislatures did not review or revise their partial-birth abortion bans to conform with *Stenberg*'s criteria. Why did Congress finally enact the "partial-birth" abortion ban after the Court's decision in *Stenberg*?

7. *Sources.* The abortion debate is reflected in a large volume of scholarship; recent articles include The Supreme Court, 2005 Term, Abortion Rights — Remedy for Unconstitutionality, 120 Harv. L. Rev. 293 (2006); Symposium, The Legacy of Roe: The Constitution, Reproductive Rights, and Feminism, 6 U. Pa. J. Const. L. 684-843 (2004); Symposium on Twenty-five Years of Roe v. Wade: The Legal Evolution of Reproductive Freedom and Prenatal Rights, 62 Alb. L. Rev. 801 (1999).

Notes: Thirty-five Years of Abortion Jurisprudence

1. *Regulation of Abortion Providers.* The Supreme Court held in *Roe*, at least by implication, that states could require that first-trimester abortions be performed by physicians. 410 U.S. 113, 163 (1973). The state's interest in the health of a pregnant woman would become compelling at the point where the risks of the abortion outweigh the risks of carrying the pregnancy to term, or at the end of the first trimester. After this point, "a state may regulate the abortion procedure to the extent that the regulation reasonably relates to the preservation and protection of maternal health." States may establish requirements for providers and facilities. At the point of fetal viability, sometime around the end of the second trimester, a state may assert its compelling interest in protecting fetal life by prohibiting abortion, except where the procedure was necessary to preserve the life or health of the pregnant woman. Id. The Supreme Court confirmed that states may require that physicians perform abortions in Mazurek v. Armstrong, 520 U.S. 968 (1997) (rejecting contention that requirement placed an undue burden on access to abortion).

In recent years some states have increased reporting and inspection requirements for abortion providers. Although many regulations will be upheld given the Supreme Court's explicit authorization of certain forms of state provider regulation, providers and activists have successfully challenged some of these new regulatory provisions. See, e.g., Northwestern Memorial Hospital v. Ashcroft, 362 F.3d 923 (7th Cir. 2004) (affirming a district court order quashing a subpoena requiring a hospital to produce the medical records of patients who had undergone a particular late-term abortion procedure); Aid for Women et al. v. Foulston et al., 427 F. Supp. 2d 1093 (2006) (finding that Kansas's reporting statute does not require reporting of consensual underage sexual activity and that contrary reading of statute would violate minors' limited right of informational privacy). See also Note, 56 Duke L.J. 583 (2006); Note, 105 Colum. L. Rev. 1563 (2005); Jodi Rudoren, Kansas' Top Court Limits Abortion Record Search, N.Y. Times, Feb. 4, 2006, at A7.

2. *Government Funding for Abortion.* Restrictions on government funding for abortions were the first real political and legal successes for abortion opponents. In Maher v. Roe, 432 U.S. 464 (1977), the Supreme Court upheld the

constitutional validity of a Connecticut welfare rule that provided Medicaid recipients with coverage for pregnancy services but not for non-therapeutic abortion services. In Harris v. McRae, 448 U.S. 297 (1980), the Court upheld the "Hyde Amendment," which prohibited the use of federal funds contributed to the Medicaid program to reimburse the cost of most abortions even when they were medically necessary. The Court found that state and federal funding restrictions did not violate the due process or equal protection clause because, while women had a constitutional right to choose abortion, they did not have a constitutional right to make the government pay for it. The government, the Court held, was free to establish programs that provided pregnancy benefits while denying coverage for abortion:

> But, regardless of whether the freedom of a woman to choose to terminate her pregnancy for health reasons lies at the core or the periphery of the due process liberty recognized in [Roe v. Wade], it simply does not follow that a woman's freedom of choice carries with it a constitutional entitlement to the financial resources to avail herself of the full range of protected choices. . . . [A]lthough government may not place obstacles in the path of a woman's exercise of her freedom of choice, it need not remove those not of its own creation. Indigence falls in the latter category. The financial constraints that restrict an indigent woman's ability to enjoy the full range of constitutionally protected freedom of choice are the product not of governmental restrictions on access to abortions, but rather of her indigence. Although Congress has opted to subsidize medically necessary services generally, but not certain medically necessary abortions, the fact remains that the Hyde Amendment leaves an indigent woman with at least the same range of choice in deciding whether to obtain a medically necessary abortion as she would have had if Congress had chosen to subsidize no health care costs at all. We are thus not persuaded that the Hyde Amendment impinges on the constitutionally protected freedom of choice recognized in [Roe]. 448 U.S. at 316-317.

Federal funding for abortion is the subject of regular congressional debate, and the abortion coverage exclusion occasionally expands and narrows as the result of political campaigns waged by pro-choice and pro-life forces. For a decision involving the federal government's refusal to pay for an abortion in a case involving a fetal abnormality, see Britell v. United States, 372 F.3d 1370 (Fed. Cir. 2004) (under the federal CHAMPUS program).

State courts have sometimes found a state constitutional right to Medicaid funding for abortions, requiring that states fund these services even in the absence of federal assistance. See, e.g., State Department of Health & Human Services v. Planned Parenthood of Alaska, Inc., 28 P.3d 904 (Alaska 2001). Other states have statutory or constitutional provisions that *prohibit* expenditure of state funds on abortions. These jurisdictions have been confronted with something of a dilemma because federal law requires that states provide funding for abortion in some limited circumstances, and federal law of course is supreme, even when weighed against a state constitutional provision. See Dalton v. Little Rock Family Planning Services, 516 U.S. 474 (1996).

Government funding returned as a controversial issue in the late 1980s with the adoption of new regulations implementing federal funding of family planning clinics under Title X of the Public Health Service Act, 42 U.S.C. §§300 to 300a-6.

The Act specified that federal funds could not be "used in programs where abortion is a method of family planning." Id. §300a-6. The regulations placed three different conditions on recipients of Title X federal funds. The first, and most controversial, set of provisions came to be known as the "gag clause." Title X providers were prohibited from counseling about abortion or providing abortion referrals as a method of family planning. The Title X project was forbidden from providing an abortion referral even when specifically requested by a patient. Project personnel were permitted to say that "the project does not consider abortion an appropriate method of family planning and therefore does not counsel or refer for abortion." 42 C.F.R. §59.8(b)(5) (1989). The regulations also restricted Title X projects from encouraging, promoting, or advocating abortion as a method of family planning through lobbying, educational programs, or other activities. 42 C.F.R. §59.10(a) (1989). Finally, Title X projects had to be organized so that they were "physically and financially separate" from abortion activities. 42 C.F.R. §59.9 (1989). The Supreme Court rejected claims that the regulations violated the First Amendment in Rust v. Sullivan, 500 U.S. 173 (1991). The Court relied on the Harris v. McRae line of federal funding cases to hold that the regulations merely implemented a permissible governmental objective: ensuring that federal funds were used only for family planning purposes, not the promotion of abortion. Id. at 192-200. The gag rule was rescinded during the Clinton administration. See Standards of Compliance for Abortion-Related Services in Family Services Projects, 65 Fed. Reg. 41,270 (2000).

3. *Minors and Abortion*. Does the right established in Roe v. Wade apply to minors as well? Even if one accepts the proposition that women have a right to choose abortion, it does not necessarily follow that minor women should be given the right to secure an abortion without parental notification or even consent. The Supreme Court has supported a minor's right of access to contraceptives, but the risks associated with an abortion clearly outweigh those created by the use of condoms. Parents ordinarily must give consent for their children to undergo medical procedures, absent an emergency, and abortion is a morally and religiously sensitive medical procedure. Notifying a parent of a child's pregnancy can, additionally, give parents important information about a child's participation in risky sexual activities. On the other hand, children have constitutional rights in many circumstances. As a policy matter, many minors have the maturity to make their own abortion determinations. Further, a minor's right to make these decisions free from parental interference may be an important issue in abusive or incestuous homes.

The post-*Roe* Supreme Court struggled to determine whether and when a minor had a right to choose abortion. See, e.g., Ohio v. Akron Center for Reproductive Health, 497 U.S. 502 (1990); Hodgson v. Minnesota, 497 U.S. 417 (1990). These decisions were marked by deep divisions within the Court, with a majority of Justices upholding state parental notification or consent rules so long as they were accompanied by a judicial bypass procedure that permitted a mature minor to obtain judicial approval of her decision. The *Casey* court affirmed the continuing validity of *Hodgson* and *Akron* by upholding Pennsylvania's parental consent/judicial bypass procedure. More recently, the United States Supreme Court found that New Hampshire's parental notification law, prohibiting physicians from performing abortions on minors without prior written notice to a parent or guardian, could be unconstitutional in a medical emergency. The matter was remanded to the Court of Appeals for a determination of whether the remedy could be narrowed to prevent invalidation of the entire legislation. Planned Parenthood v. Heed, 390 F.3d 53, *cert. granted* sub nom. Ayotte v. Planned Parenthood, 546 U.S. 320 (2006).See Note, 119 Harv. L. Rev. 2552 (2006).

May states require minors to prove they are mature enough to make a decision about abortion by clear and convincing evidence? See In the Matter of B. S., 74 P.3d 285 (Ariz. App. 2003) (applying this standard). For a summary of the law involving minors and abortion, see Carol Sanger, Regulating Teenage Abortion in the United States: Politics and Policy, 18 Int'l J.L. Pol'y & Fam. 305 (2004); and National Conference of State Legislatures, Parental Consent or Notification for Abortion (available at NCSL Web site). See also Theodore Joyce et al., Changes in Abortions and Births and the Texas Parental Notification Law, 354 New Eng. J. Med. 1031 (2006) (analysis of data to determine impact of law on abortion rates).

4. *Informed Consent and Waiting Periods*. A number of state legislatures have sought to regulate the informed consent process for abortions in two ways. First, states have sought to require the provision of specific types of information, such as fetal age, fetal development, and the availability of paternity support actions under state law. Second, states have enacted "waiting periods," under which women are required to wait some statutorily established period of time between being given information about the abortion procedure and undergoing the procedure itself. Before *Casey*, courts generally invalidated attempts to dictate the specifics of what doctors must disclose to their patients — particularly scripts that were blatant attempts to discourage the procedure. See Akron v. Akron Center for Reproductive Health, 462 U.S. 416 (1983) (striking requirement that woman be informed, inter alia, that "the unborn child is a human life from the moment of conception").

The *Casey* decision reopened this avenue for state regulation, by upholding a Pennsylvania informed consent provision and 24-hour waiting rule because they did not impose an "undue burden" on women seeking an abortion. See, e.g., Cincinnati Women's Services, Inc. v. Taft, 468 F.3d 361 (6th Cir. 2006) (upholding Ohio's requirement of an informed consent process with physician 24 hours before procedure); A Woman's Choice — East Side Women's Clinic v. Newman, 305 F.3d 684 (7th Cir. 2002) (permitting enforcement of Indiana informed consent rule that required women to make two trips to the clinic or hospital); Karlin v. Foust, 188 F.3d 446 (7th Cir. 1999) (upholding Wisconsin abortion informed consent statute). See also Annotation, 119 A.L.R.5th 315 (2004). The *Gonzales* decision is likely to reinforce the trend toward permitting states to impose significant message-oriented informed consent provisions.

For a new variation on state informed consent statutes, see Fetal Pain Legislation: Subordinating Sound Medical Findings to Moral and Political Agendas, 27 J. Leg. Med. 459 (2006); Note, The Science, Law, and Politics of Fetal Pain Legislation, 115 Harv. L. Rev. 2010 (2002) (discussing "Fetal Pain Prevention Act," under which physicians, with some exceptions, would be required to inform women seeking late-term abortions that the fetus may feel pain and to offer the choice of performing the procedure using analgesics for the fetus).

Physicians have always had a duty to disclose information to women undergoing the abortion procedure. The ordinary rules governing disclosure, see Chapter 3.C, apply unless a state has enacted a specific informed consent procedure for abortion. As you recall, the two major disclosure standards are the "malpractice" standard and the "material risk" standard. There are few reported decisions in which patients have brought informed consent claims against their physicians. See, e.g., Humes v. Clinton, 792 P.2d 1032 (Kan. 1990) (no recovery for emotional distress caused by physician's failure to disclose risks where no physical injury occurs); Boes v. Deschu, 768 S.W.2d 205 (Mo. Ct. App. 1989) (plaintiff subjected to coercive "anti-abortion" counseling states claim for intentional infliction of emotional distress); Acuna v. Turkish, 894 A.2d 1208 (N.J. Super. 2006) (informed consent claim arising from abortion survives motion for summary judgment); Rodriguez v. Epstein, 664 N.Y.S.2d 20 (App. Div. 1997) (physicians not required to refer patients in counseling on alternatives to elective abortion); Spencer v. Seikel, 742 P.2d 1126 (Okla. 1987) (physician not liable for failing to inform plaintiff that late-term abortion might be available in other states).

Some have argued that women undergoing abortions are likely to experience significant emotional reactions to the procedure, akin to post-traumatic stress disorder. Do physicians have a duty to warn patients about the "abortion trauma syndrome"? Does it matter whether a jurisdiction follows the "material risk" or "professional" standard of disclosure? See Emily Bazelon, Is There a Post-Abortion Syndrome?, N.Y. Times Magazine, Jan. 21, 2006, at 41; Nada L. Stotland, The Myth of the Abortion Trauma Syndrome, 268 JAMA 2078 (1992); A. N. Broen et al., Predictors of Anxiety and Depression Following Pregnancy Termination: A Longitudinal Five-Year Follow-up Study, 85 Acta Obstet. Gynecol. Scand. 317 (2006). See also Bendar v. Rosen, 588 A.2d 1264 (N.J. Super. Ct. App. Div. 1991) (facts are as complex as those found in the typical Torts final; court upholds jury award for psychological trauma following an abortion). Does Justice Kennedy's opinion in *Gonzales* open the door to new state legislation mandating that physicians disclose the risk of post-abortion trauma?

5. *Spousal Notification/Consent.* In Planned Parenthood of Central Missouri v. Danforth, 428 U.S. 52 (1976), the Supreme Court appeared to eliminate any question about whether putative fathers have an interest in blocking an abortion. There, the Court invalidated a requirement that the spouse consent to a woman's abortion unless necessary to save her life. The Court reasoned that

> the state cannot delegate to a spouse a veto power which the state itself is absolutely and totally prohibited from exercising. . . . [W]hen the wife and the husband disagree on this decision, the view of only one of the two marriage partners can prevail. Inasmuch as it is the woman who physically bears the child and who is the more directly and immediately affected by the pregnancy, as between the two, the balance weighs in her favor.

Courts generally refuse to give genetic fathers any right to prevent an abortion. Annotation, 62 A.L.R.3d 1097 (1975). For a recent example of the issue see Adam Liptak, Ex-Boyfriend Loses Bid to Halt an Abortion, N.Y. Times, Aug. 6, 2002, at A10, col. 1. The *Casey* plurality struck down Pennsylvania's spousal notification requirement using the undue burden standard.

6. *Conscience Provisions.* Generally, private facilities and actors are not required to participate in abortions. See Lisa C. Ikemoto, When a Hospital Becomes Catholic, 47 Mercer L. Rev. 1087 (1996). Under federal law, private hospitals, which are not state actors, are free to decide for themselves not to perform abortions. See 20 U.S.C. §1688 ("Nothing in this chapter shall be construed to require or prohibit any person, or public or private entity, to provide or pay for any benefit or service, including the use of facilities, related to abortion."). But see Doe v. Bridgeton Hospital Ass'n Inc., 389 A.2d 526 (N.J. Super. Ct. Law Div. 1978) (private hospitals required to provide access to abortions under state constitution).

Consider also the rights of individual health care practitioners (as opposed to facilities) to refuse to participate in abortions. Following *Roe*, Congress and many state legislatures moved quickly to enact so-called conscience clause statutes that protect physicians, nurses, and other medical personnel from retaliatory measures for refusing to participate in abortions. See 42 U.S.C. §300a-7 (known as the "Church Amendment"); Shelton v. University of Medicine & Dentistry of New Jersey, 223 F.3d 220 (3d Cir. 2000) (hospital provided reasonable accommodations to nurse's religious beliefs regarding abortions); Judith F. Daar, A Clash at the Bedside: Patient Autonomy v. A Physician's Professional Conscience, 44 Hastings L.J. 1241, 1274 (1993) (comparing protection for physician conscience in death and dying and abortion cases). The FDA's approval of RU-486 and emergency contraception (which some have argued serves as an abortifacient) generated claims that pharmacists should have a similar right of conscience. Julie Cantor & Ken Baum, The Limits of Conscientious Objection — May Pharmacists Refuse to Fill Prescriptions for Emergency Contraception?, 351 New Eng. J. Med. 2008 (2004); Leslie C. Griffin, Conscience and Emergency Contraception, 6 Hous. J. Health L. & Pol'y 299 (2006); Comment, 54 UCLA L. Rev. 709 (2007). Justice Kennedy's opinion in *Gonzales*, supra, notes that states have the power to regulate abortion "to protect[ ] the integrity and ethics of the medical profession."

7. *Abortion Protesters.* Courts and legislatures have also struggled to resolve the controversies created by abortion protesters. Anti-abortion protesters regularly block clinic doors and engage in "sidewalk counseling" of women attempting to gain access to abortion clinics. Theoretically, protesters might be charged with violation of state trespass laws. Compare Joan Teshima, Annotation, Trespass: State Prosecution for Unauthorized Entry or Occupation, for Public Demonstration Purposes, of Business, Industrial, or Utility Premises, 41 A.L.R.4th 773 (1985) with James O. Pearson, Jr., Annotation, "Choice of Evils," Necessity, Duress, or Similar Defense to State or Local Criminal Charges Based on Acts of Public Protest, 3 A.L.R.5th 521 (1992). Abortion clinics and their supporters have also sought to use the federal Racketeer Influenced and Corrupt Organizations Act (RICO). In Scheidler v. National Organization of Women, 547 U.S. 9 (2006), the Supreme Court rejected efforts to use RICO and the Hobbs Act's extortion provisions in a class action brought by NOW against individuals and organizations involved in anti-abortion protests.

State and local officials often have seemed overwhelmed by the numbers and commitment of protesters. Judges issue injunctions designed to create a "buffer zone" around clinics, attempting to balance the need to protect free speech against the harms protesters inflict on the clinics and their patients. The Supreme

Court opinions in this area are complex. See, e.g., Schenck v. Pro-Choice Network of Western New York, 519 U.S. 357 (1997) (upholding "fixed" 15-foot buffer zones but striking down "floating" buffer zone established around people and vehicles; floating buffer zones unnecessarily burdened speech); Madsen v. Women's Health Center, 512 U.S. 753 (1994) ("In evaluating a content-neutral injunction, the governing standard is whether the injunction's challenged provisions burden no more speech than necessary to serve a significant government interest."); McGuire v. Reilly, 386 F.3d 45 (1st Cir. 2004) (upholding a statute regulating speech and activities in buffer zone around facilities performing abortions), *cert. denied*, 125 S. Ct. 1827 (2005). See also Bray v. Alexandria Women's Health Clinic, 506 U.S. 263 (1993) (42 U.S.C. §1985 does not protect women seeking abortion from the concerted activities of abortion protesters).

Clinic defenders turned to other forums for additional relief. Congress enacted statutory protections for clinics in 1994, in the Freedom of Access to Clinic Entrances Act of 1994. 18 U.S.C. §248. Several federal circuit courts of appeal have upheld the constitutionality of the Act. See, e.g., United States v. Gregg, 226 F.3d 253 (3d Cir. 2000) (Act is valid exercise of commerce clause power), *cert. denied*, 532 U.S. 971 (2001); United States v. Bird, 401 F.3d 633 (5th Cir. 2005) (Act is valid exercise of commerce clause power); United States v. Hart, 212 F.3d 1067 (8th Cir. 2000) (Act does not violate First Amendment), *cert. denied*, 531 U.S. 1114 (2001); United States v. Balint, 201 F.3d 928 (7th Cir. 2000) (Act not unconstitutionally vague); Terry v. Reno, 101 F.3d 1412 (D.C. Cir. 1996), *cert. denied*, 520 U.S. 1264 (1997) (upholding Act's constitutionality). See also Planned Parenthood of Columbia/Willamette, Inc. v. American Coalition of Life Activists, 422 F.3d 949 (9th Cir. 2005), *cert. denied*, 126 S. Ct. 1912 (2006) (publication of names and addresses of abortion providers through "guilty" posters and Internet Web site are "threat[s] of force" giving rise to liability for punitive damages under FACE; amount reduced).

Problem: Late-Trimester Abortions

Suppose that Annie Grey is 28 weeks pregnant when she discovers that she is carrying a fetus with anencephaly. She does not want to give birth to a child who will have no higher brain functions and who will have little chance of surviving past the first few weeks of life. She wants to undergo a late-term abortion. Consider the relevant federal and state statutes. Are abortions for women in Annie's situation legal in your state? If they are legal, are there any physicians who are willing to perform the procedure? How would you find out? If they are not legal, is there any mechanism to prevent Annie from traveling to another state or country where the procedure would be legal? Susan Frelich Appleton, Gender, Abortion, and Travel After Roe's End, 51 St. Louis U. L.J. 655 (2007). Who would have standing to bring such a claim? Could you argue that medical providers who permit the use of testing to identify and abort fetuses likely to be born with disabilities have violated the ADA? Would public health institutions engaging in the policy violate the equal protection clause? Would you have to show that a fetus was a "person"? Martha A. Field, Killing the "Handicapped" — Before and After Birth, 16 Harv. Women's L.J. 79 (1993).

C. STATE OR FEDERAL RECOGNITION
   OF FETAL INTERESTS

1. Introduction

This section considers what steps government can take to protect potential life, apart from restricting abortions. There are a variety of alternative legal mechanisms for protecting fetal interests. Tort law could be used to recover damages for fetal injuries and to deter conduct that puts fetuses at risk of injury. Criminal law could be used to punish those who injure fetuses. Governments also may establish the importance of fetal interests via proclamations and even by the allocation of public funds.

The Supreme Court's procreation jurisprudence presents no barrier to the preferential allocation of public funds toward childbearing rather than abortion or to the development of a particularized abortion informed consent statute. See supra at pages 470-473. Yet *Skinner, Roe,* and *Casey* do not resolve the validity of other governmental efforts to value and protect fetal interests. *Skinner* suggested that individuals have a fundamental liberty interest in deciding to procreate. *Roe* held that a fetus was not a "person" entitled to protection under the Fourteenth Amendment and prohibited the state from adopting a definition of fetal personhood that would infringe on a woman's right to choose abortion. However, *Casey* suggests that the Supreme Court will be much more deferential toward a state's asserted desire to protect fetuses, at least so long as the measures taken to protect the fetus do not "unduly" infringe a woman's abortion option. Furthermore, *Casey* reiterates *Roe*'s holding that a state's interest in fetal life becomes compelling at the point of viability. At viability, the state may prohibit abortion completely unless the procedure is necessary for the health or life of the pregnant woman. The Supreme Court's decision in *Gonzales* may refine or even realign the government's ability to promote fetal interests and to define the scope of what might be medically appropriate, but it is unlikely that the Court will ever explicitly permit states to value the fetus's potential life more than the life of the pregnant woman.

This brief summary demonstrates that the abortion cases are not very helpful in establishing the scope of governmental power to protect fetal life outside of the abortion context, when the risk to the fetus comes from something other than the pregnant woman's right to choose abortion. Courts have struggled to determine the appropriate constitutional balance between a state's interest in protecting fetal life and a woman's right to engage in activities that might put her fetus at risk. The first part of this section briefly summarizes state and federal recognition of fetal interests. The second part of the section focuses on two of the most difficult areas for courts and commentators: forced medical treatment for pregnant women and criminal prosecution of pregnant women for conduct presenting a risk to their fetus.

a. State Law and Fetal Personhood

State law protections for fetal interests have grown in recent years in areas ranging from tort law, to criminal law, to medical research. State courts generally resolve the question of a fetus's personhood by interpreting and applying the words of statutes or precedents rather than searching for a unitary definition of personhood that could be applied to fetuses in all areas of the law. Does this strike you as the correct approach? What prevents states from adopting a unitary concept of personhood that could be applied across different areas of law? Wouldn't such an approach comport more closely with the centrality of personhood to most ethical, moral, and jurisprudential theories? See, e.g., Note, What We Talk about When We Talk about Persons: The Language of a Legal Fiction, 114 Harv. L. Rev. 1745 (2001). See also In the Matter of the Unborn Child of Starks, 18 P.3d 342 (Okla. 2001).

States have been particularly quick to recognize fetal interests in tort law. The old black-letter rule was that fetuses could recover for injuries sustained in utero only if they were born alive; parents could not recover for the wrongful death of their unborn children. These tort rules have undergone significant revision. A majority of states now permit suits on behalf of injured fetuses, even when stillborn, if the injury was sustained after the point of viability. Farley v. Sartin, 466 S.E.2d 522, 528 n.13 (W. Va. 1995) (listing 37 jurisdictions that recognize a wrongful death cause of action for viable fetuses); see also Mamta K. Shah, Note, Inconsistencies in the Legal Status of an Unborn Child: Recognition of a Fetus as Potential Life, 29 Hofstra L. Rev. 931, 933-949 (2001) (summarizing tort rules). A few states even permit tort claims where the injury was sustained prior to viability. See, e.g., Nealis v. Baird, 996 P.2d 438 (Okla. 1999) (wrongful death statute covers nonviable fetus born alive); Wiersma v. Maple Leaf Farms, 543 N.W.2d 787 (S.D. 1996) (wrongful death statute provides cause of action for loss of nonviable unborn child).

Tort claims involving fetal injury often involve substantial causation issues: the plaintiff must prove that the tortfeasor actually caused legally cognizable harm. This burden of proof may be difficult to meet where the pregnancy is in the earliest stages at the time of the fetal injury because of the significant rate of spontaneous abortion or miscarriage during this period. See Roland F. Chase, Annot., Liability for Prenatal Injuries, 40 A.L.R.3d 1222 (1971); Sheldon R. Shapiro, Annot., Right to Maintain Action or to Recover Damages for Death of Unborn Child, 84 A.L.R.3d 411 (1978). See also Agota Peterfy, Commentary, Fetal Viability as a Threshold to Personhood: A Legal Analysis, 16 J. Leg, Med. 607 (1995).

Does a fetus have similar rights to be free of injuries caused by its mother? There are several problems with these claims: the parental immunity doctrine will protect the pregnant woman in some jurisdictions; there are difficulties establishing the appropriate standard of care; and there are also public policy concerns with imposing liability for maternal conduct. See Thomas M. Fleming, Annot., Right of Child to Action against Mother for Infliction of Prenatal Injuries, 78 A.L.R.4th 1082 (1991). Only a handful of courts have even considered the issue; litigation of this sort typically arises only when mothers arrange to have their children sue them in order to draw resources from their homeowners' or automobile insurance policies. Most courts have rejected the claims. See Stallman v. Youngquist, 531 N.E.2d 355 (Ill. 1988) (car accident); Remy v. MacDonald, 801 N.E.2d 260 (Mass. 2004) (car accident; summarizing case law); Chenault v. Huie, 989 S.W.2d 474 (Tex. App. 1999) (grossly negligent use of illicit drugs). But see Grodin v. Grodin, 301 N.W.2d 869 (Mich. Ct. App. 1981) (child's mother liable to child for prenatal injuries as would be a third party). The *Stallman* court's criticism of the liability claim was pointed:

It is clear that the recognition of a legal right to begin life with a sound mind and body on the part of a fetus which is assertable after birth against its mother would have serious ramifications for all women and their families, and for the way in which society views women and women's reproductive abilities. The recognition of such a right by a fetus would necessitate the recognition of a legal duty on the part of the woman who is the mother; a legal duty, as opposed to a moral duty, to effectuate the best prenatal environment possible. . . . Any action which negatively impacted on fetal development would be a breach of the pregnant woman's duty to her developing fetus. Mother and child would be legal adversaries from the moment of conception until birth. . . .

The relationship between a pregnant woman and her fetus is unlike the relationship between any other plaintiff and defendant. No other plaintiff depends exclusively on any other defendant for everything necessary for life itself. No other defendant must go through biological changes of the most profound type, possibly at the risk of her own life, in order to bring forth an adversary into the world. It is, after all, the whole life of the pregnant woman which impacts on the development of the fetus. As opposed to the third-party defendant, it is the mother's every waking and sleeping moment which, for better or worse, shapes the prenatal environment which forms the world for the developing fetus. 531 N. E.2d at 359-360.

A few courts have considered whether maternal negligence should be imputed to her child in the child's action against third parties for prenatal conduct. See, e.g., Hogle v. Hall, 916 P.2d 814 (Nev. 1996) (no).

States may also use the criminal law to protect fetal interests. Criminal prosecutions against "strangers" have generally fallen into two categories: (1) traditional crimes and (2) special criminal statutes protecting fetuses. Attempts to prosecute third parties for traditional crimes such as murder or manslaughter typically fail. Homicide convictions, for example, require the death of a "person," usually defined as a person born alive. A defendant who violently assaults a pregnant woman might be prosecuted for a homicide if the fetus is born alive but then dies as a result of the criminal conduct. Cf. Mamta K. Shah, Note, Inconsistencies in the Legal Status of an Unborn Child: Recognition of a Fetus as Potential Life, 29 Hofstra L. Rev. 931, 933-949 (2001). See also State v. Horne, 319 S.E.2d 703 (S.C. 1984) (death of unborn viable fetus supports manslaughter conviction).

A number of states have enacted special statutes designed to criminalize conduct related to fetuses. Feticide statutes are a common example. Prosecutions under these provisions are less controversial, in part because legislative intent is clear. The statutes generally include specific exceptions for a woman exercising her right to choose abortion and for abortion providers. Mamta K. Shah, supra; Alan S. Wasserstrom, Annot., Homicide Based on Killing of Unborn Child, 64 A. L.R.5th 671 (1998). See also People v. Davis, 872 P.2d 591 (Cal. 1994). Many states reviewed and revised criminal laws governing fetuses in the aftermath of some highly publicized cases involving the murder of pregnant women. Kirk Johnson, Harm to Fetuses Becomes Issue in Utah and Elsewhere, N.Y. Times, March 27, 2004, at A9, col. 1 (summarizing state proposals). See also National Conference of State Legislatures, Fetal Homicide Laws (NCSL Web site). Do feticide statutes demonstrate irreconcilable conflicts in the law given that third parties can be subjected to criminal penalties for conduct permissible when undertaken by the pregnant woman? See Carolyn B. Ramsey, Restructuring the Debate Over Fetal Homicide Laws, 67 Ohio St. L.J. 721 (2006) (arguing that abortion rights are not inconsistent with feticide prosecutions). Criminal prosecution of women for risky prenatal activity is a controversial area that will be considered in more detail below.

States can also show respect for fetuses, and indirectly disfavor abortion, by restricting the use of fetal tissue produced in spontaneous or planned abortions. A number of state legislatures have prohibited the use of fetal remains in medical research or have otherwise attempted to restrict fetal experimentation. Violators may be criminally prosecuted. See, e.g., Mo. Ann. Stat. §188.036 (purports to ban abortions performed to obtain fetal material for experimentation); N.D. Cent. Code §14-02.2-02 (fetal experimentation restrictions); 18 Pa. Cons. Stat. Ann. §3216 (fetal experimentation restrictions). These statutes may be implicated in stem cell research, discussed infra at page 556.

b. Federal Recognition of Fetal Interests

The federal government has had fewer opportunities to show its interest in fetal well-being, but federal activity is prominent in three areas: (1) the allocation of funds designed to protect fetal health; (2) the adoption of legislation designed to criminally or civilly penalize risky conduct; and (3) the dramatic debates about the permissibility of embryonic stem cell research.

The federal government wields enormous power through its capacity to tie the expenditure of federal dollars to particular policy objectives. For many years, the eligibility rules for the federal-state Medicaid program were the most important federal expression of interest in fetal well-being through the provision of Medicaid coverage for pregnant women. Coverage for pregnant women near or below the federal poverty level has expanded over the past two decades. See 42 U.S.C. §§1396a(a)(10)(A)(III), 1396d(n). Health insurance coverage for pregnant women is an indirect indication of the value of fetal life. See also 42 C.F.R. §457.10 (unborn children eligible for health coverage under State Children's Health Insurance Program). Federal funding for stem cell research, which raises the specter of the use and destruction of embryos, will be discussed in the final section of this chapter, at page 556.

Congress has also sought to recognize and to protect fetal interests more directly. The federal Partial-Birth Abortion Ban Act of 2003 discussed supra, at page 459, recognizes a private cause of action to protect fetal interests. The Act gives certain relatives of a fetus subjected to the prohibited procedure a right to recover civil damages. 18 U.S.C.A. §1531. Congress also expanded federal criminal law to recognize the distinct offense of injuring or killing a fetus.

The federal Unborn Victims of Violence Act of 2004, 18 U.S.C.A. §1841, was enacted in the aftermath of a highly publicized murder of a pregnant woman. The Act provides:

(a)(1) Whoever engages in conduct that violates any of [certain enumerated] . . . provisions of law . . . and thereby causes the death of, or bodily injury . . . [to] a child, who is in utero at the time the conduct takes place, is guilty of a separate offense under this section.

(2)(A) Except as otherwise provided in this paragraph, the punishment for that separate offense is the same as the punishment provided under Federal law for that conduct had that injury or death occurred to the unborn child's mother.

(B) An offense under this section does not require proof that

(i) the person engaging in the conduct had knowledge or should have had knowledge that the victim of the underlying offense was pregnant; or

(ii) the defendant intended to cause the death of, or bodily injury to, the unborn child.

(C) If the person engaging in the conduct thereby intentionally kills or attempts to kill the unborn child, that person shall instead of being punished under subparagraph (A), be punished as provided under . . . for intentionally killing or attempting to kill a human being.

(D) Notwithstanding any other provision of law, the death penalty shall not be imposed for an offense under this section. . . .

Constitutionally protected abortion procedures are exempted. Id. See generally, Carolyn B. Ramsey, Restructuring the Debate Over Fetal Homicide Laws, 67 Ohio St. L.J. 721 (2006)

2. Pregnant Women and Forced Medical Treatment

A pregnant woman presents a unique dilemma for health care providers. The woman's autonomy interests must be fully recognized as a matter of law and medical ethics. Yet the woman's decisions about medical treatment can have an immediate impact on the fetus, whose interests also demand respect. The health care professional's legal and ethical obligations to the fetus, as a being separate and distinct from her mother, are a matter of greater controversy. Should a physician's obligation to the fetus ever override the obligation to a pregnant patient? When and how should courts or legislatures intervene in this potential conflict? Are the rules developed in this area truly *sui generis*, or should they be applied to situations in which third parties make demands for biological support from other persons? Compare the following material, for instance, with the discussion in Chapter 6 of whether people can be forced to donate life-saving organs or tissue at little risk to themselves.

■ IN RE A.C.
573 A.2d 1235 (D.C. App. 1990) (en banc)

TERRY, Associate Judge.

I

. . . This case came before the trial court when George Washington University Hospital petitioned the emergency judge in chambers for declaratory relief as to how it should treat its patient, A.C., who was close to death from cancer and was twenty-six and one-half weeks pregnant with a viable fetus. After a hearing lasting approximately three hours, which was held at the hospital (though not in A.C.'s room), the court ordered that a cesarean section be performed on A. C. to deliver the fetus. Counsel for A.C. immediately sought a stay in this court, which was unanimously denied by a hastily assembled division of three judges. In re A.C., 533 A.2d 611 (D.C. 1987). The cesarean was performed, and a baby girl, L.M.C., was delivered. Tragically, the child died within two and one-half hours, and the mother died two days later.

Counsel for A.C. now maintain that A.C. was competent and that she made an informed choice not to have the cesarean performed. Given this view of the facts, they argue that it was error for the trial court to weigh the state's interest in preserving the potential life of a viable fetus against A.C.'s interest in having her decision respected. They argue further that, even if the substituted judgment procedure had been followed, the evidence would necessarily show that A.C. would not have wanted the cesarean section. Under either analysis, according to these arguments, the trial court erred in subordinating A.C.'s right to bodily integrity in favor of the state's interest in potential life. . . .

II

[A.C. had suffered from cancer for 14 years. During a period of remission, she married and conceived a child. At 25 weeks in her pregnancy, her doctors found a terminal, inoperable tumor in her lung. She decided to continue her pregnancy and to receive palliative treatment, apparently with the desire to extend her life at least to the twenty-eighth week of pregnancy, when the prognosis for the fetus would be much better if intervention were necessary. However, as her condition worsened during her twenty-sixth week, her stated desire to have the baby became more equivocal. Her mother opposed the operation, but her husband "was too distraught to testify and uttered only a few words at the hearing."]

After hearing this testimony and the arguments of counsel, the trial court made oral findings of fact. It found, first, that A.C. would probably die, according to uncontroverted medical testimony, "within the next twenty-four to forty-eight hours"; second, that A.C. was "pregnant with a twenty-six and a half week viable fetus who, based upon uncontroverted medical testimony, has approximately a 50 to 60 percent chance to survive if a cesarean section is performed as soon as possible"; third, that because the fetus was viable, "the state has [an] important and legitimate interest in protecting the potentiality of human life"; and fourth, that there had been some testimony that the operation "may very well hasten the death of [A.C.]," but that there had also been testimony that delay would greatly increase the risk to the fetus and that "the prognosis is not great for the fetus to be delivered post-mortem. . . ." Most significantly, the court found:

> The court is of the view that it does not clearly know what [A.C.'s] present views are with respect to the issue of whether or not the child should live or die. She's presently unconscious. As late as Friday of last week, she wanted the baby to live. As late of yesterday, she did not know for sure.

Having made these findings of fact and conclusions of law, and expressly relying on In re Madyun, 114 Daily Wash. L. Rptr. 2233 (D.C. Super. Ct. July 26, 1986),[5] the court ordered that a cesarean section be performed to deliver A.C.'s child. . . .

[After the judge's order was communicated to A.C. by her doctors, she at first agreed to the operation, but shortly later she refused. Although she appeared lucid, her doctors differed in their opinions as to whether she had reached a truly competent and informed decision one way or the other.] After hearing this new evidence, the court found that it was "still not clear what her intent is" and again ordered that a cesarean section be performed. . . . The operation took place, but the baby lived for only a few hours, and A.C. succumbed to cancer two days later.

IV

A. INFORMED CONSENT AND BODILY INTEGRITY

A number of learned articles have been written about the propriety or impropriety of court-ordered cesarean sections. E.g., Johnsen, The Creation of Fetal Rights: Conflicts with Women's Constitutional Rights to Liberty, Privacy, and Equal Protection, 95 Yale L.J. 599 (1986); Kolder, Gallagher & Parsons, Court-Ordered Obstetrical Interventions, 316 New Eng. J. Med. 1192 (1987) (hereafter Obstetrical Interventions); Rhoden, The Judge in the Delivery Room: The Emergence of Court-Ordered Caesareans, 74 Cal. L. Rev. 1951 (1986); Robertson, Procreative Liberty and the Control of Conception, Pregnancy, and Childbirth, 69 Va. L. Rev. 405 (1983). Commentators have also considered how medical decisions for incompetent persons which may involve some detriment or harm to them should be made. . . . These and other articles demonstrate the complexity of medical intervention cases, which become more complex with the steady advance of medical technology. From a recent national survey, it appears that over the five years preceding the survey there were 36 attempts to override maternal refusals of proposed medical treatment, and that in 15 instances where court orders were sought to authorize cesarean interventions, 13 such orders were granted. Obstetrical Interventions, supra, 316 New Eng. J. Med. at 1192-1193. . . . Nevertheless, there is only one published decision from an appellate court that deals with the question of when, or even whether, a court may order a cesarean section: Jefferson v. Griffin Spalding County Hospital Authority, 247 Ga. 86, 274 S.E.2d 457 (1981).

Jefferson is of limited relevance, if any at all, to the present case. In *Jefferson* there was a competent refusal by the mother to undergo the proposed surgery, but the evidence showed that performance of the cesarean was in the medical interests of both the mother and the fetus.[7] . . .

---

[5] Madyun was affirmed by this court in an unreported order. See also n.23, infra.

[7] Because the patient in *Jefferson* had a placenta previa which blocked the birth canal, doctors estimated that without cesarean intervention there was a 99 percent chance that her full-term fetus would perish and a 50 percent chance that the mother would die as well. The mother was unquestionably competent to make her own treatment decisions, but refused a cesarean because of her religious beliefs. A trial court gave custody of the fetus to state human resources officials and ordered a cesarean section; the Georgia Supreme Court denied the parents' motion for a stay. [Nevertheless, the mother went into hiding, and both she and the child survived without the operation.]

[O]ur analysis of this case begins with the tenet common to all medical treatment cases: that any person has the right to make an informed choice, if competent to do so, to accept or forego medical treatment. . . .

[C]ourts do not compel one person to permit a significant intrusion upon his or her bodily integrity for the benefit of another person's health. See, e.g., . . . McFall v. Shimp, 10 Pa. D. & C.3d 90 (Allegheny County Ct. 1978). In *McFall* the court refused to order Shimp to donate bone marrow which was necessary to save the life of his cousin, McFall:

> The common law has consistently held to a rule which provides that one human being is under no legal compulsion to give aid or to take action to save another human being or to rescue. . . . For our law to compel defendant to submit to an intrusion of his body would change every concept and principle upon which our society is founded. To do so would defeat the sanctity of the individual, and would impose a rule which would know no limits, and one could not imagine where the line would be drawn.

Id. at 91. [This case is excerpted and discussed at page 381.] Even though Shimp's refusal would mean death for McFall, the court would not order Shimp to allow his body to be invaded. It has been suggested that fetal cases are different because a woman who "has chosen to lend her body to bring [a] child into the world" has an enhanced duty to assure the welfare of the fetus, sufficient even to require her to undergo cesarean surgery. Robertson, Procreative Liberty, supra, 69 Va. L. Rev. at 456. Surely, however, a fetus cannot have rights in this respect superior to those of a person who has already been born.[8] . . .

In those rare cases in which a patient's right to decide her own course of treatment has been judicially overridden, courts have usually acted to vindicate the state's interest in protecting third parties, even if in fetal state. . . .

We hold, however, that without a competent refusal from A.C. to go forward with the surgery, and without a finding through substituted judgment that A.C. would not have consented to the surgery, it was error for the trial court to proceed to a balancing analysis, weighing the rights of A.C. against the interests of the state.

There are two additional arguments against overriding A.C.'s objections to caesarean surgery. First . . . [court orders diminish the patient's trust in her physician and may deter women from seeking care]. . . . Second, and even more compellingly, any judicial proceeding in a case such as this will ordinarily take place — like the one before us here — under time constraints so pressing that it is difficult or impossible for the mother to communicate adequately with counsel, or for counsel to organize an effective factual and legal presentation in defense of her liberty and privacy interests and bodily integrity. . . .

---

[8] There are also practical consequences to consider. What if A.C. had refused to comply with a court order that she submit to a cesarean? Under the circumstances she obviously could not have been held in civil contempt and imprisoned or required to pay a daily fine until compliance. . . . Enforcement could be accomplished only through physical force or its equivalent. A.C. would have to be fastened with restraints to the operating table, or perhaps involuntarily rendered unconscious by forcibly injecting her with an anesthetic, and then subjected to unwanted major surgery. Such actions would surely give one pause in a civilized society, especially when A.C. had done no wrong. Cf. Rochin v. California, 342 U.S. 165, 169, 72 S. Ct. 205, 208, 96 L. Ed. 183 (1952).

In this case A.C.'s court-appointed attorney was unable even to meet with his client before the hearing. By the time the case was heard, A.C.'s condition did not allow her to be present, nor was it reasonably possible for the judge to hear from her directly. The factual record, moreover, was significantly flawed because A.C.'s medical records were not before the court and because Dr. Jeffrey Moscow, the physician who had been treating A.C. for many years, was not even contacted and hence did not testify.[17] . . .

C. THE TRIAL COURT'S RULING. . . .

What a trial court must do in a case such as this is to determine, if possible, whether the patient is capable of making an informed decision about the course of her medical treatment. If she is, and if she makes such a decision, her wishes will control in virtually all cases. If the court finds that the patient is incapable of making an informed consent (and thus is incompetent), then the court must make a substituted judgment. This means that the court must ascertain as best it can what the patient would do if faced with the particular treatment question. Again, in virtually all cases the decision of the patient, albeit discerned through the mechanism of substituted judgment, will control. We do not quite foreclose the possibility that a conflicting state interest may be so compelling that the patient's wishes must yield, but we anticipate that such cases will be extremely rare and truly exceptional. This is not such a case.

Having said that, we go no further. We need not decide whether, or in what circumstances, the state's interests can ever prevail over the interests of a pregnant patient. We emphasize, nevertheless, that it would be an extraordinary case indeed in which a court might ever be justified in overriding the patient's wishes and authorizing a major surgical procedure such as a cesarean section.[23]

. . . If the substituted judgment procedure were to be followed, there is evidence going both ways as to what decision A.C. would have made, and we see no point in requiring the court now to make that determination when it can have no practical effect on either A.C. or L.M.C.

Accordingly, we vacate the order of the trial court and remand the case for such further proceedings as may be appropriate.

---

[17] In an affidavit filed after the hearing, Dr. Moscow said that if he had been notified of the proceedings, he would have come to the hospital immediately and would have testified that a cesarean section was medically inadvisable *both for A.C. and for the fetus*. Dr. Moscow also viewed the hospital's handling of A.C.'s case as deficient in several other significant respects. In these circumstances we think it unfortunate that Dr. Moscow was not called by representatives of the hospital and made available to the court when the hospital decided to seek judicial guidance.

[23] In particular, we stress that nothing in this opinion should be read as either approving or disapproving the holding in In re Madyun, supra. There are substantial factual differences between *Madyun* and the present case. In this case, for instance, the medical interests of the mother and the fetus were in sharp conflict; what was good for one would have been harmful to the other. In *Madyun*, however, there was no real conflict between the interests of mother and fetus; on the contrary, there was strong evidence that the proposed cesarean would be beneficial to both. Moreover, in *Madyun* the pregnancy was at full term, and Mrs. Madyun had been in labor for two and a half days; in this case, however, A.C. was barely two-thirds of the way through her pregnancy, and there were no signs of labor. If another *Madyun*-type case ever comes before this court, its result may well depend on facts that we cannot now foresee. For that reason (among others), we defer until another day any discussion of whether *Madyun* was rightly or wrongly decided. [Elsewhere the court also limited its reasoning to those cases involving "a major bodily invasion," reserving judgment on when "lesser invasions" would be permitted and on "where the line should be drawn between 'major' and 'minor' surgery."]

BELSON, Associate Judge, concurring in part and dissenting in part.

I agree with much of the majority opinion, but I disagree with its ultimate ruling that the trial court's order must be set aside, and with the narrow view it takes of the state's interest in preserving life and the unborn child's interest in life. . . . I would hold that in those instances, fortunately rare, in which the viable unborn child's interest in living and the state's parallel interest in protecting human life come into conflict with the mother's decision to forgo a procedure such as a cesarean section, a balancing should be struck in which the unborn child's and the state's interests are entitled to substantial weight.

It was acknowledged in Roe v. Wade, 410 U.S. 113 (1973), that the state's interest in potential human life becomes compelling at the point of viability. . . . When the unborn child reaches the state of viability, the child becomes a party whose interests must be considered. . . .

The balancing test should be applied in instances in which women become pregnant and carry an unborn child to the point of viability. This is not an unreasonable classification because, I submit, a woman who carries a child to viability is in fact a member of a unique category of persons. Her circumstances differ fundamentally from those of other potential patients for medical procedures that will aid another person, for example, a potential donor of bone marrow for transplant. This is so because she has undertaken to bear another human being, and has carried an unborn child to viability. Another unique feature of the situation we address arises from the singular nature of the dependency of the unborn child upon the mother. A woman carrying a viable unborn child is not in the same category as a relative, friend, or stranger called upon to donate bone marrow or an organ for transplant. Rather, the expectant mother has placed herself in a special class of persons who are bringing another person into existence, and upon whom that other person's life is totally dependent. Also, uniquely, the viable unborn child is literally captive within the mother's body. No other potential beneficiary of a surgical procedure on another is in that position.

For all of these reasons, . . . I cannot agree that in cases where a viable unborn child is in the picture, it would be extremely rare, within that universe, to require that the mother accede to the vital needs of the viable unborn child.[8]

For the reasons stated above, I would affirm.

Notes: Forced Medical Treatment

1. *Abortion and Cesareans.* How should the state's interest in protecting viable fetuses, recognized in *Roe, Casey,* and subsequent case law affect a woman's right to control her own medical treatment? Should these decisions be limited to the abortion context in which they arose? Does the underlying reasoning — that the state's compelling interest can override a woman's constitutionally protected right

---

[8] To the contrary, it appears that a majority of courts faced with this issue have found that the state's compelling interest in protection of the unborn child should prevail. See Noble-Allgire, Court-Ordered Cesarean Sections, 10 J. Legal Med. 211, 236 (1989). I add that in mapping this uncharted area of the law, we can draw lines, and a line I would draw would be to preclude the use of physical force to perform an operation. The force of the court order itself as well as the use of the contempt power would, I think, be adequate in most cases. See id. at 243.

to choose abortion — seem transferable where the constitutional interests at stake are a woman's right to choose her own medical care and to be free from extreme invasions to her bodily integrity? Recall that Cruzan v. Director, Missouri Department of Health, 497 U.S. 261 (1990), suggests that the right to control end-of-life treatment decisions has a constitutional dimension. If a state interest is compelling in one circumstance, wouldn't it be compelling in the other? In which cases would the In re A.C. court permit forced medical interventions to preserve the fetus?

2. *Moral or Legal Obligations to Protect Fetuses?* Generations of law students have considered the hypothetical of the champion swimmer who observes a person drowning offshore. The bystander is said to have a moral, but not a legal, obligation to attempt to save the drowning swimmer. Is the pregnant woman in the same position as the expert swimmer? Which of the following factors should be considered ethically or legally relevant to the resolution of these cases: Whether the woman became pregnant by choice? Whether she intends to carry the fetus to term? The gestational age of the fetus? The probability of harm to the fetus? The degree of harm to the fetus? The probability and degree of harm confronted by the pregnant woman? Whether the proposed medical treatment would benefit the woman as well as the fetus? The nature of the intrusion into the woman's autonomy? The rationale for the woman's refusal of treatment? What other factors might you consider? Do pregnant women have an ethical duty to protect their fetuses from harm? Should pregnant women have a legal obligation to protect their fetuses from harm, just as parents have a legal obligation to safeguard their children?

For a detailed analysis of the ethical and legal aspects of these cases, see David Orentlicher, Matters of Life and Death: Making Moral Theory Work in Medical Ethics and the Law 91-120 (2001) (arguing that pregnant women may have both a moral and a legal obligation to protect their fetuses, at least under some circumstances, but noting that the creation of a legal obligation could create a perverse incentive for pregnant women to avoid prenatal care). For thoughtful expositions of other views, and citations to numerous other commentaries, see April L. Cherry, The Free Exercise Rights of Pregnant Women Who Refuse Medical Treatment, 69 Tenn. L. Rev. 563 (2002); Daniel R. Levy, The Maternal Conflict: The Right of a Woman to Refuse a Cesarean Section Versus the State's Interest in Saving the Life of the Fetus, 108 W. Va. L. Rev. 97 (2005); Michelle Oberman, Mothers and Doctors' Orders: Unmasking the Doctor's Fiduciary Role in Maternal-Fetal Conflicts, 94 Nw. U. L. Rev. 451 (2000). See also Kirk Johnson, Harm to Fetuses Becomes Issue in Utah and Elsewhere, N.Y. Times, March 27, 2004, at A9, col. 1 (discussing attempted murder charge brought against woman who refused cesarean section).

3. *Court-Ordered Medical Interventions.* The *A.C.* court implies, in dicta, that the state's interest in fetal life might override a woman's interest in avoiding some minimally intrusive medical interventions. Should the state's interest in preserving the life of a viable fetus outweigh a woman's right to refuse routine prenatal care? Antibiotics? A physician's recommendation of complete bed rest for three months? The use of forceps? A cesarean section delivery?

Most of the reported cases involve cesareans. The Kolder study described by the *A.C.* court also found:

> Among 21 cases in which court orders were sought, the orders were obtained in 86 percent; in 88 percent of those cases, the orders were received within six hours. Eighty-one percent of the women involved were black, Asian, or Hispanic, 44 percent were unmarried, and 24 percent did not speak English as their primary language. All the women were treated in a teaching-hospital clinic or were receiving public assistance. . . . Veronica E. Kolder et al., Court-Ordered Obstetrical Interventions, 316 New Eng. J. Med. 1192, 1192 (1987).

The In re A.C. decision is regarded by most law review commentators as the dominant judicial approach, at least at the appellate level. See also In re Baby Boy Doe, a Fetus, 632 N.E.2d 326, 330 (Ill. App. Ct. 1994) (Illinois courts should not balance the rights of the viable fetus against the woman's right to control her treatment; "a woman's competent choice in refusing medical treatment as invasive as a cesarean section . . . must be honored, even in circumstances where the choice may be harmful to her fetus."). But see Pemberton v. Tallahassee Memorial Regional Center, 66 F. Supp. 2d 1247 (N.D. Fla. 1999).

In *Pemberton*, a woman subjected to a state-court-ordered cesarean section brought §1983 and §1985 claims in federal court against the regional hospital, claiming that its actions had violated her constitutional rights to "bodily integrity . . . to refuse unwanted medical treatment . . . to make important personal and family decisions without undue governmental interference . . . [and] her right to religious freedom." Id. at 1251. The court rejected the claims, noting:

> Ms. Pemberton was at full term and actively in labor. It was clear that one way or the other, a baby would be born (or stillborn) very soon, certainly within hours. Whatever the scope of Ms. Pemberton's personal constitutional rights . . . they clearly did not outweigh the interests of the State of Florida in preserving the life of the unborn child. . . . Bearing an unwanted child is surely a greater intrusion on the mother's constitutional interests than undergoing a caesarean section to deliver a child that the mother affirmatively desires to deliver. [Id. at 1251-1252.]

Cases involving less intrusive measures are more uncommon. See, e.g., Barbara F. v. Bristol Division of the Juvenile Court Department, 745 N.E.2d 357 (Mass. 2000) (discussing case involving protective custody of pregnant woman who had religious objections to prenatal care); Taft v. Taft, 446 N.E.2d 395 (Mass. 1983) (rejecting husband's effort to obtain a court order requiring pregnant wife to undergo "purse string" operation on cervix). Clashes between optimal fetal development and basic lifestyle choices such as whether to smoke, what to eat, and how to conduct childbirth are likely to arise with much greater frequency in the future due to rapid advances of medical science on three fronts: (1) understanding the fetal developmental process; (2) refining diagnostic techniques that detect fetal problems; and (3) developing modes of surgical and medical intervention that allow *in utero* therapy.

A maternal-fetal conflict may also arise when a woman needs medication that can negatively impact her fetus. See, e.g., Guardianship of J.D.S., 864 So. 2d 534 (Fla. App. 2004) (state law does not permit appointment of guardian for a fetus in case involving incompetent pregnant women whose medications posed risk to fetus). See also Linda C. Fentiman, The New "Fetal Protection": The Wrong

Answer to the Crisis of Inadequate Health Care for Women and Children, 84 Denv. U. L. Rev. 537 (2006); April L. Cherry, Roe's Legacy: The Nonconsensual Medical Treatment of Pregnant Women and Implications for Female Citizenship, 6 U. Pa. J. Const. L. 723 (2004).

4. *Medical Predictions and Medical Ethics.* In a surprising number of the reported cases, such as the principal case and *Jefferson,* described in n.7 of the opinion, the doctors' predictions of the need for fetal intervention proved completely wrong. Sometimes the strength of the medical evidence appears to be exaggerated by the court. See *Pemberton,* 66 F. Supp. at 1250 n.2 (noting that the underlying court order exaggerated the degree of certainty of the underlying medical testimony).

The absence of predictive certainty has played at least some role in the development of the ethical guidelines of medical societies. See, e.g., Committee on Ethics Opinion, American College of Obstetricians and Gynecologists, Maternal Decision Making, Ethics, and the Law, No. 321 (Nov. 2005) (noting limitation of medical knowledge and predictions; concluding that "[e]fforts to use the legal system to protect the fetus by constraining pregnant women's decision making or punishing them erode a woman's basic rights to privacy and bodily integrity and are not justified"), available at http://www.acog.org/from_home/publications/ethics/co321.pdf. The American Medical Association House of Delegates-approved policy provides:

> Court Ordered Medical Treatments And Legal Penalties For Potentially Harmful Behavior By Pregnant Women: (1) Judicial intervention is inappropriate when a woman has made an informed refusal of a medical treatment designed to benefit her fetus. If an exceptional circumstance could be found in which a medical treatment poses an insignificant or no health risk to the woman, entails a minimal invasion of her bodily integrity, and would clearly prevent substantial and irreversible harm to her fetus, it might be appropriate for a physician to seek judicial intervention. However, the fundamental principle against compelled medical procedures should control in all cases which do not present such exceptional circumstances. AMA, H-420.969 Legal Interventions During Pregnancy, available through: http://www.ama-assn.org/ama/noindex/category/11760.html.

5. *State or Private Interests.* Should it matter whether the action to force a cesarean is brought by private parties or by the state? In re A.C. was initiated by a hospital, which sought a declaratory judgment permitting the surgery. In re Baby Boy Doe, supra note 3, was pursued by the Illinois state attorney's office. Should the hospital be able to assert the state's interest in protecting fetuses? In the employment context, the Supreme Court has held that policies purportedly designed to protect fetuses that discriminate against fertile women constitute impermissible sex discrimination under Title VII of the Civil Rights Act. Int'l Union, United Automobile, Aerospace and Agricultural Implement Workers of America, UAW v. Johnson Controls, 499 U.S. 187 (1991). Johnson Controls argued that its policy of discriminating against fertile woman was justified as a "bona fide occupational qualification [BFOQ] necessary to the normal operation" of its business. The Court rejected the claim, holding that "Johnson Controls'

professed moral and ethical concerns about the welfare of the next generation do not suffice to establish a BFOQ of female sterility." The Civil Rights Act provisions apply only to employment, not to a hospital's treatment of its patients, but the Court's reasoning suggests that private third parties might be restricted from discriminating against women in order to protect fetuses. For more information on the *Johnson Controls* decision, see Mary Becker, Reproductive Hazards after *Johnson Controls*, 31 Hous. L. Rev. 43 (1994); Elaine Draper, Reproductive Hazards and Fetal Exclusion Policies after *Johnson Controls*, 12 Stan. L. & Pol'y Rev. 117 (2001).

6. *Testing and Medical Treatment for HIV Transmission.* Many women with HIV infection are pregnant or hope to become pregnant. Pregnant women who take anti-retroviral drugs and deliver through cesarean section can reduce the risk of HIV transmission from 25-30 percent to a little over 2 percent. Is the risk of HIV transmission from woman to child sufficient to support a program of mandatory HIV testing for pregnant women? Does your answer depend on the use to be made of the test information? What if it is used to "encourage" HIV-infected pregnant women to abort? To get treatment for themselves or their children? Many states have enacted statutes designed to encourage the use of "routine" HIV testing for pregnant women. See Leslie E. Wolf, Bernard Lo & Lawrence O. Gostin, Legal Barriers to Implementing Recommendations for Universal Routine Prenatal HIV Testing, 32 J.L. Med. & Ethics 137 (2004). The federal Centers for Disease Control and Prevention has issued new guidelines encouraging HIV screening for pregnant women. Bernard M. Branson et al., Revised Recommendations for HIV Testing of Adults, Adolescents, and Pregnant Women in Health Care Settings, 55 MMWR Recomm. Rep. 1 (2006) (RR-14) (recommending directive counseling); and Lawrence O. Gostin, HIV Screening in Health Care Settings: Public Health and Civil Liberties in Conflict?, 296 JAMA 2023 (2006). See discussion at page 637.

Should women with HIV infection be forced to take antiretroviral therapy? Is this the type of "lesser" invasion of liberty that a court might accept? Cheryl Amana, Drugs, AIDS and Reproductive Choice: Maternal-State Conflict Continues into the Millennium, 28 N.C. Cent. L.J. 32 (2005); Michael A. Grizzi, Compelled Antiviral Treatment of HIV Positive Women, 5 UCLA Women's L.J. 473 (1995). You should reconsider these problems after reading Chapter 6's discussion of public health laws under which people can be screened for diseases and forced to undergo treatment to protect the health of third parties. See pages 627-650. Are the rules governing forced medical treatment for pregnant women consistent with other public health policies? Are any differences explained by the lesser weight given to the state's interest in protecting fetuses, even viable ones?

7. *Brain Death and Pregnancy.* Are there any legal or ethical problems associated with maintaining a brain-dead woman on life support to permit her fetus to mature with the hope that it can be delivered alive? See Daniel Sperling, Maternal Brain Death, Am. J.L. & Med. 453 (2004). See also David R. Field et al., Maternal Brain Death Pregnancy, 260 JAMA 816 (1988) (patient maintained in a brain-dead state for nine weeks at a cost of $217,784 before delivery of an infant weighing about 3 pounds); AP, Brain-Dead Woman's Fetus Passes Milestone in Development, N.Y. Times, July 21, 2005, at A17, col. 1; AP, Brain-Dead Woman Has Baby, N.Y. Times, Aug. 3, 2005, at A17, col. 2.

Problem: Pregnancy and Living Wills

Janet Kuan was 24 weeks pregnant when an aneurysm burst in her brain. She was rushed to the hospital and into surgery, but she experienced extensive brain damage. Although her brain stem is still functioning—and she can breathe without a respirator—all of her higher brain functions have irreversibly ceased. Janet's physicians agree that she is in a permanent vegetative state.

Two years ago, Janet filled out a living will form provided to her by her physician. The form indicated that the she wished to refuse "life sustaining treatments" if she were reliably diagnosed as suffering from a "terminal condition," which was defined to include a "permanent vegetative state." The form also included the following language: "Pursuant to state law, this document becomes null and void and will be given no effect if I am pregnant at the time I am diagnosed with the terminal condition." Janet had crossed out this language in the form and written: "I do not wish to be treated if I am terminally ill and pregnant."

Janet's husband, Nick, wants Janet to be kept alive using a feeding tube and whatever other means are necessary. He hopes that the child can be delivered alive. Janet's parents are repelled by the thought of their child being used as an incubator. What should Janet's physicians do? If the courts become involved, how should they rule and for what reasons?

Many states have enacted living will statutes that purport to restrict the ability of pregnant women to refuse life sustaining treatment. Assess the validity of these statutes under *Cruzan*, supra at pages 237 and 274, and the majority and dissenting opinions in *A.C.* Should it matter whether the fetus is viable? Would the In re A.C. majority approve the application of the statute to void a pregnant woman's decision not to pursue life sustaining treatment under the theory that the treatment would extend rather than diminish her life expectancy? Should it matter whether the life sustaining treatment is more or less invasive than a cesarean section? For a discussion of these issues, see Timothy J. Burch, Incubator or Individual?: The Legal and Policy Deficiencies of Pregnancy Clauses in Living Will and Advanced Health Care Directive Statutes, 54 Md. L. Rev. 528 (1995); Fentiman, supra; Note, 84 Minn. L. Rev. 971 (2000); Katherine A. Taylor, Compelling Pregnancy at Death's Door, 7 Colum. J. Gender & L. 85 (1997).

Problem: Cesarean Deliveries

Conflicts over cesarean births are also connected to debates about whether women who have had a cesarean delivery may subsequently deliver vaginally without undue risk to themselves or to their children. See, e.g., E. Lieberman et al., Results of the National Study of Vaginal Birth After Cesarean in Birth Centers, 104 Obstet. Gynecol. 933 (2004). Concerns about the risks have led physicians and hospitals to refuse to offer vaginal delivery as an option to women who have had a cesarean section delivery in the past. See, e.g., Denise Grady, Trying to Avoid a 2nd Caesarean, Many Find the Choice Isn't Theirs, N.Y. Times, Nov. 29, 2004, at A1. Should a woman who has previously had a cesarean delivery have a right to give birth vaginally despite the increased risk? Is this a matter that can and should be dealt with using the informed consent process? If the informed consent process is legally adequate, would there be any heightened malpractice risk for the health care providers? See AMA, H-420.969 Legal Interventions During Pregnancy, supra. Can the woman waive her child's right to bring a claim for damages? Is the woman's right to choose vaginal birth related in any way to her right to refuse life sustaining treatment?

Problem: Access to Drugs Associated with Birth Defects

How should the FDA regulate medications that could have a negative impact on fetuses if taken by pregnant women? Accutane® (used to treat acne), thalidomide (used to treat leprosy), and other products are associated with a significant risk of severe birth defects. Should the products be banned for all, prescribed only for those women who are willing to demonstrate that they are not pregnant and will not become pregnant, or prescribed for anyone with suitable warnings? See Ami E. Doshi, The Cost of Clear Skin: Balancing the Social and Safety Costs of IPledge with the Efficacy of Accutane (Isotretinoin), 37 Seton Hall L. Rev. 625 (2007); Richard A. Epstein, Regulatory Paternalism in the Market for Drugs: Lessons from Vioxx and Celebrex, 5 Yale J. Health Pol'y L. & Ethics 741 (2005); Lars Noah, Ambivilent Commitments to Federalism in Controlling the Practice of Medicine, 53 U. Kan. L. Rev. 149 (2004).

3. Pregnant Women and Drug Use

■ WHITNER v. SOUTH CAROLINA
492 S.E.2d 777 (S.C. 1997), cert. denied, 523 U.S. 1145 (1998)

TOAL, Justice.

This case concerns the scope of the child abuse and endangerment statute in the South Carolina Children's Code (the Code), S.C. Code Ann. §20-7-50 (1985) [the "statute"]. We hold the word child as used in that statute includes viable fetuses.

On April 20, 1992, Cornelia Whitner (Whitner) pled guilty to criminal child neglect for causing her baby to be born with cocaine metabolites in its system by reason of Whitner's ingestion of crack cocaine during the third trimester of her pregnancy. The circuit court judge sentenced Whitner to eight years in prison. Whitner did not appeal her conviction.

Thereafter, Whitner filed a petition for Post Conviction Relief (PCR), pleading the circuit court's lack of subject matter jurisdiction to accept her guilty plea. . . .

Under South Carolina law, a circuit court lacks subject matter jurisdiction to accept a guilty plea to a nonexistent offense. For the sentencing court to have had subject matter jurisdiction to accept Whitner's plea, criminal child neglect would have to include an expectant mother's use of crack cocaine after the fetus is viable. . . .

[The statute] provides:

> Any person having the legal custody of any child or helpless person, who shall, without lawful excuse, refuse or neglect to provide . . . the proper care and

attention for such child or helpless person, so that the life, health or comfort of such child or helpless person is endangered or is likely to be endangered, shall be guilty of a misdemeanor and shall be punished within the discretion of the circuit court.

The state contends this section encompasses maternal acts endangering or likely to endanger the life, comfort, or health of a viable fetus.

Under the Children's Code, "child" means a "person under the age of 18." The question for this Court, therefore, is whether a viable fetus is a "person" for purposes of the Children's Code.

In interpreting a statute, this court's primary function is to ascertain the intent of the legislature. Of course, where a statute is complete, plain, and unambiguous, legislative intent must be determined from the language of the statute itself. We should consider, however, not merely the language of the particular clause being construed, but the word and its meaning in conjunction with the purpose of the whole statute and the policy of the law. Finally, there is a basic presumption that the legislature has knowledge of previous legislation as well as of judicial decisions construing that legislation when later statutes are enacted concerning related subjects.

South Carolina law has long recognized that viable fetuses are persons holding certain legal rights and privileges. . . . [The court summarized the treatment of fetuses under state tort law, noting that the state wrongful death statute had been interpreted to permit actions brought on behalf of viable fetuses even where they were not born alive.]

More recently, we held the word *person* as used in a criminal statute includes viable fetuses. State v. Horne, 319 S.E.2d 703 (S.C. 1984), concerned South Carolina's murder statute, S.C. Code Ann. §16-3-10 (1976). The defendant in that case stabbed his wife, who was nine months' pregnant, in the neck, arms, and abdomen. Although doctors performed an emergency cesarean section to deliver the child, the child died while still in the womb. The defendant was convicted of voluntary manslaughter and appealed his conviction on the ground South Carolina did not recognize the crime of feticide.

This court disagreed. In a unanimous decision, we held it would be "grossly inconsistent . . . to construe a viable fetus as a 'person' for the purposes of imposing civil liability while refusing to give it a similar classification in the criminal context." 319 S.E.2d at 704. Accordingly, the court recognized the crime of feticide with respect to viable fetuses.

Similarly, we do not see any rational basis for finding a viable fetus is not a "person" in the present context. Indeed, it would be absurd to recognize the viable fetus as a person for purposes of homicide laws and wrongful death statutes but not for purposes of statutes proscribing child abuse. Our holding . . . that a viable fetus is a person rested primarily on the plain meaning of the word *person* in light of existing medical knowledge concerning fetal development. We do not believe that the plain and ordinary meaning of the word *person* has changed in any way that would now deny viable fetuses status as persons.

The policies enunciated in the Children's Code also support our plain meaning reading of "person." . . . The abuse or neglect of a child at any time during childhood can exact a profound toll on the child herself as well as on society as a whole. However, the consequences of abuse or neglect which takes place after birth often pale in comparison to those resulting from abuse suffered by the viable fetus before birth. This policy of prevention supports a reading of the word *person* to include viable fetuses. Furthermore, the scope of the Children's Code is quite broad. It applies "to all children who have need of services." When coupled with the comprehensive remedial purposes of the Code, this language supports the inference that the legislature intended to include viable fetuses within the scope of the Code's protection.

Whitner advances several arguments against an interpretation of "person" as used in the Children's Code to include viable fetuses. We shall address each of Whitner's major arguments in turn.

Whitner's first argument concerns the number of bills introduced in the South Carolina General Assembly in the past five years addressing substance abuse by pregnant women. . . . We disagree with Whitner's conclusion about the significance of the proposed legislation. Generally, the legislature's subsequent acts "cast no light on the intent of the legislature which enacted the statute being construed." . . .

Whitner also argues an interpretation of the statute that includes viable fetuses would lead to absurd results obviously not intended by the legislature. Specifically, she claims if we interpret "child" to include viable fetuses, every action by a pregnant woman that endangers or is likely to endanger a fetus, whether otherwise legal or illegal, would constitute unlawful neglect under the statute. For example, a woman might be prosecuted . . . for smoking or drinking during pregnancy. Whitner asserts these "absurd" results could not have been intended by the legislature and, therefore, the statute should not be construed to include viable fetuses.

We disagree for a number of reasons. First, the same arguments against the statute can be made whether or not the child has been born. After the birth of a child, a parent can be prosecuted . . . for an action that is likely to endanger the child without regard to whether the action is illegal in itself. For example, a parent who drinks excessively could, under certain circumstances, be guilty of child neglect or endangerment even though the underlying act—consuming alcoholic beverages—is itself legal. Obviously, the legislature did not think it "absurd" to allow prosecution of parents for such otherwise legal acts when the acts actually or potentially endanger the "life, health or comfort" of the parents' born children. We see no reason such a result should be rendered absurd by the mere fact the child at issue is a viable fetus.

Moreover, we need not address this potential parade of horribles advanced by Whitner. In this case, which is the only case we are called upon to decide here, certain facts are clear. Whitner admits to having ingested crack cocaine during the third trimester of her pregnancy, which caused her child to be born with cocaine in its system. Although the precise effects of maternal crack use during pregnancy are somewhat unclear, it is well documented and within the realm of public knowledge that such use can cause serious harm to the viable unborn child. . . . There can be no question here Whitner endangered the life, health, and comfort of her child. We need not decide any cases other than the one before us.

We are well aware of the many decisions from other states' courts throughout the country holding maternal conduct before the birth of the child does not give rise to criminal prosecution under state child abuse/endangerment or drug distribution statutes. . . . Many of these cases were prosecuted under statutes forbidding delivery or distribution of illicit substances and depended on statutory construction of the terms "delivery" and "distribution." . . . Obviously, such cases are inapplicable to the present situation. The cases concerning child endangerment statutes or construing the terms *child* and *person* are also distinguishable, because the states in which these cases were decided have entirely different bodies of case law from South Carolina. . . .

[Previous tort and criminal law cases] were decided primarily on the basis of the meaning of "person" as understood in the light of existing medical knowledge, rather than based on any policy of protecting the relationship between mother and child. As a homicide case, *Horne* also rested on the state's — not the mother's — interest in vindicating the life of the viable fetus. Moreover, the United States Supreme Court has repeatedly held that the states have a compelling interest in the life of a viable fetus [citing *Roe* and *Casey*]. . . . If, as Whitner suggests we should, we read *Horne* only as a vindication of the mother's interest in the life of her unborn child, there would be no basis for prosecuting a mother who kills her viable fetus by stabbing it, by shooting it, or by other such means, yet a third party could be prosecuted for the very same acts. We decline to read *Horne* in a way that insulates the mother from all culpability for harm to her viable child. . . .

[T]he dissent implies that we have ignored the rule of lenity requiring us to resolve any ambiguities in a criminal statute in favor of the defendant. The dissent argues that "[a]t most, the majority only suggests that the term *child* . . . is ambiguous," and that the ambiguity "is created not by reference to our decisions under the Children's Code or by reference to the statutory language and applicable rules of statutory construction, but by reliance on decisions in two different fields of the law, civil wrongful death and common law feticide."

Plainly, the dissent misunderstands our opinion. First, we do not believe the statute is ambiguous and, therefore, the rule of lenity does not apply. Furthermore, our interpretation of the statute is based primarily on the plain meaning of the word *person* as contained in the statute. We need not go beyond that language. However, because our prior decisions . . . support our reading of the statute, we have discussed the rationale underlying those holdings. We conclude that both statutory language and case law compel the conclusion we reach. We see no ambiguity. . . .

C. CONSTITUTIONAL ISSUES

[The court quickly disposed of any constitutional impediments to child endangerment prosecutions of drug-using pregnant women. It rejected Whitner's "notice" claim because the statute clearly and unambiguously covered viable fetuses and Whitner therefore had notice of the potential for prosecution. The court also rejected Whitner's claim that prosecution improperly violated her Fourteenth Amendment "privacy" interests. The court found that the statute merely created an additional penalty for conduct that was already illegal — use of crack cocaine — and did not improperly penalize Whitner for choosing to carry her pregnancy to term.]

Waller and Burnett, JJ., concur.

FINNEY, Chief Justice.

I respectfully dissent, and would affirm the grant of post-conviction relief to respondent Whitner.

The issue before the court is whether a fetus is a "child" within the meaning of . . . a statute which makes it a misdemeanor for a "person having legal custody of any child or helpless person" to unlawfully neglect that child or helpless person. Since this is a penal statute, it is strictly construed against the state and in favor of respondent.

The term *child* . . . is defined as a "person under the age of 18" unless a different meaning is required by the circumstances. . . . More importantly, it is apparent from a reading of the entire statute that the word *child* . . . means a child in being and not a fetus. A plain reading of the entire child neglect statute demonstrates the intent to criminalize only acts directed at children, and not those which may harm fetuses. First, [the statute] . . . does not impose criminal liability on every person who neglects a child, but only on a person having legal custody of that child. The statutory requirement of legal custody is evidence of intent to extend the statute's reach only to children, because the concept of legal custody is simply inapplicable to a fetus. Second, [the statute refers to other statutory sections] . . . for the definition of neglect. [These sections] . . . define[ ] a neglected child as one harmed or threatened with harm, and further defines harm. The vast majority of acts which constitute statutory harm under [these provisions] are acts which can only be directed against a child, and not towards a fetus.[2] . . .

At most, the majority only suggests that the term *child* as used in [the child neglect statute at issue] is ambiguous. This suggestion of ambiguity is created not by reference to our decisions under the Children's Code or by reference to the statutory language and applicable rules of statutory construction, but by reliance on decisions in two different fields of the law, civil wrongful death and common law feticide. Even if these wrongful death, common law, and Children's Code decisions are sufficient to render the term *child* in [the statute] . . . ambiguous, it is axiomatic that the ambiguity must be resolved in respondent's favor.

I would affirm.

MOORE, A.J.

I concur with the dissent in this case but write separately to express my concerns with today's decision. In my view, the repeated failure of the legislature to pass proposed bills addressing the problem of drug use during pregnancy is evidence the child abuse and neglect statute is not intended to apply in this instance. This court should not invade what is clearly the sole province of the legislative branch. At the very least, the legislature's failed attempts to enact a statute regulating a pregnant woman's conduct indicate the complexity of this issue. While the majority opinion is perhaps an argument for what the law should be, it is for the General Assembly, and not this court, to make that determination by means of a clearly drawn statute. With today's decision, the majority not only

---

[2] Examples include condoning delinquency, using excessive corporal punishment, committing sexual offenses against the child, and depriving her of adequate food, clothing, shelter or education.

ignores legislative intent but embarks on a course rejected by every other court to address the issue. . . .

■ FERGUSON v. CITY OF CHARLESTON
532 U.S. 67 (2001)

STEVENS, J.

In this case, we must decide whether a state hospital's performance of a diagnostic test to obtain evidence of a patient's criminal conduct for law enforcement purposes is an unreasonable search if the patient has not consented to the procedure. More narrowly, the question is whether the interest in using the threat of criminal sanctions to deter pregnant women from using cocaine can justify a departure from the general rule that an official nonconsensual search is unconstitutional if not authorized by a valid warrant.

I

In the fall of 1988, staff members at the public hospital operated in the city of Charleston by the Medical University of South Carolina (MUSC) became concerned about an apparent increase in the use of cocaine by patients who were receiving prenatal treatment. In response to this perceived increase, as of April 1989, MUSC began to order drug screens to be performed on urine samples from maternity patients who were suspected of using cocaine. If a patient tested positive, she was then referred by MUSC staff to the county substance abuse commission for counseling and treatment. However, despite the referrals, the incidence of cocaine use among the patients at MUSC did not appear to change.

Some four months later, Nurse Shirley Brown, the case manager for the MUSC obstetrics department, heard a news broadcast reporting that the police in Greenville, South Carolina, were arresting pregnant users of cocaine on the theory that such use harmed the fetus and was therefore child abuse.[1] Nurse Brown discussed the story with MUSC's general counsel, Joseph C. Good, Jr., who then contacted Charleston Solicitor Charles Condon in order to offer MUSC's cooperation in prosecuting mothers whose children tested positive for drugs at birth.

After receiving Good's letter, Solicitor Condon took the first steps in developing the policy at issue in this case. . . . [the policy is called] "POLICY M-7," dealing with the subject of "Management of Drug Abuse During Pregnancy." . . .

The first three pages of Policy M-7 set forth the procedure to be followed by the hospital staff to "identify/assist pregnant patients suspected of drug abuse." . . . The first section, entitled the "Identification of Drug Abusers," provided that a patient should be tested for cocaine through a urine drug screen if she met one or more of nine criteria . . . [including no or late prenatal care]. It also stated that a chain of custody should be followed when obtaining and testing urine samples, presumably to

---

[1] Under South Carolina law, a viable fetus has historically been regarded as a person; in 1995, the South Carolina Supreme Court held that the ingestion of cocaine during the third trimester of pregnancy constitutes criminal child neglect. Whitner v. South Carolina, 492 S.E.2d 777 (S.C. 1995), cert. denied, 523 U.S. 1145 (1998).

make sure that the results could be used in subsequent criminal proceedings. The policy also provided for education and referral to a substance abuse clinic for patients who tested positive. Most important, it added the threat of law enforcement intervention that "provided the necessary 'leverage' to make the [p]olicy effective." . . . That threat was, as respondents candidly acknowledge, essential to the program's success in getting women into treatment and keeping them there.

The threat of law enforcement involvement was set forth in two protocols, the first dealing with the identification of drug use during pregnancy, and the second with identification of drug use after labor. Under the latter protocol, the police were to be notified without delay and the patient promptly arrested. Under the former, after the initial positive drug test, the police were to be notified (and the patient arrested) only if the patient tested positive for cocaine a second time or if she missed an appointment with a substance abuse counselor. . . . [However, at least one patient was arrested after an initial positive drug screen.] In 1990, however, the policy was modified at the behest of the solicitor's office to give the patient who tested positive during labor, like the patient who tested positive during a prenatal care visit, an opportunity to avoid arrest by consenting to substance abuse treatment.

The last six pages of the policy contained forms for the patients to sign, as well as procedures for the police to follow when a patient was arrested. The policy also prescribed in detail the precise offenses with which a woman could be charged, depending on the stage of her pregnancy [with the charges as well as their nature and severity changing with each stage]. . . . Other than the provisions describing the substance abuse treatment to be offered to women who tested positive, the policy made no mention of any change in the prenatal care of such patients, nor did it prescribe any special treatment for the newborns.

II

Petitioners are 10 women who received obstetrical care at MUSC and who were arrested after testing positive for cocaine. Four of them were arrested during the initial implementation of the policy; they were not offered the opportunity to receive drug treatment as an alternative to arrest. The others were arrested after the policy was modified in 1990; they either failed to comply with the terms of the drug treatment program or tested positive for a second time. Respondents include the city of Charleston, law enforcement officials who helped develop and enforce the policy, and representatives of MUSC.

Petitioners' complaint challenged the validity of the policy under various theories, including the claim that warrantless and nonconsensual drug tests conducted for criminal investigatory purposes were unconstitutional searches. Respondents advanced two principal defenses to the constitutional claim: (1) that, as a matter of fact, petitioners had consented to the searches; and (2) that, as a matter of law, the searches were reasonable, even absent consent, because they were justified by special non-law-enforcement purposes. . . . The District Court rejected the second defense because the searches in question "were not done by the medical university for independent purposes. [Instead,] the police came in and there was an agreement reached that the positive screens would be shared with the police." . . . Accordingly, the District Court submitted the factual defense to the jury with instructions that required a verdict in favor of petitioners unless the jury found consent. . . . The jury found for respondents.

Petitioners appealed, arguing that the evidence was not sufficient to support the jury's consent finding. The Court of Appeals for the Fourth Circuit affirmed, but without reaching the question of consent. . . .

We granted certiorari, 528 U.S. 1187 (2000), to review the appellate court's holding on the "special needs" issue. Because we do not reach the question of the sufficiency of the evidence with respect to consent, we necessarily assume for purposes of our decision — as did the Court of Appeals — that the searches were conducted without the informed consent of the patients. We conclude that the judgment should be reversed and the case remanded for a decision on the consent issue.

III

Because MUSC is a state hospital, the members of its staff are government actors, subject to the strictures of the Fourth Amendment. . . . Moreover, the urine tests conducted by those staff members were indisputably searches within the meaning of the Fourth Amendment. Skinner v. Railway Labor Executives' Assn., 489 U.S. 602, 617 (1989). . . . Neither the District Court nor the Court of Appeals concluded that any of the nine criteria used to identify the women to be searched provided either probable cause to believe that they were using cocaine, or even the basis for a reasonable suspicion of such use. Rather, the District Court and the Court of Appeals viewed the case as one involving MUSC's right to conduct searches without warrants or probable cause. . . . Furthermore, given the posture in which the case comes to us, we must assume for purposes of our decision that the tests were performed without the informed consent of the patients. . . .

Because the hospital seeks to justify its authority to conduct drug tests and to turn the results over to law enforcement agents without the knowledge or consent of the patients, this case differs from the four previous cases in which we have considered whether comparable drug tests "fit within the closely guarded category of constitutionally permissible suspicionless searches." Chandler v. Miller, 520 U.S. 305, 309 (1997). . . .

In each of . . . [the prior] cases, we employed a balancing test that weighed the intrusion on the individual's interest in privacy against the "special needs" that supported the program. As an initial matter, we note that the invasion of privacy in this case is far more substantial than in those cases. In the previous four cases, there was no misunderstanding about the purpose of the test or the potential use of the test results, and there were protections against the dissemination of the results to third parties. . . . The reasonable expectation of privacy enjoyed by the typical patient undergoing diagnostic tests in a hospital is that the results of those tests will not be shared with nonmedical personnel without her consent. . . . [2]

---

[2] There are some circumstances in which state hospital employees, like other citizens, may have a duty to provide law enforcement officials with evidence of criminal conduct acquired in the course of routine treatment, see, e.g., S.C. Code Ann. §20-7-510 (2000) (physicians and nurses required to report to child welfare agency or law enforcement authority "when in the person's professional capacity the person" receives information that a child has been abused or neglected). While the existence of such laws might lead a patient to expect that members of the hospital staff might turn over evidence acquired in the course of treatment to which the patient had consented, they surely would not

In none of our prior cases was there any intrusion upon that kind of expectation.[3]

The critical difference between those four drug-testing cases and this one, however, lies in the nature of the "special need" asserted as justification for the warrantless searches. In each of those earlier cases, the "special need" that was advanced as a justification for the absence of a warrant or individualized suspicion was one divorced from the State's general interest in law enforcement. . . . In this case, however, the central and indispensable feature of the policy from its inception was the use of law enforcement to coerce the patients into substance abuse treatment. This fact distinguishes this case from circumstances in which physicians or psychologists, in the course of ordinary medical procedures aimed at helping the patient herself, come across information that under rules of law or ethics is subject to reporting requirements, which no one has challenged here. See, e.g., Council on Ethical and Judicial Affairs, American Medical Association, PolicyFinder, Current Opinions E-5.05 (2000) (requiring reporting where "a patient threatens to inflict serious bodily harm to another person or to him or herself and there is a reasonable probability that the patient may carry out the threat"). . . .

Respondents argue in essence that their ultimate purpose — namely, protecting the health of both mother and child — is a beneficent one. . . . In looking to the programmatic purpose, we consider all the available evidence in order to determine the relevant primary purpose. . . . Tellingly, the document codifying the policy incorporates the police's operational guidelines. It devotes its attention to the chain of custody, the range of possible criminal charges, and the logistics of police notification and arrests. Nowhere, however, does the document discuss different courses of medical treatment for either mother or infant, aside from treatment for the mother's addiction.

Moreover, throughout the development and application of the policy, the Charleston prosecutors and police were extensively involved in the day-to-day administration of the policy. . . .

While the ultimate goal of the program may well have been to get the women in question into substance abuse treatment and off of drugs, the immediate objective of the searches was to generate evidence for law enforcement purposes . . . in order to reach that goal. . . . The threat of law enforcement may ultimately have been intended as a means to an end, but the direct and primary purpose of MUSC's policy was to ensure the use of those means. In our opinion, this distinction is critical. Because law enforcement involvement always serves some broader social purpose or objective, under respondents' view, virtually any nonconsensual suspicionless search could be immunized under the special needs doctrine by defining the search solely in terms of its ultimate, rather than immediate, purpose. . . . Such an approach is inconsistent with the Fourth Amendment. Given the primary purpose of the Charleston program, which was to use the threat of arrest and prosecution in order to force women into treatment, and given the extensive involvement of law enforcement officials at every stage of

---

lead a patient to anticipate that hospital staff would intentionally set out to obtain incriminating evidence from their patients for law enforcement purposes.

[3] In fact, we have previously recognized that an intrusion on that expectation may have adverse consequences because it may deter patients from receiving needed medical care. . . .

the policy, this case simply does not fit within the closely guarded category of "special needs."[4]

The fact that positive test results were turned over to the police does not merely provide a basis for distinguishing our prior cases applying the "special needs" balancing approach to the determination of drug use. It also provides an affirmative reason for enforcing the strictures of the Fourth Amendment. While state hospital employees, like other citizens, may have a duty to provide the police with evidence of criminal conduct that they inadvertently acquire in the course of routine treatment, when they undertake to obtain such evidence from their patients for the specific purpose of incriminating those patients, they have a special obligation to make sure that the patients are fully informed about their constitutional rights, as standards of knowing waiver require. . . .

As respondents have repeatedly insisted, their motive was benign rather than punitive. Such a motive, however, cannot justify a departure from Fourth Amendment protections, given the pervasive involvement of law enforcement with the development and application of the MUSC policy. The stark and unique fact that characterizes this case is that Policy M-7 was designed to obtain evidence of criminal conduct by the tested patients that would be turned over to the police and that could be admissible in subsequent criminal prosecutions. While respondents are correct that drug abuse both was and is a serious problem, "the gravity of the threat alone cannot be dispositive of questions concerning what means law enforcement officers may employ to pursue a given purpose." . . . The Fourth Amendment's general prohibition against nonconsensual, warrantless, and suspicionless searches necessarily applies to such a policy. . . .

Accordingly, the judgment of the Court of Appeals is reversed, and the case is remanded for further proceedings consistent with this opinion.

It is so ordered.

KENNEDY, J., concurring:

I agree that the search procedure in issue cannot be sustained under the Fourth Amendment. My reasons for this conclusion differ somewhat from those set forth by the Court, however, leading to this separate opinion. . . .

In my view, it is necessary and prudent to be explicit in explaining the limitations of today's decision. The beginning point ought to be to acknowledge the legitimacy of the State's interest in fetal life and of the grave risk to the life and health of the fetus, and later the child, caused by cocaine ingestion. Infants whose mothers abuse cocaine during pregnancy are born with a wide variety of physical and neurological abnormalities. . . . There should be no doubt that South Carolina can impose punishment upon an expectant mother who has so little regard for her own unborn that she risks causing him or her lifelong damage and suffering. The State, by taking special measures to give rehabilitation and training to expectant mothers with this tragic addiction or weakness, acts well within its powers and its civic obligations.

---

[4] It is especially difficult to argue that the program here was designed simply to save lives. Amici claim a near consensus in the medical community that programs of the sort at issue, by discouraging women who use drugs from seeking prenatal care, harm, rather than advance, the cause of prenatal health. . . .

The holding of the Court, furthermore, does not call into question the validity of mandatory reporting laws such as child abuse laws which require teachers to report evidence of child abuse to the proper authorities, even if arrest and prosecution is the likely result. . . . [W]e must accept the premise that the medical profession can adopt acceptable criteria for testing expectant mothers for cocaine use in order to provide prompt and effective counseling to the mother and to take proper medical steps to protect the child. If prosecuting authorities then adopt legitimate procedures to discover this information and prosecution follows, that ought not to invalidate the testing. . . .

Scalia, J., dissenting:

There is always an unappealing aspect to the use of doctors and nurses, ministers of mercy, to obtain incriminating evidence against the supposed objects of their ministration — although here, it is correctly pointed out, the doctors and nurses were ministering not just to the mothers but also to the children whom their cooperation with the police was meant to protect. But whatever may be the correct social judgment concerning the desirability of what occurred here, that is not the issue in the present case. . . . The question before us is a narrower one: whether, whatever the desirability of this police conduct, it violates the Fourth Amendment's prohibition of unreasonable searches and seizures. In my view, it plainly does not. . . .

It is rudimentary Fourth Amendment law that a search which has been consented to is not unreasonable. There is no contention in the present case that the urine samples were extracted forcibly. The only conceivable bases for saying that they were obtained without consent are the contentions (1) that the consent was coerced by the patients' need for medical treatment, (2) that the consent was uninformed because the patients were not told that the tests would include testing for drugs, and (3) that the consent was uninformed because the patients were not told that the results of the tests would be provided to the police. . . .

Until today, we have never held — or even suggested — that material which a person voluntarily entrusts to someone else cannot be given by that person to the police, and used for whatever evidence it may contain. . . . Today's holding would be remarkable enough if the confidential relationship violated by the police conduct were at least one protected by state law. . . . But today's holding goes even beyond that, since there does not exist any physician-patient privilege in South Carolina. . . .

There remains to be considered the first possible basis for invalidating this search, which is that the patients were coerced to produce their urine samples by their necessitous circumstances, to-wit, their need for medical treatment of their pregnancy. If that was coercion, it was not coercion applied by the government — and if such nongovernmental coercion sufficed, the police would never be permitted to use the ballistic evidence obtained from treatment of a patient with a bullet wound. And the Fourth Amendment would invalidate those many state laws that require physicians to report gunshot wounds, . . . evidence of spousal abuse, . . . and (like the South Carolina law relevant here, see S.C. Code Ann. §20-7-510 (2000)) evidence of child abuse. . . .

I think it clear, therefore, that there is no basis for saying that obtaining of the urine sample was unconstitutional. The special-needs doctrine is thus quite irrelevant, since it operates only to validate searches and seizures that are otherwise unlawful. In the ensuing discussion, however, I shall assume (contrary to legal precedent) that the taking of the urine sample was (either because of the patients' necessitous circumstances, or because of failure to disclose that the urine would be tested for drugs, or because of failure to disclose that the results of the test would be given to the police) coerced. Indeed, I shall even assume (contrary to common sense) that the testing of the urine constituted an unconsented search of the patients' effects. On those assumptions, the special-needs doctrine would become relevant; and, properly applied, would validate what was done here. . . .

The cocaine tests started in April 1989, neither at police suggestion nor with police involvement. Expectant mothers who tested positive were referred by hospital staff for substance-abuse treatment . . . — an obvious health benefit to both mother and child. . . . Thus, in their origin—before the police were in any way involved—the tests had an immediate, not merely an "ultimate," . . . purpose of improving maternal and infant health. Several months after the testing had been initiated . . . [the hospital invited police involvement.] . . . Why would there be any reason to believe that, once this policy of using the drug tests for their "ultimate" health benefits had been adopted, use of them for their original, immediate, benefits somehow disappeared, and testing somehow became in its entirety nothing more than a "pretext" for obtaining grounds for arrest?

In sum, there can be no basis for the Court's purported ability to "distinguish this case from circumstances in which physicians or psychologists, in the course of ordinary medical procedures aimed at helping the patient herself, come across information that . . . is subject to reporting requirements." . . .

But as far as the Fourth Amendment is concerned: There was no unconsented search in this case. And if there was, it would have been validated by the special-needs doctrine. For these reasons, I respectfully dissent.

Notes: Maternal Substance Abuse

1. *Prevalence and Effect of Maternal Substance Abuse.* Thousands of children are born each year to women who have used tobacco, alcohol, or illegal drugs during pregnancy. In 2004-2005, 3.9 percent of all pregnant women age 15-44 reported using illicit drugs in the last month. Drug use was more prevalent in young pregnant women (12.3 percent for young women age 15-17 compared to 1.6 percent for women age 26-44). Seventeen percent of pregnant women age 15-44 reported using tobacco products within the past month. More than 12 percent of pregnant women in this age range reported drinking alcohol. Substance Abuse and Mental Health Services Administration, U.S. Dept. Health and Human Services, 2005 National Survey on Drug Use and Health, available at http://www.oas.samhsa.gov. The type of substance used varies by race and socioeconomic status, although there is some evidence that the overall use of potentially injurious substances is consistent across all groups. See S. L. Hans, Demographic and Psychosocial Characteristics of Substance-Abusing Pregnant Women, 26 Clin. Perinatology 55 (1999).

Illicit drugs, alcohol, tobacco, and other substances can injure developing fetuses. Research findings include higher rates of prematurity, lower birth weights, and cognitive/behavioral abnormalities. It is important to recognize, however, that other related factors may contribute to some of these problems, including inadequate diet, poor prenatal care, and a less than optimal developmental environment. See, e.g., Seetha Shankaran et al., Impact of Maternal Substance Use During Pregnancy on Childhood Outcome, 12 Sem. Fetal & Neonatal Med. 143 (2007) (summarizing studies). Should policies developed to deal with the use of illicit drugs by pregnant women be applied to the use of harmful, but legal, substances? The *Whitner* court suggests that such prosecutions are possible but potentially problematic from a constitutional standpoint.

2. *Two Views on Legislative Intent.* Determining whether traditional child endangerment, drug delivery, or other statutes apply to the problem of risky prenatal conduct is initially a problem of statutory interpretation. Does the statute apply to fetuses explicitly or will a court find that the legislature intended for the provision to apply to fetuses? The vast majority of states that have considered the statutory interpretation questions in the criminal context have found that the legislature did not intend to include fetuses. For an excellent review of the relevant cases, see Linda C. Fentiman, The New "Fetal Protection": The Wrong Answer to the Crisis of Inadequate Health Care for Women and Children, 84 Denv. U. L. Rev. 537 (2006); Editorial Staff of the Yale Journal of Health Policy, Law, and Ethics, Synopsis of State Case and Statutory Law, 1 Yale J. Health Pol'y L. & Ethics 215 (2001) [hereinafter Synopsis of State Case and Statutory Law]. See also State v. Ikerd, 850 A.2d 516 (N.J. Super. 2004) (holding that "a pregnant, drug-addicted woman who has violated the conditions of her probation cannot be sentenced to prison for the avowed purpose of safeguarding the health of her fetus."). *Whitner*, therefore, represents the minority view. The decision could still be "right" for purposes of South Carolina law. Do you agree that the state legislature intended that the child endangerment statute be applied to a pregnant woman's behavior toward her fetus? Why would the legislature attempt to enact legislation on the subject if the child endangerment statute already provided a remedy? How persuasive is the majority's statutory interpretation? Is the legislature likely to "correct" the court if it is wrong?

South Carolina continues to follow the *Whitner* approach. In State v. McKnight, 576 S.E.2d 168 (S.C.), *cert. denied*, 540 U.S. 819 (2003), the South Carolina Supreme Court cited *Whitner* in affirming a defendant's conviction of homicide by child abuse through prenatal use of cocaine. The defendant gave birth to a stillborn child estimated to be at 34-37 weeks of gestation; metabolites of cocaine were found during an autopsy of the fetus. The defendant was sentenced to a twenty year term of imprisonment. See Fentiman, supra, at 537.

The defendant in *Whitner* argued that South Carolina's recognition of tort and criminal law actions arising from fetal injuries was an attempt to protect a woman's relationship with her fetus rather than an effort to protect a fetal right to be free from harm. The court rejected the argument, finding that state case law was based on the definition of "person" and noting the state's compelling interest in protecting fetal life. Other courts have accepted the defendant's view and have restricted actions brought against the woman, as opposed to some third party, on the theory that the state's interest is in protecting the woman's interest in the fetus.

State ex rel. Angela M.W. v. Kruzicki, 561 N.W.2d 729 (Wis. 1997), is typical of the majority approach. Angela M.W.'s obstetrician reported her to county authorities because of her persistent drug use during pregnancy. The county filed a motion to take Angela's unborn child (and, by necessity, Angela herself) into custody; the order was granted by the juvenile court. The county then filed a petition asserting that the unborn child was a "child in need of protection or services" under state law because Angela was endangering her fetus's health. The relevant statute defined "child" as a "person who is less than 18 years of age." Angela brought and lost an action in the court of appeals, seeking her release or a stay of the juvenile court proceedings. In the course of these proceedings, Angela gave birth to a baby boy.

The Wisconsin Supreme Court reversed the court of appeals, with three justices dissenting. 561 N.W.2d 729 (Wis. 1997) (The court issued its decision despite the child's birth and Angela's release from confinement under an exception to the mootness doctrine often used in litigation involving pregnancy. See Roe v. Wade, supra.) The court agreed that the definition of "child" was ambiguous under the statutory scheme but held that the legislature had not intended to include unborn fetuses in the definition. The court noted, for example, that the statute used "child" in a number of ways that were inconsistent with the inclusion of viable fetuses. The majority did not reach the constitutional issues because it was able to overturn the custodial order on statutory interpretation grounds alone.

Note that some states have attempted to prosecute pregnant drug users under statutes that make it a criminal offense to "deliver" drugs to another "person." The prosecutions proceeded on the theory that a pregnant woman who had ingested illegal drugs within a few days of giving birth was capable of transmitting drug metabolites to her newborn during the brief time period between birth and the cutting of the umbilical cord—when the child was a "person." Courts have rejected these prosecutions, holding that the legislatures did not intend this application of the drug delivery statutes. See, e.g., Synopsis of State Case and Statutory Law, supra; Johnson v. State, 602 So. 2d 1288 (Fla. 1992).

3. *The Constitution and the Prosecution of Pregnant Women.* Most attempted prosecutions have failed on the basis of statutory interpretation and legislative intent. Courts, therefore, have rarely reached the constitutional objections to the prosecution of pregnant women. Of course a state legislature could easily surmount the statutory interpretation obstacles to criminal prosecution by enacting legislation that clearly imposes criminal punishments on pregnant women who injure their fetuses. Courts reviewing this type of legislation would be forced to confront potential due process and equal protection challenges. How would you frame the constitutional questions?

The *Whitner* court's constitutional analysis was cursory. The majority defended child endangerment prosecutions from constitutional attack by noting that the underlying drug use was already criminal. Would it be unconstitutional to prosecute pregnant women for conduct that, while potentially injurious, was otherwise legal? How would you analyze the prosecution of a woman for smoking tobacco after fetal viability? The dissenting justices in State ex rel. Angela M.W. seemed to argue that such prosecutions would also be permissible under the due process and equal protection clauses:

Angela next contends that the custodial effect of the protective order violated her due process liberty interest under the United States Constitution. . . . In regard to the state interest implicated here, the United States Supreme Court has determined [that] . . . the state's interest in protecting the life and health of an unborn child becomes compelling and dominant once the fetus reaches viability. . . . In the present case, there is no dispute that Angela's child was a viable fetus when the petition was filed, that Angela was actively using cocaine, and that the use of cocaine put the child at substantial risk of great bodily harm or possibly death. As such, the state has a compelling state interest to protect Angela's fetus under *Roe* [and] *Casey*. . . . [If *Roe* stands for the proposition that the state's interest in a viable fetus can override a woman's wish to terminate the pregnancy, why shouldn't the state be able to] protect the viable fetus from maternal conduct which functionally presents the same risk and portends the same result, the death of the viable fetus? . . .

The next issue therefore is whether the infringement on Angela's liberty is narrowly tailored to further the compelling state interest. I conclude that it is. The Children's Code specifies the procedures necessary to further the state's compelling interest in the protection of children. These procedures must be complied with before the state can exercise its right to detain and ultimately protect a child. [The procedures include a post-detention hearing to determine whether there is probable cause to exercise jurisdiction over the child and whether the child will be "subject to injury if . . . not taken into protective custody."] . . . In light of all the statutorily imposed procedures necessary to detain a child, it is clear that the means by which the state's compelling interest is served are narrowly tailored to [meet the state's interest in protecting children]. . . .

Finally, Angela argues that if the state is allowed to intervene when the mother ingests cocaine, this will "open the door" for the state to intervene whenever a mother acts in any manner that is potentially harmful to her viable fetus. Angela cites as examples the possibility of state intervention if a mother smokes or refuses to take her prenatal vitamins. This argument is not a realistic one because [the statute] . . . contains the necessary protections against unreasonable or unjustified intervention by the state. . . . Clearly, the Children's Code enables the state to intervene only when a child faces substantial risk. Thus, [the statute] . . . contains the necessary stopping point to protect against Angela's slippery slope argument. In fact, if this were not true, then the same argument would have validity under the Children's Code even if the child has been born [citing Whitner v. State, supra]. State ex rel. Angela M.W. v. Kruzicki, 561 N.W.2d 729, 747-749 (Wis. 1997) (Crooks, J., dissenting).

Do you agree with the dissent's disposition of the constitutional questions? Do the abortion cases stand for the proposition that the state's compelling interest in fetal life can outweigh more than a woman's right to terminate her pregnancy? How would you characterize the nature of the pregnant woman's interests? Is the use of forced confinement and drug treatment a measure narrowly tailored to achieve the state's objectives? Compare the dissent's analysis with the majority and dissenting opinions in In re A.C. See also Nancy Ehrenreich, The Colonization of the Womb, 43 Duke L.J. 492 (1993).

4. *Medical Care for Pregnant Women and the Fourth Amendment.* The *Ferguson* case might be viewed as the natural outgrowth of the criminalization of drug use by pregnant women. Note that the Court does not find fault with the state law

criminalizing prenatal drug abuse. What were the constitutional defects of the hospital policy in *Ferguson*? State law often requires health care providers to report matters such as child abuse and gunshot wounds. Do reports under these statutes present the same Fourth Amendment problems as the hospital policy in *Ferguson*? For a summary of state testing and reporting rules, see Synopsis of State Case and Statutory Law, supra.

On remand in *Ferguson*, the United States Court of Appeals for the Fourth Circuit issued a lengthy opinion holding that: (1) a mother's Fourth Amendment interests are not implicated by newborn urine testing; (2) the MUSC's policy of testing patients' urine for evidence of cocaine was not designed to further medical care; (3) the hospital's consent forms did not adequately inform patients about the use of urine tests for law enforcement purposes; and (4) patients who presented themselves to the hospital for treatment could not be said to have impliedly consented to the urine search policy. Ferguson v. City of Charleston, South Carolina, 308 F.3d 380 (4th Cir. 2002). The court also held that two patients had sufficient knowledge of the law enforcement purposes of the testing to imply consent. Id. Could a state require welfare recipients to undergo warrantless, suspicionless drug testing as a condition of receiving benefits? Marchwinski v. Howard, 113 F. Supp. 2d 1134 (E.D. Mich. 2000) (no), upheld on rehearing en banc, 60 Fed. Appx. 601 (6th Cir. 2003) (judgment of the district court reinstated by equally divided vote of the appeals court en banc).

5. *The Criminal Model vs. the Treatment Model.* Punitive prenatal substance abuse policies clearly might deter drug-addicted women from seeking prenatal care. Not surprisingly, the AMA's policy favors treatment over criminal liability: "Criminal sanctions or civil liability for harmful behavior by the pregnant woman toward her fetus are inappropriate. . . . Pregnant substance abusers should be provided with rehabilitative treatment appropriate to their specific physiological and psychological needs." AMA, H-420.969 Legal Interventions During Pregnancy, available through http://www.ama-assn.org/ama/noindex/category/11760.html. Critics of the criminal model also note that drug treatment centers have often refused to permit pregnant women to participate in treatment programs because of health and liability concerns. See, e.g., Elaine W. v. Joint Diseases North General Hospital (N.Y. 1993).

Whitner and *Ferguson* were followed by a new wave of legislation focused on the therapeutic solution to risky maternal conduct. See Synopsis of State Case and Statutory Law, supra; Laura E. Gomez, Misconceiving Mothers: Legislators, Prosecutors, and the Politics of Prenatal Drug Exposure (1997); Lynn M. Paltrow, Governmental Responses to Pregnant Women Who Use Alcohol or Other Drugs, 8 DePaul J. Health Care L. 461 (2005); Jean Reith Schroedel & Pamela Fiber, Punitive Versus Public Health Oriented Responses to Drug Use by Pregnant Women, 1 Yale J. Health Pol'y L. & Ethics 217 (2001).

One possible non-criminal approach to prenatal substance abuse is civil commitment. See pages 663-664. Does this approach avoid any of the drawbacks of criminal prosecution? See David F. Chavkin, "For Their Own Good": Civil Commitment of Alcohol and Drug-Dependent Women, 37 S.D. L. Rev. 224 (1991/ 1992); Fentiman, supra, 84 Denv. U. L. Rev. at 545-546.

D. USING REPRODUCTIVE TECHNOLOGIES TO CREATE NEW FAMILIES

Technological advances in reproduction have cast into question some long-established legal doctrines. Who is the father of a child conceived through artificial insemination? Who is the mother of a child born through the use of in vitro fertilization techniques and surrogacy? Is it possible to have two fathers or two mothers? These questions are intrinsically important because of the joys, legal rights, and obligations that go along with parenthood. Yet the answers to these questions also can have important consequences for our ideas of what "fatherhood" or "motherhood" mean.

Some of the issues considered in this section build upon those discussed in section A of this chapter. Litigants often assert their constitutional right to control procreation, for example, in arguing for particular legal treatment of a reproductive technology. Moreover, the struggle for control between individuals and the state is a consistent theme of the cases in section A and in this section. Nonetheless, there are important differences in the cases in these sections.

In the earlier section, the state's attempt to control most often took the form of regulations or of outright prohibition of the use of the technology itself, such as state attempts to restrict access to abortion. In this section, we are concerned primarily with state attempts to control outcome rather than use. Only with respect to cloning, discussed in the final section of this chapter, have states begun to impose blanket prohibitions on the use of reproductive technologies to facilitate reproduction. Most state regulation focuses on the manner in which the technology is used and seeks to establish the legal status of participants in the process. These efforts have been resisted by individuals who have sought to use contractual agreements or existing statutory mechanisms to establish legal status and relationships. The primary issue therefore has been whether individuals or the state controls the legal status of participants in reproductive ventures.

1. Parenting Possibilities

■ ASSISTED REPRODUCTIVE TECHNOLOGY AND THE FAMILY*
John A. Robertson**
47 Hastings L.J. 911 (1996)

More than one in eight married couples in the United States suffer from infertility (defined as a lack of pregnancy after a year of unprotected intercourse). Although some couples adopt or choose to remain childless, many turn to physicians for help in forming families. The list of assisted reproductive techniques (ARTs) available for treating infertility now includes intrauterine insemination (IUI), ovulation induction, in vitro fertilization (IVF), intracytoplasmic sperm injection, sperm donation, egg donation, embryo donation, and gestational surrogacy.

The growth of the contemporary infertility industry has been largely spurred by the development of IVF. The first American birth resulting from in vitro fertilization occurred in 1981. By 1988, 15,000 stimulated IVF cycles occurred in more than 100 clinics. In 1994, more than 300 clinics performed more than 35,000 cycles, resulting in more than 6,000 births.[1] More than 200 programs now provide donor eggs, and thousands of obstetricians and gynecologists provide IUI, donor sperm, and ovulation induction in office settings. Twenty to thirty thousand children are born each year as a result of these techniques, with the vast majority of them produced by artificial insemination with partner or donor sperm. . . .

The use of assisted reproductive techniques by infertile couples is a family-centered act, reflecting couples' desire to form families with biologically related offspring. Although adoption and foster parenting can provide parenting experiences, only ARTs enable one or both partners to have some biologic tie, either genetic or gestational, to their children. While some critics of ARTs disapprove of the emphasis these technologies place on genetic ties, our culture, our law, and our social and psychological understandings of reproduction and parenting define parental and offspring roles largely though not exclusively in genetic or biologic terms. In this context, the development of safe and effective ARTs appears to be positive: It reduces the suffering of childless couples by making it possible for them to realize their procreative goals.

Yet many people have doubts about ARTs and the industry that has grown up around them. Some of these doubts concern the morality and consequences of interfering with nature or manipulating the earliest stages of life. Others focus on the consequences for offspring, for participants (including the couples directly involved and the collaborating donors and surrogates), and for women and families generally. Some have criticized the industry's emphasis on profits and its lack of regulation — which has recently received considerable attention because of allegations of the theft of eggs and embryos by leading doctors at a California fertility center. . . .

My basic premise is that ARTs support the traditional notion of the family, even though they depart from the conventional method of producing children through coital conception. Despite the differences in the method of conception, the goal of an ART is a child biologically related to one or both rearing parents — a goal similar to that sought through coital conception. The family project in each case should be treated equally. The use of gamete donors and surrogates, however, requires special attention because of the potential problems that the resulting desegregation of the genetic, gestational, and social aspects of procreation pose for participants and offspring. . . .

ARTs, Freedom, and the Family

Before addressing current policy issues, it is useful to consider briefly the connection between the use of ARTs and personal and procreative liberty. Critics

---

[1] Ed. Note: "In 2003, a total of 122,872 ART procedures were reported to CDC. These procedures resulted in 35,785 live-birth deliveries and 48,746 infants. Nationwide, 74% of ART procedures used freshly fertilized embryos from the patients' eggs; 14% used thawed embryos from the patient's eggs; 8% used freshly fertilized embryos from donor eggs; and 4% used thawed embryos from donor eggs. . . . Approximately 1% of U.S. infants born in 2003 were conceived through ART." Victoria Clay Wright et al., Assisted Reproductive Technology Surveillance — United States, 2003, 55 MMWR 1 (2006) (Surveillance Summary No. 4); and John A. Robertson, Commerce and Regulation in the Assisted Reproduction Industry, 85 Tex. L. Rev. 665, 665 (2007) (approximately 200,000 ART births worldwide).

of ARTs have often called for prohibition or regulation without realizing the impact such restrictions would have on procreative freedom, a freedom that is highly valued in other contexts. Yet the right of infertile couples to use these techniques is as important as their right to conceive coitally or to avoid reproduction once pregnancy has occurred. The argument in support of the rights of infertile couples to use ARTs to form families can be briefly stated.

Although it is not mentioned explicitly in the Constitution, courts would no doubt recognize as fundamental the right of a married couple to reproduce coitally, because of the traditional association of reproduction and childbearing with marriage, and the independent importance of reproduction in people's lives. Since an infertile couple or individual has the same interest in bearing and rearing offspring as a fertile couple does, their right to use noncoital techniques to treat infertility should have equivalent respect. This is clearest when the couple's own gametes will be involved, such as IUI and IVF, but it should also be recognized when one partner does not contribute genetically or gestationally to reproduction. Thus laws that restrict or prohibit access to ARTs should be judged under the same exacting standard that would apply to direct restrictions on coital reproduction — the need to show a compelling state interest not achievable by less restrictive means. Under this standard, most objections to ARTs are insufficient to justify banning or unduly burdening their use, though there is considerable room for reasonable regulation designed to assure that consumers fully understand and freely choose the particular ART at issue. . . .

■ WHAT DOES IT MEAN TO BE A "PARENT"? THE CLAIMS OF BIOLOGY AS THE BASIS FOR PARENTAL RIGHTS
John Lawrence Hill
66 N.Y.U. L. Rev. 353, 355 (1991)

Charting Parental Possibilities: A Sampling of Alternative Reproductive Technologies*

Number	Source of gametes		Site of fertilization	Site of pregnancy	Intended parent(s)	Notes
	Male	*Female*				
1	H	W	W	W	H, W	Traditional artificial insemination by husband (AIH)

* Information updated and revised from chart found in John Lawrence Hill, What Does It Mean to Be a "Parent"? The Claims of Biology as the Basis for Parental Rights, 66 N.Y.U. L. Rev. 353, 355 (1991) (citing William B. Weil, Jr., & LeRoy Walters, Editor's Introduction, 10 J. Med. & Phil. 209, 210 (1985)). See also Roger J. Chin, Assisted Reproductive Technologies: Legal Issues in Procreation, 8 Loy. Consumer L. Rev. 190 (1996).

Number	Source of gametes		Site of fertilization	Site of pregnancy	Intended parent(s)	Notes
	Male	*Female*				
2	D	W	W	W	H, W	AID
3	D	F	F	F	F, F + P	AI, single F or single F with unmarried partner
4	H	W	L	W	H, W	IVF
5	D	W	L	W	H, W	IVF with donated sperm
6	H	D	L	W	H, W	IVF with donated egg
7	D_m	D_f	L	W	H, W	IVF with donated gametes (or embryo)
8	H	D_f	FS (or D)	W	H, W	AIH with donor egg in vivo, embryo extraction
9	D_m	D_f	FS (or D_f)	W	H, W	AID with donor egg in vivo, embryo extraction
10	H	W	W, L, S	GS	H, W	gestational surrogacy
11	D	W	W, L, S	GS	H, W	AID + gestational surrogacy
12	H	D_f	L, S	GS	H, W	donor egg, gestational surrogacy
13	H	D_f	L, S	DGS	H,W	full surrogacy (egg and womb)
14	D_m	D_f	L, S	DGS	H,W	AID + full surrogacy
15	M	D_f	S, DGS	GS, DGS	M, M + P	use of surrogacy for single M or M with unmarried partner

Number	Source of gametes		Site of fertilization	Site of pregnancy	Intended parent(s)	Notes
	Male	*Female*				
16	D_m	D_f	S, DGS	GS, DGS	M, M + P	AID + surrogacy for single M or M with unmarried partner
17	D_m	F	F, L, S, DGS	GS, DGS	F, F + P	use of surrogacy for single F or F with unmarried partner
18	D_m	D_f	L, S, DGS	GS, DGS	F, F + P	AI + egg donation + surrogacy for single F or F with unmarried partner

H = Husband; W = Wife; P = Partner (no legal marriage); M = Male; F = Female; D = Donor; S = Fertilization Surrogate; GS = Gestational Surrogate; DGS = Egg Donor + Gestational Surrogate; L = Laboratory.

Notes: Parenting Possibilities

1. *Parenting as an Emotional and Constitutional Subject.* Professor Robertson reviews the prevalence of infertility in our society. An estimated 10 percent of the reproductive-age population is infertile, that is, unable to conceive after a year of unprotected intercourse. Allen A. Mitchell, Infertility Treatment—More Risks and Challenges, New Eng. J. Med. 769 (2002); Bradley J. Van Voorhis, In Vitro Fertilization, New Eng. J. Med. 379 (2007). How important is it to have a child? How important is it to have a child that is genetically related to you or to your partner? See L. Jill Halman et al., Attitudes about Infertility Interventions among Fertile and Infertile Couples, 82 Am. J. Pub. Health 191 (1992); Gina Kolata, The Heart's Desire, N.Y. Times, May 11, 2004, at D1, col. 1 (discussing costs and methods of treating fertility). Robertson suggests that constitutional protection of the right to procreate extends to the use of new reproductive technologies, even where the resulting child will not be biologically related to the intended parents. Do you agree?

While the language in *Skinner* (page 427) is broad and general, the Supreme Court has been disinclined in recent years to find constitutional protection for activities not deeply rooted in history and tradition. See Troxel v. Granville, 530 U.S. 57 (2000) (parents have fundamental right to make childrearing decisions;

Constitution limits state's ability to presume interaction with grandparents is in the best interests of a child); Michael H. v. Gerald D., 491 U.S. 110 (1989) (rejecting claim of married woman's male lover that he had constitutional right to establish a parenting relationship with his genetic child, born of his lover during her marriage to another man). Will courts find that procreative liberty is limited to "natural" procreation, via sexual reproduction? What will be the limits of constitutional protection for procreative liberty? Does our right to procreative liberty extend beyond genetic parenting, to include the use of donated gametes? If genetic parenting is constitutionally significant, will cloning be given any constitutional protection?

2. *Technology and Parenting Possibilities.* Examine the chart at pages 509-511, which does not purport to be a comprehensive summary of the wide range of present or future reproductive technologies. Cf. Alternative Sources of Gametes: Reality or Science Fiction, 15 Human Repro. 988 (2000). Note also that the chart makes certain assumptions about the legal significance of particular aspects of assisted reproduction. The chart assumes, for example, that the place of fertilization is not as likely to be a legally significant factor as the place of gestation, the genetic heritage of the child, or the intent of the parties.

With these caveats in mind, examine each reproductive alternative and consider who you think should be considered to be the "legal" parent(s) of the child produced by this arrangement. What factors motivate your judgments? Should it matter whether the parties have some legal relationship, e.g., are married? Can you think of any alternatives not listed in this scheme? The chart begins with the presumption that procreation revolves around a married couple (note the emphasis on "husbands" and "wives"). Should single men and women, gay couples, or unmarried heterosexual partners be able to use alternative reproductive technologies? Are there situations in which the law should recognize more than two parents? See Alison Harvison Young, Reconceiving the Family: Challenging the Paradigm of the Exclusive Family, 6 Am. U. J. Gender & L. 505 (1998); John A. Robertson, Gay and Lesbian Access to Assisted Reproductive Technology, 55 Case W. Res. L. Rev. 323 (2004). See also John Bowe, Gay Donor or Gay Dad?, N.Y. Times Magazine, Nov. 19, 2006, at 66. The situation is made even more complex by the potential for human cloning, discussed infra in section E.

3. *Regulation.* ART regulation involves the intersection of matters typically regulated at the state level (family law, medical practice) with issues amenable to federal regulation (interstate commerce, human subjects research, the donation and use of human cells). Not surprisingly, regulation in the United States has been piecemeal with significant regulatory gaps. Courts occasionally have been forced to step in to resolve the implications of new reproductive technologies. See generally, David Adamson, Regulation of Assisted Reproductive Technologies in the United States, 39 Fam. L.Q. 727 (2005).

Commissions and other advisory groups have issued numerous recommendations. See National Conference of the Commissioners on Uniform State Laws, Uniform Parentage Act (2000); New York State Task Force on Life and the Law, Assisted Reproductive Technologies: Analysis and Recommendations for Public Policy (1998); President's Council on Bioethics, Reproduction and Responsibility: The Regulation of New Biotechnologies (2004).

Professional societies and organizations have issued guidelines. The American College of Obstetricians and Gynecologists (ACOG) and the American Society for Reproductive Medicine (ASRM) both have issued ethical guidelines regarding the use of alternative reproductive technologies. Baruch A. Brody et al., Medical Ethics: Codes, Opinions, and Statements 409-476, 881-973 (2000). See also the Society for Assisted Reproductive Technology available at http://www.sart.org/.

The President's Council recommended that Congress consider a package of legislative initiatives that would prohibit certain human-nonhuman hybrids, the use of women's uteruses for anything other than human reproduction, the use of certain methods to create children, the use of embryos after a designated stage of development, and the commercialization of embryos. The Council also recommended that professional organizations act to ensure that members follow the organization's guidelines. President's Council on Bioethics, Reproduction and Responsibility: The Regulation of New Biotechnologies 205-224 (2004).

4. *International Developments.* The use of ARTs has also been controversial around the world. Several countries have enacted comprehensive legislation designed to cover the use of ARTs and new genetic technologies such as cloning. As an example, Italy enacted legislation banning the use of donated sperm and eggs and restricting the use and methods of in vitro fertilization in 2004. See Fabio Turone, Italy to Pass New Law on Assisted Reproduction, 328 Brit. Med. J. 9 (2004); and John A. Robertson, Protecting Embryos and Burdening Women: Assisted Reproduction in Italy, 19 Human Repro. 1693 (2004). An effort to change the legislation by referendum failed in 2005. Ian Fisher, Italian Vote to Ease Fertility Law Fails for Want of Voters, N.Y. Times, June 14, 2005, at A11, col. 1. Canada enacted the Assisted Human Reproduction Act in 2004. One major purpose of the Act is to prevent the commercialization of reproductive technologies. Thus, the Act prohibits payment for sperm or egg donors. Critics argue that the decommercialization will reduce the supplies of sperm and eggs available for use. Canada has established a new Agency to administer the Act. The legislation can be found at http://laws.justice.gc.ca/en/A-13.4/. See also the U.K.'s Human Fertilisation & Embryology Authority, at http://www.hfea.gov.uk/en/default.html. Differences in regulatory environments might affect the success

rates of IVF procedures in different countries. See Norbert Gleicher, Andrea Weghofer & David Barad, A Formal Comparison of the Practice of Assisted Reproductive Technologies between Europe and the USA, 21 Human Repro. 1945 (2006) (noting differences in ART success rates and suggesting relationship to difference in regulatory environments). See also June Carbone & Paige Gottheim, Markets, Subsidies, Regulation and Trust: Building Ethical Understandings into the Market for Fertility Services, 9 J. Gender Race & Just. 509 (2006); Alicia Ouelette et al., Lessons Across the Pond: Assisted Reproductive Technology in the United Kingdom and the United States, 31 Am. J.L. & Med. 419 (2005); Ellen Waldman, Cultural Priorities Revealed: The Development and Regulation of Assisted Reproduction in the United States and Israel, 16 Health Matrix 65 (2006). Differences in ART regulation have led to concerns about an international trade in reproductive services. See Note, 15 Minn. J. Int'l L. 263 (2006); Richard F. Storrow, Quests for Conception: Fertility Tourists, Globalization, and Feminist Legal Theory, 57 Hastings L.J. 295 (2005).

5. *Commentaries.* This is yet another area rich with commentaries. An early, influential article is John A. Robertson, Procreative Liberty and the Control of Conception, Pregnancy, and Childbirth, 69 Va. L. Rev. 405 (1983). Some more recent commentaries include R. Alta Charo, And Baby Makes Three — or Four, or Five, or Six: Redefining the Family After the Reprotech Revolution, 15 Wis. Women's L.J. 231 (2000); Janet L. Dolgin, Choice, Tradition, and the New Genetics: The Fragmentation of the Ideology of Family, 32 Conn. L. Rev. 523 (2000); Thomas H. Murray, What Are Families For? Getting to an Ethics of Reproductive Technology, Hastings Center Rep. 41 (May-June 2002) (suggesting that emphasis on procreative liberty risks disregard for the interests of children); Dorothy E. Roberts, Race and the New Reproduction, 47 Hastings L.J. 935 (1996); John A. Robertson, Children of Choice: Freedom and the New Reproductive Technologies (1994); John A. Robertson, Procreative Liberty and Harm to Offspring in Assisted Reproduction, 30 Am. J.L. & Med. 7 (2004); John A. Robertson, Procreative Liberty in the Era of Genomics, 29 Am. J.L. & Med. 439 (2003); E. Gary Spitko, The Constitutional Function of Biological Paternity: Evidence of Biological Mother's Consent to the Biological Father's Co-Parenting of Her Child, 48 Ariz. L. Rev. 97 (2006) (advancing a proposed rule for determining the parental status of participants in various assisted reproductive endeavors).

Notes: Genetics and Reproduction

1. *Genetic Testing.* Reproductive and genetic technologies can be combined, with interesting policy dilemmas as one major consequence. As noted supra, at page 431, the Human Genome Research Project reached an important milestone in 2000 with the completion of a draft map of the human genome. Researchers, ethicists, legislators, and regulators must now manage a rapid acceleration of the process of translating basic genetic information into new genetic tests, new genetic therapies, and new genetic possibilities. The identification of a particular gene's

action or impact on humans is often followed, at some later point, by a test designed to identify persons at risk for the trait or condition. Tests for sickle-cell anemia, Tay-Sachs disease, and cystic fibrosis are examples. Genetic tests can be a double-edged sword. They can provide important information to persons who are concerned with their own future health or who are considering whether to reproduce. The tests also create the possibility for discrimination by private actors, such as employers or insurers, and for coercive state interventions. Testing can also occur at various stages in reproduction, with ethical and religious concerns generally increasing at each stage. Individuals can be tested before donating their gametes, the pre-embryo can be tested after conception but before implantation, or the embryo and fetus can be tested after implantation. Genetic testing after implantation clearly raises the possibility of abortion, with all the attendant controversy.

A number of commentators have written about genetic testing and reproduction. See, e.g., Lori B. Andrews, Future Perfect (2001); Before Birth: Understanding Prenatal Screening (E. M. Ettorre ed., 2001); Carolyn Jacobs Chachkin, What Potent Blood: Non-Invasive Prenatal Genetic Diagnosis and the Transformation of Modern Prenatal Care, 33 Am. J.L. & Med. 9 (2007); Bob Heyman & Mette Henriksen, Risk, Age and Pregnancy: A Case Study of Prenatal Genetic Screening and Testing (2001); Barbara Katz Rothman, The Tentative Pregnancy: Prenatal Diagnosis and the Future of Motherhood (1986); President's Council on Bioethics, Reproduction and Responsibility: The Regulation of New Biotechnologies (2004); Sonia Mateu Suter, The Routinization of Prenatal Testing, 28 Am. J.L. & Med. 233 (2002); Symposium: Legal Liability in the Frontier of Genetic Testing, Parts I and II, 41 Jurimetrics 1-260 (2000-2001) (two issues).

2. *"Negative" vs. "Positive" Eugenics.* Persons who take advantage of prenatal screening may use information about their child's genetic characteristics in deciding whether to continue the pregnancy to term. See Dorothy C. Wertz et al., Attitudes toward Abortion among Parents of Children with Cystic Fibrosis, 81 Am. J. Pub. Health 992 (1991). Preimplantation genetic screening can be combined with IVF so that only genetically desirable embryos are implanted in a woman's uterus. See Amy Harmon, The DNA Age: Choosing Genes, Couples Cull Embryos to Halt Heritage of Cancer, N.Y. Times, Sept. 6, 2006, at sec. 1, pg. 1. Could a state restrict access to genetic screening tests in order to further its interest in protecting fetal life? The state would not restrict abortion per se, but merely limit parental access to information.

Should it matter whether parents are engaging in "negative" versus "positive" eugenics? In the first, parents seek to avoid some abnormal and seriously disabling genetic condition. In the second, they hope to acquire a child with some particularly socially desirable traits. Would a "negative" eugenic program discriminate against fetuses on the basis of their disability? Michael Malinowski, Coming into Being: Law, Ethics, and the Practice of Prenatal Genetic Screening, 45 Hastings L.J. 1435 (1994); Note, Regulating Preimplantation Genetic Diagnosis: The Pathologization Problem, 118 Harv. L. Rev. 2770 (2005). What if the parents sought to use these technologies to choose the gender of their child, perhaps by implanting only the embryos of the "correct" gender? Compare the discussion of sex selection and abortion, supra, page 431, and Judith F. Daar, ART and the Search for Perfectionism: On Selecting Gender, Genes, and Gametes, 9 J. Gender Race & Just. 241 (2005); Susannah Baruch et al., Genetic Testing of Embryos: Practices and Perspectives of U.S. IVF Clinics, Fertility and Sterility (July 10, 2007) (majority of surveyed IVF clinics will participate in sex selection at parental request).

3. *Genetic Engineering and Genetic Therapy.* At some future point, effective genetic engineering and genetic therapy technologies may be developed. While the terms are not always used consistently, "gene therapy" most often refers to treating a genetic disorder, either through traditional medical or genetic means. Genetic engineering typically refers to altering an individual's genes. Somatic genetic engineering or therapy involves changing the genetic content of a person's non-reproductive cells. Germ-line genetic engineering or therapy involves changing the genetic content of a person's reproductive cells or gametes. Germ-line genetic engineering could be very appealing to those who have serious genetic conditions that limit their ability or desire to reproduce. Yet the scientific risks and ethical concerns related to genetic engineering are greatest when the "treatment," perhaps more realistically called an "experiment," also involves future generations.

Should the federal government or state governments restrict access to these technologies? Should regulation distinguish between somatic cell therapy and germ-line therapy, assuming that researchers are able to confidently predict whether germ-line cells will be affected by a treatment? How should regulation proceed, perhaps with a permanent, total ban on germ-line research? See, e.g., George J. Annas et al., Protecting the Endangered Human: Toward an International Treaty Prohibiting Cloning and Inheritable Alterations, 28 Am. J. L. & Med. 151 (2002); Allen Buchanan et al., From Chance to Choice: Genetics and Justice (2002); Michael J. Reiss, What Sort of People Do We Want? The Ethics of Changing People through Genetic Engineering, 13 Notre Dame J.L. Ethics & Pub. Pol'y 63 (1999); Michael Sandal, The Case Against Perfection: Ethics in an Age of Genetic Engineering (2007).

Assuming that research goes forward, are you concerned about equality of access to genetic screening tests and/or genetic therapies? What if access to genetic technologies could reify class differences—permitting the wealthy to ensure the future success of their offspring through positive genetic engineering? Is this any different from current practices that permit the wealthy to send their children to expensive, private schools? See generally LeRoy Walters & Julie Palmer, The Ethics of Human Gene Therapy (1996).

4. *Genetic Enhancement.* Advances in genetics may also empower humans to "enhance" their offspring. Enhancement may occur by taking genes associated with desirable traits from third parties for incorporation into one's gametes or embryos. "Enhancement" might also be achieved through the use of non-human genetic materials or engineered materials. Although all such research would be controversial, incorporation of novel genes into the germ line once again would be the most risky, controversial, and morally problematic. See, e.g., Harry Adams, A Human Germline Modification Scale, 32 J.L. Med & Ethics 164 (2004); Roberta M. Berry, Genetic Enhancement in the Twenty-first Century: Three Problems in

Legal Imagining, 34 Wake Forest L. Rev. 715 (1999); Maxwell J. Mehlman, Any DNA to Declare? Regulating Offshore Access to Genetic Enhancement, 28 Am. J. L. & Med. 179 (2002); Maxwell J. Mehlman, The Law of Above Averages: Leveling the New Genetic Enhancement Playing Field, 34 Wake Forest L. Rev. 561 (1999); Symposium on Manufactured Humanity: The Ethics and Legality of Stem Cell Research, Bioengineering, and Human Cloning, 65 Alb. L. Rev. 587-855 (2002); Daniel L. Tobey, What's Really Wrong with Genetic Enhancement: A Second Look at Our Posthuman Future, 6 Yale J.L. & Tech. 54 (2003-2004).

2. Gamete Donation

The donation of gametes — sperm and ova — encompasses old and new uses of reproductive technology. Artificial insemination (AI), also known as intrauterine insemination (IUI), is the oldest assisted reproductive technique; in its simplest form, it requires no medical expertise or specialized equipment. The two major types of IUI used today involve (1) using the sperm of the husband or male partner (AIH); or (2) using the sperm of a third-party donor (AID). AIH can compensate for certain types of male infertility. AID provides a substitute source of male gametes in the case of profound male infertility or compensates for the absence of a male partner for single heterosexual women or lesbians. See Walter Wadlington, Artificial Insemination: The Dangers of a Poorly Kept Secret, 64 Nw. U. L. Rev. 777 (1970). Most of the legal and policy debates have focused on AID. In the Internet age, it should not be surprising that sperm banks offer information about potential donors online. Couples or single women searching for a suitable donor may select various donor characteristics, may hear an audiotape of the donor's voice, and may even be able to see a donor's baby picture. See Jennifer Egan, Wanted: A Few Good Sperm, N.Y. Times Magazine, March 19, 2006, at 46.

Donation of an egg (also called an oocyte) is much more medically complex and invasive. Prospective donors must undergo medical treatment to stimulate their ovaries to produce multiple eggs. The donor is monitored through ultrasound exams and blood tests to determine whether there are a sufficient number of eggs to warrant harvesting. The eggs must be retrieved from inside the woman's body using an ultrasound-guided needle or through a laparoscopic procedure. Donated eggs typically are fertilized in the laboratory (using in vitro fertilization (IVF)), creating a preembryo that can either be frozen or implanted in a woman's uterus. (The legal and ethical aspects of embryo donation and use will be discussed in great detail below, at pages 522-530.) Researchers recently have begun to have success freezing and thawing ova for use in later fertilization procedures, but the technological problems associated with freezing unfertilized eggs are still significant. John K. Jain & Richard Paulson, Oocyte Preservation, 86 Fertility & Sterility 1037 (2006). There are as yet no "egg banks" on the Internet, although there are Web sites offering to match infertile women with prospective egg donors having certain characteristics.

Gamete donation is governed by federal regulations adopted in 2004 and the voluntary guidelines of professional organizations. 21 C.F.R. §§1271.45-1271.90 (2006) (donor eligibility and screening rules); and American Society for

Reproductive Medicine (ASRM), 2006 Guidelines for Gamete and Embryo Donation, 85 Fertility & Sterility S38 (Supp. 4 2006) The federal regulations require entities that provide ART to register with the government; organizations that participate in gamete donation are subject to inspection and other oversight. The regulations and guidelines generally require evaluation and testing of the gamete donor for certain communicable and genetic conditions. The ASRM guidelines also require screening and evaluation of potential gamete recipients. Are health care providers who refuse to provide reproductive technology services to persons with hereditary conditions or disabilities engaged in impermissible disability-based discrimination under the ADA? See Carl H. Coleman, Conceiving Harm: Disability Discrimination in Assisted Reproductive Technologies, 50 UCLA L. Rev. 17 (2002).

Who is the father of a child produced through IUI? Should a child produced within a marriage be presumed to be the child of the husband? Should genetic parentage govern over social norms or the parties' expectations? The artificial insemination provisions of the 1973 version of the Uniform Parentage Act (UPA), adopted in some form or another in most states, were designed to eliminate ambiguity and to relieve prospective donors of the risk of unwanted paternity. National Conference of Commissioners on Uniform State Laws (NCCUSL), UPA §5 (1973). The 1973 Act provided a legal mechanism for recognizing the infertile husband as the father of a child born through insemination of his wife using donor sperm. The husband was required to give written consent, the procedure had to be performed under the supervision of a physician, and the records were subject to inspection by a court upon a showing of good cause. Under the 1973 UPA, the sperm donor was not considered the father so long as the sperm was provided to a licensed physician for insemination of a "married woman." This restrictive language placed the donor at risk if the sperm was used in the insemination of a woman who was not legally married — and consequently made IUI for single or lesbian women difficult to obtain in some states. Other states adopted a version of the rule that simply omitted the word "married," eliminating the legal barrier to the use of IUI for unmarried women. Many providers nonetheless continued to deny access to these services to unmarried women. See Holly J. Harlow, Paternalism without Paternity: Discrimination against Single Women Seeking Artificial Insemination by Donor, 6 S. Cal. Rev. L. & Women's Stud. 173 (1996).

Until recently, the law presumed that the woman who gave birth to a child was the child's mother. The 1973 UPA did not consider the legal consequences of egg donation, IVF, or gestational surrogacy. Courts were forced to resolve the first disputes without the assistance of special legislation. NCCUSL adopted a Uniform Act on the Status of Children of Assisted Conception in the late 1980s; the Act treated egg and sperm donation roughly equivalently. States began to enact gamete and embryo donation provisions in the early 1990s.

The Uniform Parentage Act has been significantly revised. The 2002 Act provides:

> **§701. Scope of Article.** This [article] does not apply to the birth of a child conceived by means of sexual intercourse[, or as the result of a [lawful] gestational agreement . . .].

§702. Parental Status of Donor. A donor is not a parent of a child conceived by means of assisted reproduction.

§703. Paternity of Child of Assisted Reproduction. A man who provides sperm for, or consents to, assisted reproduction by a woman as provided in Section 704 with the intent to be the parent of her child, is a parent of the resulting child.

§704. Consent to Assisted Reproduction.

(a) Consent by a woman, and a man who intends to be a parent of a child born to the woman by assisted reproduction must be in a record signed by the woman and the man. This requirement does not apply to a donor.

(b) Failure [sic] a man to sign a consent required by subsection (a), before or after birth of the child, does not preclude a finding of paternity if the woman and the man, during the first two years of the child's life resided together in the same household with the child and openly held out the child as their own.

The Act also limits the period of time in which the husband can challenge his paternity following the use of assisted conception, with some exceptions. UPA §705 (2002), available at http://www.law.upenn.edu/bll/ulc/upa/final2002.pdf.

Notes: Gamete Donation

1. *Gamete Donation.* The trend in the law is to treat the donation of sperm and eggs as legally similar. Do you agree? Should the greater degree of medical and physical intrusion involved in egg donation have any legal significance? See generally Anne Reichman Schiff, Solomonic Decisions in Egg Donation: Unscrambling the Conundrum of Legal Maternity, 80 Iowa L. Rev. 265 (1995). Should it be permissible to compensate gamete donors? The 2002 UPA provides that a "donor" is "an individual who produces eggs or sperm used for assisted reproduction, whether or not for consideration." UPA §102(8) (2002). Sperm donors typically are compensated less than $100 per deposit; egg donors might receive $3,500 to $5,000 per cycle, plus expenses. Should the amount of the compensation be regulated? Ethics Committee of the ASRM, Financial Incentives in Recruitment of Oocyte Donors, 74 Fertility & Sterility 216 (2000) (suggesting that payments over $5,000 require justification and that payments over $10,000 are inappropriate) See also Barbara L. Atwell, The Modern Age of Informed Consent, 40 U. Rich. L. Rev. 591 (2006) (expressing concern about sale of eggs by college-aged women); John A. Robertson, Compensation and Egg Donation for Research, 86 Fertility & Sterility 1573 (2006) (summarizing current rules and practices). For a discussion of restrictions on the recruitment of gamete donors in other countries, see the sources cited supra at page 513.

Both the 1973 and 2002 versions of the UPA refuse to apply the "donation" rules when the child is conceived through sexual intercourse. See UPA §701 (2002). Why doesn't the UPA permit the parties to execute a document indicating that the sexual activity is for the purpose of donating gametes? The Pennsylvania Supreme Court granted an appeal in a complex case involving a donor whose sperm was used for in vitro fertilization. Among other things, the decision may directly confront the possible conflict between the treatment of sperm donors and the usual rule providing that parents cannot bargain away the support rights of their children. See Ferguson v. McKiernan, 855 A.2d 121 (Pa. Super. 2004), appeal granted in part, 868 A.2d 378 (Pa. 2005). How should courts and legislatures treat embryo donations?

2. *Difficulties in the Application of the 1973 UPA Approach.* The 1973 UPA imposed a variety of requirements, such as physician supervision and written consent by the husband. Where the criteria were not satisfied, the donor might be given — or forced to accept — parental rights and obligations. Cf. Jhordan C. v. Mary K., 224 Cal. Rptr. 530 (Cal. Ct. App. 1986); Weaver v. Guinn, 31 P.3d 1119 (Or. Ct. App. 2001). Where there have been technical violations of the statute, in a manner agreed to by both husband and wife, courts sometimes reached the statutory results through equitable doctrines such as estoppel or ratification. See, e. g., K.B. v. N.B., 811 S.W.2d 634 (Tex. Ct. App. 1991), *cert. denied*, 504 U.S. 918 (1992). Adherence to the criteria, on the other hand, did not necessarily shield the participants from the claims of donors seeking parental rights. See McIntyre v. Crouch, 780 P.2d 239 (Or. Ct. App. 1989) (termination of donor's parental rights might be unconstitutional where "donor" argues that sperm was provided with understanding that he would be considered father). See generally Annotation, 83 A.L.R.4th 295 (1991).

In recent years, there has been a resurgence of litigation surrounding some of the implications of IUI for nontraditional families. The use of IUI by lesbian couples created a new wave of litigation testing the legal recognition of the nonbiological lesbian parent of the resulting child. See, e.g., Kristine H. v. Lisa R., 117 P.3d 690 (Cal. 2005) (birth mother estopped from contesting maternity of her former partner with whom she had previously obtained a stipulated judgment declaring that both were the parents of a child born through AI); K.M. v. E.G., 117 P.3d 673 (Cal. 2005) (woman who provided ova to her female partner for in vitro fertilization is a legal parent of the children born through this arrangement along with the birth mother; law terminating parental rights of sperm donor not applied to the partner who donated ova); Elisa B. v. The Superior Court of El Dorado County, 117 P.3d 660 (Cal. 2005) (woman is legally a parent despite lack of biological connection based on conduct holding the children born to her female partner through AI as her own). See E. Gary Spitko, The Constitutional Function of Biological Paternity: Evidence of the Biological Mother's Consent to the Biological Father's Co-Parenting of Her Child, 48 Ariz. L. Rev. 97 (2006).

3. *Changes in the 2002 UPA.* The 2002 UPA had been adopted by five states as of early 2007; it may or may not be adopted by other states. If adopted, it will help to resolve some, but not all, of the issues that have arisen under the 1973 UPA. The 2002 UPA makes clear that a donor is not the legal parent whether or not the assisted reproduction participants are married. The revised UPA also provides that donors have no parental rights and no right to seek such rights, UPA §702 cmt., yet the language is unlikely to deter courts from resolving fraud or misrepresentation claims brought by sperm donors who want to maintain a relationship with their biological offspring. See note 2, supra. The new Act also eliminates the requirement that the donor provide his sperm to a physician. UPA §102(8) (2002). The 2002 UPA continues the presumption that a woman who gives birth to a child is

the mother of the child, unless the child is conceived as a part of a gestational surrogacy contract authorized and approved under state law. UPA §201 (2002). This presumption provides additional protection for egg donors, by emphasizing that the woman who gives birth is the mother rather than the donor. Would you suggest any additional changes to the UPA? Does the right to procreate noted in *Skinner* have any impact on the enforceability of any aspect of the UPA?

4. *Tort and Criminal Liability.* Will a physician be liable for genetically defective semen? Current guidelines suggest screening donors for family histories of genetic disorders as well as for sexually transmitted diseases such as HIV. See American Society for Reproductive Medicine (ASRM), 2006 Guidelines for Gamete and Embryo Donation, 85 Fertility & Sterility S38 (Supp. 4 2006). Tort claims can be difficult to assert if donors can remain anonymous. But see Johnson v. Superior Court, 95 Cal. Rptr. 2d 864 (2000) (tort action claiming failure to disclose sperm donor had family history of autosomal dominant polycystic kidney disease; court compels donor's deposition and record production). There are occasional errors in the donation process. See, e.g., Harnicher v. University of Utah Medical Center, 962 P.2d 67 (Utah 1998) (defendants allegedly used wrong donor's sperm, resulting in triplets; insufficient proof of negligent infliction of emotional distress); Cynthia R. Mabry, "Who Is My Real Father?" The Delicate Task of Identifying a Father and Parenting Children Created from an In Vitro Mix-Up, 18 Nat'l Black L.J. 1 (2004-2005). Could a physician be held liable in tort for a violation of the old UPA's provisions requiring a husband's consent to IUI? See Shin v. Kong, 95 Cal. Rptr. 2d 304 (Ct. App. 2000) (no). For three bizarre cases, see James v. Jacobson, 6 F.3d 233 (4th Cir. 1993) (noting criminal prosecution of physician who used his own sperm in providing AI services to more than seventy women); Judy Siegel-Itkovich, Doctor's Licence Suspended After He Admitted Removing Ova Without Consent, 334 Brit. Med. J. 557 (2007) (physician removed hundreds of ova without patient consent for use in ART); Stone v. Regents, University of California, 92 Cal. Rptr. 2d 94 (Ct. App. 1999) (physician allegedly engaged in "egg stealing"). Should sperm banks be held liable for the negligent destruction of donated sperm? How would you measure the damages? See Kurchner v. State Farm Fire & Casualty Co., 858 So. 2d 1220 (Fla. App. 2003) (destruction of sperm not "bodily injury" and loss not covered under insurance policy).

5. *Posthumous Reproduction.* The ability to donate and store gametes (and embryos) means that it is possible to parent a child after one's death. What ethical and legal issues are raised by this possibility? One key question involves control—who has the right to decide whether to use stored gametes for reproductive purposes? See Hecht v. Superior Court, 59 Cal. Rptr. 2d 222 (Ct. App. 1996), *review denied* (Cal. 1997) (after a six-year battle, a deceased man's frozen sperm were awarded to his girlfriend as designated in his will, over the objection of the decedent's adult children); John A. Robertson, Posthumous Reproduction, 69 Ind. L.J. 1027 (1994); Anne Reichman Schiff, Arising from the Dead: Challenges of Posthumous Procreation, 75 N.C. L. Rev. 901 (1997); Carson Strong, Ethical and Legal Aspects of Sperm Retrieval after Death or Persistent Vegetative State, 27 J.L. Med. & Ethics 347 (1999).

The posthumous birth raises another set of issues: should the child be considered the legal child of the decedent? What is the impact on the child's ability to inherit or to take part in family/survivors benefits programs? The traditional rule is that a man cannot be the father of a child born more than nine to ten months after his death. The 2002 UPA provides:

§707. **Parental Status of Deceased Individual.** If an individual who consented in a record to be a parent by assisted reproduction dies before placement of eggs, sperm, or embryos, the deceased individual is not a parent of the resulting child unless the deceased spouse consented in a record that if assisted reproduction were to occur after death, the deceased individual would be a parent of the child.

See also Woodward v. Commissioner of Social Security, 760 N.E.2d 257 (Mass. 2002) (eligibility of posthumously conceived children for federal social security survivor benefits depends on state inheritance law; Massachusetts court holds that children can inherit if wife establishes genetic relationship and decedent's consent to posthumous reproduction and support); Gillett-Netting v. Barnhart, 371 F.3d 593 (9th Cir. 2004) (posthumously conceived children were "children" under Social Security Act and were presumed dependent on deceased for purposes of entitlement to child's insurance benefits). See also James E. Bailey, An Analytic Framework for Resolving the Issues Raised by the Interaction between Reproductive Technology and the Law of Inheritance, 47 DePaul L. Rev. 743 (1998); Sharona Hoffman & Andrew P. Morriss, Birth After Death: Perpetuities and the New Reproductive Technologies, 38 Ga. L. Rev. 575 (2004); Michael K. Elliott, Tales of Parenthood from the Crypt: The Predicament of the Posthumously Conceived Child, 39 Real Prop. Prob. & Tr. J. 47 (2004).

6. *Anonymity.* Artificial insemination has a long history, and the early presumption was that anonymity was a necessary part of the arrangement. Anonymity helped to ensure that the sperm donor would not be held liable for child support in an era of ambiguous obligations. Anonymity also allowed the receiving couple to both claim parentage over the child born as a result of AI and could help to conceal the male partner's infertility in a less sympathetic era. Yet the legal and social climate has changed considerably in the past few decades. Adopted children and those who have given children up for adoption have pushed for the creation of mechanisms that allow adopted children to learn the identity of their birth parents. See Elizabeth J. Samuels, The Idea of Adoption: An Inquiry into the History of Adult Adoptee Access to Birth Records, 53 Rutgers L. Rev. 367 (2001). Should the open adoption and adoption registry concepts be mirrored in the world of gamete donation? Ethics Committee of the American Society for Reproductive Medicine, 81 Fertility & Sterility 527 (2004); Amy Harmon, Are You My Sperm Donor? Few Clinics Will Say, N.Y. Times, Jan. 20, 2006, at A1; Note, 80 Tex. L. Rev. 365 (2001).

3. In Vitro Fertilization and Frozen Embryos

In vitro fertilization (IVF) involves the fertilization of eggs by sperm in a laboratory setting. The first known "test tube" baby was born in the late 1970s.

The birth was controversial. A congressional committee held hearings on the topic of federal funding for related research projects. See, e.g., Walter Wadlington, Artificial Conception: The Challenge for Family Law, 69 Va. L. Rev. 465 (1983). Critics argued that IVF was unnatural, that it supplanted God in the creation of new life, that it could lead to embryo farms, and that children born from IVF might have genetic or other health problems. Thirty years later, IVF has become an accepted infertility procedure. More than 100,000 cycles of IVF were performed in 2003, resulting in the birth of nearly 50,000 children. Does this illustrate what philosopher Bertrand Russell once observed (in An Outline of Intellectual Rubbish: A Hilarious Catalogue of Organized and Individual Stupidity 20 (1943)), that "every advance in civilization has been denounced as unnatural while it was recent"?

IVF is physically and emotionally taxing for participants. The woman providing the eggs (who may either be a donor or the intended parent) must undergo the hormone therapy and egg extraction procedures described supra at page 535. These hormone treatments cause ovarian hyperstimulation syndrome in "less than 5% of IVF cycles"; the syndrome ordinarily resolves within a few weeks but in very rare cases can lead to death. Bradley J. Van Voorhis, In Vitro Fertilization, 356 New Eng. J. Med. 379, 382 (2007) (video of oocyte extraction available online). The man providing the sperm (either the donor or the intended parent) must undergo screening and sample collection. The intended carrier of the embryo — either the gestational surrogate or the intended mother — must undergo treatment to ensure that her uterus is prepared to receive the embryo at the time of implantation (which may occur soon after fertilization or after unfreezing stored embryos). There are two additional, related forms of treatment that are less commonly used: GIFT (gamete intrafallopian transfer), in which the gametes are placed in the fallopian tube, where it is hoped that fertilization will occur; and ZIFT (zygote intrafallopian transfer), in which a fertilized egg is given an opportunity to undergo cell division to become a zygote in the laboratory before being placed in the fallopian tube.

"Multiple births are the most frequent complication of IVF, contributing to a virtual epidemic of multiple gestations in the United States." Bradley J. Van Voorhis, supra, at 382. IVF is associated with multiple births because physicians seeking to achieve a pregnancy often transfer multiple embryos in one cycle in hopes that at least one will be retained and the pregnancy brought to term. Multiple gestations are more risky for both the pregnant woman and the resulting children, who may be born with low birth weight and other special medical needs. Yet even singleton pregnancies induced through IVF are associated with higher rates of complications and "some studies have suggested that assisted reproductive technology is associated with an increased risk of birth defects." Id; Allen A. Mitchell, Infertility Treatment — More Risks and Challenges, 346 New Eng. J. Med. 769 (2002) (discussing recent studies). Recent developments include a trend toward reducing the number of embryos transferred or transferring a later-stage embryo called a blastocyst.

These procedures are fairly expensive. A single cycle of IVF can cost $10,000 or more. Given a 28 percent success rate per cycle, expenses of $40,000 to $50,000 per live birth are common. Van Voorhis, supra; Tarun Jain et al., Insurance Coverage and Outcomes of In Vitro Fertilization, 347 New Eng. J. Med.

661 (2002). Many people would not be able to afford IVF if required to pay out of pocket; health insurance coverage for IVF is therefore an important issue. Historically, insurance companies argued that IVF procedures were excluded as "experimental" or that they were not covered "treatments" because they did not address the underlying medical condition of infertility and required "treatment" of third parties (such as the sperm donor). The more common current technique is to include a specific exclusion for infertility treatment within the health insurance plan or contract. Peter J. Neumann, Should Health Insurance Cover IVF? Issues and Options, 22 J. Health Pol. Pol'y & L. 1215 (1997); Edward L. Raymond, Jr., Annot., Coverage of Artificial Insemination Procedures or Other Infertility Treatments by Health, Sickness, or Hospitalization Insurance, 80 A.L.R.4th 1059 (1990). A few states require that insurance contracts sold within the state provide coverage for IVF, although this requirement cannot be applied to self-insured employee benefit plans. Neumann, supra, at 1217. Do health plans limiting or denying coverage for infertility treatment violate the Americans with Disabilities Act or the Pregnancy Discrimination Act? See Saks v. Franklin Covey Co., 316 F.3d 337 (2nd Cir. 2003) (holding that exclusions of coverage for male and female infertility treatments did not violate the Pregnancy Discrimination Act or Title VII's ban on sex discrimination). For an article on whether infertility treatment costs can be deducted as a medical expense under the Internal Revenue Code, see Katherine T. Pratt, Inconceivable? Deducting the Costs of Fertility Treatment, 89 Cornell L. Rev. 1121 (2004).

Consumers of infertility services may be vulnerable to unscrupulous practitioners. Congressional concern with this problem led to passage of the Fertility Clinic Success Rate and Certification Act of 1992, Pub. L. No. 102-493, codified at 42 U.S.C.A. §§263a-1 to -7 (2006). Clinic success rates are available online. See, e.g., http://www.cdc.gov/mmwr/preview/mmwrhtml/ss5504a1.htm. See also Judith Daar, Regulating Reproductive Technologies: Panacea or Paper Tiger, 34 Hous. L. Rev. 609 (1997); President's Council on Bioethics, Reproduction and Responsibility: The Regulation of New Biotechnologies 210-214 (2004) (recommendations designed to strengthen Act).

Problems: Ethical Aspects of IVF

- *The Risk of Failure vs. the Risk of Sextuplets.* How many embryos should be transferred to a woman's uterus at one time? Should the number be set by individual physicians, ethical guidelines, or a standard of care enforceable in a malpractice action? The problem arises in part because of the relatively high expense and low success rate of IVF. Physicians might transfer two to four embryos in hopes of achieving a single live birth, depending on the age of the woman and other factors. But multiple embryo transfers increase the risk of a multiple pregnancy, which brings greater health risks for the woman and fetuses. The "remedy" is selective abortion, discussed supra at pages 448-449. Should the birth of sextuplets become prima facie evidence of unethical or negligent conduct by an infertility center? See Practice Committee of the Society for Assisted Reproductive Technology and the Practice Committee of the American

Society for Reproductive Medicine, Guidelines on Number of Embryos Transferred, 86 Fertility & Sterility S51 (Supp. 4 2006); President's Council on Bioethics, Reproduction and Responsibility: The Regulation of New Biotechnologies 215-216 (2004) (recommending a reduction "in the incidence of multiple embryo transfers and resulting multiple births, a known source of high risk and discernible harm to the resulting children") (emphasis omitted)

- *Postmenopausal Reproduction.* Should access to IVF be restricted based on the age of the intended mother? Researchers can use hormone therapy to sustain a pregnancy even after menopause. See Shari Roan, Woman Gives Birth at 63, L.A. Times, Apr. 24, 1997, at A1 (USC physicians announce birth of baby girl to 63-year-old woman). The USC pregnancy was produced using a donor egg; the recipient's own ovaries stopped producing new eggs at menopause. Is the ethical analysis the same for men and women seeking to reproduce later in life? See Ethics Committee of the American Society for Reproductive Medicine, Oocyte Donation to Postmenopausal Women, 82 Fertility & Sterility S254 (Supp. 1 2004); I. Goold, Should Older and Postmenopausal Women Have Access to Assisted Reproductive Technology?, 24 Monash Bioethics Rev. 27 (2005).

- *Preimplantation Genetic Diagnosis.* Genetic tests can be used to select which preembryos will be implanted. Much of the commentary by ethicists has focused on the use of tests to avoid the implantation of embryos with disabling genetic conditions or to select offspring of a certain sex. See page 516. Are there any limits on parental ability to select for traits that might be considered to be disabilities? Should it be permissible for deaf parents to use PGD to ensure that they have deaf offspring? Consider the "rights-based" analysis of reproduction, which focuses on the right of the parent to reproduce and to use technology to achieve a healthy child. Under a rights-based approach, when may the state interfere with parental reproductive choices? Could a parent be held liable for intentionally selecting an injurious genetic characteristic for their child? Now consider an ethics-based approach to the problems of reproduction. What ethical norms would you apply to a parent's use of reproductive technologies? How would you capture the interests of the child and society? See Susannah Baruch et al., Genetic Testing of Embryos: Practices and Perspectives of U.S. IVF Clinics, Fertility and Sterility (July 10, 2007) (small percentage of surveyed IVF clinics reported receiving such requests); Carina Dennis, Deaf by Design, 431 Nature 894 (2004); M. Häyry, There Is a Difference Between Selecting a Deaf Embryo and Deafening a Hearing Child, 30 J. Med. Ethics 510 (2004).

- *Children of the Unborn.* Tissue from the ovaries of aborted female fetuses can be used to create a new life. Other than the obvious opportunities for impossible brain teasers, is there any moral or policy problem with being the child of someone who was never born? Would *Roe* and *Casey* bar state attempts to restrict the use of fetal reproductive tissue? See Jonathan Hersey, Comment, Enigma of the Unborn Mother: Legal and Ethical Considerations of Aborted Fetal Ovarian Tissue and Ova Transplantations, 43 UCLA L. Rev. 159 (1995); John A. Robertson, Ethical Issues in

Ovarian Transplantation and Donation, 73 Fertility & Sterility 443, 445 (2000).

- *Embryo "Cloning" or "Twinning."* This type of "cloning" differs from that discussed infra at pages 560-565 because it begins with an egg that has been fertilized by sperm. Early embryos can be stimulated to divide and can be separated to create artificial identical twins. One of the twin's embryos could be frozen, allowing the twin to be born long after its genetically identical sibling. Does this process present any ethical or legal dilemmas? See Andrea L. Bonnicksen, Ethical and Policy Issues in Human Embryo Twinning, 4 Cambridge Q. Healthcare Ethics 268 (1995).

■ J.B. v. M.B. & C.C.
783 A.2d 707 (N.J. 2001)

PORITZ, C.J.

In this case, a divorced couple disagree about the disposition of seven preembryos . . . that remain in storage after the couple, during their marriage, undertook in vitro fertilization procedures. We must first decide whether the husband and wife have entered into an enforceable contract that is now determinative on the disposition issue. If not, we must consider how such conflicts should be resolved by our courts.

Although the reproductive technology to accomplish in vitro fertilization has existed since the 1970s, there is little case law to guide us in our inquiry. . . .

J.B. and M.B. were married in February 1992. After J.B. suffered a miscarriage early in the marriage, the couple encountered difficulty conceiving a child and sought medical advice from the Jefferson Center for Women's Specialties. Although M.B. did not have infertility problems, J.B. learned that she had a condition that prevented her from becoming pregnant. On that diagnosis, the couple decided to attempt in vitro fertilization at the Cooper Center for In Vitro Fertilization, P.C. (the Cooper Center). . . .

The Cooper Center's consent form describes the procedure . . . . The consent form also contains language discussing the control and disposition of the preembryos. . . .

The in vitro fertilization procedure was carried out in May 1995 and resulted in eleven preembryos. Four were transferred to J.B. and seven were cryopreserved. J.B. became pregnant . . . and gave birth to the couple's daughter on March 19, 1996. In September 1996, however, the couple separated, and J.B. informed M.B. that she wished to have the remaining preembryos discarded. M.B. did not agree.

J.B. filed a complaint for divorce on November 25, 1996, in which she sought an order from the court "with regard to the . . . frozen embryos." In a counterclaim filed on November 24, 1997, M.B. demanded judgment compelling his wife "to allow the . . . frozen embryos currently in storage to be implanted or donated to other infertile couples." J.B. filed a motion for summary judgment on the preembryo issue in April 1998 alleging, in a certification filed with the motion, that she had intended to use the preembryos solely within her marriage to M.B. She stated . . . "I endured the in vitro process and agreed to preserve the preembryos for our use in the context of an intact family." . . . M.B., in a cross-motion filed in

July 1998, described his understanding very differently. . . . His certification stated: . . . "For me, as a Catholic, the I.V.F. procedure itself posed a dilemma. We discussed this issue extensively and had agreed that no matter what happened the eggs would be either utilized by us or by other infertile couples." . . .

The couple's final judgment of divorce, entered in September 1998, resolved all issues except disposition of the preembryos. Shortly thereafter, the trial court granted J.B.'s motion for summary judgment on that issue. . . . Because the husband was "fully able to father a child," and because he sought control of the preembryos "merely to donate them to another couple," the court concluded that the wife had "the greater interest and should prevail."

The Appellate Division affirmed. . . . We . . . now modify and affirm the judgment of the Appellate Division. . . .

M.B. contends that the judgment of the court below violated his constitutional rights to procreation and the care and companionship of his children. He also contends that his constitutional rights outweigh J.B.'s right not to procreate because her right to bodily integrity is not implicated, as it would be in a case involving abortion. He asserts that religious convictions regarding preservation of the preembryos, and the State's interest in protecting potential life, take precedence over his former wife's more limited interests. Finally, M.B. argues that the Appellate Division should have enforced the clear agreement between the parties to give the preembryos a chance at life. He believes that his procedural due process rights have been violated because he was not given an opportunity to introduce evidence demonstrating the existence of that agreement, and because summary judgment is inappropriate in a case involving novel issues of fact and law.

J.B. argues that the Appellate Division properly held that any alleged agreement between the parties to use or donate the preembryos would be unenforceable as a matter of public policy. She contends that New Jersey has "long recognized that individuals should not be bound by agreements requiring them to enter into family relationships or [that] seek to regulate personal intimate decisions relating to parenthood and family life." J.B. also argues that in the absence of an express agreement establishing the disposition of the preembryos, a court should not imply that an agreement exists. It is J.B.'s position that requiring use or donation of the preembryos would violate her constitutional right not to procreate. Discarding the preembryos, on the other hand, would not significantly affect M.B.'s right to procreate because he is fertile and capable of fathering another child. . . .

M.B. contends that he and J.B. entered into an agreement to use or donate the preembryos, and J.B. disputes the existence of any such agreement. As an initial matter, then, we must decide whether this case involves a contract for the disposition of the cryopreserved preembryos resulting from in vitro fertilization. We begin, therefore, with the consent form provided to J.B. and M.B. by the Cooper Center. . . . That form states, among other things:

> The control and disposition of the embryos belongs to the Patient and her Partner. You will be asked to execute the attached legal statement regarding control and disposition of cryopreserved embryos.

The attachment, executed by J.B. and M.B., provides further detail in respect of the parties' "control and disposition":

> I, J.B. (patient), and M.B. (partner) agree that all control, direction, and ownership of our tissues will be relinquished to the IVF Program under the following circumstances:
>
> 1. A dissolution of our marriage by court order, unless the court specifies who takes control and direction of the tissues, or
> 2. In the event of death of both of the above named individuals, or unless provisions are made in a Will, or
> 3. When the patient is no longer capable of sustaining a normal pregnancy, however, the couple has the right to keep embryos maintained for up to two years before making a decision [regarding a] "host womb" or
> 4. At any time by our/my election which shall be in writing, or
> 5. When a patient fails to pay periodic embryo maintenance payment.

The consent form, and more important, the attachment, do not manifest a clear intent by J.B. and M.B. regarding disposition of the preembryos in the event of "[a] dissolution of [their] marriage." Although the attachment indicates that the preembryos "will be relinquished" to the clinic if the parties divorce, it carves out an exception that permits the parties to obtain a court order directing disposition of the preembryos. . . . Clearly, the thrust of the document signed by J.B. and M.B. is that the Cooper Center obtains control over the preembryos unless the parties choose otherwise in a writing, or unless a court specifically directs otherwise in an order of divorce.

The conditional language employed in the attachment stands in sharp contrast to the language in the informed consents provided by the hospital in Kass v. Kass, 696 N.E.2d 174 (N.Y. 1998). . . . In *Kass*, the New York Court of Appeals enforced a couple's memorialized decision to donate their preembryos for scientific research when they could not agree on disposition. . . . The court found that the parties had signed an unambiguous contract to relinquish control of their preembryos to the hospital for research purposes in the event of a dispute. . . . In that case, the parties executed several forms before undergoing in vitro fertilization. . . . Informed Consent No. 2 stated: "In the event of divorce, we understand that legal ownership of any stored . . . [preembryos] must be determined in a property settlement and will be released as directed by order of a court of competent jurisdiction." Addendum No. 2-1 further elaborated:

> In the event that we . . . are unable to make a decision regarding the disposition . . . we now indicate our desire for the disposition of . . . [preembryos] and direct the IVF Program to (choose one):
>
>> Our frozen pre-zygotes may be examined by the IVF Program for biological studies and be disposed of by the IVF Program for approved research investigation as determined by the IVF Program.

Moreover, before the parties divorced, they drafted and signed an "'uncontested divorce' agreement" indicating that their preembryos "should be disposed of [in] the manner outlined in our consent form and [neither party] will lay claim to custody of these . . . [preembryos]." . . .

The *Kass* court found that the parties had agreed to donate their preembryos for IVF research if they could not together decide on another disposition. . . . That holding is based on language entirely different from the language in the form in this case. Here, the parties have agreed that on the dissolution of their marriage the Cooper Center obtains control of the preembryos unless the court specifically makes another determination. Under that provision, the parties have sought another determination from the court.

M.B. asserts, however, that he and J.B. jointly intended another disposition. Because there are no other writings that express the parties' intentions, M.B. asks the Court either to remand for an evidentiary hearing on that issue or to consider his certified statement. . . .

We find no need for a remand to determine the parties' intentions at the time of the in vitro fertilization process. Assuming that it would be possible to enter into a valid agreement at that time irrevocably deciding the disposition of preembryos in circumstances such as we have here, a formal, unambiguous memorialization of the parties' intentions would be required to confirm their joint determination. The parties do not contest the lack of such a writing. We hold, therefore, that J.B. and M.B. never entered into a separate binding contract providing for the disposition of the cryopreserved preembryos now in the possession of the Cooper Center.

In essence, J.B. and M.B. have agreed only that on their divorce the decision in respect of control, and therefore disposition, of their cryopreserved preembryos will be directed by the court. In this area, however, there are few guideposts for decision-making. Advances in medical technology have far outstripped the development of legal principles to resolve the inevitable disputes arising out of the new reproductive opportunities now available. For infertile couples, those opportunities may present the only way to have a biological family. Yet, at the point when a husband and wife decide to begin the in vitro fertilization process, they are unlikely to anticipate divorce or to be concerned about the disposition of preembryos on divorce. As they are both contributors of the genetic material comprising the preembryos, the decision should be theirs to make. See generally Davis v. Davis, 842 S.W.2d 588, 597 (Tenn. 1992) (stating that donors should retain decision-making authority with respect to their preembryos). . . .

But what if, as here, the parties disagree. Without guidance from the Legislature, we must consider a means by which courts can engage in a principled review of the issues presented in such cases in order to achieve a just result. Because the claims before us derive, in part, from concepts found in the Federal Constitution and the Constitution of this State, we begin with those concepts.

Both parties . . . invoke the right to privacy in support of their respective positions. More specifically, they claim procreational autonomy as a fundamental attribute of the privacy rights guaranteed by both the Federal and New Jersey Constitutions. Their arguments are based on various opinions of the United States Supreme Court that discuss the right to be free from governmental interference with procreational decisions. . . . In Skinner v. Oklahoma [supra at page 427], the Court spoke of that most "basic liberty[ ]" when rejecting, on equal protection grounds, an Oklahoma statute that required sterilization of certain repeat criminal offenders. 316 U.S. at 541. . . .

This Court also has recognized the fundamental nature of procreational rights [when we] observed . . . that "the rights of personal intimacy, of marriage, of sex, of family, of procreation . . . are fundamental rights protected by both the federal and state Constitutions." . . .

Those decisions provide a framework within which disputes over the disposition of preembryos can be resolved. In *Davis, supra,* for example, a divorced couple could not agree on the disposition of their unused, cryopreserved preembryos. . . . [842 S.W.2d 588, 589 (Tenn. 1992)]. The Tennessee Supreme Court balanced the right to procreate of the party seeking to donate the preembryos (the wife), against the right not to procreate of the party seeking destruction of the preembryos (the husband). . . .

We agree with the Tennessee Supreme Court that "ordinarily, the party wishing to avoid procreation should prevail." . . . M.B.'s right to procreate is not lost if he is denied an opportunity to use or donate the preembryos. M.B. is already a father and is able to become a father to additional children, whether through natural procreation or further in vitro fertilization. In contrast, J.B.'s right not to procreate may be lost through attempted use or through donation of the preembryos. Implantation, if successful, would result in the birth of her biological child and could have life-long emotional and psychological repercussions.[7] . . . Her fundamental right not to procreate is irrevocably extinguished if a surrogate mother bears J.B.'s child. We will not force J.B. to become a biological parent against her will.

The court below "concluded that a contract to procreate is contrary to New Jersey public policy and is unenforceable." . . . That determination follows the reasoning of the Massachusetts Supreme Judicial Court in A.Z. v. B.Z., wherein an agreement to compel biological parenthood was deemed unenforceable as a matter of public policy. 725 N.E.2d 1051, 1057-58 (2000). The Massachusetts court likened enforcement of a contract permitting implantation of preembryos to other contracts to enter into familial relationships that were unenforceable under the laws of Massachusetts, i.e., contracts to marry or to give up a child for adoption prior to the fourth day after birth. . . .

[T]he laws of New Jersey also evince a policy against enforcing private contracts to enter into or terminate familial relationships. . . . [8]

---

[7] The legal consequences for J.B. also are unclear. See N.J.A.C. 8:2-1.4(a) (stating "the woman giving birth shall be recorded as a parent"). We note without comment that a recent case before the Chancery Division in Bergen County concluded that seventy-two hours must pass before a non-biological surrogate mother may surrender her parental rights and the biological mother's name may be placed on the birth certificate. A.H.W. v. G.H.B., 772 A.2d 948 (2000). In Arizona, an appellate court determined that a statute allowing a biological father but not a biological mother to prove paternity violated the Equal Protection Clause. Soos v. Superior Court, 897 P.2d 1356, 1361 (1995). In California, the legal mother is the person who "intended to bring about the birth of a child that she intended to raise as her own." Johnson v. Calvert, 851 P.2d 776, 782 (Cal. 1993), cert. denied, 510 U.S. 874, and cert. dismissed, Baby Boy J. v. Johnson, 510 U.S. 938 (1993).

[8] Currently, a minority of states have passed legislation addressing in vitro fertilization. See, e.g., Cal. Penal Code §?367g (West 1999) (permitting use of preembryos only pursuant to written consent form); Fla. Stat. ch. 742.17 (1997) (establishing joint decision-making authority regarding disposition of preembryos); La. Rev. Stat. Ann. §§9:121 to 9:133 (West 1991) (establishing fertilized human ovum as a biological human being that cannot be intentionally destroyed); Okla. Stat. Ann. tit. 10, §?556 (West 2001) (requiring written consent for embryo transfer); Tex. Family Code Ann. §151.103 (West 1996) (establishing parental rights over child resulting from preembryo).

Enforcement of a contract that would allow the implantation of preembryos at some future date in a case where one party has reconsidered his or her earlier acquiescence raises similar issues. If implantation is successful, that party will have been forced to become a biological parent against his or her will.

We note disagreement on the issue both among legal commentators and in the limited caselaw on the subject. *Kass,* supra, held that "agreements between progenitors, or gamete donors, regarding disposition of their . . . [preembryos] should generally be presumed valid and binding, and enforced in a dispute between them. . . . " 696 N.E.2d at 180. The New York court emphasized that such agreements would "avoid costly litigation," "minimize misunderstandings and maximize procreative liberty by reserving to the progenitors the authority to make what is in the first instance a quintessentially personal private decision."[9] . . . Yet, as discussed above, the Massachusetts Supreme Judicial Court as well as our Appellate Division have declared that when agreements compel procreation over the subsequent objection of one of the parties, those agreements are violative of public policy. *A.Z., supra,* 725 N.E.2d at 1057-58; *J.B., supra,* 331 N.J. Super. at 234. . . .

We recognize that persuasive reasons exist for enforcing preembryo disposition agreements. Both the *Kass* and *Davis* decisions pointed out the benefits of enforcing agreements between the parties. . . . We also recognize that in vitro fertilization is in widespread use, and that there is a need for agreements between the participants and the clinics that perform the procedure. We believe that the better rule, and the one we adopt, is to enforce agreements entered into at the time in vitro fertilization is begun, subject to the right of either party to change his or her mind about disposition up to the point of use or destruction of any stored preembryos.

The public policy concerns that underlie limitations on contracts involving family relationships are protected by permitting either party to object at a later date to provisions specifying a disposition of preembryos that that party no longer accepts. Moreover, despite the conditional nature of the disposition provisions, in the large majority of cases the agreements will control, permitting fertility clinics and other like facilities to rely on their terms. Only when a party affirmatively notifies a clinic in writing of a change in intention should the disposition issue be reopened. Principles of fairness dictate that agreements provided by a clinic should be written in plain language, and that a qualified clinic representative should review the terms with the parties prior to execution. Agreements should not be signed in blank, as in *A.Z., supra,* 725 N.E.2d at 1057, or in a manner suggesting that the parties have not given due consideration to the disposition question. Those and other reasonable safeguards should serve to limit later disputes.

Finally, if there is disagreement as to disposition because one party has reconsidered his or her earlier decision, the interests of both parties must be evaluated. . . . Because ordinarily the party choosing not to become a biological

---

[9] The Supreme Court of Tennessee, in dicta, also stated "that an agreement regarding disposition of any untransferred preembryos in the event of contingencies (such as the death of one or more of the parties, divorce, financial reversals, or abandonment of the program) should be presumed valid and should be enforced as between the progenitors." *Davis, supra,* 842 S.W.2d at 597.

parent will prevail, we do not anticipate increased litigation as a result of our decision. In this case, after having considered that M.B. is a father and is capable of fathering additional children, we have affirmed J.B.'s right to prevent implantation of the preembryos. We express no opinion in respect of a case in which a party who has become infertile seeks use of stored preembryos against the wishes of his or her partner, noting only that the possibility of adoption also may be a consideration, among others, in the court's assessment.

Under the judgment of the Appellate Division, the seven remaining preembryos are to be destroyed. It was represented to us at oral argument, however, that J.B. does not object to their continued storage if M.B. wishes to pay any fees associated with that storage. M.B. must inform the trial court forthwith whether he will do so; otherwise, the preembryos are to be destroyed.

The judgment of the Appellate Division is affirmed as modified.

VERNIERO, J., concurring.

I join in the disposition of this case and in all but one aspect of the Court's opinion. I do not agree with the Court's suggestion, in dicta, that the right to procreate may depend on adoption as a consideration. . . . I also write to express my view that the same principles that compel the outcome in this case would permit an infertile party to assert his or her right to use a preembryo against the objections of the other party, if such use were the only means of procreation. In that instance, the balance arguably would weigh in favor of the infertile party absent countervailing factors of greater weight. I do not decide that profound question today, and the Court should not decide it or suggest a result, because it is absent from this case.

[Justice Zazzali's concurring opinion is omitted.]

Notes: Frozen Embryo Disputes

1. *Family, Property, or Contract Law?* Should preembryos be treated as the property or as the children of one or both parents? The *Davis* litigation, cited in *J.B.*, has influenced all subsequent decisions. Davis v. Davis, 842 S.W.2d 588 (Tenn. 1992), on rehearing in part, 1992 WL 341632 (Tenn. 1992), *cert. denied* sub nom. Stowe v. Davis, 507 U.S. 911 (1993). As in most frozen embryo disputes, the litigants were divorcing and could not agree on the disposition of their frozen embryos, which had been produced in more hopeful times. The *Davis* trial court resolved the frozen embryo dispute as though the embryos were children of the marriage. 842 S.W.2d at 589. The wife was awarded "custody" so that she could arrange to have the embryos implanted. The trial court's holding was exceedingly controversial — in part because it implicitly challenged the characterization of embryos and fetuses as nonpersons in abortion law — and the decision was promptly appealed. The Tennessee Supreme Court rejected the notion that the preembryos were "persons," finding instead that the preembryos had a special status:

> To our way of thinking, the most helpful discussion on this point is found . . . in the ethical standards set by The American Fertility Society. . . .

> [T]he preembryo deserves respect greater than that accorded to human tissue but not the respect accorded to actual persons. The preembryo is due greater respect than other human tissue because of its potential to become a person and because of its symbolic meaning for many people. Yet, it should not be treated as a person, because it has not yet developed the features of personhood, is not yet established as developmentally individual, and may never realize its biologic potential. . . .

We conclude that preembryos are not, strictly speaking, either "persons" or "property," but occupy an interim category that entitles them to special respect because of their potential for human life. It follows that any interest that [the genetic parents] . . . have in the preembryos in this case is not a true property interest. However, they do have an interest in the nature of ownership, to the extent that they have decisionmaking authority concerning disposition of the preembryos, within the scope of policy set by law. . . . *Davis*, 842 S.W.2d at 596.

What does it mean to give the embryos "special respect" because of their potential for human life? What are the practical implications of this "respect"? What does it mean to say that the progenitors have decisional authority, particularly since most disputes arise because the genetic parents disagree about the decision to make? Post-*Davis*, the Iowa Supreme Court has "identified three primary approaches to resolving disputes over the disposition of frozen embryos . . . (1) the contractual approach; (2) the contemporaneous mutual consent model; and (3) the [interests] balancing test [used in *J.B.* and in *Davis* where the parties had not executed an agreement]." In re Witten, 672 N.W.2d 768 (Iowa 2003).

2. *Disposing of Frozen Embryos by Contract or Mutual Agreement?* As noted in the *J.B.* decision, supra, there is substantial disagreement about whether the parties can contractually bind themselves to a particular form of embryo disposition even after one or both parties changes his or her preference. Does the *J.B.* court enforce the agreement signed by the parties? The informed consent form/disposition agreement appears to give the Cooper Center control over the embryos upon the divorce of the parties, absent a court order or a written agreement of the parties. Perhaps the court's decision actually fulfills the contract's terms. What about the alleged additional agreement between the parties, the one that M.B. claimed that he should have a right to prove? Why doesn't M.B. have a right to present evidence about his agreement with his wife regarding the disposition of the embryos? The court appears to impose a judicially constructed "statute of frauds," requiring that such agreements be written.

The New Jersey court also holds that "[w]e believe that the better rule, and the one we adopt, is to enforce agreements entered into at the time in vitro fertilization is begun, subject to the right of either party to change his or her mind about disposition up to the point of use or destruction of any stored preembryos." *J.B.*, supra. Does this mean that the court favors the use of binding predisposition contracts? Probably not, given that the court will only enforce agreements so long as the parties don't change their minds: This certainly is not the traditional legal approach to the enforcement of contracts.

It appears that other courts might enforce disposition agreements in some circumstances. The *Davis* court noted in dicta, for example:

> We believe, as a starting point, that an agreement regarding disposition of any untransferred preembryos in the event of contingencies (such as the death of one or more of the parties, divorce, financial reversals, or abandonment of the program) should be presumed valid and should be enforced as between the progenitors. This conclusion is in keeping with the proposition that the progenitors, having provided the gametic material giving rise to the preembryos, retain decisionmaking authority as to their disposition.
>
> At the same time, we recognize that life is not static, and that human emotions run particularly high when a married couple is attempting to overcome infertility problems. It follows that the parties' initial "informed consent" to IVF procedures will often not be truly informed because of the near impossibility of anticipating, emotionally and psychologically, all the turns that events may take as the IVF process unfolds. Providing that the initial agreements may later be modified by agreement will, we think, protect the parties against some of the risks they face in this regard. But, in the absence of such agreed modification, we conclude that their prior agreements should be considered binding. *Davis*, 842 S. W.2d at 597.

See also Kass v. Kass, 696 N.E.2d 174 (N.Y. 1998) (enforcing dispositional terms of signed consents, which assigned preembryos for research purposes); Roman v. Roman, 193 S.W.3d 40 (2006) (embryo agreement terms should be enforced).

The contractual approach has been described as "[t]he currently prevailing view." In re Witten, 672 N.W.2d 768, 776 (Iowa 2003) (noting that New York, Tennessee, and Washington will employ the contractual approach in some circumstances). The *Witten* court nonetheless rejected the contractual approach because it provides "'insufficient[ ] protect[ion for] the individual and societal interests at stake.'" Id. at 777. The court agreed with critics of contractual approach who argued that preferences regarding embryo disposition cannot be known in advance. Id. The court noted:

> We have considered and rejected the arguments of some commentators that embryo disposition agreements are analogous to antenuptial agreements and divorce stipulations, which courts generally enforce. . . . Whether embryos are viewed as having life or simply has having the potential for life, this characteristic or potential renders embryos fundamentally distinct from the chattels, real estate, and money that are the subjects of antenuptial agreements. Divorce stipulations are also distinguishable. While such agreements may address custody issues, they are contemporaneous with the implementation of the stipulation, an attribute noticeably lacking in disposition agreements. In re Witten, 672 N.W.2d at 781-782.

The court rejected the balancing of interests approach because it would require the court to make sensitive value judgments about procreation particularly within the dominion of individuals. The court thus adopted the contemporaneous agreement standard: "A better principle to apply . . . is the requirement of contemporaneous mutual consent. Under that model, no transfer, release, disposition, or use of the embryos can occur without the signed authorization of both donors. If a stalemate results, the status quo would be maintained. . . . Thus, any expense [for embryo storage] should logically be borne by the person opposing destruction." Id. at 783. See also A.Z. v. B.Z., 725 N.E.2d 1051 (Mass. 2000) (court expresses doubt about whether informed consent forms offered by clinic and signed by parties reflected their intent).

3. *Frozen Embryos and the Constitution.* Frozen embryos occupy a peculiar position under the law. Who should have power to exercise control over the embryos? Are these questions answered by an analysis of the "right to procreate" or the "right not to procreate"? Women invest more "sweat equity" in in vitro reproduction than men. Women must undergo arduous hormone therapy and ovum retrieval procedures. Men must produce a sperm sample, typically under less harrowing conditions. Should this difference in investments affect the outcome? See Ruth Colker, Pregnant Men Revisited or Sperm Is Cheap, Eggs Are Not, 47 Hastings L.J. 1063 (1996). If procreation had occurred in the ordinary fashion, a man's ability to decline the opportunity of fatherhood would have ended with the procreative act itself. A man cannot require that a woman undergo an abortion, for example; see page 473. Should courts use a similar analogy when considering frozen embryo disputes, denying genetic parents the opportunity to reject parenthood once they have committed their gametes to the enterprise? See Kass v. Kass, 1995 WL 110368 (N.Y. Sup. Ct.) (unpublished opinion), *rev'd*, 663 N.Y.S.2d 581 (App. Div. 1997).

Instead, courts following the balancing of interests approach have favored the right not to procreate. In *J.B.*, supra, for example, the court anticipates that the party who does not wish to procreate will "ordinarily . . . prevail." The *Davis* court reached a similar result for cases not governed by a pre-existing contractual agreement:

> If no prior agreement exists, then the relative interests of the parties in using or not using the preembryos must be weighed. Ordinarily, the party wishing to avoid procreation should prevail, assuming that the other party has a reasonable possibility of achieving parenthood by means other than use of the preembryos in question. If no other reasonable alternatives exist, then the argument in favor of using the preembryos to achieve pregnancy should be considered. However, if the party seeking control of the preembryos intends merely to donate them to another couple, the objecting party obviously has the greater interest and should prevail. But the rule does not contemplate the creation of an automatic veto, and in affirming the judgment of the court of appeals, we would not wish to be interpreted as so holding. . . .

842 S.W.2d at 604. See also A.Z. v. B.Z., 725 N.E.2d 1051 (Mass. 2000) (husband's interest in avoiding procreation outweighed defendant's interest in having additional children; husband should not be forced to become a parent). When, if ever, would these courts authorize the use of embryos over the objection of one of the parties? What is the significance of the dispute between the majority and concurring opinions in *J.B.* regarding the ability to adopt?

4. *Genetic Parenthood and Frozen Embryo Disputes.* In In re Litowitz, the Washington Supreme Court confronted a frozen embryo dispute in which one of the parties was not genetically related to the embryos. 48 P.3d 261 (Wash. 2002),

opinion amended, 53 P.3d 516 (2002), *cert. denied* sub nom. Litowitz v. Litowitz, 537 U.S. 1191 (2003). Becky M. Litowitz was unable to produce oocytes or to bear a child. She and her then husband David J. Litowitz entered into an agreement with an egg donor to obtain eggs that could be fertilized with David's sperm and then implanted in a gestational surrogate. The Litowitz marriage crumbled before the birth of their first child produced according to this arrangement. The parties could not agree to the disposition of the remaining frozen embryos. The trial court gave the embryos to the husband for implantation in another surrogate "based on the best interest of the child." Id. at 264.

The Washington Supreme Court took a different approach. The court held that Becky Litowitz's rights would be determined by contract because she had no biological connection to the preembryos. Id. at 267. Becky argued that she and David had equal rights to the embryos because the egg donor contract provided that the "intended parents" were the owners of the donated eggs. Id. at 267-268. The court rejected this claim, holding that the egg donor contract did not apply once the eggs had been fertilized. Id. at 268. The court then turned to the cryopreservation contract the parties entered into with the fertility clinic. That contract provided that the preembryos should be "thawed out and not allowed to undergo further development" after five years. Id. at 271. Given that the five years had expired, the court suggested that the embryos might already have been destroyed or could be destroyed in accordance with the parties' expressed wishes.

5. *Legislation.* Several states have enacted legislation establishing special consent and dispute resolution rules for the allocation of frozen embryos. See, e.g., National Conference of State Legislatures, Gamete (Egg/Sperm) and Embryo Distribution (available on NCSL Web site). Some jurisdictions focus on regulating the informed consent process. See, e.g., Cal. Health & Safety Code §125315 (patients must be given options for disposition in the event of separation or divorce). Other jurisdictions given the partner wishing to avoid procreation the right to withdraw consent any time before the use of the embryos. See, e.g., Colo. Rev. Stat. §19-4-106. Several states have enacted rules governing embryo adoption. See National Conference of State Legislatures, supra. Legislation may be helpful in some circumstances but is not likely to resolve the need for judicial determinations completely. How should courts resolve embryo disputes when the parties have failed to execute an agreement about the disposition of embryos as required by state law?

6. *Commentators.* Professor Robertson is the leading commentator on frozen embryo disputes; he served as an expert in the *Davis* trial and has written extensively on the subject. See, e.g., John A. Robertson, Precommitment Strategies for Disposition of Frozen Embryos, 50 Emory L.J. 990 (2001). See also Jessica Berg, Owning Persons: The Application of Property Theory to Embryos and Fetuses, 40 Wake Forest L. Rev. 159 (2005); Carl H. Coleman, Procreative Liberty and Contemporaneous Choice: An Inalienable Rights Approach to Frozen Embryo Disputes, 84 Minn. L. Rev. 55 (1999) (frequently cited by the court in In re Witten); Janet L. Dolgin, The "Intent" of Reproduction: Reproductive Technologies and the Parent-Child Bond, 26 Conn. L. Rev. 1261 (1994); Annot., 87 A.L.R.5th 253 (2001); Ellen Waldman, The Parent Trap: Uncovering the Myth of "Coerced Parenthood" in Frozen Embryo Disputes, 53 Am. U. L. Rev. 1021 (2004) (discusses and critiques the dominance of the right to

not procreate in frozen embryo disputes). See generally New York State Task Force on Life & the Law, Assisted Reproductive Technologies: Analysis and Recommendations for Public Policy (1998).

7. *Lost Embryos; Donated Embryos.* Should couples be permitted to sue infertility centers that lose or destroy frozen embryos? See Jeter v. Mayo Clinic Arizona, 121 P.3d 1256 (Ariz. 2005) (rejecting wrongful death claim but permitting certain other claims to go forward). See also Charles P. Kindregan, Jr., & Maureen McBrien, Embryo Donation: Unresolved Legal Issues in the Transfer of Surplus Cryopreserved Embryos, 49 Vill. L. Rev. 169 (2004); Gretchen Ruethling, Couple Can Sue Over Lost Embryos, N.Y. Times, Feb. 8, 2005, at A18, col. 1 (trial judge authorizes wrongful death action because Illinois legislature has established that life begins at conception).

4. Womb and Ovum Donors

■ R.R. v. M.H.
689 N.E.2d 790 (Mass. 1998)

Wilkins, C.J.

On a report by a judge in the Probate and Family Court, we are concerned with the validity of a surrogacy parenting agreement between the plaintiff (father) and the defendant (mother). Both the mother and the father are married but not to each other. A child was conceived through artificial insemination of the mother with the father's sperm, after the mother and father had executed the surrogate parenting agreement. The agreement provided that the father would have custody of the child. During the sixth month of her pregnancy and after she had received funds from the father pursuant to the surrogacy agreement, the mother changed her mind and decided that she wanted to keep the child.

The father thereupon brought this action. . . . The question of the enforceability of the surrogacy agreement is before us and, although we could defer any ruling until there is a final judgment entered, the issue is one on which we elect to comment because it is fully briefed and is of importance to more than the parties. This court has not previously dealt with the enforceability of a surrogacy agreement. . . .

The baby girl who is the subject of this action was born on August 15, 1997. . . . The defendant mother and the plaintiff father are her biological parents. The father and his wife, who live in Rhode Island, were married in June, 1989. The wife is infertile. Sometime in 1994, she and the father learned of an egg donor program but did not pursue it because the procedure was not covered by insurance and had a relatively low success rate. Because of their ages (they were both in their forties), they concluded that pursuing adoption was not feasible. In April, 1996, responding to a newspaper advertisement for surrogacy services, they consulted a Rhode Island attorney who had drafted surrogacy contracts for both surrogates and couples seeking surrogacy services. On the attorney's advice, the father and his wife consulted the New England Surrogate Parenting Advisors (NESPA), a for-profit corporation that helps infertile couples find women willing to act as surrogate mothers. They entered into a contract with NESPA in

September, 1996, and paid a fee of $6,000. Meanwhile, in the spring of 1996, the mother, who was married and had two children, responded to a NESPA advertisement. She reported to NESPA that her family was complete and that she desired to allow others less fortunate than herself to have children. The mother submitted a surrogacy application to NESPA. The judge found that the mother was motivated to apply to NESPA by a desire to be pregnant, in order to earn money, and to help an infertile couple.

In October, Dr. Angela Figueroa of NESPA brought the mother together with the father and his wife. They had a seemingly informative exchange of information and views. The mother was advised to seek an attorney's advice concerning the surrogacy agreement. Shortly thereafter, the mother, the father, and his wife met again to discuss the surrogacy and other matters. The mother also met with a clinical psychologist as part of NESPA's evaluation of her suitability to act as a surrogate. The psychologist, who also evaluated the father and his wife, advised the mother to consult legal counsel, to give her husband a chance to air his concerns, to discuss arrangements for contact with the child, to consider and discuss her expectations concerning termination of the pregnancy, and to arrange a meeting between her husband and the father and his wife. The psychologist concluded that the mother was solid, thoughtful, and well grounded, that she would have no problem giving the child to the father, and that she was happy to act as a surrogate. The mother told the psychologist that she was not motivated by money, although she did plan to use the funds received for her children's education. The mother's husband told the psychologist by telephone that he supported his wife's decision.

The mother signed the surrogate parenting agreement and her signature was notarized on November 1. The father signed on November 18. The agreement stated that the parties intended that the "Surrogate shall be inseminated with the semen of Natural Father" and "that, on the birth of the child or children so conceived, Natural Father, as the Natural Father, will have the full legal parental rights of a father, and surrogate will permit Natural Father to take the child or children home from the hospital to live with he [sic] and his wife." The agreement acknowledged that the mother's parental rights would not terminate if she permitted the father to take the child home and have custody, that the mother could at any time seek to enforce her parental rights by court order, but that, if she attempted to obtain custody or visitation rights, she would forfeit her rights under the agreement and would be obligated to reimburse the father for all fees and expenses paid to her under it. . . .

The agreement provided for compensation to the mother in the amount of $10,000 "for services rendered in conceiving, carrying and giving birth to the Child." Payment of the $10,000 was to be made as follows: $500 on verification of the pregnancy; $2,500 at the end of the third month; $3,500 at the end of the sixth month; and $3,500 at the time of birth "and when delivery of child occurs." The agreement stated that no payment was made in connection with adoption of the child, the termination of parental rights, or consent to surrender the child for adoption. The father acknowledged the mother's right to determine whether to carry the pregnancy to term, but the mother agreed to refund all payments if, without the father's consent, she had an abortion that was not necessary for her physical health. The father assumed various expenses of the pregnancy, including tests, and had the right to name the child. The mother would be obliged, however, to repay all expenses and fees for services if tests showed that the father was not the biological father of the child, or if the mother refused to permit the father to take the child home from the hospital. The agreement also provided that the mother would maintain some contact with the child after the birth. The judge found that the mother entered into the agreement on her own volition after consulting legal counsel. There was no evidence of undue influence, coercion, or duress. The mother fully understood that she was contracting to give custody of the baby to the father. She sought to inseminate herself on November 30 and December 1, 1996. The attempt at conception was successful.

The lawyer for the father sent the mother a check for $500 in December, 1996, and another for $2,500 in February. In May, the father's lawyer sent the mother a check for $3,500. She told the lawyer that she had changed her mind and wanted to keep the child. She returned the check uncashed in the middle of June. The mother has made no attempt to refund the amounts that the father paid her, including $550 that he paid for pregnancy-related expenses.

Approximately two weeks after the mother changed her mind and returned the check for $3,500, and before the child was born, the father commenced this action against the mother seeking to establish his paternity, alleging breach of contract, and requesting a declaration of his rights under the surrogacy agreement. Subsequently, the wife's husband was added as a defendant. The judge appointed a guardian ad litem to represent the interests of the unborn child. Proceedings were held on . . . the mother's motion to determine whether surrogacy contracts are enforceable in Massachusetts. . . .

A significant minority of States have legislation addressing surrogacy agreements. Some simply deny enforcement of all such agreements. . . . Others expressly deny enforcement only if the surrogate is to be compensated. . . . Some States have simply exempted surrogacy agreements from provisions making it a crime to sell babies. . . . A few States have explicitly made unpaid surrogacy agreements lawful. . . . Florida, New Hampshire, and Virginia require that the intended mother be infertile. . . . New Hampshire and Virginia place restrictions on who may act as a surrogate and require advance judicial approval of the agreement. . . . Last, Arkansas raises a presumption that a child born to a surrogate mother is the child of the intended parents and not the surrogate. . . .

There are few appellate court opinions on the enforceability of traditional surrogacy agreements. . . .

The best known opinion is that of the Supreme Court of New Jersey in *Matter of Baby M.*, 537 A.2d 1227 (N.J. 1988), where the court invalidated a compensated surrogacy contract because it conflicted with the law and public policy of the State. . . . The Baby M surrogacy agreement involved broader concessions from the mother than the agreement before us because it provided that the mother would surrender her parental rights and would allow the father's wife to adopt the child. . . . The agreement, therefore, directly conflicted with a statute prohibiting the payment of money to obtain an adoption and a statute barring enforcement of an agreement to adoption made prior to the birth of the child. . . . The court acknowledged that an award of custody to the father was in the best interests of the child, but struck down orders terminating the mother's parental rights and authorizing the adoption of the child by the husband's wife. . . . The court added that it found no "legal prohibition against surrogacy when the surrogate mother volunteers, without any payment, to act as a surrogate and is given the right to change her mind and to assert her parental rights." ...

The case before us concerns traditional surrogacy, in which the fertile member of an infertile couple is one of the child's biological parents. Surrogate fatherhood, the insemination of the fertile wife with sperm of a donor, often an anonymous donor, is a recognized and accepted procedure. ... If the mother's husband consents to the procedure, the resulting child is considered the legitimate child of the mother and her husband. *G. L. c. 46, §4B.* ... Section 4B does not comment on the rights and obligations, if any, of the biological father, although inferentially he has none. In the case before us, the infertile spouse is the wife. No statute decrees the consequences of the artificial insemination of a surrogate with the sperm of a fertile husband. This situation presents different considerations from surrogate fatherhood because surrogate motherhood is never anonymous and her commitment and contribution is unavoidably much greater than that of a sperm donor.[10]

We must face the possible application of *G. L. c. 46, §4B,* to this case. Section 4B tells us that a husband who consents to the artificial insemination of his wife with the sperm of another is considered to be the father of any resulting child. In the case before us, the birth mother was married at the time of her artificial insemination. ... It is doubtful, however, that the Legislature intended §4B to apply to the child of a married surrogate mother. ...

Policies underlying our adoption legislation suggest that a surrogate parenting agreement should be given no effect if the mother's agreement was obtained prior to a reasonable time after the child's birth or if her agreement was induced by the payment of money. Adoption legislation is, of course, not applicable to child custody, but it does provide us with some guidance. Although the agreement makes no reference to adoption and does not concern the termination of parental rights or the adoption of the child by the father's wife, the normal expectation in the case of a surrogacy agreement seems to be that the father's wife will adopt the child with the consent of the mother (and the father). Under *G. L. c. 210, §2,* adoption requires the written consent of the father and the mother but, in these circumstances, not the mother's husband. Any such consent, written, witnessed, and notarized, is not to be executed "sooner than the fourth calendar day after the date of birth of the child to be adopted." Id. That statutory standard should be interpreted as providing that no mother may effectively agree to surrender her child for adoption earlier than the fourth day after its birth, by which time she better knows the strength of her bond with her child. Although a consent to surrender custody has less permanency than a consent to adoption, the legislative judgment that a mother should have time after a child's birth to reflect on her wishes concerning the child weighs heavily in our consideration whether to give effect to a prenatal custody agreement. No private agreement concerning

---

[10] A situation which involves considerations different from those in the case before us arises when the birth mother has had transferred to her uterus an embryo formed through in vitro fertilization of the intended parents' sperm and egg. This latter process in which the birth mother is not genetically related to the child (except coincidentally if an intended parent is a relative) has been called gestational surrogacy. ...

adoption or custody can be conclusive in any event because a judge, passing on custody of a child, must decide what is in the best interests of the child.[11]

Adoptive parents may pay expenses of a birth parent but may make no direct payment to her. See *G. L. c. 210, §11A*. . . . Even though the agreement seeks to attribute that payment of $10,000, not to custody or adoption, but solely to the mother's services in carrying the child, the father ostensibly was promised more than those services because, as a practical matter, the mother agreed to surrender custody of the child. She could assert custody rights, according to the agreement, only if she repaid the father all amounts that she had received and also reimbursed him for all expenses he had incurred. The statutory prohibition of payment for receiving a child through adoption suggests that, as a matter of policy, a mother's agreement to surrender custody in exchange for money (beyond pregnancy-related expenses) should be given no effect in deciding the custody of the child.

The mother's purported consent to custody in the agreement is ineffective because no such consent should be recognized unless given on or after the fourth day following the child's birth. In reaching this conclusion, we apply to consent to custody the same principle which underlies the statutory restriction on when a mother's consent to adoption may be effectively given. Moreover, the payment of money to influence the mother's custody decision makes the agreement as to custody void. Eliminating any financial reward to a surrogate mother is the only way to assure that no economic pressure will cause a woman, who may well be a member of an economically vulnerable class, to act as a surrogate. It is true that a surrogate enters into the agreement before she becomes pregnant and thus is not presented with the desperation that a poor unwed pregnant woman may confront. However, compensated surrogacy arrangements raise the concern that, under financial pressure, a woman will permit her body to be used and her child to be given away.

There is no doubt that compensation was a factor in inducing the mother to enter into the surrogacy agreement and to cede custody to the father. If the payment of $10,000 was really only compensation for the mother's services in carrying the child and giving birth and was unrelated to custody of the child, the agreement would not have provided that the mother must refund all compensation paid (and expenses paid) if she should challenge the father's right to custody. Nor would the agreement have provided that final payment be made only when the child is delivered to the father. We simply decline, on public policy grounds, to apply to a surrogacy agreement of the type involved here the general principle that an agreement between informed, mature adults should be enforced absent proof of duress, fraud, or undue influence.

We recognize that there is nothing inherently unlawful in an arrangement by which an informed woman agrees to attempt to conceive artificially and give birth to a child whose father would be the husband of an infertile wife. We suspect that many such arrangements are made and carried out without disagreement.

---

[11] In the case of a divorce, a judge may approve an agreement between parents concerning child custody unless the judge makes specific findings that the agreement would not be in the best interests of the child. *G. L. c. 208, §31*.

If no compensation is paid beyond pregnancy-related expenses and if the mother is not bound by her consent to the father's custody of the child unless she consents after a suitable period has passed following the child's birth, the objections we have identified in this opinion to the enforceability of a surrogate's consent to custody would be overcome. Other conditions might be important in deciding the enforceability of a surrogacy agreement, such as a requirement that (a) the mother's husband give his informed consent to the agreement in advance; (b) the mother be an adult and have had at least one successful pregnancy; (c) the mother, her husband, and the intended parents have been evaluated for the soundness of their judgment and for their capacity to carry out the agreement; (d) the father's wife be incapable of bearing a child without endangering her health; (e) the intended parents be suitable persons to assume custody of the child; and (f) all parties have the advice of counsel. The mother and father may not, however, make a binding best-interests-of-the-child determination by private agreement. Any custody agreement is subject to a judicial determination of custody based on the best interests of the child.

The conditions that we describe are not likely to be satisfactory to an intended father because, following the birth of the child, the mother can refuse to consent to the father's custody even though the father has incurred substantial pregnancy-related expenses. A surrogacy agreement judicially approved before conception may be a better procedure, as is permitted by statutes in Virginia and New Hampshire. A Massachusetts statute concerning surrogacy agreements, pro or con, would provide guidance to judges, lawyers, infertile couples interested in surrogate parenthood, and prospective surrogate mothers.

We do not reach but comment briefly on the mother's argument that the agreement was unconscionable. She actively sought to become a surrogate and entered into the surrogacy agreement voluntarily, advised by counsel, not under duress, and fully informed. Unconscionability is not apparent on this record.

A declaration shall be entered that the surrogacy agreement is not enforceable. Such further orders as may be appropriate, consistent with this opinion, may be entered in the Probate and Family Court.

■ CULLITON v. BETH ISRAEL DEACONESS MEDICAL CENTER
756 N.E.2d 1133 (Mass. 2001)

GREANEY, J.

We transferred this case here on our own motion to decide whether a judge in the Probate and Family Court had authority to act on the plaintiffs' complaint that sought declaratory and injunctive relief by way of a judgment ordering the defendant Beth Israel Deaconess Medical Center (hospital) "to enter MARLA CULLITON as the mother, and STEVEN CULLITON as the father [,] on the birth certificates of unborn Baby A and unborn Baby B." The children, twins, were born while the case was pending appeal. They are the genetic children of the plaintiffs, who had embryos . . . that had been created from the plaintiff Steven Culliton's sperm . . . and the plaintiff Marla Culliton's ova . . . implanted into the uterus of the defendant Melissa Carroll, who agreed to act as a gestational carrier for the plaintiffs pursuant to a gestational carrier contract with them. The judge ordered the entry of a judgment dismissing the complaint because of a "lack of clarity and certainty as to this court's authority" to grant the relief sought. We conclude that the judge had authority to decide the merits of the complaint. We also conclude that, on the facts of this case, a judgment should enter declaring that the plaintiffs are the legal parents of the children, and ordering the hospital, through its reporters, to place the plaintiffs' names on all "record[s] of birth" created pursuant to G. L. c. 46, §§1, 3, 3A, listing the plaintiffs as the mother and father, respectively, of the children.

The facts of this case are undisputed. We now summarize those facts and provide an overview of the case's procedural background. The plaintiffs and the defendant Melissa Carroll (gestational carrier), a single woman over the age of twenty-one years who had "at least one previous live birth," entered into a gestational carrier contract. Pursuant to the contract, the gestational carrier agreed to have implanted into her uterus embryos that were created from the sperm of Steven Culliton and the ova of Marla Culliton; to carry and deliver any child resulting from the embryo implantation; and, upon the birth of any child resulting from the embryo implantation, to permit the plaintiffs to have sole physical and legal custody of the child or children. For her role, the gestational carrier was to receive certain financial compensation.[6] The contract appears to have been executed because Marla "is capable of conceiving a child, but incapable of bearing and giving birth to a child without unreasonable risk to her health."

The gestational carrier underwent the embryo implantation and became pregnant with twins. A few months later, the plaintiffs filed a verified complaint in the Probate and Family Court seeking a declaration of paternity and maternity, as well as a prebirth order directing the hospital at which the gestational carrier was expected to deliver to designate the plaintiffs as the father and mother of the children on their birth certificates. Together with the complaint, the plaintiffs and the gestational carrier filed a stipulation for the entry of judgment in the plaintiffs' favor. . . .

A judge in the Probate and Family Court, concluding that he did not have the authority to issue a prebirth order of parentage, ordered the entry of a judgment of dismissal. . . . The plaintiffs filed a notice of appeal, and the case was entered in the Appeals Court. That court, on motion by the plaintiffs, entered a preliminary injunction enjoining the hospital from issuing birth certificates until resolution of the appeal. The day before we transferred the case here, the twins were born. After transfer, we entered an order continuing the injunction in effect. . . .

The judge acted prudently in seeking to place this case before us as quickly as possible because, as he correctly noted, there is no direct legal "authority for issuing a pre-birth order regarding parentage under the facts of this case." Authority elsewhere is sparse and not altogether consistent [citing cases from Ohio, New Jersey, New York, and California].

---

[6] Under the contract, the plaintiffs agreed to pay the gestational carrier for certain medical expenses, maternity clothing, travel expenses, childcare expenses, legal expenses, telephone expenses, medically necessitated lost wages, psychological counselling expenses, health insurance expenses, and living expenses. According to the contract, payment of these expenses was not conditioned "upon the termination of any parental rights or the placement of the child with [the plaintiffs]."

The pregnancy in issue is not governed by the statutes referred to by the [trial] judge. General Laws c. 209C, for instance, establishes procedures for determining paternity and maternity for children "born out of wedlock." See G. L. c. 209C, §1. . . . While the twins technically were born out of wedlock, because the gestational carrier was not married when she gave birth to them, it is undisputed that the twins were conceived by a married couple. In these circumstances the children should be presumed to be the children of marriage. . . . Conversely, problems would have arisen if the gestational carrier had been married at the time of birth, for, in those circumstances, under G. L. c. 209C, her husband would be presumed to be the father of the children to whom she gave birth. . . . Additionally, under the statute, in contested cases, one method of proving paternity involves soliciting testimony from one parent concerning the occurrence of "sexual intercourse" with the other party during the "probable period of conception." . . . As shown by the facts of this case, reproductive advances have eliminated the necessity of having sexual intercourse in order to procreate. It is apparent, after examining the paternity statute in detail, that the statute is simply an inadequate and inappropriate device to resolve parentage determinations of children born from this type of gestational surrogacy.

Nor does the adoption statute, G. L. c. 210, furnish any better guidance. While this court has previously looked to the adoption statute in deciding whether to enforce a traditional surrogacy agreement, . . . see [citing R.R. v. M.H., supra], the court did so "to assure that no economic pressure will cause a woman . . . to act as a surrogate. . . . Compensated surrogacy arrangements raise the concern that, under financial pressure, a woman will permit her body to be used and her child to be given away." . . . In such an arrangement, the surrogate is both the genetic mother of the child and the mother who carries the child through pregnancy and delivery. The child is thus, undisputedly, "her" child to be surrendered for adoption. Here, where it is undisputed that the plaintiffs were not donating an embryo or embryos to the gestational carrier, and that the twins have no genetic relation to the gestational carrier, the concerns are different. . . . Also, in these circumstances, applying the four-day waiting period of G. L. c. 210, §2, to this gestational carrier arrangement would work unintended, and possibly detrimental, results. The duties and responsibilities of parenthood (for example, support and custody) would lie with the gestational carrier for at least four days; the gestational carrier could be free to surrender the children for adoption; and the genetic parents of the children would be forced to go through the adoption process, possibly having to wait as long as six months, see G. L. c. 210, §5A . . . , before becoming the legal parents of the children. As is evident from its provisions, the adoption statute was not intended to resolve parentage issues arising from gestational surrogacy agreements.

Contrary to the plaintiffs' contention, G. L. c. 46, §4B, does not authorize the relief sought in this case. That statute provides that "any child born to a married woman as a result of artificial insemination with the consent of her husband, shall be considered the legitimate child of the mother and such husband." G. L. c. 46, §4B. As we explained in R.R. v. M.H., supra at 510, §4B "seems to concern the status of a child born to a fertile mother whose husband, presumably infertile, consented to her artificial insemination with the sperm of another man so that the couple could have a child biologically related to the mother." The situation that §4B addresses is not present here. The statute does not apply. . . .

Here, where (a) the plaintiffs are the sole genetic sources of the twins; (b) the gestational carrier agrees with the orders sought; (c) no one, including the hospital, has contested the complaint or petition; and (d) by filing the complaint and stipulation for judgment the plaintiffs agree that they have waived any contradictory provisions in the contract (assuming those provisions could be enforced in the first place), we conclude that pursuant to the Probate and Family Court's general equity jurisdiction under G. L. c. 215, §6, the judge had authority to consider the merits of the relief sought here.[9]

This conclusion acknowledges the importance of establishing the rights and responsibilities of parents as soon as is practically possible. By enacting G. L. c. 46, which contains provisions establishing a process for the issuance of accurate birth certificates on which the "parents" of a newly born child are listed, the Legislature has also recognized and addressed, in some measure, this concern. Delays in establishing parentage may, among other consequences, interfere with a child's medical treatment in the event of medical complications arising during or shortly after birth; may hinder or deprive a child of inheriting from his legal parents should a legal parent die intestate before a postbirth action could determine parentage; may hinder or deprive a child from collecting Social Security benefits under 42 U.S.C. §402(d) (Supp. 1999); and may result in undesirable support obligations as well as custody disputes (potentially more likely in situations where the child is born with congenital malformations or anomalies, or medical disorders and diseases). . . . Our holding provides that such consequences, at least in some circumstances, can be minimized or avoided, thus furnishing a measure of stability and protection to children born through such gestational surrogacy arrangements. See E.N.O. v. L.M.M., 711 N.E.2d 886 (Mass. 1999), cert. denied, 528 U.S. 1005 (1999) ("the court's duty as parens patriae necessitates that its equitable powers extend to protecting the best interests of children.").

[W]e suggested [in a previous case] that a protocol for these types of cases be established. Such a protocol becomes increasingly necessary as infertile couples, and others, take advantage of existing and emerging assisted reproductive technologies, and as children are conceived and born through these technologies. . . . While responding to some parentage issues arising through artificial insemination, see G. L. c. 46, §4B, the Legislature has not enacted laws to determine parentage of children born from other methods of reproductive technologies or assisted conception. The Legislature is the most suitable forum to deal with the questions involved in this case, and other questions as yet unlitigated, by providing a comprehensive set of laws that deal with the medical, legal, and ethical aspects of these practices. . . .

---

[9] This conclusion takes into account a fact apparently overlooked by the plaintiffs, namely, that a hospital's reporters do not "issue" birth certificates. Rather, they furnish certain information pursuant to G. L. c. 46, §§1, 3, 3A, including the identity of the "parents" of the child born, which, in turn, is used by city and town clerks to "record" a complete "return of birth," which is commonly known as a person's birth certificate, see G. L. c. 46, §§1, 3, 3A, 4A. City or town clerks, the Commissioner of Public Health, or the State Registrar of Vital Records and Statistics may then furnish or "issue" a certified copy of the birth record to a parent. See G. L. c. 46, §§2A, 19, 19B, 19C.

The judgment of dismissal is vacated. The preliminary injunction enjoining the hospital from complying with its statutory obligations for the children is dissolved. A judgment is to enter declaring the plaintiffs as the legal parents of the children and ordering the hospital, through its reporters, to place the plaintiffs' names on its "record[s] of birth" created pursuant to G. L. c. 46, §§1, 3, 3A, listing the plaintiffs as the mother and father, respectively, of the children.

So ordered.

Notes: Traditional and Gestational Surrogacy

1. *One Plus One Equals Three?* Do *R.R.* and *Culliton* give consistent treatment to the legal "weight" of genetic parenthood and gestational parenthood? The modern approach is to treat egg donation and sperm donation as equivalent legal acts with equivalent consequences. See supra at page 519. A gamete donor is thus legally permitted to terminate his or her parental rights at the time of the donation. According to *Culliton*, a gestational surrogate may also enter into a binding agreement to forgo whatever parental rights she might have before the birth of the child. What prevents an egg donor who is also a gestational surrogate from entering into a binding agreement to forgo her parental rights? Why does the *R.R.* court turn instead to the laws governing adoption for standards to be applied in traditional surrogacy cases?

Perhaps the distinction is that the parties in *Culliton* sought an agreed court order and there was no dispute that required a court to weigh the gestational surrogate's interests? See Steven H. Snyder & Mary Patricia Byrn, The Use of Prebirth Parentage Orders in Surrogacy Proceedings, 39 Fam. L.Q. 633 (2005). The *Culliton* court does note the gestational carrier's agreement. Is there a legal or ethical basis for reaching a different result if the gestational carrier does not agree? In Johnson v. Calvert, 851 P.2d 776 (Cal. 1993) (en banc), *cert. denied*, 510 U.S. 874 (1993), cert. dismissed by Baby Boy J. v. Johnson, 510 U.S. 938 (1993), the California Supreme Court rejected a claim by a gestational surrogate that she should be recognized as the mother of the resulting child and given visitation privileges. The court found that state laws addressing the determination of maternity were ambiguous and held that the original intent of the parties should determine the outcome:

> Because two women each have presented acceptable proof of maternity, we do not believe this case can be decided without enquiring into the parties' intentions as manifested in the surrogacy agreement. . . . Mark and Crispina are a couple who desired to have a child of their own genetic stock but are physically unable to do so without the help of reproductive technology. . . . The parties' aim was to bring Mark's and Crispina's child into the world, not for Mark and Crispina to donate a zygote to Anna. . . . No reason appears why Anna's later change of heart should vitiate the determination that Crispina is the child's natural mother.
>
> We conclude that although the Act recognizes both genetic consanguinity and giving birth as means of establishing a mother and child relationship, when the two means do not coincide in one woman, she who intended to procreate the child—that is, she who intended to bring about the birth of a child that she

intended to raise as her own — is the natural mother under California law. . . . 851 P.2d at 782.

The court rejected Anna's claim that the surrogacy contract violated public policy, noting that gestational surrogacy is distinguishable from adoption and that public policy favored giving women the same right to enter into contracts as men. See also Todd M. Krim, Beyond *Baby M*: International Perspectives on Gestational Surrogacy and the Demise of the Unitary Biological Mother, 5 Ann. Health L. 193 (1996). The end result in practice is that infertile couples split the biological and legal transactions into two parts by using an egg donor and a different gestational surrogate.

Some women who are incapable of producing suitable ova may seek to bear and rear children created with donor ova. In this circumstance, the parties intend that the gestational mother serve as the legal mother, even though she has no genetic relationship with the child. The physical arrangements in these two situations are similar (woman gives birth to a child with whom she has no genetic relationship), but the parties' preliminary intentions differ. How should the courts treat disputes arising out of these arrangements? Note that the 2002 UPA contains the presumption, found in most state laws, that a woman who gives birth to a child is the child's mother. UPA §201(a)(1) (2002). The Act also includes alternate provisions applicable in states that permit gestational surrogacy. Id. §201(a)(1), (4). In addition, the UPA provides that mechanisms for challenging paternity may also be used to challenge maternity. Id. §106; see also Soos v. Superior Court, County of Maricopa, 897 P.2d 1356 (Ariz. Ct. App. 1995) (statute that allowed biological father to prove paternity while denying genetic mother that right violates equal protection clause). Does this provision lessen the maternal security of an intended mother who gives birth to a baby produced from a donor egg? Could the woman argue that she did not "donate" the egg? See supra at page 519 note 2.

The Tennessee Supreme Court considered a case questioning the legal status of a woman who gave birth to triplets conceived using IVF, donor eggs, and her male partner's sperm. In re C.K.G., 173 S.W.3d 714 (Tenn. 2005). The woman sought custody of the children when the couple separated. Her former partner objected, asserting that the woman was not the mother or a legal parent of the children because she was merely a gestational surrogate with no genetic or legally enforceable tie to the children. The trial court held that the woman was the birth mother and legal mother; the appeals court affirmed using the intent of the parties as the legally relevant test, see Johnson v. Calvert, supra. The Tennessee Supreme Court affirmed that the woman was the legal mother on different grounds. The court rejected the intent test as straying too far from Tennessee's statutory framework and the genetics test because it would reach unintended results in cases involving egg donors. 173 S.W.3d at 724-725. The court instead adopted a "narrow" ruling limited to the specific facts and focusing on several factors: genetics, intent, gestation, and the "absence of controversy between the gestator and the genetic 'mother.'" Based on its analysis of these factors, the court decided that the woman who gave birth to the triplets was the legal mother and entitled to share custody with the genetic father. Id at 730.

2. *Constitutional Considerations.* How does the right to procreate apply to surrogacy arrangements? Does the Massachusetts court in *R.R.* consider whether

infertile couples have a constitutionally protected interest in the enforcement of their surrogacy arrangement? In *Baby M*, the court considered and rejected the genetic father's constitutional claims:

> Both parties argue that the Constitutions — state and federal — mandate approval of their basic claims. The source of their constitutional arguments is essentially the same: the right of privacy, the right to procreate, the right to the companionship of one's child, those rights flowing either directly from the Fourteenth Amendment or by its incorporation of the Bill of Rights, or from the Ninth Amendment, or through the penumbra surrounding all of the Bill of Rights. They are the rights of personal intimacy, of marriage, of sex, of family, of procreation. . . . The right asserted by the Sterns is the right of procreation; that asserted by Mary Beth Whitehead is the right to the companionship of her child. We find that the right of procreation does not extend as far as claimed by the Sterns. . . . The right to procreate very simply is the right to have natural children, whether through sexual intercourse or artificial insemination. It is no more than that. Mr. Stern has not been deprived of that right. Through artificial insemination of Mrs. Whitehead, Baby M is his child. The custody, care, companionship, and nurturing that follow birth are not parts of the right to procreation; they are rights that may also be constitutionally protected, but that involve many considerations other than the right of procreation. . . .
>
> Mrs. Whitehead, on the other hand, asserts a claim that falls within the scope of a recognized fundamental interest protected by the Constitution. As a mother, she claims the right to the companionship of her child. This is a fundamental interest, constitutionally protected. Furthermore, it was taken away from her by the action of the court below. Whether that action under these circumstances would constitute a constitutional deprivation, however, we need not and do not decide. By virtue of our decision Mrs. Whitehead's constitutional complaint — that her parental rights have been unconstitutionally terminated — is moot. . . . In re Baby M, 537 A.2d 1227, 1253-1255 (N.J. 1988).

3. *Traditional Surrogacy Contracts.* Why does the *R.R.* court refuse to enforce the surrogacy contract? Is there a way to write an enforceable traditional surrogacy contract in Massachusetts? Are the factors the court suggests ones that a court or legislature should devise? Why does the court reject the surrogate's claim that the contract was unconscionable? What is the legal distinction between refusing to enforce a contract and declaring it unconscionable?

What explains discomfort with surrogacy contracts? The development of private law in the nineteenth century can be viewed, under one theory, as the movement from status to contract. See H. Maine, Ancient Law (1939) (originally published in 1884). Many years before the development of doctrines tested on today's bar exam, an individual was born into a network of social relationships that established his or her legal rights and duties to others and to the state. This status-based idea of legal relationships is reflected in matters ranging in time from feudal law to the old law of master and servant to modern family law. Surrogacy contracts could be viewed as part of a continued assault on status-based law by contractarian principles. See, e.g., Janet L. Dolgin, Status and Contract in Surrogate Motherhood: An Illumination of the Surrogacy Debate, 38 Buff. L. Rev. 515 (1990).

Discomfort with traditional surrogacy arrangements is intertwined with concerns about economic exploitation. The *Baby M* court issued the classic statement regarding the need for courts to protect surrogates:

> Intimated, but disputed, is the assertion that surrogacy will be used for the benefit of the rich at the expense of the poor. See, e.g., Radin, Market Inalienability, 100 Harv. L. Rev. 1849, 1930 (1987). In response it is noted that the Sterns are not rich and the Whiteheads not poor. Nevertheless, it is clear to us that it is unlikely that surrogate mothers will be as proportionately numerous among those women in the top 20 percent income bracket as among those in the bottom 20 percent. Ibid. Put differently, we doubt that infertile couples in the low-income bracket will find upper income surrogates. . . .
>
> The point is made that Mrs. Whitehead agreed to the surrogacy arrangement, supposedly fully understanding the consequences. Putting aside the issue of how compelling her need for money may have been, and how significant her understanding of the consequences, we suggest that her consent is irrelevant. There are, in a civilized society, some things that money cannot buy. In America, we decided long ago that merely because conduct purchased by money was "voluntary" did not mean that it was good or beyond regulation and prohibition. West Coast Hotel Co. v. Parrish, 300 U.S. 379 (1937). Employers can no longer buy labor at the lowest price they can bargain for, even though that labor is "voluntary," 29 U.S.C. §206 (1982), or buy women's labor for less money than paid to men for the same job, 29 U.S.C. §206(d), or purchase the agreement of children to perform oppressive labor, 29 U.S.C. §212, or purchase the agreement of workers to subject themselves to unsafe or unhealthful working conditions, 29 U.S.C. §§651 to 678. (Occupational Safety and Health Act of 1970). There are, in short, values that society deems more important than granting to wealth whatever it can buy, be it labor, love, or life. . . .
>
> The surrogacy contract is based on principles that are directly contrary to the objectives of our laws. It guarantees the separation of a child from its mother; it looks to adoption regardless of suitability; it totally ignores the child; it takes the child from the mother regardless of her wishes and her maternal fitness; and it does all of this, it accomplishes all of its goals, through the use of money.
>
> Beyond that is the potential degradation of some women that may result from this arrangement. In many cases, of course, surrogacy may bring satisfaction, not only to the infertile couple, but to the surrogate mother herself. The fact, however, that many women may not perceive surrogacy negatively but rather see it as an opportunity does not diminish its potential for devastation to other women.
>
> In sum, the harmful consequences of this surrogacy arrangement appear to us all too palpable. In New Jersey the surrogate mother's agreement to sell her child is void. Its irrevocability infects the entire contract, as does the money that purports to buy it. . . . In re Baby M., 537 A.2d 1227, 1249-1250 (N.J. 1988).

How would you describe the court's attitude toward women who wish to become surrogates? Empowering? Respectful? Paternalistic? *Baby M*'s analysis of the evils of surrogacy can be compared with the pro-contract views of the proponents of law and economics and the views of some feminists. See, e.g., Lori Andrews, Beyond Doctrinal Boundaries: A Legal Framework for Surrogate Motherhood, 81 Va. L. Rev. 2343 (1995); Richard Epstein, Surrogacy: The Case for Full Contractual Enforcement, 81 Va. L. Rev. 2305 (1995); Richard A. Posner,

The Ethics and Economics of Enforcing Contracts of Surrogate Motherhood, 5 J. Contemp. Health L. & Pol'y 21, 31 (1989).

4. *The 2002 UPA and Gestational Surrogacy.* As noted in *R.R.*, fewer than half the states regulate surrogacy agreements, most enacting prohibitions or bans on payment. See Charts, 33 Fam. L.Q. 908 (2000) (no author). Are you surprised by this legislative response? Why have so many states prohibited surrogacy agreements? Note that a ban on surrogacy agreements is not technically a ban on surrogacy itself; the ban merely impedes the creation of enforceable agreements in which money is paid to the surrogate. While this undoubtedly has the effect of diminishing the business of surrogacy, surrogate arrangements are still possible between family members, for example, who are motivated by nonmonetary factors. Where contractual models have been adopted, they are largely applicable only to gestational surrogacy, where the surrogate has no genetic relationship with the resulting child. Are contractual models the appropriate mechanism for dealing with gestational disputes? What if major contractual terms were never decided by the parties — such as payment, visitation rights, and so forth? Should a court fill in these terms?

The revised UPA offers the choice of recognizing gestational surrogacy agreements as an alternative rather than as the uniform consensus approach:

§801. Gestational Agreement Authorized.

(a) A prospective gestational mother, her husband if she is married, a donor or the donors, and the intended parents may enter into a written agreement providing that:

(1) the prospective gestational mother agrees to pregnancy by means of assisted reproduction;

(2) the prospective gestational mother, her husband if she is married, and the donors relinquish all rights and duties as the parents of a child conceived through assisted reproduction; and

(3) the intended parents become the parents of the child.

(b) The man and the woman who are the intended parents must both be parties to the gestational agreement.

(c) A gestational agreement is enforceable only if validated as provided in Section 803.

(d) A gestational agreement does not apply to the birth of a child conceived by means of sexual intercourse.

(e) A gestational agreement may provide for payment of consideration.

(f) A gestational agreement may not limit the right of the gestational mother to make decisions to safeguard her health or that of the embryos or fetus. . . .

§803. Hearing to Validate Gestational Agreement.

(a) If the requirements of subsection (b) are satisfied, a court may issue an order validating the gestational agreement and declaring that the intended parents will be the parents of a child born during the term of the agreement.

(b) The court may issue an order under subsection (a) only on finding that:

(1) the residence requirements of Section 802 have been satisfied and the parties have submitted to the jurisdiction of the court under the jurisdictional standards of this [Act];

(2) unless waived by the court, the [relevant child-welfare agency] has made a home study of the intended parents and the intended parents meet the standards of fitness applicable to adoptive parents;

(3) all parties have voluntarily entered into the agreement and understand its terms;

(4) adequate provision has been made for all reasonable health-care expense associated with the gestational agreement until the birth of the child, including responsibility for those expenses if the agreement is terminated; and

(5) the consideration, if any, paid to the prospective gestational mother is reasonable.

§806. *Termination of Gestational Agreement.*

(a) After issuance of an order under this [article], but before the prospective gestational mother becomes pregnant by means of assisted reproduction, the prospective gestational mother, her husband, or either of the intended parents may terminate the gestational agreement by giving written notice of termination to all other parties.

(b) The court for good cause shown may terminate the gestational agreement.

(c) An individual who terminates a gestational agreement shall file notice of the termination with the court. On receipt of the notice, the court shall vacate the order issued under this [article]. An individual who does not notify the court of the termination of the agreement is subject to appropriate sanctions.

(d) Neither a prospective gestational mother nor her husband, if any, is liable to the intended parents for terminating a gestational agreement pursuant to this section.

§807. *Parentage Under Validated Gestational Agreement.*

(a) Upon birth of a child to a gestational mother, the intended parents shall file notice with the court that a child has been born to the gestational mother within 300 days after assisted reproduction. Thereupon, the court shall issue an order:

(1) confirming that the intended parents are the parents of the child;

(2) if necessary, ordering that the child be surrendered to the intended parents; and

(3) directing the [agency maintaining birth records] to issue a birth certificate naming the intended parents as parents of the child. . . .

(c) If the intended parents fail to file notice required under subsection (a), the gestational mother or the appropriate State agency may file notice with the court that a child has been born to the gestational mother within 300 days after assisted reproduction. Upon proof of a court order issued pursuant to Section 803 validating the gestational agreement, the court shall order the intended parents are the parents of the child and are financially responsible for the child.

§809.   Effect of Nonvalidated Gestational Agreement.

(a) A gestational agreement, whether in a record or not, that is not judicially validated is not enforceable.

(b) If a birth results under a gestational agreement that is not judicially validated as provided in this [article], the parent-child relationship is determined as provided in [Article] 2.

(c) Individuals who are parties to a nonvalidated gestational agreement as intended parents may be held liable for support of the resulting child, even if the agreement is otherwise unenforceable. The liability under this subsection includes assessing all expenses and fees. . . .

The UPA offers a strong judicial review model for gestational surrogacy arrangements. Note the many terms and conditions placed on the gestational surrogacy contract. Are any of the requirements ethically or legally dubious? Should a gestational surrogate have the same right to freely make an abortion decision as other pregnant women? See Kevin Yamamoto & Shelby A.D. Moore, A Trust Analysis of a Gestational Carrier's Right to Abortion, 70 Fordham L. Rev. 93 (2001). What is the practical effect of §809?

Challenges to state surrogacy legislation are relatively rare. In J.R. v. Utah, 261 F. Supp. 2d 1268 (2003), the plaintiffs sought to establish that the biological parents were the legal parents of twins born as a result of a gestational surrogacy agreement, despite a state law which appeared to make the birth mother the legal mother of the resulting child. The district court found that the plaintiffs lacked standing to challenge one portion of the Utah statute:

> The Utah surrogacy statute, Utah Code Ann. §76-7-204 (1999), does *not* prohibit use of gestational surrogacy as a procreative method, or deny persons access to that medical technology. . . . It is uncontroverted that plaintiffs utilized this method to accomplish the birth of twin children, and to that extent, have effectively exercised their rights to procreate.

Id. at 1279. The plaintiffs did not have standing to challenge Utah's ban on enforcing surrogacy agreements because their complaint did not actually ask the court to enforce any particular provision of their gestational surrogacy contract. The court did permit the plaintiffs to challenge another key aspect of the statutory scheme — the provision which appeared to make the birth mother the legal mother of the child, even where the parties intended a gestational surrogacy arrangement:

> Utah Code Ann. §76-7-204(3)(a) provides that "the surrogate mother is the mother of the child for all legal purposes, and her husband, if she is married, is the father of the child for all legal purposes." In contrast to §76-7-204(2), this provision may bear directly upon the question whether J.R. and M.R. may be "legally . . . acknowledged as parents of their own children." (Pltfs' Reply/Resp. Mem. at 3 P. 7.) Plaintiffs have alleged the requisite "injury in fact" that affords them standing to pursue their constitutional challenge to this statutory presumption.

Id. at 1280.

5. *Surrogacy and Intentional Parenting.* In In re Buzzanca, a California court considered the impact of assisted reproduction involving a donated embryo and a gestational surrogate. 72 Cal. Rptr. 2d 280 (Ct. App. 1998). Luanne and John Buzzanca agreed to create a child by using a donor embryo implanted into a gestational surrogate. John filed for divorce shortly before the birth of Jaycee. John alleged that the couple did not have children; Luanne contended that they were expecting their first child from the surrogate. Id. at 282. The surrogate did not want to parent the child. The trial court found that Jaycee did not have any parents. Id. at 283. The appellate court rejected this conclusion, finding that the artificial insemination statute applied to both intended parents and that John became Jaycee's father by causing the child's conception. Id. at 284-288, 292. The intent of the parties was only relevant to a point, however, as John was barred from asserting that Luanne had promised to assume responsibility for Jaycee's care. Id. at 292. See also Doe v. Doe, 710 A.2d 1297 (Conn. 1998) (nonbiological mother given custody of child conceived as a result of a surrogacy arrangement in which her husband's sperm had been used to impregnate a third party).

6. *Tort Law Implications of Surrogacy Arrangements.* What tort claims might arise from these arrangements? Could the parents in *R.R.* sue the fertility clinic or psychologist for failure to appropriately screen surrogates for latent traditionally maternal instincts? What would be the damages? Could the fertility clinic be liable if a child from a surrogacy arrangement is born with a genetic defect?

7. *Womb Transplants.* Womb transplants may provide an alternative to gestational surrogacy for some women. See Roni Rabin, Prospect of Womb Transplant Raises Hopes and Red Flags, N.Y. Times, Jan. 1, 2007, at F5. What are the advantages and disadvantages of this approach? The uterus can be obtained from deceased donors much like other organs. Womb transplants impose significant surgical risks on the recipient, including the need to take immunosuppressive drugs and the risk of rejection. Fetuses carried in the transplanted uterus would also be exposed to additional risk. Should these risks be considered "unnecessary" because of the available alternative of surrogacy? Id.

8. *Commentaries.* The surrogate motherhood controversy has generated profuse commentary in legal, medical, philosophical, and popular journals. In addition to the books and articles cited above, see Margaret Friedlander Brinig, A Maternalistic Approach to Surrogacy, 81 Va. L. Rev. 2377 (1995); R. Alta Charo, And Baby Makes Three — or Four, or Five, or Six: Redefining the Family after the Reprotech Revolution, 15 Wis. Women's L.J. 231 (2000); Rachel Cook et al., eds., Surrogate Motherhood: International Perspectives (2003); Janet L. Dolgin, An Emerging Consensus: Reproductive Technology and the Law, 23 Vt. L. Rev. 225 (1998); Janet L. Dolgin, Choice, Tradition, and the New Genetics: The Fragmentation of the Ideology of Family, 32 Conn. L. Rev. 523 (2000); Helene S. Shapo, Assisted Reproduction and the Law: Disharmony on a Socially Divisive Issue, 100 Nw. U. L. Rev. 465 (2006); Molly J. Walker Wilson, Precommitment in Free-Market Procreation: Surrogacy, Commissioned Adoption, and Limits on Human Decision Making Capacity, 31 J. Legis. 329 (2005); see also Danny R. Veilleux, Annot., Validity and Construction of Surrogate Parenting Agreement, 77 A.L.R.4th 70 (1989).

Problems: Determining Parentage

The explosive growth of reproductive technologies creates an almost bewildering array of parenting possibilities. The statutes and cases in this section demonstrate that the rules governing the determination of parentage are still in flux. The most established technology — artificial insemination or IUI — is regulated by statutes that attempt to allocate parenting rights and responsibilities. Consumers of donated sperm nonetheless confront some legal uncertainties. Technologies designed to provide the female components of the reproductive process — eggs and a uterus — are less well regulated, and significant areas of legal uncertainty still remain. States appear to be moving toward treating egg donation as the equivalent of sperm donation. See 2002 UPA. Conflicts over the disposition of frozen embryos also can be difficult to resolve, with courts suggesting that they will enforce the prior agreements of progenitors but balking at the imposition of parenthood on a presently unwilling individual. Gestational surrogates appear to have fewer legally protected interests than traditional surrogates (in which both egg and uterus are provided by one donor). The state of legal confusion, however, does not prevent these transactions from going forward. Consumers and sellers of reproductive services, and their lawyers, attempt to meet the objectives of the parties within whatever legal framework is available. A poor use of reproductive technology can result in substantial emotional and financial costs for the participants, as well as in professional disciplinary or malpractice liability for the health care providers and attorneys.

1. *Sperm Donation and IUI*. Assume you are in a jurisdiction that has adopted the 2002 version of Uniform Parentage Act's provisions governing gamete donation (see page 550). Melissa and Julie wish to have and raise a child together. Their friend, David, volunteers to provide sperm that will be used to artificially inseminate Julie. How should the transaction be structured to ensure that David will not have any parental rights and obligations? How could the parties use IUI and ensure that David will be considered to be the resulting child's legal father? Will Melissa have any legally recognized relationship with the child? Could such a relationship be created?

2. *Egg Donation and Surrogacy*. Latisha and Michael Bates have been married for eight years. Pregnancy and/or the hormonal treatments necessary for egg harvesting would injure Latisha's health. The couple still want very much to have a child, preferably one that is genetically related to Michael. They have heard about surrogacy arrangements and would like to hire a surrogate to bear their child. Assume you are in a jurisdiction with laws like those in Massachusetts. Could the Bateses enter into a surrogacy agreement with their neighbor, Paula? What should be the terms? Will the agreement be enforceable? What type of compensation, if any, will the Bateses be able to give Paula? Who will be the parents of the resulting child? Can the parties do anything to ensure that Latisha and Michael will be considered to be the parents?

Now assume that the Bateses make a separate arrangement with an egg donor, Ala Truistic, whose egg would be fertilized with Michael's sperm and implanted in Paula's uterus for gestation. Could Ala be paid any compensation for undergoing the procedures necessary for egg donation? Could Paula be compensated for enduring the pregnancy? Who would be the mother? Consider this question first based under the Massachusetts cases, supra at pages 537-542. Then consider the 2002 UPA approach. Who would be considered to be the legal parents of any resulting child?

Suppose that Ala donates several eggs that are fertilized with Michael's sperm. The eggs are donated pursuant to a written agreement that provides that Ala is donating the eggs "for use by Michael and Latisha Bates, a married couple, for use in raising the resulting child in a loving home." Latisha files for divorce from Michael after the eggs are fertilized and the resulting embryos are frozen but before implantation into Paula. Suppose that Ala now wants to control the disposition of the frozen embryos on the theory that the donation contract has been breached. Could you make any arguments on her behalf? Suppose that Michael wants to control the disposition of the embryos on the theory that Ala's ability to exercise reproductive choices ended with her donation?

E. ETHICAL AND LEGAL IMPLICATIONS OF ADVANCES IN GENETICS

1. Introduction

The fifth and final section of the chapter explores the legal implications of advances in genetics and the regulation of genetic technologies. In some senses these advances have already played a significant role in the chapter's coverage of reproduction: advances in understanding heredity and genetics undercut the scientific foundation for the eugenics theories underlying the laws challenged in Buck v. Bell, supra at page 425, and Skinner v. Oklahoma, supra at page 427. Genetic testing provides the technical capacity for parents to identify the sex of a fetus and to learn whether the fetus has certain genetic anomalies; the woman carrying the fetus may decide to abort based on the results of these tests. See page 448 and the discussion of intentional parenting. The process greatly increases the possibility of using genetic information to shape offspring. This can be seen in Internet Web sites for sperm and egg donors, which appear to offer recipients the ability to select donors based on characteristics commonly understood to have a genetic component such as height, hair and eye color, and intelligence. IVF provides an even more direct opportunity to perform genetic testing on the preembryos and to use the results to determine which embryos will be selected for transplantation. Genetic testing can be used to screen for disabling genetic conditions as well as to select for some characteristics. See page 515.

This section of the chapter will focus more directly on the implications of scientific discoveries in this area. Should cloning and related procedures be allowed for reproductive, research, or therapeutic purposes? Should scientists be permitted to patent life forms and genes? How should society balance the positive incentives created from intellectual property ownership rules with the need to ensure equitable access to important new developments?

2. Stem Cell Research

One of the most significant current debates for federal and state governments concerned with the recognition of fetal interests involves embryonic stem cells. Understanding the debate requires familiarity with some basic biology. The human body contains hundreds of different types of specialized cells capable of performing different functions. Heart muscle cells, nerve cells (neurons), and liver cells all perform different functions. Certain types of stem cells are "undifferentiated" (they have not yet become specialized cells), "pluripotent" (they have the capacity to become any type of specialized cell), and "self-replicating" (they can replicate in a proper laboratory setting). Stem cells can be found in all stages of human development from embryos (up to about seven weeks of development), fetuses (from the eighth week of development to birth), children, and adults. Embryonic stem cells currently are easier to harvest and considered more likely to be pluripotent than stem cells from older organisms. See generally Helen Frankish, Researchers Question Ability of Stem Cells to Generate Multiple Cell Types, 359 Lancet 951 (2002) (focusing on problems with adult stem cells); Konrad Hochedlinger & Rudolf Jaenisch, Nuclear Transplantation, Embryonic Stem Cells, and the Potential for Cell Therapy, 349 New Eng. J. Med. 275 (2003); National Institutes of Health, Regenerative Medicine 2006, available at http://stemcells.nih.gov/info/scireport/2006report.htm; and National Institutes of Health, Stem Cell Information, available at http://stemcells.nih.gov/.

There are several uses for stem cells. At a basic level, researchers hope to use embryonic stem cells to understand more about the process by which stem cells are able to differentiate into one of hundreds of specialized cells in the human body. Once more is understood about this process, it is possible that researchers will be able to develop clinical uses for stem cells by, for example, using stem cells to generate differentiated cells that could be used to replace heart muscle injured in a heart attack, nerve cells for those who have suffered spinal cord injuries, or insulin-producing cells for persons with diabetes. Stem cell research thus offers the tantalizing possibility of enormous tangible benefits to persons suffering from cardiovascular disease, diabetes, or spinal cord injuries, along with other conditions. Some scientists argue that mastery of the process of cellular differentiation, combined with a ready supply of embryonic stem cells, could halt or reverse the progress of these diseases. See National Institutes of Health, Regenerative Medicine 2006, available at http://stemcells.nih.gov/info/scireport/2006report.htm.

Stem cell research is tied to the ongoing debates about cloning. The use of ordinary stem cells for treatment could give rise to an immune reaction in the recipient of the stem cells as the body treats the cells as foreign matter. This reaction might be avoided by using somatic cell nuclear transplantation (often referred to as SCNT in the scientific literature). This technique involves taking the genetic materials from a somatic cell[1] and transplanting this material into an oocyte (a human egg cell) that has had its original genetic material removed. The oocyte is then manipulated into beginning the process of cell division and the creation of an embryo. The embryo will contain stem cells that could be extracted and used to create specialized cells that would no longer be viewed as foreign by the recipient

---

[1] Somatic cells are ordinary cells from the body containing a full complement of genes as opposed to germ-line cells (sperm and egg cells), which contain only half of a person's genes.

and thus would not create the risk of tissue rejection and the need for the recipient to take immune-suppressing drugs. This procedure is known as "therapeutic" cloning because, as in reproductive cloning, an embryo is created with virtually the same genetic identity as another human being.[2] Therapeutic cloning is different from reproductive cloning because the resulting embryo is never implanted in a uterus with the hope of producing a human being; instead the goal is to provide a therapeutic treatment using embryonic stem cells. The following diagram compares natural reproduction, therapeutic cloning, and reproductive cloning:

Stem cell research implicates debates about fetal interests because most scientists have argued that embryonic stem cells offer more benefit to researchers than adult stem cells, and the acquisition of embryonic stem cells has been associated with the destruction of the embryo. To those who believe that personhood begins at the union of a sperm and egg, research using embryonic stem cells involves the sacrifice of human life for scientific progress. Furthermore, the successful development of treatments using embryonic stem cells might require the commercialized production and exploitation of human embryos.

The use of fetal stem cells implicates strongly held views regarding the status of embryos and fetuses and the degree to which they command special respect

Normal Reproduction, Reporductive Cloning, and Therapeutic Cloning[3]

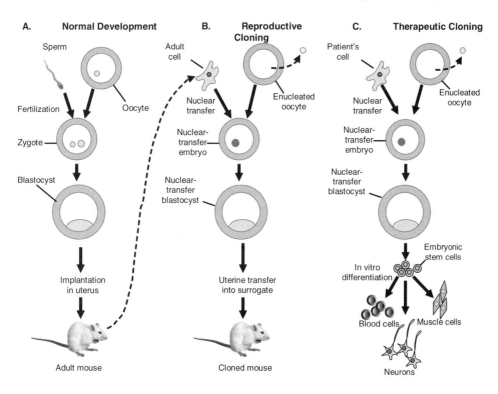

---

[2] The cloned embryo will not be completely identical because the genetic material found in the oocyte's mitochondria is not removed; mitochondrial DNA from the donor oocyte therefore will be reproduced in the embryo.

[3] Adapted from Konrad Hochedlinger & Rudolf Jaenisch, Nuclear Transplantation, Embryonic Stem Cells, and the Potential for Cell Therapy, 349 New Eng. J. Med. 275 (2003).

and concern. Many ethicists and others object to the creation of potential human life solely for the purpose of producing stem cells. Many also object to the extraction of stem cells from embryos or fetuses originally created for other purposes, such as through ordinary pregnancy or the use of in vitro fertilization, even if the potential for human life will never be realized because of a woman's right to choose to terminate her pregnancy or because embryos created for assisted human reproduction are no longer needed for this purpose.

The federal debate about stem cell research has focused on funding for research. For over a decade, Congress has imposed a limitation on the use of federal funds for certain types of research involving embryos, including research in which "human embryos are destroyed . . . or knowingly subjected to a risk of injury or death greater than that allowed for research on fetuses in utero" under federal regulations. The provision appeared, perhaps inadvertently, to allow federal funding for research involving the use of stem cell lines that had been created via the destruction of embryos at some point in the past. See President's Council on Bioethics, Monitoring Stem Cell Research 24-28 (2004). See also 42 U.S.C.A. §289g, 289g-1 (restrictions on fetal research and transplantation of fetal tissue). The Clinton administration issued guidelines authorizing the use of federal funds for stem cell research late in his presidency; the guidelines represented an effort to expand federal funding while recognizing the special status of fetal tissue. See 65 Fed. Reg. 51,976 (2000); 65 Fed. Reg. 69,951 (2000). The guidelines were withdrawn by the Bush administration. 66 Fed. Reg. 57,107 (2001). See generally Case Studies, Should the Federal Government Fund Embryonic Stem Cell Research?, 2 Yale J. Health Pol'y L. & Ethics 143-206 (2001) (commentaries by leading academicians and politicians).

In August 2001, after a protracted public debate, President Bush issued new guidelines permitting the limited use of federal funds to study embryonic stem cells. One major restriction was that researchers could only use embryonic stem cell lines established prior to the president's decision that were derived from embryos originally created for use in assisted reproduction but which were no longer going to be used for this purpose. Despite concerns that there would be insufficient stem cell material of appropriate quality to pursue an aggressive research agenda, Bush rejected suggestions that federal funding be allocated to research on new tissue lines to be created in a similar manner. The Bush administration also favored continued research into whether adult stem cells could provide some of the same benefits without the moral dilemma.

Stem cell research continued to attract considerable public attention in the early 2000s, driven in part by public pleas from prominent individuals such as Christopher Reeve, an actor paralyzed in a riding accident; Michael J. Fox, an actor with Parkinson's disease; and former First Lady Nancy Reagan, whose husband, former President Ronald Reagan, eventually died from Alzheimer's disease. In July 2006 the U.S. Senate joined the House in voting to expand access to federal funding for human embryonic stem cell research, eliciting President Bush's first use of his veto power. Sheryl Gay Stolberg, First Bush Veto Maintains Limits on Stem Cell Use, N.Y. Times, July 20, 2006.

The federal funding debate has sparked a parallel debate in the states. The gap in federal funding sparked concerns that important stem cell research projects and leading researchers might leave the United States for other, more hospitable jurisdictions around the world. Some argued that the United States might lose access to important and potentially lucrative scientific developments. Stem cell activists began to promote state funding of stem cell research as a method of ensuring that U.S. researchers could remain at the forefront of the field. The National Conference of State Legislatures tracks state legislation related to stem cell research. See www.ncsl.org/programs/health/genetics.htm. Several states have had successful voter or legislative initiatives designed to provide funding and support for stem cell research, including embryonic stem cell research. See, e.g., the Web site for the California Institute for Regenerative Medicine, established as result of a voter initiative, at http://www.cirm.ca.gov/.

Notes: Stem Cell Research

1. *Resources on Stem Cell Research.* Stem cell research has attracted an enormous amount of commentary from individuals and specialized, expert committees or groups. For more information about stem cell research and the implications for law and ethics see, e.g., Janet L. Dolgin, Embryonic Discourse: Abortion, Stem Cells, and Cloning, 31 Fla. St. L. Rev. 101 (2003); Russell Korobkin, Stem Cell Century: Law and Policy for a Breakthrough Technology (forthcoming 2007); President's Council on Bioethics, Monitoring Stem Cell Research (2004), available at http://www.bioethics.gov/reports/stemcell/index. html; Committee on Guidelines for Human Embryonic Stem Cell Research, National Research Council, Guidelines for Human Embryonic Stem Cell Research (2005), available at http://www.nap.edu/catalog/11278.html; Human Embryonic Stem Cell Research Advisory Committee, National Research Council, 2007 Amendments to the National Academies' Guidelines for Human Embryonic Stem Cell Research, available at http://www.nap.edu/catalog/11278.html/11871.html; National Academies/Institute of Medicine, Stem Cells and the Future of Regenerative Medicine (2002); John Robertson, Embryo Culture and the "Culture of Life" Constitutional Issues in the Embryonic Stem Cell Debate, 2006 Chi. Legal F. 1; Russell Korobkin, Embryonic Histrionics: A Critical Evaluation of the Bush Stem Cell Funding Policy and the Congressional Alternative, 47 Jurimetrics J. 1 (Fall 2006); Irving L. Weissman, Stem Cells — Scientific, Medical, and Political Issues, 346 New Eng. J. Med. 1576 (2002).

2. *The Destruction of Preexisting Embryos.* Existing stem cell lines have largely been derived from embryos originally created as a part of assisted human reproduction but are no longer needed for that purpose. Should both genetic contributors be required to consent to the use of the embryo in research? Should this rule apply even when the embryo was created through a gamete donation? Is it enough if the consent document contains a reference to "use in research," or should there be a specific, detailed consent relating to the creation of stem cell lines? Should the "intended parents" of an embryo be required to consent to the use of the embryo even it was created solely through the use of donor gametes? See Guidelines for Human Embryonic Stem Cell Research (2005), supra, at 9 (consent required); Guidelines for Human Embryonic Stem Cell Research (2007), supra (rejecting request to modify rules to allow use of embryos created with anonymous donor sperm where donors had not specifically consented to use of embryo for research).

3. *The Creation of Embryos for Stem Cell Research.* President Bush authorized federal funding for research using existing stem cell lines derived from embryos created for reproduction, but refused to expand funding to newly created stem cell lines derived in the same manner. Is there an ethical basis for the distinction between stem cell lines existing in 2001 and those that might be created today? President's Council on Bioethics, Monitoring Stem Cell Research, supra, at 30.

May researchers nonetheless create new embryonic stem cell lines so long as they are willing to forgo federal funding and so long as their research does not violate state law? See page 478. See Guidelines for Human Embryonic Stem Cell Research (2005), supra, at 3 (yes). Should the gamete donors involved in embryonic stem cell research be required to give their full informed consent even though they are not the true subjects of the research? Stem cell research may someday lead to enormously valuable therapeutic discoveries. Would it be permissible to offer donors a financial incentive to participate? Id. at 9 (yes; no).

Oocyte donation is an invasive and potentially risky procedure. Is it unethical to ask women who will receive no direct medical or financial benefit to bear the risks of oocyte donation? See Committee on Assessing the Medical Risks of Human Oocyte Donation for Stem Cell Research, Assessing the Medical Risks of Human Oocyte Donation for Stem Cell Research: Workshop Report, available at http:www.nap.edu/catalog/11832.html; Debora Spar, The Egg Trade—Making Sense of the Market for Human Oocytes, 356 New Eng. J. Med. 1289 (2007) (noting inconsistency in permitting payment to oocyte donors for reproduction but not for research); Robert Steinbrook, Egg Donation and Human Embryonic Stem-Cell Research, 354 New Eng. J. Med. 324 (2006).

4. *Alternatives to the Destruction of the Embryo.* Should researchers explore the possibility of removing embryonic stem cells from embryos without destroying them? The living embryo could then either be refrozen and stored or implanted for reproduction. This technique, if scientifically viable, might eliminate the ethical concerns about the destruction of embryonic life. Does it raise other concerns? Even attempting to research better methods of extracting stem cells without destruction of the embryo would involve an increased risk to embryonic development not associated with any direct benefit to the embryo or fetus. See President's Council on Bioethics, Alternative Sources of Human Pluripotent Stem Cells: A White Paper (2005), available at http://www.bioethics.gov/reports/stemcell/index.html.

5. *Therapeutic Cloning.* Part of the controversy surrounding therapeutic cloning arises from the fact that it involves the creation of embryos that are then destroyed to extract embryonic stem cells. Should the fact that the embryos are cloned create any additional ethical concerns? Is the line between therapeutic and reproductive cloning, as clear as Diagram 1 would suggest? The next section will explore the cloning debate in more detail.

3. Human Cloning

Scientists reported the first successful reproductive cloning of a mammal early in 1997. Wilmut et al., Viable Offspring Derived from Fetal and Adult Mammalian Cells, 385 Nature 810 (1997). Reproductive cloning essentially involves the creation of a sort of time-delayed, nearly identical twin. An ovum's nucleus is replaced by the nucleus of a mature adult cell that contains the core genetic identity of an individual being. The ovum is induced to divide and to produce living offspring that have virtually the same genetic identity as the donor of the original genetic material ("virtually," because cloning does not now involve the transfer of genetic material found outside the nucleus in the mitochondria. Cf. R. Sanders Williams, Another Surprise from the Mitochondrial Genome, 347 New Eng. J. Med. 609 (2002) (brief summary of knowledge regarding mitochondrial DNA)).

This is not the "cloning" of late-night science fiction films—a single cell does not grow in a laboratory and give rise to an adult being with the same memories and abilities as the original being. See Nancy L. Segal, Human Cloning: Insights from Twins and Twin Research, 53 Hastings L.J. 1073 (2002). Neither Hitler nor Gandhi could be absolutely replicated. But the development of mammalian cloning nonetheless has raised the significant possibility that people might now be able to pass on their genetic heritage to future generations without engaging in the shuffling and mixing of genes that occurs in sexual reproduction. This could be an important tool for persons who do not have gametes or who cannot reproduce sexually within their relationships. David Orentlicher, Beyond Cloning: Expanding Reproductive Options for Same-Sex Couples, 66 Brook. L. Rev. 651 (2001).

The immediate response to the birth of Dolly, the cloned sheep, was largely negative. The FDA reacted swiftly, asserting jurisdiction over clinical research using cloning technology for human reproduction in 1998. Researchers were warned not to pursue human reproductive cloning without following the FDA's investigational new drug (IND) regulations. See U.S. FDA, Use of Cloning Technology to Clone a Human Being, available at http://www.fda.gov/cber/genetherapy/clone.htm.

Commentators argued that research into human cloning should be banned for a number of reasons. Would cloning stifle the normal evolutionary process, which depends on new combinations of genes created through sexual reproduction? Would cloning encourage unduly egocentric reproduction—perhaps the creation of fifty genetic copies of a wealthy real estate developer or writer of health law casebooks? Would cloning encourage reproduction for profit—fifty genetic copies of Michael Jordan or Bill Gates? Perhaps cloning would be used to create genetically identical persons who could provide "spare parts," such as organs or tissue for their creator. See, e.g., Human Cloning Requires a Moratorium, Not a Ban, 386 Nature 1 (1997); Elizabeth Pennisi & Nigel Williams, Will Dolly Send in the Clones?, 275 Science 1415 (1997). If nothing else, negative responses to the possibility of human reproductive cloning have revealed our fears about genetic determinism and our belief that "normal" reproduction represents something different—and better—than selfish egotism.

Scientific and ethical advisory boards weighed in on reproductive cloning in the early 2000s. See, e.g., President's Council on Bioethics, Human Cloning and Human Dignity: An Ethical Inquiry (2002), available at http://www.bioethics.gov/reports/cloningreport/index.html; National Research Council, Scientific and Medical Aspects of Human Reproductive Cloning (2002) (focusing on medical risks that make the procedure unsafe for participants and offspring). These advisory groups uniformly recommended at least a moratorium if not a permanent ban on human cloning for reproduction. The virtual uniformity of views regarding the inadvisability of human cloning reflected the fact that mammalian cloning appeared to be extraordinarily difficult to achieve and to entail significant risks of genetic and other abnormalities. This raises the possibility that the debate may become less one sided if human cloning should ever become less medically risky. When and how would researchers determine the safety of human cloning if the practice is banned?

Therapeutic cloning, discussed supra, does not directly raise the risks of reproductive cloning as there is no effort or intent to implant the cloned embryos and to achieve a live birth. The issues are nonetheless tied together in many public debates. Ethicists are divided on whether cloning for biomedical research purposes — i.e., embryonic stem cell research — should be banned or regulated along with cloning for reproduction. President Bush's Council on Bioethics issued a majority and minority view on these issues in 2002:

> **Majority Recommendation:** Ten Members of the Council recommend a ban on cloning-to-produce-children combined with a four-year moratorium on cloning-for-biomedical-research. We also call for a federal review of current and projected practices of human embryo research, pre-implantation genetic diagnosis, genetic modification of human embryos and gametes, and related matters, with a view to recommending and shaping ethically sound policies for the entire field. . . .
> **Minority Recommendation:** Seven Members of the Council recommend a ban on cloning-to-produce-children, with regulation of the use of cloned embryos for medical research.

President's Council on Bioethics, Human Cloning and Human Dignity: An Ethical Inquiry 11-12 (2002) (Executive Summary, online version) [hereinafter President's Council Human Cloning Report].

The conflation of reproductive and therapeutic cloning has continued for lawmakers as well. Congress began efforts to ban reproductive cloning in the early 2000s. The proposed bills uniformly prohibited reproductive cloning and imposed substantial criminal penalties on persons associated with reproductive cloning. Despite virtually uniform agreement that reproductive cloning should be prohibited, congressional action was stymied, in large part because of the clash between lawmakers who favored permitting therapeutic cloning and those who believed that therapeutic and reproductive cloning were indistinguishable misuses of human embryos. See, e.g., George J. Annas, Cloning and the U.S. Congress, 346 New Eng. J. Med. 1599 (2002). Lawmakers who opposed both forms of cloning were for a time unwilling to compromise to deliver legislation that would have distinguished between therapeutic and reproductive cloning. See discussion of therapeutic cloning and federal legislation, supra at pages 556-559.

State legislatures have also been quite active, with more substantial if widely varying results. National Conference of State Legislatures, State Embryonic and Fetal Research Laws (available at www.ncsl.org). Reproductive cloning is uniformly prohibited in the states that have addressed the issue. About six states prohibit research on therapeutic cloning, while five states permit therapeutic cloning. Id.

The cloning debate continues to attract worldwide attention. Despite unanimous support for a treaty to ban human cloning for reproduction in the

U.N. General Assembly, the treaty effort failed due to disagreements about whether and how to ban cloning for research purposes and therapeutic cloning. Instead of pursuing the treaty, the United States agreed to a compromise declaration against human reproductive cloning. Warren Hoge, U.S. Drops Effort for Treaty Banning Cloning, N.Y. Times, Nov. 20, 2004, at A3, col. 1. The final declaration, adopted by the General Assembly in 2005, urged nations to ban human cloning in terms broad enough to encompass both reproductive and therapeutic cloning. Compliance with the declaration is voluntary. The declaration sparked sharp debate and "no" votes from countries choosing to regulate rather than to ban therapeutic human cloning. United Nations Declaration on Human Cloning at http://www.un.org/News/Press/docs/2005/ga10333.doc.htm.

Notes: Human Reproductive Cloning

1. *Cloning as Procreation?* Reproductive cloning would produce a child who, from a genetic standpoint, would be similar to an identical twin of the genetic progenitor. From one genetic perspective, the child would not be the "child" of anyone, because reproduction involves the mixing of parental genes, not the duplication of those genes. Could you even develop an argument that the U.S. Constitution's protection of procreative liberty includes a right to cloning? See generally John A. Robertson, Liberty, Identity, and Human Cloning, 76 Tex. L. Rev. 1371 (1998); Cass R. Sunstein, Is There a Constitutional Right to Clone?, 53 Hastings L.J. 987 (2002). What about the treatment of a cloned child under state law — to whom would the UPA assign parental rights?

2. *The Ethics of Cloning.* The President's Bioethics Advisory Council unanimously found that human reproductive cloning is unethical. President's Council Human Cloning Report, ch. 5 (2002). The Council viewed human cloning as a particularly risky type of human experimentation in which it is impossible to obtain the consent of the party at the most risk, the cloned child. Unlike other groups, the Council found that "safety is not a temporary ethical concern. It is rather an enduring moral concern that might not be surmountable and should thus preclude work toward the development of cloning techniques to produce children." Id. at 14. The President's Council identified several "specific ethical issues and objections to cloning human children: (1) problems of identity and individuality; (2) concerns regarding manufacture; (3) the prospects of a new eugenics; (4) troubled family relations; and (5) effects on society [through, e.g., permitting dehumanizing practices]." Id. at 18. How would you weigh these ethical objections? How many of them do you think apply to other uses of reproductive technology?

3. *Scientific Fraud.* As noted above, efforts to clone mammals have been fraught with difficulty, and the results in non-humans have been mixed. Is human cloning scientifically feasible? A South Korean research team announced through articles in leading journals that it had successfully created stem cell lines from therapeutic human cloning in the early 2000s. The results suggested that the significant scientific barriers to human cloning are not insurmountable. In 2005 the lead South Korean scientist, Woo Suk Hwang, was forced to admit that his research results had been fabricated. He also revealed that the research had used

oocytes "donated" by junior researchers in his lab as well as from paid donors. See Evan Snyder & Jeanne Loring, Beyond Fraud — Stem Cell Research Continues, 354 New Eng. J. Med. 321 (2006); and Robert Steinbrook, Egg Donation and Human Embryonic Stem-Cell Research, 354 New Eng. J. Med. 324 (2006). The repercussions were significant. First, it appeared that the hurdles to successful human cloning remain high. Second, the ethical and legal issues associated with the regulation of cloning research became much more salient, beginning with concerns about the exploitation of donors. Third, the incident vividly demonstrated the risk of misconduct arising from high-profile scientific research.

4. *Comparing Regulatory Regimes*. Several countries have enacted comprehensive legislation designed to address assisted reproductive technologies, embryo research, and cloning. Are there any lessons in this legislation for the United States? Australia has two separate acts for stem cell research and cloning: Prohibition of Human Cloning 2002 (http://www.nhmrc.gov.au/publications/_files/prohibit.pdf) and the Research Involving Human Embryos Act 2002 (http://www.nhmrc.gov.au/publications/_files/embryact.pdf). The Prohibition of Human Cloning bans human reproductive cloning; creating an embryo for a purpose other than for achieving pregnancy; creating an embryo with more than two genetic donors; keeping an embryo alive for more than 14 days; using cells from a human embryo to create another human embryo; creating heritable alterations to the genome; chimeras; and commercial trading in human eggs, sperm, or embryos. The Research Involving Human Embryos Act regulates certain uses of excess ART embryos. The National Health and Medical Research Council Licensing Committee licenses the use of the excess ART embryos and monitors compliance.

Canada's Assisted Human Reproduction Act prohibits germ-line engineering, the creation of chimeras, human reproductive cloning, sex selection unless it is being used to treat or prevent a sex-linked disease, and creation of human embryos solely for research; and payment of surrogates or payment for gametes. http://laws.justice.gc.ca/en/A-13.4/.

The United Kingdom has had legislation in place since 1990. The Human Fertilization and Embryology Act creates the Human Fertilization and Embryology Authority, whose responsibilities include licensing ART clinics and gamete and embryo storage facilities, and licensing and monitoring human embryo research. The Act prohibits using embryos older than 14 days for research, implanting a human embryo into an animal, somatic cell nuclear transfer, and genetic alteration while a cell is part of an embryo. The Authority prohibits human reproductive cloning but authorizes therapeutic cloning research. See www.opsi. gov.uk/acts/acts1990/Ukpga_19900037_en_1.htm (the Act); and http://www.hfea. gov.uk/ (Web site for the Authority).

5. *Commentaries*. Commentaries on cloning are becoming as voluminous as those found in other areas of reproductive health law. In addition to the sources noted above, see Ronald Chester, Cloning Embryos from Adult Human Beings: The Relative Merits of Reproductive, Research and Therapeutic Uses, 39 New Eng. L. Rev. 583 (2004-2005); Rudolf Jaenisch, Human Cloning — The Science and Ethics of Nuclear Transplantation, 351 New Eng. J. Med. 2786 (2004); Leon R. Kass & James Q. Wilson, The Ethics of Human Cloning (1998); Symposium on

Human Cloning: Legal, Social, and Moral Perspectives for the Twenty-first Century, 27 Hofstra L. Rev. 473-668 (1999).

Problem: Human Cloning

Your client, Chris Jacobs, wants to create a child through cloning. Chris is preparing to go to an unnamed foreign country where experts believe they have perfected the process. The nucleus from some of Chris's cells will be inserted into a donor's eggs, whose nuclei have been removed. The eggs will be stimulated into developing into embryos, which will then be implanted into a gestational surrogate. The surrogate will then relinquish the child to Chris. Chris hopes to be a parent within a year. How would you counsel Chris? Do you have any ethical, professional disciplinary, or malpractice concerns? Assume that Chris brings a child back to this country. How would you go about attempting to establish that Chris is the child's parent? Examine the relevant statutes in your state. Who is the child's parent?

4. Intellectual Property and the Ownership of Genetic Discoveries

▮ DIAMOND v. CHAKRABARTY
447 U.S. 303 (1980)

Burger, C.J.

We granted certiorari to determine whether a live, human-made microorganism is patentable subject matter under 35 U.S.C. § 101.

In 1972, respondent Chakrabarty, a microbiologist, filed a patent application, assigned to the General Electric Co. The application asserted 36 claims related to Chakrabarty's invention of "a bacterium from the genus *Pseudomonas* containing therein at least two stable energy-generating plasmids, each of said plasmids providing a separate hydrocarbon degradative pathway."[2] This human-made, genetically engineered bacterium is capable of breaking down multiple components of crude oil. Because of this property, which is possessed by no naturally occurring bacteria, Chakrabarty's invention is believed to have significant value for the treatment of oil spills.

Chakrabarty's patent claims were of three types: first, process claims for the method of producing the bacteria; second, claims for an inoculum comprised of a carrier material floating on water, such as straw, and the new bacteria; and third, claims to the bacteria themselves. The patent examiner allowed the claims falling

---

[2] Plasmids are hereditary units physically separate from the chromosomes of the cell. In prior research, Chakrabarty and an associate discovered that plasmids control the oil degradation abilities of certain bacteria. In particular, the two researchers discovered plasmids capable of degrading camphor and octane, two components of crude oil. In the work represented by the patent application at issue here, Chakrabarty discovered a process by which four different plasmids, capable of degrading four different oil components, could be transferred to and maintained stably in a single *Pseudomonas* bacterium, which itself has no capacity for degrading oil.

into the first two categories, but rejected claims for the bacteria. His decision rested on two grounds: (1) that micro-organisms are "products of nature," and (2) that as living things they are not patentable subject matter. . . . [T]he Patent Office Board of Appeals . . . affirmed the Examiner on the second ground. Relying on the legislative history of the 1930 Plant Patent Act, in which Congress extended patent protection to certain asexually reproduced plants, the Board concluded that §101 was not intended to cover living things such as these laboratory created micro-organisms. . . .

[The case went through a circuitous appeal process finally resulting in a decision by Court of Customs and Patent Appeals reversing the patent examiner and Board of Appeals.] The Commissioner of Patents and Trademarks . . . sought certiorari, and we granted the writ. . . .

II

The Constitution grants Congress broad power to legislate to "promote the Progress of Science and useful Arts, by securing for limited Times to Authors and Inventors the exclusive Right to their respective Writings and Discoveries." Art. I, §8, cl. 8. The patent laws promote this progress by offering inventors exclusive rights for a limited period as an incentive for their inventiveness and research efforts. . . . The authority of Congress is exercised in the hope that "[t]he productive effort thereby fostered will have a positive effect on society through the introduction of new products and processes of manufacture into the economy, and the emanations by way of increased employment and better lives for our citizens" [Kewanee Oil Co. v. Bicron Corp., 416 U.S. 470, 480 (1974)].

The question before us in this case is a narrow one of statutory interpretation requiring us to construe 35 U.S.C. §101, which provides: "Whoever invents or discovers any new and useful process, machine, manufacture, or composition of matter, or any new and useful improvement thereof, may obtain a patent therefore, subject to the conditions and requirements of this title." [ ] Specifically, we must determine whether respondent's micro-organism constitutes a "manufacture" or "composition of matter" within the meaning of the statute.[3] . . .

III

. . . Guided by [ ] canons of construction, this Court has read the term "manufacture" in §101 in accordance with its dictionary definition to mean "the production of articles for use from raw or prepared materials by giving to these materials new forms, qualities, properties, or combinations, whether by hand-labor or by machinery." American Fruit Growers, Inc. v. Brogdex Co., 283 U.S. 1 (1931). . . . In choosing such expansive terms as "manufacture" and "composition of matter," modified by the comprehensive "any," Congress plainly contemplated that the patent laws would be given wide scope.

The relevant legislative history also supports a broad construction. The Patent Act of 1793, authored by Thomas Jefferson, defined statutory subject

---

[3] This case does not involve the other "conditions and requirements" of the patent laws, such as novelty and nonobviousness. 35 U.S.C. §§101, 103.

matter as "any new and useful art, machine, manufacture, or composition of matter, or any new or useful improvement [thereof]." The Act embodied Jefferson's philosophy that "ingenuity should receive a liberal encourage-ment." . . . In 1952, when the patent laws were recodified, Congress replaced the word "art" with "process," but otherwise left Jefferson's language intact. The Committee Reports accompanying the 1952 Act inform us that Congress intended statutory subject matter to "include anything under the sun that is made by man."

This is not to suggest that §101 has no limits or that it embraces every discovery. The laws of nature, physical phenomena, and abstract ideas have been held not patentable. . . . Thus, a new mineral discovered in the earth or a new plant found in the wild is not patentable subject matter. Likewise, Einstein could not patent his celebrated law that $E = mc^2$; nor could Newton have patented the law of gravity. Such discoveries are "manifestations of . . . nature, free to all men and reserved exclusively to none."

Judged in this light, respondent's micro-organism plainly qualifies as patentable subject matter. His claim is not to a hitherto unknown natural phenomenon, but to a non-naturally occurring manufacture or composition of matter—a product of human ingenuity "having a distinctive name, character [and] use." The point is underscored dramatically by comparison of the invention here with that in [Funk Brothers Seed Co. v. Kalo Inoculant Co, 333 U.S. 127, 130 (1948)]. There, the patentee had discovered that there existed in nature certain species of root-nodule bacteria which did not exert a mutually inhibitive effect on each other. He used that discovery to produce a mixed culture capable of inoculating the seeds of leguminous plants. Concluding that the patentee had discovered "only some of the handiwork of nature," the Court ruled the product nonpatentable:

> Each of the species of root-nodule bacteria contained in the package infects the same group of leguminous plants which it always infected. No species acquires a different use. The combination of species produces no new bacteria, no change in the six species of bacteria, and no enlargement of the range of their utility. Each species has the same effect it always had. The bacteria perform in their natural way. Their use in combination does not improve in any way their natural functioning. They serve the ends nature originally provided and act quite independently of any effort of the patentee."

Here, by contrast, the patentee has produced a new bacterium with markedly different characteristics from any found in nature and one having the potential for significant utility. His discovery is not nature's handiwork, but his own; accordingly it is patentable subject matter under §101.

IV

Two contrary arguments are advanced, neither of which we find persuasive. [The Court discussed arguments that congressional enactment of the] . . . 1930 Plant Patent Act, which afforded patent protection to certain asexually reproduced plants, and the 1970 Plant Variety Protection Act, which authorized protection for certain sexually reproduced plants but excluded bacteria from its protection . . .

[indicated] congressional understanding that the terms "manufacture" or "composition of matter" do not include living things; if they did, the petitioner argues, neither Act would have been necessary. . . . [The Court rejected these claims, noting that] Congress . . . explained at length its belief that the work of the plant breeder "in aid of nature" was patentable invention. . . .

Congress thus recognized that the relevant distinction was not between living and inanimate things, but between products of nature, whether living or not, and human-made inventions. Here, respondent's micro-organism is the result of human ingenuity and research. Hence, the passage of the Plant Patent Act affords the Government no support. . . .

In particular, we find nothing in the exclusion of bacteria from plant variety protection to support the petitioner's position. . . . The legislative history gives no reason for this exclusion. As the Court of Customs and Patent Appeals suggested, it may simply reflect congressional agreement with [that court's previous holding that "bacteria were not plants for the purposes of the 1930 Act"]. . . . Or it may reflect the fact that prior to 1970 the Patent Office had issued patents for bacteria under §101.[9] . . .

The petitioner's second argument is that . . . genetic technology was unforeseen when Congress enacted §101. From this it is argued that resolution of the patentability of inventions such as respondent's should be left to Congress. The legislative process, the petitioner argues, is best equipped to weigh the competing economic, social, and scientific considerations involved, and to determine whether living organisms produced by genetic engineering should receive patent protection. . . . The subject-matter provisions of the patent law have been cast in broad terms to fulfill the constitutional and statutory goal of promoting "the Progress of Science and the useful Arts" with all that means for the social and economic benefits envisioned by Jefferson. Broad general language is not necessarily ambiguous when congressional objectives require broad terms. . . . Congress employed broad general language in drafting §101 precisely because such inventions are often unforeseeable.[10]

To buttress his argument, the petitioner, with the support of *amicus*, points to grave risks that may be generated by research endeavors such as respondent's. The briefs present a gruesome parade of horribles. Scientists, among them Nobel laureates, are quoted suggesting that genetic research may pose a serious threat to the human race, or, at the very least, that the dangers are far too substantial to permit such research to proceed apace at this time. We are told that genetic research and related technological developments may spread pollution and disease, that it may result in a loss of genetic diversity, and that its practice may tend to depreciate the value of human life. These arguments are forcefully, even passionately, presented; they remind us that, at times, human ingenuity seems

---

[9] In 1873, the Patent Office granted Louis Pasteur a patent on "yeast, free from organic germs of disease, as an article of manufacture." And in 1967 and 1968, immediately prior to the passage of the Plant Variety Protection Act, that Office granted two patents which, as the petitioner concedes, state claims for living micro-organisms.

[10] Even an abbreviated list of patented inventions underscores the point: telegraph (Morse, No. 1,647); telephone (Bell, No. 174,465); electric lamp (Edison, No. 223,898); airplane (the Wrights, No. 821,393); transistor (Bardeen & Brattain, No. 2,524,035); neutronic reactor (Fermi & Szilard, No. 2,708,656); laser (Schawlow & Townes, No. 2,929,922). See generally Revolutionary Ideas, Patents & Progress in America, United States Patent and Trademark Office (1976).

unable to control fully the forces it creates—that with Hamlet, it is sometimes better "to bear those ills we have than fly to others that we know not of."

It is argued that this Court should weigh these potential hazards in considering whether respondent's invention is patentable subject matter under §101. We disagree. The grant or denial of patents on micro-organisms is not likely to put an end to genetic research or to its attendant risks. The large amount of research that has already occurred when no researcher had sure knowledge that patent protection would be available suggests that legislative or judicial fiat as to patentability will not deter the scientific mind from probing into the unknown any more than Canute could command the tides. Whether respondent's claims are patentable may determine whether research efforts are accelerated by the hope of reward or slowed by want of incentives, but that is all.

What is more important is that we are without competence to entertain these arguments—either to brush them aside as fantasies generated by fear of the unknown, or to act on them. The choice we are urged to make is a matter of high policy for resolution within the legislative process after the kind of investigation, examination, and study that legislative bodies can provide and courts cannot. That process involves the balancing of competing values and interests, which in our democratic system is the business of elected representatives. . . .

Congress is free to amend §101 so as to exclude from patent protection organisms produced by genetic engineering. . . . Or it may choose to craft a statute specifically designed for such living things. But, until Congress takes such action, this Court must construe the language of §101 as it is. The language of that section fairly embraces respondent's invention. Accordingly, the judgment of the Court of Customs and Patent Appeals is *affirmed*.

BRENNAN, J., dissenting [joined by Justices White, Marshall, and Powell].

I agree with the Court that the question before us is a narrow one. Neither the future of scientific research, nor even, the ability of respondent Chakrabarty to reap some monopoly profits from his pioneering work, is at stake. Patents on the processes by which he has produced and employed the new living organism are not contested. The only question we need decide is whether Congress, exercising its authority under Art. I, §8, of the Constitution, intended that he be able to secure a monopoly on the living organism itself, no matter how produced or how used. Because I believe the Court has misread the applicable legislation, I dissent.

The patent laws attempt to reconcile this Nation's deep seated antipathy to monopolies with the need to encourage progress. . . . Given the complexity and legislative nature of this delicate task, we must be careful to extend patent protection no further than Congress has provided. . . . [W]e are not dealing—as the Court would have it—with the routine problem of "unanticipated inventions." . . . In [the two Plant Acts] . . . Congress has addressed the general problem of patenting animate inventions and has chosen carefully limited language granting protection to some kinds of discoveries, but specifically excluding others. . . .

Because Congress thought it had to legislate in order to make agricultural "human-made inventions" patentable and because the legislation Congress enacted is limited, it follows that Congress never meant to make items outside the scope of the legislation patentable.

Second, the 1970 Act clearly indicates that Congress has included bacteria within the focus of its legislative concern, but not within the scope of patent protection. Congress specifically excluded bacteria from the coverage of the 1970 Act. The Court's attempts to supply explanations for this explicit exclusion ring hollow. . . . It is the role of Congress, not this Court, to broaden or narrow the reach of the patent laws. This is especially true where, as here, the composition sought to be patented uniquely implicates matters of public concern.

■ HARVARD COLLEGE v. CANADA (COMMISSIONER OF PATENTS)
2002 SCC 76, 219 D.L.R. (4th) 577 (Supreme Court of Canada 2002)

BASTARACHE J.: . . .

This appeal raises the issue of the patentability of higher life forms within the context of the *Patent Act*, R.S.C. 1985, C. P-4. The respondent, the President and Fellows of Harvard College, seeks to patent a mouse that has been genetically altered to increase its susceptibility to cancer, which makes it useful for cancer research. The patent claims also extend to all non-human mammals which have been similarly altered. . . .

The Commissioner of Patents upheld the Patent Examiner's refusal to grant the patent. This decision was in turn upheld by the Federal Court Trial Division, but was overturned by a majority of the Federal Court of Appeal. . . . To refuse a patent, the Commissioner must be satisfied that the applicant is not "by law" entitled to the patent, wording which indicates that the Commissioner has no discretion independent of the *Patent Act* to consider the public interest when granting or denying a patent. . . . [Therefore], the sole question is whether Parliament intended the definition of invention, and more particularly the words "manufacture" or "composition of matter", within the context of the *Patent Act*,[7] to encompass higher life forms such as the oncomouse [so-called in reference to "oncology" or cancer].

II. FACTUAL BACKGROUND. . . .

On June 21, 1985, the respondent, the President and Fellows of Harvard College ("Harvard"), applied for a patent on an invention entitled "transgenic animals". The invention aims to produce animals with a susceptibility to cancer for purposes of animal carcinogenic studies. The animals can be used to test a material suspected of being a carcinogen by exposing them to the material and seeing if tumours develop. Because the animals are already susceptible to tumour development, . . . the animals will be expected to develop tumours in a shorter time period. The animals can also be used to test materials thought to confer protection against the development of cancer. . . .

---

7 . . . [According to the] *Patent Act*, R.S.C. 1985, c. P-4: . . . "invention" means any new and useful art, process, machine, manufacture or composition of matter, or any new and useful improvement in any art, process, machine, manufacture or composition of matter. . . .

The technology by which a cancer-prone mouse ("oncomouse") is produced is described in the patent application disclosure. The oncogene (the cancer-promoting gene) is obtained from the genetic code of a non-mammal source, such as a virus. A vehicle for transporting the oncogene into the mouse's chromosomes is constructed using a small piece of bacterial DNA referred to as a plasmid. The plasmid, into which the oncogene has been "spliced", is injected into fertilized mouse eggs, preferably while they are at the one-cell stage. The eggs are then implanted into a female host mouse, or "foster mother", and permitted to develop to term. . . . [T]hose [offspring] that contain the oncogene are called "founder" mice. . . .

In its patent application, the respondent seeks to protect both the process by which the oncomice are produced and the end product of the process, i.e., the founder mice and the offspring whose cells are affected by the oncogene. The process and product claims also extend to all non-human mammals. . . .

V. ANALYSIS . . .

The sole question in this appeal is whether the words "manufacture" and "composition of matter", in the context of the *Patent Act* [see footnote 7 above], are sufficiently broad to include higher life forms. If these words are not sufficiently broad to include higher life forms, it is irrelevant whether this Court believes that higher life forms such as the oncomouse ought to be patentable. . . .

Having considered the relevant factors, I conclude that Parliament did not intend to include higher life forms within the definition of invention found in the *Patent Act*. . . . I do not believe that a higher life form such as the oncomouse is easily understood as either a "manufacture" or a "composition of matter". For this reason, I am not satisfied that the definition of "invention" in the *Patent Act* is sufficiently broad to include higher life forms. This conclusion is supported by the fact that the patenting of higher life forms raises unique concerns which do not arise in respect of non-living inventions and which are not addressed by the scheme of the Act. Even if a higher life form could, scientifically, be regarded as a "composition of matter", . . . the patenting of higher life forms is a highly contentious and complex matter that raises serious practical, ethical and environmental concerns. [Therefore,] [a]bsent explicit legislative direction, the Court should not order the Commissioner to grant a patent on a higher life form. . . .

In *Chakrabarty*, the majority [of the U.S. Supreme Court] attributed the widest meaning possible to the phrases "composition of matter" and "manufacture" for the reason that inventions are, necessarily, unanticipated and unforeseeable. . . . I agree that the definition of invention in the *Patent Act* is broad. Because the Act was designed in part to promote innovation, it is only reasonable to expect the definition of invention to be broad enough to encompass unforeseen and unanticipated technology. I cannot however agree with the suggestion that the definition is unlimited in the sense that it includes "anything under the sun that is made by man". In drafting the *Patent Act*, Parliament chose to adopt an exhaustive definition that limits invention to any "art, process, machine, manufacture or composition of matter". Parliament did not define "invention" as "anything new and useful made by man". By choosing to define invention in this way, Parliament signalled a clear intention to include certain subject matter as patentable and to exclude other subject matter as being outside the confines of the Act. . . .

[T]he word ["manufacture"] would commonly be understood to denote a non-living mechanistic product or process. . . . In *Chakrabarty*, . . . "manufacture" was defined as "the production of articles for use from raw or prepared materials by giving to these materials new forms, qualities, properties, or combinations, whether by hand-labor or by machinery." . . . Is a mouse an "article" [or] "material" . . . ? In my view, while a mouse may be analogized to a "manufacture" when it is produced in an industrial setting, the word in its vernacular sense does not include a higher life form. . . .

As regards the meaning of the words "composition of matter", I believe that they must be defined more narrowly than was the case in *Chakrabarty*. . . . It [ ] is significant that the word "matter" captures but one aspect of a higher life form. As defined by the *Oxford English Dictionary* . . . "matter" is a "[p]hysical or corporeal substance in general, . . . contradistinguished from immaterial or incorporeal substance (spirit, soul, mind), and from qualities, actions, or conditions". . . . Higher life forms are generally regarded as possessing qualities and character-istics that transcend the particular genetic material of which they are composed. A person whose genetic make-up is modified by radiation does not cease to be him or herself. Likewise, the same mouse would exist absent the injection of the oncogene into the fertilized egg cell; it simply would not be predisposed to cancer. The fact that it has this predisposition to cancer that makes it valuable to humans does not mean that the mouse, along with other animal life forms, can be defined solely with reference to the genetic matter of which it is composed. The fact that animal life forms have numerous unique qualities that transcend the particular matter of which they are composed makes it difficult to conceptualize higher life forms as mere "composition[s] of matter". It is a phrase that seems inadequate as a description of a higher life form. . . . It simply does not follow from the objective of promoting ingenuity that all inventions must be patentable. . . .

The respondent . . . submits that there is . . . no evidentiary or legal basis for the distinction the Patent Office has made between lower life forms such as bacteria, yeast and moulds, and higher life forms such as plants and animals. . . . [T]he issue of whether a lower life form is a "composition of matter" or "manufacture" was never challenged in the courts in this country and . . . it is now accepted in Canada that lower life forms are patentable. Nonetheless, I agree with the appellant that this does not necessarily lead to the conclusion that higher life forms are patentable, at least in part for the reasons that it is easier to conceptualize a lower life form as a "composition of matter" or "manufacture" than it is to conceptualize a higher life form in these terms. . . .

[I]t is up to Parliament and not the courts to assess the validity of the distinction drawn by the Patent Office between higher life forms and lower life forms. Yet, even if this Court were to alter the *status quo* and find higher life forms patentable, it would be unable to avoid engaging in line-drawing. The majority of the Federal Court of Appeal, which found that the *Patent Act* did apply to higher life forms, was nonetheless compelled to draw a distinction between higher life forms and human beings. In doing so, it merely substituted one line, that between humans and animals, for the line preferred by the Patent Office, that between higher and lower life forms. In my opinion, the decision to move the line in this manner was ill-advised. As I stated earlier when considering the definition of invention, the patenting of all plants and animals, and not just human beings, raises several concerns that are not appropriately dealt with in the *Patent Act*. In addition, a judicially crafted exception from patentability for human beings does not adequately address issues such as what defines a human being and whether parts of the human body as opposed to the entire person would be patentable. . . .

Appeal allowed.

[Justice Binnie's dissenting opinion omitted. The Justices were split 5-4.]

Notes on Ownership

1. *Intellectual Property Doctrine.* As noted in *Chakrabarty*, the Patent Act establishes a broad right to patent "any new and useful [invention], . . . subject to the conditions and requirements of this title." 35 U.S.C.A. §101. Although not emphasized in *Chakrabarty*, these conditions require that the invention be "novel," "non-obvious," and "adequately enabled and described." A patent gives an inventor a monopoly over the use of the discovery for a twenty-year period. The owner can profit from the discovery directly or through "licensing" the use of the discovery to third parties who pay the inventor a "royalty." The Patent Act gives patent holders the right to bring a civil action against infringers for injunctive relief and damages (usually at least what would have been the reasonable royalty payments, but treble damages are possible in cases of intentional infringement). 35 U.S.C.A. §§281-287.

Ownership of intellectual property creates incentives for innovation, but this also can result in barriers to accessing the invention itself and to innovation in related areas. The patent owner has the right to exclude others from using the invention. If the patent holder does not make use of the patent or offer other users licenses at a reasonable fee, then the innovation may not be available to the public, defeating the overriding purpose of offering patent protection in the first place. Patent law attempts to balance these competing policy considerations.

The field of intellectual property is vast, and there are numerous books, articles, and treatises. Some basic reference works are Donald S. Chisum, Patents: A Treatise on the Law of Patentability, Validity, and Infringement (this 26-volume loose-leaf publication demonstrates the breadth of the field); Janice M. Mueller, Introduction to Patent Law (2006); Craig Allen Nord, David Barnes & Michael J. Madison, The Law of Intellectual Property (2006). For an international perspective, see Oliver Mills, Biotechnological Innovation, Moral Rights and Patent Law (2005). For an example of especially relevant articles, see Rebecca S. Eisenberg, Patents and the Progress of Science, 56 U. Chi. L. Rev. 1017 (1989); Arti K. Rai & Rebecca S. Eisenberg, Bayh-Dole Reform and the Progress of Biomedicine, 66 Law & Contemp. Probs. 289 (Spring 2003); Dan Burk & Mark Lemley, Policy Levers in Patent Law, 89 Va. L. Rev. 1575 (2003).

2. *Developments in the United States and Canada.* The *Chakrabarty* decision was a 5-4 decision involving a closely contested question of federal statutory interpretation. Congress did not accept the Court's implicit invitation to override its decision. See Anna Lumelsky, Diamond v. Chakrabarty: Gauging Congress's

Response to Dynamic Statutory Interpretation by the Supreme Court, 39 U.S.F. L. Rev. 641 (2005).

The Supreme Court of Canada's 5-4 decision in the Harvard Mouse case was equally controversial. As Justice Binnie noted in his dissent, "the oncomouse has been held patentable, and is now patented" in sixteen jurisdictions, including the United States. Two additional countries have issued patents for similar inventions. "Indeed, we were not told of any country with a patent system comparable to Canada's (or otherwise) in which a patent on the oncomouse had been applied for and been refused." 2002 SCC 76 at ¶2. The Canadian Parliament has not acted to clarify the law. The Supreme Court of Canada revisited the patentability of life forms in another 5-4 decision upholding patents for plants genetically modified to resist application of an herbicide used to control weeds. Schmeiser v. Monsanto, 2004 SCC 34 (2004).

3. *Human Gene and Stem Cell Patents.* A topic hinted at toward the end of the Canadian case—patents for human genes—is now a pressing controversy in the United States. There are thousands of researchers, companies, and universities involved in a new race to patent genes discovered as an outgrowth of efforts to map the entire human genome:

> Companies and universities have obtained patents on more than 4,000 human genes, almost 20 percent of the roughly 24,000 human genes. Whether human genes should be patentable is hotly contested. Some oppose the patenting of human genes on moral grounds, arguing that human beings should not be the subject of property rights. Others object that DNA sequences should not be patentable because they are discoveries of nature that are the common heritage of all rather than man-made inventions. Nevertheless, current U.S. policy . . . permits patents on human genes [as "composition[s] of matter."] . . . While newly-discovered plants, minerals, and other natural phenomena cannot be patented because they exist without human intervention, isolated and purified versions of naturally occurring substances are patentable. Gene patents lie at the intersection of these two lines of precedent because they involve isolated and purified DNA sequences from living organisms.

Michael J. Malinowski & Radhika Rao, Legal Limits on Genetic Research and the Commercialization of Its Results, 54 Am. J. Comp. L. 45, 47-49 (2006).

The tidal wave of applications for human gene patents was generated by the lenient initial rulings on the first set of gene patents considered by the Patent and Trademark Office (PTO). This led to widespread criticism that premature gene patents were preventing even more productive research efforts. Although the PTO's gene patenting policies have not been formally rejected in court, these concerns caused the PTO to toughen its standards on the secondary considerations required for patentability (such as utility, nonobviousness, and adequate description), even though it continues to view human genes as inherently patentable subject matter. For instance, the PTO requires applicants to precisely identify the gene, what useful functions it controls, and perhaps also the molecular details of the proteins coded for by the gene and how they relate to these functions. See U.S. Patent Trademark Office, Utility Examination Guidelines, 66 Fed. Reg. 1092 (2001) (revised guidelines governing gene patents); Helen M. Berman & Rochelle Dreyfuss, Reflections on the Science and Law of Structural

Biology, Genomics, and Drug Development, 53 UCLA L. Rev. 871 (2006); National Research Council of the Nat'l Academies, Reaping the Benefits of Genomic and Proteomic Research: Intellectual Property Rights, Innovation, and Public Health 140-144 (2006); Rebecca S. Eisenberg, How Can You Patent Genes?, 2(3) Am. J. Bioethics 3 (Summer 2002). See also Lori B. Andrews & Jordan Paradise, Gene Patents: The Need for Bioethics Scrutiny and Legal Change, 5 Yale J. Health Pol'y L. & Ethics 403 (2005); Dianne Nicol, On the Legality of Gene Patents, 29 Melb. U. L. Rev. 809 (2005) (Australia, the United States, and United Kingdom); J. Jason Williams, Protecting the Frontiers of Biotechnology Beyond the Genome: The Limits of Patent Law in the Face of the Proteomics Revolution, 58 Vand. L. Rev. 955 (2005); Symposium, 77 Acad. Med. 1301 (2002).

Human stem cells have also been patented in the United States. Jeanne F. Loring & Cathryn Campbell, Intellectual Property and Human Embryonic Stem Cell Research, 311 Science 1716 (2006); Mark L. Rohrbaugh, Intellectual Property of Human Pluripotent Stem Cells at 53-54, in National Institutes of Health, Regenerative Medicine (2006); Symposium, 39 New Eng. L. Rev. 501 (2004-2005). This has also been controversial, not only because the patents involve human cells, but also because patent holders have been accused of limiting the ability of researchers to pursue potentially important research of great public benefit. The holders of patents covering two of the most useful lines of human stem cells (WARF and Geron) claim that their patents cover all similar human stem cells even if they are derived from other sources, and they have imposed significant licensing costs on researchers, including the right to receive royalties if the research results in additional products with commercial value.

Again, the U.S. Patent and Trademark Office, rather than relenting on whether human stem cells are fundamentally patentable subject matter, has begun to question stem cell patents on more technical grounds. For example, in 2007 it revoked three such patents previously issued to the University of Wisconsin because the cells "appeared to be the same as, or obvious variations of, cells described in earlier scientific papers or in patents issued to others." Andrew Pollack, 3 Patents on Stem Cells Are Revoked in Initial Review, N.Y. Times, April 3, 2007, at C2, col. 1. See also Fiona Murray, The Stem-Cell Market—Patents and the Pursuit of Scientific Progress, 356 New Eng. J. Med. 2341 (2007). The treatment of these matters in other countries is not yet clear.

If human genes, cells, and tissues can be patented, should courts also allow the patenting of human beings? See Seán M. Coughlin, The Newman Application and the USPTO's Unnecessary Response: Patentability of Humans and Human Embryos, 5 Chi.-Kent J. Intell. Prop. 90 (2006) (no).

4. *IP and the Access Debate.* Intellectual property ownership rules give patent holders monopoly power to extract significant profits from their inventions, or to block others from using, or even experimenting with, their inventions. When medical technologies are involved, these rights generate considerable controversy if they threaten to retard biomedical research or block access to essential life-saving innovations. An example of this problem can be found in Chapter 4.B.2's discussion of Greenberg v. Miami Children's Hospital Research Institute, Inc., 264 F. Supp. 2d 1064 (S.D. Fla. 2003), at page 398, which involves a patent on the gene that causes Canavan's disease—a fatal brain disorder that is most prevalent

in children of eastern and central European Jewish descent. Families affected with the disease who had provided biological samples to the researchers who discovered the gene sued (unsuccessfully) to block enforcement of patent rights because they felt the owners were obstructing access to the gene test in order to increase their profits. Patent law addresses concerns such as these in several ways.

(a) *"March-in" Rights and Compulsory Licensing.* First, patents can be over-ridden for pressing public policy considerations. Without going into details here, various sources of law allow (1) the U.S. government to "march in" and reclaim pharmaceutical patents from private entities whose research the government funded, if the private patent holder fails to develop or market the product; (2) courts to refuse to enjoin patent infringement where the infringement serves an important public purpose; and (3) in some countries, compulsory licensing to protect public health, meaning that the government can force companies to sell essential patented medical products at reasonable prices. Exercises of these special powers are rare and controversial, however. See National Research Council of the Nat'l Academies, Reaping the Benefits of Genomic and Proteomic Research: Intellectual Property Rights, Innovation, and Public Health 146-147 (2006); Kevin Outterson, Patent Buy-outs for Global Disease Innovations for Low- and Middle-Income Countries, 32 Am. J.L. & Med. 159 (2006); Simone A. Rose, On Purple Pills, Stem Cells, and Other Market Failures: A Case for a Limited Compulsory Licensing Scheme for Patent Property, 48 How. L.J. 579 (2005).

(b) *Access to Research Materials.* There have been numerous reports of IP-fueled restrictions on access to biomedical research materials such as cell lines, cancer drugs, or gene-altered mice. U.S. law only dimly recognizes a vague research exemption to patent rights, similar to, but much narrower than, the "fair use" exception under copyright law. Comment, 113 Yale L.J. 261 (2003). These concerns have resulted in various studies and recommendations, either for a more explicit research exemption in the law, or for biomedical patent holders to adopt "best practices" in their licensing and patent enforcement practices for researchers. See, e.g., Principles and Guidelines for Recipients of NIH Research Grants and Contracts on Obtaining and Disseminating Biomedical Research Resources, 62 Fed. Reg. 72090 (1999); NIH, Best Practices for the Licensing of Genomic Inventions, 70 Fed. Reg. 18413 (2005); National Research Council of the Nat'l Academies, Reaping the Benefits of Genomic and Proteomic Research: Intellectual Property Rights, Innovation, and Public Health 140-144 (2006).

(c) *Medical Process Patents.* For public policy reasons, many countries bar patents for medical processes, such as innovations in surgical procedures or medical protocols. This is not the law in the United States. Instead, medical processes are inherently patentable, if other requirements are met (such as novelty, nonobviousness, etc.). However, medical ethics disfavor seeking patent protection, and a special statutory amendment (35 U.S.C. 287(c)) prevents patent holders from enforcing their rights against health care practitioners, making such patents generally not worth the effort. See Aaron Kesselheim & Michelle Mello, Medical-Process Patents: Monopolizing the Delivery of Health Care, 355 New Eng. J. Med. 2036 (2006); Note, 18 Cardozo L. Rev. 1527 (1997);

Comment, 5 Geo. Mason L. Rev. 227, 265 (1997); Note, 91 Minn. L. Rev. 1088 (2007).

Problem: Patenting Human Genes

The Genomic Research and Accessibility Act was introduced in the U.S. House of Representatives by a Republican and a Democratic sponsor early in 2007. The Act provides:

> Notwithstanding any other provision of law, no patent may be obtained for a nucleotide sequence, or its functions or correlations, or the naturally occurring products it specifies. H.R. 977, 110th Cong., 1st Sess. (2007).

Would you support the bill? Are you concerned about promoting innovation, ensuring access, the moral or ethical aspects of humanity, or other factors? See Michael Crichton, Patenting Life, N.Y. Times, Feb. 13, 2007, at A19 (op-ed supporting the bill).

Note: Concluding Thoughts

This chapter has examined the state's right to regulate individual reproductive capacity and the implications of advances in genetic technology. You are now in a position to assess whether the legal treatment of reproductive issues is united by any common constitutional theme or policy, or whether this chapter's topics are united only by their biological underpinnings. For interesting commentary that takes this perspective, see Note, Guiding Regulatory Reform in Reproduction and Genetics, 120 Harv. L. Rev. 574 (2006) (comparing and contrasting regulatory approaches to reproduction and genetics). You might also have developed some views on whether the Supreme Court has arrived at a firmer constitutional basis for judicial review of state legislation than in the *Lochner* debacle. You can appreciate the role that advances in genetics have played in reproduction along with some of the larger issues raised by the intersection of those advances with intellectual property law. You can look forward to being able to place the reproductive case law in context with material in other chapters. What is the nature of a person's interest in controlling reproduction? Do we have a constitutional right to control procreative capacity that is distinguishable from the right to control medical treatment? See Chapters 2 and 3. How is state regulation to protect the health of pregnant women or to safeguard fetal life similar to or different from other types of state regulation? See Chapter 6.

6

■

Public Health Law

Our lives are a tenuous gift, subject to revocation by injury, illness, and death. What is the proper role of government in safeguarding people from illness or injury? Should this responsibility be exercised by federal, state, or local government? To what extent should the need to protect public health outweigh the interests of persons subjected to coercive regulation? This chapter will consider these important questions.

Section A introduces some traditional public health strategies designed to reduce the transmission of disease and to protect individuals from injury. It is important to understand the potential scope of these measures before considering their legal implications. Medical and legal approaches to solving public health threats often seem to conflict, or at least to operate with different assumptions. Even the "simple" process of identifying and assessing the severity of public health threats can raise a number of important legal and policy questions.

Section B provides a sketch of legal underpinnings for state or federal attempts to protect public health. Traditionally, states have had the primary authority and responsibility for public health under their "police power," whether exercised directly or delegated to local governmental authorities. The federal government does not have any constitutional authority to regulate to protect the public health. Instead, its power comes from the authority to regulate the relationship between the United States and foreign countries, to regulate interstate commerce, and to spend to promote the public welfare. U.S. Const. art. 1, §8. This basic constitutional division of authority has blurred over time. These constitutional rules are supplemented by some important statutory developments, particularly the widespread effect of statutes that prohibit discrimination against persons with disabilities.

What distinguishes "public health" law from other categories of legal regulation? It can be difficult to discern a unifying theme. Consider licensing requirements for restaurants, funding for waste treatment plants, food and drug regulations, federal support of the Centers for Disease Control and Prevention and the National Institutes of Health, rules governing quarantines and civil commitments, licensure of health care providers, and environmental regulation. It is hard to imagine a more diverse set of policies. Yet each is founded upon governmental interests in protecting health. Seen in this light, many of the topics discussed in other chapters could be considered specific examples of "public health law." State or federal attempts to control the physician-patient relationship, to control the dying process, or to regulate organ transplantation, abortion, and reproductive technologies can be justified by the need to protect the health of members of our society. The major distinction between these topics and those traditionally considered the domain of "public health law" is the identification of the "public" protected. Government regulations considered elsewhere in this book are concerned mainly with protecting the individual patient. In contrast, public health policies traditionally have protected society "at large" from threats to public health.

The range of potential public health topics is so large that only a small subset of public health policies has been selected for consideration here. In this chapter, we focus on the three major types of public health regulation that affect the treatment relationship:

- The role of the federal government in regulating pharmaceuticals, alcohol and tobacco;
- The constitutional and statutory basis for state disease testing and reporting statutes; and
- The constitutional and statutory bases for quarantine, commitment, and mandatory treatment.

The main theme that connects these different topics is the attempt to balance the state's interest in protecting the public at large with an individual's right to freedom from coercion or constraint. As you read these materials, consider whether the balance struck between public needs and individual rights is appropriate. Will the state's interest in public health always outweigh the assertion of individual interests? What role will the courts take in ensuring that the threat to health is real and that the public health measures employed are likely to reduce the risk?

Consider also the wide range of threats to public health that public health entities must address. Can the same government agencies and statutory/regulatory framework be used to address the public health risks presented by avian influenza, bioterrorism, and obesity?

A. PUBLIC HEALTH STRATEGIES

1. Medical and Legal Views of Public Health

What does it mean to protect the public's health? Health professionals tend to give a four-step answer to this question. First, potential threats to public health must be understood. Scientists work to identify "injuries" to public health and to connect those harms with their causes. Suppose that your fellow law students suddenly began to experience high fevers, swelling of their extremities, lung congestion, unconsciousness, and then rapid death. Part of the medical response would be to identify the cause of this problem — perhaps exposure to a contagious disease or an environmental toxin. Similarly, suppose that scientists observed increasing rates of morbidity and mortality from lung cancer or heart disease in society. They might then attempt to identify the causes of these conditions, such as use of tobacco products or ingestion of a diet high in fat.

The second task is to identify a mechanism for eliminating or reducing the threat. Identifying a "cure" for the malady afflicting your classmates might be a part of this task. But researchers might also try to reduce exposure to the causal agent. If the disease is spread by exposure to rodent feces, for example, public health officials would probably develop recommendations to minimize exposure to this source and to safely clean your law school's food service areas. Similarly, medical authorities might develop educational or regulatory campaigns designed to discourage smoking or to encourage consumption of low-fat foods.

The third step is implementation. The protective mechanisms developed in step two must be implemented — often with the financial help of governmental authorities and/or the creation of legal obligations. In this stage, scientists must work with other groups in society, such as political interest groups, trade associations, lobbyists, public health officials, and legislators.

The fourth step, at least ideally, involves evaluation of the policy's outcomes. Have the new rules regarding food service sanitation actually reduced the premature death rate? Do people actually have a better diet and smoke less? If not, how can these policies be improved?

■ HISTORY OF CDC
Centers for Disease Control
45 MMWR 526 (1996)

. . . When CDC's name changed in 1970, from the Communicable Disease Center to the Centers for Disease Control, CDC scientists were poised to accept new challenges. The most notable of the agency's many achievements in the following ten years was its role in global smallpox eradication, a program that finally succeeded because of the application of scientific principles of surveillance to a complex problem. In the realm of infectious diseases, CDC maintained its preeminence, identifying the Ebola virus and the sexual transmission of hepatitis B, and isolating the hepatitis C virus and the bacterium causing Legionnaires disease. The Study of the Effectiveness of Nosocomial Infection Control (SENIC) was the most expensive study the agency had ever undertaken and proved for the first time the effectiveness of recommended infection-control practices. Other studies included identification of the association of Reye's syndrome with aspirin use, the relation between liver cancer and occupational exposure to vinyl chloride, and the harmful effects of the popular liquid protein diet.

The 1980s institutionalized what is considered to be a critically important scientific activity at CDC — the collaboration of laboratorians and epidemiologists.

The decade began with the national epidemic of toxic-shock syndrome, documentation of the association with a particular brand of tampons, and the subsequent withdrawal of that brand from the market. CDC collaboration with the National Center for Health Statistics (NCHS) resulted in the removal of lead from gasoline, which in turn has markedly decreased this exposure in all segments of the population. The major public health event of the 1980s was the emergence of AIDS. CDC helped lead the response to this epidemic, including characterization of the syndrome and defining risk factors for disease. . . .

The 1990s have been characterized by continuing applications of CDC's classic field-oriented epidemiology, as well as by the development of new methodologies. For example, the disciplines of health economics and decision sciences were merged to create a new area of emphasis — prevention effectiveness — as an approach for making more rational choices for public health interventions. In 1993, the investigation of hantavirus pulmonary syndrome required a melding between field epidemiology and the need for sensitivity to and involvement of American Indians and their culture. Similarly, the response to global problems with Ebola virus and plague underscore the importance of adapting these new methodologies. Other major CDC contributions to the world's health include global polio eradication efforts and efforts to prevent neural tube defects. Finally, in October 1992, Congress changed CDC's official name to the Centers for Disease Control and Prevention, to recognize CDC's leadership role in prevention. Today, CDC is both the nation's prevention agency and a global leader in public health. As the world enters the new millennium, CDC will remain the agency ready to address the challenges to its vision of healthy people in a healthy world through prevention.

■ **SUMMARY OF NOTIFIABLE DISEASES — UNITED STATES, 2005**
Scott J. N. McNabb et al., Division of Integrated Surveillance Systems and Services, National Center for Public Health Informatics, Coordinating Center for Health Information and Service, CDC
54(53) MMWR 2-3, 18-19 (March 30, 2007)

The *Summary of Notifiable Diseases — United States, 2005* contains the official statistics, in tabular and graphic form, for the reported occurrence of nationally notifiable infectious diseases in the United States for 2005. . . . Part 1 contains tables showing incidence data for the nationally notifiable infectious diseases during 2005.* . . .

A notifiable disease is one for which regular, frequent, and timely information regarding individual cases is considered necessary for the prevention

---

* Because no cases of . . . [a variety of notifiable diseases such as anthrax and smallpox were reported in 2005] these diseases do not appear in the tables in Part 1. . . . Data on human immunodeficiency virus (HIV) infections are not included because HIV infection (not acquired immunodeficiency syndrome [AIDS]) reporting has been implemented on different dates and using different methods than for AIDS case reporting. . . .

and control of the disease. A brief history of the reporting of nationally notifiable infectious diseases in the United States is available at http://www.cdc.gov/epo/dphsi/nndsshis.htm. In 1961, CDC assumed responsibility for the collection and publication of data on nationally notifiable diseases. [The National Notifiable Diseases Surveillance System] is neither a single surveillance system nor a method of reporting. . . .

Notifiable disease reporting at the local level protects the public's health by ensuring the proper identification and follow-up of cases. Public health workers ensure that persons who are already ill receive appropriate treatment; trace contacts who need vaccines, treatment, quarantine, or education; investigate and halt outbreaks; eliminate environmental hazards; and close premises where spread has occurred. Surveillance of notifiable conditions helps public health authorities to monitor the impact of notifiable conditions, measure disease trends, assess the effectiveness of control and prevention measures, identify populations or geographic areas at high risk, allocate resources appropriately, formulate prevention strategies, and develop public health policies. Monitoring surveillance data enables public health authorities to detect sudden changes in disease occurrence and distribution, identify changes in agents and host factors, and detect changes in health-care practices.

The list of nationally notifiable infectious diseases is revised periodically. A disease might be added to the list as a new pathogen emerges, or a disease might be deleted as its incidence declines. Public health officials at state health departments and CDC collaborate in determining which diseases should be nationally notifiable. [The Council of State and Territorial Epidemiologists], with input from CDC, makes recommendations annually for additions and deletions. Although disease reporting is mandated by legislation or regulation at the state and local levels, state reporting to CDC is voluntary. Reporting completeness of notifiable diseases is highly variable and related to the condition or disease being reported. The list of diseases considered notifiable varies by state and year.

All states report conditions that were designated as internationally quarantinable and notifiable (i.e., cholera, plague, and yellow fever) in compliance with the International Health Regulations (IHR) issued by the World Health Organization (WHO).[1] In May 2005, the World Health Assembly adopted revised IHR. The current IHR will be replaced by the 2005 IHR when it becomes official on June 15, 2007. . . . On December 13, 2006, the United States formally accepted the 2005 IHR and is taking steps to implement these new international rules. . . .

---

[1] Editor's Note: for information on the IHR, see David P. Fidler and Lawrence O. Gostin, The New International Health Regulations: An Historic Development for International Law and Public Health, 34 J.L. Med. & Ethics 85 (2006).

TABLE 1. Reported cases of notifiable diseases,* by month — United States, 2005

Disease	Jan	Feb	Mar	Apr	May	Jun	Jul	Aug	Sep	Oct	Nov	Dec	Total
AIDS†	2,905	2,695	4,274	3,130	3,255	3,877	3,631	3,219	3,353	3,963	2,943	3,875	41,120
Botulism													
foodborne	1	—	—	—	—	1	2	9	1	—	2	3	19
infant	4	4	5	4	10	10	9	8	8	10	3	10	85
other (wound & unspecified)	1	1	1	3	3	1	1	4	3	5	2	6	31
Brucellosis	3	8	8	11	12	8	13	14	7	12	9	15	120
Chancroid§	2	2	2	2	1	1	—	—	—	1	2	4	17
Chlamydia§¶	67,989	76,735	76,283	91,530	75,649	72,200	91,765	75,576	71,290	94,206	70,134	113,088	976,445
Cholera	—	—	—	1	—	1	—	2	—	2	1	1	8
Coccidioidomycosis	360	335	251	304	326	295	328	510	319	584	565	2,365	6,542
Cryptosporidiosis	129	138	147	212	175	179	394	947	1,495	874	354	615	5,659
Cyclosporiasis	2	2	6	44	229	123	79	20	7	2	13	16	543
Domestic arboviral diseases**													
California serogroup													
neuroinvasive	—	—	—	1	1	5	15	20	20	11	—	—	73
nonneuroinvasive	—	—	—	—	—	—	1	5	1	—	—	—	7
eastern equine, neuroinvasive	—	—	—	—	—	2	4	11	3	1	—	—	21
Powassan, neuroinvasive	—	—	—	—	—	—	—	1	—	—	—	—	1
St. Louis													
neuroinvasive	—	—	—	—	—	—	—	1	5	—	1	—	7
nonneuroinvasive	—	—	—	—	—	1	1	1	3	—	—	—	6
West Nile													
neuroinvasive	—	—	1	—	1	21	191	590	407	91	6	1	1,309
nonneuroinvasive	1	1	1	1	10	39	326	849	402	54	7	—	1,691
Ehrlichiosis													
human granulocytic	—	4	7	29	36	97	175	96	96	68	32	146	786
human monocytic	4	5	10	8	16	35	87	66	72	59	34	110	506
human (other & unspecified)	2	2	2	1	5	23	38	10	9	10	2	8	112
Enterohemorrhagic *Escherichia coli* infection													
O157:H7	58	73	87	127	116	190	317	338	367	451	181	316	2,621
Shiga toxin-positive													
non-O157	13	17	14	18	22	29	58	53	55	68	31	123	501
not serogrouped	14	11	8	22	19	12	29	62	56	61	26	87	407
Giardiasis	1,047	1,179	1,284	1,579	1,242	1,261	1,899	1,916	2,096	2,464	1,365	2,401	19,733
Gonorrhea§	25,339	24,520	24,706	29,739	23,995	24,610	33,106	27,189	26,335	33,221	25,012	41,821	339,593
Haemophilus influenzae, invasive disease													
all ages, serotypes	182	205	220	255	208	192	186	113	146	158	129	308	2,304
age <5 yrs													
serotype b	—	—	—	1	1	1	—	—	2	—	1	3	9
nonserotype b	3	15	19	9	10	9	10	13	11	16	3	17	135
unknown serotype	14	24	24	22	17	16	13	20	14	13	13	27	217
Hansen disease (leprosy)	2	2	4	6	5	19	6	6	3	7	3	24	87
Hantavirus pulmonary syndrome	—	2	—	1	4	5	5	2	3	1	1	2	26
Hemolytic uremic syndrome, postdiarrheal	4	11	9	17	10	17	17	33	22	24	10	47	221
Hepatitis, viral, acute													
A	267	331	278	337	262	276	344	362	482	498	272	779	4,488
B	331	382	341	469	343	337	468	352	367	454	334	941	5,119
C	33	32	39	47	38	50	63	45	58	70	42	135	652

* No cases of anthrax; diphtheria; domestic arboviral disease, western equine encephalitis virus, neuroinvasive and nonneuroinvasive, eastern equine nonneuroinvasive, and Powassen nonneuroinvasive; severe acute respiratory syndrome–associated coronavirus (SARS-CoV) disease; smallpox; or yellow fever were reported in 2005. Data on chronic hepatitis B and hepatitis C virus infection (past or present) are not included because they are undergoing data quality review. Data on human immunodeficiency virus (HIV) infections are not included because HIV infection reporting has been implemented on different dates and using different methods than for acquired immunodeficiency syndrome (AIDS) case reporting.

† Total number of AIDS cases reported to the Division of HIV/AIDS Prevention, National Center for HIV/AIDS, Viral Hepatitis, STD, and TB Prevention (NCHHSTP) (proposed), through December 31, 2005.

§ Totals reported to the Division of STD Prevention, NCHHSTP (proposed), as of May 5, 2006.

¶ Chlamydia refers to genital infections caused by *Chlamydia trachomatis.*

** Totals reported to the Division of Vector-Borne Infectious Diseases, National Center for Zoonotic, Vector-Borne, and Enteric Diseases (NCZVED) (proposed) (ArboNET Surveillance), as of June 23, 2006.

TABLE 1. *(Continued)* Reported cases of notifiable diseases,* by month — United States, 2005

Disease	Jan	Feb	Mar	Apr	May	Jun	Jul	Aug	Sep	Oct	Nov	Dec	Total
Influenza-associated pediatric mortality[††]	4	10	10	4	4	3	3	1	1	—	1	4	45
Legionellosis	95	76	78	88	96	141	348	250	284	319	222	304	2,301
Listeriosis	40	34	42	47	38	54	114	109	98	130	79	111	896
Lyme disease	448	377	470	562	784	2,293	5,929	3,965	2,124	1,957	1,211	3,185	23,305
Malaria	105	79	80	99	90	118	173	150	146	127	96	231	1,494
Measles	3	4	3	5	1	2	33	2	4	—	3	6	66
Meningococcal disease, invasive													
all serogroups	102	121	142	129	108	115	82	55	59	81	78	173	1,245
serogroup A, C, Y, & W-135	26	31	39	34	29	30	15	14	14	17	16	32	297
serogroup B	12	12	16	16	10	16	11	4	8	12	6	33	156
other serogroup	5	4	3	4	2	2	1	2	1	—	1	2	27
serogroup unknown	59	74	84	75	67	67	55	35	36	52	55	106	765
Mumps	18	28	19	25	26	26	27	52	15	19	23	36	314
Pertussis	1,724	1,630	1,196	1,598	1,816	1,819	2,508	2,137	1,974	2,584	1,879	4,752	25,616
Plague	—	—	—	—	2	—	2	1	2	—	—	1	8
Poliomyelitis, paralytic[§§]	—	—	—	—	—	—	—	—	—	1	—	—	1
Psittacosis	—	1	—	5	—	1	4	1	1	1	—	2	16
Q fever	6	2	6	10	14	24	19	14	12	14	3	12	136
Rabies													
animal	485	291	464	732	551	466	565	582	550	525	332	372	5,915
human	1	—	—	—	—	—	—	—	1	—	—	—	2
Rocky Mountain spotted fever	41	40	35	57	81	185	243	290	234	192	168	370	1,936
Rubella	—	1	1	2	1	1	2	1	—	—	—	2	11
Rubella, congenital syndrome	—	—	1	—	—	—	—	—	—	—	—	—	1
Salmonellosis	1,745	1,730	2,009	2,731	3,154	3,777	5,585	5,149	5,016	5,589	3,384	5,453	45,322
Shigellosis	655	790	918	1,071	1,092	1,195	1,574	1,485	1,641	2,060	1,322	2,365	16,168
Streptococcal disease, invasive, group A	345	421	469	600	436	362	378	260	215	294	265	670	4,715
Streptococcal toxic-shock syndrome	13	14	22	31	12	9	6	3	2	2	5	10	129
Streptococcus pneumoniae, invasive disease													
drug resistant, all ages	223	268	335	371	263	207	161	93	99	161	194	621	2,996
age <5 yrs	94	112	167	164	155	118	80	48	45	103	117	292	1,495
Syphilis[¶¶]													
all stages***	2,056	2,370	2,489	3,392	2,660	2,662	3,156	2,631	2,326	3,268	2,429	3,839	33,278
congenital (age <1 yr)	25	32	25	26	27	36	28	24	28	21	20	37	329
primary & secondary	532	612	562	880	699	675	830	716	592	916	672	1,039	8,724
Tetanus	—	2	3	1	3	3	3	1	2	2	1	6	27
Toxic-shock syndrome	8	6	7	6	8	10	9	6	8	1	3	18	90
Trichinellosis	1	—	—	1	1	2	5	2	2	—	—	2	16
Tuberculosis[†††]	589	799	1,116	1,036	1,103	1,334	1,110	1,174	1,231	1,146	1,150	2,309	14,097
Tularemia	1	—	2	3	7	31	24	26	18	20	4	18	154
Typhoid fever	20	10	19	25	17	24	32	29	39	51	14	44	324
Vancomycin-intermediate *Staphylococcus aureus*	—	—	—	—	—	—	—	—	1	—	1	—	2
Vancomycin-resistant *Staphylococcus aureus*	—	—	—	2	—	—	—	—	—	1	—	—	3
Varicella (chickenpox)	1,869	2,261	2,851	3,180	2,813	2,401	1,776	1,211	1,363	3,167	2,924	6,426	32,242
Varicella (deaths)[§§§]	—	—	—	1	1	—	—	—	—	—	1	—	3

[††] Totals reported to the Influenza Division, National Center for Immunization and Respiratory Diseases (NCIRD) (proposed), as of December 31, 2005.
[§§] Cases of vaccine-associated paralytic polio (VAPP) caused by polio vaccine virus.
[¶¶] Totals reported to the Division of STD Prevention, NCHHSTP (proposed), as of May 5, 2006.
[***] Includes the following categories: primary, secondary, latent (including early latent, late latent, and latent syphilis of unknown duration), neurosyphilis, late (including late syphilis with clinical manifestations other than neurosyphilis), and congenital syphilis.
[†††] Totals reported to the Division of TB Elimination, NCHHSTP (proposed), as of May 12, 2006.
[§§§] Death counts provided by the Division of Viral Diseases, NCIRD (proposed), as of December 31, 2005.

■ THE LAW AND THE PUBLIC'S HEALTH: A STUDY OF INFECTIOUS DISEASE LAW IN THE UNITED STATES*

Lawrence O. Gostin, Scott Burris, and Zita Lazzarini

99 Colum. L. Rev. 59 (1999)

Public health is typically regarded as a scientific pursuit, and, undoubtedly, our understanding of the etiology and response to disease is heavily influenced by scientific inquiry. Less well understood is the role of law in public health. Law is an essential part of public health practice. Law defines the jurisdiction of public

* Reprinted with permission. Lawrence O. Gostin is a law professor at Georgetown University. Scott Burris is a law professor at Temple University's Beasley School of Law. Zita Lazzarini is a professor and Director of the Division of Medical Humanities, Health Law & Ethics at the University of Connecticut School of Medicine.

health officials and specifies the manner in which they may exercise their authority. The law is a tool in public health work, which is used to establish norms for healthy behavior and to help create the social conditions in which people can be healthy. The most important social debates about public health take place in legal fora—legislatures, courts, and administrative agencies—and in the law's language of rights, duties, and justice. . . .

The Institute of Medicine (IOM), in its foundational 1988 report, "The Future of Public Health" (the IOM Report), agreed that law was essential to public health, but cast serious doubt on the soundness of public health's legal basis in the United States. . . . [2]

Communicable disease control has occupied American governments from the earliest years of European settlement, and it was in response to epidemics that formal health agencies were first created. Throughout the history of the United States, each state, through the exercise of its police powers, has enacted a web of legislation to control infectious disease. These laws range from generic statutes establishing powers relating to communicable and sexually transmitted disease, to disease-specific laws relating, for example, to tuberculosis or HIV/AIDS. Although the threat of communicable diseases in America has declined throughout the last century, new diseases such as AIDS, hepatitis C, and hantavirus have emerged as major threats, and old diseases such as tuberculosis and E. coli have returned with new virulence.

Communicable disease law has deep historical roots, yet remains centrally important to legal institutions and to the public's health. Our approach to reform, however, is based on a broader notion of the determinants of health and the role of the state in promoting it, a view in which the distinction between communicable and noncommunicable health threats is, in many ways, unimportant. Thus, many of our points about communicable disease law apply to public health regulation as a whole.

Our frankly utilitarian premise is that public health law ought to be as effective as possible in helping public health agencies create the conditions necessary for health. To do this, the law must reflect our best understanding of how public health agencies work to promote health, as well as the political conditions in which these agencies operate. . . .

The essential job of public health agencies is to identify what makes us healthy and what makes us sick, and then to take the steps necessary to make sure we encounter a maximum of the former and a minimum of the latter. At first glance, this would seem to be a rather uncontroversial goal, but we will show that the pursuit of public health creates fundamental social disputes virtually by definition. Public health is rooted in the biomedical and social sciences, but from the moment of asserting some collective responsibility for the population's health, through the process of defining the determinants of health and disease, to the implementation of programs, the practice of public health entails judgments that challenge deeply ingrained social attitudes and practices.

Three distinct accounts of disease and health are widely used in public health practice today. . . . The microbial model focuses on the pathogens that are the immediate causes of many illnesses. The microbial model produces interventions

---

[2] Committee for the Study of the Future of Public Health, IOM, Nat'l Acad. of Sci., The Future of Public Health 1-6 (1988). . . .

designed to kill the pathogen or isolate it from human beings; it also tends to produce political disputes about the proper scope and exercise of the state's power to attack the pathogen by controlling the human being who carries it. The behavioral model looks primarily at the behavior that exposes us to pathogens or that otherwise tends to produce illness and premature death. The idea that behavior is an important factor in health and disease is widely accepted, but health efforts on the behavioral model are nonetheless often controversial. When the government gives advice about how to have safer sex or how to reduce the risk of drug injection, many people see an official endorsement of what they regard as deviant behavior. When the state uses its power to discourage smoking, to require a motorcycle helmet, or even to prevent dental caries through water fluoridation, many people see unacceptable paternalism. The ecological model takes the broadest view of what makes people ill or well, seeking the causes of disease in the way society organizes itself, produces and distributes wealth, and interacts with the natural environment. Such an approach operates unavoidably as a critique of the status quo, pointing to such fundamental social causes of disease as poverty, racism, and severe income inequality. The ecological model also implicates our collective responsibility for unhealthy behavior, suggesting the importance of social factors in producing, for example, the levels of drug abuse and unsafe sex that fuel the HIV and hepatitis epidemics. Each of these models of disease and health is rooted in the sciences of medicine and epidemiology and provides complementary ways of understanding and fighting disease, but each also entails judgments about who is responsible for illness and who must change to produce health. . . .

We name five perennially significant political problems inherent in modern public health practice. The first is the problem of popular apathy about public health programs. Much of what public health agencies do is to prevent injury and disease, often by getting people at low risk to refrain from behaviors they enjoy or profit from. . . .

Second, public health agencies have a jurisdiction problem. Many societal and environmental factors that influence public health are beyond the reach of health agencies. Occupational safety, environmental protection, food safety, and the prevention of violence and accidents are normally the province of other agencies, and much of the behavior that public health tries to change — eating a diet high in fat, for example — is not subject to direct legal regulation at all.

Third, public health agencies must confront the problem of stigma and social hostility. Communicable disease control has traditionally had to deal with barriers thrown up by the social reaction to disease. In their time, diseases like cholera, yellow fever, tuberculosis, and syphilis were all attributed to sin or vice, and the shame and social risk of having such conditions often led the sick to conceal their illness and to avoid medical and public health services. The problem of stigma and social hostility has been an important factor in HIV prevention since the earliest days of the epidemic.

The fourth problem involves the legitimacy of government action in certain realms of human behavior. The problem of legitimacy arises whenever public health measures are perceived to exceed the bounds of proper government action. Whether framed in terms of paternalism, endorsement, neutrality, or simple libertarianism, the legitimacy issue turns on the belief that there are certain things government simply ought not do, no matter how laudable its objectives.

Finally, health agencies face a problem of trust. Because so much of what public health does depends upon voluntary cooperation by those at risk and the support of the population at large, health officials must appear credible in the advice they render and trustworthy in their practices. If the public perceives health officials as simply the tool of an overreaching government or suspects that they have been captured by "special interests," their ability to win compliance and support is compromised.

As if these built-in challenges were not enough, communicable disease control faces economic and structural barriers: the decline in the public health infrastructure for monitoring and controlling disease; the transformation of the health care system, including expansion of managed care and integrated delivery systems; and the emergence and resurgence of infectious disease threats. . . .

"Public health" refers both to a goal for the health of a population and to professional practices aimed at its attainment. . . . At a minimum, the goal of public health is to attain the highest level and widest distribution of physical and mental health that a society reasonably can achieve within the limits of the resources it chooses to devote to the task. . . .

Even this carefully narrowed definition places the goal of public health at the intersection of deep social fault lines. First, it posits that public health is a function of the health of populations, not individuals. Geoffrey Rose has brilliantly described the practical implications of this difference for disease prevention, including most notably the "prevention paradox." This is the apparently iron law holding that those measures that have the greatest potential for improving public health (like seatbelt use) offer little absolute benefit to any individual, while measures that heroically save individual lives (like heart transplants) make no significant contribution to the population's health. Public health, in other words, has as its chief duty the unenviable tasks of providing common goods and controlling negative externalities, both difficult at best. . . .

The ability of public health work to attract support is, however, essential to its success, for, as the definition of public health also reminds us, public health operates in a world of choices in the allocation of limited resources. The great sanitarian Herman Biggs famously remarked that "public health is purchasable," but because there will always be limits on how much we are willing to buy, public health will always turn on allocational decisions. Thus, public health, as both a goal and a practice, is as inherently political (i.e., concerned with the allocation of resources in society) as it is technological (i.e., concerned with the deployment of professional knowledge of illness).

Finally, public health's desire for optimally healthy populations builds into the definition a concern for distributive justice that must, on occasion, challenge the current distribution of wealth. A society in which the more prosperous segment of the population enjoys health conditions that are as good as any in the world, but where many are living substantially below the norm, is not a nation with good public health. . . .

Nineteenth-century sanitarians focused on providing clean water, adequate sewers, pure food, safe workplaces, and hygienic dwellings to the urban poor who were at greatest risk for the most common communicable diseases. Toward this end, boards of health were created and given increasingly broad powers to investigate and abate nuisances endangering health, and an administrative and legal infrastructure was built of food safety laws, building codes, social welfare programs, and water bureaus. But as early as the turn of this century, the escalating success of biomedical science was changing public health, moving its center away from a broad social, environmental focus to a more individualized, medical one based on germ theory. Health leaders . . . pushed for the legal authority to deploy modern "epidemiological methods" of disease control, in which pathogens were to be identified through individual testing or population screening and reporting, and then eliminated through vaccination, treatment, isolation, or quarantine. With good diagnostic tools and surveillance, disease outbreaks could be spotted early. With quick and effective treatments, patients could be rendered noninfectious with little disruption to their lives or society's business. The pathogen, not social conditions, was thought to be the problem, and through modern methods like these, the pathogen could be defeated. Health authorities sought the power to test suspected carriers, screen populations (such as marriage license applicants and newborns), trace partners, and require treatment. The social vision and reform agenda that had focused sanitary reformers on slums and sewer lines was replaced with a concern for biomedical research, vaccination, and timely medical treatment. It was in the early- to mid-twentieth century, the heyday of the microbial model of disease, that communicable disease law assumed the form in which it largely exists to this day.

Health departments are influenced by this history, even as they try to adapt to changes in social conditions and threats to health. Health departments today are generally organized to serve four "core functions": health promotion and disease prevention; assessment, data collection, and data analysis; medical services; and leadership and policy development. . . .

The main job of health agencies is to directly promote good health and prevent illness. To this end, modern public health practice deploys measures based on all three of the major models of disease causation. Health departments continue to employ traditional measures aimed at finding and controlling pathogens (e.g., testing, screening, reporting, contact tracing, vaccination, compulsory treatment, and isolation). Health departments also oversee the purity of water supplies and the hygienic conditions of food service establishments. Law provides both jurisdiction over the problem and the authority to require compliance. Law, in the form of privacy rules and due process requirements, also helps assure that measures involving the control of individuals are, and are perceived to be, rational, fair, and as harmless to the individual as possible.

Health departments also devote significant resources to changing behavior in the population. As chronic, nonmicrobial diseases such as cancer and heart disease came to dominate the mortality tables, public health focused its attention on risk-enhancing behavior such as smoking, high-fat diets, and inactivity. Significant behavioral sources of traumatic injury and death, such as teen violence and drunken driving, have also been treated as public health problems. Changing behavior has, of course, become crucial in controlling communicable diseases like HIV, as well. Risk-factor screening (for cholesterol or high blood pressure, for example), individualized counseling, and health education are standard tools of behavior change, but so is the law. Law is used to reduce unsafe behavior by both direct (e.g., helmet laws for motorcyclists and drunk driving laws) and indirect (e.g., taxes and subsidies) means, the goals of which are to make healthier behavior less costly and unhealthy behavior more expensive.

Influenced by ecological thinking about disease, public health workers have recognized the importance of addressing the social causes of unhealthy individual behavior. Individual choices depend in substantial part on the options provided by society and on the behavioral cues with which individual decisionmakers are bombarded in any social setting. They also depend upon material conditions, like the distribution of wealth and government policies. Health workers now routinely design interventions that attempt to address social factors such as stigma, discrimination, and sexism. Public health officials have become advocates of policies, such as the elimination of legal barriers to sterile hypodermic syringes and needles, that make it possible for individuals to make healthier choices. Using tools of economics and marketing, public health authorities have begun to develop programs to influence individual behavior choices by changing the prevailing social norms.

Ecological strategies address environmental problems, land use, patterns of commerce, and medical and commercial use of antimicrobials, as well as social, political, and economic conditions that influence population movement and changes in standards of living. With such broad targets, health measures aimed at ecological causes of disease quickly bring health agencies to the outer bounds of their statutory jurisdiction. . . .

Notes: Traditional Public Health Strategies

1. *Sources of Information.* There are a broad range of measures designed to improve public health, ranging from improved sanitation to vaccination, screening programs, and education about health threats such as tobacco. There are different sources of information on all of these public health topics. The Centers for Disease Control and Prevention (CDC) is a world leader in identifying threats to public health and in developing recommendations to reduce health risks. Its publication, the aptly named *Morbidity and Mortality Weekly Report* (MMWR), is a major source of data on a variety of threats to public health, but particularly for data on contagious diseases. The publication is not for the fainthearted or for those with any tendencies toward hypochondria. The MMWR's pages are regularly filled with detailed case descriptions of everything from infectious diseases to the disastrous effects of exposure to carbon monoxide from poorly vented furnaces. The CDC maintains extensive online resources. See, e.g., CDC homepage, http://www.cdc.gov/; MMWR homepage, http://www.cdc.gov/mmwr/.

2. *Conflicts Between Medical and Legal Norms.* Medical or scientific authorities and lawyers tend to have somewhat different perspectives on public health strategies. Historically, public health officials focused on the medical or scientific aspects of public health policies and paid little attention to their impact on individual liberty. The article by Professors Gostin, Burris, and Lazzarini is one part of a massive project to study and to reform public health law. The CDC now includes a public health law program, see http://www2a.cdc.gov/phlp/ and

provides funding for academic study, see http://www.publichealthlaw.net/. Professor Gostin is a leader in the reform of public health law. See Lawrence O. Gostin, Public Health Law: Power, Duty, Restraint (2000). Where should public health policies be developed—in legislative bodies, in administrative agencies, or somewhere else? Should physicians or lawyers have primary control over the development and implementation of public health strategies? What role should the courts take in overseeing public health measures?

3. *Fear.* What is the public response to threats to its health? In your free time you might consider renting one of the many movies focusing on public health topics. See, e.g., *Outbreak* (1995) (starring Dustin Hoffman). Those with a more literary bent might want to read *The Plague*, by Albert Camus, or the portions of the Bible dealing with plagues and public reactions to contagious diseases (especially Exodus, Deuteronomy, and Amos).

What would be your response to an apparently serious, contagious illness spreading among your classmates? Dangerous contagious diseases can create a state euphemistically called "anxiety," better known as fear or panic. Fear can motivate a wide range of responses, some helpful from a public health standpoint, but some not. What should be the role of public health officials in addressing public concerns? Should courts worry more about too weak or too vigilant public health responses? See also Cass R. Sunstein, Laws of Fear: Beyond the Precautionary Principle (2005); Luc Bonneux & Wim Van Damme, An Iatrogenic Pandemic of Panic, 332 Brit. Med. J. 786 (2006); Laurie Garrett, The Coming Plague: Newly Emerging Diseases in a World Out of Balance (1994); Nancy Khardori, Bioterrorism Preparedness: Medicine, Public Health, Policy (2006); Fred A. Mettler Jr. & George L. Voelz, Major Radiation Exposure—What to Expect and How to Respond, 346 New Eng. J. Med. 1554, 1560 (2002) (noting high rates of psychological distress that would be associated with terrorist radiation attack).

4. *Other Resources.* There are a number of excellent books and articles on public health measures from medical and legal perspectives. In addition to the sources noted above, see Dan Beauchamp, The Health of the Republic: Epidemics, Medicine, and Moralism as Challenges to Democracy (1988); Allan M. Brandt, No Magic Bullet: A Social History of Venereal Disease in the United States Since 1880 (1985); Davis P. Fidler, International Law and Infectious Diseases (2005); Frank P. Grad, Public Health Law Manual (2004); Kenneth R. Wing, The Law and the Public's Health (6th ed. 2003); Scott Burris, Emerging Issues in Public Health Law: Law as a Structural Factor in the Spread of Communicable Disease, 36 Hous. L. Rev. 1755 (1999); Wendy K. Mariner, Law and Public Health: Beyond Emergency Preparedness, 38 J. Health L. 247 (2005); Alexandra Minna Stern & Howard Markel, International Efforts to Control Infectious Diseases, 1851 to the Present, 292 JAMA 1474 (2004); Symposium, The State of Public Health, 25 Health Aff. 898-1061 (2006); Symposium, Public Health in Law, 10 J. Health Care L. & Pol'y 1 (2007).

5. *Assessing Public Health Threats.* What are the greatest threats to public health? Infectious conditions? Bioterrorism? Environmental hazards? Dietary and lifestyle choices? How would you identify the "greatest" threat? By number of persons affected? By the severity of the harm? Now consider the appropriate role of government in responding to the risks you have identified. Should the

government develop a response to one or more of these risks? What type of response seems justified: public education or using regulations to reduce risks? Where should governments apply their scarce resources and why? The next case addresses some of these issues, in the context of OSHA regulation. Although the Occupational Safety and Health Administration is not considered one of the classic public health agencies, the following case focuses on a workplace health risk peculiar to hospitals—contagious disease—that is at the core of classic public health regulation. Moreover, this case explains the fundamentals of risk assessment that are the basis for all public health measures.

2. Risk Assessment and Regulatory Competence

■ AMERICAN DENTAL ASSOCIATION v. MARTIN
984 F.2d 823 (7th Cir. 1993)

POSNER, Circuit Judge.

In 1991 the Occupational Safety and Health Administration promulgated a rule on occupational exposure to bloodborne pathogens. 29 C.F.R. §1910.1030. The rule is designed to protect health care workers from viruses, particularly those causing Hepatitis B and AIDS, that can be transmitted in the blood of patients. Promulgated after a protracted notice-and-comment rulemaking proceeding, the rule and its supporting reasons occupy 178 densely packed pages in the Federal Register. Most employers in the health care industry have accepted the rule, which in essence requires compliance with procedures for health care workers recommended by the Centers for Disease Control (since renamed the Centers for Disease Control and Prevention), the federal agency responsible for the control of contagious diseases. Many of these employers, indeed, had adopted the procedures as soon as the CDC recommended them. Three employer groups, however, challenge the rule—dentists, represented by the American Dental Association, and medical-personnel and home-health employers, both represented by the Home Health Services and Staffing Association. Medical-personnel firms supply health care workers on a temporary basis to hospitals and nursing homes, while home-health firms supply such workers to patients at home.

As of 1991, there had been only 24 confirmed cases of U.S. health care workers infected with the AIDS virus by patients since AIDS was first diagnosed in 1981. Hepatitis B is a far more common disease than AIDS, though less scary, publicized, or stigmatized. . . . Although most infected persons recover uneventfully, about 1 percent die and about 6 to 10 percent of adult (and a much higher percentage of child) victims of Hepatitis B become carriers. . . . Nonetheless, because of the greater virulence of the Hepatitis B virus (HBV) and the fact that many health care workers are not vaccinated, patient-communicated Hepatitis B kills about 200 health workers in the U.S. per year—roughly 100 times the number of such workers infected by patient-communicated HIV [human immunodeficiency virus]. The precautions against infection of health care workers by the two viruses is similar, except that the vaccine against HBV offers a protection that has no counterpart with regard to HIV, and contaminated laundry poses a danger of spreading HBV that also has no counterpart with regard to HIV.

OSHA's rule reflects the public-health philosophy of "universal precautions," which means precautions against the blood of every patient, not just the blood of patients known or believed likely to be carriers of HBV or HIV. The precautions are various. They include engineering controls (such as requirements for the location of sinks), work practice controls (such as standards of care in handling contaminated sharp instruments, such as needles), requirements for personal protective equipment such as gloves, masks, goggles, and gowns, requirements for housekeeping (covering such things as the cleaning of contaminated surfaces and laundry and the disposal of contaminated waste), reporting requirements, and provisions for medical care. The rule requires the employer to offer employees who are at risk of exposure to the blood of patients the Hepatitis B vaccine at the employer's own expense, though it allows the employees to decline to be vaccinated. An employee who is involved in an "exposure incident," such as being stuck with a contaminated needle, must be offered at the employer's expense a confidential blood test for HBV and HIV; that is, only the employee is entitled to the result of the test.

In deciding to impose this extensive array of restrictions on the practice of medicine, nursing, and dentistry, OSHA did not (indeed is not authorized to) compare the benefits with the costs and impose the restrictions on finding that the former exceeded the latter. Instead it asked whether the restrictions would materially reduce a significant workplace risk to human health without imperiling the existence of, or threatening massive dislocation to, the health care industry. For this is the applicable legal standard. 29 U.S.C. §655(b)(5); Industrial Union Dept., AFL-CIO v. American Petroleum Institute, 448 U.S. 607, 642-645, 655-656 (1980) (the "benzene" case) (plurality opinion); American Textile Mfrs. Institute, Inc. v. Donovan, 452 U.S. 490, 509-512, 530-536 (1981) (the "cotton dust" case). The agency focused on HBV rather than on HIV because of the minute number of health care workers who have been infected by the latter virus. It estimated that the rule would eliminate between 113 and 129 annual deaths of health care workers from Hepatitis B, and a somewhat higher figure (187 to 197) if deaths of nonworkers infected by health-care workers who (but for the rule) would be carriers are factored in as well. (In making this additional calculation, OSHA expressed an uncharacteristic, but as it seems to us commendable, concern with the indirect effects of its rule. On the other hand it did not consider the reduction in medical care that might result from the rule's effect in making the practice of medicine more costly — more on this shortly.) Most of these deaths would be avoided by the vaccine, but by no means all, because the vaccine is not a hundred percent effective and, more important, because many health care workers refuse to be vaccinated. Hence the other parts of the rule would have a positive effect even on Hepatitis B; and there is no vaccine (or cure) for AIDS.

OSHA's evaluation of the effects of the rule, relying as it does on the undoubted expertise of the Centers for Disease Control, cannot seriously be faulted, at least by judges. Hence we cannot say that the rule, viewed as a whole, flunks the test of material reduction of a significant risk to workplace health. As for the impact on the health care industry, OSHA estimated the total cost of compliance with the rule at $813 million a year, clearly not enough to break the multi-hundred-billion-dollar healthcare industry. The rule's implicit valuation of a life is high — about $4 million — but not so astronomical, certainly by regulatory standards, . . . as to call the rationality of the rule seriously into question, especially when we consider that neither Hepatitis B nor AIDS is a disease of old people. . . . Nor is death the only consequence of these diseases. AIDS causes protracted pain and disability before death, and Hepatitis B causes pain and disability and often permanent liver damage, even when the patient "recovers."

No doubt the agency's $813 million estimate is an underestimate. It ignores . . . many or most time costs. . . . But the petitioners made no effort in the rulemaking proceeding to quantify these costs or to provide any basis for supposing them to be huge.

OSHA also exaggerated the number of lives likely to be saved by the rule by ignoring lives likely to be sacrificed by it, since the increased cost of medical care, to the extent passed on to consumers, will reduce the demand for medical care, and some people may lose their lives as a result. The agency's consideration of the indirect costs of the rule is thus incomplete. How many lives the rule is likely to sacrifice, however, we do not know; and again the petitioners make no effort to come up with a number. So while $4 million doubtless underestimates the agency's implicit valuation of each life actually likely to be saved by the rule, we do not know how great the underestimate is and we cannot resolve our doubts against the agency. We add that the $4 million ignores the benefits to workers who will be spared illness — remember that 99 times as many people get Hepatitis B as die from it.

As an original matter we might have been inclined to think that the regulation of the safety of the medical and dental workplace could be left largely to the market, that doctors, dentists, and other health care workers have a stronger incentive than the government to protect themselves from health hazards at reasonable cost, that their employees are compensated in their wages for what is after all a modest risk, and that health care workers who refuse to be vaccinated against Hepatitis B are knowingly assuming the risk and should be left to bear the consequences without government interference. But the occupational safety and health law is constructed on different premises that we are not free to question, and perhaps the infectious character of HIV and HBV warrants even on narrowly economic grounds more regulation than would be necessary in the case of a noncommunicable disease. . . .

So in the main the [bloodborne pathogen] rule must be upheld. Which is not to say that it is a good rule. It may be unnecessary; it may go too far; its costs may exceed its benefits. . . . But our duty as a reviewing court of generalist judges is merely to patrol the boundary of reasonableness, and . . . OSHA's bloodborne-pathogens rule — accepted as it has been by most health care industries and based as it is on the recommendations of the nation's, perhaps the world's, leading repository of knowledge about the control of infectious diseases — does not cross it. . . .

COFFEY, Circuit Judge, concurring in part, dissenting in part.

Section 3(8) of the Occupational Safety and Health Act defines "occupational safety and health standard" as a standard which requires the adoption of practices "reasonably necessary or appropriate to provide safe or healthful employment and places of employment." 29 U.S.C. §652(8). . . .

The rule adopted can best be classified as an attempt to try to kill a fly with a sledgehammer. The rule was drafted partially in response to the public hysteria surrounding AIDS. . . . The rule was not drafted in response to an established significant risk of harm to employees. The dangers of transmitting the blood-borne pathogen hepatitis B have been well-established for years yet for reasons unexplained OSHA did not concern itself with that risk in the workplace prior to November 1987. . . . The rule unduly burdens health care employers, including but not limited to dentists, doctors and hospitals, while offering but minimal benefit to their employees, and furthermore it is estimated that it will increase health care costs some $817 million annually. Additionally, the rule duplicates the scientifically based and well-reasoned guidelines of the Centers for Disease Control and Prevention (CDC) a governmental agency medically and scientifically qualified to determine and evaluate if there is in fact a significant risk in the health care area and, if so, propose reasonable, efficient guidelines. . . .

I suggest that the United States Congress must address the question of whether there is a need to duplicate the education, investigation and prevention efforts of the CDC and state health agencies, thus increasing health care costs, and whether OSHA is the proper agency to regulate health care given their lack of experience, knowledge and expertise in comparison to the CDC and state health agencies. In the alternative, the entire rule should be remanded to OSHA. . . .

I am cognizant of the need for dental and medical regulations and safeguards to insure and prevent the spread of infection, but fail to understand why OSHA must assert authority over the health care field when it lacks the required medical knowledge, training, and experience, much less expertise. . . . There is no need for four separate entities (OSHA, CDC, state agencies, and professional organizations) to regulate the health care industry. . . . One qualified entity can most effectively and efficiently regulate the health care profession. I see no reason why the respective states are unable to continue to regulate the medical and dental profession as the states have traditionally done in the past and presently do in many other professional fields including but not limited to law, engineering and architecture. . . .

Finally, there is little doubt that lobbyists and the media in all probability have greatly impacted OSHA's rulemaking.

Notes: Risk Assessment by Legislatures, Agencies, and Courts

1. *Is Any Action Required?* Identify the risk the bloodborne pathogen rule was designed to reduce. Was this a risk in need of reduction? How would you answer that question? Posner contends, in dictum, that the whole concept of an occupational safety and health statute is unnecessary because it is in workers' own interests to practice safe work habits and because workers in unsafe workplaces may be choosing to risk injury in exchange for higher wages. Judge Coffey criticizes the bloodborne pathogen standard from a different standpoint; he argues that it provides little marginal benefit over guidelines already issued by the Centers for Disease Control and Prevention that were already being implemented in most workplaces. In your view, is the bloodborne pathogen standard necessary and appropriate? Should the answer be influenced by the fact

that the rule was precipitated by a fear of HIV even though the long-standing risk of hepatitis was much more serious? Is this a case of overreaction to irrational hysteria, or was HIV simply the impetus to take action that was long overdue?

2. *Administrative Competence.* Assuming some action was necessary, is OSHA the correct agency to act? OSHA's bloodborne pathogen rule was a departure from OSHA's historical focus on traditional sources of risk in the workplace such as machinery and chemicals. What do you think of Judge Coffey's contention that the states or the CDC are better able to regulate the health care professions? See Paula E. Berg, When the Hazard Is Human: Irrationality, Inequity, and Unintended Consequences in Federal Regulation of Contagion, 75 Wash. U. L.Q. 1367 (1997). OSHA attempted to regulate workplace exposure to tuberculosis in the late 1990s, but the initiative ultimately failed. See 62 Fed. Reg. 54160 (1997) (proposed regulations); Institute of Medicine, Tuberculosis in the Workplace (2001) (study of whether OSHA regulations necessary in light of CDC guidelines); and 68 Fed. Reg. 75768-01 (2003) (withdrawal of proposed TB regulations).

3. *Risk Assessment Literature.* The vast academic literature on risk assessment explores how and why society chooses to respond to some risks but not others, and at what costs. For a small sampling, see Stephen Breyer, Breaking the Vicious Cycle: Toward Effective Risk Regulation (1993); Disease Mapping and Risk Assessment for Public Health (Andrew Lawson et al. eds., 1999); Lawrence O. Gostin, Public Health Law: Power, Duty, Restraint 94-99 (2000); Paul Slovic, The Perception of Risk (2000); Kip Viscusi, Fatal Tradeoffs: Public and Private Responsibilities for Risk (1992); Cass R. Sunstein, Laws of Fear: Beyond the Precautionary Principle (2005); Matthew D. Adler, Against "Individual Risk": A Sympathetic Critique of Risk Assessment, 153 U. Pa. L. Rev. 1121 (2005); R. Keeney, Decisions about Life-Threatening Risks, 331 New Eng. J. Med. 193 (1994).

Problem: State Law, Disaster Planning, and Bioterrorism Preparedness

The United States was fortunate not to experience many large-scale public health disasters for nearly 80 years after the influenza epidemic in the early part of the 1900s. Concerns about terrorism and bioterrorism spurred public health officials and researchers to review the ability of state and local governments to respond to public health emergencies in the early 2000s. Medical journals increased their coverage of illnesses and injuries associated with potential terrorist attacks. See, e.g., Luciana Borio et al., Consensus Statement, Hemorrhagic Fever Viruses and Biological Weapons: Medical and Public Health Management, 287 JAMA 2391 (2002); Julie Louise Gerberding et al., Bioterrorism Preparedness and Response: Clinicians and Public Health Agencies as Essential Partners, 287 JAMA 898 (2002); Fred A. Metterl & George L. Voelz, Major Radiation Exposure—What to Expect and How to Respond, 346 New Eng. J. Med. 1554 (2002). See also Judith Miller et al., Germs: Biological Weapons and America's Secret War (2001).

Concerns about large-scale public health threats continued to grow during the 2000s, though the nature of the potential threat varied. Concerns about the ability of the public health system to respond to large events were reinforced in the aftermath of natural disasters, such as the Indian Ocean tsunami in 2004 and Hurricane Katrina in 2005. See Symposium, 25 Health Aff. 898 (2006); Symposium, 2 J. Health & Biomed. L. 157 (2006); Symposium, 58 Admin. L. Rev. 551 (2006). The prospect of a new avian influenza pandemic was also occupying the news headlines and the minds of public health officials as this book went to press in 2007. See, e.g., Lawrence Gostin, Public Health Strategies for Pandemic Influenza, 295 JAMA 1700 (2006); and the CDC Web site devoted to pandemic influenza, at http://www.pandemicflu.gov/. According to some estimates, a new pandemic influenza could cause global mortality of 62 million people, with many of the deaths occurring in the developing world. C. J. Lopez, Estimation of Potential Global Pandemic Influenza Mortality on the Basis of Vital Registry Data from the 1918-1920 Pandemic: A Quantitative Analysis, 368 Lancet 2211 (2006).

Professor Lawrence Gostin and the Center for Law and the Public's Health at Georgetown and Johns Hopkins universities prepared the Model State Emergency Health Powers Act to facilitate discussion of the legal aspects of disaster preparedness, available at www.publichealthlaw.net (vers. Dec. 21, 2001) (hereinafter MSEHPA). The Web site includes information about state legislation related to the model act. See also Lawrence O. Gostin et al., The Model State Emergency Health Powers Act: Planning for and Response to Bioterrorism and Naturally Occurring Infectious Diseases, 288 JAMA 622 (2002); William Martin, Legal and Public Policy Responses of States to Bioterrorism, 94 Am. J. Pub. Health 1093 (2004); N. Pieter M. O'Leary, Bioterrorism or Avian Influenza: California, the Model State Emergency Health Powers Act, and Protecting Civil Liberties During a Public Health Emergency, 42 Cal. W. L. Rev. 249 (2006).

The Model Act includes rules and procedures designed to improve detection of a public health emergency and then establishes rules and procedures that take effect only in a public health emergency. The definition of "public health emergency" is therefore critical to the Act's operation:

> A "public health emergency" is an occurrence or imminent threat of an illness or health condition that:
> (1) is believed to be caused by any of the following:
> (i) bioterrorism;
> (ii) the appearance of a novel or previously controlled or eradicated infectious agent or biological toxin;
> (iii) [a natural disaster]
> (iv) [a chemical attack or accidental release; or]
> (v) [a nuclear attack or accident] . . . and
> (2) poses a high probability of any of the following harms;
> (i) a large number of deaths in the affected population;
> (ii) a large number of serious or long-term disabilities in the affected population; or
> (iii) widespread exposure to an infectious or toxic agent that poses a significant risk of substantial future harm to a large number of people in the affected population.

MSEHPA §104(m) (emphasis omitted; items in brackets are optional provisions). Note that the Act attempts to give states the option of creating a single legal framework for the public health response to a wide range of crises. As you review the Act's provisions through the remainder of this chapter, consider whether you would advise a state to adopt a single framework. Should the same rules apply in a bioterrorism incident as in a natural disaster? Does that Act—created in the shadow of 9/11—give adequate and appropriate guidance for other types of health emergencies?

B. THE SOURCE AND LIMIT OF AUTHORITY TO PROTECT PUBLIC HEALTH

This section explores the fundamental source and scope of the government's authority to pursue various public health measures. The first case is an historical one that establishes the constitutional basis for constraining individual liberties. The second case looks at the limits imposed by the more contemporary concern about disability discrimination. Although each case focuses on a specific public health measure, the general principles these cases establish permeate all of the public health topics that we encounter in the remainder of the chapter.

1. Constitutional Principles

■ JACOBSON v. COMMONWEALTH OF MASSACHUSETTS
197 U.S. 11 (1905)

HARLAN, J.

This case involves the validity, under the Constitution of the United States, of certain provisions in the statutes of Massachusetts relating to vaccination.

[A Massachusetts statute permitted cities to require vaccination and revaccination of all inhabitants of a city; noncompliant citizens over the age of 21 could be charged a fine of $5.00. The city of Cambridge adopted a smallpox vaccination regulation under this statute. Jacobson refused to be vaccinated for smallpox and these proceedings were instituted against him. He was found guilty and jailed until he paid the $5.00 fine.] . . .

The authority of the state to enact this statute is to be referred to what is commonly called the police power,—a power which the state did not surrender when becoming a member of the Union under the Constitution. Although this court has refrained from any attempt to define the limits of that power, yet it has distinctly recognized the authority of a state to enact quarantine laws and "health laws of every description"; indeed, all laws that relate to matters completely within its territory and which do not by their necessary operation affect the people of other states. According to settled principles, the police power of a state must be held to embrace, at least, such reasonable regulations established directly by legislative enactment as will protect the public health and the public safety. It is equally true that the state may invest local bodies called into existence for purposes of local administration with authority in some appropriate way to safeguard the public health and the public safety. The mode or manner in which those results are to be accomplished is within the discretion of the state, subject, of course, so far as federal power is concerned, only to the condition that no rule prescribed by a state, nor any regulation adopted by a local governmental agency acting under the sanction of state legislation, shall contravene the Constitution of the United States, nor infringe any right granted or secured by that instrument. A local enactment or regulation, even if based on the acknowledged police powers of a state, must always yield in case of conflict with the exercise by the general government of any power it possesses under the Constitution, or with any right which that instrument gives or secures.

We come, then, to inquire whether any right given or secured by the Constitution is invaded by the statute as interpreted by the state court. The defendant insists that his liberty is invaded when the state subjects him to fine or imprisonment for neglecting or refusing to submit to vaccination; that a compulsory vaccination law is unreasonable, arbitrary, and oppressive, and, therefore, hostile to the inherent right of every freeman to care for his own body and health in such way as to him seems best; and that the execution of such a law against one who objects to vaccination, no matter for what reason, is nothing short of an assault upon his person. But the liberty secured by the Constitution of the United States to every person within its jurisdiction does not import an absolute right in each person to be, at all times and in all circumstances, wholly freed from restraint. There are manifold restraints to which every person is necessarily subject for the common good. . . .

Applying these principles to the present case, it is to be observed that the legislature of Massachusetts required the inhabitants of a city or town to be vaccinated only when, in the opinion of the board of health, that was necessary for the public health or the public safety. The authority to determine for all what ought to be done in such an emergency must have been lodged somewhere or in some body; and surely it was appropriate for the legislature to refer that question, in the first instance, to a board of health composed of persons residing in the locality affected, and appointed, presumably, because of their fitness to determine such questions. To invest such a body with authority over such matters was not an unusual, nor an unreasonable or arbitrary, requirement. Upon the principle of self-defense, of paramount necessity, a community has the right to protect itself against an epidemic of disease which threatens the safety of its members. It is to be observed that when the regulation in question was adopted smallpox, according to the recitals in the regulation adopted by the board of health, was prevalent to some extent in the city of Cambridge, and the disease was increasing. If such was the situation, — and nothing is asserted or appears in the record to the contrary, — if we are to attach, any value whatever to the knowledge which, it is safe to affirm, in common to all civilized peoples touching smallpox and the methods most usually employed to eradicate that disease, it cannot be adjudged that the present regulation of the board of health was not necessary in order to protect the public health and secure the public safety. Smallpox being prevalent and increasing at Cambridge, the court would usurp the functions of another branch of government if it adjudged, as matter of law, that the mode adopted under the sanction of the state, to protect the people at large was arbitrary, and not justified by the necessities of the case. We say necessities of the case, because it might be that an acknowledged power of a local community to protect itself against an epidemic threatening the safety of all might be exercised in particular circumstances and in reference to particular persons in such an arbitrary, unreasonable manner, or might go so far beyond what was reasonably required for the safety of the public, as to authorize or compel the courts to interfere for the protection of such persons. . . .

There is, of course, a sphere within which the individual may assert the supremacy of his own will, and rightfully dispute the authority of any human government, — especially of any free government existing under a written constitution, to interfere with the exercise of that will. But it is equally true that in every well-ordered society charged with the duty of conserving the safety of its members the rights of the individual in respect of his liberty may at times, under the pressure of great dangers, be subjected to such restraint, to be enforced by reasonable regulations, as the safety of the general public may demand. . . . [Citing rules governing the quarantine of persons exposed to contagious diseases and mandatory military service.] It is not, therefore, true that the power of the public to guard itself against imminent danger depends in every case involving the control of one's body upon his willingness to submit to reasonable regulations established by the constituted authorities, under the sanction of the state, for the purpose of protecting the public collectively against such danger. . . .

Looking at the propositions embodied in the defendant's rejected offers of proof, it is clear that they are more formidable by their number than by their inherent value. . . . We must assume that, when the statute in question was passed, the legislature of Massachusetts was not unaware of these opposing theories [about the safety and efficacy of vaccination], and was compelled, of necessity, to choose between them. . . . Upon what sound principles as to the relations existing between the different departments of government can the court review this action of the legislature? If there is any such power in the judiciary to review legislative action in respect of a matter affecting the general welfare, it can only be when that which the legislature has done comes within the rule that, if a statute purporting to have been enacted to protect the public health, the public morals, or the public safety, has no real or substantial relation to those objects, or is, beyond all question, a plain, palpable invasion of rights secured by the fundamental law, it is the duty of the courts to so adjudge, and thereby give effect to the Constitution. Mugler v. Kansas, 123 U.S. 623, 661.

Whatever may be thought of the expediency of this statute, it cannot be affirmed to be, beyond question, in palpable conflict with the Constitution. Nor, in view of the methods employed to stamp out the disease of smallpox, can anyone confidently assert that the means prescribed by the state to that end has no real or substantial relation to the protection of the public health and the public safety. Such an assertion would not be consistent with the experience of this and other countries whose authorities have dealt with the disease of smallpox. . . .

[T]he police power of a state, whether exercised directly by the legislature, or by a local body acting under its authority, may be exerted in such circumstances, or by regulations so arbitrary and oppressive in particular cases, as to justify the interference of the courts to prevent wrong and oppression. Extreme cases can be readily suggested. Ordinarily such cases are not safe guides in the administration of the law. It is easy, for instance, to suppose the case of an adult who is embraced by the mere words of the act, but yet to subject whom to vaccination in a particular condition of his health or body would be cruel and inhuman in the last degree. We are not to be understood as holding that the statute was intended to be applied to such a case, or, if it was so intended, that the judiciary would not be competent to interfere and protect the health and life of the individual concerned. . . . Until otherwise informed by the highest court of Massachusetts, we are not inclined to hold that the statute establishes the absolute rule that an adult must be vaccinated if it be apparent or can be shown with reasonable certainty that he is not at the time a fit subject of vaccination, or that vaccination, by reason of his then condition, would seriously impair his health, or probably cause his death. No such case is here presented. It is the cause of an adult who, for aught that appears, was himself in perfect health and a fit subject of vaccination, and yet, while remaining in the community, refused to obey the statute and the regulation adopted in execution of its provisions for the protection of the public health and the public safety, confessedly endangered by the presence of a dangerous disease.

We now decide only that the statute covers the present case, and that nothing clearly appears that would justify this court in holding it to be unconstitutional and inoperative in its application to the plaintiff in error. The judgment of the court below must be affirmed. It is so ordered. Mr. Justice Brewer and Mr. Justice Peckham dissent.

Notes: The State Police Power and Federalism

1. *Delegation.* The police power is the power of the "state" to protect its citizens. The power is most often initially invested in the state legislature by the state constitution. The legislature therefore may pass statutes designed to protect the public. The state legislature also can delegate the power in at least two different directions. It may establish some administrative agency in the executive branch, such as a state health department, which will be given statutory authority to oversee some aspects of public health. The legislature may also delegate some portion of its authority to other political entities within the state, such as to counties, cities, or local health entities.

As an initial matter, it is important to determine whether the entity exercising the police power has the constitutional authority to do so. See Wong Wai v. Williamson, 103 F. 1 (C.C. N.D. Cal. 1900) (court notes that the San Francisco Board of Supervisors, rather than the Board of Health, was the entity with authority to issue ordinances to protect public health). Other, related questions include examining the delegation of authority from the legislature to the entity to ensure that the entity has not exceeded or improperly exercised its authority under the terms of the grant. In *Jacobson*, for example, the Court noted that the state may give some public health authority to local bodies, and that, in this case, the Massachusetts legislature had delegated to the local Board of Health the determination of when vaccinations were necessary. The delegation itself can also be challenged as "standardless" or as not providing sufficient guidance to the entity given the authority to exercise the police power.

2. *Interpreting* Jacobson. The *Jacobson* case, while ancient in constitutional law terms, is often cited as the authoritative statement of the scope of the state's police power. See, e.g., Planned Parenthood of Southeastern Pennsylvania v. Casey, 505 U.S. 833 (1992); Cruzan v. Director, Missouri Department of Health, 497 U.S. 261 (1990). Professor Larry Gostin argues that:

> *Jacobson* established a floor of constitutional protection. Public health powers are constitutionally permissible only if they are exercised in conformity with four standards . . . [:]
>
> *Public Health Necessity.* Public health powers are exercised under the theory that they are necessary to prevent an avoidable harm. . . . [T]he standard of public health necessity requires, at a minimum, that the subject of the compulsory intervention must actually pose a threat to the community. . . .
>
> *Reasonable Means.* . . . The methods used . . . must be designed to prevent or ameliorate the threat. The *Jacobson* Court adopted a means/ends test that required a reasonable relationship between the public health intervention and the achievement of a legitimate public health objective. . . . [T]he methods adopted must have a "real and substantial relation" to protection of the public health, and cannot be "a plain, palpable invasion of rights."
>
> *Proportionality.* . . . [A] public health regulation is unconstitutional if the human burden imposed is wholly disproportionate to the expected benefit. . . .
>
> *Harm Avoidance.* . . . The control measure itself . . . should not pose a health risk to its subject.

Lawrence O. Gostin, Public Health Law: Power, Duty, Restraint 68-69 (2000) [hereinafter "Public Health Law"]. Do you agree with this analysis of *Jacobson*? Is the end result consistent with the current approach to judicial review under the rational basis standard? Gostin and others have argued that courts should apply a somewhat heightened scrutiny to public health measures that would ordinarily be tested under the highly deferential rational basis standard. Id. at 82-83. Commentators agree that public health measures will elicit even greater judicial scrutiny if they infringe on fundamental rights or operate based on suspect or quasi-suspect classifications.

Do individuals have a liberty interest in avoiding vaccination? Do individuals have a protected liberty interest in engaging in behaviors that could help spread disease? Or do individuals have a fundamental right to bodily integrity that is outweighed by the state's compelling interest in protecting public health? *Jacobson*'s discussion of these issues seems a little murky to the modern eye. The Court suggests at times that there simply is no liberty interest in conduct that puts others at risk. Yet the Court's analysis ultimately is consistent with the more modern balancing approach: Whatever liberty interest individuals have can be outweighed where the state has a compelling interest in protecting public health, assuming the public health measure is appropriately tailored to meet that objective. Under what facts could Jacobson have avoided vaccination without penalty? For more on *Jacobson*'s relevance today, see Wendy Parmet, Richard Goodman & Amy Farber, Individual Rights Versus the Public's Health — 100 Years After *Jacobson v. Massachusetts*, 352 New Eng. J. Med. 652 (2005). See also

Coshow v City of Escondido, 34 Cal. Rptr. 3d 19 (2005) (rejecting substantive due process challenge to fluoridation of drinking water).

3. *Due Process and Equal Protection.* Courts in the early 1900s were extremely deferential to a state's power to protect public health. Thus, courts would uphold a state's public health action so long as it was not "arbitrary" or "unreasonable" or "unnecessary" to protect public health. See *Jacobson,* supra. Under current constitutional law doctrines, individuals have a protected liberty interest in maintaining their own bodily integrity and in exercising at least some decision-making power with respect to their medical treatment. See Chapters 3-5, especially the discussions of *Cruzan* (pages 237 and 269) and *Casey* (page 449). Persons subjected to coercive state policies may also assert their First Amendment right to the free exercise of religion and their Fourth Amendment right to be free from unreasonable searches and seizures. Under the modern approach, a state may infringe a fundamental right to serve a compelling state interest only so long as the infringement is narrowly tailored to meet that interest. Consider whether and how this standard has been incorporated into modern public health decisions as you read the remaining cases in this chapter. See also Public Health Law at 63-64.

Under the equal protection clause, class-based legislation will be reviewed under one of three standards: (1) suspect classifications (those based on race, for example, or those that intrude on other fundamental rights) will be subjected to strict scrutiny; (2) quasi-suspect classifications (such as gender) will receive intermediate scrutiny; and (3) all other legislative classifications will be reviewed under the rational basis standard. There is some suggestion that the Supreme Court will apply a heightened rational basis review standard (sometimes called "rational basis with bite") to some classifications, see, e.g., Romer v. Evans, 517 U.S. 620 (1996) (Court uses "rational basis" standard to strike down state measure that specifically prejudiced persons seeking legislative bans on discrimination against homosexuals); City of Cleburne v. Cleburne Living Center, 473 U.S. 432 (1985) (Court invalidates application of zoning ordinance to group home for mentally retarded under "rational basis" standard).

4. *Statutory Construction.* Courts generally follow the rule of statutory construction that exhorts that ambiguous statutes should be construed to avoid constitutional defects. In *Jacobson,* for example, the Court grafts an exception onto the vaccination rule. What constitutional defect is remedied by this procedure?

5. *Compulsory Vaccination and Religious Objections.* Compulsory smallpox vaccination opened the door to broader immunization campaigns. Later programs were targeted at early vaccination of children prior to attending public school. In another classic decision, the U.S. Supreme Court held that parental religious objections to vaccination would not justify avoiding vaccination of children despite the First Amendment's protection of religious freedom. See Prince v. Massachusetts, 321 U.S. 158 at 166-167 (1944). On religious objection to health measures generally, see Timothy J. Aspinwall, Religious Exemptions to Childhood Immunization Statutes: Reaching for a More Optimal Balance Between Religious Freedom and Public Health, 29 Loy. U. Chi. L.J. 109, 127 (1997); Annot., 94 A.L.R.5th 613 (2001). Low immunization rates have been tied to outbreaks of preventable disease. Daniel A. Salmon et al., Health Consequences of Religious and Philosophical Exemptions from Immunization Laws, 282 JAMA 47 (1999).

6. *Vaccine Safety.* Childhood vaccinations continue to be controversial, despite the unified efforts of public health authorities to reassure the public about the safety and efficacy of the vaccinations. See, e.g., the CDC's National Vaccine Program Office Web site, http://www.hhs.gov/nvpo/immun.htm, and the Web site for the Institute for Vaccine Safety at Johns Hopkins University, http://www.vaccinesafety.edu/. Use your favorite Internet search engine to find information by combining "vaccine" with "risks" or "danger." Do the "official" Web sites provide sufficient information to counteract the "scary" vaccine Web sites?

7. *Vaccine Production and Distribution.* Vaccines must be developed, manufactured, and distributed if they are to be used to protect public health. Much of this activity occurs in the private sector as pharmaceutical companies work to discover and develop vaccines, to secure governmental approval for their use, and to establish economically beneficial manufacturing and distribution arrangements. There are substantial concerns about whether this system is capable of meeting the public health needs of the United States and other countries. Much of the publicity has involved the yearly influenza vaccine. See, e.g., James G. Hodge Jr. & Jessica P. O'Connell, The Legal Environment Underlying Influenza Vaccine Allocation and Distribution Strategies, 12 J. Pub. Health Mgmt. Prac. 340 (2006); Anthony B. Iton, Rationing Influenza Vaccine: Legal Strategies and Considerations for Local Health Officials, 12 J. Pub. Health Mgmt. Prac. 349 (2006); Michelle M. Mello & Troyen A. Brennan, Legal Concerns and the Influenza Vaccine Shortage, 294 JAMA 1817 (2005); Paul A. Offit, Why Are Pharmaceutical Companies Gradually Abandoning Vaccines?, 24 Health Aff. 622 (2005); James Ranson, Another Year of Influenza Vaccine Supply and Distribution Problems: Why Does This Keep Happening and What Can Be Done About It?, 12 J. Pub. Health Mgmt. Prac. 210 (2006).

8. *Federal Authority Over Public Health.* These days we are most likely to see the federal government as a pervasive force in our lives, with its influence—for good or for bad—exerted over everything from the national defense, to the organization of our health care system, to the problem of educational standards in our local schools. Constitutionally speaking, the national government has limited powers and may exercise authority only in those areas ceded by the states to the federal government within that document. Somewhat surprisingly, given the undeniable breadth and scope of federal health and safety regulation, the federal government does not have any direct constitutional authority to protect the public health. Congress and the executive branch have not been deterred by this gap in authority. Instead, Congress has achieved many of the same objectives through the exercise of its powers to regulate the relationship between the United States and foreign countries, to regulate interstate commerce, and to spend to promote the public welfare. U.S. Const. art. 1, §8. For a sampling of federal public health initiatives, see Public Health Law at 42-45 (Table 1). See also James Hodge, Lawrence O. Gostin & Jon S. Vernick, The Pandemic and All-Hazards Preparedness Act: Improving Public Health Emergency Response, 297 JAMA 1708 (2007) (evaluating impact of new federal legislation, including impact on states).

9. *State vs. Federal Authority.* A state's power to regulate in order to protect the public health can also be limited by conflicts with federal authority over interstate or international matters. States often attempt to establish standards that can have

a negative impact on interstate commerce. Should a state or local government be permitted to legislate to improve roadway safety within its borders? City of Columbus v. Ours Garage & Wrecker Service, Inc., 536 U.S. 424 (2002) (preserving local tow truck rule from federal preemption despite generally broad federal preemptive authority). In general, state power in areas impinging on interstate commerce is severely restricted by federal supremacy and preemption.

10. *Modern Approaches to Vaccination.* For recent updates on vaccine safety and public health policy, see Ciro A. de Quadros, The Century of Vaccines, 94 Am. J. Pub. Health 910 (2004); Roger Bernier & Karen Midthun, Getting the Science Right and Doing the Right Science in Vaccine Safety, 94 Am. J. Pub. Health 914 (2004); Walter A. Orenstein et al., Immunizations in the United States: Success, Structure, and Stress, 24 Health Aff. 599 (2005); Wendy E. Parmet, Informed Consent and Public Health: Are They Compatible When It Comes to Vaccines?, 8 J. Health Care L. & Pol'y 71 (2005); Rosemary B Quigley, Uncertain Benefit: The Public Policy of Approving Smallpox Vaccine Research, 94 Am. J. Pub. Health 943 (2004); Daniel A. Salmon, Lawrence H. Moulton & Neal A. Halsey, Enhancing Public Confidence in Vaccines Through Independent Oversight of Postlicensure Vaccine Safety, 94 Am. J. Pub. Health 947 (2004).

Problem: Bioterrorism and Smallpox Vaccination

Routine vaccination for smallpox ended in the early 1970s, when it appeared that the only smallpox virus on earth was safely contained in scientific laboratories in the United States and Russia. The federal government began to reconsider its vaccination policies in 2001, amidst growing concern about the threat that smallpox would be used as a weapon of bioterrorism. The initial problem was the production of new smallpox vaccine. The federal government arranged to purchase several hundred million doses of vaccine. The second issue involved the appropriate distribution strategy. The smallpox vaccine carries a significant risk of disease or death for persons with compromised immune systems (e.g., persons with HIV, or transplant recipients) as well as for people with a history of eczema or atopic dermatitis. A massive vaccination program could put millions at risk, whether or not they underwent vaccination directly, because of the live viral particles that would be shed from the vaccination site of those who did receive the vaccine. Yet delaying vaccination programs until after the first case of smallpox could result in thousands of preventable deaths.

What smallpox vaccine distribution policy do you favor? Use Web-based public health resources to find the federal government's current smallpox vaccination strategy. What ethical and/or legal constraints should govern the development and implementation of mandatory or voluntary vaccination policies?

See generally CDC Smallpox, available at http://www.bt.cdc.gov/agent/smallpox/, for the most current federal plans for the distribution of smallpox vaccine in the event of a confirmed case. For a discussion of the failure of the federal government's initial smallpox vaccination campaign see Jay Gold Rathbun, The Smallpox Vaccination Campaign of 2003: Why Did It Fail and What Are the Lessons for Bioterrorism Preparedness?, 64 La. L. Rev. 851 (2004).

Problem: HPV Vaccination

The FDA approved a new vaccine to prevent infection by human papillomavirus (HPV) in 2006. HPV is the most common sexually transmitted disease, with infection rates of 40-50 percent among sexually active young people. While apparently harmless in many cases, HPV does cause cervical cancer in women, other cancers in men and women, genital warts, and warts in the respiratory tract. See the CDC's HPV Vaccine Fact Sheet at http://www.cdc.gov/nip/publications/vis/vis-hpv.pdf. The vaccine requires three separate doses, administered before the recipient has been exposed to the disease during sexual activity, and costs nearly $400. The federal government's Advisory Committee on Immunization Practices adopted recommendations providing for routine use of the HPV vaccine for girls 11-12 years old. Lauri E. Markowitz et al., Quadrivalent Human Papillomavirus Vaccine: Recommendations of the Advisory Committee on Immunization Practices (ACIP), 56 MMWR 1 (2007) (RR-2). This opened the door to consideration of whether states should add the vaccine to the list of mandatory childhood vaccinations. What factors do you think should be relevant to this decision? Assuming efficacy studies demonstrate that the vaccine is effective in males, would there be any problem with mandating a vaccine for girls (who face the risk of cervical cancer) but not boys (who can transmit the disease and face the risk of other medical conditions from HPV)? For more information on the controversy, see R. Alto Charo, Politics, Parents, and Prophylaxis — Mandating HPV Vaccination in the United States, 356 New Eng. J. Med. 1905 (2007); Lawrence O. Gostin & Catherine D. DeAngelis, Mandatory HPV Vaccination: Public Health vs. Private Wealth, 297 JAMA 1921 (2007); Stephanie Saule & Andrew Pollack, Furor on Rush to Require Cervical Cancer Vaccine, N.Y. Times, Feb. 17, 2007, at A1, col. 2; George F. Sawaya & Karen Smith-McCune, HPV Vaccination — More Answers, More Questions, 356 New Eng. J. Med. 1991 (2007).

2. Disability Discrimination

Despite its age, *Jacobson* still sets the basic framework for debating the constitutional legitimacy of various public health interventions. That debate has expanded in recent years, however, to incorporate a new concern, one that has a statutory origin: disability discrimination. The following case explains how concepts of disability discrimination relate to contagious diseases. As with *Jacobson*, the case's relevance extends far beyond the particular dispute since it establishes broad principles that apply throughout the public health arena.

■ SCHOOL BOARD OF NASSAU COUNTY v. ARLINE
480 U.S. 273 (1987)

BRENNAN, Justice.

Section 504 of the Rehabilitation Act of 1973, 29 U.S.C. §794 (Act), prohibits a federally funded state program from discriminating against a handicapped individual solely by reason of his or her handicap. This case presents the questions whether a person afflicted with tuberculosis, a contagious disease, may be considered a "handicapped individual" within the meaning of §504 of the Act, and, if so, whether such an individual is "otherwise qualified" to teach elementary school.

I

From 1966 until 1979, respondent Gene Arline taught elementary school in Nassau County, Florida. She was discharged in 1979 after suffering a third relapse of tuberculosis within two years. After she was denied relief in state administrative proceedings, she brought suit in federal court, alleging that the school board's decision to dismiss her because of her tuberculosis violated §504 of the Act . . . [which] reads in pertinent part:

> No otherwise qualified handicapped individual . . . shall, solely by reason of his handicap, be excluded from participation in, be denied the benefits of, or be subjected to discrimination under any program or activity receiving Federal financial assistance. . . .

29 U.S.C. §794. In 1974 Congress expanded the definition of "handicapped individual" for use in §504 to read as follows:

> [A]ny person who (i) has a physical or mental impairment which substantially limits one or more of such person's major life activities, (ii) has a record of such an impairment, or (iii) is regarded as having such an impairment.

The amended definition reflected Congress' concern with protecting the handicapped against discrimination stemming not only from simple prejudice, but also from "archaic attitudes and laws" and from "the fact that the American people are simply unfamiliar with and insensitive to the difficulties confront[ing] individuals with handicaps." S. Rep. No. 93-1297, p.50 (1974), U.S. Code Cong. & Admin. News 1974, p.6400. To combat the effects of erroneous but nevertheless prevalent perceptions about the handicapped, Congress expanded the definition of "handicapped individual" so as to preclude discrimination against "[a] person who has a record of, or is regarded as having, an impairment [but who] may at present have no actual incapacity at all." Southeastern Community College v. Davis, 442 U.S. 397, 405-406, n.6 (1979).

Petitioners concede that a contagious disease may constitute a handicapping condition to the extent that it leaves a person with "diminished physical or mental capabilities," and concede that Arline's hospitalization for tuberculosis in 1957 demonstrates that she has a record of a physical impairment. Petitioners maintain, however, that Arline's record of impairment is irrelevant in this case, since the school board dismissed Arline not because of her diminished physical capabilities, but because of the threat that her relapses of tuberculosis posed to the health of others.

We do not agree with petitioners that, in defining a handicapped individual under §504, the contagious effects of a disease can be meaningfully distinguished from the disease's physical effects on a claimant in a case such as this. Arline's contagiousness and her physical impairment each resulted from the same underlying condition, tuberculosis. It would be unfair to allow an employer to seize upon the distinction between the effects of a disease on others and the effects of a disease on a patient and use that distinction to justify discriminatory treatment.

Allowing discrimination based on the contagious effects of a physical impairment would be inconsistent with the basic purpose of §504, which is to ensure that handicapped individuals are not denied jobs or other benefits because of the prejudiced attitudes or the ignorance of others. By amending the definition of "handicapped individual" to include not only those who are actually physically impaired, but also those who are regarded as impaired and who, as a result, are substantially limited in a major life activity, Congress acknowledged that society's accumulated myths and fears about disability and disease are as handicapping as are the physical limitations that flow from actual impairment. Few aspects of a handicap give rise to the same level of public fear and misapprehension as contagiousness. Even those who suffer or have recovered from such noninfectious diseases as epilepsy or cancer have faced discrimination based on the irrational fear that they might be contagious. . . . We conclude that the fact that a person with a record of a physical impairment is also contagious does not suffice to remove that person from coverage under §504.

IV

The remaining question is whether Arline is otherwise qualified for the job of elementary schoolteacher. To answer this question in most cases, the district court will need to conduct an individualized inquiry and make appropriate findings of fact. Such an inquiry is essential if §504 is to achieve its goal of protecting handicapped individuals from deprivations based on prejudice, stereotypes, or unfounded fear, while giving appropriate weight to such legitimate concerns of grantees as avoiding exposing others to significant health and safety risks. The basic factors to be considered in conducting this inquiry are well established. In the context of the employment of a person handicapped with a contagious disease, we agree with amicus American Medical Association that this inquiry should include:

> [findings of] facts, based on reasonable medical judgments given the state of medical knowledge, about (a) the nature of the risk (how the disease is transmitted), (b) the duration of the risk (how long is the carrier infectious), (c) the severity of the risk (what is the potential harm to third parties) and (d) the probabilities the disease will be transmitted and will cause varying degrees of harm.

In making these findings, courts normally should defer to the reasonable medical judgments of public health officials. The next step in the "otherwise-qualified" inquiry is for the court to evaluate, in light of these medical findings, whether the employer could reasonably accommodate the employee. . . .

Because of the paucity of factual findings by the district court, we, like the court of appeals, are unable at this stage of the proceedings to resolve whether Arline is "otherwise qualified" for her job. . . .

We remand the case to the district court to determine whether Arline is otherwise qualified for her position. The judgment of the court of appeals is Affirmed.

[The dissenting opinion of Chief Justice Rehnquist and Justice Scalia is omitted.]

Notes: Balancing Risk Reduction with Other Values

1. *Disability Discrimination Law.* The *Arline* case was decided under the federal Rehabilitation Act of 1973, which prohibits disability-based discrimination by the federal government, federal contractors, and recipients of federal funds. 29 U.S. C. §§701-796. Congress later enacted the Americans with Disabilities Act (ADA), 42 U.S.C. §§12101-12213 to expand protection against discrimination by private employers, public entities, and public accommodations. Thus, these disability discrimination principles apply to virtually all of the different public health measures encountered in this chapter.

The two Acts have similar definitions of disability: A person is disabled under the statutes if she (1) has a physical or mental impairment that substantially limits her ability to engage in one or more major life activities; (2) has a record of such an impairment; or (3) is regarded as being impaired. 42 U.S.C. §12102(2). A person who meets one of these three tests will be protected from discrimination so long as she meets the essential qualifications and does not present a "direct threat" or a "significant risk" to the health or safety of others, with or without reasonable accommodation. See, e.g., id. at §12111(3) (defining direct threat) and §12113(b) (direct threat defense). Thus, as in *Arline*, persons with contagious diseases are protected from discrimination unless they present a significant risk to others. See generally, Peter David Blanck et al., Disability Civil Rights Law and Policy (2003).

How should employers and the courts assess the degree and probability of risk? In *Arline*, the Supreme Court suggested that "courts normally should defer to the reasonable medical judgments of public health officials." In Bragdon v. Abbott, the Court described a more nuanced approach:

> In assessing the reasonableness of [a defendant's] actions, the views of public health authorities such as the U.S. Public Health Service, CDC, and the National Institutes of Health, are of special weight and authority. *Arline*, [480 U.S.] at 288; 28 C.F.R. pt. 36, App. B, p. 626 (1997). The views of these organizations are not conclusive, however. A health care professional who disagrees with the prevailing medical consensus may refute it by citing a credible scientific basis for deviating from the accepted norm.

524 U.S. 624, 650 (1998). See also Samuel R. Bagenstos, The Americans with Disabilities Act as Risk Regulation, 101 Colum. L. Rev. 1479 (2001).

2. *TB, HIV, and "Disability."* On remand, the district court found that Arline did not present a significant risk to the health and safety of others. Arline v. School Board of Nassau County, 692 F. Supp. 1286 (M.D. Fla. 1988). Although Arline was infected with TB, the decision was clearly potentially relevant to discrimination against persons with HIV infection or AIDS. The next question, however, is whether a person with HIV infection has a "disability" as defined in the statutes. The Supreme Court finally addressed this question in Bragdon v. Abbott, 524 U.S. 624 (1998). Sidney Abbott was infected with HIV but appeared otherwise healthy. Bragdon refused to fill Abbott's cavity in his dental office, offering to do so in a local hospital if Abbott would pay the hospital charges. Abbott brought a disability-based discrimination claim. The Court held that Abbott was a person with a disability because she had a physical impairment that substantially limited her ability to engage in the major life activity of reproduction. The "substantial limitation" was not physical inability to reproduce but the fact that HIV could be transmitted to her sexual partner or to her offspring in the process.

3. *Direct Threat.* Employers, public entities, and places of public accommodation are permitted to discriminate against a person with a disability where that person poses a significant risk to the health or safety of others. Employers have successfully relied upon the "direct threat" exclusion in a number of cases. See, e.g., Turco v. Hoechst Celanese Corp., 101 F.3d 1090 (5th Cir. 1996) (diabetic presents direct threat in workplace with heavy machinery and dangerous chemicals). In most cases involving HIV infection, courts have rejected "direct threat" claims asserted by employers or others. See, e.g., Chalk v. United States District Court Central District of California, 840 F.2d 701 (9th Cir. 1988). The risk of HIV transmission within health care settings has provoked the greatest policy debate. Should HIV-infected health care providers be permitted to continue to practice? See Waddell v. Valley Force Dental Associates, 276 F.3d 1275 (11th Cir.), *cert. denied*, 122 S. Ct. 2293 (2001) (HIV-infected dental hygienist posed a direct threat to patients that could not be eliminated with reasonable accommodations). Should health care providers be permitted to discriminate against HIV-infected patients? Bragdon v. Abbott, 524 U.S. 624 (1998) (HIV-infected patient did not pose significant risk to health and safety of dentist through filling of cavity). Where should the burden of proof lie in "direct threat" litigation? Compare McKenzie v. Benton, 388 F.3d 1342 (10th Cir. 2004) (plaintiff has burden of proving she did not pose a direct threat), *cert. denied* 544 U.S. 1048 (2005), with Branham v. Snow, 392 F.3d 896 (7th Cir. 2004) (defendant has burden of proof for the defense of direct threat).

4. *Other State and Local Laws.* Virtually every state has its own disability discrimination statutes. The great majority have already declared AIDS and HIV infection covered under these state laws. There are also more general antidiscrimination laws in most states related to public accommodations and private housing. About half the states have enacted HIV-specific statutes, either as independent new provisions or as amendments to existing legislation. How will other contagious diseases be treated under these statutes?

5. *The Americans with Disabilities Act and State Public Health Regulation. Jacobson* seemed to stand for the proposition that the state had broad powers to regulate to protect the public health, even when those regulations intruded on personal

liberty. You might predict that courts would use a very loose standard of review when considering the constitutional validity of state public health regulation. Does the ADA fundamentally change this understanding of the relative power of the state and the judiciary in public health matters? Should the ADA's prohibition of disability-based discrimination apply to actions by state public health authorities?

Many commentators have argued that the federal laws prohibiting disability-based discrimination prevent states from discriminating against persons with disabilities in public services (under the ADA) or in federally funded programs (under the Rehabilitation Act). See, e.g., Scott Burris, Rationality Review and the Politics of Public Health, 34 Vill. L. Rev. 933 (1989).

The Supreme Court's decision in Board of Trustees of the University of Alabama v. Garrett, 531 U.S. 356 (2001), cast doubt on whether and how the ADA might be applied to the states. In *Garrett*, the Court held that Congress had exceeded its Fourteenth Amendment authority in attempting to abrogate states' Eleventh Amendment immunity under Title I of the ADA. State employees were denied the ability to bring actions for money damages under the ADA in federal court. Id. Injunctive and declaratory relief remain available.

Similar concerns are raised by Title II of the ADA's prohibition against disability-based discrimination in public services. See Ruth Colker & Adam Milani, The Post-*Garrett* World: Insufficient State Protection against Disability Discrimination, 53 Ala. L. Rev. 1075 (2002); Lawrence O. Gostin, Public Health Theory and Practice in the Constitutional Design, 11 Health Matrix 265 (2001).

In Tennessee v. Lane, 124 S. Ct. 1978 (2004), the Court held that Title II could be used to recover money damages in cases involving a valid exercise of congressional power to enforce the Fourteenth Amendment. See City of Boerne v. Flores, 521 U.S. 507 (1997) (setting forth test used to determine whether a congressional enactment is a valid effort to enforce the Fourteenth Amendment). Abrogation of state immunity was upheld in *Lane* because the action contested under Title II involved a fundamental right—access to the courts. In United States v. Georgia et al., the Court held that Title II of the ADA validly abrogates state sovereign immunity "for conduct that actually violates the Fourteenth Amendment." 546 U.S. 151 (2006) (emphasis omitted). See also Phiffer v. Columbia River Correction Inst., 384 F.3d 791 (9th Cir. 2004), *cert. denied*,126 S. Ct. 1140 (2006) (inmate suffering from osteoarthritis and osteoporosis denied accommodation for his disabilities; state not entitled to Eleventh Amendment immunity from the inmate's suit under Title II of the ADA).

Case law must be monitored to determine whether and how Title II might be applied in other public health cases. The Rehabilitation Act's provisions prohibiting disability-based discrimination by recipients of federal funds might grow in importance if *Lane* signals sharp restrictions in the application of Title II of the ADA to cases involving state public services. See, e.g., Constantine v. Rectors and Visitors of George Mason University, 411 F.3d 474 (4th Cir. 2005).

6. *Summary.* Persons seeking to challenge the validity of public health measures may look to the federal Constitution, federal statutes such as the ADA and Rehabilitation Act, state constitutions, state statutes, and state regulations. You may wish to consider each of these potential limitations on public health initiatives throughout the remainder of this chapter.

C. REGULATING MEDICAL TREATMENT TO PROTECT PUBLIC HEALTH

There are many types of governmental intervention into the treatment relationship. Much of the discussion in previous chapters might be characterized, one way or another, as governmental regulation of this important relationship. The policies examined in this section are distinguished from those studied before, however, by their explicit and unique grounding in a governmental interest in protecting the community's health, along with the health of the individual. The analytical focus here is the sacrifice of individual autonomy to serve the public health. How much of a sacrifice can be exacted? In what circumstances? With what level of judicial oversight?

1. Restricting Consumer Choice to Protect Public Health

a. The FDA, Pharmaceutical Regulation, and the Constitution

■ **UNITED STATES v. RUTHERFORD**
442 U.S. 544 (1979)

MARSHALL, J., delivered the opinion for a unanimous Court.

The question presented in this case is whether the Federal Food, Drug, and Cosmetic Act precludes terminally ill cancer patients from obtaining Laetrile, a drug not recognized as "safe and effective" within the meaning of ... 21 U.S.C. §321(p)(1) ["the statute"].

I

[T]he Federal Food, Drug, and Cosmetic Act ... prohibits interstate distribution of any "new drug" unless the Secretary of Health, Education, and Welfare approves an application supported by substantial evidence of the drug's safety and effectiveness.[11] As defined ... [by the statute], the term "new drug" includes

---

[11] Section 505, as set forth in 21 U.S.C. §355, provides in part:

(a) ... No person shall introduce or deliver for introduction into interstate commerce any new drug, unless an approval of an application filed pursuant to subsection (b) of this section is effective with respect to such drug.

(b) ... Any person may file with the Secretary an application with respect to any drug subject to the provisions of subsection (a) of this section. Such person shall submit to the Secretary as a part of the application (1) full reports of investigations which have been made to show whether or not such drug is safe for use and whether such drug is effective in use. ...

(d) ... If the Secretary finds ... that (1) the investigations ... required to be submitted to the Secretary ... do not include adequate tests by all methods reasonably applicable to show whether or not such drug is safe for use under the conditions prescribed, recommended, or suggested in the proposed labeling thereof; (2) the results of such tests show that such drug is unsafe for use under such conditions or do not show that such drug is safe for use under such conditions; ... (4) ... he has insufficient

[a]ny drug . . . not generally recognized, among experts qualified by scientific training and experience to evaluate the safety and effectiveness of drugs, as safe and effective for use under the conditions prescribed, recommended, or suggested in the labeling. . . .

In 1975, terminally ill cancer patients and their spouses brought this action to enjoin the government from interfering with the interstate shipment and sale of Laetrile, a drug not approved for distribution under the Act. Finding that Laetrile, in proper dosages, was nontoxic and effective, the district court ordered the government to permit limited purchases of the drug by one of the named plaintiffs. [T]he court of appeals for the Tenth Circuit . . . instructed the district court to remand the case to the Food and Drug Administration for determination whether Laetrile was a "new drug" under [the statute]. . . . After completion of administrative hearings, the Commissioner . . . determined first that no uniform definition of Laetrile exists; rather, the term has been used generically for chemical compounds similar to, or consisting at least in part of, amygdalin, a glucoside present in the kernels or seeds of most fruits. The Commissioner further found that Laetrile in its various forms constituted a "new drug" . . . because it was not generally recognized among experts as safe and effective for its prescribed use. . . .

On review of the Commissioner's decision, the district court sustained his determination that Laetrile, because not generally regarded as safe or effective, constituted a new drug. . . . [T]he court held that, by denying cancer patients the right to use a nontoxic substance in connection with their personal health, the Commissioner had infringed constitutionally protected privacy interests.

The court of appeals addressed neither the statutory nor the constitutional rulings of the district court. Rather, the Tenth Circuit held that "the 'safety' and 'effectiveness' terms used in the statute have no reasonable application to terminally ill cancer patients." Since those patients, by definition, would "die of cancer regardless of what may be done," the court concluded that there were no realistic standards against which to measure the safety and effectiveness of a drug

---

information to determine whether such drug is safe for use under such conditions; or (5) . . . there is a lack of substantial evidence that the drug will have the effect it purports or is represented to have under the conditions of use prescribed, recommended, or suggested in the proposed labeling thereof; or (6) based on a fair evaluation of all material facts, such labeling is false or misleading in any particular; he shall issue an order refusing to approve the application. . . . As used in this subsection . . . , the term "substantial evidence" means evidence consisting of adequate and well-controlled investigations, including clinical investigations, by experts qualified by scientific training and experience to evaluate the effectiveness of the drug involved, on the basis of which it could fairly and responsibly be concluded by such experts that the drug will have the effect it purports or is represented to have under the conditions of use prescribed, recommended, or suggested in the labeling or proposed labeling thereof.

(i) . . . The Secretary shall promulgate regulations for exempting from the operation of the foregoing subsections of this section drugs intended solely for investigational use by experts qualified by scientific training and experience to investigate the safety and effectiveness of drugs. . . .

The Secretary has delegated his approval authority to the Commissioner of the Food and Drug Administration. See 21 CFR §5.10(a)(1) (1978).

for that class of individuals. The court of appeals therefore approved the district court's injunction permitting use of Laetrile by cancer patients certified as terminally ill. . . .

II

The Federal Food, Drug, and Cosmetic Act makes no special provision for drugs used to treat terminally ill patients. By its terms, . . . the Act requires premarketing approval for "any new drug" unless it is intended solely for investigative use or is exempt under one of the Act's grandfather provisions. And . . . [the statute] defines "new drug" to encompass "[a]ny drug . . . not generally recognized . . . as safe and effective for use under the conditions prescribed, recommended, or suggested in the labeling." . . .

In the instant case, we are persuaded by the legislative history and consistent administrative interpretation of the Act that no implicit exemption for drugs used by the terminally ill is necessary to attain congressional objectives or to avert an unreasonable reading of the terms *safe* and *effective*. . . .

Nothing in the history of the 1938 Food, Drug, and Cosmetic Act, which first established procedures for review of drug safety, or of the 1962 Amendments, which added the current safety and effectiveness standards in . . . [the statute],[12] suggests that Congress intended protection only for persons suffering from curable diseases. To the contrary, in deliberations preceding the 1938 Act, Congress expressed concern that individuals with fatal illnesses, such as cancer, should be shielded from fraudulent cures. See, e.g., 79 Cong. Rec. 5023 (1935). . . .

In implementing the statutory scheme, the FDA has never made exception for drugs used by the terminally ill. As this Court has often recognized, the construction of a statute by those charged with its administration is entitled to substantial deference. . . .

In the court of appeals' view, an implied exemption from the Act was justified because the safety and effectiveness standards set forth in . . . [the statute] could have "no reasonable application" to terminally ill patients. 582 F.2d, at 1236. We disagree. . . . Only when a literal construction of a statute yields results so manifestly unreasonable that they could not fairly be attributed to congressional design will an exception to statutory language be judicially implied. Here, however, we have no license to depart from the plain language of the Act, for Congress could reasonably have intended to shield terminal patients from ineffectual or unsafe drugs.

A drug is effective within the meaning of . . . [the statute] if there is general recognition among experts, founded on substantial evidence, that the drug in fact produces the results claimed for it under prescribed conditions. Contrary to the court of appeals' apparent assumption, effectiveness does not necessarily denote capacity to cure. In the treatment of any illness, terminal or otherwise, a drug is

---

[12] Under the 1938 Act, a "new drug" was one not generally recognized by qualified experts as safe for its recommended use. §201(p)(1), 52 Stat. 1041. The Drug Amendments of 1962, Pub. L. 87-781, 76 Stat. 789, redefined the term to include drugs not generally recognized as effective or safe for their intended use. §201(p)(1), 21 U.S.C. §321(p)(1). . . . In addition, the Amendments provided that no new drug application may be approved absent substantial evidence that the drug is effective as well as safe under prescribed conditions. §505(d), 21 U.S.C. §355(d). See n.11, supra.

effective if it fulfills, by objective indices, its sponsor's claims of prolonged life, improved physical condition, or reduced pain. . . .

Thus, the Commissioner generally considers a drug safe when the expected therapeutic gain justifies the risk entailed by its use. For the terminally ill, as for anyone else, a drug is unsafe if its potential for inflicting death or physical injury is not offset by the possibility of therapeutic benefit. . . .

[Further,] if an individual suffering from a potentially fatal disease rejects conventional therapy in favor of a drug with no demonstrable curative properties, the consequences can be irreversible. . . . The FDA's practice also reflects the recognition, amply supported by expert medical testimony in this case, that with diseases such as cancer it is often impossible to identify a patient as terminally ill except in retrospect. Cancers vary considerably in behavior and in responsiveness to different forms of therapy.[13] Even critically ill individuals may have unexpected remissions and may respond to conventional treatment. Thus, as the Commissioner concluded, to exempt from the Act drugs with no proved effectiveness in the treatment of cancer "would lead to needless deaths and suffering among . . . patients characterized as 'terminal' who could actually be helped by legitimate therapy."

It bears emphasis that although the court of appeals' ruling was limited to Laetrile, its reasoning cannot be so readily confined. To accept the proposition that the safety and efficacy standards of the Act have no relevance for terminal patients is to deny the Commissioner's authority over all drugs, however toxic or ineffectual, for such individuals. If history is any guide, this new market would not be long overlooked. Since the turn of the century, resourceful entrepreneurs have advertised a wide variety of purportedly simple and painless cures for cancer, including liniments of turpentine, mustard, oil, eggs, and ammonia; peat moss; arrangements of colored floodlamps; pastes made from glycerin and limburger cheese; mineral tablets; and "Fountain of Youth" mixtures of spices, oil, and suet. In citing these examples, we do not, of course, intend to deprecate the sincerity of Laetrile's current proponents, or to imply any opinion on whether that drug may ultimately prove safe and effective for cancer treatment. But this historical experience does suggest why Congress could reasonably have determined to protect the terminally ill, no less than other patients, from the vast range of self-styled panaceas that inventive minds can devise.

We note finally that construing . . . [the statute] to encompass treatments for terminal diseases does not foreclose all resort to experimental cancer drugs by patients for whom conventional therapy is unavailing. . . . [Another section of the Act] exempts from premarketing approval drugs intended solely for investigative use if they satisfy certain preclinical testing and other criteria. An application for clinical testing of Laetrile by the National Cancer Institute is now pending before the Commissioner. That the Act makes explicit provision for carefully regulated use of certain drugs not yet demonstrated safe and effective reinforces our

---

[13] The Commissioner noted that these unexpected behavior patterns may account for anecdotal claims of Laetrile's effectiveness. Users of Laetrile who experience spontaneous remissions or delayed responses to conventional therapy after its abandonment may ascribe their improvement to Laetrile without any objective basis for that attribution. . . . Particularly since accepted cancer treatments such as chemotherapy and radiation often have painful side effects, the Commissioner concluded that patients who subjectively perceive improvement after substituting Laetrile for these modes of therapy may erroneously believe that their condition has been arrested or ameliorated.

conclusion that no exception for terminal patients may be judicially implied. Whether, as a policy matter, an exemption should be created is a question for legislative judgment, not judicial inference. The judgment of the court of appeals is reversed. . . .

Notes: The Scope and Constitutionality of Pharmaceutical Regulation

1. *Federal and State Regulation of Pharmaceuticals.* The federal government has enacted a complex web of food, drug, and medical device regulations under the federal authority to regulate interstate commerce. The power to regulate interstate commerce includes the power to regulate commerce to protect public health. For a thorough overview of regulation, see Kenneth R. Piña & Wayne L. Pines (eds.), A Practical Guide to Food and Drug Law and Regulation (2d ed. 2002); Richard Merrill, The Architecture of Government Regulation of Medical Products, 82 Va. L. Rev. 1753 (1996). See also Philip J. Hilts, Protecting America's Health: The FDA, Business, and One Hundred Years of Regulation (2003).

2. *The Drug Approval Process.* As noted in *Rutherford*, new drugs must be proven to be "safe" and "effective" in treating a particular condition. 21 U.S.C. §355. The approval process typically requires the completion of three phases of drug trials:

> (a) Phase 1.
>   (1) Phase 1 studies are typically closely monitored and may be conducted in patients or normal volunteer subjects. These studies are designed to determine the metabolism and pharmacologic actions of the drug in humans, the side effects associated with increasing doses, and, if possible, to gain early evidence on effectiveness. . . .
>   (b) Phase 2. Phase 2 includes the controlled clinical studies conducted to evaluate the effectiveness of the drug for a particular indication or indications in patients with the disease or condition under study and to determine the common short-term side effects and risks associated with the drug. Phase 2 studies are typically well controlled, closely monitored, and conducted in a relatively small number of patients, usually involving no more than several hundred subjects.
>   (c) Phase 3. Phase 3 studies are expanded controlled and uncontrolled trials. They are performed after preliminary evidence suggesting effectiveness of the drug has been obtained, and are intended to gather the additional information about effectiveness and safety that is needed to evaluate the overall benefit-risk relationship of the drug and to provide an adequate basis for physician labeling. Phase 3 studies usually include from several hundred to several thousand subjects. [21 C.F.R. §312.21.]

3. *FDA Regulation of Drugs Used to Treat Terminal Illness.* Note that the *Rutherford* opinion is almost solely concerned with the issue of whether the FDA's statutorily granted power to regulate the safety and effectiveness of drugs could be applied to drugs used to treat terminal conditions. Phrased in this way, this question of statutory interpretation almost answers itself. The language of the Act

appears broad enough to cover these drugs. Congress had been concerned about fraudulent exploitation of the seriously ill, the drugs had always been regulated under FDA policy, and no implied exemption was required by history or logic. The Court therefore held that Congress intended for these drugs to be regulated under the Food, Drug, and Cosmetic Act and that the FDA's policy did not exceed its statutory mandate.

Under current federal regulations, patients with serious or life-threatening illnesses may be given access to certain types of investigational new drugs under some circumstances. 21 C.F.R. §312.34. Patients with serious illnesses typically will obtain access only after the drug has cleared Phase 3 or after all clinical trials have been completed. Patients who have immediately life-threatening diseases may obtain access before Phase 3 trials have been completed, "but ordinarily not earlier than Phase 2." Id. Despite this compassionate use regulation, the FDA has generally refused to allow terminally ill patients access to new drugs that have tested only through Phase 1 trials.

4. *Pharmaceutical Choice as a Constitutional Right?* Why did the *Rutherford* Court not consider whether the FDA's regulation of laetrile violates the constitutional rights of terminally ill cancer patients? Shouldn't a terminally ill patient—for whom traditional, accepted treatments have failed—have the right to choose unapproved treatments? The district court had found a constitutional violation, but the Tenth Circuit Court of Appeals had decided the case on other grounds. On remand from the Supreme Court decision, the Tenth Circuit confronted and rejected this claim, holding that "the decision by the patient whether to have a treatment or not is a protected right, but his selection of a particular treatment, or at least a medication, is within the area of governmental interest in protecting public health." Rutherford v. United States, 616 F.2d 455, 457 (10th Cir. 1980).

The issue dramatically reemerged with the D.C. Circuit's initial decision in Abigail Alliance for Better Access to Developmental Drugs and Washington Legal Foundation v. Eschenbach, 445 F.3d 470 (2006), reversed en banc 495 F.3d 695 (D.C. Cir. 2007). The plaintiffs sought "to enjoin the FDA from enforcing the policy barring the sale of post-Phase I investigational new drugs to terminally ill patients not in Phase II trials." Id. at 473-474. A panel of the D.C. Circuit initially held that the trial court had erred in dismissing the complaint, finding that:

> where there are no alternative government-approved treatment options, a terminally ill, mentally competent adult patient's informed access to potentially life-saving investigational new drugs determined by the FDA after Phase I trials to be sufficiently safe for expanded human trials warrants protection under the Due Process Clause. The prerogative asserted by the FDA—to prevent a terminally ill patient from using potentially life-saving medication to which those in Phase II clinical trials have access—thus impinges upon an individual liberty deeply rooted in our Nation's history and tradition of self-preservation. . . . [W]e remand the case . . . to determine whether the FDA's policy . . . is narrowly tailored to serve a compelling governmental interest. Id. at 486.

On rehearing, the en banc court reversed, ruling that the plaintiffs' claim did not involve any fundamental constitutionally protected right and that the FDA's approach would easily survive rational basis review:

Although terminally ill patients desperately need curative treatments, . . . their deaths can certainly be hastened by the use of a potentially toxic drug with no proven therapeutic benefit. . . . [P]rior to the distribution of a drug outside of controlled studies, the Government has a rational basis for ensuring that there is a scientifically and medically acceptable level of knowledge about the risks and benefits of the drug. We therefore hold that the FDA's policy of limiting access to investigational drugs is rationally related to the legitimate state interest. . . . Id. at 713.

Compare Seeley v. Washington State, 940 P.2d 604 (Wash. 1997) (terminally ill cancer patient has no constitutional right to use marijuana to control nausea).

Is restricting access to potential treatments for terminally ill patients consistent with the jurisprudence governing the termination of life-sustaining treatment? See Chapter 3. With case law on a woman's right to choose abortion? See Chapter 5.B.2. See Eugene Volokh, Medical Self-Defense, Prohibited Experimental Therapies, and Payment for Organs, 120 Harv. L. Rev. 1813 (2007).

5. *The FDA and Drug Development Efforts.* The FDA has been criticized for unnecessary delays in the approval of important drugs. The laetrile dispute in the 1970s paved the way for vigorous protests by AIDS activists in the 1980s and 1990s. Congress sought to speed up the development of new drugs by providing additional incentives to pharmaceutical firms. Under the Orphan Drug Act, Pub. L. No. 97-414, 96 Stat. 2049 (1983), as amended, those companies are encouraged to develop and market drugs for rare illnesses, where the relatively small number of persons affected might otherwise not constitute a sufficient market to sustain the research and development costs of providing treatment. In 1997, Congress also enacted the Food and Drug Administration Modernization Act, Pub. L. No. 105-115, 111 Stat. 2296 (1997) (reforms included codification of fast-track and other measures designed to improve access to drugs). See Thomas Roberts Jr. & Bruce Chabner, Beyond Fast Track for Drug Approvals, 351 New Eng. J. Med. 501 (2004); Eve Slater, Today's FDA, 352 New Eng. J. Med. 293 (2005).

Any effort to speed up the approval of new drugs inevitably creates the risk that truncated studies and review will result in the release of drugs with unknown hazards and effectiveness; the current debate focuses on whether the reform of the drug approval process has gone too far or not far enough. See Steven R. Salbu, The FDA and Public Access to New Drugs: Appropriate Levels of Scrutiny in the Wake of HIV, AIDS, and the Diet Drug Debacle, 79 B.U. L. Rev. 93 (1999). See also David Healy, Did Regulators Fail Over Selective Serotonin Reuptake Inhibitors?, 333 Brit. Med. J. 92 (2006); Karen E. Lasser et al., Timing of New Black Box Warnings and Withdrawals for Prescription Medications, 287 JAMA 2215 (2002) (research reveals that serious adverse drug reactions emerged in 10 percent of new drugs approved by FDA between 1975 and 1999; drug must be on the market for many years before true level of safety is known); Susan Okiel, What Ails the FDA? 352 New Eng. J. Med. 1063 (2005); Eric J. Topol, Failing the Public Health — Rofecoxib, Merck, and the FDA, 351 New Eng. J. Med. 1707 (2004).

6. *Women and Minorities in Drug Research.* As noted in Chapter 2's discussion of human experimentation, at page 227, medical research has at least sometimes

been advanced at the expense of minorities and other disadvantaged groups. Ironically, in recent years medical researchers have also been subjected to criticism for excluding women and minorities from participation in important research efforts. Researchers sometimes kept women from participating in drug research trials because of fears that women could expose fetuses to potentially unsafe drugs during pregnancy. See Seminar on Women in Clinical Trials of FDA-Regulated Products: Who Participates and Who Decides?, 48 Food & Drug L.J. 161 et seq. (1993). The exclusion of minorities often stemmed from the methodology used to attract research subjects. See C. Bartlett et al., The Causes and Effects of Socio-Demographic Exclusions from Clinical Trials, 9(38) Health Tech. Assess. iii (2005) (comparing U.S. and U.K. data)

The exclusion of woman and minorities from drug research has had two results: (1) excluded groups did not have access to potentially effective (though possibly risky and ineffective) experimental treatments, and (2) researchers failed to gather data on whether there were group-related variations in the effectiveness of the experimental drugs. Congress responded to these concerns with the NIH Revitalization Act of 1993. The statute requires researchers to include women and minorities in NIH-funded research and, where practicable, to include sufficient numbers to determine whether the studied drug is as effective in these groups. 42 U.S.C. §289a-2; http://grants1.nih.gov/grants/funding/women_min/women_min.htm. See also Karen L. Baird, The New NIH and FDA Medical Research Policies, 24 J. Health Pol. Pol'y & L. 531 (1999); Allen L. Gifford et al., Participation in Research and Access to Experimental Treatments by HIV-Infected Patients, 346 New Eng. J. Med. 1373 (2002); Asefeh Heiat, Cary P. Gross & Harlan M. Krumholz, Representation of the Elderly, Women, and Minorities in Heart Failure Clinical Trials, 162 Arch. Intern. Med. 1682 (2002); Lisa C. Ikemoto, In the Shadow of Race: Women of Color in Health Disparities Policy, 39 U.C. Davis L. Rev. 1023 (2006); T. E. King Jr., Racial Disparities in Clinical Trials, 346 New Eng. J. Med. 1400 (2002); and Symposium, The Responsible Use of Racial and Ethnic Categories in Biomedical Research: Where Do We Go from Here?, J.L. Med. & Ethics 483-558 (2006).

7. *Drug Labeling, "Off-Label Use," and the Learned Intermediary Doctrine.* Under the regulatory policy of the FDA, each prescription drug carries a package-insert label with quite elaborate information on the methods of administering the drug, conditions for which the drug is recommended, as well as warnings about contraindications for use and about known dangers and side effects. The package inserts have considerable, although not totally controlling, influence over the proper standard of accepted patient care related to the drug. Physicians may, and often do, prescribe drugs for "off-label" uses, although there has been controversy in recent years about insurance reimbursement for such use. The FDA has also been concerned about whether manufacturers should be permitted to disseminate information about off-label uses to physicians. The agency initially took the view that these communications should be severely restricted to prevent circumvention of the labeling process. The Food and Drug Administration Modernization Act of 1997 authorizes manufacturers to inform physicians about off-label scientific research studies in some cases. See Lars Noah, Medicine's Epistemology: Mapping the Haphazard Diffusion of Knowledge in the Biomedical Community, 44 Ariz. L. Rev. 373, 443-447 (2002) (summarizing history and noting argument

that restrictions violate First Amendment). See also Madlen Gazarian, Off-Label Use of Medicines: Consensus Recommendations for Evaluating Appropriateness, 185 Med. J. Aust. 544 (2006); David C. Radley, Stan N. Finkelstein & Randall S. Stafford, Off-Label Prescribing Among Office-Based Physicians, 166 Arch. Intern. Med. 1021 (2006).

In the prescription drug field, the courts have quite uniformly accepted the package-insert warnings to physicians as meeting the drug manufacturers' legal obligation. The physician is expected to be a "learned intermediary" between the company and the patient in protecting the patient and in providing direct information about the drug to the patient. The retail pharmacist is also a source of advice for drug consumers. These assumptions have been shaken somewhat by the expansion of direct-to-consumer (DTC) advertising by pharmaceutical companies. See, e.g., Prescription-Drug Advertisements, 21 C.F.R. §202.1 (2006); Meredith Rosenthal et al., Promotion of Prescription Drugs to Consumers, 346 New Eng. J. Med. 498 (2002) (DTC advertising tripled from 1996 to 2000, though still merely 15 percent of total sum spent on drug promotion); Sidney M. Wolfe, Direct-to-Consumer Advertising—Education or Emotion Promotion, 346 New Eng. J. Med. 524 (2002). For a discussion about direct-to-consumer advertising in the context of the Vioxx controversy, see Ernst Bernt, To Inform or Persuade? Direct-to-Consumer Advertising of Prescription Drugs, 352 New Eng. J. Med. 325 (2005); Henry Waxman, The Lessons of Vioxx—Drug Safety and Sales, 352 New Eng. J. Med. 2576. (2005); Susan Okie, Raising the Safety Bar—The FDA's Coxib Meeting, 352 New Eng. J. Med. 1283 (2005).

8. *The FDA and New Regulatory Challenges: Dietary Supplements and Genetic Tests*. The FDA regularly finds itself in controversies about the scope of its regulatory authority. One major controversy, involving the agency's attempt to regulate tobacco, is discussed in the next subsection at page 623. The regulation of dietary supplements has been controversial, in part because of industry claims that the supplements are more like food than they are like classic pharmaceuticals. The FDA's suggestion that it might regulate supplements as though they were drugs prompted congressional action in the form of the Dietary Supplement Health and Education Act of 1994, Pub. L. No. 103-417, 108 Stat. 4325 (1994) (DSHEA). The DSHEA gives the FDA the authority to "regulate[] vitamins, minerals, herbs, amino acids, and other dietary substances. Dietary supplements are generally regulated in a manner similar to food and the FDA is authorized to prevent adulterated products from entering the market." Nutraceutical v. von Eschenbach, 459 F.3d 1033, 1035 (2006) (interpreting DSHEA; upholding FDA ban on ephedrine-alkaloid dietary supplements). A dietary supplement is adulterated if it "presents a significant or unreasonable risk of illness or injury" under suggested or ordinary use. 21 U.S.C. §342(f)(1). See Symposium, The Dietary Supplement Health and Education Act: Regulation at the Crossroads, 31 Am. J.L. & Med. 147-363 (2005); Lars Noah & Barbara Noah, A Drug by Any Other Name . . . ? Paradoxes in Dietary Supplement Risk Regulation, 17 Stan. L. & Pol'y Rev. 165 (2006); Institute of Medicine, Dietary Supplements: A Framework for Evaluating Safety (2005).

The regulation of genetic tests is also controversial. Are genetics tests best regulated as medical devices? Laboratory procedures and standards? Clinical practice? See David C. Bonnin, The Need for Increased Oversight of Genetic Testing: A Detailed Look at the Genetic Testing Process, 4 Hous. J. Health L. & Pol'y 149 (2003); Douglas A. Grimm, FDA, CLIA, or a "Reasonable Combination of Both": Toward Increased Regulatory Oversight of Genetic Testing, 41 U.S.F. L. Rev. 107 (2006); Anny Huang, FDA Regulation of Genetic Testing: Institutional Reluctance and Public Guardianship, 53 Food & Drug L.J. 555 (1998); Neil A. Holtzman, FDA and the Regulation of Genetic Tests, 41 Jurimetrics J. 53 (2000); Richard A. Merrill, Genetic Testing: A Role for the FDA?, 41 Jurimetrics J. 63 (2000).

b. Federal-State Conflicts: State Regulation and Medicinal Marijuana

The Food and Drug Administration (FDA) does not have jurisdiction over wholly intrastate manufacture and distribution of drugs, which may be regulated by the state. The intrastate exception to federal regulation is rarely applicable. See Texas State Board of Medical Examiners v. Burzynski, 917 S.W.2d 365 (Tex. Ct. App. 1996). States criminalize the sale of unapproved drugs and subject licensed health care professionals who prescribe or administer unapproved drugs to disciplinary action. See, e.g., People v. Privitera, 591 P.2d 919 (Cal. 1979) (defendants convicted of felony conspiracy to sell and prescribe laetrile).

Several states enacted "medicinal marijuana" laws in the early 2000s, for the most part through voter referenda. These state laws purported to shield from prosecution persons involved in prescribing, using, or possessing marijuana for specified medical purposes. The California initiative is typical:

§11362.5. Medical use. . . .

(b)(1) The people of the State of California hereby find and declare that the purposes of the Compassionate Use Act of 1996 are as follows:

(A) To ensure that seriously ill Californians have the right to obtain and use marijuana for medical purposes where that medical use is deemed appropriate and has been recommended by a physician who has determined that the person's health would benefit from the use of marijuana in the treatment of cancer, anorexia, AIDS, chronic pain, spasticity, glaucoma, arthritis, migraine, or any other illness for which marijuana provides relief.

(B) To ensure that patients and their primary caregivers who obtain and use marijuana for medical purposes upon the recommendation of a physician are not subject to criminal prosecution or sanction.

(C) To encourage the federal and state governments to implement a plan to provide for the safe and affordable distribution of marijuana to all patients in medical need of marijuana.

(2) Nothing in this section shall be construed to supersede legislation prohibiting persons from engaging in conduct that endangers others, nor to condone the diversion of marijuana for nonmedical purposes.

(c) Notwithstanding any other provision of law, no physician in this state shall be punished, or denied any right or privilege, for having recommended marijuana to a patient for medical purposes.

(d) . . . [State criminal laws], relating to the possession of marijuana, and . . . relating to the cultivation of marijuana, shall not apply to a patient, or to a patient's primary caregiver, who possesses or cultivates marijuana for the personal medical purposes of the patient upon the written or oral recommendation or approval of a physician.

(e) For the purposes of this section, "primary caregiver" means the individual designated by the person exempted under this section who has consistently assumed responsibility for the housing, health, or safety of that person. Cal. Health & Safety Code Ann. §11362.5.

See also People v. Mower, 49 P.3d 1067 (Cal. 2002) (interpreting key elements).

Proponents argued that the drug could be used to treat glaucoma and to reduce nausea and weight loss for persons undergoing chemotherapy. Opponents noted that marijuana is regulated by the federal Controlled Substances Act (CSA) and that federal law trumps state law. Controlled Substances Act, 21 U.S.C. §§801-971 (2006); U.S. Const. art. VI cl. 2. In Gonzales, Attorney General, et al. v. Raich et al. 545 U.S. 1 (2005), the Supreme Court ruled that congressional authority to regulate interstate commerce includes the power to prohibit the local cultivation and use of marijuana for medical purposes, even in the eleven states that permit it. See Susan Okie, Medical Marijuana and the Supreme Court, 353 New Eng. J. Med. 648 (2005); George J. Annas, Jumping Frogs, Endangered Toads, and California's Medical Marijuana Law, 353 New Eng. J. Med. 2291 (2005); Lawrence Gostin, Medical Marijuana, American Federalism, and the Supreme Court, 294 JAMA 842 (2005); Note, 118 Harv. L. Rev. 1985 (2005).

Problem: Drug Importation

Drugs approved for sale in the United States are often available at lower prices in other countries. Should senior citizens and the chronically ill be able to organize drug shopping trips to Canada and Mexico and bring drugs back into the United States? What if the bargain hunters can demonstrate that they hold a valid prescription for the drugs and that the drugs have been approved for sale in the United States? Would state legislation authorizing or facilitating the importation be invalid?

The FDA Web site includes a page devoted to the topic, see http://www.fda. gov/importeddrugs/. See also United States v. Rx Depot, Inc., 438 F.3d 1052 (10th Cir.), cert. denied, 127 S. Ct. 80 (2006) (disgorgement order related to reimportation profits upheld); and 21 U.S.C §381(d)(1). For commentary on the reimportation issue, see generally Abigail Zuger, Rx: Canadian Drugs, 349 New Eng. J. Med. 2188 (2003); Richard Frank. Prescription Drug Prices, 351 New Eng. J. Med. 1375 (2004); and Kevin Outersson, Pharmaceutical Arbitrage: Balancing Access and Innovation in International Prescription Drug Markets, 5 Yale J. Health Pol'y L. & Ethics 193 (2005).

c. The Regulation of Alcohol and Tobacco to Promote Public Health

Alcohol has been a sensitive regulatory area for more than 100 years. The repeal of the Prohibition amendment left much, but not all, of the regulation of alcohol with states and local governments. U.S. Const. Amendment XXI; Elizabeth D. Lauzon, Interplay Between Twenty-first Amendment and Commerce Clause Concerning State Regulation of Intoxicating Liquors, 116 A.L.R.5th 149 (2004).

Federal law does require a "warning label" on alcoholic beverages. See 27 U.S.C. §205(e). What should such labels say? Should they warn against the adverse health effects of all drinking? Should they warn only of "excessive drinking"? Should warnings be specific for particular health risks or diseases? Should the labeling be limited to warnings relating to safety, such as the dangers of drinking and then operating motor vehicles, power boats, or airplanes? Congress actually required that the following warning — and only this warning — be given:

Government Warning

(1) According to the Surgeon General, women should not drink alcoholic beverages during pregnancy because of the risk of birth defects. (2) Consumption of alcoholic beverages impairs your ability to drive a car or operate machinery and may cause health problems. 27 U.S.C. §§215, 216.

Do you think that the warning is effective? Some states and municipalities require posted warnings in bars or restaurants serving alcohol. The warnings typically focus on the risk of alcohol to the developing fetus. See, e.g., Ga. Stat. 3-1-5. Should federal or state law forbid the sale of alcohol to visibly pregnant women?

Cigarette smoking, cigar smoking, and tobacco chewing are associated with various forms of cancer and heart disease. Nearly all campaigns against tobacco have the goal of complete abstinence. Smokers who quit can gain better health and more favorable long-term projected life expectancies, even if they have smoked heavily for many years. Indeed, the prevalence of cigarette smoking has declined in the United States since the first strong case was made against tobacco in the 1964 Surgeon General's report. Up to 1965, more than half of American men and about one-third of American women smoked.

In 2005 only about 20.9 percent of adults smoked, with smoking slightly more popular among men than women. CDC, Tobacco Use Among Adults, 2005, 55 MMWR 1145 (2006). Smoking is more prevalent among the poor and less educated. Id. (nearly 30 percent of those with incomes below the poverty line smoked; 43.2 percent of all adults with GED educational attainment smoked). About 42.5 percent of the adult population has had over 100 cigarettes during their lifetime; about 50 percent of these individuals are now nonsmokers. Id. About 42 percent of current smokers had given up cigarettes for at least a day in the past year in an effort to quit smoking Id. See also Nancy A. Rigotti, Treatment of Tobacco Use and Dependence, 346 New Eng. J. Med. 506 (2002).

Public health authorities have issued guidelines on the treatment of tobacco dependence. Should physicians be held liable for malpractice if they fail to suggest treatment for tobacco dependence to their patients? Randy M Torrijos & Stanton A Glantz, The US Public Health Service "Treating Tobacco Use and Dependence Clinical Practice Guidelines" as a Legal Standard of Care, 15 Tobacco Control 447 (2006).

The labels currently on cigarette packages warn of a variety of fatal and disabling conditions resulting from smoking. 15 U.S.C. §1333. See also 15 U.S.C. §4402 (smokeless tobacco warning label). Federal regulation came shortly after the Surgeon General's 1964 report. Ironically, tobacco companies were able to use the publicity surrounding the Surgeon General's report and the federal warning requirements as part of their defense in products liability claims for more than 20 years.

Tobacco litigation groups, state attorneys general, and private litigants continued the tort assault on tobacco companies despite years of defensive victories. Juries began to award damages to plaintiffs in tobacco litigation suits in the mid-1990s. States began to pursue claims against tobacco companies for billions of dollars of medical care provided under Medicaid for illnesses alleged to be tobacco-related. Tobacco companies were eager to settle these claims so long as they could preserve the financial viability of the industry. The companies entered into a Master Settlement Agreement in 1998. Master Settlement Agreement, available at http://caag.state.ca.us/tobacco/msa.htm.

Under the Master Settlement Agreement, tobacco companies agreed to pay states billions of dollars and to refrain from a wide range of tobacco-marketing activities. Tobacco advertisements were removed from billboards across the country. Despite the hopes of anti-tobacco advocates, most states used the settlement revenue for general budgetary or health purposes; few took advantage of the opportunity to fund massive anti-smoking campaigns. A summary of tobacco-related lawsuits and an analysis of the voluminous Master Settlement Agreement can be found at a Web site maintained by the Tobacco Control Resource Center, Inc., and The Tobacco Products Liability Project at Northeastern University School of Law, www.tobacco.neu.edu. See also Hai-Yen Sung et al., A Major State Tobacco Tax Increase, the Master Settlement Agreement, and Cigarette Consumption: The California Experience, 95 Am. J. Pub. Health 1030 (2005); Steven Schroeder, Tobacco Control in the Wake of the 1998 Master Settlement Agreement, 350 New Eng. J. Med. 293 (2004).

In 1996 FDA officials began to speak of regulating tobacco as a drug. The proposal was controversial. See Lawrence O. Gostin et al., FDA Regulation of Tobacco Advertising and Youth Smoking: Historical, Social, and Constitutional Perspectives, 277 JAMA 410 (1997); David A. Kessler et al., The Legal and Scientific Basis for FDA's Assertion of Jurisdiction over Cigarettes and Smokeless Tobacco, 277 JAMA 405 (1997); Nicotine in Cigarettes and Smokeless Tobacco Is a Drug and These Products Are Nicotine Delivery Devices under the Federal Food, Drug, and Cosmetic Act: Jurisdictional Determination, 61 Fed. Reg. 44,619 (Aug. 28, 1996); Regulations Restricting the Sale and Distribution of Cigarettes and Smokeless Tobacco to Protect Children and Adolescents, 61 Fed. Reg. 44,396 (Aug. 28, 1996).

The Supreme Court rejected the FDA's assertion of jurisdiction over tobacco regulation in Food & Drug Administration v. Brown & Williamson Tobacco Corp., 529 U.S. 120 (2000), finding that the agency had exceeded its statutory authority. Among other things, the Court pointed out that the attempt to regulate tobacco was inconsistent with the FDA's mandate to regulate the distribution of drugs so that their therapeutic benefit outweighed their risks. Under this regime, tobacco should be banned rather than regulated because its manufacturers offered no therapeutic justification for its use. See also Margaret Gilhooley, Tobacco Unregulated: Why the FDA Failed, and What to Do Now, 111 Yale L.J. 1179 (2002).

State and local governments have joined in the fight against tobacco use and the threat of "secondhand" smoke. Many jurisdictions prohibit smoking in most public buildings, with tobacco users often forced to enjoy their habit outside in the elements or in ill-appointed "fishbowl" smoking rooms. Anti-smoking regulations have changed the "atmosphere" in bars and restaurants across North America.

The Supreme Court marked the limits of state and local anti-tobacco regulations in Lorillard Tobacco Co. v. Reilly, 533 U.S. 525 (2001). Massachusetts had enacted comprehensive and restrictive regulations governing the sale, promotion, and labeling of tobacco products. The Court first held that the regulations governing cigarette advertising were preempted by the Federal Cigarette Labeling and Advertising Act, 15 U.S.C. §§1331 et seq. (2000). Lorillard, 533 U.S. at 550-551. The Court then analyzed the constitutionality of the advertising restrictions for smokeless tobacco and cigars, holding that the billboard and point-of-sale restrictions violated the First Amendment. Id. at 565-566. The Court upheld regulations requiring that tobacco products be placed behind counters so that customers had to interact with sales personnel before the purchase. Id. at 569-570.

What rules govern smoking behavior, tobacco advertising and tobacco sales in your jurisdiction? Are additional measures under consideration?

For a comprehensive examination of tobacco issues in the United States, see Allan M. Brandt, The Cigarette Century: The Rise, Fall, and Deadly Persistence of the Product That Defined America (2007). For a global perspective on tobacco, see Ruth Roemer, Allyn Taylor & Jean Lariviere, Origins of the WHO Framework Convention of Tobacco Control, 95 Am. J. Pub. Health 936 (2005).

Problem: Motorcycle Helmets and the Law

Common sense suggests, and epidemiological data confirm, that motorcycle helmets can dramatically reduce the risk of injury or death associated with the use of motorcycles. Yet public debate about state helmet laws demonstrates that the reduction of deaths or injuries is not always sufficient to justify restrictions on individual liberty. What arguments can you marshal favoring or opposing the imposition of a mandatory helmet law? Should it matter whether the law is designed to protect the safety of the motorcyclist or of others? Should this be a matter for state or federal lawmakers? What constitutional analysis would you apply to a law requiring motorcyclists and their passengers to wear helmets? For an excellent survey of the issues, see Marian Moser Jones & Ronald Bayer, Paternalism and Its Discontents: Motorcycle Helmet Laws, Libertarian Values, and Public Health, 97 Am. J. Pub. Health 208 (2007).

Problem: Public Health and the Crushing Problem of Obesity

Obesity and overweight are often discussed in terms reminiscent of the tobacco debate. Americans are allegedly "addicted" to high-fat, high-calorie, processed foods that offer "empty calories" rather than balanced nutritional value. Food companies, restaurants, and TV cooking classes promote the eating of too many calories even as modern conveniences have reduced our caloric needs.

The result is a demonstrable increase in the prevalence of obesity in children and adults. See Rachel Tolbert Kimbro, Jeanne Brooks-Gunn & Sara McLanahan, Racial and Ethnic Differences in Overweight and Obesity Among 3-Year-Old Children, 97 Am. J. Pub. Health 298 (2007). While obesity is sometimes viewed as an evil on its own, public health advocates typically decry increasing rates of obesity and overweight because of associated negative health conditions. Obesity can be related to specific problems such as diabetes and cardiovascular disease. Some types of foods, such as those containing "trans fats," are targeted as particularly harmful. See generally Committee on Progress in Preventing Childhood Obesity, Institute of Medicine, Progress in Preventing Childhood Obesity: How Do We Measure Up? (2007); Susan Okie, New York to Trans Fats: You're Out!, 356 New Eng. J. Med. 2017 (2007). Despite the pervasive public accounts of crisis, there are critics of the medicalization of food and weight. See Michael Gard & Jan Wright (eds.), The Obesity Epidemic: Science and Ideology (2005). Much as in the case of tobacco, the obesity debate has a strong moral overlay: overweight individuals are sometimes portrayed as morally blameworthy while efforts to hold the manufacturers or distributors of food products legally responsible are laughingly dismissed.

What should be the role of law, and of public health law in particular, in combating the "epidemic" of obesity? What should be the roles of the federal and state governments? What should be the balance between regulations designed to ensure that consumers have the information to make good food choices versus restrictive regulations diminishing access to certain types of foods versus regulations designed to enhance exercise (requiring exercise periods in schools, for example)? Is there any role for tort law claims? See generally, Lawrence O. Gostin, Law as a Tool to Facilitate Healthier Lifestyles and Prevent Obesity, 297 JAMA 87 (2007); Michelle M. Mello et al., Obesity — The New Frontier of Public Health Law, 354 New Eng. J. Med. 2601 (2006); Sarah Taylor Roller, Theodore Voorhees Jr. & Ashley K. Lunkenheimer, Obesity, Food Marketing and Consumer Litigation: Threat or Opportunity?, 61 Food & Drug L.J. 419 (2006); Joseph P. McMenamin & Andrea D. Tiglio, Not the Next Tobacco: Defenses to Obesity Claims, 61 Food & Drug L.J. 445 (2006); Symposium, Childhood Obesity, 35 J.L. Med. & Ethics 7-157 (2007).

2. Testing and Public Health

Section A, supra, discusses primary public health techniques, including the identification of threats to public health and the development of strategies to address those threats. Traditionally, public health authorities have used five strategies to respond to certain types of contagious diseases. *Testing* is used to identify persons who are infected with the disease. The individual might then be *treated*, if any treatment is available, or might be *confined* to protect others from the disease. *Reporting* allows state and federal public health officials to gather specific information about people who have been infected and also permits general epidemiological research into the rate and distribution of infection within a population of people. *Contact tracing* is used to alert people who have had contact with an infected person of the possibility of exposure to the disease. If such an individual tests positive for the relevant condition, a new round of testing, reporting, and tracing can begin.

Each of these public health strategies entails some risk to individual liberty. Mandatory testing can be physically intrusive; it also violates the concept of individual autonomy and control over one's medical care. Reporting violates the norms of confidentiality and can expose an individual to the risk of additional, more intrusive public health interventions. Contact tracing might threaten the confidentiality of the "source" individual, and can lead to additional harms. Should courts weigh the protection of public health against individual liberties in determining the validity of public health programs? These traditional public health strategies have never been employed for all contagious conditions, instead they have been reserved for particularly serious and particularly transmissible conditions. How should public health authorities determine whether and when to employ these techniques? Mandatory reporting will be explored in section C.3. Treatment and confinement will be considered in sections C.4 and C.5.

■ PEOPLE v. ADAMS
597 N.E.2d 574 (Ill. 1992)

MILLER, C.J.

In separate proceedings in the circuit court of Cook County, the defendants, Henrietta Adams and Peggy Madison, were convicted of prostitution. Pursuant to §5-5-3(g) of the Unified Code of Corrections ["the statute"], the defendants were ordered to undergo medical testing to determine whether they were carriers of the human immunodeficiency virus (HIV), the cause of acquired immunodeficiency syndrome (AIDS). Rather than submit to the court-ordered tests, the defendants filed motions challenging the constitutionality of [the statute]. Following a hearing, the trial judge determined that the testing procedure represented an illegal search and seizure and denied the defendants equal protection. Because the statute was declared unconstitutional, the state's appeal from that ruling lies directly to this court. For the reasons that follow, we reverse the judgment of the circuit court and remand these consolidated actions for further proceedings. . . .

[The relevant statute provides that a defendant convicted of prostitution or soliciting for prostitution]

> shall undergo medical testing to determine whether the defendant has any sexually transmissible disease, including a test for infection with human immunodeficiency virus (HIV). . . . Except as otherwise provided by law, the results of such test shall be kept strictly confidential by all medical personnel involved in the testing and must be personally delivered in a sealed envelope to the judge of the court in which the conviction was entered for the judge's inspection in camera. Acting in accordance with the best interests of the victim and the public, the judge shall have the discretion to determine to whom, if anyone, the results of the testing may be revealed. The court shall order that the cost of any such test shall be paid by the county and may be taxed as costs against the convicted defendant. . . .

[The defendants were convicted of prostitution and were ordered to undergo HIV testing as a condition of probation. They refused, contending that the testing] . . . violated their rights to privacy, to freedom from unreasonable searches and seizures, and to the equal protection of the laws, as guaranteed by the United States and Illinois and, in addition, that the testing requirement was cruel and unusual punishment, in violation of the Eighth Amendment of the United States Constitution. . . .

[T]he defendants presented the testimony of three expert witnesses, who questioned the utility of the testing requirement for persons convicted of prostitution. . . . These witnesses believed that mandatory HIV testing of sex offenders is ineffective and may even be counterproductive to the effort to stop the spread of AIDS, particularly among women in prostitution. . . . The trial judge . . . ruled that the HIV testing statute violated the Fourth Amendment's guarantee against unreasonable searches and seizures and denied the defendants their Fourteenth Amendment right to equal protection of the laws. . . . The trial judge rejected the defendants' contention that the testing requirement constituted cruel and unusual punishment under the Eighth Amendment. In light of his conclusion that the testing requirement was an invalid search, the trial judge found it unnecessary to rule on the defendants' additional contention that the statute violated their right to privacy. Because the trial judge found the testing requirement unconstitutional, he removed it from the terms of the defendants' probationary orders.

The state has appealed the trial judge's ruling directly to this court. . . . The parties present two issues for our review: whether the HIV testing requirement found in . . . [the statute] constitutes an invalid search and seizure, and whether the statute denies the defendants equal protection of the laws.

I

. . . The present statute took effect on January 1, 1988. It was among a series of laws enacted by our General Assembly in response to the growing AIDS crisis. A companion provision . . . contains a similar requirement for mandatory HIV testing of persons convicted of certain offenses under the Hypodermic Syringes and Needles Act. . . . Together, then, . . . [these statutes] target, for purposes of mandatory testing, two major groups at risk of contracting AIDS: sex offenders and intravenous drug users. We note, too, that a number of other states have enacted similar laws imposing mandatory testing on persons convicted of certain offenses involving sexual misconduct. [Omitted are citations to laws in California, Colorado, Florida, Kentucky, Nevada, Virginia, and Washington.] . . . The California statute was upheld against similar constitutional challenge in Love v. Superior Court (1990), 226 Cal. App. 3d 736, 276 Cal. Rptr. 660. . . . [T]he present cases involve only that portion of the statute requiring that persons convicted of prostitution undergo testing for HIV, and we limit our discussion accordingly.

As a general principle, legislative enactments are presumed to be constitutional, and a party challenging a statute has the burden of establishing its invalidity. Doubts concerning a statute's constitutionality will be resolved in favor of its validity. Our task here is to determine only whether the challenged legislation is constitutional, and not whether it necessarily provides the best or most effective means of curtailing the spread of the disease. . . . [The defendants argue that the testing is an unreasonable search and seizure and that it violates equal protection.]

II

The trial judge found that the personal intrusion required by the HIV testing statute is unreasonable under the Fourth Amendment because the statute fails to require any individualized suspicion that the person to be tested is a carrier of HIV and, furthermore, because the intended social benefits of the testing mandate are outweighed by the individual privacy interests infringed by the statute's operation.

As an initial matter, we note that the challenged provision is a public health measure and thus involves a field in which the states exercise broad regulatory and administrative powers. Like other measures intended to enhance public health and community well-being, governmental action designed to control the spread of disease falls within the scope of the state's police powers. Traditionally, the states have been allowed broad discretion in the formulation of measures designed to protect and promote public health [citing *Jacobson*, supra]. . . . The protections afforded by the Fourth Amendment are not limited to investigations of criminal conduct but may apply to governmental activities in civil contexts as well. Thus, the governmental action challenged here, even though it is carried out for a purpose unrelated to routine criminal investigation, may still raise Fourth Amendment concerns.

The defendants argue, and the state agrees, that the taking and testing of a blood sample from an individual pursuant to the present statute is a search under the Fourth Amendment. The test required by the statute implicates the Fourth Amendment in two separate respects. First, the drawing of the blood sample is itself an intrusion on the individual's bodily integrity. Second, the performance of the test on the sample also implicates Fourth Amendment interests.

Thus, the statutorily authorized blood test at issue in this case is a search for Fourth Amendment purposes, and the governmental action in administering the test must therefore satisfy the applicable Fourth Amendment requirements if the statute is to survive constitutional scrutiny. "[T]he Fourth Amendment does not proscribe all searches and seizures, but only those that are unreasonable." [Skinner v. Railway Labor Executives Ass'n, 489 U.S. 602, 619 (1989).] Accordingly, we must determine whether the intrusion mandated by the HIV testing statute is a reasonable one, when it is measured against the applicable Fourth Amendment standards. . . .

A warrant and individualized suspicion are not always necessary, however, to sustain the validity of a governmental intrusion challenged on Fourth Amendment grounds. Special governmental needs, beyond the normal needs of law enforcement, may in appropriate cases justify a Fourth Amendment intrusion conducted without either of those traditional safeguards. . . . To resolve this question, we must balance the importance of the state's interest to be achieved under the statute against the nature and scope of this intrusion on individuals' Fourth Amendment interests.

The challenged statute concerns matters lying at the heart of the state's police power. There are few, if any, interests more essential to a stable society than the health and safety of its members. Toward that end, the state has a compelling interest in protecting and promoting public health and, here, in adopting measures reasonably designed to prevent the spread of AIDS. . . .

The HIV testing statute is designed to serve a public health goal, rather than the ordinary needs of law enforcement. The manifest purpose of . . . [the statute] is to help control the spread of AIDS by identifying persons infected with the causative virus. . . . Once persons who are carriers of the virus have been identified, the victims of their conduct and the offenders themselves can receive necessary treatment, and, moreover, can adjust their conduct so that other members of the public do not also become exposed to HIV. In this way, the spread of AIDS through the community at large can be slowed, if not halted. We believe that the HIV testing requirement advances a special governmental need.

Having identified the important governmental purpose served by the statute, we must next balance that interest against the intrusion on personal freedom effected by the statute. The requirement of a warrant protects individual privacy "by assuring citizens subject to a search or seizure that such intrusions are not the random or arbitrary acts of government agents." (Skinner, 489 U.S. at 621-622.) In addition, the warrant requirement interposes between government and citizen the neutral judgment of a magistrate, charged with the independent assessment of the facts and circumstances assertedly justifying the particular intrusion. (Id. at 622.) We do not believe that these purposes would be served by imposing here a separate requirement that the state secure a warrant before subjecting an individual to a test pursuant to the statute. . . .

The testing requirement is automatically triggered upon a defendant's conviction for one of the offenses enumerated in the provision; in that case, the defendant must undergo testing for HIV, as well as for other sexually transmissible diseases. . . . Thus, . . . [the statute] affords the court no discretion in determining whom to test. Under this statutory regimen, there would be nothing for the presiding judge, or other magistrate, to weigh if issuance of a warrant were to be required. The only discretionary function allowed by the statute lies in determining to whom the results of the test may be revealed. As the statute makes clear, however, that determination must be made by the court.

Even if a warrant is not required, probable cause, or some individualized suspicion, generally will be necessary to sustain the validity of a search or seizure challenged on fourth amendment grounds. (Id. at 624.) . . .

As we have stated, the purpose of the HIV testing statute is to protect public health by preventing the spread of AIDS among the members of the community. In this context, when the challenged intrusion is intended to prevent the spread of a dangerous condition providing few articulable grounds for a search, other than categories of risk, and thus advances an important function that is related to administrative concerns of public health and safety, rather than to the concerns of criminal investigation, individualized suspicion may become less important. . . .

The aim of . . . [the statute] is not to ferret out evidence of misconduct but rather to provide reliable information concerning the HIV status of sex offenders, and possibly their victims. In view of this important public health mission, we consider that the state's interest in conducting suspicionless testing outweighs the individual's interest in requiring some degree of individualized suspicion. The actual physical intrusion required by the HIV testing statute is relatively slight and poses no threat to the health or safety of the individual tested. The procedure involves the drawing of a sample of blood, and the test may be performed "only by appropriately licensed medical practitioners." . . .

As an additional circumstance reducing the impact of the intrusion on individual privacy interests, we note that the test results may be disclosed only to the person tested, and to others, as directed by the trial judge, and otherwise must remain confidential. Thus, we conclude that the intrusion . . . is comparatively slight.

We recognize that the information obtained as the result of a positive HIV test may have a devastating impact on individuals who would prefer not to know their true status. In addition, persons with AIDS are often stigmatized and subject to social disapproval. These matters are indications of the seriousness of the AIDS problem. We do not agree with the defendants, however, that these consequences make the test more objectionable for Fourth Amendment purposes, for the focus of the Fourth Amendment inquiry must remain primarily on the actual physical intrusion caused by the search. Moreover, the statute at issue here requires that the test results remain confidential; they are subject to disclosure only upon court order.

In addition, we note that [convicted] offenders necessarily have reduced expectations of personal privacy. . . .

Finally, we believe that the general requirement that a search be conducted only upon probable cause or some other showing of individualized suspicion would be impracticable here, for often there are no outward manifestations of the disease, or of a person's status as a carrier of HIV, apart from the individual's membership in a high-risk group. Thus, requiring individualized suspicion would only jeopardize the state's goal of accurately identifying HIV carriers among those members of the population who are primarily at risk of exposure to the virus. . . .

The central focus of the defendants' challenge to the HIV testing statute is their argument that mandatory testing, even of high-risk groups, is not an effective means of combating the spread of AIDS. The defendants observe that many eminent public health authorities have declared their opposition to mandatory HIV testing. The defendants contend that mandatory testing is ineffective because the test results are not always accurate, whether through the variable latency of the virus, which can elude detection even though it is present in the body of the person tested, or through limitations on the sensitivity and specificity of the tests themselves. . . .

Based on the evidence introduced in the circuit court, the defendants further assert that many of the sexual practices most frequently performed in prostitution do not involve activity having a high risk of HIV transmission. In addition, the defendants suggest that if a program of mandatory testing is going to be adopted, it should be limited to cases in which an offender has committed an act having some demonstrable risk of transmitting the disease. The defendants note that no sexual activity occurred in the present cases, and they conclude that their intended partners—undercover police officers—thus had no risk of exposure to the virus. . . .

[T]he issue before us is not whether the state has chosen what all or even most experts would consider to be the best or most effective means of combating the disease, but whether the means chosen by the state can withstand constitutional scrutiny. It is clear that unprotected sexual activity is a major means of transmitting AIDS. According to testimony presented in the court below, women in prostitution have on average 20 sexual encounters each week. Whether or not the statutory scheme provides the most effective means of dealing with the AIDS problem, we do not believe that its program of mandatory testing of certain groups of offenders is constitutionally infirm. In sum, the challenged statute serves a compelling state interest, one that we believe is a special governmental need rendering unnecessary the traditional fourth amendment safeguards of a warrant and individualized suspicion. The testing procedure is activated by court order, but the statute affords the presiding judge no discretion in determining who must be tested. Accordingly, there would be little purpose served by separately requiring the issuance of a warrant. The governmental interest at stake here, and the type of statute involved, similarly militate against imposing a requirement of individualized suspicion. . . . [W]e conclude that the challenged statute is not an unreasonable search and seizure under the provisions of the United States and Illinois Constitutions.

III

[The defendants argue that the HIV testing statute violates the equal protection clause because] . . . the measure is both overinclusive and under-inclusive in scope. The defendants believe that the statute is overinclusive in scope because it includes within its scope offenses [such as solicitation] having no risk of AIDS transmission. . . . The defendants maintain that the statute is underinclusive in scope because it fails to require HIV testing for certain criminal and noncriminal conduct [such as adultery, fornication, and bigamy] that is as likely to result in the transmission of AIDS as prostitution, the offense charged here. . . . The defendants contend that the extent to which the challenged statute is alternately overinclusive and underinclusive demonstrates the absence of any legitimate governmental purpose that would sustain it. . . .

The present statute does not impinge upon the exercise of a fundamental right or operate against a suspect class. Thus, under the standard of review appropriate here, the statute need not establish a perfect fit between the desired end and the means chosen to achieve that end. . . . [The testing] requirement bears a rational relationship to the state interest in combating the spread of AIDS. In sum, we conclude that the testing provision, as applied to the present defendants, does not deny them equal protection of the laws, under either the federal or state Constitutions. . . .

Notes: Testing Programs

1. *Voluntary Screening*. Voluntary screening programs raise the fewest constitutional objections. A voluntary program is consistent with the norms of patient consent for medical treatment. In practice, a voluntary program can operate along a spectrum of voluntariness and consent: A patient may have an opportunity to give specific, sometimes written consent after a discussion of the test's risks and benefits. A patient can be told that testing is "routine" and will be performed unless the patient "opts out" or objects. Finally, a patient's consent to medical treatment can be deemed to cover a particular test without any specific discussion or explicit opportunity to object.

A voluntary screening program can be established through the development of professional norms of practice or through governmental intervention. When the link between maternal age and Down syndrome was recognized, for example, prenatal screening for the condition became widespread. In part because of the risk of malpractice liability, physicians began to routinely advise women of the risk of Down syndrome and to offer prenatal screening.

Governmental bodies have also required that certain screening tests be offered to selected populations. For example, newborn screening programs for phenylketonuria (PKU) and other conditions are often established under state law. See Celia I. Kaye and the Committee on Genetics, Introduction to the Newborn Screening Fact Sheets, 118 Pediatrics 1304 (2006) (including summary of state testing requirements). Some of these programs, while officially voluntary, can as a practical matter result in coercive testing. This is particularly so where individuals either do not understand that testing is being performed or do not understand their right to refuse the procedure. For an interesting case dealing with the liability implications of state newborn screening programs, see Creason v. State Dep't of Health Services, 957 P.2d 1323 (Cal. 1998).

Genetic screening is an extremely controversial area. Some genetic screening is already in place, see discussion of newborn screening, supra. With the completion of the map of the human genome, see supra at page 431, the expansion of genetic testing is highly probable. While most testing is likely to be voluntary, a number of commentators are concerned about the potential misuse of genetic testing in public health. See, e.g., Lori B. Andrews, A Conceptual Framework for Genetic Policy: Comparing the Medical, Public Health, and Fundamental Rights Models, 79 Wash. U. L.Q. 221 (2001); Ellen Wright Clayton, The Complex Relationship of Genetics, Groups, and Health: What It Means for Public Health, 30 J.L. Med. & Ethics 290 (2002); Mark A. Rothstein, Rethinking the Meaning of Public Health, 30 J.L. Med. & Ethics 144 (2002). See also Elizabeth B. Cooper, Testing for Genetic Traits: The Need for a New Legal Doctrine of Informed Consent, 58 Md. L. Rev. 346 (1999).

2. *"Conditional" Screening.* Conditional screening programs occupy an uneasy middle ground between voluntary and mandatory testing programs. Conditional screening occurs where testing is required as a condition of participation in some activity or for the receipt of some benefit. Conditional screening seems most like voluntary screening where the activity or benefit is of little consequence to the individual to be tested. A rule that requires HIV screening of blood donors, for example, seems more like a voluntary testing program because no one is compelled to donate blood and the benefits of donation are largely emotional. See Cal. Health & Safety Code §§1603.3, 1644.5 (HIV screening of blood and tissue donors).

Conditional screening seems much more like mandatory screening where the activity or benefit is of great importance. Rules that require testing marriage license applicants for sexually transmitted diseases or that impose HIV testing on hospital patients or in the context of employment seem closer to mandatory testing. Certainly, a person can avoid testing, but only by refraining from participating in a valuable activity. For that reason, the legal analysis of these programs is likely to be similar to that employed for traditional mandatory screening programs.

3. *Premarital Screening.* Various jurisdictions have conditioned issuance of a marriage license on submission of evidence that the participants have undergone a premarital examination and testing for certain diseases. See, e.g., Therese Hesketh, Getting Married in China: Pass the Medical Test First, 326 Brit. Med. J. 277 (2003). Some jurisdictions have repealed their premarital testing provisions, often because they were considered to be inefficient: not many cases of infection were identified, and transmission would often already have been accomplished via premarital sexual activity. See, e.g., N.Y. Dom. Rel. §13-a. Repealed. L. 1985, 674, §1, eff. Aug. 1, 1985. Should states consider expanding their premarital testing statutes to include mandatory HIV screening or, as science advances, genetic screening? See Michael Closen, Robert Gamrath & Dem Hopkins, Mandatory Premarital HIV Testing: Political Exploitation of the AIDS Epidemic, 69 Tul. L. Rev. 71 (1994). Illinois and Louisiana adopted mandatory premarital screening for HIV in the early stages of the epidemic; both soon repealed their provisions. See Ill. Rev. Stat. ch. 40, §204 (1987) (repealed).

How would you analyze the constitutionality of a statute requiring premarital testing for some sexually transmitted disease? Is the right to marry fundamental? See Loving v. Virginia, 388 U.S. 1 (1967). Would a testing statute impermissibly intrude on this right? What is the compelling state interest? Is the measure narrowly tailored to achieve public health objectives? Utah for a time prohibited persons with HIV infection from marrying. Would a ban on marriage by HIV-infected persons be considered constitutional? Would it violate the Americans with Disabilities Act (ADA)? See T.E.P. & K.J.C. v. Leavitt, 840 F. Supp. 110 (C.D. Utah 1993) (Utah marriage ban violates the ADA; court did not reach constitutional issues).

4. *Medical Testing in Private and Public Employment.* Should private entities be entitled to screen individuals for unwanted medical conditions? The ADA regulates employer use of medical examinations. The Act sets up three different rules. Employers may not impose medical exams or ask questions designed to ferret out applicants' disabilities during the pre-offer stage. Employers may ask

whether an applicant will be able to perform the essential functions of a job, with or without reasonable accommodations. After extending a conditional offer of employment, the employer may require that all prospective employees undergo a medical screening exam. The exam does not need to be job-related, but the employer must offer a nondiscriminatory rationale for retracting a job offer after an employment physical. Once employed, an individual may only be subjected to mandatory medical exams that are job-related and consistent with business necessity. See, e.g., Deborah F. Buckman, Construction and Application of §102(d) of Americans with Disabilities Act (42 U.S.C.A. §12112(d)), pertaining to medical examinations and inquiries, 159 A.L.R. Fed. 89 (2000).

The government-as-employer often must comply with certain constitutional rules, including those protecting individual rights as well as the ADA. The federal government uses HIV screening tests for some state department and all military applicants and personnel. The government asserts that these testing programs are justified because of the special nature of the employment settings, which require worldwide deployment away from adequate health care, or, in the military, the need for battlefield transfusions. The testing programs have been held to be constitutional. See Local 1812, American Federation of Government Employees v. Department of State, 662 F. Supp. 50 (D.D.C. 1987). But see Norman-Bloodsaw v. Lawrence Berkeley Laboratory, 135 F.3d 1260 (9th Cir. 1998) (noting that employees had a protected privacy interest in intimate personal matters such as syphilis, sickle-cell trait, and pregnancy; case remanded for further fact finding regarding employee authorization and government's need for information). The state department's HIV policy is currently facing challenge under the federal Rehabilitation Act, see page 609. Taylor v. Rice, 451 F.3d 898 (D.C. Cir. 2006) (claim survives summary judgment).

5. *Mandatory Screening.* Mandatory screening programs impose testing on all persons who fit within some defined group. Examples of current mandatory screening programs include premarital testing for sexually transmitted diseases; mandatory drug testing of certain employees; mandatory HIV or other testing for those convicted of sexual offenses; and mandatory TB screening for prisoners. In each of these cases, states have sought to enhance safety or health by identifying those who might present a risk to others. Does the rationale applied in *Adams* suggest that each of these programs will be found to be constitutional under the Fourth Amendment and the equal protection clause? Can you think of any other constitutional objections? For a discussion of issues related to immigration, see Amy L. Fairchild, Policies of Inclusion: Immigrants, Disease, Dependency, and American Immigration Policy at the Dawn and Dusk of the 20th Century, 94 Am. J. Pub. Health 528 (2004).

6. *STD Testing for Persons Convicted of Sexual Crimes.* What public health objectives are served by testing persons convicted of sexual crimes for sexually transmitted diseases (STDs)? Will the testing program necessarily prevent future transmission of disease? Does the disclosure of the test result to the survivor of a sexual assault provide useful information? Unfortunately, some test results are at best ambiguous: (1) A negative HIV test result may mean that the defendant was infected with HIV but had not yet established an immune response to the virus. (2) A positive HIV test result does not mean that the virus was transmitted to the crime victim and may not be available in time to guide the victim's decisionmaking about

prophylactic treatment options. Despite these criticisms, testing convicted defendants is very popular among legislators. See, e.g., N.Y. Crim. Proc. Law §390.15. See also Michael P. Bruyere, Damage Control for Victims of Physical Assault — Testing the Innocent for AIDS, 21 Fla. St. U. L. Rev. 945 (1994); Steven Eisenstat, An Analysis of the Rationality of Mandatory Testing for the HIV Antibody: Balancing the Governmental Public Health Interests with the Individual's Privacy Interest, 52 U. Pitt. L. Rev. 327 (1991).

As discussed in *Adams*, mandatory testing programs generally are held to implicate the Fourth Amendment's right to be free from unreasonable searches and seizures. The Fourth Amendment requires that searches be reasonable, balancing the government's interest in the search against the individual's liberty interests. Not all searches require a warrant or individualized suspicion. Courts have developed the "special governmental needs" exception to the warrant requirement. Under this approach, applied in *Adams*, a warrantless search may be upheld where it serves some special governmental purpose important enough to outweigh an individual's reasonable expectation of privacy. As the *Adams* court noted, concerns about public health and safety easily fall within the category of "special needs." What public health objectives were supported by coercive testing of persons convicted of prostitution? Why does the court hold that the intrusion into individual liberty is "minimal" when balanced against the governmental need? What types of personal interests are at stake? Which is most important, the physical intrusion of the blood test? The use of an HIV antibody test? The disclosure of the test result to others? Do you agree with the court's balancing analysis? See also Ferguson v. City of Charleston at page 496.

Several other courts have upheld mandatory testing of convicted criminal defendants. See, e.g., Adams v. State, 498 S.E.2d 268 (Ga. 1998). People v. McVickers, 13 Cal. Rptr. 2d 850 (Cal. 1992). See also Government of Virgin Islands v. Roberts, 756 F. Supp. 898 (D.V.I. 1991) (permitting mandatory testing of person indicted for offense capable of transmitting HIV).

7. *TB and HIV Testing in Prisons.* Contagious diseases also present complex constitutional issues within prisons. Prisoners do not lose all of their constitutional rights by virtue of their confinement. Prisoners may thus assert their right to be free from unreasonable searches, to make medical decisions, to pursue their religious beliefs, and to be free from cruel and unusual punishment. U.S. Const. amends. I, V, VIII, XIV. Prisoners may also be able to assert statutory claims, such as prohibitions against disability-based discrimination. 29 U.S.C. §794 (Rehabilitation Act provisions prohibiting disability-based discrimination by federal entities or recipients of federal funds); 42 U.S.C. §12132 (ADA prohibition of disability-based discrimination by public entities). But see pages 611-612. Prison officials are nonetheless given considerable latitude in devising prison rules that, while impinging on individual liberties, are considered reasonable in light of the prison's legitimate penological goals. See Turner v. Safely, 482 U.S. 78, 89 (1987); and Johnson v. California, 543 U.S. 499 (2005) (*Turner* applies to restriction of rights that are inconsistent with incarceration but not to policies contravening racial equality). See also Thompson v. City of Los Angeles, 885 F.2d 1439, 1447 (9th Cir. 1989) (prison officials have compelling interest in disease prevention).

Should correctional facilities be permitted to test inmates for the presence of contagious conditions? Most courts have answered affirmatively. See, e.g., Moore

v. Mabus, 976 F.2d 268 (5th Cir. 1992) ("identification and segregation of HIV-positive prisoners obviously serves a legitimate penological purpose"); Hasenmeier-McCarthy v. Rose, 986 F. Supp. 464 (S.D. Ohio 1998) (forcible administration of TB test performed pursuant to legitimate penological interest in detecting and controlling communicable disease).

A number of commentators have written on the problems of HIV and TB in correctional facilities. See Scott Burris, Prisons, Law and Public Health: The Case Coordinated Response to Epidemic Disease Behind Bars, 47 U. Miami L. Rev. 291 (1992); Lawrence O. Gostin, Tuberculosis and the Power of the State: Toward the Development of Rational Standards for the Review of Compulsory Public Health Powers, 2 U. Chi. L. Sch. Roundtable 219 (1995); John V. Jacobi, Prison Health, Public Health: Obligations and Opportunities, 31 Am. J.L. & Med. 447 (2005).

Persons who knowingly put others at risk for HIV transmission, through sexual or other activity, can be prosecuted for assault, attempted murder, or for violation of HIV-specific criminal statutes. Zita Lazzarini et al., Evaluating the Impact of Criminal Laws on HIV Risk Behavior, 30 J.L. Med. & Ethics 239 (2002). Prosecution is difficult unless it can be shown that the defendant knew that he or she was HIV-infected. Should test results obtained from convicted defendants or prisoners be used in subsequent prosecutions to prove that the defendant must have known of his or her HIV status at the time of the risky act? See State ex rel. J.G., 701 A.2d 1260 (N.J. 1997) (no). See also Amanda Weiss, Criminalizing Consensual Transmission of HIV, 2006 Chi. Legal F. 389

Problem: HIV Screening for Pregnant Women and Newborns

The risk of HIV transmission from woman to child during pregnancy is less than 30 percent. Proponents of mandatory or routine HIV testing for pregnant women note that the risk of HIV transmission through pregnancy can be reduced significantly. Transmission rates can drop to less than 2 percent if pregnant women are aware of their infection, take antiretroviral therapies, and use special procedures during birth and during the newborn's first days and months of life. Even so, "an estimated 144-236 HIV-infected infants were born in the United States in 2002." CDC, Reduction in Perinatal Transmission of HIV Infection — United States, 1985-2005, 55 MMWR 586, 593 (2006); Edward M. Connor et al., Reduction of Maternal-Infant Transmission of Human Immunodeficiency Virus Type 1 with Zidovudine Treatment, 331 New Eng. J. Med. 1173 (1994).

Should states impose mandatory HIV testing for pregnant women? Would mandatory testing be constitutional? See Suzanne M. Malloy, Comment, Mandatory HIV Screening of Newborns: A Proposition Whose Time Has Not Yet Come, 45 Am. U. L. Rev. 1185 (1996). Would a program of routine testing (with an "opt out" provision) achieve the same or better results? See, e.g., Tex. Health & Safety Code §81.090. Would there be any difficulty with encouraging physicians to use directive counseling — urging pregnant women to undergo testing rather than merely listing the benefits and burdens of testing? Bernard M. Branson et al., Revised Recommendations for HIV Testing of Adults, Adolescents, and Pregnant Women in Health Care Settings, 55 MMWR Recomm. Rep. 1 (2006) (RR-14) (recommending directive counseling); and Lawrence O. Gostin, HIV Screening in Health Care Settings: Public Health and Civil Liberties in Conflict?, 296 JAMA 2023 (2006). Should women who refuse retroviral therapy for themselves or their newborns be charged with child neglect? Cf. Doe v. Division of Youth & Family Services, 148 F. Supp. 2d 462 (D.N.J. 2001) (complaint alleging improper HIV testing of pregnant woman along with effort to coerce perinatal antiretroviral therapy).

Problem: Routine HIV Screening for All

Should mandatory or routine HIV testing be imposed for all adults and adolescents? What would be the benefits and risks of such testing program? The CDC recently moved to recommend routine HIV testing for adolescents and adults in health care settings. The recommendations specify that patients should be told about the testing and be given an opportunity to decline. Do you agree with this approach? Bernard M. Branson et al., Revised Recommendations for HIV Testing of Adults, Adolescents, and Pregnant Women in Health Care Settings, 55 MMWR Recomm. Rep. 1 (2006) (RR-14). Examine your jurisdiction's rules regarding HIV testing. Could the CDC's recommendations be adopted without legislative changes?

The CDC's new recommendations are advisory, but could they serve to establish a new standard of care in medical practice with respect to HIV screening? Should physician failure to implement HIV screening lead to liability for failure to diagnose HIV infection? Should states act to establish the standard via legislation? For a discussion about HIV screening see Paltiel et al., Expanded Screening for HIV in the United States—An Analysis of Cost-Effectiveness, 352 New Eng. J. Med. 586 (2005); see also Samuel Bossette, Routine Screening for HIV Infection—Timely and Cost-Effective, 352 New Eng. J. Med. 620 (2005).

Problem: State Law, Disaster Planning, and Bioterrorism Preparedness

The Model State Emergency Health Powers Act (MSEHPA), described supra at page 597, includes rules and procedures designed to improve detection of a public health emergency and then establishes rules and procedures that take effect only in a public health emergency. As noted above, a public health emergency is one that is caused by bioterrorism, novel infectious agents, natural disasters, or certain other enumerated events.

The Model Act includes provisions authorizing mandatory medical examinations and tests:

> Medical examination and testing. During a state of public health emergency the public health authority may perform physical examinations and/or tests as necessary for the diagnosis or treatment of individuals.

(a) Medical examinations or tests may be performed by any qualified person authorized to do so by the public health authority.

(b) Medical examinations or tests must not be such as are reasonably likely to lead to serious harm to the affected individual.

(c) The public health authority may isolate or quarantine, pursuant to Section 604 [discussed infra at page 668], any person whose refusal of medical examination or testing results in uncertainty regarding whether he or she has been exposed to or is infected with a contagious or possibly contagious disease or otherwise poses a danger to public health. MSEHPA §602.

Evaluate the constitutionality of the Model Act's testing provisions. Should it matter how a public health emergency is declared and whether there can be judicial review of the decision? Should it matter whether public health authorities have any reason to suspect that an individual has been exposed to a contagious disease or transmissible condition? Compare the Model Act's provisions to the relevant public health statute in your own state. Do the public health authorities in your state have explicit authority to mandate medical tests or examinations? If so, do you see any similarities or differences between your state law and the Model Act? Which seems better from a legal or policy standpoint? Should the same testing rules apply in bioterrorism incidents as during natural disasters or a natural epidemic such as avian influenza? Would you recommend the adoption of the Model Act's testing provision?

3. Confidentiality, Reporting, and Contact Tracing

Testing programs, whether public or private, create opportunities for additional public health interventions. What use should be made of a test result? One possibility is that the individual tested could be counseled about the significance of the test result and given information about how to safeguard her own health or the health of others with whom she may have contact. Testing can thus be an opportunity to improve public health through targeted education. See Lawrence O. Gostin, Public Health Law: Power, Duty, Restraint 187-199 (2000).

Other public health interventions might proceed along a different path. State reporting statutes require specified entities to report information to state health authorities. Common examples of reporting statutes include those that govern gunshot wounds, suspected child abuse, and certain diseases, such as plague or HIV. In some cases, reporting statutes are an "early warning" system that can alert public health officials to serious epidemics. More prosaically, the information could promote better health budgeting as states reallocate funds and personnel to emerging health threats. Public health officials could follow up case reports with notices about treatment or other options. Finally, the information could be used to protect those exposed to disease. Contact tracing programs attempt to identify and notify persons who have been exposed to a person with a contagious condition.

Each of these public health strategies begins with the disclosure of an individual's health status to others. Do individuals have a right to confidentiality that protects them from disclosures about their health status? The answer may depend on the nature of the information and the public interest asserted in its disclosure.

■ WHALEN v. ROE
429 U.S. 589 (1977)

STEVENS, J.

The constitutional question presented is whether the state of New York may record, in a centralized computer file, the names and addresses of all persons who have obtained, pursuant to a doctor's prescription, certain drugs for which there is both a lawful and an unlawful market.

The district court enjoined enforcement of the portions of the New York State Controlled Substances Act of 1972 which require such recording on the ground that they violate appellees' constitutionally protected rights of privacy. We noted probable jurisdiction of the appeal by the Commissioner of Health, 424 U.S. 907, and now reverse.

Many drugs have both legitimate and illegitimate uses. In response to a concern that such drugs were being diverted into unlawful channels, in 1970 the New York legislature created a special commission to evaluate the state's drug-control laws. The commission found the existing laws deficient in several respects. There was no effective way to prevent the use of stolen or revised prescriptions, to prevent unscrupulous pharmacists from repeatedly refilling prescriptions, to prevent users from obtaining prescriptions from more than one doctor, or to prevent doctors from over-prescribing, either by authorizing an excessive amount in one prescription or by giving one patient multiple prescriptions. In drafting new legislation to correct such defects, the commission consulted with enforcement officials in California and Illinois where central reporting systems were being used effectively.

The new New York statute classified potentially harmful drugs in five schedules.[7] Drugs, such as heroin, which are highly abused and have no recognized medical use, are in Schedule I; they cannot be prescribed. Schedules II through V include drugs which have a progressively lower potential for abuse but also have a recognized medical use. Our concern is limited to Schedule II which includes the most dangerous of the legitimate drugs.[8]

With an exception for emergencies, the Act requires that all prescriptions for Schedule II drugs be prepared by the physician in triplicate on an official form. The completed form identifies the prescribing physician; the dispensing pharmacy; the drug and dosage; and the name, address, and age of the patient. One copy of the form is retained by the physician, the second by the pharmacist, and the third is forwarded to the New York State Department of Health in Albany.

---

[7] These five schedules conform in all material aspects with the drug schedules in the Federal Comprehensive Drug Abuse Prevention and Control Act of 1970. 21 U.S.C. §801 et seq.

[8] These include opium and opium derivatives, cocaine, methadone, amphetamines, and methaqualone. Pub. Health Law §3306. These drugs have accepted uses in the amelioration of pain and in the treatment of epilepsy, narcolepsy, hyperkinesia, schizo-affective disorders, and migraine headaches.

A prescription made on an official form may not exceed a 30-day supply, and may not be refilled.

The district court found that about 100,000 Schedule II prescription forms are delivered to a receiving room at the Department of Health in Albany each month. They are sorted, coded, and logged and then taken to another room where the data on the forms is recorded on magnetic tapes for processing by a computer. Thereafter, the forms are returned to the receiving room to be retained in a vault for a five-year period and then destroyed as required by the statute. . . .

A few days before the Act became effective, this litigation was commenced by a group of patients regularly receiving prescriptions for Schedule II drugs, by doctors who prescribe such drugs, and by two associations of physicians. After various preliminary proceedings, a three-judge district court conducted a one-day trial. Appellees offered evidence tending to prove that persons in need of treatment with Schedule II drugs will from time to time decline such treatment because of their fear that the misuse of the computerized data will cause them to be stigmatized as "drug addicts."

I

The district court found that the state had been unable to demonstrate the necessity for the patient-identification requirement on the basis of its experience during the first 20 months of administration of the new statute. . . .

State legislation which has some effect on individual liberty or privacy may not be held unconstitutional simply because a court finds it unnecessary, in whole or in part. For we have frequently recognized that individual states have broad latitude in experimenting with possible solutions to problems of vital local concern.

The New York statute challenged in this case represents a considered attempt to deal with such a problem. It is manifestly the product of an orderly and rational legislative decision. It was recommended by a specially appointed commission which held extensive hearings on the proposed legislation, and drew on experience with similar programs in other states. There surely was nothing unreasonable in the assumption that the patient-identification requirement might aid in the enforcement of laws designed to minimize the misuse of dangerous drugs. For the requirement could reasonably be expected to have a deterrent effect on potential violators as well as to aid in the detection or investigation of specific instances of apparent abuse. At the very least, it would seem clear that the state's vital interest in controlling the distribution of dangerous drugs would support a decision to experiment with new techniques for control. For if an experiment fails — if in this case experience teaches that the patient-identification requirement results in the foolish expenditure of funds to acquire a mountain of useless information — the legislative process remains available to terminate the unwise experiment. It follows that the legislature's enactment of the patient-identification requirement was a reasonable exercise of New York's broad police powers. The district court's finding that the necessity for the requirement had not been proved is not, therefore, a sufficient reason for holding the statutory requirement unconstitutional.

II

Appellees contend that the statute invades a constitutionally protected "zone of privacy." The cases sometimes characterized as protecting "privacy" have in fact involved at least two different kinds of interests. One is the individual interest in avoiding disclosure of personal matters, and another is the interest in independence in making certain kinds of important decisions. Appellees argue that both of these interests are impaired by this statute. The mere existence in readily available form of the information about patients' use of Schedule II drugs creates a genuine concern that the information will become publicly known and that it will adversely affect their reputations. This concern makes some patients reluctant to use, and some doctors reluctant to prescribe, such drugs even when their use is medically indicated. It follows, they argue, that the making of decisions about matters vital to the care of their health is inevitably affected by the statute. Thus, the statute threatens to impair both their interest in the nondisclosure of private information and also their interest in making important decisions independently.

We are persuaded, however, that the New York program does not, on its face, pose a sufficiently grievous threat to either interest to establish a constitutional violation.

Public disclosure of patient information can come about in three ways. Health Department employees may violate the statute by failing, either deliberately or negligently, to maintain proper security. A patient or a doctor may be accused of a violation and the stored data may be offered in evidence in a judicial proceeding. Or, thirdly, a doctor, a pharmacist, or the patient may voluntarily reveal information on a prescription form.

The third possibility existed under the prior law and is entirely unrelated to the existence of the computerized data bank. Neither of the other two possibilities provides a proper ground for attacking the statute as invalid on its face. There is no support in the record, or in the experience of the two states that New York has emulated, for an assumption that the security provisions of the statute will be administered improperly. And the remote possibility that judicial supervision of the evidentiary use of particular items of stored information will provide inadequate protection against unwarranted disclosures is surely not a sufficient reason for invalidating the entire patient-identification program.

Even without public disclosure, it is, of course, true that private information must be disclosed to the authorized employees of the New York Department of Health. Such disclosures, however, are not significantly different from those that were required under the prior law. Nor are they meaningfully distinguishable from a host of other unpleasant invasions of privacy that are associated with many facets of health care. Unquestionably, some individuals' concern for their own privacy may lead them to avoid or to postpone needed medical attention. Nevertheless, disclosures of private medical information to doctors, to hospital personnel, to insurance companies, and to public health agencies are often an essential part of modern medical practice even when the disclosure may reflect unfavorably on the character of the patient. Requiring such disclosures to representatives of the state having responsibility for the health of the community, does not automatically amount to an impermissible invasion of privacy.

Appellees also argue, however, that even if unwarranted disclosures do not actually occur, the knowledge that the information is readily available in a computerized file creates a genuine concern that causes some persons to decline needed medication. The record supports the conclusion that some use of Schedule II drugs has been discouraged by that concern; it also is clear, however, that about 100,000 prescriptions for such drugs were being filled each month prior to the entry of the district court's injunction. Clearly, therefore, the statute did not deprive the public of access to the drugs.

Nor can it be said that any individual has been deprived of the right to decide independently, with the advice of his physician, to acquire and to use needed medication. Although the state no doubt could prohibit entirely the use of particular Schedule II drugs, it has not done so. This case is therefore unlike those in which the Court held that a total prohibition of certain conduct was an impermissible deprivation of liberty. Nor does the state require access to these drugs to be conditioned on the consent of any state official or other third party. Within dosage limits which appellees do not challenge, the decision to prescribe, or to use, is left entirely to the physician and the patient.

We hold that neither the immediate nor the threatened impact of the patient-identification requirements in the New York State Controlled Substances Act of 1972 on either the reputation or the independence of patients for whom Schedule II drugs are medically indicated is sufficient to constitute an invasion of any right or liberty protected by the Fourteenth Amendment. . . .

Reversed.

Notes: Informational Privacy

1. *Informational vs. Decisional Privacy.* Does *Whalen* clearly establish that we have a fundamental constitutional right to maintain the privacy of our medical information? To the contrary, the Court upholds the validity of a state public health statute that required physicians to report sensitive information about individual prescription drug use. The constitutional protection of confidentiality is at best found in the margins of the decision, in the Court's suggestion that a constitutional right to privacy might have been implicated if the state's reporting mechanism had failed to protect patient information from improper disclosure. Justice Brennan concurred in the Court's opinion with the understanding that constitutional norms were implicated and that widespread dissemination of private information could only be justified by a compelling governmental objective. Justice Stewart's concurrence rested on his understanding that the opinion did not establish a constitutional right to privacy.

2. *Nomenclature. Whalen* suggests that the "right to privacy" encompasses both decisional and informational privacy. In recent years, the Supreme Court has retreated from the use of "privacy" as a basis for protecting individual decisionmaking from governmental intrusion. Most Justices now tend to refer to a "protected liberty interest" in making certain types of decisions free from unwarranted governmental interference. The Court has not taken the opportunity to revisit and more clearly delineate an individual's protected liberty interest in the privacy of information. But see Ferguson v. City of Charleston at page 496.

3. *Confidentiality in the Courts of Appeal.* Despite *Whalen*'s unstable foundation, some courts have begun to erect a constitutional confidentiality doctrine. The

debate has centered on the standard of review to be applied to state measures that intrude on individual privacy. The Tenth Circuit requires a compelling state interest for privacy intrusions. Stidham v. Peace Officer Standards & Training, 265 F.3d 1144 (10th Cir. 2001). A few federal courts of appeal have adopted an intermediate standard of review, employing a balancing test to weigh an individual's interest in privacy against the governmental objective. See Overstreet v. Lexington-Fayette Urban County Government, 305 F.3d 566 (6th Cir. 2002) (balancing test applies only when disclosure implicates fundamental rights); Denius v. Dunlap, 209 F.3d 944 (7th Cir. 2000) (noting relevance of type of information); Doe v. Southeastern Pennsylvania Transportation Authority, 72 F.3d 1133 (3d Cir. 1995) (balancing test includes consideration of seven factors); Doe v. City of New York, 15 F.3d 264 (2d Cir. 1994) (balancing test required a "substantial" state interest when balanced against an individual's right to confidentiality of his HIV status). Some courts of appeal apply only a rational basis standard of review. See also National Federation of Federal Employees v. Greenberg, 983 F.2d 286, 293-294 (D.C. Cir. 1993) (critique of *Whalen*'s "uncharted terrain").

Which of the following measures would likely withstand constitutional attack in which jurisdictions?

1. A state statute requiring physicians to report the names and addresses of persons diagnosed with AIDS.
2. A statute requiring disclosure of a surgeon's HIV status to her patients.
3. A statute requiring persons with TB to post the information on their doors in at least 12-point type.

Commentators have argued that individual privacy is increasingly at risk because of a number of trends, including expanded governmental involvement in health care and the resurgence of dangerous contagious diseases such as HIV and TB. Some interesting sources include: Lawrence O. Gostin, Public Health Law: Power, Duty, Restraint 113-142 (2000); Seth F. Kreimer, Sunlight, Secrets, and Scarlett Letters: The Tension Between Privacy and Disclosure in Constitutional Law, 140 U. Pa. L. Rev. 1 (1991); Neil M. Richards, Essay, The Information Privacy Law Project, 94 Geo. L.J. 1087 (2006); Daniel J. Solove, A Taxonomy of Privacy, 154 U. Penn. L. Rev. 477 (2006).

4.*Statutory and Common Law Protections*. The confidentiality of health-related information is protected by statute and common law as well. Yet none of these sources of protection is absolute. Each has an extensive list of express or implied exceptions. Typically, for example, physicians are permitted to disclose confidential medical information if "*required or authorized by law*," such as by a state reporting statute. See, e.g., Tex. Occ. Code Ann. §159.004.

■ **MIDDLEBROOKS v. STATE BOARD OF HEALTH**
    710 So. 2d 891 (Ala. 1998)

MADDOX, Justice.
This case presents the issue whether §22-11A-2, Ala. Code 1975, which requires physicians, dentists, and certain other persons to report cases or suspected

cases of "notifiable diseases" and health conditions, such as HIV infections and AIDS cases, to the Alabama State Board of Health, is discriminatory and therefore violates the Equal Protection Clause of the Fourteenth Amendment to the Constitution of the United States.

Dr. Mark Middlebrooks, a physician practicing in Jefferson County, specializes in infectious diseases. Through his practice, Dr. Middlebrooks diagnoses and treats patients who are infected with HIV and AIDS. Under the provisions of §22-11A-2, Dr. Middlebrooks is within the class of persons required to report all cases of HIV infection and AIDS to the State Board of Health. The required reports are to include the names and addresses of persons infected.[1]

In July 1993, Dr. Middlebrooks was contacted by officials of the Jefferson County Health Department, who requested that he comply with the reporting mandate of the statute and with the rules of the State Board of Health. . . . Dr. Middlebrooks provided certain statistical data, as the statute and regulatory rules required, but he refused to provide the names and addresses of his patients.

On September 8, 1994, the State Board of Health filed this action against Dr. Middlebrooks, seeking to compel him to disclose the names and addresses of his HIV and AIDS patients, as required by statute and rule. On March 13, 1996, the trial court entered an order compelling disclosure; Dr. Middlebrooks appealed.

Dr. Middlebrooks primarily contends that the statutory and regulatory scheme violates the Equal Protection Clause of the Fourteenth Amendment because persons or entities not listed in the statute are authorized by regulations adopted by the Federal Food and Drug Administration to sell confidential HIV-testing kits and the sellers of those kits are not required to report the names and addresses of the purchasers. Dr. Middlebrooks argues that he is subjected to discriminatory treatment because he is required to report the names and addresses of his HIV and AIDS patients while those who sell the testing kits and out-of-state testing laboratories that evaluate the test results are not required to report the names and addresses of those persons who test positive.

In order to address Dr. Middlebrooks's arguments, we believe it essential to discuss briefly the right of privacy in regard to disclosure of medical information relating to diseases such as HIV and AIDS.

---

[1] Section 22-11A-2 provides, in part:

> Each physician, dentist, nurse, medical examiner, hospital administrator, nursing home administrator, laboratory director, school principal, and day care center director shall be responsible to report cases or suspected cases of notifiable diseases and health conditions. The report shall contain such information, and be delivered in such a manner, as may be provided for from time to time by the rules of the state board of health. All medical and statistical information and reports required by this chapter shall be confidential and shall not be subject to the inspection, subpoena, or admission into evidence in any court, except proceedings brought under this chapter to compel the examination, testing, commitment or quarantine of any person or upon the written consent of the patient, or if the patient is a minor, his parent or legal guardian. Any physician or other person making any report required by this chapter or participating in any judicial proceeding resulting therefrom shall, in doing so, be immune from any civil or criminal liability, that might otherwise be incurred or imposed.

The rules of the State Board of Health define HIV and AIDS as "notifiable diseases" and require the reporting person to give the patient's name and address and certain laboratory data. *Alabama Administrative Code*, Chapter 420-4-1 et seq.

The United States Supreme Court has stated:

> [D]isclosures of private medical information to doctors, to hospital personnel, to insurance companies, and to public health agencies are often an essential part of modern medical practice even when the disclosure may reflect unfavorably on the character of the patient. Requiring such disclosures to representatives of the State having responsibility for the health of the community, does not automatically amount to an impermissible invasion of privacy.

Whalen v. Roe, 429 U.S. 589, 602 (1977). In United States v. Westinghouse Electric Corp., 638 F.2d 570, 578 (3d Cir.1980), the United States Court of Appeals for the Third Circuit established factors for a court to consider when determining "whether an invasion into an individual's records is justified." Those factors are:

> the type of record requested, the information it does or might contain, the potential for harm in any subsequent nonconsensual disclosure, the injury from disclosure to the relationship in which the record was generated, the adequacy of safeguards to prevent unauthorized disclosure, the degree of need for access, and whether there is an express statutory mandate, articulated public policy, or other recognizable public interest militating toward access. [Id.]

After weighing the *Westinghouse* factors, we hold that the prevention of the spread of HIV and AIDS is a legitimate governmental interest, and that, even in regard to HIV and AIDS, where, in some situations, the disclosure may reflect unfavorably on the character of the patient, . . . the State can require disclosure to representatives of the State having responsibility for the health of the community, and that the disclosure required by §22-11A-2 does not amount to an impermissible invasion of privacy. The statute and the regulatory rules adopted pursuant thereto have adequate safeguards to protect the medical records from unauthorized disclosure.

Now that we have determined that §22-11A-2 does not violate the right to privacy, we must decide whether Dr. Middlebrooks's constitutional right to equal protection is violated by the fact that §22-11A-2 does not apply to the stores that market and sell at-home HIV testing kits and out-of-state testing labs that analyze the results of the tests.

The purpose of the Equal Protection Clause is to prevent states from enacting legislation that treats persons "similarly situated" differently. City of Cleburne v. Cleburne Living Center, Inc., 473 U.S. 432, 439 (1985). "It does not, however, require that a statute necessarily apply equally to all persons or require that things different in fact be treated in law as though they were the same." McClendon v. Shelby County, 484 So. 2d 459, 464 (Ala. Civ. App.1985).

We conclude that the State has made a reasonable classification in this instance. It appears to us that the out-of state testing labs that analyze the results of the testing kits are not, as to those required to report HIV and AIDS cases under §22-11A-2, similarly situated.[3]

---

[3] We note, from the Board's brief, that Alabama, like other states, is attempting to get a waiver of the federal rule that permits the sale of testing kits within the state. In any event, it appears to us that the out-of-state testing labs do not know the identity of the persons that are being tested. The vendors

We conclude that the trial judge properly ordered Dr. Middlebrooks to disclose to the State Board of Health the names of his patients infected with HIV and AIDS. The judgment is, therefore, affirmed.

Notes: Reporting and Contact Tracing

1. Middlebrooks *Analysis*. What standard of review does the court apply to Dr. Middlebrooks's constitutional claims? Given the standard of review, could Dr. Middlebrooks have relied on public health experts who question whether states should require name-specific HIV reporting? Note that public health officials have strongly supported names-based reporting. See, e.g., CDC, Guidelines for National Human Immunodeficiency Virus Case Surveillance, Including Monitoring for Human Immunodeficiency Infection and Acquired Immunodeficiency Syndrome, 48 MMWR 1 (1999) (RR-13). Most states now require physicians and others to report the names of persons tested for HIV. Centers for Disease Control and Prevention, 17 HIV/AIDS Surveillance Report, 2005 5 (2006). Why isn't the state reporting scheme irrational under the equal protection clause? Does it help or hurt the equal protection clause analysis if state residents can obtain anonymous HIV antibody testing at clinics in the state or if individuals are permitted to use false names when registering for testing?

2. *Reporting Requirements*. States currently require physicians to report a wide range of health conditions to public health authorities. New reporting requirements are typically added piecemeal and spread throughout the state's code of laws. See, e.g., Cal. Health & Safety Code §120250 (duty to report infectious, contagious, or communicable diseases); Cal. Penal Code §11166 (duty to report child abuse); Cal. Welf. & Inst. Code §15630 (duty to report elder or dependent adult abuse).

3. *Contact Tracing*. Contact tracing programs provide a mechanism for the notification of persons who may have been exposed to a contagious or transmissible condition. These programs have a long history, particularly for sexually transmitted diseases such as syphilis and gonorrhea. They are now being applied to persons exposed to HIV infection. See, e.g., G. L. Dolbear et al., Named Reporting and Mandatory Partner Notification in New York State: The Effect on Consent for Perinatal HIV Testing, 79 J. Urb. Health 238 (2002) (preliminary data indicates that introduction of named reporting and mandatory partner notification reduced willingness to undergo perinatal testing); Mary R. Reichler et al., Evaluation of Investigations Conducted to Detect and Prevent Transmission of Tuberculosis, 287 JAMA 991 (2002) (reviewing data and concluding that improvements are needed in TB contact investigation techniques).

Contact tracing programs for HIV may require even greater attention if the CDC's new guidelines promoting routine HIV screening are implemented (see supra at page 637). Contact tracing programs typically are required to protect the confidentiality of the source individual. The programs nonetheless increase the risk that an individual's identity will be disclosed to third parties. Suppose, for

---

of the testing kits are not similarly situated, because they merely sell the kits and have no information on whether a particular purchaser is HIV- or AIDS-positive.

example, that an individual notified about possible exposure to a sexually transmitted disease has had only one sexual partner. Consider Iowa's approach to the issues:

141A.5. Partner Notification Program — HIV.

1. The department shall maintain a partner notification program for persons known to have tested positive for the HIV infection.

2. The department shall initiate the program at alternative testing and counseling sites and at sexually transmitted disease clinics.

3. In administering the program, the department shall provide for the following:

a. A person who tests positive for the HIV infection shall receive posttest counseling, during which time the person shall be encouraged to refer for counseling and HIV testing any person with whom the person has had sexual relations or has shared drug injecting equipment.

b. The physician or other health care provider attending the person may provide to the department any relevant information provided by the person regarding any person with whom the tested person has had sexual relations or has shared drug injecting equipment. The department disease prevention staff shall then conduct partner notification in the same manner as that utilized for sexually transmitted diseases consistent with the provisions of this chapter.

c. Devise a procedure, as a part of the partner notification program, to provide for the notification of an identifiable third party who is a sexual partner of or who shares drug injecting equipment with a person who has tested positive for HIV, by the department or a physician, when all of the following situations exist:

(1) A physician for the infected person is of the good faith opinion that the nature of the continuing contact poses an imminent danger of HIV infection transmission to the third party.

(2) When the physician believes in good faith that the infected person, despite strong encouragement, has not and will not warn the third party and will not participate in the voluntary partner notification program.

Notwithstanding subsection 4, the department or a physician may reveal the identity of a person who has tested positive for the HIV infection pursuant to this subsection only to the extent necessary to protect a third party from the direct threat of transmission. . . . The department shall adopt rules. . . . The rules shall provide a detailed procedure by which the department or a physician may directly notify an endangered third party.

4. In making contact the department shall not disclose the identity of the person who provided the names of the persons to be contacted and shall protect the confidentiality of persons contacted. . . . Iowa Code Ann. §141A.5.

Will this provision apply if a patient is tested in a private physician's office? Does the statute reach an appropriate balance between individual liberties and public health? What can or should be done if a person refuses to name his or her contacts? See also Lawrence O. Gostin & James G. Hodge Jr., Piercing the Veil of Secrecy in HIV/AIDS and Other Sexually Transmitted Diseases: Theories of Privacy and Disclosure in Partner Notification, 5 Duke J. Gender L. & Pol'y 9 (1998); Nancy E. Kass & Andrea Carlson Gielen, The Ethics of Contact Tracing Programs and Their Implications for Women, 5 Duke J. Gender L. & Pol'y 89

(1998); Sharon Salmon, The Name Game: Issues Surrounding New York State's HIV Partner Notification Law, 16 N.Y.L. Sch. J. Hum. Rts. 959 (2000).

Problem: Reporting, and Contact Tracing Under the MSEHPA

The MSEHPA also includes reporting and tracking provisions. The following sections are in effect whether or not a public health emergency has been declared:

Article III. Measures to Detect and Track Public Health Emergencies

Section 301. Reporting.

(a) **Illness or health condition.** A health care provider, coroner, or medical examiner shall report all cases of persons who harbor any illness or health condition that may be potential causes of a public health emergency. Reportable illnesses and health conditions include, but are not limited to, the diseases caused by the biological agents listed in 42 C.F.R. §72, app. A (2000) and any illnesses or health conditions identified by the public health authority.

(b) **Pharmacists.** In addition to the foregoing requirements for health care providers, a pharmacist shall report any unusual or increased prescription rates, unusual types of prescriptions, or unusual trends in pharmacy visits that may be potential causes of a public health emergency. . . .

(c) **Manner of reporting.** The report shall be made electronically or in writing within [*twenty-four (24) hours*] to the public health authority. The report shall include as much of the following information as is available: the specific illness or health condition that is the subject of the report; the patient's name, date of birth, sex, race, occupation, and current home and work addresses (including city and county); the name and address of the health care provider, coroner, or medical examiner and of the reporting individual, if different; and any other information needed to locate the patient for follow-up. For cases related to animal or insect bites, the suspected locating information of the biting animal or insect, and the name and address of any known owner, shall be reported.

(d) **Animal diseases.** Every veterinarian, livestock owner, veterinary diagnostic laboratory director, or other person having the care of animals shall report animals having or suspected of having any diseases that may be potential causes of a public health emergency. . . .

(f) **Enforcement.** The public health authority may enforce the provisions of this Section in accordance with existing enforcement rules and regulations. . . .

Section 302. Tracking. The public health authority shall ascertain the existence of cases of an illness or health condition that may be potential causes of a public health emergency; investigate all such cases for sources of infection and to ensure that they are subject to proper control measures; and define the distribution of the illness or health condition. To fulfill these duties, the public health authority shall identify exposed individuals as follows—

(a) **Identification of individuals.** Acting on information developed in accordance with Section 301 of this Act, or other reliable information, the public health authority shall identify all individuals thought to have been exposed to an illness or health condition that may be a potential cause of a public health emergency.

(b) **Interviewing of individuals.** The public health authority shall counsel and interview such individuals where needed to assist in the positive identification of exposed individuals and develop information relating to the source and spread of the illness or health condition. Such information includes the name and address (including city and county) of any person from whom the illness or health condition may have been contracted and to whom the illness or health condition may have spread.

(c) **Examination of facilities or materials.** The public health authority shall, for examination purposes, close, evacuate, or decontaminate any facility or decontaminate or destroy any material when the authority reasonably suspects that such facility or material may endanger the public health.

(d) **Enforcement.** The public health authority may enforce the provisions of this Section in accordance with existing enforcement rules and regulations. An order of the public health authority given to effectuate the purposes of this Section shall be enforceable immediately by the public safety authority. . . .

Section 303. Information sharing.

(a) Whenever the public safety authority or other state or local government agency learns of a case of a reportable illness or health condition, an unusual cluster, or a suspicious event that may be the cause of a public health emergency, it shall immediately notify the public health authority.

(b) Whenever the public health authority learns of a case of a reportable illness or health condition, an unusual cluster, or a suspicious event that it reasonably believes has the potential to be caused by bioterrorism, it shall immediately notify the public safety authority, tribal authorities, and federal health and public safety authorities.

(c) Sharing of information on reportable illnesses, health conditions, unusual clusters, or suspicious events between public health and safety authorities shall be restricted to the information necessary for the treatment, control, investigation, and prevention of a public health emergency. MSEHPA §§301-303, available at www.publichealthlaw.net (Dec. 21, 2001 version).

Evaluate the constitutionality of the Model Act's reporting and tracking provisions. Does the constitutionality of the provisions depend on the identification of a serious threat of bioterrorism or other public health emergency? Note that section 303 explicitly permits public health authorities to share information with public safety officials, before the declaration of a public health emergency. Does this entanglement of public health and police functions complicate your analysis? See Ferguson v. City of Charleston, 532 U.S. 67 (2001), supra at page 496. Would the disclosures be permissible under the federal HIPAA privacy rule? Julie Bruce, Bioterrorism Meets Privacy: An Analysis of the Model State Health Powers Act and the HIPAA Privacy Rule, 12 Annals Health L. 75 (2003); and Janlori Goldman, Balancing in a Crisis? Bioterrorism, Public Health and Privacy, 38 J. Health L. 481 (2005). What does it mean to "counsel and interview" persons under MSEHPA §302(b)? Is the reference to enforcement powers in §302(d) meant to suggest that individuals might be compelled to disclose information about possible sources and contacts?

Compare the Model Act's provisions to the relevant public health statute in your own state. Do health care providers in your state have an obligation to report diseases related to bioterrorism? What about pharmacists? How are these measures enforced? May public health authorities and law enforcement share information? If so, do you see any similarities or differences between your state law and the Model Act? Which seems better from a legal or policy standpoint? If not, would you recommend the adoption of the Model Act's provisions? See also Lawrence Gostin, When Terrorism Threatens Health: How Far Are Limitations on Personal and Economic Liberties Justified? 55 Fla. L. Rev. 1105 (2003).

4. Isolation and Quarantine

■ WONG WAI v. WILLIAMSON
103 F. 1 (C.C.N.D. Cal. 1900)

Morrow, Circuit Judge.

[A Chinese resident of San Francisco brought suit against various governmental officers, challenging the application of rules that (1) required persons of Chinese ancestry to undergo inoculation against the bubonic plague by a "serum known as 'Haffkine Prophylactic,'" and (2) prohibited uninoculated Chinese residents from traveling outside the city.] . . .

Upon the filing of the bill of complaint, together with affidavits supporting the allegations therein contained, the court issued an order to the defendants to show cause why an injunction should not issue, restraining the defendants from committing the acts and carrying into execution the threats set forth in the bill of complaint. To the order to show cause no return has been made as required by the rules of practice in equity cases, but in lieu thereof the defendants . . . composing the board of health of the city and county of San Francisco, have produced a copy of a resolution adopted by the board on May 18, 1900, as follows:

> Resolved, that it is the sense of this board that bubonic plague exists in the city and county of San Francisco, and that all necessary steps already taken for the prevention of its spread be continued, together with such additional measures as may be required.

The defendant J. J. Kinyoun, the acting quarantine officer of the United States at the port of San Francisco, in response to the order has produced the following telegram:

Washington, D.C., May 21, 1900.
Surgeon Kinyoun, Angel Island, California: By direction of the president, secretary of treasury has promulgated the following regulations under act of congress March twenty-seventh, eighteen ninety: First, during the existence of plague at any point in the United States the surgeon general, marine hospital service, is authorized to forbid the sale or donation of transportation by common carriers to Asiatics or other races liable to the disease; second, no common carrier shall accept for transportation any person suffering with plague, or any article

infected therewith, nor shall common carriers accept for transportation any class of persons who may be designated by the surgeon general of the marine hospital service as being likely to convey the risk of plague contagion to other communities, and said common carriers shall be subject to inspection. Inform transportation companies, and direct them, under above regulations, to refuse transportation to Asiatics, except on your certificate, and instruct bonded inspectors to inspect trains and prevent Asiatics leaving state without your certificate.

Wyman, Surgeon General Marine Hospital Service.

No objections being offered to these documents as constituting the return of the defendants, they will be so considered. . . .

The defendants constituting the board of health of the city and county of San Francisco contend that they are justified in their action with respect to the matter in controversy under their authority as a board, acting pursuant to the resolution of the board of May 18, 1900. The charter of the city and county of San Francisco provides, in article 10, for a department of public health, under the management of a board of health. . . . Section 4 provides, among other things, that the board shall enforce all ordinances, rules, and regulations which may be adopted by the supervisors for the carrying out and enforcement of a good sanitary condition in the city and county, and for the protection of the public health; and the board is required to submit to the supervisors, from time to time, a draft of such ordinances, rules, and regulations as it may deem necessary to promote the objects mentioned in the section. . . . [The charter provides, however, that the Board of Supervisors is the legislative body of the city with the power to enact ordinances.]

It thus appears that suitable provision has been made in the city charter for the necessary legislation providing rules and regulations to secure proper sanitary conditions in the city and for the protection of the public health, but we are not advised that the board of supervisors has taken any action whatever in that direction; and the resolution of the board of health furnished to the court fails to disclose the method it has adopted for that purpose, under the conditions it has declared to exist. We need not, however, dwell upon the manifest lack of legislative authority to enable the board of health to deal with this important subject. It is sufficient for the present purpose to mention the fact, as one of the features of the situation to be considered in connection with the regulations which the complainant alleges have been imposed upon him and other Chinese residents of the city by the defendants.

It appears that there are about 25,000 Chinese residents in the city of San Francisco, and, while it is well known that a large number of these people are domiciled within the area designated as the "Chinese Quarter," nevertheless there are a great many scattered over the city, engaged in various employments. No restrictions have been placed upon any of the Chinese residents in passing from one part of the city to the other; nor has any house, block, or section of the city been declared infected or unsanitary. There is, therefore, no fact established by the board of supervisors or by the board of health from which an inference might be drawn that any particular class of persons, or persons occupying a particular district, were liable to develop, or in danger of developing, the plague. The restriction is that no Chinese person shall depart from the city without being inoculated with the serum called "Haffkine Prophylactic." The city has a population of about 350,000, but the restriction does not apply to any of the inhabitants other than Chinese or Asiatics, and the inhabitants other than Chinese or Asiatics are permitted to depart from and return to the city without being subject to the inoculation imposed upon the Chinese inhabitants. This restriction, it is alleged, discriminates unreasonably against the complainant and other Chinese residents, confines them within the territorial limits of the city and county, and deprives them of their liberty, causing them great and irreparable loss and injury.

The conditions of a great city frequently present unexpected emergencies affecting the public health, comfort, and convenience. Under such circumstances, officers charged with the duties pertaining to this department of the municipal government should be clothed with sufficient authority to deal with the conditions in a prompt and effective manner. Measures of this character, having a uniform operation, and reasonably adapted to the purpose of protecting the health and preserving the welfare of the inhabitants of a city, are constantly upheld by the courts as valid acts of legislation, however inconvenient they may prove to be, and a wide discretion has also been sanctioned in their execution. But when the municipal authority has neglected to provide suitable rules and regulations upon the subject, and the officers are left to adopt such methods as they may deem proper for the occasion, their acts are open to judicial review, and may be examined in every detail to determine whether individual rights have been respected in accordance with constitutional requirements. This proposition is too clear to require discussion. . . .

In the light of these well-established principles, the action of the defendants as described in the bill of complaint cannot be justified. The regulations they have adopted appear to be without legislative authority, but assuming that they have the sanction of a general authority under the resolution of May 18, 1900, still they cannot be sustained. They are not based upon any established distinction in the conditions that are supposed to attend this plague, or the persons exposed to its contagion, but they are boldly directed against the Asiatic or Mongolian race as a class, without regard to the previous condition, habits, exposure to disease, or residence of the individual; and the only justification offered for this discrimination was a suggestion made by counsel for the defendants in the course of argument, that this particular race is more liable to the plague than any other. No evidence has, however, been offered to support this claim, and it is not known to be a fact. This explanation must therefore be dismissed as unsatisfactory. . . .

It follows from these considerations that the defendants have failed to justify their action in the premises, and that an injunction must issue as prayed for in the bill of complaint.

Notes: Isolation and Quarantine

1. *Definitions and History.* "Isolation" and "quarantine" are technically different public health approaches, though the two terms are often used interchangeably to describe separating those who are or may be infected from

those who are believed to be unaffected. Isolation is used to separate infected people with communicable conditions from others until the period of communicability passes. Quarantine is used to detain those who have been exposed to a disease for the incubation period of that disease so that contact with uninfected persons can be avoided.

However denominated, the concept of separation has ancient roots. In earlier centuries, the victims of disease who were believed to be dangerous to the public through some human contact (which then included most of the known afflictions of humans) were banished from the community and abandoned, beyond the campfire, the village, or the wall of the city. In urbanized areas in the Middle Ages, the practice of "quarantine" began. Voyagers were held on board ship; the local afflicted were confined to their homes. As hospitals and detention houses were developed, they were used for isolation or quarantine when other quarters were not available. With no available treatment, isolation for a temporary period until the person recovered and was no longer infectious, or until death, was the most humane alternative. In the nineteenth century and the early twentieth century, quarantine and isolation were the most common means of disease control. For a comprehensive historical analysis of the sweep of diseases and plagues from ancient times, see a wonderfully enlightening and exciting review by a leading American historian, William Hardy McNeill, Plagues and Peoples (1998) along with the excellent, Norman F. Cantor, In the Wake of the Plague: The Black Death and the World It Made (2002). The plague can now be treated effectively with antibiotics. Modern contagious diseases that spark a similar level of fear include the Ebola virus and smallpox, see page 605 supra.

2. Wong Wai. The public health measures adopted in *Wong Wai* combined a form of vaccination with a quarantine order barring uninoculated Asians from leaving San Francisco. The court decision is relatively unique in its detailed examination and rejection of a measure asserted to involved protection of the public health. What explains the result?

Consider the large number of evidentiary and legal defects cited by the court. Should it matter whether there was evidence that the bubonic plague was present within the city? (The opinion casts doubt on this factor; others have suggested that cases of plague had been reported.) Were the quarantine and inoculation orders issued by the appropriate governmental authorities? The court suggests that the orders should have been passed as ordinances by the Board of Supervisors rather than issued by the city Board of Health. What should be the effect of finding the orders to be *ultra vires*? Why were the inoculation and quarantine orders applicable only to those of Asian heritage? What standard of review would a modern court apply to an order of this type? What types of evidence would be necessary to support a public health measure applied only to persons of a particular racial or ethnic background? See also Jew Ho v. Williamson, 103 F. 10 (C.C.N.D. Cal. 1900).

3. *Isolation and HIV Infection.* Should persons with HIV infection be separated from the general population? Public health authorities uniformly reject the suggestion. See Lawrence O. Gostin & Zita Lazzarini, Human Rights and Public Health in the AIDS Pandemic 64-76 (1997). Segregation or isolation of persons with HIV within correctional facilities is more controversial. See, e.g., Onishea v. Hopper, 171 F.3d 1289 (11th Cir. 1999) (segregation of HIV-infected inmates

does not violate Rehabilitation Act). Uninfected prisoners have argued that the failure to segregate infected prisoners violates the Eighth Amendment's prohibition against cruel and unusual punishment. See Glick v. Henderson, 855 F.2d 536 (8th Cir. 1988). See also Annot., 162 A.L.R. Fed. 181 (2000); Scott Burris, Prisons, Law and Public Health: The Case for a Coordinated Response to Epidemic Disease Behind Bars, 47 U. Miami L. Rev. 291 (1992).

4. *Federal Quarantine Regulations.* The federal Public Health Service Act gives the Secretary of Health and Human Services authority over quarantines within federal jurisdiction:

> (a) Promulgation and enforcement by Surgeon General
> The Surgeon General, with the approval of the Secretary, is authorized to make and enforce such regulations as in his judgment are necessary to prevent the introduction, transmission, or spread of communicable diseases from foreign countries into the States or possessions, or from one State or possession into any other State or possession. . . .
>
> (b) Apprehension, detention, or conditional release of individuals
> Regulations prescribed under this section shall not provide for the apprehension, detention, or conditional release of individuals except for the purpose of preventing the introduction, transmission, or spread of such communicable diseases as may be specified from time to time in Executive orders of the President upon the recommendation of the Secretary, in consultation with the Surgeon General,
>
> (c) Application of regulations to persons entering from foreign countries
>
> Except as provided in subsection (d) of this section, regulations prescribed under this section, insofar as they provide for the apprehension, detention, examination, or conditional release of individuals, shall be applicable only to individuals coming into a State or possession from a foreign country or a possession.
>
> (d)(1) Apprehension and examination of persons reasonably believed to be infected
> Regulations prescribed under this section may provide for the apprehension and examination of any individual reasonably believed to be infected with a communicable disease in a qualifying stage and [who is a probable source of infection who is or will be moving from state to state] . . . Such regulations may provide that if upon examination any such individual is found to be infected, he may be detained for such time and in such manner as may be reasonably necessary. . . . 42 U.S.C.A. §264 (2006).

The current executive order includes SARS and influenza viruses capable of causing a pandemic. See CDC's Global Migration and Quarantine Web site, at http://www.cdc.gov/ncidod/dq/isolation_quarantine/index.htm (with links to the current Presidential Executive Order). In 2005 the CDC issued draft regulations expanding its quarantine powers under the statute. Department of Health and Human Services, Control of Communicable Diseases (Proposed Rule), 70 Fed. Reg. 71892 (2005). Some public health law experts expressed concerns about the lack of certain procedural protections in the proposed rules. See Lawrence O. Gostin, Federal Executive Power and Communicable Disease Control: CDC Quarantine Regulations, Hastings Center Rep., March-April 2006, at 10.

5.*State Quarantine Law.* State quarantine laws were little used and little discussed for decades. The situation changed with the advent of drug-resistant TB and the threats posed by bioterrorism and resurgent strains of influenza. Professor Gostin notes, "While many existing state isolation and quarantine statutes are antiquated, 27 states have modernized their laws based on the [MSEHPA]." Lawrence Gostin, Public Health Strategies for Pandemic Influenza: Ethics and the Law, 295 JAMA 1700, 1703 (2006). The relevant MSEHPA provisions are discussed in the problem found at page 668.

6.*State Quarantines and Conflicts with Federal Law.* Where does the state's power to restrict the movement of people end? Is a state permitted to enact travel restrictions that hinder interstate commerce or immigration, two areas within the domain of federal law? Federal quarantine law specifies: "(e) Nothing in this section . . . or the regulations . . . may be construed as superseding any provision under State law (including regulations and including provisions established by political subdivisions of States), except to the extent that such a provision conflicts with an exercise of Federal authority. . . . " 42 U.S.C.A. §264 (2006). Does this resolve the question?

In Compagnie Francaise de Navigation a Vapeur v. State Board of Health, Louisiana, 186 U.S. 380 (1902), the Supreme Court considered and upheld the validity of a board order barring entry of any "body or bodies of people, immigrants, soldier, or others" into cities where a quarantine had been declared. The asserted basis of this "reverse" quarantine was that the introduction of new, uninfected persons to an area would "add fuel to the flame." How would this case be decided today? What, if anything, has changed? Has Congress occupied the field more thoroughly than it had in the early 1900s? Has the Court changed its mind about the state's ability to enact public safety regulations that impede interstate commerce? Could a state pass a statute refusing to permit introduction of additional hazardous waste into its borders? See Chemical Waste Management v. Hunt, 504 U.S. 334, 346-347 (1992) (distinguishing permissible and impermissible state quarantine provisions that have an impact on interstate commerce, citing *Compagnie Francaise*). See also Annot., 86 A.L.R.4th 401 (1991). Federal laws prohibiting disability-based discrimination might also limit the permissibility of state quarantine rules in some situations. See supra at page 611.

7. *Responding to SARS.* The outbreak of Severe Acute Respiratory Syndrome (SARS) in Canada and other countries during 2003 provided a modern example of the use of quarantine and isolation. The crisis required the use of "in house" quarantine orders and sparked a number of important policy debates. Tomislav Svoboda, Public Health Measures to Control the Spread of the Severe Acute Respiratory Syndrome During the Outbreak in Toronto, 350 New Eng. J. Med. 2352 (2004). See also, Lawrence O. Gostin, Ronald Bayer & Amy L. Fairchild, Ethical and Legal Challenges Posed by Severe Acute Respiratory Syndrome: Implications for the Control of Severe Infectious Disease Threats, 290 JAMA 3229 (2003); James M. Hughes, The SARS Response—Building and Assessing an Evidence-Based Approach to Future Global Microbial Threats, 290 JAMA 3251 (2003); Xinghuo Pang et al. Evaluation of Control Measures Implemented in the Severe Acute Respiratory Syndrome Outbreak in Beijing, 2003, 290 JAMA 3215 (2003); and National Advisory Committee on SARS and Public Health, Learning from SARS: Renewal of Public Health in Canada (2003) (the Naylor Report).

8. *A New Influenza Pandemic?* How should we prepare for the possibility of a new, deadly influenza pandemic? As noted supra at page 597, an avian flu virus capable of rapid human-to-human transmission could cause millions of deaths worldwide. See also an online resource for avian and pandemic flu information managed by the Department of Health and Human Services: http://www.pandemicflu.gov/. Canada's experience with quarantine orders during the SARS outbreak suggests that isolation/quarantine might be important components of the public health response, although this will depend on the characteristics of the influenza virus. Neil M. Ferguson et al., Letter, Strategies for Mitigating an Influenza Epidemic, 442 Nature 448 (2006) (model shows that "case isolation or household quarantine could have a significant impact" on influenza pandemic). Does the current legal framework in the United States permit the use of isolation and quarantine on the scale that might be warranted from a public health standpoint? See Lawrence Gostin, Public Health Strategies for Pandemic Influenza: Ethics and the Law, 295 JAMA 1700 (2006).

5. Civil Commitment, and Mandatory Treatment

Should a state be able to promote public health by requiring medical treatment? In some sense, this form of state regulation could be viewed as the most direct and effective method of health promotion. So long as the state has correctly identified an affected individual and so long as an effective treatment is available, mandatory treatment would seem to promote both the health of the individual and of those with whom the individual interacts. The apparent simplicity of this approach is matched, of course, by the serious threat to individual liberties it entails. When should the state's interest in public health outweigh the individual's rights to freedom of movement, to bodily integrity, and to make medical treatment decisions free from state coercion? Should it matter whether the illness is mental or physical?

■ ADDINGTON v. TEXAS
441 U.S. 418 (1979)

BURGER, C.J.

[The appellant had a long history of temporary commitments as mentally ill (seven times between 1969 and 1975) to several Texas mental hospitals. In December 1975, appellant was arrested on charges of assault and threats against his mother. His mother filed a petition for indefinite commitment. A trial was held before a jury to determine whether the appellant was mentally ill and in need of treatment for his welfare and protection, or for the protection of others. The trial lasted six days. The appellant was found mentally ill and subject to commitment under the law based upon "clear, unequivocal and convincing evidence." The Texas Supreme Court upheld the commitment and the applicable standard of proof.]

The question in this case is what standard of proof is required by the Fourteenth Amendment to the Constitution in a civil proceeding brought under state law to commit an individual involuntarily for an indefinite period to a state mental hospital.

This Court repeatedly has recognized that civil commitment for any purpose constitutes a significant deprivation of liberty that requires due process protection. Moreover, it is indisputable that involuntary commitment to a mental hospital after a finding of probable dangerousness to self or others can engender adverse social consequences to the individual. Whether we label this phenomena "stigma" or choose to call it something else is less important than that we recognize that it can occur and that it can have a very significant impact on the individual.

The state has a legitimate interest under its *parens patriae* powers in providing care to its citizens who are unable because of emotional disorders to care for themselves; the state also has authority under its police power to protect the community from the dangerous tendencies of some who are mentally ill. Under the Texas Mental Health Code, however, the state has no interest in confining individuals involuntarily if they are not mentally ill or if they do not pose some danger to themselves or others. Since the preponderance standard creates the risk of increasing the number of individuals erroneously committed, it is at least unclear to what extent, if any, the state's interests are furthered by using a preponderance standard in such commitment proceedings.

The expanding concern of society with problems of mental disorders is reflected in the fact that in recent years many states have enacted statutes designed to protect the rights of the mentally ill. However, only one state by statute permits involuntary commitment by a mere preponderance of the evidence, Miss. Code Ann. §41-21-75 (1978 Supp.), and Texas is the only state where a court has concluded that the preponderance-of-the-evidence standard satisfies due process. We attribute this not to any lack of concern in those states, but rather to a belief that the varying standards tend to produce comparable results. As we noted earlier, however, standards of proof are important for their symbolic meaning as well as for their practical effect. . . .

Appellant urges the Court to hold that due process requires use of the criminal law's standard of proof—"beyond a reasonable doubt." . . .

There are significant reasons why different standards of proof are called for in civil commitment proceedings as opposed to criminal prosecutions. In a civil commitment state power is not exercised in a punitive sense. . . .

In addition, the "beyond a reasonable doubt" standard historically has been reserved for criminal cases. This unique standard of proof, not prescribed or defined in the Constitution, is regarded as a critical part of the "moral force of the criminal law," In re Winship, 397 U.S., at 364, and we should hesitate to apply it too broadly or casually in noncriminal cases.

The heavy standard applied in criminal cases manifests our concern that the risk of error to the individual must be minimized even at the risk that some who are guilty might go free. Patterson v. New York, 432 U.S. 197, 208 (1977). The full force of that idea does not apply to a civil commitment. It may be true that an erroneous commitment is sometimes as undesirable as an erroneous conviction, 5 J. Wigmore, Evidence §1400 (Chadbourn rev. 1974). However, even though an erroneous confinement should be avoided in the first instance, the layers of professional review and observation of the patient's condition, and the concern of family and friends generally will provide continuous opportunities for an erroneous commitment to be corrected. Moreover, it is not true that the release of a genuinely mentally ill person is no worse for the individual than the failure to convict the guilty. One who is suffering from a debilitating mental illness and in need of treatment is neither wholly at liberty nor free of stigma. See Chodoff, The Case for Involuntary Hospitalization of the Mentally Ill, 133 Am. J. Psychiatry 496, 498 (1976); Schwartz, Myers & Astrachan, Psychiatric Labeling and the Rehabilitation of the Mental Patient, 31 Arch. Gen. Psychiatry 329, 334 (1974). It cannot be said, therefore, that it is much better for a mentally ill person to "go free" than for a mentally normal person to be committed. . . .

The subtleties and nuances of psychiatric diagnosis render certainties virtually beyond reach in most situations. The reasonable-doubt standard of criminal law functions in its realm because there the standard is addressed to specific, knowable facts. Psychiatric diagnosis, in contrast, is to a large extent based on medical "impressions" drawn from subjective analysis and filtered through the experience of the diagnostician. This process often makes it very difficult for the expert physician to offer definite conclusions about any particular patient. Within the medical discipline, the traditional standard for "factfinding" is a "reasonable medical certainty." If a trained psychiatrist has difficulty with the categorical "beyond a reasonable doubt" standard, the untrained lay juror—or indeed even a trained judge—who is required to rely upon expert opinion could be forced by the criminal law standard of proof to reject commitment for many patients desperately in need of institutionalized psychiatric care. Such "freedom" for a mentally ill person would be purchased at a high price. . . .

We have concluded that the reasonable-doubt standard is inappropriate in civil commitment proceedings because, given the uncertainties of psychiatric diagnosis, it may impose a burden the state cannot meet and thereby erect an unreasonable barrier to needed medical treatment. Similarly, we conclude that use of the term *unequivocal* is not constitutionally required, although the states are free to use that standard. To meet due process demands, the standard has to inform the factfinder that the proof must be greater than the preponderance-of-the-evidence standard applicable to other categories of civil cases.

We noted earlier that the trial court employed the standard of "clear, unequivocal and convincing" evidence in appellant's commitment hearing before a jury. That instruction was constitutionally adequate. However, determination of the precise burden equal to or greater than the "clear and convincing" standard which we hold is required to meet due process guarantees is a matter of state law which we leave to the Texas Supreme Court. Accordingly, we remand the case for further proceedings not inconsistent with this opinion.

Vacated and remanded.

■ IN THE INTEREST OF J.A.D.

492 N.W.2d 82 (N.D. 1992)

VANDE WALLE, Justice.

J.A.D. appealed from an order of the county court of Stutsman County requiring that he be hospitalized and treated for mental illness for a period not to exceed 90 days. We reverse. . . .

Before a court can issue an order for an involuntary treatment, the petitioner must prove by clear and convincing evidence that the respondent is a person requiring treatment. NDCC §25-03.1-19. The determination that an individual is a "person requiring treatment" under the statutory definition is a two-step process: (1) the court must find that the individual is mentally ill, and (2) the court must find that there is a reasonable expectation that if the person is not hospitalized there exists a serious risk of harm to himself, others, or property.[1] NDCC §25-03.1-02(10). . . . We therefore focus on the evidence that J.A.D. was mentally ill and that there was a substantial likelihood of substantial harm to J.A.D. to determine if there is clear and convincing evidence to support the findings of the trial court. . . .

The record demonstrates that J.A.D. is suffering from a mental illness. The record also fairly indicates that without treatment, J.A.D.'s mental health would be at a substantial risk of deterioration. However, as we have previously held, the need for treatment alone is not sufficient to order hospitalization. The issue is therefore whether or not this likely deterioration of J.A.D.'s mental health will predictably result in dangerousness to himself, others, or property. . . .

The record is tenuous as to whether J.A.D. poses a danger to himself, to others, or to property. Testimony at the hearing indicates that J.A.D. may be a danger to himself, though most likely not a danger to others or to property. The concern over J.A.D.'s dangerousness to himself centered around his homelessness and his ability to take care of himself, such as his resourcefulness at getting food and proper nutrition, and his propensity to seek out shelter during the winter months. . . .

Dr. Kottke's testimony that J.A.D. was in need of treatment as defined by the statutes was not clear and convincing. Dr. Kottke's conclusion, that absent commitment to the State Hospital there exists a strong risk of harm to J.A.D., was also premised on his concern that J.A.D. would not seek appropriate shelter when winter came, as it surely will, in North Dakota.

All three witnesses expressed concern that because J.A.D. was a recent arrival from the deep South he was not aware of the severe cold which the winter season may bring to North Dakota and would not seek appropriate food and shelter. These concerns were essentially premised on isolated incidents in which J.A.D. did not take advantage of shelter the caseworker had arranged, the fact that J.A.D. took shelter in abandoned buildings, that he talked about obtaining a hotplate, and the fact that he once placed food he received from the private organization in a garbage dumpster because, according to the witness, he could not remember where he obtained the food and was afraid to eat it. . . .

---

[1] Section 25-03.1-02(10) reads:

"Person requiring treatment" means a person who is mentally ill or chemically dependent, and there is a reasonable expectation that if the person is not treated there exists a serious risk of harm to that person, others, or property. "Serious risk of harm" means a substantial likelihood of: a. Suicide as manifested by suicidal threats, attempts, or significant depression relevant to suicidal potential; b. Killing or inflicting serious bodily harm on another person or inflicting significant property damage, as manifested by acts or threats; c. Substantial deterioration in physical health, or substantial injury, disease, or death based upon recent poor self-control or judgment in providing one's shelter, nutrition, or personal care; or d. Substantial deterioration in mental health which would predictably result in dangerousness to that person, others, or property, based upon acts, threats, or patterns in the person's treatment history, current condition, and other relevant factors.

Not all homeless people are mentally ill and in need of treatment. Homelessness may in some instances be a product of mental illness, but it may also be the result of economic hardship or simply lifestyle choice. We cannot categorize homeless people as people in need of compulsory mental therapy simply because they do without a traditional home, kitchen, plumbing, or electricity. Homeless people may be very resourceful in obtaining food and shelter, as evidenced by J.A.D. seeking out the Salvation Army and social programs offered by the various state and private agencies in the community. J.A. D. has been receiving food and meals, and has sought shelter. Because he did not make use of the shelter which he was offered during the summer months is not necessarily indicative of a propensity to not seek shelter in the winter months. J.A. D. had the wherewithal to travel to North Dakota, and we can presume that he has the wherewithal to leave. In the winter, he may seek assistance for shelter as he has in the past, or simply leave the state for warmer locations. There is no presumption that J.A.D., as a homeless person, will neither be able to fend for himself during the winter months nor be able to take care of his needs. . . . [The court also expressed its concern with the trial court's failure to adequately consider appropriate, less restrictive alternatives to commitment.] . . .

Accordingly, we reverse the order for hospitalization and treatment.

ERICKSTAD, Chief Justice, specially concurring.

I respectfully, reluctantly concur in the result of the majority opinion, with great concern that, in our effort to find clear and convincing evidence of J.A.D.'s need for treatment, we have actually tried this case anew and found that evidence wanting. . . .

Through our very careful review of the facts and our analysis of the possible consequences of the facts, we may have deprived J.A.D. of treatment crucial to his future welfare, without providing him with a safety net of any kind, at a time, considering the season of the year, when survival as a homeless person in North Dakota could be hazardous to say the very least.

Notes: Mandatory Mental Health Treatment

1. *Trends in Mental Health Treatment.* The *Addington* case in the Supreme Court represented a high-water mark in efforts to raise the standard of proof for compulsory hospitalization of the mentally ill. In large measure, the laws on commitment of the mentally ill came full circle in some 200 years in the United States. The nineteenth-century laws were essentially modeled after criminal procedures. The person who was believed to be mentally ill was "arrested" and "charged" with being "insane" and at large and was "committed" to a mental institution, usually for life. On any escape, the patient was hunted down like a criminal and returned to the institution in chains.

In the middle years of the twentieth century, the laws concerning mental illness were largely decriminalized, and compulsory hospitalization was made considerably easier as an administrative action without judicial intervention. This was the case all over the world. The movement away from the informal system back to a much more structured, judicially sanctioned review procedure for compulsory hospitalization began in the 1970s and continued into the 1980s. Michael L. Perlin, The Hidden Prejudice: Mental Disability on Trial (2000); The Evolution of Mental Health Law (Lynda E. Frost & Richard Bonnie eds., 2001).

2. *Clear and Convincing Evidence.* Why does the Court impose this higher burden of proof for civil commitments? Should the burden apply to all aspects of the state's case, including both the diagnosis of mental illness and the requirement of dangerousness? Most jurisdictions answer both questions affirmatively. In addition to *J.A.D.*, supra, see Colorado v. Stevens, 761 P.2d 768 (Colo. 1988); In re Richard A., 771 A.2d 572 (N.H. 2001) (reviewing standards); In the Matter of The Commitment of N.N., 679 A.2d 1174 (N.J. 1996) (discussing the constitutional constraints applicable to the commitment of minors). In most cases, the issues of commitment and treatment are intertwined. Will the same due process protections apply to "mandatory treatment," as an issue distinct from commitment? Yes. See Wetherhorn v. Alaska Psychiatric Institute, 156 P.3d 371 (Alaska 2007); Donaldson v. District Court, 847 P.2d 632 (Colo. 1993) (en banc); In re C.E., 641 N.E.2d 345 (Ill. 1994). How do you reconcile this approach with the right to control one's own medical treatment described in Chapters 2 and 3?

A number of commentators have explored the law and policy governing mental health civil commitments. See generally Paul S. Appelbaum, Civil Mental Health Law: Its History and Its Future, 20 Mental & Physical Disability L. Rep. 599 (1996); Lawrence O. Gostin & Lance Gable, "The Human Rights of Persons with Mental Disabilities: A Global Perspective on the Application of Human Rights Principles to Mental Health." 63 Md. L. Rev. 20 (2004); Veronica J. Manahan, When Our System of Involuntary Civil Commitment Fails Individuals with Mental Illness: Russell Westin and the Case for Effective Monitoring and Medication Delivery Mechanisms, 28 Law & Psychol. Rev. 1 (2004); Bruce J. Winick, Therapeutic Jurisprudence and the Civil Commitment Hearing, 10 J. Contemp. Legal Issues 37 (1999); Annot., 97 A.L.R.3d 780 (1980).

The Americans with Disabilities Act prohibits discrimination against persons with disabilities who do not present a direct threat to health and safety. Is this consistent with state law, or does the ADA place any additional obstacles in the path of involuntary commitment? The answer will depend in part on each state's laws. In addition, courts will have to determine whether a specific claim for money damages under Title II against a state in matters involving mental health constitutes a valid exercise of Congressional power under the Fourteenth Amendment. See supra page 611. See Susan Stefan, Unequal Rights: Discrimination Against People with Mental Disabilities and the Americans with Disabilities Act (2001) (pre-*Garrett/Lane* analysis).

3. *Mental Retardation.* Does commitment based on mental retardation invoke the same constitutional concerns as commitment for mental illness? In Heller v. Doe, 509 U.S. 312 (1993), the Court considered the validity of a statutory scheme that imposed a lower burden of proof on involuntary commitments for persons who were mentally retarded. The Court's analysis was based on a rational review standard because the litigants had failed to properly present their claim that a higher level of scrutiny should be applied. A divided Court upheld the lower commitment standard, in part because of distinctions between mental retardation and mental illness. Mental retardation might be easier to diagnose, with less risk of error, for example. Similarly, Kentucky "could conclude" that mentally retarded

persons were more likely to present a danger to themselves or others. In addition, treatment for mental retardation is "much less invasive" than treatment for mental illness. Justices Souter, Blackmun, and Stevens dissented, with O'Connor joining in part. See Susan Lee, Heller v. Doe: Involuntary Civil Commitment and the "Objective" Language of Probability, 20 Am. J.L. & Med. 457 (1994). See also Atkins v. Virginia, 122 S. Ct. 2242 (2002) (capital punishment of mentally retarded violates Eighth Amendment proscription against cruel and unusual punishment); Porter v. Knickrehm, 457 F.3d 794 (8th Cir. 2006) (only minimal procedural protections required for admission of mentally retarded individual to state human development center when admission under voluntary authority of legal guardian).

4. *Civil Commitment for Substance Abuse.* Should persons addicted to drugs or alcohol be subjected to civil commitment and forced treatment? Under what circumstances would such a commitment be legitimate? Is addiction a "mental illness"? See, e.g., Melanie B. Abbott, Homelessness and Substance Abuse: Is Mandatory Treatment the Solution?, 22 Fordham Urb. L. J. 1 (1994); Mara Lynn Krongard, Comment, A Population at Risk: Civil Commitment of Substance Abusers after Kansas v. Hendricks, 90 Cal. L. Rev. 111 (2002). Several states have enacted statutes providing for civil commitment of pregnant women who have habitually or excessively used specific enumerated controlled substances. See, e.g., S.D. Codified Laws §34-20A-70; Wis. Stat. Ann. §48.193. See also the discussion of maternal-fetal conflict, supra at page 480.

5. *Involuntary Commitment of Homeless Persons.* The deinstitutionalization of mental patients in the 1970s and 1980s added to the population of homeless persons. About one-third to one-half of the homeless are estimated to be coping with some form of mental illness or addiction. H. Richard Lamb & Leona L. Bachrach, Some Perspectives on Deinstitutionalization, 52 Psychiatric Services 1039 (2001). Some jurisdictions have sought to institutionalize homeless persons on the theory that they are incapable of protecting themselves. What is your view? Are you concerned about the extent to which poverty might be misconstrued as mental illness?

6. *Involuntary Treatment of Prisoners with Psychotropic Medications.* Do *Addington*'s due process protections apply to prisoners? In Washington v. Harper, 494 U.S. 210 (1990), the Supreme Court analyzed the constitutionality of a state policy that authorized treatment of inmates with antipsychotic drugs without a judicial hearing. The Court held that prisoners do retain a protected liberty interest in avoiding unwanted treatment. It held, however, that this due process interest was subject to the reasonableness test of Turner v. Safley, 482 U.S. 78 (1987): Policies that infringe prisoner rights will be upheld so long as they are reasonably related to legitimate penological interests. Applying this standard, the Court held that "given the requirements of the prison environment, the due process clause permits the state to treat a prison inmate who has a serious mental illness with antipsychotic drugs against his will, if the inmate is dangerous to himself or others and the treatment is in the inmate's medical interest." *Harper*, 494 U.S. at 227.

The Court also considered whether Harper had been denied his right to procedural due process. See, e.g., Morrissey v. Brewer, 408 U.S. 471, 481 (1972). The state's procedure, which included determinations through administrative hearings before the institution's own mental health care personnel (although not those involved in the direct treatment of the prisoner), was deemed to be procedurally adequate. 494 U.S. at 232-236. The Court rejected contentions that the decision should be made before a judge and with the assistance of counsel. Justice Blackmun, often deferential to medical authority, concurred in the majority decision, while noting that use of a formal commitment procedure would render the debate unnecessary. Id. at 236-237. Justices Stevens, Brennan, and Marshall dissented, noting that the Court had failed to recognize and protect Harper's significant liberty interests. See also Foucha v. Louisiana, 504 U.S. 71 (1992) (person acquitted by reason of insanity who subsequently was found to be without mental illness could not be committed to mental institution based on dangerousness alone). For a discussion on forced medical treatment in order to stand trial, see George Annas, Forcible Medication for Courtroom Competence — The Case of Charles Sell, 350 New Eng. J. Med. 2297 (2004).

7. *Outpatient Commitment.* Inpatient commitment and mandatory treatment both involve substantial invasions of individual liberty. What standards should be applied to state laws permitting "outpatient commitment," under which individuals might be required to demonstrate continued adherence to medical treatment or therapy? Could outpatient commitment be used to ensure that mentally ill patients continue to take necessary medications while in the community, thus preventing relapses and the need for inpatient commitment? See Jeffrey Geller & Johnathan A. Stanley, Setting the Doubts About the Constitutionality of Outpatient Commitment, 31 New Eng. J. on Crim. & Civ. Confinement 127 (2005); Bruce J. Winick et al., Symposium, Preventive Outpatient Commitment for Person with Serious Mental Illness, 9 Psych. Pub. Pol'y & L. 8 (2003). See also In the Matter of K.L., 806 N.E.2d 480 (N.Y. 2004).

Notes: Mandatory Treatment for Contagious Diseases

1. *Mandatory Treatment of Contagious Disease. Addington*'s principles have been applied to cases involving involuntary treatment of persons for contagious disease. Recent regulations tend to include elaborate due process safeguards. The ordinance in City of New York v. Antoinette R., 630 N.Y.S.2d 1008 (N.Y. Sup. Ct. 1995), provides a typical example:

> The issue presented at this special proceeding is whether the respondent, a person with active tuberculosis, should be forcibly detained in a hospital setting to allow for the completion of an appropriate regime of medical treatment. . . .
>
> Due to a resurgence of tuberculosis, New York City recently revised the Health Code to permit the detention of individuals infected with TB who have demonstrated an inability to voluntarily comply with appropriate medical treatment. . . . The prerequisite for an order is that there is a substantial likelihood, based on the person's past or present behavior, that the individual cannot be relied upon to participate in or complete an appropriate prescribed course of medication or, if necessary, follow required contagion precautions for tuberculosis. Such behavior may include the refusal or failure to take medication or to complete treatment for tuberculosis, to keep appointments for the treatment of tuberculosis, or a disregard for contagion precautions.
>
> The statute provides certain due process safeguards when detention is ordered. For example, there are requirements for an appraisal of the risk posed to others and a review of less restrictive alternatives which were attempted or

considered. Furthermore, there must be a court review within five days at the patient's request, and court review within 60 days and at 90-day intervals thereafter. The detainee also has the right to counsel, to have counsel provided, and to have friends or relatives notified. See Richard T. Andrias, The Criminal Justice System and the Resurgent TB Epidemic, 9 Crim. Just. 2 (Spring, 1994). . . .

In *Antoinette*, the city sought to apply its mandatory treatment regime to a 33-year-old woman who had repeatedly been diagnosed with TB but who had failed to complete her course of treatment after being released from the hospital. Court-ordered "directly observed therapy" (DOT) had failed when she refused to comply. The issue in the case was whether Antoinette would be forced to remain in the hospital for the estimated seven months it would take to complete treatment or whether she would be released for treatment in the home of her mother:

> The mother of the respondent lives in a private home with four of her grandchildren and a newborn great-grandson, the grandchild of the respondent. The mother is willing to take the respondent into her home and provide cooperation should she be released from the hospital. Over the past two months the mother has visited her daughter on several occasions and talked with her over the phone on a daily basis. The mother has noticed a change in attitude in the respondent, that is, she is not as hostile. The mother attributes this change to the respondent's acceptance of religion. The respondent also contends that her attitude has been transformed and credits religion as her motivation. Since being detained at the hospital, she has joined various outpatient programs and attended parenting meetings. A nurses aide and the head nurse, who attend to the medical needs of the respondent, both verify that there has been an improvement in the respondent's demeanor. She is now cooperative while taking her medicines and on occasions has independently approached the nursing staff to request her medicines. Relying on her "change in attitude," the respondent opposes the order of detention and again requests the option of participating in Directly Observed Therapy to be conducted at her mother's place of residence. . . .
>
> The petitioner's request for enforcement of the order of the Commissioner is granted. The petitioner has demonstrated through clear and convincing evidence the respondent's inability to comply with a prescribed course of medication in a less restrictive environment. The respondent has repeatedly sought medical treatment for the infectious stages of the disease and has consistently withdrawn from medical treatment once symptoms abate. She has also exhibited a pattern of behavior which is consistent with one who does not understand the full import of her condition nor the risks she poses to others, both the public and her family. On the contrary, she has repeatedly tried to hide the history of her condition from medical personnel. Although the court is sympathetic to the fact that she has recently undergone an epiphany of sorts, there is nothing in the record which would indicate that once she leaves the controlled setting of the hospital she would have the self-discipline to continue her cooperation. Moreover, her past behavior and lack of compliance with outpatient treatment when her listed residence was her mother's house, makes it all the more difficult to have confidence that her mother's good intentions will prevail over the respondent's inclinations to avoid treatments. In any event, the court will reevaluate the progress of the respondent's ability to cooperate in a less restrictive setting during its next review of the order in 90 days.
>
> Accordingly, the respondent shall continue to be detained in a hospital setting until the petitioner or the court determines that the respondent has

completed an appropriate course of medication for tuberculosis, or a change in circumstances indicates that the respondent can be relied upon to complete the prescribed course of medication without being in detention. The petitioner is further directed, pursuant to New York City Health Code §11.47 to apply to the court within 90 days for authorization to continue respondent's detention.

Assess the evidence in *Antoinette*. If you represented Antoinette, what evidence and arguments would you want to present at the next hearing? Do you think that you would be successful?

2.*Due Process*. Is it clear to you that the clear and convincing evidence standard should be applied to commitment and treatment orders applied to persons with contagious diseases? In which ways are the consequences and proof disputes similar to those implicated in commitment for mental illness? Most jurisdictions that have considered the issue use the "clear and convincing" standard and provide other due process protections. See, e.g., Greene v. Edwards, 263 S.E.2d 661 (W. Va. 1980) ("clear and convincing" standard applied to commitment for TB treatment). See also Lawrence O. Gostin, Public Health Law: Power, Duty, Restraint 216-224 (2000). Can these cases be reconciled with the "right to die" jurisprudence developed in Chapter 3? Patients with contagious conditions presumably are competent. What explains the state's ability to override their treatment refusals?

3. *Americans with Disabilities Act*. The ADA prohibits discrimination by public entities against persons with disabilities unless those persons present a direct threat to the health or safety of others. 42 U.S.C. §12131. As noted supra at page 611, there are substantial limitations on the ability to use Title II of the ADA to bring claims for money damages against states. The potential remains, however, to consider whether the ADA could be used to limit state control measures that "discriminate" against carriers of contagious diseases. In City of Newark v. J.S., 652 A.2d 265 (N.J. Super. Ct. Law Div. 1993), for example, the court construed the state's TB commitment statute to avoid due process and ADA claims. The court held that the city had presented clear and convincing evidence of the likelihood that J.S. presented a danger to others and approved his commitment. It rejected mandatory sputum tests and treatment, however, noting that J.S. could refuse these measures, although to do so would likely render his confinement indefinite. The court's analysis of the due process and ADA issues was heavily influenced by Professor Gostin's work. Lawrence O. Gostin, Controlling the Resurgent Tuberculosis Epidemic: A Fifty-State Survey of TB Statutes and Proposals for Reform, 269 JAMA 255 (1993).

4. *Directly Observed Therapy (DOT)*. Directly observed therapy is similar to the outpatient commitment approach for persons with mental illness discussed above. DOT provides an alternative to commitment for persons with treatable contagious conditions. In DOT, an individual is ordered to undergo treatment and is monitored to ensure that treatment is taken. A person's adherence to a drug therapy regime can be monitored by requiring the individual to appear at a health clinic daily or by daily visits from a public health worker. This strategy has some obvious advantages for both the individual and the state: The procedure is less intrusive and less expensive. It still involves a significant liberty infringement, however, and, as in *Antoinette R.*, recalcitrant persons can evade monitoring. What are your views on the use of DOT? Would you object to a program of DOT designed to ensure that you take the entire dose whenever you are issued a prescription for antibiotics?

Problem: Sexually Violent Predators — Treatment or Punishment?

Suppose that you are a state legislator who is concerned about recent scientific studies that show high recidivism rates among sexually violent pedophiles. You understand public anxiety about the release of these persons into the community. Yet you also are concerned about protecting the constitutional rights of all citizens. A victims' rights group has proposed a new statute, called "The Sexually Violent Predator Act." Under the statute, the state health department could bring an action for the civil commitment of "sexually violent predators." The state would have the burden of proving, beyond a reasonable doubt, that the person to be committed (1) had committed and was likely to commit in the future certain acts of sexual violence directed against persons under age 13, and (2) that the person had a "mental abnormality" or a "personality disorder." Persons committed under the proposed statute would be confined to a special unit, physically located within a correctional facility but separately staffed with trained, non-correctional personnel. The individual's commitment would be subject to judicial review upon the motion of the individual or state, but in any event on a yearly basis. Individuals housed in the special unit would be offered group therapy, although the legislation's proponents conceded that this therapy was unlikely to cure the committed person's underlying disorder. Do you favor or oppose the proposed legislation? What additional information do you need to determine the constitutional validity of the proposal?

For further information, see Kansas v. Crane, 534 U.S. 407 (2002) (states must prove individual lacks control over dangerous behavior); Kansas v. Hendricks, 521 U.S. 346 (1997) (upholding statute). See also Monica Davey & Abby Goodnough, Doubts Rise as States Hold Sex Offenders After Prison: Costly Efforts Keep Ex-Convicts Off Streets, but Mandated Treatment Often Fails, N.Y. Times, March 4, 2007, at 1, col. 4; Annot., 96 A.L.R. 3d 840 (2005).

Problem: Public Health Emergencies, Mandatory Treatment, and Quarantine

The MSEHPA includes provisions giving state public health authorities broad powers to require treatment and to impose isolation or quarantine. These provisions undoubtedly are the most controversial in the Model Act. See, e.g., George J. Annas, Bioterrorism, Public Health, and Civil Liberties, 346 New Eng. J. Med. 1337 (2002); Lawrence O. Gostin et al., The Model State Emergency Health Powers Act: Planning for and Response to Bioterrorism and Naturally Occurring Infectious Diseases, 288 JAMA 622 (2002). See also Joseph Barbera et al., Large-Scale Quarantine Following Biological Terrorism in the United States: Scientific Examination, Logistics and Legal Limits, and Possible Consequences, 286 JAMA 2711 (2001). Review the following excerpts from the Model Act, which will become effective only when a state declares a public health emergency pursuant to the Act:

Section 603. Vaccination and treatment. During a state of public health emergency the public health authority may exercise the following emergency powers over persons as necessary to address the public health emergency —

(a) **Vaccination.** To vaccinate persons as protection against infectious disease and to prevent the spread of contagious or possibly contagious disease.

(1) Vaccination may be performed by any qualified person authorized to do so by the public health authority.

(2) A vaccine to be administered must not be such as is reasonably likely to lead to serious harm to the affected individual.

(3) To prevent the spread of contagious or possibly contagious disease the public health authority may isolate or quarantine, pursuant to Section 604, persons who are unable or unwilling for reasons of health, religion, or conscience to undergo vaccination pursuant to this Section.

(b) **Treatment.** To treat persons exposed to or infected with disease.

(1) Treatment may be administered by any qualified person authorized to do so by the public health authority.

(2) Treatment must not be such as is reasonably likely to lead to serious harm to the affected individual.

(3) To prevent the spread of contagious or possibly contagious disease the public health authority may isolate or quarantine, pursuant to Section 604, persons who are unable or unwilling for reasons of health, religion, or conscience to undergo treatment pursuant to this Section.

Section 604. Isolation and quarantine.

(a) **Authorization.** During the public health emergency, the public health authority may isolate . . . or quarantine . . . an individual or groups of individuals. This includes individuals or groups who have not been vaccinated, treated, tested, or examined pursuant to Sections 602 and 603. The public health authority may also establish and maintain places of isolation and quarantine, and set rules and make orders. Failure to obey these rules, orders, or provisions shall constitute a misdemeanor.

(b) **Conditions and principles.** The public health authority shall adhere to the following conditions and principles when isolating or quarantining individuals or groups of individuals:

(1) Isolation and quarantine must be by the least restrictive means necessary to prevent the spread of a contagious or possibly contagious disease to others and may include, but are not limited to, confinement to private homes or other private and public premises.

(2) Isolated individuals must be confined separately from quarantined individuals. . . .

(5) Isolated and quarantined individuals must be immediately released when they pose no substantial risk of transmitting a contagious or possibly contagious disease to others. . . .

(c) **Cooperation.** Persons subject to isolation or quarantine shall obey the public health authority's rules and orders; and shall not go beyond the isolation or quarantine premises. Failure to obey these provisions shall constitute a misdemeanor. . . .

Section 605. Procedures for isolation and quarantine. During a public health emergency, the isolation and quarantine of an individual or groups of individuals shall be undertaken in accordance with the following procedures.

(a) **Temporary isolation and quarantine without notice.**

(1) **Authorization.** The public health authority may temporarily isolate or quarantine an individual or groups of individuals through a written

directive if delay in imposing the isolation or quarantine would significantly jeopardize the public health authority's ability to prevent or limit the transmission of a contagious or possibly contagious disease to others.

(2) **Content of directive.** The written directive shall specify the following: (i) the identity of the individual(s) or groups of individuals subject to isolation or quarantine; (ii) the premises subject to isolation or quarantine; (iii) the date and time at which isolation or quarantine commences; (iv) the suspected contagious disease if known; and (v) a copy of Article 6 and relevant definitions of this Act.

(3) **Copies.** A copy of the written directive shall be given to the individual to be isolated or quarantined or, if the order applies to a group of individuals and it is impractical to provide individual copies, it may be posted in a conspicuous place in the isolation or quarantine premises.

(4) **Petition for continued isolation or quarantine.** Within ten (10) days after issuing the written directive, the public health authority shall file a petition pursuant to Section 605(b) for a court order authorizing the continued isolation or quarantine of the isolated or quarantined individual or groups of individuals.

(b) **Isolation or quarantine with notice.**

(1) **Authorization.** The public health authority may make a written petition to the trial court for an order authorizing the isolation or quarantine of an individual or groups of individuals.

(2) **Content of petition.** A petition under subsection (b)(1) shall specify the following: (i) the identity of the individual(s) or groups of individuals subject to isolation or quarantine; (ii) the premises subject to isolation or quarantine; (iii) the date and time at which isolation or quarantine commences; (iv) the suspected contagious disease if known; (v) a statement of compliance with the conditions and principles for isolation and quarantine of Section 604(b); and (vi) a statement of the basis upon which isolation or quarantine is justified in compliance with this Article. The petition shall be accompanied by the sworn affidavit of the public health authority attesting to the facts asserted in the petition, together with any further information that may be relevant and material to the court's consideration.

(3) **Notice.** Notice to the individuals or groups of individuals identified in the petition shall be accomplished within twenty-four (24) hours in accordance with the rules of civil procedure.

(4) **Hearing.** A hearing must be held on any petition filed pursuant to this subsection within five (5) days of filing of the petition. In extraordinary circumstances and for good cause shown the public health authority may apply to continue the hearing date on a petition filed pursuant to this Section for up to ten (10) days, which continuance the court may grant in its discretion giving due regard to the rights of the affected individuals, the protection of the public's health, the severity of the emergency and the availability of necessary witnesses and evidence.

(5) **Order.** The court shall grant the petition if, by a preponderance of the evidence, isolation or quarantine is shown to be reasonably necessary to prevent or limit the transmission of a contagious or possibly contagious disease to others. . . .

(e) **Court to appoint counsel and consolidate claims.**

(1) **Appointment.** The court shall appoint counsel at state expense to represent individuals or groups of individuals who are or who are about to be

isolated or quarantined pursuant to the provisions of this Act and who are not otherwise represented by counsel. . . . MSEHPA §§603-605, available at www.publichealthlaw.net (Dec. 21, 2001, version).

Evaluate the constitutionality of the Model Act's vaccination, treatment, and quarantine provisions. Note that the "penalty" for refusing vaccination or treatment under §603 is isolation or quarantine pursuant to §604. Is the threatened loss of liberty more or less constitutionally problematic than the fine in *Jacobson*, supra at page 598? Note that the Act anticipates that licensed health care providers might not be available to care for all and merely requires states to use "qualified" persons. Section 604 describes the conditions of isolation/quarantine, while §605 focuses on the procedural prerequisites. Both sections take into account the possibility that a massive public health emergency might preclude individualized determinations and care. Public authorities are authorized to maintain "places" for quarantine, for example, and notices may be posted if individual notice is impractical. The penalty for violating the Act's quarantine/ isolation provisions is a misdemeanor. Would this preclude criminal prosecution for attempted murder, for example, if a person with smallpox escaped from isolation? Should it? Section 605 permits public health authorities to impose isolation and quarantine without notice. A petition for a court order must be filed within ten days. The Act also provides a mechanism for public health authorities to secure a court order before implementing isolation/quarantine. What standard of proof is required?

Compare the Model Act's provisions to the relevant public health statute in your own state. Does your state law permit public health officials to order vaccination or treatment? Does it include provisions for isolation/quarantine, with or without a court order? If your state has comprehensive public health laws covering these issues, do you see any similarities or differences between your state law and the Model Act? Which seems better from a legal or policy standpoint? If your state does not have such laws, would you recommend the adoption of the Model Act's provisions?

D. CONCLUSION

This chapter is a capstone in our focus on bioethical aspects of the treatment relationship. As you conclude this section, consider whether the rules developed in Chapters 3-6 consistently deal with the conflict between personal freedom and social interests. You may conclude that the chapters represent a progression of sorts, in which individuals' interests are measured against successively "weightier" social interests. In Chapter 3, the primary state interest is simply society's interest in preserving the life of the individual patient. Chapter 4 begins to look at situations where lives other than the patient's are at stake. In Chapter 5, the stakes are raised even higher on both sides of the conflict. On one side there is the notion that the individual herself owes an obligation of protection for the potential life of her fetus, and on the other side we recognize special constitutional protection for reproductive freedom. In this chapter, the state asserts the broadest interest, one that attempts to protect the health of the community as a whole. Do you think there is a matching pattern in the courts' rulings across these chapters? In other words, do individuals have consistently less freedom as the state's interests become progressively stronger?

Are the cases in this chapter united by any other common themes? Public health cases are often viewed in isolated groupings, identified by the specific public health strategy employed rather than by broader themes. Section C considered a wide range of state interventions into the treatment relationship. Does grouping these interventions together bring any clarification to your understanding of the law?

Public health challenges continue to elicit new strategies and new legal challenges to those strategies. These challenges may intensify in the future. Some scientists predict widespread outbreaks of highly lethal, antibiotic-resistant infections similar to the plagues that ravaged Europe centuries earlier. If this were to occur, would you predict greater or lesser recognition of personal liberty interests in public health matters?

Glossary of Organizational Terms and Acronyms

In previous generations, it was necessary to learn a specialized vocabulary to study law and medicine. This is still true, but in the past that vocabulary was purely medical. Today, it includes many obscure organizational terms as well. This is a selected glossary of organizational terms and acronyms, adapted from Prospective Payment Assessment Commission, 1996 Report to Congress.

AFDC	Aid to Families with Dependent Children
AHA	American Hospital Association
AHRQ	Agency for Health Care Research and Quality
AMA	American Medical Association
CDHC	Consumer-Directed (or Driven) Health Care
CMS	Center for Medicare and Medicaid Services
COBRA	Consolidated Omnibus Budge Reconciliation Act of 1985
CON	Certificate of Need
DRG	Diagnosis-Related Group
DHHS	See HHS
ERISA	Employee Retirement Income Security Act of 1974
ESRD	End-Stage Renal Disease
FDA	Food and Drug Administration
HCFA	Health Care Financing Administration, now CMS
HHS	Health and Human Services, Department of
HIPAA	Health Insurance Portability and Accountability Act
HIV	Human Immunodeficiency Virus
HRA or HSA	Healthcare Reimbursement or Health Savings Account (see also MSA)

HMO	Health Maintenance Organization
IDS	Integrated Delivery System
IPA	Independent Practice Association
JCAHO	Joint Commission on Accreditation of Healthcare Organizations
MSA	Medical Savings Account
MSO	Management Services Organization
NCQA	National Committee for Quality Assurance
OBRA	Omnibus Budget Reconciliation Act
PHO	Physician-Hospital Organization
POS	Point of Service
PPO	Preferred Provider Organization
PPS	Prospective Payment System
PRO	Peer Review Organization
RBRVS	Resource-Based Relative Value Scale
SNF	Skilled Nursing Facility
SSI	Supplemental Security Income
TEFRA	Tax Equity and Fiscal Responsibility Act of 1982
UR/UM	Utilization Review, or Utilization Management

Community Rating—A method of determining an insurance premium structure that reflects expected utilization by the population as a whole, rather than by specific groups.

Consumer-Driven Health Care—An alternative to managed care, which seeks to activate patients to be cost-conscious consumers at the point of treatment, by requiring them to pay more out of pocket, and by providing better information about treatment options and costs.

Cost Shifting—Increasing revenues from some payers to offset uncompensated care losses and lower net payments from other payers.

Diagnosis-Related Groups (DRGs)—A system for determining case mix, used for payment under Medicare's PPS and by some other payers. The DRG system classifies patients into groups based on the principal diagnosis, type of surgical procedure, presence or absence of significant comorbidities or complications, and other relevant criteria. DRGs are intended to categorize patients into groups that are clinically meaningful and homogeneous with respect to resource use. Medicare's PPS currently uses 490 mutually exclusive DRGs, each of which is assigned a relative weight that compares its costlines to the average for all DRGs.

Fee-for-Service—A method of reimbursing health care providers in which payment is made for each unit of service rendered.

Health Maintenance Organization (HMO)—A managed care plan that integrates financing and delivery of a comprehensive set of health care services to an enrolled population. HMOs may contract with, directly employ, or own participating health care providers. Enrollees are usually required to choose from among these providers and in return have limited copayments. Providers may be paid through capitation, salary, per diem, or prenegotiated fee-for-service rates.

Health Savings Account (HSA)—A tax-sheltered account, similar to an IRA, and also known as a Healthcare Reimbursement Account (HRA) or Medical Savings Account (MSA), that is used to pay for medical expenses. It is coupled with high-deductible or "catastrophic" insurance, such that the HSA can pay for most ordinary expenses and insurance is used only for very expensive treatment.

Integrated Delivery System (IDS)—Any number of different arrangements among doctors, hospitals, other medical facilities, and insurers in which a full range of medical services is offered to employers, subscribers, or insurers. Includes conventional arrangements such as HMOs, as well as more innovative arrangements known as PHOs, PSNs, or MSOs, which are discussed in Chapter 10.

Managed Care—Any system of health service payment or delivery arrangements in which the health plan or provider attempts to control or coordinate health service use to contain health expenditures, improve quality, or both. Arrangements often involve a defined delivery system of providers having some form of contractual relationship with the plan.

Peer Review Organization (PRO)—An organization that contracts with HCFA to investigate the quality of health care furnished to Medicare beneficiaries and to educate beneficiaries and providers. PROs also conduct limited review of medical records and claims to evaluate the appropriateness of care provided.

Physician-Hospital Organization (PHO)—A joint venture or affliation among one or more hospitals and physicians or physician groups. The venture might encompass the full range of medical services, or only one or a few services.

Point-of-Service (POS)—A health plan allowing the enrollee to choose to receive a service from a participating or a nonparticipating provider, with different benefit levels associated with one or the other types of providers.

Preferred Provider Organization (PPO)—A health plan with a network of providers whose services are available to enrollees at lower cost than the services of nonnetwork providers. PPO enrollees may self-refer to any network provider at any time.

Prospective Payment—A method of paying health care providers in which rates are established in advance. Providers are paid these rates regardless of the costs they actually incur.

Prospective Payment System (PPS)—Medicare's acute care hospital payment method for inpatient care. Prospective per case payment rates are set at a level intended to cover operating costs for treating a typical inpatient in a given diagnosis-related group. Payments for each hospital are adjusted for differences in area wages, teaching activity, care to the poor, and other factors.

Relative Value Scale—An index that assigns weights to each medical service; the weights represent the relative amount to be paid for each service. The relative value scale used in the development of the Medicare Physician Fee Schedule consists of three cost components, physician work, practice expense, and malpractice expense.

Risk Adjustment—Increases or reductions in the amount of payment made to a health plan on behalf of a group of enrollees to compensate for health care expenditures that are expected to be higher or lower than average.

Uncompensated Care—Care rendered by hospitals or other providers without payment from the patient or a government-sponsored or private insurance program. It includes both charity care, which is provided without the expectation of payment, and bad debts, for which the provider has made an unsuccessful effort to collect payment due from the patient.

Utilization Review (UR)—A review of services delivered by a health care provider to evaluate the appropriateness, necessity, and quality of the prescribed services. The review can be performed on a prospective, concurrent, or retrospective basis.

Table of Cases

Principal cases are in italics. Cases cited in excerpted materials are not listed here.

Index